California Probate Code and Related Provisions

ASPEN PUBLISHERS

California Probate Code and Related Provisions

With Commentary

2007–2008

D. Kelly Weisberg
Professor of Law
Hastings College of the Law
University of California

AUSTIN BOSTON CHICAGO NEW YORK THE NETHERLANDS

Aspen Publishers
Attn: Permissions Department
76 Ninth Avenue, 7th Floor
New York, NY 10011-5201

To contact Customer Care, e-mail customer.care@aspenpublishers.com, call 1-800-234-1660, fax 1-800-901-9075, or mail correspondence to:

Aspen Publishers
Attn: Order Department
PO Box 990
Frederick, MD 21705

Printed in the United States of America.

2 3 4 5 6 7 8 9 0

ISBN 978-0-7355-7116-7

About Wolters Kluwer Law & Business

Wolters Kluwer Law & Business is a leading provider of research information and workflow solutions in key specialty areas. The strengths of the individual brands of Aspen Publishers, CCH, Kluwer Law International and Loislaw are aligned within Wolters Kluwer Law & Business to provide comprehensive, in-depth solutions and expert-authored content for the legal, professional and education markets.

CCH was founded in 1913 and has served more than four generations of business professionals and their clients. The CCH products in the Wolters Kluwer Law & Business group are highly regarded electronic and print resources for legal, securities, antitrust and trade regulation, government contracting, banking, pension, payroll, employment and labor, and healthcare reimbursement and compliance professionals.

Aspen Publishers is a leading information provider for attorneys, business professionals and law students. Written by preeminent authorities, Aspen products offer analytical and practical information in a range of specialty practice areas from securities law and intellectual property to mergers and acquisitions and pension/benefits. Aspen's trusted legal education resources provide professors and students with high-quality, up-to-date and effective resources for successful instruction and study in all areas of the law.

Kluwer Law International supplies the global business community with comprehensive English-language international legal information. Legal practitioners, corporate counsel and business executives around the world rely on the Kluwer Law International journals, loose-leafs, books and electronic products for authoritative information in many areas of international legal practice.

Loislaw is a premier provider of digitized legal content to small law firm practitioners of various specializations. Loislaw provides attorneys with the ability to quickly and efficiently find the necessary legal information they need, when and where they need it, by facilitating access to primary law as well as state-specific law, records, forms and treatises.

Wolters Kluwer Law & Business, a unit of Wolters Kluwer, is headquartered in New York and Riverwoods, Illinois. Wolters Kluwer is a leading multinational publisher and information services company.

Summary of Contents

Contents

PREFACE AND ACKNOWLEDGMENTS

California Probate Code and Related Provisions with Commentary, 2007-2008 Edition, provides an authoritative guide to California probate law tailored to the unique needs of the law student. It furnishes explanations of fundamental legal principles, background on statutes (including those that have been repealed), commentary on selected statutes, notations on important case law developments, citations to recent law review articles, and a Glossary explaining key terminology. It also elucidates current legal developments in the cutting-edge areas of domestic partnerships and the right to die. The book is designed primarily for use in courses in Wills and Trusts.

This book, however, goes far beyond the study of state law by illuminating important legislation on many tangential areas that are relevant to probate law and by including pertinent model legislation. Part I includes a selective presentation of statutes from a variety of California codes. Parts II and III explore relevant provisions of the Restatement (Third) of Property: Wills and Other Donative Transfers, vol. 1 (1999) and vol. 2 (2003), as well as the Restatement of Trusts, vols. 1 and 2 (2003). The Restatements of the Law are drafted by the American Law Institute, an influential group of lawyers, law professors, and judges, and constitute a law reform project to clarify underlying principles and make policy recommendations. Part IV includes provisions and commentary from the Uniform Principal and Income Act (1997, rev. 2002), and Part V sets forth provisions of the Uniform Probate Code, Article II (1990). Part VI contains provisions and commentary from the Uniform Prudent Investor Act (1994). Part VII includes provisions and commentary from the Uniform Trust Code (2000, rev. 2003).

This book is intended to be especially user friendly. Unlike traditional codes, which are targeted to practitioners with some knowledge of the underlying substantive law and its statutory provisions, this Code is written for students. It assumes that the readers have little or no prior knowledge of the field and therefore provides essential explanations, commentary, and definitions. In addition, it is organized topically, rather than chronologically, enabling readers to find a given statute easily. All statutes addressing a given topic—probate code provisions as well as family law provisions, for example—are included in one location. Thus, if a reader is interested in learning about the legal regulation of California marital property at death, he or she will quickly locate pertinent statutory provisions from various California Codes all set forth in the same place. Headings to the statutes distill the content of the provisions, and legislative histories include essential information. A Table of Cases, a Table of Statutes, and a detailed Index also help students navigate the material.

Equally important, the substantive material is presented in a logical progression. That is, the framework of this Code reflects the same theoretical structure as the basic Wills and Trusts law course. Thus, the coverage of the California Probate Code explores intestate succession, family protection, the formalities of will execution, testamentary capacity, will doctrines (integration, incorporation by reference, republication by codicil, acts of independent significance, extrinsic evidence, and mistake), revocation of wills, will contracts, and will substitutes. Then the book turns to trusts, including discussion of trust creation and validity, modification and termination of trusts, trustees, beneficiaries, charitable trusts, and fiduciary administration. Finally, it addresses problems of construction (classification of testamentary gifts, ademption, satisfaction, abatement, exoneration, lapse, and class gifts) and health care decisionmaking (planning for disability and death).

In the preparation of this book, I would like to acknowledge the invaluable assistance of Professor Ed Halbach, University of California at Berkeley, Boalt Hall School of Law, for his advice regarding the selection of relevant provisions and commentary from the Restatements and the Uniform Trust Code. Also appreciated was the research assistance of the following Hastings students: Derek Deavenport, Kristen Driskell, and Kenny Jue.

For permission to reprint from other works, I would like to thank the publishers:

PREFACE AND ACKNOWLEDGMENTS

I invite you to contact me at weisberg@uchastings.edu with any comments, criticisms, and suggestions.

D. Kelly Weisberg
Hastings College of the Law
University of California

California Probate Code and Related Provisions

PART I

~

CALIFORNIA PROBATE CODE

I
INTESTATE SUCCESSION

This chapter explores the inheritance laws that apply when a person dies without a will (or without a valid will that affects all of the person's property). First, the chapter explains key definitions and terminology, jurisdictional issues, and issues regarding the disposition of the decedent's remains and personal effects. Second, the chapter explores patterns of estate distribution for the surviving spouse, children, and other relatives. Third, it focuses on questions of status (posthumous children, aliens, adoptees, nonmarital children, and disqualification for misconduct). Finally, it addresses problems of simultaneous death and prior transactions of the decedent (such as advancements, releases, and assignments).

I. Introduction

A. Definitions and Terminology

This section sets forth the definitions of key terms that appear elsewhere in this Code. It also provides an explanation of essential terminology.

The term "probate" has multiple meanings. The term refers to a process, procedure, and court. First, probate refers to the process of administration of an estate. It also signifies the procedure of proving that a will is valid (i.e., admitting the will to probate). Finally, it refers to the court that both admits the will to probate and supervises the administration of the estate.

The probate estate is the estate that is subject to administration. Note that property that passes outside of probate (i.e., "nonprobate property" such as joint tenancy property, life insurance, payable on death accounts at financial institutions) is not considered part of the probate estate. Administration is the process of collecting and managing the decedent's property, paying creditors' claims and, finally, distributing the remaining property to the heirs or beneficiaries.

At common law, "descent" referred to the passage of real property to the heirs of a person who died intestate. "Distribution" referred to the passage of personal property to the intestate's next of kin. In modern usage, the rules regarding both types of property (real and personal) are the same.

At common law, the term "heir" referred to those who took the intestate's realty, whereas those who inherited the intestate's personal property were "next of kin." Today, the term refers to persons who take real and/or personal property of the intestate. (A person who dies without a will is an intestate; one who dies with a will dies testate.) At common law, the surviving spouse of an intestate decedent was not considered an heir (i.e., the surviving spouse could not inherit the decedent's real property). Today most courts construe "heirs" to include spouses because most modern intestacy statutes give spouses a share of the intestate estate. William M. McGovern, Jr., & Sheldon F. Kurtz, Wills, Trusts and Estates Including Taxation and Future Interests §2.4 at 64-65 (3d ed., 2004) [hereinafter McGovern & Kurtz].

According to the Restatement (Third) of Property: Wills and Other Donative Transfers §2.1(b) (1999) [hereinafter Restatement (Third) of Property], the decedent's intestate estate "consisting of that part of the decedent's net probate estate that is not disposed of by a valid will, passes at the decedent's death to the decedent's heirs as provided by statute." (The Restatements are a product of the American Law Institute, an eminent organization of lawyers, law professors, and judges involved in codifying and explaining the interrelationship between statutory and decisional law.)

The California Probate Code was first adopted in 1931 (Stats. 1931, ch. 281). It was substantially revised in 1983 (Stats. 1983, ch. 842) to eliminate some of the technical requirements regarding will execution (discussed in Chapter III, Section II *infra*). The 1983 revisions adopted a large portion (but not all) of the Uniform Probate Code. The state legislature enacted the current California Probate Code in 1990 (Stats. 1990, ch. 79 (A.B. 759), §14, effective July 1, 1991). The former Probate Code, previously enacted in 1931, was repealed at that time (Stats. 1990, ch. 79 (A.B. 759), §13, effective July 1, 1991).

All property, real or personal, is classified as community, quasi-community, or separate property. Both the California Probate Code and Family Code provide definitions of community property, quasi-community property, and separate property of married persons who are California domiciliaries. However, only the California Probate Code regulates succession of such property. For purposes of dissolution and death, California treats quasi-community property as community property. For further explanation of these concepts, see Chapter II, Section IIC *infra*.

In a series of cases, California courts explored the modern meaning of "property" in the face of reproductive technological

advances—specifically, whether an individual has a property interest in sperm that would permit him to direct their distribution. See Hecht v. Superior Court, 20 Cal. Rptr. 2d 275 (Ct. App. 1993); Kane v. Superior Court, 44 Cal. Rptr. 2d 578 (Ct. App. 1995); Hecht v. Superior Court, 59 Cal. Rptr. 2d 222 (Ct. App. 1996). Decedent William Kane lived with his partner Deborah Hecht for 5 years. During that time he bequeathed to her 15 vials of sperm that he had frozen in hopes that she might one day bear his child. After Kane committed suicide, Hecht sought to recover Kane's sperm from the sperm bank. Kane's adult children from a prior marriage sought to prevent her from doing so.

The appellate court explored the traditional definition of property and then examined whether the definition applied to sperm. Reasoning that the decedent had "an interest in the nature of ownership" (20 Cal. Rptr. 2d at 281) in the sperm vials, the court asserted that the sperm should be distributed according to the decedent's intent. The court then examined evidence of that intent (i.e., the testamentary bequest of sperm, another will provision explaining his wishes, the decedent's contract with the sperm bank that released the sperm vials to Hecht). Given the overwhelming evidence of the decedent's intent, the court granted Hecht possession of the sperm vials.

The Uniform Probate Code (UPC), promulgated by the National Conference of Commissioners on Uniform State Laws (NCCUSL), has had a significant influence on the law of succession, including that of California. (Specific provisions are discussed throughout this Code.) The UPC is model legislation that was completed by the NCCUSL in 1969, and substantially revised in 1975, 1982, 1987, 1989, 1990, and 1991. The UPC was the product of a collaboration between the NCCUSL and the Real Property, Probate and Trust Law Section of the American Bar Association. NCCUSL is an organization of lawyers, judges, and law professors, appointed by the states to draft proposals for uniform and model laws and to work toward their enactment. The original version of the UPC was enacted in 18 states but was enacted in part in many additional states (including California). In 1990, NCCUSL reformulated Article II of the UPC to respond to developments in the law of gratuitous transfers. According to a Prefatory Note to those revisions, these developments consisted of:

> (1) the decline of formalism in favor of intent-serving policies; (2) the recognition that will substitutes and other inter vivos transfers have so proliferated that they now constitute a major, if not the major, form of wealth transmission; (3) the advent of the multiple-marriage society, resulting in a significant fraction of the population being married more than once and having step-children and children by previous marriages and in the acceptance of a partnership or marital-sharing theory of marriage.

Unif. Prob. Code art. II, Prefatory Note (1990, amended 1993).

CALIFORNIA PROBATE CODE

§1. Title

This code shall be known as the Probate Code.

(Stats. 1990 (A.B. 759), ch. 79, §14, effective July 1, 1991.)

§21. "Account," defined

"Account," when used to mean a contract of deposit of funds between a depositor and a financial institution, includes a checking account, savings account, certificate of deposit, share account, mutual capital certificate, and other like arrangements.

(Stats. 1990 (A.B. 759), ch. 79, §14, effective July 1, 1991.)

§24. "Beneficiary," defined

"Beneficiary" means a person to whom a donative transfer of property is made or that person's successor in interest, and:

(a) As it relates to the intestate estate of a decedent, means an heir.

(b) As it relates to the testate estate of a decedent, means a devisee.

(c) As it relates to a trust, means a person who has any present or future interest, vested or contingent.

(d) As it relates to a charitable trust, includes any person entitled to enforce the trust.

(Stats. 1990 (A.B. 759), ch. 79, §14, effective July 1, 1991.)

§26. "Child," defined

"Child" means any individual entitled to take as a child under this code by intestate succession from the parent whose relationship is involved.

(Stats. 1990 (A.B. 759), ch. 79, §14, effective July 1, 1991.)

§28. "Community property," defined

"Community property" means:

(a) Community property heretofore or hereafter acquired during marriage by a married person while domiciled in this state.

(b) All personal property wherever situated, and all real property situated in this state, heretofore or hereafter acquired during the marriage by a married person while domiciled elsewhere, that is community property, or a substantially equivalent type of marital property, under the laws of the place where the acquiring spouse was domiciled at the time of its acquisition.

(c) All personal property wherever situated, and all real property situated in this state, heretofore or hereafter acquired during the marriage by a married person in exchange for real or personal property, wherever situated that is community property, or a substantially equivalent type of marital property, under the laws of the place where the acquiring spouse was domiciled at the time the property so exchanged was acquired.
(Stats. 1990 (A.B. 759), ch. 79, §14, effective July 1, 1991.)

§32. "Devise," defined

"Devise," when used as a noun, means a disposition of real or personal property by will, and, when used as a verb, means to dispose of real or personal property by will.
(Stats. 1990 (A.B. 759), ch. 79, §14, effective July 1, 1991.)

§34. "Devisee," defined

(a) "Devisee" means any person designated in a will to receive a devise.

(b) In the case of a devise to an existing trust or trustee, or to a trustee on trust described by will, the trust or trustee is the devisee and the beneficiaries are not devisess.
(Stats. 1990 (A.B. 759), ch. 79, §14, effective July 1, 1991.)

§37. "Domestic partner" defined for probate purposes

(a) "Domestic partner" means one of two persons who have filed a Declaration of Domestic Partnership with the Secretary of State pursuant to Division 2.5 (commencing with Section 297) of the Family Code, provided that the domestic partnership has not been terminated pursuant to Section 299 of the Family Code.

(b) Notwithstanding Section 299 of the Family Code, if a domestic partnership is terminated by the death of one of the parties and Notice of Termination was not filed by either party prior to the date of death of the decedent, the domestic partner who survives the deceased is a surviving domestic partner, and shall be entitled to the rights of a surviving domestic partner as provided in this code.
(Enacted Stats. 2001 (A.B. 25), ch. 893, §13.)

§38. "Family allowance," defined

"Family allowance" means an allowance provided for In Chapter 4 (commencing with Section 6540) of Part 3 of Division 6.
(Stats. 1990 (A.B. 759), ch. 79, §14, effective July 1, 1991.)

§39. "Fiduciary," defined

"Fiduciary" means personal representative, trustee, guardian, conservator, attorney-in-fact under a power of attorney, custodian under the California Uniform Transfer To Minors Act (Part 9 (commencing with Section 3900) of Division 4) or other legal representative subject to this code.
(Stats. 1990 (A.B. 759), ch. 79, §14, effective July 1, 1991. Amended by Stats. 1997 (A.B. 1172), ch. 724, §2.)

§44. "Heir," defined

"Heir" means any person, including the surviving spouse, who is entitled to take property of the decedent by intestate succession under this code.
(Stats. 1990 (A.B. 759), ch. 79, §14, effective July 1, 1991.)

§48. "Interested person," defined

(a) Subject to subdivision (b), "interested person" includes any of the following:

(1) An heir, devisee, child, spouse, creditor, beneficiary, and any other person having a property right in or claim against a trust estate or the estate of a decedent which may be affected by the proceeding.

(2) Any person having priority for appointment as personal representative.

(3) A fiduciary representing an interested person.

(b) The meaning of "interested person" as it relates to particular persons may vary from time to time and shall be determined according to the particular purposes of, and matter involved in, any proceeding.
(Stats. 1990 (A.B. 759), ch. 79, §14, effective July 1, 1991.)

§50. "Issue," defined

"Issue" of a person means all his or her lineal descendants of all generations, with the relationship of parent and child at each generation being determined by the definitions of child and parent.
(Stats. 1990 (A.B. 759), ch. 79, §14, effective July 1, 1991.)

§54. "Parent," defined

"Parent" means any individual entitled to take as a parent under this code by intestate succession from the child whose relationship is involved.
(Stats. 1990 (A.B. 759), ch. 79, §14, effective July 1, 1991.)

§58. "Personal representative," defined

(a) "Personal representative" means executor, administrator, administrator with the will annexed, special administrator, successor personal representative, public administrator acting pursuant to Section 7660, or a person who performs substantially the same function under the law of another jurisdiction governing the person's status.

(b) "General personal representative" excludes a special administrator unless the special administrator has the powers, duties, and obligations of a general personal representative under Section 8545.
(Stats. 1990 (A.B. 759), ch. 79, §14, effective July 1, 1991; Stats. 2004 (A.B. 2687), ch. 888, §1, effective January 1, 2005.)

§59. "Predeceased spouse," defined

"Predeceased spouse" means a person who died before the decedent while married to the decedent, except that the term does not include any of the following:

(a) A person who obtains or consents to a final decree or judgment of dissolution of marriage from the decedent or a final decree or judgment of annulment of their marriage, which decree or judgment is not recognized as valid in this state, unless they (1) subsequently participate in a marriage ceremony purporting to marry each to the other or (2) subsequently live together as husband and wife.

(b) A person who, following a decree or judgment of dissolution or annulment of marriage obtained by the decedent, participates in a marriage ceremony to a third person.

(c) A person who was a party to a valid proceeding concluded by an order purporting to terminate all marital property rights.

(Stats. 1990 (A.B.759), ch. 79, §14, effective July 1, 1991.)

§60. "Probate homestead," defined

"Probate homestead" means a homestead provided for in Chapter 3 (commencing with Section 6520) of Part 3 of Division 6.

(Stats. 1990 (A.B. 759), ch. 79, §14, effective July 1, 1991.)

§62. "Property," defined

"Property" means anything that may be the subject of ownership and includes both real and personal property and any interest therein.

(Stats. 1990 (A.B. 759), ch. 79, §14, effective July 1, 1991.)

§66. "Quasi-community property," defined

"Quasi-community property" means the following property, other than community property as defined in Section 28:

(a) All personal property wherever situated, and all real property situated in this state, heretofore or hereafter acquired by a decedent while domiciled elsewhere that would have been the community property of the decedent and the surviving spouse if the decedent had been domiciled in this state at the time of its acquisition.

(b) All personal property wherever situated, and all real property situated in this state, heretofore or hereafter acquired in exchange for real or personal property, wherever situated, that would have been the community property of the decedent and the surviving spouse if the decedent had been domiciled in this state at the time the property so exchanged was acquired.

(Stats. 1990 (A.B. 759), ch. 79, §14, effective July 1, 1991.)

§76. "Subscribing witness," defined

A "subscribing witness" to a will means a witness who signs the will as provided in Section 6110.

(Stats. 1990 (A.B. 759), ch. 79, §14, effective July 1, 1991.)

§78. "Surviving spouse," exclusions

"Surviving spouse" does not include any of the following:

(a) A person whose marriage to the decedent has been dissolved or annulled, unless, by virtue of a subsequent marriage, the person is married to the decedent at the time of death.

(b) A person who obtains or consents to a final decree or judgment of dissolution of marriage from the decedent or a final decree or judgment of annulment of their marriage, which decree or judgment is not recognized as valid in this state, unless they (1) subsequently participate in a marriage ceremony purporting to marry each to the other or (2) subsequently live together as husband and wife.

(c) A person who, following a decree or judgment of dissolution or annulment of marriage obtained by the decedent, participates in a marriage ceremony with a third person.

(d) A person who was a party to a valid proceeding concluded by an order purporting to terminate all marital property rights.

(Stats.1990 (A.B. 759), ch. 79, §14, effective July 1, 1991.)

§6400. Property subject to intestacy provisions

Any part of the estate of a decedent not effectively disposed of by will passes to the decedent's heirs as prescribed in this part.

(Stats. 1990 (A.B. 759), ch. 79, §14, effective July 1, 1991.)

§7000. Passage of decedent's property

Subject to Section 7001, title to a decedent's property passes on the decedent's death to the person to whom it is devised in the decedent's last will or, in the absence of such a devise, to the decedent's heirs as prescribed in the laws governing intestate succession.

(Stats. 1990 (A.B. 759), ch. 79, §14, effective July 1, 1991.)

§7001. Limitations on passage of decedent's property

The decedent's property is subject to administration under this code, except as otherwise provided by law, and is subject to the rights of beneficiaries, creditors, and other persons as provided by law.

(Stats. 1990 (A.B. 7), ch. 79, §14, effective July 1, 1991.)

CALIFORNIA FAMILY CODE

§125. "Quasi-community property," defined

"Quasi-community property" means all real or personal property, wherever situated, acquired before or after the operative date of this code in any of the following ways:

(a) By either spouse while domiciled elsewhere which would have been community property if the spouse who acquired the property had been domiciled in this state at the time of its acquisition.

(b) In exchange for real or personal property, wherever situated, which would have been community property if the spouse who acquired the property so exchanged had been domiciled in this state at the time of its acquisition.

(Stats. 1992 (A.B. 2650), ch. 162, §10, effective January 1, 1994.)

§760. "Community property," defined

Except as otherwise provided by statute, all property, real or personal, wherever situated, acquired by a married person during the marriage while domiciled in this state is community property.

(Stats. 1992 (A.B. 2650), ch. 162, §10, effective January 1, 1994.)

§770. "Separate property," defined

(a) Separate property of a married person includes all of the following:

(1) All property owned by the person before marriage.

(2) All property acquired by the person after marriage by gift, bequest, devise, or descent.

(3) The rents, issues, and profits of the property described in this section.

(b) A married person may, without the consent of the person's spouse, convey the person's separate property.

(Stats. 1992 (A.B. 2650), ch. 162, §10, effective January 1, 1994.)

§771. Separate property includes earnings and accumulations when spouses live apart

(a) The earnings and accumulations of a spouse and the minor children living with, or in the custody of, the spouse, while living separate and apart from the other spouse, are the separate property of the spouse.

(b) Notwithstanding subdivision (a), the earnings and accumulations of an unemancipated minor child related to a contract of a type described in Section 6750 shall remain the sole legal property of the minor child.

(Stats. 1992 (A.B. 2650), ch. 162, §10, effective January 1, 1994. Amended by Stats. 1999 (S.B. 1162), ch. 940, §1.)

§772. Separate property includes earnings or accumulations after legal separation

After entry of a judgment of legal separation of the parties, the earnings or accumulations of each party are the separate property of the party acquiring the earnings or accumulations.

(Stats. 1992 (A.B. 2650), ch. 162, §10, effective January 1, 1994.)

§780. Community property includes personal injury awards if claim arose during marriage

Except as provided in Section 781 and subject to the rules of allocation set forth in Section 2603, money and other property received or to be received by a married person in satisfaction of a judgment for damages for personal injuries, or pursuant to an agreement for the settlement or compromise of a claim for such damages, is community property if the cause of action for the damages arose during the marriage.

(Stats. 1992 (A.B. 2650), ch. 162, §10, effective January 1, 1994.)

§781. Separate property includes personal injury awards if claim arose after divorce or separation

(a) Money or other property received or to be received by a married person in satisfaction of a judgment for damages for personal injuries, or pursuant to an agreement for the settlement or compromise of a claim for those damages, is the separate property of the injured person if the cause of action for the damages arose as follows:

(1) After the entry of a judgment of dissolution of a marriage or legal separation of the parties.

(2) While either spouse, if he or she is the injured person, is living separate from the other spouse.

(b) Notwithstanding subdivision (a), if the spouse of the injured person has paid expenses by reason of the personal injuries from separate property or from the community property, the spouse is entitled to reimbursement of the separate property or the community property for those expenses from the separate property received by the injured person under subdivision (a).

(c) Notwithstanding subdivision (a), if one spouse has a cause of action against the other spouse which arose during the marriage of the parties, money or property paid or to be paid by or on behalf of a party to the party's spouse of that marriage in satisfaction of a judgment for damages for personal injuries to that spouse, or pursuant to an agreement for the settlement or compromise of a claim for the damages, is the separate property of the injured spouse.

(Stats. 1992 (A.B. 2650), ch. 162, §10, effective January 1, 1994.)

§2502. Separate property does not include quasi-community property

"Separate property" does not include quasi-community property.

(Stats. 1992 (A.B. 2650), ch. 162, §10, effective January 1, 1994.)

B. Jurisdiction and Venue

A person who desires to prove a will or probate an estate must bring the action in the proper court, i.e., the court that has jurisdiction over such matters. The court that performs the functions of proving a will to be valid (i.e., "admitting the will to probate") and supervising the administration of the estate is called the "probate court." Sometimes, the court performing these functions is the probate division of the court of general jurisdiction in the state. In some states, the probate court is known by other names, such as the Surrogate's Court in New York or the Orphan's Court in Pennsylvania.

In addition, the action must be brought in a court that has venue over the matter. Generally, for purposes of administration of an estate, venue is based on the decedent's domicile at the time of death (Cal. Prob. Code §7051). For trust purposes, venue is normally based on the residence of the trustee or the location where the trust is administered. See Uniform Trust Code §204 (2000, as amended 2001).

CALIFORNIA PROBATE CODE

§7050. Jurisdiction of superior court

The superior court has jurisdiction of proceedings under this code concerning the administration of the decedent's estate.
(Stats. 1990 (A.B. 759), ch. 79, §14, effective July 1, 1991. Amended Stats. 1994 (A.B. 3686), ch. 806, §22.)

§7051. Venue where decedent domiciled in this state

If the decedent was domiciled in this state at the time of death, the proper county for proceedings concerning administration of the decedent's estate is the county in which the decedent was domiciled, regardless of where the decedent died.
(Stats. 1990 (A.B. 759), ch. 79, §14, effective July 1, 1991.)

C. Disposition of Decedent's Remains

According to the weight of authority in this country, a person possesses a sufficient proprietary interest in his or her body to make a valid direction as to the place and manner of burial. Such directions, provided that they are reasonable, may be judicially enforced. In re Henderson's Estate, 57 P.2d 212, 214 (Cal. Ct. App. 1936). Both case law and statutory law recognize a person's right to dispose of his or her remains.

Early British common law recognized a property interest in dead bodies. Remigius N. Nwabueze, Biotechnology and the New Property Regime in Human Bodies and Body Parts, 24 Loy. L.A. Int'l & Comp. L. Rev. 19, 22 (2002). Thus, before the nineteenth century, creditors could seize the body of a deceased debtor for debts owed.

By the mid-nineteenth century, public sentiment had changed sufficiently that a new rule developed. Blackstone previously enunciated this rule (called "a no-property rule in dead bodies") by stating:

> [t]hough the heir has a property interest in the monuments and escutcheons of his ancestors, he has none in their bodies or ashes; nor can he bring any civil action . . . against their bodies or ashes or violate their remains.

Cited in id. at 23.

American courts rejected the British no-property-in-dead-bodies rule. One court denounced the rule as follows:

> The dogma of the English ecclesiastical law, that a child has no such claim, no such exclusive power, no peculiar interest in the dead body of its parent, is so utterly inconsistent with every enlightened perception of personal right, so inexpressibly repulsive to every proper moral sense, that its adoption would be an eternal disgrace to American jurisprudence.

Ritter v. Couch, 76 S.E. 428, 430 (W. Va. 1912) (cited in Nwabueze, *supra*, at 28).

Prior to the 1970s, few states had statutes providing that a person could direct the manner of disposal of his or her body. Frank D. Wagner, Annot., Enforcement of Preference Expressed by Decedent as to Disposition of His Body After Death, 54 A.L.R.3d 1037 §2(a)(1973 & Supp. 2005). Many states now do so. California law provides that the decedent has the right to govern the disposition of personal remains. Specifically, according to California Health and Safety Code §7100.1, a person may direct in writing the disposition of his or her remains and specify the funeral goods and services to be provided. If the decedent has not expressed such wishes, then the right to control the disposition of the decedent's remains (as well as the location and conditions of burial and funeral arrangements) vests in statutorily designated persons (who are accorded priority in cases of disputes) (Cal. Health & Safety Code §7100).

According to California statute, an agent under a power of attorney for health care is given first priority in controlling the disposition of the decedent's remains (Cal. Health & Safety Code §7100(a)(1)). A surviving spouse is accorded the next priority. See, e.g., Melican v. Regents of the University of California, 2007 WL 1502155 (Cal. Ct. App. 2007) (affirming denial of claim of decedent's children for alleged mishandling of decedent's remains because his widow, who was the sole dispositional rights holder with authority to decide whether to donate his body, was not a plaintiff in the case); Ross v. Forest Lawn Memorial Park, 203 Cal. Rptr. 468 (Ct. App. 1984) (holding that the surviving spouse's paramount right not only to the custody of the dead body, but also to determine the time and place of burial, excludes the rights of the next of kin).

Also, in Newman v. Sathyavaglswaran, 287 F.3d 786 (9th Cir. 2002), the Ninth Circuit Court of Appeal held that family members have a constitutional right to the body of a deceased relative that is entitled to due process protection. In *Newman*, the parents of deceased children brought an action pursuant to 42 U.S.C. §1983, alleging a taking of their property without due process because their deceased children's corneas were removed by the Los Angeles County Coroner's office without notice or consent. The Court of Appeals held that common law rights, combined with a statutory right under California law to control the disposition of their children's bodies, created in the parents a property interest in their children's corneas that was protected by the Due Process Clause.

Several highly publicized disputes surfaced recently in California, Michigan, and Nevada among divorced parents concerning the disposition of the remains of their children who were soldiers killed in the war in Iraq. See Rodney Foo, Mom Appealing Ruling in Soldier's Burial Battle, San Jose Mercury News, Jan. 20, 2006, at B2.

Sometimes, a spouse or family member wishes to disinter and reinter the remains of another family member. Pursuant to California Health and Safety Code §7525, the remains of a deceased person may be removed from a cemetery plot with the consent of both the cemetery authority and the surviving spouse. If the cemetery withholds consent, then the petitioner may seek judicial authorization. Cal. Health & Safety Code §7526. In Maffei v. Woodlawn Memorial Park, 29 Cal. Rptr. 3d 679 (Ct. App. 2005), the appellate court affirmed the trial court order denying the surviving spouse's petition to disinter and reinter his wife's remains. The court reasoned that the trial court had not abused its discretion because the surviving spouse originally consented to the interment and did not mention an alternative burial plan until 20 years after the interment.

CALIFORNIA HEALTH & SAFETY CODE §7100. Right to control the disposition of decedent's remains

(a) The right to control the disposition of the remains of a deceased person, the location and conditions of interment, and arrangements for funeral goods and services to be provided, unless other directions have been given by the decedent pursuant to Section 7100.1, vests in, and the duty of disposition and the liability for the reasonable cost of disposition of the remains devolves upon, the following in the order named:

(1) An agent under a power of attorney for health care who has the right and duty of disposition under Division 4.7 (commencing with Section 4600) of the Probate Code, except that the agent is liable for the costs of disposition only in either of the following cases:

(A) Where the agent makes a specific agreement to pay the costs of disposition.

(B) Where, in the absence of a specific agreement, the agent makes decisions concerning disposition that incur costs, in which case the agent is liable only for the reasonable costs incurred as a result of the agent's decisions, to the extent that the decedent's estate or other appropriate fund is insufficient.

(2) The competent surviving spouse.

(3) The sole surviving competent adult child of the decedent, or if there is more than one competent adult child of the decedent, the majority of the surviving competent adult children. However, less than the majority of the surviving competent adult children shall be vested with the rights and duties of this section if they have used reasonable efforts to notify all other surviving competent adult children of their instructions and are not aware of any opposition to those instructions by the majority of all surviving competent adult children.

(4) The surviving competent parent or parents of the decedent. If one of the surviving competent parents is absent, the remaining competent parent shall be vested with the rights and duties of this section after reasonable efforts have been unsuccessful in locating the absent surviving competent parent.

(5) The sole surviving competent adult sibling of the decedent, or if there is more than one surviving competent adult sibling of the decedent, the majority of the surviving competent adult siblings. However, less than the majority of the surviving competent adult siblings shall be vested with the rights and duties of this section if they have used reasonable efforts to notify all other surviving competent adult siblings of their instructions and are not aware of any opposition to those instructions by the majority of all surviving competent adult siblings.

(6) The surviving competent adult person or persons respectively in the next degrees of kinship, or if there is more than one surviving competent adult person of the same degree of kinship, the majority of those persons. Less than the majority of surviving competent adult persons of the same degree of kinship shall be vested with the rights and duties of this section if those persons have used reasonable efforts to notify all other surviving competent adult persons of the same degree of kinship of their instructions and are not aware of any opposition to those instructions by the majority of all surviving competent adult persons of the same degree of kinship.

(7) The public administrator when the deceased has sufficient assets.

(b)(1) If any person to whom the right of control has vested pursuant to subdivision (a) has been charged with first or second degree murder or voluntary manslaughter in connection with the decedent's death and those charges are known to the funeral director or cemetery authority, the right of control is relinquished and passed on to the next of kin in accordance with subdivision (a).

(2) If the charges against the person are dropped, or if the person is acquitted of the charges, the right of control is returned to the person.

(3) Notwithstanding this subdivision, no person who has been charged with first or second degree murder or voluntary manslaughter in connection with the decedent's death to whom the right of control has not been returned pursuant to paragraph (2) shall have any right to control disposition pursuant to subdivision (a) which shall be applied, to the extent the funeral director or cemetery authority know about the charges, as if that person did not exist.

(c) A funeral director or cemetery authority shall have complete authority to control the disposition of the remains, and to proceed under this chapter to recover usual and customary charges for the disposition, when both of the following apply:

(1) Either of the following applies:

(A) The funeral director or cemetery authority has knowledge that none of the persons described in paragraphs (1) to (6), inclusive, of subdivision (a) exists.

(B) None of the persons described in paragraphs (1) to (6), inclusive, of subdivision (a) can be found after reasonable inquiry, or contacted by reasonable means.

(2) The public administrator fails to assume responsibility for disposition of the remains within seven days after having been given written notice of the facts. Written notice may be delivered by hand, U.S. mail, facsimile transmission, or telegraph.

(d) The liability for the reasonable cost of final disposition devolves jointly and severally upon all kin of the decedent in the same degree of kinship and upon the estate of the decedent. However, if a person accepts the gift of an entire body under subdivision (a) of Section 7155.5, that person, subject to the terms of the gift, shall be liable for the reasonable cost of final disposition of the decedent.

(e) This section shall be administered and construed to the end that the expressed instructions of the decedent or the person entitled to control the disposition shall be faithfully and promptly performed.

(f) A funeral director or cemetery authority shall not be liable to any person or persons for carrying out the instructions of the decedent or the person entitled to control the disposition.

(g) For purposes of this section, "adult" means an individual who has attained 18 years of age, "child" means a natural or adopted child of the decedent, and "competent" means an individual who has not been declared incompetent by a court of law or who has been declared competent by a court of law following a declaration of incompetence.

(Stats. 1939 (A.B. 598), ch. 60, p. 673, §7100. Amended by Stats. 1947, ch. 125, p. 646, §1; Stats. 1957, ch. 933, p. 2144, §1; Stats. 1965, ch. 654, p. 2021, §1; Stats. 1968, ch. 926, p. 1758, §1; Stats. 1969, ch. 999, p. 1971, §1; Stats. 1970, ch. 960, §3; Stats. 1970, ch. 1006, §1.5; Stats. 1970, ch. 1006, p. 1809, §1.5; Stats. 1993, ch. 1232, §22; Stats. 1994 (A.B. 1392), ch. 570, §8; Stats. 1997 (A.B. 1546), ch. 475, §23; Stats. 1998 (S.B. 1360), ch. 253, §1; Stats. 1999 (A.B. 1677), ch. 657, §36; Stats. 1999 (A.B. 891), ch. 658, §5.5, effective July 1, 2000; Stats. 2001 (A.B. 1278), ch. 230, §1; Stats. 2004 (A.B. 2811), ch. 307, §1, effective January 1, 2005.)

§7100.1. Decedent may direct the disposition of his or her remains

(a) A decedent, prior to death, may direct, in writing, the disposition of his or her remains and specify funeral goods and services to be provided. Unless there is a statement to the contrary that is signed and dated by the decedent, the directions may not be altered, changed, or otherwise amended in any material way, except as may be required by law, and shall be faithfully carried out upon his or her death, provided both of the following requirements are met: (1) the directions set forth clearly and completely the final wishes of the decedent in sufficient detail so as to preclude any material ambiguity with regard to the instructions; and, (2) arrangements for payment through trusts, insurance, commitments by others, or any other effective and binding means, have been made, so as to preclude the payment of any funds by the survivor or survivors of the deceased that might otherwise retain the right to control the disposition.

(b) In the event arrangements for only one of either the cost of interment or the cost of the funeral goods and services are made pursuant to this section, the remaining wishes of the decedent shall be carried out only to the extent that the decedent has sufficient assets to do so, unless the person or persons that otherwise have the right to control the disposition and arrange for funeral goods and services agree to assume the cost. All other provisions of the directions shall be carried out.

(c) If the directions are contained in a will, they shall be immediately carried out, regardless of the validity of the will in other respects or of the fact that the will may not be offered for or admitted to probate until a later date.

(Stats. 1997 (A.B. 1546), ch. 475, §24. Amended by Stats. 1998 (S.B. 1360), ch. 253, §2.)

§7525. Required consent to disinter remains

The remains of a deceased person may be removed from a plot in a cemetery with the consent of the cemetery authority and the written consent of one of the following in the order named:

(a) The surviving spouse.

(b) The surviving children.

(c) The surviving parents.

(d) The surviving brothers or sisters.

(Stats.1939, ch. 60, p. 684, §7525.)

§7526. Permission of court in absence of consent

If the required consent can not be obtained,
permission by the superior court of the county where the cemetery is situated is sufficient.

(Stats.1939, ch. 60, p. 685, § 7526.)

D. Disposition of Decedent's Personal Effects

Upon the death of the decedent, California law specifies that certain agencies or institutions may deliver the decedent's personal effects and other tangible personal property to family members and others. California Probate Code §330 provides that the hospital in which the decedent died and the decedent's employer (among others) may deliver such property directly to the decedent's surviving spouse, relative, or conservator or guardian of the decedent's estate (provided that the conservator or guardian of the estate is acting in that capacity at the time of the decedent's death). The specified agencies and officials may act

immediately and need not wait 40 days after the decedent's death (as required for the use of the affidavit procedure pursuant to California Probate Code §13100) to deliver these personal effects and other tangible personal property. The agency or official is not liable if the agency or official relies for proof of identity on a document described in California Probate Code §13104(d) (such as an ID card or driver's license issued by the California Department of Motor Vehicles, American or foreign passport, driver's license or ID card of another state, or an ID card issued by the armed forces).

CALIFORNIA PROBATE CODE

§330. Delivery of decedent's personal effects

(a) Except as provided in subdivision (b), a public administrator, government official, law enforcement agency, the hospital or institution in which a decedent died, or the decedent's employer, may, without the need to wait 40 days after death, deliver the tangible personal property of the decedent in its possession, including keys to the decedent's residence, to the decedent's surviving spouse, relative, or conservator or guardian of the estate acting in that capacity at the time of death.

(b) A person shall not deliver property pursuant to this section if the person knows or has reason to believe that there is a dispute over the right to possession of the property.

(c) A person that delivers property pursuant to this section shall require reasonable proof of the status and identity of the person to whom the property is delivered, and may rely on any document described in subdivision (d) of Section 13104 as proof of identity.

(d) A person that delivers property pursuant to this section shall, for a period of three years after the date of delivery of the property, keep a record of the property delivered and the status and identity of the person to whom the property is delivered.

(e) Delivery of property pursuant to this section does not determine ownership of the property or confer any greater rights in the property than the recipient would otherwise have and does not preclude later proceedings for administration of the decedent's estate. If proceedings for administration of the decedent's estate are commenced, the person holding the property shall deliver it to the personal representative on request by the personal representative.

(f) A person that delivers property pursuant to this section is not liable for loss or damage to the property caused by the person to whom the property is delivered.

(Stats. 1990 (A.B. 759), ch. 79, §14, effective July 1, 1991.)

II. Intestacy

A. Share of Surviving Spouse and Issue

The term "testate succession" refers to the passage of property under a decedent's will. "Intestate succession" refers to the passage of property of a decedent who dies without a valid will.

At common law, the distribution of personal property and the descent of land were handled differently. The bulk of wealth consisted of real property. Land could not be devised by will until the Statute of Wills in 1540. However, a widow had a right to a portion of her husband's real property in the form of "dower." The husband's correlative right in his deceased wife's estate was termed "curtesy." The common law rights of surviving spouses are explained further in Chapter II, Section IIA *infra*.

In regard to personal property, at common law a husband acquired title to the wife's personal property upon marriage. Therefore, upon the wife's death, the law had no need to provide for the husband's inheritance of the wife's personal property. At the husband's death, ecclesiastical courts distributed his personal property to his widow and children. McGovern & Kurtz, *supra*, §3.2 at 130. According to the Statute of Distribution of 1670, a widow inherited one-third of her husband's personal property if he left surviving issue but one-half if he did not. Id., §2.1 at 49.

Most jurisdictions today have abolished dower and curtesy. See, e.g., Cal. Prob. Code §6412 (abolishing dower and curtesy in California). The few jurisdictions that retain these marital estates make no distinction between the rights of a surviving wife or husband in recognition of equal protection issues. Most jurisdictions have replaced dower with the forced share. For further discussion of forced share, see Chapter II, Section IIB *infra*.

Jurisdictions utilize various approaches today to compute the intestate share of a surviving spouse. According to the Restatement (Third) of Property §2.2, "An intestate decedent's surviving spouse takes a share of the intestate estate as provided by statute. The exact share differs among the states. . . ."

Statutes generally take into consideration the existence and number of surviving children and, if no children or their descendants survive, the existence of other close relatives. In addition, many jurisdictions reflect the influence of the Uniform Probate Code by taking into consideration whether the decedent or the surviving spouse had children from prior relationships or whether all the decedent's surviving descendants are also descendants of the surviving spouse.

According to the basic intestacy scheme in all jurisdictions, a decedent's intestate estate passes first to the surviving spouse. If the decedent dies without leaving a spouse surviving (e.g., if the decedent dies as a single

person or if the decedent's spouse predeceases), then the decedent's entire intestate estate passes to his or her descendants. If the decedent dies without having either a surviving spouse or any surviving descendants, then the decedent's ancestors and collateral relatives take the decedent's estate.

In California, it is necessary to distinguish between community property and separate property to determine the surviving spouse's right to the decedent's intestate estate. A married decedent's intestate estate consists of *all of his or her separate property* and *one-half of the couple's community property* (the marital property shared by the spouses). That is, in a community property jurisdiction such as California, the decedent has testamentary disposition only over his or her half of the community property in addition to his or her separate property. The decedent does not have testamentary disposition over the entire community property because, from the date of the marriage, half of the community property belongs to the other spouse.

If the decedent fails to exercise testamentary disposition over his or her half of the *community property*, the decedent's share of that community property passes to the surviving spouse (Cal. Prob. Code §6401). Thus, in the event of a decedent dying intestate, the decedent's surviving spouse acquires the decedent's one-half of the community property. Because that surviving spouse already owns one-half of the community property (as of the date of the marriage), the survivor then holds an interest in the entire community property. This result occurs from an application of California Probate Code §6401(a) together with California Probate Code §100.

Many community property states (such as California) also recognize the concept of *quasi-community* property (i.e., foreign-acquired property that would have been community property had the parties been domiciled in California at the time of acquisition). In California, the surviving spouse also acquires the intestate's half of the quasi-community property (Cal. Prob. Code §6401(b)).

The surviving spouse in community property jurisdictions also is entitled to a share of the decedent's *separate property* if the decedent dies intestate. Pursuant to California Probate Code §6401(c)(1), the surviving spouse takes all of the intestate's separate property if the decedent did not leave any surviving issue, parent, sibling, or issue of a deceased sibling. However, if the decedent died intestate leaving surviving issue, then the number of the decedent's children (or issue of those children) affects the surviving spouse's share of the decedent's separate property. That is, the surviving spouse takes one-half of the intestate's separate property if there is only one child (or issue of that child) or where the decedent leaves no issue but leaves a parent or parents or their issue. On the other hand, the surviving spouse takes one-third of the intestate's separate property if the decedent left more than one child, or left one child plus surviving issue of another deceased child, or left issue of two or more deceased children (Cal. Prob. Code §6401). The surviving spouse's share diminishes as the number of children increases in order for the children to have an enlarged share.

After determining the share of the surviving spouse, California law turns to a determination of the share of surviving issue. The term "issue" is synonymous with the term "descendants" and includes children, grandchildren, great-grandchildren, etc. See Cal. Prob. Code §50 (defining issue as "all [of a person's] lineal descendants of all generations").

The portion of the intestate decedent's estate that does not pass to the surviving spouse under California Probate Code §6401 (or the entire intestate estate of a decedent who has no surviving spouse), passes as follows: (1) to the decedent's issue and all such issue take equally if they are related in the same degree of kinship to the decedent (if not, those of more remote degree inherit as provided in California Probate Code §240) (Cal. Prob. Code §6401(a)); (2) if the decedent left no issue surviving, then the remaining intestate property passes to the decedent's parent or parents equally (Cal. Prob. Code §6401(b)); (3) if the decedent left no surviving issue or parent, then the remainder of the decedent's intestate estate passes to the issue of the parents (or the issue of either of them) and such issue take equally if they are all of the same degree of kinship to the decedent, but, if of unequal degree, then those of more remote degree take as provided in California Probate Code §240 (Cal. Prob. Code §6401(c)).

If the decedent is not survived by issue or a parent (or the issue of a parent) but is survived by one or more grandparents (or the issue of grandparents), then the remainder of the decedent's intestate estate passes to that grandparent or grandparents (or to the issue of such grandparents if there is no surviving grandparent). Again, the issue take equally if they are all of the same degree of kinship to the decedent, but if of unequal degree, those of more remote degree take as provided in California Probate Code §240 (Cal. Prob. Code §6402(d)).

The California Probate Code also takes into consideration affinal relationships. (*Affinity* refers to relationships by marriage; *consanguinity* refers to relationships by blood.)

Specifically, if the decedent is not survived by a surviving spouse, issue, a parent (or issue of a parent), a grandparent (or issue of a grandparent), but is survived by the issue of a predeceased spouse, then the remainder of the decedent's intestate estate (except for the decedent's property subject to California Probate §6402.5) passes to the issue of that predeceased spouse. Again, such issue take equally if they are all of the same degree of kinship to the predeceased spouse, but if of unequal degree, then those of more remote degree take as provided in California Probate Code §240 (Cal. Prob. Code §6402(e)). (Note that California Probate Code §6402.5 has separate rules for distribution of real property and personal property to the issue of a predeceased spouse as well as different durational requirements that apply to the timing of a predeceased spouse's death.) If the decedent is not survived by any of the preceding persons, but is survived by next of kin (those relatives not previously specified by statute), then the decedent's estate passes to the next of kin in equal degree—but if there are two or more collateral kindred in equal degree who claim through different ancestors, those who claim through the nearest ancestor are preferred to those claiming through an ancestor more remote (Cal. Prob. Code §6402(f)). Note that those persons related to the decedent solely by affinity, such as issue of a predeceased spouse, do not inherit under the Uniform Probate Code (UPC) (with the exception, of course, of the surviving spouse).

Finally, if the decedent is not survived by next of kin or by the issue of a predeceased spouse, but is survived by parents of a predeceased spouse (or the issue of such parents), then the remainder of the decedent's intestate estate passes to such parent or parents equally (or to their issue if both are deceased) and such issue take equally if they are all of the same degree of kinship to the predeceased spouse, but if of unequal degree those of more remote degree take as provided by California Probate Code §240 (Cal. Prob. Code §6402(g)). If none of the aforementioned relatives survive the decedent, then principles of escheat apply. For discussion of escheat, see Section IIC *infra*.

The Uniform Probate Code operates somewhat differently, although the goal of providing adequately for the surviving spouse is the same. The UPC provides that the intestate share of a decedent's surviving spouse is the entire intestate estate if the decedent leaves no descendant or parent surviving or if all of the decedent's surviving descendants are also descendants of the surviving spouse (and there are no other descendants of the surviving spouse who survive the decedent) (UPC §2-102(1)(i), (ii)).

However, if the decedent dies survived by a spouse and at least one parent, then the surviving spouse receives the first $200,000 plus three-fourths of the balance (UPC §2-102(2)). (The $200,000 figure is a suggested amount and may be modified by jurisdictions adopting the UPC.) If the decedent is survived by a spouse and their issue (i.e., issue of both parties), plus the surviving spouse has descendants who are not descendants of the decedent (such as children from a prior marriage of the surviving spouse), then the surviving spouse takes the first $150,000, plus one-half the balance of the estate. If the decedent leaves surviving issue who are not descendants of the surviving spouse (such as children from the decedent's prior marriage), then the surviving spouse takes $100,000 plus one-half the balance. In this manner, the UPC takes into account the modern reconstituted family. (Article II of the UPC is set forth in Part V of this Code.)

In some cases, an intestate dies without a surviving spouse (i.e., if the decedent has never married or the decedent's spouse predeceased). Generally, the estate then passes to the decedent's descendants. If all of the decedent's children are alive, each child receives an equal share (i.e., a "per capita" distribution). However, if some of the decedent's children predeceased the intestate but left children who survive the intestate, the division of the estate may be: (1) per stirpes, (2) per capita with representation, or (3) per capita at each generation (discussed *infra*).

Note that the California Probate Code permits inheritance by very remote relatives (including relatives of the decedent's predeceased spouse), whereas the Uniform Probate Code disallows inheritance after the issue of the decedent's grandparents (and does not permit inheritance by relatives of a decedent's predeceased spouse) (UPC §2-103(4)).

California Probate Code §105 limits the application of Probate Code §§100-104 to situations in which the decedent died on or after January 1, 1985 (the date this part of the Code became effective).

1. Intestate Share of Surviving Spouse

The intestate share of the surviving spouse, according to California law, is set forth below. Statutory provisions regulate the disposition of the survivor's share in the decedent's community property, quasi-community property, and separate property.

The probate administration process may be avoided when the surviving spouse succeeds to the decedent's entire estate. The court may

distribute, via summary proceedings, the community, quasi-community, and separate property that pass outright to the surviving spouse. Specifically, the California Probate Code provides for a summary procedure for "confirming" or "determining" the surviving spouse's right to the estate's community, quasi-community, and separate probate. This process is called a "spousal set-aside." The procedure obviates the need for probate administration of the decedent's property regardless of the size of the estate.

This optional procedure is available to the surviving spouse regardless of whether the property passes by will or intestate succession or already "belongs to" the surviving spouse. According to California Probate Code §13650, property qualifying for the set-aside may be "determined" (i.e., for property that passes to the surviving spouse) and "confirmed" (i.e., for an interest in community or quasi-community property that already belongs to the surviving spouse) without the need for probate administration. Although the set-aside procedure is optional, it is desirable to clear title, clarify the property subject to administration, and determine the value of property for purposes of establishing the extent of the surviving spouse's liability to creditors. Bruce S. Ross & Isabella Horton Grant, California Practice Guide: Probate §4:54, at 4-25 (2002) [hereinafter Ross & Grant].

In California, spouses can take title to property as "community property" or as "community property with right of survivorship." (The latter concept is explored further in Chapter VIII on Will Substitutes *infra*.) In the latter case, when the first spouse dies, such property passes to the surviving spouse as if it were joint tenancy property. Thus, it passes without the need for probate administration or a spousal property set-aside pursuant to California Civil Code §682.1.

California law also provides for inheritance rights in cases of intestacy for a surviving spouse who qualifies as a "putative spouse." A putative spouse is a person who enters into an invalid marriage with a good faith belief that the marriage is valid. A putative marriage might arise if the parties undergo a marriage ceremony but, because of some legal impediment (for example, one party's prior divorce was not yet final or the marriage was not properly formalized), the marriage is not valid. In such a case, one of the parties may have committed bigamy. See, e.g., Estate of Vargas, 111 Cal. Rptr. 779 (Ct. App. 1974) (holding that the second wife of a man who led a double life with two separate families had the status of a putative spouse; hence, equal division of his estate between the two wives was proper).

Note that the California Family Code does not define "putative marriage," but specifies only that a court declare the status of a "putative spouse." 32 Cal. Jur.3d Family Law §93. The Family Code gives a putative spouse "quasi-marital property" rights when the putative marriage is ended by death or divorce. Thus, property that would have been community property or quasi-community property had the marriage been valid is regarded as "quasi-marital property" and is divided equally as if it were community property (Cal. Fam. Code §2251(a)(2)).

A putative spouse not only has the right to share in the distribution of marital property upon dissolution of the marriage (Cal. Fam. Code §2251), but also has a right to spousal support at dissolution (Cal. Fam. Code §§2254, 4455), and standing to sue for wrongful death (Cal. Code Civ. Proc. §377.60). See also Kunahoff v. Woods, 332 P.2d 773 (Ct. App. 1958) (holding that putative wife who participated in marriage ceremony and lived with putative husband for 31 years before his death, was an "heir" within the meaning of the wrongful death statute and thereby was entitled to bring an action, even though no marriage license had been obtained, and minister did not file a record of the marriage); Estate of DePasse, 118 Cal. Rptr. 2d 143 (Ct. App. 2002) (denying alleged husband one-half interest in decedent-wife's estate because husband's awareness of license requirement was sufficient to show that he did not have a good faith belief that his marriage was lawful, as required to confer putative spouse status).

If the surviving spouse qualifies as a putative spouse, the probate court may declare that the putative spouse has intestate succession rights (i.e., the right to succeed to the entire quasi-marital estate, and the right to succeed to the separate estate under California Probate Code §6401). On the other hand, if there are two "surviving spouses" (as in a bigamous marriage), the court may apply equitable principles to distribute the decedent's intestate property. See Estate of Hafner, 229 Cal. Rptr. 676 (Cal. 1986) (holding that, as between surviving innocent legal wife and children of bigamous husband, and surviving innocent putative spouse, one-half of estate would go to surviving legal wife and children, and the other half would go to surviving putative spouse as quasi-marital property); Estate of Leslie, 207 Cal. Rptr. 561, 566-569 (Ct. App. 1984) (holding that surviving putative husband was entitled to a share of

decedent's separate property). The California Family Code provisions on bigamy are included *infra*.

A recent California case addressed the right of a domestic partner to sue for wrongful death of her partner. Bouley v. Long Beach Memorial Medical Center, 127 Cal. App. 4th 501 (Ct. App. 2005), held that the 2004 amendment to the wrongful death statute (Cal. Code Civ. Proc. §377.60) applied retroactively to grant a surviving partner standing to sue for wrongful death when the deceased partner's death from medical malpractice occurred prior to 2002 despite the fact that the partnership was not registered at the time.

CALIFORNIA PROBATE CODE

§100. Community property: disposition upon death

(a) Upon the death of a married person, one-half of the community property belongs to the surviving spouse and the other half belongs to the decedent.

(b) Notwithstanding subdivision (a), a husband and wife may agree in writing to divide their community property on the basis of a non pro rata division of the aggregate value of the community property or on the basis of a division of each individual item or asset of community property, or partly on each basis. Nothing in this subdivision shall be construed to require this written agreement in order to permit or recognize a non pro rata division of community property.

(Stats. 1990 (A.B. 759), ch. 79, §14, effective July 1, 1991. Amended by Stats. 1998 (A.B. 2069), ch. 682, §2.)

§101. Quasi-community property: disposition upon death

(a) Upon the death of a married person domiciled in this state, one-half of the decedent's quasi-community property belongs to the surviving spouse and the other half belongs to the decedent.

(b) Notwithstanding subdivision (a), a husband and wife may agree in writing to divide their quasi-community property on the basis of a non pro rata division of the aggregate value of the quasi-community property, or on the basis of a division of each individual item or asset of quasi-community property, or partly on each basis. Nothing in this subdivision shall be construed to require this written agreement in order to permit or recognize a non pro rata division of quasi-community property.

(Stats. 1990 (A.B. 759), ch. 79, §14, effective July 1, 1991. Amended by Stats. 1998 (A.B. 2069), ch. 682, §3.)

§104. Exception: community property held in revocable trust is governed by trust provisions

Notwithstanding Section 100, community property held in a revocable trust described in Section 761 of the Family Code is governed by the provisions, if any, in the trust for disposition in the event of death.

(Stats. 1990 (A.B. 759), ch. 79, §14, effective July 1, 1991. Amended by Stats. 1992 (A.B. 2641), ch. 163, §119, effective January 1, 1994.)

§104.5. For transfers of property to revocable trusts: presumption arises regarding character of assets

Transfer of community and quasi-community property to a revocable trust shall be presumed to be an agreement, pursuant to Sections 100 and 101, that those assets retain their character in the aggregate for purposes of any division provided by the trust. This section shall apply to all transfers prior to, on, or after January 1, 2000.

(Stats. 1999 (A.B. 1051), ch. 263, §1.)

§105. Application of Part

This part does not apply where the decedent died before January 1, 1985, and the law applicable prior to January 1, 1985, continues to apply where the decedent died before January 1, 1985.

(Stats. 1990 (A.B. 759), ch. 79, §14, effective July 1, 1991.)

§6401. Intestate share of surviving spouse or surviving domestic partner

(a) As to community property, the intestate share of the surviving spouse is the one-half of the community property that belongs to the decedent under Section 100.

(b) As to quasi-community property, the intestate share of the surviving spouse is the one-half of the quasi-community property that belongs to the decedent under Section 101.

(c) As to separate property, the intestate share of the surviving spouse or surviving domestic partner, as defined in subdivision (b) of Section 37, is as follows:

(1) The entire intestate estate if the decedent did not leave any surviving issue, parent, brother, sister, or issue of a deceased brother or sister.

(2) One-half of the intestate estate in the following cases:

(A) Where the decedent leaves only one child or the issue of one deceased child.

(B) Where the decedent leaves no issue but leaves a parent or parents or their issue or the issue of either of them.

(3) One-third of the intestate estate in the following cases:

(A) Where the decedent leaves more than one child.

(B) Where the decedent leaves one child and the issue of one or more deceased children.

(C) Where the decedent leaves issue of two or more deceased children.

(Stats. 1990 (A.B. 759), ch. 79, §14, effective July 1, 1991. Amended by Stats. 2002 (A.B. 2216), ch. 447, §1, effective July 1, 2003.)

§6402.5. Portion of decedent's estate that passes to issue of decedent's predeceased spouse

(a) For purposes of distributing real property under this section if the decedent had a predeceased spouse who died not more than 15 years before the decedent and there is no surviving spouse or issue of the decedent, the portion of the decedent's estate attributable to the decedent's predeceased spouse passes as follows:

(1) If the decedent is survived by issue of the predeceased spouse, to the surviving issue of the predeceased spouse; if they are all of the same degree of kinship to the predeceased spouse they take equally, but if of unequal degree those of more remote degree take in the manner provided in Section 240.

(2) If there is no surviving issue of the predeceased spouse but the decedent is survived by a parent or parents of the predeceased spouse, to the predeceased spouse's surviving parent or parents equally.

(3) If there is no surviving issue or parent of the predeceased spouse but the decedent is survived by issue of a parent of the predeceased spouse, to the surviving issue of the parents of the predeceased spouse or either of them, the issue taking equally if they are all of the same degree of kinship to the predeceased spouse, but if of unequal degree those of more remote degree take in the manner provided in Section 240.

(4) If the decedent is not survived by issue, parent, or issue of a parent of the predeceased spouse, to the next of kin of the decedent in the manner provided in Section 6402.

(5) If the portion of the decedent's estate attributable to the decedent's predeceased spouse would otherwise escheat to the state because there is no kin of the decedent to take under Section 6402, the portion of the decedent's estate attributable to the predeceased spouse passes to the next of kin of the predeceased spouse who shall take in the same manner as the next of kin of the decedent take under Section 6402.

(b) For purposes of distributing personal property under this section if the decedent had a predeceased spouse who died not more than five years before the decedent, and there is no surviving spouse or issue of the decedent, the portion of the decedent's estate attributable to the decedent's predeceased spouse passes as follows:

(1) If the decedent is survived by issue of the predeceased spouse, to the surviving issue of the predeceased spouse; if they are all of the same degree of kinship to the predeceased spouse they take equally, but if of unequal degree those of more remote degree take in the manner provided in Section 240.

(2) If there is no surviving issue of the predeceased spouse but the decedent is survived by a parent or parents of the predeceased spouse, to the predeceased spouse's surviving parent or parents equally.

(3) If there is no surviving issue or parent of the predeceased spouse but the decedent is survived by issue of a parent of the predeceased spouse, to the surviving issue of the parents of the predeceased spouse or either of them, the issue taking equally if they are all of the same degree of kinship to the predeceased spouse, but if of unequal degree those of more remote degree take in the manner provided in Section 240.

(4) If the decedent is not survived by issue, parent, or issue of a parent of the predeceased spouse, to the next of kin of the decedent in the manner provided in Section 6402.

(5) If the portion of the decedent's estate attributable to the decedent's predeceased spouse would otherwise escheat to the state because there is no kin of the decedent to take under Section 6402, the portion of the decedent's estate attributable to the predeceased spouse passes to the next of kin of the predeceased spouse who shall take in the same manner as the next of kin of the decedent take under Section 6402.

(c) For purposes of disposing of personal property under subdivision (b), the claimant heir bears the burden of proof to show the exact personal property to be disposed of to the heir.

(d) For purposes of providing notice under any provision of this code with respect to an estate that may include personal property subject to distribution under subdivision (b), if the aggregate fair market value of tangible and intangible personal property with a written record of title or ownership in the estate is believed in good faith by the petitioning party to be less than ten thousand dollars ($10,000), the petitioning party need not give notice to the issue or next of kin of the predeceased spouse. If the personal property is subsequently determined to have an aggregate fair market value in excess of ten thousand dollars ($10,000), notice shall be given to the issue or next of kin of the predeceased spouse as provided by law.

(e) For the purposes of disposing of property pursuant to subdivision (b), "personal property" means that personal property in which there is a written record of title or ownership and the value of which in the aggregate is ten thousand dollars ($10,000) or more.

(f) For the purposes of this section, the "portion of the decedent's estate attributable to the decedent's predeceased spouse" means all of the following property in the decedent's estate:

(1) One-half of the community property in existence at the time of the death of the predeceased spouse.

(2) One-half of any community property, in existence at the time of death of the predeceased spouse, which was given to the decedent by the predeceased spouse by way of gift, descent, or devise.

(3) That portion of any community property in which the predeceased spouse had any incident of ownership and which vested in the decedent upon the death of the predeceased spouse by right of survivorship.

(4) Any separate property of the predeceased spouse which came to the decedent by gift, descent, or devise of the predeceased spouse or which vested in the decedent upon the death of the predeceased spouse by right of survivorship.

(g) For the purposes of this section, quasi-community property shall be treated the same as community property.

(h) For the purposes of this section:

(1) Relatives of the predeceased spouse conceived before the decedent's death but born thereafter inherit as if they had been born in the lifetime of the decedent.

(2) A person who is related to the predeceased spouse through two lines of relationship is entitled to only a single share based on the relationship which would entitle the person to the larger share.

(Stats. 1990 (A.B. 759) ch. 79, §14, effective July 1, 1991.)

§6412. Abolition of dower and curtesy

Except to the extent provided in Section 120 [establishing a surviving spouse's right to elect against the decedent's will regarding non-community real property, located in California, of a nondomiciliary decedent], the estates of dower and curtesy are not recognized.

(Stats. 1990 (A.B. 759), ch. 79, §14, effective July 1, 1991.)

§13501. Property that is subject to administration

Except as provided in Chapter 6 (commencing with Section 6600) of Division 6 and in Part 1 (commencing with Section 13000) of this division, the following property of the decedent is subject to administration under this code:

(a) Property passing to someone other than the surviving spouse under the decedent's will or by intestate succession.

(b) Property disposed of in trust under the decedent's will.

(c) Property in which the decedent's will limits the surviving spouse to a qualified ownership. For the purposes of this subdivision, a devise to the surviving spouse that is conditioned on the spouse surviving the decedent by a specified period of time is not a "qualified ownership" interest if the specified period of time has expired.

(Stats. 1990 (A.B. 759), ch. 79, §14, effective July 1, 1991.)

§13656. No administration is necessary if all of decedent's property passes to surviving spouse

(a) If the court finds that all of the estate of the deceased spouse is property passing to the surviving spouse, the court shall issue an order describing the property, determining that the property is property passing to the surviving spouse, and determining that no administration is necessary. The court may issue any further orders which may be necessary to cause delivery of the property or its proceeds to the surviving spouse.

(b) If the court finds that all or part of the estate of the deceased spouse is not property passing to the surviving spouse, the court shall issue an order (1) describing any property which is not property passing to the surviving spouse, determining that that property does not pass to the surviving spouse and determining that that property is subject to administration under this code and (2) describing the property, if any, which is property passing to the surviving spouse, determining that that property passes to the surviving spouse, and determining that no administration of that property is necessary. If the court determines that property passes to the surviving spouse, the court may issue any further orders which may be necessary to cause delivery of that property or its proceeds to the surviving spouse.

(c) If the petition filed under this chapter includes a description of the interest of the surviving spouse in the community or quasi-community property, or both, which belongs to the surviving spouse pursuant to Section 100 or 101 and the court finds that the interest belongs to the surviving spouse, the court shall issue an order describing the property and confirming the ownership of the surviving spouse and may issue any further orders which may be necessary to cause ownership of the property to be confirmed in the surviving spouse.

(Stats. 1990 (A.B. 759), ch. 79, §14, effective July 1, 1991.)

CALIFORNIA CIVIL CODE

§682.1. Community property of husband and wife shall pass to the survivor without administration

(a) Community property of a husband and wife, when expressly declared in the transfer document to be community property with right of survivorship, and which may be accepted in writing on the face of the document by a statement signed or initialed by the grantees, shall, upon the death of one of the spouses, pass to the survivor, without administration, pursuant to the terms of the instrument, subject to the same procedures, as property held in joint tenancy. Prior to the death of either spouse, the right of survivorship may be terminated pursuant to the same procedures by which a joint tenancy may be severed. Part I (commencing with Section 5000) of Division 5 of the Probate Code and Chapter 2 (commencing with Section 13540), Chapter 3 (commencing with Section 13550) and Chapter 3.5 (commencing with Section 13560) of Part 2 of Division 8 of the Probate Code apply to this property.

(b) This section does not apply to a joint account in a financial institution to which Part 2 (commencing with Section 5100) of Division 5 of the Probate Code applies.

(c) This section shall become operative on July 1, 2001, and shall apply to instruments created on or after that date.

(Stats. 2000 (A.B. 2913), ch. 645, §1, effective July 1, 2001.)

CALIFORNIA CODE OF CIVIL PROCEDURE

§377.60. Persons with standing to sue for wrongful death of family member

A cause of action for the death of a person caused by the wrongful act or neglect of another may be asserted by any of the following persons or by the decedent's personal representative on their behalf:

(a) The decedent's surviving spouse, domestic partner, children, and issue of deceased children, or, if there is no surviving issue of the decedent, the persons, including the surviving spouse or domestic partner, who would be entitled to the property of the decedent by intestate succession.

(b) Whether or not qualified under subdivision (a), if they were dependent on the decedent, the putative spouse, children of the putative spouse, stepchildren, or parents. As used in this subdivision, "putative spouse" means the surviving spouse of a void or voidable marriage who is found by the court to have believed in good faith that the marriage to the decedent was valid.

(c) A minor, whether or not qualified under subdivision (a) or (b), if, at the time of the decedent's death, the minor resided for the previous 180 days in the decedent's household and was dependent on the decedent for one-half or more of the minor's support.

(d) This section applies to any cause of action arising on or after January 1, 1993.

(e) The addition of this section by Chapter 178 of the Statutes of 1992 was not intended to adversely affect the standing of any party having standing under prior law, and the standing of parties governed by that version of this section as added by Chapter 178 of the Statutes of 1992 shall be the same as specified herein as amended by Chapter 563 of the Statutes of 1996.

(f)(1) For the purpose of this section, "domestic partner" means a person who, at the time of the decedent' s death, was the domestic partner of the decedent in a registered domestic partnership established in accordance with subdivision (b) of Section 297 of the Family Code.

(2) Notwithstanding paragraph (1), for a death occurring prior to January 1, 2002, a person may maintain a cause of action pursuant to this section as a domestic partner of the decedent by establishing the factors listed in paragraphs (1) to (6), inclusive, of subdivision (b) of Section 297 of the Family Code, as it read pursuant to Section 3 of Chapter 893 of the Statutes of 2001, prior to its becoming inoperative on January 1, 2005.

(3) The amendments made to this subdivision during the 2003-04 Regular Session of the Legislature are not intended to revive any cause of action that has been fully and finally adjudicated by the courts, or that has been settled, or as to which the applicable limitations period has run.

(Stats. 1992 (S.B. 1496), ch. 178, §20. Amended by Stats. 1996 (S.B. 392), ch. 563, §1; Stats. 1997 (S.B. 449), ch. 13, §1, effective May 23, 1997; Stats. 2001 (A.B. 25), ch. 893, §2; Stats. 2004 (A.B. 2580), ch. 947 §1, effective January 1, 2005.)

CALIFORNIA FAMILY CODE

§751. Spouses' interests in community property are present, existing, and equal

The respective interests of the husband and wife in community property during continuance of the marriage relation are present, existing, and equal interests.

(Stats. 1992 (A.B. 2650), ch. 162, §10, effective January 1, 1994.)

§752. Neither spouse has interest in other's separate property

Except as otherwise provided by statute, neither husband nor wife has any interest in the separate property of the other.

(Stats. 1992 (A.B. 2650), ch. 162, §10, effective January 1, 1994.)

§2251. Status of "putative spouse"

(a) If a determination is made that a marriage is void or voidable and the court finds that either party or both parties believed in good faith that the marriage was valid, the court shall:

(1) Declare the party or parties to have the status of a putative spouse.

(2) If the division of property is in issue, divide, in accordance with Division 7 (commencing with Section 2500), that property acquired during the union which would have been community property or quasi-community property if the union had not been void or voidable. This property is known as "quasi-marital property".

(b) If the court expressly reserves jurisdiction, it may make the property division at a time after the judgment.

(Stats. 1992 (A.B. 2650), ch. 162, §10, effective January 1, 1994.)

§2254. Court may order support for putative spouse

The court may, during the pendency of a proceeding for nullity of marriage or upon judgment of nullity of marriage, order a party to pay for the support of the other party in the same manner as if the marriage had not been void or voidable if the party for whose benefit the order is made is found to be a putative spouse.

(Stats. 1992 (A.B. 2650), ch. 162, §10, effective January 1, 1994.)

CALIFORNIA PENAL CODE

§281. "Bigamy" defined

(a) Every person having a husband or wife living, who marries any other person, except in the cases specified in Section 282, is guilty of bigamy.

(b) Upon a trial for bigamy, it is not necessary to prove either of the marriages by the register, certificate, or other record evidence thereof, but the marriages may be proved by evidence which is admissible to prove a marriage in other cases; and when the second marriage took place out of this state, proof of that fact, accompanied with proof of cohabitation thereafter in this state, is sufficient to sustain the charge.

(Enacted 1872. Amended by Stats. 1987, ch. 828, §17; Stats. 1989, ch. 897, §18.)

§282. Bigamy: exceptions

Section 281 does not extend to any of the following:

(a) To any person by reason of any former marriage whose husband or wife by such marriage has been absent for five successive years without being known to such person within that time to be living.

(b) To any person by reason of any former marriage which has been pronounced void, annulled, or dissolved by the judgment of a competent court.

(Enacted 1872. Amended by Stats.1987, c. 828, §18.)

§283. Bigamy: punishment

Bigamy is punishable by a fine not exceeding ten thousand dollars ($10,000) or by imprisonment in a county jail not exceeding one year or in the state prison.

(Enacted 1872. Amended by Stats. 1905, ch. 272, p. 245, §1; Stats. 1949, ch. 1252, p. 2205, §1; Stats. 1976, ch. 1139, p. 5110, §172, effective July 1, 1977; Stats. 1983, ch. 1092, §264, urgency, effective September 27, 1983, operative January 1, 1984.)

2. Intestate Share of Surviving Domestic Partner

In 1999, California passed its first statewide domestic partnership law (Stats. 1999 (A.B. 26), ch. 588). Subsequent legislation (explained below) significantly expanded the scope of benefits provided to state domestic partners.

California's domestic partnership law applies to same-sex couples and also to those opposite-sex couples in which one partner is over the age of 62. The latter provision was included in order to redress shortcomings of the Social Security Act that result in the elderly losing survivor benefits by remarrying. On the policy rationale for expanding domestic partnerships to include older opposite-sex couples, see Megan E. Callan, Comment, The More, The Not Marry-er: In Search of a Policy Behind Eligibility for California Domestic Partnerships, 40 San Diego L. Rev. 427 (2003).

In adopting domestic partnership legislation, California is among the small but growing number of states that recognize the rights of same-sex couples. In May 2007, Oregon became the ninth state to offer either civil unions or domestic partnerships. In addition to California, the other states are Connecticut, Hawaii, Maine, New Hampshire, New Jersey, Vermont, and Washington. The District of Columbia also offers protection to same-sex partners. However, whereas some of these jurisdictions grant same-sex couples exactly the same legal rights as spouses, other states offer more limited rights to domestic partners.

In 2003, Massachusetts became the first state to recognize same-sex marriage. Several countries also recognize the rights of same-sex couples to marry, including Belgium, Canada, the Netherlands, South Africa, and Spain. Israel recognizes the validity of marriages of same-sex couples entered into in foreign jurisdictions.

For probate purposes in California, domestic partners are defined by reference to Family Code section 297 (Cal. Prob. Code §37; Cal. Fam. Code §297(a)). In addition to sharing the same residence, each partner must not be married to another person or currently in another domestic partnership, must not be related to the other partner by blood, must be at least 18 years old, and must be capable of consent (Cal. Fam. Code §297(b)(1) - (4) and (6)). To formally register as domestic partners, a couple must file a notarized Declaration of Domestic Partnership with the Secretary of State (Cal. Fam. Code §§297(b), 298.5(a)).

Beginning in 2001, state statutes explicitly gave domestic partners most of the same rights as spouses with respect to conservatorships, intestate succession, will revocation, use of statutory wills, and estate administration (Stats. 2001 (A.B. 25), ch. 893; Stats. 2002 (A.B. 2216), ch. 447, effective July 1, 2003). In July 2003, California domestic partners obtained the same right as spouses to inherit a partner's separate property in case of intestacy (Cal. Prob. Code §6401(c)).

The legislation establishing that right was spearheaded by Keith Bradkowski, the domestic partner of a male flight attendant aboard one of the planes that struck the World Trade Center on September 11, 2001. The couple had registered as domestic partners with the Secretary of State but the decedent had not executed a will, leaving Bradkowski unable to inherit any of his deceased partner's estate. Ann E. Marimow, A State Extends Inheritance Rights: San Carlos Man Who Lost Partner Helped Pass Bill, S.J. Mercury News, September 11, 2002, at 19. See also Nancy J. Knauer, The September 11 Attacks and Surviving Same-Sex Partners: Defining Family Through Tragedy, 75 Temple L. Rev. 31 (2002).

As of January 1, 2005, California legislation (A.B. 205) vastly expanded the rights and responsibilities of domestic partners. It explicitly granted domestic partners "the same rights, protections, and benefits," and imposed upon them "the same responsibilities, obligations, and duties under law, whether they derive from statutes, administrative regulations, court rules, government policies, common law, or any other provisions or sources of law, as are granted to and imposed upon spouses" (Cal. Fam. Code §297.5(a)). In addition, it made former or surviving domestic partners legally equivalent to former or surviving spouses; and with respect to a child of either partner, it made domestic partners subject to the same rights and obligations as spouses (Cal. Fam. Code

§297.5(b), (c) and (d)). Furthermore, the Family Code states that all state laws referring to spouses shall be construed to apply to domestic partners as well (Cal. Fam. Code §297.5(l)).

This broad grant of rights notably includes state laws relating to community property (Cal. Fam. Code §§297.5(a)-(c), (g), (m), 299(a)(6)-(7), and 299.3). For couples who entered into state domestic partnerships before January 1, 2005 (the effective date of A.B. 205), the laws of community property apply retroactively to the date that the couple entered into the domestic partnership (Cal. Fam. Code §297.5(m)(1)). Prior to January 1, 2005, the provisions of Probate Code section 6401(a) and (b), which allow a spouse to inherit the decedent's entire community and quasi-community property, did not apply to domestic partners. However, now that domestic partners are entitled to community property and have the same rights and responsibilities as spouses, sections 6401(a) and (b) would allow domestic partners as well to inherit community and quasi-community property. In 2006, the state legislature enacted legislation permitting registered domestic partners to file income tax returns jointly or separately on the same terms as spouses, and also recognized the earned income of registered domestic partners as community property (S.B. 1827, amending Cal. Fam. Code §297.5 and Cal. Rev. & Tax. Code §§17024.5, 18521).

CALIFORNIA PROBATE CODE

§37. Domestic partner defined for probate purposes

(a) "Domestic partner" means one of two persons who have filed a Declaration of Domestic Partnership with the Secretary of State pursuant to Division 2.5 (commencing with Section 297) of the Family Code, provided that the domestic partnership has not been terminated pursuant to Section 299 of the Family Code.

(b) Notwithstanding Section 299 of the Family Code, if a domestic partnership is terminated by the death of one of the parties and Notice of Termination was not filed by either party prior to the date of death of the decedent, the domestic partner who survives the deceased is a surviving domestic partner, and shall be entitled to the rights of a surviving domestic partner as provided in this code.

(Stats. 2001 (A.B. 25), ch. 893, §13.)

§6401. Intestate share of surviving spouse or surviving domestic partner

(a) As to community property, the intestate share of the surviving spouse is the one-half of the community property that belongs to the decedent under Section 100.

(b) As to quasi-community property, the intestate share of the surviving spouse is the one-half of the quasi-community property that belongs to the decedent under Section 101.

(c) As to separate property, the intestate share of the surviving spouse or surviving domestic partner, as defined in subdivision (b) of Section 37, is as follows:

(1) The entire intestate estate if the decedent did not leave any surviving issue, parent, brother, sister, or issue of a deceased brother or sister.

(2) One-half of the intestate estate in the following cases:

(A) Where the decedent leaves only one child or the issue of one deceased child.

(B) Where the decedent leaves no issue but leaves a parent or parents or their issue or the issue of either of them.

(3) One-third of the intestate estate in the following cases:

(A) Where the decedent leaves more than one child.

(B) Where the decedent leaves one child and the issue of one or more deceased children.

(C) Where the decedent leaves issue of two or more deceased children.

(Enacted Stats. 1990 (A.B. 759), ch. 79, §14, effective July 1, 1991. Amended Stats. 2002 (A.B. 2216), ch. 447, §1, effective July 1, 2003.)

§6402. Intestate share of surviving issue, parents, grandparents, predeceased spouse and next of kin

Except as provided in Section 6402.5, the part of the intestate estate not passing to the surviving spouse or surviving domestic partner, as defined in subdivision (b) of Section 37, under Section 6401, or the entire intestate estate if there is no surviving spouse or domestic partner, passes as follows:

(a) To the issue of the decedent, the issue taking equally if they are all of the same degree of kinship to the decedent, but if of unequal degree those of more remote degree take in the manner provided in Section 240.

(b) If there is no surviving issue, to the decedent's parent or parents equally.

(c) If there is no surviving issue or parent, to the issue of the parents or either of them, the issue taking equally if they are all of the same degree of kinship to the decedent, but if of unequal degree those of more remote degree take in the manner provided in Section 240.

(d) If there is no surviving issue, parent or issue of a parent, but the decedent is survived by one or more grandparents or issue of grandparents, to the grandparent or grandparents equally, or to the issue of those grandparents if there is no surviving grandparent, the issue taking equally if they are all of the same degree of kinship to the decedent, but if of unequal degree those of more remote degree take in the manner provided in Section 240.

(e) If there is no surviving issue, parent or issue of a parent, grandparent or issue of a grandparent, but the decedent is survived by the issue of a predeceased spouse, to that issue, the issue taking equally if they are all of the same degree of kinship to the predeceased spouse, but if of unequal degree those of more remote degree take in the manner provided in Section 240.

(f) If there is no surviving issue, parent or issue of a parent, grandparent or issue of a grandparent, or issue of a predeceased spouse, but the decedent is survived by next of kin, to the next of kin in equal degree, but where there are two or more collateral kindred in equal degree who claim through different ancestors, those who claim through the nearest ancestor are preferred to those claiming through an ancestor more remote.

(g) If there is no surviving next of kin of the decedent and no surviving issue of a predeceased spouse of the decedent, but the decedent is survived by the parents of a predeceased spouse or the issue of those parents, to the parent or parents equally, or to the issue of those parents if both are deceased, the issue taking equally if they are all of the same degree of kinship to the predeceased spouse, but if of unequal degree those of more remote degree take in the manner provided in Section 240.

(Stats. 1990 (A.B. 759), ch. 79, §14, effective July 1, 1991. Amended by Stats. 2002 (A.B. 2216), ch. 447, §2, effective July 1, 2003.)

CALIFORNIA FAMILY CODE

§297. Requirements to establish domestic partnership

(a) Domestic partners are two adults who have chosen to share one another's lives in an intimate and committed relationship of mutual caring.

(b) A domestic partnership shall be established in California when both persons file a Declaration of Domestic Partnership with the Secretary of State pursuant to this division, and, at the time of filing, all of the following requirements are met:

(1) Both persons have a common residence.

(2) Neither person is married to someone else or is a member of another domestic partnership with someone else that has not been terminated, dissolved, or adjudged a nullity.

(3) The two persons are not related by blood in a way that would prevent them from being married to each other in this state.

(4) Both persons are at least 18 years of age.

(5) Either of the following:

(A) Both persons are members of the same sex.

(B) One or both of the persons meet the eligibility criteria under Title II of the Social Security Act as defined in 42 U.S.C. Section 402(a) for old-age insurance benefits or Title XVI of the Social Security Act as defined in 42 U.S.C. Section 1381 for aged individuals. Notwithstanding any other provision of this section, persons of opposite sexes may not constitute a domestic partnership unless one or both of the persons are over the age of 62.

(6) Both persons are capable of consenting to the domestic partnership.

(c) "Have a common residence" means that both domestic partners share the same residence. It is not necessary that the legal right to possess the common residence be in both of their names. Two people have a common residence even if one or both have additional residences. Domestic partners do not cease to have a common residence if one leaves the common residence but intends to return.

(Stats. 1999 (A.B. 26), ch. 588, §2. Amended by Stats. 2001 (A.B. 25), ch. 893, §3; Stats. 2003 (A.B. 205), ch. 421, §3, effective January 1, 2005.)

§297.5. Registered domestic partners shall have the same rights and responsibilities as spouses

(a) Registered domestic partners shall have the same rights, protections, and benefits, and shall be subject to the same responsibilities, obligations, and duties under law, whether they derive from statutes, administrative regulations, court rules, government policies, common law, or any other provisions or sources of law, as are granted to and imposed upon spouses.

(b) Former registered domestic partners shall have the same rights, protections, and benefits, and shall be subject to the same responsibilities, obligations, and duties under law, whether they derive from statutes, administrative regulations, court rules, government policies, common law, or any other provisions or sources of law, as are granted to and imposed upon former spouses.

(c) A surviving registered domestic partner, following the death of the other partner, shall have the same rights, protections, and benefits, and shall be subject to the same responsibilities, obligations, and duties under law, whether they derive from statutes, administrative regulations, court rules, government policies, common law, or any other provisions or sources of law, as are granted to and imposed upon a widow or a widower.

(d) The rights and obligations of registered domestic partners with respect to a child of either of them shall be the same as those of spouses. The rights and obligations of former or surviving registered domestic partners with respect to a child of either of them shall be the same as those of former or surviving spouses.

(e) To the extent that provisions of California law adopt, refer to, or rely upon, provisions of federal law in a way that otherwise would cause registered domestic partners to be treated differently than spouses, registered domestic partners shall be treated by California law as if federal law recognized a domestic partnership in the same manner as California law.

(f) Registered domestic partners shall have the same rights regarding nondiscrimination as those provided to spouses.

(g) No public agency in this state may discriminate against any person or couple on the ground that the person is a registered domestic partner rather than a spouse or that the couple are registered domestic partners rather than spouses, except that nothing in this section applies to modify eligibility for long-term care plans pursuant to Chapter 15 (commencing with Section 21660) of Part 3 of Division 5 of Title 2 of the Government Code.

(h) This act does not preclude any state or local agency from exercising its regulatory authority to implement statutes providing rights to, or imposing responsibilities upon, domestic partners.

(i) This section does not amend or modify any provision of the California Constitution or any provision of any statute that was adopted by initiative.

(j) Where necessary to implement the rights of registered domestic partners under this act, gender-specific terms referring to spouses shall be construed to include domestic partners.

(k)(1) For purposes of the statutes, administrative regulations, court rules, government policies, common law, and any other provision or source of law governing the rights, protections, and benefits, and the responsibilities, obligations, and duties of registered domestic partners in this state, as effectuated by this section, with respect to community property, mutual responsibility for debts to third parties, the right in particular circumstances of either partner to seek financial support from the other following the dissolution of the partnership, and other rights and duties as between the partners concerning ownership of property, any reference to the date of a marriage shall be deemed to refer to the date of registration of a domestic partnership with the state.

(2) Notwithstanding paragraph (1), for domestic partnerships registered with the state before January 1, 2005, an agreement between the domestic partners that the partners intend to be governed by the requirements set forth in Sections 1600 to 1620, inclusive, and which complies with those sections, except for the agreement's effective date, shall be enforceable as provided by Sections 1600 to 1620, inclusive, if that agreement was fully executed and in force as of June 30, 2005.

(Stats. 2003 (A.B. 205), ch. 421, §4, effective January 1, 2005; Stats. 2004 (A.B. 2580), ch. 947, §2; Stats. 2006 (S.B. 1827), ch. 802, §2.)

§298. Requisite forms to establish and terminate domestic partnerships

(a)(1) The Secretary of State shall prepare forms entitled "Declaration of Domestic Partnership" and "Notice of Termination of Domestic Partnership" to meet the requirements of this division. These forms shall require the signature and seal of an acknowledgment by a notary public to be binding and valid.

(2) When funding allows, the Secretary of State shall include on the form notice that a lesbian, gay, bisexual, and transgender specific domestic abuse brochure is available upon request.

(b)(1) The Secretary of State shall distribute these forms to each county clerk. These forms shall be available to the public at the office of the Secretary of State and each county clerk.

(2) The Secretary of State shall, by regulation, establish fees for the actual costs of processing each of these forms, and the cost for preparing and sending the mailings and notices required pursuant to Section 299.3, and shall charge these fees to persons filing the forms.

(3) There is hereby established a fee of twenty-three dollars ($23) to be charged in addition to the existing fees established by regulation to persons filing domestic partner registrations pursuant to Section 297 for development and support of a lesbian, gay, bisexual, and transgender curriculum for training workshops on domestic violence, conducted pursuant to Section 13823.15 of the Penal Code, and for the support of a minigrant program to promote healthy nonviolent relationships in the lesbian, gay, bisexual, and transgender community. This paragraph shall not apply to persons of opposite sexes filing a domestic partnership registration and who meet the qualifications described in subparagraph (B) of paragraph (5) of subdivision (b) of Section 297.

(4) The fee established by paragraph (3) shall be deposited in the Equality in Prevention and Services for Domestic Abuse Fund, which is hereby established. The fund shall be administered by the Office of Emergency Services, and expenditures from the fund shall be used to support the purposes of paragraph (3).

(c) The Declaration of Domestic Partnership shall require each person who wants to become a domestic partner to (1) state that he or she meets the requirements of Section 297 at the time the form is signed, (2) provide a mailing address, (3) state that he or she consents to the jurisdiction of the Superior Courts of California for the purpose of a proceeding to obtain a judgment of dissolution or nullity of the domestic partnership or for legal separation of partners in the domestic partnership, or for any other proceeding related to the partners' rights and obligations, even if one or both partners ceases to be a resident of, or to maintain a domicile in, this state, (4) sign the form with a declaration that representations made therein are true, correct, and contain no material omissions of fact to the best knowledge and belief of the applicant, and (5) have a notary public acknowledge his or her signature. Both partners' signatures shall be affixed to one Declaration of Domestic Partnership form, which form shall then be transmitted to the Secretary of State according to the instructions provided on the form. Filing an intentionally and materially false Declaration of Domestic Partnership shall be punishable as a misdemeanor.

(Stats. 1999 (A.B. 26), ch. 588, §2; Stats. 2003 (A.B. 205), ch. 421, §5, effective January 1, 2005; Stats. 2006 (A.B. 2051), ch. 856, §2.)

§298.5. Procedure for filing and registering the requisite form for establishment of a domestic partnership

(a) Two persons desiring to become domestic partners may complete and file a Declaration of Domestic Partnership with the Secretary of State.

(b) The Secretary of State shall register the Declaration of Domestic Partnership in a registry for those partnerships, and shall return a copy of the registered form and a Certificate of Registered Domestic Partnership, and except for those opposite sex domestic partners who meet the qualifications described in subparagraph (B) of paragraph (5) of subdivision

(b) of Section 297, a copy of the brochure that is made available to county clerks and the Secretary of State by the State Department of Health Services pursuant to Section 358 and distributed to individuals receiving a confidential marriage license pursuant to Section 503, to the domestic partners at the mailing address provided by the domestic partners.

(c) No person who has filed a Declaration of Domestic Partnership may file a new Declaration of Domestic Partnership or enter a civil marriage with someone other than their registered domestic partner unless the most recent domestic partnership has been terminated or a final judgment of dissolution or nullity of the most recent domestic partnership has been entered. This prohibition does not apply if the previous domestic partnership ended because one of the partners died.

(d) When funding allows, the Secretary of State shall print and make available upon request, pursuant to Section 358, a lesbian, gay, bisexual, and transgender specific domestic abuse brochure developed by the State Department of Health Services and made available to the Secretary of State to domestic partners who qualify pursuant to Section 297. *(Stats. 1999 (A.B. 26), ch. 588, §2; Stats. 2003 (A.B. 205), ch. 421, §6, effective January 1, 2005; Stats. 2006 (A.B. 2051), ch. 856, §3.)*

§299. Procedures for terminating a domestic partnership

(a) A registered domestic partnership may be terminated without filing a proceeding for dissolution of domestic partnership by the filing of a Notice of Termination of Domestic Partnership with the Secretary of State pursuant to this section, provided that all of the following conditions exist at the time of the filing:

(1) The Notice of Termination of Domestic Partnership is signed by both registered domestic partners.

(2) There are no children of the relationship of the parties born before or after registration of the domestic partnership or adopted by the parties after registration of the domestic partnership, and neither of the registered domestic partners, to their knowledge, is pregnant.

(3) The registered domestic partnership is not more than five years in duration.

(4) Neither party has any interest in real property wherever situated, with the exception of the lease of a residence occupied by either party which satisfies the following requirements:

(A) The lease does not include an option to purchase.

(B) The lease terminates within one year from the date of filing of the Notice of Termination of Domestic Partnership.

(5) There are no unpaid obligations in excess of the amount described in paragraph (6) of subdivision (a) of Section 2400, as adjusted by subdivision (b) of Section 2400, incurred by either or both of the parties after registration of the domestic partnership, excluding the amount of any unpaid obligation with respect to an automobile.

(6) The total fair market value of community property assets, excluding all encumbrances and automobiles, including any deferred compensation or retirement plan, is less than the amount described in paragraph (7) of subdivision (a) of Section 2400, as adjusted by subdivision (b) of Section 2400, and neither party has separate property assets, excluding all encumbrances and automobiles, in excess of that amount.

(7) The parties have executed an agreement setting forth the division of assets and the assumption of liabilities of the community property, and have executed any documents, title certificates, bills of sale, or other evidence of transfer necessary to effectuate the agreement.

(8) The parties waive any rights to support by the other domestic partner.

(9) The parties have read and understand a brochure prepared by the Secretary of State describing the requirements, nature, and effect of terminating a domestic partnership.

(10) Both parties desire that the domestic partnership be terminated.

(b) The registered domestic partnership shall be terminated effective six months after the date of filing of the Notice of Termination of Domestic Partnership with the Secretary of State pursuant to this section, provided that neither party has, before that date, filed with the Secretary of State a notice of revocation of the termination of domestic partnership, in the form and content as shall be prescribed by the Secretary of State, and sent to the other party a copy of the notice of revocation by first-class mail, postage prepaid, at the other party's last known address. The effect of termination of a domestic partnership pursuant to this section shall be the same as, and shall be treated for all purposes as, the entry of a judgment of dissolution of a domestic partnership.

(c) The termination of a domestic partnership pursuant to subdivision (b) does not prejudice nor bar the rights of either of the parties to institute an action in the superior court to set aside the termination for fraud, duress, mistake, or any other ground recognized at law or in equity. A court may set aside the termination of domestic partnership and declare the termination of the domestic partnership null and void upon proof that the parties did not meet the requirements of subdivision (a) at the time of the filing of the Notice of Termination of Domestic Partnership with the Secretary of State.

(d) The superior courts shall have jurisdiction over all proceedings relating to the dissolution of domestic partnerships, nullity of domestic partnerships, and legal separation of partners in a domestic partnership. The dissolution of a domestic partnership, nullity of a domestic partnership, and legal separation of partners in a domestic partnership shall follow the same procedures, and the partners shall possess the same rights, protections, and benefits, and be subject to the same responsibilities, obligations, and duties, as apply to the dissolution of marriage, nullity of marriage, and legal separation of spouses in a marriage, respectively, except as provided in subdivision (a), and except that, in accordance with the consent acknowledged by domestic partners in the Declaration of Domestic Partnership form, proceedings for dissolution, nullity, or legal separation of a domestic partnership registered in this state may be filed in the superior courts of this state even if neither domestic partner is a resident of, or maintains a domicile in, the state at the time the proceedings are filed.

(Stats. 2003 (A.B. 205), ch. 421, §8, effective January 1, 2005. Amended by Stats. 2004 (A.B. 2580), ch. 947, §3.)

§299.2. Recognition of other states' same-sex unions

A legal union of two persons of the same sex, other than a marriage, that was validly formed in another jurisdiction, and that is substantially equivalent to a domestic partnership as defined in this part, shall be recognized as a valid domestic partnership in this state regardless of whether it bears the name domestic partnership.

(Stats. 2003 (A.B. 205), ch. 421, §9, effective January 1, 2005.)

§299.3. Notice to registered domestic partners and potential applicants regarding change in law

(a) On or before June 30, 2004, and again on or before December 1, 2004, and again on or before January 31, 2005, the Secretary of State shall send the following letter to the mailing address on file of each registered domestic partner who registered more than one month prior to each of those dates:

"Dear Registered Domestic Partner:

This letter is being sent to all persons who have registered with the Secretary of State as a domestic partner.

Effective January 1, 2005, California's law related to the rights and responsibilities of registered domestic partners will change (or, if you are receiving this letter after that date, the law has changed, as of January 1, 2005). With this new legislation, for purposes of California law, domestic partners will have a great many new rights and responsibilities, including laws governing community property, those governing property transfer, those regarding duties of mutual financial support and mutual responsibilities for certain debts to third parties, and many others. The way domestic partnerships are terminated is also changing. After January 1, 2005, under certain circumstances, it will be necessary to participate in a dissolution proceeding in court to end a domestic partnership.

Domestic partners who do not wish to be subject to these new rights and responsibilities MUST terminate their domestic partnership before January 1, 2005. Under the law in effect until January 1, 2005, your domestic partnership is automatically terminated if you or your partner marry or die while you are registered as domestic partners. It is also terminated if you send to your partner or your partner sends to you, by certified mail, a notice terminating the domestic partnership, or if you and your partner no longer share a common residence. In all cases, you are required to file a Notice of Termination of Domestic Partnership.

If you do not terminate your domestic partnership before January 1, 2005, as provided above, you will be subject to these new rights and responsibilities and, under certain circumstances, you will only be able to terminate your domestic partnership, other than as a result of your domestic partner's death, by the filing of a court action.

Further, if you registered your domestic partnership with the state prior to January 1, 2005, you have until June 30, 2005, to enter into a written agreement with your domestic partner that will be enforceable in the same manner as a premarital agreement under California law, if you intend to be so governed.

If you have any questions about any of these changes, please consult an attorney. If you cannot find an attorney in your locale, please contact your county bar association for a referral.

Sincerely,

The Secretary of State"

(b) From January 1, 2004, to December 31, 2004, inclusive, the Secretary of State shall provide the following notice with all requests for the Declaration of Domestic Partnership form. The Secretary of State also shall attach the Notice to the Declaration of Domestic Partnership form that is provided to the general public on the Secretary of State's Web site:

"NOTICE TO POTENTIAL DOMESTIC PARTNER REGISTRANTS

As of January 1, 2005, California's law of domestic partnership will change.

Beginning at that time, for purposes of California law, domestic partners will have a great many new rights and responsibilities, including laws governing community property, those governing property transfer, those regarding duties of mutual financial support and mutual responsibilities for certain debts to third parties, and many others. The way domestic partnerships are terminated will also change. Unlike current law, which allows partners to end their partnership simply by filing a "Termination of Domestic Partnership" form with the Secretary of State, after January 1, 2005, it will be necessary under certain circumstances to participate in a dissolution proceeding in court to end a domestic partnership.

If you have questions about these changes, please consult an attorney. If you cannot find an attorney in your area, please contact your county bar association for a referral."

(Stats. 2003 (A.B. 205), ch. 421, §10; Amended by Stats. 2004 (A.B. 2580), ch. 947, §4; Stats. 2005, (S.B. 1108), ch. 22, §59.)

§299.6. Preemption of local ordinances or laws

(a) Any local ordinance or law that provides for the creation of a "domestic partnership" shall be preempted on and after July 1, 2000, except as provided in subdivision (c).

(b) Domestic partnerships created under any local domestic partnership ordinance or law before July 1, 2000, shall remain valid. On and after July 1, 2000, domestic partnerships previously established under a local ordinance or law shall be governed by this division and the rights and duties of the partners shall be those set out in this division, except as provided in subdivision (c), provided a Declaration of Domestic Partnership is filed by the domestic partners under Section 298.5.

(c) Any local jurisdiction may retain or adopt ordinances, policies, or laws that offer rights within that jurisdiction to domestic partners as defined by Section 297 or as more broadly defined by the local jurisdiction's ordinances, policies, or laws, or that impose duties upon third parties regarding domestic partners as defined by Section 297 or as more broadly defined by the local jurisdiction's ordinances, policies, or laws, that are in addition to the rights and duties set out in this division, and the local rights may be conditioned upon the agreement of the domestic partners to assume the additional obligations set forth in this division.
(Enacted Stats. 1999 (A.B. 26), ch. 588 §2.)

CALIFORNIA GOVERNMENT CODE

§14771. Notice to state agencies of need to include references to domestic partners on state forms

(a) The director [of the Department of General Services], through the forms management center, shall do all of the following:

(1) Establish a State Forms Management Program for all state agencies, and provide assistance in establishing internal forms management capabilities.

(2) Study, develop, coordinate and initiate forms of interagency and common administrative usage, and establish basic state design and specification criteria to effect the standardization of public-use forms.

(3) Provide assistance to state agencies for economical forms design and forms artwork composition and establish and supervise control procedures to prevent the undue creation and reproduction of public-use forms.

(4) Provide assistance, training, and instruction in forms management techniques to state agencies, forms management representatives, and departmental forms coordinators, and provide direct administrative and forms management assistance to new state organizations as they are created.

(5) Maintain a central cross index of public-use forms to facilitate the standardization of these forms, to eliminate redundant forms, and to provide a central source of information on the usage and availability of forms.

(6) Utilize appropriate procurement techniques to take advantage of competitive bidding, consolidated orders, and contract procurement of forms, and work directly with the Office of State Publishing toward more efficient, economical and timely procurement, receipt, storage, and distribution of state forms.

(7) Coordinate the forms management program with the existing state archives and records management program to ensure timely disposition of outdated forms and related records.

(8) Conduct periodic evaluations of the effectiveness of the overall forms management program and the forms management practices of the individual state agencies, and maintain records which indicate net dollar savings which have been realized through centralized forms management.

(9) Develop and promulgate rules and standards to implement the overall purposes of this section.

(10) Create and maintain by July 1, 1986, a complete and comprehensive inventory of public-use forms in current use by the state.

(11) Establish and maintain, by July 1, 1986, an index of all public-use forms in current use by the state.

(12) Assign, by January 1, 1987, a control number to all public-use forms in current use by the state.

(13) Establish a goal to reduce the existing burden of state collections of public information by 30 percent by July 1, 1987, and to reduce that burden by an additional 15 percent by July 1, 1988.

(14) Notwithstanding any other provision of law, including, but not limited to, Section 14774, provide notice to state agencies, forms management representatives, and departmental forms coordinators, that in the usual course of reviewing and revising all public-use forms that refer to or use the terms spouse, husband, wife, father, mother, marriage, or marital status, that appropriate references to state-registered domestic partner, parent, or state-registered domestic partnership are to be included.

(15) Delegate implementing authority to state agencies where the delegation will result in the most timely and economical method of accomplishing the responsibilities set forth in this section.

The director, through the forms management center, may require any agency to revise any public-use form which the director determines is inefficient.

(b) Due to the need for tax forms to be available to the public on a timely basis, all tax forms, including returns, schedules, notices, and instructions prepared by the Franchise Tax Board for public use in connection with its administration of the Personal Income Tax Law, Senior Citizens Property Tax Assistance and Postponement Law, Bank and Corporation Tax Law, and the Political Reform Act of 1974 and the State Board of Equalization's administration of county assessment standards, state-assessed property, timber tax, sales and use tax, hazardous substances tax, alcoholic beverage tax, cigarette tax, motor vehicle fuel license tax, use fuel tax, energy resources surcharge, emergency telephone users surcharge, insurance tax, and universal telephone service tax shall be exempt from subdivision (a), and, instead, each board shall do all of the following:

(1) Establish a goal to standardize, consolidate, simplify, efficiently manage, and, where possible, reduce the number of tax forms.

(2) Create and maintain, by July 1, 1986, a complete and comprehensive inventory of tax forms in current use by the board.

(3) Establish and maintain, by July 1, 1986, an index of all tax forms in current use by the board.

(4) Report to the Legislature, by January 1, 1987, on its progress to improve the effectiveness and efficiency of all tax forms.

(c) The director, through the forms management center, shall develop and maintain, by December 31, 1995, an ongoing master inventory of all nontax reporting forms required of businesses by state agencies, including a schedule for notifying each state agency of the impending expiration of certain report review requirements pursuant to subdivision (b) of Section 14775.

(Stats. 1975, ch. 398 §1, effective July 1, 1976. Amended by Stats. 1982, ch. 1118 §4; Stats. 1985 ch. 1263 §3; Stats. 1994 (S.B. 1898), ch. 769 § 2; Stats. 2003 (A.B. 205), ch. 421 §12; Stats. 2004 (A.B. 2580), ch. 947 §5.)

CALIFORNIA CODE OF CIVIL PROCEDURE

§377.60. Persons who have standing to sue for wrongful death of family member

A cause of action for the death of a person caused by the wrongful act or neglect of another may be asserted by any of the following persons or by the decedent's personal representative on their behalf:

(a) The decedent's surviving spouse, domestic partner, children, and issue of deceased children, or, if there is no surviving issue of the decedent, the persons, including the surviving spouse or domestic partner, who would be entitled to the property of the decedent by intestate succession.

(b) Whether or not qualified under subdivision (a), if they were dependent on the decedent, the putative spouse, children of the putative spouse, stepchildren, or parents. As used in this subdivision, "putative spouse" means the surviving spouse of a void or voidable marriage who is found by the court to have believed in good faith that the marriage to the decedent was valid.

(c) A minor, whether or not qualified under subdivision (a) or (b), if, at the time of the decedent's death, the minor resided for the previous 180 days in the decedent's household and was dependent on the decedent for one-half or more of the minor's support.

(d) This section applies to any cause of action arising on or after January 1, 1993.

(e) The addition of this section by Chapter 178 of the Statutes of 1992 was not intended to adversely affect the standing of any party having standing under prior law, and the standing of parties governed by that version of this section as added by Chapter 178 of the Statutes of 1992 shall be the same as specified herein as amended by Chapter 563 of the Statutes of 1996.

(f)(1) For the purpose of this section, "domestic partner" means a person who, at the time of the decedent' s death, was the domestic partner of the decedent in a registered domestic partnership established in accordance with subdivision (b) of Section 297 of the Family Code.

(2) Notwithstanding paragraph (1), for a death occurring prior to January 1, 2002, a person may maintain a cause of action pursuant to this section as a domestic partner of the decedent by establishing the factors listed in paragraphs (1) to (6), inclusive, of subdivision (b) of Section 297 of the Family Code, as it read pursuant to Section 3 of Chapter 893 of the Statutes of 2001, prior to its becoming inoperative on January 1, 2005.

(3) The amendments made to this subdivision during the 2003-04 Regular Session of the Legislature are not intended to revive any cause of action that has been fully and finally adjudicated by the courts, or that has been settled, or as to which the applicable limitations period has run.

(Stats. 1992 (S.B. 1496), ch. 178, §20. Amended by Stats. 1996 (S.B. 392), ch. 563, §1; Stats. 1997 (S.B. 449), ch. 13, §1, effective May 23, 1997; Stats. 2001 (A.B. 25), ch. 893, §2; Stats. 2004 (A.B. 2580), ch. 947 §1, effective January 1, 2005.)

3. Intestate Share of Surviving Issue

Intestacy schemes generally provide that descendants take the portion of a decedent's intestate estate that does not pass to the surviving spouse (or all of the intestate estate if the decedent is single at the time of death). However, if more than one descendant survives, a determination must be made regarding the applicable method of dividing the decedent's property. If all of the decedent's children are alive, the decedent's property generally passes to them in equal shares (a per capita distribution). But, if some (or all) of the decedent's children predecease the intestate and those dead children leave issue surviving the decedent, then jurisdictions apply one of three different methods of property division:

- **per stirpes,**
- **per capita with representation, or**
- **per capita at each generation.**

The common law adopted a method of division called *per stirpes*. McGovern & Kurtz, *supra*, §2.2 at 53. In this system, the ultimate takers of the intestate's estate are determined by roots or stocks. Under the principle of "representation," a descendant takes the share (or stands in the shoes) of his or her immediate, predeceased ancestor. Note that this method is subject to two principles: (1) a descendant who is related to the decedent more remotely than his or her immediate ancestor cannot inherit intestate if that immediate ancestor is still alive; and (2) in many states, if all the issue are of the same degree of kinship to the decedent (i.e., all are grandchildren), then these issue share equally (see, e.g., Cal. Prob. Code §6402(a)).

To illustrate, suppose the decedent had two children (A and B). One of those children (B) predeceased the decedent, leaving two children (C and D). When the decedent's intestate estate is divided according to a traditional per stirpes

distribution, A would take one-half of the estate, but C and D would each take one-fourth (because they would share their dead parent B's share).

On the other hand, suppose that no child survives a decedent; rather, the decedent is survived only by grandchildren and great-grandchildren. Then, the central question becomes: Which generation shall be the "root generation" or the generation at which the estate is first divided? Under the minority approach announced by Maud v. Catherwood, 155 P.2d 111 (Cal. Ct. App. 1945), the root generation is the generation nearest to the decedent, provided that some members of that generation died leaving issue now surviving (regardless of whether there are any members of the nearest generation who are alive at the decedent's death).

Current California law (Cal. Prob. Code §240) changes that rule. The root generation is the closest generation to the decedent where there are any living takers. Thus, if all of the decedent's children predeceased the decedent, then those children are ignored in the distribution of the intestate estate. Assuming that some of the decedent's children died leaving children surviving, then the first division of the estate takes place at the generation of the grandchildren.

The current California rule (Cal. Prob. Code §240) is based on the original version of UPC §2-106 and, as explained, changed the rule of *Maud*. Note that California Probate Code §240 applies only for decedents who die intestate, or for the makers of wills or trusts, who die on or after January 1, 1985. That is, the *Maud* rule still applies to instruments of testators or settlors who died before January 1, 1985 (Cal. Prob. Code §241).

The current California division (Cal. Prob. Code §240) is sometimes referred to as "per capita with representation." Under this approach if the ultimate takers are related to the decedent in different generations, then the shares are determined by the number of surviving persons in the nearest generation with any living taker plus the number of deceased persons in that generation who left issue surviving.

The UPC no longer follows the "per capita with representation" approach. Rather, as of 1990, the UPC adopted the approach of "per capita at each generation." Under this approach, the root generation is the nearest generation to the decedent with any living takers (i.e., the first generation in which one or more members survived). Then, the shares of the deceased members of that generation who left issue surviving are combined and drop down to the next generation, to be distributed per capita among the takers of that more remote generation.

The current version of the UPC was influenced by the view of Professor Lawrence Waggoner who disapproved of the result (that was possible under the approach of per capita with representation) in which persons in the same generation would take unequal shares. McGovern & Kurtz, *supra*, §2.2 at 53. That is, suppose a decedent had three children (A, B, and C). The decedent dies, leaving C surviving, but A and B have predeceased. A predeceased the decedent, leaving three children surviving (A1, A2, and A3). B predeceased the decedent, leaving one child surviving (B1). Although A1, A2, A3, and B1 are all grandchildren of the decedent, they would not take equal shares under the per-capita-with-representation approach. That is, A1, A2, and A3 would have to divide the one-third share of their deceased parent (A), thereby taking one-ninth respectively of their grandparent's estate. B1, on the other hand, would take one-third (as would C).

Under the approach of "per capita at each generation" as applied to the same fact pattern, C would take one-third of the decedent's estate. Then, the shares of the predeceased children (A and B) who died leaving issue surviving (that is, the other two-thirds of the decedent's estate) would be combined and drop down to the next generation—to be distributed per capita among the takers of the grandchildren's level. That would mean that A1, A2, A3, and B1 would each take one-sixth of the decedent's estate.

Note that the California Probate Code permits the maker of a will, trust, or other instrument to alter the basic distribution scheme of California Probate Code §240. That is, Probate Code §246 permits a will, trust, or other instrument to specify distribution by means of the Maud v. Catherwood approach (by explicit use of the terms "per stirpes" or "by representation" or "by right of representation" or by explicit reference to California Probate Code §246). And California Probate Code §247 permits a will, trust, or other instrument to specify distribution based on the approach of "per capita at each generation" (by use of that specific term or by explicit reference to that particular Code section).

CALIFORNIA PROBATE CODE

§240. Basic method of intestate distribution of shares

If a statute calls for property to be distributed or taken in the manner provided in this section, the property shall be divided into as many equal shares as there are living members of the nearest generation of issue then living and deceased members of that generation who leave issue then

living, each living member of the nearest generation of issue then living receiving one share and the share of each deceased member of that generation who leaves issue then living being divided in the same manner among his or her then living issue.
(Stats. 1990 (A.B. 759), ch. 79, §14, effective July 1, 1991.)

§241. Section 240 applicable to estates of decedents dying on or after January 1, 1985

Section 240 does not apply where the death of the decedent in the case of intestate succession or of the testator, settlor, or other transferor occurred before January 1, 1985, and the law applicable prior to January 1, 1985, shall continue to apply where the death occurred before January 1, 1985.
(Stats. 1990 (A.B. 759), ch. 79, §14, effective July 1, 1991.)

§245. Distribution of shares if instrument fails to specify

(a) Where a will, trust, or other instrument calls for property to be distributed or taken "in the manner provided in Section 240 of the Probate Code," or where a will, trust, or other instrument that expresses no contrary intention provides for issue or descendants to take without specifying the manner, the property to be distributed shall be distributed in the manner provided in Section 240.

(b) Use of the following words without more, as applied to issue or descendants, is not an expression of contrary intention:

(1) "Per capita" when living members of the designated class are not all of the same generation.

(2) Contradictory wording, such as "per capita and per stirpes" or "equally and by right of representation."

(Stats. 1990 (A.B. 759), ch. 79, §14, effective July 1, 1991.)

§246. Distribution of shares if instrument specifies division "by representation" or "per stirpes"

(a) Where a will, trust, or other instrument calls for property to be distributed or taken "in the manner provided in Section 246 of the Probate Code," the property to be distributed shall be divided into as many equal shares as there are living children of the designated ancestor, if any, and deceased children who leave issue then living. Each living child of the designated ancestor is allocated one share, and the share of each deceased child who leaves issue then living is divided in the same manner.

(b) Unless the will, trust, or other instrument expressly provides otherwise, if an instrument executed on or after January 1, 1986, calls for property to be distributed or taken "per stirpes," "by representation," or "by right of representation," the property shall be distributed in the manner provided in subdivision (a).

(c) If a will, trust, or other instrument executed before January 1, 1986, calls for property to be distributed or taken "per stirpes," "by representation," or by "right of representation," the property shall be distributed in the manner provided in subdivision (a), absent a contrary intent of the transferor.
(Stats. 1990 (A.B. 759), ch. 79, §14, effective July 1, 1991.)

§247. Distribution of shares if instrument specifies division "per capita at each generation"

(a) Where a will, trust, or other instrument calls for property to be distributed or taken "in the manner provided in Section 247 of the Probate Code," the property to be distributed shall be divided into as many equal shares as there are living members of the nearest generation of issue then living and deceased members of that generation who leave issue then living. Each living member of the nearest generation of issue then living is allocated one share, and the remaining shares, if any, are combined and then divided and allocated in the same manner among the remaining issue as if the issue already allocated a share and their descendants were then deceased.

(b) Unless the will, trust, or other instrument expressly provides otherwise, if an instrument executed on or after January 1, 1986, calls for property to be distributed or taken "per capita at each generation," the property shall be distributed in the manner provided in subdivision (a).

(c) If a will, trust, or other instrument executed before January 1, 1986, calls for property to be distributed or taken "per capita at each generation," the property shall be distributed in the manner provided in subdivision (a), absent a contrary intent of the transferor.
(Stats. 1990 (A.B. 759), ch. 79, §14, effective July 1, 1991.)

§6402. Intestate share of heirs who take after a surviving spouse or domestic partner

Except as provided in Section 6402.5 [i.e., governing the portion of a decedent's real property attributable to decedent's predeceased spouse who died not more than 15 years before the decedent], the part of the intestate estate not passing to the surviving spouse or surviving domestic partner, as defined in subdivision (b) of Section 37, under Section 6401, or the entire intestate estate if there is no surviving spouse or domestic partner, passes as follows:

(a) To the issue of the decedent, the issue taking equally if they are all of the same degree of kinship to the decedent, but if of unequal degree those of more remote degree take in the manner provided in Section 240.

(b) If there is no surviving issue, to the decedent's parent or parents equally.

(c) If there is no surviving issue or parent, to the issue of the parents or either of them, the issue taking equally if they are all of the same degree of kinship to the decedent, but if of unequal degree those of more remote degree take in the manner provided in Section 240.

(d) If there is no surviving issue, parent or issue of a parent, but the decedent is survived by one or more grandparents or issue of grandparents, to the grandparent or grandparents equally, or to the issue of those grandparents if there is no surviving grandparent, the issue taking equally if they are all of the same degree of kinship to the decedent, but if of unequal degree those of more remote degree take in the manner provided in Section 240.

(e) If there is no surviving issue, parent or issue of a parent, grandparent or issue of a grandparent, but the decedent is survived by the issue of a predeceased spouse, to that issue, the issue taking equally if they are all of the same degree of kinship to the predeceased spouse, but if of unequal degree those of more remote degree take in the manner provided in Section 240.

(f) If there is no surviving issue, parent or issue of a parent, grandparent or issue of a grandparent, or issue of a predeceased spouse, but the decedent is survived by next of kin, to the next of kin in equal degree, but where there are two or more collateral kindred in equal degree who claim through different ancestors, those who claim through the nearest ancestor are preferred to those claiming through an ancestor more remote.

(g) If there is no surviving next of kin of the decedent and no surviving issue of a predeceased spouse of the decedent, but the decedent is survived by the parents of a predeceased spouse or the issue of those parents, to the parent or parents equally, or to the issue of those parents if both are deceased, the issue taking equally if they are all of the same degree of kinship to the predeceased spouse, but if of unequal degree those of more remote degree take in the manner provided in Section 240.

(Stats. 1990 (A.B.759), ch. 79, §14, effective July 1, 1991. Amended by Stats. 2002 (A.B. 2216), ch. 447, §2, effective July 1, 2003.)

§6402.5. Portion of decedent's estate that passes to issue of decedent's predeceased spouse

(a) For purposes of distributing real property under this section if the decedent had a predeceased spouse who died not more than 15 years before the decedent and there is no surviving spouse or issue of the decedent, the portion of the decedent's estate attributable to the decedent's predeceased spouse passes as follows:

(1) If the decedent is survived by issue of the predeceased spouse, to the surviving issue of the predeceased spouse; if they are all of the same degree of kinship to the predeceased spouse they take equally, but if of unequal degree those of more remote degree take in the manner provided in Section 240.

(2) If there is no surviving issue of the predeceased spouse but the decedent is survived by a parent or parents of the predeceased spouse, to the predeceased spouse's surviving parent or parents equally.

(3) If there is no surviving issue or parent of the predeceased spouse but the decedent is survived by issue of a parent of the predeceased spouse, to the surviving issue of the parents of the predeceased spouse or either of them, the issue taking equally if they are all of the same degree of kinship to the predeceased spouse, but if of unequal degree those of more remote degree take in the manner provided in Section 240.

(4) If the decedent is not survived by issue, parent, or issue of a parent of the predeceased spouse, to the next of kin of the decedent in the manner provided in Section 6402.

(5) If the portion of the decedent's estate attributable to the decedent's predeceased spouse would otherwise escheat to the state because there is no kin of the decedent to take under Section 6402, the portion of the decedent's estate attributable to the predeceased spouse passes to the next of kin of the predeceased spouse who shall take in the same manner as the next of kin of the decedent take under Section 6402.

(b) For purposes of distributing personal property under this section if the decedent had a predeceased spouse who died not more than five years before the decedent, and there is no surviving spouse or issue of the decedent, the portion of the decedent's estate attributable to the decedent's predeceased spouse passes as follows:

(1) If the decedent is survived by issue of the predeceased spouse, to the surviving issue of the predeceased spouse; if they are all of the same degree of kinship to the predeceased spouse they take equally, but if of unequal degree those of more remote degree take in the manner provided in Section 240.

(2) If there is no surviving issue of the predeceased spouse but the decedent is survived by a parent or parents of the predeceased spouse, to the predeceased spouse's surviving parent or parents equally.

(3) If there is no surviving issue or parent of the predeceased spouse but the decedent is survived by issue of a parent of the predeceased spouse, to the surviving issue of the parents of the predeceased spouse or either of them, the issue taking equally if they are all of the same degree of kinship to the predeceased spouse, but if of unequal degree those of more remote degree take in the manner provided in Section 240.

(4) If the decedent is not survived by issue, parent, or issue of a parent of the predeceased spouse, to the next of kin of the decedent in the manner provided in Section 6402.

(5) If the portion of the decedent's estate attributable to the decedent's predeceased spouse would otherwise escheat to the state because there is no kin of the decedent to take under Section 6402, the portion of the decedent's estate attributable to the predeceased spouse passes to the next of kin of the predeceased spouse who shall take in the same manner as the next of kin of the decedent take under Section 6402.

(c) For purposes of disposing of personal property under subdivision (b), the claimant heir bears the burden of proof to show the exact personal property to be disposed of to the heir.

(d) For purposes of providing notice under any provision of this code with respect to an estate that may include personal property subject to distribution under subdivision (b), if the aggregate fair market value of tangible and intangible personal property with a written record of title or ownership in the estate is believed in good faith by the petitioning party to be less than ten thousand dollars

($10,000), the petitioning party need not give notice to the issue or next of kin of the predeceased spouse. If the personal property is subsequently determined to have an aggregate fair market value in excess of ten thousand dollars ($10,000), notice shall be given to the issue or next of kin of the predeceased spouse as provided by law.

(e) For the purposes of disposing of property pursuant to subdivision (b), "personal property" means that personal property in which there is a written record of title or ownership and the value of which in the aggregate is ten thousand dollars ($10,000) or more.

(f) For the purposes of this section, the "portion of the decedent's estate attributable to the decedent's predeceased spouse" means all of the following property in the decedent's estate:

(1) One-half of the community property in existence at the time of the death of the predeceased spouse.

(2) One-half of any community property, in existence at the time of death of the predeceased spouse, which was given to the decedent by the predeceased spouse by way of gift, descent, or devise.

(3) That portion of any community property in which the predeceased spouse had any incident of ownership and which vested in the decedent upon the death of the predeceased spouse by right of survivorship.

(4) Any separate property of the predeceased spouse which came to the decedent by gift, descent, or devise of the predeceased spouse or which vested in the decedent upon the death of the predeceased spouse by right of survivorship.

(g) For the purposes of this section, quasi-community property shall be treated the same as community property.

(h) For the purposes of this section:

(1) Relatives of the predeceased spouse conceived before the decedent's death but born thereafter inherit as if they had been born in the lifetime of the decedent.

(2) A person who is related to the predeceased spouse through two lines of relationship is entitled to only a single share based on the relationship which would entitle the person to the larger share.

(Stats. 1990 (A.B. 759), ch. 79, §14, effective July 1, 1991.)

B. Shares of Ascendants and Collateral Relatives

In the event that the intestate dies without leaving any surviving spouse or descendants, then the decedent's ancestors and collateral relatives succeed to the intestate's estate. Ascendants (or ancestors) are those persons who are related to the intestate in the ascending line (e.g., the decedent's parents or grandparents). Collateral relatives are those who are related to the decedent through an ancestor such as a parent or grandparent. Collateral relatives would include the decedent's brothers, sisters, nieces, nephews, cousins, etc. Under the intestacy scheme of all states, descendants (those related in a descending line or issue) are preferred to ascendants and collateral relatives.

According to the general intestate scheme (and in California as well), the parent or parents of an intestate take the portion of the intestate's estate that does not pass to the surviving spouse, provided that the decedent died without surviving issue. See, e.g., Cal. Prob. Code §6402(b). In California, if neither issue nor parent survive, then the portion of the intestate's estate that does not pass to the surviving spouse passes to *issue* of the parent(s) (Cal. Prob. Code §6402(c)). In the event that there are no surviving issue, parent, or issue of a parent, but the decedent left surviving grandparents (or issue of grandparents), then the intestate estate passes to the grandparent or grandparents equally or to their issue (Cal. Prob. Code §6402(d)). Upon the failure of grandparents or the issue of grandparents to take, the intestate estate passes to issue of a predeceased spouse (Cal. Prob. Code §6402(e)). Upon the failure of issue of a predeceased spouse to take, then the estate passes to the "next-of-kin" (Cal. Prob. Code §6402(f)) and thereafter (upon the failure of the next-of-kin to take) to the parents of a predeceased spouse or the issue of such parents (Cal. Prob. Code §6402(g)).

The process of determining who are the "next of kin" of an intestate varies among the different jurisdictions. Four primary methods exist:

- **the civil law system,**
- **the modified civil law system,**
- **the canon law system, and**
- **the parentelic system.**

First, the *civil law system* requires counting the total number of steps (generations) from the decedent up to the nearest common ancestor and then from the nearest common ancestor down to the claimant. ("Common" here refers to the ancestor who is common between the decedent and claimant.) The claimant (or claimants) with the lowest degree count is (are) entitled to take the decedent's estate. The modified civil law system follows the same procedure but provides that if several heirs are equally related to the decedent, then preference is given to the heirs who share the nearest common ancestor with the intestate.

The *canon law system* determines next of kin by counting the number of steps from the intestate to the nearest common ancestor and then counts the number of steps from the nearest common ancestor to the claimant. However, instead of adding these two sums together (as in the civil law system), the relevant degree of kinship is the larger of the two numbers (of the two lines of kinship). The claimant with the smallest degree count here

takes the intestate estate. This system was used by eccleasiastic courts to determine prohibited degrees of kinship for purposes of marriage. For marital purposes, the largest degree count was preferable; however, for inheritance purposes, the smaller degree count is preferable.

The final system, the *parentelic system*, dispenses with the necessity for counting degrees of kinship. Rather, the intestate estate is divided into two shares. One portion passes to the maternal grandparents and the other portion to the paternal grandparents. If one of two maternal (or paternal) grandparents is deceased, then that share passes to that grandparent's spouse. If both maternal (or both paternal) grandparents are deceased, then that half share of the decedent's estate passes to that grandparents' issue (the decedent's aunts, uncles, etc. on that side). Some state statutes (but not California) then provide that if none of these takers survive, the estate is then divided among the great-grandparents or their issue in a similar manner.

The California statute (Cal. Prob. Code §6402) reflects a parentelic approach in terms of its distribution to relatives as distantly related as grandparents or the issue of grandparents (Cal. Prob. Code §§6402(d) and (e)). After those takers, California law incorporates affinal relatives by permitting issue of a predeceased spouse to take (Cal. Prob. Code §6402(f)), followed by parent(s) of a predeceased spouse (Cal. Prob. Code §6402(g)).

UPC §2-103 also reflects a parentelic approach. However, the UPC (like California) disallows inheritance by any persons more remote than grandparents and their issue. (Unlike California, the UPC makes no provision for those issue or parents of a predeceased spouse.)

CALIFORNIA PROBATE CODE

§6402. Intestate share of heirs who take after a surviving spouse (ascendants, collaterals)

Except as provided in Section 6402.5, the part of the intestate estate not passing to the surviving spouse under Section 6401, or the entire intestate estate if there is no surviving spouse, passes as follows:

(a) To the issue of the decedent, the issue taking equally if they are all of the same degree of kinship to the decedent, but if of unequal degree those of more remote degree take in the manner provided in Section 240.

(b) If there is no surviving issue, to the decedent's parent or parents equally.

(c) If there is no surviving issue or parent, to the issue of the parents or either of them, the issue taking equally if they are all of the same degree of kinship to the decedent, but if of unequal degree those of more remote degree take in the manner provided in Section 240.

(d) If there is no surviving issue, parent or issue of a parent, but the decedent is survived by one or more grandparents or issue of grandparents, to the grandparent or grandparents equally, or to the issue of such grandparents if there is no surviving grandparent, the issue taking equally if they are all of the same degree of kinship to the decedent, but if of unequal degree those of more remote degree take in the manner provided in Section 240.

(e) If there is no surviving issue, parent or issue of a parent, grandparent or issue of a grandparent, but the decedent is survived by the issue of a predeceased spouse, to such issue, the issue taking equally if they are all of the same degree of kinship to the predeceased spouse, but if of unequal degree those of more remote degree take in the manner provided in Section 240.

(f) If there is no surviving issue, parent or issue of a parent, grandparent or issue of a grandparent, or issue of a predeceased spouse, but the decedent is survived by next of kin, to the next of kin in equal degree, but where there are two or more collateral kindred in equal degree who claim through different ancestors, those who claim through the nearest ancestor are preferred to those claiming through an ancestor more remote.

(g) If there is no surviving next of kin of the decedent and no surviving issue of a predeceased spouse of the decedent, but the decedent is survived by the parents of a predeceased spouse or the issue of such parents, to the parent or parents equally, or to the issue of such parents if both are deceased, the issue taking equally if they are all of the same degree of kinship to the predeceased spouse, but if of unequal degree those of more remote degree take in the manner provided in Section 240.

(Stats. 1990 (A.B. 759), ch. 79, §14, effective July 1, 1991.)

C. Escheat

Escheat applies if there is no taker of the decedent's intestate estate. If the decedent leaves no heirs to take his or her estate (or any portion of it), then the unclaimed property goes to the state. Specifically, according to California statute, when the probate court makes an order for final distribution of the decedent's estate, any balance that is not distributed to known heirs or beneficiaries is distributed to the state (Cal. Prob. Code §11900(a)). If the property remains unclaimed for a designated period of time, title vests ("escheats") in the state (Cal. Prob. Code §§6404, 6800 et seq.).

The property that escheats is subject to the statutory provisions relating to unclaimed property generally. See, e.g., Cal. Code Civ. Proc. §§1300 et seq. (unclaimed property); Cal. Govt. Code §182 (property as belonging or reverting to the state). For escheat of the estates of Native Americans dying intestate without heirs, see 25 U.S.C. §§373a, 373b (2000).

Most states allow inheritance by very remote relatives (known as "laughing heirs" because they are so distantly related as to feel no sorrow at the decedent's death). Most jurisdictions prefer inheritance by distant relatives rather than having the property escheat to the state. McGovern & Kurtz, *supra*, §2.2 at 59. The policy against escheat was reflected in In re Estate of Jetter, 570 N.W.2d 26 (S.D. 1997). Two unmarried brothers executed wills leaving their respective property to the surviving brother and expressly disinherited all other relatives. The will failed to make a disposition of the property upon the death of the last surviving brother (and contained no residuary clause). As a result, at the death of the surviving brother, the court was faced with a choice: enforcement of the negative will provision or escheat to the state. Based on the policy disfavoring escheat (and interpreting the escheat statute narrowly so as to apply only when no heir could be found), the court determined that the $3.2 million estate passed by intestate succession to the disinherited heirs. See also Julia M. Melius, Note, Was South Dakota Deprived of $3.2 Million? Intestacy, Escheat and the Statutory Power to Disinherit in the Estate of Jetter, 44 S.D. L. Rev. 49 (1999).

CALIFORNIA PROBATE CODE

§6404. Escheat applies if there is no taker

Part 4 (commencing with Section 6800) (escheat) applies if there is no taker of the intestate estate under the provisions of this part.

(Stats. 1990 (A.B. 759), ch. 79, §14, effective July 1, 1991.)

§6800. Escheat of property of decedent: conditions

(a) If a decedent, whether or not the decedent was domiciled in this state, leaves no one to take the decedent's estate or any portion thereof by testate succession, and no one other than a government or governmental subdivision or agency to take the estate or a portion thereof by intestate succession, under the laws of this state or of any other jurisdiction, the same escheats at the time of the decedent's death in accordance with this part.

(b) Property that escheats to the state under this part, whether held by the state or its officers, is subject to the same charges and trusts to which it would have been subject if it had passed by succession and is also subject to the provisions of Title 10 (commencing with Section 1300) of Part 3 of the Code of Civil Procedure relating to escheated estates.

(Stat. 1990 (A.B. 759), ch. 79, §14, effective July 1, 1991.)

§6801. Escheat of real property in this state

Real property in this state escheats to this state in accordance with Section 6800.

(Stats. 1990 (A.B. 759), ch. 79, §14, effective July 1, 1991.)

§6802. Escheat of tangible personal property customarily kept in this state

All tangible personal property owned by the decedent, wherever located at the decedent's death, that was customarily kept in this state prior to the decedent's death, escheats to this state in accordance with Section 6800.

(Stats. 1990 (A.B. 759), ch. 79, §14, effective July 1, 1991.)

§6803. Tangible personal property subject to control of superior court in this state

(a) Subject to subdivision (b), all tangible personal property owned by the decedent that is subject to the control of a superior court of this state for purposes of administration under this code escheats to this state in accordance with Section 6800.

(b) The property described in subdivision (a) does not escheat to this state but goes to another jurisdiction if the other jurisdiction claims the property and establishes all of the following:

(1) The other jurisdiction is entitled to the property under its law.

(2) The decedent customarily kept the property in that jurisdiction prior to the decedent's death.

(3) This state has the right to escheat and take tangible personal property being administered as part of a decedent's estate in that jurisdiction if the decedent customarily kept the property in this state prior to the decedent's death.

(Stats. 1990 (A.B. 759), ch. 79, §14, effective July 1, 1991.)

§6804. Intangible personal property of decedent domiciled in this state

All intangible property owned by the decedent escheats to this state in accordance with Section 6800 if the decedent was domiciled in this state at the time of the decedent's death.

(Stats. 1990 (A.B. 759), ch. 79, §14, effective July 1, 1991.)

§6805. Intangible personal property subject to control of superior court in this state

(a) Subject to subdivision (b), all intangible property owned by the decedent that is subject to the control of a superior court of this state for purposes of administration under this code escheats to this state in accordance with Section 6800 whether or not the decedent was domiciled in this state at the time of the decedent's death.

(b) The property described in subdivision (a) does not escheat to this state but goes to another jurisdiction if the other jurisdiction claims the property and establishes all of the following:

(1) The other jurisdiction is entitled to the property under its laws.

(2) The decedent was domiciled in that jurisdiction at the time of the decedent's death.

(3) This state has the right to escheat and take intangible property being administered as part of a

decedent's estate in that jurisdiction if the decedent was domiciled in this state at the time of the decedent's death.
(Stats. 1990 (A.B. 759), ch. 79, §14, effective July 1, 1991.)

§6806. Benefits distributable from certain trusts

Notwithstanding any other provision of law, a benefit consisting of money or other property distributable from a trust established under a plan providing health and welfare, pension, vacation, severance, retirement benefit, death benefit, unemployment insurance or similar benefits does not pass to or escheat to the state under this part but goes to the trust or fund from which it is distributable, subject to the provisions of Section 1521 of the Code of Civil Procedure. However, if such plan has terminated and the trust or fund has been distributed to the beneficiaries thereof prior to distribution of such benefit from the estate, such benefit passes to the state and escheats to the state under this part.
(Stats. 1990 (A.B. 759), ch. 79, §14, effective July 1, 1991.)

§11900. Court shall order undistributed property to the state and convert such property to money if practicable

(a) The court shall order property that is not ordered distributed to known beneficiaries to be distributed to the state.

(b) Insofar as practicable, any real property or tangible personal property shall be converted to money before distribution to the state.
(Stats. 1990 (A.B. 759), ch. 79, §14, effective July 1, 1991.)

CALIFORNIA CODE OF CIVIL PROCEDURE

§1410. Procedure to establish title of state by escheat

The Attorney General shall, from time to time, commence actions on behalf of the state for the purpose of having it adjudged that title to unclaimed property to which the state has become entitled by escheat has vested in the state, and for the purpose of having it adjudged that property has been actually abandoned or that the owner thereof has died and there is no person entitled thereto and the same has escheated and vested in the state. Such actions shall be brought in the Superior Court for the County of Sacramento; except that if any real property covered by the petition is not situated in the County of Sacramento, an action respecting the real property shall be commenced in the superior court for the county in which such real property or any part thereof is situated. The Attorney General shall cause to be recorded in the office of the county recorder of the county in which the real property is situated, a notice of the pendency of the petition containing the names of the parties, and the object of the action and a description of the property in the county affected thereby. From the time of filing such notice for record only, shall a purchaser or encumbrancer of the property affected thereby be deemed to have constructive notice of the pendency of the action, and only of the pendency against parties designated by their real names.

Such action shall be commenced by filing a petition. The provisions of Section 1420, relating to the facts to be set forth in the petition, joinder of parties and causes of action, and the provisions of Section 1423, relating to appearances and pleadings, shall be applicable to any proceeding had under this section.

Upon the filing of the petition, the court shall make an order requiring all persons interested in the property or estate to appear on a day not more than 90 days nor less than 60 days from the date of the order and show cause, if any they have, why title to the property should not vest in the State of California.

Service of process in such actions shall be made by delivery of a copy of the order, together with a copy of the petition, to each person who claims title to any property covered by the petition and who is known to the Attorney General or the Controller or who has theretofore filed in the office of the Controller a written request for such service of process, stating his name and address, including street number, or postoffice box number, if any, and by publishing the order at least once a week for two consecutive weeks in a newspaper published in the county in which the action is filed, the last publication to be at least 10 days prior to the date set for the hearing.

Upon completion of the service of process, as provided in this section, the court shall have full and complete jurisdiction over the estate, the property, and the person of everyone having or claiming any interest in the property, and shall have full and complete jurisdiction to hear and determine the issues therein, and to render an appropriate judgment.

In addition to the foregoing publication of the order, a notice shall be given by publication, at least once a week for two successive weeks in a newspaper published in the county from which the property was forwarded to the State Treasury or is situated, of each estate and item of property from such county or situated in such county in excess of one thousand dollars ($1,000). Such notice shall state that a petition has been filed and an order made as hereinbefore provided and shall list each estate and item in excess of one thousand dollars ($1,000) and show the amount of the property, if money, or a description thereof, if other than money, and the name of the owner or claimant and his last known address. Any omission or defect in the giving of such additional notice shall not affect the jurisdiction of the court.

If it appears from the facts found or admitted that the state is entitled to the property or any part thereof mentioned in the petition, judgment shall be rendered that title to such property or part thereof, as the case may be, has vested in the state by escheat.

No costs of suit shall be allowed against any party in any action or proceeding had under this section.
(Stats. 1951, ch. 1708, p. 3946, §5. Amended by Stats. 1951, ch. 1738, p. 4146, §2; Stats. 1965, ch. 2066, p. 4810, §2;

Stats. 1972, ch. 856, p. 1521, §1, effective January 1, 1973; Stats. 1984, ch. 268, §1, effective June 30, 1984.)

§1415. Escheat of money or personal property valued at $1,000 or less

Whenever any money or other personal property of a value of one thousand dollars ($1,000) or less has heretofore been, or is hereafter, deposited in the State Treasury and the same is subject to being declared escheated to the state or being declared vested in the state as abandoned property, or otherwise, under any laws of this state, in lieu of the procedure provided for elsewhere in this chapter, the Controller may, from time to time, prepare a return listing such property and give notice thereof in the manner hereinafter provided. Such return shall list each item and show (1) the amount of the property, if money, or a description thereof if other than money; (2) the name of the owner or claimant and his last known address, if known; (3) the name and address of the person delivering the property to the State Treasury, if known but where the property is received from an estate, only the name of the decedent together with the name of the county and the number of the proceeding need be given; (4) the facts and circumstances by virtue of which it is claimed the property has escheated or vested in the state; and (5) such other information as the Controller may desire to include to assist in identifying each item.

When such return has been completed, the Controller shall prepare, date, and attach thereto a notice that the property listed in the return has escheated or vested in the state. Copies of such return and notice shall then be displayed and be open to public inspection during business hours in at least three offices of the Controller, one in the City of Sacramento, one in the City and County of San Francisco, and one in the City of Los Angeles.

The Controller shall then cause notice to be given by publication in one newspaper of general circulation published in the City of Sacramento, and also by publication in one newspaper of general circulation published in the City and County of San Francisco, and also by publication in one newspaper of general circulation published in the City of Los Angeles, at least once each calendar week for two consecutive weeks, that said return and notice that the property listed in the return has escheated or vested in the state has been prepared and is on display and open to public inspection during business hours, giving the addresses and room numbers of the locations where the same may be inspected.

Such publication shall be made within 90 days after attaching the notice to the return. Notice by such publication shall be deemed completed 120 days after attaching the notice to the return.

Within five years after such notice by publication is completed, any person entitled to such property may claim it in the manner provided in Chapter 3 [Section 1335 et seq.] of this title. All persons who fail to make such claim within the time limited are forever barred; saving, however, to infants and persons of unsound mind, the right to appear and claim such property at any time within the time limited, or within one year after their respective disabilities cease.
(Stats. 1951, ch. 1708, p. 3947, §5. Amended by Stats. 1965, ch. 1350, p. 3237, §1; Stats. 1984, ch. 268, §2, effective June 30, 1984.)

§1420. Commencement of action after two years following decedent's death

At any time after two years after the death of any decedent who leaves property to which the state is entitled by reason of it having escheated to the state, the Attorney General shall commence a proceeding on behalf of the state in the Superior Court for the County of Sacramento to have it adjudged that the state is so entitled. Such action shall be commenced by filing a petition, which shall be treated as the information elsewhere referred to in this title.

There shall be set forth in such petition a description of the property, the name of the person last possessed thereof, the name of the person, if any, claiming such property, or portion thereof, and the facts and circumstances by virtue of which it is claimed the property has escheated.

Upon the filing of such petition, the court must make an order requiring all persons interested in the estate to appear and show cause, if any they have, within 60 days from the date of the order, why such estate should not vest in the state. Such order must be published at least once a week for four consecutive weeks in a newspaper published in said County of Sacramento, the last publication to be at least 10 days prior to the date set for the hearing. Upon the completion of the publication of such order, the court shall have full and complete jurisdiction over the estate, the property, and the person of everyone having or claiming any interest in the said property, and shall have full and complete jurisdiction to hear and determine the issues therein, and render the appropriate judgment thereon.

If proceedings for the administration of such estate have been instituted, a copy of such order must be filed with the papers in such estate. If proceedings for the administration of any estate of any such decedent have been instituted and none of the persons entitled to succeed thereto have appeared and made claim to such property or any portion thereof, before the decree of final distribution therein is made, or before the commencement of such proceeding by the Attorney General, or if the court shall find that such persons as have appeared are not entitled to the property of such estate, or any portion thereof, the court shall, upon final settlement of the proceedings for the administration of such estate, after the payment of all debts and expenses of administration, distribute all moneys and other property remaining to the State of California.

In any proceeding brought by the Attorney General under this chapter, any two or more parties and any two or more causes of action may be joined in the same proceedings and in the same petition without being separately stated; and it shall be sufficient to allege in the petition that the decedent left no heirs to take the estate and the failure of heirs to appear and set up their claims in any such proceeding, or in any proceedings for the administration of such estate, shall be sufficient proof upon which to base the judgment in any such proceeding or such decree of distribution.

Where proceedings for the administration of any estate have not been commenced within six months from the death of any decedent the Attorney General may direct the public administrator to commence the same forthwith.

(Stats. 1951, ch. 1708, p. 3949, §5. Amended by Stats. 2002 (S.B. 1316), ch. 784, §83.)

D. Other

1. Share of Half-Blood Relatives

Half-blood relatives are related to each other through one common ancestor (such as through the same mother or the same father). In contrast, persons related by whole blood share the same common ancestors (i.e., share the same mother and father).

Most modern intestacy statutes do not make any distinctions between the inheritance rights of relatives of the whole-blood and those of the half-blood. See, e.g., Cal. Prob. Code §6406; UPC §2-107. A few states, however, give half-blood relatives only half as much as a whole-blood relative. McGovern & Kurtz, *supra*, §2.2 at 58. For a recent reform proposal, see Ralph C. Brashier, Consanguinity, Sibling Relationships, and the Default Rules of Inheritance Law: Reshaping Half-Blood Statutes to Reflect the Evolving Family, 58 SMU L. Rev.137 (2005) (suggesting that states should invest probate courts with discretion in determining the intestate shares of half-blood relatives).

CALIFORNIA PROBATE CODE

§6406. Intestate share of half-blood relatives

Except as provided in Section 6451[whole-blood sibling (or the sibling's issue) of an adopted person inherits from or through the adopted person], relatives of the half-blood inherit the same share they would inherit if they were of the whole-blood.

(Stats. 1990 (A.B. 759), ch. 79, §14, effective July 1, 1991. Amended by Stats. 1993 (A.B. 1137), ch. 529, §3.)

§6451. Effect of adoption: severance of biological parent-child relationship and exceptions

(a) An adoption severs the relationship of parent and child between an adopted person and a natural parent of the adopted person unless both of the following requirements are satisfied:

(1) The natural parent and the adopted child lived together at any time as parent and child, or the natural parent was married to or cohabiting with the other natural parent at the time the person was conceived and died before the person's birth.

(2) The adoption was by the spouse of either of the natural parents or after the death of either of the natural parents.

(b) Neither a natural parent nor a relative of a natural parent, except for a wholeblood brother or sister of the adopted person or the issue of that brother or sister, inherits from or through the adopted person on the basis of a parent and child relationship between the adopted person and the natural parent that satisfies the requirements of paragraphs (1) and (2) of subdivision (a), unless the adoption is by the spouse or surviving spouse of that parent.

(c) For the purpose of this section, a prior adoptive parent and child relationship is treated as a natural parent and child relationship.

(Stats. 1993 (A.B. 1137), ch. 529, §5.)

2. Bar on Double Inheritance by Some Relatives

An heir who is related to the decedent through two lines of relationship is entitled to only a single share. Suppose, for example, that the biological parents of a child (X) die in an automobile accident. X subsequently is adopted by a sister of X's biological mother (e.g., an aunt). If the aunt were to predecease X's grandmother, then when the grandmother dies intestate, X would be both a biological and an adopted grandchild of the parents of the biological mother (Cal. Prob. Code §6413). However, X would be barred from double inheritance.

CALIFORNIA PROBATE CODE

§6413. Person related to decedent through two lines of relationships: bar on double inheritance

A person who is related to the decedent through two lines of relationship is entitled to only a single share based on the relationship which would entitle the person to the larger share.

(Stats. 1990 (A.B. 759), ch. 79, §14, effective July 1, 1991.)

3. Share of Foster Child or Stepchild

A stepparent-child relationship arises when a child's biological parent remarries. The new spouse of the child's biological parent becomes the child's stepparent. Under the general rule in most jurisdictions, only a stepchild who is adopted by the new spouse may inherit from or through the stepparent.

However, some stepchildren have greater rights under California's intestacy scheme than in either the UPC or the majority of other states. Kim A. Feigenbaum, Note, The Changing Family Structure: Challenging Stepchildren's Lack of

Inheritance Rights, 66 Brook. L. Rev. 167, 170 (2000). California provides for an intestate share for stepchildren under certain circumstances (Cal. Prob. Code §6454). Specifically, a stepchild may inherit from a stepparent if: (1) the parent-child relationship began while the child was a minor, (2) the relationship continued throughout the joint lives of the stepparent and child, and (3) the stepparent would have adopted the stepchild but for a legal barrier. Note that the statute does not define the term "parent-child relationship" (leaving the matter to the court's discretion), and also presents a formidable obstacle to recognition of a stepchild's right to inherit in the form of the "legal-barrier requirement." This last requirement necessitates proof that the stepparent wanted to adopt the child but was unable to do so (often for the reason that the noncustodial biological parent refused consent).

The California Supreme Court has interpreted the legal-barrier condition to require that the legal barrier to adoption must exist throughout the relationship and continue until the time the stepparent dies. Estate of Joseph, 70 Cal. Rptr. 2d 619 (Cal. 1998). (Note that the California statute does not permit a foster parent or stepparent to inherit from the child and does not create rights in more distant relatives.)

The statute has been criticized by commentators. Professor Susan Gary points to the limited usefulness of the statute stemming from the "legal barrier" requirement. She notes that the common legal barrier of parental refusal of consent to adoption vanishes when the stepchild reaches majority. However, parents are less likely to feel the need to adopt when a child reaches majority. Thus, according to Gary, the statute may be useful only when a stepparent dies while the stepchild is a minor. Susan N. Gary, The Parent-Child Relationship Under Intestacy Statutes, 32 U. Memp. L. Rev. 643, 671-674 (2002).

Professor Margaret Mahoney criticizes the "legal barrier" requirement from a different perspective. She urges that the requirement be replaced with a functional determination (based on the common law in loco parentis doctrine) of the parent-child relationship for intestacy purposes. Margaret M. Mahoney, Stepfamilies in the Law of Intestate Succession and Wills, 22 U.C. Davis L. Rev. 917, 931-936 (1989). See also Gary, *supra*, at 673-674 (criticizing Mahoney's proposal as being too narrow because it is predicated on a marital relationship and because it still requires that the parent-child relationship begin while the child was a minor).

Regarding stepchildren, the UPC creates an exception to the general rule that for purposes of inheritance by, from, or through the child, an adopted child is the child of the adopting parents and not of the child's biological parents. According to UPC §2-114(b)(ii), a stepparent adoption does not preclude the adopted stepchild's right to inherit from and through the child's noncustodial biological parent. However, that subsection does not permit correlative inheritance: it does not establish the right of the noncustodial biological parent (and that parent's relatives) to inherit from and through the adopted stepchild. For a discussion of Adoption, see Section IIIC *infra*. For a discussion of Estate of Ford, 8 Cal. Rptr. 3d 541 (Cal. 2004) (holding that a foster child was not equitably adopted), see Section III C4 *infra*.

CALIFORNIA PROBATE CODE

§6454. Foster parent or stepparent: intestate succession from or through such parent

For the purpose of determining intestate succession by a person or the person's issue from or through a foster parent or stepparent, the relationship of parent and child exists between that person and the person's foster parent or stepparent if both of the following requirements are satisfied:

(a) The relationship began during the person's minority and continued throughout the joint lifetimes of the person and the person's foster parent or stepparent.

(b) It is established by clear and convincing evidence that the foster parent or stepparent would have adopted the person but for a legal barrier.

(Stats. 1993 (A.B. 1137), ch. 529, §5.)

III. Questions of Status

A. Posthumous Children

State intestacy statutes generally make provisions for posthumous heirs. A posthumous heir is an heir who was conceived while the intestate was alive but born after the intestate's death. At common law and according to UPC §2-108, posthumous heirs inherit as if they had been born during the decedent's lifetime.

California treats posthumous heirs (defined broadly as afterborn "relatives" of the decedent) as though they were alive at the time of death; thus they share in the estate (Cal. Prob. Code §6407). The UPC requires that posthumous heirs must survive at least 120 hours after birth in order to qualify (UPC §2-108).

The inheritance rights of posthumous children arose in the case of Woodward v. Commissioner of Social Services, 760 N.E.2d 257 (Mass. 2002). A woman gave birth to twin daughters after being artificially impregnated by the sperm of her late husband who had died of leukemia. She then applied for Social Security survivor benefits for the twins. The Social

Security Administration denied benefits on the basis of an administrative judge's findings that the children did not qualify as intestate heirs because they were neither born nor in utero at the husband's death. The wife appealed. The United States District Court for the District of Massachusetts certified to the Supreme Court of Massachusetts the question of whether posthumous children enjoy the inheritance rights of natural children under state intestate succession law. The Supreme Judicial Court held that the children could inherit if the wife established their genetic relationship with the decedent and that the decedent consented both to reproduce posthumously and to support any resulting child. See generally Amy L. Komoroski, Comment, After Woodward v. Commissioner of Social Services: Where Do Posthumously Conceived Children Stand in the Line of Descent?, 11 B.U. Pub. Int. L.J. 297 (2002).

In a similar case regarding posthumous children's claims for survivor benefits with the Social Security Administration, a New Jersey Superior Court judge held that, in circumstances where the decedent left no estate and an adjudication of parentage did not unfairly intrude on the rights of others or cause "serious problems" with the orderly administration of estates, the children could inherit under state intestacy law. In re Estate of Kolacy, 753 A.2d 1257 (N.J. Super. Ch. 2000).

In the most recent case involving Social Security benefits, Gillett-Netting v. Barnhart, 371 F.3d 593 (9th Cir. 2004), a widow sought review of the Commissioner of Social Security's denial of her claim for survivors' benefits that she filed on behalf of her twins who were conceived by in vitro fertilization after her husband's death. The district court granted summary judgment for the Commissioner, and the widow appealed. The Ninth Circuit Court of Appeals held that the posthumously conceived twins were "children" within the definition of the Social Security Act, and that the children were presumed dependent for purposes of entitlement to survivors' benefits because they were legitimate under applicable state law.

Only a few state statutes address the issue of the inheritance rights of posthumously conceived children. Some of these statutes grant rights to such children if the deceased parent gave consent during his lifetime. However, the nature of that consent varies. Compare La. Rev. Stat. Ann. §9:391.1(A) (West 2004) (requiring the deceased's authorization that his spouse use his gametes), with Tex. Fam. Code Ann. §160.707 (Vernon 2001) (requiring that the deceased spouse "consented in a record that if assisted reproduction were to occur after death the deceased spouse would be a parent of the child"). The latter provision is modeled after Uniform Parentage Act §707, 9B U.L.A. 43 (Supp. 2005). See also Human Fertilisation and Embryology (Deceased Fathers) Act 2003, Ch. 24 s.1 (Eng.) (recognizing decedent as father if he previously consented in writing, the woman elects within 42 days of the birth for the decedent to be treated as the father, and no other person is to be treated as the father).

The issue of the inheritance rights of posthumously conceived children first arose in California in Hecht v. Superior Court, 20 Cal. Rptr. 2d 275 (Ct. App. 1993), where the appellate court considered whether a decedent's sperm should be considered as "property" that could be bequeathed to the decedent's girlfriend. In answering in the affirmative, the court noted, in dicta, that, under the provisions of California's Probate Code (e.g., Cal. Prob. Code §6407 *infra*), "it is unlikely that the estate would be subject to claims with respect to any such children" resulting from insemination of the girlfriend with the decedent's sperm. *Hecht*, 20 Cal. Rptr. 2d at 290. See generally Christine E. Kirk, Assisted Reproduction: Children Conceived Posthumously Entitled to Inheritance Rights, 30 J.L. Med. & Ethics 109 (2002).

California enacted legislation in 2004 (effective January 1, 2006) to provide inheritance rights for posthumously conceived children by the addition of Sections 249.5, 249.6, 249.7, and 249.8 to the Probate Code. The legislation provides that a posthumously conceived child will be deemed to have been born in the decedent's lifetime if the child or the child's representative proves by clear and convincing evidence that certain conditions are satisfied (specifically, the decedent provides written consent to the posthumous use of his genetic material, designates a person to control the use of his/her genetic material, and the child was in utero within two years of the decedent's death).

CALIFORNIA PROBATE CODE

§249.5. Posthumous child's inheritance rights

For purposes of determining rights to property to be distributed upon the death of a decedent, a child of the decedent conceived and born after the death of the decedent shall be deemed to have been born in the lifetime of the decedent, and after the execution of all of the decedent's testamentary instruments, if the child or his or her representative proves by clear and convincing evidence that all of the following conditions are satisfied:

(a) The decedent, in writing, specifies that his or her genetic material shall be used for the posthumous conception of a child of the decedent, subject to the following:

(1) The specification shall be signed by the decedent and dated.

(2) The specification may be revoked or amended only by a writing, signed by the decedent and dated.

(3) A person is designated by the decedent to control the use of the genetic material.

(b) The person designated by the decedent to control the use of the genetic material has given written notice by certified mail, return receipt requested, that the decedent's genetic material was available for the purpose of posthumous conception. The notice shall have been given to a person who has the power to control the distribution of either the decedent's property or death benefits payable by reason of the decedent's death, within four months of the date of issuance of a certificate of the decedent's death or entry of a judgment determining the fact of the decedent's death, whichever event occurs first.

(c) The child was in utero using the decedent's genetic material and was in utero within two years of the date of issuance of a certificate of the decedent's death or entry of a judgment determining the fact of the decedent's death, whichever event occurs first. This subdivision does not apply to a child who shares all of his or her nuclear genes with the person donating the implanted nucleus as a result of the application of somatic nuclear transfer technology commonly known as human cloning.

(Stats. 2004 (A.B. 1910), ch. 775, §5. Amended by Stats. 2005 (A.B. 204), ch. 285, §1, effective January 1, 2006.)

§249.6. Notice of availability of genetic material for posthumous conception

(a) Upon timely receipt of the notice required by Section 249.5 or actual knowledge by a person who has the power to control the distribution of either the decedent's property or death benefits payable by reason of the decedent's death, that person may not make a distribution of property or pay death benefits payable by reason of the decedent's death before two years following the date of issuance of a certificate of the decedent's death or entry of a judgment determining the fact of decedent's death, whichever event occurs first.

(b) Subdivision (a) does not apply to, and the distribution of property or the payment of benefits may proceed in a timely manner as provided by law with respect to, any property if the birth of a child or children of the decedent conceived after the death of the decedent will not have an effect on any of the following:

(1) The proposed distribution of the decedent's property.

(2) The payment of death benefits payable by reason of the decedent's death.

(3) The determination of rights to property to be distributed upon the death of the decedent.

(4) The right of any person to claim a probate homestead or probate family allowance.

(c) Subdivision (a) does not apply to, and the distribution of property or the payment of benefits may proceed in a timely manner as provided by law with respect to, any property if the person named in subdivision (a) of Section 249.5 sends written notice by certified mail, return receipt requested, that the person does not intend to use the genetic material for the posthumous conception of a child of a decedent. This notice shall be signed by the person named in paragraph (3) of subdivision (a) of Section 249.5 and at least one competent witness, and dated.

(d) A person who has the power to control the distribution of either the decedent's property or death benefits payable by reason of the decedent's death, shall incur no liability for making a distribution of property or paying death benefits if that person made a distribution of property or paid death benefits prior to receiving notice or acquiring actual knowledge of the existence of genetic material available for posthumous conception purposes or the written notice required by subdivision (b) of Section 249.5.

(e) Each person to whom payment, delivery, or transfer of the decedent's property is made is personally liable to a person who, pursuant to Section 249.5, has a superior right to the payment, delivery, or transfer of the decedent's property. The aggregate of the personal liability of a person shall not exceed the fair market value, valued as of the time of the transfer, of the property paid, delivered, or transferred to the person under this section, less the amount of any liens and encumbrances on that property at that time.

(f) In addition to any other liability a person may have pursuant to this section, any person who fraudulently secures the payment, delivery, or transfer of the decedent's property pursuant to this section shall be liable to the person having a superior right for three times the fair market value of the property.

(g) An action to impose liability under this section shall be barred three years after the distribution to the holder of the decedent's property, or three years after the discovery of fraud, whichever is later. The three-year period specified in this subdivision may not be tolled for any reason.

(Stats. 2004 (A.B. 1910), ch. 775, § 6. Amended by Stats. 2005 (A.B. 204), ch. 285, § 2, effective January 1, 2006.)

§249.7. Failing to give notice of available genetic material

If the written notice required pursuant to Section 249.5 is not given in a timely manner to any person who has the power to control the distribution of either the decedent's property or death benefits payable by reason of the decedent's death, that person may make the distribution in the manner provided by law as if any child of the decedent conceived after the death of the decedent had predeceased the decedent without heirs. Any child of a decedent conceived after the death of the decedent, or that child's representative, shall be barred from making a claim against either the person making the distribution or the recipient of the distribution when the claim is based on wrongful distribution and written notice has not been given in a timely manner pursuant to Section 249.5 to the person making that distribution.

(Stats. 2004 (A.B. 1910), ch. 775, § 7, effective January 1, 2005.)

§249.8. Who may file petition requesting delayed distribution of property

Notwithstanding Section 249.6, any interested person may file a petition in the manner prescribed in Section 248 or 17200 requesting a distribution of property of the decedent or death benefits payable by reason of decedent's death that are subject to the delayed distribution provisions of Section 249.6. The court may order distribution of all, or a portion of, the property or death benefits, if at the hearing it appears that distribution can be made without any loss to any interested person, including any loss, either actual or contingent, to a decedent's child who is conceived after the death of the decedent. The order for distribution shall be stayed until any bond required by the court is filed.

(Stats. 2004, ch. 775 (A.B. 1910), §8. Amended by Stats. 2005, c. 285 (A.B. 204), §3.)

§6407. Posthumous relatives of decedent

Relatives of the decedent conceived before the decedent's death but born thereafter inherit as if they had been born in the lifetime of the decedent.

(Stats. 1990 (A.B. 759), ch. 79, §14, effective July 1, 1991.)

B. Aliens

At common law, an alien could not inherit real property in England. The modern trend reverses this presumption so that unless a statute provides otherwise, noncitizens are able to inherit property generally. McGovern & Kurtz, *supra*, §2.2 at 60.

At one time, many states had "reciprocity statutes," providing that an alien could not inherit from a United States citizen unless the alien's nation granted reciprocal rights to American citizens. In Zschernig v. Miller, 389 U.S. 429 (1968), the United States Supreme Court analyzed the constitutionality of an Oregon statute that stated conditions under which an alien not residing in the United States or its territories could take property in Oregon through testate or intestate succession. *Zschernig* involved proceedings by East German next-of-kin of an Oregon intestate against the administrator and Oregon officials for determination of heirship. The Oregon State Board argued that the property should escheat to the state. Invalidating the law, Justice Douglas held that the Oregon statute constituted an intrusion by the state into the field of foreign affairs, which the Constitution entrusts to the President and Congress. Shortly thereafter, a California court of appeal held a similar law unconstitutional in In re Kraemer's Estate, 81 Cal. Rptr. 287 (Ct. App. 1969).

A few states (Nebraska, North Carolina, Oklahoma, Virginia, and Wyoming) still have reciprocity statutes. Restatement (Third) of Property, *supra*, §1.3, Statutory Note 2. Some states have "retention" statutes that "require or permit retention by the state of the inheritance if it appears unlikely that the beneficiary will be able to enjoy that property." Id., §1.3, Statutory Note 3 (citing Connecticut, Maryland, Massachusetts, Nebraska, New Jersey, and New York). Still other states have prohibitions or restrictions on ownership of *real property* by nonresident aliens. Id., §1.3, Statutory Note 4 (citing Alaska, District of Columbia, Indiana, Iowa, Kentucky, Mississippi, Missouri, Oklahoma, Pennsylvania, South Carolina, and South Dakota).

Today, the California Probate Code follows the Uniform Probate Code in eliminating this bar on inheritance. See Cal. Prob. Code §6411; UPC §2-111. See also Restatement (Third) of Property, *supra*, at §1.3. The Restatement provision is codified in the original and revised Uniform Probate Code. Restatement (Third) of Property, *supra*, at §1.3 cmt. a.

On the historical xenophobic practice of state courts in withholding bequests to legatees residing in Communist countries, see Harold J. Berman, Soviet Heirs in American Courts, 62 Colum. L. Rev. 257 (1962); Chaitkin, The Rights of Residents of Russia and Its Satellites to Share in Estates of American Decedents, 25 S. Cal. L. Rev. 297 (1952); William B. Wong, Comment, Iron Curtain Statutes, Communist China, and the Right to Devise, 32 UCLA L. Rev. 643 (1985).

CALIFORNIA PROBATE CODE

§6411. Aliens: not disqualified to take

No person is disqualified to take as an heir because that person or a person through whom he or she claims is or has been an alien.

(Stats. 1990 (A.B. 759), ch. 79, §14, effective July 1, 1991.)

C. Adoption

The common law did not recognize adoption, which originated in the Roman and civil law systems. As a result, adoption in the United States is entirely a creation of statutory law. Massachusetts adopted the first comprehensive adoption statute in 1851. McGovern & Kurtz, *supra*, §2.10 at 100n.4.

Historically, same-sex couples in California were unable to adopt children jointly, nor was one partner able to adopt the children of his or her partner. However, California now permits joint adoption by gay or lesbian couples based on case law and statute.

Sharon S. v. Superior Court, 31 Cal. 4th 417 (2003), upheld the validity of second-parent adoptions. Sharon S. and Annette F. were in a relationship for 11 years but never registered as domestic partners. Sharon gave birth to two sons through artificial insemination during the relationship. Annette adopted the older boy and was in the process of adopting the younger boy when the couple broke up. Annette then petitioned for adoption of the younger child. Sharon withdrew her consent and maintained that the adoption was not authorized because Family Code section 8617 requires the birth parent (i.e., Sharon) to relinquish all rights to the child before giving it up for adoption. The California Supreme Court disagreed, holding that termination of a birth parent's rights is not a mandatory prerequisite to every adoption and that second-parent adoptions are valid under California's independent adoption law.

While the case was pending, California's domestic partnership law went into effect, permitting the use of the stepparent adoption procedures of Family Code §9000 by registered gay and lesbian partners (Stats. 2001 (A.B. 25), ch. 893)).

Outside California, a few state statutes limit adoption by homosexuals or same-sex couples. Florida was the first state to ban adoptions by homosexuals in 1977 (Fla. Stat. Ann. §63.042(3)). See also Conn. Gen. Stat. Ann. §45a-726a (2004) (sexual orientation may be considered and nothing shall require placement with a prospective adoptive or foster parent who is homosexual or bisexual); Miss. Ann. Code §93-17-3(2)(2004)(adoption by couples of the same gender is prohibited). New Hampshire formerly banned homosexual adoption, but lifted that ban in 2001. Martin R. Gardner, Adoption by Homosexuals in the Wake of Lawrence v. Texas, 6 J. L. Fam. Stud. 19, 30 (2004).

Utah bans adoption by unmarried, cohabiting couples (Utah Ann. Code §78-30-1(3)(b)(2002)), which by definition includes all same-sex couples. In practice, even in states without a statutory ban, many state courts do not allow adoption by homosexuals or same-sex couples, either because courts maintain that such adoptions would be contrary to the best interests of the child, or because parental termination statutes prevent the practice. Gardner, *supra*, at 23.

In Lofton v. Secretary of the Department of Children and Family Services, 358 F.3d 804 (11th Cir. 2004), *cert. denied,* 543 U.S. 1081 (2005), gay and lesbian foster parents and guardians challenged the constitutionality of Florida's prohibition against homosexual adoption. The federal district court granted summary judgment for the state. The Eleventh Circuit affirmed, holding that relationships involving foster and legal guardian families did not create a liberty interest in family integrity under the Due Process Clause of the Fourteenth Amendment and also that the statute did not violate the Amendment's Equal Protection Clause. See also Cox v. Florida Department of Health and Rehabilitative Services, 656 So. 2d 902 (Fla. 1995) (holding that the Florida ban on gay adoptions did not violate *state* constitutional rights to privacy or due process and was not unconstitutionally vague, but failing to reach the equal protection issue because of an insufficient record).

More recently, two men who were registered domestic partners in California filed a federal suit (based on diversity jurisdiction) against the Arizona operators of an adoption Web site after the Web site operators rejected the partners' application to post a profile to adopt a child. The plaintiffs alleged violations of California's Unruh Civil Rights Act, which forbids businesses from discriminating against customers based on sexual orientation and marital status. The federal district court denied defendants' motion for summary judgment, holding that fact issues existed regarding whether their policy of not allowing unmarried couples to post profiles on their Web site amounted to marital status, sexual orientation, or gender discrimination. Butler v. Adoption Media, LLC, 2007 WL 963159 (N.D. Cal. 2007).

In general, the inheritance rights of adopted children focus on four issues: (1) the inheritance rights of adopted children to inherit by, from, and through their adoptive parents; (2) the inheritance rights of biological parents to inherit by, from, and through their adopted-away child; (3) adult adoption, and (4) equitable adoption.

1. Inheritance By, From, and Through Adoptive Parents

Today, the general rule is that adoptive children inherit from their adoptive parents but not from their biological parents. This result follows because adoption severs all legal ties of the adoptive child to the biological family. Thus, an adopted child inherits by, from, or through the adoptive parents. See, e.g., UPC §2-114 ("for purposes of intestate succession by, through, or from a person . . . an adopted individual is the child or his or her adopting parents"). See also McGovern & Kurtz, *supra*, §2.10 at 100-101.

The last area to be liberalized was the right of adopted children to inherit *through* their adoptive parents. Thus, if an adoptive parent's parent dies, the adopted child might not be considered as "issue" of a predeceased parent because a third party (such as a grandparent) is sometimes considered "a stranger to the adoption" (i.e., not a party to the adoption contract). The policy rationale is that the grandparent would not want an adopted child "foisted on" the grandparent. The same problem exists in terms of a will or trust leaving a class gift to "grandchildren." An adopted grandchild might not take because of similar "stranger to the adoption" reasoning. See McGovern & Kurtz, *supra*, §2.10 at 103. The modern trend, however, recognizes increased acceptance of adoption, and treats adopted children the same as their biological counterparts.

2. Inheritance By, From, and Through Biological Parents

The corollary to the general rule that adoptees can inherit by, from, and through their adoptive parents is that inheritance rights are cut off by, from, and through the biological parents. This result flows from the fact that adoption severs legal ties to the biological parents. Restatement (Third) of Property, *supra*, at §2.5, cmt. e.

The general rule that adoptees cannot inherit from their biological parents is subject to exceptions in some cases in which children continue to have contact with their biological parents. See UPC §2-114(b). The most common exception occurs with stepparent adoptions in which a child is adopted by the spouse of a biological parent. Many jurisdictions provide that in such a case, the child does not lose the right to inherit from the noncustodial biological parent. For example, California law provides that an adopted-away child does not lose the right to inherit from the (noncustodial) biological parent so long as (1) the child and biological parent lived together "at any time" as parent and child, or "the natural parent was married to or cohabiting with the other natural parent at the time the person was conceived and died before the person's birth" and (2) the adoption was by the spouse of either of the natural parents or after the death of either of the natural parents (Cal. Prob. Code §6451(a)(1), and (2)). For discussion of the inheritance rights of stepchildren, see also Section III D3 *supra*.

3. Adult Adoption

Adult adoption enables one adult to adopt another adult and thereby to create a legally recognized family relationship. Persons may resort to adult adoption not only to create inheritance rights, but also to obtain decision-making authority regarding a partner in cases of emergency or incapacity, secure visitation rights upon hospitalization or imprisonment, and permit recovery in tort actions and beneficiary privileges under insurance policies, retirement funds, and employee benefit packages. Angie Smokla, Note, That's the Ticket: A New Way of Defining Family, 10 Cornell J.L. & Pub. Pol'y 629, 638 (2001). The practice does have some disadvantages: The adoption is irrevocable and destroys the adoptee's legal relationship with the natural parents (thereby terminating inheritance rights vis à vis the natural parent). Id. at 639.

All states except Alabama and Nebraska permit adult adoption, although many states restrict the practice in various ways. Id. at 638-639. Some states require that the adoptee be younger than the adopter (or a certain number of years younger), the adoptee be a specified relative, the adoptee lived with the adopter a specified number of years during the adoptee's minority or had a filial relationship with the adopter during minority, or that the adoptee must be disabled or mentally retarded. Id.

As aforementioned, a few states expressly restrict adoption by same-sex couples. Such bans apply to adult adoptions as well as adoption of minors.)

4. Equitable Adoption

Equitable adoption (also called "virtual adoption," "de facto adoption," or "adoption by estoppel") is a judicially created equitable remedy that protects the interests of a child whose foster parents or stepparents agree to adopt the child but never finalize the adoption. The issue of equitable adoption arises most often when the foster parent or stepparent dies intestate without legally adopting the child. Application of the doctrine results in enabling the child to inherit from the deceased parent's estate. See, e.g., Estate of Wilson, 168 Cal. Rptr. 533 (Ct. App. 1980). Currently, at least 28 states recognize equitable adoption. Kristine S. Knaplund, Grandparents Raising Grandchildren and the Implications for Inheritance, 48 Ariz. L. Rev. 1, 6, (2006).

Case law reflects two theoretical bases for the doctrine: (1) contract theory, and (2) estoppel theory.

According to the contract theory, courts "presuppose that the foster parent as promisor has contracted to effect a legal adoption and that by granting relief the court is specifically enforcing that contract." Jan Ellen Rein, Relatives by Blood, Adoption, and Association: Who Should Get What and Why (The Impact of Adoptions, Adult Adoptions, and Equitable Adoptions on Intestate Succession and Class Gifts), 37 Vand. L. Rev. 711, 770 (1984). On the other hand, courts using the estoppel theory "stress the child's performance of filial services for the foster parent and purport to protect the child 'against the fraud of the adoptive parents' neglect or design in failing to do that which he in equity was obligated to do.'" Id. at 771. Under the latter theory, courts emphasize that the parent

(or their heirs) is estopped from asserting the invalidity of the adoption proceeding when the child "performed" filial responsibilities and the adoptive parents received all the benefits and, in fact, induced the child's performance based on representations as to the existence of the adoption. Rein criticizes that case law often fails to distinguish between the contract or estoppel analysis (id. at 771), and that the facts of most cases do not fit either of these legal theories well (id. at 772).

Most jurisdictions apply the doctrine in limited situations. In most states, the doctrine does not extend beyond the child. That is, a parent may not inherit from an equitably adopted child. Rebecca C. Bell, Comment, Virtual Adoption: The Difficulty of Creating an Exception to the Statutory Scheme, 29 Stetson L. Rev. 415, 416 (1999). See also In Estate of Furia, 126 Cal. Rptr. 2d 384 (Ct. App. 2002) (denying the right of an equitably adopted child to share in her foster grandmother's estate as "issue" of her late foster father); Jolley v. Seamco Laboratories, Inc., 828 So. 2d 1050 (Fla. Dist. Ct. App. 2002) (holding that an equitably adopted child was not a "survivor" for purposes of maintaining a suit for wrongful death).

In Estate of Ford, 8 Cal. Rptr. 3d 541 (Cal. 2004), a foster child claimed a right to inherit the intestate estate of his foster father (who died without issue or a surviving spouse). The California Supreme Court held that, although the evidence revealed a close family relationship (the child lived with his foster parents from the ages of 2 to 22), there was insufficient proof that the family ever made an attempt to adopt him or stated an intent to do so, as required by California Probate Code §6455. (The trial court had ruled that the requirement of a "legal barrier" to the adoption was not met under California Probate Code §6454, and therefore the foster son appealed only on the equitable adoption claim.) See also Restatement (Third) of Property, *supra*, at §2.5 cmt. k (discussing equitable adoption); Tracy Bateman Farrell, Annotation, Modern Status of Law as to Equitable Adoption or Adoption by Estoppel, 122 A.L.R.5th 205 §3(a) (2004).

CALIFORNIA PROBATE CODE

§6451. Legal consequences of adoption

(a) An adoption severs the relationship of parent and child between an adopted person and a natural parent of the adopted person unless both of the following requirements are satisfied:

(1) The natural parent and the adopted person lived together at any time as parent and child, or the natural parent was married to or cohabiting with the other natural parent at the time the person was conceived and died before the person's birth.

(2) The adoption was by the spouse of either of the natural parents or after the death of either of the natural parents.

(b) Neither a natural parent nor a relative of a natural parent, except for a wholeblood brother or sister of the adopted person or the issue of that brother or sister, inherits from or through the adopted person on the basis of a parent and child relationship between the adopted person and the natural parent that satisfies the requirements of paragraphs (1) and (2) of subdivision (a), unless the adoption is by the spouse or surviving spouse of that parent.

(c) For the purpose of this section, a prior adoptive parent and child relationship is treated as a natural parent and child relationship.

(Stats. 1993 (A.B. 1137), ch. 529, §5.)

§6455. Judicial doctrine of equitable adoption is not affected by this chapter

Nothing in this chapter affects or limits application of the judicial doctrine of equitable adoption for the benefit of the child or the child's issue.

(Stats. 1993 (A.B. 1137), ch. 529, §5.)

D. Nonmarital Children

Historically, children born out of wedlock (now termed "nonmarital children") were considered illegitimate and ineligible to inherit under intestacy laws. Gradually, the law permitted nonmarital children to inherit from their mother. McGovern & Kurtz, *supra*, §2.9 at 93 (pointing out that several American statutes so provided by the early nineteenth century).

The nonmarital child's right to inherit by, from, and through the biological father has been more problematic because of problems of proof of paternity. Many states impose a higher standard of proof or require particular kinds of proof in order for nonmarital children to inherit from their fathers. Id. at 94. The United States Supreme Court has held that, in order for a nonmarital child to inherit from a noncustodial biological father, a state may require a higher level of proof in the form of a judicial declaration of paternity (Lalli v. Lalli, 439 U.S. 259 (1978)), but may not require that the child's parents subsequently marry after the child's birth (Trimble v. Gordon, 430 U.S. 762 (1977)). As explained *infra*, this area of the law has been liberalized.

Another area of inheritance law and nonmarital children concerns the rights of parents of those children to inherit by, from, and through the child. Most states today allow parents of a nonmarital child and their relatives to inherit from the child. McGovern & Kurtz, *supra*, §2.9 at 97. The UPC, however, imposes limitations on the parents' ability to inherit from and through a nonmarital child. Specifically, UPC

§2-114(c) provides that the parent of a nonmarital child and that parent's kin do not inherit from and through the nonmarital child unless that natural parent openly treated the child as his or her child, and provided child support during the child's minority. California law mirrors this provision, requiring acknowledgment and financial contribution (Cal. Prob. Code §6452).

Today, most jurisdictions recognize the inheritance rights of nonmarital children. Many states have done so by adopting the Uniform Parentage Act (UPA), approved by NCCUSL in 1973. The UPA was the most important of the various uniform laws adopted by NCCUSL that addressed the rights of illegitimates. (Other uniform acts included: the Uniform Illegitimacy Act in 1922, the Uniform Blood Tests To Determine Paternity Act in 1952, and the Uniform Paternity Act in 1960, the Uniform Putative and Unknown Fathers Act in 1988, and the Uniform Status of Children of Assisted Conception Act in 1988.)

As of December 2000, the original version of the UPA was in effect in 19 states, and several additional states had enacted significant portions of it. The original UPA declared that all children should be treated equally without regard to the marital status of their parents, and established a set of rules for presumptions of parentage. When the UPC underwent substantial revision in 1990, it conferred additional importance on the Uniform Parentage Act by adopting similar language, providing that children have the right to inherit from their biological parents "without regard to the parents' marital status" (UPC §2-114(a)), and also providing that the parent and child relationship will be determined under the state's Parentage Act or other appropriate legislation.

NCCUSL promulgated a revised UPA in 2000 and amended it in 2002. The revised UPA replaces all earlier uniform acts dealing with parentage (not only the original UPA but also all subsequent acts). As explained above, the original UPA established several presumptions to facilitate the determination of paternity. The revised and amended UPA retains these presumptions of paternity with minor modifications. Thus, a man is presumed to be the father of a child if: (1) the child was born during the father's marriage to the child's mother; (2) the child was conceived during the marriage but born within 300 days after its termination (by death, annulment, declaration of invalidity, or divorce); (3) the child was conceived or born during an invalid marriage or within 300 days after its termination by the aforementioned methods; (4) the child was born before a valid or invalid marriage accompanied by other facts indicating that the husband is the father (i.e., he voluntarily acknowledged paternity in state birth records, agreed to be and is named on the child's birth certificate, or promised in a writing to support the child); or (5) for the first 2 years of the child's life, he resided in the same household with the child and openly held out the child as his own. Revised UPA §204(a).

The revised Act makes two changes to the earlier presumptions of the former Act. New subsection (5) changes former UPA §4(4) that created a presumption of paternity by "holding out" (if a man "receives the child into his home and openly holds out the child as his natural child"). The lack of a time period in the earlier Act led to uncertainty about whether the presumption could arise if the child's residence in the home occurred for a brief time or took place long after the child's birth. Revised UPA §204(a) cmt. The revised Act now includes an explicit requirement that the man reside with the child for the first 2 years of the child's life. In addition, the revised UPA eliminates a presumption in the earlier Act that created a presumption of paternity if the man "acknowledges his paternity of the child in a writing filed with [named agency] [and] the mother does not dispute the acknowledgment within a reasonable time." UPA §4(5)(1973)). This presumption was eliminated because it conflicted with a new provision on voluntary acknowledgment of paternity which now establishes actual paternity rather than merely a presumption of paternity.

According to the Restatement (Third) of Property §2.5, "An individual is the child of his or her genetic parents, whether or not they are married to each other. . . ." Exceptions to this rule are if: the child has been adopted out, results from assisted reproductive technology, or the parent has been disqualified from inheritance for certain acts of misconduct. See also McGovern & Kurtz, *supra*, §2.9 at 93-96.

Increasing recognition of the rights of nonmarital children has led to a more favorable attitude by courts and legislatures toward inclusion of such children in wills. McGovern & Kurtz, *supra*, §2.9 at 98 (citing UPC §2-705 to the effect that unless a will provides otherwise "individuals born out of wedlock and their respective descendants [are] are included in class gifts . . . .").

California law regarding the rights of nonmarital children to inherit reflects the views of the UPC and Uniform Parentage Act. California statute expressly provides that children may inherit intestate by, through, or from a natural parent "regardless of the marital status of the natural parents" (Cal. Prob. Code §6450). For purposes of determining whether a

person qualifies as a "natural parent," the California Probate Code refers to the original Uniform Parentage Act.

See generally Ralph C. Brashier, Inheritance Law and the Evolving Family 121-147 (2004).

CALIFORNIA PROBATE CODE

§6450. Conditions for existence of "parent-child relationship"

Subject to the provisions of this chapter, a relationship of parent and child exists for the purpose of determining intestate succession by, through, or from a person in the following circumstances:

(a) The relationship of parent and child exists between a person and the person's natural parents, regardless of the marital status of the natural parents.

(b) The relationship of parent and child exists between an adopted person and the person's adopting parent or parents.

(Stats. 1993 (A.B. 1137), ch. 529, §5.)

§6452. Parent's right to inherit "from or through" nonmarital child

If a child is born out of wedlock, neither a natural parent nor a relative of that parent inherits from or through the child on the basis of the parent and child relationship between that parent and the child unless both of the following requirements are satisfied:

(a) The parent or a relative of the parent acknowledged the child.

(b) The parent or a relative of the parent contributed to the support or the care of the child.

(Stats. 1993 (A.B. 1137), ch. 529, §5. Amended by Stats. 1996 (A.B. 2751), ch. 862, §15.)

§6453. "Natural parent" defined

For the purpose of determining whether a person is a "natural parent" as that term is used in this chapter:

(a) A natural parent and child relationship is established where that relationship is presumed and not rebutted pursuant to the Uniform Parentage Act (Part 3 (commencing with Section 7600) of Division 12 of the Family Code).

(b) A natural parent and child relationship may be established pursuant to any other provisions of the Uniform Parentage Act, except that the relationship may not be established by an action under subdivision (c) of Section 7630 of the Family Code unless any of the following conditions exist:

(1) A court order was entered during the father's lifetime declaring paternity.

(2) Paternity is established by clear and convincing evidence that the father has openly held out the child as his own.

(3) It was impossible for the father to hold out the child as his own and paternity is established by clear and convincing evidence.

(c) A natural parent and child relationship may be established pursuant to Section 249.5.

(Stats. 1993 (A.B. 1137), ch. 529, §5. Amended by Stats. 2004 (A.B. 1910), ch. 775 §9, effective January 1, 2005.)

§21114. Class gift described: transfers to heirs, next of kin, relatives, etc.

(a) If a statute or an instrument provides for transfer of a present or future interest to, or creates a present or future interest in, a designated person's "heirs," "heirs at law," "next of kin," "relatives," or "family," or words of similar import, the transfer is to the persons, including the state under Section 6800, and in the shares that would succeed to the designated person's intestate estate under the intestate succession law of the transferor's domicile, if the designated person died when the transfer is to take effect in enjoyment. If the designated person's surviving spouse is living but is remarried at the time the transfer is to take effect in enjoyment, the surviving spouse is not an heir of the designated person for purposes of this section.

(b) As used in this section, "designated person" includes the transferor.

(Stats. 1994 (A.B. 3686), ch. 806, §41. Amended by Stats. 2002 (A.B. 1784), ch. 138, §23, effective January 1, 2003.)

§21115. Right of certain children to inherit based on "class gift language" in will or trust

(a) Except as provided in subdivision (b), halfbloods, adopted persons, persons born out of wedlock, stepchildren, foster children, and the issue of these persons when appropriate to the class, are included in terms of class gift or relationship in accordance with the rules for determining relationship and inheritance rights for purposes of intestate succession.

(b) In construing a transfer by a transferor who is not the natural parent, a person born to the natural parent shall not be considered the child of that parent unless the person lived while a minor as a regular member of the household of the natural parent or of that parent's parent, brother, sister, spouse, or surviving spouse. In construing a transfer by a transferor who is not the adoptive parent, a person adopted by the adoptive parent shall not be considered the child of that parent unless the person lived while a minor (either before or after the adoption) as a regular member of the household of the adopting parent or of that parent's parent, brother, sister, or surviving spouse.

(c) Subdivisions (a) and (b) shall also apply in determining:

(1) Persons who would be kindred of the transferor or kindred of a surviving, deceased, or former spouse of the transferor under Section 21110.

(2) Persons to be included as issue of a deceased transferee under Section 21110.

(3) Persons who would be the transferor's or other designated person's heirs under Section 21114.

(d) The rules for determining intestate succession under this section are those in effect at the time the transfer is to take effect in enjoyment.

(Stats. 1994 (A.B. 3686), ch. 806, §41. Amended by Stats. 2002 (A.B. 1784), ch. 138, §24, effective January 1, 2003.)

CALIFORNIA FAMILY CODE

§7611. Conditions to establish conclusive presumption of paternity

A man is presumed to be the natural father of a child if he meets the conditions provided in Chapter 1 (commencing with Section 7540) or Chapter 3 (commencing with Section 7570) of Part 2 or in any of the following subdivisions:

(a) He and the child's natural mother are or have been married to each other and the child is born during the marriage, or within 300 days after the marriage is terminated by death, annulment, declaration of invalidity, or divorce, or after a judgment of separation is entered by a court.

(b) Before the child's birth, he and the child's natural mother have attempted to marry each other by a marriage solemnized in apparent compliance with law, although the attempted marriage is or could be declared invalid, and either of the following is true:

(1) If the attempted marriage could be declared invalid only by a court, the child is born during the attempted marriage, or within 300 days after its termination by death, annulment, declaration of invalidity, or divorce.

(2) If the attempted marriage is invalid without a court order, the child is born within 300 days after the termination of cohabitation.

(c) After the child's birth, he and the child's natural mother have married, or attempted to marry, each other by a marriage solemnized in apparent compliance with law, although the attempted marriage is or could be declared invalid, and either of the following is true:

(1) With his consent, he is named as the child's father on the child's birth certificate.

(2) He is obligated to support the child under a written voluntary promise or by court order.

(d) He receives the child into his home and openly holds out the child as his natural child.

(e) [This subsection is inoperative after January 1, 1997.]

(Stats. 1992 (A.B. 2650), ch. 162, §10, effective January 1, 1994. Amended by Stats. 1993 (A.B. 1500), ch. 219, §176. Amended by Stats. 1994 (A.B. 2208), ch. 1269, §53; This section was held unconstitutional in the case of In re Jerry P., 95 Cal. App. 4th 793 (Ct. App. 2002) (holding that the statute was an unconstitutional violation of due process and equal protection as applied to a de facto father who was thwarted from holding the child out as his by the child's mother, when the father moved for family reunification services in a child dependency proceeding), modified on denial of rehearing, review granted and opinion superseded 119 Cal. Rptr. 2d 856, 46 P.3d 331, publication ordered 121 Cal. Rptr. 2d 106, 47 P.3d 988, review dismissed, cause remanded 124 Cal. Rptr. 2d 718, 53 P.3d 133.)

§7611.5. Presumption against natural father status

Where Section 7611 does not apply, a man shall not be presumed to be the natural father of a child if either of the following is true:

(a) The child was conceived as a result of an act in violation of Section 261 [rape] of the Penal Code and the father was convicted of that violation.

(b) The child was conceived as a result of an act in violation of Section 261.5 [statutory rape] of the Penal Code, the father was convicted of that violation, and the mother was under the age of 15 years and the father was 21 years of age or older at the time of conception.

(Stats. 1993 (A.B. 1500), ch. 219, §177.)

§7630. Persons who may bring action to determine existence of father-child relationship

(a) A child, the child's natural mother, a man presumed to be the child's father under subdivision (a), (b), or (c) of Section 7611, an adoption agency to whom the child has been relinquished or a prospective adoptive parent of the child may bring an action as follows:

(1) At any time for the purpose of declaring the existence of the father and child relationship presumed under subdivision (a), (b), or (c) of Section 7611.

(2) For the purpose of declaring the nonexistence of the father and child relationship presumed under subdivision (a), (b), or (c) of Section 7611 only if the action is brought within a reasonable time after obtaining knowledge of relevant facts. After the presumption has been rebutted, paternity of the child by another man may be determined in the same action, if he has been made a party.

(b) Any interested party may bring an action at any time for the purpose of determining the existence or nonexistence of the father and child relationship presumed under subdivision (d) or (f) of Section 7611.

(c) An action to determine the existence of the father and child relationship with respect to a child who has no presumed father under Section 7611 or whose presumed father is deceased may be brought by the child or personal representative of the child, the Department of Child Support Services, the mother or the personal representative or a parent of the mother if the mother has died or is a minor, a man alleged or alleging himself to be the father, or the personal representative or a parent of the alleged father if the alleged father has died or is a minor.

(d)(1) If a proceeding has been filed under Chapter 2 (commencing with Section 7820) of Part 4, an action under subdivision (a) or (b) shall be consolidated with that proceeding. The parental rights of the presumed father shall be determined as set forth in Sections 7820 through 7829, inclusive.

(2) If a proceeding pursuant to Section 7662 has been filed under Chapter 5 (commencing with Section 7660), an action under subdivision (c) shall be consolidated with that proceeding. The parental rights of the alleged natural father shall be determined as set forth in Section 7664.

(3) The consolidated action under paragraph (1) or (2) shall be heard in the court in which the proceeding is filed, unless the court finds, by clear and convincing evidence, that transferring the action to the other court poses a substantial hardship to the petitioner. Mere inconvenience does not constitute a sufficient basis for a finding of substantial hardship. If the court determines there is a substantial hardship, the consolidated action shall be heard in the court in which the paternity action is filed.

(e) A party to an assisted reproduction agreement may bring an action at any time to establish a parent and child relationship consistent with the intent expressed in that assisted reproduction agreement.

(Stats. 1992 (A.B. 2650), ch. 162, §10, effective January 1, 1994; Stats. 2000 (A.B. 1358), ch. 808, §76, effective September 28, 2000; Stats. 2001 (A.B. 538), ch. 353, §1; Stats. 2003 (S.B. 182), ch. 251, §2; Stats. 2004 (A.B. 1910), ch. 775, §2; Stats. 2005 (S.B. 302), ch. 627, §2; Stats. 2006 (S.B. 1325), ch. 806, §3.)

E. Disqualification for Misconduct

1. Slayer Disqualification

A person can lose the right to inherit under the intestacy statutes because of misconduct. The most common form of misconduct that serves as a bar to inheritance is murdering the decedent (known as the "slayer disqualification").

The common law had no slayer disqualification because felons normally forfeited all their property. Thus, many American jurisdictions permitted slayers to inherit from their victims until legislatures remedied the gap by enacting statutory bars to inheritance. Most states now have statutes that prevent a murderer from inheriting from the victim. McGovern & Kurtz, *supra*, §2.7 at 75. These statutes developed in a piecemeal fashion; therefore, many statutes initially failed to address inheritance involving insurance policies or joint tenancy property. In such cases, courts sometimes used principles of constructive trust (an equitable remedy to prevent unjust enrichment) to preclude the slayer from inheriting. The policy justification is that a wrongdoer should not benefit from his or her wrong.

Some state statutes require that the slayer must have been "convicted" of murder in order to be barred from inheritance. Problems arise if the slayer has not been tried, or has been acquitted (or convicted of a lesser offense). In these jurisdictions, some courts conclude that the absence of a conviction does not prevent them from precluding the slayer from inheriting. In cases where a slayer has been acquitted (or convicted of a lesser offense), some courts nonetheless justify the preclusion on the ground that the standard in a civil proceeding is lower than the reasonable doubt standard required for a criminal conviction. McGovern & Kurtz, *supra*, §2.7 at 77-78.

The Uniform Probate Code bars inheritance by an individual who "feloniously and intentionally kills the decedent" (UPC §2-803). The UPC extends the slayer disqualification to beneficiaries of many types of property (including joint tenancies and life insurance) (id.). In terms of joint tenancy property, the UPC terminates the right of survivorship but permits the slayer to retain his or her half-interest in the property (id. at §2-803(c)(2)). Moreover, the UPC also provides that the policy of preclusion can apply even if the particular property interest is not explicitly specified (id. at §2-803(f)).

If the slayer is disqualified, the property is distributed generally as if the slayer predeceased the victim. McGovern & Kurtz, *supra*, §2.7 at 80; UPC §2-803 (property is distributed as if the killer disclaimed). As a result, the children of the slayer may inherit the property, either by representation in the intestacy situation or under an anti-lapse statute in the testate situation.

However, the new Restatement of Restitution provides for a different result in slayer disqualification cases: the property will be distributed by statute or, in the absence of statute, to "the person with the paramount equitable claim." Such a person generally is:

(a) the person at whose expense the slayer has been unjustly enriched,

(b) the person intended by the victim to take the assets in question, or

(c) the person who succeeds to legal ownership of the property on elimination of the slayer's interest.

If no such "paramount claim" can be identified, the court has discretion to divide the property "between persons whose equitable claims are of equal rank." Restatement (Third) of Restitution (Tent. Draft No. 5 (March 12, 2007)), §45 (3).

Like the UPC, California law precludes a person who "feloniously and intentionally" kills the decedent from inheriting any property, interest, or benefit under the decedent's will, or a trust created by or for the benefit of the decedent or in which the decedent has an interest (Cal. Prob. Code §250). All aforementioned property interests pass as if the slayer predeceased the decedent, and statutory provisions substituting the slayer's issue do not apply (Cal. Prob. Code §250(b)(1)). Furthermore, the slayer is precluded from inheriting from the decedent by intestate succession (Cal. Prob. Code §250(a)(2)), and from inheriting any of the decedent's quasi-community property (Cal. Prob. Code §250(a)(3)),

or any property of the decedent under family protection provisions (such as a homestead allowance, family allowance, or personal property set-aside) (Cal. Prob. Code §250(a)(5)), or gifts in view of impending death (Cal. Prob. Code §250(a)(4)).

The California slayer disqualification (Cal. Prob. Code §250) was added in 1984 (Stats. 1984, ch. 527, §3). It restated former California Probate Code §200 (Stats. 1983, ch. 842, §22, repealed by Stats. 1984, ch. 527, §1) which superseded former California Probate Code §258 (repealed by Stats. 1983, ch. 842, §19). Under former California Probate Code §258, the killer was disqualified if the killing was accidental but was within the felony murder rule. Law Revision Commission Commentary following California Probate Code §250.

The present California slayer disqualification (Cal. Prob. Code §250) is similar to UPC §2-803(a)(1987), except that the former covers various matters in more detail. Id. Also, California Probate Code §250 differs from the UPC by the addition of a provision adding references to the nomination of a conservator (Cal. Prob. Code §250(b)(3)).

A joint tenant (in real and personal property, joint and multiple-party accounts in financial institutions, etc.) who feloniously and intentionally kills another joint tenant effects a severance of the property. The decedent's share thereby passes to the decedent's heirs or beneficiaries; the slayer retains his or her interest but takes no rights by survivorship (Cal. Prob. Code §251). For discussion of joint tenancy, see Chapter VIII *infra*. Similarly, beneficiaries of a bond, life insurance policy, or other contractual arrangement, who slay the insured are precluded from taking any benefit thereunder (Cal. Prob. Code §252).

The California Probate Code has a "catch-all" provision, similar to the UPC, regarding the acquisition of property interests or benefits that have not been previously specified. California Probate Code §253 specifies that any property, interests, or benefits that have not been previously described will be treated "in accordance with principles of this part."

For purposes of determining whether a killing was "felonious and intentional," the statute specifies that a final judgment of conviction is conclusive. In the absence of such a judgment, the court may determine by a preponderance of evidence whether the killing was felonious and intentional. An acquittal has no effect in a subsequent civil proceeding to establish that the killing was felonious and intentional.

In California, a slayer who is charged with murder or voluntary manslaughter also loses the right to control the disposition of a decedent's remains. Cal. Health & Safety Code §7100.

For classic articles on the slayer disqualification, see Mary Louise Fellows, The Slayer Rule: Not Solely a Matter of Equity, 71 Iowa L. Rev. 489 (1986); William M. McGovern, Jr., Homicide and Succession to Property, 68 Mich. L. Rev. 65 (1969); Jeffrey G. Sherman, Mercy Killing and the Right to Inherit, 61 U. Cin. L. Rev. 803 (1993).

For recent commentary, see Julie Waller Hampton, Comment, The Need for a New Slayer Disqualification Statute in North Carolina, 24 Campbell L. Rev. 295 (2002); Julie J. Olenn, Comment, 'Til Death Do Us Part: New York's Slayer Rule and In re Estates of Covert, 49 Buff. L. Rev. 1341 (2001).

2. Other Unworthy Heir Statutes

States have a variety of other "unworthy heir" statutes. Professor Frances Foster points out that many jurisdictions disqualify spouses who abandon the decedent, or disqualify parents who abandon or refuse to support their children. Frances H. Foster, The Family Paradigm of Inheritance Law, 80 N.C. L. Rev. 199, 207 n. 38 (2001). See also UPC §2-114(c) (permitting inheritance only if the parent has openly treated the child as belonging to the parent, and has not refused to support the child); Restatement (Third) of Property, *supra*, at §2.5(5) (barring a parent from inheriting from or through a child, if the parent "has refused to acknowledge or has abandoned his or her child, or a person whose parental rights have been terminated"). The common law barred an adulterous wife from claiming dower. McGovern & Kurtz, *supra*, §2.11 at 112.

An interesting case involving an unworthy heir statute is In re Estate of Lunsford, 547 S.E.2d 483 (N.C. Ct. App. 2001), *vacated and remanded*, 556 S.E.2d 292 (N.C. 2001). A mother obtained a wrongful death award on behalf of the estate of her 17-year-old daughter who was killed in an automobile accident. Because wrongful death proceeds in North Carolina are paid to surviving family members in accordance with intestate succession law (which bars a parent who abandons a child from inheriting), the court prevented the father from inheriting half of the proceeds. (The father had paid only $100 in child support and had visited the daughter rarely in 15 years.) The case was remanded for a determination of whether the father was eligible under one of two statutory exceptions (where the abandoning parent resumes care and maintenance at least one year prior to the child's death or where the parent was deprived of the

custody under a court order but substantially complied with all court orders for child support). See generally Heyward D. Armstrong, Comment, In re Estate of Lunsford and Statutory Ambiguity: Trying to Reconcile Child Abandonment and the Intestate Succession Act, 81 N.C. L. Rev. 1149 (2003). But cf. Hotarek v. Benson, 557 A.2d 1259 (Conn. 1989)(permitting a mother to inherit from her 15-year-old son despite the mother's neglect and failure to provide financial support).

California is the first state to disqualify an heir from inheritance through intestate succession, elective share, homestead allowance, or any other statutory allowances for manifesting a pattern of physical violence directed toward the decedent. Thomas H. Shepherd, Comment, It's the 21st Century . . . Time for Probate Codes to Address Family Violence: A Proposal that Deals with the Realities of the Problem, 20 St. Louis U. Pub. L. Rev. 449, 450 (2001). Specifically, California law precludes persons from exercising their inheritance rights if they physically abuse or neglect an elder or dependent adult. In such cases, the abuser is considered to have predeceased the decedent in the determination of shares of the estate (Cal. Prob. Code §259). Abuse is broadly defined to include physical abuse and neglect, false imprisonment, and fiduciary abuse. See generally Kymberleigh N. Korpus, Note, Extinguishing Inheritance Rights: California Breaks New Ground in the Fight Against Elder Abuse But Fails to Build an Effective Foundation, 52 Hastings L.J. 537 (2001); Robin L. Preble, Family Violence and Family Property: A Proposal For Reform, 13 Law & Ineq . 401 (1995).

For commentary advocating law reform that would deny intestate shares to persons who abandon, fail to support, or maltreat a decedent, see Frances H. Foster, Towards a Behavior-Based Model of Inheritance?: The Chinese Experiment, 32 U.C. Davis L. Rev. 77 (1998); Paula A. Monopoli, "Deadbeat Dads": Should Support and Inheritance Be Linked?, 49 U. Miami L. Rev. 257 (1994); Preble, *supra*; Anne-Marie E. Rhodes, Abandoning Parents Under Intestacy: Where We Are, Where We Need to Go, 27 Ind. L. Rev. 517 (1994).

CALIFORNIA PROBATE CODE

§250. Slayer disqualification: wills, trusts, intestate succession, and family protection

(a) A person who feloniously and intentionally kills the decedent is not entitled to any of the following:

(1) Any property, interest, or benefit under a will of the decedent, or a trust created by or for the benefit of the decedent or in which the decedent has an interest, including any general or special power of appointment conferred by the will or trust on the killer and any nomination of the killer as executor, trustee, guardian, or conservator or custodian made by the will or trust.

(2) Any property of the decedent by intestate succession.

(3) Any of the decedent's quasi-community property the killer would otherwise acquire under Section 101 or 102 upon the death of the decedent.

(4) Any property of the decedent under Part 5 (commencing with Section 5700) of Division 5.

(5) Any property of the decedent under Part 3 (commencing with Section 6500) of Division 6.

(b) In the cases covered by subdivision (a):

(1) The property interest or benefit referred to in paragraph (1) of subdivision (a) passes as if the killer had predeceased the decedent and Section 21110 does not apply.

(2) Any property interest or benefit referred to in paragraph (1) of subdivision (a) which passes under a power of appointment and by reason of the death of the decedent passes as if the killer had predeceased the decedent, and Section 1389.4 of the Civil Code does not apply.

(3) Any nomination in a will or trust of the killer as executor, trustee, guardian, conservator, or custodian which becomes effective as a result of the death of the decedent shall be interpreted as if the killer had predeceased the decedent.

(Stats. 1990 (A.B. 759), ch. 79, §14, effective July 1, 1991. Amended by Stats. 1991 (S.B. 271), ch. 1055, §13; Stats. 1992 (A.B. 2975), ch. 871, §2; Stats. 1997 (A.B. 1172), ch. 724, §3.)

§251. Slayer disqualification: joint tenancy property

A joint tenant who feloniously and intentionally kills another joint tenant thereby effects a severance of the interest of the decedent so that the share of the decedent passes as the decedent's property and the killer has no rights by survivorship. This section applies to joint tenancies in real and personal property, joint and multiple-party accounts in financial institutions, and any other form of coownership with survivorship incidents.

(Stats. 1990 (A.B .759), ch. 79, §14, effective July 1, 1991.)

§252. Slayer disqualification: bonds, life insurance and other beneficiary designations

A named beneficiary of a bond, life insurance policy, or other contractual arrangement who feloniously and intentionally kills the principal obligee or the person upon whose life the policy is issued is not entitled to any benefit under the bond, policy, or other contractual arrangement, and it becomes payable as though the killer had predeceased the decedent.

(Stats. 1990 (A.B. 759), ch. 79, §14, effective July 1, 1991.)

§253. Slayer disqualification extends to similar cases not controlled by other provisions

In any case not described in Section 250, 251, or 252 in which one person feloniously and intentionally kills another, any acquisition of property, interest, or benefit by the killer as a result of the killing of the decedent shall be treated in accordance with the principles of this part.

(Stats. 1990 (A.B. 759), ch. 79, §14, effective July 1, 1991.)

§254. Determination of "felonious and intentional" killing: conviction required

(a) A final judgment of conviction of felonious and intentional killing is conclusive for purposes of this part.

(b) In the absence of a final judgment of conviction of felonious and intentional killing, the court may determine by a preponderance of evidence whether the killing was felonious and intentional for purposes of this part. The burden of proof is on the party seeking to establish that the killing was felonious and intentional for the purposes of this part.

(Stats. 1990 (A.B. 759), ch. 79, §14, effective July 1, 1991.)

§255. Rights of good faith purchasers are unaffected

This part does not affect the rights of any person who, before rights under this part have been adjudicated, purchases from the killer for value and without notice property which the killer would have acquired except for this part, but the killer is liable for the amount of the proceeds or the value of the property.

(Stats. 1990 (A.B. 759), ch. 79, §14, effective July 1, 1991.)

§256. Protection of obligors for payments previously made

An insurance company, financial institution, or other obligor making payment according to the terms of its policy or obligation is not liable by reason of this part, unless prior to payment it has received at its home office or principal address written notice of a claim under this part.

(Stats. 1990 (A.B. 759), ch. 79, §14, effective July 1, 1991.)

§257. Effective date of application of part

This part does not apply where the decedent was killed before January 1, 1985; and the law applicable prior to January 1, 1985, continues to apply where the decedent was killed before January 1, 1985.

(Stats. 1990 (A.B. 759), ch 79, §14, effective July 1, 1991.)

§258. Slayer is not entitled to bring wrongful death action

A person who feloniously and intentionally kills the decedent is not entitled to bring an action for wrongful death of the decedent or to benefit from the action brought by the decedent's personal representative. The persons who may bring an action for wrongful death of the decedent and to benefit from the action are determined as if the killer had predeceased the decedent.

(Stats. 1992 (S.B. 1496), ch. 178, §29.5.)

§259. Disqualification by persons liable for elder abuse or abuse of dependent adult

(a) Any person shall be deemed to have predeceased a decedent to the extent provided in subdivision (c) where all of the following apply:

(1) It has been proven by clear and convincing evidence that the person is liable for physical abuse, neglect, or fiduciary abuse of the decedent, who was an elder or dependent adult.

(2) The person is found to have acted in bad faith.

(3) The person has been found to have been reckless, oppressive, fraudulent, or malicious in the commission of any of these acts upon the decedent.

(4) The decedent, at the time those acts occurred and thereafter until the time of his or her death, has been found to have been substantially unable to manage his or her financial resources or to resist fraud or undue influence.

(b) Any person shall be deemed to have predeceased a decedent to the extent provided in subdivision (c) if that person has been convicted of a violation of Section 236 of the Penal Code or any offense described in Section 368 of the Penal Code.

(c) Any person found liable under subdivision (a) or convicted under subdivision (b) shall not

(1) receive any property, damages, or costs that are awarded to the decedent's estate in an action described in subdivision (a) or (b), whether that person's entitlement is under a will, a trust, or the laws of intestacy; or

(2) serve as a fiduciary as defined in Section 39, if the instrument nominating or appointing that person was executed during the period when the decedent was substantially unable to manage his or her financial resources or resist fraud or undue influence. This section shall not apply to a decedent who, at any time following the act or acts described in paragraph (1) of subdivision (a), or the act or acts described in subdivision (b), was substantially able to manage his or her financial resources and to resist fraud or undue influence within the meaning of subdivision (b) of Section 1801 of the Probate Code and subdivision (b) of Section 39 of the Civil Code.

(d) For purposes of this section, the following definitions shall apply:

(1) Physical abuse as defined in Section 15610.63 of the Welfare and Institutions Code.

(2) Neglect as defined in Section 15610.57 of the Welfare and Institutions Code.

(3) False imprisonment as defined in Section 368 of the Penal Code.

(4) Fiduciary abuse as defined in Section 15610.30 of the Welfare and Institutions Code.

(e) Nothing in this section shall be construed to prohibit the severance and transfer of an action or proceeding to a separate civil action pursuant to Section 801.
(Stats. 1998 (S.B. 1715), ch. 935, §4.)

CALIFORNIA HEALTH AND SAFETY CODE §7100. Right to control the disposition of decedent's remains

(a) The right to control the disposition of the remains of a deceased person, the location and conditions of interment, and arrangements for funeral goods and services to be provided, unless other directions have been given by the decedent pursuant to Section 7100.1, vests in, and the duty of disposition and the liability for the reasonable cost of disposition of the remains devolves upon, the following in the order named:

(1) An agent under a power of attorney for health care who has the right and duty of disposition under Division 4.7 (commencing with Section 4600) of the Probate Code, except that the agent is liable for the costs of disposition only in either of the following cases:

(A) Where the agent makes a specific agreement to pay the costs of disposition.

(B) Where, in the absence of a specific agreement, the agent makes decisions concerning disposition that incur costs, in which case the agent is liable only for the reasonable costs incurred as a result of the agent's decisions, to the extent that the decedent's estate or other appropriate fund is insufficient.

(2) The competent surviving spouse.

(3) The sole surviving competent adult child of the decedent, or if there is more than one competent adult child of the decedent, the majority of the surviving competent adult children. However, less than the majority of the surviving competent adult children shall be vested with the rights and duties of this section if they have used reasonable efforts to notify all other surviving competent adult children of their instructions and are not aware of any opposition to those instructions by the majority of all surviving competent adult children.

(4) The surviving competent parent or parents of the decedent. If one of the surviving competent parents is absent, the remaining competent parent shall be vested with the rights and duties of this section after reasonable efforts have been unsuccessful in locating the absent surviving competent parent.

(5) The sole surviving competent adult sibling of the decedent, or if there is more than one surviving competent adult sibling of the decedent, the majority of the surviving competent adult siblings. However, less than the majority of the surviving competent adult siblings shall be vested with the rights and duties of this section if they have used reasonable efforts to notify all other surviving competent adult siblings of their instructions and are not aware of any opposition to those instructions by the majority of all surviving competent adult siblings.

(6) The surviving competent adult person or persons respectively in the next degrees of kinship, or if there is more than one surviving competent adult person of the same degree of kinship, the majority of those persons. Less than the majority of surviving competent adult persons of the same degree of kinship shall be vested with the rights and duties of this section if those persons have used reasonable efforts to notify all other surviving competent adult persons of the same degree of kinship of their instructions and are not aware of any opposition to those instructions by the majority of all surviving competent adult persons of the same degree of kinship.

(7) The public administrator when the deceased has sufficient assets.

(b)(1) If any person to whom the right of control has vested pursuant to subdivision (a) has been charged with first or second degree murder or voluntary manslaughter in connection with the decedent's death and those charges are known to the funeral director or cemetery authority, the right of control is relinquished and passed on to the next of kin in accordance with subdivision (a).

(2) If the charges against the person are dropped, or if the person is acquitted of the charges, the right of control is returned to the person.

(3) Notwithstanding this subdivision, no person who has been charged with first or second degree murder or voluntary manslaughter in connection with the decedent's death to whom the right of control has not been returned pursuant to paragraph (2) shall have any right to control disposition pursuant to subdivision (a) which shall be applied, to the extent the funeral director or cemetery authority know about the charges, as if that person did not exist.

. . .

(Stats. 1939, ch. 60, p. 673, §7100. Amended by Stats. 1947, ch. 125, p. 646, §1; Stats. 1957, ch. 933, p. 2144, §1; Stats. 1965, ch. 654, p. 2021, §1; Stats. 1968, ch. 926, p. 1758, §1; Stats. 1969, ch. 999, p. 1971, §1; Stats. 1970, ch. 960, §3; Stats. 1970, ch. 1006, §1.5; Stats. 1970, ch. 1006, p. 1809, §1.5; Stats. 1993 (A.B. 598), ch. 1232, §22; Stats. 1994 (A.B. 1392), ch. 570; Stats. 1997 (A.B. 1546), ch. 475, §23; Stats. 1998 (S.B. 1360), ch. 253, §1; Stats. 1999 (A.B. 1677), ch. 657, §36; Stats. 1999 (A.B. 891), ch. 658, §5.5, effective July 1, 2000; Stats. 2001 (A.B. 1278), ch. 230, §1; Stats. 2004 (A.B. 2811), ch. 307, §1, effective January 1, 2005.)

IV. Simultaneous Death

A basic tenet of inheritance law is that an heir must outlive the intestate (or a beneficiary must outlive a testator) in order to inherit from the decedent. The issue of survival of family members is cast into doubt when persons die simultaneously (technically, nearly simultaneously). This event occurs with increasing frequency because of the death of

multiple family members in airplane crashes and automobile accidents. Simultaneous death poses a problem not merely for intestate succession but also for testate succession. Provisions in trusts also may lead to questions regarding the order of death.

The common law required survival only for an instant for inheritance purposes. That standard led to considerable litigation involving family members who attempted to prove that one family member had outlived another by manifesting even the slightest signs of life.

The original version of the Uniform Simultaneous Death Act first addressed the issue in 1940. That widely adopted Act required "sufficient evidence" to prove that two persons died otherwise than simultaneously. Uniform Simultaneous Death Act §2 (1940). The UPC now also requires survival for 120 hours and mandates a clear and convincing burden of proof. UPC §2-702(b). A beneficiary who fails to survive for the requisite period is deemed to have predeceased the decedent. A subsequent version of the Uniform Simultaneous Death Act also substantially eliminated problems of proof by requiring that a person must survive by 120 hours in order to inherit from the decedent. Uniform Simultaneous Death Act §4 (1993).

California law provides rules for determining the sequence of deaths and establishes a procedure for applying these rules (Cal. Prob. Code §§220-234). According to California Probate Code §220, if title to property depends upon a person surviving another and the fact of survival cannot be established by clear and convincing evidence, the property of each is to be distributed as if that person had survived the other. On the other hand, if clear and convincing evidence as to the order of death does exist, then the statute is not applicable.

Mirroring the UPC provision, California's *clear and convincing* standard is coupled with a requirement of *survival by at least 120 hours*. This standard applies for a person to inherit as an *intestate heir* (Cal. Prob. Code §6403) or as the beneficiary of a statutory will (Cal. Prob. Code §6211). Thus, if a decedent (D) died intestate leaving X as his heir, or left a statutory will bequeathing his property to X, then in the event that D and X died together in a car crash, X's representative would have to prove by clear and convincing evidence that X survived the decedent by at least 120 hours in order for D's property to pass to X's estate. If X's representative is unable to make that showing, then D is treated as having survived X and D's estate passes to D's heirs (or to alternative beneficiaries under D's statutory will).

The community and quasi-community property of a husband and wife who die simultaneously is distributed pursuant to California Probate Code §103. Thus, for example, if husband (H) and wife (W) die together in an airplane crash, their community (and/or quasi-community property) passes as follows: one-half is distributed as if H survived W and as if that half belonged to H; the other half is distributed as if W survived H and that half belonged to W (Cal. Prob. Code §103). In the event that the sequence of death cannot be established by clear and convincing evidence and the property involves a life or accident insurance policy which is community or quasi-community property (and there is no alternative beneficiary except the estate or personal representative of the insured), the proceeds are distributed as community property under this section as well (i.e., half the proceeds pass as if the insured survived and the other half as if the beneficiary survived) (Cal. Prob. Code §224).

If a will (or other instrument) contains a survivorship condition, California Probate Code §21109(c) applies. California Probate Code §6403 applies in cases of intestate succession, and California Probate Code §6211 determines the sequence of death under a statutory will containing a survivorship condition. If property is owned in joint tenancy and there is no clear and convincing evidence that one joint tenant survived the other, the property is distributed as if each joint tenant survived the other (i.e., one-half passes to one joint tenant's heirs or beneficiaries and the other half passes to the other joint tenant's heirs or beneficiaries) (Cal. Prob. Code §223(b)).

The provisions of California Probate §§220 et seq. do not apply in cases of a trust, deed, insurance contract, or other situation if the instrument makes a different provision for dealing with simultaneous death, or if a provision requires survival for a stated period in order to take property, or provides for a presumption as to survivorship that results in a distribution of property different from that provided by this chapter (Cal. Prob. Code §221(b)).

The proceedings for an order determining survival are commenced by a personal representative (executor or administrator), beneficiary, heir at law, or even creditor (Cal. Prob. Code §231). The petition must allege the petitioner's standing, date of death, reason for determining survival, circumstances of death, and lack of sufficient evidence regarding survival, plus (in an intestate or statutory will situation) an allegation that the simultaneously deceased heir or beneficiary survived the decedent by at least 120 hours. See generally Ross & Grant, *supra*, at §14-34.14-14:150.

CALIFORNIA PROBATE CODE

§103. Effect on community property if clear and convincing evidence of survival is absent

Except as provided by Section 224, if a husband and wife die leaving community or quasi-community property and it cannot be established by clear and convincing evidence that one spouse survived the other:

(a) One-half of the community property and one-half the quasi-community property shall be administered or distributed, or otherwise dealt with, as if one spouse had survived and as if that half belonged to that spouse.

(b) The other half of the community property and the other half of the quasi-community property shall be administered or distributed, or otherwise dealt with, as if the other spouse had survived and as if that half belonged to that spouse.

(Stats. 1990 (A.B. 759), ch. 79, §14, effective July 1, 1991.)

§220. Requirement of proof of survival by clear and convincing evidence

Except as otherwise provided in this chapter, if the title to property or the devolution of property depends upon priority of death and it cannot be established by clear and convincing evidence that one of the persons survived the other, the property of each person shall be administered or distributed, or otherwise dealt with, as if that person had survived the other.

(Stats. 1990 (A.B. 759), ch. 79, §14, effective July 1, 1991.)

§221. Exceptions: if certain instruments provide otherwise

(a) This chapter does not apply in any case where Section 103, 6146, 6211, or 6403 applies.

(b) This chapter does not apply in the case of a trust, deed, or contract of insurance, or any other situation, where (1) provision is made dealing explicitly with simultaneous deaths or deaths in a common disaster or otherwise providing for distribution of property different from the provisions of this chapter or (2) provision is made requiring one person to survive another for a stated period in order to take property or providing for a presumption as to survivorship that results in a distribution of property different from that provided by this chapter.

(Stats. 1990 (A.B. 759), ch. 79, §14, effective July 1, 1991. Amended by Stats. 1990 (S.B. 1775), ch. 710, §1, effective July 1, 1991.)

§222. Exception: if testate beneficiary's inheritance is conditioned on survival

(a) If property is so disposed of that the right of a beneficiary to succeed to any interest in the property is conditional upon surviving another person and it cannot be established by clear and convincing evidence that the beneficiary survived the other person, the beneficiary is deemed not to have survived the other person.

(b) If property is so disposed of that one of two or more beneficiaries would have been entitled to the property if he or she had survived the others, and it cannot be established by clear and convincing evidence that any beneficiary survived any other beneficiary, the property shall be divided into as many equal portions as there are beneficiaries and the portion of each beneficiary shall be administered or distributed, or otherwise dealt with, as if that beneficiary had survived the other beneficiaries.

(Stats. 1990 (A.B. 759), ch. 79, §14, effective July 1, 1991.)

§223. Simultaneous death of joint tenants

(a) As used in this section, "joint tenants" includes owners of property held under circumstances that entitled one or more to the whole of the property on the death of the other or others.

(b) If property is held by two joint tenants and both of them have died and it cannot be established by clear and convincing evidence that one survived the other, the property held in joint tenancy shall be administered or distributed, or otherwise dealt with, one-half as if one joint tenant had survived and one-half as if the other joint tenant had survived.

(c) If property is held by more than two joint tenants and all of them have died and it cannot be established by clear and convincing evidence that any of them survived the others, the property held in joint tenancy shall be divided into as many portions as there are joint tenants and the share of each joint tenant shall be administered or distributed, or otherwise dealt with, as if that joint tenant had survived the other joint tenants.

(Stats. 1990 (A.B. 759), ch. 79, §14, effective July 1, 1991.)

§224. Simultaneous death of insured and beneficiary under life or accident insurance

If the insured and a beneficiary under a policy of life or accident insurance have died and it cannot be established by clear and convincing evidence that the beneficiary survived the insured, the proceeds of the policy shall be administered or distributed, or otherwise dealt with, as if the insured had survived the beneficiary, except if the policy is community or quasi-community property of the insured and the spouse of the insured and there is no alternative beneficiary except the estate or personal representative of the insured, the proceeds shall be distributed as community property under Section 103.

(Stats. 1990 (A.B. 759), ch. 79 §14, effective July 1, 1991.)

§226. Chapter inapplicable if death occurs prior to January 1, 1985

This chapter does not apply where a person the priority of whose death is in issue died before January 1, 1985, and the law applicable prior to January 1, 1985, continues to apply where none of the persons the priority of whose death is in issue died on or after January 1, 1985.

(Stats. 1990 (A.B. 759), ch. 79, §14, effective July 1, 1991.)

§230. Petition for purpose of determining order of survival

A petition may be filed under this chapter for any one or more of the following purposes:

(a) To determine for the purposes of Section 103, 220, 222, 223, 224, 6146, 6147, 6211, 6242, 6243, 6244, or 6403, or other provision of this code whether one person survived another.

(b) To determine for the purposes of Section 1389.4 of the Civil Code whether issue of an appointee survived the donee.

(c) To determine for the purposes of Section 24606 of the Education Code whether a person has survived in order to receive benefits payable under the system.

(d) To determine for the purposes of Section 21371 of the Government Code whether a person has survived in order to receive money payable under the system.

(e) To determine for the purposes of a case governed by former Sections 296 to 296.8, inclusive, repealed by Chapter 842 of the Statutes of 1983, whether persons have died other than simultaneously.

(Stats. 1990 (A.B. 759), ch. 79, §14, effective July 1, 1991. Amended by Stats. 1990 (S.B. 1775), ch. 710, §2, effective July 1,1991.)

§231. Persons authorized to petition

A petition may be filed under this chapter by any of the following:

(a) The personal representative of any person the priority of whose death is in issue under the applicable provision referred to in Section 230.

(b) Any other person interested in the estate of any such person.

(Stats. 1990 (A.B. 759), ch. 79, §14, effective July 1, 1991.)

§232. Court where petition may be filed

(a) The petition shall be filed in the estate proceeding in which the person filing the petition received his or her appointment or in the estate proceeding for the estate in which the person filing the petition claims an interest.

(b) The court that first acquires jurisdiction under this section has exclusive jurisdiction for the purposes of this chapter.

(Stats. 1990 (A.B. 759), ch. 79, §14, effective July 1, 1991.)

§233. Notice of hearing shall be given to certain persons

Notice of the hearing on the petition shall be given as provided in Section 1220 to all of the following persons:

(a) The personal representative of each person the priority of whose death is in issue if there is a personal representative for the person.

(b) Each known devisee of each person the priority of whose death is in issue.

(c) Each known heir of each person the priority of whose death is in issue.

(d) All persons (or their attorneys if they have appeared by attorneys) who have requested special notice as provided in Section 1250 in the proceeding in which the petition is filed or who have given notice of appearance in person or by attorney in that proceeding.

(Stats. 1990 (A.B. 759), ch. 79, §14, effective July 1, 1991.)

§234. Court shall make a determination and order

If the court determines that the named persons are dead and that it has not been established by clear and convincing evidence that one person survived another, the court shall make an order to that effect. If the court determines that the named persons are dead and that there is clear and convincing evidence that one person survived another, the court shall make an order setting forth the order in which the persons died. The order, when it becomes final, is a binding determination of the facts set forth in the order and is conclusive as against the personal representatives of the deceased persons named in the order and against all persons claiming by, through, or under any of the deceased persons.

(Stats. 1990 (A.B. 759), ch. 79, §14, effective July 1, 1991.)

§6211. Survival for purposes of a statutory will: 120 hours, clear and convincing evidence

Reference to a person "if living" or who "survives me" means a person who survives the decedent by 120 hours. A person who fails to survive the decedent by 120 hours is deemed to have predeceased the decedent for the purpose of a California statutory will, and the beneficiaries are determined accordingly. If it cannot be established by clear and convincing evidence that a person who would otherwise be a beneficiary has survived the decedent by 120 hours, it is deemed that the person failed to survive for the required period. The requirement of this section that a person who survives the decedent must survive the decedent by 120 hours does not apply if the application of the 120-hour survival requirement would result in the escheat of property to the state.

(Stats. 1991 (S.B. 271), ch. 1055, §20.)

§6403. Survival for purposes of intestate succession: 120 hours, clear and convincing evidence

(a) A person who fails to survive the decedent by 120 hours is deemed to have predeceased the decedent for the purpose of intestate succession, and the heirs are determined accordingly. If it cannot be established by clear and convincing evidence that a person who would otherwise be an heir has survived the decedent by 120 hours, it is deemed that the person failed to survive for the required period. The requirement of this section that a person who survives the decedent must survive the decedent by 120 hours does not apply if the application of the 120-hour survival requirement would result in the escheat of property to the state.

(b) This section does not apply to the case where any of the persons upon whose time of death the disposition of property depends died before January 1, 1990, and such case

continues to be governed by the law applicable before January 1, 1990.
(Stats. 1990 (A.B. 759), ch. 79, §14, effective July 1, 1991.)

§21109. Survival for purposes of testate succession or succession under another instrument: 120 hours, clear and convincing evidence

(a) A transferee who fails to survive the transferor or until any future time required by the instrument does not take under the instrument.

(b) If it cannot be established by clear and convincing evidence that the transferee has survived the transferor, it is deemed that the beneficiary did not survive the transferor.

(c) If it cannot be established by clear and convincing evidence that the transferee survived until a future time required by the instrument, it is deemed that the transferee did not survive until the required future time.
(Stats. 1994 (A.B. 3636), ch. 806, §41.)

V. Advancements, Releases, and Assignments

Some transactions by the decedent prior to death may affect the share of an heir to the decedent's intestate estate. An *advancement* is an inter vivos gift of real or personal property that anticipates the recipient's inheritance. If the gift is considered an advancement, then the donee's share of the donor's estate is reduced to compensate for the advancement. The process of equalization is referred to as "hotchpot."

Whether or not a gift is considered an advancement on an inheritance depends on the intent of the donor. McGovern & Kurtz, *supra*, at §2.6 at 70. The common law assumed a gift was an advancement, presuming that a decedent would wish to deal with all children equally. California law on advancements, derived from the UPC, reverses this presumption, and thereby requires a writing to evidence the donor's intent to treat a gift as an advancement on inheritance. Specifically, a gift will be treated as an advancement only (1) if the *decedent declares in a contemporaneous writing* that the gift is to be deducted from the heir's share of the estate or that the gift is an advancement against the heir's share of the estate, or (2) if *the heir acknowledges in writing* that the gift is to be so deducted or is an advancement (Cal. Prob. Code §6409).

At common law, the doctrine applied only to children. According to the UPC, hotchpot is required whenever an "heir" receives an advancement (UPC §2-109).

Valuation of the advanced property occurs at the time the heir came into possession or enjoyment of the property or at the time of death of the decedent, whichever occurs first (Cal. Prob. Code §6409 (b)). However, if the decedent or heir specifies the value of the property advanced (in the contemporaneous writing of the decedent, or in an acknowledgment of the heir made contemporaneously with the advancement), then that value is conclusive (Cal. Prob. Code §6409(c)).

An issue sometimes arises regarding whether the donee's issue will be charged with the advancement if the donee predeceases the decedent. California law, like that of the UPC, specifies that the donee's issue are not charged with the advancement unless the donor's declaration or donee's acknowledgment provides otherwise (Cal. Prob. Code §6409(d)). See generally 40 Cal. Jur.3d Intestate Succession §10 (Advancements).

Note that the advancement doctrine operates in the intestate situation. A comparable rule as to gifts in the testate situation (i.e., a gift by a testator to a potential beneficiary after execution of a will) is referred to as the "satisfaction" doctrine, or "ademption by satisfaction" (Cal. Prob. Code §21135). The Restatement (Third) of Property §2.6 adheres to the UPC rule. Restatement (Third) of Property, *supra*, §2.6 cmt. b.

Other transactions prior to the decedent's death that affect inheritance rights of the heirs are assignments of an expectancy interest and releases. An assignment occurs when a potential heir assigns his or her expectancy interest in the decedent's estate to someone other than the intestate for fair and adequate consideration. The term "expectancy interest" means that the assignor is giving away something he or she does not yet have. Therefore, because the interest is an expectancy and not a vested right, an assignment is not binding on the assignor's issue.

A *release* is similar to an assignment, except that, in exchange for consideration, the potential heir transfers his or her interest in certain property owned by the intestate to the intestate. For example, a parent quitclaims a deed for Blackacre to a child in exchange for a release of the child's share of the parent's estate. The effect of a release differs from that of an assignment. In the release situation, the child's issue (such as a grandchild) are bound by the release and will not share in the parent's estate. The policy rationale is that, unlike in the assignment situation, the parent is on notice that the release has occurred and can take steps to bring the grandchild into the estate plan.

On releases and assignments, see generally Katheleen R. Guzman, Releasing the Expectancy, 34 Ariz. St. L.J. 775 (2002) (examining the differences between releases and assignments within traditional succession

doctrine and proposing reform in release law). For a case involving the assignment of an expectancy, see Diaz v. Rood, 851 So. 2d 843 (Fla. Dist. Ct. App. 2003) (holding that trial court applied an incorrect standard to determine whether "fair and sufficient" consideration existed to support the husband's assignment to his separated wife of a half interest of any future inheritance he would receive from his father's estate).

CALIFORNIA PROBATE CODE

§6409. Advancements: requirements, valuation, effect on donee's issue if donee predeceases

(a) If a person dies intestate as to all or part of his or her estate, property the decedent gave during lifetime to an heir is treated as an advancement against that heir's share of the intestate estate only if one of the following conditions is satisfied:

(1) The decedent declares in a contemporaneous writing that the gift is to be deducted from the heir's share of the estate or that the gift is an advancement against the heir's share of the estate.

(2) The heir acknowledges in writing that the gift is to be so deducted or is an advancement.

(b) Subject to subdivision (c), the property advanced is to be valued as of the time the heir came into possession or enjoyment of the property or as of the time of death of the decedent, whichever occurs first.

(c) If the value of the property advanced is expressed in the contemporaneous writing of the decedent, or in an acknowledgment of the heir made contemporaneously with the advancement, that value is conclusive in the division and distribution of the intestate estate.

(d) If the recipient of the property advanced fails to survive the decedent, the property is not taken into account in computing the intestate share to be received by the recipient's issue unless the declaration or acknowledgment provides otherwise.

(Stats. 1990 (A.B. 759), ch. 79, §14, effective July 1, 1991.)

§21135. Satisfaction doctrine: inter vivos gifts in testate context

(a) Property given by a transferor during his or her lifetime to a person is treated as a satisfaction of an at-death transfer to that person in whole or in part only if one of the following conditions is satisfied:

(1) The instrument provides for deduction of the lifetime gift from the at-death transfer.

(2) The transferor declares in a contemporaneous writing that the gift is in satisfaction of the at-death transfer or that its value is to be deducted from the value of the at-death transfer.

(3) The transferee acknowledges in writing that the gift is in satisfaction of the at-death transfer or that its value is to be deducted from the value of the at-death transfer.

(4) The property given is the same property that is the subject of a specific gift to that person.

(b) Subject to subdivision (c), for the purpose of partial satisfaction, property given during lifetime is valued as of the time the transferee came into possession or enjoyment of the property or as of the time of death of the transferor, whichever occurs first.

(c) If the value of the gift is expressed in the contemporaneous writing of the transferor, or in an acknowledgment of the transferee made contemporaneously with the gift, that value is conclusive in the division and distribution of the estate.

(d) If the transferee fails to survive the transferor, the gift is treated as a full or partial satisfaction of the gift, as the case may be, in applying Sections 21110 and 21111 unless the transferor's contemporaneous writing provides otherwise.

(Stats. 1994 (A.B. 3686), ch. 806, §41. Amended by Stats. 2002 (A.B. 1784), ch. 138, §36.)

II
FAMILY PROTECTION: POLICY LIMITATIONS ON FREEDOM OF TESTATION

This chapter focuses on policy limitations on the freedom of testation. One of the foremost considerations for limiting the power of testamentary disposition is family protection, i.e., the protection of the surviving spouse and children of the decedent. Protection of these family members takes the form of (1) allowances and exemptions, and (2) additional common law and statutory rights.

I. Allowances and Exemptions

Administration of an estate (whether testate or intestate) often is lengthy and costly. As a result, most jurisdictions provide certain minimal statutory rights for the surviving spouse (and often children) during the period of estate administration.

State statutes provide protection for family members in the form of: (1) family allowances, (2) homestead exemptions, and (3) personal property exemptions. Sometimes these exemptions are referred to as "set-asides" because, upon granting of a petition, the court sets aside certain assets that are then unavailable for distribution to the heirs or beneficiaries. These statutory rights serve several purposes: They provide the spouse, minor, and dependent children of the decedent with a roof over their heads; provide these persons money with which to live while the estate is in administration (although sometimes for a shorter period); and give the dependents designated tangible property owned by the decedent.

The California family protection statutes are set forth in California Probate Code §§6540-6545 (family allowance) and §§6500-6528 (dealing with temporary possession of the family dwelling and exempt personal property, and setting aside exempt property and a probate homestead).

A. Family Allowance

Many jurisdictions permit the court to grant an allowance for the support of the surviving spouse and surviving children for the period during which the estate is in administration. A family allowance often is necessary because the decedent's assets are frozen during probate administration and also because death deprives dependent family members of the decedent's support. The policy is sometimes conceptualized as an extension of the husband's or father's duty of support. 24 Cal. Jur.3d Decedents' Estates §341 (citing authority to that effect).

According to California law, the family allowance is payable to the surviving spouse, minor children, and adult children in some circumstances (discussed *infra*). At one time, men were excluded from petitioning for a family allowance by statute (Hills v. Superior Court of Los Angeles County, 279 P. 805 (Cal. 1929)).

In addition, the court has discretion to award a family allowance to a parent of a decedent who was dependent on the decedent for support (Cal. Prob. Code §6540(b)). That statutory provision was at issue in Estate of Herrera v. Farrell Construction Co., 12 Cal. Rptr.2d 751 (Ct. App. 1992), in which an intestate decedent's mother filed a claim for a family allowance of $1000 per month for herself and her husband. An accounting showed that she had already received payments of $20,000 and that payment of the family allowance would render the estate insolvent. A creditor (Farrell Construction Co.) objected to the mother's petition. The California Court of Appeal affirmed the trial court's denial of the allowance despite the fact that such allowances generally have priority over creditors' claims. The appellate court distinguished between "mandatory" and "discretionary" allowances under California Probate Code §6540(b). Whereas a spouse or children are entitled to the allowance, the award of an allowance to the decedent's parents is discretionary. Given the mother's conduct, the appellate court held that the denial of the family allowance was within the trial court's discretion.

Many state statutes provide support only for minor children. However, some states permit support for adult children in limited circumstances. For example, California law authorizes an allowance for "adult children of the decedent who are physically or mentally incapacitated from earning a living and were actually dependent in whole or in part upon the decedent for support" (Cal. Prob. Code §6540(a)), and gives the court discretion to award an allowance to other adult dependent children (Cal. Prob. Code §6540(b)(1)). The UPC protects "minor children whom the decedent was obligated to support and children who were in fact being supported by him" (UPC §2-404).

The family allowance is a cash allotment payable from the decedent's estate. Generally, nonprobate assets are not reachable to satisfy the family allowance. For example, California law authorizes the payment of the family allowance "*out of the estate* . . . during administration of the estate" (Cal. Prob. Code §6540(a)) (emphasis added). In Parson v. Parson, 56 Cal. Rptr.2d 686 (Ct. App. 1996), the court denied a family allowance to a surviving, but disinherited, spouse on the basis that there was no "estate" from which to distribute it because the decedent had placed all of his assets in a revocable trust. The UPC permits some nonprobate assets to be reached if the estate is insolvent (UPC §6-102).

Payments cease upon the recipient's death or remarriage. 24 Cal. Jur.3d Decedents' Estates §339. Note, however, that in some states, any unpaid family allowance passes to the recipient's estate. McGovern & Kurtz, *supra*, §3.4 at 137.

The amount of the allowance varies from jurisdiction to jurisdiction. Some states fix the amount, whereas other states leave the amount to the court's discretion. The California Probate Code provides that specified family members are entitled to "such *reasonable* family allowance out of the estate as is necessary for their maintenance according to their circumstances during administration" (Cal. Prob. Code §6540(a) (emphasis added). California thereby reflects the influence of the original UPC, which provides for a "reasonable allowance" and advises that "account should be taken of the previous standard of living" (UPC §2-404). Following revisions in 1990, the UPC set a ceiling, permitting the family allowance not to exceed $18,000, or $1500 per month for a period not to exceed one year (UPC §2-405 cmt.).

Many jurisdictions, similar to California, provide that the family allowance may be paid for the entire period that the estate is in administration.

The purpose of the family allowance is to place the welfare of the decedent's family above the interests of creditors, heirs, legatees, and devisees. As a result, payment of the allowance is given priority over other debts (Cal. Prob. Code §§11420(a), 11421).

Family members may claim a family allowance in either the testate or intestate situations. In the testate situation, family members generally may claim both the family allowance as well as their share under the decedent's will (unless the will specifies otherwise). They may claim the allowance even if the decedent disinherits them. McGovern & Kurtz, *supra*, §3.4 at 138.

In some cases, the court may consider the recipient's need in determining the amount of the family allowance. According to California law, if only one family member claims the allowance, the court may authorize the allowance even though the recipient has other means of support. However, in the case of several eligible claimants, if one claimant has reasonable maintenance from other sources, the family allowance must be granted only to those persons who do not have a reasonable maintenance from other sources (Cal. Prob. Code §6540(c)).

CALIFORNIA PROBATE CODE

§38. "Family allowance," defined

"Family allowance" means an allowance provided for in Chapter 4 (commencing with Section 6540) of Part 3 of Division 6.

(Stats. 1990 (A.B. 759), ch. 79, §14, effective July 1, 1991.)

§6540. Eligible recipients of the family allowance

(a) The following are entitled to such reasonable family allowance out of the estate as is necessary for their maintenance according to their circumstances during administration of the estate:

(1) The surviving spouse of the decedent.

(2) Minor children of the decedent.

(3) Adult children of the decedent who are physically or mentally incapacitated from earning a living and were actually dependent in whole or in part upon the decedent for support.

(b) The following may be given such reasonable family allowance out of the estate as the court in its discretion determines is necessary for their maintenance according to their circumstances during administration of the estate: (1) Other adult children of the decedent who were actually dependent in whole or in part upon the decedent for support.

(2) A parent of the decedent who was actually dependent in whole or in part upon the decedent for support.

(c) If a person otherwise eligible for family allowance has a reasonable maintenance from other sources and there are one or more other persons entitled to a family allowance, the family allowance shall be granted only to those who do not have a reasonable maintenance from other sources.

(Stats. 1990 (A.B. 759), ch. 79, §14, effective July 1, 1991.)

§6541. Procedure for granting or modifying family allowance

(a) The court may grant or modify a family allowance on petition of any interested person.

(b) With respect to an order for the family allowance provided for in subdivision (a) of Section 6540:

(1) Before the inventory is filed, the order may be made or modified either (A) ex parte or (B) after notice of the hearing on the petition has been given as provided in Section 1220.

(2) After the inventory is filed, the order may be made or modified only after notice of the hearing on the petition has been given as provided in Section 1220.

(c) An order for the family allowance provided in subdivision (b) of Section 6540 may be made only after notice of the hearing on the petition has been given as provided in Section 1220 to all of the following persons:

(1) Each person listed in Section 1220.

(2) Each known heir whose interest in the estate would be affected by the petition.

(3) Each known devisee whose interest in the estate would be affected by the petition.

(Stats. 1990 (A.B. 759), ch. 79, §14, effective July 1, 1991.)

§6542. Commencement of family allowance

A family allowance commences on the date of the court's order or such other time as may be provided in the court's order, whether before or after the date of the order, as the court in its discretion determines, but the allowance may not be made retroactive to a date earlier than the date of the decedent's death.

(Stats. 1990 (A.B. 759), ch. 79, §14, effective July 1, 1991.)

§6543. Termination of family allowance: upon distribution or one year for insolvent estates

(a) A family allowance shall terminate no later than the entry of the order for final distribution of the estate or, if the estate is insolvent, no later than one year after the granting of letters.

(b) Subject to subdivision (a), a family allowance shall continue until modified or terminated by the court or until such time as the court may provide in its order.

(Stats. 1990 (A.B. 759), ch. 79, §14, effective July 1, 1991.)

§6544. Cost shall be paid as an expense of estate administration

The costs of proceedings under this chapter shall be paid by the estate as expenses of administration.

(Stats. 1990 (A.B. 759), ch. 79, §14, effective July 1, 1991.)

§6545. No stay on appeal

Notwithstanding Chapter 2 (commencing with Section 916) of Title 13 of Part 2 of the Code of Civil Procedure, the perfecting of an appeal from an order made under this chapter does not stay proceedings under this chapter or the enforcement of the order appealed from if the person in whose favor the order is made gives an undertaking in double the amount of the payment or payments to be made to that person. The undertaking shall be conditioned that if the order appealed from is modified or reversed so that the payment or any part thereof to the person proves to have been unwarranted, the payment or part thereof shall, unless deducted from any preliminary or final distribution ordered in favor of the person, be repaid and refunded into the estate within 30 days after the court so orders following the modification or reversal, together with interest and costs.

(Stats. 1990 (A.B. 759), ch. 79, §14, effective July 1, 1991.)

B. Homestead Exemption

Many jurisdictions provide for a homestead exemption to surviving family members. The homestead exemption generally protects the principal family residence or a percentage of the equity in the residence (dependent on statute) from attachment by creditors. Protection for the homestead rights of a surviving spouse and children stems from a surviving spouse's common law right to a dower or curtesy interest in the deceased spouse's real property. Gregory J. Duncan, Home Sweet Home? Litigation Aspects to Minnesota's Descent of Homestead, 29 Wm. Mitchell L. Rev. 185, 188 (2002).

States take four approaches to the homestead allowance:

- **some follow the UPC approach;**
- **some have constitutional or statutory descent homesteads;**
- **others permit residency during probate proceedings or at the discretion of the court; and**
- **still others follow miscellaneous approaches.**

***Id.*, at 196-198. These approaches are explored below.**

First, some states follow the UPC approach. The UPC provides a homestead allowance in the amount of $15,000 that is protected from creditors' claims. If the decedent left no surviving spouse, then each minor child and dependent child is entitled to an equal share of the $15,000 allowance (UPC §2-402). Under the UPC, the homestead allowance is exempt from creditors' claims against the estate and is added to any share passing by will, intestate succession, or elective share. Among states that follow the UPC by providing a fixed amount, those amounts range from $7500 to $27,000. Duncan, *supra*, at 195 n.57.

Second, some states provide, either by statute or state constitutional provision, that the surviving spouse and children shall have a life estate or fee simple right in the homestead. Other states following this approach provide that close family members have a superior right to occupy the homestead (rather than vest in them a life estate). In the latter case specifying a right to occupancy, when the surviving spouse ceases to occupy the homestead, the survivor's rights terminate and the property descends according to the laws of descent. *Id.* at 196 n. 69.

Third, still other states permit a surviving spouse to possess and occupy the homestead during probate administration or for an indefinite period of time at the court's discretion. *Id.* at 197.

Finally, a few states use a combination of the aforementioned approaches. That is, some

permit a cash award but, depending on the value of the property, may set off the homestead to the persons entitled to it. *Id.* at 197-198.

California law provides that the probate homestead shall be set apart for the use of the surviving spouse and minor children (Cal. Prob. Code §6521). The period of time for which the property may be set aside shall not exceed the lifetime of the surviving spouse or the minority of a child (Cal. Prob. Code §6524).

The court must consider certain factors in setting apart the probate homestead. These factors include: the needs of surviving family members, any liens and encumbrances on the property, creditors' claims, the needs of the decedent's heirs or devisees, and the decedent's intent regarding the estate property and estate plan (as expressed in inter vivos and testamentary transfers or by other means) (Cal. Prob. Code §6523(a)).

Generally, the court awards the principal family residence as the probate homestead. However, according to California statute, the court has discretion, in light of the aforementioned factors, to select other property. That is, the court must select "the most appropriate property available that is suitable for that use, including in addition to the dwelling itself such adjoining property as appears reasonable" (Cal. Prob. Code §6523(b)(1)). The court normally selects property that is free from liens and encumbrances, even if it is not the principal family residence. Ross & Grant, *supra*, §7:34 at 7-9.

Property that is eligible for the homestead set-aside includes only *property that is subject to probate administration* (i.e., only property before the probate court, which is included in the inventory). That is, joint tenancy property or property passing under summary administration procedure is not eligible because it is not part of the probate estate. There is no ceiling on the value of property to be set aside. *Id.*, *supra*, §7:34-3 at 7-9. However, the court must follow the statutory order of preference, giving preference to community and quasi-community property of the decedent and the person entitled to the homestead (Cal. Prob. Code §6522).

The decedent's testate beneficiaries or intestate heirs take their property subject to the homestead. "[I]n effect, they have remainder interests." Ross & Grant, *supra*, §7:47 at 7-12. Furthermore, although the homesteaded property may be used to satisfy decedent's debts, any sale is subject to the right of occupancy in the homestead recipient (Cal. Prob. Code §6526(a)).

California law also protects the survivors' right to temporary possession of the family home and exempt personal property. That is, the surviving spouse and minor children (without a court order) may remain in temporary possession of the family dwelling, as well as of the wearing apparel, household furniture, and other exempt personal property of the decedent. According to California Probate Code §6500, the surviving family members may remain in temporary possession until the filing of the inventory for the estate and for 60 days thereafter ("or for such other period as may be ordered by the court for good cause on petition therefor").

The case of Estate of Liccardo, 283 Cal. Rptr. 839 (Ct. App. 1993), illustrates the operation of California's probate homestead law. A surviving spouse petitioned the probate court to set aside a probate homestead for her and her three minor children. The property she requested was the family's home in Saratoga (appraised at $1.8 million). That property had passed to her when she earlier petitioned the probate court for a community property spousal set-aside order, determining property passing to the surviving spouse without administration pursuant to California Probate Code §13500 (*infra*) and confirming property belonging to the surviving spouse pursuant to §§100 and 101. Creditors of her late husband, who had claims exceeding $2.5 million, opposed her petition to set aside the family home as the homestead. The court denied the widow's petition, holding that the statutory scheme permitting property to pass to the surviving spouse without administration also kept such property out of the probate estate, and thus precluded judicial selection of such property for a homestead.

CALIFORNIA PROBATE CODE

§60. "Probate homestead," defined

"Probate homestead" means a homestead provided for in Chapter 3 (commencing with Section 6520) of Part 3 of Division 6.

(Stats. 1990 (A.B. 759), ch. 79, §14, effective July 1, 1991.)

§6500. Surviving family members have temporary right to remain in possession

Until the inventory is filed and for a period of 60 days thereafter, or for such other period as may be ordered by the court for good cause on petition therefor, the decedent's surviving spouse and minor children are entitled to remain in possession of the family dwelling, the wearing apparel of the family, the household furniture, and the other property of the decedent exempt from enforcement of a money judgment.

(Stats. 1990 (A.B. 759), ch. 79, §14, effective July 1, 1991.)

§6501. Interested persons may file petition for order

A petition for an order under Section 6500 may be filed by any interested person. Notice of the hearing on the petition shall be given as provided in Section 1220.
(Stats. 1990 (A.B. 759), ch. 79, §14, effective July 1, 1991.)

§6510. Court may set aside exempt property for surviving spouse and minor children

Upon the filing of the inventory or at any subsequent time during the administration of the estate, the court in its discretion may on petition therefor set apart all or any part of the property of the decedent exempt from enforcement of a money judgment, other than the family dwelling, to any one or more of the following:

(a) The surviving spouse.

(b) The minor children of the decedent.

(Stats. 1990 (A.B. 759), ch. 79, §14, effective July 1, 1991.)

§6520. Court may select and set aside probate homestead

Upon the filing of the inventory or at any subsequent time during the administration of the estate, the court in its discretion may on petition therefor select and set apart one probate homestead in the manner provided in this chapter. *(Stats. 1990 (A.B. 759), ch. 79, §14, effective July 1, 1991.)*

§6521. Eligible persons for whom homestead may be set apart

The probate homestead shall be set apart for the use of one or more of the following persons:

(a) The surviving spouse.

(b) The minor children of the decedent.

(Stats. 1990 (A.B. 759), ch. 79, §14, effective July 1, 1991.)

§6522. Particular property from which homestead may be selected

(a) The probate homestead shall be selected out of the following property, giving first preference to the community and quasi-community property of, or property owned in common by, the decedent and the person entitled to have the homestead set apart:

(1) If the homestead is set apart for the use of the surviving spouse or for the use of the surviving spouse and minor children, out of community property or quasi-community property.

(2) If the homestead is set apart for the use of the surviving spouse or for the use of the minor children or for the use of the surviving spouse and minor children, out of property owned in common by the decedent and the persons entitled to have the homestead set apart, or out of the separate property of the decedent or, if the decedent was not married at the time of death, out of property owned by the decedent.

(b) The probate homestead shall not be selected out of property the right to possession of which is vested in a third person unless the third person consents thereto. As used in this subdivision, thirdperson means a person whose right to possession of the property (1) existed at the time of the death of the decedent or came into existence upon the death of the decedent and (2) was not created by testate or intestate succession from the decedent.
(Stats. 1990 (A.B. 759), ch. 79, §14, effective July 1, 1991; Stats. 1990 (S.B. 1775), ch. 710, §17, effective July 1, 1991.)

§6523. Court shall consider certain factors in setting apart homestead

(a) In selecting and setting apart the probate homestead, the court shall consider the needs of the surviving spouse and minor children, the liens and encumbrances on the property, the claims of creditors, the needs of the heirs or devisees of the decedent, and the intent of the decedent with respect to the property in the estate and the estate plan of the decedent as expressed in inter vivos and testamentary transfers or by other means.

(b) The court, in light of subdivision (a) and other relevant considerations as determined by the court in its discretion, shall:

(1) Select as a probate homestead the most appropriate property available that is suitable for that use, including in addition to the dwelling itself such adjoining property as appears reasonable.

(2) Set the probate homestead so selected apart for such a term and upon such conditions (including, but not limited to, assignment by the homestead recipient of other property to the heirs or devisees of the property set apart as a homestead) as appear proper.

(Stats. 1990 (A.B. 759), ch. 79, §14, effective July 1, 1991.)

§6524. Homestead shall be set apart only for spouse's lifetime or child's minority

The property set apart as a probate homestead shall be set apart only for a limited period, to be designated in the order, and in no case beyond the lifetime of the surviving spouse, or, as to a child, beyond its minority. Subject to the probate homestead right, the property of the decedent remains subject to administration including testate and intestate succession. The rights of the parties during the period for which the probate homestead is set apart are governed, to the extent applicable, by the Legal Estates Principal and Income Law, Chapter 2.6 (commencing with Section 731) of Title 2 of Part 1 of Division 2 of the Civil Code. *(Stats. 1990 (A.B. 759), ch. 79, §14, effective July 1, 1991.)*

§6526. Liability of property set aside as probate homestead

(a) Property of the decedent set apart as a probate homestead is liable for claims against the Estate of the decedent, subject to the probate homestead right. The probate homestead right in property of the decedent is liable for claims that are secured by liens and encumbrances on the property at the time of the decedent's death but is exempt to the extent of the homestead exemption as to any claim that would have been subject to a homestead exemption at the time of the decedent's death under Article 4 (commencing with Section 704.710) of Chapter 4 of Division 2 of Title 9 of Part 2 of the Code of Civil Procedure.

(b) The probate homestead right in the property of the decedent is not liable for claims against the person for whose use the probate homestead is set apart.

(c) Property of the decedent set apart as a probate homestead is liable for claims against the testate or intestate successors of the decedent or other successors to the property after administration, subject to the probate homestead right.

(Stats. 1990 (A.B. 759), ch. 79, §14, effective July 1, 1991.)

§6527. Court may modify or terminate homestead right

(a) The court may by order modify the term or conditions of the probate homestead right or terminate the probate homestead right at any time prior to entry of an order for final distribution of the decedent's estate if in the court's discretion to do so appears appropriate under the circumstances of the case.

(b) A petition for an order under this section may be filed by any of the following:

(1) The person for whose use the probate homestead is set apart.

(2) The testate or intestate successors of the decedent or other successors to the property set apart as a probate homestead.

(3) Persons having claims secured by liens or encumbrances on the property set apart as a probate homestead.

(c) Notice of the hearing on the petition shall be given to all the persons listed in subdivision (b) as provided in Section 1220.

(Stats. 1990 (A.B. 759), ch. 79, §14, effective July 1, 1991.)

§6528. Effect of section is declaratory

Nothing in this chapter terminates or otherwise affects a declaration of homestead by, or for the benefit of, a surviving spouse or minor child of the decedent with respect to the community, quasi-community, or common interest of the surviving spouse or minor child in property in the decedent's estate. This section is declaratory of, and does not constitute a change in, existing law.

(Stats. 1990 (A.B. 759), ch. 79, §14, effective July 1, 1991.)

§13500. Passage of property to surviving spouse of an intestate without administration (i.e., property not available for probate homestead)

Except as provided in this chapter, when a husband or wife dies intestate leaving property that passes to the surviving spouse under Section 6401, or dies testate and by his or her will devises all or a part of his or her property to the surviving spouse, the property passes to the survivor subject to the provisions of Chapter 2 (commencing with Section 13540) and Chapter 3 (commencing with Section 13550), and no administration is necessary.

(Stats. 1990 (A.B.759), ch. 79, §14, effective July 1, 1991.)(Stats. 1990 (A.B.759), ch. 79, §14, effective July 1, 1991.)

C. Personal Property Exemption

Many jurisdictions provide for a modest amount of exempt property (sometimes called "personal property set-asides") to pass to the decedent's surviving spouse and/or surviving children. Exempt personal property generally consists of such items as home furnishings, food, clothes, jewelry, firearms, sporting equipment, cars not used for income, certain quantities of farm animals, and household pets. Gerry W. Beyer, Wills, Trusts and Estates 242-243 (2d. ed. 2002). This property is exempt from distribution to heirs and beneficiaries, as well as from sale by creditors. It is available in both testate and intestate situations. Personal property exemptions (like homestead exemptions and family allowances) take precedence over creditors' claims and the decedent's will. McGovern & Kurtz, *supra*, §3.4 at 138. Under the UPC, exempt property passes to the surviving spouse. Only in the event that no surviving spouse survives do the children take the property. UPC §2-403 imposes a limit of $10,000 as the maximum value of the exemption (which is in addition to the homestead allowance and the family allowance).

In California, the court may set aside exempt property for the use and benefit of the surviving spouse and/or minor children (Cal. Prob. Code §6510). Property eligible for set-aside includes any of the decedent's property "exempt from enforcement of a money judgment" (Cal. Prob. Code §§6500, 6510), including all personal property exempt from execution under California Code of Civil Procedure §§704.010-704.210.

Those specific items of property subject to such exemption (as specified in designated provisions of the Code of Civil Procedure) include: motor vehicles; household furnishings, appliances, provisions, wearing apparel, and personal effects; materials for repair or improvement of principal residence; jewelry, heirlooms, and works of art; health aids (including prosthetic and orthopedic appliances); personal property used in a trade, business, or profession; recently paid wages and earnings which are traceable to deposit accounts or are in the form of cash or its equivalent; deposit account containing Social Security payments directly deposited by the government; prisoner's funds held in an inmate's trust or similar account; life insurance, annuity, or endowment policies; and benefits

from matured policies necessary for support; public retirement and related benefits and contributions; public employee vacation credits; private retirement and related benefits and contributions necessary for support; unemployment and unemployment disability funds and strike benefits payable by a labor union; disability and health insurance benefits; personal injury cause of action and damages award or settlement; wrongful death cause of action and award or settlement; workers' compensation claim, award, or payment; public assistance benefits and financial aid from a charity or fraternal benefit society; relocation benefits for displacement from a dwelling, paid pursuant to federal or state law; student financial aid; cemetery plot; property not subject to enforcement of a money judgment. Ross & Grant, *supra*, §7:4 at 7-2.

CALIFORNIA PROBATE CODE

§6501. Interested persons may file petition for order

A petition for an order under Section 6500 may be filed by any interested person. Notice of the hearing on the petition shall be given as provided in Section 1220.

(Stats. 1990 (A.B. 759), ch. 79, §14, effective July 1, 1991.)

§6510. Court may set aside exempt property for surviving spouse and minor children

Upon the filing of the inventory or at any subsequent time during the administration of the estate, the court in its discretion may on petition therefor set apart all or any part of the property of the decedent exempt from enforcement of a money judgment, other than the family dwelling, to any one or more of the following:

(a) The surviving spouse.

(b) The minor children of the decedent.

(Stats. 1990 (A.B. 759), ch. 79, §14, effective July 1, 1991.)

§6511. Procedure to set aside exempt personal property

A petition for an order under Section 6510 may be filed by any interested person. Notice of the hearing on the petition shall be given as provided in Section 1220.*(Stats. 1990 (A.B. 759), ch. 79, §14, effective July 1, 1991.)*

II. Minimum Rights of the Surviving Spouse

The law protects a surviving spouse from disinheritance by the decedent. Two justifications (the support rationale and the marital contribution rationale) exist for limiting testamentary freedom in the context of spousal disinheritance. First, the decedent has a moral duty to support a surviving spouse even after the decedent's death. Second, it is considered unfair to allow a decedent to deprive the surviving spouse of the latter's contribution to the acquisition of the decedent's assets. Andra J. Hedrick, Note, Protection Against Spousal Disinheritance: A Critical Analysis of Tennessee's New Forced Share System, 28 U. Mem. L. Rev. 561, 562-563 (1998).

Surviving spouses enjoy different levels of protection against disinheritance depending on the law of the state exercising jurisdiction over the decedent's estate. *Id.* at 563. Such protections include dower, statutory forced share, and community property rights.

A. Dower

At common law, a surviving wife was protected from disinheritance by the concept of dower. The widow's dower interest consisted of *a life estate in one-third of all real property* of which her husband was seised (owned) at any time during the marriage (regardless of whether the husband actually owned the property at his death). Dower guaranteed the widow a share of the decedent's *real property,* which could not be defeated by the husband's will or his inter vivos conveyances. That is, the grantee or devisee took the real property subject to the widow's dower right. Dower was an inchoate right, dependent on the wife's surviving her husband.

The husband's correlative right in his deceased wife's estate was termed curtesy. Curtesy consisted of a life estate in all (not simply one-third) the lands of which his wife was seised at any time during the marriage. However, the husband only acquired his curtesy right if he fathered a child with his wife (regardless of whether that child survived).

The primary differences between dower and curtesy at common law may be summarized as follows: (1) curtesy entitled the husband to an estate in all the wife's inheritable freeholds, whereas dower entitled the widow to an interest in only one-third of the husband's; (2) curtesy attached to the wife's equitable as well as legal interests, whereas dower applied only to the husband's legal estates; (3) a requirement for curtesy was the birth of issue, whereas no such requirement pertained to the dower right; and (4) before the wife's death, curtesy was a present estate, whereas dower was only a protected expectancy before the husband's death. Hedrick, *supra*, at 570 n. 38 (citing George L. Haskins, Curtesy in the United States, 100 U. Pa. L. Rev. 196, 197 (1951)).

Gender-based distinctions regarding the rights of the surviving spouse have been found to violate equal protection. See, e.g., Stokes v. Stokes, 613 S.W.2d 372 (Ark. 1981) (finding dower statute violative of equal protection); Boan v. Watson, 316 S.E.2d 401 (S.C. 1984) (same). Today, a small number of states continue to protect the survivor's dower rights, but the rights are available to both men and women.

At one time, some states differentiated between the dower rights of state residents versus nonresidents. In Ferry v. Spokane, P. & S. Ry., 258 U.S. 314 (1922), the Supreme Court found that such a statute did not violate the privileges and immunities or equal protection clauses of the Constitution. The court upheld the constitutionality of an Oregon statute providing for dower, if the wife was an Oregon resident, in all of the lands of which the husband was seised at any time during the marriage, but restricting dower to the lands of which the husband died seised if the widow was a resident of another state. The statute was repealed in 1969 (Laws 1969, ch. 591, §305).

As mentioned above, dower protected the surviving spouse from disinheritance and from creditors (i.e., beneficiaries and creditors took property subject to her dower right). However, dower had many disadvantages. It applies only to the decedent's real property and not to personal property. Dower provides only a life estate for the surviving spouse and not a fee interest. Finally, it is a clog on title. As a result, many states have abolished dower. See, e.g., Cal. Prob. Code §6412; UPC §2-113 (abolishing dower and curtesy). The abolition of dower and curtesy was attributable in large part to the transformation from an agrarian to an industrialized society. Hedrick, *supra*, at 571 n. 39.

CALIFORNIA PROBATE CODE

§6412. Abolition of dower and curtesy

Except to the extent provided in Section 120 [establishing a surviving spouse's right to elect against the decedent's will regarding non-community real property, located in California, of a nondomiciliary decedent], the estates of dower and curtesy are not recognized.

(Stats. 1990 (A.B. 759), ch. 79, §14, effective July 1, 1991.)

B. Forced Share and the Surviving Spouse's Election

Most jurisdictions today have replaced dower with the concept of a forced (or elective) share. A forced share enables the surviving spouse to take a certain portion of the decedent's estate if the decedent disinherits the spouse or fails to bequeath a minimum amount to the survivor. The surviving spouse has the right to take a statutory share of the decedent's estate in lieu of the share that the survivor would have taken under the decedent's will. Thus, if a husband bequeaths his wife only a small portion of his estate, the wife has a choice: (1) to take the share given to her under the decedent's will or (2) refuse that testamentary gift and, instead, take her statutory share. Generally, the surviving spouse will choose whichever option yields a larger amount.

The amount of the forced share varies from jurisdiction to jurisdiction. Some jurisdictions simply specify that the surviving spouse's elective share is the "intestate share." Other jurisdictions provide:

- a fixed percentage of the net probate estate (ranging from one-third to one-half);
- a fixed percentage (e.g., ranging from one-third to one-half) of the net probate estate depending on the number of children (the more children, the smaller the share);
- a minimum dollar amount plus a fixed percentage of any additional property in the net probate estate (e.g., the first $100,000 plus one-half the balance) (reflecting the influence of the pre-1990 UPC);
- a percentage of the estate varying with the length of the marriage (reflecting the influence of the current UPC).

The majority of forced-share jurisdictions provide for a statutory share that is equal to a fixed fraction of the decedent's estate. "The modern approach, however, is to determine the surviving spouse's statutory share according to the length of time in which the decedent and surviving spouse were married to each other, taking into account their individual and marital wealth." Hedrick, *supra*, at 565. These latter states are called "accrual-type elective share systems" and reflect the influence of the UPC, as revised in 1990, to include a redesigned forced-share system. By revising the forced-share provision, the drafters of the 1990 UPC attempted to take into account the partnership theory of marriage.

The forced share is distinguishable from dower in several ways. Unlike dower, the surviving spouse takes the elective share in fee. Also, the forced share applies to both real and personal property. However, in many states the elective share includes only assets that the decedent owned at death, i.e., the net probate estate. If the decedent made significant inter vivos gifts to third persons and thereby depleted the probate estate, the surviving spouse has no claim to those assets. Also, the elective share is subject to the claims of creditors. Recall that dower protected the surviving spouse from the husband's inter vivos conveyances and creditors' claims.

Some states protect the surviving spouse from the decedent's inter vivos transfers by applying the elective share to certain asserts that pass outside probate. This approach (called the "augmented estate") is influenced by UPC §§2-201 et seq. The problem of the best manner of protecting the surviving spouse against the decedent's nonprobate transfers is discussed in Section IV of this chapter *infra*.

The surviving spouse generally must exercise the election within a fixed time period. For example, the UPC provides that the surviving spouse must make the election no later than either 9 months after the decedent's death or 6 months after the decedent's will was admitted to probate (whichever is later) (UPC §2-211).

Note that when the surviving spouse makes an election, that election may upset the decedent's estate plan. As a result, some of the legacies may have to be reduced (or abated) to provide for the surviving spouse's share. For a discussion of abatement, see Chapter XV, Section IIC *infra*.

Community property jurisdictions generally do not provide for forced shares because the surviving spouse does not need protection from disinheritance. That is, because of the nature of the community property system (explained in Section IIC *infra*), the surviving spouse acquires one-half of the community property as of the date of the marriage. That half is not subject to the other spouse's testamentary disposition and is protected against inter vivos transfers without consent.

C. Community Property Rights

Community property states offer the most protection to surviving spouses. There are nine community property states (i.e., Arizona, California, Idaho, Louisiana, Nevada, New Mexico, Texas, Washington, and Wisconsin).

In community property states, each spouse has an undivided interest in any property acquired from spousal earnings during the marriage. During the marriage, the spouses' interests in the community property are present, existing, and equal (Cal. Fam. Code §751). That is, at the death of the decedent, the surviving spouse already has ownership of half of the marital property dating from the beginning of the marriage. A decedent has testamentary disposition only over the decedent's half of the community property (as well as over the decedent's half of the quasi-community property and all the decedent's separate property, discussed *infra*). Because of these protective rules, the forced share is an unnecessary safeguard against disinheritance.

The California Family Code and Probate Code contain similar definitions of "community property." Community property includes: all property (real property within the state and personal property wherever situated) acquired during the marriage by a California domiciliary (except for gift or inheritance), as well as property acquired in exchange for community property (Cal. Fam. Code §760; Cal. Prob. Code §28).

Note that a presumption operates in California regarding property acquired by the spouses during the marriage in joint tenancy (or other joint form). Such jointly acquired property is considered community property for purposes or dissolution or legal separation (Cal. Fam. Code §2581), but not death.

See, e.g., Dorn v. Solomon, 67 Cal. Rptr.2d 311 (Ct. App. 1997) (holding that, because title to the family home was acquired in joint tenancy and the parties were not divorcing or legally separated, there was a presumption that the title passed to the estranged husband when the wife died one day after executing a quitclaim deed purporting to transfer the home to an irrevocable trust to enable her to bequeath her share to her daughter from a prior marriage); Estate of Levine, 178 Cal. Rptr. 275 (Ct. App. 1981) (affirming denial of executor's petition to declare real property as community property of decedent and wife to enable decedent to bequeath his interest to his son, reasoning that where decedent never communicated his intention to his wife that the marital home was to be considered community property although title was taken in joint tenancy and where there was no agreement that property would be other than joint tenancy, property would be distributed upon husband's death as joint tenancy property). For a discussion of joint tenancy, see Chapter VIII *infra*.

Some community property states, like California, protect the rights of a surviving spouse when the couple has changed domicile from a common law marital property state to a community property state. This protection takes the form of quasi-community property. In California, quasi-community property consists of all personal property (in California as well as outside the state), and all real property located in California, that is acquired by a decedent while domiciled elsewhere that would have been the community property of the decedent and the surviving spouse if the decedent had been domiciled in California at the time of its acquisition (Cal. Prob. Code §66).

In California, separate property is that property owned by a person before marriage and all property acquired thereafter by gift, bequest, devise, or descent, together with the rents, issues, and profits thereof (i.e., property acquired with separate property funds) (Cal. Fam. Code §770(a)). It also includes property "transmuted" by written agreement from community to separate property (Cal. Fam. Code §§850-853), or property acquired while the spouses were "separated" (Cal. Fam. Code §771). Each spouse has testamentary disposition over his or her separate property (Cal. Prob. Code §6101(a)). However, any of the decedent's separate property that is not disposed of by will passes to the surviving spouse and issue. For a discussion of these concepts, see Chapter I, Section IIA *supra*.

The spouses can change the characterization of their property by *transmutation*. That is, property may be transmuted by a written agreement from community property to separate property or vice versa (Cal. Fam. Code §§850-853). A transmutation of real or personal property must be made in writing by an express declaration that is made or accepted by the spouse whose interest in the property is adversely affected (Cal. Fam. Code §852(a)).

The community property system also provides protection for the surviving spouse from inter vivos transfers that were made without the survivor's consent. This protection stems from the spouse's fiduciary duty vis à vis each other. During their marriage, the spouses are subject to a fiduciary duty similar to that required of persons in confidential relationships. Each spouse owes the other a duty of the "highest good faith and fair dealing," and neither may take unfair advantage of the other (Cal. Fam. Code §721(b)). For example, statutes place restrictions on gifts of community property by one spouse (Cal. Fam. Code §1100) and on nonprobate transfers of quasi-community property (Cal. Prob. Code §102). See generally William P. Hogoboom & Donald B. King, Family Law (Chapter 8); Ross & Grant, *supra*, at §§4:14:51.21.

Most community property jurisdictions (including California) follow *a rule of equal management and control* whereby either spouse may manage community property without the other's consent (Cal. Fam. Code §§1100(a), 1102(a)) (subject to various limitations). By so providing, California changed an entrenched common law principle that the husband was master of the household—a rule that formerly was reflected in the community property system because statutes placed management of community property in the husband's hands with limited exceptions. The United States Supreme Court marked the end of such gender-based rules in Kirchberg v. Feenstra, 450 U.S. 455 (1981), which invalidated, on equal protection grounds, a Louisiana statute designating the husband as "head and master" of the community. California had provided for equal management rights in 1975, several years prior to the Supreme Court ruling. Today, in the management and control of the community property, each spouse has certain obligations:

- to provide access (for inspection purposes) to the other spouse regarding any record of transactions;
- to give, upon request, information to the other spouse regarding transactions concerning the community property; and
- to account to each other (and hold as a trustee) any benefit derived from a community property transaction without the consent of the other spouse (Cal. Fam. Code §721(b)(1),(2) & (3)).

In addition, spouses must make full disclosure of information regarding the existence, characterization, and valuation of all assets in which the community has or may have an interest (Cal. Fam. Code §1100(e)). They must provide full disclosure regarding debts for which the community is or may be liable, as well as provide access (upon request) to information regarding the value and character of assets and liabilities. *Id.* See also In re Marriage of Rossi, 108 Cal. Rptr.2d 270 (Ct. App. 2001) (holding that ex-wife breached fiduciary duty to husband by her failure to disclose lottery proceeds which were community property and therefore ex-husband was entitled to the entire amount).

Breach of a spouse's fiduciary duty in the management of the community estate (such as by a spouse's conveyance of community property to a third party without the other spouse's consent) enables the aggrieved spouse to *restore one-half of the unauthorized community property transfer* (Cal. Fam. Code §1101(g)), either by:

(1) bringing a common law action (a "set-aside suit") against the transferee; or

(2) proceeding against the transferor-spouse's estate.

Ross & Grant, *supra*, §§4:19.1a & 4:19.2. Note that if an aggrieved spouse seeks relief against the transferee at any time *during the marriage*, the former may void the transaction *entirely*. Cal. Fam. Code §1101(h); Ross & Grant, *supra*, at §4:19.1a.

Certain exceptions exist to the rule permitting either spouse the right of management and control: (1) a spouse operating a community property business has the primary management of that business (Cal. Fam. Code §1100(d)); (2) a spouse who holds a bank or savings and loan account in his or her name may manage that account (Cal. Fam. Code §851); and (3) some special transactions (e.g., sales of community furniture, household furnishings, clothing of the nonseller spouse, clothing of the children) require the consent of both spouses

(Cal. Fam. Code §1100(c)). Additional exceptions to the equal-management-and-control rule include situations in which community property is held in trust, in which the power to revoke may be exercised by either spouse acting alone (Cal. Fam. Code §761), or in which a spouse is under a conservatorship or lacks legal capacity (Cal. Fam. Code §1103).

Community real property is also subject to the equal management rule. However, by statute (Cal. Fam. Code §1102), both spouses must join in conveyances, encumbrances, or leases for more than one year of community realty. This rule serves as an additional protection against spousal disinheritance.

In addition, a surviving spouse has a statutory *right to recapture* (i.e., restore to the decedent's estate) *one-half of the quasi-community property* (in which the surviving spouse had an expectancy) that the decedent transferred to a third party (Cal. Prob. Code §102). For the surviving spouse to take advantage of this statutory protection, the decedent must have: (1) died a California domiciliary, (2) made the transfer without substantial consideration, (3) made the transfer without the spouse's written consent or joinder, and (4) retained (at the time of death) possession, enjoyment, or income rights in the property; some power to revoke the transfer or to consume, invade, or dispose of the principal for his or her own benefit, or held property at the decedent's death with another with the right of survivorship. These recapture provisions are not applicable to life or accident insurance, a joint annuity, or a pension payable to other than the surviving spouse. 24 Cal. Jur.3d Decedents' Estates §4.

Finally, the decedent's nonprobate transfer of community property without the other spouse's consent is not effective as to the nonconsenting spouse's interest. That is, such an unauthorized transfer does not affect the nonconsenting spouse's disposition on death of that spouse's interest in the community property by will, intestate succession, or nonprobate transfer (Cal. Prob. Code §5020).

CALIFORNIA PROBATE CODE

§28. "Community property," defined

"Community property" means:

(a) Community property heretofore or hereafter acquired during marriage by a married person while domiciled in this state.

(b) All personal property wherever situated, and all real property situated in this state, heretofore or hereafter acquired during the marriage by a married person while domiciled elsewhere, that is community property, or a substantially equivalent type of marital property, under the laws of the place where the acquiring spouse was domiciled at the time of its acquisition.

(c) All personal property wherever situated, and all real property situated in this state, heretofore or hereafter acquired during the marriage by a married person in exchange for real or personal property, wherever situated that is community property, or a substantially equivalent type of marital property, under the laws of the place where the acquiring spouse was domiciled at the time the property so exchanged was acquired.

(Stats. 1990 (A.B. 759), ch. 79, §14, effective July 1, 1991.)

§66. "Quasi-community property," defined

"Quasi-community property" means the following property, other than community property as defined in Section 28:

(a) All personal property wherever situated, and all real property situated in this state, heretofore or hereafter acquired by a decedent while domiciled elsewhere that would have been the community property of the decedent and the surviving spouse if the decedent had been domiciled in this state at the time of its acquisition.

(b) All personal property wherever situated, and all real property situated in this state, heretofore or hereafter acquired in exchange for real or personal property, wherever situated, that would have been the community property of the decedent and the surviving spouse if the decedent had been domiciled in this state at the time the property so exchanged was acquired.

(Stats. 1990 (A.B. 759), ch. 79, §14, effective July 1, 1991.)

§100. Community property: disposition upon death

(a) Upon the death of a married person, one-half of the community property belongs to the surviving spouse and the other half belongs to the decedent.

(b) Notwithstanding subdivision (a), a husband and wife may agree in writing to divide their community property on the basis of a non pro rata division of the aggregate value of the community property or on the basis of a division of each individual item or asset of community property, or partly on each basis. Nothing in this subdivision shall be construed to require this written agreement in order to permit or recognize a non pro rata division of community property.

(Stats. 1990 (A.B. 759), ch. 79, §14, effective July 1, 1991; Stats. 1998 (A.B. 2069), ch. 682, §2.)

§101. Quasi-community property: disposition upon death§101.

(a) Upon the death of a married person domiciled in this state, one-half of the decedent's quasi-community property belongs to the surviving spouse and the other half belongs to the decedent.

(b) Notwithstanding subdivision (a), a husband and wife may agree in writing to divide their quasi-community property on the basis of a non pro rata division of the aggregate value of the quasi-community property, or on the

basis of a division of each individual item or asset of quasi-community property, or partly on each basis. Nothing in this subdivision shall be construed to require this written agreement in order to permit or recognize a non pro rata division of quasi-community property.
(Stats. 1990 (A.B. 759), ch. 79, §14, effective July 1, 1991; Stats. 1998 (A.B. 2069), ch. 682, §3.)

§102. Surviving spouse may recapture some quasi-community property

(a) The decedent's surviving spouse may require the transferee of property in which the surviving spouse had an expectancy under Section 101 [quasi-community property] at the time of the transfer to restore to the decedent's estate one-half of the property if the transferee retains the property or, if not, one-half of its proceeds or, if none, one-half of its value at the time of transfer, if all of the following requirements are satisfied:

(1) The decedent died domiciled in this state.

(2) The decedent made a transfer of the property to a person other than the surviving spouse without receiving in exchange a consideration of substantial value and without the written consent or joinder of the surviving spouse.

(3) The transfer is any of the following types:

(A) A transfer under which the decedent retained at the time of death the possession or enjoyment of, or the right to income from, the property.

(B) A transfer to the extent that the decedent retained at the time of death a power, either alone or in conjunction with any other person, to revoke or to consume, invade, or dispose of the principal for the decedent's own benefit.

(C) A transfer whereby property is held at the time of the decedent's death by the decedent and another with right of survivorship.

(b) Nothing in this section requires a transferee to restore to the decedent's estate any life insurance, accident insurance, joint annuity, or pension payable to a person other than the surviving spouse.

(c) All property restored to the decedent's estate under this section belongs to the surviving spouse pursuant to Section 101 as though the transfer had not been made.
(Stats. 1990 (A.B. 759), ch. 79, §14, effective July 1, 1991.)

§104. Exception: community property held In revocable trust is governed by trust provisions

Notwithstanding Section 100, community property held in a revocable trust described in Section 761 of the Family Code is governed by the provisions, if any, in the trust for disposition in the event of death.
(Stats. 1990 (A.B. 759), ch. 79, §14, effective July 1, 1991; Stats. 1992 (A.B. 2641), ch. 163, §119, effective January 1, 1994.)

§104.5. For transfers of property to revocable trusts: presumption arises regarding character of assets

Transfer of community and quasicommunity property to a revocable trust shall be presumed to be an agreement, pursuant to Sections 100 and 101, that those assets retain their character in the aggregate for purposes of any division provided by the trust. This section shall apply to all transfers prior to, on, or after January 1, 2000.
(Stats. 1999 (A.B. 1051), ch. 263, §1.)

§105. Application

This part does not apply where the decedent died before January 1, 1985, and the law applicable prior to January 1, 1985, continues to apply where the decedent died before January 1, 1985.
(Stats. 1990 (A.B. 759), ch. 79, §14, effective July 1, 1991.)

§5020. Nonprobate transfer of community property without spouse's consent is not effective as to nonconsenting spouse's interest

A provision for a nonprobate transfer of community property on death executed by a married person without the written consent of the person's spouse (1) is not effective as to the nonconsenting spouse's interest in the property and (2) does not affect the nonconsenting spouse's disposition on death of the nonconsenting spouse's interest in the community property by will, intestate succession, or nonprobate transfer.
(Stats.1992 (A.B. 1719), ch. 51, §6.)

§5023. "Modification" of provision of nonprobate transfer, defined

(a) As used in this section modification means revocation of a provision for a nonprobate transfer on death in whole or part, designation of a different beneficiary, or election of a different benefit or payment option. As used in this section, modification does not mean, and this section does not apply to, the exercise of a power of appointment under a trust.

(b) If a married person executes a provision for a nonprobate transfer of community property on death with the written consent of the person's spouse and thereafter executes a modification of the provision for transfer of the property without written consent of the spouse, the modification is effective as to the person's interest in the community property and has the following effect on the spouse's interest in the community property:

(1) If the person executes the modification during the spouse's lifetime, the modification revokes the spouse's previous written consent to the provision for transfer of the property.

(2) If the person executes the modification after the spouse's death, the modification does not affect the spouse's previous written consent to the provision for transfer of the property, and the spouse's interest in the

community property is subject to the nonprobate transfer on death as consented to by the spouse.

(3) If a written expression of intent of a party in the provision for transfer of the property or in the written consent to the provision for transfer of the property authorizes the person to execute a modification after the spouse's death, the spouse's interest in the community property is deemed transferred to the married person on the spouse's death, and the modification is effective as to both the person's and the spouse's interests in the community property.

(Stats. 1992 (A.B. 1719), ch. 51, §6; Stats. 1993 (A.B. 908), ch. 527, §3.)

§5031. Revocation of consent to nonprobate transfer of community property

(a) If a married person executes a provision for a nonprobate transfer of community property on death with the written consent of the person's spouse, the consenting spouse may revoke the consent by a writing, including a will, that identifies the provision for transfer of the property being revoked, and that is served on the married person before the married person's death.

(b) Revocation of a spouse's written consent to a provision for a nonprobate transfer of community property on death does not affect the authority of the holder of the property to transfer the property in compliance with the provision for transfer of the property to the extent provided in Section 5003.

(Stats. 1992 (A.B. 1719), ch. 51, §6.)

§5032. Revocation of consent to nonprobate transfer of community property: effect on transfers

On revocation of a spouse's written consent to a nonprobate transfer of community property on death, the property passes in the same manner as if the consent had not been given.

(Stats. 1992 (A.B. 1719), ch. 51, §6.)

§13540. Right of surviving spouse to dispose of real property

(a) Except as provided in Section 13541, after 40 days from the death of a spouse, the surviving spouse or the personal representative, guardian of the estate, or conservator of the Estate of the surviving spouse has full power to sell, convey, lease, mortgage, or otherwise deal with and dispose of the community or quasi-community real property, and the right, title, and interest of any grantee, purchaser, encumbrancer, or lessee shall be free of rights of the Estate of the deceased spouse or of devisees or creditors of the deceased spouse to the same extent as if the property had been owned as the separate property of the surviving spouse.

(b) The surviving spouse or the personal representative, guardian of the estate, or conservator of the Estate of the surviving spouse may record, prior to or together with the instrument that makes a disposition of property under this section, an affidavit of the facts that establish the right of the surviving spouse to make the disposition.(c) Nothing in this section affects or limits the liability of the surviving spouse under Sections 13550 to 13553, inclusive, and Chapter 3.5 (commencing with Section 13560).

(Enacted Stats. 1990 (A.B. 759), ch. 79, §14, effective July 1, 1991; Stats. 1991 (S.B. 271), ch. 1055, §54; Stats. 1994 (A.B. 3686), ch. 806, §36.)

§13541. Recording notice of interest in property

(a) Section 13540 does not apply to a sale, conveyance, lease, mortgage, or other disposition that takes place after a notice that satisfies the requirements of this section is recorded in the office of the county recorder of the county in which real property is located.

(b) The notice shall contain all of the following:

(1) A description of the real property in which an interest is claimed.

(2) A statement that an interest in the property is claimed by a named person under the will of the deceased spouse.

(3) The name or names of the owner or owners of the record title to the property.

(c) There shall be endorsed on the notice instructions that it shall be indexed by the recorder in the name or names of the owner or owners of record title to the property, as grantor or grantors, and in the name of the person claiming an interest in the property, as grantee.

(d) A person shall not record a notice under this section for the purpose of slandering title to the property. If the court in an action or proceeding relating to the rights of the parties determines that a person recorded a notice under this section for the purpose of slandering title, the court shall award against the person the cost of the action or proceeding, including a reasonable attorney's fee, and the damages caused by the recording. *(Stats. 1990 (A.B. 759), ch. 79, §14, effective July 1, 1991; Stats. 1991 (S.B. 271), ch. 1055, §55.)*

CALIFORNIA FAMILY CODE

§721. Contracts with each other and third parties; fiduciary relationship

(a) Subject to subdivision (b), either husband or wife may enter into any transaction with the other, or with any other person, respecting property, which either might if unmarried.

(b) Except as provided in Sections 143, 144, 146, 16040 and 16047 of the Probate Code [regarding waivers of a surviving spouse's rights to a deceased spouse's estate], in transactions between themselves, a husband and wife are subject to the general rules governing fiduciary relationships which control the actions of persons occupying confidential relations with each other. This confidential relationship imposes a duty of the highest good faith and fair dealing on each spouse, and neither shall take any unfair advantage of the other. This confidential relationship is a fiduciary relationship subject to the same rights and duties of nonmarital business partners, as provided in Sections 16403,

16404, and 16503 of the Corporations Code, including, but not limited to, the following:

(1) Providing each spouse access at all times to any books kept regarding a transaction for the purposes of inspection and copying.

(2) Rendering upon request, true and full information of all things affecting any transaction which concerns the community property. Nothing in this section is intended to impose a duty for either spouse to keep detailed books and records of community property transactions.

(3) Accounting to the spouse, and holding as a trustee, any benefit or profit derived from any transaction by one spouse without the consent of the other spouse which concerns the community property.

(Stats. 1992 (A.B. 2650), ch. 162, §10, effective January 1, 1994; Stats. 2002 (S.B. 1936), ch. 310, §1.)

§751. Spouses' interests in community property are present, existing, and equal

The respective interests of the husband and wife in community property during continuance of the marriage relation are present, existing, and equal interests.

(Stats. 1992 (A.B. 2650), ch. 162, §10, effective January 1, 1994.)

§771. Earnings and accumulations are separate property when spouses live apart

(a) The earnings and accumulations of a spouse and minor children living with, or in the custody of, the spouse, while living separate and apart from the other spouse, are the separate property of the spouse.

(b) Notwithstanding subdivision (a), the earnings and accumulations of an unemancipated minor child related to a contract of a type described in Section 6750 [entertainment contracts] shall remain the sole legal property of the minor child.

(Stats. 1992 (A.B. 2650), ch. 162, §10, effective January 1, 1994.)

§1100. Each spouse has equal right to management and control of community personal property; exceptions for gifts and sales

(a) Except as provided in subdivisions (b), (c), and (d) and Sections 761 and 1103, either spouse has the management and control of the community personal property, whether acquired prior to or on or after January 1, 1975, with like absolute power of disposition, other than testamentary, as the spouse has of the separate Estate of the spouse.

(b) A spouse may not make a gift of community personal property, or dispose of community personal property for less than fair and reasonable value, without the written consent of the other spouse. This subdivision does not apply to gifts mutually given by both spouses to third parties and to gifts given by one spouse to the other spouse.

(c) A spouse may not sell, convey, or encumber community personal property used as the family dwelling, or the furniture, furnishings, or fittings of the home, or the clothing or wearing apparel of the other spouse or minor children which is community personal property, without the written consent of the other spouse.

(d) Except as provided in subdivisions (b) and (c), and in Section 1102, a spouse who is operating or managing a business or an interest in a business that is all or substantially all community personal property has the primary management and control of the business or interest. Primary management and control means that the managing spouse may act alone in all transactions but shall give prior written notice to the other spouse of any sale, lease, exchange, encumbrance, or other disposition of all or substantially all of the personal property used in the operation of the business (including personal property used for agricultural purposes), whether or not title to that property is held in the name of only one spouse. Written notice is not, however, required when prohibited by the law otherwise applicable to the transaction.

Remedies for the failure by a managing spouse to give prior written notice as required by this subdivision are only as specified in Section 1101. A failure to give prior written notice shall not adversely affect the validity of a transaction nor of any interest transferred.

(e) Each spouse shall act with respect to the other spouse in the management and control of the community assets and liabilities in accordance with the general rules governing fiduciary relationships which control the actions of persons having relationships of personal confidence as specified in Section 721, until such time as the assets and liabilities have been divided by the parties or by a court. This duty includes the obligation to make full disclosure to the other spouse of all material facts and information regarding the existence, characterization, and valuation of all assets in which the community has or may have an interest and debts for which the community is or may be liable, and to provide equal access to all information, records, and books that pertain to the value and character of those assets and debts, upon request.

(Stats. 1992 (A.B. 2650), ch. 162, §10, effective January 1, 1994; Stats.1993 (A.B. 1500), ch. 219, §100.8.)

§1101. Remedies for spouse's breach of fiduciary duty

(a) A spouse has a claim against the other spouse for any breach of the fiduciary duty that results in impairment to the claimant spouse's present undivided one-half interest in the community estate, including, but not limited to, a single transaction or a pattern or series of transactions, which transaction or transactions have caused or will cause a detrimental impact to the claimant spouse's undivided one-half interest in the community estate.

(b) A court may order an accounting of the property and obligations of the parties to a marriage and may determine the rights of ownership in, the beneficial enjoyment of, or access to, community property, and the classification of all property of the parties to a marriage.

(c) A court may order that the name of a spouse shall be added to community property held in the name of the other spouse alone or that the title of community property held in some other title form shall be reformed to reflect its community character, except with respect to any of the following:

(1) A partnership interest held by the other spouse as a general partner.

(2) An interest in a professional corporation or professional association.

(3) An asset of an unincorporated business if the other spouse is the only spouse involved in operating and managing the business.

(4) Any other property, if the revision would adversely affect the rights of a third person.

(d)(1) Except as provided in paragraph (2), any action under subdivision (a) shall be commenced within three years of the date a petitioning spouse had actual knowledge that the transaction or event for which the remedy is being sought occurred.

(2) An action may be commenced under this section upon the death of a spouse or in conjunction with an action for legal separation, dissolution of marriage, or nullity without regard to the time limitations set forth in paragraph (1).

(3) The defense of laches may be raised in any action brought under this section.

(4) Except as to actions authorized by paragraph (2), remedies under subdivision (a) apply only to transactions or events occurring on or after July 1, 1987.

(e) In any transaction affecting community property in which the consent of both spouses is required, the court may, upon the motion of a spouse, dispense with the requirement of the other spouse's consent if both of the following requirements are met:

(1) The proposed transaction is in the best interest of the community.

(2) Consent has been arbitrarily refused or cannot be obtained due to the physical incapacity, mental incapacity, or prolonged absence of the nonconsenting spouse.

(f) Any action may be brought under this section without filing an action for dissolution of marriage, legal separation, or nullity, or may be brought in conjunction with the action or upon the death of a spouse.

(g) Remedies for breach of the fiduciary duty by one spouse, including those set out in Sections 721 and 1100, shall include, but not be limited to, an award to the other spouse of 50 percent, or an amount equal to 50 percent, of any asset undisclosed or transferred in breach of the fiduciary duty plus attorney's fees and court costs. The value of the asset shall be determined to be its highest value at the date of the breach of the fiduciary duty, the date of the sale or disposition of the asset, or the date of the award by the court.

(h) Remedies for the breach of the fiduciary duty by one spouse, as set forth in Sections 721 and 1100, when the breach falls within the ambit of Section 3294 of the Civil Code shall include, but not be limited to, an award to the other spouse of 100 percent, or an amount equal to 100 percent, of any asset undisclosed or transferred in breach of the fiduciary duty.

(Stats. 1992 (A.B. 2650), ch. 162, §10, effective January 1, 1994; Stats. 2001 (A.B. 583), ch. 703, §1.)

§1102. Exception to equal-management-and-control rule for transfers of community real property

(a) Except as provided in Sections 761 and 1103, either spouse has the management and control of the community real property, whether acquired prior to or on or after January 1, 1975, but both spouses, either personally or by a duly authorized agent, must join in executing any instrument by which that community real property or any interest therein is leased for a longer period than one year, or is sold, conveyed, or encumbered.

(b) Nothing in this section shall be construed to apply to a lease, mortgage, conveyance, or transfer of real property or of any interest In real property between husband and wife.

(c) Notwithstanding subdivision (b):

(1) The sole lease, contract, mortgage, or deed of the husband, holding the record title to community real property, to a lessee, purchaser, or encumbrancer, in good faith without knowledge of the marriage relation, shall be presumed to be valid if executed prior to January 1, 1975.

(2) The sole lease, contract, mortgage, or deed of either spouse, holding the record title to community real property to a lessee, purchaser, or encumbrancer, in good faith without knowledge of the marriage relation, shall be presumed to be valid if executed on or after January 1, 1975.

(d) No action to avoid any instrument mentioned in this section, affecting any property standing of record in the name of either spouse alone, executed by the spouse alone, shall be commenced after the expiration of one year from the filing for record of that instrument in the recorder's office in the county in which the land is situated.

(e) Nothing in this section precludes either spouse from encumbering his or her interest in community real property, as provided in Section 2033, to pay reasonable attorney's fees in order to retain or maintain legal counsel in a proceeding for dissolution of marriage, for nullity of marriage, or for legal separation of the parties.

(Stats. 1992 (A.B. 2650), ch. 162, §10, effective January 1, 1994; Stats. 1993 (A.B. 1500), ch. 219, §101.)

§1103. Exception to equal-management-and-control rule for spouses lacking capacity

(a) Where one or both of the spouses either has a conservator of the estate or lacks legal capacity to manage and control community property, the procedure for management and control (which includes disposition) of the community property is that prescribed in Part 6 (commencing with Section 3000) of Division 4 of the Probate Code.

(b) Where one or both spouses either has a conservator of the estate or lacks legal capacity to give consent to a gift of community personal property or a disposition of community personal property without a valuable consideration as required by Section 1100 or to a sale, conveyance, or encumbrance of community personal property for which a consent is required by Section 1100, the procedure for that gift, disposition, sale, conveyance, or encumbrance is that prescribed in Part 6 (commencing with Section 3000) of Division 4 of the Probate Code.

(c) Where one or both spouses either has a conservator of the estate or lacks legal capacity to join in executing a lease, sale, conveyance, or encumbrance of community real property or any interest therein as required by Section 1102, the procedure for that lease, sale, conveyance, or encumbrance is that prescribed in Part 6 (commencing with Section 3000) of Division 4 of the Probate Code.

(Stats. 1992 (A.B. 2650), ch. 162, §10, effective January 1, 1994.)

§2581. Community property presumption that operates upon dissolution of marriage or legal separation

For the purpose of division of property on dissolution of marriage or legal separation of the parties, property acquired by the parties during marriage in joint form, including property held in tenancy in common, joint tenancy, or tenancy by the entirety, or as community property, is presumed to be community property. This presumption is a presumption affecting the burden of proof and may be rebutted by either of the following:

(a) A clear statement in the deed or other documentary evidence of title by which the property is acquired that the property is separate property and not community property.

(b) Proof that the parties have made a written agreement that the property is separate property.

(Stats. 1993 (A.B. 1500), ch. 219, §111.7.)

CALIFORNIA CIVIL CODE

§3294. Exemplary damages: conditions for awarding

(a) In an action for the breach of an obligation not arising from contract, where it is proven by clear and convincing evidence that the defendant has been guilty of oppression, fraud, or malice, the plaintiff, in addition to the actual damages, may recover damages for the sake of example and by way of punishing the defendant.

(b) An employer shall not be liable for damages pursuant to subdivision (a), based upon acts of an employee of the employer, unless the employer had advance knowledge of the unfitness of the employee and employed him or her with a conscious disregard of the rights or safety of others or authorized or ratified the wrongful conduct for which the damages are awarded or was personally guilty of oppression, fraud, or malice. With respect to a corporate employer, the advance knowledge and conscious disregard, authorization, ratification or act of oppression, fraud, or malice must be on the part of an officer, director, or managing agent of the corporation.

(c) As used in this section, the following definitions shall apply:

(1) "Malice" means conduct which is intended by the defendant to cause injury to the plaintiff or despicable conduct which is carried on by the defendant with a willful and conscious disregard of the rights or safety of others.

(2) "Oppression" means despicable conduct that subjects a person to cruel and unjust hardship in conscious disregard of that person's rights.

(3) "Fraud" means an intentional misrepresentation, deceit, or concealment of a material fact known to the defendant with the intention on the part of the defendant of thereby depriving a person of property or legal rights or otherwise causing injury.

(d) Damages may be recovered pursuant to this section in an action pursuant to Chapter 4 (commencing with Section 377.10) of Title 3 of Part 2 of the Code of Civil Procedure based upon a death which resulted from a homicide for which the defendant has been convicted of a felony, whether or not the decedent died instantly or survived the fatal injury for some period of time. The procedures for joinder and consolidation contained in Section 377.62 of the Code of Civil Procedure shall apply to prevent multiple recoveries of punitive or exemplary damages based upon the same wrongful act.

(e) The amendments to this section made by Chapter 1498 of the Statutes of 1987 apply to all actions in which the initial trial has not commenced prior to January 1, 1988.

(Enacted 1872; Stats. 1905, ch. 463, p. 621, §1; Stats. 1980, ch. 1242, p. 4217, §1; Stats. 1982, ch. 174, §1; Stats. 1983, ch. 408, §1; Stats. 1987, ch. 1498, §5; Stats. 1988, ch. 160, §17; Stats. 1992 (S.B. 1496), ch. 178, §5.)

III. Waiver by the Surviving Spouse

A spouse may renounce ("disclaim") any statutory rights in the other's estate. Spouses may do so either by a premarital agreement (sometimes called an "antenuptial agreement") or by an agreement executed during the marriage. Often, the marital parties agree to waive inheritance rights in order to protect the respective spouses' children from prior marriages.

California law specifies the rules by which the surviving spouse may waive rights in the decedent's estate. According to the California Probate Code (§§140-147), a surviving spouse may renounce (in whole or part) specified rights that she or he is entitled to upon the decedent's death. California Probate Code §141(a) provides that such a waiver may be executed *before or during the marriage*. If the waiver is executed before the marriage, it is subject to the California version of the Uniform Premarital Agreements

Act (see Cal. Fam. Code §§1600 et seq.). The waiver must be voluntary, informed, and in writing (Cal. Prob. Code §142(a)).

The California Probate Code provides that the following rights may be waived:

- **the right to inherit property by intestate or testate succession (provided that the will was executed before the waiver) (Cal. Prob. Code §141(a)(1), (2));**
- **rights pursuant to family protection statutes, such as the right to a family allowance, probate homestead, and the right to exempt personal property (Cal. Prob. Code §141(a)(3), (4), (5));**
- **the right to a small estate set-aside provided by California Probate Code §§6600-6615 (Cal. Prob. Code §141(a)(6));**
- **the right to elect to take community or quasi-community property against the decedent's will (Cal. Prob. Code §141(a)(7));**
- **the right to take the statutory share of an omitted spouse (Cal. Prob. Code §141(a)(8));**
- **the right to be appointed personal representative of the decedent's estate (Cal. Prob. Code §141(a)(9)); and**
- **an interest in property that is the subject of a nonprobate transfer on death (Cal. Prob. Code §141(a)(10)).**

The UPC, similarly, provides that spouses may waive property rights by premarital or marital agreements. Such agreements must be in writing, voluntary, and not unconscionable (UPC §2-213(a)). Spouses may also waive the family protection allowances and exemptions (UPC §2-213(a)). To contest such a waiver, the surviving spouse must show that the waiver was not executed voluntarily or that it was unconscionable at the time of execution and lacked fair disclosure (UPC §2-213(b)). See also Restatement (Third) of Property, *supra*, at §9.4.

CALIFORNIA PROBATE CODE

§120. Surviving spouse may elect to take share of California land of nondomiciliary decedent

If a married person dies not domiciled in this state and leaves a valid will disposing of real property in this state which is not the community property of the decedent and the surviving spouse, the surviving spouse has the same right to elect to take a portion of or interest in such property against the will of the decedent as though the property were located in the decedent's domicile at death.

(Stats. 1990 (A.B. 759), ch. 79, §14, effective July 1, 1991.)

§140. "Waiver," defined

As used in this chapter, "waiver" means a waiver by the surviving spouse of any of the rights listed in subdivision (a) of Section 141, whether signed before or du..ng marriage.

(Stats. 1990 (A.B. 759), ch. 79, §14, effective July 1, 1991.)

§141. Surviving spouse may waive enumerated rights

(a) The right of a surviving spouse to any of the following may be waived in whole or in part by a waiver under this chapter:

(1) Property that would pass from the decedent by intestate succession.

(2) Property that would pass from the decedent by testamentary disposition in a will executed before the waiver.

(3) A probate homestead.

(4) The right to have exempt property set aside.

(5) Family allowance.

(6) The right to have an estate set aside under Chapter 6 (commencing with Section 6600) of Part 3 of Division 6.

(7) The right to elect to take community or quasi-community property against the decedent's will.

(8) The right to take the statutory share of an omitted spouse.

(9) The right to be appointed as the personal representative of the decedent's estate.

(10) An interest in property that is the subject of a nonprobate transfer on death under Part 1 (commencing with Section 5000) of Division 5.

(b) Nothing in this chapter affects or limits the waiver or manner of waiver of rights other than those referred to in subdivision (a), including, but not limited to, the right to property that would pass from the decedent to the surviving spouse by nonprobate transfer upon the death of the decedent, such as the survivorship interest under a joint tenancy, a Totten trust account, or a pay-on-death account.

(Stats. 1990 (A.B. 759), ch. 79, §14, effective July 1, 1991; Stats. 1992 (A.B. 1719), ch. 51, §2.)

§142. Waiver shall be in writing and signed; defenses

(a) A waiver under this chapter shall be in writing and shall be signed by the surviving spouse.

(b) Subject to subdivision (c), a waiver under this chapter is enforceable only if it satisfies the requirements of subdivision (a) and is enforceable under either Section 143 or Section 144.

(c) Enforcement of the waiver against the surviving spouse is subject to the same defenses as enforcement of a contract, except that:

(1) Lack of consideration is not a defense to enforcement of the waiver.

(2) A minor intending to marry may make a waiver under this chapter as if married, but the waiver becomes effective only upon the marriage.

(Stats. 1990 (A.B. 759), ch. 79, §14, effective July 1, 1991.)

§143. Waiver is enforceable unless survivor proves lack of fair disclosure or counsel

(a) Subject to Section 142, a waiver is enforceable under this section unless the surviving spouse proves either of the following:

(1) A fair and reasonable disclosure of the property or financial obligations of the decedent was not provided to the surviving spouse prior to the signing of the waiver unless the surviving spouse waived such a fair and reasonable disclosure after advice by independent legal counsel.

(2) The surviving spouse was not represented by independent legal counsel at the time of signing of the waiver.

(b) Subdivision (b) of Section 721 of the Family Code does not apply if the waiver is enforceable under this section.

(Stats. 1990 (A.B. 759), ch. 79, §14, effective July 1, 1991; Stats. 1992 (A.B. 2641), ch. 163, §120, effective January 1, 1994.)

§144. Waiver is enforccable unless unconscionable at time of enforcement

(a) Except as provided in subdivision (b), subject to Section 142, a waiver is enforceable under this section if the court determines either of the following:

(1) The waiver at the time of signing made a fair and reasonable disposition of the rights of the surviving spouse.

(2) The surviving spouse had, or reasonably should have had, an adequate knowledge of the property and financial obligations of the decedent and the decedent did not violate the duty imposed by subdivision (b) of Section 721 of the Family Code.

(b) If, after considering all relevant facts and circumstances, the court finds that enforcement of the waiver pursuant to subdivision (a) would be unconscionable under the circumstances existing at the time enforcement is sought, the court may refuse to enforce the waiver, enforce the remainder of the waiver without the unconscionable provisions, or limit the application of the unconscionable provisions to avoid an unconscionable result.

(c) Except as provided in paragraph (2) of subdivision (a), subdivision (b) of Section 721 of the Family Code does not apply if the waiver is enforceable under this section.

(Stats. 1990, ch. 79, §14 (A.B. 759), effective July 1, 1991; Stats. 1992, ch. 163, §121 (A.B. 2641), effective January 1, 1994.)

§145. General waivers of "all rights" and also property settlements are effective

Unless the waiver or property settlement provides to the contrary, a waiver under this chapter of "all rights" (or equivalent language) in the property or Estate of a present or prospective spouse, or a complete property settlement entered into after or in anticipation of separation or dissolution or annulment of marriage, is a waiver by the spouse of the rights described in subdivision (a) of Section 141.

(Stats. 1990 (A.B. 759), ch. 79, §14, effective July 1, 1991.)

§146. Waiver may only be amended or revoked by written agreement

(a) As used in this section, "agreement" means a written agreement signed by each spouse or prospective spouse altering, amending, or revoking a waiver under this chapter.

(b) Except as provided in subdivisions (c) and (d) of Section 147, unless the waiver specifically otherwise provides, a waiver under this chapter may not be altered, amended, or revoked except by a subsequent written agreement signed by each spouse or prospective spouse.

(c) Subject to subdivision (d), the agreement is enforceable only if it satisfies the requirements of subdivision (b) and is enforceable under either subdivision (e) or subdivision (f).

(d) Enforcement of the agreement against a party to the agreement is subject to the same defenses as enforcement of any other contract, except that:

(1) Lack of consideration is not a defense to enforcement of the agreement.

(2) A minor intending to marry may enter into the agreement as if married, but the agreement becomes effective only upon the marriage.

(e) Subject to subdivision (d), an agreement is enforceable under this subdivision unless the party to the agreement against whom enforcement is sought proves either of the following:

(1) A fair and reasonable disclosure of the property or financial obligations of the other spouse was not provided to the spouse against whom enforcement is sought prior to the signing of the agreement unless the spouse against whom enforcement is sought waived such a fair and reasonable disclosure after advice by independent legal counsel.

(2) The spouse against whom enforcement is sought was not represented by independent legal counsel at the time of signing of the agreement.

(f) Subject to subdivisions (d) and (g), an agreement is enforceable under this subdivision if the court determines that the agreement at the time of signing made a fair and reasonable disposition of the rights of the spouses.

(g) If, after considering all relevant facts and circumstances, the court finds that enforcement of the agreement pursuant to subdivision (f) would be unconscionable under the circumstances existing at the time enforcement is sought, the court may refuse to enforce the agreement, enforce the remainder of the agreement without the unconscionable provisions, or limit the application of the unconscionable provisions to avoid an unconscionable result.

(h) Subdivision (b) of Section 721 of the Family Code does not apply if the agreement is enforceable under this section.

(Stats. 1990 (A.B. 759), ch. 79, §14, effective July 1, 1991; Stats. 1992 (A.B. 2641), ch. 163, §122, effective January 1, 1994.)

§147. Validity of waivers and agreements under prior law

(a) Subject to subdivisions (c) and (d), a waiver, agreement, or property settlement made after December 31, 1984, is invalid insofar as it affects the rights listed in subdivision (a) of Section 141 unless it satisfies the requirements of this chapter.

(b) Nothing in this chapter affects the validity or effect of any waiver, agreement, or property settlement made prior to January 1, 1985, and the validity and effect of such waiver, agreement, or property settlement shall continue to be determined by the law applicable to the waiver, agreement, or settlement prior to January 1, 1985.

(c) Nothing in this chapter affects the validity or effect of any premarital property agreement, whether made prior to, on, or after January 1, 1985, insofar as the premarital property agreement affects the rights listed in subdivision (a) of Section 141, and the validity and effect of such premarital property agreement shall be determined by the law otherwise applicable to the premarital property agreement. Nothing in this subdivision limits the enforceability under this chapter of a waiver made under this chapter by a person intending to marry that is otherwise enforceable under this chapter.

(d) Nothing in this chapter limits any right one spouse otherwise has to revoke a consent or election to disposition of his or her half of the community or quasi-community property under the will of the other spouse.

(Stats. 1990 (A.B. 759), ch. 79, §14, effective July 1, 1991.)

CALIFORNIA FAMILY CODE

§721. Spouses may contract with each other and are subject to rules regarding fiduciary relationships

(a) Subject to subdivision (b), either husband or wife may enter into any transaction with the other, or with any other person, respecting property, which either might if unmarried.

(b) Except as provided in Sections 143, 144, 146, 16040, and 16047 of the Probate Code, in transactions between themselves, a husband and wife are subject to the general rules governing fiduciary relationships which control the actions of persons occupying confidential relations with each other. This confidential relationship imposes a duty of the highest good faith and fair dealing on each spouse, and neither shall take any unfair advantage of the other. This confidential relationship is a fiduciary relationship subject to the same rights and duties of nonmarital business partners, as provided in Sections 16403, 16404, and 16503 of the Corporations Code, including, but not limited to, the following:

(1) Providing each spouse access at all times to any books kept regarding a transaction for the purposes of inspection and copying.

(2) Rendering upon request, true and full information of all things affecting any transaction which concerns the community property. Nothing in this section is intended to impose a duty for either spouse to keep detailed books and records of community property transactions.

(3) Accounting to the spouse, and holding as a trustee, any benefit or profit derived from any transaction by one spouse without the consent of the other spouse which concerns the community property.

(Stats. 1992 (A.B. 2650), ch. 162, §10, effective January 1, 1994; Stats. 2002 (S.B.1936), ch. 310 , §1.)

Editor's note:

In enacting the 2002 amendments (S.B. 1936), the legislature provided:

[SEC. 2. It is the intent of the Legislature in enacting this act to clarify that Section 721 of the Family Code provides that the fiduciary relationship between spouses includes all of the same rights and duties in the management of community property as the rights and duties of unmarried business partners managing partnership property, as provided in Sections 16403, 16404, and 16503 of the Corporations Code, and to abrogate the ruling in In re Marriage of Duffy (2001) 91 Cal. App.4th 923, to the extent that it is in conflict with this clarification." In Duffy, the California Court of Appeal held that, in a marital dissolution proceeding, the evidence was insufficient to support a finding that the former husband breached his fiduciary duty of full disclosure upon request and also that the former husband did not owe a duty of care to his former wife in investing the community assets.]

IV. Attempts to Defeat the Spouse's Statutory Rights

A. Generally

A significant problem in forced-share jurisdictions is the protection of the surviving spouse's right to nonprobate assets (i.e., those assets that are not part of the probate estate). Such nonprobate assets often consist of joint tenancy property that passes by right of survivorship or life insurance proceeds. In some cases, testators use such assets as probate avoidance techniques—i.e., by holding joint property with someone other than the spouse or making life insurance proceeds payable to someone other than the spouse.

States approach this problem in different ways. Some states subject the decedent's inter vivos transfers to the "illusory transfer" test. These states subject property whose transfer is deemed illusory to the surviving spouse's elective share. McGovern & Kurtz, *supra*, §3.7 at 150. The Restatement (Second) of Property (Donative Transfers) §34.1(3)(1990), as well as the Restatement (Third) of Trusts §25, cmt. d (1996), both permit a surviving spouse to reach assets of a revocable trust created by the decedent (cited in McGovern & Kurtz, *supra*, at 150).

Other states invalidate those nonprobate transfers that are made fraudulently with an intent to deprive the surviving spouse of the elective share. *Id.* at 150-151. Other states simply

include certain nonprobate assets when computing the elective share. *Id.* at 151. This last approach reflects the influence of the UPC (discussed *infra*).

B. UPC Augmented Estate

The UPC also provides for an elective share for the surviving spouse. The elective share applies to protect surviving spouses of decedents who were domiciled at death in a state that adopted the UPC. A surviving spouse may elect to take a designated percentage of the "augmented estate" (UPC §2-202). The augmented estate is an estate that is conceptualized for the purpose of calculating the value of the surviving spouse's elective share. The concept signifies that the probate estate is "augmented" (increased) by certain inter vivos transfers of the decedent.

Specifically, the augmented estate takes into account:

- the decedent's gross probate estate minus creditors' claims, funeral expenses and expenses of administration, and family protection allowances and exemptions (UPC §2-204);
- decedent's nonprobate transfers to others to the extent the decedent retained interests (such as a joint tenancy with right of survivorship, a revocable trust, life insurance owned by the decedent on the decedent's life, multiple-party accounts held in decedent's name with a right of survivorship in a third party, and powers of appointment) (UPC §2-205(1)); or irrevocable transfers by the decedent to third persons within two years before death that would have been included in this category (UPC §2-205(3));
- the surviving spouse's property which consisted of the decedent's nonprobate property that was derived from the decedent by reason of the latter's death (e.g., life insurance benefits, retirement plan benefits) (UPC §2-206); and
- the surviving spouse's assets (i.e., assets earned during the marriage, acquired prior to marriage, and assets derived from the decedent and other persons) (UPC §2-207(a)). The purpose of including the last two categories (assets derived from the decedent as a result of death and the surviving spouse's personal assets) in the augmented estate is to ensure that the augmented estate concept does not benefit surviving spouses with substantial personal assets.

The original version of the UPC (promulgated in 1969) specified that the surviving spouse would take a fixed share (a one-third share) of the augmented estate. However, subsequent revisions in 1990 altered the percentage to take into consideration the length of the marriage. Spouses married at least 1 year may take 3 percent of the augmented estate; those married at least 5 years take 15 percent of the augmented estate; and those married 15 years or more are entitled to 50 percent of the augmented estate. Further, the Code suggests a minimum monetary amount of $50,000 regardless of the length of the marriage. The policy rationale for the 1990 UPC provisions is that marriage is a partnership in which each spouse earns an increasing interest in the estate of the other. The UPC expands the spouses' interest to all assets of both spouses and not merely marital property (unlike in community property states in which the spouse's one-half interest applies only to property acquired during the marriage).

C. Election Will

Sometimes, a testator attempts to bequeath or devise property that belongs to a beneficiary of the will (i.e., property that does not belong to the testator). Such situations commonly arise in wills of spouses who live in community property states (although the use of such election wills is not limited to marital partners).

For example, one spouse may attempt to effectuate a testamentary scheme that involves a testamentary gift of all of the community property (not merely the testator's half but the half that belongs to the other spouse). Because the decedent-spouse only has the right of testamentary disposition over the decedent's half of the community property (and the decedent's separate property), the act of bequeathing all of the community property may serve to put the surviving spouse to an election.

The surviving spouse then has a choice: (1) to elect against the will (thereby retaining the survivor's property that was the subject of the testator's testamentary gift but renouncing any testamentary gift), or (2) to take under the will (thereby acquiescing in the testator's testamentary gift of the surviving spouse's property to another party). Clearly, the surviving spouse will choose the alternative that is financially most beneficial.

Most jurisdictions favor a construction that does not lead to an election by the surviving spouse. That is, if the testator's will bequeaths "all my property," courts are likely to interpret that bequest to encompass only the property over which the decedent has testamentary disposition (i.e., the testator's half of the community property and all of his or her separate property).

V. Protection from Disinheritance

A testator has the power to disinherit family members. This ability is inherent in the power of testamentary disposition. In order to disinherit an heir, the testator must execute a will that expressly disinherits the heir. The will must also dispose of all of the testator's property because any property that is not devised by the will may pass to the heir by the laws of intestate succession.

If the decedent attempts to disinherit a spouse, the surviving spouse may claim an elective share. The surviving spouse may claim that share regardless of whether the decedent's will disinherits the survivor entirely or bequeaths to the survivor part of the decedent's estate.

In some cases, a testator may unintentionally disinherit a family member. Given the jurisdiction, such family members may be protected from some types of unintentional disinheritance (discussed *infra*).

A. Spouses

Many jurisdictions protect certain family members (e.g., spouses, children) against unintentional disinheritance. These statutes are known as "pretermitted" (or omitted) heir statutes. American pretermission statutes date from the eighteenth century. McGovern & Kurtz, *supra*, §3.5 at 140.

The share given to an omitted spouse in many jurisdictions is the same as the intestate share. However, most omitted spouse statutes give a share of only the net probate estate and do not include nonprobate property (such as trust property). *Id.*, §3.7 at 147. Cf. Cal. Prob. Code §21610 which applies to "testamentary instruments" meaning both wills and trusts.

Note that California Probate Code §§21600 et seq. govern the rights of omitted spouses and children of decedents who die on or after January 1, 1998. Former California Probate Code §§6560 et seq., applicable to estates of decedents who die before that date, applies only to property that passes by will.

The most common situation that results in unintentional omission of a spouse is the antenuptial will, i.e., a spouse who marries a testator after the testator executes a will. The English Wills Act of 1837 provided that marriage revoked the will of a spouse, and many jurisdictions follow this rule. McGovern & Kurtz, *supra*, §3.6 at 145. Other jurisdictions revoke a will only if the testator both marries and has a child. *Id.*

The California statute specifies the manner of satisfying the share of an omitted spouse. If a decedent omits a surviving spouse who married the decedent after the execution of all of the decedent's testamentary instruments, the survivor shall receive: (a) the one-half of the community property that belonged to the decedent spouse; (b) one-half of the quasi-community property that belonged to the decedent spouse; (c) a share of the separate property that would equal that which the surviving spouse would have received had the decedent died intestate, but this cannot exceed more than one-half of the separate property (Cal. Prob. Code §21610). However, for purposes of determining the omitted spouse's share, a court has held that the decedent's estate does not include funds held in a Totten trust account. Estate of Allen, 16 Cal. Rptr.2d 352 (Ct. App. 1993).

The current California omitted spouse statute replaces the common law doctrine of implied revocation by a subsequent marriage. 64 Cal. Jur.3d Wills §328. For discussion of revocation of wills by operation of law, see Chapter VII *infra*.

Omitted California spouses do not receive a share of the estate when the decedent's failure to provide for the spouse is clearly intentional as evident from the testamentary instruments, or the decedent provided for the spouse by way of a transfer intended as a substitute for a devise, or if the surviving spouse waived such rights (Cal. Prob. Code §21611). The intent to disinherit the spouse must be explicit. That is, courts have held that some general provisions (i.e., those excluding "heirs living at the time of the testator's death" or "any legal heir of mine" or "all my heirs who are not specifically mentioned herein") were not sufficient to evidence the requisite intent to disinherit an omitted spouse. 64 Cal. Jur.3d Wills §338. See also Estate of Katleman, 16 Cal. Rptr.2d 468, 474-475 (Ct. App. 1993) (holding that a no-contest clause may not defeat the pretermission claims unless the contestant spouse is mentioned in the clause with the same specificity required of a general disinheritance clause). (The case was decided under a former pretermitted spouse statute.)

A putative spouse qualifies as an omitted spouse under California Probate Code §21610 and is entitled to succeed to a share of the decedent's estate. See, e.g., Estate of Sax, 263 Cal. Rptr. 190 (Ct. App. 1989) (holding that the statute does not require the marriage to be valid). However, the statutory definition of

surviving spouse does not include a person whose marriage has been dissolved or annulled. 64 Cal. Jur.3d Wills §331.

California law is similar in some regards to the UPC. The UPC provides for an intestate share to a spouse in the antenuptial will situation (UPC §2-301), and does not permit the omitted spouse to take if evidence establishes that the omission was intentional (such as if the will shows an express intent to exclude the spouse from a subsequent marriage, or if the surviving spouse received transfers outside the will that were intended to be in lieu of a testamentary gift) (*id.*). However, the UPC has an additional provision precluding an omitted spouse that is not present in the California statute: An omitted spouse cannot take if the will (or the evidence) indicates that the will was executed in "contemplation" of the marriage (UPC §2-301(a)(1)). California law falls to incorporate this provision because the California statute was based on an earlier version of the UPC. McGovern & Kurtz, *supra*, §3.6 at 145 n. 8. (Note that an expressly disinherited spouse can still take an elective share in many jurisdictions; however, that share may be smaller than the share provided for an omitted spouse. For example, under the UPC, the size of the elective share depends on the duration of the marriage.)

A common scenario in antenuptial will situations occurs when a testator executes a will with a small provision for a "friend." Later, the testator marries the friend. "Most courts have held that such a devise does not bar an omitted spouse's claim unless the will was made in contemplation of the marriage, but there are also contrary decisions." McGovern & Kurtz, *supra*, §3.6, at 146.

CALIFORNIA PROBATE CODE

§21610. Share of omitted spouse in antenuptial will situation

Except as provided in Section 21611, if a decedent fails to provide in a testamentary instrument for the decedent's surviving spouse who married the decedent after the execution of all of the decedent's testamentary instruments, the omitted spouse shall receive a share in the decedent's estate, consisting of the following property in said estate:

(a) The one-half of the community property that belongs to the decedent under Section 100 [set forth in Section II C supra this Chapter];

(b) The one-half of the quasi-community property that belongs to the decedent under Section 101 [set forth in Section II C supra this Chapter].

(c) A share of the separate property of the decedent equal in value to that which the spouse would have received if the decedent had died without having executed a testamentary instrument, but in no event is the share to be more than one-half the value of the separate property in the estate.

(Stats. 1997 (A.B. 1172), ch. 724, §34.)

§21611. Exceptions to omitted spouse's protection in antenuptial will situation

The spouse shall not receive a share of the estate under Section 21610 if any of the following is established:

(a) The decedent's failure to provide for the spouse in the decedent's testamentary instruments was intentional and that intention appears from the testamentary instruments.

(b) The decedent provided for the spouse by transfer outside of the estate passing by the decedent's testamentary instruments and the intention that the transfer be in lieu of a provision in said instruments is shown by statements of the decedent or from the amount of the transfer or by other evidence.

(c) The spouse made a valid agreement waiving the right to share in the decedent's estate.

(Stats. 1997 (A.B. 1172), ch. 724, §34.)

§21612. Manner of satisfying spouse's share; order of abatement

(a) Except as provided in subdivision (b), in satisfying a share provided by this chapter:

(1) The share will first be taken from the decedent's estate not disposed of by will or trust, if any.

(2) If that is not sufficient, so much as may be necessary to satisfy the share shall be taken from all beneficiaries of decedent's testamentary instruments in proportion to the value they may respectively receive. The proportion of each beneficiary's share that may be taken pursuant to this subdivision shall be determined based on values as of the date of the decedent's death.

(b) If the obvious intention of the decedent In relation to some specific gift or devise or other provision of a testamentary instrument would be defeated by the application of subdivision (a), the specific devise or gift or provision may be exempted from the apportionment under subdivision (a), and a different apportionment, consistent with the intention of the decedent, may be adopted.

(Stats. 1997 (A.B. 1172), ch. 724, §34. Amended by Stats. 2003 (A.B. 167), ch. 32, §17, effective January 1, 2004.)

B. Children

Pretermitted heir statutes protect not only omitted spouses but also omitted children. However, children receive far less protection than spouses. Pretermitted heir statutes generally provide a share for an omitted child born to the testator after the testator executed a will. The rationale for inclusion is based on presumed intent (i.e., the idea that a testator would have wanted to provide a share for such a child). Jurisdictions are more restrictive in their

treatment of those omitted children who were *alive* at the time of the will execution.

Disinheritance of a child may stem from several reasons. The most common is inadvertence—either a child is unintentionally omitted from the will or no will is written after the child is born. Brian C. Brennan, Note, Disinheritance of Dependent Children: Why Isn't America Fulfilling Its Moral Obligation?, 14 Quinnipiac Prob. L.J. 125, 128-129 (1999). Intentional disinheritance on the other hand, may result from some parents' belief that disinheriting a child will force the child to work harder in life "to become a better person and a more contributing member of society," or the mistaken belief that existing legal provisions (family allowances, homestead exemptions, and personal property exemptions) will protect the child. *Id.* at 129-131. Finally, the increasing rate of divorce and remarriage leads to more frequent disinheritance of children from prior marriages as testators balance the needs of current families against those of previous ones. *Id.* at 131-132.

Only one state (Louisiana) guarantees children a forced share in their parents' estate. Policy reasons underlying this concept of forced heirship include: furthering state interests in warding off intra-family litigation, promoting family solidarity, and preventing excessive concentrations of wealth. Brennan, *supra*, at 155. Louisiana adopted the French law of inheritance (the Napoleonic Code of 1803) in 1825, guaranteeing children a forced share. The concept was enshrined in the state constitution. See La. Const. (art. XII, §5) (providing "no law shall abolish forced heirship"). In 1989-1990, the Louisiana state legislature placed restrictions on forced heirship in terms of age and competency. See La. Civ. Code art. 1493 (as amended in 1989 and 1990) (extinguishing forced heirship for persons who upon the decedent's death are competent and 23 years of age or older). The Louisiana Supreme Court subsequently declared these restrictions unconstitutional (Succession of Lauga, 624 So.2d 1156 (La. 1993); Succession of Terry, 624 So.2d 1201 (La. 1993)).

In 1995, however, by constitutional amendment, the Louisiana state legislature deleted the language "no law shall abolish forced heirship" and required the legislature to implement legislation restricting forced heirship to those children age 23 or younger but also permitting forced shares to those issue (of any age) who were incompetent. See La. Constit. art. XII, §5 (amended by Acts 1995, No. 1321, Section 1, approved Oct. 21, 1995, effective Nov. 23, 1995) (cited in Brennan, *supra*, at 156 n. 228).

Statutory guidelines in Louisiana currently permit disinheritance of a child only in limited circumstances. A parent must disinherit the child expressly and with "just cause." According to Louisiana Civil Code Art. 1621(A)(1)-(8), a parent has just cause if: (1) the child has struck a parent or attempted to do so; (2) the child has been guilty, toward a parent, of cruel treatment, crime, or grievous injury; (3) the child has attempted to take the parent's life; (4) the child, without any reasonable basis, has accused a parent of committing a capital crime; (5) the child has used force to prevent a parent from executing a will; (6) a minor child has married without the parent's consent; (7) the child has been convicted of a capital crime; and (8) the child, after majority, has failed to communicate with the parent without just cause for a period of two years, unless the child was on active military duty. However, satisfying just cause merely creates a rebuttable presumption (i.e., the heir may prove that the cause did not exist or that a reconciliation occurred after the disinheritance).

In other states, pretermitted heir statutes differ as to: (1) the existence of protection for living versus after-born children (i.e., some statutes only cover children born after the will was executed); (2) protection for children versus other relatives of the testator (i.e., some statutes cover grandchildren as well, although UPC §2-302 protects children only and not other relatives); and (3) the type of evidence admissible to prove intention to disinherit (i.e., some statutes provide that only evidence on the face of the will is admissible whereas other states admit extrinsic evidence as well).

Some statutes provide that the will is revoked by the subsequent birth of children. The majority of states, however, permit the pretermitted heir to take an intestate share.

California law protects children who were born to or adopted by the decedent *after* execution of all of the decedent's testamentary instruments (will or trust). In this regard, the California statute shares a similarity with the UPC approach. According to the California statute, such a child receives the share that he or she would have received if the decedent had died intestate (Cal. Prob. Code §21620). However, omitted children will receive no share if the testamentary instruments reveal that the exclusion was the intent of the decedent, or the decedent devised or directed the disposition of his estate to the other parent of the omitted child, or provided for the child by way of a transfer intended to substitute for a devise (Cal. Prob. Code §21621). See also UPC §2-302.

California statutory guidelines protect *some* children who were living at the time of will execution. That is, if the decedent failed to provide for a living child whom he erroneously believed to be dead, or of whom he was not

aware, the child shall receive the share that he or she would have received had the decedent died intestate (Cal. Prob. Code §21622). These provisions do not apply if the decedent died before January 1, 1998 (Cal. Prob. Code §21630). See also Estate of Della Sala, 86 Cal. Rptr.2d 569 (Ct. App. 1999) (affirming denial of pretermitted status to son, holding that the son failed to carry his burden of proving that the sole reason for his pretermission was the testator's mistaken belief that he was dead; evidence that the testator had misled executrix into believing that he had no living relatives did not establish that testator thought his son was dead).

An issue of recent interest is whether a father can disinherit his child to defeat his child support obligations. In L.W.K. v. E.R.C., 735 N.E.2d 359, 364 (Mass. 2000), the Massachusetts Supreme Judicial Court held that a testator charged with an obligation to support his child cannot nullify that legal obligation by disinheriting the child. The court reasoned that a legally enforceable obligation to pay child support, like other financial obligations of the testator, takes precedence over testamentary dispositions and must be satisfied prior to any distribution of assets under the will. The court also provided that the assets of an inter vivos trust established by the decedent (under which he was the sole beneficiary, and which he solely retained the power to modify, alter, or revoke), had to be included in his estate and, as such, had to be made available to satisfy his child support obligations.

Note that the California rules that govern the manner of satisfying the omitted child's share (Cal. Prob. Code §21623) are analogous to those applying to satisfying the pretermitted spouse's share (Cal. Prob. Code §21612, *supra*). On the rules of abatement, see Chapter XV, Section IIC, *infra*.

On disinheritance, see generally Susanna Blumenthal, The Deviance of the Will, Policing the Bounds of Testamentary Freedom in Nineteenth-Century America, 119 Harv. L. Rev. 959 (2006); Richard Lewis Brown, Undeserving Heirs? The Case of the "Terminated Parent," 40 U. Rich. L. Rev. 547 (2006).

CALIFORNIA PROBATE CODE

§21620. Pretermitted child: born or adopted after will execution; share of such children

Except as provided in Section 21621, if a decedent fails to provide in a testamentary instrument for a child of decedent born or adopted after the execution of all of the decedent's testamentary instruments, the omitted child shall receive a share in the decedent's estate equal in value to that which the child would have received if the decedent had died without having executed any testamentary instrument.

(Stats. 1997 (A.B. 1172), ch. 724, §34.)

§21621. Child shall not receive a share in some cases

A child shall not receive a share of the estate under Section 21620 if any of the following is established:

(a) The decedent's failure to provide for the child in the decedent's testamentary instruments was intentional and that intention appears from the testamentary instruments.

(b) The decedent had one or more children and devised or otherwise directed the disposition of substantially all of the estate to the other parent of the omitted child.

(c) The decedent provided for the child by transfer outside of the estate passing by the decedent's testamentary instruments and the intention that the transfer be in lieu of a provision in said instruments is shown by statements of the decedent or from the amount of the transfer or by other evidence.

(Stats.1997 (A.B. 1172), ch. 724, §34.)

§21622. Protection of some living children

If, at the time of the execution of all of decedent's testamentary instruments effective at the time of decedent's death, the decedent failed to provide for a living child solely because the decedent believed the child to be dead or was unaware of the birth of the child, the child shall receive a share in the estate equal in value to that which the child would have received if the decedent had died without having executed any testamentary instruments.

(Stats. 1997 (A.B. 1172), ch. 724, §34.)

§21623. Omitted child's share; role of decedent's intention

(a) Except as provided in subdivision (b), in satisfying a share provided by this chapter:

(1) The share will first be taken from the decedent's estate not disposed of by will or trust, if any.

(2) If that is not sufficient, so much as may be necessary to satisfy the share shall be taken from all beneficiaries of decedent's testamentary instruments in proportion to the value they may respectively receive. The proportion of each beneficiary's share that may be taken pursuant to this subdivision shall be determined based on values as of the date of the decedent's death.

(b) If the obvious intention of the decedent In relation to some specific gift or devise or other provision of a testamentary instrument would be defeated by the application of subdivision (a), the specific devise or gift or provision of a testamentary instrument may be exempted from the apportionment under subdivision (a), and a different apportionment, consistent with the intention of the decedent, may be adopted.

(Stats.1997 (A.B. 1172), ch. 724, §34. Amended by Stats. 2003 (A.B. 167), ch. 32, §16, effective January 1, 2004.)

§21630. Date of application of part

This part does not apply if the decedent died before January 1, 1998. The law applicable prior to January 1, 1998, applies if the decedent died before January 1, 1998.
(Stats. 1997 (A.B. 1172), ch. 724, §34.)

C. Mortmain Statutes

Historically, some jurisdictions restricted the decedent's dispositions to charity. Such restrictions were called "mortmain" statutes. These statutes date to the thirteenth century in England. John R. Cunningham, Mortmain Statutes: The Dead Hand Still Survives, 27 Idaho L. Rev. 49 (1990/1991).

Mortmain (meaning "dead hand") statutes refers to the perpetual ownership of land by charitable organizations. "In thirteenth century England, the Crown was deeply concerned about the ownership of land by ecclesiastical and lay corporations." *Id.* Among the problems such ownership posed were: "(1) the loss of feudal incidents to the crown and lords because of the transfer of land from one generation to another, (2) the consequential restraint on the free alienability of land, and (3) the inability of religious organizations and persons to perform certain feudal burdens attaching to land ownership." *Id.* at 49-50.

In response, Parliament enacted forfeiture and mortmain statutes which provided that real property held by religious organizations had to be forfeited to the overlord and, if he refused, to the Crown. David Villar Patton, The Queen, the Attorney General, and the Modern Charitable Fiduciary: A Historical Perspective on Charitable Enforcement Reform, 11 U. Fla. J.L. & Pub. Pol'y 131, 134 (2000).

The first comprehensive mortmain statute (the Statute of Mortmain) was enacted by Parliament in 1279. One commentator explained the reasons for its enactment: "Perhaps there was justification for the early English Mortmain statutes since at one time in England the church and other religious societies possessed nearly half of the real property in England." Shirley Norwood Jones, The Demise of Mortmain in the United States, 12 Miss. C. L. Rev. 407, 408 (1992).

Religious charities found a loophole by the conveyance of land to individuals for the use of a religious order. "By the 1390s, however, the mortmain statutes were expanded to include conveyances to individuals, and the loophole was closed." Patton, *supra*, at 134. Parliament enacted subsequent legislation in the eighteenth century (9 Geo. 2, c. 36 (1736)), providing that all gifts of land to charity had to be made by a deed, sealed and delivered at least 12 months before the donor's death. McGovern & Kurtz, *supra*, §3.10 at 176.

Although the English Mortmain Statute was not widely adopted in this country, many American jurisdictions enacted similar restrictions. Statutes were of two types. Some jurisdictions provided that charitable testamentary gifts were invalid unless the will was executed a specified *time before death*. The policy underlying this type of statute was "to prevent the testator from being unduly influenced while under fear of impending death." Atkinson, *supra*, §35 at 136. Other jurisdictions enacted limitations on the *proportion of the estate* which might be devoted to charitable purposes. *Id.* at 135. Some state statutes incorporated both provisions. Statutes generally required that the testator had to be survived by certain close relatives who were the sole persons eligible to object.

In the nineteenth century, California law incorporated a mortmain statute granting certain of the decedent's heirs the right to avoid testamentary gifts to charity in excess of one-third of the decedent's estate (Cal. Civ. Code §1313, replaced by Cal. Prob. Code §41). The California Mortmain Statute (Cal. Prob. Code §41) was repealed by the legislature on November 4, 1971, effective March 4, 1972. See also Estate of Hinckley, 58 Cal. 457 (Cal. 1881) (holding that the mortmain statute recognized the right to convey property for charitable uses); Estate of Taylor, 108 Cal. Rptr. 778 (Ct. App. 1973) (holding that, where Cal. Prob. Code §41 limiting bequests to charities to one-third of estate if the testator was survived by certain heirs was in effect at time of testator's death but that statute was repealed prior to the assertion of rights by testator's son, testator's son had no rights under statute).

The California Mortmain Statute (1931 Cal. Stat. ch. 281, §§40-43, now repealed) provided that a devise or bequest could not be made to charity within 30 days of death if the testator was survived by named relatives; even prior to the 30 days, the devises and bequests could not exceed one-third of the estate if certaln relatives survived or there was a pro rata reduction. Devises and bequests to state, municipal, county, or political subdivisions within the state were excepted. Jones, *supra*, at 411. By case law and statute, California successively restricted the mortmain statute until its repeal in 1971. *Id.* at 412.

As of 1970, 11 states had a mortmain statute. Restatement (Third) of Property, v. 2, §9.6, Reporter's Note cmt. 3. By 1992, only three states had such statutes. Jones, *supra*, at 410. Today, all mortmain statutes have been repealed by statute or declared unconstitutional (on equal protection and/or due process grounds).

Restatement (Third) of Property, v. 2, §9.6 cmt. c. See also Estate of French v. Doyle, 365 A.2d 621 (D.C. App. 1976) (declaring statute unconstitutional on due process and equal protection grounds); Shriner's Hosp. for Crippled Children v. Zrillic, 564 So. 2d 64 (Fla. 1990) (declaring statute unconstitutional under equal protection grounds of the state and federal constitutions); Estate of Kinyon, 615 P.2d 174 (Mont. 1980); Shriner's Hosp. for Crippled Children v. Hester, 492 N.E.2d 153 (Ohio 1986) (declaring statute unconstitutional on equal protection grounds of the state and federal constitutions); Estate of Cavill, 329 A.2d 503 (Pa. 1974) (declaring statute unconstitutional on substantive due process grounds).

Idaho was one of the last states to repeal its statute following a case addressing the constitutionality of the statute. In Estate of Kirk, 907 P.2d 794 (Idaho 1995), a testator wrote handwritten charitable dispositions on the back of a check stub within 120 days of her death, raising the question whether this disposition violated the Idaho Mortmain Statute. The Idaho Supreme Court declined to rule on the constitutionality of the statute, holding that the mortmain statute only applied to wills and testamentary trusts (and not to this disposition which included amendments to an inter vivos trust), and consequently were not governed by the statute. The Idaho statute, codified at Idaho Code §15-2-615(a), was later repealed (S.L. 1994, ch. 359, §1). See generally Elizabeth Barker Brandt, Estate of Kirk: Mortmain, Perpetuities, Extrinsic Evidence, Aaargh!, 39 Advocate (Idaho) 21 (July 1996).

CALIFORNIA PROBATE CODE

§41. Mortmain statute: restrictions on charitable devises (repealed)

No estate, real or personal, may be bequeathed or devised to any charitable or benevolent society or corporation, or to any person or persons in trust for charitable uses, by a testator who leaves a spouse, brother, sister, nephew, niece, descendant or ancestor surviving him, who, under the will, or the laws of succession, would otherwise have taken the property so bequeathed or devised, unless the will was duly executed at least 30 days before the death of the testator. If so executed at least 30 days before death, such devises and legacies shall be valid, but they may not collectively exceed one-third of the testator's estate as against his spouse, brother, sister, nephew, niece, descendant or ancestor, who would otherwise, as aforesaid, have taken the excess over one-third, and if they do, a pro rata deduction from such devises and legacies shall be made so as to reduce the aggregate thereof to one-third of the estate.

All property bequeathed or devised contrary to the provisions of this section shall go to the spouse, brother, sister, nephew, niece, descendant or ancestor of the testator, if and to the extent that they would have taken said property as aforesaid but for such devises or legacies; otherwise the testator's estate shall go in accordance with his will and such devises and legacies shall be unaffected.

Nothing herein contained is intended to, or shall be deemed or construed to vest any property devised or bequeathed to charity or in trust for a charitable use, in any person who is not a relative of the testator belonging to one of the classes mentioned herein, or in any such relative, unless and then only to the extent that such relative takes the same under a substitutional or residuary bequest or devise in the will or under the laws of succession because of the absence of other effective disposition in the will.

(Repealed by Stats. 1971, ch. 1395, p. 2747, §1; Stats. 1931, ch. 281, p. 589, §41, as amended Stats. 1937, ch. 480, p. 1435, §1; Stats. 1943, ch. 305, p. 1296, §1.)

D. Negative Beneficiaries

A testator may desire to disinherit a particular person (so-called negative beneficiary). According to the common law rule, such a disinheritance provision is ineffective unless the testator makes an affirmative disposition of the entire estate. Thus, if a negative beneficiary becomes the testator's heir and some property passes intestate (because the testator has not named beneficiaries for all his or her property), the negative beneficiary will take an intestate share of that property. Frederic S. Schwartz, Models of the Will and Negative Disinheritance, 48 Mercer L. Rev. 1137, 1137-1138 (1997).

The Restatement (Third) of Property (§2.7) provides that a will may "expressly exclude or limit the right of an individual or class to succeed to property" passing by intestate succession. This provision thereby reverses the common law rule. The Restatement also addresses the effect of a negative will provision on the distribution of the intestate property. That is, if the testator expressly excludes or limits the right of an individual or class to take by intestate succession, any share of the decedent's intestate estate (that would have passed to the disinherited person or class), passes as if the person or class made a disclaimer. Thus, for example, if the decedent provided that his only brother would take "$50 and no more," the brother is entitled to the $50. However, any share of the decedent's intestate share that would have passed to the brother instead passes to the brother's descendants by representation. *Id.* at §2.7, cmt. c. The revised UPC (§2-101) also authorizes negative wills.

III
WILL EXECUTION

All states require that the testator must comply with certain formalities in order for a will to be valid. This chapter explores these formal requirements. First, the chapter addresses the historical background and policies underlying the formalities. Second, it explores testamentary capacity and testamentary intent. Third, it examines requirements regarding a writing and the testator's signature. Fourth, it focuses on the rules regarding attestation by witnesses. Finally, it explores various types of wills (including holographic wills, oral wills, conditional wills, statutory wills, foreign and international wills, and the self-proved will).

I. Introduction

A. Terminology

A will disposes of property owned at death. A will may be one of the following types:

- formally executed (also called "attested" or "witnessed");
- handwritten ("holographic"); or
- oral ("nuncupative").

To be valid, a will must comply with certain statutory formalities (discussed *infra*). It is not essential that a document be called a "will" in order for it to serve as a will.

A codicil is a document that amends a will. In some cases, a codicil may do nothing more than revoke a prior will. A valid codicil must be executed with the requisite statutory formalities. If a codicil complies with the statutory requirements, it may be probated as a will (for example, if the will to which it is attached is not effective). It is not required that a codicil must call itself a "codicil" (or a "will") in order to serve as a testamentary instrument.

According to California statute, the term "will" may include a codicil (Cal. Prob. Code §88). In addition, the term "will" may include a testamentary instrument which does no more than: (1) appoint an executor, (2) revoke a will, or (3) change another will. *Id.* That is, a will or codicil need not be dispositive.

The UPC recognizes several different wills: (1) the witnessed will (UPC §2-502(a)), (2) the holographic will (UPC §2-502(b)), (3) the foreign will (UPC §2-506), (4) the international will (UPC Art. II, Pt. 10, Uniform International Wills Act), and (5) the self-proved will (UPC §2-504). California recognizes (1) witnessed wills (Cal. Prob. Code §§6110 et seq.), (2) holographic wills (Cal. Prob. Code §6111), (3) statutory wills (Cal. Prob. Code §§6200 et seq.), and (4) international wills (Cal. Prob. Code §§6380 et seq.). Until 1982, California recognized oral wills (former Cal. Prob. Code §§54, 55).

The term "personal representative" generally signifies an executor (the person who administers a testate estate) or administrator (the person who administers an intestate estate). The term "fiduciary" includes both a personal representative and trustee (as well as a conservator, guardian, attorney-in-fact under a power of attorney, and custodian under the Uniform Transfer to Minors Act). Cal. Prob. Code §39.

In California, an "executor" is the person who administers the estate of a decedent who dies with a formally executed will, holographic will, or even a statutory will (Cal. Prob. Code §6203). A "testator," similarly, is the person who executes a formally executed will, holographic will, or even a statutory will (Cal. Prob. Code §6201).

CALIFORNIA PROBATE CODE

§32. "Devise," defined

"Devise," when used as a noun, means a disposition of real or personal property by will, and, when used as a verb, means to dispose of real or personal property by will.

(Stats. 1990 (A.B. 759), ch. 79, §14, effective July 1, 1991.)

§34. "Devisee," defined

(a) "Devisee" means any person designated in a will to receive a devise.

(b) In the case of a devise to an existing trust or trustee, or to a trustee on trust described by will, the trust or trustee is the devisee and the beneficiaries are not devisees.

(Stats. 1990 (A.B. 759), ch. 79, §14, effective July 1, 1991.)

§45. "Instrument," defined

"Instrument" means a will, trust, deed, or other writing that designates a beneficiary or makes a donative transfer of property.

(Stats. 1990 (A.B. 759), ch. 79, §14, effective July 1, 1991.)

§88. "Will," defined

"Will" includes codicil and any testamentary instrument which merely appoints an executor or revokes or revises another will.

(Stats. 1990 (A.B. 759), ch. 79, §14, effective July 1, 1991.)

§6101. Will may dispose of testator's half of community property and half of quasi-community property, but all of testator's separate property

A will may dispose of the following property:

(a) The testator's separate property.

(b) The one-half of the community property that belongs to the testator under Section 100.

(c) The one-half of the testator's quasi-community property that belongs to the testator under Section 101.

(Stats. 1990 (A.B. 759), ch. 79, §14, effective July 1, 1991.)

§6102. Eligible beneficiaries of a will

A will may make a disposition of property to any person, including but not limited to any of the following:

(a) An individual.

(b) A corporation.

(c) An unincorporated association, society, lodge, or any branch thereof.

(d) A county, city, city and county, or any municipal corporation.

(e) Any state, including this state.

(f) The United States or any instrumentality thereof.

(g) A foreign country or a governmental entity therein.

(Stats. 1990 (A.B. 759), ch. 79, §14, effective July 1, 1991.)

§6105. Validity of conditional will

A will, the validity of which is made conditional by its own terms, shall be admitted to probate or rejected, or denied effect after admission to probate, in conformity with the condition.

(Stats. 1990 (A.B. 759), ch. 79, §14, effective July 1, 1991.)

§6113. Will execution and choice of law

A written will is validly executed if its execution complies with any of the following:

(a) The will is executed in compliance with Section 6110 or 6111 or Chapter 6 (commencing with Section 6200) (California statutory will) or Chapter 11 (commencing with Section 6380) (Uniform International Wills Act).

(b) The execution of the will complies with the law at the time of execution of the place where the will is executed.

(c) The execution of the will complies with the law of the place where at the time of execution or at the time of death the testator is domiciled, has a place of abode, or is a national.

(Stats. 1990 (A.B. 759), ch. 79, §14, effective July 1, 1991.)

§6200. Application of these definitions

Unless the provision or context clearly requires otherwise, these definitions and rules of construction govern the construction of this chapter.

(Stats. 1991 (S.B. 271), ch. 1055, §20.)

§6201. "Testator," defined

"Testator" means a person choosing to adopt a California statutory will.

(Stats. 1991 (S.B. 271), ch. 1055, §20.)

§6203. "Executor," defined

"Executor" means both the person so designated in a California statutory will and any other person acting at any time as the executor or administrator under a California statutory will.

(Stats. 1991 (S.B. 271), ch. 1055, §20.)

§6204. "Trustee," defined

"Trustee" means both the person so designated in a California statutory will and any other person acting at any time as the trustee under a California statutory will.

(Stats. 1991 (S.B. 271), ch. 1055, §20.)

§6205. "Descendants," defined

"Descendants" mean children, grandchildren, and their lineal descendants of all generations, with the relationship of parent and child at each generation being determined as provided in Section 21115. A reference to "descendants" in the plural includes a single descendant where the context so requires.

(Stats. 1991 (S.B. 271), ch. 1055, §20. Amended by Stats. 2002 (A.B. 1784), ch. 138, §7, effective January 1, 2003.)

§6206. References in statutory will to UGMA or UTMA

A reference in a California statutory will to the "Uniform Gifts to Minors Act of any state" or the "Uniform Transfers to Minors Act of any state" includes both the Uniform Gifts to Minors Act of any state and the Uniform Transfers to Minors Act of any state. A reference to a "custodian" means the person so designated in a California statutory will or any other person acting at any time as a custodian under a Uniform Gifts to Minors Act or Uniform Transfers to Minors Act.

(Stats. 1991 (S.B. 271), ch. 1055, §20.)

§6207. Pronouns and plural nouns

Masculine pronouns include the feminine, and plural and singular words include each other, where appropriate.

(Stats. 1991 (S.B. 271), ch. 1055, §20.)

§6208. Meaning of "shall" or "may"

(a) If a California statutory will states that a person shall perform an act, the person is required to perform that act.

(b) If a California statutory will states that a person may do an act, the person's decision to do or not to do the act shall be made in the exercise of the person's fiduciary powers.

(Stats. 1991 (S.B. 271), ch. 1055, §20.)

§6209. Distribution to "descendants"

Whenever a distribution under a California statutory will is to be made to a person's descendants, the property shall be divided into as many equal shares as there are then living descendants of the nearest degree of living descendants and

deceased descendants of that same degree who leave descendants then living; and each living descendant of the nearest degree shall receive one share and the share of each deceased descendant of that same degree shall be divided among his or her descendants in the same manner.
(Stats. 1991 (S.B. 271), ch. 1055, §20.)

§6210. "Person," defined

"Person" includes individuals and institutions.
(Stats. 1991 (S.B. 271), ch. 1055, §20.)

B. Historical Background

English common law reflected a different evolution for the distribution of personal property and the descent of real property. In the Middle Ages, ecclesiastical courts permitted distribution of personalty via oral wills called "testaments" (generally dictated to clerics) to a decedent's spouse, child, or another person of the decedent's choice. On the other hand, "primogeniture" governed inheritance of real property, i.e., land passed automatically to the eldest son. Individuals could not devise real property until the Statute of Wills of 1540. The Statute of Wills permitted wills of real property, provided that such instruments were in writing (although equity enforced oral devisees of uses before that time). McGovern & Kurtz, *supra*, §4.1 at 182.

The subsequent Statute of Frauds of 1677 specified various formalities for the execution of wills (such as the requirement that devises of land be signed by the testator and subscribed by witnesses) and also limited the use of oral wills. The Statute of Wills ("Wills Act") of 1837 permitted persons to dispose of all real and personal property owned at death provided that certain formalities of execution were met. For the first time, the requirements for disposition of real and personal property were the same. The Wills Act also established a minimum age requirement for testamentary capacity, and specified rules for amendments and revocation of wills.

Currently, all states have legislation on will execution that have been derived from the English Statute of Frauds of 1677 and the Wills Act of 1837. Christopher J. Caldwell, Comment, Should "E-Wills" Be Wills: Will Advances in Technology Be Recognized for Will Execution?, 63 U. Pitt. L. Rev. 467, 467 (2002).

See generally Carole Shammas et al., Inheritance in America from Colonial Times to the Present (1987); David A. Thomas, AngloAmerican Land Law: Diverging Developments from a Shared History—Part I: The Shared History, 34 Real Prop. Prob. & Tr. J. 143 (1999); David A. Thomas, Anglo-American Land Law: Diverging Developments from a Shared History—Part II: How Anglo-American Land Law Diverged After American Colonization are [*sic*] Independence, 34 Real Prop. Prob. & Tr. J. 295 (1999); David A. Thomas, Anglo-American Land Law: Diverging Developments from a Shared History—Part III: 34 British and American Real Property Law and Practice—A Contemporary Comparison, 34 Real Prop. Prob. & Tr. J. 443 (1999).

II. Formalities of Will Execution

Every jurisdiction has a Wills Act that requires certain formalities for executing a valid will. All statutes mandate a writing, signature, and attestation by witnesses. Most jurisdictions require strict compliance with these statutory requirements. Such rigid adherence to formalism often has led to harsh results and a defeat of testators' intent.

In an influential law review article in 1975, Professor John Langbein proposed liberalization of the formal requirements for will execution by means of a doctrine of "substantial compliance." John H. Langbein, Substantial Compliance with the Wills Act, 88 Harv. L. Rev. 489, 489 (1975). He advocated liberal judicial interpretation of jurisdictions' Wills Acts: fatally defective wills should still be admitted to probate if will proponents could prove that the functions of the will formalities were satisfied.

Subsequently, Langbein modified his proposal, influenced by a statute enacted in South Australia. John H. Langbein, Excusing Harmless Errors in the Execution of Wills: A Report on Australia's Tranquil Revolution in Probate Law, 87 Colum. L. Rev. 1, 9 n. 31 (1987) (citing Wills Act Amendment Act (No. 2 of 1975), §9 amending Wills Act of 1936, §12(2), (8 S. Austral. Stat. 665)). That statute authorized probate courts to employ a "dispensing power" that excuses harmless errors. Probate courts could disregard the formal statutory requirements if the courts were satisfied beyond a reasonable doubt that "the document embodies the unequivocal intent of the testator." Langbein, Excusing Harmless Errors, *supra*, at34.

Langbein termed the South Australian statute "a triumph of law reform." *Id.* at 1. He evaluated the operation of the Australian legislation by reviewing a decade of case law (41 cases) involving attestation problems (i.e., testators who had not signed in the presence of witnesses present at the same time), or signature problems (i.e., testators who either had not signed wills or not signed at the end of the will), or defective alteration cases. He concluded that courts were applying the doctrine effectively and that the new legislation had not undermined the Wills Act. He recommended that the United States enact similar legislation but with two improvements: (1) the reform should extend to revocation formalities, and (2) the standard of proof should be lowered to clear and convincing evidence. *Id.* at 53.

Langbein's influence was reflected in subsequent revisions to the Uniform Probate Code and in the Restatement (Third) of Property on Donative Transfers. The 1990 revisions to Article II of the Uniform Probate Code (UPC §2-503) permitted courts to dispense with some statutory formalities (although which formalities are not specified) provided that the will proponents establish by clear and convincing evidence that the testator intended the instrument to constitute his or her will:

> Although a document or writing added upon a document was not executed in compliance with Section 2-502, the document or writing is treated as if it had been executed in compliance with that section if the proponent of the document or writing establishes by clear and convincing evidence that the decedent intended the document or writing to constitute . . . the decedent's will. . . .

(UPC §2-503). The UPC thereby permitted the admission of extrinsic evidence to prove testamentary intent. California has no provision similar to UPC §2-503. See Cal. Prob. Code §6110, Law Revision Commission Comment, Commentary. (However, California Probate Code §6226(b) does permit extrinsic evidence to prove testamentary intent regarding statutory wills.) For further discussion of the "harmless error rule," see Sean P. Milligan, Comment, The Effect of a Harmless Error in Executing a Will: Why Texas Should Adopt Section 2-503 of the Uniform Probate Code, 36 St. Mary's L.J. 787 (2005).

The Restatement (Third) of Property (Wills and Other Donative Transfers) §3.3 (1999), reflects a similar liberalizing trend by providing for a "harmless error" rule: "A harmless error in executing a will may be excused if the proponent establishes by clear and convincing evidence that the decedent adopted the document as his or her will."

Note that the 1990 revisions to the UPC reflected liberalization of other technical requirements for will execution. Specifically, the revisions included: codification of the conscious presence requirement, the change for holographs from "material provisions" to "material portions," and the allowance of a signature by the witnesses within a reasonable time after witnessing the testator's signing or acknowledgment. (These revisions are discussed *infra*.)

The California Probate Code was significantly revised in 1983 to eliminate some of the formal requirements that previously invalidated wills. The 1983 revisions adopted a major portion of the UPC. In the 1983 revisions, the Legislature added California Probate Code §6110 that eliminated the following requirements:

- the testator's signature must be "at the end" of the will,
- the testator must "declare" to witnesses that the instrument is his or her will,
- the witnesses' signatures must be "at the end" of the will,
- the testator must "request" the witnesses to sign the will, and
- the witnesses must sign the will in the testator's presence.

14 Witkin, Summary of California Law (10th ed. 2005), Ch. XXI, Wills and Probate, §137, p. 203 [hereinafter Witkin, Summary, Wills]. See also former Cal. Prob. Code §50, repealed Stats. 1983, ch. 842, §18, p. 3024.

However, California Probate Code §6110 retained some requirements of former California Probate Code §50:

- the will must be in writing,
- the will must be signed by the testator or by a proxy who signs the testator's name in the testator's presence and by the testator's direction,
- the testator must sign or acknowledge his or her signature in the presence of two witnesses, and
- the witnesses must sign the will.

See Estate of Eugene, 128 Cal. Rptr. 2d 622, 624-625 (Ct. App. 2002) (explaining this history).

In 1990, the California legislature undertook another significant revision of the Probate Code. However, the legislature re-enacted without change the provision on the formalities of will execution (Cal. Prob. Code §6110) (Stats. 1990, ch. 79, §14, pp. 463, 684). In 1996, California Probate Code §6110 was amended to authorize a conservator, pursuant to a court order, to execute a will for the testator (Stats. 1996, ch. 563, §20).

A. Function of the Formalities

Several purposes explain the formalities for will execution. In a classic article, two commentators identified three functions of will formalities:

- a ritual or cautionary function (which reinforces the instrument as a will to the decedent as a deliberate and final decision);
- an evidentiary function (which provides the court with reliable evidence of testamentary intent); and
- a protective function (which safeguards the testator from improper acts by others of coercion, fraud, or undue influence).

Ashbel G. Gulliver & Catherine J. Tilson, Classification of Gratuitous Transfers, 51 Yale L.J. 1, 3-6 (1941). Subsequently, Professor John Langbein identified a fourth function:

- the channeling function (which identifies the instrument as a will in the larger community).

Langbein, Substantial Compliance, *supra*, at 491-498 (discussing the channeling function). The channeling function of law originated with Lon Fuller who suggested that the formalities of contract law provide "channels for the legally effective expression of intention." Lon L. Fuller, Consideration and Form, 41 Colum. L. Rev. 799, 801 (1941). See also Estate of Eugene, 128 Cal. Rptr.2d 622, 627 (Ct. App. 2002) (discussing the purpose underlying the attestation rules of the prevention of fraud and concluding that an inadvertent mistake that led to the attorney's failure to sign a will should not vitiate the testator's intent).

B. Testamentary Capacity

The Statute of Wills of 1540 permitted devises of real property by minors. However, Parliament soon amended the Statute to require that the testator of a devise of real property must be 21 years of age. Thomas Atkinson, Wills §50, at 230 (2d ed. 1953). Regarding testamentary capacity for the disposition of personal property, the civil law rule was that a boy had to be at least 14 years old and a girl at least 12 years old. *Id.* at 229. That rule was adopted by the ecclesiastical courts. *Id.* However, the Wills Act of 1837 established age 21 as the minimum age for both male and female testators and for dispositions of both real and personal property. *Id.* at 230.

Statutes in all jurisdictions now establish capacity to make a will. Most jurisdictions require that a testator be an adult and mentally competent. Minimum ages range from 14 to 21, with the majority of jurisdictions requiring that a testator be at least 18 years of age. Age 18 is also the minimum specified by UPC §2-501.

Some jurisdictions establish age 18 as the minimum, but permit certain exceptions. Thus, for example, in some states persons in military service or married persons may make wills, regardless of age.

A few states permit minors below age 18 to make wills. For example, Louisiana permits minors to execute a will at age 16, while Georgia and Puerto Rico permit minors to do so at age 14. Many jurisdictions set the minimum age simply as the statutory age of majority. McKen V. Carrington, Estate Planning for the Non-Taxable Estate, 21 St. Mary's L.J. 367, 370-372 (1989) (surveying minimum age for will execution in different jurisdictions).

California Probate Code §6100 requires that the testator be at least 18 years of age and "of sound mind." However, California provides an exception for an emancipated minor. An emancipated minor is considered an adult for some purposes, including making or revoking a will (Cal. Fam. Code §7050). See Law Revision Commission, Comment to California Probate Code §6100.

The requirement in California Probate Code §6100 regarding age and "sound mind" (but not the conservatorship provision) is identical to UPC §2-501. A statutory amendment in California in 1995 added subdivision (b), authorizing a conservator to make a will for a conservatee. According to California Probate Code §6100, a conservator may make a will on behalf of a conservatee who lacks testamentary capacity, provided the conservator first obtains court approval in a "substituted judgment" proceeding pursuant to California Probate Code §2580 (Cal. Prob. Code §2580(b)(13)). A conservatee who is later deemed "mentally competent to make a will" may amend or revoke the will that was executed by the conservator or make a new, inconsistent will (Cal. Prob. Code §6100(b)). Prior to the 1995 amendment, California case law held that a conservator, conservator's attorney, and the probate court had no authority to execute a will on behalf of a conservator. Conservatorship of Romo, 235 Cal. Rptr. 377 (Ct. App. 1987).

Testamentary capacity (issues of mental capacity, undue influence, fraud, etc.) is explored further in Chapter IV *infra*.

CALIFORNIA PROBATE CODE

§6100. Persons eligible to make a will

(a) An individual 18 or more years of age who is of sound mind may make a will.

(b) A conservator may make a will for the conservatee if the conservator has been so authorized by a court order pursuant to Section 2580. Nothing in this section shall impair the right of a conservatee who is mentally competent to make a will from revoking or amending a will made by the conservator or making a new and inconsistent will.

(Stats. 1990 (A.B. 759), ch. 79, §14, effective July 1, 1991. Amended by Stats. 1995 (A.B. 1466), ch. 730, §7.)

CALIFORNIA FAMILY CODE

§7050. Emancipated minors are considered adults for specified purposes

An emancipated minor shall be considered as being an adult for the following purposes:

(a) The minor's right to support by the minor's parents.

(b) The right of the minor's parents to the minor's earnings and to control the minor.

(c) The application of Sections 300 and 601 of the Welfare and Institutions Code.

(d) Ending all vicarious or imputed liability of the minor's parents or guardian for the minor's torts. Nothing in this section affects any liability of a parent, guardian, spouse, or employer imposed by the Vehicle Code, or any vicarious liability that arises from an agency relationship.

(e) The minor's capacity to do any of the following:

(1) Consent to medical, dental, or psychiatric care, without parental consent, knowledge, or liability.

(2) Enter into a binding contract or give a delegation of power.

(3) Buy, sell, lease, encumber, exchange, or transfer an interest In real or personal property, including, but not limited to, shares of stock in a domestic or foreign corporation or a membership in a nonprofit corporation.

(4) Sue or be sued in the minor's own name.

(5) Compromise, settle, arbitrate, or otherwise adjust a claim, action, or proceeding by or against the minor.

(6) Make or revoke a will.

(7) Make a gift, outright or in trust.

(8) Convey or release contingent or expectant interests in property, including marital property rights and any right of survivorship incident to joint tenancy, and consent to a transfer, encumbrance, or gift of marital property.

(9) Exercise or release the minor's powers as donee of a power of appointment unless the creating instrument otherwise provides.

(10) Create for the minor's own benefit or for the benefit of others a revocable or irrevocable trust.

(11) Revoke a revocable trust.

(12) Elect to take under or against a will.

(13) Renounce or disclaim any interest acquired by testate or intestate succession or by inter vivos transfer, including exercise of the right to surrender the right to revoke a revocable trust.

(14) Make an election referred to in Section 13502 of, or an election and agreement referred to in Section 13503 of, the Probate Code.

(15) Establish the minor's own residence.

(16) Apply for a work permit pursuant to Section 49110 of the Education Code without the request of the minor's parents.

(17) Enroll in a school or college.

(Stats. 1992 (A.B. 2650), ch. 162, §10, effective January 1, 1994.)

C. Testamentary Intent

A testator must have the requisite intent to execute a valid will. Testamentary intent must be present at the time the testator signed the testamentary instrument. "Testamentary intent" refers to the testator's general intent that a particular document serve as a disposition of his or her property to be effective on death. See also Estate of Smith, 71 Cal. Rptr.2d 424, 431 (Ct. App. 1996). See generally Emily Sherwin, Clear and Convincing Evidence of Testamentary Intent: The Search for a Compromise Between Formality and Adjudicative Justice, 34 Conn. L. Rev. 453 (2002).

D. Writing Requirement

All states require that a will be in writing. The California Probate Code requires that a will must be in writing, as well as signed and attested (Cal. Prob. Code §6110(a)). The written will may be either witnessed or holographic. California no longer permits oral (nuncupative) wills. Oral wills were permitted until 1982 (former Cal. Prob. Code §§54, 55). For further discussion, see "Oral Wills," Section H *infra.*

California courts have given effect to wills that were written in foreign languages. 64 Cal. Jur. 3d Wills §236 (citing Bruck v. Tucker, 42 C. 346 (1971) (Spanish); In re Estate of Alexander, 85 P. 308 (1906) (German); In re Estate of Jepson, 172 P. 1107 (1918) (German)).

Interestingly, California Probate Code §6100 does not require that the writing be by the testator. Thus, courts have admitted to probate printed will forms and mimeographed forms distributed at a military installation. 64 Cal. Jur. 3d Wills §252 (citing authority). Wills even have been admitted to probate in which another person wrote the body of the will or guided the testator's hand in writing because the testator was physically unable to do so. *Id.*

Currently, no state allows probate of a videotaped will. See Estate of Reed, 672 P.2d 829 (Wyo.1983) (holding that a tape-recorded will was not "in writing"). Some commentators, however, advocate videotaping the will execution ceremony to provide evidence of testamentary capacity and due execution for the probate process. Caldwell, *supra,* at 475. In 1985 Indiana became the first state to authorize by statute the admission of a videotaped will execution ceremony to show that the statutory requirements for execution were satisfied. John A. Warnick, The Ungrateful Living: An Estate Planner's Nightmare—The Trial Attorney's Dream, 24 Land & Water L. Rev. 401, 423 n. 114 (1989) (citing Ind. Code Ann. §29-1-5-3(d)). However, the section was repealed in 1989 by P.L. 262-1989, Sec. 1.

The issue of whether e-mail messages or a web site could qualify as a valid will has not yet arisen in case law. Warnick, *supra,* at 476. For further discussion, see "Electronic Signatures," Section E3 *infra.*

See generally Gerry W. Beyer, Video Requiem: Thy Will Be Done, Tr. & Est., July 1985, at 24; Gerry W. Beyer & William R. Buckley, Videotape and the Probate Process: The Nexus Grows, 42 Okla. L. Rev. 43 (1989); Lisa L. McGarry, Note, Videotaped Wills: An Evidentiary Tool or a Written Will Substitute?, 77 Iowa L. Rev. 1187, 1187 (1992); Terry Zickefoose, Videotaped Wills: Ready for Prime Time, 9 Prob. L.J. 139 (1989).

CALIFORNIA PROBATE CODE

§6110. Will shall be in writing, signed and witnessed

(a) Except as provided in this part, a will shall be in writing and satisfy the requirements of this section.

(b) The will shall be signed by one of the following:

(1) By the testator.

(2) In the testator's name by some other person in the testator's presence and by the testator's direction.

(3) By a conservator pursuant to a court order to make a will under Section 2580.

(c) The will shall be witnessed by being signed by at least two persons each of whom (1) being present at the same time, witnessed either the signing of the will or the testator's acknowledgment of the signature or of the will and (2) understand that the instrument they sign is the testator's will.

(Stats. 1990 (A.B. 759), ch. 79, §14, effective July 1, 1991. Amended by Stats. 1996 (S.B. 392), ch. 563, §20.)

E. Testator's Signature

A valid will requires the testator's signature. The Statute of Frauds of 1677 required that the will be signed by the testator but did not require a particular place for the signature. Atkinson, *supra*, §64 at 301. A few years later, the case of Lemayne v. Stanley, 3 Lev.1, 83 Eng. Rep. 545 (1681), held that the testator's name could appear at the top, bottom, or margin of the will and upheld the validity of a will that provided, "I, John Stanley, make this my last will."

All state wills legislation include the requirement of a testator's signature. See also UPC §2-502(a)(1). However, most American jurisdictions follow the rule of Lemayne v. Stanley in failing to specify the place for that signature. Atkinson, *supra.*, §64 at 301.

Although the will must be signed by the testator, the testator need not write a full or correct name. If a testator cannot write his signature (whether for reasons of illiteracy or illness), the testator's mark will suffice if intended by the testator as a "complete act" to authenticate the instrument. *Id.* §64 at 297.

In California, if a testator is unable to write, the testator may sign by means of a mark. However, the witness must write the testator's name "near" the mark and the witness must write his or her name as well. 64 Cal. Jur.3d Wills §239 (citing Cal. Civ. Code §14; Cal. Code Civ. Proc. §17). The purpose of requiring the testator's name "near" the mark is to clarify which name the mark represents. *Id.* (citing Estate of Gooch, 26 Cal. Rptr. 835, 837 (Ct. App. 1962)). A California court has liberally construed this requirement. Estate of McCabe, 274 Cal. Rptr. 43, 44-45 (Ct. App. 1990) (validating the will under the "substantial compliance" doctrine).

Some states require that the testator sign in the witnesses' presence. Many states, however, require that the testator sign OR acknowledge the testator's signature or will in the witnesses' presence. Thus, the testator could simply acknowledge the testator's signature to the witnesses or could simply acknowledge that the instrument before the witnesses is indeed the testator's will. This situation commonly arises if the testator previously signed the will. See the discussion of Acknowledgment vs. Publication, Section F4 *infra*.

CALIFORNIA CIVIL CODE

§14. Words and phrases; signature includes a mark when person cannot write

Words used in this Code in the present tense include the future as well as the present; words used in the masculine gender include the feminine and neuter; the singular number includes the plural, and the plural the singular; the word person includes a corporation as well as a natural person; county includes city and county; writing includes printing and typewriting; oath includes affirmation or declaration; and every mode of oral statement, under oath or affirmation, is embraced by the term "testify," and every written one in the term "depose"; signature or subscription includes mark, when the person cannot write, his name being written near it, by a person who writes his own name as a witness; provided, that when a signature is by mark it must in order that the same may be acknowledged or may serve as the signature to any sworn statement be witnessed by two persons who must subscribe their own names as witnesses thereto. The following words have in this Code the signification attached to them in this section, unless otherwise apparent from the context:

1. The word "property" includes property real and personal;
2. The words "real property" are coextensive with lands, tenements, and hereditaments;
3. The words "personal property" include money, goods, chattels, things in action, and evidences of debt;
4. The word "month" means a calendar month, unless otherwise expressed;
5. The word "will" includes codicil;
6. The word "section" whenever hereinafter employed refers to a section of this Code, unless some other Code or statute is expressly mentioned.

(Enacted 1872. Amended by Code Am.1873-74, ch. 612, p. 181, §1; Stats. 1903, ch. 281, p. 407, §1.)

CALIFORNIA CODE OF CIVIL PROCEDURE

§17. Words and phrases: meanings; signature may include mark when person cannot write

(a) Words used in this Code in the present tense include the future as well as the present; words used in the masculine gender include the feminine and neuter; the singular number includes the plural and the plural the singular; the word "person" includes a corporation as well as a natural person; the word "county" includes "city and county"; writing includes printing and typewriting; oath includes affirmation or declaration; and every mode of oral statement, under oath or affirmation, is embraced by the term "testify," and every written one in the term "depose"; signature or subscription includes mark, when the person cannot write, his or her name being written near it by a person who writes his or her own name as a witness; provided, that when a signature is by mark it must, in order that the same may be acknowledged or may serve as the signature to any sworn statement, be witnessed by two persons who must subscribe their own names as witness thereto.

(b) The following words have in this Code the signification attached to them in this section, unless otherwise apparent from the context:

(1) The word "property" includes both real and personal property.

(2) The words "real property" are coextensive with lands, tenements, and hereditaments.

(3) The words "personal property" include money, goods, chattels, things in action, and evidences of debt.

(4) The word "month" means a calendar month, unless otherwise expressed.

(5) The word "will" includes codicil.

(6) The word "writ" signifies an order or precept in writing, issued in the name of the people, or of a court or judicial officer, and the word "process" signifies a writ or summons issued in the course of judicial proceedings.

(7) The word "state," when applied to the different parts of the United States, includes the District of Columbia and the territories, and the words "United States" may include the district and territories.

(8) The word "section," whenever hereinafter employed, refers to a section of this Code, unless some other Code or statute is expressly mentioned.

(9) The word "affinity," when applied to the marriage relation, signifies the connection existing in consequence of marriage, between each of the married persons and the blood relatives of the other.

(10) The word "sheriff" shall include "marshal."

(Enacted 1872. Amended by Code Am.1873-74, ch. 383, p. 280, §3; Stats. 1903, ch. 123, p. 134, §1; Stats. 1933, ch. 742, p. 1804, §1; Stats. 1951, ch. 1737, p. 4081, §1, effective January 1, 1952; Stats. 1996 (A.B. 3472), ch. 872, §5; Stats. 2002 (S.B. 1316), ch. 784, §21; Stats. 2003 (S.B. 600), ch. 62, §21, effective January 1, 2004.)

CALIFORNIA PROBATE CODE
§6110. Will shall be in writing, signed and witnessed

(a) Except as provided in this part, a will shall be in writing and satisfy the requirements of this section.

(b) The will shall be signed by one of the following:

(1) By the testator.

(2) In the testator's name by some other person in the testator's presence and by the testator's direction.

(3) By a conservator pursuant to a court order to make a will under Section 2580.

(c) The will shall be witnessed by being signed by at least two persons each of whom (1) being present at the same time, witnessed either the signing of the will or the testator's acknowledgment of the signature or of the will and (2) understand that the instrument they sign is the testator's will.

(Stats. 1990 (A.B. 759), ch. 79, §14, effective July 1, 1991. Amended Stats. 1996 (S.B. 392), ch. 563, §20.)

1. Proxy Signature

Generally, a will must be written and signed by the testator. However, some states permit the will to be signed either by the testator or by another person (a proxy). E.g., Cal. Prob. Code §6110(b)(1), (2)). In California, if a proxy signs the testator's name, that signature must be in the testator's presence and at the testator's direction (Cal. Prob. Code §6110(b)(2)). A person who forges a signature on a testamentary instrument is subject to criminal liability (Cal. Penal Code §470).

The Uniform Probate Code also allows a will to be signed by the testator or by another on the testator's behalf. UPC §2-502. The 1990 revisions to the Uniform Probate Code adopted the rule that the proxy who signs the will at the testator's request must sign in the conscious presence of the testator (rather than requiring actual presence) (UPC §2-502(a)(2)).

Neither California nor the UPC specify the location on the will where the signature need appear (UPC §2-501, Cal. Prob. Code §6110). On California's former subscription requirement, see Section E2 *infra*. On the "presence" requirement, see Section E5 *infra*.

CALIFORNIA PROBATE CODE
§6110. Will shall be in writing, signed and witnessed

(a) Except as provided in this part, a will shall be in writing and satisfy the requirements of this section.

(b) The will shall be signed by one of the following:

(1) By the testator.

(2) In the testator's name by some other person in the testator's presence and by the testator's direction.

(3) By a conservator pursuant to a court order to make a will under Section 2580.

(c) The will shall be witnessed by being signed by at least two persons each of whom (1) being present at the same time, witnessed either the signing of the will or the testator's acknowledgment of the signature or of the will and (2) understand that the instrument they sign is the testator's will.

(Stats. 1990 (A.B. 759), ch. 79, §14, effective July 1, 1991. Amended by Stats. 1996 (S.B. 392), ch. 563, §20.)

CALIFORNIA PENAL CODE

§470. Criminal liability for person who forges a will, codicil, conveyance or other instrument

(a) Every person who, with the intent to defraud, knowing that he or she has no authority to do so, signs the name of another person or of a fictitious person to any of the items listed in subdivision (d) is guilty of forgery.

(b) Every person who, with the intent to defraud, counterfeits or forges the seal or handwriting of another is guilty of forgery.

(c) Every person who, with the intent to defraud, alters, corrupts, or falsifies any record of any will, codicil, conveyance, or other instrument, the record of which is by law evidence, or any record of any judgment of a court or the return of any officer to any process of any court, is guilty of forgery.

(d) Every person who, with the intent to defraud, falsely makes, alters, forges, or counterfeits, utters, publishes, passes or attempts or offers to pass, as true and genuine, any of the following items, knowing the same to be false, altered, forged, or counterfeited, is guilty of forgery: any check, bond, bank bill, or note, cashier's check, traveler's check, money order, post note, draft, any controller's warrant for the payment of money at the treasury, county order or warrant, or request for the payment of money, receipt for money or goods, bill of exchange, promissory note, order, or any assignment of any bond, writing obligatory, or other contract for money or other property, contract, due bill for payment of money or property, receipt for money or property, passage ticket, lottery ticket or share purporting to be issued under the California State Lottery Act of 1984, trading stamp, power of attorney, certificate of ownership or other document evidencing ownership of a vehicle or undocumented vessel, or any certificate of any share, right, or interest in the stock of any corporation or association, or the delivery of goods or chattels of any kind, or for the delivery of any instrument of writing, or acquittance, release or discharge of any debt, account, suit, action, demand, or any other thing, real or personal, or any transfer or assurance of money, certificate of shares of stock, goods, chattels, or other property whatever, or any letter of attorney, or other power to receive money, or to receive or transfer certificates of shares of stock or annuities, or to let, lease, dispose of, alien, or convey any goods, chattels, lands, or tenements, or other estate, real or personal, or falsifies the acknowledgment of any notary public, or any notary public who issues an acknowledgment knowing it to be false; or any matter described in subdivision (b).

(e) Upon a trial for forging any bill or note purporting to be the bill or note of an incorporated company or bank, or for passing, or attempting to pass, or having in possession with intent to pass, any forged bill or note, it is not necessary to prove the incorporation of the bank or company by the charter or act of incorporation, but it may be proved by general reputation; and persons of skill are competent witnesses to prove that the bill or note is forged or counterfeited.

(Stats. 1998 (A.B. 2008), ch. 468, §2. Amended by Stats. 2005 (A.B. 361), ch. 295, §5, effective January 1, 2006.)

2. Subscription Requirement

The Statute of Frauds, as explained above, required that a will disposing of real property be signed, but did not specify the location for the testator's signature. In contrast, the English Wills Act of 1837 required that the will must be subscribed, i.e., signed at the "end." In 1982, England eliminated the subscription requirement. Nonetheless, some states still retain this requirement. McGovern & Kurtz, *supra*, §4.2 at 187-188.

In jurisdictions with a subscription requirement, troublesome cases sometimes arose regarding whether a will was subscribed if material appeared after the testator's signature. This problem necessitated judicial exploration of the "end" requirement. Case law formulated two tests: the logical end and the physical end. *Id.* at 174.

At one time, California law required that the testator's signature must be subscribed ("at the end") of the will and, similarly, that the witnesses' signatures be "at the end" of the will. However, in 1983 the state legislature added California Probate Code §6110 eliminating these requirements. See Cal. Prob. Code, former §50, repealed Stats. 1983, ch. 842, §18, p. 3024; 12 Witkin, Summary, Wills, *supra*, at §§4-5, pp. 39-41, quoting 16 Cal. Law Revision Com. Rep., pp. 2318-2319.

The UPC requires that the will be signed but does not require that the signature appear in any particular place. See UPC §2-502 (specifying merely that the will must be signed by the testator or by a proxy).

3. Electronic Signatures

In an effort to make the law responsive to technological developments by protecting electronic transactions, Congress enacted the Electronic Signatures in Global and National Commerce Act (or "E-Sign Act"), Pub. L. No. 106-229, 114 Stat. 464 (2000). The Act does not require acceptance of electronic signatures but rather provides that such signatures may not be denied legal effect because they are in electronic form (i.e., not paper-based). However, the Act excludes electronic signatures that are used in testamentary instruments such as wills or testamentary trusts. Chandel Gauthreaux Hall, A Cursory Look at the E-Sign Act, 48 La. B.J. 452 (2001).

Similarly, the Uniform Electronic Transactions Act (UETA), 7A U.L.A. 20 (Supp. 2000), promulgated by NCCUSL, in 1999 also excludes wills and trusts. That Uniform Act provides:

Section 3. Scope

(a) Except as otherwise provided in subsection (b), this [Act] applies to electronic records and electronic signatures relating to a transaction.

(b) This [Act] does not apply to a transaction to the extent it is governed by:

(1) a law governing the creation and execution of wills, codicils, or testamentary trusts;

. . .

F. Witnesses

1. Generally

The Wills Acts of the various jurisdictions require that a will must be attested (i.e., witnessed) by several persons. The Statute of Frauds required "three or four credible" witnesses. McGovern & Kurtz, *supra*, §4.3 at 189. The Wills Act of 1837 required only two. *Id.* Today, almost all states (including California, as well as the Uniform Probate Code) require that a will be signed by two witnesses. Cal. Prob. Code §6110(c); UPC §2-505(a).

Most states require that the witnesses be "competent" or capable of giving testimony in court. See, e.g., Cal. Prob. Code §6110. In other words, the witness must understand the significance of taking an oath. See also the discussion of Competence vs. Interest, Section IIF3 *infra*.

Only a few states have minimum age requirements for witnesses. McGovern & Kurtz, *supra*, §4.3 at 189.

Often, witnesses' signatures appear in an "attestation clause" or "testimonium clause." Such a clause declares that the instrument is a will, specifies the number of pages, recites the statutory requirements for execution, and includes the date of execution. Although no state requires such a clause, many states hold that the presence of such a clause raises a rebuttable presumption that the will was duly executed. Restatement (Third) of Property, *supra*, at §3.1, cmt. q.

Some statutes and case law address the order of the testator's signature and witnesses' attestation. That is, some jurisdictions require that the testator sign prior to attestation by witnesses. Most states, however, follow the "continuous transaction" approach and consider the attestation valid provided that the testator signs and the witnesses attest as part of a continuous transaction. The UPC requires that the attestation occurs within a reasonable time after either (1) the witness observes the testator sign, (2) the testator acknowledges his or her signature, or (3) the testator acknowledges the will (UPC §2-502(a)(3)).

The procedure for admitting a will to probate in California requires admission of the evidence of only one witness (Cal. Prob. Code §8220(a)). Although California statute requires two witnesses for execution of a valid will (Cal. Prob. Code §6110), that requirement does not extend to proving the will (i.e., admitting the will to probate). The requirements for due execution (including the two-witness requirement) "exist to protect the testator from fraud or undue influence when the will is executed." Estate of Burdette, 97 Cal. Rptr.2d 263 (Ct. App. 2000).

Proof by one witness at probate is required to establish the will's validity by showing that the will was executed "in all particulars as prescribed by law" (Cal. Prob. Code §8220(a)). Witnesses need not appear at the probate hearing. Rather, proof may be received by:

- "self-proving wills" (i.e., an affidavit or a declaration under oath contained in the will that includes the attestation clause) (Cal. Prob. Code §8220(b)) [see Section IIL *infra*];
- an affidavit or declaration under oath with an attached photographic copy of the will (Cal. Prob. Code §§8220(b), 1022); or
- a deposition (Cal. Prob. Code §8220(c)).

Ross & Grant, Cal. Probate Prac. Ch.3-E, 3:2273:299.

If no subscribing witnesses are available, then the Probate Code authorizes an alternative method of proof provided that "the will on its face conforms to all requirements of law." California Probate Code §8221 permits proof of the testator's handwriting plus one of the following: handwriting of one subscribing witness, or receipt into evidence of one of two documents: either a writing in the will bearing all the subscribing witnesses' signatures or an affidavit of a person with knowledge of the circumstances of will execution.

Three different issues arise regarding "presence" during an attestation by witnesses: (1) must the testator sign in the witnesses' presence? (2) must the witnesses sign in the testator's presence? and (3) must the witnesses sign in the presence of each other? These issues are discussed *infra*.

2. Testator's Signature in the Witnesses' Presence

Most states do not require that the testator actually sign the will while in the witnesses' presence. That is, most states permit the testator to acknowledge his or her signature to the witnesses. This situation is likely to arise when the testator previously affixes a signature to the will and then subsequently shows the instrument to the witnesses while asking them to serve as witnesses. The testator's acknowledgment can be by statements or gestures.

The California Probate Code requires that the testator sign or acknowledge his or her signature in the presence of two witnesses (Cal. Prob. Code §6110). The testator's act of either signing the will or else acknowledging his or her signature of the will must occur in the presence of at least two witnesses who are present at the same time. Thus, for example, a will would be invalid if the testator's acknowledgment is made one morning to one witness but later that same day to the other witness. In re Emart's Estate, 165 P. 707 (Cal. 1917). The witnesses must also understand that the instrument they sign is the testator's will. Cal. Prob. Code §6110(c)(2).

In 1983 when the Probate Code was revised, the legislature repealed some of the technical formalities for will execution (i.e., publication, subscription, etc.). However, the legislature retained (in Cal. Prob. Code §6110) the requirement of former Code §50 that the testator sign or acknowledge his or her signature in the presence of two witnesses.

3. Competence vs. Interest

a. Definition

Generally, statutes require that witnesses be "competent" or "credible" at the time of the execution of the will. This requirement refers to the witness's ability to give testimony in court to establish the validity of the will. The requirement was reflected in the Statute of Frauds and the UPC. The Statute of Frauds required that wills be attested by "credible" witnesses. McGovern & Kurtz, *supra*, §4.3 at 189. The UPC specifies that "any person generally competent to be a witness may act as a witness to a will" (UPC §2-505(a)). The UPC rule is the prevailing view. McGovern & Kurtz, *supra*. California law provides that any person generally competent to be a witness may act as a witness to a will (Cal. Prob. Code §6112(a)).

Competence is required at the time of execution. If a witness is competent at the time of the execution of the will but subsequently becomes incompetent, the will is nonetheless valid.

At common law, an interested witness was not considered competent to testify. An interested witness is someone who stands to take a pecuniary interest under the testator's will, such as a beneficiary. At common law (and in some states today), the spouse of a beneficiary was considered an interested witness (based on the doctrine of coverture in which the wife's legal identity merged with that of her husband's). An executor generally is not considered an interested witness, because the executor receives fees pursuant to statutory authority (i.e. not prescribed by the will).

b. Effect on the Will

An important issue is the effect on the will of having an interested witness. At common law, attestation by an essential interested witness rendered the entire will void. (However, the presence of an extra or "supernumerary" witness could validate the will.)

The Model Probate Code (the predecessor to the Uniform Probate Code) provided for a purging statute. Under that approach, the essential interested witness forfeited any benefit under the will, but a witness who was an heir of the testator's could take the lesser of: the beneficiary's share under the will or the beneficiary's intestate share in the decedent's estate.

> [A]n interested witness shall, unless the will is also attested by two disinterested witnesses forfeit so much of the provisions therein made for him as in the aggregate exceeds in value, as of the date of the testator's death, what he would have received had the testator died intestate.

Model Probate Code §46(b). However, the will was not invalidated if attested by an interested witness. Many states still follow this approach.

Currently, in California there is a rebuttable presumption affecting the burden of proof that an essential interested witness procured his or her devise by duress, menace, fraud, or undue influence (Cal. Prob. Code §6112). The presumption does not operate if the will is subscribed by at least two other disinterested witnesses. Also, the presumption does not apply to witnesses who are given a devise solely in their fiduciary capacity, such as to a trustee (Cal. Prob. Code §6112(c)). Ross & Grant, *supra*, §3:247 at 3-68. If the essential interested witness fails to rebut the presumption, the witness may still take his or her intestate share (Cal. Prob. Code §6112(d)).

The UPC follows a rule of nonforfeiture in terms of the effect on the will of having an interested witness. An essential interested witness does not forfeit his or her share under the will (UPC §2-505(b)). Nor does having an interested witness invalidate the will. Rather, issues of undue influence are left to will contests.

CALIFORNIA PROBATE CODE

§6112. Witnesses: competency and Interest

(a) Any person generally competent to be a witness may act as a witness to a will.

(b) A will or any provision thereof is not invalid because the will is signed by an interested witness.

(c) Unless there are at least two other subscribing witnesses to the will who are disinterested witnesses, the fact that the will makes a devise to a subscribing witness creates a presumption that the witness procured the devise by duress, menace, fraud, or undue influence. This presumption is a presumption affecting the burden of proof. This presumption does not apply where the witness is a person to whom the devise is made solely in a fiduciary capacity.

(d) If a devise made by the will to an interested witness fails because the presumption established by subdivision (c) applies to the devise and the witness fails to rebut the presumption, the interested witness shall take such proportion of the devise made to the witness in the will as does not exceed the share of the estate which would be distributed to the witness if the will were not established. Nothing in this subdivision affects the law that applies where it is established that the witness procured a devise by duress, menace, fraud, or undue influence.

(Stats. 1990 (A.B. 759), ch. 79, §14, effective July 1, 1991.)

4. Acknowledgment vs. Publication

As explained above, many states do not require that the testator sign in the witnesses' presence and instead permit the testator to "acknowledge" the testator's will or signature. Thus, the testator could simply confirm his or her signature to the witnesses or confirm that the instrument before the witnesses is indeed the testator's will. This situation might arise if the testator previously signed the will. Acknowledgment does not require any specific words; gestures may suffice.

Acknowledgment is different from publication. Some jurisdictions require that the testator "publish" his or her will. By publication, the testator declares to the witnesses that the instrument is his or her will and requests them to sign it. In jurisdictions with a publication requirement, there is no requirement that the witnesses have to know the *contents* of the will.

In California, the Probate Code was revised in 1983 to eliminate some of the formal requirements that previously invalidated wills. At that time, the legislature eliminated the requirements that the testator must "declare" to witnesses that the instrument is his or her will and must "request" the witnesses to sign the will. See Cal. Prob. Code, former §50, repealed Stats. 1983, ch. 842, §18, p. 3024. Now, the witnesses must "understand that the instrument they sign is the testator's will" (Cal. Prob. Code §6110)(c)(2)). They can acquire that understanding by any means (i.e., from the testator's conduct and surrounding circumstances). 64 Cal. Jur. 3d Wills §258.

The UPC requires that the witnesses see either (1) the testator's signing or (2) the testator's acknowledgment of that signature or acknowledgment of the will (UPC §2-502(a)(3)). The UPC has no publication requirement.

5. Witnesses' Signature in the Testator's Presence: Line of Sight vs. Conscious Presence Tests

Most statutes today require that witnesses sign the will "in the presence of the testator." The requirement derives from the Statute of Frauds's mandate that the witnesses sign a will devising real property in the testator's presence. McGovern & Kurtz, *supra*, §4.3 at 192.

Considerable controversy exists about the meaning of "presence." In the famous case of Cunningham v. Cunningham, 83 N.W. 58 (Minn. 1900), an ill testator signed his will while sitting on the edge of his bed. Two physicians, whom he requested to serve as witnesses, then witnessed the will at a table in an adjoining room (out of the testator's sight). When the contestants argued that the will was invalid because the attestation was outside the testator's "presence," as the statute required, the Minnesota Supreme Court disagreed. In upholding the will, the court explained the tests for presence:

- the line-of-sight test, and
- the conscious presence test.

Under the former test, the testator must see the attestation by witnesses or could have seen the attestation without a material change of his position. Under the latter test, the witnesses must sign within the testator's hearing, knowledge, and understanding. The *Cunningham* court adopted the more liberal conscious presence test because, based on the circumstances (the testator knew what was being done, the attestation lasted only a few minutes, and he approved their signatures afterward), there was no possibility of fraud and the denial of probate would defeat the testator's intent.

In California, the Probate Code was significantly revised in 1983 to eliminate many of the formal requirements that previously invalidated wills. At that time, the legislature added California Probate Code §6110 which deleted (among other requirements) the rule of former Probate Code §50 that the witnesses actually must sign the will in the testator's presence (thereby allowing them to acknowledge the testator's signature or the will). See Cal. Prob. Code, former §50, repealed Stats. 1983, ch. 842, §18, p. 3024. For a statutory will, however, the Probate Code still requires that the witnesses sign in the testator's presence (Cal. Prob. Code §6221).

Although the two witnesses need not sign the will in the testator's presence in California, they must sign before the testator's death. In re Estate of Saueressig, 136 P.3d 201 (Cal. 2006), the California supreme court held that subscription of a witness after the testator's death will not satisfy the two-witness requirement of Cal. Prob. Code §6110(c)) because it would "erode the efficacy of the witnessing requirement as a safeguard against fraud or mistake." The court specifically disapproved Estate of Eugene, 128 Cal. Rptr. 2d 622 (Ct. App. 2002) (holding that, on the facts of the case, a scrivener-witness who inadventently failed to sign a will at the time of execution could sign after the testator's death).

Post-death attestation also has been rejected by a number of other jurisdictions. *Saueressig*, supra (surveying case law). However, the UPC would permit post-death attestation so long as the signing occurs "within a reasonable time" (UPC §2-502(a)(3), Comment). The UPC does not require the witnesses to sign in the testator's presence.

Must the witnesses sign at the same time? Most states do not require that the witnesses be together when they affix their signatures to the will. (Recall, however, that some jurisdictions, including California, require that the witnesses be all together when the testator either signs or acknowledges his or her signature on the will.)

The California Probate Code does not require that the witnesses sign in the presence of each other. 64 Cal. Jur.3d Wills §254 (citing Law Revision Commission Comment to Cal. Prob. Code §6110). Nor does the UPC require that the witnesses sign in each other's presence. Note that, unlike wills legislation in many states permitting a testator to acknowledge a previously affixed signature, statutes generally do not permit witnesses to do so.

CALIFORNIA PROBATE CODE

§76. "Subscribing witness" defined

A "subscribing witness" to a will means a witness who signs the will as provided in Section 6110.

(Stats. 1990 (A.B. 759), ch. 79, §14, effective July 1, 1991.)

§6110. Will shall be in writing, signed and witnessed

(a) Except as provided in this part, a will shall be in writing and satisfy the requirements of this section.

(b) The will shall be signed by one of the following:

(1) By the testator.

(2) In the testator's name by some other person in the testator's presence and by the testator's direction.

(3) By a conservator pursuant to a court order to make a will under Section 2580.

(c) The will shall be witnessed by being signed by at least two persons each of whom (1) being present at the same time, witnessed either the signing of the will or the testator's acknowledgment of the signature or of the will and (2) understand that the instrument they sign is the testator's will.

(Stats. 1990 (A.B. 759), ch. 79, §14, effective July 1, 1991. Amended Stats. 1996 (S.B. 392), ch. 563, §20.)

§6111.5. Extrinsic evidence is admissibility in some cases

Extrinsic evidence is admissible to determine whether a document constitutes a will pursuant to Section 6110 or 6111, or to determine the meaning of a will or a portion of a will if the meaning is unclear.

(Stats. 1990 (S.B. 1775), ch. 710, §14, effective July 1, 1991.)

§6112. Witnesses: competency and interest

(a) Any person generally competent to be a witness may act as a witness to a will.

(b) A will or any provision thereof is not invalid because the will is signed by an interested witness.

(c) Unless there are at least two other subscribing witnesses to the will who are disinterested witnesses, the fact that the will makes a devise to a subscribing witness creates a presumption that the witness procured the devise by duress, menace, fraud, or undue influence. This presumption is a presumption affecting the burden of proof. This presumption does not apply where the witness is a person to whom the devise is made solely in a fiduciary capacity.

(d) If a devise made by the will to an interested witness fails because the presumption established by subdivision (c) applies to the devise and the witness fails to rebut the presumption, the interested witness shall take such proportion of the devise made to the witness in the will as does not exceed the share of the estate which would be distributed to the witness if the will were not established. Nothing in this subdivision affects the law that applies where it is established that the witness procured a devise by duress, menace, fraud, or undue influence.

(Stats. 1990 (A.B. 759), ch. 79, §14, effective July 1, 1991.)

§6221. Method of executing a statutory will

A California statutory will shall be executed only as follows:

(a) The testator shall complete the appropriate blanks and shall sign the will.

(b) Each witness shall observe the testator's signing and each witness shall sign his or her name in the presence of the testator.

(Stats. 1991 (S.B. 271), ch. 1055, §20.)

§6222. Execution of attestation clause

The execution of the attestation clause provided in the California statutory will by two or more witnesses satisfies Section 8220.

(Stats. 1991 (S.B. 271), ch. 1055, §20.)

§8220. Proof of will based on evidence of subscribing witnesses

Unless there is a contest of a will:

(a) The will may be proved on the evidence of one of the subscribing witnesses only, if the evidence shows that the will was executed in all particulars as prescribed by law.

(b) Evidence of execution of a will may be received by an affidavit of a subscribing witness to which there is attached a photographic copy of the will, or by an affidavit in the original will that includes or incorporates the attestation clause.

(c) If no subscribing witness resides in the county, but the deposition of a witness can be taken elsewhere, the court may direct the deposition to be taken. On the examination, the court may authorize a photographic copy of the will to be made and presented to the witness, and the witness may be asked the same questions with respect to the photographic copy as if the original will were present.

(Stats. 1990 (A.B. 759), ch. 79, §14, effective July 1, 1991.)

§8221. Proof by handwriting if no subscribing witness is available

If no subscribing witness is available as a witness within the meaning of Section 240 of the Evidence Code, the court may, if the will on its face conforms to all requirements of law, permit proof of the will by proof of the handwriting of the testator and one of the following:

(a) Proof of the handwriting of any one subscribing witness.

(b) Receipt in evidence of one of the following documents reciting facts showing due execution of the will:

(1) A writing in the will bearing the signatures of all subscribing witnesses.

(2) An Affidavit of a person with personal knowledge of the circumstances of the execution.

(Stats. 1990 (A.B. 759), ch. 79, §14, effective July 1, 1991.)

§8253. Court may admit evidence of other witnesses if subscribing witnesses are unavailable

At the trial, each subscribing witness shall be produced and examined. If no subscribing witness is available as a witness within the meaning of Section 240 of the Evidence Code, the court may admit the evidence of other witnesses to prove the due execution of the will.

(Stats. 1990 (A.B. 759), ch. 79, §14, effective July 1, 1991.)

G. Holographic Wills

A holographic (sometimes called "olographic") will is a handwritten will. Holographic wills were permitted in English ecclesiastic courts beginning around 1600, but were abolished by the English Wills Act of 1837. R. H. Helmholz, The Origin of Holographic Wills in English Law, 15 J. Leg. Hist. 97 (1994). See also Gail B. Bird, Sleight of Handwriting: The Holographic Will in California, 21 Hast. L.J. 605 (1981).

Holographs are valid in over half the states, including Alaska, Arizona, Arkansas, California, Colorado, Hawaii, Idaho, Kentucky, Louisiana, Oklahoma, Maine, Maryland, Michigan, Mississippi, Montana, Nebraska, Nevada, New Jersey, New York, North Carolina, North Dakota, South Dakota, Tennessee, Texas, Utah, West Virginia, and Wyoming. Restatement (Third) of Property, *supra*, at §§3.1, 3.2. However, Maryland and New York limit holographic wills to persons in the armed services. *Id.* Holographic wills are also recognized by UPC §2-502(b).

A holographic will is valid in California if "the signature and the material provisions are in the handwriting of the testator" (Cal. Prob. Code §6111). There is no requirement in California that a handwritten will carry a date. However, if the holograph contains no date and that fact leads to doubt as to which will is controlling, then "the holographic will is invalid to the extent of the inconsistency unless the time of its execution is established to be after the date of execution of the other will" (Cal. Prob. Code §6111(b)(1)). Until 1982, California law required a date for holographic wills. (See former Cal. Prob. Code §53, repealed by Stats. 1982, ch. 187, §2, p. 570.) However, under prior law, wills were not invalidated if the date was incorrect. Bird, *supra*, at 612.

The fact that the will is in the testator's handwriting serves as a mark of the will's authenticity. As a result, witnesses are not required for holographic wills. However, the attestation of a holographic will does not destroy its validity in California. 64 Cal. Jur. 3d Wills §264.

A controversial issue in many jurisdictions is the requirement that the holographic will must be "entirely" in the testator's handwriting. Litigation has addressed whether printed or typewritten words will invalidate a holographic will (because then the will is no longer "entirely" in the testator's handwriting). Courts have applied two theories to determine whether printed matter invalidated a holographic will: (1) the intent theory and (2) the surplusage theory. Under the former, courts denied probate to a holographic will if the testator intended the nonholographic material to be part of the will. On the other hand, the surplusage theory overlooks nonholographic (printed) matter which is surplusage (nonessential) and considers only what the testator wrote.

California courts reflected a law reform movement from strict construction to the intent theory and, finally, to the surplusage theory.

Early California cases interpreted strictly the statutory requirement that the will must be entirely handwritten. Under former California Civil Code §1277, "[a] [h]olographic will is one that is entirely written, dated and signed by the hand of the testator himself. It is subject to no other form, . . . and need not be witnessed." In Estate of Thorn, 192 P. 19 (Cal. 1920), the California Supreme Court denied probate to a holographic will, despite the testator's express wishes, because the testator used a rubber stamp to print the name of a parcel of real property within the body of the will.

Gradually, the California courts began following an intent approach. That is, courts emphasized whether the particular testator intended to include the printed matter as part of his or her will. In 1931, the legislature re-enacted California Civil Code §1277 as California Probate Code §53, adding a new provision: "No address, date or other matter written, printed or stamped upon the document, which is not incorporated in the provisions which are in the handwriting of the decedent, shall be considered as any part of the will." The new provision codified the rule in Estate of DeCaccia, 273 P.552 (Cal. 1928). *DeCaccia* reversed a trial court order denying probate to a holographic will that was written under a printed letterhead stating, "Oakland, California." The court reasoned that the location of the printed address on the same line as the testator's handwritten date was not evidence of the testator's intent to include the printed address as part of the will.

Subsequent California cases modified the intent theory as an objective test. As a commentator explains:

> The court [became] less concerned with the subjective intent of the testator than with whether the printed matter should reasonably be viewed as relevant or essential: would a reasonably prudent testator, having in mind the requisites of Probate Code section 53, have intended that these obviously insignificant printed words be part of his or her will?

Bird, *supra*, at 623. This new approach reflected "dubious logic" (*id.*) because the inevitable answer to the previous question was "Of course not; the will is therefore valid." *Id.*

A subsequent case wrestled with the application of the intent-to-incorporate approach involving a holographic will written on a stationer's form. In Estate of Black, 181 Cal. Rptr. 222 (Cal. 1982), the decedent wrote her will on three printed one-page will forms, inserting her signature and place of domicile, her executor, the date and the place where she executed it. She deleted or ignored some of the printed language (e.g., regarding residuary gifts, witnesses, a testimonium clause). The trial court denied probate because the testatrix incorporated some of the printed language. The California Supreme Court reversed, reasoning that none of the incorporated material was either material to the substance of the will or essential to its validity.

The California Supreme Court thereby judicially adopted the surplusage theory. Under the surplusage theory, courts give effect to the handwritten portions of the will if such portions make sense standing alone, thereby disregarding immaterial nonholographic portions. Restatement (Third) of Property §3.2 cmt. b.

A year later, in 1983, the legislature replaced California Probate Code §53 with California Probate Code §6111. That section codified the surplusage approach (influenced by the original UPC §2-503) by requiring that the signature and material provisions must be in the testator's handwriting. In 1990, the California legislature added subdivision (c) to recognize preprinted form wills.

Note that the revised UPC holographic will provision differs slightly from that of the current California statute. The revised UPC requires that the "material portions" of the will be in the testator's handwriting (UPC §2-502(b)). (The words "material portions" differ from the California requirement of "material provisions.")

In California, a photocopy of the testator's handwritten dispositions satisfies the holographic will formalities. Estate of Brenner, 91 Cal. Rptr. 2d 149 (Ct. App. 1999).

The Restatement (Third) of Property describes the law reform movement regarding holographic wills by identifying holographic will statutes as "first generation," "second generation," and "third generation." First-generation holographic will statutes require that the will be entirely written, dated, and signed in the testator's handwriting. Second-generation holographic will statutes, those modeled on the original UPC §2-503, specify that valid holographic wills require that the signature and material provisions must be in the testator's handwriting. Third-generation holographic will statutes, modeled after the revised UPC, require that the "material portions" of the holographic will be in the testator's handwriting.

> The purpose of changing from "material provisions" to "material portions" was to leave no doubt about the validity of a will in which immaterial parts of dispositive provisions—such as "I give, devise, and bequeath"—are not in the testator's handwriting. The material portion of a dispositive provision—which must be in the testator's handwriting under the Revised UPC—are the words identifying the property and the devisee.

Restatement (Third) of Property, §3.2 cmt. b.

CALIFORNIA PROBATE CODE

§6111. Holographic will: requirements for validity

(a) A will that does not comply with Section 6110 is valid as a holographic will, whether or not witnessed, if the signature and the material provisions are in the handwriting of the testator.

(b) If a holographic will does not contain a statement as to the date of its execution and:

(1) If the omission results in doubt as to whether its provisions or the inconsistent provisions of another will are controlling, the holographic will is invalid to the extent of the inconsistency unless the time of its execution is established to be after the date of execution of the other will.

(2) If it is established that the testator lacked testamentary capacity at any time during which the will might have been executed, thc will is invalid unless it is established that it was executed at a time when the testator had testamentary capacity.

(c) Any statement of testamentary intent contained in a holographic will may be set forth either in the testator's own handwriting or as part of a commercially printed form will.

(Stats. 1990 (A.B. 759), ch. 79, §14, effective July 1, 1991. Amended Stats. 1990 (S.B. 1775), ch. 710, §13, effective July 1, 1991.)

§8220. Evidence of subscribing witness

Unless there is a contest of a will:

(a) The will may be proved on the evidence of one of the subscribing witnesses only, if the evidence shows that the will was executed in all particulars as prescribed by law.

(b) Evidence of execution of a will may be received by an affidavit of a subscribing witness to which there is attached a photographic copy of the will, or by an affidavit in the original will that includes or incorporates the attestation clause.

(c) If no subscribing witness resides in the county, but the deposition of a witness can be taken elsewhere, the court may direct the deposition to be taken. On the examination, the court may authorize a photographic copy of the will to be made and presented to the witness, and the witness may be asked the same questions with respect to the photographic copy as if the original will were present.

(Stats. 1990 (A.B. 759), ch. 79, §14, effective July 1, 1991.)

§8221. Proof where subscribing witnesses are all unavailable

If no subscribing witness is available as a witness within the meaning of Section 240 of the Evidence Code, the court may, if the will on its face conforms to all requirements of law, permit proof of the will by proof of the handwriting of the testator and one of the following:

(a) Proof of the handwriting of any one subscribing witness.

(b) Receipt in evidence of one of the following documents reciting facts showing due execution of the will:

(1) A writing in the will bearing the signatures of all subscribing witnesses.

(2) An Affidavit of a person with personal knowledge of the circumstances of the execution.

(Stats. 1990 (A.B. 759), ch. 79, §14, effective July 1, 1991.)

§8222. Proof of holographic will

A holographic will may be proved in the same manner as other writings.

(Stats. 1990 (A.B. 759), ch. 79, §14, effective July 1, 1991.)

H. Oral Wills

An oral or nuncupative will is a will that is spoken rather than written. Two general types of oral wills exist: the oral will that is uttered during the testator's last illness and the soldiers'/sailors' will. The former is an oral will that was spoken by the testator during his or her last illness before witnesses and soon afterward reduced to writing. A soldiers'/sailors' will is an oral will in which a soldier or sailor disposes of his personalty without the necessity for the usual formalities of will execution.

Oral wills date to Roman law when they were permitted for soldiers. McGovern & Kurtz, *supra*, §4.4 at 200. Historically, such wills were permitted for soldiers either as a reward for military service or because soldiers in active service could not comply easily with testamentary formalities. *Id.*

The Statute of Frauds of 1676 (which required wills of real property to be in writing) also regulated oral wills. By the Statute of Frauds, Parliament created a number of substantive requirements for the validity of oral wills of personal property valued in excess of £30. Lloyd Bonfield, Reforming the Requirements for Due Execution of Wills: Some Guidance from the Past, 70 Tul. L. Rev. 1893 (1996). The Statute of Frauds required that three persons (who acted at the testator's request) must "bear witness" that the testator's statements were his will. The testator must have spoken the statements during a last illness. And, the statements had to be spoken in the decedent's "habitation or dwelling, or where he or she hath been resident for the space of ten days or more next before the making of such Will, except where such person was surprised or taken sick, being from his own home, and died before he returned to the place of his or her dwelling." Cited in *id.* at 1911.

The Statute of Frauds also regulated the probate procedure for nuncupative wills. Church courts had to receive testimony proving the validity of such wills within six months, unless the testimony or its substance was reduced to writing shortly after utterance (i.e., within six days). *Id.* at 1912. The Statute also limited the

ability to revoke orally a clause, devise, or bequest in a written will. *Id.* The English Wills Act of 1837 abolished oral wills except for those of soldiers in active military service or sailors at sea (regarding disposition of personal property). McGovern & Kurtz, *supra*, §4.4 at 200.

The majority of states (including California) and the UPC (UPC §2-506) do not recognize oral wills. The reasons for nonrecognition may be summarized as follows:

> It is well known that oral (nuncupative) wills are . . . made difficult to execute properly for there is too much room for mistake, fraud, and perjury where a will is dependent entirely on the attention, intelligence, memory, and honesty of those gathered around the bedside of an honest person. . . .

Sarajane Love, 3 Redfearn's Wills and Administration in Georgia 50-51 (5th ed. 1988) (cited in Mary F. Radford & F. Skip Sugarman, Georgia's New Probate Code, 13 Ga. St. U. L. Rev. 605, 670 n. 307 (1997)).

In those few states that permit oral wills today, courts require the evidence of an oral will to be clear and convincing and insist on strict compliance with the statutory requirements. McGovern & Kurtz, *supra*, §4.4 at 200. The UPC does not recognize oral wills.

Typically, those few jurisdictions that continue to recognize oral wills limit them to personal property and sometimes set a value on the property. Many of these states require that the oral will must be put into writing within a short period of time after the spoken will and, similarly, must be probated within a short period of time after the testator's death. Finally, many statutes have witnessing requirements.

I. Conditional Wills

A conditional will is a will whose validity is subject to a condition. That is, the effectiveness of the will is conditional upon an event, such as death from a particular disease or operation. If the condition does not occur, then the will is not effective. 14 Witkin, Summary, Wills, *supra*, at §114. California Probate Code §6105 provides that a conditional will shall be admitted to or denied probate "in conformity with the condition."

Traditionally, courts have been reluctant to find wills conditional, preferring to find that the condition merely expresses the testator's motivation for executing the will. The issue is whether the testator intended to make the occurrence of an event as a condition precedent to the operation of the will (in which case the instrument is denied probate if the condition is not fulfilled), or whether the testator stated the possibility of the event merely as the motive leading to execution of the will (in which case the will becomes effective on the testator's death even if the event never took place). Witkin, *supra*, at §170.

In a famous case, Estate of Taylor, 259 P.2d 1014 (Cal. 1953), the testator (Clark Taylor) was in the Navy when he wrote to a Mr. Lindsay, saying that in case "Davie Jones gets me out in the South Pacific," he wanted his "Bonds, and cash in the bank also the pay I will have coming" to go to an old friend Betty Black. *Id.* at 1015-1016. After Taylor left the Navy, he lived with the Black's family. He mentioned the letter repeatedly. At Taylor's death, Lindsay filed the letter for probate; an aunt of Taylor's contested it. The court held that the possibility of the testator's dying at sea was an inducement rather than a condition, reasoning that the preferred construction was to uphold an informal will of a decedent in the armed services. The court was influenced by the facts that the testator (1) delivered the letter to a third person; (2) directed its preservation after the apparent condition failed; and (3) no will was subsequently executed, and this document was not revoked. Witkin, *supra*, at §170.

For conditional will cases, see In re Crowell, 154 S.W.3d 556 (Tenn. Ct. App. 2004) (concluding that a provision was not a motive or inducement but rather a condition precedent to the will's operation); In re Estate of Franklin, 2001 WL 896635 (Tenn. Ct. App. 2001) (remanding consideration of a will that specified a disposition "in case I die on my way to & from Jersey" in light of the following relevant factors: (1) the circumstances surrounding execution; (2) the decedent's statements following execution; (3) the manner of preservation of the document after lapse of the purported contingency; (4) the decedent's education and knowledge of the law; (5) the presence or absence of subsequent testamentary documents; (6) whether the contingency bears a reasonable relation to the disposition of the decedent's property; (7) whether a finding of a conditional will means that the deceased died intestate; (8) whether effectuating the terms of the will would be equitable under the circumstances; and (9) any other relevant factors); In re Estate of Bem, 637 N.W.2d 506 (Mich. Ct. App. 2001) (admitting testator's holographic will, holding that it was not valid only if the testator died on the specified trip but rather it referred to his reason for writing the will).

CALIFORNIA PROBATE CODE

§6105. Validity of conditional will

A will, the validity of which is made conditional by its own terms, shall be admitted to probate or rejected, or denied effect after admission to probate, in conformity with the condition.

(Stats. 1990 (A.B. 759), ch. 79, §14, effective July 1, 1991.)

J. Statutory Will

A small number of states (California, Maine, Massachusetts, Michigan, New Mexico, and Wisconsin) have enacted a statutory will. Captain Theresa A. Bruno, The Deployment Will, 47 A.F. L. Rev. 211, 225 (1999). California was the first of these states to enact statutory will legislation in the 1980s. *Id.*

The statutory will (a type of "fill-in-the-blank" will) is a legislative effort to accommodate the large numbers of persons who would otherwise die intestate. Statutory wills permit testators to fill in blank spaces for beneficiaries, guardians for children, trustees, and executors of the estate. "The positive attributes of the statutory fill-in-the-blank will are the relative ease with which a person can complete the document and the ability to consider, in the comfort of one's own home, the division of personal items." Bruno, *supra*, at 225. See also Major Peterson, Estate Planning Note: Uniform Statutory Will Act, 1993-JUL Army Law. 46, 46 (1993) (urging greater use of the statutory will for army personnel).

Statutory wills were used first in the 1920s in England. The National Conference of Commissioners on Uniform State Laws (NCCUSL) enacted the Uniform Statutory Will Act in the United States in 1984 (Unif. Stat. Will Act, 8A U.L.A. 385 (West Supp. 1992)). However, the Act was not widely adopted. *Bruno, supra*, at 225. In 1996, NCCUSL removed the Uniform Statutory Will Act from the list of uniform state laws. *Id.* at 225 n.88 (citing Minutes of the Third Meeting of the Executive Committee of the National Conference of Commissioners on Uniform State Laws (July 16, 1996)). Only two states (New Mexico and Massachusetts) continue to follow the Act. *Id.* at 225. (The other aforementioned statutory will states have different legislation.)

The California legislature authorized statutory will forms in 1983 (Stats. 1983, ch. 842, effective January 1, 1985). 64 Cal. Jur.3d Wills §284. In enacting the statutory will, the California legislature recognized two different forms (a statutory will, and a statutory will with trust). The statutory will with trust provision was repealed in 1991 (Stats. 1991, ch. 1055, §19, p. 4883). (For the text of the statutory will with trust, see former Cal. Prob. Code, §6241; Stats. 1990, ch. 79, §14, p. 700; Stats. 1983, ch. 842, §55, p. 3063.) See generally 14 Witkin, Summary, Wills, *supra*, at §115. See also Estate of Smith, 71 Cal. Rptr. 2d 424 (Ct. App. 1998*), review denied* (May 27, 1998) (holding that duly executed statutory will with trust would not be denied admission to probate based on a finding that the testator was mistaken as to how the will would dispose of property).

According to current California law, any individual of sound mind who is over age 18 may execute a statutory will (Cal. Prob. Code §6220). The testator must complete the appropriate blanks and sign the will. The will also must be signed by two or more witnesses. Each witness must observe the testator signing, and each witness must sign his or her name in the testator's presence (Cal. Prob. Code §6221(b)). 64 Cal. Jur.3d Wills §285. Testators often make mistakes in completing the statutory will. However, such mistakes do not necessarily invalidate the will. In the first case on California statutory wills, someone other than the testator had filled in the blanks on a statutory will, although the will was properly signed and witnessed. Estate of Perry, 58 Cal. Rptr. 2d 797 (Ct. App.1996). Reversing a grant of summary judgment to the contestants, the court ruled that a statutory will failing to meet the requirements of California Probate Code §6221 may still be admitted to probate if it complies with the general requirements for execution of wills provided in California Probate Code §6110 (a writing, signed by the testator or by another at his direction, with the signatures of two witnesses).

Beginning in 2001, a domestic partner has had the same right as a spouse to make a statutory will that names his or her partner (Cal. Prob. Code §6240).

CALIFORNIA PROBATE CODE

§6221. Execution of statutory will: testator's and witnesses' signatures

A California statutory will shall be executed only as follows:

(a) The testator shall complete the appropriate blanks and shall sign the will.

(b) Each witness shall observe the testator's signing and each witness shall sign his or her name in the presence of the testator.

(Stats. 1991 (S.B. 271), ch. 1055, §20.)

§6222. Execution of attestation clause in statutory will

The execution of the attestation clause provided in the California statutory will by two or more witnesses satisfies Section 8220.

(Stats. 1991 (S.B. 271), ch. 1055, §20.)

§6223. Contents of a California statutory will

(a) There is only one California statutory will.

(b) The California statutory will includes all of the following:

(1) The contents of the California statutory will form set out in Section 6240, excluding the questions and answers at the beginning of the California statutory will.

(2) By reference, the full texts of each of the following:

(A) The definitions and rules of construction set forth in Article 1 (commencing with Section 6200).

(B) The property disposition clauses adopted by the testator. If no property disposition clause is adopted, Section 6224 shall apply.

(C) The mandatory clauses set forth in Section 6241.

(c) Notwithstanding this section, any California statutory will or California statutory will with trust executed on a form allowed under prior law shall be governed by the law that applied prior to January 1, 1992.

(Stats. 1991 (S.B. 271), ch. 1055, §20.)

§6224. Testator's selection of more than one property disposition clause

If more than one property disposition clause appearing in paragraphs 2 or 3 of a California statutory will is selected, no gift is made. If more than one property disposition clause in paragraph 5 of a California statutory will form is selected, or if none is selected, the residuary Estate of a testator who signs a California statutory will shall be distributed to the testator's heirs as if the testator did not make a will.

(Stats. 1991 (S.B. 271), ch. 1055, §20.)

§6225. Text of property disposition clause is controlling

Only the texts of property disposition clauses and the mandatory clauses shall be considered in determining their meaning. Their titles shall be disregarded.

(Stats. 1991 (S.B. 271), ch. 1055, §20.)

§6240. California statutory will form

QUESTIONS AND ANSWERS ABOUT THIS CALIFORNIA STATUTORY WILL

The following is the California Statutory Will form:

The following information, in question and answer form, is not a part of the California Statutory Will. It is designed to help you understand about Wills and to decide if this Will meets your needs. This Will is in a simple form. The complete text of each paragraph of this Will is printed at the end of the Will.

1. What happens if I die without a Will? If you die without a Will, what you own (your "assets") in your name alone will be divided among your spouse, domestic partner, children, or other relatives according to state law. The court will appoint a relative to collect and distribute your assets.

2. What can a Will do for me? In a Will you may designate who will receive your assets at your death. You may designate someone (called an "executor") to appear before the court, collect your assets, pay your debts and taxes, and distribute your assets as you specify. You may nominate someone (called a "guardian") to raise your children who are under age 18. You may designate someone (called a "custodian") to manage assets for your children until they reach any age from 18 to 25.

3. Does a Will avoid probate? No. With or without a Will, assets in your name alone usually go through the court probate process. The court's first job is to determine if your Will is valid.

4. What is community property? Can I give away my share in my Will? If you are married and you or your spouse earned money during your marriage from work and wages, that money (and the assets bought with it) is community property. Your Will can only give away your one-half of community property. Your Will cannot give away your spouse's one-half of community property.

5. Does my Will give away all of my assets? Do all assets go through probate? No. Money in a joint tenancy bank account automatically belongs to the other named owner without probate. If your spouse, domestic partner, or child is on the deed to your house as a joint tenant, the house automatically passes to him or her. Life insurance and retirement plan benefits may pass directly to the named beneficiary. A Will does not necessarily control how these types of "nonprobate" assets pass at your death.

6. Are there different kinds of Wills? Yes. There are handwritten Wills, typewritten Wills, attorney-prepared Wills, and statutory Wills. All are valid if done precisely as the law requires. You should see a lawyer if you do not want to use this Statutory Will or if you do not understand this form.

7. Who may use this Will? This Will is based on California law. It is designed only for California residents. You may use this form if you are single, married, a member of a domestic partnership, or divorced. You must be age 18 or older and of sound mind.

8. Are there any reasons why I should NOT use this Statutory Will? Yes. This is a simple Will. It is not designed to reduce death taxes or other taxes. Talk to a lawyer to do tax planning, especially if (i) your assets will be worth more than $600,000 or the current amount excluded from estate tax under federal law at your death, (ii) you own business-related assets, (iii) you want to create a trust fund for your children's education or other purposes, (iv) you own assets in some other state, (v) you want to disinherit your spouse, domestic partner, or descendants, or (vi) you have valuable interests in pension or profit-sharing plans. You should talk to a lawyer who knows about estate planning if this Will does not meet your needs. This Will treats most adopted children like natural children. You should talk to a lawyer if you have stepchildren or foster children whom you have not adopted.

9. May I add or cross out any words on this Will? No. If you do, the Will may be invalid or the court may ignore the crossed out or added words. You may only fill in the blanks. You may amend this Will by a separate document (called a codicil). Talk to a lawyer if you want to do something with your assets which is not allowed in this form.

10. May I change my Will? Yes. A Will is not effective until you die. You may make and sign a new Will. You may change your Will at any time, but only by an amendment (called a codicil). You can give away or sell your assets before your death. Your Will only acts on what you own at death.

11. Where should I keep my Will? After you and the witnesses sign the Will, keep your Will in your safe deposit box or other safe place. You should tell trusted family members where your Will is kept.

12. When should I change my Will? You should make and sign a new Will if you marry, divorce, or terminate your domestic partnership after you sign this Will. Divorce, annulment, or termination of a domestic partnership automatically cancels all property stated to pass to a former husband, wife, or domestic partner under this Will, and revokes the designation of a former spouse or domestic partner as executor, custodian, or guardian. You should sign a new Will when you have more children, or if your spouse or a child dies, or a domestic partner dies or marries. You may want to change your Will if there is a large change in the value of your assets. You may also want to change your Will if you enter a domestic partnership or your domestic partnership has been terminated after you sign this Will.

13. What can I do if I do not understand something in this Will? If there is anything in this Will you do not understand, ask a lawyer to explain it to you.

14. What is an executor? An "executor" is the person you name to collect your assets, pay your debts and taxes, and distribute your assets as the court directs. It may be a person or it may be a qualified bank or trust company.
15. Should I require a bond? You may require that an executor post a "bond." A bond is a form of insurance to replace assets that may be mismanaged or stolen by the executor. The cost of the bond is paid from the estate's assets.
16. What is a guardian? Do I need to designate one? If you have children under age 18, you should designate a guardian of their "persons" to raise them.
17. What is a custodian? Do I need to designate one? A " custodian" is a person you may designate to manage assets for someone (including a child) who is under the age of 25 and who receives assets under your Will. The custodian manages the assets and pays as much as the custodian determines is proper for health, support, maintenance, and education. The custodian delivers what is left to the person when the person reaches the age you choose (from 18 to 25). No bond is required of a custodian.
18. Should I ask people if they are willing to serve before I designate them as executor, guardian, or custodian? Probably yes. Some people and banks and trust companies may not consent to serve or may not be qualified to act.
19. What happens if I make a gift in this Will to someone and that person dies before I do? A person must survive you by 120 hours to take a gift under this Will. If that person does not, then the gift fails and goes with the rest of your assets. If the person who does not survive you is a relative of yours or your spouse, then certain assets may go to the relative's descendants.
20. What is a trust? There are many kinds of trusts, including trusts created by Wills (called "testamentary trusts") and trusts created during your lifetime (called "revocable living trusts"). Both kinds of trusts are long-term arrangements in which a manager (called a "trustee") invests and manages assets for someone (called a " beneficiary") on the terms you specify. Trusts are too complicated to be used in this Statutory Will. You should see a lawyer if you want to create a trust.
21. What is a domestic partner? You have a domestic partner if you have met certain legal requirements and filed a form entitled "Declaration of Domestic Partnership" with the Secretary of State. Notwithstanding Section 299.6 of the Family Code, if you have not filed a Declaration of Domestic Partnership with the Secretary of State, you do not meet the required definition and should not use the section of the Statutory Will form that refers to domestic partners even if you have registered your domestic partnership with another governmental entity. If you are unsure if you have a domestic partner or if your domestic partnership meets the required definition, please contact the Secretary of State's office.

INSTRUCTIONS

1. READ THE WILL. Read the whole Will first. If you do not understand something, ask a lawyer to explain it to you.
2. FILL IN THE BLANKS. Fill in the blanks. Follow the instructions in the form carefully. Do not add any words to the Will (except for filling in blanks) or cross out any words.
3. DATE AND SIGN THE WILL AND HAVE TWO WITNESSES SIGN IT. Date and sign the Will and have two witnesses sign it. You and the witnesses should read and follow the Notice to Witnesses found at the end of this Will.[see illustration or form in printed copy]

(Stats. 1991 (S.B. 271), ch. 1055, §20. Amended by Stats. 2001 (A.B. 25), ch. 893, §52; Stats. 2003 (A.B. 167), ch. 32, §5, effective January 1, 2004.)

§6241. Mandatory clauses specified

The mandatory clauses of the California statutory will form are as follows:

(a) Intestate Disposition. If the testator has not made an effective disposition of the residuary estate, the executor shall distribute it to the testator's heirs at law, their identities and respective shares to be determined according to the laws of the State of California in effect on the date of the testator's death relating to intestate succession of property not acquired from a predeceased spouse.

(b) Powers of Executor.

(1) In addition to any powers now or hereafter conferred upon executors by law, including all powers granted under the Independent Administration of Estates Act, the executor shall have the power to:

(A) Sell estate assets at public or private sale, for cash or on credit terms.

(B) Lease estate assets without restriction as to duration.

(C) Invest any surplus moneys of the estate In real or personal property, as the executor deems advisable.

(2) The executor may distribute estate assets otherwise distributable to a minor beneficiary to one of the following:

(A) The guardian of the minor's person or estate.

(B) Any adult person with whom the minor resides and who has the care, custody, or control of the minor.

(C) A custodian of the minor under the Uniform Transfers to Minors Act as designated in the California statutory will form.

The executor is free of liability and is discharged from any further accountability for distributing assets in compliance with the provisions of this paragraph.

(3) On any distribution of assets from the estate, the executor shall have the discretion to partition, allot, and distribute the assets in the following manner:

(A) In kind, including undivided interest in an asset or in any part of it.

(B) Partly in cash and partly in kind.

(C) Entirely in cash.

If a distribution is being made to more than one beneficiary, the executor shall have the discretion to distribute assets among them on a pro rata or non pro rata basis, with the assets valued as of the date of distribution.

(c) Powers of Guardian. A guardian of the person nominated in the California statutory will shall have the same authority with respect to the person of the ward as a parent having legal custody of a child would have. All powers wanted to guardians in this paragraph may be exercised without court authorization.

(Stats. 1991 (S.B. 271), ch. 1055, §20.)

§6242. Statutory will shall include only clauses as existing on date of execution

(a) Except as specifically provided in this chapter, a California statutory will shall include only the texts of the property disposition clauses and the mandatory clauses as they exist on the day the California statutory will is executed.

(b) Sections 6205, 6206, and 6227 apply to every California statutory will, including those executed before January 1, 1985. Section 6211 applies only to California statutory wills executed after July 1, 1991.

(c) Notwithstanding Section 6222, and except as provided in subdivision (b), a California statutory will is governed by the law that applied prior to January 1, 1992, if the California statutory will is executed on a form that (1) was prepared for use under former Sections 56 to 56.14, inclusive, or former Sections 6200 to 6248, inclusive, of the Probate Code, and (2) satisfied the requirements of law that applied prior to January 1, 1992.

(d) A California statutory will does not fail to satisfy the requirements of subdivision (a) merely because the will is executed on a form that incorporates the mandatory clauses of Section 6241 that refer to former Section 1120.2. If the will incorporates the mandatory clauses with a reference to former Section 1120.2, the trustee has the powers listed in Article 2 (commencing with Section 16220) of Chapter 2 of Part 4 of Division 9.

(Stats. 1991 (S.B. 271), ch. 1055, §20. Amended by Stats. 2004 (A.B. 3082), ch. 183, §279, effective January 1, 2005.)

§6243. Application of law

Except as specifically provided in this chapter, the general law of California applies to a California statutory will.

(Stats. 1991 (S.B. 271), ch. 1055, §20.)

K. Foreign and International Wills

Sometimes, a testator executes a will in a state or country that is different from that of the testator's domicile or place of death. Many states have statutes that recognize such wills. The Uniform Probate Code includes two statutory approaches to validate such wills. The first solution recognizes the foreign will that has been executed according to the requirements of other states or countries through a special choice of law rule (UPC §2-506). The second solution is the Uniform International Wills Act, which authorizes a special procedure (UPC §§10-1001 to 10-1010) and specifies that wills executed pursuant to that procedure (in jurisdictions that have enacted the Act or that are signatories to an international convention) will be given effect in other jurisdictions.

To facilitate the probate of foreign wills, the UPC proposes a liberal rule regarding choice of law. UPC §2-506 recognizes the validity of any foreign instrument executed according to any of the UPC's provisions, but also provides that a written will is valid if executed in compliance with the law of any of the following jurisdictions:

- **the place of execution,**
- **the testator's domicile at the time of execution,**
- **the testator's place of abode at the time of execution,**
- **the place of the testator's nationality at the time of execution,**
- **the testator's domicile at the time of death,**
- **the testator's place of abode at the time of death, or**
- **the testator's nationality at the time of death.**

Like the UPC choice of law rule for foreign wills, the Uniform International Wills Act is an attempt to provide validity to wills probated in other nations. However, the Uniform International Wills Act proposes an execution procedure that is intended to validate wills in all jurisdictions that recognize the legislation. The Act is incorporated in the Uniform Probate Code, (Article II, Part 10) and was promulgated by the National Conference of Commissioners on Uniform State Laws (NCCUSL) in 1977. Under the Act, a will is valid if it complies with the requirements of the Act, regardless of the place where it was executed, the location of the assets, or the nationality, domicile, or residence of the testator. The Act also implements an international convention calling for all countries and states to adopt a uniform formality for executing wills. The Act has been adopted by Alaska, California, Colorado, Connecticut, Delaware, District of Columbia, Hawaii, Illinois, Minnesota, Montana, New Mexico, North Dakota, Pennsylvania, and Virginia.

California enacted the Uniform International Wills Act separately from the Uniform Probate Code. California's version of the Uniform International Wills Act is found at California Probate Code §§6380 et seq.

According to California law, for an international will to be valid,

- **it must be in writing (although the writing may be in any language) (Cal. Prob. Code §6382(a));**
- **the testator must declare that the document is his or her will and know the contents thereof (Cal. Prob. Code §6382(b));**
- **the testator's declaration must be in the presence of three persons, i.e., two witnesses and a special authorized person (Cal. Prob. Code §6382(b)) who is defined as someone who has been admitted to practice law in California and is in good standing or who has been empowered by federal law to supervise the execution of international wills (e.g., members of the diplomatic and consular service of the United States designated by Foreign Service Regulations) (Cal. Prob. Code §§6380(b), 6388);**
- **the testator (or a proxy) must sign the will or acknowledge the testator's signature in the presence of these three**

persons (Cal. Prob. Code §6382(b)&(c)); and

- **the witnesses and authorized person must attest the will by signing it in the testator's presence (Cal. Prob. Code §6382(e)).**

The Act also provides that a certificate must be signed by the authorized person, reciting the requirements for valid execution of an international will, and which is conclusive of the validity of the instrument as a will (Cal. Prob. Code §6384).

Compliance with some statutory requirements for international wills is mandatory, whereas noncompliance with other requirements will not affect the validity of the international will. Requirements that fall into the latter category are: (1) signatures must be at the end of the will; (2) each sheet must be signed (and numbered) by the testator, a proxy, or authorized person; (3) the will must be dated at the end by the authorized person; and (4) the authorized person must ask the testator whether the testator wishes to make a declaration concerning the safekeeping of the will and if so, the certificate (Cal. Prob. Code §6384) must mention the place where the will is being kept (Cal. Prob. Code §6383). Note that if a will is invalid as an international will, it still may be valid as another kind of will (Cal. Prob. Code §6381(b)).

The statute also provides for a registry system, established by the Secretary of State, where information about international wills is kept. Such information is confidential until the death of the testator, at which time it is available to a person who presents a death certificate or other "satisfactory evidence" of the testator's death (Cal. Prob. Code §6389).

On the probate of wills in foreign languages, see California Probate Code §8002 *infra* (requiring that English translations be attached).

Federal legislation authorizes military testamentary instruments. Congress created a new will, the military testamentary instrument, by the enactment of the National Defense Authorization Act for 2001, Floyd D. Spence National Defense Authorization Act for Fiscal Year 2001, §551, Pub. L. No. 106-398, 114 Stat. 1654, 1654A-123 to -125 (2000) (codified as amended at 10 U.S.C. §1044d). The statute enables the military attorney to provide testamentary instruments that are valid in every U.S. jurisdiction.

CALIFORNIA PROBATE CODE

§6380. Definitions

In this chapter:

(a) "International will" means a will executed in conformity with Sections 6381 to 6384, inclusive.

(b) "Authorized person" and "person authorized to act in connection with international wills" means a person who by Section 6388, or by the laws of the United States including members of the diplomatic and consular service of the United States designated by Foreign Service Regulations, is empowered to supervise the execution of international wills. *(Stats. 1990 (A.B. 759), ch. 79, §14, effective July 1, 1991.)*

§6381. Validity of international wills complying with requirements of chapter

(a) A will is valid as regards form, irrespective particularly of the place where it is made, of the location of the assets and of the nationality, domicile, or residence of the testator, if it is made in the form of an international will complying with the requirements of this chapter.

(b) The invalidity of the will as an international will does not affect its formal validity as a will of another kind.

(c) This chapter docs not apply to the form of testamentary dispositions made by two or more persons in one instrument. *(Stats. 1990 (A.B. 759), ch. 79, §14, effective July 1, 1991.)*

§6382. Mandatory requirements: writing, declaration, signature, three witnesses

(a) The will shall be made in writing. It need not be written by the testator himself or herself. It may be written in any language, by hand or by any other means.

(b) The testator shall declare in the presence of two witnesses and of a person authorized to act in connection with international wills that the document is the testator's will and that the testator knows the contents thereof. The testator need not inform the witnesses, or the authorized person, of the contents of the will.

(c) In the presence of the witnesses, and of the authorized person, the testator shall sign the will or, if the testator has previously signed it, shall acknowledge his or her signature.

(d) If the testator is unable to sign, the absence of the testator's signature does not affect the validity of the international will if the testator indicates the reason for his or her inability to sign and the authorized person makes note thereof on the will. In that case, it is permissible for any other person present, including the authorized person or one of the witnesses, at the direction of the testator, to sign the testator's name for the testator if the authorized person makes note of this also on the will, but it is not required that any person sign the testator's name for the testator.

(e) The witnesses and the authorized person shall there and then attest the will by signing in the presence of the testator. *(Stats. 1990 (A.B. 759), ch. 79, §14, effective July 1, 1991.)*

§6383. Optional requirements: subscription; date; declaration concerning safekeeping

(a) The signatures shall be placed at the end of the will. If the will consists of several sheets, each sheet shall be signed by the testator or, if the testator is unable to sign, by the person signing on his or her behalf or, if there is no such person, by the authorized person. In addition, each sheet shall be numbered.

(b) The date of the will shall be the date of its signature by the authorized person. That date shall be noted at the end of the will by the authorized person.

(c) The authorized person shall ask the testator whether the testator wishes to make a declaration concerning the safekeeping of the will. If so and at the express request of the testator, the place where the testator intends to have the will kept shall be mentioned in the certificate provided for in Section 6384.

(d) A will executed in compliance with Section 6382 is not invalid merely because it does not comply with this section.
(Stats. 1990 (A.B. 759), ch. 79, §4, effective July 1, 1991.)

§6384. Certificate establishing compliance with statutory requirements

The authorized person shall attach to the will a certificate to be signed by the authorized person establishing that the requirements of this chapter for valid execution of an international will have been fulfilled. The authorized person shall keep a copy of the certificate and deliver another to the testator. The certificate shall be substantially in the following form:

CERTIFICATE
(Convention of October 26, 1973)
1. I,
_______________________________________,
(name, address, and capacity)
a person authorized to act in connection with international wills,
2. certify that on _________ (date) at _________ (place)
3.
____
(testator) (name, address, date and place of birth)
in my presence and that of the witnesses
4. (a)
____
(name, address, date and place of birth)
(b)
____
(name, address, date and place of birth)
has declared that the attached document is his will and that he knows the contents thereof.
5. I furthermore certify that:
6. (a) in my presence and in that of the witnesses
(1) the testator has signed the will or has acknowledged his signature previously affixed.
(2) following a declaration of the testator stating that he was unable to sign his will for the following reason ___________,
I have mentioned this declaration on the will, [FN*] and the signature has been affixed by
____
(name and address) [FN*]
7. (b) the witnesses and I have signed the will;
8. (c) each page of the will has been signed by
_____________________ and numbered; [FN*]
9. (d) I have satisfied myself as to the identity of the testator and of the witnesses as designated above;
10. (e) the witnesses met the conditions requisite to act as such according to the law under which I am acting;
11. (f) the testator has requested me to include the following statement concerning the safekeeping of his will: [FN*]
____
12. PLACE OF EXECUTION
13. DATE
14. SIGNATURE and, if necessary, SEAL
[FN*] to be completed if appropriate

(Stats. 1990 (A.B. 759), ch. 79, §14, effective July 1, 1991.)

§6385. Certificate of authorized person is conclusive of validity

In the absence of evidence to the contrary, the certificate of the authorized person is conclusive of the formal validity of the instrument as a will under this chapter. The absence or irregularity of a certificate does not affect the formal validity of a will under this chapter.
(Stats. 1990 (A.B. 759), ch. 79, §14, effective July 1, 1991.)

§6386. Methods of revocation

The international will is subject to the ordinary rules of revocation of wills.
(Stats. 1990 (A.B. 759), ch. 79, §14, effective July 1, 1991.)

§6387. Application of chapter

Sections 6380 to 6386, inclusive, derive from Annex to Convention of October 26, 1973, Providing a Uniform Law on the Form of an International Will. In interpreting and applying this chapter, regard shall be had to its international origin and to the need for uniformity in its interpretation.
(Stats. 1990 (A.B. 759), ch. 79, §14, effective July 1, 1991.)

§6388. "Authorized persons" defined

Individuals who have been admitted to practice law before the courts of this state and who are in good standing as active law practitioners of this state are authorized persons In relation to international wills.
(Stats. 1990 (A.B. 759), ch. 79, §14, effective July 1, 1991.)

§6389. Registry system for international wills

The Secretary of State shall establish a registry system by which authorized persons may register in a central information center information regarding the execution of international wills, keeping that information in strictest confidence until the death of the maker and then making it available to any person desiring information about any will who presents a death certificate or other satisfactory evidence of the testator's death to the center. Information that may be received, preserved in confidence until death, and reported as indicated is limited to the name, social security or other individual identifying number established by law, if any, address, date and place of birth of the testator, and the intended place of deposit or safekeeping of the instrument pending the death of the maker. The Secretary of State, at the request of the authorized person,

may cause the information it receives about execution of any international will to be transmitted to the registry system of another jurisdiction as identified by the testator, if that other system adheres to rules protecting the confidentiality of the information similar to those established in this state.
(Stats. 1990 (A.B. 759), ch. 79, §14, effective July 1, 1991.)

§6390. Chapter continues former law

After December 31, 1984, a reference in a written instrument, including a will, to the former law (repealed by Chapter 892 of the Statutes of 1984) shall be deemed to be a reference to the corresponding provision of this chapter.
(Stats. 1990 (A.B. 759), ch. 79, §14, effective July 1, 1991.)

L. Self-Proved Wills

Some states and UPC §2-504 provide for a "self-proved will" which consists of a witnessed will with a notarized affidavit in which the testator and witnesses affirm under oath that all the statutory requirements have been fulfilled. A self-proving affidavit resembles an attestation clause. However, because of the addition of the notarized statement under oath, a self-proved will facilitates probate by enabling the will to be admitted without the necessity of testimony by the subscribing witnesses.

Almost all states permit self-proving affidavits in connection with a will or codicil. Betsy Dupree-Kyle, Comment, Michigan Self-Proved Wills: What Are They and How Do They Work?, 2000 L. Rev. Mich. St. U. Det. C.L. 829, 830 (2000).

Jurisdictions differ as to whether the self-proving affidavit is incorporated into the will, serving as a substitute for the attestation clause (thereby requiring one set of signatures), or instead a two-step procedure requiring execution of a will and a separate affidavit (thereby requiring two sets of signatures). According to the majority approach, one set of signatures is sufficient to witness a will and to self-prove it. See, e.g., Estate of Dellinger, 793 N.E.2d 1041 (Ind. 2003). The UPC includes alternative forms. One form permits the affidavit to be a part of the will itself, i.e., the testator and witnesses execute both the affidavit and will simultaneously (UPC §2-504(a)). The second form requires a separate execution of the will and affidavit (UPC §2-504(b)).

UPC provisions for the self-proved will specify additional requirements (not required for the witnessed will generally): the testator must declare to witnesses that this will is the testator's last will, and the witnesses must sign in the testator's presence and hearing (UPC §2-504).

Sometimes, problems have arisen when testator or witnesses sign only the self-proving affidavit and not the will. Courts in some jurisdictions have held that a signature on the self-proving affidavit does not constitute a signature on the will. As a result, NCCUSL added subsection (c) to UPC §2-504 to provide that a signature on the self-proving affidavit is considered a signature affixed to the will. Most states now permit the signatures on the self-proving affidavit "to bootstrap the otherwise invalid will." Beyer, Wills, Trusts, and Estates, *supra*, §5.4.2.4, at 94.

California law provides that evidence of execution of a will may be received by affidavit. Evidence of execution may be received by (1) an affidavit of the subscribing witness with a photographic copy of the will attached, or (2) an affidavit in the original will that includes or incorporates the attestation clause (Cal. Prob. Code §8220). 14 Witkin, Summary, Wills, *supra*, at §545.

Note that California statutory wills are self-proving. That is, execution of the attestation clause by two or more competent witnesses is sufficient proof of the will for admission to probate (Cal. Prob. Code §§6222, 6240, 8220).

On the history of self-proved wills, see Dupree-Kyle, *supra*, at 835-838. See also Bruce H. Mann, Self-Proving Affidavits and Formalism in Wills Adjudication, 63 Wash. U.L.Q. 39 (1985).

CALIFORNIA PROBATE CODE

§8220. Subscribing witnesses and affidavit

Unless there is a contest of a will:

(a) The will may be proved on the evidence of one of the subscribing witnesses only, if the evidence shows that the will was executed in all particulars as prescribed by law.

(b) Evidence of execution of a will may be received by an affidavit of a subscribing witness to which there is attached a photographic copy of the will, or by an affidavit in the original will that includes or incorporates the attestation clause.

(c) If no subscribing witness resides in the county, but the deposition of a witness can be taken elsewhere, the court may direct the deposition to be taken. On the examination, the court may authorize a photographic copy of the will to be made and presented to the witness, and the witness may be asked the same questions with respect to the photographic copy as if the original will were present.
(Stats. 1990 (A.B. 759), ch. 79, §14, effective July 1, 1991.)

M. Limitations on Transfers to Beneficiaries who Serve as Drafters

California law invalidates donative transfers to certain classes of persons. These persons

include: drafters of the instrument as well as persons related by blood or marriage to the drafter, cohabitants of the drafter, employees of the drafter, and care custodians of dependent adults. The issue of donative transfers to beneficiaries who serve as drafters raises the specter of conflicts of interest and undue influence. On Undue Influence, see Chapter IV, Section IV.

In 1993, the California legislature enacted California Probate Code §§21350 to 21356, and substantially amended those provisions in 1995. The legislature enacted the 1993 legislation In response to reports that an Orange County attorney representing a large number of elderly residents had drafted numerous wills and trusts under which he was a major beneficiary, and had abused his position as trustee or conservator to benefit himself or his law partners. Rice v. Clark, 47 P.3d 300, 304 (Cal. 2002) (explaining legislative history) (citing Assem. Com. on Judiciary, Analysis of Assem. Bill No. 21 (1993-1994 Reg. Sess.) as amended Feb. 4, 1993, p. 1). In 2003, the legislature added the category of "domestic partner of the drafter" to the list of prohibited transferees.

California Probate Code §21351 states exceptions, exempting transfers to relatives and cohabitants of the transferor, instruments reviewed by an independent attorney who counsels the transferor and executes a specified certificate, and transfers approved by the court on petition of a conservator. Subdivision (d) of that provision permits a transferee, other than the drafter, to rebut the presumption of disqualification by showing upon clear and convincing evidence that the transfer was not the product of fraud, menace, duress, or undue influence.

A recent case addressed whether there was a "personal friend" exception to the rule. That is, in Bernard v. Foley, 138 P.3d 1196 (Cal. 2006), relatives who were beneficiaries of the decedent's revocable living trust filed a petition to invalidate a trust amendment, which was executed by the decedent three days before she died, designating decedent's longtime friends as residual beneficiaries. The California Supreme Court held that personal friends who are providing health services to a decedent are not excepted from the statutory scheme presumptively disqualifying "care custodians" from receiving testamentary transfers.

California Probate Code §21353 provides that the disqualified person is treated as having predeceased the transferor, but may still receive his or her intestate share in the transferor's estate. The prohibition applies despite any contrary provisions in the instrument (Cal. Prob. Code §21352).

The 1993 legislation applies to all donative transfers by instrument, not only to wills and other testamentary transfers (as in prior law). Also, the 1993 legislation invalidates gifts to drafters and to fiduciaries (and to persons close to them) who transcribe the instrument or cause it to be transcribed. Under prior law, the transferee had to receive an "undue" benefit in order to raise the presumption of invalidity. Also, a transferee now bears an elevated burden of proof. That is, to rebut the presumption of invalidity, the transferee must show the absence of undue influence, fraud, or duress by clear and convincing evidence, and without reliance on the testimony of any presumptively disqualified person (Cal. Prob. Code §21351(d)).

According to California Probate Code §21351(e)(B), the presumption of disqualification is conclusive as to a drafter-transferee (i.e., an attorney who drafts a client's will to benefit himself). However, the presumption is rebuttable if an attorney drafts a will so as to benefit a relative or law partner, but only by clear and convincing evidence other than the drafter's testimony that the client freely chose that disposition (Cal. Prob. Code §21351(d), (e)). Rice v. Clark, *supra*, at 305 (explaining legislative history).

As originally enacted, California Probate Code §21350(a)(1) disqualified any person, including attorneys and other fiduciaries, who "drafted, transcribed, or caused to be drafted or transcribed, the instrument." In 1995, the legislature amended the provision to retain the disqualification of all drafters but expressly limit the disqualification of transcribers, and those who cause the instrument to be transcribed, to fiduciaries (Cal. Prob. Code §21350 (a)(4)). Also, the 1995 amendments eliminated any reference to a person who "caused [the instrument] to be drafted." Rice v. Clark, *supra*, at 305 (explaining legislative history).

California regulations pertaining to professional conduct (Rule 4-400) also prohibit a lawyer from inducing a client to make a substantial gift to the lawyer (or the lawyer's family) unless the lawyer is related to the client. This prohibition reflects the influence of the ABA Model Rules on conflict of interest (*infra*). The presence of a substantial gift by a client to an attorney raises a presumption of undue influence. See, e.g., McGee v. State Bar, 24 Cal. Rptr. 839 (Cal. 1962) (holding that attorney's conduct in drafting will that named him as residuary beneficiary of elderly client's estate overcame presumption and did not merit discipline because he made an affirmative showing that justified his actions by having another attorney review the will with the client).

In Rice v. Clark, 47 P.3d 300 (Cal. 2002), the California Supreme Court explored the issue whether the class of prohibited transferees includes a person (i.e., a handyman who performed maintenance and errands for the testatrix and helped her with her finances) who provides necessary information in the

instrument's preparation and who encourages the donor to execute it, but who does not direct or otherwise participate in the instrument's transcription to final written form. The court permitted the bequest, concluding that the category of persons disqualified under California Probate Code §21350 (a)(4) was not so broad. See also Estate of Swetmann, 102 Cal. Rptr. 2d 457 (Ct. App. 2000) (holding that the testator's conservator did not "cause" the decedent's will to be transcribed, reasoning that a person who "causes" a document to be transcribed, for purposes of California Probate Code §21350(a) restricting transfers to a fiduciary who transcribes an instrument or causes it to be transcribed, is one who directs the drafted document to be written out in its final form and is in a position to subvert the true intent of the testator).

CALIFORNIA PROBATE CODE

§21350. Prohibited transferees

(a) Except as provided in Section 21351, no provision, or provisions, of any instrument shall be valid to make any donative transfer to any of the following:

(1) The person who drafted the instrument.

(2) A person who is related by blood or marriage to, is a domestic partner of, is a cohabitant with, or is an employee of, the person who drafted the instrument.

(3) Any partner or shareholder of any law partnership or law corporation in which the person described in paragraph (1) has an ownership interest, and any employee of that law partnership or law corporation.

(4) Any person who has a fiduciary relationship with the transferor, including, but not limited to, a conservator or trustee, who transcribes the instrument or causes it to be transcribed.

(5) A person who is related by blood or marriage to, is a domestic partner of, is a cohabitant with, or is an employee of a person who is described in paragraph (4).

(6) A care custodian of a dependent adult who is the transferor.

(7) A person who is related by blood or marriage to, is a domestic partner of, is a cohabitant with, or is an employee of, a person who is described in paragraph (6).

(b) For purposes of this section, "a person who is related by blood or marriage" to a person means all of the following:

(1) The person's spouse or predeceased spouse.

(2) Relatives within the third degree of the person and of the person's spouse.

(3) The spouse of any person described in paragraph (2).

In determining any relationship under this subdivision, Sections 6406, 6407, and Chapter 2 (commencing with Section 6450) of Part 2 of Division 6 shall be applicable.

(c) For purposes of this section, the term "dependent adult" has the meaning as set forth in Section 15610.23 of the Welfare and Institutions Code and also includes those persons who (1) are older than age 64 and (2) would be dependent adults, within the meaning of Section 15610.23, if they were between the ages of 18 and 64. The term "care custodian" has the meaning as set forth in Section 15610.17 of the Welfare and Institutions Code.

(d) For purposes of this section, "domestic partner" means a domestic partner as defined under Section 297 of the Family Code.

(Stats. 1993 (A.B.21), ch. 193, §8. Amended by Stats. 1995 (A.B. 1466), ch. 730, §12; Stats. 1996 (S.B. 392), ch. 563, §34; Stats. 1996 (A.B. 2751), ch. 862, §47; Stats. 1997, c. 724 (A.B. 1172), ch. 724, §33. Stats. 2003 (A.B. 1349), ch. 444, §1, effective January 1, 2004.)

§21350.5. "Disqualified person," definition

For purposes of this part, "disqualified person" means a person specified in subdivision (a) of Section 21350, but only in cases where Section 21351 does not apply.

(Stats. 1995 (A.B. 1466), ch. 730, §13.)

§21351. Exemptions: familial relationship between transferor and draftsperson, or independent review

Section 21350 does not apply if any of the following conditions are met:

(a) The transferor is related by blood or marriage to, is a cohabitant with, or is the registered domestic partner, pursuant to Division 2.5 (commencing with Section 297) of the Family Code, of the transferee or the person who drafted the instrument. For purposes of this section, "cohabitant" has the meaning set forth in Section 13700 of the Penal Code. This subdivision shall retroactively apply to an instrument that becomes irrevocable on or after July 1, 1993.

(b) The instrument is reviewed by an independent attorney who (1) counsels the client (transferor) about the nature and consequences of the intended transfer, (2) attempts to determine if the intended consequence is the result of fraud, menace, duress, or undue influence, and (3) signs and delivers to the transferor an original certificate in substantially the following form, with a copy delivered to the drafter:

"CERTIFICATE OF INDEPENDENT REVIEW

I, ______________________________, have reviewed
(attorney's name)

______________________________ and counseled my client,
(name of instrument)

______________________________, on the nature and conse-
(name of client)

quences of the transfer, or transfers, of property to

____
(name of potentially disqualified person)

contained in the instrument. I am so disassociated from the interest of the transferee as to be in a position to advise my client independently, impartially, and confidentially as to the consequences of the transfer. On the basis of this counsel, I conclude that the transfer, or transfers, in the instrument that otherwise might be invalid under Section 21350 of the Probate Code are valid because the transfer, or transfers, are not the product of fraud, menace, duress, or undue influence.

_______________________________ ______________"

(Name of Attorney) (Date)

Any attorney whose written engagement signed by the client is expressly limited solely to the preparation of a certificate under this subdivision, including the prior counseling, shall not be considered to otherwise represent the client.

(c) After full disclosure of the relationships of the persons involved, the instrument is approved pursuant to an order under Article 10 (commencing with Section 2580) of Chapter 6 of Part 4 of Division 4.

(d) The court determines, upon clear and convincing evidence, but not based solely upon the testimony of any person described in subdivision (a) of Section 21350, that the transfer was not the product of fraud, menace, duress, or undue influence. If the court finds that the transfer was the product of fraud, menace, duress, or undue influence, the disqualified person shall bear all costs of the proceeding, including reasonable attorney's fees.

(e) Subdivision (d) shall apply only to the following instruments:

(1) Any instrument other than one making a transfer to a person described in paragraph (1) of subdivision (a) of Section 21350.

(2) Any instrument executed on or before July 1, 1993, by a person who was a resident of this state at the time the instrument was executed.

(3) Any instrument executed by a resident of California who was not a resident at the time the instrument was executed.

(f) The transferee is a federal, state, or local public entity, an entity that qualifies for an exemption from taxation under Section 501(c)(3) or 501(c)(19) of the Internal Revenue Code, or a trust holding an interest for this entity, but only to the extent of the interest of the entity, or the trustee of this trust. This subdivision shall retroactively apply to an instrument that becomes irrevocable on or after July 1, 1993.

(g) For purposes of this section, "related by blood or marriage" shall include persons within the fifth degree or heirs of the transferor.

(h) The transfer does not exceed the sum of three thousand dollars ($3,000). This subdivision shall not apply if the total value of the property in the Estate of the transferor does not exceed the amount prescribed in Section 13100.

(i) The transfer is made by an instrument executed by a nonresident of California who was not a resident at the time the instrument was executed, and that was not signed within California.

(Stats. 1993 (A.B. 21), ch. 293, §8. Amended by Stats. 1994 (A.B. 797), ch. 40, §4, effective April 19, 1994; Stats. 1995 (A.B. 1466), ch. 730, §14; Stats. 2002 (S.B. 1575), ch. 412, §1.)

§21352. Liability for making prohibited transfers

No person shall be liable for making any transfer pursuant to an instrument that is prohibited by this part unless that person has received actual notice of the possible invalidity of the transfer to the disqualified person under Section 21350 prior to making the transfer. A person who receives actual notice of the possible invalidity of a transfer prior to the transfer shall not be held liable for failing to make the transfer unless the validity of the transfer has been conclusively determined by a court.

(Stats. 1993 (A.B. 21), ch. 293, §8.)

§21353. Effect on instrument of a failed transfer

If a transfer fails under this part, the transfer shall be made as if the disqualified person predeceased the transferor without spouse or issue, but only to the extent that the value of the transfer exceeds the intestate interest of the disqualified person.

(Stats. 1993 (A.B. 21), ch. 293, §8. Amended by Stats. 1995 (A.B. 1466), ch. 730, §15.)

§21354. Application of Part despite contrary provision in instrument

This part applies notwithstanding a contrary provision in the instrument.

(Stats. 1993 (A.B.21), ch. 293, §8.)

§21356. Commencement of action to establish invalidity of prohibited transfer

An action to establish the invalidity of any transfer described in Section 21350 can only be commenced within the periods prescribed in this section as follows:

(a) In case of a transfer by will, at any time after letters are first issued to a general representative and before an order for final distribution is made.

(b) In case of any transfer other than by will, within the later of three years after the transfer becomes irrevocable or three years from the date the person bringing the action discovers, or reasonably should have discovered, the facts material to the transfer.

(Stats. 1995 (A.B. 1466), ch. 730, §17.)

CALIFORNIA BUSINESS & PROFESSIONS CODE

§6103.6. Violation of prohibition on donative transfers shall be grounds for discipline

Violation of Section 15687 of the Probate Code [restrictions on compensation for attorneys acting as trustee], or of Part 3.5 (commencing with Section 21350) of Division 11 of the Probate Code [limitations on donative transfers], shall be grounds for discipline, if the attorney knew or should have known of the facts leading to the violation. This section shall only apply to violations that occur on or after January 1, 1994.

(Stats. 1993 (A.B. 21), ch. 293, §1. Amended by Stats. 1995 (A.B. 1466), ch. 730, §1.)

CALIFORNIA RULES OF PROFESSIONAL CONDUCT

Rule 4-400. Gifts From Client

A member shall not induce a client to make a substantial gift, including a testamentary gift, to the member or to the member's parent, child, sibling, or spouse, except where the client is related to the member.

(Adopted November 28, 1988, effective May 27, 1989.)

ABA MODEL RULES

Rule 1.8: Conflict of Interest

. . .

(c) A lawyer shall not solicit any substantial gift from a client, including a testamentary gift, or prepare on behalf of a client an instrument giving the lawyer or a person related to the lawyer any substantial gift unless the lawyer or other recipient of the gift is related to the client. For purposes of this paragraph, related persons include a spouse, child, grandchild, parent, grandparent or other relative or individual with whom the lawyer or the client maintains a close, familial relationship.

. . . .

IV
TESTAMENTARY CAPACITY

This chapter addresses issues of capacity to make a will. These issues include legal and mental capacity, fraud, duress, and undue influence. Such issues are grounds for contest of a will. Will contests are also discussed in Chapter XIV, Section IIID *infra*.

I. Mental Capacity

A person must have legal capacity and mental capacity to execute a will. Most jurisdictions require that a testator be an adult and mentally competent. Statutes in all jurisdictions establish the minimum age to make a will. The majority of jurisdictions require that a testator be at least 18 years of age. Age 18 is also the minimum specified by the Uniform Probate Code (§2-501). Some jurisdictions permit exceptions for persons in military service, married persons, or emancipated minors. See, e.g., Cal. Probate Code §6100 (discussed *infra*). For discussion of the requirements for will execution, see Chapter III, Section IIB *supra*.

The issue of a minor's testamentary capacity arose in Sisco v. Cosgrove, Michelizzi, Schwabacher, Ward & Bianchi, 59 Cal. Rptr. 2d 647 (Ct. App. 1996). The mother of a teenage boy (who died in a car crash at age 16), who had received a settlement in a sexual molestation action, brought a malpractice action against her son's attorneys, alleging that they were negligent in failing to ensure that she would be sole beneficiary of her son's settlement proceeds upon his death, and that such negligence allowed the decedent's estranged father (from whom she had separated due to domestic violence) to inherit half of the proceeds. The appellate court affirmed the superior court's dismissal of the action, reasoning that the decedent could not have designated his mother as beneficiary of his will or of his annuity because a minor cannot make a will under California Probate Code §6100. As such, the minor died intestate, and his estate (including the settlement proceeds) was distributed to his parents equally.

In addition to legal capacity, a testator must have the mental capacity to execute a will. The first case to develop a doctrinal test for testamentary capacity was Pawlet, Marquess of Winchester's Case, 77 Eng. Rep. 287 (K.B. 1601), in which a testator's legitimate son challenged his father's will bequeathing the bulk of his estate to nonmarital children. Eunice L. Ross & Thomas J. Reed, Will Contests §2:6 (2d ed. 2003).

The modern test for testamentary capacity, with its three-pronged requirement, derives from two subsequent English cases. Ross & Reed, *supra*, at §2:6. Greenwood v. Greenwood, 163 Eng. Rep. 930 (K.B. 1790), involved a challenge by the decedent's brother to the validity of title to real estate devised in the decedent's will. The decedent's brother argued that the will was the product of an unsound mind, claiming that the decedent was violent and insane at the time he made the will. Lord Kenyon charged the jury on the law of testamentary capacity, requiring that the testator must understand: (1) what he possessed, and (2) who were the natural objects of his bounty. Later, Harwood v. Baker, 13 Eng. Rep. 117 (P.C. 1840), added the third requirement of the test for testamentary capacity—i.e., the testator must be able to form an intelligent distribution plan. *Harwood* involved a will contest by children of the decedent's first marriage who had been disinherited in favor of the decedent's second wife.

American statutes include the requirement that the testator must be "of sound mind." That term is generally not defined. See, e.g., Cal. Prob. Code §6100 (requiring that the testator be at least 18 years of age and "of sound mind"). However, California provides an exception for an emancipated minor. An emancipated minor is considered an adult for some purposes, including making or revoking a will (Cal. Fam. Code §7050). See Law Revision Commission, Comment to California Probate Code §6100.

The California requirement regarding age and "sound mind" is identical to UPC §2-501, except for a provision added by statutory amendment in California in 1995, authorizing a conservator to make a will for a conservatee. Specifically, a conservator may make a will on behalf of the conservatee who lacks testamentary capacity, provided the conservator first obtains court approval in a "substituted judgment" proceeding pursuant to California Probate Code §2580 (Cal. Prob. Code §2580(b)(13)). A conservatee who is later deemed "mentally competent to make a will" may subsequently amend or revoke the will that was previously executed by the conservator or make a new, inconsistent will (Cal. Prob. Code §6100(b)).

The 1995 statutory amendment changed prior case law. Prior to that amendment, California case law held that a conservator, conservator's attorney, and the probate court had no authority to execute a will on behalf of a conservator. Conservatorship of Romo, 235 Cal. Rptr. 377 (Ct. App. 1987).

Mental competency is determined at the time of execution of the will. Evidence as to mental condition before or after the execution of the will is important only insofar as it sheds light on the testator's mental condition at the time of execution. 14 Witkin, Summary, Wills, *supra*, at §122. The burden of proof is on the party asserting the testator's mental incapacity. Evidence by subscribing witnesses and intimate acquaintances is admissible on the subject of mental capacity. Psychiatric evidence also is admissible. *Id.*

Mental derangement also is a ground for invalidating a will based on lack of capacity. The doctrinal rule for "insane delusion" derives from mid-nineteenth century case law. Ross & Reed, *supra*, at §2:9. In Dew v. Clark, 162 Eng. Rep. 410 (Prerog. 1826), a testator took a violent, unreasonable dislike to his daughter from his first marriage and disinherited her. His third wife subsequently committed him to an insane asylum. *Dew* announced the doctrine that invalidates a will because all or part of it is the product of the testator's insane delusion about a family member. Ross & Reed, *supra*, at §2:7.

The insane delusion doctrine was first adopted by Maryland in 1848 and shortly thereafter by New York and Pennsylvania. *Id.* However, the most frequently cited insane delusion case is American Seaman's Friends Society v. Hopper, 33 N.Y. 619, 1865 WL 4050 (1865), in which the decedent bequeathed his residuary estate to the American Seaman's Friends Society and disinherited his wife and blood relatives, including two nephews. A few years before his death, the decedent began to suspect his wife (then in her sixties) of carrying on an affair with several ministers (who were elderly and beyond reproach). He also believed that his nephews were involved with his wife in a conspiracy to murder him and that one nephew had caused him to fall against a hot stove (the nephew was not present in the house at the time). The appellate court denied probate of the decedent's will. *Hooper* set forth the requirement that the insane delusion must affect the dispositive provisions of the will.

California law on testamentary capacity includes requirements regarding mental capacity and mental derangement. According to California Probate Code §6100.5, a person is not mentally competent to make a will if either:

- the individual does not have sufficient mental capacity to be able to (A) understand the nature of the testamentary act, (B) understand and recollect the nature and situation of his or her property, or (C) remember and understand his or her relations to his or her living descendants, spouse, and parents, and those whose interests are affected by the will; or
- the individual suffers from a mental disorder with symptoms including delusions or hallucinations, which delusions or hallucinations result in the person's devising his or her property in a way which, except for the existence of the delusions or hallucinations, he or she would not have done.

A contestant must satisfy only one of the above tests for mental incapacity in order for a court to invalidate a will. Under the second prong above, if a testator suffers hallucinations or delusions, the will is invalid only if the hallucinations or delusions cause the testator to devise property in a manner that he or she would not have done without the delusions (Cal. Prob. Code §6100.5(a)(2)). Hallucinations or delusions unrelated to the testamentary act do not evidence mental incompetency.

California Probate Code §6100.5 codified the standards for testamentary capacity derived from California case law. The standards were first set forth in Estate of Perkins, 235 P. 45 (Cal. 1925), in which a widow left an estate valued at $57,000. Her will bequeathed sums ranging from $250 to $5000 to various relatives (including her sister and two brothers) and the residue to a young man whom she had known for 2 years while he was in military service. Her sister and one brother challenged the will on the ground of lack of capacity and undue influence. The court held that the contestants failed to prove that the testatrix was of unsound mind at the time of execution. According to the court, the evidence revealed that her hallucinations and delusions (that she and her brother were leaving for Europe or Iowa, that her nightdress was torn when it was not, that she was going to be married, etc.) were temporary, arose in response to pain caused by her illness, and did not influence her testamentary act. The court reasoned that the will reaffirmed the testatrix's previous testamentary plan because she had previously executed a holographic will with the same plan and explained her reasons for naming her residuary beneficiary (because she loved him like a son and he had shown her many kindnesses). The proper test, according to the court, to establish mental derangement is whether the abnormality of mind had a direct influence on the testamentary act.

The issue of a testator's mental capacity, based on a claim that the decedent suffered delusions, arose in several subsequent California cases. In Goodman v. Zimmerman, 32 Cal. Rptr. 2d 419 (Ct. App. 1994), the testator's son filed a petition for revocation of probate. The testator left the son a $2 million bequest, whereas he left his two daughters most of his

$100 million estate. The son argued that the testator suffered from a delusion pertaining to the son and claimed that none of his father's reasons for disinheriting him could withstand reasonable scrutiny. The appellate court denied the petition, holding that the trial court's finding that the testator was not suffering from a delusional disorder was supported by evidence that the son had mistreated his sisters and also held that the testator was not delusional in his criticism of his son's management of the family business.

In In re Estate of Schmidt, 1999 WL 33494419 (unpublished/noncitable) (Cal. Ct. App. 1999), the beneficiaries, executors, and trustees contested the validity of a prior will alleging lack of testamentary capacity. The appellate court affirmed the trial court finding that the testator manifested delusions (at the time the 1991 will was executed) about his second wife's nephew (i.e., that the nephew had stolen $1 million from the decedent's sister's mattress and had taken pictures of the decedent doing lewd acts), and that these delusions were so irrational that they constituted evidence of the testator's lack of testamentary capacity. However, the appellate court remanded on the issue whether the testator's insane delusions caused him to exclude his wife's nephew from inheritance. The appellate court criticized the trial court for failing to find a causal relationship between any particular delusion and the exclusion of the nephew because the record contained many explanations for the decision to exclude the nephew that were unrelated to the testator's irrational beliefs about the nephew.

Schmidt also shed light on the meaning of the term "insane delusion":

> [C]ourts used the term "insane delusion" to describe the type of delusion that can be said to vitiate testamentary capacity. The modern trend, reflected in section 6100.5, is to avoid characterizing individuals who suffer from debilitating delusions and hallucinations as insane. . . . Nevertheless, the same guidelines apply. To constitute a delusion under section 6100.5(a)(2), a false belief must have the following characteristics: Its source must be the mind of the testator. There can be no fact or belief based on fact to support it. And, it must be firmly held in the face of unequivocal evidence to the contrary.

Id. at 15.

California case law has held that the following, alone, do not establish mental incapacity: illiteracy, old age, illness, physical weakness, committing suicide, lapses of memory, inability to transact business, idiosyncrasies and peculiarities of behavior, acute alcoholism, cruelty or unfriendly acts toward family, or prejudices or false beliefs concerning relatives. 14 Witkin, Summary, Wills, *supra*, at §120. A prior adjudication of insanity or incompetency in another proceeding affords only an inference of lack of capacity as of its date and cannot support a finding of incapacity for a will that was executed subsequently. *Id.* at §128.

Some examples of delusions that have resulted in courts' denying probate to a will include: the testator's groundless belief that his wife is unfaithful, his child is illegitimate, his brother is robbing and harassing him, and that his recently employed nurse (named a legatee) is actually a long-term friend. *Id.* at §185. Some cases involve spiritualism, i.e., testators' obeying supposed communications from deceased relatives that induce the testator to make particular testamentary dispositions. *Id.*

For a recent proposal to improve assessments of testamentary capacity, see Pamela Champine, Expertise and Instinct in the Assessment of Testamentary Capacity, 51 Vill. L. Rev. 25(2006) (urging formulation of a new test on testamentary capacity to be administered by psychologists).

CALIFORNIA PROBATE CODE

§810. Legislative findings regarding legal capacity

The Legislature finds and declares the following:

(a) For purposes of this part, there shall exist a rebuttable presumption affecting the burden of proof that all persons have the capacity to make decisions and to be responsible for their acts or decisions.

(b) A person who has a mental or physical disorder may still be capable of contracting, conveying, marrying, making medical decisions, executing wills or trusts, and performing other actions.

(c) A judicial determination that a person is totally without understanding, or is of unsound mind, or suffers from one or more mental deficits so substantial that, under the circumstances, the person should be deemed to lack the legal capacity to perform a specific act, should be based on evidence of a deficit in one or more of the person's mental functions rather than on a diagnosis of a person's mental or physical disorder.

(Stats. 1995 (S.B. 730), ch. 842, §2. Amended by Stats. 1998 (A.B. 2801), ch. 581, §19.)

§811. Evidence to support a determination of unsound mind or incapacity

(a) A determination that a person is of unsound mind or lacks the capacity to make a decision or do a certain act, including, but not limited to, the incapacity to contract, to make a conveyance, to marry, to make medical decisions, to execute wills, or to execute trusts, shall be supported by evidence of a deficit in at least one of the following mental functions, subject to subdivision (b), and evidence of a correlation between the deficit or deficits and the decision or acts in question:

(1) Alertness and attention, including, but not limited to, the following:

(A) Level of arousal or consciousness.

(B) Orientation to time, place, person, and situation.

(C) Ability to attend and concentrate.

(2) Information processing, including, but not limited to, the following:

(A) Short- and long-term memory, including immediate recall.

(B) Ability to understand or communicate with others, either verbally or otherwise.

(C) Recognition of familiar objects and familiar persons.

(D) Ability to understand and appreciate quantities.

(E) Ability to reason using abstract concepts.

(F) Ability to plan, organize, and carry out actions in one's own rational self-interest.

(G) Ability to reason logically.

(3) Thought processes. Deficits in these functions may be demonstrated by the presence of the following:

(A) Severely disorganized thinking.

(B) Hallucinations.

(C) Delusions.

(D) Uncontrollable, repetitive, or intrusive thoughts.

(4) Ability to modulate mood and affect. Deficits in this ability may be demonstrated by the presence of a pervasive and persistent or recurrent state of euphoria, anger, anxiety, fear, panic, depression, hopelessness or despair, helplessness, apathy or indifference, that is inappropriate in degree to the individual's circumstances.

(b) A deficit in the mental functions listed above may be considered only if the deficit, by itself or in combination with one or more other mental function deficits, significantly impairs the person's ability to understand and appreciate the consequences of his or her actions with regard to the type of act or decision in question.

(c) In determining whether a person suffers from a deficit in mental function so substantial that the person lacks the capacity to do a certain act, the court may take into consideration the frequency, severity, and duration of periods of impairment.

(d) The mere diagnosis of a mental or physical disorder shall not be sufficient in and of itself to support a determination that a person is of unsound mind or lacks the capacity to do a certain act.

(e) This part applies only to the evidence that is presented to, and the findings that are made by, a court determining the capacity of a person to do a certain act or make a decision, including, but not limited to, making medical decisions. Nothing in this part shall affect the decisionmaking process set forth in Section 1418.8 of the Health and Safety Code, nor increase or decrease the burdens of documentation on, or potential liability of, health care providers who, outside the judicial context, determine the capacity of patients to make a medical decision.

(Stats. 1996 (S.B. 1650), ch.78, §3. Amended by Stats. 1998 (A.B. 2801), ch. 581, §20.)

§812. Capacity to make a decision: elements

Except where otherwise provided by law, including, but not limited to, Section 813 and the statutory and decisional law of testamentary capacity, a person lacks the capacity to make a decision unless the person has the ability to communicate verbally, or by any other means, the decision, and to understand and appreciate, to the extent relevant, all of the following:

(a) The rights, duties, and responsibilities created by, or affected by the decision.

(b) The probable consequences for the decisionmaker and, where appropriate, the persons affected by the decision.

(c) The significant risks, benefits, and reasonable alternatives involved in the decision.

(Stats. 1996 (S.B. 1650), ch. 178, §5.)

§813. Capacity to give informed consent to medical treatment: elements

(a) For purposes of a judicial determination, a person has the capacity to give informed consent to a proposed medical treatment if the person is able to do all of the following:

(1) Respond knowingly and intelligently to queries about that medical treatment.

(2) Participate in that treatment decision by means of a rational thought process.

(3) Understand all of the following items of minimum basic medical treatment information with respect to that treatment:

(A) The nature and seriousness of the illness, disorder, or defect that the person has.

(B) The nature of the medical treatment that is being recommended by the person's health care providers.

(C) The probable degree and duration of any benefits and risks of any medical intervention that is being recommended by the person's health care providers, and the consequences of lack of treatment.

(D) The nature, risks, and benefits of any reasonable alternatives.

(b) A person who has the capacity to give informed consent to a proposed medical treatment also has the capacity to refuse consent to that treatment.

(Stats. 1995 (S.B. 730), ch. 842, §5. Amended by Stats. 1996 (S.B. 1650), ch. 178. §6.)

§6100. Persons who are eligible to make will

(a) An individual 18 or more years of age who is of sound mind may make a will.

(b) A conservator may make a will for the conservatee if the conservator has been so authorized by a court order pursuant to Section 2580. Nothing in this section shall impair the right of a conservatee who is mentally competent

to make a will from revoking or amending a will made by the conservator or making a new and inconsistent will.
(Stats. 1990 (A.B. 759), ch. 79, §14, effective July 1, 1991. Amended by Stats. 1995 (A.B. 1466), ch. 730, §7.)

§6100.5. Persons who are not mentally competent to make a will

(a) An individual is not mentally competent to make a will if at the time of making the will either of the following is true:

(1) The individual does not have sufficient mental capacity to be able to (A) understand the nature of the testamentary act, (B) understand and recollect the nature and situation of the individual's property, or (C) remember and understand the individual's relations to living descendants, spouse, and parents, and those whose interests are affected by the will.

(2) The individual suffers from a mental disorder with symptoms including delusions or hallucinations, which delusions or hallucinations result in the individual's devising property in a way which, except for the existence of the delusions or hallucinations, the individual would not have done.

(b) Nothing in this section supersedes existing law relating to the admissibility of evidence to prove the existence of mental incompetence or mental disorders.

(c) Notwithstanding subdivision (a), a conservator may make a will on behalf of a conservatee if the conservator has been so authorized by a court order pursuant to Section 2580.
(Stats. 1990 (A.B. 759), ch. 79, §14, effective July 1, 1991. Amended by Stats. 1995 (A.B. 1466), ch. 730, §8.)

§6220. Persons who may execute a statutory will

Any individual of sound mind and over the age of 18 may execute a California statutory will under the provisions of this chapter.
(Stats. 1991 (S.B. 271), ch. 1055, §20.)

§8252. Proponents have burden of proof of due execution; contestants have burden of proof of lack of capacity

(a) At the trial, the proponents of the will have the burden of proof of due execution. The contestants of the will have the burden of proof of lack of testamentary intent or capacity, undue influence, fraud, duress, mistake, or revocation. If the will is opposed by the petition for probate of a later will revoking the former, it shall be determined first whether the later will is entitled to probate.

(b) The court shall try and determine any contested issue of fact that affects the validity of the will.
(Stats. 1990 (A.B. 759), ch. 79, §14, effective July 1, 1991.)

CALIFORNIA EVIDENCE CODE

§870. Witness may state opinion as to sanity

A witness may state his opinion as to the sanity of a person when:

(a) The witness is an intimate acquaintance of the person whose sanity is in question;

(b) The witness was a subscribing witness to a writing, the validity of which is in dispute, signed by the person whose sanity is in question and the opinion relates to the sanity of such person at the time the writing was signed; or

(c) The witness is qualified under Section 800 or 801 to testify in the form of an opinion.
(Stats. 1965, ch. 299, §2, effective January 1, 1967.)

II. Fraud

Fraud is a ground for invalidating a will. "A will is invalid if the testator has been wilfully deceived by the beneficiary as to the character or contents of the instrument, or as to extrinsic facts which are material to the disposition and in fact caused it." Atkinson, *supra*, §56 at 263.

Testamentary fraud takes many forms. Such fraud may consist of fraudulent concealment (by a statement or conduct) of relevant facts, knowingly with the intent to mislead, that prevents the decedent from acquiring knowledge of the truth. Or, the deceiver may fraudulently fail to reveal facts (fraudulent nondisclosure) to the testator, who (had he or she known the true facts) would have made a different disposition. Fraudulent concealment or fraudulent nondisclosure also operates when the wrongdoer has a fiduciary duty to disclose facts to the testator. Ross & Reed, *supra*, at §8:13.

"Scienter" is an essential element to prove fraud. Scienter requires that the deceiver made the misrepresentation either with knowledge of its falsity or with reckless disregard of the truth so as to induce the deceased to perform some testamentary act in reliance on the misrepresentation. *Id.*

Fraud may occur in the execution or inducement of a will. Either form of fraud can invalidate the entire will or only certain provisions. "Fraud in execution generally occurs when deceit is practiced upon decedent as to the character, nature, identity of contents of the document executed." Ross & Reed, *supra*, at §8:10. *Fraud in the execution* involves situations where the decedent is deceived into executing a particular document which he or she believes is another document. Or, pages of a document may be fraudulently substituted. *Id.*

In contrast, *fraud in the inducement* refers to a misrepresentation or concealment of a material fact that induces the decedent to make a will other than that which he or she intended. See, e.g., In re Young, 738 N.Y.S.2d 100 (App. Div. 2001) (holding that there was no admissible evidence to support the claim of the testatrix's son that his sister exerted fraud upon the testatrix to the effect that a disposition to the

mentally disabled son would cause him to lose his Social Security benefits).

In the days before no-fault divorce, fraud cases frequently involved a spouse in a bigamous marriage with the testator. "The causation question then arises whether, had the testator not been deceived as to the bigamous marriage, a bequest would have been made to the deceitful spouse." Ross & Reed, *supra*, at §8:11. See, e.g., Estate of Carson, 194 P. 5 (Cal. 1920) (stating that if the bequest to the bigamous husband were the direct fruit of his fraud, such bequest is void, and concluding that it was not an unreasonable inference, from the fact that the wife had been so recently married when the will was made, that she left the bulk of her estate to her husband because she believed he was her lawful husband, and would not have done so if she had believed otherwise). Misrepresentations also may relate to the alleged death of a beneficiary or to facts about a beneficiary that would lead to an estrangement. If proven, the ensuing will may be invalidated.

In an interesting will contest case, Estate of Supple, 55 Cal. Rptr. 542 (Ct. App. 1966), the contestant argued that the charitable beneficiaries named in the will (the Catholic Church and its agencies) had influenced the making of the will by teaching the testator certain religious beliefs which were in fact untrue and which they had no reason to believe were true, and that the testator executed his will in reliance upon such representations. The contestant alleged that:

> all of the above representations were in fact false and untrue, constituting childish superstitions incompatible with man's advanced position in science and technology, and that the charitable beneficiaries who made these representations were guilty of unduly influencing the testator and were also guilty of fraud because they had made positive assertions which, although they believed them to be true, were not warranted by the information which they had and because they had breached a duty which, without an actually fraudulent intent, gained them an advantage by misleading the testator to his prejudice and the prejudice of his heirs at law.

Id. at 544. The appellate court concluded that the claim did not state a cause of action which was susceptible of proof within the limits of the First Amendment.

Note that courts are more willing to admit extrinsic evidence in the proof of fraud than in the case of mistake. Ross & Reed, *supra*, at §8:14.

According to California law, the execution or revocation of a will (or part of a will) is ineffective if the act was procured by duress, menace, fraud, or undue influence (Cal. Prob. Code §6104). In California, the law governing fraud in the contract context also applies to wills. 64 Cal. Jur.3d, *supra*, at §167. The California Civil Code recognizes two types of fraud: actual fraud and constructive fraud (Cal. Civ. Code §§1572–1573). Actual fraud consists of acts or conduct by a party to a contract that are performed with the intent to deceive the other party. In contrast, constructive fraud comprises all acts, omissions, and concealments involving a breach of legal or equitable duty, trust, or confidence, and resulting in damage to another. In re Arbuckle's Estate, 220 P.2d 950 (Cal. Ct. App. 1950) (holding that the contestant was able to establish a prima facie case that he was an interested person entitled to contest a will by showing that testator's trusted agent accepted custody of decedent's prior will and codicil, and then destroyed will "fraudulently" within meaning of statute, without the testator's knowledge or consent).

If only one beneficiary is involved in the purported fraud, then only the testamentary provisions involving that beneficiary will be invalidated. Estate of Carson, 194 P. 5, 8 (Cal. 1920) ("[O]nly the portions of the will in favor of [the alleged wrongdoer] whose probate should be revoked in case the contestants should succeed, the remaining portions continuing as a valid expression of the testatrix's testamentary intention").

Several remedies exist for fraudulently procured actions or inactions by testators (i.e., fraudulent procured revocation of a will, wrongful prevention of revocation, or fraudulent procurement of a new will). A tort remedy (termed "wrongful interference with the expectation of a bequest") may exist for fraudulent prevention of the execution of a will or codicil. The elements of the tort require plaintiff to prove: (1) the existence of the expectancy; (2) the defendants' intentional interference with that expectancy; (3) the interference involved tortious conduct such as fraud, duress, or undue influence; and (4) there is a reasonable certainty that the devise to plaintiff would have been received but for defendant's interference. Ross & Reed, *supra*, at §8:8 (citing case law).

In cases of fraudulent revocation of a testator's will, the will may be probated as a lost will. If execution or revocation of a will is prevented by fraud, the disappointed legatee may be the beneficiary of a constructive trust even though the will cannot be probated. If fraud induced a revocation and new will, similarly, courts might probate the former will and impose a constructive trust or reform the substituted legacy. *Id.*

The new Restatement of Restitution provides for a restitutionary claim against a wrongdoer or a third person on behalf of an intended donee regarding wrongfully diverted donative transfers. Section 46 sets forth the claim for "wrongful interference with donative transfer" that is applicable if assets that would have passed by donative transfer are diverted as a result of fraud, duress, undue influence, or "other wrongful interference." The recipient is liable for the extent of unjust enrichment. The rule applies to any type of donative transfer, including inter vivos gift, gift by survivorship, by will or inheritance, trust, insurance proceeds, retirement funds, or "similar assets." Restatement (Third) of Restitution and Unjust Enrichment (Tent. Draft No. 5, March 12, 2007), §46 (1), (2).

In jurisdictions that recognize the tort of wrongful interference with an expectation of a bequest, the claimant may have a choice between an action for damages and an action for restitution. As the commentary to the Restatement explains:

> The choice [in many cases] may make no practical difference. Yet the liabilities in tort and restitution are not coextensive. Whereas an action for tort damages will not be available against the innocent beneficiary of a third party's wrongful interference, the rule of §46 (like the law of restitution generally) allows a claim in unjust enrichment against innocent donees.... In other circumstances, an action in restitution may offer decisive advantages through the availability of specific relief (typically constructive trust) or the applicable period of limitations.

Id. at §46 cmt.

A recent United States Supreme Court decision addressed the issue of tortious interference with an expectation of an inheritance. In Marshall v. Marshall, 126 S.Ct. 1735 (2006), a widow (Anna Nicole Smith) brought a proceeding in her Chapter 11 bankruptcy case to recover for her stepson's alleged tortious interference with her expectation of inheritance from her deceased husband (Howard Marshall) who died without providing for her in his will. Finding that it had jurisdiction over Smith's claim, the bankruptcy court entered a judgment in her favor and awarded her $449 million in compensatory damages and $25 million in punitive damages.

Marshall's son filed a posttrial motion to dismiss for lack of subject-matter jurisdiction, asserting that Smith's claim for tortious interference was beyond the bankruptcy court's jurisdiction pursuant to the "probate exception" to federal court diversity jurisdiction, and therefore could only be tried in the Texas state probate court proceedings. The Ninth Circuit Court of Appeal agreed, finding that the probate exception applied to bar federal jurisdiction with respect to Smith's claim.

The United States Supreme Court reversed, holding that the probate exception did not apply to deprive the bankruptcy court of jurisdiction over Smith's claim. The Court reasoned that Smith's claim did not involve the administration of the probate estate, the probate of a will, or any other "purely" probate matter. In construing the probate exception narrowly, the Court ruled that (assuming diversity exists), federal district courts instead of the state probate court have jurisdiction over such a claim. At the same time, the Court rejected prior rulings of the Texas probate court that Marshall's will was valid and that the state probate court had exclusive jurisdiction over all of the widow's claims.

At one time California recognized the tort of wrongful interference with an expected inheritance. In re Estate of Legeas, 258 Cal. Rptr. 858 (Cal. Ct. App. 1989). However, the California Supreme Court denied review, denied a rehearing, and ordered the opinion depublished.

In California, witnesses to a will are required to allege that, to their knowledge, the decedent executed the will free from "duress, menace, fraud or undue influence" (Cal. Prob. Code §6104).

For discussion of the requirements pertaining to will execution, see Chapter III *supra*.

CALIFORNIA CIVIL CODE

§1572. "Actual fraud," defined

ACTUAL FRAUD, WHAT. Actual fraud, within the meaning of this Chapter, consists in any of the following acts, committed by a party to the contract, or with his connivance, with intent to deceive another party thereto, or to induce him to enter into the contract:

1. The suggestion, as a fact, of that which is not true, by one who does not believe it to be true;
2. The positive assertion, in a manner not warranted by the information of the person making it, of that which is not true, though he believes it to be true;
3. The suppression of that which is true, by one having knowledge or belief of the fact;
4. A promise made without any intention of performing it; or,
5. Any other act fitted to deceive.

(Enacted 1872.)

§1573. "Constructive fraud," defined

CONSTRUCTIVE FRAUD. Constructive fraud consists:

1. In any breach of duty which, without an actually fraudulent intent, gains an advantage to the person in fault, or

any one claiming under him, by misleading another to his prejudice, or to the prejudice of any one claiming under him; or,

2. In any such act or omission as the law specially declares to be fraudulent, without respect to actual fraud.

(Enacted 1872.)

CALIFORNIA PROBATE CODE

§6104. Effect of duress, menace, fraud, or undue influence

The execution or revocation of a will or a part of a will is ineffective to the extent the execution or revocation was procured by duress, menace, fraud, or undue influence.

(Stats. 1990 (A.B. 759), ch. 79, §14, effective July 1, 1991.)

III. Duress

Duress is also a ground to invalidate a will. Duress typically includes violence or threats of violence which thereby induce the testator to make a will in favor of the wrongdoer or a third party. Originally, duress signified threats involving life or limb, unjust civil imprisonment, criminal prosecution, imprisonment of decedent or a close relative, or wrongful seizure or damage to decedent's property. Subsequently, duress was broadened to include economic duress or business compulsion. Ross & Reed, *supra*, at §8:15.

Evidence establishing duress must be clear and convincing. In addition, causation must be proved—i.e., that the decedent's action or inaction would not have been undertaken but for the coercion. *Id.* at §8:17.

> The issue in duress is not whether a brave or firm decedent would have resisted the compulsion or been in fear from the threats, but whether the particular deceased undertook the testamentary action or inaction through compulsion or such fear as to preclude the exercise of free will and judgment.

***Id.* at §8:15.**

Duress requires an "unlawful" threat. For example, in Rubenstein v. Sela, 672 P.2d 491 (Ariz. Ct. App. 1983), the court refused to permit a wife to invalidate a deed on the ground of duress because the husband's threat to leave her if she did not was not an unlawful act. McGovern & Kurtz, *supra*, §7.3 at 284.

Courts sometimes blur the lines between duress and undue influence. The former refers to a physical compulsion or threat-induced fear; the latter refers to unfair persuasion. Ross & Reed, *supra*, at §8:16.

Duress in the will context sometimes involves situations in which the decedent is prevented from executing a will, changing a will, or revoking a will. See, e.g., Blakeley v. Blakeley, 298 F.2d 635 (7th Cir. 1962); Pope v. Garrett, 211 S.W.2d 559 (Tex. 1948). Duress also encompasses the wrongdoer's actions aimed at procuring the decedent's total or partial intestacy.

Restitutionary principles dictate the remedy for duress. The Restatement of Restitution specifies the remedy depending on the nature of the wrong. Ross & Reed, *supra*, at §8:14 (citing Restatement of Restitution §184, cmts. g, h). For example, if the wrongdoer's duress prevents execution of a will, the probate court cannot admit the will to probate. However, a court (probate court or equity court, depending on which court has jurisdiction) might impress a constructive trust against all the heirs in favor of the intended legatee(s). If the wrongdoer uses duress to induce a revocation of a will and substitution of a new will, the new will might be denied probate or a constructive trust imposed in favor of legatees under the prior will. If the wrongdoer uses duress to prevent the revocation of a will and execution of a new will, the will may be probated with the imposition of a construction trust in favor of the disappointed legatees.

Duress cases arise infrequently. For example, in Wells v. Estate of Wells, 922 S.W.2d 715 (Ark. 1996), the state supreme court denied probate to a will that was offered for probate by decedent's stepson. Evidence revealed that the stepson isolated the decedent from her relatives when she was hospitalized for a heart attack (shortly before the will was executed), that the decedent telephoned her attorney claiming that her stepson had made her a prisoner, that he made her sign a bunch of papers, and that she did not know what she had signed. A neighbor and niece testified that the stepson and his wife mistreated the decedent, and she feared him. The court found that the evidence supported a finding of duress and undue influence by the stepson.

Recall that California law precludes persons from exercising their inheritance rights if they physically abuse or neglect an elder or dependent adult. In such cases, the abuser is considered to have predeceased the decedent in the determination of shares of the estate (Cal. Prob. Code §259). Abuse is broadly defined to include physical abuse and neglect, false imprisonment, and fiduciary abuse.

CALIFORNIA PROBATE CODE

§259. Disqualification by persons liable for elder abuse or abuse of dependent adult

(a) Any person shall be deemed to have predeceased a decedent to the extent provided in subdivision (c) where all of the following apply:

(1) It has been proven by clear and convincing evidence that the person is liable for physical abuse, neglect, or fiduciary abuse of the decedent, who was an elder or dependent adult.

(2) The person is found to have acted in bad faith.

(3) The person has been found to have been reckless, oppressive, fraudulent, or malicious in the commission of any of these acts upon the decedent.

(4) The decedent, at the time those acts occurred and thereafter until the time of his or her death, has been found to have been substantially unable to manage his or her financial resources or to resist fraud or undue influence.

(b) Any person shall be deemed to have predeceased a decedent to the extent provided in subdivision (c) if that person has been convicted of a violation of Section 236 of the Penal Code or any offense described in Section 368 of the Penal Code.

(c) Any person found liable under subdivision (a) or convicted under subdivision (b) shall not

(1) receive any property, damages, or costs that are awarded to the decedent's estate in an action described in subdivision (a) or (b), whether that person's entitlement is under a will, a trust, or the laws of intestacy; or

(2) serve as a fiduciary as defined in Section 39, if the instrument nominating or appointing that person was executed during the period when the decedent was substantially unable to manage his or her financial resources or resist fraud or undue influence. This section shall not apply to a decedent who, at any time following the act or acts described in paragraph (1) of subdivision (a), or the act or acts described in subdivision (b), was substantially able to manage his or her financial resources and to resist fraud or undue influence within the meaning of subdivision (b) of Section 1801 of the Probate Code and subdivision (b) of Section 39 of the Civil Code.

(d) For purposes of this section, the following definitions shall apply:

(1) Physical abuse as defined in Section 15610.63 of the Welfare and Institutions Code.

(2) Neglect as defined in Section 15610.57 of the Welfare and Institutions Code.

(3) False imprisonment as defined in Section 368 of the Penal Code.

(4) Fiduciary abuse as defined in Section 15610.30 of the Welfare and Institutions Code.

(e) Nothing in this section shall be construed to prohibit the severance and transfer of an action or proceeding to a separate civil action pursuant to Section 801.

(Stats. 1998, ch. 935, §4 (S.B. 1715).)

§6104. Effect of duress, menace, fraud, or undue influence

The execution or revocation of a will or a part of a will is ineffective to the extent the execution or revocation was procured by duress, menace, fraud, or undue influence.

(Stats. 1990 (A.B. 759), ch. 79, §14, effective July 1, 1991.)

IV. Undue Influence

Undue influence, in conjunction with lack of mental capacity, is the most frequent ground for invalidating a will. Ray D. Madoff, Unmasking Undue Influence, 81 Minn. L. Rev. 571, 574 (1997). The wills of many famous people (e.g., Doris Duke, Georgia O'Keeffe, J. Seward Johnson, and Pearl S. Buck) have been challenged based on undue influence. *Id.* at 573.

Undue influence doctrine is similar to, and yet different from, the doctrines of fraud and duress. Like the doctrines of fraud and duress, the undue influence doctrine attempts to protect testators' rights to dispose freely of their property. *Id.* at 576. However, the doctrines reveal several inherent differences.

> The doctrine of fraud prevents a will from being given effect when the will is brought about through lies told to the testator. The doctrine of duress prevents a will from being given effect when the will is brought about through threats of harm to the testator. The undue influence doctrine is broader than each of these in that it invalidates a will when it is the result of any action that subverts the will of the testator and replaces the will of the testator with that of the one influencing.

***Id.* at 579-580.**

Another difference between the doctrine of undue influence and mental capacity is that mental incapacity generally invalidates the entire will. However, a finding of undue influence may invalidate only that portion of the will that was unduly influenced. See 64 Cal. Jur.3d, *supra*, at 176 (citing In re Estate of Everts 125 P. 1058 (Cal. 1912)). See also Cal. Prob. Code §6104.

The law of undue influence dates to an eighteenth-century English case. Ross & Reed, *supra*, at §2:8. In Mountain v. Bennet, 29 Eng. Rep. 1200 (Ex. 1787), the testator devised real property to his wife, whom he had secretly married shortly before executing his will. His heirs objected to admission of the will to probate on the ground that the wife unduly influenced the decedent to make a will in her favor. Based in part on the widow's letter to her subsequent husband in which she gloated about the control she yielded over the decedent, the jury denied probate.

The law of undue influence continued to develop in a subsequent will contest case, Kinleside v. Harrison, 161 Eng. Rep. 1196 (Prerog. 1818), which announced the doctrine that a confidential relationship between the testator and a person who benefits from the will raises a presumption of undue influence. Ross & Reed, *supra*, at §2:8. Finally, in 1828, the Prerogative Court decided Williams v. Goude,

162 Eng. Rep. 682 (Prerog. 1828), which announced the modern test for undue influence. In *Williams*, the testator's will preferred his wife's nephews over his only heirs, two nephews. Testator's nephews argued that the widow had urged him to favor her nephews. In upholding the testator's will, the court explained:

> The influence to vitiate an act must amount to force and coercion destroying free—it must not be the influence of affection and attachment—it must not be the mere desire of gratifying the wishes of another. . . . there must be proof that the act was obtained by this coercion—by importunity which could not be resisted. . . .

Id. at 684. These cases formed the basis for American legal doctrine on undue influence. Ross & Reed, *supra*, at §2:8.

The first noteworthy American case on undue influence involved the will of a South Carolina planter who disinherited his relatives in favor of his mistress (a slave) and their nonmarital son. O'Neall ads. Farr, 30 S.C.L. 80, 1 Rich. 80 (S.C. 1844) (discussed in Ross & Reed, *supra*, at §2:10). The South Carolina Supreme Court reversed a jury verdict in favor of the relatives, and stated the law on undue influence which was similar to that of Williams v. Goude, *supra*.

By the 1860s, American law of undue influence required that any person who gained a benefit from the will of another by importuning or manipulating a confidential relationship could lose the testamentary gift, particularly if the beneficiary was not the natural object of the testator's bounty. Ross & Reed, *supra*, at §2:10. Early American cases attempted to determine the influence that was "undue" and tended to define such influence by its absence (i.e., as not mere advice or persuasion). However, most courts viewed manipulation in a confidential relationship as "extremely suspicious" conduct leading to findings of undue influence. On the other hand, courts were reluctant to find that importuning by spouses, children, or other close relatives was abuse of a confidential relationship leading to a finding of undue influence. *Id.*

Undue influence may be proven by one of two methods:

- a showing of (1) susceptibility to undue influence, (2) opportunity to exert such influence, (3) a disposition to influence unduly to procure an improper favor, and (4) an unnatural result that is the effect of the supposed influence; or
- a showing of a confidential relationship and suspicious circumstances.

Courts frequently wrestle with what makes a disposition "natural." "[W]hat one frequently finds in the case law is a surprisingly straightforward and objective response to the question of what constitutes a 'natural' disposition: a 'natural' disposition is one which provides for a testator's heirs at law." Madoff, *supra*, at 590.

The presence of a confidential relationship plus "suspicious circumstances" gives rise to a presumption of undue influence. McGovern & Kurtz, *supra*, §7.3 at 306-308. The Restatement (Third) of Property (Wills and Other Donative Transfers) §8.3, cmt. g, also uses the term "suspicious circumstances" as an element raising the presumption. The Restatement mentions participation in procurement as one of several suspicious circumstances.

The classic confidential relationships are doctor-patient, pastor-parishioner, guardian-ward, priest-penitent, nurse-companion, and attorney-client. A relationship between family members is not necessarily a confidential relationship. "[T]he undue influence doctrine only categorizes family relationships as 'confidential' in very limited circumstances." Madoff, *supra*, at 584. Rather, a confidential relationship refers to a relationship in which one party dominates the other or in which one party depends on the other, such as for business decisionmaking. A confidential relationship "is generally defined as a relationship of trust and reliance whereby the testator reasonably believed that the confidant was acting in the testator's best interest." *Id.* at 583.

According to California law, the execution or revocation of a will is ineffective to the extent it is procured by undue influence (Cal. Prob. Code §6104). The contestant must prove that the undue influence destroyed the testator's free agency. 64 Cal. Jur.3d §173 (citing Estate of Welch, 272 P.2d 512 (Cal. 1954); Estate of Niquette, 71 Cal. Rptr. 83 (Ct. App. 1968)). Undue influence is present where a testator makes a disposition that differs from, or is contrary to, the one the testator would have made had he or she exercised free will. 64 Cal. Jur.3d §174 (citing In re Estate of Greuner 87 P.2d 872 (Ct. App. 1939); Estate of Hettermann, 119 P.2d 788 (Cal. Ct. App. 1941)).

Indications of undue influence include: (1) dispositions in the will inconsistent with the testator's expressed intentions, (2) unnatural provisions present in the will, (3) a relationship between a chief beneficiary and the testator such that the beneficiary had an opportunity to control the testamentary act, (4) weakness in the testator's mental and physical condition, (5) a beneficiary's undue profit, (6) a beneficiary's active role in the testamentary act, and (7) a confidential relationship between a testator and chief beneficiary. 64 Cal. Jur. 3d §180.

Recall that undue influence plays a role in the determination of an "interested witness." An interested witness may still take under the will if the witness satisfies the burden of proving that the devise was not procured by duress, menace, fraud, or undue influence. The presumption applies only to the devise of the interested witness. Also, the presumption does not apply unless the witness is essential. That is, if there are two other witnesses to the will who are disinterested witnesses, the presumption does not apply. On the requirements for will execution, see also Chapter III *supra*.

Undue influence may also lead to invalidation of inter vivos transfers. See McGovern & Kurtz, *supra*, §7.3 at 302-303. See generally Madoff, *supra* (providing critique of traditional undue influence doctrine).

CALIFORNIA PROBATE CODE

§6104. Effect of duress, menace, fraud, or undue influence

The execution or revocation of a will or a part of a will is ineffective to the extent the execution or revocation was procured by duress, menace, fraud, or undue influence.

(Stats. 1990 (A.B. 759), ch. 79, §14, effective July 1, 1991.)

§6112. Witnesses: presumption that devise to interested witness was procured by duress, menace, fraud or undue influence

(a) Any person generally competent to be a witness may act as a witness to a will.

(b) A will or any provision thereof is not invalid because the will is signed by an interested witness.

(c) Unless there are at least two other subscribing witnesses to the will who are disinterested witnesses, the fact that the will makes a devise to a subscribing witness creates a presumption that the witness procured the devise by duress, menace, fraud, or undue influence. This presumption is a presumption affecting the burden of proof. This presumption does not apply where the witness is a person to whom the devise is made solely in a fiduciary capacity.

(d) If a devise made by the will to an interested witness fails because the presumption established by subdivision (c) applies to the devise and the witness fails to rebut the presumption, the interested witness shall take such proportion of the devise made to the witness in the will as does not exceed the share of the estate which would be distributed to the witness if the will were not established. Nothing in this subdivision affects the law that applies where it is established that the witness procured a devise by duress, menace, fraud, or undue influence.

(Stats. 1990 (A.B. 759), ch. 79, §14, effective July 1, 1991.)

V. Right to Jury Trial in Will Contests

At common law, the right to demand a trial by jury in probate proceedings did not exist. 24 Cal. Jur.3d Decedents' Estates §227. Because probate matters were subject to ecclesiastic jurisdiction, a jury trial was not granted as a matter of right. *Id.* (citing In re Estate of Dolbeer, 96 P. 266 (Cal. 1908)). Nor is the right to a jury trial in probate proceedings constitutionally required. According to Estate of Escover, 292 P. 167 (Cal. 1930), the provision of the California constitution (Art. I, §7) guaranteeing the right to trial by jury does not apply to probate. See also Estate of Gardner, 2 Cal. Rptr. 2d 664 (Ct. App. 1991) (holding that the right to a jury trial in probate proceedings is statutory and not constitutional and therefore, unless a statute specifically provides for a jury trial, the contestants have no such right).

Prior to 1988, jury trials were permitted in California in will contest actions, when requested by the contestants, according to statutory authority pursuant to California Probate Code §371. That provision was repealed in 1988 (Stats. 1988, ch. 1199, §42) and replaced by California Probate Code §8252 (Stats. 1988, ch. 1199, §81.5) that eliminated the right to a jury trial in will contests. According to Law Revision Commission Commentary to Probate Code §8252,

> Under former law, there was a high percentage of reversals on appeal of jury verdicts, with the net result that the whole jury and appeal process served mainly to postpone enjoyment of the estate, enabling contestants as a practical matter to force compromise settlements to which they would not otherwise be entitled.

Currently, the California Probate Code authorizes a jury trial only where that right is expressly granted by a particular statute. That is, pursuant to California Probate Code §825, added in 1999, there is no right to a jury trial in proceedings under the Probate Code unless "expressly provided" in the Code. In addition, according to California Probate Code §8252(b), the court shall determine any contested issue of fact that affects the validity of a will. The right to a jury trial in probate proceedings also is limited by general rules of practice (Cal. Prob. Code §1000).

CALIFORNIA PROBATE CODE

§825. Right to jury trial

Except as expressly otherwise provided in this code, there is no right to a jury trial in proceedings under this code.

(Stats. 1999 (A.B. 239), ch. 175, §1.)

§1000. Civil action rules generally applicable in probate

Except to the extent that this code provides applicable rules, the rules of practice applicable to civil actions, including discovery proceedings and proceedings under Title 3a (commencing with Section 391) of Part 2 of the Code of Civil Procedure, apply to, and constitute the rules of practice in, proceedings under this code. All issues of fact joined in probate proceedings shall be tried in conformity with the rules of practice in civil actions.

(Stats. 1990 (A.B.759), ch. 79, §14, effective July 1, 1991. Amended by Stats. 1994 (A.B. 3686), ch. 806, §5; Stats. 1997 (A.B. 1172), ch. 724, §4; Stats. 2002 (A.B. 1938), ch. 1118, §5.)

§8252. Court shall try contested issues of fact affecting will's validity

(a) At the trial, the proponents of the will have the burden of proof of due execution. The contestants of the will have the burden of proof of lack of testamentary intent or capacity, undue influence, fraud, duress, mistake, or revocation. If the will is opposed by the petition for probate of a later will revoking the former, it shall be determined first whether the later will is entitled to probate.

(b) The court shall try and determine any contested issue of fact that affects the validity of the will.

(Stats. 1990 (A.B. 759), ch. 79, §14, effective July 1, 1991.)

V

WILL DOCTRINES, EXTRINSIC EVIDENCE, AND MISTAKE

I. Introduction

Will provisions must be interpreted and construed before the terms can be put into effect. The primary concern in interpreting a will is the determination of the testator's intent. Discovery of the testator's intention is the "basic rule" of interpretation of donative instruments. 14 Witkin, Summary, Wills, *supra*, at §184.

Because of the difficulty of discovering the unexpressed intent of the testator, courts tend to emphasize the importance of reliance on the language used by the testator in the will. Thus, for example, California Probate Code §21101(a) provides: "The intention of the transferor *as expressed in the instrument* controls the legal effect of the dispositions made in the instrument" (emphasis added).

If the language in the will is not conclusive, courts may resort to an examination of the surrounding circumstances and extrinsic evidence. However, if these efforts in turn are not successful, then courts conclude the process of interpretation of the instrument and employ instead various legal presumptions or rules of construction. 14 Witkin, Summary, Wills, *supra*, at §184. Thus, for example, California Probate Code §21101(b) provides: "The rules of construction expressed in this part apply where the intention of the transferor is not indicated by the instrument." See generally William M. McGovern, Facts and Rules in the Construction of Wills, 26 UCLA L. Rev. 285 (1978).

The construction rule in the original version of the UPC (§2-603) emphasized that the court must rely on "the intention of the testator as expressed in his will." However, a subsequent revision in 1990 broadened this provision by providing that courts were no longer limited to reliance on the words of the testator's will if evidence of a "contrary intention" exists (UPC §2-601). (An important issue in the determination of the testator's intent is the admission of extrinsic evidence. For discussion of this topic, see Section III *infra*.)

In sum, *interpretation* is the process of determining the testator's intent, usually by reliance on the language of the will and/or extrinsic evidence. When a court's attempt at interpretation fails (i.e., when the testator's intent cannot be determined), courts may resort to *construction*. Construction is the process of assigning a meaning to a testamentary provision when the testator's intent cannot be ascertained.

Some common rules of construction include: every expression in a will should be given effect if possible (Cal. Prob. Code §21120), preference should be given to an interpretation of a will that will avoid intestacy (*id.*), and all parts of an instrument should be construed as a whole (Cal. Prob. Code §21121).

Another common rule of construction is that words of a will are to be given their ordinary meaning unless a different intention can be ascertained (Cal. Prob. Code §21122). Thus, for example, in Estate of Verdisson, 6 Cal. Rptr. 2d 363 (Ct. App. 1992), the court held that the word "properties" as used by a testatrix of French descent meant both her real and personal property, and the word "money" included cash derived from a returned life insurance premium (occasioned by the testatrix's suicide under the policy) but did not include her interest in a mutual fund.

On the rules of construction applicable to survival (the lapse doctrine) and class gifts, see Chapter XV, Sections A and B, respectively.

The California statutory provisions governing the construction of wills (Cal. Prob. Code §§6140 et seq.) were repealed in 1994. However, the legislature enacted similar provisions (Cal. Prob. Code §§21102 et seq. *infra*) that applied more broadly—not only to wills, but also to trusts, deeds, and other instruments recognized by the Probate Code.

CALIFORNIA PROBATE CODE

§21102. Intention of testator is controlling

(a) The intention of the transferor as expressed in the instrument controls the legal effect of the dispositions made in the instrument.

(b) The rules of construction in this part apply where the intention of the transferor is not indicated by the instrument.

(c) Nothing in this section limits the use of extrinsic evidence, to the extent otherwise authorized by law, to determine the intention of the transferor.

(Stats. 1994 (A.B. 3686), ch. 806, §41. Amended by Stats. 2002 (A.B. 1784), ch. 138, §11, effective January 1, 2003.)

§21103. Meaning and legal effect of a testamentary disposition: choice of law

The meaning and legal effect of a disposition in an instrument is determined by the local law of a particular state selected by the transferor in the instrument unless the application of that law is contrary to the rights of the surviving spouse to community and quasi- community property, to any other public policy of this state applicable to the disposition, or, in the case of a will, to Part 3 (commencing with Section 6500) of Division 6.

(Stats. 1994 (A.B. 3686), ch. 806, §41. Amended by Stats. 2002 (A.B. 1784), ch. 138, §12, effective January 1, 2003.)

§21104. "At Death Transfer" defined

As used in this part, "at-death transfer" means a transfer that is revocable during the lifetime of the transferor, but does not include a joint tenancy or joint account with right of survivorship.

(Stats. 1994 (A.B. 3686), ch. 806, §41. Amended by Stats. 2002 (A.B. 1784), ch. 138, §13, effective January 1, 2003.)

§21105. Will passes all property, including after-acquired property

Except as otherwise provided in Sections 641 and 642, a will passes all property the testator owns at death, including property acquired after execution of the will.

(Stats. 1994 (A.B. 3686), ch. 806, §41. Amended by Stats. 2002 (A.B. 1784), ch. 138, §14, effective January 1, 2003.)

§21106. Transfer to more than one person vests property in owners in common [repealed]

A transfer of property to more than one person vests the property in them as owners in common.

(Stats. 1994 (A.B. 3686), ch. 806, §41. Repealed as incomplete and unnecessary by Stats. 2002 (A.B. 1784), ch. 138, §15, effective January 1, 2003.)

§21107. Effect of a testamentary direction to convert real property to money

If an instrument directs the conversion of real property into money at the transferor's death, the real property and its proceeds shall be deemed personal property from the time of the transferor's death.

(Stats. 1994 (A.B. 3686), ch. 806, §41. Amended by Stats. 2002 (A.B. 1784), ch. 138, §16, effective January 1, 2003.)

§21108. Abolition of doctrine of worthier title

The law of this state does not include (a) the common law rule of worthier title that a transferor cannot devise an interest to his or her own heirs or (b) a presumption or rule of interpretation that a transferor does not intend, by a transfer to his or her own heirs or next of kin, to transfer an interest to them. The meaning of a transfer of a legal or equitable interest to a transferor's own heirs or next of kin, however designated, shall be determined by the general rules applicable to the interpretation of instruments.

(Stats. 1994 (A.B. 3686), ch. 806, §41. Amended by Stats. 2002 (A.B. 1784), ch. 138, §17, effective January 1, 2003.)

§21109. Transferee who fails to survive does not take (construction of "survival")

(a) A transferee who fails to survive the transferor of an at-death transfer or until any future time required by the instrument does not take under the instrument.

(b) If it cannot be determined by clear and convincing evidence that the transferee survived until a future time required by the instrument, it is deemed that the transferee did not survive until the required future time.

(Stats. 1994 (A.B. 3686), ch. 806, §41. Amended by Stats. 2002 (A.B. 1784), ch. 138, §18, effective January 1, 2003.)

§21110. Antilapse statute substitutes issue for transferee

(a) Subject to subdivision (b), if a transferee is dead when the instrument is executed, or fails or is treated as failing to survive the transferor or until a future time required by the instrument, the issue of the deceased transferee take in the transferee's place in the manner provided in Section 240. A transferee under a class gift shall be a transferee for the purpose of this subdivision unless the transferee's death occurred before the execution of the instrument and that fact was known to the transferor when the instrument was executed.

(b) The issue of a deceased transferee do not take in the transferee's place if the instrument expresses a contrary intention or a substitute disposition. A requirement that the initial transferee survive the transferor or survive for a specified period of time after the death of the transferor constitutes a contrary intention. A requirement that the initial transferee survive until a future time that is related to the probate of the transferor's will or administration of the estate of the transferor constitutes a contrary intention.

(c) As used in this section, "transferee" means a person who is kindred of the transferor or kindred of a surviving, deceased, or former spouse of the transferor.

(Stats. 1994 (A.B. 3686), ch. 806, §41. Amended by Stats. 2002 (A.B. 1784), ch. 138, §19, effective January 1, 2003.)

§21111. Effect of failed transfer

(a) Except as provided in subdivision (b) and subject to Section 21110, if a transfer fails for any reason, the property is transferred as follows:

(1) If the transferring instrument provides for an alternative disposition in the event the transfer fails, the property is transferred according to the terms of the instrument.

(2) If the transferring instrument does not provide for an alternative disposition but does provide for the transfer of a residue, the property becomes a part of the residue transferred under the instrument.

(3) If the transferring instrument does not provide for an alternative disposition and does not provide for the transfer of a residue, or if the transfer is itself a residuary gift, the property is transferred to the decedent's estate.

(b) Subject to Section 21110, if a residuary gift or a future interest is transferred to two or more persons and the share of a transferee fails for any reason, and no alternative disposition is provided, the share passes to the other transferees in proportion to their other interest in the residuary gift or the future interest.

(c) A transfer of "all my estate" or words of similar import is a residuary gift for purposes of this section.

(d) If failure of a future interest results in an intestacy, the property passes to the heirs of the transferor determined pursuant to Section 21114.

(Stats. 1994 (A.B. 3686), ch. 806, §41. Amended Stats. 1996 (S.B. 392), ch. 563, §32; Stats. 2001 (A.B. 873), ch. 417, §11. Amended by Stats. 2002 (A.B. 1784), ch. 138, §20, effective January 1, 2003.)

§21112. Construction of "issue" involving condition in a transfer of interest

A condition in a transfer of a present or future interest that refers to a person's death "with" or "without" issue, or to a person's "having" or "leaving" issue or no issue, or a condition based on words of similar import, is construed to refer to that person's being dead at the time the transfer takes effect in enjoyment and to that person either having or not having, as the case may be, issue who are alive at the time of enjoyment.

(Stats. 1994 (A.B. 3686), ch. 806, §41. Amended by Stats. 2002 (A.B. 1784), ch. 138, §21, effective January 1, 2003.)

§21113. Construction of "transfer of an interest to a class" [repealed]

(a) A transfer of a present interest to a class includes all persons answering the class description at the transferor's death.

(b) A transfer of a future interest to a class includes all persons answering the class description at the time the transfer is to take effect in enjoyment.

(c) A person conceived before but born after the transferor's death or after the time the transfer takes effect in enjoyment takes if the person answers the class description.

(Stats. 1994 (A.B. 3686), ch. 806, §41. Repealed as unnecessary by Stats. 2002 (A.B. 1784), ch. 138, §22, effective January 1, 2003.)

[Note: The statute was repealed because it was unnecessary and also because it inadequately codified the common law rule of convenience by its failure to include the common law exceptions.]

§21114. Class gift to "heirs," "next of kin," "relatives," etc.

(a) If a statute or an instrument provides for transfer of a present or future interest to, or creates a present or future interest in, a designated person's "heirs," "heirs at law," "next of kin," "relatives," or "family," or words of similar import, the transfer is to the persons, including the state under Section 6800, and in the shares that would succeed to the designated person's intestate estate under the intestate succession law of the transferor's domicile, if the designated person died when the transfer is to take effect in enjoyment. If the designated person's surviving spouse is living but is remarried at the time the transfer is to take effect in enjoyment, the surviving spouse is not an heir of the designated person for purposes of this section.

(b) As used in this section, "designated person" includes the transferor.

(Stats. 1994 (A.B. 3686), ch. 806, §41. Amended by Stats. 2002 (A.B. 1784), ch. 138, §23, effective January 1, 2003.)

§21115. Inclusion of half-bloods, adoptees, nonmarital persons, stepchildren, and foster children

(a) Except as provided in subdivision (b), halfbloods, adopted persons, persons born out of wedlock, stepchildren, foster children, and the issue of these persons when appropriate to the class, are included in terms of class gift or relationship in accordance with the rules for determining relationship and inheritance rights for purposes of intestate succession.

(b) In construing a transfer by a transferor who is not the natural parent, a person born to the natural parent shall not be considered the child of that parent unless the person lived while a minor as a regular member of the household of the natural parent or of that parent's parent, brother, sister, spouse, or surviving spouse. In construing a transfer by a transferor who is not the adoptive parent, a person adopted by the adoptive parent shall not be considered the child of that parent unless the person lived while a minor (either before or after the adoption) as a regular member of the household of the adopting parent or of that parent's parent, brother, sister, or surviving spouse.

(c) Subdivisions (a) and (b) shall also apply in determining:

(1) Persons who would be kindred of the transferor or kindred of a surviving, deceased, or former spouse of the transferor under Section 21110.

(2) Persons to be included as issue of a deceased transferee under Section 21110.

(3) Persons who would be the transferor's or other designated person's heirs under Section 21114.

(d) The rules for determining intestate succession under this section are those in effect at the time the transfer is to take effect in enjoyment.

(Stats. 1994 (A.B. 3686), ch. 806, §41. Repealed by Stats. 2002 (A.B. 1784), ch. 138, §25, effective January 1, 2003.)

§21116. Presumption that disposition vests at transferor's death [repealed]

A testamentary disposition by an instrument, including a transfer to a person on attaining majority, is presumed to vest at the transferor's death.

(Stats. 1994 (A.B. 3686), ch. 806, §41. Repealed by Stats. 2002 (A.B. 1784), ch. 138, §26, effective January 1, 2003.)

[Note: The statute was repealed because its presumption in favor of early vesting was inconsistent with the rule of deferred vesting applicable in some circumstances. See, e.g., Section 21114 (class gifts to heirs, next of kin, relatives, etc.).]

§21120. Policy of giving some effect to every expression and avoiding intestacy

The words of an instrument are to receive an interpretation that will give every expression some effect, rather than one that will render any of the expressions inoperative. Preference is to be given to an interpretation of an instrument that will prevent intestacy or failure of a transfer, rather than one that will result in an intestacy or failure of a transfer.

(Stats. 1994 (A.B. 3686), ch. 806, §41. Amended by Stats. 2002 (A.B. 1784), ch. 138, §28, effective January 1, 2003.)

§21121. Policy of construing instrument as whole

All parts of an instrument are to be construed in relation to each other and so as, if possible, to form a consistent whole. If the meaning of any part of an instrument is ambiguous or doubtful, it may be explained by any reference to or recital of that part in another part of the instrument.

(Stats. 1994 (A.B. 3686), ch. 806, §41. Amended by Stats. 2002 (A.B. 1784), ch. 138, §29, effective January 1, 2003.)

§21122. Policy of giving words their ordinary meaning

The words of an instrument are to be given their ordinary and grammatical meaning unless the intention to use them in another sense is clear and their intended meaning can be ascertained. Technical words are not necessary to give effect to a disposition in an instrument. Technical words are to be considered as having been used in their technical sense unless (a) the context clearly indicates a contrary intention or (b) it satisfactorily appears that the instrument was drawn solely by the transferor and that the transferor was unacquainted with the technical sense.

(Stats. 1994 (A.B. 3686), ch. 806, §41. Amended by Stats. 2002 (A.B. 1784), ch. 138, §30, effective January 1, 2003.)

II. Will Doctrines

A. Integration

Generally, when a testator executes a will, the document consists of several pages. The testamentary scheme might even include several different documents (e.g., wills, codicils, and other testamentary instruments such as trusts). Sometimes, it is difficult for courts to ascertain which instruments were intended to be part of the will. Integration involves the process of establishing which writings were intended by the testator to be part of his or her will.

Integration has two elements. First, the doctrine requires that the testator *intended* the separate writings to be part of the will. For example, one court held that two or more handwritten documents that did not refer to one another, nonetheless, might be admitted to probate when it was clear that the testator intended them to constitute his will (Estate of Phippen, 47 Cal. Rptr. 648 (Ct. App. 1965)). Second, the separate writings must have been *present at the time of execution* of the will. Thus, a court held that a letter written after the execution of a holographic will could not be integrated with the will. Estate of Fritz, 227 P.2d 539 (Cal. Ct. App. 1951).

In California, integration has been applied to probate a single codicil from two separate writings (Estate of Morrison, 220 P.2d 413 (Cal. Ct. App. 1950)), and to validate separately addressed letters written on the same piece of paper (In re Estate of Henderson, 238 P. 938 (Cal. 1925)). However, courts have refused to apply Integration to part of a holographic codicil that was written on the back of the page on which the testator's signature appears (Estate of Archer, 239 Cal. Rptr. 137 (Ct. App. 1987)), and to alter the distributive portion of a valid will by way of an invalid codicil (Estate of Twohig, 223 Cal. Rptr. 352 (Ct. App. 1986)). See generally 64 Cal. Jur.3d §248 (citing authority).

Integration is facilitated by several techniques of execution. For example, the testator and witnesses might initial each page, or each page of the will might be numbered in reference to the whole (i.e., "one of ten pages," "two of ten pages," etc.), or sentences could spill over from one page to the next (rather than each page having self-contained paragraphs), or the same format (ink, type) could be used throughout, or the will might contain an attestation clause that refers to the number of pages in the entire document.

Extrinsic evidence is admissible to prove the testator's intent to integrate two or more writings into a single will. *Fritz*, 227 P.2d 539 (holding that, where extrinsic evidence is lacking of the testator's intention to have his will consist of various pages, the pages will not be so regarded by the court unless the context indicates such a coherency as to constitute one continuous composition). See generally 64 Cal. Jur.3d §250; Restatement (Third) of Property, *supra*, at §3.5, cmt. d.

Integration problems frequently arise with holographic wills because such wills often are written informally. Sometimes, courts will validate several writings as one holographic will by allowing the name of the decedent placed on any of the writings to constitute a signature of the whole will (Estate of Moody, 257 P.2d 709

(Cal. Ct. App. 1953); *Phippen*, 47 Cal. Rptr. 648. See generally 64 Cal. Jur.3d §250.

Cases are divided as to whether a signature on an envelope containing sheets of papers with will provisions can be integrated into a valid will. Restatement (Third) of Property, *supra*, at §3.5. The Restatement adopts the "better view" that integration should be permitted in such cases. *Id.*

B. Incorporation by Reference

Incorporation by reference occurs when a testamentary instrument refers to a separate and distinct writing in an effort to give the latter testamentary significance. For example, by a will dated June 10, 2003, Testator (T) leaves $10,000 to "the person whose name I shall write in a letter dated this date and enclosed in an envelope with this will. I also leave the residue of my estate to my wife Wilma." T dies survived by Wilma but no issue or parents. A letter is found at T's death in his safe, physically attached to the will and dated June 10, 2003, with the name of T's niece Nancy. If T's will successfully incorporates the letter by reference, then Nancy will take the $10,000 and Wilma will take the residue. On the other hand, if T's attempted incorporation by reference fails, then the $10,000 gift to Nancy fails and Wilma takes the entire estate.

Language in the will must manifest the intent to incorporate the extrinsic document by reference. The will must be a valid testamentary instrument for the doctrine of incorporation by reference to apply. *Twohig*, 223 Cal. Rptr. 352 (unsigned holographic codicil cannot incorporate formally attested will).

Note that only writings may be incorporated, not physical objects. Estate of Blain, 295 P.2d 898 (Cal. Ct. App. 1956) (holding that holographic will may not incorporate a ring that was attached). 64 Cal. Jur.3d §240.

Pursuant to the incorporation by reference doctrine, the extrinsic writing generally has not been executed with the requisite testamentary formalities and need not be testamentary in character. Thus, the writing sought to be incorporated does not have to be signed or witnessed as required for a will.

Incorporation by reference has several requirements:

- the testator must have intended to incorporate the extrinsic writing into the will;
- the extrinsic writing must be in existence when the testator executed the will;
- the will must sufficiently describe the extrinsic writing so that it is identified and conforms to the description in the will.

The second requirement above is sometimes referred to as *"the existing document rule."* Thus, a testator generally cannot incorporate by reference a *future* document. *Twohig*, 223 Cal. Rptr. 352 (holding that a valid 1973 will could not incorporate an unsigned 1983 codicil). Some courts require that the will refer to the extrinsic document as being an existing document when the will was executed, although UPC §2-510 does not hold to this strict requirement. McGovern & Kurtz, *supra*, §6.2 at 273. See also Restatement (Third) of Property, *supra*, at §3.6 (explaining that this additional requirement was imposed at common law but, because it is "intent-defeating," the Restatement does not adopt it as a requirement).

The effect of incorporation by reference is that the extrinsic document then becomes part of the will. 64 Cal. Jur.3d Wills §246. But cf. Restatement (Third) of Property, *supra*, at §3.6, cmt. h (stating that the incorporated document is "treated as part of the will for purposes of" distributing the estate, but "need not be offered for probate nor be made part of the public record") (cited in McGovern & Kurtz, *supra*, §6.2 at 272 n.2).

Incorporation by reference is distinguishable from integration. Integration occurs when the testator intends separate writings to be part of one testamentary instrument. However, under the integration doctrine, the will does not specifically refer to any extraneous documents or writings (as in incorporation by reference). Estate of McCarty, 27 Cal. Rptr. 94 (Ct. App. 1962). See generally 64 Cal. Jur.3d Wills §249.

Early California courts had difficulty permitting incorporation by reference of nonholographic material (i.e., material not in the testator's handwriting) into a holographic will. Courts reasoned that incorporating by reference nonholographic material would violate the rule (since repealed) that a holographic will must be entirely written, dated, and signed in the hand of the testator. See, e.g., Estate of Caruch, 293 P.2d 514 (Cal. Ct. App. 1956). California Probate Code §6130 does not expressly authorize or prohibit incorporation by reference in such cases. 64 Cal. Jur.3d Wills §274. Note that a valid codicil may incorporate by reference a defectively executed will.

A will may incorporate by reference the will of another person. In re Estate of Martin, 88 P.2d 234 (Cal. Ct. App. 1939) (affirming a decree admitting a husband's will to probate and incorporating by reference a will executed by his deceased wife).

In addition, California Probate Code §6300 permits pour-over wills provided that the trust is executed before, or concurrently with, the execution of the pour-over will. A pour-over will is a will that makes a devise to a (generally, previously executed) trust. California Probate Code §6300 recognizes pour-overs to trusts by means of the doctrine of incorporation by reference provided that: (1) the trust is identified in the testator's will and (2) the trust terms are set forth in a written instrument. The Uniform Testamentary Additions to Trusts Acts (UTATA) (Cal. Prob. Code §§6300 et seq.) now regulates these devises. UTATA was approved by NCCUSL in 1960, and has been widely adopted. California adopted it in 1965 as former California Probate Code §§170 et seq., now California Probate Code §§6300 et seq. NCCUSL adopted a revised Uniform Act in 1991 (8B U.L.A. 355). 14 Witkin, Summary, Wills, *supra*, at §170.

Law Revision Commission Commentary to California Probate Code §6130 points out that the provision permitting pour-overs to trusts that may be amended after the will is executed is "hard to reconcile" with the "existing document" rule. For further discussion of pour-over devises to trusts, see Chapter IX *infra*.

California Probate Code §6130 codifies the common law doctrine of incorporation by reference. Law Revision Commission Comment to Probate Code §6130. Extrinsic evidence is admissible to facilitate the identification of incorporated documents. 64 Cal. Jur.3d §242. California Probate Code §6130 is the same as UPC §2-510.

When California initially enacted California Probate Code §6130, the legislature did not adopt the related UPC provision (§2-513) which was intended to relax execution formalities, especially for people who change their will frequently and informally by making lists of tangible personal property. Specifically, UPC §2-513 allows a list of tangible personal property to be incorporated by reference even if the list was prepared *after* the will was executed (emphasis added). Law Revision Commission Comment to Probate Code §6130. According to UPC §2-513, under limited circumstances, a separate writing may dispose of certain property even if the writing does not satisfy the traditional formulation of the incorporation by reference doctrine (because the writing came into existence after the execution of the will) or the doctrine of events of independent significance (because the writing may not have independent significance). Lawrence H. Averill, Uniform Probate Code in a Nutshell 166 (3d ed. 1993). For the separate writing to be effective under the UPC, the writing must be signed by the testator, the items and devisees must be described sufficiently, the items must be personal property (and must not otherwise be disposed of by the testator's will), and there must be a reference to this writing in a valid will of the testator. The provision precludes its use for testamentary disposition of money. UPC Commentary also bars its use to transmit writings of indebtedness, documents of title, securities, and property used in trade or business. Unsigned holographic writings do not qualify under the provision. Averill, *supra*, at 167.

To illustrate, Testator executes a will on September 2, 2003, that leaves pieces of jewelry to "each of four friends whose name I will write on a piece of paper and enclose with this will. I leave the residue of my estate to my brother Bob." A piece of paper is found among Testator's papers at his death that is dated December 10, 2003. It is signed and lists the names of four of Testator's friends. How will Testator's estate be distributed? Note that the list cannot be incorporated by reference into the will because the list was not in existence at the time that the will was executed. Nor does the list have any independent significance because it exists only to dispose of property at Testator's death. The only possibility to give the list testamentary effect would be if the jurisdiction has adopted UPC §2-513.

In 2006, the California legislature enacted California Probate Code §6132 (influenced by UPC §2-513) that permits a will to refer to a writing executed in the future that directs the disposition of tangible personal property not otherwise disposed of by the will. The writing must be written or signed by the testator before *or after* the execution of the will and need not have substantial independent significance. The term "tangible personal property" exempts cash (Cal Prob. Code §6132(a)). The value of the property disposed of by such a writing may not exceed $5,000 for any particular item; the total value of such property may not exceed $25,000 (Cal. Prob. Code §6132(g)).

CALIFORNIA PROBATE CODE

§6130. Doctrine of incorporation by reference

A writing in existence when a will is executed may be incorporated by reference if the language of the will manifests this intent and describes the writing sufficiently to permit its identification.

(Stats. 1990 (A.B. 759), ch. 79, §14, effective July 1, 1991.)

§6132. Writings that direct disposition of a testator's tangible personal property

(a) Notwithstanding any other provision, a will may refer to a writing that directs disposition of tangible personal property not otherwise specifically disposed of by the will, except for money that is common coin or currency and property used primarily in a trade or business. A writing directing disposition of a testator's tangible personal property is effective if all of the following conditions are satisfied:

(1) An unrevoked will refers to the writing.

(2) The writing is dated and is either in the handwriting of, or signed by, the testator.

(3) The writing describes the items and the recipients of the property with reasonable certainty.

(b) The failure of a writing to conform to the conditions described in paragraph (2) of subdivision (a) does not preclude the introduction of evidence of the existence of the testator's intent regarding the disposition of tangible personal property as authorized by this section.

(c) The writing may be written or signed before or after the execution of the will and need not have significance apart from its effect upon the dispositions of property made by the will. A writing that meets the requirements of this section shall be given effect as if it were actually contained in the will itself, except that if any person designated to receive property in the writing dies before the testator, the property shall pass as further directed in the writing and, in the absence of any further directions, the disposition shall lapse.

(d) The testator may make subsequent handwritten or signed changes to any writing. If there is an inconsistent disposition of tangible personal property as between writings, the most recent writing controls.

(e)(1) If the writing directing disposition of tangible personal property omits a statement as to the date of its execution, and if the omission results in doubt whether its provisions or the provisions of another writing inconsistent with it are controlling, then the writing omitting the statement is invalid to the extent of its inconsistency unless the time of its execution is established to be after the date of execution of the other writing.

(2) If the writing directing disposition of tangible personal property omits a statement as to the date of its execution, and it is established that the testator lacked testamentary capacity at any time during which the writing may have been executed, the writing is invalid unless it is established that it was executed at a time when the testator had testamentary capacity.

(f)(1) Concurrent with the filing of the inventory and appraisal required by Section 8800, the personal representative shall also file the writing that directs disposition of the testator's tangible personal property.

(2) Notwithstanding paragraph (1), if the writing has not been found or is not available at the time of the filing of the inventory and appraisal, the personal representative shall file the writing no later than 60 days prior to filing the petition for final distribution pursuant to Section 11640.

(g) The total value of tangible personal property identified and disposed of in the writing shall not exceed twenty-five thousand dollars ($25,000). If the value of an item of tangible personal property described in the writing exceeds five thousand dollars ($5,000), that item shall not be subject to this section and that item shall be disposed of pursuant to the remainder clause of the will. The value of an item of tangible personal property that is disposed of pursuant to the remainder clause of the will shall not be counted towards the twenty-five thousand dollar ($25,000) limit described in this subdivision.

(h) As used in this section, the following definitions shall apply:

(1) "Tangible personal property" means articles of personal or household use or ornament, including, but not limited to, furniture, furnishings, automobiles, boats, and jewelry, as well as precious metals in any tangible form, such as bullion or coins and articles held for investment purposes. The term "tangible personal property" does not mean real property, a mobilehome as defined in Section 798.3 of the Civil Code, intangible property, such as evidences of indebtedness, bank accounts and other monetary deposits, documents of title, or securities.

(2) "Common coin or currency" means the coins and currency of the United States that are legal tender for the payment of public and private debts, but does not include coins or currency kept or acquired for their historical, artistic, collectable, or investment value apart from their normal use as legal tender for payment.

(Stats. 2006 (A.B.2568), ch. 280, §1.)

C. Republication by Codicil

A codicil is a document that amends or modifies a will. Sometimes, a codicil may do no more than appoint an executor or revoke an earlier will (Cal. Prob. Code §88). That is, a codicil does not have to make testamentary gifts. In order for a codicil to be valid, it must meet the same formal requirements as a will. Note that a California statutory will can be amended by codicil in the same manner as other wills (Cal. Prob. Code §6226).

A codicil that refers to an earlier will "republishes" it. McGovern & Kurtz, *supra*, §6.2 at 272. See also Restatement (Third) of Property, *supra*, at §3.6, cmt. d. That is, the will is considered to be executed at the later date of the codicil. This doctrine only applies to validly executed wills (i.e., a will cannot "speak again" if it never "spoke" once).

The origins of the doctrine are traced to the common law rule that a will could not dispose of land acquired after the will was executed. (A will could bequeath personal property, but not real property, that was acquired after the execution of the will. Only after the Wills Act of 1837 did English law permit a will to operate on real property that was acquired after the execution of the will.) Restatement (Third) of Property, *supra*, at §3.4. The doctrine of republication by codicil developed to overcome this rule.

Republication by codicil may serve to validate a writing that cannot be incorporated by reference. In the famous case of Simon v. Grayson, 102 P.2d 1081 (Cal. 1940), at the decedent's death, his safe deposit contained a

will, a codicil, and a letter to his executors. The will (executed on March 25, 1932) left $6000 to his executors to be paid as he directed in a letter "that will be found in my effects [and] shall be dated March 25, 1932." Although a letter was found in the safe deposit box with a bequest to a Mrs. Esther Cohn, it was dated July 3, 1933. The will thus purported to incorporate the letter by reference. Testator also had executed a codicil on November 25, 1933 which (inter alia) confirmed that the earlier will would remain in force. The residuary legatees contended that the attempted incorporation-by-reference was ineffective because it failed the "existing document rule." However, the California Supreme Court held that, although the letter was not in existence when the will was executed, the subsequent republication of the will by codicil satisfied the existing document rule and incorporated the letter by reference.

Republication by codicil is a rule of construction designed to carry out the testator's probable intention. The doctrine will not be applied "where the result would be so inequitable as to appear contrary to that intention." 14 Witkin, Summary, Wills, *supra*, at §161. In In re McCauley's Estate, 71 P. 512 (Cal. 1903), a testatrix executed a will on February 12, 1900, leaving gifts to charitable institutions. She executed a codicil on March 16, 1900, and died on April 14, 1900. Her date of death was 28 days after the codicil. A mortmain statute (Cal. Civ. Code §1313), in effect at the time, invalidated any bequests or devises to charity that were made within 30 days of death. The court declined to apply republication of the codicil, which would have invalidated the charitable bequests, because to do so would have defeated the testatrix's intent.

The doctrine of republication by codicil is "rarely codified." Restatement (Third) of Property, *supra*, at §3.4 (Statutory Note).

CALIFORNIA PROBATE CODE

§88. "Will" defined

"Will" includes codicil and any testamentary instrument which merely appoints an executor or revokes or revises another will.

(Stats. 1990 (A.B. 759), ch. 79, §14, effective July 1, 1991.)

§6226. Revocation and amendment of statutory wills

(a) A California statutory will may be revoked and may be amended by codicil in the same manner as other wills.

(b) Any additions to or deletions from the California statutory will on the face of the California statutory will form, other than in accordance with the instructions, shall be given effect only where clear and convincing evidence shows that they would effectuate the clear intent of the testator. In the absence of such a showing, the court either may determine that the addition or deletion is ineffective and shall be disregarded, or may determine that all or a portion of the California statutory will is invalid, whichever is more likely to be consistent with the intent of the testator.

(c) Notwithstanding Section 6110, a document executed on a California statutory will form is valid as a will if all of the following requirements are shown to be satisfied by clear and convincing evidence:

(1) The form is signed by the testator.

(2) The court is satisfied that the testator knew and approved of the contents of the will and intended it to have testamentary effect.

(3) The testamentary intent of the maker as reflected in the document is clear.

(Stats. 1991 (S.B. 271), ch. 1055, §20.)

D. Acts of Independent Significance

Reference to events of independent significance allows the testator to make testamentary dispositions based on the occurrence or nonoccurrence of specified acts or facts. For example, Testator executes a will that contains a bequest of $10,000 "to the person who is my housekeeper at my death."

The doctrine permits a court to admit certain extrinsic evidence (evidence outside the will) in order to determine certain beneficiaries and certain property that pass under the testator's will. "A statement of its principle is that if a fact, be it an act or event, has significance other than to pass property at death, this significance entitles that fact to control and to determine the disposition of the property." Averill, *supra*, at 165.

Under the doctrine of incorporation by reference (discussed *supra*), a testator cannot affect his will by a *future* writing because only existing documents may be incorporated by reference into a will. However, by the doctrine of acts of independent significance, the testator may make a valid testamentary disposition based on future acts (e.g., future acts of a third person or the testator). For the doctrine to apply, these acts must have a significance distinct from their effect on the will (i.e., independent significance). 14 Witkin, Summary, Wills, *supra*, at §169.

The doctrine of acts of independent significance is usually not codified. Averill, *supra*, at 165. However, following promulgation of the UPC, many jurisdictions enacted statutes addressing the doctrine. California Probate Code §6131 codifies the doctrine. That statute is identical to UPC §2-512. Law Revision Commission Comment to California Probate Code §6131.

Under this doctrine, courts have allowed devises of the contents of a house or safe deposit box but not an unattested writing of the testator. McGovern & Kurtz, *supra*, §6.2 at 274.

The UPC made a significant change in prior law by permitting the referenced act to occur *before or after the execution of the will or before or after the testator's death* (emphasis added) (UPC §2-512). This change (which California adopted) may allow a pour-over into a trust that is not even in existence when the will is executed. Law Revision Commission Comment to California Probate Code §6131. (Note that California Probate Code §6300, set forth in Chapter IX *infra*, permits pour-overs to trusts that are executed *before or concurrently* with the execution of the pour-over will.) See also Restatement (Third) of Property, *supra*, at §3.7.

Recall that the UPC adopted a liberal rule (UPC §2-513) that was intended to relax execution formalities, especially for people who change their will frequently and informally by making lists of tangible personal property. UPC §2-513 permits, under limited circumstances, a separate writing to dispose of certain personal property even if the writing does not satisfy the traditional formulation of the doctrine of events of independent significance (because the writing may not have independent significance). Averill, *supra*, at 166. To be effective under the UPC, the writing must be signed by the testator, the items and devisees must be described sufficiently, the items must be personal property (and must not otherwise be disposed of by the testator's will), and there must be a reference to this writing in a valid will of the testator.

As explained above, the California legislature recently enacted California Probate Code §6132 (reprinted in Section IIB supra) that was influenced by UPC §2-513. The new statute permits a will to refer to a writing executed in the future in order to direct the disposition of tangible personal property not otherwise disposed of by the will. The writing must be written or signed by the testator, either before *or after* the execution of the will, and need not have substantial independent significance. The statute imposes limitations on the value of any personal property that may be disposed of by such an informal writing.

CALIFORNIA PROBATE CODE

§6131. Doctrine of Acts of Independent Significance

A will may dispose of property by reference to acts and events that have significance apart from their effect upon the dispositions made by the will, whether the acts and events occur before or after the execution of the will or before or after the testator's death. The execution or revocation of a will of another person is such an event.

(Stats. 1990 (A.B. 759), ch. 79, §14, effective July 1, 1991.)

III. Extrinsic Evidence and Mistake

A central issue in the determination of the testator's intent is the admissibility of extrinsic evidence. Several bases exist for excluding evidence of the testator's intent that is not in writing, signed, and attested. McGovern & Kurtz, *supra*, §6.1 at 259. The Parol Evidence Rule provides that oral evidence shall not be admitted to vary the written terms of an agreement, such as a contract, a deed, or a will. The Statute of Frauds requires transfers of real property to be in writing. And, wills legislation in all jurisdictions requires that testamentary instruments must comport with various statutory requirements. Unlike disputes involving contracts, when disputes arise regarding wills, one of the parties (i.e., the testator) is no longer alive to present evidence of intent. For this reason, as a general rule, courts are reluctant to admit extrinsic evidence. Despite this general rule, however, courts will admit extrinsic evidence of the testator's intent in limited circumstances (discussed *infra*).

According to California law, extrinsic evidence may be admissible to determine whether a document constitutes a will (formally attested or holographic) or to determine the meaning of the will or an unclear portion of a will (Cal. Prob. Code §6111.5). However, extrinsic evidence is not available to contradict or vary the terms of a will.

Even though courts admit extrinsic evidence in some circumstances, they are still reluctant to admit testimony regarding oral declarations of the testator.

Testators sometimes execute wills based on a mistaken belief. Mistakes in wills take several forms: (1) mistake in omission, (2) mistake in execution, (3) mistake in misdescription, and (4) mistake in the inducement.

A *mistake in omission* results when the testator intends to make a particular gift or a gift to a particular beneficiary but fails to do so. According to the traditional rule, courts will not remedy a mistake in omission. In such situations, courts probate the will as written, refusing to correct the testator's mistake. "Correction would require the addition of a new provision, and the court cannot add anything to the will; a testamentary gift can only be made by the testator in writing." 14 Witkin, Summary, Wills, *supra*, at §236. Courts justify their reluctance to add omitted provisions either by reference to the Parol Evidence Rule (i.e., the addition of words would violate the Parol Evidence Rule) or the Statute of Wills (permitting an unnamed beneficiary to take, or unnamed property to pass, would permit a testamentary gift that violates the Statute of Wills). The primary concern here is with the possibility of fraud.

For example, in Estate of De Moulin, 225 P.2d 303 (Cal. Ct. App. 1950), the testator dictated a will, leaving $100 each to his son and daughter, and appointing his wife executrix. Due to the testator's secretary's mistake, the residuary clause contained a blank where the testator had intended to insert his wife as residuary beneficiary. The appellate court refused to reform the document, holding that the intention of the testator must be resolved from the words of the will itself. The court refused to admit the oral declarations of the testator or to apply the exception to the general rule that would admit instructions to a draftsman to clarify an imperfect description of a beneficiary (saying that the exception did not apply where there is a total failure to name a beneficiary). See also Estate of Townsend, 34 Cal. Rptr. 275 (Ct. App. 1963) (holding that, although the will evidenced a clear intent to provide for appellant, testimony of the attorney who drew the will to the effect that decedent had instructed him that the residue go to appellant was inadmissible for the reason that any defect in the will was one of omission and not of ambiguity, and the court may not remedy a mistake in omission).

A *mistake in execution* occurs when the testator is mistaken about the particular instrument being executed. Mistake in execution frequently arises when spouses execute mutual and reciprocal wills. Thus, a husband mistakenly executes a wife's will, and the wife mistakenly executes the husband's will. Traditionally, courts refuse to remedy a mistake in execution, finding that the requisite testamentary intent was lacking. (Recall that testamentary intent requires that the testator intend this instrument to operate as his or her will.) Courts explain that the husband did not intend for his wife's will to operate as his will; nor did the wife intend for her husband's will to operate as her will. See, e.g., In re Pavlinko's Estate, 148 A.2d 528 (Pa. 1959) (refusing to admit the will of the wife as the will of the husband).

However, in recent years, courts have been more willing to correct such mistakes. For example, in In re Snide, 418 N.E.2d 656 (N.Y. 1981), a husband and wife mistakenly executed each other's will. The husband died first without realizing his mistake. The widow then introduced to probate the will that the husband had executed. The Surrogate decreed that the husband's will could be reformed to substitute the husband's name wherever the wife's name appeared. The Appellate Division reversed, refusing to admit the document based on the traditional rule. The New York Court of Appeals reversed, granting relief through reformation, reasoning that the will was executed with the requisite formalities, the wills of husband and wife were identical, and the denial of relief would frustrate the testator's intent.

Mistakes in misdescription have several variations. Sometimes, the will reveals a mistake regarding a beneficiary's name. For example, a testatrix left property to "the French Orphans of France." No such society existed. Instead, the Fraternite Franco-Americaine, claiming the property as the successor to the "French War Orphans Relief," attempted to show that the decedent had dealt with its organization in the past. In response, the court corrected the provision to permit the charity to take. Estate of Regnler, 11 P.2d 639 (Cal. 1932). The traditional rule in such cases was termed "the plain meaning rule." That is, if the meaning was clearly expressed in the document, courts refused to admit extrinsic evidence to vary the description in the will (and permitted the property to pass intestate if the institution could not be identified). 14 Witkin, Summary, Wills, *supra*, at §128 (citing Estate of Zilke, 1 P.2d 475 (Cal. 1931)).

In a famous case, an English court refused to remedy a mistake in misdescription in a bequest to a children's welfare organization. A Scottish testator mistakenly bequeathed a legacy to the "National Society for the Prevention of Cruelty to Children" (an organization headquartered in London with which he was unfamiliar) when he actually intended to bequeath the legacy to a different organization ("the Scottish National Society for the Prevention of Cruelty to Children") that was headquartered in Edinburgh where the testator lived. Scottish Nat'l Soc'y for the Prevention of Cruelty to Children, 111 L.T.R. 869 (1915).

The distinction between latent and patent ambiguity becomes especially relevant in misdescription cases. A *latent ambiguity* is an ambiguity that emerges in attempting to apply the will provision(s) to a particular person or property. At that point, it becomes apparent that no person or property conforms to the misdescription in the will. For example, a testatrix bequeathed her residuary estate to "my nephew Raymond and his wife Mabel." At the time the will was executed, the testator's nephew Raymond was married to Evelyn and divorced from his former wife Mabel. The latent ambiguity emerged when it became apparent that "Mabel" was not "Raymond's wife." Breckheimer v. Kraft, 273 N.E.2d 468 (Ill. App. Ct. 1971) (holding that parol evidence was admissible to explain the latent ambiguity).

A *patent ambiguity* is an ambiguity that is apparent on the face of the will. An example would be the same devise given to two different people. "I give Blackacre to A; I give Blackacre to B."

Under the traditional rule, courts admit extrinsic evidence to resolve a latent ambiguity but not a patent ambiguity. As one court explains:

> It is settled doctrine that, as a latent ambiguity is only disclosed by extrinsic evidence, it may be removed by extrinsic evidence. Such an ambiguity may arise upon a will, either when it names a person as the object of a gift, or a thing as the subject of it, and there are two persons or things that answer the name or description. . . .

In re Zilke's Estate, 1 P.2d 475, 476 (Cal. Ct. App. 1931) (quoting Taylor v. McCowen, 99 P. 351, 353 (Cal. 1909)).

Many misdescription cases reveal judicial reliance on the distinction between latent versus patent ambiguities. Thus, for example in Patch v. White, 117 U.S. 210 (1886), the testator devised to his brother real property that was described as: "Lot #6 in Square 403." In fact, the testator owned, and intended to devise, Lot #3 in Square 406. Extrinsic evidence revealed a latent ambiguity: a conflict between the description contained in the will and the subject matter of the gift. Adhering to the rule that if a latent ambiguity is only disclosed by extrinsic evidence, it may be removed by extrinsic evidence, the court held that extrinsic evidence was admissible to reveal the parcel that the testator actually owned. The court added that since the instrument revealed the testator's intention to dispose of all his property, the clause would be reformed.

Traditionally, courts were reluctant to admit extrinsic evidence unless the will revealed some ambiguity. That is, according to the general rule, only when the language of a will was ambiguous or uncertain could courts resort to extrinsic evidence in order to ascertain the intention of the testator. However, the California Supreme Court announced a change in that policy in Estate of Russell, 70 Cal. Rptr. 561 (Cal. 1968). *Russell* involved a residuary gift to the testatrix's long-term male companion and to her dog. The question arose as to whether the companion was to receive the entire estate in order to care for the dog, or whether the estate should be distributed in equal shares to the companion and pet. The California Supreme Court held that, in light of evidence of the testatrix's intent, the gift could not reasonably be construed as an absolute gift of the entire residue to her companion who would then use whatever proportion necessary for the dog. The court determined that when language in a will is uncertain, resort may be had to extrinsic evidence to ascertain the testator's intention. The case, therefore, turned the traditional no-extrinsic-evidence rule on its head. Whereas under prior law, the court had to find an ambiguity before it could allow the admission of extrinsic evidence, *Russell* permitted the introduction of extrinsic evidence to show that, under the circumstances of a particular case, the seemingly clear language of a will describing a beneficiary or gift may actually embody a latent ambiguity "for it is only by the introduction of extrinsic evidence that existence of such an ambiguity can be shown." *Id.* at 566.

By the beginning of the 1980s, legal scholars announced that appellate courts in California, New Jersey, and New York had decided several cases that "may presage the abandonment of the ancient 'no-reformation' rule" (i.e., the rule that courts would not reform wills on the basis of mistake). John H. Langbein & Lawrence W. Waggoner, Reformation of Wills on the Ground of Mistake: Change of Direction in American Law?, 130 U. Pa. L. Rev. 521, 521 (1982).

A *mistake in the inducement* is a mistake that induces the testator to execute a will. Such a mistake can arise from the testator's incorrect belief about the conduct of, or assets owed to, a beneficiary. The testator makes a will based on that mistaken belief.

Traditionally, courts are reluctant to remedy mistakes in the inducement of wills. According to the general rule, mistakes in the inducement, "relating as they do to facts outside the will itself, cannot be proved because such mistakes are wholly subjective in nature, and the question of what the testator would have done had he not been mistaken is too conjectural to be undertaken on the basis of extrinsic evidence." Max A. Yageman, Mistake in the Inducement in Wills, 1 Am. Jur. Proof of Facts 2d 323 (2002).

Early cases developed a common law exception to the general rule. According to this exception, some courts grant relief for mistakes in the inducement if: (1) the mistake is on the face of the will, and (2) the alternative disposition is also apparent on the face of the will. Thus, in Gifford v. Dyer, 2 R.I. 99 (R.I. 1852), the testatrix executed a will bequeathing her property to her brother-in-law and two nephews, stemming from her belief that her only son was dead. Her son had left home 10 years before and had not been heard from since. The court held that the appearance of the son did not revoke the will because the will contained no express mention

of the testator's mistaken belief and any alternative disposition had she known the truth.

Courts are more willing to remedy fraud in the inducement than mistake in the inducement. In the former, a third party induces the testator to make a will or devise by fraudulently misrepresenting a material fact.

Note that, according to the modern trend, courts are more willing to admit extrinsic evidence, even in cases of patent ambiguity. See, e.g., Matter of Estate of Frietze, 966 P.2d 183 (N.M. Ct. App. 1998) (holding that extrinsic evidence was properly admitted to resolve an ambiguity posed by the testator's devising the same piece of real property, with two different legal descriptions, to two different beneficiaries, although declining to admit extrinsic evidence regarding another parcel where the will was not ambiguous).

On mistakes in the inducement of revocation of a will, see Chapter VI, Section III *infra*.

CALIFORNIA PROBATE CODE

§6111.5. Admissibility of extrinsic evidence: to determine if document is a will or its meaning

Extrinsic evidence is admissible to determine whether a document constitutes a will pursuant to Section 6110 or 6111, or to determine the meaning of a will or a portion of a will if the meaning is unclear.

(Stats. 1990 (S.B. 1775), ch. 710, §14, effective July 1, 1991.)

CALIFORNIA CODE OF CIVIL PROCEDURE

§1856. Written terms intended as a final expression of agreement may not be contradicted by parol evidence; exceptions

(a) Terms set forth in a writing intended by the parties as a final expression of their agreement with respect to such terms as are included therein may not be contradicted by evidence of any prior agreement or of a contemporaneous oral agreement.

(b) The terms set forth in a writing described in subdivision (a) may be explained or supplemented by evidence of consistent additional terms unless the writing is intended also as a complete and exclusive statement of the terms of the agreement.

(c) The terms set forth in a writing described in subdivision (a) may be explained or supplemented by course of dealing or usage of trade or by course of performance.

(d) The court shall determine whether the writing is intended by the parties as a final expression of their agreement with respect to such terms as are included therein and whether the writing is intended also as a complete and exclusive statement of the terms of the agreement.

(e) Where a mistake or imperfection of the writing is put in issue by the pleadings, this section does not exclude evidence relevant to that issue.

(f) Where the validity of the agreement is the fact in dispute, this section does not exclude evidence relevant to that issue.

(g) This section does not exclude other evidence of the circumstances under which the agreement was made or to which it relates, as defined in Section 1860, or to explain an extrinsic ambiguity or otherwise interpret the terms of the agreement, or to establish illegality or fraud.

(h) As used in this section, the term agreement includes deeds and wills, as well as contracts between parties.

(Enacted 1872. Amended by Stats. 1978, ch. 150, p. 374, §1.)

VI
REVOCATION OF WILLS

This chapter addresses the revocation of wills. First, it explores the different methods of revocation. Then, it examines the common law doctrine of dependent relative revocation that permits a revocation to be disregarded. Next, it focuses on revival, the process of reinstating a revoked will. It turns to a common law presumption regarding the revocation of a will. Finally, it examines limitations on the probate of a lost or destroyed will.

I. Introduction

A testator may revoke his or her will at any time after executing it. The methods of revocation are specified by state statute. The primary methods of revocation are: (1) revocation by operation of law, (2) revocation by physical act, and (3) revocation by subsequent written instrument.

To revoke a will, a testator (1) must have an intent to revoke (called *animus revocandi*), and (2) must comply with the statutory requirements regarding the methods of revocation. If a testator does not have the requisite intent and/or fails to comply with the statutory formalities, the revocation will be ineffective.

The intent to revoke and the actual revocation of the will must be concurrent. Note that if an attempted revocation is not effective, then the decedent's estate passes according to the will. In Estate of Silva, 145 P. 1015 (Cal. 1915), the court held that the testator's will was not revoked where the testator's wife fraudulently destroyed the envelope of the will and not the will itself, despite the testator's request, because the intent to revoke was not concurrent with a revocation. However, the court noted that the petitioners might seek alternative relief in equity via a constructive trust. *Id.* at 1017.

California Probate Code §6120 specifies the requisite methods for revocation. First, a will may be revoked by a subsequent will that revokes the prior will in part or in total (Cal. Prob. Code §6120(a)). Second, a testator may revoke a will by burning, tearing, canceling, obliterating, or otherwise destroying it, provided that the testator did so with the intent to revoke (Cal. Prob. Code §6120(b)). California Probate Code §6122 provides for revocation by operation of law if the testator's marriage is dissolved or annulled. The revocation of a will is invalid if procured by duress, menace, fraud, or undue influence (Cal. Prob. Code §6104).

Many jurisdictions recognize partial revocation of a will, following the Statute of Frauds provision that neither the will *nor any part thereof* may be revoked except in the prescribed manner (emphasis added). Atkinson, *supra*, §86 at 444. For example, California Probate Code §6120 provides: "A will *or any part thereof* is revoked by any of the following [methods] (emphasis added)." See also UPC §2-507.

Many states do not permit partial revocation by physical act (i.e., they permit partial revocation only by subsequent instrument). Atkinson, *supra*, §86 at 444-445. The policy underlying such a prohibition is a concern with fraud (i.e., the fear that an interested beneficiary, rather than the testator, revoked the will in part). If a jurisdiction does not recognize partial revocation, then the partial revocation is ineffective and the will is admitted to probate unchanged.

CALIFORNIA PROBATE CODE

§6104. Revocation is ineffective if procured by duress, menace, fraud, or undue influence

The execution or revocation of a will or a part of a will is ineffective to the extent the execution or revocation was procured by duress, menace, fraud, or undue influence.

(Stats. 1990 (A.B. 759), ch. 79, §14, effective July 1, 1991.)

§6120. Revocation by subsequent will or by physical act

A will or any part thereof is revoked by any of the following:

(a) A subsequent will which revokes the prior will or part expressly or by inconsistency.

(b) Being burned, torn, canceled, obliterated, or destroyed, with the intent and for the purpose of revoking it, by either (1) the testator or (2) another person in the testator's presence and by the testator's direction.

(Stats. 1990 (A.B. 759), ch. 79, §14, effective July 1, 1991.)

§6121. Methods of revoking a duplicate will

A will executed in duplicate or any part thereof is revoked if one of the duplicates is burned, torn, canceled, obliterated, or destroyed, with the intent and for the purpose of revoking it, by either (1) the testator or (2) another person in the testator's presence and by the testator's direction.

(Stats. 1990 (A.B. 759), ch. 79, §14, effective July 1, 1991.)

§6122. Revocation by operation of law: dissolution or annulment

(a) Unless the will expressly provides otherwise, if after executing a will the testator's marriage is dissolved or annulled, the dissolution or annulment revokes all of the following:

(1) Any disposition or appointment of property made by the will to the former spouse.

(2) Any provision of the will conferring a general or special power of appointment on the former spouse.

(3) Any provision of the will nominating the former spouse as executor, trustee, conservator, or guardian.

(b) If any disposition or other provision of a will is revoked solely by this section, it is revived by the testator's remarriage to the former spouse.

(c) In case of revocation by dissolution or annulment:

(1) Property prevented from passing to a former spouse because of the revocation passes as if the former spouse failed to survive the testator.

(2) Other provisions of the will conferring some power or office on the former spouse shall be interpreted as if the former spouse failed to survive the testator.

(d) For purposes of this section, dissolution or annulment means any dissolution or annulment which would exclude the spouse as a surviving spouse within the meaning of Section 78. A decree of legal separation which does not terminate the status of husband and wife is not a dissolution for purposes of this section.

(e) Except as provided in Section 6122.1, no change of circumstances other than as described in this section revokes a will.

(f) Subdivisions (a) to (d), inclusive, do not apply to any case where the final judgment of dissolution or annulment of marriage occurs before January 1, 1985. That case is governed by the law in effect prior to January 1, 1985.

(Stats. 1990 (A.B. 759), ch. 79, §14, effective July 1, 1991. Amended Stats. 2001 (A.B. 25), ch. 893, §50; Stats. 2002 (A.B. 25), ch. 664, §179, effective January 1, 2003.)

§6122.1. Revocation by operation of law: termination of domestic partnership

(a) Unless the will expressly provides otherwise, if after executing a will the testator's domestic partnership is terminated, the termination revokes all of the following:

(1) Any disposition or appointment of property made by the will to the former domestic partner.

(2) Any provision of the will conferring a general or special power of appointment on the former domestic partner.

(3) Any provision of the will nominating the former domestic partner as executor, trustee, conservator, or guardian.

(b) If any disposition or other provision of a will is revoked solely by this section, it is revived by the testator establishing another domestic partnership with the former domestic partner.

(c) In case of revocation by termination of a domestic partnership:

(1) Property prevented from passing to a former domestic partner because of the revocation passes as if the former domestic partner failed to survive the testator.

(2) Other provisions of the will conferring some power or office on the former domestic partner shall be interpreted as if the former domestic partner failed to survive the testator.

(d) This section shall apply only to wills executed on or after January 1, 2002.

(Stats. 2001 (A.B. 25), ch. 893, §51.)

§6123. Anti-revival doctrine: effect of revocation of a revoking instrument

(a) If a second will which, had it remained effective at death, would have revoked the first will in whole or in part, is thereafter revoked by acts under Section 6120 or 6121, the first will is revoked in whole or in part unless it is evident from the circumstances of the revocation of the second will or from the testator's contemporary or subsequent declarations that the testator intended the first will to take effect as executed.

(b) If a second will which, had it remained effective at death, would have revoked the first will in whole or in part, is thereafter revoked by a third will, the first will is revoked in whole or in part, except to the extent it appears from the terms of the third will that the testator intended the first will to take effect.

(Stats. 1990 (A.B. 759), ch. 79, §14, effective July 1, 1991.)

§6124. Presumption of revocation for a lost will that was last traced to the testator's possession

If the testator's will was last in the testator's possession, the testator was competent until death, and neither the will nor a duplicate original of the will can be found after the testator's death, it is presumed that the testator destroyed the will with intent to revoke it. This presumption is a presumption affecting the burden of producing evidence.

(Stats. 1990 (A.B. 759), ch. 79, §14, effective July 1, 1991.)

§6226. Revocation of a statutory will

(a) A California statutory will may be revoked and may be amended by codicil in the same manner as other wills.

(b) Any additions to or deletions from the California statutory will on the face of the California statutory will form, other than in accordance with the instructions, shall be given effect only where clear and convincing evidence shows that they would effectuate the clear intent of the testator. In the absence of such a showing, the court either may determine that the addition or deletion is ineffective and shall be disregarded, or may determine that all or a portion of the California statutory will is invalid, whichever is more likely to be consistent with the intent of the testator.

(c) Notwithstanding Section 6110, a document executed on a California statutory will form is valid as a will if all of the following requirements are shown to be satisfied by clear and convincing evidence:

(1) The form is signed by the testator.

(2) The court is satisfied that the testator knew and approved of the contents of the will and intended it to have testamentary effect.

(3) The testamentary intent of the maker as reflected in the document is clear.

(Stats. 1991 (S.B. 271), ch. 1055, §20.)

§8252. Proponents of will have burden of proof of due execution; contestants have burden of proof of lack of testamentary intent or capacity

(a) At the trial, the proponents of the will have the burden of proof of due execution. The contestants of the will have the burden of proof of lack of testamentary intent or capacity, undue influence, fraud, duress, mistake, or revocation. If the will is opposed by the petition for probate of a later will revoking the former, it shall be determined first whether the later will is entitled to probate.

(b) The court shall try and determine any contested issue of fact that affects the validity of the will.

(Stats. 1990 (A.B. 759), ch. 79, §14, effective July 1, 1991.)

II. Methods of Revocation

A. Revocation by Operation of Law

Certain events may trigger a revocation of a will by operation of law. The purpose of statutes providing for revocation by operation of law is to effectuate the presumed intent of the testator. The most common triggering events are: marriage, the birth of issue, and divorce.

The English Wills Act of 1837 (7 Wm. IV & 1 Vict., c. 26, §§xviii, xix) provided that marriage revoked the will of either spouse. Atkinson, *supra*, §85 at 423. By this Wills Act, Parliament changed the former gender-based common law rule that a woman's will was revoked upon marriage (based on the fact that a married woman was under a common law disability preventing her from being able to make a will), but a man's will was not revoked unless he also had after-born children. *Id.* at 422, 424.

Many states today provide, similarly, that marriage will revoke a will. In some states, a marriage does not revoke the will if the will was in contemplation of the marriage or if the spouse was provided for in the will or by nonprobate transfers with the intent that such transfers be in lieu of a testamentary share. Also, of course, a spouse may waive the right to inherit property from the decedent. In addition, many state statutes provide that divorce (now called "dissolution") revokes any testamentary dispositions to the former spouse.

Most states revoke a *portion* of a testator's will if the will does not provide a minimal amount to the surviving spouse. In such cases, statute provides that the surviving spouse receives a forced or elective share of the decedent's estate. For discussion of the forced share, see Chapter II, Section IIB *supra*.

California law provides some protection for an omitted spouse and children (see Chapter II, Section IVA and B *supra*.) Although a spouse and/or children may receive an intestate share in some cases, this does not have the effect of revoking the testator's will. (The will is still probated and its provisions effectuated insofar as possible.)

On the other hand, a dissolution or annulment of a marriage serves to revoke the following: any testamentary dispositions to a former spouse; will provisions conferring a general or special power of appointment on the former spouse; and any will provision nominating the former spouse as executor, trustee, conservator, or guardian (Cal. Prob. Code §6122). Dissolution or annulment of a marriage also revokes a statutory will (Cal. Prob. Code §6227). However, a legal separation does not serve to exclude a former spouse (Cal. Prob. Code §6122(d)) from a will because a legal separation does not terminate the marital status of the parties. 40 Cal. Jur.3d Intestate Succession §17.

Termination of a domestic partnership (similar to dissolution of marriage) serves to revoke any bequest to a former domestic partner (Cal. Prob. Code §§6122(a)(1), 6122.1(a)(1)). Termination of the relationship also revokes any provision conferring upon the former domestic partner any power of appointment or nomination of the former partner as an executor, trustee, conservator, or guardian (Cal. Prob. Code §6122.1(a)(3)).

Probate Code Section 6122(d) states that for spouses, the will revocation provisions of section 6122 do not apply in the case of legal separation, but only in the case of dissolution or annulment. Section 6122.1, respecting domestic partners, makes no such distinction. California adopted Section 6122.1 in 2001, at which time, domestic partners lacked the ability to obtain an annulment or legal separation, but only had the option to terminate their partnership (see former Cal. Fam. Code §299, effective through December 31, 2004).

Since A.B. 205 went into effect on January 1, 2005, domestic partners, like spouses, may annul their partnership or obtain a legal separation (Cal Fam. Code §299(d)). Because of

that change in the law, and also because A.B. 205 gave domestic partners all the same rights and responsibilities as spouses under the law (Cal. Fam. Code §297.5(a)), the exception of Probate Code section 6122(d) now presumably applies to domestic partners as well. That is, if domestic partners are legally separated, the law would not recognize the domestic partnership as terminated for the purposes of will revocation.

Probate Code section 6122.1 applies only to wills executed on or after January 1, 2002. State domestic partnerships have been available in California since January 1, 2000 (Stats. 1999 (A.B. 26), ch. 588). A.B. 205, which went into effect on January 1, 2005, significantly expanded the state's domestic partnership law by granting domestic partners "the same rights, protections, and benefits," as well as "the same responsibilities, obligations, and duties," as spouses (Cal. Fam. Code §297.5(a)). After A.B. 205 was adopted, but before it took effect, the state notified members of couples who had already registered as domestic partners of the new changes in the law and gave them the opportunity to dissolve the partnership or enter into a prenuptial-like agreement (Cal. Fam. Code §299.3).

When a will provision is revoked by dissolution, the property that would have passed to the former spouse or domestic partner passes instead as if the former spouse or domestic partner predeceased the testator (Cal. Prob. Code §§6122(c), 6122.1(c)). Similarly, if a will provision confers an office or power upon a former spouse or domestic partner, that provision must be interpreted as if the former spouse or domestic partner had died before the testator.

Some spouses or domestic partners reconcile after having dissolved their relationship. Remarriage or re-entry into a domestic partnership relationship revives those parts of the will formerly revoked by the divorce or domestic partnership termination (Cal. Prob. Code §§6122(b), 6122.1(b)).

According to the Restatement Third of Property (Wills & Other Donative Transfers) section 4.2(c), "A testamentary provision that was revoked by dissolution of the testator's marriage is revived if: (i) the testator remarried the former spouse, reexecuted the will, or executed a codicil indicating an intent to revive the previously revoked provision; or (ii) the dissolution of the marriage is nullified." The part of the Restatement that deals with the revocation of wills does not specifically address domestic partnerships. Restatement (Third) of Property, *supra*, Div. 1, Ch. 4. However, other parts of the Restatement suggest that where state law treats domestic partners as the legal equivalent of a spouse, the same probate laws should apply to both. See, e.g., Restatement (Third) of Property, *supra*, at §2.2, cmt. g; §8.1, cmt. c.

An interesting issue is whether the revocation-by-dissolution provision (Cal. Prob. Code §6122) also applies to revoke testamentary bequests made to the former spouse's *children*. See, e.g., In re Estate of Jones, 18 Cal. Rptr. 3d 637 (Ct. App. 2004) (ruling that testator's former stepdaughter lost her status as a residuary beneficiary following her mother's divorce because, when a testator provides for his spouse's children, he normally intends to exclude such children of an ex-spouse after a dissolution, absent a contrary intent); Estate of Hermon, 46 Cal. Rptr. 2d 577 (Ct. App. 1995) (holding that devises to "my spouse's children" and "my spouse's issue" were revoked upon dissolution, absent a contrary intent in the will, and reversing the trial court determination that the former spouse's children were entitled to share in the estate as members of a class that continued to exist after the dissolution). Note that revised UPC §2-804 revokes testamentary bequests to the former spouse as well as bequests to the former spouse's relatives.

CALIFORNIA PROBATE CODE

§6122. Revocation by operation of law: dissolution or annulment

(a) Unless the will expressly provides otherwise, if after executing a will the testator's marriage is dissolved or annulled, the dissolution or annulment revokes all of the following:

(1) Any disposition or appointment of property made by the will to the former spouse.

(2) Any provision of the will conferring a general or special power of appointment on the former spouse.

(3) Any provision of the will nominating the former spouse as executor, trustee, conservator, or guardian.

(b) If any disposition or other provision of a will is revoked solely by this section, it is revived by the testator's remarriage to the former spouse.

(c) In case of revocation by dissolution or annulment:

(1) Property prevented from passing to a former spouse because of the revocation passes as if the former spouse failed to survive the testator.

(2) Other provisions of the will conferring some power or office on the former spouse shall be interpreted as if the former spouse failed to survive the testator.

(d) For purposes of this section, dissolution or annulment means any dissolution or annulment which would exclude the spouse as a surviving spouse within the meaning of Section 78. A decree of legal separation which does not terminate the status of husband and wife is not a dissolution for purposes of this section.

(e) Except as provided in Section 6122.1, no change of circumstances other than as described in this section revokes a will.

(f) Subdivisions (a) to (d), inclusive, do not apply to any case where the final judgment of dissolution or annulment of marriage occurs before January 1, 1985. That case is governed by the law in effect prior to January 1, 1985.

(Stats. 1990 (A.B. 759), ch. 79, §14, effective July 1, 1991. Amended Stats. 2001 (A.B. 25), ch. 893, §50; Stats. 2002 (A.B. 25), ch. 664, §179, effective January 1, 2003.)

§6122.1. Revocation by operation of law: termination of domestic partnership

(a) Unless the will expressly provides otherwise, if after executing a will the testator's domestic partnership is terminated, the termination revokes all of the following:

(1) Any disposition or appointment of property made by the will to the former domestic partner.

(2) Any provision of the will conferring a general or special power of appointment on the former domestic partner.

(3) Any provision of the will nominating the former domestic partner as executor, trustee, conservator, or guardian.

(b) If any disposition or other provision of a will is revoked solely by this section, it is revived by the testator establishing another domestic partnership with the former domestic partner.

(c) In case of revocation by termination of a domestic partnership:

(1) Property prevented from passing to a former domestic partner because of the revocation passes as if the former domestic partner failed to survive the testator.

(2) Other provisions of the will conferring some power or office on the former domestic partner shall be interpreted as if the former domestic partner failed to survive the testator.

(d) This section shall apply only to wills executed on or after January 1, 2002.

(Stats. 2001 (A.B. 25), ch. 893, §51.)

§6227. Revocation of a statutory will by dissolution or annulment

(a) If after executing a California statutory will the testator's marriage is dissolved or annulled, the dissolution or annulment revokes any disposition of property made by the will to the former spouse and any nomination of the former spouse as executor, trustee, guardian, or custodian made by the will. If any disposition or nomination is revoked solely by this section, it is revived by the testator's remarriage to the former spouse.

(b) In case of revocation by dissolution or annulment:

(1) Property prevented from passing to a former spouse because of the revocation passes as if the former spouse failed to survive the testator.

(2) Provisions nominating the former spouse as executor, trustee, guardian, or custodian shall be interpreted as if the former spouse failed to survive the testator.

(c) For purposes of this section, dissolution or annulment means any dissolution or annulment that would exclude the spouse as a surviving spouse within the meaning of Section 78. A decree of legal separation which does not terminate the status of husband and wife is not a dissolution or annulment for purposes of this section.

(d) This section applies to any California statutory will, without regard to the time when the will was executed, but this section does not apply to any case where the final judgment of dissolution or annulment of marriage occurs before January 1, 1985; and, if the final judgment of dissolution or annulment of marriage occurs before January 1, 1985, the case is governed by the law that applied prior January 1, 1985.

(Stats. 1991 (S.B. 271), ch. 1055, §20.)

§21610. Share of omitted spouse in antenuptial will situation

Except as provided in Section 21611, if a decedent fails to provide in a testamentary instrument for the decedent's surviving spouse who married the decedent after the execution of all of the decedent's testamentary instruments, the omitted spouse shall receive a share in the decedent's estate, consisting of the following property in said estate:

(a) The one-half of the community property that belongs to the decedent under Section 100 [set forth in Section II C supra this Chapter];

(b) The one-half of the quasi-community property that belongs to the decedent under Section 101 [set forth in Section II C supra this Chapter].

(c) A share of the separate property of the decedent equal in value to that which the spouse would have received if the decedent had died without having executed a testamentary instrument, but in no event is the share to be more than one-half the value of the separate property in the estate.

(Stats. 1997 (A.B. 1172), ch. 724, §34.)

§21611. Exceptions to omitted spouse's protection in antenuptial will situation

The spouse shall not receive a share of the estate under Section 21610 if any of the following is established:

(a) The decedent's failure to provide for the spouse in the decedent's testamentary instruments was intentional and that intention appears from the testamentary instruments.

(b) The decedent provided for the spouse by transfer outside of the estate passing by the decedent's testamentary instruments and the intention that the transfer be in lieu of a provision in said instruments is shown by statements of the decedent or from the amount of the transfer or by other evidence.

(c) The spouse made a valid agreement waiving the right to share in the decedent's estate.
(Stats. 1997 (A.B. 1172), ch. 724, §34.)

§21612. Manner of satisfying spouse's share; order of abatement

(a) Except as provided in subdivision (b), in satisfying a share provided by this chapter:

(1) The share will first be taken from the decedent's estate not disposed of by will or trust, if any.

(2) If that is not sufficient, so much as may be necessary to satisfy the share shall be taken from all beneficiaries of decedent's testamentary instruments in proportion to the value they may respectively receive. This value shall be determined as of the date of the decedent's death.

(b) If the obvious intention of the decedent in relation to some specific gift or devise or other provision of a testamentary instrument would be defeated by the application of subdivision (a), the specific devise or gift or provision may be exempted from the apportionment under subdivision (a), and a different apportionment, consistent with the intention of the decedent, may be adopted.
(Stats. 1997 (A.B. 1172), ch. 724, §34. Amended by Stats. 2003 (A.B. 167), ch. 32, §17, effective January 1, 2004.)

CALIFORNIA FAMILY CODE

§2024. Petitions for dissolution or annulment shall contain a notice informing parties of legal effect on will

(a) A petition for dissolution of marriage, nullity of marriage, or legal separation of the parties, or a joint petition for summary dissolution of marriage, shall contain the following notice:

"Dissolution or annulment of your marriage may automatically cancel your spouse's rights under your will, trust, retirement benefit plan, power of attorney, pay on death bank account, transfer on death vehicle registration, survivorship rights to any property owned in joint tenancy, and any other similar thing. It does not automatically cancel your spouse's rights as beneficiary of your life insurance policy. If these are not the results that you want, you must change your will, trust, account agreement, or other similar document to reflect your actual wishes.

Dissolution or annulment of your marriage may also automatically cancel your rights under your spouse's will, trust, retirement benefit plan, power of attorney, pay on death bank account, transfer on death vehicle registration, and survivorship rights to any property owned in joint tenancy, and any other similar thing. It does not automatically cancel your rights as beneficiary of your spouse's life insurance policy.

You should review these matters, as well as any credit cards, other credit accounts, insurance policies, retirement benefit plans, and credit reports to determine whether they should be changed or whether you should take any other actions in view of the dissolution or annulment of your marriage, or your legal separation. However, some changes may require the agreement of your spouse or a court order (see Part 3 (commencing with Section 231) of Division 2 of the Family Code)."

(b) A judgment for dissolution of marriage, for nullity of marriage, or for legal separation of the parties shall contain the following notice:

"Dissolution or annulment of your marriage may automatically cancel your spouse's rights under your will, trust, retirement benefit plan, power of attorney, pay on death bank account, transfer on death vehicle registration, survivorship rights to any property owned in joint tenancy, and any other similar thing. It does not automatically cancel your spouse's rights as beneficiary of your life insurance policy. If these are not the results that you want, you must change your will, trust, account agreement, or other similar document to reflect your actual wishes.

Dissolution or annulment of your marriage may also automatically cancel your rights under your spouse's will, trust, retirement benefit plan, power of attorney, pay on death bank account, transfer on death vehicle registration, survivorship rights to any property owned in joint tenancy, and any other similar thing. It does not automatically cancel your rights as beneficiary of your spouse's life insurance policy.

You should review these matters, as well as any credit cards, other credit accounts, insurance policies, retirement benefit plans, and credit reports to determine whether they should be changed or whether you should take any other actions in view of the dissolution or annulment of your marriage, or your legal separation."
(Stats. 1992 (A.B. 2650), ch. 162, §10, effective January 1, 1994. Amended by Stats. 1993 (A.B. 1500), ch. 219, §105; Stats. 2001 (A.B. 873), ch. 417, §1.)

B. Revocation by Physical Act

State statutes generally require that the physical act of revocation must be performed with concurrent intent to revoke. Statutes specify the nature of the physical act that is legally sufficient to revoke a will. Many states reflect the influence of the Statute of Frauds that permitted "burning, canceling, tearing, or obliterating." The UPC and some states extend the necessary physical acts by the addition of language permitting "burning, tearing, canceling, obliterating, or *destroying the will*. . . ." (UPC §2-507) (emphasis added).

If the physical act is not legally sufficient, it will not constitute a revocation. In such cases, the will or will provision is still effective.

Note that "canceling" implies marking through the words but leaving them legible, such as by drawing lines through the words or writing "VOID" across the face of the will; however, "obliterating" the words renders them illegible.

At common law, any act of cancellation had to touch a *material* part of the will. Atkinson, *supra*, §86 at 439. The modern trend liberalizes this requirement so that any act of burning, tearing, or cancellation is sufficient. According to UPC §2-507(a)(2), "A burning, tearing, or canceling is a 'revocatory act on the will,' whether or not the burn, tear, or cancellation touched any of the words on the will."

In some states, such as California, the revocation does not have to be performed by the testator. It may be accomplished by a proxy (a third party), provided that the proxy revokes the will "in the testator's presence and by the testator's direction" (Cal. Prob. Code §6120(b)). Proxies, thus, are permitted for revocation as well as for execution of a will (compare Cal. Prob. Code §6110(b)(2)).

Some states require witnesses for a proxy revocation. Under prior California law (former Cal. Prob. Code §74), two witnesses were necessary to prove revocation of a will by a proxy. Law Revision Commission Comment to California Probate Code §6120. This requirement was subsequently repealed (by Stats. 1983, ch. 842, §18).

CALIFORNIA PROBATE CODE

§6120. Revocation by subsequent will or by physical act

A will or any part thereof is revoked by any of the following:

(a) A subsequent will which revokes the prior will or part expressly or by inconsistency.

(b) Being burned, torn, canceled, obliterated, or destroyed, with the intent and for the purpose of revoking it, by either (1) the testator or (2) another person in the testator's presence and by the testator's direction.

(Stats. 1990 (A.B. 759), ch. 79, §4, effective July 1, 1991.)

§6121. Revocation of duplicate

A will executed in duplicate or any part thereof is revoked if one of the duplicates is burned, torn, canceled, obliterated, or destroyed, with the intent and for the purpose of revoking it, by either (1) the testator or (2) another person in the testator's presence and by the testator's direction.

(Stats. 1990 (A.B. 759), ch. 79, §14, effective July 1, 1991.)

§6124. Presumption of revocation for a will last traced to the testator's possession

If the testator's will was last in the testator's possession, the testator was competent until death, and neither the will nor a duplicate original of the will can be found after the testator's death, it is presumed that the testator destroyed the will with intent to revoke it. This presumption is a presumption affecting the burden of producing evidence.

(Stats. 1990 (A.B. 759), ch. 79, §14, effective July 1, 1991.)

C. Revocation by Subsequent Written Instrument

A subsequent will may revoke a prior will in two ways: (1) expressly or (2) by implication. An express revocation by subsequent instrument may be entire or partial. UPC §2-507(a)(1). An example of an express revocation would be: "I, Jane Smith, do hereby revoke all prior wills and codicils."

A subsequent will also may revoke a prior will by implication, such as by inconsistency. For example, if Testator gave Blackacre to A in his first will but his second will gave Blackacre to B, then the devise of Blackacre to A has been revoked by inconsistency.

To constitute an effective revocation, the subsequent instrument must be valid, i.e., it must comply with the statutory formalities. However, the subsequent instrument does not have to be dispositive; it may do nothing more than revoke the prior will. Also, a holographic will may revoke a formally attested will, provided that the jurisdiction recognizes holographic instruments. McGovern & Kurtz, *supra*, §5.1 at 235-236.

The Restatement (Third) of Property permits testators to make a handwritten alteration of a holographic will without re-signing the document. Restatement (Third) of Property, *supra*, at §3.2, cmt. f. The Restatement (Third) of Property also permits testators to make handwritten alterations of a previously executed attested will "if he or she signs the alteration and, if the statute so requires, dates it." *Id.*, cmt. g. The handwritten alteration of the formally attested will, then, is regarded as a holographic codicil.

According to the UPC, if a testator makes a complete disposition of his or her estate in a subsequent will, a presumption applies that the testator intended to revoke the prior will (rather than merely supplement it) (UPC §2-507(c)) (cited in McGovern & Kurtz, *supra*, §5.1 at 236).

CALIFORNIA PROBATE CODE

§6120. Revocation by subsequent will or by act

A will or any part thereof is revoked by any of the following:

(a) A subsequent will which revokes the prior will or part expressly or by inconsistency.

(b) Being burned, torn, canceled, obliterated, or destroyed, with the intent and for the purpose of revoking it, by either (1) the testator or (2) another person in the testator's presence and by the testator's direction.
(Stats. 1990 (A.B. 759), ch. 79, §14, effective July 1, 1991.)

III. Dependent Relative Revocation

Dependent relative revocation is a common law doctrine that permits a court to disregard a valid revocation of a will in some cases. The situation generally arises when a testator makes a will but later revokes the will (or will provision) in order to effectuate a subsequent testamentary scheme. If the revocation of the will (or will provision) was dependent on, and relative to, a mistake, a court may disregard the revocation based on the testator's presumed intent.

A classic case of dependent relative revocation arises in the situation involving partial revocation by physical act. For example, the testator makes a bequest of $10,000 to each of the three children (A, B, and C) of his best friend. Later, he crosses out the $10,000 bequest to A and inserts instead $15,000. If the jurisdiction recognizes partial revocation by physical act, the testator's cancellation of the $10,000 to A is an effective revocation. However, the $15,000 "codicil" fails because it does not comply with the statute of wills (either as a formally attested will or as a holographic instrument). A court might apply dependent relative revocation based on the testator's presumed intent. That is, the court might disregard the testator's revocation of the $10,000 gift to A in the belief that the revocation was dependent on and relative to a mistake (the effectiveness of the larger bequest). The presumed intent would be that the testator would clearly prefer for A to take $10,000 rather than zero.

Some jurisdictions impose a restriction on the doctrine and apply dependent relative revocation only where Will #1 was revoked by physical act, based on the theory that such revocations are inherently ambiguous.

In In re Kaufman's Estate, 155 P.2d 831 (Cal. 1945), the testator executed a will in New York. When he later moved to California, he executed a new will naming a new executor and repeating the same dispositive plan. In both wills, the Second Church of Christ, Scientist, of New York City, was the residuary legatee. When the testator died within 30 days after executing the second will, California's Mortmain Statute (discussed in Chapter II, Section VC *supra*, and Chapter XIII, Section VII, *infra*) invalidated the bequest to the church. The church filed a petition to have the earlier will admitted to probate. The court held that the earlier will should be admitted to probate under the doctrine of dependent relative revocation, on the ground that the testator revoked the first will only because the second duplicated its purpose and the testator would have preferred the first will to dying intestate as to a substantial part of his estate.

In a subsequent dependent relative revocation case, a testatrix executed a will that exercised a testamentary power of appointment over a portion of a trust created by her deceased husband. She exercised the power of appointment in favor of her daughter from a prior marriage (thereby preferring her daughter to her late husband's five sons and/or grandchildren). Later, testatrix executed another will that inadvertently failed to exercise the power of appointment. After her death, the executrix petitioned to admit to probate the later will and that portion of the earlier will exercising the power of appointment. One of the testatrix's step-grandchildren initiated a will contest and objected to the admission of any portion of the earlier will.

The appellate court held that: (1) the second will, which revoked all former wills, also revoked the exercise of the power of appointment in the first will, unless the doctrine of dependent relative revocation applied; (2) the doctrine of dependent relative revocation applies even where the decedent's last will is not wholly or partially invalid if, as a result of a mistake on the testator's part, his last will purports to revoke a prior will and fails in a material way to distribute the estate in accordance with the testator's intent; and (3) the doctrine of dependent relative revocation was applicable in the present case. In re Estate of Anderson, 65 Cal. Rptr. 2d 307 (Ct. App. 1997).

IV. Revival of a Revoked Will

Revival is the process of reinstating a revoked will. The testator may *intentionally* revive a revoked will in two ways: (1) by re-executing the former will so that it complies with all the statutory formalities, or (2) by executing a new testamentary instrument (in accordance with statutory formalities) expressly providing that the former will is effective.

Revival becomes more problematic if the following sequence of events occurs:

- the testator executes a will (Will #1) and then revokes it by a subsequent written instrument (Will #2);
- the testator then revokes the subsequent revoking instrument (Will #2) by physical act (tearing up Will #2).

This sequence of events may lead to uncertainty regarding the testator's intent: Did the testator wish the first will to be revived or did the testator wish to die intestate?

Courts have different responses to this situation. The common law followed a rule of *automatic revival*. That is, upon the revocation of a revoking instrument (Will #2), the former will (Will #1) was automatically revived. The theory for this approach was that a will was not effective until death. Therefore, Will #1 was never revoked by Will #2 because Will #2, having been revoked prior to death, was never effective. At the testator's death, Will #1 is given effect because it is the only will then in existence.

The majority of states now follow a *rebuttable presumption of anti-revival*. Under this approach, the former will (Will #1) is not revived unless evidence reveals that the testator intended this effect. (If no evidence of intent to revive the former will is apparent, then the court determines that the testator died intestate.) This approach is derived from the English Wills Act of 1837 limiting the circumstances in which a former will can be revived—only by re-execution or "by a duly executed codicil expressing an intention to revive it." Cited in McGovern & Kurtz, *supra*, §5.4 at 244. Many American jurisdictions adopted this rule but required that the testator's intent to revive had to be evidenced by the "terms" of the revoking instrument. That is, courts limited evidence of intent to the face of the will; therefore, statements by the testator regarding revival were inadmissible. This approach reflected an unwillingness to admit extrinsic evidence because of the possibility of fraud.

The UPC follows the anti-revival rule. However, the UPC liberalized the rule regarding the admission of extrinsic evidence that is sufficient to revive an earlier will. Under the UPC, revocation of a revoking instrument will revive the former will if the testator's intent to revive is evident "from the circumstances of the revocation of the subsequent will or from the testator's *contemporaneous or subsequent* declarations" (UPC §2-509(a) (emphasis added)). Thus, the UPC admits oral statements of the testator, including those that were made contemporaneously with the revocation as well as those that occurred after the revocation.

The UPC's dispensing power concept also might permit admission of extrinsic evidence. The dispensing power under UPC §2-503 applies to execution, revocation, alteration, and revival of wills. "A document, writing or even interlineation on a will might be treated as executed in compliance with the [UPC]'s will statute, if proponents of the document, writing or interlineation prove by clear and convincing evidence that the testator desired it to constitute a revival of a prior revoked clause or will." Averill, *supra*, at 156. The application of this provision has not yet been explored by the drafters or the courts. *Id.* For discussion of the dispensing power generally, see Chapter IV, Section II *supra*.

The UPC has a provision somewhat analogous to the common law automatic revival doctrine in regard to remarriage of the decedent to a prior spouse. Upon the testator's remarriage to a previously divorced spouse (or in cases of remarriage following an annulment), the provisions for that former spouse are automatically revived by operation of law (UPC §2-804(d)). See also Cal. Prob. Code §§6122(b), 6122.1(b).

California law (Cal. Prob. Code §6123) regarding revocation of a second will is identical to UPC §2-509 and follows the approach of the anti-revival presumption with the liberal admission of extrinsic evidence. Note that former California Probate Code §75 (repealed in 1983 and replaced by former California Probate Code §6123 which was identical to the current 1990 version of §6123) also contained a presumption against revival. However, former California Probate Code §75 limited the possibility of revival to those situations involving revocation of the revoking instrument by physical act, stemming from the belief that physical acts of destruction of a revoking instrument cause the most uncertainty.

Current California law also provides that if the testator executes a *third* will revoking the second will, then the first will will only be revived to the extent "it appears from the terms of the third will that the testator intended the first will to take effect" (Cal. Prob. Code §6123(b)).

Like the UPC's dispensing power standard, the Restatement (Third) of Property requires "clear and convincing" evidence of the testator's intent to revive. Restatement (Third) of Property, *supra*, at §4.2, cmt. i.

The Restatement (Third) of Property §4.2 specifies different methods of revival based on the method of will revocation. A will revoked by physical act may be revived "if the testator: (i) reexecuted the will; (ii) executed a codicil indicating an intent to revive the previously revoked will; or (iii) performed an act on the will that clearly and convincingly demonstrates an intent to reverse the revocation." *Id.* at §4.2(b). However, a will revoked by a subsequent will may be revived "if the testator: (i) reexecuted the previously revoked will; (ii) executed a codicil indicating an intent to revive the previously revoked will; (iii) revoked the revoking will by act intending to revive the previously revoked will; or (iv) revoked the revoking will by another, later will whose terms indicate an intent to revive the previously revoked will." *Id.* at §4.2(a).

A will revoked by divorce is revived "if: (i) the testator remarried the former spouse, reexecuted the will, or executed a codicil indicating an intent to revive the previously revoked provision; or (ii) the dissolution of the marriage is nullified." *Id.* at §4.2(c).

Note that it is important, in applying the doctrine of revival, to determine whether the subsequent revoking instrument revoked the prior will entirely or partially. If the prior will is only revoked partially (i.e., the revoking instrument merely supersedes it), then the revocation of the revoking instrument automatically reinstates the superseded disposition. See also UPC §2-509(b).

In In re Estate of Garrett, 2002 WL 1288765 (Cal. Ct. App. 2002) (nonpublished/noncitable), a testator executed a will that devised one-half of his estate to his nephew and one-half to his sister-in-law. A later codicil devised the entire estate to his nephew. A second will confirmed that much of his estate would pass to the nephew (via a living trust that he previously executed). Some time later, the testator told his lawyer that he no longer wanted to leave his estate to the nephew because of the nephew's personal problems. The lawyer explained that if the testator failed to name another beneficiary, his estate would pass by intestate succession. Testator then revoked the living trust and second will.

On the testator's death, the nephew filed a petition for probate of the first will and codicil, arguing that the testator intended to revive the will because it was found in a bag containing his important papers and had the words "Last" and "Good" written on it. The trial court considered extrinsic evidence (testimony of witnesses and various letters) to determine whether "it is evident from the circumstances of the revocation of the [Second Will] or from [the testator's] contemporary or subsequent declarations that [the testator] intended the [First Will] to take effect as executed" (Cal. Prob. Code §6123 (a)). The appellate court affirmed the trial court's finding that the testator did not intend to revive the first will when he revoked the second will. The appellate court reasoned that even if the handwriting on the first will was the testator's, there was no evidence showing when those words were written. Moreover, those words were not conclusive proof that the testator intended to revive the first will upon revocation of the second will. Furthermore, the court reasoned that the fact that the testator included the first will with his important papers did not show an intent to revive the first will. The court held that he intended to die intestate.

CALIFORNIA PROBATE CODE

§6123. Anti-revival doctrine: effect of revocation of a revoking instrument

(a) If a second will which, had it remained effective at death, would have revoked the first will in whole or in part, is thereafter revoked by acts under Section 6120 or 6121, the first will is revoked in whole or in part unless it is evident from the circumstances of the revocation of the second will or from the testator's contemporary or subsequent declarations that the testator intended the first will to take effect as executed.

(b) If a second will which, had it remained effective at death, would have revoked the first will in whole or in part, is thereafter revoked by a third will, the first will is revoked in whole or in part, except to the extent it appears from the terms of the third will that the testator intended the first will to take effect.

(Stats. 1990 (A.B. 759), ch. 79, §14, effective July 1, 1991.)

V. Presumptions

A. Presumption of Revocation

At common law, if a will could not be found at the testator's death and was last traced to the testator's possession, the law presumed that the testator destroyed the will with the requisite intent. Many jurisdictions continue to apply this rebuttable presumption. Some jurisdictions also apply the presumption if the will is found in a mutilated condition in the testator's possession at death. Once the presumption applies, the proponent of the will must introduce evidence to overcome it.

Duplicate originals often present problems in terms of the application of this presumption. A duplicate will is one that meets all the statutory formalities (i.e., signed, attested, etc.). Some testators execute duplicate wills in the belief that such an act ensures against loss.

In some cases, only one of the duplicate originals is traced to the testator's possession. If the other duplicate cannot be found, a rebuttable presumption exists that the testator destroyed it with the intention of revoking both it and any other duplicates. 79 Am. Jur.2d Wills §575. However, if both duplicate original wills are found at the testator's death, but only one of them has been canceled, then courts apply a presumption that the will is not revoked. The rationale is that if testator intended revocation, he or she would have canceled both copies. *Id.*

California Probate Code §6124 codifies the common law presumption, provided that "the testator was competent until death" and that "neither the will nor a duplicate original of the will can be found."

A recent case interpreted the meaning of the term "duplicate original" in California Probate Code §6124 to invoke the application of the presumption of revocation. Testator, who was survived by neither wife nor issue, left a devise of real property to plaintiff and her children. The original will could not be found at his death, but an unexecuted photocopy was found among his possessions. In a will contest, the court determined that the term "duplicate original" as used in Cal. Prob. Code §6124 does *not* include an unexecuted photocopy, and therefore, the presumption that the testator destroyed his will with the intent to revoke it would apply. Lauermann v. Superior Court, 26 Cal. Rptr. 3d 258 (Ct. App. 2005).

CALIFORNIA PROBATE CODE
§6124. Presumption of revocation for a lost will last traced to the testator's possession

If the testator's will was last in the testator's possession, the testator was competent until death, and neither the will nor a duplicate original of the will can be found after the testator's death, it is presumed that the testator destroyed the will with intent to revoke it. This presumption is a presumption affecting the burden of producing evidence.
(Stats. 1990 (A.B. 759), ch. 79, §14, effective July 1, 1991.)

B. Lost and Destroyed Will Statutes

A validly executed will that has been lost or destroyed may still be given effect in some circumstances. When a will cannot be found at death, several possibilities arise: (1) the will has been lost, (2) the will has been destroyed by the testator, or (3) the will has been destroyed by another person. At common law, ecclesiastical courts probated valid wills that were lost or destroyed when real property was involved and when proof of the contents could be established. Atkinson, *supra*, §97, at 506.

Today, in cases when a will cannot be found at death and it was last traced to the testator's possession (and, in California, if the testator was competent), the presumption of revocation operates (see Section A *supra*). However, because of the concern that the loss of the will may be attributable to wrongdoing, jurisdictions permit probate of a lost or destroyed will under some circumstances.

Many jurisdictions have lost or destroyed will statutes that specify the requirements for probate of such wills. Generally, "a will lost, or mutilated without intent thereby to revoke, may be admitted to probate upon satisfactory proof of its contents and due execution." Atkinson, *supra*, §97, at 506. Many jurisdictions require proof of the contents and the facts of due execution by clear and convincing evidence.

Proof of the contents may consist of testimony by witnesses, or production of a copy, draft, or memorandum of the will made by the testator. *Id.*, §97 at 511. Proof of the facts of due execution may be by attesting witnesses or by proof of the witnesses' handwriting. *Id.*, §97 at 509. If the decedent's attorney had a copy of the will, that copy could be offered in evidence or oral testimony by the attorney could establish its terms. 14 Witkin, Summary, Wills, *supra*, at §551. Declarations of the testator, made before or after the execution, may serve as corroboration of the contents (although not proof of the provisions) or the facts of due execution. Atkinson, *supra*, §97 at 511.

California's lost and destroyed will statute (formerly California Probate Code §350) was based on an earlier statute that was adopted by the California legislature in 1850 (Stats. 1850, chap. 129, sec. 38, p. 379). The 1850 statute was identical to a New York statute that was enacted in 1827 (1 R.L. 364, Title I, Art. Third, sec. 89; New York Rev. Stats. 1846, Vol. 2, p. 133). The original California (and New York) statute read:

> No will . . . shall be allowed to be proved as a lost or destroyed will, unless the same shall be proved to have been in existence at the time of the death of the testator; or be shown to have been fraudulently

destroyed, in the lifetime of the testator; nor unless its provisions shall be clearly and distinctly proved by at least two credible witnesses, a correct copy or draft being deemed equivalent to one witness.

Prior to 1850, New York courts maintained that the fraudulent destruction of a will did not amount to a revocation, and that if the contents of the will could be satisfactorily shown, the will would be admitted to probate. In re Arbuckle's Estate, 220 P.2d 950, 956 (Cal. Ct. App. 1950) (explaining history of California statute). New York courts interpreted the term "fraudulent" liberally. They required neither actual fraud, nor an intention to profit by the destruction of the will. They interpreted "fraudulent" to mean "constructive fraud." "The destruction of the will, without the knowledge or consent of the testatrix, in disregard of her intention and to the injury of the objects of her bounty, constitutes constructive fraud, and becomes a fraudulent destruction, within the meaning of section 143 of the Surrogate's Court Act." ***Id.*** **at 957.**

In California, the San Francisco Earthquake and subsequent fire in 1906 highlighted the need for a statutory amendment to the lost and destroyed will statute because so many wills in attorneys' offices and financial institutions were destroyed. At that time, the California lost and destroyed will statute (Cal. Code Civ. Proc. §1339) provided:

No will shall be proven as a lost or destroyed will, unless the same is proved to have been in existence at the time of the death of the testator, or is shown to have been fraudulently destroyed in the lifetime of the testator, nor unless its provisions are clearly and distinctly proved by at least two credible witnesses.

In 1907, the legislature amended the statute to enable probate of lost or destroyed wills that "have been fraudulently or ***by public calamity*** **destroyed. . . ." (Stats. 1907, ch. 100, p. 122) (emphasis added). Provisions of such wills still had to be proven by clear and convincing evidence and by at least two credible witnesses. See also In re Patterson's Estate, 102 P. 941 (Cal. 1909) (holding that the statutory amendment should be applied liberally to give effect to a will destroyed in the 1906 fire).**

The current statute (Cal. Prob. Code §8223) continues former California Probate Code §8223 (of the same number) unchanged. Former California Probate Code §8223 (added by Stats. 1988, ch. 1199, §81.5) replaced a prior statute (Cal. Prob. Code §350) requiring that a missing will must be clearly and distinctly proved by at least two credible witnesses. In 1982, the Law Revision Commission recommended repeal of this strict level of proof (i.e., the clear and convincing standard and two-credible-witnesses requirement) and replacement with a preponderance standard and no minimum number of witnesses. These changes were subsequently enacted. Currently, California Probate Code §8223 requires merely that the petition for probate of a lost or destroyed will shall include a written statement of the testamentary words or their substance.

For many years, many state statutes, similar to those of California and New York, adhered to the requirement that the will must have been "fraudulently destroyed." Under such provisions, there was no need to prove actual fraud. Courts interpreted the language as requiring that the will must have been destroyed by a third party without the decedent's knowledge. See, e.g., In re Fox's Will, 174 N.E.2d 499 (N.Y. 1961) (holding that a will that had been destroyed in a Berlin bombing in 1944 could be admitted to probate, reasoning that the phrase "fraudulently destroyed" had nothing to do with the motive for destruction but solely with the agency of destruction, i.e., it was destroyed by someone other than the testator and without his authorization or direction).

The proponent of a will that has been lost or destroyed need not prove the exact words of the original will. Proof of the substance of the will is sufficient. See, e.g., In re Camp's Estate, 66 P.227 (Cal. 1901) (holding that where the testimony of two witnesses coincides as to the provisions in a lost portion of a will, the court is authorized to establish such provisions, although such witnesses may differ as to the exact language used by the testator). Also, if witnesses recall only a substantial portion of the will but not its entire contents, that portion could be admitted to probate. ***Patterson's Estate, supra.***

CALIFORNIA PROBATE CODE

§8223. Lost or destroyed wills: requirements to probate

The petition for probate of a lost or destroyed will shall include a written statement of the testamentary words or their substance. If the will is proved, the provisions of the will shall be set forth in the order admitting the will to probate.

(Stats. 1990 (A.B. 759), ch. 79, §14, effective July 1, 1991.)

VII
CONTRACTS TO MAKE WILL

I. Introduction

A. Types of Contracts

A will contract is an agreement that requires a testator to make a particular testamentary disposition of property. It thereby restricts the testator's ability to make a different disposition.

Several types of will contracts exist:

- contracts to make a will;
- contracts to make a particular devise or bequest;
- contracts to die intestate;
- contracts to revoke a will;
- contracts not to revoke a will; and
- contracts not to contest a will.

Will contracts arise most frequently in two situations. First, a testator promises to make a bequest or devise in favor of a third person in consideration for the latter's services. Often such services involve caretaking for the testator for the remainder of his or her life. Such contracts are sometimes referred to as "life-care contracts." Second, two testators (generally spouses) make joint or mutual wills with reciprocal provisions that contain (or allegedly contain) a contract not to revoke their respective wills.

In the former case, the contract is breached when the testator fails to make the agreed-upon will (or the agreed-upon provision in a will). The party who has rendered services in reliance on the testator's promise discovers this fact after the testator's death. In the joint or mutual will situation, the surviving spouse breaches the agreement by disposing of his or her estate differently than previously promised. Jeff G. Carchidi, California Oral Will Contracts: The Decline of Testator Intent in the Shadow of Equitable Estoppel, 39 Santa Clara L. Rev. 1187, 1190 (1999). The latter case is "representative of much of California's judicial history on this subject." *Id.* at 1206.

Will contracts are governed by the law of contracts and not the law of succession. Thus, assume that a testator (T) makes a promise to leave his or her home to X. When T dies, X discovers that T left his home to Y, instead of to X, in breach of the contract. T's will will be probated (provided that it conforms to all the statutory requirements); X must pursue a remedy under the jurisdiction's applicable contract law.

B. Historical Background

The law has long recognized the right of a person to enter into a contract to make a particular testamentary disposition. The only bar to such contracts was the Statute of Frauds' requirement that a contract regarding the transfer of real property must be in writing. However, even in cases where the Statute of Frauds was applicable, courts commonly admitted extrinsic evidence and applied exceptions (e.g., part performance doctrine, etc., discussed *infra*) to permit proof of oral will contracts.

California has a history of recognition of will contracts. Carchidi, *supra*, at 1192. Prior to January 1, 1985, a contract to make a will was regulated by California Civil Code §1624(6) (*infra*) which required that an agreement to devise or bequeath property by will was invalid unless that agreement "or some note or memorandum thereof" was in writing and signed by the party to be charged. See In re Estate of Murphy, 2001 WL 1640734 at 4 n.8 (Cal. Ct. App. 2001) (unpublished/noncitable) (reviewing the history of California law).

The California legislature recodified the law on will contracts with the enactment of California Probate Code §150 (now repealed), effective January 1, 1985 (set forth *infra*). The codification responded to a widespread concern about the willingness of courts to admit extrinsic evidence to determine the contractual nature of a will. California Probate Code §150 listed three methods to prove a will contract, all of which required some type of writing evidencing the contract. Section 150 specified that a contract to make a will was enforceable only when: (1) the will contained the material provisions of the contract; (2) the will made an express reference to the contract; or (3) there was a writing signed by the decedent evidencing the contract. Will contracts were defined as those agreements to make a will or devise, not to revoke a will or devise, or to die intestate. In enacting California Probate Code §150, the legislature chose language identical to that of the UPC (former UPC §2-701) (pre-1990 art. 2).

California Probate Code §150 made two important changes to prior case law: It clarified the evidence necessary to prove a will contract and also provided that joint wills or mutual wills did not raise the presumption of a will contract (this latter contribution is discussed *infra*). "With the enactment of section 150(a)(3), the Legislature allowed proof by a writing signed by the decedent evidencing the contract. It did not state that the contract itself must be in writing." *Murphy, supra,* at 3. As the *Murphy* court explains, case law "implicitly accepted the interpretation" that California Probate Code §150 was satisfied by written evidence of a contract as distinguished from a written contract. *Id.* at 3 (citing Juran v. Epstein, 28 Cal. Rptr. 2d 588 (Ct. App. 1994) (rejecting two documents purportedly evidencing a will contract between plaintiff's mother and stepfather because the documents did not provide sufficient evidence of the contract)). The court in *Murphy* continues:

> In its analysis the *Juran* court noted the Law Revision Commission's concern that alleged beneficiaries might fabricate oral agreements after the alleged promisor is dead, and it quoted the Commission's statement that "[s]ound policy requires some form of written evidence that such an agreement actually exists." (16 Cal. Law Revision Com. Rep. (Dec. 1982) p. 2349, italics added.)

Murphy, supra, at 3. The change wrought by California Probate Code §150 reflected a legislative concern with permitting only the strongest allegations of will contracts: those in which the contestants could produce a writing evidencing the contract.

Section 150 was derived from former UPC §2-701 (now UPC §2-514). Commentary to UPC §2-701 stated that its purpose was to reduce the amount of litigation over oral contracts not to revoke wills, by "tighten[ing] the methods by which contracts concerning succession may be proved." UPC §2-514 cmt. (cited in *Murphy, supra,* at 3 n.7). Professor William Fratcher, a reporter for the UPC, actually advocated a stricter policy regarding proof of will contracts. He believed that will contracts were

> rarely desirable as estate planning devices and they are likely to cause much suffering if entered into without competent advice as to their effects. Consequently, it seems desirable to impose [formal] requirements upon the making of such contracts that are so difficult that they cannot be met without the advice of counsel.

William F. Fratcher, Toward Uniform Succession Legislation, 41 N.Y.U. L. Rev. 1037, 1081 (1966) (commenting on the First Reporter's Draft of the Uniform Probate Code) (cited in Adam J. Hirsch, Inheritance and Inconsistency, 57 Ohio St. L.J. 1057, 1081 n.71(1996)). To that end, a working draft of the UPC specified that parties should make will contracts "in the manner hereinafter prescribed for the execution of attested written wills." UPC §234 (First Reporter's Draft, Aug. 1966) (cited in Hirsch, *supra,* at 1082 n.76). That recommendation to make will contracts conform to the jurisdictions' statute of wills was never adopted.

It is important to note that even prior to the enactment of California Probate Code §150, California courts permitted contestants to obtain relief for breach of an alleged oral contract via equitable remedies "if enforcement of the Statute of Frauds would cause unconscionable injury to the plaintiff or the unjust enrichment of the defendant." *Murphy, supra,* at 3. As one commentator criticizes the law (post-California Probate Code §150), courts were too willing to grant relief to plaintiffs who proved that they had materially relied on a promise without requiring plaintiffs to prove the existence of the contract by clear and convincing evidence. Carchidi, *supra,* at 1209-1210.

In response to case law developments, the California legislature revised the provision on will contracts in 2000 (Stats. 2000, ch. 17 (A.B. 1491)) to codify a narrow exception to the rule requiring a writing. California Probate Code §21700 added two new methods to prove a will contract: (1) clear and convincing evidence of an agreement between the decedent and the claimant or a promise by the decedent to the claimant that is enforceable in equity; and (2) clear and convincing evidence of an agreement between the decedent and another person for the benefit of the claimant or a promise by the decedent to another person for the benefit of the claimant that is enforceable in equity (Cal. Prob. Code §21700(4), (5)). Thus, the current statute retains the former methods of proof that require a writing but now permits the admission of extrinsic evidence provided that it reaches the level of clear and convincing evidence of an agreement.

The new Probate Code provision on will contracts also broadened the application of the statute. California Probate Code §21700 now extends to agreements or promises to make or not to revoke other commonly used testamentary instruments such as trusts.

As explained above, the former California statute (Cal. Prob. Code §150), was modeled on the UPC. However, the most recent revision (Cal. Prob. Code §21700, allowing an oral agreement to be proved by clear and convincing evidence) adopts a policy that is more liberal than the current UPC.

II. Proof of the Contract

The foremost problem in litigation involving will contracts is proof of the contract. This issue is especially important because one of the

parties to the contract (the decedent) is no longer available to testify as to his or her understanding of the situation. Courts are worried that, after the death of the testator, self-interested relatives will fabricate evidence of a contract by the testator to leave them his or her property.

A. Joint and Mutual Wills

Problems of proof arise most frequently in connection with joint and mutual wills. A joint will is a single document that is the will of two or more persons. In this situation, the same testamentary instrument is probated on the death of each of the testators. The joint will is frequently used by husbands and wives. Mutual wills are the separate testamentary documents of two persons that contain reciprocal provisions. For that reason, they are sometimes referred to as "reciprocal wills."

Joint wills and mutual wills are notorious litigation breeders because of the likelihood that such wills are contractual. That is, the fact that joint wills and mutual wills contain identical provisions raises the inference that such wills were executed pursuant to a contract not to revoke. For example, a husband's will may leave all his property to his wife if she survives him; but if she does not survive him (or after her death, if she does survive him), the property shall pass to the children of his prior marriage. The wife's will contains identical language: all the wife's property to the husband if he survives her; but if he does not survive her (or after his death, if he does survive her), then the property shall pass to the children of her prior marriage.

The fact that each will contains the same disposition indicates the possibility that the testators entered into an agreement as to the method of distribution of their estates and that they wanted the survivor to be bound by that agreement. The problem arises after the death of the first spouse. At that time, the surviving spouse may change his or her will to provide only for his or her respective children. Then, the issue becomes whether the parties' mutual or reciprocal wills were based on a contract not to revoke their respective wills.

Joint wills and mutual wills in California are governed not only by Probate Code provisions (see Section IIB *infra*), but also by family law rules pertaining to transfers between spouses (Cal. Fam. Code §721(b)). Regarding transfers between spouses, see also Chapter II *supra*.

CALIFORNIA FAMILY CODE

§721. Spouses may contract with each other and are subject to rules regarding fiduciary relationships

(a) Subject to subdivision (b), either husband or wife may enter into any transaction with the other, or with any other person, respecting property, which either might if unmarried.

(b) Except as provided in Sections 143, 144, 146, 16040, and 16047 of the Probate Code, in transactions between themselves, a husband and wife are subject to the general rules governing fiduciary relationships which control the actions of persons occupying confidential relations with each other. This confidential relationship imposes a duty of the highest good faith and fair dealing on each spouse, and neither shall take any unfair advantage of the other. This confidential relationship is a fiduciary relationship subject to the same rights and duties of nonmarital business partners, as provided in Sections 16403, 16404, and 16503 of the Corporations Code, including, but not limited to, the following:

(1) Providing each spouse access at all times to any books kept regarding a transaction for the purposes of inspection and copying.

(2) Rendering upon request, true and full information of all things affecting any transaction which concerns the community property. Nothing in this section is intended to impose a duty for either spouse to keep detailed books and records of community property transactions.

(3) Accounting to the spouse, and holding as a trustee, any benefit or profit derived from any transaction by one spouse without the consent of the other spouse which concerns the community property.

(Stats. 1992 (A.B. 2650), ch. 162, §10, effective January 1, 1994. Amended by Stats. 2002 (S.B. 1936), ch. 310, §1.)

Editor's note:

In enacting the 2002 amendments (S.B. 1936), the legislature provided:

[SEC. 2. It is the intent of the Legislature in enacting this act to clarify that Section 721 of the Family Code provides that the fiduciary relationship between spouses includes all of the same rights and duties in the management of community property as the rights and duties of unmarried business partners managing partnership property, as provided in Sections 16403, 16404, and 16503 of the Corporations Code, and to abrogate the ruling in In re Marriage of Duffy (2001) 91 Cal. App.4th 923, to the extent that it is in conflict with this clarification. In Duffy, the California Court of Appeal held that, in a marital dissolution proceeding, the evidence was insufficient to support a finding that the former husband breached his fiduciary duty of full disclosure upon request and also that the former husband did not owe a duty of care to his former wife in investing the community assets.]

B. Majority View: No Presumption of a Contract Not to Revoke

When two parties execute joint wills or mutual wills that contain identical provisions, some states presume that such wills are executed pursuant to a contract. However, under the majority view (followed by California and the UPC), the execution of a joint will or mutual will does not create the presumption of a contract not to revoke the will or wills (Cal. Prob. Code §21700; UPC §2-514).

A significant contribution of the UPC (former §2-701, now §2-514) was to eliminate the presumption that the execution of a joint will or reciprocal wills constitutes a contract not to revoke. The California legislature adopted this provision in California Probate Code §150 (the precursor to California Probate Code §21700). This provision resolved an issue that had been the subject of considerable prior litigation. See, e.g., Daniels v. Bridges, 267 P.2d 343 (Cal. Ct. App. 1954) (holding that the mere fact that a joint will contains reciprocal, similar, or identical provisions is not of itself sufficient evidence of a contract nor enough to establish a legal obligation to forebear revocation); Lynch v. Lichtenthaler, 193 P.2d 77 (Cal. Ct. App. 1948) (holding that the mere concurrent execution of mutual wills with full knowledge of their contents by both testators is not enough to prove a legal obligation to forebear revocation, in the absence of a valid contract); In re Crawford's Estate, 160 P.2d 64 (Cal. Ct. App. 1945) (holding that reciprocal wills executed by husband and wife, standing alone, do not prove the existence of an alleged collateral agreement between the spouses not to revoke).

CALIFORNIA PROBATE CODE
§150. Will contracts [repealed]

(a) A contract to make a will or devise, or not to revoke a will or devise, or to die intestate, if made after December 31, 1984, can be established only by one of the following:

(1) Provisions of a will stating material provisions of a contract.

(2) An express reference in a will to the contract and extrinsic evidence proving the terms of the contract.

(3) A writing signed by the decedent evidencing the contract.

(b) The execution of a joint will or mutual will does not create a presumption of a contract not to revoke the will or wills.

(c) A contract to make a will or devise, or not to revoke a will or devise, or to die intestate, if made on or before December 31, 1984, can be established only under the law applicable to the contract on December 31, 1984.

CALIFORNIA PROBATE CODE
§21700. Will contracts: proof, effect of execution of joint or mutual wills

(a) A contract to make a will or devise or other instrument, or not to revoke a will or devise or other instrument, or to die intestate, if made after the effective date of this statute, can be established only by one of the following:

(1) Provisions of a will or other instrument stating the material provisions of the contract.

(2) An expressed reference in a will or other instrument to a contract and extrinsic evidence proving the terms of the contract.

(3) A writing signed by the decedent evidencing the contract.

(4) Clear and convincing evidence of an agreement between the decedent and the claimant or a promise by the decedent to the claimant that is enforceable in equity.

(5) Clear and convincing evidence of an agreement between the decedent and another person for the benefit of the claimant or a promise by the decedent to another person for the benefit of the claimant that is enforceable in equity.

(b) The execution of a joint will or mutual wills does not create a presumption of a contract not to revoke the will or wills.

(c) A contract to make a will or devise or other instrument, or not to revoke a will or devise or other instrument, or to die intestate, if made prior to the effective date of this section, shall be construed under the law applicable to the contract prior to the effective date of this section.

(Stats. 2000 (A.B. 1491), ch. 17, §8.)

III. Breach

A. After Promisor's Death

Generally, claims on will contracts are brought after the promisor's death. Such claims may be brought either against the promisor's estate or against a third party (often a third party who has received benefits under the decedent's will).

As previously explained, the most common breaches of will contracts occur in two situations. First, a surviving spouse receives a disposition under the deceased spouse's will that was allegedly executed pursuant to a will contract. The surviving spouse subsequently revokes his or her will in breach of that contract and executes a new testamentary disposition. See, e.g., *Juran*, 28 Cal. Rptr. 2d 588 (holding that testatrix's letters, stating that she "hoped" testator would abide by her wishes, that testator would have "use" of wife's personal property until he died, and that her will and that of testator were "identical," did not expressly or impliedly refer to agreement not to revoke mutual wills and, thus, were insufficient to meet writing

requirement of probate code provision governing such agreements); Brown v. Superior Court, 212 P.2d 878 (Cal. 1949) (holding that relative of deceased husband could bring an action against a widow, who conveyed all the property to her second husband, to enforce a contract between the decedent and his wife to execute mutual wills bequeathing half of their combined estates, on the death of the surviving spouse, to the relatives of each).

It is important to note that the surviving spouse has the ability to revoke his or her will even though doing so would constitute a breach of the will contract. Furthermore, the probate court will not deny admission to probate of a will merely because of the existence of a will contract calling for a different testamentary scheme. Rather, the plaintiff's remedy is under contract law not the law of succession.

In the second common breach of a will contract, a caregiver provides caretaking services for the decedent for many years in reliance on an alleged will contract that bequeaths or devises to the caregiver a significant portion of the decedent's estate. At the decedent's death, the caregiver discovers that the decedent died intestate or, alternatively, that the decedent's testamentary plan was not in conformity with the will contract.

In Schultz v. Almond, 2002 WL 1340963 (Cal. Ct. App. 2002), (unpublished/noncitable), Jacqueline Schultz, a licensed vocational nurse, took care of a neighbor, Ellis Bell, for 6 years until the latter's death at age 93. Bell suggested to Schultz in 1994 that he would leave his estate to her when he died, if she would look after him and run his errands, thereby enabling him to remain in his home rather than in a nursing home. Agreeing to his proposal, Schultz took him grocery shopping and ran errands for him weekly. She took him to medical appointments and monitored his treatments and nutrition. Bell referred to their agreement at least once per month. When Bell died intestate, Schultz brought an action against the estate for breach of contract and a constructive trust. The appellate court affirmed the trial court award of the entire estate to Schultz and the imposition of a constructive trust on the estate assets. See also Estate of Housley, 65 Cal. Rptr. 2d 628 (Ct. App. 1997) (son provided services for 30 years); Estate of Brenzikofer, 57 Cal. Rptr. 2d 401 (Ct. App. 1996) (tenants provided caretaking services for 26 years).

Among the legal and equitable remedies which are available for a breach of a will contract are: a breach of contract action, specific performance (sometimes called quasi-specific performance on the theory that specific performance is not possible after the death of one of the contracting parties); a constructive trust to prevent unjust enrichment (by someone who has received a benefit under the will which was allegedly in breach of the contract); and a claim for quantum meruit for the reasonable value of the services rendered to the decedent.

The procedure in California is that the personal representative or any other "interested party" may file a petition requesting that the court make an order in a case where the decedent binds himself or herself or his or her personal representative by a contract in writing to convey real property or to transfer personal property at death and the contract is one which can be specifically enforced (Cal. Prob. Code §850, formerly Cal. Prob. Code §9860, repealed by Stats. 2001, ch. 49 (S.B. 669), §4).

B. During Lifetimes of Contracting Parties

An issue which sometimes arises is whether the contracting parties can revoke their will contract while both parties are alive. Most authorities allow either party to repudiate the will contract unilaterally at any time before performance. McGovern & Kurtz, *supra*, §4.9 at 229.

Thus, according to the majority view, a contract is unilaterally revocable during the lifetimes of all the contracting parties. However, some states require that the breaching party give notice to the other so that the latter has the opportunity to change his or her will.

Note, however, that courts generally will not enforce contracts to make a will until the promisor's death. Thus, a promisee cannot bring an action before the promisor's death to compel compliance with the will contract. In re Marriage of Edwards, 45 Cal. Rptr. 2d 138 (Ct. App. 1995), involved a dispute concerning whether the former husband was in compliance with a provision of a marital settlement agreement requiring his testamentary disposition of one-half of his net estate to the parties' children. The former wife sought to compel production of documents (i.e., the beneficiaries of his IRA account) to verify the husband's compliance. The trial court denied enforcement. The appellate court affirmed, holding that the wife could not seek specific performance of the husband's promise to make the testamentary disposition during the husband's lifetime, absent a showing of bad faith inter vivos transfers.

CALIFORNIA PROBATE CODE

§850. Persons who may petition for court orders

(a) The following persons may file a petition requesting that the court make an order under this part:

(1) A guardian, conservator, or any claimant, in the following cases:

(A) Where the conservatee is bound by a contract in writing to convey real property or to transfer personal property, executed by the conservatee while competent or executed by the conservatee's predecessor in interest, and the contract is one that can be specifically enforced.

(B) Where the minor has succeeded to the interest of a person bound by a contract in writing to convey real property or to transfer personal property, and the contract is one that can be specifically enforced.

(C) Where the guardian or conservator or the minor or conservatee is in possession of, or holds title to, real or personal property, and the property or some interest therein is claimed to belong to another.

(D) Where the minor or conservatee has a claim to real or personal property title to or possession of which is held by another.

(2) The personal representative or any interested person in any of the following cases:

(A) Where the decedent while living is bound by a contract in writing to convey real property or to transfer personal property and dies before making the conveyance or transfer and the decedent, if living, could have been compelled to make the conveyance or transfer.

(B) Where the decedent while living binds himself or herself or his or her personal representative by a contract in writing to convey real property or to transfer personal property upon or after his or her death and the contract is one which can be specifically enforced.

(C) Where the decedent died in possession of, or holding title to, real or personal property, and the property or some interest therein is claimed to belong to another.

(D) Where the decedent died having a claim to real or personal property, title to or possession of which is held by another.

(3) The trustee or any interested person in any of the following cases:

(A) Where the trustee is in possession of, or holds title to, real or personal property, and the property, or some interest, is claimed to belong to another.

(B) Where the trustee has a claim to real or personal property, title to or possession of which is held by another.

(C) Where the property of the trust is claimed to be subject to a creditor of the settlor of the trust.

(b) The petition shall set forth facts upon which the claim is based.

(Stats. 2001 (S.B. 669), ch. 49, §1.)

IV. Defenses

A. Statute of Frauds

A fundamental problem regarding enforcement of will contracts is that the Statute of Frauds requires contracts of real property to be in writing. Courts have interpreted contracts to devise land to fall under this provision. McGovern & Kurtz, *supra*, §4.9 at 227.

California courts traditionally have held that equitable doctrines are available (under former California Probate Code §150 as well as former Civil Code §1624(b)) to bar defendants from relying on the Statute of Frauds as a defense in cases involving oral allegations of will contracts. *Housley*, 65 Cal. Rptr. 2d at 637. As the *Housley* court explains:

> There are thus two alternative circumstances in which equitable principles may be applied by a court to estop a promisor from relying on the statute of frauds to avoid an oral agreement to make a will or devise. First, equitable estoppel may apply where the promisor had induced the promisee to make a serious change of position in reliance on the oral agreement, commonly known as "detrimental reliance," and a failure to enforce the oral agreement would have caused an unconscionable injury to the promisee. Alternatively, equitable estoppel may apply where the promisor would be unjustly enriched by receiving the benefit of the promisee's performance if the promisor were allowed to invoke the statute of frauds.

***Id.* at 633.**

The part performance doctrine is often applicable in the life-care situation. The acts of the promisee generally consist of the performance of personal services for the promisor, providing a home, food and shelter, companionship, and nursing care. In some cases, the promisee may leave work, move, and make significant accommodations to provide care in return for the promised benefit. Such acts may satisfy the court as to the existence of a will contract and demonstrate hardship if the promisee does not obtain the promised benefit. That is, the performance of these acts by the promisee serve to corroborate the oral testimony as to the existence of the will contract. Given that such services are not normally rendered without expectation of reward, the promisee must have provided services based on the existence of a will contract. "This would be especially probable if no compensation was paid during the life of the alleged promisor." George Gleason Bogert et al., Trusts and Trustees: Constructive Trusts §480 (rev. 2d ed. 2002) [hereinafter Bogert].

The basis of an award of specific performance is to give the promisee the property for which he or she contracted. As a prerequisite to granting specific performance, courts require that the plaintiff's remedy at law be inadequate. Sometimes, courts prefer to use the remedy of constructive trust, rather than specific

performance, because some courts reject the view that there can be a decree for specific performance of a contract to make a will that is in effect until death (i.e., courts are reluctant to issue decrees that require someone to do an act or to supervise personal matters). *Id.*

Several California cases have addressed the application of the Statute of Frauds as a defense in claims involving will contracts. In *Housely, supra*, one of the testator's children lived with the testator for a 30-year period. During that time, the son provided daily care for his father and paid for his father's living expenses. The father had executed a will and inter vivos trust that named the son as a beneficiary. However, before his death, the father executed a codicil to the will and amended the trust to remove the son as a beneficiary. After the father's death, the latter will and codicil were admitted to probate. The son filed a petition seeking imposition of a constructive trust on the father's estate and an order declaring the son to be a beneficiary of the trust based on the son's detrimental reliance on the father's alleged promises to leave all of his property to the son. The son alleged that he would not have cared for the father and paid many of his expenses had the father not promised that he would leave him all his property.

In response, the testator's other child (his daughter who was serving as executrix) alleged that the purported oral contract was invalid under the Statute of Frauds. The son countered that she was estopped from relying on the Statute of Frauds because a failure to enforce the oral agreement would result in an unconscionable injury to him. Reversing the trial court's grant of summary judgment for the executrix, the Court of Appeal held that: (1) a fact question existed as to date of alleged oral agreement; (2) equitable estoppel could be used to estop a Statute of Frauds defense, regardless of whether the alleged agreement was made before or after 1985; and (3) a fact question existed as to whether equitable estoppel should apply. The court remanded for a determination of these issues.

In Marston v. Marston, 2002 WL 31032732 (Cal. Ct. App. 2002)(unpublished, noncitable), the testator's daughter-in-law brought an action for quasi-specific enforcement of her alleged oral contract with the testator to make a will. She claimed that she had agreed to marry the testator's son (who had a history of mental problems that made him unemployable) in exchange for the testator's promise of financial support during the marriage and a one-third share of his estate. (When the father died, he left $150,000 in trust only to the son.) The daughter-in-law sought quasi-specific performance of the contract to make a will and also sought to impose a constructive trust on a one-third interest in the decedent's estate.

The trial court granted the motion for summary judgment of the defendants (other family members of the decedent). Reversing, the appellate court held that: (1) a genuine issue of fact existed as to whether the daughter-in-law made an oral contract with the testator; and (2) a genuine issue of fact existed as to whether the doctrine of equitable estoppel barred the Statute of Frauds defense. Specifically, the court held that the daughter-in-law had introduced evidence sufficient to create a triable issue of fact regarding whether the oral contract induced her to make a serious change of position. The court reasoned that a trier of fact could find that reliance on the will contract induced her to make a serious change of position by her marriage to the testator's son, requiring her to assume personal and legal obligations to care and support a spouse with mental and emotional problems, and foreclosed her marriage to someone else. The court added that a trier of fact could also conclude that she would suffer an "unconscionable" injury if the lack of a written contract caused the testator's oral promise to be unenforceable.

In *Brenzikofer*, 57 Cal. Rptr. 2d 401, tenants (a husband and wife) filed a petition seeking specific performance of their landlord's alleged oral agreement to convey to them the house that they were renting from her. They alleged that the landlord had orally promised to convey them the house in return for their care of her (for 26 years) and of her many cats. The trial court granted the administrator's summary judgment motion. Reversing and remanding, the appellate court held that: (1) a fact question as to whether the landlord promised to devise her home to tenants precluded summary judgment for the administrator; (2) the tenants' petition was not time barred; and (3) unjust enrichment was an issue for trial. The appellate court found that an oral agreement existed between the plaintiff and the deceased based on extrinsic evidence consisting of affidavits from four nonparty witnesses. The court also reasoned that if the defendant was permitted to assert the Statute of Frauds as a defense, plaintiffs would suffer an unconscionable injury.

See generally Vartuhi Torounian, Chapter 17: An Attempt to Improve the Existing Probate Law, 32 McGeorge L. Rev. 681 (2001) (discussing California case law involving will contracts).

B. Statute of Limitations

Another possible defense to a claim for breach of a will contract is that the claim is

barred by the statute of limitations. Jurisdictions have different statutes of limitation that apply to will contract claims. For example, California law applies a 1-year statute of limitations on all actions (contract, tort, etc.) against a decedent on which the statute of limitations otherwise applicable has not run at the time of death (Cal. Code Civ. Proc. §366.2). California has a 2-year statute of limitations for breaches of oral contracts (Cal. Code Civ. Proc. §339). See also Potter v. Bland, 288 P.2d 569 (Cal. Ct. App. 1955); Keefe v. Keefe, 125 P. 929 (Cal. Ct. App. 1912). However, a 4-year statute of limitations may apply in some cases (for example, in claims seeking constructive trust or based on resulting trust). See *Brenzikofer*, 57 Cal. Rptr. 2d at 405.

Generally, a cause of action on a contract to make a will generally does not come into existence until the promisor dies. The applicable statute of limitations begins running at that point. However, this general rule is subject to an exception—if the promisor makes an inter vivos transfer of property in violation of a contract to make will. In such a case, the promisee may seek equitable relief against the promisor during the promisor's lifetime. A party may be equitably estopped from asserting the statute of limitations as a defense if his or her conduct has induced another not to bring suit within the applicable limitations period. These principles are illustrated in Battuello v. Battuello, 75 Cal. Rptr. 2d 548 (Ct. App. 1998).

In *Battuello*, a son filed suit against his mother, both individually and in her capacity as trustee of family trust, and against his father's estate to establish an interest in the family vineyard on the basis of his father's oral contract to make a will conveying the property to him. His mother demurred, arguing that the complaint was barred by the 1-year statute of limitations. The appellate court held that the son made sufficient allegations to support his claim of equitable estoppel that would preclude assertion of the 1-year limitations period. Specifically, he alleged that his mother convinced him not to file a timely breach of contract suit within 1 year of the promisor's death by her promising him, during settlement negotiations, that he would receive the property notwithstanding its conveyance to family trust.

Amendments to the Code of Civil Procedure in 2000 address the statute of limitations for actions on will contracts. Specifically, California Code of Civil Procedure §366.3 provides that the statute of limitation for bringing a will contract action is 1 year from the date of the testator's death. As one commentator notes:

> [The new provision] gives added assurance that the estate of the deceased will not endure unending contests. . . . Since most estates and trusts are distributed within 18 months after the date of death, a coherent statute of limitations that will run one year from date of death will grant beneficiaries peace of mind that their inheritance is not subject to challenge in the future. Moreover, a statute of limitations for all claims against an estate will give greater assurance to fiduciaries in administering estates.

Torounian, *supra*, at 690. In addition, amendments in 2000 to the California Probate Code extended the application of the statute to agreements or promises to make or not to revoke other commonly used testamentary instruments such as trusts. *Id.* at 689-690.

CALIFORNIA CODE OF CIVIL PROCEDURE

§339. Statute of limitations for actions upon an oral contract: two years

Within two years: 1. An action upon a contract, obligation or liability not founded upon an instrument of writing, except as provided in Section 2725 of the Commercial Code or subdivision 2 of Section 337 of this code; or an action founded upon a contract, obligation or liability, evidenced by a certificate, or abstract or guaranty of title of real property, or by a policy of title insurance; provided, that the cause of action upon a contract, obligation or liability evidenced by a certificate, or abstract or guaranty of title of real property or policy of title insurance shall not be deemed to have accrued until the discovery of the loss or damage suffered by the aggrieved party thereunder.

2. An action against a sheriff or coroner upon a liability incurred by the doing of an act in an official capacity and in virtue of office, or by the omission of an official duty including the nonpayment of money collected in the enforcement of a judgment.

3. An action based upon the rescission of a contract not in writing. The time begins to run from the date upon which the facts that entitle the aggrieved party to rescind occurred. Where the ground for rescission is fraud or mistake, the time does not begin to run until the discovery by the aggrieved party of the facts constituting the fraud or mistake.

(Enacted 1872. Amended by Code Am. 1873-74, ch. 383, p. 291, §33; Stats. 1905, ch. 258, p. 231, §1; Stats. 1906, ch. 1, p. 5, §2; Stats. 1907, ch. 323, p. 599, §2; Stats. 1913, ch. 187, p. 332, §1; Stats. 1917, ch. 203, p. 299, §2; Stats. 1961, ch. 589, p. 1736, §7; Stats. 1980, ch. 1307, §1; Stats. 1982, ch. 497, p. 2154, §31, effective July 1, 1983; Stats. 1996 (A.B. 3472), ch. 872, §11.)

§366.2. Statute of limitations upon death of person against whom action may be brought: one year after death

(a) If a person against whom an action may be brought on a liability of the person, whether arising in contract, tort, or otherwise, and whether accrued or not accrued, dies before the expiration of the applicable limitations period, and the cause of action survives, an action may be commenced within one year after the date of death, and the limitations period that would have been applicable does not apply.

(b) The limitations period provided in this section for commencement of an action shall not be tolled or extended for any reason except as provided in any of the following, where applicable:

(1) Sections 12, 12a, and 12b of this code.

(2) Part 4 (commencing with Section 9000) of Division 7 of the Probate Code (creditor claims in administration of estates of decedents).

(3) Part 8 (commencing with Section 19000) of Division 9 of the Probate Code (payment of claims, debts, and expenses from revocable trust of deceased settlor).

(4) Part 3 (commencing with Section 21300) of Division 11 of the Probate Code (no contest clauses).

(c) This section applies to actions brought on liabilities of persons dying on or after January 1, 1993.

(Stats. 1992 (S.B. 1496), ch. 178, §8. Amended by Stats. 1993 (A.B. 1704), ch. 151, §2, effective July 19, 1993; Stats. 1994 (A.B. 797), ch. 40, §1, effective January 1, 1995; Stats. 1996 (A.B. 2751), ch. 862, §1; Stats. 1998 (A.B. 2801), ch. 581, §1; Stats. 2006 (A.B. 2864), ch. 221, §1.)

§366.3. Statute of limitations for claims arising from promise or agreement relating to distribution from estate or trust or under other instrument

(a) If a person has a claim that arises from a promise or agreement with a decedent to distribution from an estate or trust or under another instrument, whether the promise or agreement was made orally or in writing, an action to enforce the claim to distribution may be commenced within one year after the date of death, and the limitations period that would have been applicable does not apply.

(b) The limitations period provided in this section for commencement of an action shall not be tolled or extended for any reason except as provided in Sections 12, 12a, and 12b of this code and Part 3 (commencing with Section 21300) of Division 11 of the Probate Code.

(c) This section applies to actions brought on claims concerning persons dying on or after the effective date of this section.

(Stats. 2000 (A.B. 1491), ch. 17, §1; Stats. 2006 (A.B. 2864), ch. 221, §2.)

VIII
WILL SUBSTITUTES

This chapter addresses nontestamentary devices that enable property to be transferred at death without administration. States permit testators to dispose of their property at death through either testamentary dispositions or nontestamentary devices (called "will substitutes" or "nonprobate transfers"). Common will substitutes include life insurance, multiple-party accounts, joint tenancy, deeds, gifts, and inter vivos trusts. (Inter vivos trusts are discussed in Chapter IX *infra.*)

I. Nonprobate Transfers Generally

A. Introductory Provisions: Validity, Restrictions, Protection of Property Holder

A nonprobate transfer is a will substitute. A will substitute permits the property owner to enjoy rights of ownership during his or her lifetime while enabling the property to avoid the subsequent costs and delay of the probate process. California legislation (Cal. Prob. Code §5000) validates a large number of written instruments that provide for nonprobate transfers on death. The section adopts the substance of UPC §6-201 (1987). It is broader than the repealed California statute (former Cal. Prob. Code §160) because of its inclusion of such nonprobate transfers as: a certificated or uncertificated security, account agreement, custodial agreement, compensation plan, individual retirement plan, employee benefit plan, deed of gift, and marital property agreement. The statutory enumeration of written instruments is not intended to be exclusive. Also, the statute provides that an instrument making a nonprobate transfer need not comply with the formalities required for a will. Law Revision Commission Commentary following California Probate Code §5000.

The holder of property involving a nonprobate transfer need not recognize claims (unless required by federal law) by persons who are not authorized by the instrument to execute a provision for transfer of the property (e.g., a nonemployee-spouse under an employee benefit plan or a nonowner-spouse under an insurance policy) (Cal. Prob. Code §5002). Law Revision Commission Commentary following California Probate Code §5002.

The California legislation provides some protection to holders of property that is the subject of a nonprobate transfer. The holder of property is not required to ascertain the respective separate, community, and quasi-community property interests of the spouses in the property or whether the transfer is consistent with the rights of the person named as beneficiary (such as if the surviving spouse is no longer a "surviving spouse" because of a dissolution or annulment under California Probate Code §5600) (Cal. Prob. Code §5003).

The California Law Revision Commission is considering the enactment of a revocable transfer on death (TOD) deed for real property (also called a "beneficiary deed") based on the belief that such a deed would be preferable to existing donative transfer devices. After a comprehensive review of the practice in nine jurisdictions, the Commission has determined to introduce implementing legislation in 2007. Further information is available at http://www.clrc.ca.gov (last visited July 5, 2007).

CALIFORNIA PROBATE CODE

§5000. Validity of nonprobate transfers on death despite noncompliance with requirements for execution of will

(a) A provision for a nonprobate transfer on death in an insurance policy, contract of employment, bond, mortgage, promissory note, certificated or uncertificated security, account agreement, custodial agreement, deposit agreement, compensation plan, pension plan, individual retirement plan, employee benefit plan, trust, conveyance, deed of gift, marital property agreement, or other written instrument of a similar nature is not invalid because the instrument does not comply with the requirements for execution of a will, and this code does not invalidate the instrument.

(b) Included within subdivision (a) are the following:

(1) A written provision that money or other benefits due to, controlled by, or owned by a decedent before death shall be paid after the decedent's death to a person whom the decedent designates either in the instrument or in a separate writing, including a will, executed either before or at the same time as the instrument, or later.

(2) A written provision that money due or to become due under the instrument shall cease to be payable in event of the death of the promisee or the promisor before payment or demand.

(3) A written provision that any property controlled by or owned by the decedent before death that is the subject of the instrument shall pass to a person whom the decedent designates either in the instrument or in a separate writing, including a will, executed either before or at the same time as the instrument, or later.

(c) Nothing in this section limits the rights of creditors under any other law.

(Stats. 1990 (A.B. 759), ch. 79, §14, effective July 1, 1991.)

§5002. Holder of property need not receive, hold or transfer property to unauthorized persons

Notwithstanding any other provision of this part, a holder of property under an instrument of a type described in Section 5000 is not required to receive, hold, or transfer the property in compliance with a provision for a nonprobate transfer on death executed by a person who has an interest in the property if either (1) the person is not authorized by the terms of the instrument to execute a provision for transfer of the property, or (2) the provision for transfer of the property does not otherwise satisfy the terms of the instrument.

(Stats. 1992 (A.B. 1719), ch. 51, §4.)

§5003. Holder of property need not ascertain ownership interests or status of beneficiaries; exceptions

(a) A holder of property under an instrument of a type described in Section 5000 may transfer the property in compliance with a provision for a nonprobate transfer on death that satisfies the terms of the instrument, whether or not the transfer is consistent with the beneficial ownership of the property as between the person who executed the provision for transfer of the property and other persons having an interest in the property or their successors, and whether or not the transfer is consistent with the rights of the person named as beneficiary.

(b) Except as provided in this subdivision, no notice or other information shown to have been available to the holder of the property affects the right of the holder to the protection provided by subdivision (a). The protection provided by subdivision (a) does not extend to a transfer made after either of the following events:

(1) The holder of the property has been served with a contrary court order.

(2) The holder of the property has been served with a written notice of a person claiming an adverse interest in the property. However, this paragraph does not apply to a pension plan to the extent the transfer is a periodic payment pursuant to the plan.

(c) The protection provided by this section does not affect the rights of the person who executed the provision for transfer of the property and other persons having an interest in the property or their successors in disputes among themselves concerning the beneficial ownership of the property.

(d) The protection provided by this section is not exclusive of any protection provided the holder of the property by any other provision of law.

(e) A person shall not serve notice under paragraph (2) of subdivision (b) in bad faith. If the court in an action or proceeding relating to the rights of the parties determines that a person has served notice under paragraph (2) of subdivision (b) in bad faith, the court shall award against the person the cost of the action or proceeding, including a reasonable attorney's fee, and the damages caused by the service.

(Stats. 1992 (A.B. 1719), ch. 51, §5. Amended by Stats. 2001 (A.B. 873), ch. 417, §7.)

B. Nonprobate Transfers of Community Property

1. General Provisions

California legislation also governs nonprobate transfers of community property at death. In 1992 the state legislature enacted new legislation addressing such transfers (Cal. Prob. Code §§5010 et seq.).

The most significant features of California Probate Code §§5010 et seq. include: (1) a nonprobate transfer of community property at death is voidable without the written consent of the spouse, and the court has flexibility in fashioning a remedy for a transfer without consent; (2) consent to a nonprobate transfer of community property at death is not ordinarily a transmutation of the property into the separate property of the other spouse; rather, the property retains its community character; (3) a nonprobate transfer of community property remains revocable until death, provided the

revocation is in writing and the other spouse is informed of the revocation before death; (4) the surviving spouse may not change the disposition of the decedent's share of the community property unless the decedent's consent to do so is explicit. 14 Witkin, Summary, Wills, §308.

Written consent to a provision for a nonprobate transfer includes a written joinder in the provision, i.e., joint action by both spouses in writing (Cal. Prob. Code §5010). To be effective, a written consent need not satisfy the statutory requirements for transmutation (Cal. Prob. Code §5022). The validity of a written consent is subject to common law and statutory defenses (e.g., fraud, undue influence, misrepresentation, violation of the special fiduciary duty applicable in transactions between spouses). Law Revlslon Commission Commentary following California Probate Code §5010.

The applicable rules in this section are not intended to override either other state statutes that govern rights under specific instruments or federal law (such as the Employee Retirement Income Security Act or ERISA) (Cal. Prob. Code §5011). Law Revision Commission Commentary following California Probate Code §5011.

CALIFORNIA PROBATE CODE

§5010. "Written consent" defined

As used in this chapter, "written consent" to a provision for a nonprobate transfer of community property on death includes a written joinder in such a provision.

(Stats. 1992 (A.B. 1719), ch. 51, §6.)

§5011. Rights of parties in nonprobate transfers are subject to terms of instrument, state law, and intent

Notwithstanding any other provision of this part, the rights of the parties in a nonprobate transfer of community property on death are subject to all of the following:

(a) The terms of the instrument under which the nonprobate transfer is made.

(b) A contrary state statute specifically applicable to the instrument under which the nonprobate transfer is made.

(c) A written expression of intent of a party in the provision for transfer of the property or in a written consent to the provision.

(Stats. 1992 (A.B. 1719), ch. 51, §6.)

§5012. Provisions do not affect obligations of holders of community property

A provision of this chapter concerning rights between a married person and the person's spouse in community property is relevant only to controversies between the person and spouse and their successors and does not affect the obligation of a holder of community property under an instrument of a type described in Section 5000 to hold, receive, or transfer the property in compliance with a provision for a nonprobate transfer on death, or the protection provided the holder by Section 5003.

(Stats. 1992 (A.B. 1719), ch. 51, §6.)

§5013. Surviving spouse's waiver of rights in community property unaffected

Nothing in this chapter limits the effect of a surviving spouse's waiver of rights in community property under Chapter 1 (commencing with Section 140) of Part 3 of Division 2 or other instrument or agreement that affects a married person's interest in community property.

(Stats. 1992 (A.B. 1719), ch. 51, §6.)

§5014. Application of chapter and effective date

(a) Except as provided in subdivision (b), this chapter applies to a provision for a nonprobate transfer of community property on the death of a married person, regardless of whether the provision for transfer of the property was executed by the person, or written consent to the provision for transfer of the property was given by the person's spouse, before, on, or after January 1, 1993.

(b) Subdivision (c) of Section 5030 does not apply, and the applicable law in effect on the date of death does apply, to revocation of a written consent given by a spouse who died before January 1, 1993.

(Stats. 1992 (A.B. 1719), ch. 51, §6.)

§5015. Common law and statutory defenses (fraud, etc.) are still effective

Nothing in this chapter limits the application of principles of fraud, undue influence, duress, mistake, or other invalidating cause to a written consent to a provision for a nonprobate transfer of community property on death.

(Stats. 1992 (A.B. 1719), ch. 51, §6.)

2. Consent to Provision for Nonprobate Transfers of Community Property

Written consent is required for a nonprobate transfer of community property. Specifically, a provision for a nonprobate transfer of community property that is executed by one

spouse without the written consent of the other spouse is not effective as to the nonconsenting spouse's interest in that property. Nor does such a transfer affect the nonconsenting spouse's disposition of his or her interest on death by will, intestate succession, or nonprobate transfer (Cal. Prob. Code §5020). California Probate Code §5020 codifies the case law rule that the statutory community property gift limitations apply to nonprobate transfers such as beneficiary designations in trusts and accounts.

A spouse can modify a nonprobate transfer of community property after initial consent is given. Such modifications (e.g., designation of beneficiaries, revocation, election of a different benefit or payment option) are governed by California Probate Code §5023. If one spouse acquires the other spouse's consent initially, but the former subsequently modifies a provision without the other spouse's consent, the modification is effective as to the modifying spouse's interest (Cal. Prob. Code §5023(b)). However, certain rules apply regarding the nonconsenting spouse's interest, depending on whether the modification was executed before or after the nonconsenting spouse's death:

(1) If the modification is executed during the nonconsenting spouse's lifetime, it revokes that spouse's original written consent (Cal. Prob. Code §5023(b)(1)). In the absence of consent, that nonconsenting spouse's interest passes with his or her estate or as otherwise disposed of.
(2) If the modification is executed after the nonconsenting spouse's death, it does not affect that spouse's original written consent (which is treated as irrevocable). However, the deceased spouse's interest is subject to the transfer based on the terms of the original consent (Cal. Prob. Code §5023(b)(2)).
(3) If the provision for transfer of the original written consent authorizes modification after the surviving spouse's death, the modification is effective (Cal. Prob. Code §5023(b)(3)).

14 Witkin, Summary, Wills, §310.

A court can set aside a nonprobate transfer of community property made under a provision executed by one spouse without the written consent of the other (Cal. Prob. Code §5021(a)).

A spouse's written consent is not a transmutation (Cal. Prob. Code §5022). According to Law Revision Commission Commentary, the statute is consistent with Estate of MacDonald, 794 P.2d 911 (Cal. 1990) (holding that a spouse's written consent to transmutation of community property must contain language that expressly states that a change in the characterization or ownership is being made, and therefore the wife's consent to her husband's designation of a trust as beneficiary of his individual retirement accounts was insufficient).

> A consent to a nonprobate transfer is in effect a consent to a future gift of the person's interest in community property. . . . Until the gift is complete, however, it remains community property and is part of the community estate for purposes of division of property at dissolution of marriage until the consent becomes irrevocable by the death of either spouse.

Law Revision Commission Commentary following California Probate Code §5022.

CALIFORNIA PROBATE CODE

§5020. Spouse's written consent is required for effectiveness of nonprobate transfer of community property

A provision for a nonprobate transfer of community property on death executed by a married person without the written consent of the person's spouse (1) is not effective as to the nonconsenting spouse's interest in the property and (2) does not affect the nonconsenting spouse's disposition on death of the nonconsenting spouse's interest in the community property by will, intestate succession, or nonprobate transfer.

(Stats. 1992 (A.B. 1719), ch. 51, §6.)

§5021. Court shall set aside nonprobate transfers of community property without written consent

(a) In a proceeding to set aside a nonprobate transfer of community property on death made pursuant to a provision for transfer of the property executed by a married person without the written consent of the person's spouse, the court shall set aside the transfer as to the nonconsenting spouse's interest in the property, subject to terms and conditions or other remedies that appear equitable under the circumstances of the case, taking into account the rights of all interested persons.

(b) Nothing in subdivision (a) affects any additional remedy the nonconsenting spouse may have against the person's estate for a nonprobate transfer of community property on death without the spouse's written consent.

(Stats. 1992 (A.B. 1719), ch. 51, §6.)

§5022. Spouse's written consent is not a transmutation; exception

(a) Except as provided in subdivision (b), a spouse's written consent to a provision for a nonprobate transfer of community property on death is not a transmutation of the consenting spouse's interest in the property.

(b) This chapter does not apply to a spouse's written consent to a provision for a nonprobate transfer of community property on death that satisfies Section 852 of the Family Code. Such a consent is a transmutation and is governed by the law applicable to transmutations.

(Stats. 1992 (A.B. 1719), ch. 51, §6. Amended by Stats. 1993 (A.B. 1500), ch. 219, §224.3.)

§5023. Modifications of nonprobate transfers without written consent of spouse

(a) As used in this section "modification" means revocation of a provision for a nonprobate transfer on death in whole or part, designation of a different beneficiary, or election of a different benefit or payment option. As used in this section, "modification" does not mean, and this section does not apply to, the exercise of a power of appointment under a trust.

(b) If a married person executes a provision for a nonprobate transfer of community property on death with the written consent of the person's spouse and thereafter executes a modification of the provision for transfer of the property without written consent of the spouse, the modification is effective as to the person's interest in the community property and has the following effect on the spouse's interest in the community property:

(1) If the person executes the modification during the spouse's lifetime, the modification revokes the spouse's previous written consent to the provision for transfer of the property.

(2) If the person executes the modification after the spouse's death, the modification does not affect the spouse's previous written consent to the provision for transfer of the property, and the spouse's interest in the community property is subject to the nonprobate transfer on death as consented to by the spouse.

(3) If a written expression of intent of a party in the provision for transfer of the property or in the written consent to the provision for transfer of the property authorizes the person to execute a modification after the spouse's death, the spouse's interest in the community property is deemed transferred to the married person on the spouse's death, and the modification is effective as to both the person's and the spouse's interests in the community property.

(Stats. 1992 (A.B. 1719), ch. 51, §6. Amended by Stats. 1993 (A.B. 908), ch. 527, §3.)

3. Revocation of Consent to Provision for Nonprobate Transfer of Community Property

A spouse may revoke written consent to a provision for a nonprobate transfer of community property on death. The revocation may occur either at any time during the marriage (Cal. Prob. Code §5030(a)) or else upon dissolution or legal separation (Cal. Prob. Code §5030(b)). The revocation may be by any writing, including a will, that is served on the other spouse before the other spouse's death (Cal. Prob. Code §5031(b)). According to Law Revision Commission Commentary, "The will provision would change existing law as to life insurance by allowing the beneficiary designation to be overridden by an express provision in a will." Law Revision Commission Commentary following California Probate Code §5031. On "blockbuster wills," see Section IIA2 *infra*. If a spouse has revoked consent in accordance with statutory requirements, the property passes "in the same manner as if the consent had not been given" (Cal. Prob. Code §5032).

CALIFORNIA PROBATE CODE

§5030. Spouse's written consent to nonprobate transfer of community property on death is revocable

(a) A spouse's written consent to a provision for a nonprobate transfer of community property on death is revocable during the marriage.

(b) On termination of the marriage by dissolution or on legal separation, the written consent is revocable and the community property is subject to division under Division 7 (commencing with Section 2500) of the Family Code or other disposition on order within the jurisdiction of the court.

(c) On the death of either spouse, the written consent is irrevocable.

(Stats. 1992 (A.B. 1719), ch. 51, §6. Amended by Stats. 1993 (A.B. 1500), ch. 219, §224.5.)

§5031. Form and service of revocation of consent for a nonprobate transfer of community property

(a) If a married person executes a provision for a nonprobate transfer of community property on death with the written consent of the person's spouse, the consenting spouse may revoke the consent by a writing, including a will, that identifies the provision for transfer of the property being revoked, and that is served on the married person before the married person's death.

(b) Revocation of a spouse's written consent to a provision for a nonprobate transfer of community property on death does not affect the authority of the holder of the property to transfer the property in compliance with the provision for transfer of the property to the extent provided in Section 5003.

(Stats. 1992 (A.B. 1719), ch. 51, §6.)

§5032. Revocation of consent to nonprobate transfer of community property: effect on transfers

On revocation of a spouse's written consent to a nonprobate transfer of community property on death, the property passes in the same manner as if the consent had not been given.

(Stats. 1992 (A.B. 1719), ch. 51, §6.)

II. Contracts

Some contracts contain provisions that direct the disposition of property at death. Property subject to such contracts generally passes directly to the designated recipient rather than through probate. Sometimes, family members of a decedent challenge the validity of contracts as "testamentary" documents, which thereby fail to comply with a given jurisdiction's statute of wills. Such challenges arise because the legislation of many states fails to define a "will." Today, however, contracts providing for at-death transfers (like many other will substitutes) have achieved considerable acceptance.

A. Life Insurance

1. General Characteristics

A life insurance policy is a contract. As such, its provisions are construed according to contract law. The insured (generally the owner of the policy) purchases life insurance from an insurance company (the insurer) by paying premiums. At the insured's death, the insurer pays the proceeds to the person(s) whom the insured has designated.

The insured may make the proceeds of a life insurance policy payable either to a designated beneficiary or to the insured's estate. In the latter case, the proceeds will be subject to claims of the decedent's creditors. Insurance proceeds also may become part of the decedent's estate upon the failure of the primary and secondary beneficiaries to survive the decedent, or upon the disclaimer of the beneficiary or beneficiaries. Law Revision Commission Commentary following California Probate Code §13005.

An insured also may put the proceeds of life insurance in trust (called a "life insurance trust"). This may be accomplished by several methods. An insured can have the proceeds paid directly to trustees who have been designated in the insured's will. Or, the insured could create an inter vivos trust and designate the trust as the beneficiary of the insurance policy. Life insurance trusts are especially useful for beneficiaries who are minors, avoiding the cost and burden involved in property management by a guardian.

Life insurance has several advantages: (1) it is a valuable asset insofar as the proceeds are insulated from creditors' claims because they pass outside the probate estate; (2) it provides substitute income replacing the decedent's wages; (3) the beneficiary is not required to pay income tax on the proceeds; and (4) the proceeds provide a source of liquidity enabling heirs and beneficiaries to pay immediate expenses at the decedent's death (funeral, medical, taxes, etc.). Beyer, *supra*, §17.2 at 288-289.

The primary types of life insurance are term life and whole life. In a term life policy, the insurer pays proceeds to a beneficiary if the insured dies within a term specified by the

policy. The policy is generally renewable but at an increased cost as the insured ages. In contrast, whole life insurance provides protection for a set amount of premiums or the insured's entire life and also builds up a cash reserve that may be used by the insured. Universal life insurance is a variation of whole life insurance that builds up a cash reserve but provides a better rate of return. *Id.* at 289-290.

An early concern reflected in case law was that life insurance was "testamentary" and therefore invalid for failure to comply with the Statute of Wills. Case law and statute now have eliminated this concern. See, e.g., Kansas City Life Ins. Co. v. Rainey, 182 S.W.2d 624 (Mo. 1944) (upholding the beneficiary designation under an annuity as a contract for the benefit of a third party and rejecting the claim that the policy was invalid as a testamentary disposition).

An annuity is a contract between an individual (the annuitant) and an insurance company or annuity provider for a guaranteed interest bearing policy with guaranteed income options. Generally, the beneficiary is the annuitant during his or her lifetime and (at the annuitant's death) the annuitant's surviving spouse and children.

California Probate Code §5000 specifies that a provision in an insurance policy "is not invalid because the instrument does not comply with the requirements for execution of a will." That provision is intended to validate written instruments that provide for nonprobate transfers on death; the listing is not intended to be exclusive. The provision adopts the substance of UPC §6-201 (1987). Law Revision Commission Commentary following §5000. See also UPC §6-101 (providing that nonprobate transfers on death such as insurance policies, pension retirement plans, trusts, gifts, etc. are nontestamentary).

Life insurance policies generally exempt the insurer from liability in case of death of the insured by suicide. The suicide exclusion is of longstanding origin and appears in all types of life insurance. The exclusion eliminates any recovery under the policy, aside from a refund of premiums paid, if the insured dies by suicide. Lee Hugh Goodman, Litigating the Suicide Exclusion in Life Insurance Policies, 20 Am. Jur. Proof of Facts 3d 227 (2002). The insurance company has the burden of establishing the affirmative defense of suicide. The insurer must prove that the act causing death was committed with suicidal intent. 39 Cal. Jur.3d Insurance Contracts and Coverage §259.

The purchaser of life insurance on a person's life must have an "insurable interest" in the person's life. A person has an insurable interest in his or her own life, as well as that of a spouse, child, and parent. After purchasing the policy, the purchaser may transfer ownership to a third party who does not have an insurable interest in the insured. For example, the California Insurance Code provides that life insurance may pass by transfer, will, or succession to any person, whether or not the transferee has an insurable interest, and that the transferee recovers on the policy whatever the insured might have recovered (Cal. Insur. Code §10130).

CALIFORNIA PROBATE CODE

§279. Requirements for effective disclaimer; scope includes interest in life insurance

(a) A disclaimer to be effective shall be filed within a reasonable time after the person able to disclaim acquires knowledge of the interest.

(b) In the case of any of the following interests, a disclaimer is conclusively presumed to have been filed within a reasonable time if it is filed within nine months after the death of the creator of the interest or within nine months after the interest becomes indefeasibly vested, whichever occurs later:

(1) An interest created under a will.

(2) An interest created by intestate succession.

(3) An interest created pursuant to the exercise or nonexercise of a testamentary power of appointment.

(4) An interest created by surviving the death of a depositor of a Totten trust account or P.O.D. account.

(5) An interest created under a life insurance or annuity contract.

(6) An interest created by surviving the death of another joint tenant.

(7) An interest created under an employee benefit plan.

(8) An interest created under an individual retirement account, annuity, or bond.

(c) In the case of an interest created by a living trust, an interest created by the exercise of a presently exercisable power of appointment, an outright inter vivos gift, a power of appointment, or an interest created or increased by succession to a disclaimed interest, a disclaimer is conclusively presumed to have been filed within a reasonable time if it is filed within nine months after whichever of the following times occurs latest:

(1) The time of the creation of the trust, the exercise of the power of appointment, the making of the gift, the creation of the power of appointment, or the disclaimer of the disclaimed property.

(2) The time the first knowledge of the interest is acquired by the person able to disclaim.

(3) The time the interest becomes indefeasibly vested.

(d) In case of an interest not described in subdivision (b) or (c), a disclaimer is conclusively presumed to have been filed within a reasonable time if it is filed within nine months after whichever of the following times occurs later:

(1) The time the first knowledge of the interest is acquired by the person able to disclaim.

(2) The time the interest becomes indefeasibly vested.

(e) In the case of a future estate, a disclaimer is conclusively presumed to have been filed within a reasonable time if it is filed within whichever of the following times occurs later:

(1) Nine months after the time the interest becomes an estate in possession.

(2) The time specified in subdivision (b), (c), or (d), whichever is applicable.

(f) If the disclaimer is not filed within the time provided in subdivision (b), (c), (d), or (e), the disclaimant has the burden of establishing that the disclaimer was filed within a reasonable time after the disclaimant acquired knowledge of the interest.

(Stats. 1990 (A.B. 759), ch. 79, §14, effective July 1, 1991.)

§1501. Nomination of minor's guardian as to particular property (including life insurance benefits)

Subject to Section 1502, a parent or any other person may nominate a guardian for property that a minor receives from or by designation of the nominator (whether before, at the time of, or after the nomination) including, but not limited to, property received by the minor by virtue of a gift, deed, trust, will, succession, insurance, or benefits of any kind.

(Stats. 1990 (A.B. 759), ch. 79, §14, effective July 1, 1991.)

§5000. Written instrument, such as life insurance, is not invalid for failure to comply with requirements for execution of wills

(a) A provision for a nonprobate transfer on death in an insurance policy, contract of employment, bond, mortgage, promissory note, certificated or uncertificated security, account agreement, custodial agreement, deposit agreement, compensation plan, pension plan, individual retirement plan, employee benefit plan, trust, conveyance, deed of gift, marital property agreement, or other written instrument of a similar nature is not invalid because the instrument does not comply with the requirements for execution of a will, and this code does not invalidate the instrument.

(b) Included within subdivision (a) are the following:

(1) A written provision that money or other benefits due to, controlled by, or owned by a decedent before death shall be paid after the decedent's death to a person whom the decedent designates either in the instrument or in a separate writing, including a will, executed either before or at the same time as the instrument, or later.

(2) A written provision that money due or to become due under the instrument shall cease to be payable in event of the death of the promisee or the promisor before payment or demand.

(3) A written provision that any property controlled by or owned by the decedent before death that is the subject of the instrument shall pass to a person whom the decedent designates either in the instrument or in a separate writing, including a will, executed either before or at the same time as the instrument, or later.

(c) Nothing in this section limits the rights of creditors under any other law.

(Stats. 1990 (A.B. 759), ch. 79, §14, effective July 1, 1991.)

§13005. "Property of the decedent" defined

"Property of the decedent," "decedent's property," "money due the decedent," and similar phrases, include property that becomes part of the decedent's estate on the decedent's death, whether by designation of the estate as beneficiary under an insurance policy on the decedent's life or under the decedent's retirement plan, or otherwise.

(Stats. 1991 (S.B. 271), ch. 1055, §33.)

CALIFORNIA FAMILY CODE

§1612. Subject matter of premarital agreements may include life insurance benefits

(a) Parties to a premarital agreement may contract with respect to all of the following:

(1) The rights and obligations of each of the parties in any of the property of either or both of them whenever and wherever acquired or located.

(2) The right to buy, sell, use, transfer, exchange, abandon, lease, consume, expend, assign, create a security interest in, mortgage, encumber, dispose of, or otherwise manage and control property.

(3) The disposition of property upon separation, marital dissolution, death, or the occurrence or nonoccurrence of any other event.

(4) The making of a will, trust, or other arrangement to carry out the provisions of the agreement.

(5) The ownership rights in and disposition of the death benefit from a life insurance policy.

(6) The choice of law governing the construction of the agreement.

(7) Any other matter, including their personal rights and obligations, not in violation of public policy or a statute imposing a criminal penalty.

(b) The right of a child to support may not be adversely affected by a premarital agreement.

(c) Any provision in a premarital agreement regarding spousal support, including, but not limited to, a waiver of it, is not enforceable if the party against whom enforcement of the spousal support provision is sought was not represented by independent counsel at the time the agreement containing the provision was signed, or if the provision regarding spousal support is unconscionable at the time of enforcement. An otherwise unenforceable provision in a premarital agreement regarding spousal support may not become enforceable solely because the party against whom enforcement is sought was represented by independent counsel.

(Stats. 1992 (A.B. 2650), ch. 162), §10, effective January 1, 1994; Stats. 2001 (S.B. 78), ch. 286, §1.)

§4360. Determination of spousal support may include amount for life insurance on obligor

(a) For the purposes of Section 4320 [i.e., court's authority to order spousal support], where it is just and reasonable in view of the circumstances of the parties, the court, in determining the needs of a supported spouse, may include an amount sufficient to purchase an annuity for the supported spouse or to maintain insurance for the benefit of the supported spouse on the life of the spouse required to make the payment of support, or may require the spouse required to make the payment of support to establish a trust to provide for the support of the supported spouse, so that the supported spouse will not be left without means for support in the event that the spousal support is terminated by the death of the party required to make the payment of support.

(b) Except as otherwise agreed to by the parties in writing, an order made under this section may be modified or terminated at the discretion of the court at any time prior to the death of the party required to make the payment of support.

(Stats. 1992, ch. 162, §10, effective January 1, 1994.)

CALIFORNIA INSURANCE CODE

§101. "Life insurance" includes insurance and annuities

Life insurance includes insurance upon the lives of persons or appertaining thereto, and the granting, purchasing, or disposing of annuities.

(Stats. 1935, ch. 145, p. 500, §101.)

§303. Change of interest by death of insured does not avoid insurance

A change of interest by will or succession, on the death of the insured, does not avoid insurance; and his interest in the insurance passes to the person taking his interest in the subject matter insured.

(Stats. 1935, ch. 145, p. 504, §303.)

§10111.5. Liability of insurer depends on whether death was accidental or suicide

An insurer shall not be liable for payments claimed under an individual or group policy of life insurance if the duty to make those payments depends upon a factual determination of whether the death of the insured was an accident or a suicide and that fact cannot be established without an autopsy and the autopsy is prohibited under Section 27491.43 of the Government Code. Insurers refusing or delaying payments in those circumstances in good faith shall not be liable for exemplary or punitive damages.

(Stats. 1984, ch. 1731, §2.)

§10130. Insured may assign policy but transferee only acquires interest of insured

A life or disability policy may pass by transfer, will or succession to any person, whether or not the transferee has an insurable interest. Such transferee may recover upon it whatever the insured might have recovered.

(Stats. 1935, ch. 145, p. 638, §10130.)

§10170. Payment events that trigger payment of life insurance or annuity

An insurance upon life may be made payable:

(a) On the death of the insured.

(b) On his surviving a specified period.

(c) Periodically as long as he lives.

(d) Otherwise contingently on the continuance or determination of life.

(e) Upon such terms and conditions and subject to such restrictions as to revocation by the policyholder and control by beneficiaries as shall have been agreed to in writing by the insurer and the policyholder. If no terms and conditions have been agreed to by the insurer and the policyholder during the insured's lifetime then upon such terms and conditions and subject to such restrictions as may be agreed to in writing by the insurer and the beneficiaries. Any such agreement may be rescinded or amended by the parties thereto without the consent of any beneficiary therein designated unless the rights of any such beneficiary have been expressly declared to be irrevocable. No such agreement hereafter made shall vest in the insurer discretion as to the conditions, time, amount, manner or method of payment. The relationship between the insurer and the policyholder or beneficiaries under any such agreement shall be that of debtor and creditor and the insurer shall not be required to segregate funds so held but shall hold them as a part of its general corporate assets.

(Stats. 1935, ch. 145, p. 639, §10170. Amended by Stats. 1943, ch. 533, p. 2082, §1; Stats .1949, ch. 307, p. 595, §1.)

§10172. Payment in accordance with policy serves to discharge insurer

Notwithstanding Sections 751 and 1100 of the Family Code and Section 249.5 of the Probate Code, when the proceeds of, or payments under, a life insurance policy become payable and the insurer makes payment thereof in accordance with the terms of the policy, or in accordance with the terms of any written assignment thereof if the policy has been assigned, that payment shall fully discharge the insurer from all claims under the policy unless, before that payment is made, the insurer has received, at its home office, written notice by or on behalf of some other person that the other person claims to be entitled to that payment or some interest in the policy.

(Stats. 1935, ch. 145, p. 639, §10172. Amended by Stats. 1941, ch. 272, p. 1382, §2; Stats. 1972, ch. 194, p. 417, §1; Stats. 1992 (A.B. 2641), ch. 163, §98, effective January 1, 1994; Stats. 2004 (A.B. 1910), ch. 775, §3, effective January 1, 2005.)

§10172.5. Insurer must pay promptly after death of insured or else pay interest

(a) Notwithstanding any other provision of law, each insurer admitted to transact life insurance, credit life insurance, or accidental death insurance in this state that fails or refuses to pay the proceeds of, or payments under, any policy of life insurance issued by it within 30 days after the date of death of the insured shall pay interest, at a rate not less than the then current rate of interest on death proceeds left on deposit with the insurer computed from the date of the insured's death, on any moneys payable and unpaid after the expiration of the 30-day period. This section shall apply only to deaths of insureds which occur on or after January 1, 1976.

(b) Nothing in this section shall be construed to allow any insurer admitted to transact life insurance, credit life insurance, or accidental death insurance in this state to withhold payment of money payable under a life insurance policy to any beneficiary for a period longer than reasonably necessary to transmit that payment. Whenever possible payment shall be made within 30 days after the date of death of the insured.

(c) In any case in which interest on the proceeds of, or payments under, any policy of life insurance, credit life insurance, or accidental death insurance becomes payable pursuant to subdivision (a), the insurer shall notify the named beneficiary or beneficiaries at their last known address that interest will be paid on the proceeds of, or payments under, that policy from the date of death of the named insured. That notice shall specify the rate of interest to be paid. In any case where the notice required by Section 249.5 of the Probate Code has been given to a life insurer, that insurer is not required to provide the notice required by this section until after it has been notified that a child has actually been born within two years of the death of the decedent. The obligation shall be deemed satisfied by giving notice to the person who first provides proof to the insurer that the child has been born alive.

(d) This section shall not require the payment of interest in any case in which the beneficiary elects in writing delivered to the insurer to receive the proceeds of, or payments under, the policy by any means other than a lump-sum payment thereof.

(Stats. 1975, ch. 876, p. 1956, §1. Amended by Stats. 2004 (A.B. 1910), ch. 775, §4.5, effective January 1, 2005.)

§10173. Effect of assignment of life insurance policy

When a policy of life insurance is assigned in writing the insurer may deal with the assignee in any manner not inconsistent with the terms of said assignment until the insurer has received at its home office written notice by or on behalf of some other person that such other person claims to be entitled to some interest in such policy.

(Stats. 1941, ch. 272, p. 1383, §3.)

2. Change of Beneficiary

Occasionally, an insured may wish to revoke the prior designation of a beneficiary. Life

insurance policies generally reserve to the insured the right to change the beneficiary. During the insured's lifetime, the beneficiary therefore has an expectancy of an inchoate gift that is revocable at the wish of the insured. The beneficiary only acquires a vested right if the policy reserves no right to change its terms. 13 Witkin, Summary, Personal Property, §138.

However, to effect any change of beneficiary, the insured must comply with the policy requirements. For example, the insured generally cannot alter the designation of beneficiary by means of a will. The life insurance company normally specifies the method of changing beneficiaries, such as by requiring a request from the insured that is filed with the insurer and indorsement of the change on the policy by the insurer. Some cases have held that the indorsement by the insurer or issuance of a new certificate is merely a ministerial act that need not be completed before the insured's death (although not dispensing with the insured's need to inform the insurance company of the change). See, e.g., Estate of Burnett, 118 P.2d 298 (Cal. 1941) (holding that letters written by the insured to the home office of insurance companies requesting a change of beneficiary were effective, regardless of the fact that insured died after the letters were mailed but before they were received, so that proceeds of policies never became assets of insured's estate subject to creditors' claims).

Case law recognizes some exceptions to the general rule that the method of changing the beneficiary specified in an insurance policy must be followed "substantially." These exceptions include situations in which: (1) the carrier has waived its own rules and, pursuant to the request of the insured, issued a new certificate; (2) it was beyond the power of the insured to comply with the formalities; or (3) the insured has pursued the policy requirements and has done everything possible to change the beneficiary, but before the new policy is actually issued, the insured dies. 39 Cal. Jur.3d Insurance Contracts and Coverage §379 (citing Pimentel v. Conselho Supremo de Uniao Portugueza do Estado, 57 P.2d 131 (Cal. 1936)).

Note, however, that a written notification of a change of beneficiary does not constitute a will. In Estate of Wheatley, 193 P. 934 (Cal. 1920), the court held that a witnessed letter addressed to the Metropolitan Life Insurance Company, stating that decedent wanted to bequeath the money in the Metropolitan policy to proponent in the event that decedent died on a trip, was not admissible as a will because it was not testamentary in character.

At common law, and in absence of statute today, divorce does not revoke the designation of the former spouse as a life insurance beneficiary. Thus, where the insured dies without changing the designation of the former spouse as beneficiary, the rights of the former spouse-beneficiary cannot be abrogated by the insured's will. According to the majority rule, any attempt to change the beneficiary of a life insurance policy by means of a will is ineffective. Even if the insured person remarries after a divorce, but neglects to change the name of his or her former spouse as beneficiary of his life insurance policy, then the former spouse (and not the surviving spouse) will be beneficiary of the policy. See Jenkins v. Jenkins, 297 P. 56 (Cal. 1931); 39 Cal. Jur.3d Insurance Contracts and Coverage §364. However, some states (including California, discussed *infra*) have enacted legislation that extends their automatic revocation statute to nontestamentary transfers.

California Probate Code §6122 provides that divorce or annulment revoke the following probate transfers and nominations to a former spouse: (1) any disposition or appointment of property made by the will to the former spouse; (2) any provision of the will conferring a general or special power of appointment on the former spouse; and (3) any provision of the will nominating the former spouse as executor, trustee, conservator, or guardian. California Probate Code §6122.1 provides that termination of a domestic partnership has the same effect (see Chapter VI, II, A for more detail.)

In 2001, the state legislature enacted legislation (Cal. Prob. Code §§5600 et seq.) that also invalidates many nonprobate transfers at death to the transferor's former spouse. The statutes cover both transfers by instrument (Cal. Prob. Code §5600) and joint tenancy survivorship (Cal. Prob. Code §5601). The statutes became effective January 1, 2002, and generally apply to an instrument making a nonprobate transfer or creating a joint tenancy executed before, on, or after that date. However, prior law applies if the person making the transfer or creating the joint tenancy dies before that date or the dissolution or other event terminating the spouse's status as a surviving spouse occurs before that date (Cal. Prob. Code §5604). Thus, where a divorce occurs before January 1, 2002, that person's rights as a nonprobate transfer beneficiary or joint tenant of the decedent are not affected by California Probate Code §§5600 or 5601.

The legislation does not limit the court's authority to order a party to a dissolution or annulment to maintain the former spouse as a beneficiary of a nonprobate transfer or to preserve a joint tenancy in favor of the former spouse. (Cal. Prob. Code §5603). 14 Witkin, Summary, Wills, §317.

If a nonprobate transfer fails under California Probate Code §5600, the property subject to the transfer is treated as though the former spouse failed to survive the transferor (Cal. Prob. Code §5600(c)). Some nonprobate transfers are exceptions to the rule and do not fail if: (1) the transfer could not be revoked by the transferor at the time of death (Cal. Prob. Code §5600(b)(1)); (2) "clear and convincing evidence" exists that the transferor "intended to preserve" the transfer to the former spouse (Cal. Prob. Code §5600(b)(2)); or (3) a court order that the transfer be maintained for the former spouse is in effect at the time of death (Cal. Prob. Code §5600(b)(3)). According to Law Revision Commission Commentary, California Probate Code §5600(a) is not applicable where a nonprobate transfer is irrevocable on execution (such as an irrevocable trust) or later becomes irrevocable by the transferor for reasons other than the transferor's death or incapacity. 14 Witkin, Summary, Wills, §318. California Probate Code §5602 provides for a procedure for certifying that a person's rights to real property transferred on the death of a spouse or former spouse, by an instrument making a nonprobate transfer or by operation of joint tenancy survivorship, are not affected by this legislation.

Note that provisions in life insurance policies are excluded from California Probate Code §5600 regulating automatic revocation of will provisions for divorced spouses. See Cal. Prob. Code §5600(e). However, recent California legislation on nonprobate transfers of community property may permit will provisions to override the designation of a life insurance beneficiary in some situations. To illustrate, a spouse may revoke his or her written consent to a provision for a nonprobate transfer of community property on death. The revocation may be by any writing, including a will, that is served on the other spouse before the latter's death (Cal. Prob. Code §5031(b)). According to Law Revision Commission Commentary, "The will provision would change existing law as to life insurance by allowing the beneficiary designation to be overridden by an express provision in a will." Law Revision Commission Commentary following California Probate Code §5031. For additional discussion, see Section IB3 *supra*.

The UPC (UPC §2-804) also changes the common law rule regarding designation of the former spouse as beneficiary of an insurance policy, pension plan, or other contract. UPC §6-101 provides that if the contract permits the owner to change the beneficiary by will, then the owner may do so.

A superwill (or "blockbuster will") enables a testator to change the conditions and provisions of will substitutes through the use of testamentary instruments. Although the American Bar Association briefly considered (but rejected) a model uniform superwill in 1987, the State of Washington has enacted pioneering legislation. Washington's superwill statute (Wash. Rev. Code ch. 11.11) permits a testator to alter in a will the beneficiary designation of revocable living trusts and of joint tenancy bank accounts with right of survivorship (but not life insurance). See generally Cynthia J. Artura, Comment, Superwill to the Rescue? How Washington's Statute Falls Short of Being a Hero in the Field of Trust and Probate Law, 74 Wash. L. Rev. 799 (1999) (criticizing the statute because its definition of nonprobate asset excludes life insurance policies and retirement plans, and recommending that the state legislature broaden the definition of nonprobate asset to include all nontestamentary revocable devices).

State statutes with automatic revocation provisions may be preempted by federal laws governing employer-provided benefits. The United States Supreme Court has explored whether federal law preempted the Washington state operation-of-law-revocation statute providing that the designation of a spouse as the beneficiary of a nonprobate asset was revoked automatically upon divorce (Wash. Rev. Code §11.07.010).

In Egelhoff v. Egelhoff, 532 U.S. 141 (2001), the Supreme Court determined whether the Employee Retirement Income Security Act of 1974 (ERISA), 88 Stat. 832, 29 U.S.C. §§1001 et seq., preempts that state statute. In *Egelhoff*, the children from an intestate's first marriage sued the intestate's second wife, whose marriage to intestate had been dissolved shortly before his death, claiming entitlement to life insurance proceeds and pension plan benefits. The decedent was employed by the Boeing Company, which provided him with a life insurance policy and a pension plan—both governed by ERISA. The decedent had designated his wife as the beneficiary under both and had failed to change the designation before his death. The Supreme Court held that federal law preempted the state statute if the insured's policy was governed by ERISA. That is, benefits should be paid in accordance with federal, rather than state, law.

CALIFORNIA PROBATE CODE

§78. Persons ineligible as "surviving spouse"

"Surviving spouse" does not include any of the following:

(a) A person whose marriage to the decedent has been dissolved or annulled, unless, by virtue of a subsequent marriage, the person is married to the decedent at the time of death.

(b) A person who obtains or consents to a final decree or judgment of dissolution of marriage from the decedent or a final decree or judgment of annulment of their marriage, which decree or judgment is not recognized as valid in this state, unless they (1) subsequently participate in a marriage ceremony purporting to marry each to the other or (2) subsequently live together as husband and wife.

(c) A person who, following a decree or judgment of dissolution or annulment of marriage obtained by the decedent, participates in a marriage ceremony with a third person.

(d) A person who was a party to a valid proceeding concluded by an order purporting to terminate all marital property rights.

(Stats. 1990 (A.B. 759), ch. 79, §14, effective July 1, 1991.)

§5600. Automatic revocation on nonprobate transfer to former spouse; exceptions

(a) Except as provided in subdivision (b), a nonprobate transfer to the transferor's former spouse, in an instrument executed by the transferor before or during the marriage, fails if, at the time of the transferor's death, the former spouse is not the transferor's surviving spouse as defined in Section 78, as a result of the dissolution or annulment of the marriage. A judgment of legal separation that does not terminate the status of husband and wife is not a dissolution for purposes of this section.

(b) Subdivision (a) does not cause a nonprobate transfer to fail in any of the following cases:

(1) The nonprobate transfer is not subject to revocation by the transferor at the time of the transferor's death.

(2) There is clear and convincing evidence that the transferor intended to preserve the nonprobate transfer to the former spouse.

(3) A court order that the nonprobate transfer be maintained on behalf of the former spouse is in effect at the time of the transferor's death.

(c) Where a nonprobate transfer fails by operation of this section, the instrument making the nonprobate transfer shall be treated as it would if the former spouse failed to survive the transferor.

(d) Nothing in this section affects the rights of a subsequent purchaser or encumbrancer for value in good faith who relies on the apparent failure of a nonprobate transfer under this section or who lacks knowledge of the failure of a nonprobate transfer under this section.

(e) As used in this section, "nonprobate transfer" means a provision, other than a provision of a life insurance policy, of either of the following types:

(1) A provision of a type described in Section 5000.

(2) A provision in an instrument that operates on death, other than a will, conferring a power of appointment or naming a trustee.

(Stats. 2001 (A.B. 873), ch. 417, §9, effective January 1, 2002.)

§5601. Automatic severance of joint tenancy with former spouse; exceptions

(a) Except as provided in subdivision (b), a joint tenancy between the decedent and the decedent's former spouse, created before or during the marriage, is severed as to the decedent's interest if, at the time of the decedent's death, the former spouse is not the decedent's surviving spouse as defined in Section 78, as a result of the dissolution or annulment of the marriage. A judgment of legal separation that does not terminate the status of husband and wife is not a dissolution for purposes of this section.

(b) Subdivision (a) does not sever a joint tenancy in either of the following cases:

(1) The joint tenancy is not subject to severance by the decedent at the time of the decedent's death.

(2) There is clear and convincing evidence that the decedent intended to preserve the joint tenancy in favor of the former spouse.

(c) Nothing in this section affects the rights of a subsequent purchaser or encumbrancer for value in good faith who relies on an apparent severance under this section or who lacks knowledge of a severance under this section.

(d) For purposes of this section, property held in "joint tenancy" includes property held as community property with right of survivorship, as described in Section 682.1 of the Civil Code.

(Stats. 2001 (A.B. 873), ch. 417, §9, effective January 1, 2002.)

§5602. Affidavit procedure provides protection for purchaser or encumbrancer of real property

(a) Nothing in this part affects the rights of a purchaser or encumbrancer of real property for value who in good faith relies on an affidavit or a declaration under penalty of perjury under the laws of this state that states all of the following:

(1) The name of the decedent.

(2) The date and place of the decedent's death.

(3) A description of the real property transferred to the affiant or declarant by an instrument making a nonprobate transfer or by operation of joint tenancy survivorship.

(4) Either of the following, as appropriate:

(A) The affiant or declarant is the surviving spouse of the decedent.

(B) The affiant or declarant is not the surviving spouse of the decedent, but the rights of the affiant or declarant to the described property are not affected by Section 5600 or 5601.

(b) A person relying on an affidavit or declaration made pursuant to subdivision (a) has no duty to inquire into the truth of the matters stated in the affidavit or declaration.

(c) An affidavit or declaration made pursuant to subdivision (a) may be recorded.

(Stats. 2001 (A.B. 873), ch. 417, §9, effective January 1, 2002.)

§5603. Judicial authority still exists to order divorcing spouses to maintain former spouse as beneficiary or to preserve joint tenancy

Nothing in this part is intended to limit the court's authority to order a party to a dissolution or annulment of marriage to maintain the former spouse as a beneficiary on any nonprobate transfer described in this part, or to preserve a joint tenancy in favor of the former spouse.

(Stats. 2001 (A.B. 873), ch. 417, §9, effective January 1, 2002.)

§5604. Effective date

(a) This part is operative on January 1, 2002.

(b) Except as provided in subdivision (c), this part applies to an instrument making a nonprobate transfer or creating a joint tenancy whether executed before, on, or after the operative date of this part.

(c) Sections 5600 and 5601 do not apply, and the applicable law in effect before the operative date of this part applies, to an instrument making a nonprobate transfer or creating a joint tenancy in either of the following circumstances:

(1) The person making the nonprobate transfer or creating the joint tenancy dies before the operative date of this part.

(2) The dissolution of marriage or other event that terminates the status of the nonprobate transfer beneficiary or joint tenant as a surviving spouse occurs before the operative date of this part.

(Stats. 2001 (A.B. 873), ch. 417, §9, effective January 1, 2002.)

§6122. Revocation by operation of law: dissolution or annulment

(a) Unless the will expressly provides otherwise, if after executing a will the testator's marriage is dissolved or annulled, the dissolution or annulment revokes all of the following:

(1) Any disposition or appointment of property made by the will to the former spouse.

(2) Any provision of the will conferring a general or special power of appointment on the former spouse.

(3) Any provision of the will nominating the former spouse as executor, trustee, conservator, or guardian.

(b) If any disposition or other provision of a will is revoked solely by this section, it is revived by the testator's remarriage to the former spouse.

(c) In case of revocation by dissolution or annulment:

(1) Property prevented from passing to a former spouse because of the revocation passes as if the former spouse failed to survive the testator.

(2) Other provisions of the will conferring some power or office on the former spouse shall be interpreted as if the former spouse failed to survive the testator.

(d) For purposes of this section, dissolution or annulment means any dissolution or annulment which would exclude the spouse as a surviving spouse within the meaning of Section 78. A decree of legal separation which does not terminate the status of husband and wife is not a dissolution for purposes of this section.

(e) Except as provided in Section 6122.1, no change of circumstances other than as described in this section revokes a will.

(f) Subdivisions (a) to (d), inclusive, do not apply to any case where the final judgment of dissolution or annulment of marriage occurs before January 1, 1985. That case is governed by the law in effect prior to January 1, 1985.

(Stats. 1990 (A.B. 759), ch. 79, §14, effective July 1, 1991. Amended Stats. 2001 (A.B. 25), ch. 893, §50; Stats. 2002 (A.B. 3034), ch. 664, §179, effective January 1, 2003.)

§6122.1. Revocation by operation of law: termination of domestic partnership

(a) Unless the will expressly provides otherwise, if after executing a will the testator's domestic partnership is terminated, the termination revokes all of the following:

(1) Any disposition or appointment of property made by the will to the former domestic partner.

(2) Any provision of the will conferring a general or special power of appointment on the former domestic partner.

(3) Any provision of the will nominating the former domestic partner as executor, trustee, conservator, or guardian.

(b) If any disposition or other provision of a will is revoked solely by this section, it is revived by the testator establishing another domestic partnership with the former domestic partner.

(c) In case of revocation by termination of a domestic partnership:

(1) Property prevented from passing to a former domestic partner because of the revocation passes as if the former domestic partner failed to survive the testator.

(2) Other provisions of the will conferring some power or office on the former domestic partner shall be interpreted as if the former domestic partner failed to survive the testator.

(d) This section shall apply only to wills executed on or after January 1, 2002.

(Stats. 2001 (A.B. 25), ch. 893, §51.)

§6227. Revocation of statutory will by dissolution or annulment of marriage

(a) If after executing a California statutory will the testator's marriage is dissolved or annulled, the dissolution or annulment revokes any disposition of property made by the will to the former spouse and any nomination of the former spouse as executor, trustee, guardian, or custodian made by the will. If any disposition or nomination is revoked solely by this section, it is revived by the testator's remarriage to the former spouse.

(b) In case of revocation by dissolution or annulment:

(1) Property prevented from passing to a former spouse because of the revocation passes as if the former spouse failed to survive the testator.

(2) Provisions nominating the former spouse as executor, trustee, guardian, or custodian shall be interpreted as if the former spouse failed to survive the testator.

(c) For purposes of this section, dissolution or annulment means any dissolution or annulment that would exclude the spouse as a surviving spouse within the meaning of Section 78. A decree of legal separation which does not terminate the status of husband and wife is not a dissolution or annulment for purposes of this section.

(d) This section applies to any California statutory will, without regard to the time when the will was executed, but this section does not apply to any case where the final judgment of dissolution or annulment of marriage occurs before January 1, 1985; and, if the final judgment of dissolution or annulment of marriage occurs before January 1, 1985, the case is governed by the law that applied prior January 1, 1985.

(Stats. 1991 (S.B. 271), ch. 1055, §20.)

3. Effect of Simultaneous Death and Homicide on Life Insurance Benefits

A beneficiary who unlawfully kills the insured cannot recover benefits under the policy. According to California Probate Code §252, a beneficiary of a life insurance policy who "feloniously and intentionally" kills the insurer is not entitled to any benefit under the policy. The policy becomes payable as if the slayer predeceased the insured. On the slayer

disqualification generally, see Chapter I, Section IIIE1 *supra*.

Also, the California Probate Code provides for distribution of life insurance proceeds in cases of the simultaneous death of the insured and beneficiary. If it cannot be established by clear and convincing evidence that the beneficiary survived the insured, the proceeds of the policy are distributed as if the insured survived the beneficiary (Cal. Prob. Code §224). The provision does not apply in the case of a trust, deed, insurance contract, or any other situation, where: (1) provision is made dealing explicitly with simultaneous deaths or otherwise providing for distribution of property different from the Probate Code provisions relating to simultaneous death, or (2) provision is made requiring one person to survive another for a stated period in order to take property or providing for a presumption as to survivorship that results in a distribution of property different from that provided by the Probate Code provisions (Cal. Prob. Code §221(b)). 39 Cal. Jur.3d Insurance Contracts and Coverage §375.

CALIFORNIA PROBATE CODE

§220. Requirement of proof of survival by clear and convincing evidence

Except as otherwise provided in this chapter, if the title to property or the devolution of property depends upon priority of death and it cannot be established by clear and convincing evidence that one of the persons survived the other, the property of each person shall be administered or distributed, or otherwise dealt with, as if that person had survived the other.

(Stats. 1990 (A.B. 759), ch. 79, §14, effective July 1, 1991.)

§221. Exceptions: if certain instruments provide otherwise

(a) This chapter does not apply in any case where Section 103, 6211, or 6403 applies.

(b) This chapter does not apply in the case of a trust, deed, or contract of insurance, or any other situation, where (1) provision is made dealing explicitly with simultaneous deaths or deaths in a common disaster or otherwise providing for distribution of property different from the provisions of this chapter or (2) provision is made requiring one person to survive another for a stated period in order to take property or providing for a presumption as to survivorship that results in a distribution of property different from that provided by this chapter.

(Stats. 1990 (A.B. 759), ch. 79, §14, effective July 1, 1991. Amended Stats. 1990, ch. 710, §1; Stats. 2002, (A.B. 1784), ch. 138, §3, effective January 1, 2003.)

§224. Simultaneous death of insured and beneficiary under life or accident insurance

If the insured and a beneficiary under a policy of life or accident insurance have died and it cannot be established by clear and convincing evidence that the beneficiary survived the insured, the proceeds of the policy shall be administered or distributed, or otherwise dealt with, as if the insured had survived the beneficiary, except if the policy is community or quasi-community property of the insured and the spouse of the insured and there is no alternative beneficiary except the estate or personal representative of the insured, the proceeds shall be distributed as community property under Section 103.

(Stats. 1990 (A.B. 759), ch. 79, §14, effective July 1, 1991.)

§250. Slayer disqualification: wills, trusts, intestate succession, and family protection

(a) A person who feloniously and intentionally kills the decedent is not entitled to any of the following:

(1) Any property, interest, or benefit under a will of the decedent, or a trust created by or for the benefit of the decedent or in which the decedent has an interest, including any general or special power of appointment conferred by the will or trust on the killer and any nomination of the killer as executor, trustee, guardian, or conservator or custodian made by the will or trust.

(2) Any property of the decedent by intestate succession.

(3) Any of the decedent's quasi-community property the killer would otherwise acquire under Section 101 or 102 upon the death of the decedent.

(4) Any property of the decedent under Part 5 (commencing with Section 5700) of Division 5.

(5) Any property of the decedent under Part 3 (commencing with Section 6500) of Division 6.

(b) In the cases covered by subdivision (a):

(1) The property interest or benefit referred to in paragraph (1) of subdivision (a) passes as if the killer had predeceased the decedent and Section 21110 does not apply.

(2) Any property interest or benefit referred to in paragraph (1) of subdivision (a) which passes under a power of appointment and by reason of the death of the

decedent passes as if the killer had predeceased the decedent, and Section 673 not apply.

(3) Any nomination in a will or trust of the killer as executor, trustee, guardian, conservator, or custodian which becomes effective as a result of the death of the decedent shall be interpreted as if the killer had predeceased the decedent.

(Stats. 1990 (A.B. 759), ch. 79, §14, effective July 1, 1991. Amended Stats. 1991 (S.B. 271), ch. 1055, §13; Stats. 1992 (A.B. 2975), ch. 871, §2; Stats. 1997 (A.B. 1172), ch. 724, §3; Stats. 2002, (A.B. 1784), ch. 138, §5, effective January 1, 2003.)

§252. Slayer disqualification: bonds, life insurance and other beneficiary designations

A named beneficiary of a bond, life insurance policy, or other contractual arrangement who feloniously and intentionally kills the principal obligee or the person upon whose life the policy is issued is not entitled to any benefit under the bond, policy, or other contractual arrangement, and it becomes payable as though the killer had predeceased the decedent.

(Stats. 1990 (A.B. 759), ch. 79, §14, effective July 1, 1991.)

4. Protection of Surviving Spouse from Unauthorized Transfers

The California Family Code and Probate Code provide protection to surviving spouses from some inter vivos transfers of the decedent (see discussion Chapter II, Section IV, *supra*). For example, breach of a spouse's fiduciary duty in the management of the community estate (such as by a spouse's conveyance of community property to a third party without the other spouse's consent) enables the aggrieved spouse at dissolution or death to restore one-half of the unauthorized community property transfer (Cal. Fam. Code §1101(g)), either by bringing a common law action (a "set-aside suit") against the transferee; or proceeding against the transferor-spouse's estate. Ross & Grant, *supra*, §§4:19.1a & 4:19.2. If an aggrieved spouse seeks relief against the transferee at any time during the marriage, the former may void the transaction entirely. Cal. Fam. Code §1101(h); Ross & Grant, *supra*, at §4:19.1a. Also, the surviving spouse may require that a transferee who receives quasi-community property in which the surviving spouse had an expectancy must restore one-half of that property to the decedent's estate (Cal. Prob. Code §102). However, the transferee need not restore life insurance (or accident insurance, joint annuity, or pension) payable to a person other than the surviving spouse. *Id.* at §102(b)).

CALIFORNIA FAMILY CODE
§1101. Remedies for spouse's breach of fiduciary duty

(a) A spouse has a claim against the other spouse for any breach of the fiduciary duty that results in impairment to the claimant spouse's present undivided one-half interest in the community estate, including, but not limited to, a single transaction or a pattern or series of transactions, which transaction or transactions have caused or will cause a detrimental impact to the claimant spouse's undivided one-half interest in the community estate.

(b) A court may order an accounting of the property and obligations of the parties to a marriage and may determine the rights of ownership in, the beneficial enjoyment of, or access to, community property, and the classification of all property of the parties to a marriage.

(c) A court may order that the name of a spouse shall be added to community property held in the name of the other spouse alone or that the title of community property held in some other title form shall be reformed to reflect its community character, except with respect to any of the following:

(1) A partnership interest held by the other spouse as a general partner.

(2) An interest in a professional corporation or professional association.

(3) An asset of an unincorporated business if the other spouse is the only spouse involved in operating and managing the business.

(4) Any other property, if the revision would adversely affect the rights of a third person.

(d)(1) Except as provided in paragraph (2), any action under subdivision (a) shall be commenced within three years of the date a petitioning spouse had actual knowledge that the transaction or event for which the remedy is being sought occurred.

(2) An action may be commenced under this section upon the death of a spouse or in conjunction with an action for legal separation, dissolution of marriage, or nullity without regard to the time limitations set forth in paragraph (1).

(3) The defense of laches may be raised in any action brought under this section.

(4) Except as to actions authorized by paragraph (2), remedies under subdivision (a) apply only to transactions or events occurring on or after July 1, 1987.

(e) In any transaction affecting community property in which the consent of both spouses is required, the court may, upon the motion of a spouse, dispense with the requirement of the other spouse's consent if both of the following requirements are met:

(1) The proposed transaction is in the best interest of the community.

(2) Consent has been arbitrarily refused or cannot be obtained due to the physical incapacity, mental incapacity, or prolonged absence of the nonconsenting spouse.

(f) Any action may be brought under this section without filing an action for dissolution of marriage, legal separation, or nullity, or may be brought in conjunction with the action or upon the death of a spouse.

(g) Remedies for breach of the fiduciary duty by one spouse, including those set out in Sections 721 and 1100, shall include, but not be limited to, an award to the other spouse of 50 percent, or an amount equal to 50 percent, of any asset undisclosed or transferred in breach of the fiduciary duty plus attorney's fees and court costs. The value of the asset shall be determined to be its highest value at the date of the breach of the fiduciary duty, the date of the sale or disposition of the asset, or the date of the award by the court.

(h) Remedies for the breach of the fiduciary duty by one spouse, as set forth in Sections 721 and 1100, when the breach falls within the ambit of Section 3294 of the Civil Code shall include, but not be limited to, an award to the other spouse of 100 percent, or an amount equal to 100 percent, of any asset undisclosed or transferred in breach of the fiduciary duty.

(Stats. 1992 (A.B. 2650), ch. 162, §10, effective January 1, 1994. Amended by Stats. 2001 (A.B. 583), ch. 703, §1.)

CALIFORNIA PROBATE CODE
§102. Surviving spouse may recapture some quasi-community property; exception for life insurance payable to third party

(a) The decedent's surviving spouse may require the transferee of property in which the surviving spouse had an expectancy under Section 101 [quasi-community property] at the time of the transfer to restore to the decedent's estate one-half of the property if the transferee retains the property or, if not, one-half of its proceeds or, if none, one-half of its value at the time of transfer, if all of the following requirements are satisfied:

(1) The decedent died domiciled in this state.

(2) The decedent made a transfer of the property to a person other than the surviving spouse without receiving in exchange a consideration of substantial value and without the written consent or joinder of the surviving spouse.

(3) The transfer is any of the following types:

(A) A transfer under which the decedent retained at the time of death the possession or enjoyment of, or the right to income from, the property.

(B) A transfer to the extent that the decedent retained at the time of death a power, either alone or in conjunction with any other person, to revoke or to consume, invade, or dispose of the principal for the decedent's own benefit.

(C) A transfer whereby property is held at the time of the decedent's death by the decedent and another with right of survivorship.

(b) Nothing in this section requires a transferee to restore to the decedent's estate any life insurance, accident insurance, joint annuity, or pension payable to a person other than the surviving spouse.

(c) All property restored to the decedent's estate under this section belongs to the surviving spouse pursuant to Section 101 as though the transfer had not been made.

(Stats. 1990 (A.B. 759), ch. 79, §14, effective July 1, 1991.)

B. Multiple-Party Accounts

1. Generally

People often hold accounts in financial institutions in two or more names. These accounts are called "multiple-party accounts." Such accounts provide a simple and inexpensive method for a depositor to specify the disposition of the funds upon death.

These accounts generally take the following forms:

- **joint account (e.g., an account payable to "X or Y");**
- **trust account (e.g., an account held as "X, in trust for Y"); or**
- **POD account (e.g., an account held as "X, payable on death to Y").**

Such accounts have caused tremendous litigation concerning such issues as: validity, ownership as between the parties of the multiple-party accounts and others, alteration of rights, rights at death (of the donee and surviving spouse), rights of creditors, and the protection of financial institutions. The Uniform Probate Code

(Article VI) has addressed these issues, and many states have legislation patterned after the UPC.

In California, multiple-party accounts are governed by the California Multiple-Party Accounts Law (Cal. Fin. Code §852 and Cal. Prob. Code §§5100 et seq.). The law applies to all "financial institutions," defined as state or national banks, state or federal savings and loan associations, or credit unions, or similar organizations, as well as industrial loan companies (Cal. Prob. Code §5128). In California, a "multiple-party account" is any of the following types of accounts: a joint account, a P.O.D. account, and a Totten trust account (Cal. Prob. Code §5132).

Ownership of the account is governed by California Probate Code §5301. While the parties are alive, the deposits in a joint account belong to the parties to the account in proportion to the net contributions made by each party, absent clear and convincing evidence of a different intent (Cal. Prob. Code §5301(a)). The deposits in a P.O.D. account belong to the depositor during his or her lifetime. If there are two or more depositors, their rights are governed by the rules applicable to joint accounts (Cal. Prob. Code §5301(b)). A trust account (Totten trust account) belongs to the depositor (trustee) during his or her lifetime unless the terms of the account reveal a different intent or unless there is clear and convincing evidence of an irrevocable trust. In the case where the evidence reveals that the trust account is irrevocable, the sums on deposit belong to the beneficiary. If the trust account has two or more depositors, their rights also are governed by the rules applicable to joint accounts (Cal. Prob. Code §5301(c)). In sum, neither the P.O.D. payee nor the Totten trust beneficiary has any rights to the account during the lifetime of the depositor (in the absence of evidence of a different intent).

Survivorship rights are governed by California Probate Code §5302. For a joint account, at the death of the depositor, the balance belongs to the surviving party or parties (absent evidence of a contrary intent) (Cal. Prob. Code §5302(a)). For a P.O.D. account, at the death of the sole depositor, the balance in the account belongs to the surviving P.O.D. payee or payees (Cal. Prob. Code §5302(b)). If there is more than one original depositor for the P.O.D. account, then survivorship rights are governed by California Probate Code §5302(a). For a trust account, at the death of the sole depositor (trustee), the balance belongs to the surviving beneficiary or beneficiaries absent evidence of a contrary intent (Cal. Prob. Code §5302(c)). If only one of several trustees dies, then survivorship rights are determined by California Probate Code §5302(a). On the status of deposits by married persons as community property, see California Probate Code §5305.

Statutory provisions also provide protection for financial institutions offering multiple-party accounts. The financial institution is protected from liability if it follows the rules set forth. For example, a holder of property that is the subject of a nonprobate transfer is not obligated to ascertain the parties' interests (i.e., as separate, community, and quasi-community property) in the property. Unless the holder of property has been served with a contrary court order or notice of an adverse claim, the holder may transfer the property in accordance with the terms of the instrument. A spouse or beneficiary asserting an adverse right must make a claim against the estate of the person who executed the instrument or against the beneficiary, not against the holder of the property (Cal. Prob. Code §5003).

Also, according to California law, financial institutions can require a special power of attorney with regard to multiple-party accounts (Cal. Prob. Code §5204). The power of attorney, however, gives the agent no ownership or survivorship right in the account.

CALIFORNIA PROBATE CODE

§5100. California Multiple-Party Accounts Law

This part may be cited as the California Multiple-Party Accounts Law.

(Stats. 1990 (A.B. 759), ch. 79, §14, effective July 1, 1991.)

§5120. Definitions govern construction

Unless the provision or context otherwise requires, the definitions in this article govern the construction of this part.

(Stats. 1990 (A.B. 759), ch. 79, §14, effective July 1, 1991.)

§5122. "Account," defined

(a) "Account" means a contract of deposit of funds between a depositor and a financial institution, and includes a checking account, savings account, certificate of deposit, share account, and other like arrangement.

(b) "Account" does not include:

(1) An account established for deposit of funds of a partnership, joint venture, or other association for business purposes.

(2) An account controlled by one or more persons as the duly authorized agent or trustee for a corporation, unincorporated association, or charitable or civic organization.

(3) A regular fiduciary or trust account where the relationship is established other than by deposit agreement.

(4) An account established for the deposit of funds of the estate of a ward, conservatee, or decedent.

(Stats. 1990 (A.B. 759), ch. 79, §14, effective July 1, 1991.)

§5124. "Agent," defined

"Agent" means a person who has a present right, subject to request, to payment from an account as an attorney in fact under a power of attorney.

(Stats. 1990 (A.B. 759), ch. 79, §14, effective July 1, 1991.)

§5126. "Beneficiary," defined

"Beneficiary" means a person named in a Totten trust account as one for whom a party to the account is named as trustee.

(Stats. 1990 (A.B. 759), ch. 79, §14, effective July 1, 1991.)

§5128. "Financial institution," defined

"Financial institution" includes:

(a) A financial institution as defined in Section 40.

(b) An industrial loan company as defined in Section 18003 of the Financial Code.

(Stats. 1990 (A.B. 759), ch. 79, §14, effective July 1, 1991.)

§5130. "Joint account," defined

"Joint account" means an account payable on request to one or more of two or more parties whether or not mention is made of any right of survivorship.

(Stats. 1990 (A.B. 759), ch. 79, §14, effective July 1, 1991.)

§5132. "Multipleparty account," defined

A "multipleparty account" is any of the following types of account:

(a) A joint account.

(b) A P.O.D. account.

(c) A Totten trust account.

(Stats. 1990 (A.B. 759), ch. 79, §14, effective July 1, 1991.)

§5134. "Net contribution," defined

(a) "Net contribution" of a party to an account as of any given time is the sum of all of the following:

(1) All deposits thereto made by or for the party, less all withdrawals made by or for the party that have not been paid to or applied to the use of any other party.

(2) A pro rata share of any interest or dividends earned, whether or not included in the current balance.

(3) Any proceeds of deposit life insurance added to the account by reason of the death of the party whose net contribution is in question.

(b) In the absence of proof otherwise:

(1) Only parties who have a present right of withdrawal shall be considered as having a net contribution.

(2) The net contribution of each of the parties having a present right of withdrawal is deemed to be an equal amount.

(c) It is the intent of the Legislature in enacting this section to provide a definition for the purpose of determining ownership interests in an account as between the parties to the account, and not as between the parties and the financial institution.

(Stats. 1990 (A.B. 759), ch. 79, §14, effective July 1, 1991.)

§5136. "Party," defined

(a) "Party" means a person who, by the terms of the account, has a present right, subject to request, to payment from a multiple-party account other than as an agent.

(b) A P.O.D. payee is a party, by reason of being a P.O.D. payee, only after the account becomes payable to the payee by reason of surviving all persons named as original payees.

(c) A beneficiary of a Totten trust account is a party, by reason of being a beneficiary, only after the account becomes payable to the beneficiary by reason of surviving all persons named as trustees.

(Stats. 1990 (A.B. 759), ch. 79, §14, effective July 1, 1991.)

§5138. "Payment," defined

"Payment" of sums on deposit includes all of the following:

(a) A withdrawal, including payment on check or other directive of a party.

(b) A pledge of sums of deposit.

(c) A setoff, reduction, or other disposition of all or part of an account pursuant to a pledge.

(Stats. 1990 (A.B. 759), ch. 79, §14, effective July 1, 1991.)

§5139. "P.O.D.," defined

"P.O.D." means pay on death.

(Stats. 1990 (A.B. 759), ch. 79, §14, effective July 1, 1991.)

§5140. "P.O.D. account," defined

"P.O.D. account" means any of the following:

(a) An account payable on request to one person during the person's lifetime and on the person's death to one or more P.O.D. payees.

(b) An account payable on request to one or more persons during their lifetimes and on the death of all of them to one or more P.O.D. payees.

(Stats. 1990 (A.B. 759), ch. 79, §14, effective July 1, 1991.)

§5142. "P.O.D. payee," defined

"P.O.D. payee" means a person designated on a P.O.D. account as one to whom the account is payable on request after the death of one or more persons.

(Stats. 1990 (A.B. 759), ch. 79, §14, effective July 1, 1991.)

§5144. "Proof of death," defined

"Proof of death" includes any of the following:

(a) An original or attested or certified copy of a death certificate.

(b) A record or report that is prima facie evidence of death under Section 103550 of the Health and Safety Code, Sections 1530 to 1532, inclusive, of the Evidence Code, or another statute of this state.

(Stats. 1990 (A.B. 759), ch. 79, §14, effective July 1, 1991. Amended by Stats. 1996 (S.B. 1497), ch. 1023, §400, effective September 29, 1996.)

§5146. Order or notice "received" by institution, defined

Except to the extent the terms of the account or deposit agreement expressly provide otherwise, a financial institution "receives" an order or notice under this part when it is received by the particular office or branch office of the financial institution where the account is carried.

(Stats. 1990 (A.B. 759), ch. 79, §14, effective July 1, 1991.)

§5148. "Request" to financial institution; effect of compliance with these requirements

"Request" means a proper request for withdrawal, including a check or order for payment, that complies with all conditions of the account (including special requirements concerning necessary signatures) and regulations of the financial institution; but, if the financial institution conditions withdrawal or payment on advance notice, for purposes of this part the request for withdrawal or payment is treated as immediately effective and a notice of intent to withdraw is treated as a request for withdrawal.

(Stats. 1990 (A.B. 759), ch. 79, §14, effective July 1, 1991.)

§5150. "Sums on deposit," defined

"Sums on deposit" means both of the following:

(a) The balance payable on an account, including interest and dividends earned, whether or not included in the current balance.

(b) Any life insurance proceeds added to the account by reason of the death of a party.

(Stats. 1990 (A.B. 759), ch. 79, §14, effective July 1, 1991.)

§5152. "Withdrawal," defined

"Withdrawal" includes payment to a third person pursuant to a check or other directive of a party or an agent.

(Stats. 1990 (A.B. 759), ch. 79, §14, effective July 1, 1991.)

§5201. Application of provisions concerning beneficial ownership and liability of financial institutions

(a) The provisions of Chapter 3 (commencing with Section 5301) concerning beneficial ownership as between parties, or as between parties and P.O.D. payees or beneficiaries of multipleparty accounts, are relevant only to controversies between these persons and their creditors and other successors, and have no bearing on the power of withdrawal of these persons as determined by the terms of account contracts.

(b) The provisions of Chapter 4 (commencing with Section 5401) govern the liability of financial institutions who make payments pursuant to that chapter.

(Stats. 1990 (A.B. 759), ch. 79, §14, effective July 1, 1991.)

§5202. Fraudulent transfer law unaffected

Nothing in this part affects the law relating to transfers in fraud of creditors.

(Stats. 1990 (A.B. 759), ch. 79, §14, effective July 1, 1991.)

§5203. Creation of accounts by different wording

(a) Words in substantially the following form in a signature card, passbook, contract, or instrument evidencing an account, or words to the same effect, executed before, on, or after July 1, 1990, create the following accounts:

(1) Joint account: "This account or certificate is owned by the named parties. Upon the death of any of them, ownership passes to the survivor(s)."

(2) P.O.D. account with single party: "This account or certificate is owned by the named party. Upon the death of

that party, ownership passes to the named pay-on-death payee(s)."

(3) P.O.D. account with multiple parties: "This account or certificate is owned by the named parties. Upon the death of any of them, ownership passes to the survivor(s). Upon the death of all of them, ownership passes to the named pay-on-death payee(s)."

(4) Joint account of husband and wife with right of survivorship: "This account or certificate is owned by the named parties, who are husband and wife, and is presumed to be their community property. Upon the death of either of them, ownership passes to the survivor."

(5) Community property account of husband and wife: "This account or certificate is the community property of the named parties who are husband and wife. The ownership during lifetime and after the death of a spouse is determined by the law applicable to community property generally and may be affected by a will."

(6) Tenancy in common account: "This account or certificate is owned by the named parties as tenants in common. Upon the death of any party, the ownership interest of that party passes to the named pay-on-death payee(s) of that party or, if none, to the estate of that party."

(b) Use of the form language provided in this section is not necessary to create an account that is governed by this part. If the contract of deposit creates substantially the same relationship between the parties as an account created using the form language provided in this section, this part applies to the same extent as if the form language had been used.

(Stats. 1990 (A.B. 759), ch. 79, §14, effective July 1, 1991.)

§5204. Financial institutions can require special power of attorney

(a) In addition to a power of attorney otherwise authorized by law, a special power of attorney is authorized under this section to apply to one or more accounts at a financial institution or to one or more contracts with a financial institution concerning safe deposit services. For the purposes of this section, "account" includes checking accounts, savings accounts, certificates of deposit, savings certificates, and any other depository relationship with the financial institution.

(b) The special power of attorney under this section shall:

(1) Be in writing.

(2) Be signed by the person or persons giving the power of attorney.

(3) Explicitly identify the attorney-in-fact or attorneys-in-fact, the financial institution, and the accounts or contracts subject to the power.

(c) The special power of attorney shall contain language in substantially the following form:

"WARNING TO PERSON EXECUTING THIS DOCUMENT: This is an important legal document. It creates a power of attorney that provides the person you designate as your attorney-in-fact with the broad powers it sets forth. You have the right to terminate this power of attorney. If there is anything about this form that you do not understand, you should ask a lawyer to explain it to you."

(d) In addition to the language required by subdivision (c), special powers of attorney that are or may be durable shall also contain substantially the following language:

"These powers of attorney shall continue even if you later become disabled or incapacitated."

(e) The power of attorney granted under this section shall endure as between the grantor and grantee of the power until the earliest of the following occurs:

(1) Revocation by the grantor of the power.

(2) Termination of the account.

(3) Death of the grantor of the power.

(4) In the case of a nondurable power of attorney, appointment of a guardian or conservator of the estate of the grantor of the power.

(f) A financial institution may rely in good faith upon the validity of the power of attorney granted under this section and is not liable to the principal or any other person for doing so if (1) the power of attorney is on file with the financial institution and the transaction is made by the attorney-in-fact named in the power of attorney, (2) the power of attorney appears on its face to be valid, and (3) the financial institution has convincing evidence of the identity of the person signing the power of attorney as principal.

(g) For the purposes of subdivision (f), "convincing evidence" requires both of the following:

(1) Reasonable reliance on a document that satisfies the requirement of Section 4751.

(2) The absence of any information, evidence, or other circumstances that would lead a reasonable person to believe that the person signing the power of attorney as principal is not the individual he or she claims to be.

(h) The protection provided by subdivision (f) does not extend to payments made after written notice is received by the financial institution as to any of the events of termination of the power under subdivision (e) if the financial institution has had a reasonable time to act on the notice. No other notice or any other information shown to have been available to the financial institution shall affect its right to the protection provided by this subdivision.

(i) The attorney-in-fact acting under the power of attorney granted under this section shall maintain books or records to permit an accounting of the acts of the attorneyinfact if an accounting is requested by a legal representative of the grantor of the power.

(j) The attorney-in-fact acting under a power of attorney granted under this section is liable for any disbursement other than a disbursement to or for the benefit of the grantor of the power, unless the grantor has authorized the disbursement in writing.

(k) Nothing in this section limits the use or effect of any other form of power of attorney for transactions with a financial institution. Nothing in this section creates an implication that a financial institution is liable for acting in reliance upon a power of attorney under circumstances where the requirements of subdivision (f) are not satisfied. Nothing in this section affects any immunity that may otherwise exist apart from this section.

(l) Nothing in this section prevents the attorney-in-fact from also being designated as a P.O.D. payee.

(m) Except as otherwise provided in this section, the Power of Attorney Law, Division 4.5 (commencing with Section 4000) shall not apply to a special power of attorney under this section. Section 4130 and Part 5 (commencing with Section 4900) of Division 4.5 shall apply to a special power of attorney under this section.

(Stats. 1990 (A.B. 759), ch. 79, §14, effective July 1, 1991. Amended by Stats. 1994 (S.B. 1907), ch. 307, §17; Stats. 1995 (S.B. 984), ch. 300, §15, effective August 3, 1995.)

§5205. Application to accounts in existence on July 1, 1990

This part applies to accounts in existence on July 1, 1990, and accounts thereafter established.

(Stats. 1990 (A.B. 759), ch. 79, §14, effective July 1, 1991.)

§5301. Ownership of account during lifetime of parties

(a) An account belongs, during the lifetime of all parties, to the parties in proportion to the net contributions by each to the sums on deposit, unless there is clear and convincing evidence of a different intent.

(b) In the case of a P.O.D. account, the P.O.D. payee has no rights to the sums on deposit during the lifetime of any party, unless there is clear and convincing evidence of a different intent.

(c) In the case of a Totten trust account, the beneficiary has no rights to the sums on deposit during the lifetime of any party, unless there is clear and convincing evidence of a different intent. If there is an irrevocable trust, the account belongs beneficially to the beneficiary.

(Stats. 1990 (A.B. 759), ch. 79, §14, effective July 1, 1991.)

§5302. Ownership of sums remaining on deposit upon death of depositor

Subject to Section 5600:

(a) Sums remaining on deposit at the death of a party to a joint account belong to the surviving party or parties as against the estate of the decedent unless there is clear and convincing evidence of a different intent. If there are two or more surviving parties, their respective ownerships during lifetime are in proportion to their previous ownership interests under Section 5301 augmented by an equal share for each survivor of any interest the decedent may have owned in the account immediately before the decedent's death; and the right of survivorship continues between the surviving parties.

(b) If the account is a P.O.D. account:

(1) On death of one of two or more parties, the rights to any sums remaining on deposit are governed by subdivision (a).

(2) On death of the sole party or of the survivor of two or more parties, (A) any sums remaining on deposit belong to the P.O.D. payee or payees if surviving, or to the survivor of them if one or more die before the party, (B) if two or more P.O.D. payees survive, any sums remaining on deposit belong to them in equal and undivided shares unless the terms of the account or deposit agreement expressly provide for different shares, and (C) if two or more P.O.D. payees survive, there is no right of survivorship in the event of death of a P.O.D. payee thereafter unless the terms of the account or deposit agreement expressly provide for survivorship between them.

(c) If the account is a Totten trust account:

(1) On death of one of two or more trustees, the rights to any sums remaining on deposit are governed by subdivision (a).

(2) On death of the sole trustee or the survivor of two or more trustees, (A) any sums remaining on deposit belong to the person or persons named as beneficiaries, if surviving, or to the survivor of them if one or more die before the trustee, unless there is clear and convincing evidence of a different intent, (B) if two or more beneficiaries survive, any sums remaining on deposit belong to them in equal and undivided shares unless the terms of the account or deposit agreement expressly provide for different shares, and (C) if two or more beneficiaries survive, there is no right of survivorship in event of death of any beneficiary thereafter unless the terms of the account or deposit agreement expressly provide for survivorship between them.

(d) In other cases, the death of any party to a multiple-party account has no effect on beneficial ownership of the account other than to transfer the rights of the decedent as part of the decedent's estate.

(e) A right of survivorship arising from the express terms of the account or under this section, a beneficiary designation in a Totten trust account, or a P.O.D. payee designation, cannot be changed by will.

(Stats. 1990 (A.B. 759), ch. 79, §14, effective July 1, 1991. Amended by Stats. 2001 (A.B. 873), ch. 417, §8.)

§5303. Survivorship rights; change of terms; withdrawal can eliminate survivorship right

(a) The provisions of Section 5302 as to rights of survivorship are determined by the form of the account at the death of a party.

(b) Once established, the terms of a multiple-party account can be changed only by any of the following methods:

(1) Closing the account and reopening it under different terms.

(2) Presenting to the financial institution a modification agreement that is signed by all parties with a present right of withdrawal. If the financial institution has a form for this purpose, it may require use of the form.

(3) If the provisions of the terms of the account or deposit agreement provide a method of modification of the terms of the account, complying with those provisions.

(4) As provided in subdivision (c) of Section 5405.

(c) During the lifetime of a party, the terms of the account may be changed as provided in subdivision (b) to eliminate or to add rights of survivorship. Withdrawal of funds from the account by a party with a present right of withdrawal during the lifetime of a party also eliminates rights of survivorship upon the death of that party with respect to the funds withdrawn.

(Stats. 1990 (A.B. 759), ch. 79, §14, effective July 1, 1991.)

§5304. Validity of transfers are not determined by requirements for a will

Any transfers resulting from the application of Section 5302 are effective by reason of the account contracts involved and this part and are not to be considered as testamentary. The right under this part of a surviving party to a joint account, or of a beneficiary, or of a P.O.D. payee, to the sums on deposit on the death of a party to a multiple-party account shall not be denied, abridged, or affected because such right has not been created by a writing executed in accordance with the laws of this state prescribing the requirements to effect a valid testamentary disposition of property.

(Stats. 1990 (A.B. 759), ch. 79, §14, effective July 1, 1991.)

§5305. Contribution of marital parties is presumed to be community property; rebuttable presumption; survivorship right may not be altered by will

(a) Notwithstanding Sections 5301 to 5303, inclusive, if parties to an account are married to each other, whether or not they are so described in the deposit agreement, their net contribution to the account is presumed to be and remain their community property.

(b) Notwithstanding Sections 2581 and 2640 of the Family Code, the presumption established by this section is a presumption affecting the burden of proof and may be rebutted by proof of either of the following:

(1) The sums on deposit that are claimed to be separate property can be traced from separate property unless it is proved that the married persons made a written agreement that expressed their clear intent that the sums be their community property.

(2) The married persons made a written agreement, separate from the deposit agreement, that expressly provided that the sums on deposit, claimed not to be community property, were not to be community property.

(c) Except as provided in Section 5307, a right of survivorship arising from the express terms of the account or under Section 5302, a beneficiary designation in a Totten trust account, or a P.O.D. payee designation, may not be changed by will.

(d) Except as provided in subdivisions (b) and (c), a multiple-party account created with community property funds does not in any way alter community property rights.

(Stats. 1990 (A.B. 759), ch. 79, §14, effective July 1, 1991. Amended by Stats. 1992 (A.B. 2641), ch. 163, §131, effective January 1, 994; Stats. 1993 (A.B. 1500), ch. 219, §224.7.)

§5306. "Tenancy in common" generally involves no right of survivorship

For the purposes of this chapter, if an account is expressly described in the deposit agreement as a "tenancy in common" account, no right of survivorship arises from the terms of the account or under Section 5302 unless the terms of the account or deposit agreement expressly provide for survivorship.

(Stats. 1990 (A.B. 759), ch. 79, §14, effective July 1, 1991.)

§5307. Ownership of community property account

For the purposes of this chapter, except to the extent the terms of the account or deposit agreement expressly provide otherwise, if the parties to an account are married to each

other and the account is expressly described in the account agreement as a "community property" account, the ownership of the account during lifetime and after the death of a spouse is governed by the law governing community property generally.
(Stats. 1990 (A.B. 759), ch. 79, §14, effective July 1, 1991.)

§5401. Financial institutions may require multiple signatures for transactions; requirements regarding net contributions of party

(a) Financial institutions may enter into multiple-party accounts to the same extent that they may enter into single-party accounts. Any multiple-party account may be paid, on request and according to its terms, to any one or more of the parties or agents.

(b) The terms of the account or deposit agreement may require the signatures of more than one of the parties to a multiple-party account during their lifetimes or of more than one of the survivors after the death of any one of them on any check, check endorsement, receipt, notice of withdrawal, request for withdrawal, or withdrawal order. In such case, the financial institution shall pay the sums on deposit only in accordance with such terms, but those terms do not limit the right of the sole survivor or of all of the survivors to receive the sums on deposit.

(c) A financial institution is not required to do any of the following:

(1) Inquire as to the source of funds received for deposit to a multiple-party account, or inquire as to the proposed application of any sum withdrawn from an account, for purposes of establishing net contributions.

(2) Determine any party's net contribution.

(3) Limit withdrawals or any other use of an account based on the net contribution of any party, whether or not the financial institution has actual knowledge of each party's contribution.

(d) All funds in an account, unless otherwise agreed in writing by the financial institution and the parties to the account, remain subject to liens, security interests, rights of setoff, and charges, notwithstanding the determination or allocation of net contributions with respect to the parties.
(Stats. 1990 (A.B. 759), ch. 79, §14, effective July 1, 1991.)

§5402. Payment of sums in joint account to party, personal representative or heir

Any sums in a joint account may be paid, on request and according to its terms, to any party without regard to whether any other party is incapacitated or deceased at the time the payment is demanded; but payment may not be made to the personal representative or heirs of a deceased party unless proof of death is presented to the financial institution showing that the decedent was the last surviving party or unless there is no right of survivorship under Section 5302.
(Stats. 1990 (A.B. 759), ch. 79, §14, effective July 1, 1991.)

§5403. Payment of sums in P.O.D. account to party, personal representative, or heir

Any P.O.D. account may be paid, on request and according to its terms, to any original party to the account. Payment may be made, on request, to the P.O.D. payee or to the personal representative or heirs of a deceased P.O.D. payee upon presentation to the financial institution of proof of death showing that the P.O.D. payee survived all persons named as original payees. Payment may be made to the personal representative or heirs of a deceased original payee if proof of death is presented to the financial institution showing that the deceased original payee was the survivor of all other persons named on the account either as an original payee or as P.O.D. payee.
(Stats. 1990 (A.B. 759), ch. 79, §14, effective July 1, 1991.)

§5404. Payment of sums in Totten trust account

Any Totten trust account may be paid, on request and according to its terms, to any trustee. Unless the financial institution has received written notice that the beneficiary has a vested interest not dependent upon surviving the trustee, payment may be made to the personal representative or heirs of a deceased trustee if proof of death is presented to the financial institution showing that the deceased trustee was the survivor of all other persons named on the account either as trustee or beneficiary. A Totten trust account may be paid to a beneficiary or beneficiaries or the personal representative or heirs of a beneficiary or beneficiaries if proof of death is presented to the financial institution showing that the beneficiary or beneficiaries survived all persons named as trustees.
(Stats. 1990 (A.B. 759), ch. 79, §14, effective July 1, 1991.)

§5405. Payment in compliance with statute serves to discharge financial institution from claims

(a) Payment made pursuant to Section 5401, 5402, 5403, or 5404 discharges the financial institution from all claims for amounts so paid whether or not the payment is consistent with the beneficial ownership of the account as between parties, P.O.D. payees, or beneficiaries, or their successors.

(b) The protection provided by subdivision (a) does not extend to payments made after the financial institution has been served with a court order restraining payment. No other notice or any other information shown to have been available to a financial institution shall affect its right to the protection provided by subdivision (a).

(c) Unless the notice is withdrawn by a subsequent writing, after receipt of a written notice from any party that withdrawals in accordance with the terms of the account, other than a checking account, share draft account, or other similar thirdparty payment instrument, should not be permitted, except with the signatures of more than one of the parties during their lifetimes or of more than one of the survivors after the death of any one of the parties, the financial institution may only pay the sums on deposit in accordance with the written instructions pending determination of the rights of the parties or their successors. No liability shall attach to the financial institution for complying with the terms of any written notice provided pursuant to this subdivision.

(d) The protection provided by this section has no bearing on the rights of parties in disputes between themselves or their successors concerning the beneficial ownership of funds in, or withdrawn from, multipleparty accounts and is in addition to, and not exclusive of, any protection provided the financial institution by any other provision of law.

(Stats. 1990 (A.B. 759), ch. 79, §14, effective July 1, 1991.)

§5406. Trust account and Totten trust account

The provisions of this chapter that apply to the payment of a Totten trust account apply to an account in the name of one or more parties as trustee for one or more other persons if the financial institution has no other or further notice in writing that the account is not a Totten trust account as defined in Section 80.

(Stats. 1990 (A.B. 759), ch. 79, §14, effective July 1, 1991.)

§5407. Requirements for payment to a minor

If a financial institution is required or permitted to make payment pursuant to this chapter to a person who is a minor:

(a) If the minor is a party to a multiple-party account, payment may be made to the minor or to the minor's order, and payment so made is a valid release and discharge of the financial institution, but this subdivision does not apply if the account is to be paid to the minor because the minor was designated as a P.O.D. payee or as a beneficiary of a Totten trust account.

(b) In cases where subdivision (a) does not apply, payment shall be made pursuant to the California Uniform Transfers to Minors Act (Part 9 (commencing with Section 3900) of Division 4), or as provided in Chapter 2 (commencing with Section 3400) of Part 8 of Division 4.

(Stats. 1990 (A.B. 759), ch. 79, §14, effective July 1, 1991.)

2. Totten Trusts (Savings Account Trusts)

A savings account trust (also called a "tentative trust" or "Totten trust" named after the case of In re Totten, 71 N.E. 748 (N.Y. 1904), discussed *infra*) is a form of multiple-party bank account in which a person (a "depositor") deposits funds in the depositor's name as trustee for another person or persons. Totten trusts are valid, by case law or statute, in the majority of jurisdictions.

Savings bank trusts have been in existence since the late nineteenth century. Historically, courts have had difficulty determining the validity of such accounts at the death of the depositor. Compare Martin v. Funk, 75 N.Y. 134 (N.Y. 1878) (holding that savings bank trust was sufficient to pass title to named beneficiary) with Brabrook v. Boston Five Cents Savings Bank, 104 Mass. 228 (Mass. 1870) (denying recovery because passbooks never were in beneficiary's possession). Early courts questioned whether these arrangements were invalid for failure to comply with a given jurisdiction's wills legislation. Even if courts determined that these arrangements were valid, other concerns emerged regarding the depositor's intent. That is, did the depositor intend to create a revocable trust or an irrevocable trust? If the latter, did the depositor intend to create an immediate irrevocable trust, or an irrevocable trust as to the balance, subject to the depositor's power to revoke any funds during his or her lifetime?

The landmark case of In re Totten, *supra*, established the validity of savings account trusts and also their revocable nature. *Totten* involved a controversy between the administrator of the decedent's estate and the beneficiary of a savings account trust created by the decedent. The decedent had opened approximately 16 trust accounts (totalling approximately $40,000) and designated various beneficiaries. During her lifetime, she retained the passbooks and control of the deposits. She never stated her intention in opening these accounts. After her death, one of the beneficiaries (a nephew who had no knowledge of the accounts during decedent's lifetime) presented a claim against the estate. After surveying the law, the court concluded that the depositor of such an account establishes a trust that is revocable until the depositor dies or

makes the gift irrevocable. If the depositor predeceases the beneficiary without revoking the gift, a presumption arises that an irrevocable trust was created as to the balance. *Totten*, 71 N.E. at 752.

Unlike other trusts with no implied power to revoke, courts have specified that Totten trusts are revocable based on judicial beliefs about the expectations of the depositor. Bogert et al., *supra*, at §47.

Generally, a depositor can revoke the savings account by manifestation of such intent, by withdrawal of any part of the whole of the funds on deposit (the withdrawal operating as a revocation to the extent of such withdrawal), or by a disposition in the depositor's will of the deposit in favor of another beneficiary. (But cf. Cal. Prob. Code §5302(e) (providing that depositor cannot revoke or modify Totten trust by will).) The depositor can make the savings account trust irrevocable by manifestation of such intent, delivery of the passbook to the beneficiary, or notice to the beneficiary. Paul Coltoff et al., Express Trusts, Deposit of Money in Bank or Other Financial Institution—Tentative Trusts, 90 C.J.S. §58. The trust becomes irrevocable when the depositor predeceases the beneficiary without revocation, thereby entitling the beneficiary to the balance remaining in the account.

Totten trusts have been recognized in California since Estate of Collins, 149 Cal. Rptr. 65 (Ct. App. 1978). Prior case law found an intent to create a savings account trust, but application of the doctrine remained uncertain. See, e.g., Kosloskye v. Cis, 160 P.2d 565 (Ct. App. 1945); Brucks v. Home Fed. Savings & Loan Ass'n, 228 P.2d 545 (Cal. 1951).

In California, Totten trusts currently are governed by legislation pertaining to multiple-party accounts (Cal. Prob. Code §§5100 et seq.) *supra*. Totten trusts are defined in California Probate Code §80, which is identical to UPC §6-101(14)(1987). Although Totten trusts now are recognized in California by statute (Cal. Fin. Code §14868; Cal. Prob. Code §80), they are excluded from application of trust law (Cal. Prob. Code §82(b)(4)). See also Estate of Allen, 16 Cal. Rptr. 2d 352 (Ct. App. 1993) (holding that an omitted spouse was not entitled to include Totten trust accounts in computing her statutory share pursuant to Cal. Prob. Code §6560 because, at the time of death, the Totten trust account passed to the beneficiary of the account, not the estate).

California Probate Code §5303(c) codifies the rule that the sums on deposit in a savings account trust vest in the beneficiary upon the death of the depositor (trustee). Before the enactment of that provision, case law (discussed *supra*) specified that a Totten trust could be defeated by circumstantial evidence. California Probate Code §5303, however, added protection for the rights of the beneficiary by requiring that the trust could be attacked only by clear and convincing evidence that survivorship was not intended. Law Revision Commission Commentary following California Probate Code §5303. Further, California Probate Code §5303(e) prevents revocation or modification of the trust by will. That legislation changes the result under prior California case law (Brucks v. Home Fed. Sav. & Loan Ass'n, 228 P.2d 545 (Cal. 1951)).

Note that property in a Totten trust that is either community or quasi-community property is subject to the rights of the donor's spouse pursuant to California Family Code §1101 and California Probate Code §102. See Chapter II, Section IIC *supra*. Also, even though the funds in the Totten trust may be community property or quasi-community property, the financial institution may rely on the form of account to make payment and is protected from liability in doing so (Cal. Prob. Code §5405).

The trust also may be challenged by: creditors of the depositor, a surviving spouse to protect a statutory intestate share in the depositor's estate, and a guardian or conservator (who must petition the Probate Court for authority) where the fund is necessary for the ward's or conservatee's welfare. 13 Witkin, Summary, Trusts, §8.

CALIFORNIA PROBATE CODE

§80. "Totten trust account," defined

"Totten trust account" means an account in the name of one or more parties as trustee for one or more beneficiaries where the relationship is established by the form of the account and the deposit agreement with the financial institution and there is no subject of the trust other than the sums on deposit in the account. In a Totten trust account, it is not essential that payment to the beneficiary be mentioned in the deposit agreement. A Totten trust account does not include (1) a regular trust account under a testamentary trust or a trust agreement which has significance apart from the account or (2) a fiduciary account arising from a fiduciary relation such as attorney-client.

(Stats. 1990 (A.B. 759), ch. 79, §14, effective July 1, 1991.)

§82. "Trust" defined; exceptions

(a) "Trust" includes the following:

(1) An express trust, private or charitable, with additions thereto, wherever and however created.

(2) A trust created or determined by a judgment or decree under which the trust is to be administered in the manner of an express trust.

(b) "Trust" excludes the following:

(1) Constructive trusts, other than those described in paragraph (2) of subdivision (a), and resulting trusts.

(2) Guardianships and conservatorships.

(3) Personal representatives.

(4) Totten trust accounts.

(5) Custodial arrangements pursuant to the Uniform Gifts to Minors Act or the Uniform Transfers to Minors Act of any state.

(6) Business trusts that are taxed as partnerships or corporations.

(7) Investment trusts subject to regulation under the laws of this state or any other jurisdiction.

(8) Common trust funds.

(9) Voting trusts.

(10) Security arrangements.

(11) Transfers in trust for purpose of suit or enforcement of a claim or right.

(12) Liquidation trusts.

(13) Trusts for the primary purpose of paying debts, dividends, interest, salaries, wages, profits, pensions, or employee benefits of any kind.

(14) Any arrangement under which a person is nominee or escrowee for another.

(Stats. 1990 (A.B. 759), ch. 79, §14, effective July 1, 1991.)

CALIFORNIA FINANCIAL CODE

§14868. Totten trust deposit agreement must indicate beneficiary's address

(a) As used in this section:

(1) "Beneficiary" has the meaning given that term in Section 5126 of the Probate Code.

(2) "Totten trust account" has the meaning given that term in Section 80 of the Probate Code.

(b) In the case of a Totten trust account, the deposit agreement shall indicate the current address of each beneficiary.

(Stats. 1989, ch. 397, §18, effective July 1, 1990.)

III. Other Joint Forms of Ownership

A. Joint Tenancy

1. Characteristics

Several forms of joint ownership exist. The most common is joint tenancy. Joint tenancies may be created in both real and personal property. Atkinson, *supra*, §40 at 164. Upon the death of a joint tenant, the remaining joint tenant (or joint tenants) take the property by operation of law without the need for judicial proceedings. *Id.*, §28 at 103.

The common law presumed that a grant to two or more persons created a joint estate with the right of survivorship. However, today joint estates are disfavored. Atkinson, *supra*, §40 at 164.

At common law, a joint tenancy required four unities of interest, title, time, and possession. That is, the joint tenants must have:

- **the same and equal interests;**
- **rights that were created under a single instrument;**
- **interests that commenced at the same time; and**
- **the right to undivided possession.**

16 Cal. Jur.3d Cotenancy and Joint Ownership §5. To elaborate, "The requirement of four unities reflects the basic concept that there is but one estate that is taken jointly. . . ." *Id.*

A joint tenant cannot devise his or her interest by will. If a joint tenant wants to devise his interest to someone other than the co-tenant(s), the former must sever the tenancy during his or her lifetime. That severance converts the joint tenancy into a tenancy in common as to the share conveyed, thereby enabling the original joint tenant to devise his or her interest. Also, if one of three or more joint tenants conveys his or her interest to one of the

others, the grantee becomes a tenant in common as to the interest conveyed, but remains a joint tenant as to his or her original interest. Annot., Estates by Entirety in Personal Property, 64 ALR2d §10 (1959 & Supp. 2006).

Creation of a joint tenancy requires compliance with the relevant statutory provision. According to California law, a joint tenancy is created by a single transfer or will that expressly states the intention to create a joint tenancy (Cal. Civ. Code §683(a)). A joint tenancy cannot be created by oral agreement in either real or personal property. 16 Cal. Jur.3d Cotenancy §15. Motor vehicles may also be held in joint tenancy form in California (Cal. Veh. Code §4150.5).

In some jurisdictions, creditors cannot reach the decedent's share of joint tenancy property after the death of the joint tenant (on the theory that the decedent's share vanishes upon death, so there is no interest to attach). For example, in California, until 1993, the state could not bring a Medi-Cal claim to collect reimbursement for health care services against the decedent's property that passed via will substitutes. Citizens Action League v. Kizer, 887 F.2d 1003 (9th Cir. 1989) (joint tenancy property); Bucholtz v. Belshe, 114 F.3d 923 (9th Cir. 1997) (inter vivos trust). (Medi-Cal is the California version of the federal Medicaid program, Title XIX of the Social Security Act, codified at 42 U.S.C. §§1396 et seq., that provides health services to eligible low-income persons.)

However, in 1993, Congress significantly broadened the definition of "estate" to provide states with the authority to obtain reimbursement for medical services from beneficiaries who obtained their interest through a vast array of types of transfers, such as "joint tenancy, tenancy in common, survivorship, life estate, living trust, or other arrangement" (42 U.S.C. §1396p (b)(4)). See also Bonta v. Burke, 120 Cal. Rptr. 2d 72 (Ct. App. 2002) (holding that decedent's "estate" that was subject to a Medi-Cal claim included a remainder interest in real property that had passed to the remainder beneficiaries).

In 2001, the California legislature enacted a new method of holding property for spouses—"community property with a right of survivorship" (Stats. 2001, ch. 754 (A.B. 1697)). See Cal. Civ. Code §682.1; Cal. Fam. Code §750. According to California Civil Code §682.1, such property (when expressly declared in the transfer document) passes at death to the surviving spouse without administration, and is subject to the same procedures as property held in joint tenancy. Also, the right of survivorship may be terminated, prior to the death of either party, pursuant to the same procedures by which a joint tenancy may be severed. See also Cal. Prob. Code §5601 (providing that dissolution or annulment severs a joint tenancy between the decedent and the decedent's former spouse and that community property with right of survivorship is treated similarly).

Note that a presumption operates in California regarding property acquired by the spouses during the marriage in joint tenancy (or other joint form). Such jointly acquired property is considered community property for purposes of dissolution or legal separation (Cal. Fam. Code §2581), but not death. See, e.g., Dorn v. Solomon, 67 Cal. Rptr. 2d 311 (Ct. App. 1997) (holding that, because title to family home was acquired in joint tenancy and parties were not divorcing or legally separated, there was a presumption that the title passed to the estranged husband when the wife died one day after executing a quitclaim deed purporting to transfer the home to an irrevocable trust to enable her to bequeath her share to her daughter from a prior marriage); Estate of Levine, 178 Cal. Rptr. 275 (Ct. App. 1981) (affirming the denial of the executor's petition to declare real property as community property of the decedent and his wife to enable decedent to bequeath his interest to his son, reasoning that where decedent never communicated his intention to his wife that the marital home was to be considered community property although title was taken in joint tenancy and where there was no agreement that property would be other than joint tenancy, property would be distributed upon husband's death as joint tenancy property). See also Chapter II, Section IIC *supra.*

CALIFORNIA CIVIL CODE

§682. Forms of property ownership by several persons

The ownership of property by several persons is either:

1. Of joint interests;
2. Of partnership interests;
3. Of interests in common;
4. Of community interest of husband and wife.

(Enacted 1872.)

§682.1. Community property with right of survivorship: creation, termination of right of survivorship

(a) Community property of a husband and wife, when expressly declared in the transfer document to be community property with right of survivorship, and which may be accepted in writing on the face of the document by a statement signed or initialed by the grantees, shall, upon the death of one of the spouses, pass to the survivor, without administration, pursuant to the terms of the instrument, subject to the same procedures, as property held in joint tenancy. Prior to the death of either spouse, the right of survivorship may be terminated pursuant to the same procedures by which a joint tenancy may be severed. Part I (commencing with Section 5000) of Division 5 of the Probate Code and Chapter 2 (commencing with Section 13540), Chapter 3 (commencing with Section 13550) and Chapter 3.5 (commencing with Section 13560) of Part 2 of Division 8 of the Probate Code apply to this property.

(b) This section does not apply to a joint account in a financial institution to which Part 2 (commencing with Section 5100) of Division 5 of the Probate Code applies.

(c) This section shall become operative on July 1, 2001, and shall apply to instruments created on or after that date.

(Stats. 2000 (A.B. 2913), ch. 645, §1, effective July 1, 2001.)

§683. Joint tenancy: definition and method of creation

(a) A joint interest is one owned by two or more persons in equal shares, by a title created by a single will or transfer, when expressly declared in the will or transfer to be a joint tenancy, or by transfer from a sole owner to himself or herself and others, or from tenants in common or joint tenants to themselves or some of them, or to themselves or any of them and others, or from a husband and wife, when holding title as community property or otherwise to themselves or to themselves and others or to one of them and to another or others, when expressly declared in the transfer to be a joint tenancy, or when granted or devised to executors or trustees as joint tenants. A joint tenancy in personal property may be created by a written transfer, instrument, or agreement.

(b) Provisions of this section do not apply to a joint account in a financial institution if Part 2 (commencing with Section 5100) of Division 5 of the Probate Code applies to such account.

(Enacted 1872. Amended by Stats. 1929, ch. 93, p. 172, §1; Stats. 1931, ch. 1051, p. 2205, §1; Stats. 1935, ch. 234, p. 912, §1; Stats. 1955, ch. 178, p. 645, §1; Stats. 1983, ch. 92, §1, effective July 1, 1984; Stats. 1989, ch. 397, §1, effective July 1, 1990; Stats. 1990 (A.B. 759), ch. 79, §1, effective July 1, 1991.)

CALIFORNIA FAMILY CODE

§750. Methods of holding property by husband and wife

A husband and wife may hold property as joint tenants or tenants in common, or as community property, or as community property with a right of survivorship.

(Stats. 1992 (A.B. 2650), ch. 162, §10, effective January 1, 1994. Amended by Stats. 2001 (A.B. 1697), ch. 754, §2.)

§2581. Community property presumption operates upon joint tenancy property at dissolution of marriage or legal separation

For the purpose of division of property on dissolution of marriage or legal separation of the parties, property acquired by the parties during marriage in joint form, including property held in tenancy in common, joint tenancy, or tenancy by the entirety, or as community property, is presumed to be community property. This presumption is a presumption affecting the burden of proof and may be rebutted by either of the following:

(a) A clear statement in the deed or other documentary evidence of title by which the property is acquired that the property is separate property and not community property.

(b) Proof that the parties have made a written agreement that the property is separate property.

(Stats. 1993 (A.B. 1500), ch. 219, §111.7.)

CALIFORNIA VEHICLE CODE

§4150.5. Co-ownership on vehicle title for registration purposes

Ownership of title to a vehicle subject to registration may be held by two (or more) coowners as provided in Section 682 of the Civil Code, except that:

(a) A vehicle may be registered in the names of two (or more) persons as coowners in the alternative by the use of the word "or." A vehicle so registered in the alternative shall be deemed to be held in joint tenancy. Each coowner shall be deemed to have granted to the other coowners the absolute right to dispose of the title and interest in the vehicle. Upon the death of a coowner the interest of the decedent shall pass to the survivor as though title or interest in the vehicle was held in joint tenancy unless a contrary intention is set forth in writing upon the application for registration.

(b) A vehicle may be registered in the names of two (or more) persons as coowners in the alternative by the use of the word "or" and if declared in writing upon the application for registration by the applicants to be community property, or tenancy in common, shall grant to each coowner the absolute power to transfer the title or interest of the other coowners only during the lifetime of such coowners.

(c) A vehicle may be registered in the names of two (or more) persons as coowners in the conjunctive by the use of the word "and" and shall thereafter require the signature of each coowner or his personal representative to transfer title to the vehicle, except where title to the vehicle is set forth in joint tenancy, the signature of each coowner or his personal representative shall be required only during the lifetime of the coowners, and upon death of a coowner title shall pass to the surviving coowner.

(d) The department may adopt suitable abbreviations to appear upon the certificate of registration and certificate of ownership to designate the manner in which title to the vehicle is held if set forth by the coowners upon the application for registration.

(Stats. 1965, ch. 891, p. 2495, §1.)

§5600.5. Co-ownership on vehicle title for transfer purposes

Ownership of title to a vehicle subject to registration may be transferred to two (or more) coowners as transferee to be held provided in Section 682 of the Civil Code, except that:

(a) A vehicle may be registered in the names of two (or more) persons as coowners in the alternative by the use of the word "or." A vehicle so registered in the alternative shall be deemed to be held in joint tenancy. Each coowner shall be deemed to have granted to the other coowners the absolute right to dispose of the title and interest in the vehicle. Upon the death of a coowner the interest of the decedent shall pass to the survivor as though title or interest in the vehicle was held in joint tenancy unless a contrary intention is set forth in writing upon the request for transfer of registration.

(b) A vehicle may be registered in the names of two (or more) persons as coowners in the alternative by the use of the word "or" and if declared in writing upon the application for a transfer of registration by the applicants to be community property, or tenancy in common, shall grant to each coowner the absolute power to transfer the title or interest of the other coowners only during the lifetime of such coowners.

(c) A vehicle may be registered in the names of two (or more) persons as coowners in the conjunctive by the use of the word "and" and shall thereafter require the signature of each coowner or his personal representative to transfer title to the vehicle, except where title to the vehicle is set forth in joint tenancy, the signature of each coowner or his personal representative shall be required only during the lifetime of the coowners, and upon death of a coowner title shall pass to the surviving coowner.

(d) The department may adopt suitable abbreviations to appear upon the certificate of registration and certificate of ownership to designate the manner in which the interest in or title to the vehicle is held if set forth by the coowners upon the application for transfer of registration.

(Stats. 1965, ch. 891, p. 2496, §2.)

2. Distinguished from Tenancy in Common and Tenancy by the Entirety

Another form of co-ownership is a tenancy in common. The primary difference between a joint tenancy and a tenancy in common is that the co-tenant's interest passes into the co-tenant's probate estate. The interest then is distributed either according to the co-tenant's will or by intestate succession.

Still another form of joint ownership—similar to a joint tenancy but applicable only to spouses—is a tenancy by the entirety. That form of co-ownership is not recognized in California. 16 Cal. Jur.3d Co-tenancy and Joint Ownership, §1 (citing Delanoy v. Delanoy, 13 P.2d 513 (Cal. 1932); Swan v. Walden, 103 P. 931 (Cal. 1909)). See generally Hanoch Dagan, The Craft of Property, 91 Cal. L. Rev. 1417 (2003); Carolyn J. Frantz & Hanoch Dagan, Properties of Marriage, 104 Colum. L. Rev. 75 (2004) (both discussing forms of ownership of marital property).

3. Severance of the Joint Tenancy

Severance of the joint tenancy extinguishes the right of survivorship. Severance must be accomplished during the lifetimes of the joint tenants. A will is ineffective to change the survivorship feature of a joint tenancy. (A frequent reason to sever the joint tenancy is to ensure that the co-tenant does not take the former's share at death.) Severance of the joint tenancy converts it into a tenancy in common.

At common law, the dissolution or annulment of a marriage did not sever a joint tenancy between spouses. See Estate of Layton,

52 Cal. Rptr. 2d 251 (Ct. App. 1996) (holding that status-only dissolution judgment that merely reserved jurisdiction over community property issues did not manifest sufficient words or conduct to sever joint tenancy). However, California Probate Code §5601(a) reverses the common law rule by providing that the joint tenancy is severed if, at the time of the decedent's death, the former spouse is not the surviving spouse due to dissolution or annulment (but not legal separation). This rule is identical to the rule governing wills (see California Probate Code §§6122(d), 6227). See also Section IA2 *supra*.

For a time, California adhered to a policy of different treatment of real and personal property for severance purposes. The common law permitted unilateral severance of a joint tenancy in real or personal property. California followed this rule in regard to real property (Riddle v. Harmon, 162 Cal. Rptr. 530 (Ct. App. 1980)). However, severance in personal property was not permitted in California without the consent of the co-tenants. Fish v. Security-First Nat'l Bank, 189 P.2d 10 (Cal. 1948); Estate of Harris, 72 P.2d 873 (Cal. 1937). Finally, Estate of Propst, 788 P.2d 628 (Cal. 1990) abrogated the rule that a joint tenancy in personal property could not be severed unilaterally by one joint tenant without the consent of the other joint tenant(s).

In *Propst*, the decedent and his wife had a number of bank accounts in joint tenancy. Prior to his death, decedent withdrew all of the funds from two of these accounts, closed six additional accounts and deposited those funds in accounts in his name alone. His intent was to sever the joint tenancy, thus cutting off his wife's right of survivorship. He then executed a will that named his daughter from a prior marriage as his residuary beneficiary and died shortly thereafter. The surviving spouse sought a determination that the funds withdrawn by decedent remained joint tenancy property, and that title passed to her outside of the probate estate. The California Supreme Court held that a joint tenancy in personal property (such as joint tenancy bank accounts) could be severed by unilateral action of one joint tenant.

In addition, severance of a real property joint tenancy by unilateral act of a joint tenant does not require a "strawman" conveyance. Riddle v. Harmon, 162 Cal. Rptr. 530 (Ct. App. 1980). That is, one joint tenant can sever by deed to himself or herself. (In *Riddle*, the decedent granted to herself an undivided one-half interest in property which she formerly held in joint tenancy with her estranged husband so that she could dispose of her interest by will.) California Civil Code §683.2 (enacted in 1984) codifies this rule by abandoning the need for an intermediate conveyance. In 1985, the legislature required that, in the case of a recorded joint tenancy in real property, the severance must be recorded to be an effective termination of the right of survivorship (Cal. Civ. Code §683.2(c)). Recordation is intended to prevent fraud by precluding one joint tenant from unilaterally severing the joint tenancy without notice and then (if the other joint tenant predeceases) destroying the severing instrument so that the surviving joint tenant becomes the owner of the entire property. 12 Witkin Summary, Real Property, §62.

California Civil Code §683.2 permits a joint tenant unilaterally to sever his or her interest in real property (without the consent of the other joint tenants) by the following methods:

- execution and delivery of a deed conveying legal title to the joint tenant's interest to a third person;
- execution of a written instrument evidencing the intent to sever the joint tenancy; or
- execution of a written declaration that the joint tenancy is severed.

Severance does not terminate the right of survivorship unless the instrument effecting the severance is recorded in the county where the real property is located. The instrument may be recorded before or after the death of the severing joint tenant—but not earlier than 3 days before death or not later than 7 days after death (Cal. Civ. Code §683.2).

If a joint tenancy involves three or more joint tenants, severance by operation of California Probate Code §5601 converts the decedent's interest into a tenancy in common, but does not sever the joint tenancy as between the other joint tenants. For example, suppose that a husband, wife, and a third person create a joint tenancy during husband and wife's marriage to each other. On the husband's death, if the marriage has been terminated, then the wife is not the husband's "surviving spouse" and the joint tenancy is severed by operation of this section. The husband's one-third interest becomes a tenancy in common and does not pass by survivorship. The remaining two-thirds remain in joint tenancy as between the third person and the former wife. Law Revision Commission Commentary following California Probate Code §5601. Also, if the decedent is subject to a court order or binding agreement prohibiting severance of the joint tenancy by the decedent, then the joint tenancy is not severed by operation of California Probate Code §5601(a). *Id.*

Note that this section does not affect the community property presumption that property acquired during marriage in joint tenancy form is presumed to be community property on dissolution of marriage or legal separation (Cal. Fam. Code §2581), or property characterized as community property under that presumption. Also, the section applies to joint tenancies in both real and personal property (but does not apply to United States Savings Bonds, which are subject to federal regulation).

California Probate Code §223 specifies the distribution of joint tenancy property in cases of simultaneous death. Note that the section is based on the Uniform Simultaneous Death Act §3 (1953). Law Revision Commission Commentary after California Probate Code §223. California Probate Code §251 explains that a slayer (who "feloniously and intentionally kills another joint tenant") effects a severance of a joint tenancy such that the slayer acquires no rights by survivorship. The share of the decedent passes as the decedent's property. This provision is the same in substance as UPC §2-803(b) and is consistent with prior California law. See, e.g., Estate of Hart, 185 Cal. Rptr. 544 (Ct. App. 1982); Johansen v. Pelton, 87 Cal. Rptr. 784 (Ct. App. 1970). Law Revision Commission Commentary after California Probate Code §251.

Sometimes, difficulties arise in determining the "share of the decedent" in California Probate Code §251 that passes as decedent's property when the decedent has been killed by the co-joint tenant. In Estate of Castiglioni, 47 Cal. Rptr. 2d 288 (Ct. App. 1995), the court held that when real property held in joint tenancy becomes subject to severance due to the felonious and intentional killing of decedent by the co-joint tenant, the portion of the property that passes as decedent's property must be calculated by application of the principles of tracing and reimbursement of contributions utilized in marital dissolution cases.

On the application of the slayer disqualification to interests held in joint tenancy, see generally Charlotte K. Goldberg, Estate of Castiglioni: Spousal Murder and the Clash of Joint Tenancy and Equity in California Community Property Law, 33 Idaho L. Rev. 513 (1997). See also Chapter I, Section IIIE2 *supra*.

The rights of a good faith purchaser or encumbrancer are protected if the person relies on an apparent severance under California Probate Code §5601 or lacks knowledge of a severance under this section. The rights of such individuals also are protected if they rely on an affidavit or declaration executed pursuant to California Probate Code §5602.

CALIFORNIA PROBATE CODE

§78. "Surviving spouse" exceptions

"Surviving spouse" does not include any of the following:

(a) A person whose marriage to the decedent has been dissolved or annulled, unless, by virtue of a subsequent marriage, the person is married to the decedent at the time of death.

(b) A person who obtains or consents to a final decree or judgment of dissolution of marriage from the decedent or a final decree or judgment of annulment of their marriage, which decree or judgment is not recognized as valid in this state, unless they (1) subsequently participate in a marriage ceremony purporting to marry each to the other or (2) subsequently live together as husband and wife.

(c) A person who, following a decree or judgment of dissolution or annulment of marriage obtained by the decedent, participates in a marriage ceremony with a third person.

(d) A person who was a party to a valid proceeding concluded by an order purporting to terminate all marital property rights.

(Stats. 1990 (A.B. 759), ch. 79, §14, effective July 1, 1991.)

§223. Joint tenant: definition, proof of survivorship, property distribution

(a) As used in this section, "joint tenants" includes owners of property held under circumstances that entitled one or more to the whole of the property on the death of the other or others.

(b) If property is held by two joint tenants and both of them have died and it cannot be established by clear and convincing evidence that one survived the other, the property held in joint tenancy shall be administered or distributed, or otherwise dealt with, one-half as if one joint tenant had survived and one-half as if the other joint tenant had survived.

(c) If property is held by more than two joint tenants and all of them have died and it cannot be established by clear and convincing evidence that any of them survived the others, the property held in joint tenancy shall be divided into as many portions as there are joint tenants and the share of each joint tenant shall be administered or distributed, or otherwise dealt with, as if that joint tenant had survived the other joint tenants.

(Stats. 1990 (A.B. 759), ch. 79, §14, effective July 1, 1991.)

§251. Joint tenants: slayer effects a severance and acquires no rights of survivorship

A joint tenant who feloniously and intentionally kills another joint tenant thereby effects a severance of the interest of the decedent so that the share of the decedent passes as the decedent's property and the killer has no rights by survivorship. This section applies to joint tenancies in real and personal property, joint and multiple-party accounts in financial institutions, and any other form of coownership with survivorship incidents.

(Stats. 1990 (A.B. 759), ch. 79, §14, effective July 1, 1991.)

§5600. Automatic revocation on nonprobate transfer to former spouse; exceptions

(a) Except as provided in subdivision (b), a nonprobate transfer to the transferor's former spouse, in an instrument executed by the transferor before or during the marriage, fails if, at the time of the transferor's death, the former spouse is not the transferor's surviving spouse as defined in Section 78, as a result of the dissolution or annulment of the marriage. A judgment of legal separation that does not terminate the status of husband and wife is not a dissolution for purposes of this section.

(b) Subdivision (a) does not cause a nonprobate transfer to fail in any of the following cases:

(1) The nonprobate transfer is not subject to revocation by the transferor at the time of the transferor's death.

(2) There is clear and convincing evidence that the transferor intended to preserve the nonprobate transfer to the former spouse.

(3) A court order that the nonprobate transfer be maintained on behalf of the former spouse is in effect at the time of the transferor's death.

(c) Where a nonprobate transfer fails by operation of this section, the instrument making the nonprobate transfer shall be treated as it would if the former spouse failed to survive the transferor.

(d) Nothing in this section affects the rights of a subsequent purchaser or encumbrancer for value in good faith who relies on the apparent failure of a nonprobate transfer under this section or who lacks knowledge of the failure of a nonprobate transfer under this section.

(e) As used in this section, "nonprobate transfer" means a provision, other than a provision of a life insurance policy, of either of the following types:

(1) A provision of a type described in Section 5000.

(2) A provision in an instrument that operates on death, other than a will, conferring a power of appointment or naming a trustee.

(Stats. 2001 (A.B. 873), ch. 417, §9, effective January 1, 2002.)

§5601. Automatic severance of joint tenancy with former spouse; exceptions

(a) Except as provided in subdivision (b), a joint tenancy between the decedent and the decedent's former spouse, created before or during the marriage, is severed as to the decedent's interest if, at the time of the decedent's death, the former spouse is not the decedent's surviving spouse as defined in Section 78, as a result of the dissolution or annulment of the marriage. A judgment of legal separation that does not terminate the status of husband and wife is not a dissolution for purposes of this section.

(b) Subdivision (a) does not sever a joint tenancy in either of the following cases:

(1) The joint tenancy is not subject to severance by the decedent at the time of the decedent's death.

(2) There is clear and convincing evidence that the decedent intended to preserve the joint tenancy in favor of the former spouse.

(c) Nothing in this section affects the rights of a subsequent purchaser or encumbrancer for value in good faith who relies on an apparent severance under this section or who lacks knowledge of a severance under this section.

(d) For purposes of this section, property held in "joint tenancy" includes property held as community property with right of survivorship, as described in Section 682.1 of the Civil Code.

(Stats. 2001 (A.B. 873), ch. 417, §9, effective January 1, 2002.)

§5602. Affidavit procedure provides protection for purchaser or encumbrancer of real property

(a) Nothing in this part affects the rights of a purchaser or encumbrancer of real property for value who in good faith relies on an affidavit or a declaration under penalty of perjury under the laws of this state that states all of the following:

(1) The name of the decedent.

(2) The date and place of the decedent's death.

(3) A description of the real property transferred to the affiant or declarant by an instrument making a nonprobate transfer or by operation of joint tenancy survivorship.

(4) Either of the following, as appropriate:

(A) The affiant or declarant is the surviving spouse of the decedent.

(B) The affiant or declarant is not the surviving spouse of the decedent, but the rights of the affiant or declarant to the described property are not affected by Section 5600 or 5601.

(b) A person relying on an affidavit or declaration made pursuant to subdivision (a) has no duty to inquire into the truth of the matters stated in the affidavit or declaration.

(c) An affidavit or declaration made pursuant to subdivision (a) may be recorded.

(Stats. 2001 (A.B. 873), ch. 417, §9, effective January 1, 2002.)

§5603. Judicial authority still exists to order divorcing spouses to maintain former spouse as beneficiary or to preserve joint tenancy

Nothing in this part is intended to limit the court's authority to order a party to a dissolution or annulment of marriage to maintain the former spouse as a beneficiary on any nonprobate transfer described in this part, or to preserve a joint tenancy in favor of the former spouse.

(Stats. 2001 (A.B. 873), ch. 417, §9, effective January 1, 2002.)

§5604. Effective date

(a) This part is operative on January 1, 2002.

(b) Except as provided in subdivision (c), this part applies to an instrument making a nonprobate transfer or creating a joint tenancy whether executed before, on, or after the operative date of this part.

(c) Sections 5600 and 5601 do not apply, and the applicable law in effect before the operative date of this part applies, to an instrument making a nonprobate transfer or creating a joint tenancy in either of the following circumstances:

(1) The person making the nonprobate transfer or creating the joint tenancy dies before the operative date of this part.

(2) The dissolution of marriage or other event that terminates the status of the nonprobate transfer beneficiary or joint tenant as a surviving spouse occurs before the operative date of this part.

(Stats. 2001 (A.B. 873), ch. 417, §9, effective January 1, 2002.)

CALIFORNIA CIVIL CODE

§682.1. Community property with right of survivorship: creation, termination of right of survivorship

(a) Community property of a husband and wife, when expressly declared in the transfer document to be community property with right of survivorship, and which may be accepted in writing on the face of the document by a statement signed or initialed by the grantees, shall, upon the death of one of the spouses, pass to the survivor, without administration, pursuant to the terms of the instrument, subject to the same procedures, as property held in joint tenancy. Prior to the death of either spouse, the right of survivorship may be terminated pursuant to the same procedures by which a joint tenancy may be severed. Part I (commencing with Section 5000) of Division 5 of the Probate Code and Chapter 2 (commencing with Section 13540), Chapter 3 (commencing with Section 13550) and Chapter 3.5 (commencing with Section 13560) of Part 2 of Division 8 of the Probate Code apply to this property.

(b) This section does not apply to a joint account in a financial institution to which Part 2 (commencing with Section 5100) of Division 5 of the Probate Code applies.

(c) This section shall become operative on July 1, 2001, and shall apply to instruments created on or after that date.

(Stats. 2000 (A.B. 2913), ch. 645, §1, effective July 1, 2001.)

§683.2. Joint tenancy: severance and right of survivorship

(a) Subject to the limitations and requirements of this section, in addition to any other means by which a joint tenancy may be severed, a joint tenant may sever a joint tenancy in real property as to the joint tenant's interest without the joinder or consent of the other joint tenants by any of the following means:

(1) Execution and delivery of a deed that conveys legal title to the joint tenant's interest to a third person, whether

or not pursuant to an agreement that requires the third person to reconvey legal title to the joint tenant.

(2) Execution of a written instrument that evidences the intent to sever the joint tenancy, including a deed that names the joint tenant as transferee, or of a written declaration that, as to the interest of the joint tenant, the joint tenancy is severed.

(b) Nothing in this section authorizes severance of a joint tenancy contrary to a written agreement of the joint tenants, but a severance contrary to a written agreement does not defeat the rights of a purchaser or encumbrancer for value in good faith and without knowledge of the written agreement.

(c) Severance of a joint tenancy of record by deed, written declaration, or other written instrument pursuant to subdivision (a) is not effective to terminate the right of survivorship of the other joint tenants as to the severing joint tenant's interest unless one of the following requirements is satisfied:

(1) Before the death of the severing joint tenant, the deed, written declaration, or other written instrument effecting the severance is recorded in the county where the real property is located.

(2) The deed, written declaration, or other written instrument effecting the severance is executed and acknowledged before a notary public by the severing joint tenant not earlier than three days before the death of that joint tenant and is recorded in the county where the real property is located not later than seven days after the death of the severing joint tenant.

(d) Nothing in subdivision (c) limits the manner or effect of:

(1) A written instrument executed by all the joint tenants that severs the joint tenancy.

(2) A severance made by or pursuant to a written agreement of all the joint tenants.

(3) A deed from a joint tenant to another joint tenant.

(e) Subdivisions (a) and (b) apply to all joint tenancies in real property, whether the joint tenancy was created before, on, or after January 1, 1985, except that in the case of the death of a joint tenant before January 1, 1985, the validity of a severance under subdivisions (a) and (b) is determined by the law in effect at the time of death. Subdivisions (c) and (d) do not apply to or affect a severance made before January 1, 1986, of a joint tenancy.

(Stats. 1984, ch. 519, §1. Amended by Stats. 1985, ch. 157, §1.)

B. Joint Ownership of Safe Deposit Boxes

Often, persons lease a safe deposit box jointly. The financial institution specifies the terms of the lease of the box. Those terms generally give the parties joint access to the box but do not change title to the contents.

> [T]he rental agreement is usually prepared by the safe-deposit box company on its printed form and is designed for its protection; often it does not represent the true understanding of the lessees. For these reasons, it is reasonable to deny that a joint tenancy can be created by this method.

Atkinson, *supra*, §40, at 167. See also American Trust Co. v. Fitzmaurice, 280 P.2d 545 (Cal. Ct. App. 1955) (holding that parties' rental of safe deposit box in joint tenancy did not establish a joint tenancy in the contents of the box).

In 1949, the California legislature enacted a statute (Cal. Civ. Code §683.1) forbidding joint tenancies in safe deposit boxes. Before that time, banks permitted the use of forms providing for a joint tenancy, with right of survivorship, in the contents of the box. Courts construed such agreements to cover not only the existing contents of the box but also future deposits despite their previous sole ownership by one party. 13 Witkin Summary, Personal Property, §34.

In 1991, the legislature amended California Probate Code §331 to provide for increased access (prior to issuance of letters of administration or letters testamentary) to a decedent's safe deposit box by a person with a key for purposes of an inventory of the contents of the box and removal of burial instructions as well as wills and trusts. The person given access must deliver any wills found therein to the clerk of the superior court (Cal. Prob. Code §331). If the person seeking access does not have a key, that person must obtain letters of administration or letters testamentary to gain access to the box. In cases in which a decedent fails to provide burial instructions, the right to dispose of the decedent's remains is determined by statutory priority (i.e., the surviving spouse, children, parents, other kin, and the public administrator) subject to California Health and Safety Code §7100.

California legislation also protects the bank in cases in which the renter(s) of the box fail to pay the rental fees. California Financial Code

§§1660 et seq. provides that the bank may enforce rental liability by opening the safe deposit box, disposing of the contents, and using the proceeds of the sale to satisfy the outstanding rental fees, cost of opening the box, and sale of the contents. However, the bank first must provide notice to the renter(s) of the box (Cal. Fin. Code §1664). Use of this remedy does not preclude the bank from other remedies to enforce its claims against the renter(s) of the box (Cal. Fin. Code §1676).

CALIFORNIA CIVIL CODE

§683.1. No contract between financial institution and renter of box shall create a joint tenancy in a safe-deposit box

No contract or other arrangement made after the effective date of this section between any person, firm, or corporation engaged in the business of renting safe-deposit boxes and the renter or renters of a safe-deposit box, shall create a joint tenancy in or otherwise establish ownership in any of the contents of such safe-deposit box. Any such contract or other arrangement purporting so to do shall be to such extent void and of no effect.

(Stats. 1949, ch. 1597, p. 2845, §1.)

CALIFORNIA FINANCIAL CODE

§1660. Bank is entitled to special remedies to enforce box rental

Every bank conducting a safe-deposit business shall be entitled to the special remedies set forth in this article in enforcing the liabilities of safe-deposit box renters and of safekeeping and storage depositors.

(Stats. 1951, ch. 364, p. 913, §1660. Amended by Stats. 1973, ch. 963, p. 1839, §98.)

§1661. Bank must mail notice of nonpayment of rental

If the rental of any safe-deposit box is not paid within six months from the day it is due, the bank, or at any time thereafter and while such rental remains unpaid, may mail a notice to the person in whose name such box stands on its records stating that if the amount due for such rental is not paid on or before a specified day, which must be at least 30 days after the date of mailing such notice, the bank will cause such box to be forced open.

(Stats. 1951, ch. 364, p. 913, §1661.)

§1662. Bank may open box, remove and inventory contents

At any time after the date specified in such notice, if the rental for such safe-deposit box to the date of payment and the cost of giving such notice have not been paid, the bank, in the presence of two of its employees, one of whom shall be an officer of the bank, may cause such box to be opened and the contents thereof to be removed and inventoried. The inventory shall be signed by such persons.

(Stats. 1951, ch. 364, p. 913, §1662. Amended by Stats. 1982, ch. 220, p. 733, §1.)

§1664. Notice of sale of contents

At any time after two years from the day when a safe-deposit box has been opened pursuant to this article, the bank may mail a notice to the person in whose name such box stood on its records, stating that unless the amounts due to the bank for rental, for the cost of mailing and publishing notice of sale, and for its charges for opening the box and for custody of its contents, and any other proper charges, giving the total amount thereof, are paid, the bank will offer for sale the contents thereof at a time and place named in such notice, which time shall be at least 30 days after the mailing thereof. If the amounts specified in such notice are not paid before the time of sale designated therein, the bank may sell all or any portion of the contents of such box, other than contents of the character described in Section 1668 and other than bonds and other securities which at the time of sale are listed on an established stock exchange in the United States, at public sale at the time and place given in such notice. Notice of the time and place of sale shall be published in a newspaper of general circulation in the county in which the sale is to be held once at least five days before the date of sale, or if no such newspaper is published in the county such notice shall be posted in three public places in the county at least five days before the date of sale. Such notice need describe the property only in general terms and as the unclaimed contents of a safe-deposit box. Such sale may be postponed from time to time by public pronouncement at the time and place of sale.

(Stats. 1951, ch. 364, p. 914, §1664.)

§1672. Bank shall deduct charges and expenses from proceeds of sale

From the proceeds of the sale, the bank shall deduct all charges as stated in the final notice, together with any further charges that have accrued since the mailing thereof, and reasonable expenses for notices, advertising, and sale, and shall credit the balance of the proceeds, if any, to an account in the name of the person in whose name the receipt for such personal property was issued.

(Stats. 1951, ch. 364, p. 916, §1672.)

§1676. Remedies are not exclusive

The provisions of this article do not preclude any other remedy by action or otherwise now or hereafter existing for the enforcement of the claims of a bank against the person in whose name the safe-deposit box stood or stands, or in whose name the safekeeping or storage receipt was issued, nor bar the right of a bank to so recover, at its option, either the entire amount of the debt due to it without recourse to sale of the property, if any, or so much of the debt due to it as shall not have been paid by the proceeds of the sale of all or any portion of the property deposited with it.

(Stats. 1951, ch. 364, p. 917, §1676.)

§1678. Notices regarding safe deposit box held in joint names

(a) Whenever this article requires that notice be sent to a person, and the box stood or stands on the records of the bank or the safekeeping or storage receipt was issued in the names of two or more persons, notice addressed to either or to any one of the two or more persons shall be binding upon and effective as to the remaining person or all remaining persons, and notice addressed to the name of any deceased individual shall be binding upon his or her legal representatives and on his or her heirs and legatees.

(b) Whenever this article requires that notice be published prior to a sale, the notice shall include the name and address of the person in whose name the safe-deposit box stood on the records of the bank or the safekeeping or storage receipt was issued. The names and addresses of all persons whose property is to be sold at the same time and place may be included in a single published notice.

(c) Whenever this article requires that an amount be credited to the account of a person in whose name a safedeposit box stood on the records of the bank or a safekeeping or storage receipt was issued, and the box stood or the receipt was issued in two or more names, the account shall be in both or all the names, subject to withdrawal by or upon the written order of any one or more of those persons, or by their successors or legal representatives.

(d) Whenever this article requires that a notice shall be mailed to the person in whose name the safe-deposit box stood on the records of the bank or a safekeeping or storage receipt was issued, the notice shall be deemed to have been so mailed if it is enclosed in a sealed envelope addressed to the person in whose name the safe-deposit box stood in the office of the bank at which the records of the safe-deposit box rentals are kept, or to the person in whose name the receipt was issued, as the case may be, addressed to the person at the address or place appearing on the safe-deposit or storage records of the office, and the envelope with postage prepaid has been deposited by at least first-class mail in the United States mail.

(Stats. 1951, ch. 364, p. 917, §1678. Amended by Stats. 1996 (A.B. 3012), ch. 1063, §58.)

CALIFORNIA PROBATE CODE

§331. Safe deposit box

(a) This section applies only to a safe deposit box in a financial institution held by the decedent in the decedent's sole name, or held by the decedent and others where all are deceased. Nothing in this section affects the rights of a surviving coholder.

(b) A person who has a key to the safe deposit box may, before letters have been issued, obtain access to the safe deposit box only for the purposes specified in this section by providing the financial institution with both of the following:

(1) Proof of the decedent's death. Proof shall be provided by a certified copy of the decedent's death certificate or by a written statement of death from the coroner, treating physician, or hospital or institution where the decedent died.

(2) Reasonable proof of the identity of the person seeking access. Reasonable proof of identity is provided for the purpose of this paragraph if the requirements of Section 13104 are satisfied.

(c) The financial institution has no duty to inquire into the truth of any statement, declaration, certificate, affidavit, or document offered as proof of the decedent's death or proof of identity of the person seeking access.

(d) When the person seeking access has satisfied the requirements of subdivision (b), the financial institution shall do all of the following:

(1) Keep a record of the identity of the person.

(2) Permit the person to open the safe deposit box under the supervision of an officer or employee of the financial institution, and to make an inventory of its contents.

(3) Make a photocopy of all wills and trust instruments removed from the safe deposit box, and keep the photocopy in the safe deposit box until the contents of the box are removed by the personal representative of the estate or other legally authorized person. The financial institution may charge the person given access a reasonable fee for photocopying.

(4) Permit the person given access to remove instructions for the disposition of the decedent's remains,

and, after a photocopy is made, to remove the wills and trust instruments.

(e) The person given access shall deliver all wills found in the safe deposit box to the clerk of the superior court and mail or deliver a copy to the person named in the will as executor or beneficiary as provided in Section 8200.

(f) Except as provided in subdivision (d), the person given access shall not remove any of the contents of the decedent's safe deposit box.

(Stats. 1991 (S.B. 271), ch. 1055, §15.)

IV. Gifts

A. Inter Vivos Gifts

A gift is a gratuitous transfer of property to a donee by a donor with donative intent. Two types of gifts exist:

- **inter vivos gifts, and**
- **conditional gifts (such as gifts in contemplation of marriage and gifts in contemplation of impending death).**

A gift requires donative intent and delivery. However, courts sometimes find donative intent even without delivery. Other times, courts find that delivery is not sufficient to show donative intent. McGovern & Kurtz, *supra*, §4.5 at 204-205.

An inter vivos gift is a completed transfer. With limited exceptions (see Section B *infra*), it cannot be made revocable or conditional. Atkinson, *supra*, §45 at 200. See also Restatement (Third) Property, *supra*, at §6.1.

There are three requirements for a valid inter vivos gift:

- **donative intent, by a donor having capacity to contract, to make an unconditional gift;**
- **actual or symbolic delivery, so as to relinquish dominion and control by the donor; and**
- **acceptance by the donee (although acceptance may be presumed).**

13 Witkin Summary, Personal Property, §124.

To be valid, an inter vivos gift must take effect at once. That is, the owner must presently divest himself of ownership and control. If the donor intends for a gift to take effect in the future, it is merely a promise to make a gift. In re McEuen's Estate, 63 P.2d 332 (Ct. App. 1936).

Gifts of intangibles can be made by several methods. The first method is manual or actual delivery. However, some intangibles (i.e., certificates of deposit, bonds) may be subject to the additional rule of financial institutions that require notice of the transfer. McGovern & Kurtz, *supra*, §4.5 at 204. *Id.* Sometimes, a gift will be effective without actual delivery if the donor merely re-registers the intangibles in the donee's name even if the donee is unaware of the gift. *Id.*

The second method is delivery by a signed writing. *Id.* at 191. The writing indicates the donor's intent to give the item. In some cases, the gift will be effective if the donor gives the signed writing without delivering the item itself. *Id.*

Traditionally, signing and delivering a check to a donee is not effective as an assignment of the donor's funds if the donor dies before the check is paid. That is, the order on the bank is considered revoked by the donor's death; the check is not enforceable against the estate. Atkinson, *supra*, §45 at 199; McGovern & Kurtz, *supra*, at 205.

The third method of delivery is symbolic (sometimes called "constructive"), such as by transferring a savings account book. Atkinson, *supra*, §45 at 202-203; McGovern & Kurtz, *supra*, §4.5 at 206. The bank book serves as a symbol or evidence of the item itself.

Delivery may be made to a third person acting on behalf of a donee, provided that the donor parts with dominion and control over the gift. U.S. v. Alcaraz-Garcia, 79 F.3d 759 (9th Cir. 1996) (delivery of cash to agent to give to relatives in Mexico). If the donee already has possession of the item, delivery is unnecessary.

The Statute of Frauds requires that gifts of real property be in writing. However, courts sometimes give effect to oral gifts of land if the donee has taken possession and made valuable improvements. McGovern & Kurtz, *supra*, §4.5 at 203.

In California, interspousal gifts are subject to special rules. Some forms of interspousal gifts do not require a writing. This rule is an exception to the general rule on transmutation of property (as explained *infra*). Married persons in California may transmute (change) the nature of their property by a written agreement or transfer,

made with the consent of both spouses, with or without consideration. They may transmute community property to the separate property of one of the spouses, separate property of one spouse to community property, or transmute the separate property of one spouse to separate property of the other spouse (Cal. Fam. Code §850). This rule is subject to certain limitations. For example, a statement in a will as to the character of property is not admissible as evidence of a transmutation in a proceeding commenced before the death of the testator (Cal. Fam. Code §853).

Another limitation is that the writing requirement does not apply to certain interspousal gifts. Specifically, the rule is not applicable to a gift of "clothing, wearing apparel, jewelry, or other tangible articles of a personal nature that is used solely or principally by the donee spouse, and is not substantial in value taking into account the circumstances of the marriage" (Cal. Fam. Code §852 (c)). This exception to the writing requirement comports with the expectations of most married couples. See generally Bret Bartolotta, Transmutation of Property and the California Family Code, 11 J. Contemp. Legal Issues 209 (1999).

B. Conditional Gifts

Inter vivos gifts generally are a completed gratuitous transfer. Thus, they are neither revocable nor conditional. However, two types of gifts are conditional:

- gifts in contemplation of marriage, and
- gifts in contemplation of death (called "gifts causa mortis").
-

1. Gifts in Contemplation of Marriage

During an engagement, the parties may give gifts to each other (such as an engagement ring). Many courts hold that an engagement ring is a conditional gift. Under this theory, A's gift to B of an engagement ring is conditioned on B's performance of an act (getting married). If the condition is not fulfilled (i.e., the marriage does not take place), then A may recover the gift.

At common law, fault barred recovery or retention of the engagement ring. Thus, the man could recover the ring if the woman unjustifiably ended the engagement or if the couple mutually dissolved it, but not if he unjustifiably terminated the engagement. In most states today, whether a party must return such a gift still depends on who was responsible (at fault) for terminating the engagement.

The fault-based rule is the majority rule. See, e.g., Clippard v. Pfefferkorn, 168 S.W.3d 616 (Mo. Ct. App. 2005). See also Brian L. Kruckenberg, Comment, "I Don't": Determining Ownership of the Engagement Ring When the Engagement Terminates (Herman v. Parrish, 942 P.2d 631 (Kan. 1997), 37 Washburn L.J. 425, 434 (1998)). However, according to the modern trend, fault is irrelevant. See, e.g., Fowler v. Perry, 830 N.E.2d 97, 105 (Ind. Ct. App. 2005)); Meyer v. Mitnick, 625 N.W.2d 136 (Mich. Ct. App. 2001); Benassi v. Back and Neck Pain Clinic, 629 N.W.2d 475 (Minn. Ct. App. 2001). California takes fault into consideration both by statute (Cal. Civ. Code §1590) and case law (Simonian v. Donoian, 215 P.2d 119, 121 (Cal. Ct. App. 1950) (providing that the donee is entitled to retain possession of engagement ring when the donor breaks the engagement without any fault on the donee's part). See generally Rebecca Tushnet, Rules of Engagement, 107 Yale L.J. 2583 (1998).

CALIFORNIA CIVIL CODE

§1590. Recovery for gifts in contemplation of marriage

Where either party to a contemplated marriage in this State makes a gift of money or property to the other on the basis or assumption that the marriage will take place, in the event that the donee refuses to enter into the marriage as contemplated or that it is given up by mutual consent, the donor may recover such gift or such part of its value as may, under all of the circumstances of the case, be found by a court or jury to be just.

(Stats. 1939, ch. 128, p. 1245, §2.)

2. Gifts in Contemplation of Death (Gifts Causa Mortis)

A gift causa mortis is a gift of personal property by a person in apprehension of immediate death. Gifts causa mortis were influenced by Roman law. Atkinson, *supra*, §45 at 200 n.7. Gifts causa mortis are a hybrid type of transfer, enabling the property owner to secure most of the advantages of both a will and an inter vivos gift. *Id.* at 205.

Gifts causa mortis, like gifts generally, require donative intent and delivery. "[A]ny set of facts which would constitute good delivery for a gift inter vivos will satisfy this requirement of a gift causa mortis." *Id.* at 202. Delivery also is effective to a third person who is requested to give the property to the donee at the donor's death. *Id.*

The primary difference between gifts causa mortis and inter vivos gifts is the revocability of the former. Gifts causa mortis may be revoked by: (1) the donor's express act; (2) the donor's recovery from illness; or (3) the donor's survival of the donee. Atkinson, *supra*, §45 at 204. Also, gifts causa mortis, unlike inter vivos gifts, may be subject to creditors' claims. "In case of insolvency of the donor's estate his personal representative is entitled to recover gifts causa mortis to the extent necessary to satisfy creditors." *Id.*

Gifts causa mortis differ from wills in several ways. Wills must be in writing. Delivery is required for gifts causa mortis but not for legacies. Gifts causa mortis require immediate apprehension of death. And, wills can dispose of land but gifts causa mortis cannot. *Id.* at 205.

California legislation provides for specific methods of revocation of a gift causa mortis. According to statute, such a gift may be revoked by: (1) the donor's recovery from the illness, or escape from the peril which triggered the gift; or (2) the death of the donee before the death of the donor (Cal. Prob. Code §5704(a)(1) & (2)). Also, a donor may revoke the gift any time during his or her lifetime or by will, provided that the will expresses an intention to revoke the gift (Cal. Prob. Code §5704(b)(1) & (2)).

According to Law Revision Commission Commentary, the definition of a gift causa mortis is phrased in terms of a condition subsequent rather than a condition precedent.

> If the giver intends the gift to become absolute only upon the giver's death, with title passing at the instant of death (condition precedent), the gift is testamentary. J. Cribbett & C. Johnson, Principles of the Law of Property 156 (3d ed. 1989). In such cases, the courts hold the attempted gift in view of death to be ineffective, and the property must be restored to the decedent's estate. See Yates v. Dundas, 80 Cal.App.2d 468, 182 P.2d 305 (1947). If the condition is subsequent, with the donee's title vesting immediately on delivery, subject to revocation if the giver survives the peril, the gift is not testamentary and can be sustained. J. Cribbett & C. Johnson, *supra*. . . .

Law Revision Commission Commentary following California Probate Code §5702.

The California legislature also amended the definition of gift causa mortis (Cal. Prob. Code §5702) by codifying existing case law to define such a gift as made in contemplation, fear, or peril of "impending" death. This change in terminology "negates a possible construction that such a gift is any gift made in contemplation of death, whether imminent or remote, such as a gift to reduce estate taxes or to avoid probate." *Id.*

A gift in view of impending death is not invalid if the death is a suicide. In Berl v. Rosenberg, 336 P.2d 975 (Cal. Ct. App. 1959), the decedent wrote a letter to his securities broker stating that "I wish to make a joint ownership account with Marion Clemens . . . for sole survivor to receive all." The letter was mailed on June 18, 1956, and was delivered on June 19, 1956 before 8:30 a.m. The decedent committed suicide June 19th before 11 a.m. The appellate court affirmed the trial court ruling that the word "wish" signified a present transfer creating a valid joint tenancy in the securities and also concluded that a gift causa mortis is not invalid as a matter of public policy in case of suicide, provided that the donor complies with all the requirements of a gift.

California legislation authorizes a personal representative to recover gifts causa mortis in some cases. According to California Probate Code §9653, upon the application of a creditor, a personal representative must commence an action to recover: (1) gifts causa mortis, (2) fraudulent transfers (i.e., conveyances of property or an interest that is fraudulent as to creditors, pursuant to the Uniform Fraudulent Transfer Act California, California Civil Code §§3439 et seq.), or (3) transfers of certain motor

vehicles pursuant to California Health and Safety Code §18102.2, or California Vehicle Code §§5910.5 or 9916.5). The proceeds of the sale of any recovered property are applied to payment of costs and expenses, and then to the decedent's debts (Cal. Prob. Code §9653(c)).

Note that a gift causa mortis of either community or quasi-community property is subject to the rights of the donor's spouse pursuant to California Family Code §1101 and California Probate Code §102. See Chapter II, Section IIC *supra*.

CALIFORNIA CIVIL CODE

§1146. "Gift," defined

GIFTS DEFINED. A gift is a transfer of personal property, made voluntarily, and without consideration.

(Enacted 1872.)

§1147. Verbal gift: requirements for validity

GIFT, HOW MADE. A verbal gift is not valid, unless the means of obtaining possession and control of the thing are given, nor, if it is capable of delivery, unless there is an actual or symbolical delivery of the thing to the donee.

(Enacted 1872.)

§1148. Gift cannot be revoked; exception for gifts causa mortis

GIFT NOT REVOCABLE. A gift, other than a gift in view of impending death, cannot be revoked by the giver.

(Enacted 1872. Amended by Stats. 1991 (S.B. 271), ch. 1055, §2.)

CALIFORNIA FAMILY CODE

§850. Married persons may transmute property by agreement or transfer

Subject to Sections 851 to 853, inclusive, married persons may by agreement or transfer, with or without consideration, do any of the following:

(a) Transmute community property to separate property of either spouse.

(b) Transmute separate property of either spouse to community property.

(c) Transmute separate property of one spouse to separate property of the other spouse.

(Stats. 1992 (A.B. 2650), ch. 162, §10, effective January 1, 1994.)

§851. Transmutation is subject to fraudulent transfer laws

A transmutation is subject to the laws governing fraudulent transfers.

(Stats. 1992 (A.B. 2650), ch. 162, §10, effective January 1, 1994.)

§852. Requirements for transmutation of property; exceptions for some interspousal gifts

(a) A transmutation of real or personal property is not valid unless made in writing by an express declaration that is made, joined in, consented to, or accepted by the spouse whose interest in the property is adversely affected.

(b) A transmutation of real property is not effective as to third parties without notice thereof unless recorded.

(c) This section does not apply to a gift between the spouses of clothing, wearing apparel, jewelry, or other tangible articles of a personal nature that is used solely or principally by the spouse to whom the gift is made and that is not substantial in value taking into account the circumstances of the marriage.

(d) Nothing in this section affects the law governing characterization of property in which separate property and community property are commingled or otherwise combined.

(e) This section does not apply to or affect a transmutation of property made before January 1, 1985, and the law that would otherwise be applicable to that transmutation shall continue to apply.

(Stats. 1992 (A.B. 2650), ch. 162, §10, effective January 1, 1994.)

§853. Statement in a will as to character of property is inadmissible as evidence of transmutation in antemortem proceeding

(a) A statement in a will of the character of property is not admissible as evidence of a transmutation of the property in a proceeding commenced before the death of the person who made the will.

(b) A waiver of a right to a joint and survivor annuity or survivor's benefits under the federal Retirement Equity Act of 1984 (Public Law 98-397) is not a transmutation of the community property rights of the person executing the waiver.

(c) A written joinder or written consent to a nonprobate transfer of community property on death that satisfies Section 852 is a transmutation and is governed by the law applicable to transmutations and not by Chapter 2 (commencing with Section 5010) of Part 1 of Division 5 of the Probate Code.

(Stats. 1992 (A.B. 2650), ch. 162, §10, effective January 1, 1994. Amended by Stats. 1993 (A.B. 1500), ch. 219, §100.)

CALIFORNIA PROBATE CODE

§5700. "Gift," defined

As used in this part, "gift" means a transfer of personal property made voluntarily and without consideration.

(Stats. 1991 (S.B. 271), ch. 1055, §18.)

§5701. Gift causa mortis is subject to general law related to gifts of personal property

Except as provided in this part, a gift in view of impending death is subject to the general law relating to gifts of personal property.

(Stats. 1991 (S.B. 271), ch. 1055, §18.)

§5702. "Gift causa mortis," defined

(a) A gift in view of impending death is one which is made in contemplation, fear, or peril of impending death, whether from illness or other cause, and with intent that it shall be revoked if the giver recovers from the illness or escapes from the peril.

(b) A reference in a statute to a gift in view of death means a gift in view of impending death.

(Stats. 1991 (S.B. 271), ch. 1055, §18.)

§5703. Presumption operates that a gift under some circumstances is a gift causa mortis

A gift made during the last illness of the giver, or under circumstances which would naturally impress the giver with an expectation of speedy death, is presumed to be a gift in view of impending death.

(Stats. 1991 (S.B. 271), ch. 1055, §18.)

§5704. Gift causa mortis may be revoked by various methods

(a) A gift in view of impending death is revoked by:

(1) The giver's recovery from the illness, or escape from the peril, under the presence of which it was made.

(2) The death of the donee before the death of the giver.

(b) A gift in view of impending death may be revoked by:

(1) The giver at any time.

(2) The giver's will if the will expresses an intention to revoke the gift.

(c) A gift in view of impending death is not affected by a previous will of the giver.

(d) Notwithstanding subdivisions (a) and (b), when the gift has been delivered to the donee, the rights of a purchaser or encumbrancer, acting before the revocation in good faith, for a valuable consideration, and without knowledge of the conditional nature of the gift, are not affected by the revocation.

(Stats. 1991 (S.B. 271), ch. 1055, §18.)

§5705. Rights of donor's creditors

A gift in view of impending death is subject to Section 9653 [creditors can force the decedent's personal representative to sue to recover a gift if there are insufficient estate assets to pay creditors' claims].

(Stats. 1991 (S.B. 271), ch. 1055, §18.)

§9653. Creditor can require personal representative to begin action to recover gifts causa mortis if estate insolvent

(a) On application of a creditor of the decedent or the estate, the personal representative shall commence and prosecute an action for the recovery of real or personal property of the decedent for the benefit of creditors if the personal representative has insufficient assets to pay creditors and the decedent during lifetime did any of the following with respect to the property:

(1) Made a conveyance of the property, or any right or interest in the property, that is fraudulent as to creditors under the Uniform Fraudulent Transfer Act (Chapter 1 (commencing with Section 3439) of Title 2 of Part 2 of Division 4 of the Civil Code).

(2) Made a gift of the property in view of impending death.

(3) Made a direction to transfer a vehicle, undocumented vessel, manufactured home, mobilehome, commercial coach, truck camper, or floating home to a designated beneficiary on the decedent's death pursuant to Section 18102.2 of the Health and Safety Code, or Section 5910.5 or 9916.5 of the Vehicle Code, and the property has been transferred as directed.

(b) A creditor making application under this section shall pay such part of the costs and expenses of the suit and attorney's fees, or give an undertaking to the personal representative for that purpose, as the personal representative and the creditor agree, or, absent an agreement, as the court or judge orders.

(c) The property recovered under this section shall be sold for the payment of debts in the same manner as if the decedent had died seized or possessed of the property. The proceeds of the sale shall be applied first to payment of the costs and expenses of suit, including attorney's fees, and then to payment of the debts of the decedent in the same manner as other property in possession of the personal representative. After all the debts of the decedent have been paid, the remainder of the proceeds shall be paid to the person from whom the property was recovered. The property may be sold in its entirety or in such portion as necessary to pay the debts.

(Stats. 1990 (A.B. 759), ch. 79, §14, effective July 1, 1991. Amended by Stats. 1991 (S.B. 271), ch. 1055, §27, effective January 1, 1993.)

CALIFORNIA CIVIL CODE

§1146. "Gift," defined

GIFTS DEFINED. A gift is a transfer of personal property, made voluntarily, and without consideration.

(Enacted 1872.)

§1147. Verbal gift: requirements for validity

GIFT, HOW MADE. A verbal gift is not valid, unless the means of obtaining possession and control of the thing are given, nor, if it is capable of delivery, unless there is an actual or symbolical delivery of the thing to the donee.

(Enacted 1872.)

§1148. Gift cannot be revoked; exception for gifts causa mortis

GIFT NOT REVOCABLE. A gift, other than a gift in view of impending death, cannot be revoked by the giver.

(Enacted 1872. Amended by Stats. 1991 (S.B. 271), ch. 1055, §2.)

CALIFORNIA PROBATE CODE

§5701. Gift causa mortis is subject to general law related to gifts of personal property

Except as provided in this part, a gift in view of impending death is subject to the general law relating to gifts of personal property.

(Stats. 1991 (S.B. 271), ch. 1055, §18.)

§5702. "Gift causa mortis," defined

(a) A gift in view of impending death is one which is made in contemplation, fear, or peril of impending death, whether from illness or other cause, and with intent that it shall be revoked if the giver recovers from the illness or escapes from the peril.

(b) A reference in a statute to a gift in view of death means a gift in view of impending death.

(Stats. 1991 (S.B. 271), ch. 1055, §18.)

§5703. Presumption operates that a gift under some circumstances is a gift causa mortis

A gift made during the last illness of the giver, or under circumstances which would naturally impress the giver with an expectation of speedy death, is presumed to be a gift in view of impending death.

(Stats. 1991 (S.B. 271), ch. 1055, §18.)

§5704. Gift causa mortis may be revoked by various methods

(a) A gift in view of impending death is revoked by:

(1) The giver's recovery from the illness, or escape from the peril, under the presence of which it was made.

(2) The death of the donee before the death of the giver.

(b) A gift in view of impending death may be revoked by:

(1) The giver at any time.

(2) The giver's will if the will expresses an intention to revoke the gift.

(c) A gift in view of impending death is not affected by a previous will of the giver.

(d) Notwithstanding subdivisions (a) and (b), when the gift has been delivered to the donee, the rights of a purchaser or encumbrancer, acting before the revocation in good faith, for a valuable consideration, and without knowledge of the conditional nature of the gift, are not affected by the revocation.

(Stats. 1991 (S.B. 271), ch. 1055, §18.)

§9653. Creditor can require personal representative to begin action to recover gifts causa mortis if estate insolvent

(a) On application of a creditor of the decedent or the estate, the personal representative shall commence and prosecute an action for the recovery of real or personal property of the decedent for the benefit of creditors if the personal representative has insufficient assets to pay creditors and the decedent during lifetime did any of the following with respect to the property:

(1) Made a conveyance of the property, or any right or interest in the property, that is fraudulent as to creditors under the Uniform Fraudulent Transfer Act (Chapter 1 (commencing with Section 3439) of Title 2 of Part 2 of Division 4 of the Civil Code).

(2) Made a gift of the property in view of impending death.

(3) Made a direction to transfer a vehicle, undocumented vessel, manufactured home, mobilehome, commercial coach, truck camper, or floating home to a

designated beneficiary on the decedent's death pursuant to Section 18102.2 of the Health and Safety Code, or Section 5910.5 or 9916.5 of the Vehicle Code, and the property has been transferred as directed.

(b) A creditor making application under this section shall pay such part of the costs and expenses of the suit and attorney's fees, or give an undertaking to the personal representative for that purpose, as the personal representative and the creditor agree, or, absent an agreement, as the court or judge orders.

(c) The property recovered under this section shall be sold for the payment of debts in the same manner as if the decedent had died seized or possessed of the property. The proceeds of the sale shall be applied first to payment of the costs and expenses of suit, including attorney's fees, and then to payment of the debts of the decedent in the same manner as other property in possession of the personal representative. After all the debts of the decedent have been paid, the remainder of the proceeds shall be paid to the person from whom the property was recovered. The property may be sold in its entirety or in such portion as necessary to pay the debts.
(Stats. 1990 (A.B. 759), ch. 79, §14, effective July 1, 1991. Amended by Stats. 1991 (S.B. 271), ch. 1055, §27, effective January 1, 1993.)

C. Gifts to Minors

Because minors lack legal capacity to manage property, property ownership for children requires special provisions. Common forms of management of property for minors are guardianships and trusts. However, each type involves shortcomings. Guardianships are cumbersome. Guardians must file a bond, submit accounts to a court, and obtain judicial approval for sales, investments, and distributions. Guardianships also terminate at age 18. McGovern & Kurtz, *supra*, §9.2 at 347. Inter vivos trusts are an alternative. However, trusts are a more expensive option, involving costs for creation and administration.

A preferable system, for modest gifts to minors, is the Uniform Gifts to Minors Act (UGMA) or its successor Uniform Transfers to Minors Act (UTMA). Every state has enacted a version of UGMA or UTMA, which enables an adult to give substantial gifts of property to a child, without the child having to assume control of the property. The National Conference of Commissioners on Uniform State Laws (NCCUSL) promulgated UGMA in 1956. UGMA stemmed from model legislation sponsored by the New York Stock Exchange to create a simple and inexpensive method to make inter vivos gifts of securities to minors. Security dealers were concerned that minors' right of disaffirmance of contracts posed hazards for brokers, and therefore made it difficult to sell securities and reinvest on minors' behalf.

Initially, UGMA applied only to inter vivos gifts of money, as well as securities, to minors. When UGMA was revised in 1965 and 1966, NCCUSL expanded the definition of custodial property (to include life insurance policies and annuity contracts) and the types of financial institutions that could serve as depositories, and also facilitated the designation of successor custodians. Prefatory Note, Uniform Transfers to Minors Act, 8C U.L.A. 3-4 (2001). In addition, NCCUSL changed the title of the Act to replace the narrow term "gifts" with the broader term "transfers" to expand the types of possible transfers. Not all states enacted the 1966 revisions. Moreover, many states have revised their versions of UGMA since 1966 to include different kinds of property that are the subject of a gift and permitting transfers to custodians from other sources. As a result, considerable lack of uniformity exists. *Id.*

1. Transfer of Property into Custodianship

UTMA allows any kind of property (real or personal, tangible or intangible, and without limit), to be the subject of a transfer to a custodian for the benefit of a minor. It permits such transfers not only by inter vivos gifts, but also from such other sources as: trusts, estates, guardianships, and third-party debtors of a minor who does not have a conservator (e.g., parties against whom a minor has a tort claim or judgment, and depository institutions holding deposits or insurance companies issuing policies payable on death to a minor). *Id.*

A donor may make a transfer pursuant to UTMA by an express declaration (i.e., mentioning the Act) that the gift is made to a custodian in the name of the minor. For property that is in registered form, the transfer generally is completed by registering ownership in the name of the minor under the given jurisdiction's Uniform Transfers to Minors Act. Delivery to the

minor is not required. A custodianship may be established only for the benefit of one minor. A "transfer" is irrevocable and indefeasibly vests ownership of the property interest in the minor.

2. Custodians: Eligibility, Duties

A person is eligible to serve as custodian if he or she has reached age 21. A trust company may also act as custodian. Only one custodian may serve. Death or incapacity of, or renunciation by, a custodian does not invalidate the transfer of property into the custodianship. In such cases, UTMA provides for the appointment of successor custodians.

A custodian first must take control of custodial property, including facilitating any necessary registration or recordation of custodial property. The custodian may act, without judicial involvement, to manage and invest custodial property.

3. Custodianships: Costs, Compensation, Investments, Expenditures

The custodian must exercise authority according to a high standard of care—i.e., the standard observed by a prudent person dealing with the property of another. The custodian may choose a broad range of allowable investments. However, custodial property should not be commingled with the custodian's personal property. Also, custodial property may not be placed in joint tenancy with a right of survivorship.

Custodians have broad discretion to use the custodial property for the minor's benefit. Under UTMA §14(a), the custodian may spend according to what he or she considers "advisable" for the minor's "use and benefit." The UTMA "use and benefit" standard is broader than that of UGMA. (See UTMA §14 cmt.) Under UGMA (§4), the custodian is limited to use custodial property for the "support, maintenance, education, and benefit of the minor."

UTMA provides for reimbursement from custodial property by "reasonable compensation" for "reasonable expenses incurred in the performance of the custodian's duties." However, the custodian who is also a transferor may not receive compensation.

4. Distribution of Custodial Property

The age of distribution of custodial property depends on the manner in which the property is transferred. If property is transferred by means of an inter vivos gift, the exercise of a power of appointment, by will, or by the terms of a trust, then the property may be distributed to a minor at age 21. The age of distribution for other transfers (e.g., testamentary transfers through life insurance designation, an employee benefit plan, or a payable on death account) is tied to the age of majority in the enacting state. Paul M. Peterson, The Uniform Transfers to Minors Act: A Practitioner's Guide, 1995 Army Lawyer 3, 10 (1995). Some states (including California) allow the transferor to vary the age of distribution within a fixed range of ages (from 18 to 25). *Id.*

At the age designated for distribution, the custodianship terminates, and the custodian may distribute the property. During the course of the custodianship, custodial property is indefeasibly vested in the minor. Any income received is attributed to the minor for tax purposes (whether or not actually distributed to the minor). Uniform Transfers to Minors Act, Prefatory Note.

5. Custodian's Liability

The expansion of the type of property interests that may be held in a custodial account increases the potential personal liability for both the minor and the custodian. As a result, UTMA limits the claims of third parties against the custodial property, and insulates the minor against personal liability unless he or she is personally at fault, and also insulates the custodian unless he or she is personally at fault or fails to disclose his custodial capacity in entering into a contract. *Id.* One possible remedy against a custodian is removal and appointment of a successor custodian. Courts may require custodians to pay damages for a breach of fiduciary duty that causes a loss of custodial property as well as the minor's attorneys fees. Peterson, *supra*, at 10.

UTMA also specifies the choice of law. A transferor designates the state law of choice by referring to a given jurisdiction in creating the custodianship. Courts of that state will follow the designation provided that the state has some minimum connections with the UTMA transaction. *Id.*

If property is transferred initially by a state that has adopted UGMA, but later enacts UTMA, UTMA provides that UTMA provisions will apply. This rule operates unless the application of UTMA would deprive the minor of rights in the property or would extend the age of distribution. *Id.*

6. California Version of UTMA

The California legislature adopted UGMA in 1959 (Cal. Civ. Code §§1154 et seq.). In 1984, it repealed UGMA and replaced it with UTMA (Cal. Prob. Code §§3900 et seq.). The California version of UTMA is known as "CUTMA." At the time, however, the legislature made a number of significant revisions:

- UTMA applies to transfers for the benefit of persons who have not reached the age of 21. On the other hand, CUTMA applies to transfers for the benefit of persons who have not reached the age of 18, but provides for a later termination (age 21 or 25) in specified circumstances (Cal. Prob. Code §3901(k) (definition of minor); §3920.5 (delayed termination)).
- CUTMA authorizes a minor's conservator to serve as custodian (Cal. Prob. Code §3911(d)(e)(f)). UTMA has no comparable provision.
- CUTMA permits a transferor who is both transferor and custodian to choose to eliminate his authority as custodian to distribute property for a minor's benefit, except pursuant to a court order (Cal. Prob. Code §3914(d)). UTMA has no comparable provision.
- CUTMA provides for venue in proceedings under the Act (Cal. Prob. Code §3921), whereas UTMA has no comparable provision. If the minor resides in California, venue is the county where the minor or custodian resides. If the minor does not reside in California, venue is: (1) the county where the transferor, custodian, or parent resides; (2) where the estate of a deceased/incapacitated custodian is being administered; or (3) if none of the foregoing, then in any county.

13 Witkin, Summary, Personal Property, §140.

Note that the creation of a custodianship in California must involve an express designation of the state in order to satisfy the choice-of-law requirement of California Probate Code §3909(a) that a choice of the California Uniform Transfers to Minors Act is appropriate and effective if any of the nexus factors specified in subdivision (a) exists at the time of the transfer. In case of the relocation of parties or property, CUTMA continues to govern, and the custodian continues to be subject to personal jurisdiction in California. Law Revision Commission Commentary following California Probate Code §3902.

The different kinds of permissible CUTMA transfers are separately described in California Probate Code §§3904, 3905, 3906, and 3907. Pursuant to CUTMA, a trustee may make a transfer to a custodian for the benefit of a minor if authorized by the trust (Cal. Prob. Code §3905). Also, if the settlor or testator fails to designate a custodian, the personal representative or trustee may do so. *Id.*

A custodian is required to transfer the custodial property to the minor when the minor attains age 18 unless the transfer specifies a later time (age 21 or 25). As mentioned above, CUTMA (unlike UTMA) provides for a choice of age as to when custodial property shall be transferred to a minor. Specifically, California Probate Code §3920.5 provides a choice of termination age because many transferors desire to preserve the custodianship as long as possible. Also, this provision permits a donor to avoid the expense of creating a trust in order to retain the property under custodial management. Law Revision Commission Commentary following California Probate Code §3920.5.

California Probate Code §3922 validates transfers made before the effective date of CUTMA that mistakenly refer to CUGMA and also

validates transfers attempted under UGMA legislation of another state, provided that California has a sufficient nexus to the transaction under California Probate Code §3902.

CALIFORNIA PROBATE CODE

§3900. California Uniform Transfers to Minors Act

This part may be cited as the "California Uniform Transfers to Minors Act."

(Stats. 1990 (A.B. 759), ch. 79, §14, effective July 1, 1991.)

§3901. Definitions

In this part:

(a) "Adult" means an individual who has attained the age of 18 years.

(b) "Benefit plan" means an employer's plan for the benefit of an employee or partner.

(c) "Broker" means a person lawfully engaged in the business of effecting transactions in securities or commodities for the person's own account or for the account of others.

(d) "Conservator" means a person appointed or qualified by a court to act as general, limited, or temporary guardian of a minor's property or a person legally authorized to perform substantially the same functions.

(e) "Court" means the superior court.

(f) "Custodial property" means (1) any interest in property transferred to a custodian under this part and (2) the income from and proceeds of that interest in property.

(g) "Custodian" means a person so designated under Section 3909 or a successor or substitute custodian designated under Section 3918.

(h) "Financial institution" means a bank, trust company, savings institution, or credit union, chartered and supervised under state or federal law or an industrial loan company licensed and supervised under the laws of this state.

(i) "Legal representative" means an individual's personal representative or conservator.

(j) "Member of the minor's family" means the minor's parent, stepparent, spouse, grandparent, brother, sister, uncle, or aunt, whether of the whole or half blood or by adoption.

(k) "Minor" means:

(1) Except as provided in paragraph (2), an individual who has not attained the age of 18 years.

(2) When used with reference to the beneficiary for whose benefit custodial property is held or is to be held, an individual who has not attained the age at which the custodian is required under Sections 3920 and 3920.5 to transfer the custodial property to the beneficiary.

(l) "Person" means an individual, corporation, organization, or other legal entity.

(m) "Personal representative" means an executor, administrator, successor personal representative, or special administrator of a decedent's estate or a person legally authorized to perform substantially the same functions.

(n) "State" includes any state of the United States, the District of Columbia, the Commonwealth of Puerto Rico, and any territory or possession subject to the legislative authority of the United States.

(o) "Transfer" means a transaction that creates custodial property under Section 3909.

(p) "Transferor" means a person who makes a transfer under this part.

(q) "Trust company" means a financial institution, corporation, or other legal entity, authorized to exercise general trust powers.

(Stats. 1990 (A.B. 759), ch. 79, §14, effective July 1, 1991.)

§3902. Application of Part to particular transfers

(a) This part applies to a transfer that refers to this part in the designation under subdivision (a) of Section 3909 by which the transfer is made if at the time of the transfer, the transferor, the minor, or the custodian is a resident of this state or the custodial property is located in this state. The custodianship so created remains subject to this part despite a subsequent change in residence of a transferor, the minor, or the custodian, or the removal of custodial property from this state.

(b) A person designated as custodian under this part is subject to personal jurisdiction in this state with respect to any matter relating to the custodianship.

(c) A transfer that purports to be made and which is valid under the Uniform Transfers to Minors Act, the Uniform Gifts to Minors Act, or a substantially similar act, of another state is governed by the law of the designated state and may be executed and is enforceable in this state if at the time of the transfer, the transferor, the minor, or the custodian is a resident of the designated state or the custodial property is located in the designated state.

(Stats. 1990 (A.B. 759), ch. 79, §14, effective July 1, 1991.)

§3903. Revocable nomination of custodian

(a) A person having the right to designate the recipient of property transferable upon the occurrence of a future event may revocably nominate a custodian to receive the property for a minor beneficiary upon the occurrence of the event by naming the custodian followed in substance by the words:

"as custodian for ______________________________
(Name of Minor)
under the California Uniform Transfers to Minors Act."

The nomination may name one or more persons as substitute custodians to whom the property must be transferred, in the order named, if the first nominated custodian dies before the transfer or is unable, declines, or is ineligible to serve. The nomination may be made in a will, a trust, a deed, an instrument exercising a power of appointment, or in a writing designating a beneficiary of contractual rights which is registered with or delivered to the payor, issuer, or other obligor of the contractual rights.

(b) A custodian nominated under this section must be a person to whom a transfer of property of that kind may be made under subdivision (a) of Section 3909.

(c) The nomination of a custodian under this section does not create custodial property until the nominating instrument becomes irrevocable or a transfer to the nominated custodian is completed under Section 3909. Unless the nomination of a custodian has been revoked, upon the occurrence of the future event, the custodianship becomes effective, and the custodian shall enforce a transfer of the custodial property pursuant to Section 3909.

(Stats. 1990 (A.B. 759), ch. 79, §14, effective July 1, 1991.)

§3905. Transfer is authorized by a will or trust

(a) A personal representative or trustee may make an irrevocable transfer pursuant to Section 3909 to a custodian for the benefit of a minor as authorized in the governing will or trust.

(b) If the testator or settlor has nominated a custodian under Section 3903 to receive the custodial property, the transfer shall be made to that person.

(c) If the testator or settlor has not nominated a custodian under Section 3903, or all persons so nominated as custodian die before the transfer or are unable, decline, or are ineligible to serve, the personal representative or the trustee, as the case may be, shall designate the custodian from among those eligible to serve as custodian for property of that kind under subdivision (a) of Section 3909.

(Stats. 1990 (A.B. 759), ch. 79, §14, effective July 1, 1991.)

§3906. Transfer by fiduciaries: requirements

(a) Subject to subdivision (c), a personal representative or trustee may make an irrevocable transfer to another adult or trust company as custodian for the benefit of a minor pursuant to Section 3909, in the absence of a will or under a will or trust that does not contain an authorization to do so.

(b) Subject to subdivision (c), a conservator may make an irrevocable transfer to another adult or trust company as custodian for the benefit of the minor pursuant to Section 3909.

(c) A transfer under subdivision (a) or (b) may be made only if all of the following requirements are satisfied:

(1) The personal representative, trustee, or conservator considers the transfer to be in the best interest of the minor.

(2) The transfer is not prohibited by or inconsistent with provisions of the applicable will, trust agreement, or other governing instrument. For the purposes of this subdivision, a spendthrift provision (such as that described in Section 15300) shall not prohibit or be inconsistent with the transfer.

(3) The transfer is authorized by the court if it exceeds ten thousand dollars ($10,000) in value; provided, however, that such court authorization shall not be required when the transfer is to a custodian who is either (A) a trust company or (B) an individual designated as a trustee by the terms of a trust instrument which does not require a bond.

(Stats. 1990 (A.B. 759), ch. 79, §14, effective July 1, 1991. Amended by Stats. 1996 (A.B. 2751), ch. 862, §13.)

§3907. Transfer by an obligor for minor's benefit

(a) Subject to subdivisions (b) and (c), a person not subject to Section 3905 or 3906 who holds property of, or owes a liquidated debt to, a minor not having a conservator may make an irrevocable transfer to a custodian for the benefit of the minor pursuant to Section 3909.

(b) If a person having the right to do so under Section 3903 has nominated a custodian under that section to receive the custodial property, the transfer shall be made to that person.

(c) If no custodian has been nominated under Section 3903, or all persons so nominated as custodian die before the transfer or are unable, decline, or are ineligible to serve, a transfer under this section may be made to an adult member of the minor's family or to a trust company unless the property exceeds ten thousand dollars ($10,000) in value.

(Stats. 1990 (A.B. 759), ch. 79, §14, effective July 1, 1991.)

§3908. Custodian's acknowledgment of delivery constitutes receipt and discharge

A written acknowledgment of delivery by a custodian constitutes a sufficient receipt and discharge for custodial property transferred to the custodian pursuant to this part.

(Stats. 1990 (A.B. 759), ch. 79, §14, effective July 1, 1991.)

§3909. Creation of custodial property, transfer, designation of initial custodian, control

(a) Custodial property is created and a transfer is made whenever any of the following occurs:

(1) An uncertificated security or a certificated security in registered form is either:

(A) Registered in the name of the transferor, an adult other than the transferor, or a trust company, followed in substance by the words:

"as custodian for ______________________
(Name of Minor)
under the California Uniform Transfers to Minors Act."

(B) Delivered if in certificated form, or any document necessary for the transfer of an uncertificated security is delivered, together with any necessary endorsement to an adult other than the transferor or to a trust company as custodian, accompanied by an instrument in substantially the form set forth in subdivision (b).

(2) Money is paid or delivered, or a security held in the name of a broker, financial institution, or its nominee is transferred, to a broker or financial institution for credit to an account in the name of the transferor, an adult other than the transferor, or a trust company, followed in substance by the words:

"as custodian for ______________________
(Name of Minor)
under the California Uniform Transfers to Minors Act."

(3) The ownership of a life or endowment insurance policy or annuity contract is either:

(A) Registered with the issuer in the name of the transferor, an adult other than the transferor, or a trust company, followed in substance by the words:

"as custodian for ______________________
(Name of Minor)
under the California Uniform Transfers to Minors Act."

(B) Assigned in a writing delivered to an adult other than the transferor or to a trust company whose name in the assignment is followed in substance by the words:

"as custodian for ______________________
(Name of Minor)
under the California Uniform Transfers to Minors Act."

(4) An irrevocable exercise of a power of appointment or an irrevocable present right to future payment under a contract is the subject of a written notification delivered to the payor, issuer, or other obligor that the right is transferred to the transferor, an adult other than the transferor, or a trust company, whose name in the notification is followed in substance by the words:

"as custodian for ______________________
(Name of Minor)
under the California Uniform Transfers to Minors Act."

(5) An interest in real property is recorded in the name of the transferor, an adult other than the transferor, or a trust company, followed in substance by the words:

"as custodian for ______________________
(Name of Minor)
under the California Uniform Transfers to Minors Act."

(6) A certificate of title issued by a department or agency of a state or of the United States which evidences title to tangible personal property is either:

(A) Issued in the name of the transferor, an adult other than the transferor, or a trust company, followed in substance by the words:

"as custodian for ______________________
(Name of Minor)
under the California Uniform Transfers to Minors Act."

(B) Delivered to an adult other than the transferor or to a trust company, endorsed to that person followed in substance by the words:

"as custodian for ______________________________
(Name of Minor)
under the California Uniform Transfers to Minors Act."

(7) An interest in any property not described in paragraphs (1) through (6) is transferred to an adult other than the transferor or to a trust company by a written instrument in substantially the form set forth in subdivision (b).

(b) An instrument in the following form satisfies the requirements of subparagraph (B) of paragraph (1) and paragraph (7) of subdivision (a):

"TRANSFER UNDER THE CALIFORNIA UNIFORM TRANSFERS TO MINORS ACT
I, ____
(Name of Transferor or Name and Representative Capacity if a Fiduciary)
hereby transfer to ________________________________,
(Name of Custodian)
as custodian for __________________________________
(Name of Minor)
under the California Uniform Transfers to Minors Act, the following:
(insert a description of the custodial property sufficient to identify it).
Dated: ________________
____
(Signature)
__________________________ acknowledges receipt of the
(Name of Custodian)
property described above as custodian for the minor named above under the California Uniform Transfers to Minors Act.
Dated: ________________
____"
(Signature of Custodian)

(c) A transferor shall place the custodian in control of the custodial property as soon as practicable.
(Stats. 1990 (A.B. 759), ch. 79, §14, effective July 1, 1991. Amended by Stats. 1991 (S.B. 271), ch. 1055, §17.)

§3910. "Single custodianship," defined

A transfer may be made only for one minor, and only one person may be the custodian. All custodial property held under this part by the same custodian for the benefit of the same minor constitutes a single custodianship.
(Stats. 1990 (A.B. 759), ch. 79, §14, effective July 1, 1991.)

§3911. Validity of transfer is not affected by certain events or acts

(a) The validity of a transfer made in a manner prescribed in this part is not affected by any of the following:

(1) Failure of the transferor to comply with subdivision (c) of Section 3909.

(2) Designation of an ineligible custodian, except designation of the transferor in the case of property for which the transferor is ineligible to serve as custodian under subdivision (a) of Section 3909.

(3) Death or incapacity of a person nominated under Section 3903 or designated under Section 3909 as custodian, or the disclaimer of the office by that person.

(b) A transfer made pursuant to Section 3909 is irrevocable, and the custodial property is indefeasibly vested in the minor, but the custodian has all the rights, powers, duties, and authority provided in this part, and neither the minor nor the minor's legal representative has any right, power, duty, or authority with respect to the custodial property except as provided in this part.

(c) By making a transfer, the transferor incorporates in the disposition all the provisions of this part and grants to the custodian, and to any third person dealing with a person designated as custodian, the respective powers, rights, and immunities provided in this part.

(d) A person is not precluded from being a custodian for a minor under this part with respect to some property because the person is a conservator of the minor with respect to other property.

(e) A person who is the conservator of the minor is not precluded from being a custodian for a minor under this part because the custodial property has or will be transferred to the custodian from the guardianship estate of the minor. In such case, for the purposes of Section 3909, the custodian shall be deemed to be "an adult other than the transferor."

(f) In the cases described in subdivisions (d) and (e), with respect to the property transferred to the custodian, this part applies to the extent it would apply if the person to whom the custodial property is transferred were not and had not been a conservator of the minor.
(Stats. 1990 (A.B. 759), ch. 79, §14, effective July 1, 1991.)

§3912. Custodian's duties and standard of care

(a) A custodian shall do all of the following:

(1) Take control of custodial property.

(2) Register or record title to custodial property if appropriate.

(3) Collect, hold, manage, invest, and reinvest custodial property.

(b) In dealing with custodial property, a custodian shall observe the standard of care that would be observed by a prudent person dealing with property of another and is not limited by any other statute restricting investments by fiduciaries except that:

(1) If a custodian is not compensated for his or her services, the custodian is not liable for losses to custodial property unless they result from the custodian's bad faith, intentional wrongdoing, or gross negligence, or from the custodian's failure to maintain the standard of prudence in investing the custodial property provided in this section.

(2) A custodian, in the custodian's discretion and without liability to the minor or the minor's estate, may retain any custodial property received from a transferor.

(c) A custodian may invest in or pay premiums on life insurance or endowment policies on (1) the life of the minor only if the minor or the minor's estate is the sole beneficiary or (2) the life of another person in whom the minor has an insurable interest only to the extent that the minor, the minor's estate, or the custodian in the capacity of custodian, is the irrevocable beneficiary.

(d) A custodian at all times shall keep custodial property separate and distinct from all other property in a manner sufficient to identify it clearly as custodial property of the minor. Custodial property consisting of an undivided interest is so identified if the minor's interest is held as a tenant in common and is fixed. Custodial property subject to recordation is so identified if it is recorded, and custodial property subject to registration is so identified if it is either registered, or held in an account designated, in the name of the custodian, followed in substance by the words:

"as custodian for ______________________________
(Name of Minor)
under the California Uniform Transfers to Minors Act."

(e) A custodian shall keep records of all transactions with respect to custodial property, including information necessary for the preparation of the minor's tax returns, and shall make them available for inspection at reasonable intervals by a parent or legal representative of the minor or by the minor if the minor has attained the age of 14 years.

(Stats. 1990 (A.B. 759), ch. 79, §14, effective July 1, 1991.)

§3913. Custodian's rights, powers, authority and liability

(a) A custodian, acting in a custodial capacity, has all the rights, powers, and authority over custodial property that unmarried adult owners have over their own property, but a custodian may exercise those rights, powers, and authority in that capacity only.

(b) This section does not relieve a custodian from liability for breach of Section 3912.

(Stats. 1990 (A.B. 759), ch. 79, §14, effective July 1, 1991.)

§3914. Use of custodial property for minor's benefit

(a) A custodian may deliver or pay to the minor or expend for the minor's benefit as much of the custodial property as the custodian considers advisable for the use and benefit of the minor, without court order and without regard to (1) the duty or ability of the custodian personally, or of any other person, to support the minor or (2) any other income or property of the minor which may be applicable or available for that purpose.

(b) On petition of an interested person or the minor if the minor has attained the age of 14 years, the court may order the custodian to deliver or pay to the minor or expend for the minor's benefit so much of the custodial property as the court considers advisable for the use and benefit of the minor.

(c) A delivery, payment, or expenditure under this section is in addition to, not in substitution for, and does not affect, any obligation of a person to support the minor.

(d) In lieu of the powers and duties described in subdivision (a), a transferor who is also the custodian may elect to govern his or her custodial powers and duties under this subdivision. If such election is made, the custodian shall not pay over to the minor for expenditure by the minor, and shall not expend for the minor's use or benefit, any part of the custodial property for any purpose prior to the time specified in Section 3920, except by order of the court upon a showing that the expenditure is necessary for the support, maintenance, or education of the minor. When the powers and duties of the custodian are governed by this subdivision, the transferor custodian shall file with the clerk of the court a declaration in substantially the following form:

Declaration Under the California Uniform Transfers to Minors Act

I, ______________________________,
(Name of Transferor-Custodian)
as custodian for ______________________________
(Name of Minor)

under the California Uniform Transfers to Minors Act, hereby irrevocably elect to be governed under subdivision (d) of Section 3914 of the Probate Code in my custodial capacity over the following described property

____

____

____

____________________.

(Description of Custodial Property)

I declare under penalty of perjury that the foregoing is true and correct.

Dated: ______________, 19____

____

___

(Signature of Transferor-Custodian)

(Stats. 1990 (A.B. 759), ch. 79, §14, effective July 1, 1991.)

§3915. Custodian's expenses, reimbursement, compensation and bond

(a) A custodian is entitled to reimbursement from custodial property for reasonable expenses incurred in the performance of the custodian's duties.

(b) Except for one who is a transferor under Section 3904, a custodian has a noncumulative election during each calendar year to charge reasonable compensation for services performed during that year.

(c) Except as provided in subdivision (f) of Section 3918, a custodian need not give a bond.

(Stats. 1990 (A.B. 759), ch. 79, §14, effective July 1, 1991.)

§3916. Exemption of third person from liability for acting on custodian's instructions

A third person in good faith and without court order may act on the instructions of, or otherwise deal with, any person purporting to make a transfer or purporting to act in the capacity of a custodian and, in the absence of knowledge, is not responsible for determining any of the following:

(a) The validity of the purported custodian's designation.

(b) The propriety of, or the authority under this part for, any act of the purported custodian.

(c) The validity or propriety under this part of any instrument or instructions executed or given either by the person purporting to make a transfer or by the purported custodian.

(d) The propriety of the application of any property of the minor delivered to the purported custodian.

(Stats. 1990 (A.B. 759), ch. 79, §14, effective July 1, 1991.)

§3917. Limitations on the liability of custodians

(a) A claim based on (1) a contract entered into by a custodian acting in a custodial capacity, (2) an obligation arising from the ownership or control of custodial property, or (3) a tort committed during the custodianship, may be asserted against the custodial property by proceeding against the custodian in the custodial capacity, whether or not the custodian or the minor is personally liable therefor.

(b) A custodian is not personally liable for either of the following:

(1) On a contract properly entered into in the custodial capacity unless the custodian fails to reveal that capacity and to identify the custodianship in the contract.

(2) For an obligation arising from control of custodial property or for a tort committed during the custodianship unless the custodian is personally at fault.

(c) A minor is not personally liable for an obligation arising from ownership of custodial property or for a tort committed during the custodianship unless the minor is personally at fault.

(Stats. 1990 (A.B. 759), ch. 79, §14, effective July 1, 1991.)

§3918. Nomination of substitute and successor custodians

(a) A person nominated under Section 3903 or designated under Section 3909 as custodian may decline to serve by delivering a valid disclaimer under Part 8 (commencing with Section 260) of Division 2 to the person who made the nomination or to the transferor or the transferor's legal representative. If the event giving rise to a transfer has not occurred and no substitute custodian able, willing, and eligible to serve was nominated under Section 3903, the person who made the nomination may nominate a substitute custodian under Section 3903; otherwise the transferor or the transferor's legal representative shall designate a substitute custodian at the time of the transfer, in either case from among the persons eligible to serve as custodian for that kind of property under subdivision (a) of Section 3909. The custodian so designated has the rights of a successor custodian.

(b) A custodian at any time may designate a trust company or an adult other than a transferor under Section 3904 as successor custodian by executing and dating an instrument of designation before a subscribing witness other than the successor. If the instrument of designation does not contain or is not accompanied by the resignation of the custodian, the designation of the successor does not take effect until the custodian resigns, dies, becomes incapacitated, or is removed. The transferor may designate one or more persons as successor custodians to serve, in the designated order of priority, in case the custodian originally designated or a prior successor custodian is unable, declines, or is ineligible to serve or resigns, dies, becomes incapacitated, or is removed. The designation either (1) shall be made in the same transaction and by the same document by which the transfer is made or (2) shall be made by executing and dating a separate instrument of designation before a subscribing witness other than a successor as a part of the same transaction and contemporaneously with the execution of the document by which the transfer is made. The designation is made by setting forth the successor custodian's name, followed in substance by the words: "is designated [first, second, etc., where applicable] successor custodian." A successor custodian designated by the transferor may be a trust company or an adult other than a transferor under Section 3904. A successor custodian effectively designated by the transferor has priority over a successor custodian designated by a custodian.

(c) A custodian may resign at any time by delivering written notice to the minor if the minor has attained the age of 14 years and to the successor custodian and by delivering the custodial property to the successor custodian.

(d) If the transferor has not effectively designated a successor custodian, and a custodian is ineligible, dies, or becomes incapacitated without having effectively designated a successor and the minor has attained the age of 14 years, the minor may designate as successor custodian, in the manner prescribed in subdivision (b), an adult member of the minor's family, a conservator of the minor, or a trust company. If the minor has not attained the age of 14 years or fails to act within 60 days after the ineligibility, death, or incapacity, the conservator of the minor becomes successor custodian. If the minor has no conservator or the conservator declines to act, the transferor, the legal representative of the transferor or of the custodian, an adult member of the minor's family, or any other interested person may petition the court to designate a successor custodian.

(e) A custodian who declines to serve under subdivision (a) or resigns under subdivision (c), or the legal representative of a deceased or incapacitated custodian, as soon as practicable, shall put the custodial property and records in the possession and control of the successor custodian. The successor custodian by action may enforce the obligation to deliver custodial property and records and becomes responsible for each item as received.

(f) A transferor, the legal representative of a transferor, an adult member of the minor's family, a guardian of the person of the minor, the conservator of the minor, or the minor if the minor has attained the age of 14 years, may petition the court to remove the custodian for cause and to designate a successor custodian other than a transferor under Section 3904 or to require the custodian to give appropriate bond.

(g) At least 15 days before the hearing on a petition under subdivision (d) or (f), the petitioner shall serve notice by mail or personal delivery on each of the following persons:

(1) The minor.

(2) The parent or parents of the minor.

(3) The transferor.

(h) Upon consideration of the petition under subdivision (d) or (f), the court may grant the relief that the court finds to be in the best interests of the minor.

(Stats. 1990 (A.B. 759), ch. 79, §14, effective July 1, 1991. Amended by Stats. 1992 (A.B. 2975), ch. 871, §7.)

§3919. Persons eligible to petition for accounting; removal of custodian

(a) A minor who has attained the age of 14 years, the minor's guardian of the person or legal representative, an adult member of the minor's family, a transferor, or a transferor's legal representative may petition the court for any of the following:

(1) An accounting by the custodian or the custodian's legal representative.

(2) A determination of responsibility, as between the custodial property and the custodian personally, for claims against the custodial property unless the responsibility has been adjudicated in an action under Section 3917 to which the minor or the minor's legal representative was a party.

(b) A successor custodian may petition the court for an accounting by the predecessor custodian.

(c) The court, in a proceeding under this part or in any other proceeding, may require or permit the custodian or the custodian's legal representative to account.

(d) If a custodian is removed under subdivision (f) of Section 3918, the court shall require an accounting and order delivery of the custodial property and records to the successor custodian and the execution of all instruments required for transfer of the custodial property.

(e) The right to petition for an accounting shall continue for one year after the filing of a final accounting by the custodian or the custodian's legal representative and delivery of the custodial property to the minor or the minor's estate. (Stats. 1990 (A.B. 759), ch. 79, §14, effective July 1, 1991.)

§3920. Termination of custodianship: age 18 unless transfer is delayed under Section 3920.5

The custodian shall transfer in an appropriate manner the custodial property to the minor or to the minor's estate upon the earlier of the following:

(a) The minor's attainment of 18 years of age unless the time of transfer of the custodial property to the minor is delayed under Section 3920.5 to a time after the time the minor attains the age of 18 years.

(b) The time specified in the transfer pursuant to Section 3909 if the time of transfer of the custodial property to the minor is delayed under Section 3920.5 to a time after the time the minor attains the age of 18 years.

(c) The minor's death.

(Stats. 1990 (A.B. 759), ch. 79, §14, effective July 1, 1991.)

§3920.5. Custodianship can last until minor attains age 25

(a) Subject to the requirements and limitations of this section, the time for transfer to the minor of custodial property transferred under or pursuant to Section 3903, 3904, 3905, or 3906, may be delayed until a specified time after the time the minor attains the age of 18 years, which time shall be specified in the transfer pursuant to Section 3909.

(b) To specify a delayed time for transfer to the minor of the custodial property, the words

"as custodian for ______________________
(Name of Minor)
until age ______________________
(Age for Delivery of Property to Minor)
under the California Uniform Transfers to Minors Act" shall be substituted in substance for the words
"as custodian for ______________________
(Name of Minor)
under the California Uniform Transfers to Minors Act" in making the transfer pursuant to Section 3909.

(c) The time for transfer to the minor of custodial property transferred under or pursuant to Section 3903 or 3905 may be delayed under this section only if the governing will or trust or nomination provides in substance that the custodianship is to continue until the time the minor attains a specified age, which time may not be later than the time the minor attains 25 years of age, and in that case the governing will or trust or nomination shall determine the time to be specified in the transfer pursuant to Section 3909.

(d) The time for transfer to the minor of custodial property transferred by the irrevocable exercise of a power of appointment under Section 3904 may be delayed under this section only if the transfer pursuant to Section 3909 provides in substance that the custodianship is to continue until the time the minor attains a specified age, which time may not be later than the time the minor attains 25 years of age.

(e) The time for transfer to the minor of custodial property transferred by irrevocable gift under Section 3904 may be delayed under this section only if the transfer pursuant to Section 3909 provides in substance that the custodianship is to continue until the time the minor attains a specified age, which time may not be later than the time the minor attains 21 years of age.

(f) The time for transfer to the minor of custodial property transferred by a trustee under Section 3906 may be delayed under this section only if the transfer pursuant to Section 3909 provides that the custodianship is to continue until a specified time not later than the time the minor attains 25 years of age or the time of termination of all present beneficial interests of the minor in the trust from which the custodial property was transferred, whichever is to occur first.

(g) If the transfer pursuant to Section 3909 does not specify any age, the time for the transfer of the custodial property to the minor under Section 3920 is the time when the minor attains 18 years of age.

(h) If the transfer pursuant to Section 3909 provides in substance that the duration of the custodianship is for a time longer than the maximum time permitted by this section for the duration of a custodianship created by that type of transfer, the custodianship shall be deemed to continue only until the time the minor attains the maximum age permitted by this section for the duration of a custodianship created by that type of transfer.

(Stats. 1990 (A.B. 759), ch. 79, §14, effective July 1, 1991. Amended by Stats. 1996 (A.B. 2751), ch. 862, §14.)

§3921. Venue of proceedings

Subject to the power of the court to transfer actions and proceedings as provided in the Code of Civil Procedure, a petition filed under this part shall be heard and proceedings thereon held in the superior court in the proper county, which shall be determined as follows:

(a) If the minor resides in this state, in either of the following counties:

(1) Where the minor resides.

(2) Where the custodian resides.

(b) If the minor does not reside within this state, in any of the following counties:

(1) Where the transferor resides.

(2) Where the custodian resides.

(3) Where the estate of a deceased or legally incapacitated custodian is being administered.

(4) Where a parent of the minor resides.

(c) If neither the minor, nor the transferor, nor any parent resides within this state, and no estate of a deceased or legally incapacitated custodian is being administered within this state, in any county.

(Stats. 1990 (A.B. 759), ch. 79, §14, effective July 1, 1991.)

§3922. Transfers to minors under Uniform Acts of another state

This part applies to a transfer within the scope of Section 3902 made on or after January 1, 1985, if either of the following requirements is satisfied:

(a) The transfer purports to have been made under the California Uniform Gifts to Minors Act.

(b) The instrument by which the transfer purports to have been made uses in substance the designation "as custodian under the Uniform Gifts to Minors Act" or "as custodian under the Uniform Transfers to Minors Act" of any other state, and the application of this part is necessary to validate the transfer.

(Stats. 1990 (A.B. 759), ch. 79, §14, effective July 1, 1991.)

§3923. Application to existing custodianships

(a) As used in this section, "California Uniform Gifts to Minors Act" means former Article 4 (commencing with Section 1154) of Chapter 3 of Title 4 of Part 4 of Division 2 of the Civil Code.

(b) Any transfer of custodial property, as now defined in this part, made before January 1, 1985, is validated, notwithstanding that there was no specific authority in the California Uniform Gifts to Minors Act for the coverage of custodial property of that kind or for a transfer from that source at the time the transfer was made.

(c) This part applies to all transfers made before January 1, 1985, in a manner and form prescribed in the California Uniform Gifts to Minors Act, except insofar as the application impairs constitutionally vested rights.

(d) To the extent that this part, by virtue of subdivision (c), does not apply to transfers made in a manner prescribed in the California Uniform Gifts to Minors Act or to the powers, duties, and immunities conferred by transfers in that manner upon custodians and persons dealing with custodians, the repeal of the California Uniform Gifts to Minors Act does not affect those transfers or those powers, duties, and immunities.

(Stats. 1990 (A.B. 759), ch. 79, §14, effective July 1, 1991.)

§3925. Act is not exclusive method for making gifts or transfers to minors

This part shall not be construed as providing an exclusive method for making gifts or other transfers to minors.

(Stats. 1990 (A.B. 759), ch. 79, §14, effective July 1, 1991.)

IX
TRUST CREATION AND VALIDITY

This chapter focuses on the requirements for the creation of a valid trust. Trusts may be created expressly by an owner of property who intends to create a trust, or may be created by operation of law. The former trusts consist of private express trusts and charitable trusts (discussed in Chapter XIII *infra*). Trusts created by operation of law consist of constructive trusts and resulting trusts.

I. Introduction

A. Definitions

A trust is an arrangement in which the legal title to property is held by a trustee, but the equitable interest in the property belongs to a beneficiary or beneficiaries. According to the Restatement (Third) of Trusts §2 (2001) [hereinafter Restatement (Third) Trusts], a trust is:

> a fiduciary relationship with respect to property, arising from a manifestation of intention to create that relationship and subjecting the person who holds title to the property to duties to deal with it for the benefit of charity or for one or more persons, at least one of whom is not the sole trustee.

The cardinal features of the trust are (1) the separation of legal and equitable interests, and (2) the fiduciary duty imposed on the trustee (the holder of legal title) to deal with the property for the benefit of the beneficiary (the holder of the equitable title).

The owner of the property is called the "trustor," "settlor," "grantor," or "donor." (The Restatement (Third) of Trusts §3 uses the term "settlor.") The person or corporation holding legal title is the "trustee." The third party who owns the equitable interest in the property is the "beneficiary" or "cestui que trust." The trust property is called the "corpus" or "res."

In California, a valid private express trust must meet the following requirements:

- the settlor must have capacity (60 Cal. Jur.3d Trusts §14; Uniform Trust Code §402(a)(1));
- the settlor must manifest a proper intent to create the trust (Cal. Prob. Code §15201);
- the trust must have property (Cal. Prob. Code §15202);
- the trust must have a beneficiary (Cal. Prob. Code §15205);
- the trust must have a purpose that is not illegal or against public policy (Cal. Prob. Code §15203).

CALIFORNIA PROBATE CODE

§24. "Beneficiary," defined

"Beneficiary" means a person to whom a donative transfer of property is made or that person's successor in interest, and:

(a) As it relates to the intestate estate of a decedent, means an heir.

(b) As it relates to the testate estate of a decedent, means a devisee.

(c) As it relates to a trust, means a person who has any present or future interest, vested or contingent.

(d) As it relates to a charitable trust, includes any person entitled to enforce the trust.

(Stats. 1990 (A.B. 759), ch. 79, §14, effective July 1, 1991.)

§45. "Instrument," defined

"Instrument" means a will, trust, deed, or other writing that designates a beneficiary or makes a donative transfer of property.

(Stats. 1990 (A.B. 759), ch. 79, §14, effective July 1, 1991.)

§56. "Person," defined

"Person" means an individual, corporation, government or governmental subdivision or agency, business trust, estate, trust, partnership, limited liability company, association, or other entity.

(Stats. 1990 (A.B. 759), ch. 79, §14, effective July 1, 1991. Amended Stats. 1994 (S.B. 2053), ch. 1010, §202.)

§62. "Property," defined

"Property" means anything that may be the subject of ownership and includes both real and personal property and any interest therein.

(Stats. 1990 (A.B. 759), ch. 79, §14, effective July 1, 1991.)

§81. "Transferor," defined

"Transferor" means the testator, settlor, grantor, owner, or other person who executes an instrument.

(Stats. 1990 (A.B. 759), ch. 79, §14, effective July 1, 1991.)

§81.5. "Transferee," defined

"Transferee" means the beneficiary, donee, or other recipient of an interest transferred by an instrument.

(Stats. 1994 (A.B. 3686), ch. 806, §2.)

§82. "Trust," defined

(a) "Trust" includes the following:

(1) An express trust, private or charitable, with additions thereto, wherever and however created.

(2) A trust created or determined by a judgment or decree under which the trust is to be administered in the manner of an express trust.

(b) "Trust" excludes the following:

(1) Constructive trusts, other than those described in paragraph (2) of subdivision (a), and resulting trusts.

(2) Guardianships and conservatorships.

(3) Personal representatives.

(4) Totten trust accounts.

(5) Custodial arrangements pursuant to the Uniform Gifts to Minors Act or the Uniform Transfers to Minors Act of any state.

(6) Business trusts that are taxed as partnerships or corporations.

(7) Investment trusts subject to regulation under the laws of this state or any other jurisdiction.

(8) Common trust funds.

(9) Voting trusts.

(10) Security arrangements.

(11) Transfers in trust for purpose of suit or enforcement of a claim or right.

(12) Liquidation trusts.

(13) Trusts for the primary purpose of paying debts, dividends, interest, salaries, wages, profits, pensions, or employee benefits of any kind.

(14) Any arrangement under which a person is nominee or escrowee for another.

(Stats. 1990 (A.B. 759), ch. 79, §14, effective July 1, 1991.)

§83. "Trust company," defined

"Trust company" means an entity that has qualified to engage in and conduct a trust business in this state.

(Stats. 1990 (A.B. 759), ch. 79, §14, effective July 1, 1991.)

§84. "Trustee," defined

"Trustee" includes an original, additional, or successor trustee, whether or not appointed or confirmed by a court.

(Stats. 1990 (A.B. 759), ch. 79, §14, effective July 1, 1991.)

B. Reasons for Establishing Trusts

Several reasons exist for establishing a trust. These include:

- **avoidance of probate with its delays and costs;**
- **providing property management for persons who are incompetent to do so or who prefer not to manage the property themselves;**
- **providing for successive enjoyment of property over several generations;**
- **securing tax benefits (by the use of irrevocable, but not revocable, trusts); and**
- **insulating trust property from the beneficiary's creditors.**

Restatement (Third) of Trusts §27, cmt. b. See generally McGovern & Kurtz, *supra*, §§9.1, 9.2 & 9.3 at 341-352.

II. Creation of a Trust

A. Common Methods

The most common methods of trust creation are: (1) a transfer or (2) a declaration of trust. The transfer of property from the owner to the trustee may be accomplished during the owner's lifetime (called an inter vivos or living trust) or may be accomplished at the owner's death by a will (called a testamentary trust). To establish a trust by a declaration, the owner declares that he or she holds property in trust for another. A declaration obviates the need for a transfer from the owner to the trustee because, in a trust created by a declaration, the owner becomes the trustee.

Other methods of trust creation also exist. According to California law, a trust may be created not only by a declaration or transfer (either inter vivos or by will), but also by the exercise of a power of appointment to another person, or an enforceable promise to create a trust (Cal. Prob. Code §15200).

Statutes on the creation, validity, modification, and termination of trusts are set forth in Part 2 of Division 9 of the California Probate Code on Trust Law. (Modification and termination of trusts are discussed in Chapter X herein; the law regarding trustees is explored in Chapter XI and the law regarding beneficiaries in Chapter XII herein.) The Trust Law was enacted by the California legislature in 1990 (effective July 1, 1991), as Division 9 of the California Probate Code (§§15000-19403). That Division also covers the law regarding trustees and beneficiaries; trust administration; judicial proceedings concerning trusts; rights of third persons; the Uniform Management of Institutional Funds Act; and payments of claims, debts, and expenses from a revocable trust of a deceased settlor. Most of the important California legislation concerning trusts is included in the Trust Law; however, various definitions are found at the beginning of the Probate Code and some other relevant provisions are located in other codes. For example, provisions on trust companies are located in California Financial Code §§1500-1591, and the Uniform Supervision of Trustees for Charitable Purposes Act is set forth in California Government Code §§12580-12598.

CALIFORNIA PROBATE CODE

§15000. Title

This division shall be known and may be cited as the Trust Law.

(Stats. 1990 (A.B. 759), ch. 79, §14, effective July 1, 1991.)

§15001. Application

Except as otherwise provided by statute:

(a) This division applies to all trusts regardless of whether they were created before, on, or after July 1, 1987.

(b) This division applies to all proceedings concerning trusts commenced on or after July 1, 1987.

(c) This division applies to all proceedings concerning trusts commenced before July 1, 1987, unless in the opinion of the court application of a particular provision of this division would substantially interfere with the effective conduct of the proceedings or the rights of the parties and other interested persons, in which case the particular provision of this division does not apply and prior law applies.

(Stats. 1990 (A.B. 759), ch. 79, §14, effective July 1, 1991.)

§15002. Common law as to trusts is law of state

Except to the extent that the common law rules governing trusts are modified by statute, the common law as to trusts is the law of this state.

(Stats. 1990 (A.B. 759), ch. 79, §14, effective July 1, 1991.)

§15003. Constructive and resulting trusts not affected

(a) Nothing in this division affects the substantive law relating to constructive or resulting trusts.

(b) The repeal of Title 8 (commencing with Section 2215) of Part 4 of Division 3 of the Civil Code by Chapter 820 of the Statutes of 1986 was not intended to alter the rules applied by the courts to fiduciary and confidential relationships, except as to express trusts governed by this division.

(c) Nothing in this division or in Section 82 is intended to prevent the application of all or part of the principles or procedures of this division to an entity or relationship that is excluded from the definition of "trust" provided by Section 82 where these principles or procedures are applied pursuant to statutory or common law principles, by court order or rule, or by contract.

(Stats. 1990 (A.B. 759), ch. 79, §14, effective July 1, 1991. Amended by Stats. 1990 (S.B. 1775), ch. 710, §43, effective July 1, 1991.)

§15004. Application to charitable trusts

Unless otherwise provided by statute, this division applies to charitable trusts that are subject to the jurisdiction of the Attorney General to the extent that the application of the provision is not in conflict with the Uniform Supervision of Trustees for Charitable Purposes Act, Article 7 (commencing with Section 12580) of Chapter 6 of Part 2 of Division 3 of Title 2 of the Government Code.

(Stats. 1990 (A.B. 759), ch. 79, §14, effective July 1, 1991.)

§15200. Methods of creating a trust

Subject to other provisions of this chapter, a trust may be created by any of the following methods:

(a) A declaration by the owner of property that the owner holds the property as trustee.

(b) A transfer of property by the owner during the owner's lifetime to another person as trustee.

(c) A transfer of property by the owner, by will or by other instrument taking effect upon the death of the owner, to another person as trustee.

(d) An exercise of a power of appointment to another person as trustee.

(e) An enforceable promise to create a trust.

(Stats. 1990 (A.B. 759), ch. 79, §14, effective July 1, 1991.)

§15208. Consideration

Consideration is not required to create a trust, but a promise to create a trust in the future is enforceable only if the requirements for an enforceable contract are satisfied.

(Stats. 1990 (A.B. 759), ch. 79, §14, effective July 1, 1991.)

B. Intent

A trust is created only if "the settlor properly manifests an intention to create a trust relationship." Restatement (Third) Trusts §13. The settlor's intention to create a trust must be express, clear, and unequivocal. Judicial determination of the settlor's intent is not limited to the writing but includes an examination of the parties' acts and declarations. Intention also may be inferred from the surrounding circumstances.

> No particular form, phraseology, or technical or formal language is required to create a trust, whether by deed or by will. [I]f the intent to create a trust is otherwise sufficiently evident, the words "trust," "trustee," or "upon trust" are not indispensable. Conversely, the use of the words "in trust" does not necessarily result in the creation of a trust, if the intention appears to be otherwise.

60 Cal. Jur.3d, Trusts, §18. According to the Restatement (Third) of Trusts §13 cmt. b, "[A] trust may be created without the settlor's use of words such as 'trust' or 'trustee'." Also, the fact that the transferor uses the words "trust" or "trustee," is not dispositive on whether the owner had the requisite intention to create a trust. *Id.* The settlor does not have to know that the relationship is called a trust or understand the characteristics of the trust relationship. *Id.* at cmt. a.

Sometimes, particular problems arise in interpreting intent when a settlor uses precatory language to create a trust. Precatory language includes expressions of desire, wish, request, etc. Precatory language is regarded as creating a trust only if it appears that the settlor intended to impose an imperative obligation on the trustee and to exclude the exercise of discretion.

If a testator expresses words of desire to an executor, courts traditionally construed such language as a command, following the English rule. Restatement (Third) of Trusts §13 cmt. d. The inference that the testator's wish is a command is no longer followed. For example, In re Estate of Marti, 61 P. 964 (Cal. 1900), the testator devised all his property to his wife but in a subsequent paragraph stated that it was his desire that his wife, on her death, should devise to his relatives one-half of the property which she received under his will. The court held that the wife was entitled to the entire estate free of trust because, while the desire of a testator for the disposition of his estate will be construed as a command when addressed to his executor, it will not when addressed to his legatee be construed as a limitation upon the estate or interest which he has given to him in absolute terms.

The Restatement (Third) of Trusts lists several circumstances that may facilitate determination of the testator's intent in the face of precatory language:

- **specific terms and tenor of the words used;**
- **definiteness (or lack thereof) of the property involved;**
- **ease (or lack thereof) of ascertaining possible trust purposes and terms;**
- **specificity (or lack thereof) of the possible beneficiaries and their interests;**
- **interests, motives, and concerns that might have influenced the transferor;**
- **transferor's prior conduct, statements, and relationships regarding the beneficiaries;**
- **personal and fiduciary relationship between the transferor and the transferee;**
- **testator's other present or past dispositions; and**
- **the likelihood that a finding of trust would be desired by the transferor.**

***Id.* at §13, cmt. d.**

CALIFORNIA PROBATE CODE

§15201. Trust requires an intention to create a trust

A trust is created only if the settlor properly manifests an intention to create a trust.

(Stats. 1990 (A.B. 759), ch. 79, §14, effective July 1, 1991.)

C. Trust Property

A valid trust requires trust property. Property may be anything that may be the subject of ownership and includes real and personal property. The trust property must be in existence when the trust is created. See, e.g., Balian v. Balian's Market, 119 P.2d 426, 429 (Ct. App. 1941) (holding that an agreement between a father and his sons that future earnings would be held by the father in trust was not enforceable "for want of a trust res, and because of the indefiniteness of the terms of the alleged trust agreement").

The owner of the property must divest himself or herself of a property interest in the property. Although an interest in property must pass to the trustee, it is not necessary that a present interest be transferred or that the beneficiary have a present right of enjoyment. That is, the beneficiary may receive a future interest because that property interest is presently vested. The reservation of a life estate by the settlor of an inter vivos trust and the retention of a power of revocation does not render a trust testamentary and invalid. See, e.g., Nichols v. Emery, 41 P. 1089 (Cal. 1895) (holding that conveyance of land to plaintiff as trustee with the provision that the grantee should sell the property within 10 months after the grantor's death and divide the proceeds among his children, was a valid, express trust, passing a present interest, subject to divestiture only by revocation, though the enjoyment of such interest was to commence in the future and that the reservation of a power of revocation did not make the trust testamentary and invalid).

Note that the settlor may not retain the full equitable and legal ownership or else the doctrine of merger applies. See, e.g., Restatement (Third) of Trusts §69 (trust terminates if the legal and equitable title "become united in one person"); Unif. Trust Code §402(a)(5) (requiring division of title).

CALIFORNIA PROBATE CODE

§15202. Trust requires trust property

A trust is created only if there is trust property.

(Stats. 1990 (A.B. 759), ch. 79, §14, effective July 1, 1991.)

D. Valid Trust Purpose

A trust requires a valid trust purpose. According to the Restatement (Third) of Trusts §27, a private trust must be for the benefit of its beneficiaries who must be identified or ascertainable.

A trust may be void for lack of certainty in its purpose or material terms. 60 Cal. Jur.3d Trusts §§21, 22. Compare Restatement (Third) of Trusts §30 specifying that a private trust (or trust provision) may be unenforceable because of impossibility or indefiniteness. However, California Probate Code §15204 provides that a court will uphold a trust for indefinite or general purposes provided that the court can determine with reasonable certainty that a particular use of the trust property comes within that purpose.

A trust is illegal if it involves the commission of a crime or tort, according to the Restatement (Third) of Trusts §29 (if the purpose is unlawful, involves the commission of a criminal or tortious act, violates rules relating to perpetuities or public policy), the Uniform Trust Code §404 (trust terms may not require the trustee to commit an act that is criminal, tortious, or contrary to public policy), and California law (Cal. Prob. Code §15203) (a trust must have a purpose that is not illegal or against public policy).

In terms of violations of public policy, a trust is invalid if it provides a financial incentive to a person for obtaining a divorce. In Hamilton v. Ferrall, 206 P.2d 663 (Cal. Ct. App. 1949), a father's will directed that half of the residue of his estate should be distributed to his son outright but the remaining half should be placed in trust for the benefit of his daughter. The will provided that the trust would terminate and the corpus would be distributed to the daughter upon the death of her husband or upon her divorce. The daughter argued that the trust was void because such a condition was contrary to "good morals and legal policy." *Hamilton*, 206 P.2d at 664. The appellate court upheld the trust, affirming the trial court opinion that the intention of the testator was not to induce the daughter to divorce but to protect her by providing financial support in the event of her husband's death or divorce. The court reasoned that "[t]he language of the trust must admit of no other reasonable construction than that of illegality before a court will declare it invalid." *Hamilton*, 206 P.2d at 665. See also 13 Witkin Summary, Trusts, *supra*, at §36.

Finally, a trust may not be created for the purpose of defrauding creditors or other persons. In In re Marriage of Dick, 18 Cal. Rptr. 2d 743 (Ct. App. 1993), an ex-husband appealed from an award of spousal support of $35,000 per month that was based on the husband's access to assets held by corporations and trusts. The court was unconvinced by the husband's declaration that he had "no positive net monthly disposable income" and found ample evidence of his ability to pay based on the assets in "a labyrinth of trusts and corporations designed by him . . . to shield and protect [him] from creditors." The court concluded that such trusts could be disregarded in determining the availability of those assets in assessing his ability to pay.

CALIFORNIA PROBATE CODE
§15203. Trust requires a valid trust purpose

A trust may be created for any purpose that is not illegal or against public policy.

(Stats. 1990 (A.B. 759), ch. 79, §14, effective July 1, 1991.)

§15204. Trust for indefinite or general purposes

A trust created for an indefinite or general purpose is not invalid for that reason if it can be determined with reasonable certainty that a particular use of the trust property comes within that purpose.

(Stats. 1990 (A.B. 759), ch. 79, §14, effective July 1, 1991.)

E. Parties

As explained above, a trust is generally created by the owner of property, who is called the "trustor," "settlor," "grantor," or "donor." The person (or corporation) who holds legal title is the "trustee." The third party who owns the equitable interest in the property is the "beneficiary" or "cestui que trust." The trustee occupies a fiduciary relationship (i.e., requiring a high standard of conduct in handling the trust property) with the beneficiary.

A trust requires a trustee to hold legal title and to deal with the property for the benefit of the beneficiaries. However, according to the basic rule, a trust will not fail, at its inception or thereafter, for want of a trustee, i.e., because of the trustee's death, incapacity, resignation, or removal. That is, a court will appoint a successor unless the terms of trust clearly specify that the trust may only continue as long as the designated trustee continues to act. For additional discussion of trustees, see Chapter XI *infra*.

A valid trust also requires a beneficiary (or beneficiaries) who holds equitable title and who has (or have) the right to enforce the trust. According to the general rule, a private express trust must have definite beneficiaries, or at least beneficiaries who will be definitely ascertainable within the period during which all interests must vest under the applicable state law pertaining to perpetuities. For additional discussion of beneficiaries, see Chapter XII *infra*. For discussion of trust duration, see *infra* this chapter, Section F.

Generally, a trust has at least three parties: a settlor, a trustee (or co-trustees), and one or more beneficiaries. However, the settlor and trustee may be the same person such as when the settlor declares himself the trustee. Note that the same person may not be the sole trustee and the sole beneficiary or else the merger doctrine applies (i.e., merger of the legal and equitable interests). See, e.g., Restatement (Third) of Trusts §69 (trust terminates if the legal and equitable title "become united in one person"). In case of merger, the beneficiary takes the property free of the trust. However, a sole trustee may be one of several beneficiaries. Similarly, one of several co-trustees may be the sole beneficiary. Below, California Probate Code §15209 states exceptions to the merger doctrine.

CALIFORNIA PROBATE CODE
§15205. Trust requires the designation of a beneficiary

(a) A trust, other than a charitable trust, is created only if there is a beneficiary.

(b) The requirement of subdivision (a) is satisfied if the trust instrument provides for either of the following:

(1) A beneficiary or class of beneficiaries that is ascertainable with reasonable certainty or that is sufficiently described so it can be determined that some person meets the description or is within the class.

(2) A grant of a power to the trustee or some other person to select the beneficiaries based on a standard or in the discretion of the trustee or other person.

(Stats. 1990 (A.B. 759), ch. 79, §14, effective July 1, 1991.)

§15209. Exception to doctrine of merger

If a trust provides for one or more successor beneficiaries after the death of the settlor, the trust is not invalid, merged, or terminated in either of the following circumstances:

(a) Where there is one settlor who is the sole trustee and the sole beneficiary during the settlor's lifetime.

(b) Where there are two or more settlors, one or more of whom are trustees, and the beneficial interest in the trust is in one or more of the settlors during the lifetime of the settlors.

(Stats. 1990 (A.B. 759), ch. 79, §14, effective July 1, 1991.)

F. Duration

In most jurisdictions, private express trusts are subject to the Rule Against Perpetuities. The purposes of the Rule are: (1) to promote alienability (to keep property productive), and (2) to limit dead hand control over property to enable trusts to respond to changing conditions (so that present property owners can use the property most productively).

According to the Rule Against Perpetuities, the duration of the trust cannot exceed a permissible period. That is, the Rule Against Perpetuities prohibits trusts in which the designation of beneficiaries will be delayed beyond a certain period of time ("the perpetuities period"). The Rule prohibits those interests that may remain contingent beyond the perpetuities period. All contingent future interests, both legal and equitable, are subject to the Rule. Future interests created in transferees (but not those retained by the transferor) are subject to the Rule.

Many states today follow the common law approach that specified the period of time as 21 years after the death of some life in being at the time of the creation of the interest, plus a period of gestation. The period begins to run, for irrevocable inter vivos trusts, from the time the settlor creates the trust (by a declaration, execution of the instrument, or delivery if required). The period begins to run, for revocable inter vivos trusts, from the time when the trust is no longer revocable (usually at the settlor's death). For testamentary trusts (similar to wills), the period begins to run from the time the settlor (or testator) dies.

Many jurisdictions have enacted reforms to the Rule Against Perpetuities. Some jurisdictions adopt a "wait-and-see" approach that looks to actual, rather than possible, events in terms of whether the contingency happens within the period of the Rule. Other jurisdictions lengthen the common law period. Some jurisdictions permit judicial reformation of existing instruments to avoid a Rule violation (via a doctrine analogous to the cy pres doctrine, discussed in Chapter XIII *infra*) to make the trust conform to the settlor's intent as closely as possible.

Many states have enacted the Uniform Statutory Rule Against Perpetuities Act (USRAP) (UPC §§2-901 to 2-905). The Act was promulgated by NCCUSL in 1986, and amended in 1990 by adding Section 1(e). Currently, 28 jurisdictions (including California) have adopted USRAP. Legislative Fact Sheet, http://nccusl.org/Updatel/uniformact_factsheets/uniformacts-fs-usrap.asp (last visited July 5, 2007). USRAP is set forth in California Probate Code §§21200-21225.

USRAP combines several of the aforementioned approaches, including the adoption of a 90-year period within which to determine whether an interest either vests or terminates after its creation. "Ninety years represents an estimate of the actual time most extended future interests will take, at the outside, to vest. If they do not vest, 90 years is a sufficient time to justify invalidating such interests." Legislative Information, Summary, Uniform Statutory Rule Against Perpetuities, http://nccusl.org/Update/uniformact_summaries/uniformacts-s-usrap.asp (last visited July 5, 2007).

Finally, a few states have abolished the Rule. On these reforms, see generally McGovern & Kurtz, *supra*, §11.4 at 465-470; Stewart E. Sterk, Jurisdictional Competition to Abolish the Rule Against Perpetuities: R.I.P. for the R.A.P., 24 Cardozo L. Rev. 2097 (2003) (criticizing abolition of the Rule); Note, Dynasty Trusts and the Rule Against Perpetuities, 116 Harv. L. Rev. 2588

(2003) (examining state trends and the academic debate about the Rule's repeal).

CALIFORNIA PROBATE CODE

§15211. Duration of trust for noncharitable purpose; Rule Against Perpetuities

A trust for a noncharitable corporation or unincorporated society or for a lawful noncharitable purpose may be performed by the trustee for only 21 years, whether or not there is a beneficiary who can seek enforcement or termination of the trust and whether or not the terms of the trust contemplate a longer duration.

(Stats. 1991 (A.B. 1577), ch. 156, §20.)

§15212. Duration of trusts for care of animals

A trust for the care of a designated domestic or pet animal may be performed by the trustee for the life of the animal, whether or not there is a beneficiary who can seek enforcement or termination of the trust and whether or not the terms of the trust contemplate a longer duration.

(Stats. 1991 (A.B. 1577), ch. 156, §20.)

§15413. Termination provision is ineffective if it violates the Rule Against Perpetuities

A trust provision, express or implied, that the trust may not be terminated is ineffective insofar as it purports to be applicable after the expiration of the longer of the periods provided by the statutory rule against perpetuities, Article 2 (commencing with Section 21205) of Chapter 1 of Part 2 of Division 11.

(Stats. 1991 (A.B. 1577), ch. 156, §20.)

§15414. Termination of trust that continues after expiration of Rule Against Perpetuities

Notwithstanding any other provision in this chapter, if a trust continues in existence after the expiration of the longer of the periods provided by the statutory rule against perpetuities, Article 2 (commencing with Section 21205) of Chapter 1 of Part 2 of Division 11, the trust may be terminated in either of the following manners:

(a) On petition by a majority of the beneficiaries.

(b) On petition by the Attorney General or by any person who would be affected by the termination, if the court finds that the termination would be in the public interest or in the best interest of a majority of the persons who would be affected by the termination.

(Stats. 1991 (A.B. 1577), ch. 156, §20.)

§21200. Title

This chapter shall be known and may be cited as the Uniform Statutory Rule Against Perpetuities.

(Stats. 1991 (A.B. 1577), ch. 156, §20.)

§21201. Common law rule against perpetuities superseded

This chapter supersedes the common law rule against perpetuities.

(Stats. 1991 (A.B. 1577), ch. 156, §20.)

§21202. Application

(a) Except as provided in subdivision (b), this part applies to nonvested property interests and unexercised powers of appointment regardless of whether they were created before, on, or after January 1, 1992.

(b) This part does not apply to any property interest or power of appointment the validity of which has been determined in a judicial proceeding or by a settlement among interested persons.

(Stats. 1991 (A.B. 1577), ch. 156, §20.)

§21205. Validity of nonvested property interests

A nonvested property interest is invalid unless one of the following conditions is satisfied:

(a) When the interest is created, it is certain to vest or terminate no later than 21 years after the death of an individual then alive.

(b) The interest either vests or terminates within 90 years after its creation.

(Stats. 1991 (A.B. 1577), ch. 156, §20.)

§21206. Validity of general power of appointment

A general power of appointment not presently exercisable because of a condition precedent is invalid unless one of the following conditions is satisfied:

(a) When the power is created, the condition precedent is certain to be satisfied or become impossible to satisfy no later than 21 years after the death of an individual then alive.

(b) The condition precedent either is satisfied or becomes impossible to satisfy within 90 years after its creation.

(Stats. 1991 (A.B. 1577), ch. 156, §20.)

§21207. Validity of nongeneral power of appointment

A nongeneral power of appointment or a general testamentary power of appointment is invalid unless one of the following conditions is satisfied:

(a) When the power is created, it is certain to be irrevocably exercised or otherwise to terminate no later than 21 years after the death of an individual then alive.

(b) The power is irrevocably exercised or otherwise terminates within 90 years after its creation.

(Stats. 1991 (A.B. 1577), ch. 156, §20.)

§21208. Possibility of posthumous births disregarded

In determining whether a nonvested property interest or a power of appointment is valid under this article, the possibility that a child will be born to an individual after the individual's death is disregarded.

(Stats. 1991 (A.B. 1577), ch. 156, §20.)

§21209. Construction of language in perpetuity saving clause

(a) If, in measuring a period from the creation of a trust or other property arrangement, language in a governing instrument (1) seeks to disallow the vesting or termination of any interest or trust beyond, (2) seeks to postpone the vesting or termination of any interest or trust until, or (3) seeks to operate in effect in any similar fashion upon, the later of (A) the expiration of a period of time not exceeding 21 years after the death of the survivor of specified lives in being at the creation of the trust or other property arrangement or (B) the expiration of a period of time that exceeds or might exceed 21 years after the death of the survivor of lives in being at the creation of the trust or other property arrangement, that language is inoperative to the extent it produces a period that exceeds 21 years after the death of the survivor of the specified lives.

(b) Notwithstanding Section 21202, this section applies only to governing instruments, including instruments exercising powers of appointment, executed on or after January 1, 1992.

(Stats. 1991 (A.B. 1577), ch. 156, §20.)

§21210. Creation of nonvested property interests or powers of appointment

Except as provided in Sections 21211 and 21212, the time of creation of a nonvested property interest or a power of appointment is determined by other applicable statutes or, if none, under general principles of property law.

(Stats. 1991 (A.B. 1577), ch. 156, §20.)

§21211. Powers exercisable by one person

For purposes of this chapter:

(a) If there is a person who alone can exercise a power created by a governing instrument to become the unqualified beneficial owner of (1) a nonvested property interest or (2) a property interest subject to a power of appointment described in Section 21206 or 21207, the nonvested property interest or power of appointment is created when the power to become the unqualified beneficial owner terminates.

(b) A joint power with respect to community property held by individuals married to each other is a power exercisable by one person alone.

(Stats. 1991 (A.B. 1577), ch. 156, §20.)

§21212. Interests or powers arising from transfer of property

For purposes of this chapter, a nonvested property interest or a power of appointment arising from a transfer of property to a previously funded trust or other existing property arrangement is created when the nonvested property interest or power of appointment in the original contribution was created.

(Stats. 1991 (A.B. 1577), ch. 156, §20.)

§21220. Reformation of disposition to most closely approximate transferor's plan

On petition of an interested person, a court shall reform a disposition in the manner that most closely approximates the transferor's manifested plan of distribution and is within the 90 years allowed by the applicable provision in Article 2 (commencing with Section 21205), if any of the following conditions is satisfied:

(a) A nonvested property interest or a power of appointment becomes invalid under the statutory rule against perpetuities provided in Article 2 (commencing with Section 21205).

(b) A class gift is not but might become invalid under the statutory rule against perpetuities provided in Article 2 (commencing with Section 21205), and the time has arrived when the share of any class member is to take effect in possession or enjoyment

. (c) A nonvested property interest that is not validated by subdivision (a) of Section 21205 can vest but not within 90 years after its creation.

(Stats. 1991 (A.B. 1577), ch. 156, §20.)

§21225. Application

Article 2 (commencing with Section 21205) does not apply to any of the following:

(a) A nonvested property interest or a power of appointment arising out of a nondonative transfer, except a nonvested property interest or a power of appointment arising out of (1) a premarital or postmarital agreement, (2) a separation or divorce settlement, (3) a spouse's election, (4) or a similar arrangement arising out of a prospective, existing, or previous marital relationship between the parties, (5) a contract to make or not to revoke a will or trust, (6) a contract to exercise or not to exercise a power of appointment, (7) a transfer in satisfaction of a duty of support, or (8) a reciprocal transfer.

(b) A fiduciary's power relating to the administration or management of assets, including the power of a fiduciary to sell, lease, or mortgage property, and the power of a fiduciary to determine principal and income.

(c) A power to appoint a fiduciary.

(d) A discretionary power of a trustee to distribute principal before termination of a trust to a beneficiary having an indefeasibly vested interest in the income and principal.

(e) A nonvested property interest held by a charity, government, or governmental agency or subdivision, if the nonvested property interest is preceded by an interest held by another charity, government, or governmental agency or subdivision.

(f) A nonvested property interest in or a power of appointment with respect to a trust or other property arrangement forming part of a pension, profit- sharing, stock bonus, health, disability, death benefit, income deferral, or other current or deferred benefit plan for one or more employees, independent contractors, or their beneficiaries or spouses, to which contributions are made for the purpose of distributing to or for the benefit of the participants or their beneficiaries or spouses the property, income, or principal in the trust or other property arrangement, except a nonvested property interest or a power of appointment that is created by an election of a participant or a beneficiary or spouse.

(g) A property interest, power of appointment, or arrangement that was not subject to the common law rule against perpetuities or is excluded by another statute of this state.

(h) A trust created for the purpose of providing for its beneficiaries under hospital service contracts, group life insurance, group disability insurance, group annuities, or any combination of such insurance, as defined in the Insurance Code.

(Stats. 1991 (A.B. 1577), ch. 156, §24. Amended by Stats. 1996 (S.B. 392), ch. 563, §33.)

III. Types of Trusts

A. Introduction

Trusts may be classified in different ways. For example, trusts can be either inter vivos or testamentary in nature. Inter vivos trusts come into effect during the settlor's lifetime. Testamentary trusts are created by will and come into effect after the settlor's death. See, e.g., Uniform Trust Code §401(1). See generally 60 Cal. Jur.3d Trusts §2.

A private trust is a trust created for noncharitable beneficiaries, whereas a charitable trust is one created for charitable purposes. For discussion of charitable trusts, see Chapter XIII *infra*.

In addition, a trust may be revocable or irrevocable. A revocable trust can be terminated by the settlor, whereas an irrevocable trust cannot. For a discussion of trust modification and termination, see Chapter X *infra*.

Trusts also can be express or created by operation of law. An express trust is one arising from the settlor's expressed intent to create the trust. The settlor's intent may be evidenced by written or spoken words. Trusts created by operation of law (by judicial intervention) include constructive and resulting trusts (discussed *infra* this chapter).

Trusts also may be active or passive. According to the Restatement (Third) of Trusts §6(1), in an active trust, the trustee has affirmative duties to perform. In contrast, the trustee's sole duty in a passive trust "is not to interfere with the enjoyment of the trust property by the beneficiaries." *Id.* A passive trust is not a valid trust. Therefore, the beneficiary is entitled to the property. *Id.* at §6(2).

B. Oral vs. Written

Pursuant to the Statute of Frauds of 1677, the conveyance of all legal interests in land (including trusts of real property) had to be manifested by a writing. Today, most American jurisdictions have adopted the Statute of Frauds' requirement that trusts of real property have to be in writing. McGovern & Kurtz, *supra*, §4.6 at 216-218.

Such a writing may be signed by the settlor or trustee, depending on the circumstances. It need not constitute the specific writing that

created the trust; rather, a subsequent written acknowledgment also suffices. *Id.* at 218.

Oral trusts of personal property are valid in most jurisdictions. However, a few jurisdictions require a writing for trusts of personal property. The primary difficulty regarding proof of oral trusts of personal property is the possibility of fraud. As a result, some jurisdictions and the Uniform Trust Code (§406) require that such trusts be established by clear and convincing evidence.

California does not recognize oral trusts of real property (Cal. Prob. Code §15206). However, oral trusts for personal property are valid if proven by clear and convincing evidence (Cal. Prob. Code §15207). The proof may be indirect, as evidenced by the circumstances surrounding the trust's creation. 60 Cal. Jur.3d Trusts §409.

CALIFORNIA PROBATE CODE

§15206. Validity of trusts of real property; Statute of Frauds' requirement

A trust in relation to real property is not valid unless evidenced by one of the following methods:

(a) By a written instrument signed by the trustee, or by the trustee's agent if authorized in writing to do so.

(b) By a written instrument conveying the trust property signed by the settlor, or by the settlor's agent if authorized in writing to do so.

(c) By operation of law.

(Stats. 1990 (A.B. 759), ch. 79, §14, effective July 1, 1991.)

§15207. Validity of oral trusts of personal property

(a) The existence and terms of an oral trust of personal property may be established only by clear and convincing evidence.

(b) The oral declaration of the settlor, standing alone, is not sufficient evidence of the creation of a trust of personal property.

(c) In the case of an oral trust, a reference in this division or elsewhere to a trust instrument or declaration means the terms of the trust as established pursuant to subdivision (a).

(Stats. 1990 (A.B. 759), ch. 79, §14, effective July 1, 1991.)

§15210. Recordation of trusts relating to real property

A trust created pursuant to this chapter which relates to real property may be recorded in the office of the county recorder in the county where all or a portion of the real property is located.

(Stats. 1990 (A.B. 759), ch. 79, §14, effective July 1, 1991.)

C. Trusts Created by Operation of Law

1. Resulting Trust

Some trusts arise by operation of law. There are two types of trusts created by operation of law: (1) resulting trusts and (2) constructive trusts.

A resulting trust is implied from the facts and circumstances of the case. 60 Cal. Jur.3d, Trusts §315. Such a trust is implied by law to carry out the parties' intentions. In a resulting trust, the transferee has the obligation to convey title to the beneficiary. However, the transferee has no other obligations. The beneficiary may be the settlor or, if the settlor has died, the settlor's successors in interest. A resulting trust may be established in personal or real property. According to the Restatement (Third) of Trusts §7, a resulting trust is a "reversionary, equitable interest implied by law in property that is held by a transferee, in whole or in part, as trustee for the transferor or the transferor's successors in interest."

A resulting trust arises in three primary situations:

- **an express trust fails,**
- **an express trust makes an incomplete disposition of the trust property, or**
- **a purchase money resulting trust.**

According to the Restatement (Third) of Trusts §8, a resulting trust arises when an express trust fails in whole or in part. The Restatement specifies two exceptions to this rule: the transferor manifested an intention that a resulting trust should not arise, or the trust fails for illegality and public policy would dictate that unjust enrichment of a transferee is preferable to giving relief to the wrongdoer. *Id.* at §8(a), (b).

The purchase money resulting trust arises when one person pays the purchase price for certain property but title to that property is taken in the name of a different person. In such a case,

a rebuttable presumption operates that the title holder holds the property on resulting trust for the person who paid the consideration. In some jurisdictions, if the title holder is a close relative (i.e., parent, child, spouse) of the property owner, then a rebuttable presumption operates that a gift took place.

According to the Restatement (Third) of Trusts §9, two exceptions exist to the purchase money resulting trust: if the transferor manifests an intention that no resulting trust should arise, or the transfer is made to accomplish an unlawful purpose, in which case a resulting trust does not arise based on public policy concerns. *Id.* at §9(1)(a), (b).

According to California Probate Code §15003(a), the provisions of the Trust Law (Cal. Prob. Code §§15000-19403) are limited in application to express trusts and do not affect trusts created by operation of law (i.e., constructive or resulting trusts). Note also that the definition of "trust" in the Probate Code (Cal. Prob. Code §82) excludes resulting trusts and most constructive trusts. 60 Cal. Jur. 3d Trusts §3.

The second type of trust created by operation of law is a constructive trust. These trusts also arise by operation of law rather than the intent of the settlor. A constructive trust is an equitable remedy imposed by a court to prevent unjust enrichment. It is a restitutionary device to prevent a wrongdoer from enjoying a beneficial interest in property that was obtained by his or her wrongful act (e.g., fraud, breach of fiduciary duty, etc.). The court impresses the constructive trust on wrongfully acquired property in order to convey that property to the person (i.e., the beneficiary) who would have owned it but for the defendant's wrongful conduct. The wrongdoer then becomes a constructive trustee with the duty to transfer the property to the plaintiff. In an action to recover the trust property, the beneficiary has the right of "tracing." That is, he or she can follow the original trust property into its product and impress a constructive trust on that product.

A plaintiff who seeks the imposition of a constructive trust must show: (1) the existence of some interest in property; (2) a right to that property; and (3) the defendant's gain of that property by fraud, mistake, undue influence, the violation of a trust, or some other wrongful act. 60 Cal. Jur. 3d, Trusts §347. The California Civil Code sets forth the circumstances under which constructive trusts arise (Cal. Civ. Code §§2223-2225).

However, a court will not impress a constructive trust for violation of an unenforceable contract. For example, a constructive trust will arise in the case of an oral agreement to convey real property (which is unenforceable under the Statute of Frauds) only when a party acquires or holds property because of fraud, mistake, or violation of some fiduciary or confidential relationship. 60 Cal. Jur.3d Trusts §357 (citing Bradley Co. v. Bradley, 131 P. 750 (Cal. 1913) (holding that, where a transfer to a grantee in a confidential relation has been induced by reliance on the grantee's oral promise to hold in trust for the grantor or another, equity will not permit the trustee to take advantage of the preexisting confidential relations in which the oral trust originated by repudiating the trust)).

See generally McGovern & Kurtz, *supra*, §6.1 at 269-270.

CALIFORNIA PROBATE CODE
§15003. Substantive law does not affect constructive and resulting trusts

(a) Nothing in this division affects the substantive law relating to constructive or resulting trusts.

(b) The repeal of Title 8 (commencing with Section 2215) of Part 4 of Division 3 of the Civil Code by Chapter 820 of the Statutes of 1986 was not intended to alter the rules applied by the courts to fiduciary and confidential relationships, except as to express trusts governed by this division.

(c) Nothing in this division or in Section 82 is intended to prevent the application of all or part of the principles or procedures of this division to an entity or relationship that is excluded from the definition of "trust" provided by Section 82 where these principles or procedures are applied pursuant to statutory or common law principles, by court order or rule, or by contract.

(Stats. 1990 (A.B. 759), ch. 79, §14, effective July 1, 1991. Amended by Stats. 1990 (S.B. 1775), ch. 710, §43, effective July 1, 1991.)

2. Constructive Trust

CALIFORNIA CIVIL CODE

§2223. "Involuntary trustee," defined

One who wrongfully detains a thing is an involuntary trustee thereof, for the benefit of the owner.

(Stats. 1986, ch. 820, §8, effective July 1, 1987.)

§2224. "Wrongful act," defined

One who gains a thing by fraud, accident, mistake, undue influence, the violation of a trust, or other wrongful act, is, unless he or she has some other and better right thereto, an involuntary trustee of the thing gained, for the benefit of the person who would otherwise have had it.

(Stats. 1986, ch. 820, §8, effective July 1, 1987.)

§2225. Constructive trust arising from proceeds from sale of story of felony

(a) As used in this section:

(1) "Convicted felon" means any person convicted of a felony, or found not guilty by reason of insanity of a felony committed in California, either by a court or jury trial or by entry of a plea in court.

(2) "Felony" means a felony defined by any California or United States statute.

(3)(A) "Representative of the felon" means any person or entity receiving proceeds or profits by designation of that felon, on behalf of that felon, or in the stead of that felon, whether by the felon's designation or by operation of law.

(B) "Profiteer of the felony" means any person who sells or transfers for profit any memorabilia or other property or thing of the felon, the value of which is enhanced by the notoriety gained from the commission of the felony for which the felon was convicted. This subparagraph shall not apply to any media entity reporting on the felon's story or on the sale of the materials, memorabilia, or other property or thing of the felon. Nor shall it apply to the sale of the materials, as the term is defined in paragraph (6), where the seller is exercising his or her first amendment rights. This subparagraph also shall not apply to the sale or transfer by a profiteer of any other expressive work protected by the First Amendment unless the sale or transfer is primarily for a commercial or speculative purpose.

(4)(A) "Beneficiary" means a person who, under applicable law, other than the provisions of this section, has or had a right to recover damages from the convicted felon for physical, mental, or emotional injury, or pecuniary loss proximately caused by the convicted felon as a result of the crime for which the felon was convicted.

(B) If a beneficiary described in subparagraph (A) has died, "beneficiary" also includes a person or estate entitled to recover damages pursuant to Chapter 4 (commencing with Section 377.10) of Title 3 of Part 2 of the Code of Civil Procedure.

(C) If a person has died and the death was proximately caused by the convicted felon as a result of the crime for which the felon was convicted, "beneficiary" also includes a person described in Section 377.60 of the Code of Civil Procedure and any beneficiary of a will of the decedent who had a right under that will to receive more than 25 percent of the value of the estate of the decedent.

(5) "Beneficiary's interest" means that portion of the proceeds or profits necessary to pay the following:

(A) In the case of a beneficiary described in subparagraph (A) or (B) of paragraph (4), those damages that, under applicable law, other than the provisions of this section, the beneficiary has or had a right to recover from the convicted felon for injuries proximately caused by the convicted felon as a result of the crime for which the felon was convicted.

(B) In the case of a beneficiary described in subparagraph (C) of paragraph (4), those damages that, under all the circumstances of the case, may be just.

(C) A beneficiary's interest shall be reduced by the following amount:

(i) Money paid to the beneficiary from the Restitution Fund because of the crime for which the felon was convicted.

(ii) Money paid to the beneficiary by the convicted felon because of a requirement of restitution imposed by a court in connection with the crime for which the felon was convicted.

(iii) Money paid to the beneficiary because of a judgment against the convicted felon based upon the crime for which the felon was convicted.

(D) In the case of an unsatisfied existing judgment or order of restitution against the convicted felon and in favor of a beneficiary, any money paid to the beneficiary pursuant to this section shall be applied to reduce the amount of the unsatisfied judgment or order.

(6) "Materials" means books, magazine or newspaper articles, movies, films, videotapes, sound recordings, interviews or appearances on television and radio stations, and live presentations of any kind.

(7) "Story" means a depiction, portrayal, or reenactment of a felony and shall not be taken to mean a passing mention of the felony, as in a footnote or bibliography.

(8) "Sale" includes lease, license, or any other transfer or alienation taking place in California or elsewhere.

(9) "Proceeds" means all fees, royalties, real property, or other consideration of any and every kind or nature received by or owing to a felon or his or her representatives for the preparation for the purpose of sale of materials, for the sale of the rights to materials, or the sale or distribution by the convicted felon of materials whether earned, accrued, or paid before or after the conviction. It includes any interest, earnings, or accretions upon proceeds, and any property received in exchange for proceeds.

(10) "Profits" means all income from anything sold or transferred by the felon, a representative of the felon, or a profiteer of the felony, including any right, the value of which thing or right is enhanced by the notoriety gained from the commission of a felony for which a convicted felon was convicted. This income may have been accrued, earned, or paid before or after the conviction. However, voluntary donations or contributions to a defendant to assist in the defense of criminal charges shall not be deemed to be "profits," provided the donation or contribution to that defense is not given in exchange for some material of value.

(b)(1) All proceeds from the preparation for the purpose of sale, the sale of the rights to, or the sale of materials that include or are based on the story of a felony for which a convicted felon was convicted, shall be subject to an involuntary trust for the benefit of the beneficiaries set forth in this section. That trust shall continue until five years after the time of payment of the proceeds to the felon or five years after the date of conviction, whichever is later. If an action is filed by a beneficiary to recover his or her interest in a trust within those time limitations, the trust character of the property shall continue until the conclusion of the action. At the end of the five-year trust period, any proceeds that remain in trust that have not been claimed by a beneficiary shall be transferred to the Controller, to be allocated to the Restitution Fund for the payment of claims pursuant to Section 13969 of the Government Code.

(2) All profits shall be subject to an involuntary trust for the benefit of the beneficiaries set forth in this section. That trust shall continue until five years after the time of payment of the profits to the felon or five years after the date of conviction, whichever is later. If an action is filed by a beneficiary to recover his or her interest in a trust within those time limitations, the trust character of the property shall continue until the conclusion of the action. At the end of the five-year trust period, any profits that remain in trust that have not been claimed by a beneficiary shall be transferred to the Controller, to be allocated to the Restitution Fund for the payment of claims pursuant to Section 13969 of the Government Code.

(3) Notwithstanding paragraph (2), in the case of a sale or transfer by a profiteer of the felony, the court in an action under subdivision (c) shall, upon an adequate showing by the profiteer of the felony, exclude from the involuntary trust that portion of the profits that represents the inherent value of the memorabilia, property, or thing sold or transferred and exclusive of the amount of the enhancement to the value due to the notoriety of the convicted felon.

(c)(1) Any beneficiary may bring an action against a convicted felon, representative of the felon, or a profiteer of a felony to recover his or her interest in the trust established by this section.

(2) That action may be brought in the superior court of the county in which the beneficiary resides, or of the county in which the convicted felon resides, or of the county in which proceeds or profits are located.

(3) If the court determines that a beneficiary is entitled to proceeds or profits pursuant to this section, the court shall order the payment from proceeds or profits that have been received, and, if that is insufficient, from proceeds or profits that may be received in the future.

(d) If there are two or more beneficiaries and if the available proceeds or profits are insufficient to pay all beneficiaries, the proceeds or profits shall be equitably apportioned among the beneficiaries taking into account the impact of the crime upon them.

Prior to any distribution of any proceeds to a beneficiary, the court shall determine whether the convicted felon has failed to pay any portion of a restitution fine or penalty fine imposed by a court, or any restitution imposed as a condition of probation. The court shall also determine whether the felon is obligated to reimburse a governmental entity for the costs of his or her defense and whether a portion of the proceeds is needed to cover his or her reasonable attorney's fees incurred in the criminal proceeding related to the felony, or any appeal or other related proceeding, or in the defense of the action brought under this section. The court shall order payment of these obligations prior to any payment to a beneficiary, except that 60 percent of the proceeds or profits shall be reserved for payment to the beneficiaries.

(e)(1) The Attorney General may bring an action to require proceeds or profits received by a convicted felon to be held in an express trust in a bank authorized to act as a trustee.

(2) An action may be brought under this subdivision within one year after the receipt of proceeds or profits by a convicted felon or one year after the date of conviction, whichever is later. That action may be brought in the superior court of any county in which the Attorney General has an office.

(3) If the Attorney General proves that the proceeds or profits are proceeds or profits from the sale of a story or thing of value that are subject to an involuntary trust pursuant to this section, and that it is more probable than not that there are beneficiaries within the meaning of this section, the court shall order that all proceeds or profits be deposited in a bank and held by the bank as trustee of the trust until an order of disposition is made by a court pursuant to subdivision (d), or until the expiration of the period specified in subdivision (b).

(4) If the Attorney General prevails in an action under this subdivision, the court shall order the payment from the proceeds or profits to the Attorney General of reasonable costs and attorney's fees.

(f)(1) In any action brought pursuant to this section, upon motion of a party the court shall grant a preliminary injunction to prevent any waste of proceeds or profits if it appears that the proceeds or profits are subject to the provisions of this section, and that they may be subject to waste.

(2) Upon motion of the Attorney General or any potential beneficiary, the court shall grant a preliminary injunction against a person against whom an indictment or information for a felony has been filed in superior court to prevent any waste of proceeds or profits if there is probable cause to believe that the proceeds or profits would be subject to an involuntary trust pursuant to this section upon conviction of this person, and that they may be subject to waste.

(g) Any violation of an order of a court made pursuant to this section shall be punishable as contempt.

(h) The remedies provided by this section are in addition to other remedies provided by law.

No period of limitations, except those provided by this section, shall limit the right of recovery under this section.

(Stats. 1986, ch. 820, §8, effective July 1, 1987. Amended by Stats. 1992 (S.B. 1496), ch. 178, §2; Stats. 1994 (S.B. 1330), ch. 556, §1, effective September 13, 1994; Stats. 1995 (S.B. 287), ch. 262, §1; Stats. 2000 (S.B. 1565), ch. 261, §2.)

[Note: The California Supreme Court held this section unconstitutional as a content-based restriction on speech in the case of Keenan v. Superior Court of Los Angeles County, 40 P.3d 718 (Cal 2002), cert. denied, 537 U.S. 818 (2002).]

CALIFORNIA PROBATE CODE

§15003. Constructive and resulting trusts

(a) Nothing in this division affects the substantive law relating to constructive or resulting trusts.

(b) The repeal of Title 8 (commencing with Section 2215) of Part 4 of Division 3 of the Civil Code by Chapter 820 of the Statutes of 1986 was not intended to alter the rules applied by the courts to fiduciary and confidential relationships, except as to express trusts governed by this division.

(c) Nothing in this division or in Section 82 is intended to prevent the application of all or part of the principles or procedures of this division to an entity or relationship that is excluded from the definition of "trust" provided by Section 82 where these principles or procedures are applied pursuant to statutory or common law principles, by court order or rule, or by contract.

(Stats. 1990 (A.B. 759), ch. 79, §14, effective July 1, 1991. Amended by Stats. 1990 (S.B. 1774), ch. 710, §43, effective July 1, 1991.)

D. Pour-Over Trusts

A pour-over is a provision in a will that makes a gift of probate assets to an existing inter vivos trust. Use of such an estate planning measure enables a testator to devise property into a trust even though the trust has been altered subsequent to the execution of the will. McGovern & Kurtz, *supra*, §6.2 at 274. Such a provision is commonly called a "pour-over" provision, and such a trust is commonly called a "pour-over" trust.

Pour-over provisions are especially common as estate planning devices because: (1) an inter vivos trust is easier to amend than a will (because an amendment to a will must conform with the jurisdiction's Statute of Wills); (2) an inter vivos trust can incorporate many types of assets (e.g, life insurance proceeds) to provide a unified dispositive scheme, and (3) the testator may pour over property into a trust that was created by a third party, such as a spouse. Beyer, *supra*, §9.6, at 177.

At common law, courts did not give effect to pour-over provisions because such provisions were thought to violate the Statute of Wills (by permitting disposition of property without compliance with the relevant wills legislation). Gradually, courts upheld pour-over dispositions based on the theories of either: (1) incorporation by reference (i.e., the will incorporates the terms of the trust by reference) or (2) facts of independent significance (i.e., the trust is a fact of independent significance). The former doctrine (incorporation) sufficed if the trust existed when the will was executed and remained unamended at the testator's death. However, if the trust had been amended since the execution of the will, then courts resorted to the doctrine of independent significance to validate the devise (because the trust, as amended, did not satisfy the preexisting document requirement of the incorporation by reference doctrine).

Subsequent legislation obviated the need for states to validate pour-over provisions by reliance on either the doctrine of incorporation by reference or facts of independent significance. Virtually all states now have adopted one of two versions of the Uniform Testamentary Additions to Trusts Act (UTATA). In 1960, the National Conference of Commissioners on Uniform State Laws promulgated the original UTATA. The original Act was adopted in 44 states. The purpose of the 1960 version was to address difficulties that arose from application of either the doctrine of incorporation by reference or the doctrine of independent significance. Under the early Act, property was governed by the trust terms in effect at the testator's death.

NCCUSL revised the Act in 1991. That version is incorporated into the Uniform Probate Code Article II as §2-511. The 1991 Act has been adopted by 15 states (not including California). The 1991 version no longer requires the trust to be in existence at the time the will is executed. The trust can be created even from property that is poured over. Moreover, the property is governed by the current terms of the trust (i.e., not the trust terms in effect at the testator's death).

For additional background on the two versions of the UTATA and the state adoptions, see http://nccusl.org/Updatel/uniformact_factsheets/uniformacts-fs-tata.asp (last visited May 27, 2007).

The California version of the UTATA is found at California Probate Code §§6300, 6301, and 6303. California Probate Code §6300 mirrors the original version of UPC §2-511 (1987), except that §6300 permits a trust to be amended after the testator's death unless the will prohibits such amendments regarding testamentary assets. See Law Revision Commission Comment following California Probate Code §6300. NCCUSL subsequently amended UPC §2-511 to permit the trust instrument to be executed "before, concurrently with, or after the execution of the testator's will."

The Restatement (Third) of Trusts §19 recognizes pour-over dispositions by will that add property to an irrevocable or revocable inter vivos trust, or that fund a trust unfunded during the testator's lifetime. According to the Restatement, such dispositions are effective if authorized by statute; validated by either the doctrine of incorporation by reference or facts of independent significance; or if the trust instrument, together with the will, either (1) "satisfies an applicable rule of substantial compliance, harmless error, or judicial dispensation," or (2) "otherwise satisfies the policies underlying the formal safeguards of the applicable Wills Act."

For discussion of the application of will doctrines (incorporation by reference, facts of independent significance) to pour-over trusts, see Chapter V *supra*.

CALIFORNIA PROBATE CODE

§6300. Testamentary additions to trusts

A devise, the validity of which is determinable by the law of this state, may be made by a will to the trustee of a trust established or to be established by the testator or by the testator and some other person or by some other person (including a funded or unfunded life insurance trust, although the settlor has reserved any or all rights of ownership of the insurance contracts) if the trust is identified in the testator's will and its terms are set forth in a

written instrument (other than a will) executed before or concurrently with the execution of the testator's will or in the valid last will of a person who has predeceased the testator (regardless of the existence, size, or character of the trust property). The devise is not invalid because the trust is amendable or revocable, or both, or because the trust was amended after the execution of the will or after the death of the testator. Unless the testator's will provides otherwise, the property so devised (1) is not deemed to be held under a testamentary trust of the testator but becomes a part of the trust to which it is given and (2) shall be administered and disposed of in accordance with the provisions of the instrument or will setting forth the terms of the trust, including any amendments thereto made before or after the death of the testator (regardless of whether made before or after the execution of the testator's will). Unless otherwise provided in the will, a revocation or termination of the trust before the death of the testator causes the devise to lapse.
(Stats. 1990 (A.B. 759), ch. 79, §14, effective July 1, 1991.)

§6301. Application to devises prior to 1965

This chapter does not invalidate any devise made by a will executed prior to September 17, 1965.
(Stats. 1990 (A.B. 759), ch. 79, §14, effective July 1, 1991.)

§6303. Citation of chapter

This chapter may be cited as the Uniform Testamentary Additions to Trusts Act.
(Stats. 1990 (A.B. 759), ch. 79, §14, effective July 1, 1991.)

E. Honorary Trusts

An honorary trust may be defined as "a noncharitable trust which has no ascertained or ascertainable beneficiaries and so is not enforceable, but one in which the court permits the trustee, if willing, to carry out the purposes of the trust." Bogert, *supra*, at §166. That is, the trustee has only a moral, and not legal, obligation to carry out an hononary trust because there is no beneficiary capable of enforcing the trust.

Although courts uphold trusts benefiting the welfare of animals, in general, trusts naming particular animals as beneficiaries cannot be upheld either as charitable trusts or as private express trusts because animals are not legal persons. *Id.* at §35. However, English courts, historically, have used the "honorary trust" theory to validate trusts for specific animals (i.e., dogs and horses). *Id.* In an honorary trust, the settlor vests in the trustee the power to care for particular animals should the trustee choose to do so. 13 Witkin, Summary, Trusts, *supra*, at §43.

Honorary trusts have been upheld in this country for the following purposes: (1) manumission of slaves; (2) erection of sepulchral monuments; (3) care of graves; and (4) care of a definite group of animals; and (5) saying of masses. William Fratcher, Bequests for Purposes, 56 Iowa L. Rev. 773, 801-802 (1971).

For a statute permitting the beneficiary of a trust to be a particular animal or animals provided that that animal or animals was or were alive during the settlor's lifetime, see Florida Statutes §736.0408(1)). Such a trust terminates on the death of the animal or (if several) the death of the last surviving animal.

An honorary trust is void generally if it can last beyond the period of the Rule Against Perpetuities. In California, trusts for the care of specific domestic pets are authorized by statute (Cal. Prob. Code §15212). The statute provides that such trusts may be performed by the trustee for the life of the animal "whether or not there is a beneficiary who can seek enforcement or termination of the trust and whether or not the terms of the trust contemplate a longer duration." *Id.*

Bogert explains the arguments in favor of, and opposed to, upholding honorary trusts:

> In support of the honorary trust theory it can be urged that their recognition will carry out the intent of the donor; that such trusts are not illegal or contrary to the public interest; that the settlor clearly intended to exclude his heirs, next of kin, and residuary legatees from any interest in the trust property and so invalidity and a consequent resulting trust for them should not be decreed; that the power of the successors of the settlor to intervene if the honorary trustee fails to carry out the provisions of the gift insures performance; and that there is some case authority for giving effect to such trusts as honorary.
>
> In opposition to honorary trusts it can be argued that a definite beneficiary and enforceability are inherent characteristics of a private trust which should not be discarded for a relatively unimportant reason; that the next of kin or heirs of a property

> owner are entitled to his property at his death, unless he gives his estate to others by will, and that in the situation under discussion there is no transfer by will of the equitable interest to any person; that a purpose or cause should not be permitted by the courts to take the place of a beneficiary in a noncharitable trust; that the carrying out of the terms of the gift is not apt to be insured by intervention by the successors of the testator, since it is unlikely that they will have the inclination or ability to watch the trustee over a period of years and go to the trouble and expense of seeking to secure the property; and that the small amount of case law approving the honorary trust is "anomalous and exceptional" and a "concession to human weakness or sentiment."

Bogert, *supra*, at §166.

CALIFORNIA PROBATE CODE
§15212. Validity of trusts for care of an animal

A trust for the care of a designated domestic or pet animal may be performed by the trustee for the life of the animal, whether or not there is a beneficiary who can seek enforcement or termination of the trust and whether or not the terms of the trust contemplate a longer duration.
(Stats. 1991 (A.B. 1577), ch. 156, §21.)

F. Secret vs. Semi-Secret Trusts

Some trusts are secret or semi-secret. In a secret trust situation, a will makes an absolute gift and is silent on whether the testator intended a trust. However, subsequent evidence reveals an agreement between the donee and the testator that the donee would hold the property in trust for a beneficiary designated by the testator. In the semi-secret trust situation, the will reveals that the testator intended a trust; however, the beneficiary is not identified in the will.

A secret trust may be enforced without a writing if proven by clear and convincing evidence. The secret trust is enforced through a constructive trust. In contrast, in the semi-secret trust situation, courts traditionally hold that the trust fails and return the purported trust property to the settlor based on a resulting trust theory. A few courts refuse to enforce semi-secret trusts.

The Restatement (Third) of Trusts (§18) recognizes secret trusts, and provides for their enforcement by constructive trust in two situations: (1) if a testator bequeaths property in reliance on the beneficiary's agreement (express or implied) to hold the property in trust for a particular purpose and person(s), and (2) if a person dies intestate and relies on an heir's agreement (express or implied) to hold property in trust for a particular purpose or person(s).

The different enforcement remedies have been criticized by commentators on various grounds. For example, one commentator notes the "pretext" of imposing equitable relief in the form of a constructive trust in the secret trust situation.

> [C]ourts have imposed an equitable constructive trust upon the named beneficiary to enforce the transfer over to the intended one. Courts thereby effectuate the testator's intent, despite her failure to comply fully with the statute of wills. The pretext for imposing a constructive trust in this case is prevention of "wrongdoing" by the beneficiary, who might otherwise break his (implicit) promise to the testator to hand over the bequest. But, as usual, this contraption comprises an imperfect antidote to the statute [of wills]: For equity can only be summoned in the event of a wrong.

Adam J. Hirsch, Inheritance Law, Legal Contraptions, and the Problem of Doctrinal Change, 79 Or. L. Rev. 527, 558 n.113 (2000).

McGovern argues out that the semi-secret trust constitutes a stronger case for relief because "the extrinsic evidence showing the intended beneficiaries is not inconsistent with the will but rather supplements it. . . ." McGovern & Kurtz, *supra*, §6.2 at 271. He points out that the Restatement of Trusts makes semi-secret trusts enforceable, and dispenses with the higher burden of proof required for constructive trusts. *Id.* (citing Restatement (Third) of Trusts §18, cmts. c, h).

X
Modification and Termination of Trusts

Once a trust is created, the provisions of the trust sometimes may be modified and even terminated. In some cases, a particular party, such as the settlor, trustee, or beneficiary, has the ability to modify the provisions of the trust. Such parties also may have the ability to terminate the trust, thereby causing distribution of the trust principal. In other cases, the court may modify the provisions of a trust or even terminate the trust if the circumstances warrant. This chapter focuses on the circumstances under which the parties and the court may alter and/or terminate a trust.

I. Settlor's Power to Modify or Revoke

A. Settlor's Power Limited by the Trust Terms

After the trust is created, a settlor might want to modify the trust by changing the beneficiaries or by altering the particular interests of the beneficiaries. Perhaps the settlor might want to terminate the trust in order to recover the trust property for the settlor's needs or to subject it to another testamentary plan. Whether the settlor is able to modify or terminate the trust generally depends on the terms of the trust instrument. If the trust instrument expressly reserves the power to modify or revoke a trust, then the settlor retains these powers. See also Restatement (Third) of Trusts §63(1) ("The settlor of an inter vivos trust has power to revoke or modify the trust to the extent the terms of the trust so provide").

A settlor either may expressly reserve a power of revocation or grant a power to terminate the trust to another (i.e., a party or nonparty to the trust). The later provision may specify that another person may exercise the power only under certain conditions, such as the occurrence of a particular event. Bogert, *supra*, at §1000.

According to California law, a trust terminates when its term expires, its purpose is fulfilled, becomes unlawful or impossible to fulfill, or, the trust is revoked (Cal. Prob. Code §15407). According to the Restatement (Third) of Trusts §61, a trust terminates (in whole or in part) upon the expiration of a period or the happening of an event as provided by the trust terms; absent such terms, the trust terminates (in whole or in part) when the purpose(s) of the trust are accomplished.

Also, recall that private express trusts are subject to the Rule Against Perpetuities. Therefore, according to California statute, if a trust has an express term specifying that the trust may not be terminated (or a similar term may be implied), such a provision is ineffective insofar as it attempts to evade the Rule (Cal. Prob. Code §15413). If a trust continues after expiration of the period under the Rule, such a trust may be terminated by a majority of the beneficiaries, the state Attorney General, or any person affected by the termination, provided that a court determines termination would be in the public interest or in the best interest of "a majority of the persons who would be affected by the termination" (Cal. Prob. Code §15414 (b)).

In addition, a trust instrument may be reformed due to fraud, duress, undue influence, or mistake. For example, if the instrument does not contain certain terms that were intended, the settlor or other interested party may seek to have the trust reformed. Also, courts have reformed trust instruments to make them irrevocable where the parties so intended (such as for tax purposes). Flitcroft v. Commission of Internal Revenue, 328 F.2d 449 (9th Cir. 1964) (holding that state court correctly found that trusts were originally intended to be irrevocable, although the original trust instruments specified they were revocable). Note that in regards to estate tax determinations, state probate court judgments do not bind federal courts. Commissioner v. Bosch, 387 U.S. 436 (1967).

The Restatement (Third) of Trusts §62 provides that a trust may be rescinded or reformed based on the same grounds as those upon which other transfers of property may be rescinded or reformed. Also, the Restatement (Third) of Property §12.2 provides for modification of donative documents to achieve the donor's tax objectives. The rationale for the latter provision is probable intention, i.e., the donor would have desired the modification if the donor had realized that the desired tax objectives would not be achieved.

On trust reformation, see also Matter of Ikuta's Estate, 639 P.3d 400 (Haw. 1981) (reforming a provision specifying that the trust was to terminate on the death of the last survivor or when the oldest child attained age 30, to change "oldest" to "youngest," because of policy against intestacy and because failure to reform the will would defeat testator's intention).

Courts may require that the party seeking to reform the trust show by clear and convincing evidence that, because of mistake or fraud, the language of the trust does not conform to the settlor's intention. See, e.g., In re Boston Regional Medical Center, Inc., 2003 WL 22019551 (Bankr. Mass. 2003). See also Restatement (Third) of Property §12.1 cmt. e (specifying that the standard of proof for reformation of donative documents to correct mistakes is clear and convincing evidence). But cf. *id.* at §12.2 cmt. c (providing that, for purposes of modifying donative documents to achieve a donor's tax objectives, proof of these objectives may be established by a preponderance of the evidence).

The settlor can relinquish the power to modify the trust, an act that is sometimes taken to avoid tax liabilities. On reformation of trusts, see generally Bogert, *supra*, at §§991-1000.

CALIFORNIA PROBATE CODE

§15407. Termination of trust: conditions

(a) A trust terminates when any of the following occurs:

(1) The term of the trust expires.

(2) The trust purpose is fulfilled.

(3) The trust purpose becomes unlawful.

(4) The trust purpose becomes impossible to fulfill.

(5) The trust is revoked.

(b) On termination of the trust, the trustee continues to have the powers reasonably necessary under the circumstances to wind up the affairs of the trust.

(Stats. 1990 (A.B. 759), ch. 79, §14, effective July 1, 1991.)

§15410. Disposition of trust property upon termination of the trust

At the termination of a trust, the trust property shall be disposed of as follows:

(a) In the case of a trust that is revoked by the settlor, as directed by the settlor.

(b) In the case of a trust that is terminated by the consent of the settlor and all beneficiaries, as agreed by the settlor and all beneficiaries.

(c) In any other case, as provided in the trust instrument or in a manner directed by the court that conforms as nearly as possible to the intention of the settlor as expressed in the trust instrument.

(d) If a trust is terminated by the trustee pursuant to subdivision (b) of Section 15408, the trust property may be distributed as determined by the trustee pursuant to the standard provided in subdivision (c) without the need for a court order. Where the trust instrument does not provide a manner of distribution at termination and the settlor's intent is not adequately expressed in the trust instrument, the trustee may distribute the trust property to the living beneficiaries on an actuarial basis.

(Stats. 1990 (A.B. 759), ch. 79, §14, effective July 1, 1991.)

§15413. Termination provision is ineffective if it violates the Rule Against Perpetuities

A trust provision, express or implied, that the trust may not be terminated is ineffective insofar as it purports to be applicable after the expiration of the longer of the periods provided by the statutory rule against perpetuities, Article 2 (commencing with Section 21205) of Chapter 1 of Part 2 of Division 11.

(Stats. 1991 (A.B. 1577), ch. 156, §22.)

§15414. Termination of trust that continues after expiration of Rule Against Perpetuities

Notwithstanding any other provision in this chapter, if a trust continues in existence after the expiration of the longer of the periods provided by the statutory rule against perpetuities, Article 2 (commencing with Section 21205) of Chapter 1 of Part 2 of Division 11, the trust may be terminated in either of the following manners:

(a) On petition by a majority of the beneficiaries.

(b) On petition by the Attorney General or by any person who would be affected by the termination, if the court finds that the termination would be in the public interest or in the best interest of a majority of the persons who would be affected by the termination.

(Stats. 1991 (A.B. 1577), ch. 156, §23.)

B. Presumptions of Revocability

Some trust instruments are silent regarding reservation of a power of modification or termination. Or the trust instrument may be unclear regarding reservation of such powers. Traditionally, in cases of ambiguity, the law often resorts to presumptions. According to the majority rule, a trust is presumed to be irrevocable unless a power of revocation is expressly reserved or may be implied from language contained in the instrument. Restatement (Second) of Trusts §330. On the other hand, a few states (including California) and the Uniform Trust Code §602 reverse the general rule: They presume that trusts are revocable unless expressly made irrevocable.

In California, until 1931, a trust was irrevocable unless the trust instrument reserved the power to revoke. 60 Cal. Jur.3d Trusts §306. Currently, California Probate Code §15400 provides that "Unless a trust is expressly made irrevocable by the trust instrument, the trust is revocable by the settlor. . . ." This provision applies only if the settlor is domiciled in California at the time of the creation of the trust, if the trust instrument is executed in this state, or if the trust instrument provides that the law of California governs the trust. *Id.*

The Restatement (Third) of Trusts §63 applies different presumptions of revocability, based on whether or not the settlor retained an interest in the trust. These presumptions apply to reflect the settlor's unstated intentions. Thus, when the settlor fails expressly to provide whether a trust may be modified or revoked, in cases in which the settlor retains no interest in the trust, it is rebuttably presumed that the settlor has no power to modify or revoke the trust. In such a case, the trust may be compared to an outright gift in which the settlor reserves no beneficial interests. The presumption of irrevocability in this case mirrors general principles regarding inter vivos gifts. Restatement (Third) of Trusts §63 at cmt. c.

However, in other cases, the settlor retains interests in the trust. If the settlor fails expressly to provide whether a trust may be modified or revoked but has retained interests in the trust, the presumption is that "the trust is revocable or amendable by the settlor." The Restatement considers the settlor's retention of a power of appointment to be a "retained interest." In these cases of retained interests, "a presumption of revocability is justified by the risk of confusion and doubts about a settlor's understanding." *Id.* at c(1). Doubts regarding the settlor's intention are resolved in favor of the settlor. A presumption of revocability also serves to protect the settlor from unanticipated, adverse tax consequences. *Id.*

As explained above, UTC §602(a) rejects the common law presumption that a trust is irrevocable. The commentary to the Restatement (Third) of Trusts points out that this UTC change is of little practical importance for professionally drafted trust instruments because such instruments specify the revocability or irrevocability of a trust. Rather, the change is important for instruments drafted by nonlawyers for which there is an inference that the trust was meant to be revocable. Cited in Restatement (Third) of Trusts §63, cmts. b, c, d.

§15400. Presumption that trust is revocable

Unless a trust is expressly made irrevocable by the trust instrument, the trust is revocable by the settlor. This section applies only where the settlor is domiciled in this state when the trust is created, where the trust instrument is executed in this state, or where the trust instrument provides that the law of this state governs the trust.

(Stats. 1990 (A.B. 759), ch. 79, §14, effective July 1, 1991.)

C. Methods of Revocation

Settlors who desire to revoke a trust must comply with the method(s) specified in the trust instrument or specified by law. If a method is specified by the instrument, that provision controls. If no method is specified, then any reasonable method may be used. Bogert, *supra*, at §1001. If the settlor vests the power of revocation in two persons, then both persons must join in the act. *Id.*

California Probate Code §15401(a)(1) and (2), for example, provides that a trust may be revoked in whole or in part by compliance with "any method of revocation provided in the trust instrument" or "by a writing (other than a will) signed by the settlor and delivered to the trustee during the lifetime of the settlor." However, if the trust instrument is explicit about the method of revocation, that direction must be followed. *Id.* at (a)(2). Note that the Uniform Trust Code §602(c)(1) liberalizes the requirement by specifying merely the need for "substantial compliance" with the prescribed method of revocation. California law also prohibits modification or revocation by an attorney in fact under a power of attorney unless expressly permitted by the trust instrument. *Id.* at (c).

If the instrument fails to specify a particular method or methods of revocation, the Restatement (Third) of Trusts §63, provides that the power to revoke "can be exercised in any way that provides clear and convincing evidence of the settlor's intention to do so."

§15401. Methods of revocation

(a) A trust that is revocable by the settlor may be revoked in whole or in part by any of the following methods:

(1) By compliance with any method of revocation provided in the trust instrument.

(2) By a writing (other than a will) signed by the settlor and delivered to the trustee during the lifetime of the settlor. If the trust instrument explicitly makes the method of revocation provided in the trust instrument the exclusive method of revocation, the trust may not be revoked pursuant to this paragraph.

(b) Unless otherwise provided in the instrument, if a trust is created by more than one settlor, each settlor may revoke the trust as to the portion of the trust contributed by that settlor, except as provided in Section 761 of the Family Code.

(c) A trust may not be modified or revoked by an attorney in fact under a power of attorney unless it is expressly permitted by the trust instrument.

(d) Nothing in this section limits the authority to modify or terminate a trust pursuant to Section 15403 or 15404 in an appropriate case.

(e) The manner of revocation of a trust revocable by the settlor that was created by an instrument executed before July 1, 1987, is governed by prior law and not by this section.

(Stats. 1990 (A.B. 759), ch. 79, §14, effective July 1, 1991. Amended by Stats. 1994 (A.B. 3686), ch. 806, §37.)

D. Notification of Irrevocability to Heirs

Until recently, California trustees were required to notify heirs and beneficiaries whenever a trust became irrevocable. Former California Probate Code §16061.7 required a trustee to notify (by providing a copy of the "terms of the trust") any heir or beneficiary whenever a trust became irrevocable for any reason. The notification was accompanied by a warning that a time limit existed on the heir's or beneficiary's ability to contest the trust. The duty to notify heirs and beneficiaries was required even if the settlor was still alive. Stemming from concern about settlors' privacy, the California legislature enacted new legislation in 2000 (amending California Probate Code §16061) to limit the circumstances requiring notification.

The new law (Cal. Prob. Code §16061.7) requires that a trustee provide a copy only if the trust becomes irrevocable for one of two reasons: (1) if the trust becomes irrevocable as a result of the death of the settlor; or (2) if the trust becomes irrevocable based on a scheme within the trust instrument that specifies a date within one year before or after the settlor's death. In support of the new legislation, one commentator writes:

> People should be able to keep their financial dealings confidential if they so desire. While other ways to give money to people during one's lifetime certainly are available, a person should be able to use a trust and keep her privacy. Of course, to notify a settlor's heirs about a settlor's financial dealings when the settlor dies makes sense, but notifying the heirs when the settlor is still alive invades the settlor's ability to keep her own financial activities private.

Erik R. Beauchamp, "It's My Money 'Til I Die": When Trustees Must Notify Heirs and Beneficiaries Concerning a Trust That Has Become Irrevocable, 32 McGeorge L. Rev. 670, 679-680 (2001).

§16061.7. Notification when trust becomes irrevocable

(a) A trustee shall serve a notification by the trustee as described in this section in the following events:

(1) When a revocable trust or any portion thereof becomes irrevocable because of the death of one or more of the settlors of the trust, or because, by the express terms of the trust, the trust becomes irrevocable within one year of the death of a settlor because of a contingency related to the death of one or more of the settlors of the trust.

(2) Whenever there is a change of trustee of an irrevocable trust. The duty to serve the notification by the trustee is the duty of the continuing or successor trustee, and any one cotrustee may serve the notification.

(b) The notification by the trustee required by subdivision (a) shall be served on each of the following:

(1) Each beneficiary of the irrevocable trust or irrevocable portion of the trust, subject to the limitations of Section 15804.

(2) Each heir of the deceased settlor, if the event that requires notification is the death of a settlor or irrevocability within one year of the death of the settlor of the trust by the express terms of the trust because of a contingency related to the death of a settlor.

(3) If the trust is a charitable trust subject to the supervision of the Attorney General, to the Attorney General.

(c) A trustee shall, for purposes of this section, rely upon any final judicial determination of heirship, known to the trustee, but the trustee shall have discretion to make a good faith determination by any reasonable means of the heirs of a deceased settlor in the absence of a final judicial determination of heirship known to the trustee.

(d) The trustee need not provide a copy of the notification by trustee to any beneficiary or heir (1) known to the trustee but who cannot be located by the trustee after reasonable diligence or (2) unknown to the trustee.

(e) The notification by trustee shall be served by mail to the last known address, pursuant to Section 1215, or by personal delivery.

(f) The notification by trustee shall be served not later than 60 days following the occurrence of the event requiring service of the notification by trustee, or 60 days after the trustee became aware of the existence of a person entitled to receive notification by trustee, if that person was not known to the trustee on the occurrence of the event requiring service of the notification. If there is a vacancy in the office of the trustee on the date of the occurrence of the event requiring service of the notification by trustee, or if that event causes a vacancy, then the 60-day period for service of the notification by trustee commences on the date the new trustee commences to serve as trustee.

(g) The notification by trustee shall contain the following information:

(1) The identity of the settlor or settlors of the trust and the date of execution of the trust instrument.

(2) The name, mailing address and telephone number of each trustee of the trust.

(3) The address of the physical location where the principal place of administration of the trust is located, pursuant to Section 17002.

(4) Any additional information that may be expressly required by the terms of the trust instrument.

(5) A notification that the recipient is entitled, upon reasonable request to the trustee, to receive from the trustee a true and complete copy of the terms of the trust.

(h) If the notification by the trustee is served because a revocable trust or any portion of it has become irrevocable because of the death of one or more settlors of the trust, or because, by the express terms of the trust, the trust becomes irrevocable within one year of the death of a settlor because of a contingency related to the death of one or more of the settlors of the trust, the notification by the trustee shall also include a warning, set out in a separate paragraph in not less than 10-point boldface type, or a reasonable equivalent thereof, that states as follows:

> "You may not bring an action to contest the trust more than 120 days from the date this notification by the trustee is served upon you or 60 days from the date on which a copy of the terms of the trust is mailed or personally delivered to you during that 120-day period, whichever is later."

(i) Any waiver by a settlor of the requirement of serving the notification by trustee required by this section is against public policy and shall be void.

(j) A trustee may serve a notification by trustee in the form required by this section on any person in addition to those on whom the notification by trustee is required to be served. A trustee is not liable to any person for serving or for not serving the notice on any person in addition to those on whom the notice is required to be served. A trustee is not required to serve a notification by trustee if the event that otherwise requires service of the notification by trustee occurs before January 1, 1998.

(Stats. 1997 (A.B. 1172), ch. 724, §23. Amended by Stats. 1998 (A.B. 2069), ch. 682, §10; Stats. 2000 (A.B. 460), ch. 34, §4; Stats. 2000 (A.B. 1628), ch. 592, §1.)

E. Settlor as Sole Beneficiary

If a court determines that the settlor is the sole beneficiary of a trust, the settlor may terminate the trust. A sole beneficiary-settlor may terminate the trust, even if the settlor has reserved no power of modification or revocation, and even if the trust is irrevocable. Bogert, *supra*, at §1004. Moreover, even if the trust purposes have not been fully accomplished or if the trust has a spendthrift provision, the settlor who is the sole beneficiary of a trust still can revoke the trust. 60 Cal. Jur.3d Trusts §312. The rationale for trust termination in such cases is that there is no problem concerning defeating the trust purpose against the settlor's wishes.

If the trust property is supposed to pass as may be specified by the settlor's *will*, and otherwise to his or her heirs, then the settlor-sole beneficiary has no right to terminate the trust during his lifetime. This result occurs because the settlor's heirs can be divested of their interests only by the exercise of the settlor's reserved power of testamentary appointment. *Id.*

See also Levy v. Crocker-Citizens Nat'l Bank, 94 Cal. Rptr. 1 (Ct. App. 1971) (holding that where trust corpus was to be distributed pursuant to the exercise of a *testamentary* general power of appointment, settlor did not have power to revoke trust because he was not the sole beneficiary since his surviving lawful issue would take in default of his exercise of power of appointment); Ammco Ornamental Iron, Inc. v. Wing, 31 Cal. Rptr. 2d 564 (Ct. App. 1994) (trustee would not be regarded as sole beneficiary of trust for purpose of terminating trust pursuant to merger doctrine).

F. Rights of Creditors in Face of Settlor's Power of Revocation

In some states, the assets of a revocable trust are subject to the claims of the settlor's creditors under specific circumstances. According to California law, creditors of the settlor may reach the trust property during the settlor's lifetime if the settlor retains the power to revoke the trust (Cal. Prob. Code §18200). The rights of creditors are limited by the maximum amount the settlor might receive. That is, the trust property is subject to creditors' claims to the extent of the power of revocation. *Id.* Compare Restatement (Second) of Trusts §330 cmt. o ("Unless it is otherwise provided by statute a power of revocation reserved by the settlor cannot be reached by his creditors [who] cannot compel him to revoke the trust for their benefit").

The Uniform Trust Code §505 also addresses creditors' claims against the settlor, both during the settlor's lifetime and after the settlor's death. According to the UTC, during the settlor's lifetime, the property of a revocable trust is subject to claims of the settlor's creditors (regardless of whether the trust contains a spendthrift provision). *Id.* at §505(a)(1). If the trust is irrevocable, a creditor or assignee of the settlor may reach the maximum amount that can be distributed to or for the settlor's benefit. *Id.* at §505(a)(2). After the settlor's death, the trust property that was revocable at the settlor's death is subject to "claims of the settlor's creditors, costs of administration of the settlor's estate, the expenses of the settlor's funeral and disposal of remains, and [statutory allowances] to a surviving spouse and children to the extent the settlor's probate estate is inadequate to satisfy those claims, costs, expenses, and [allowances]." *Id.* at §505(a)(3).

§18200. Creditors' rights during settlor's lifetime if settlor retains power of revocation

If the settlor retains the power to revoke the trust in whole or in part, the trust property is subject to the claims of creditors of the settlor to the extent of the power of revocation during the lifetime of the settlor.

(Stats. 1990 (A.B.759), ch. 79, §14, effective July 1, 1991.)

§18201. Extent of trust property subject to claims of creditors

Any settlor whose trust property is subject to the claims of creditors pursuant to Section 18200 shall be entitled to all exemptions as provided in Chapter 4 (commencing with Section 703.010) of Division 2 of Title 9 of Part 2 of the Code of Civil Procedure.

(Stats. 1998 (A.B. 2069), ch. 682, §14.)

G. Other

The power to revoke generally includes the power to amend. See, e.g., California Probate Code §15402 ("Unless the trust instrument provides otherwise, if a trust is revocable by the settlor, the settlor may modify the trust by the procedure for revocation").

Some jurisdictions, either by case law or statute, permit one of several settlors to revoke. See, e.g., California Probate Code §15401(b) ("Unless otherwise provided in the instrument, if a trust is created by more than one settlor, each settlor may revoke the trust as to the portion of the trust contributed by that settlor, except as provided in Section 761 of the Family Code").

In some cases, the trust property consists of community property. What happens to such property when the trust is revoked? California Family Code §761(b) (*infra*) establishes the presumption that either spouse acting alone may revoke the trust as to the community property. However, such a unilateral revocation does not alter the community property character of the property that results from the revocation. Note that California Family Code §761 does not provide the exclusive means by which community property may be held in trust without loss of its community character. California Law Revision Commentary following California Family Code §761. See also McGovern & Kurtz, *supra*, §5.5 at 247-248.

The reservation of a power to revoke does not affect the validity of a trust. However, note that if a settlor reserves a power of revocation that is coupled with the exercise by the settlor of a significant amount of management and control of the trust, a court may find that the trust is illusory and therefore invalid. See, e.g., Osborn v. Osborn, 226 N.E.2d 814 (Ohio Com. Pl. 1966).

See generally Gail B. Bird, Trust Termination: Unborn, Living, and Dead Hands—Too Many Fingers in the Trust Pie, 36 Hast. L.J. 563 (1985); Ronald Chester, Modification and Termination of Trusts in the 21st Century: The Uniform Trust Code Leads a Quiet Revolution, 35 Real Property, Probate & Trust Journal 697 (2001); Edward C. Halbach, Jr., Uniform Acts, Restatements, & Trends in American Trust Law at Century's End, 88 Cal. L. Rev. 1877 (2000); Julia C. Walker, Get Your Dead Hands Off Me: Beneficiaries' Right to Terminate or Modify a Trust Under the Uniform Trust Code, 67 Mo. L. Rev. 443 (2002).

§15402. Power to revoke a trust includes power to modify

Unless the trust instrument provides otherwise, if a trust is revocable by the settlor, the settlor may modify the trust by the procedure for revocation.

(Stats. 1990 (A.B. 759), ch. 79, §14, effective July 1, 1991.)

§15803. The rights of the holder of power of appointment or withdrawal

The holder of a presently exercisable general power of appointment or power to withdraw property from the trust has the rights of a person holding the power to revoke the trust that are provided by Sections 15800 to 15802, inclusive, to the extent of the holder's power over the trust property.

(Stats. 1990, ch. 79, §14 (A.B. 759), effective July 1, 1991.)

CALIFORNIA FAMILY CODE

§761. Community property transferred in trust

(a) Unless the trust instrument or the instrument of transfer expressly provides otherwise, community property that is transferred in trust remains community property during the marriage, regardless of the identity of the trustee, if the trust, originally or as amended before or after the transfer, provides that the trust is revocable as to that property during the marriage and the power, if any, to modify the trust as to the rights and interests in that property during the marriage may be exercised only with the joinder or consent of both spouses.

(b) Unless the trust instrument expressly provides otherwise, a power to revoke as to community property may be exercised by either spouse acting alone. Community property, including any income or appreciation, that is distributed or withdrawn from a trust by revocation, power of withdrawal, or otherwise, remains community property unless there is a valid transmutation of the property at the time of distribution or withdrawal.

(c) The trustee may convey and otherwise manage and control the trust property in accordance with the provisions of the trust without the joinder or consent of the husband or wife unless the trust expressly requires the joinder or consent of one or both spouses.

(d) This section applies to a transfer made before, on, or after July 1, 1987.

(e) Nothing in this section affects the community character of property that is transferred before, on, or after July 1, 1987, in any manner or to a trust other than described in this section.

(Stats. 1992 (A.B. 2650), ch. 162, §10, effective January 1, 1994.)

II. Power of the Trustee to Modify or Revoke

The trustee has the power to modify or terminate the trust only if expressly or impliedly authorized to do so by the terms of the instrument. Moreover, the trustee's power to modify or terminate must be exercised in accordance with fiduciary standards and the intent of the settlor (as expressed in the terms of the trust instrument).

Most trust instruments do not confer upon a trustee an express power to modify or revoke a trust. Even if the settlor agrees, the trustee has no power to terminate the trust unless the trust instrument expressly grants the trustee such a power. If the trustee declares the trust terminated or agrees with the settlor to do so, without authorization, the transaction is void. Bogert, *supra*, at §998.

However, in some circumstances, the trust instrument may indirectly give the trustee the authority to act in such a way that results in modification or termination of the trust. For example, the settlor might give the trustee discretion to invade principal. In that event, the exercise of the trustee's discretion to distribute all of the principal might lead to termination. Note that the trustee must believe in good faith that the invasion of the principal is necessary to fulfill the material purpose of the trust. See Estate of Ferrall, 41 Cal. 2d 166 (1953).

Alternatively, the settlor or state law might provide that if the value of the trust property falls below a certain amount, the trustee has discretion to terminate the trust and distribute the principal. For example, California Probate Code §15408 provides that a court, upon petition by a trustee or beneficiary, may order modification or termination of a trust with an uneconomically low principal, or that a trustee has the power to terminate the trust if the principal is less than $20,000.

In addition, many state statutes authorize a trustee to combine similar trusts or to divide a trust into separate trusts in order to take advantage of tax benefits (if the trusts are substantially similar), such as by permitting the trustee to make different decisions regarding taxes for each trust. See, e.g., California Probate Code §15411 (court may *combine* similar trusts upon petition by trustee or beneficiary if the court determines that administration as a single trust will not defeat or substantially impair the accomplishment of the trust purposes or the interests of the beneficiaries), §15412 (court may *divide* a trust into separate trusts upon petition by a trustee or beneficiary if the court determines that dividing the trust will not defeat or substantially impair the accomplishment of the trust purposes or the interests of the beneficiaries).

Note that whenever a trust is terminated, the trustee has a duty to act for a reasonable period in order to perform administrative tasks necessary for winding up the trust and distributing the trust property. During that period, the trustee must continue to exercise the powers granted or implied in the trust instrument that are appropriate to protect and preserve the trust property for distribution to the beneficiaries. See generally Bogert, *supra*, at §§992, 1010.

§15407. Trustee's powers on termination of trust

(a) A trust terminates when any of the following occurs:

(1) The term of the trust expires.

(2) The trust purpose is fulfilled.

(3) The trust purpose becomes unlawful.

(4) The trust purpose becomes impossible to fulfill.

(5) The trust is revoked.

(b) On termination of the trust, the trustee continues to have the powers reasonably necessary under the circumstances to wind up the affairs of the trust.

(Stats. 1990 (A.B. 759), ch. 79, §14, effective July 1, 1991.)

§15408. Court may order the modification or termination of a trust with an uneconomically low principal

(a) On petition by a trustee or beneficiary, if the court determines that the fair market value of the principal of a trust has become so low in relation to the cost of administration that continuation of the trust under its existing terms will defeat or substantially impair the accomplishment of its purposes, the court may, in its discretion and in a manner that conforms as nearly as possible to the intention of the settlor, order any of the following:

(1) Termination of the trust.

(2) Modification of the trust.

(3) Appointment of a new trustee.

(b) Notwithstanding subdivision (a), if the trust principal does not exceed twenty thousand dollars ($20,000) in value, the trustee has the power to terminate the trust.

(c) The existence of a trust provision restraining transfer of the beneficiary's interest does not prevent application of this section.

(Stats. 1990 (A.B. 759), ch. 79, §14, effective July 1, 1991.)

III. Beneficiaries' Power to Modify or Revoke

In most American jurisdictions, a trust can be modified or terminated at the beneficiaries' request, provided that (1) all the beneficiaries consent, (2) all are competent, and (3) if modification or termination will not interfere with a "material purpose" of the settlor. Under this traditional doctrine, the fact of some beneficiaries' being unborn, incompetent, or unascertainable prevents modification or termination. The material purpose requirement also has presented difficulties for beneficiaries who desire modification or termination. "Under the conventional American rule, courts defer to the settlor's intent and preserve the integrity of the trust regardless of the beneficiaries' desires." Walker, *supra*, at 447.

The traditional rule on trust modification and termination is termed the "Claflin doctrine," after the famous case of Claflin v. Claflin, 20 N.E. 545 (Mass. 1889). In *Claflin*, a testator established a trust for a son. Payments were to be made to the son at defined intervals ($10,000 at age 21, $10,000 at age 25), with the remainder to be paid when the son reached the age of 30. At age 21, the son sought termination of the trust. The court refused, reasoning that premature termination would violate the intent of the testator.

Note that an exception to the *Claflin* doctrine is if the settlor is alive and joins the beneficiaries in giving consent (even if the modification or termination is inconsistent with a material purpose of the trust). In such cases, courts are not concerned with the material purpose because the settlor has acquiesced. See also Unif. Trust Code §411(a) (permitting modification or termination of a noncharitable irrevocable trust upon consent of the settlor and all beneficiaries even if such act would be inconsistent with a material purpose of the trust).

Under the traditional doctrine, courts were troubled by the best manner of protecting the interests of those trust beneficiaries who are unborn or unascertained. Then, in 1966, the United States District Court for the District of Columbia reached a creative solution to the problem. In Hatch v. Riggs National Bank, 361 F.2d 559 (D.D.C. 1966), a settlor wanted to modify a trust, to provide herself with needed income. She had created the trust 40 years earlier. The terms of the trust directed the trustees to pay the settlor the income for her life and, upon her death, to pay the corpus according to her testamentary power of appointment and, in default of the exercise of this power of appointment, to her next of kin. The problem was whether the settlor could modify the trust in the face of a spendthrift restriction and in the face of the interests of unborn contingent beneficiaries.

The district court decided to appoint a guardian ad litem to represent the interests of the unborn or unascertained beneficiaries. The court reasoned that the appointment was in accordance with "basic principles of trust law." and the use of a guardian ad litem was recognized in other jurisdictions (although in other contexts). In addition, statutes providing for the appointment of guardians ad litem (in other contexts) were "consistent with the Anglo-American system of law and adopted to promote the objective of justice. *Hatch*, 361 F.2d. 559 at 565.

In American trust law, the *Claflin* doctrine has been liberalized by two developments: (1) some states allow vicarious consent, for example by a guardian ad litem or virtual representation, on behalf of unborn or unascertainable beneficiaries; (2) some states attempt to expand the material purpose qualification in the doctrine. Halbach, Uniform Acts, *supra,* at 1900-1901. Virtual representation is the process by which an unrepresented person (such as an unborn child) may be represented by another beneficiary with a similar beneficial interest. California's liberalization of the material purpose requirement is discussed *infra*.

American law on trust modification and termination by the beneficiaries differs from that of England. In England, a trust may be modified or terminated if all the beneficiaries are adult, legally competent, and consent. It is only necessary to show that the modification or termination is beneficial to the beneficiaries. This rule is consistent with the English view that abhors restraints on alienation.

The English rule is derived from Saunders v. Vautier, Cr. & Ph. 240 (1841), in which the court terminated a trust and awarded the balance to the beneficiary earlier than authorized by the trust instrument. Finding that the settlor had no express motivation to withhold funds until the beneficiary reached majority, the court determined that the restriction on premature termination was arbitrary. "*Saunders* epitomized the notion of freely alienable property interests and represented the majority rule in the United States [prior to adoption of the *Claflin* doctrine]." Walker, *supra*, at 448.

In the 1950s, Parliament codified the English rule on trust modification and termination. Responding to the plea of trust beneficiaries seeking to modify trusts in order to avoid tax burdens caused by reform of tax laws, Parliament enacted the Variation of Trusts Act of 1958 (6 & 7 Eliz. 2, ch. 53, §1).

The act provides that a court may consent to modification or termination of a trust on behalf of incompetent, minor, or unborn beneficiaries whenever the court finds it to the beneficiaries' advantage. The function of the court is to protect those who cannot protect themselves, considering educational and social benefits, and reduction in family dissension, as well as financial benefits. The settlor's intent is a relevant but not controlling consideration. Jesse Dukeminier & James E. Krier, The Rise of the Perpetual Trust, 50 UCLA L. Rev. 1303, 1329 (2003).

The American Law Institute in the Restatement (Third) of Trusts and NCCUSL in the Uniform Trust Code recently liberalized the *Claflin* doctrine. In cases in which all the beneficiaries desire modification or termination, both the Restatement (Third) of Trusts §65(2) and Uniform Trust Code §411(b) still require that modification or termination not be inconsistent with a material purpose of the trust. However, under the Restatement (Third) of Trusts §65, if the modification or termination would be inconsistent with a material purpose of the trust, the beneficiaries need either the settlor's consent or judicial authorization (after the settlor's death). The test for judicial authorization of modification or termination in cases of unanimous consent by the beneficiaries is if "the reason for termination or modification outweighs the material purpose." Restatement (Third) of Trusts §65(2).

The Uniform Trust Code §411(b) also permits modification or termination if all the beneficiaries consent and "if the court concludes that continuance of the trust is not necessary to achieve any material purpose of the trust." However, if not all beneficiaries consent to a proposed modification or termination, then a court may still approve modification or termination if both of the following conditions are met: (1) if all of the beneficiaries had consented, the trust could have been modified or terminated under this section; and (2) the interests of a beneficiary who does not consent will be adequately protected. Uniform Trust Code §411(e). Neither the Uniform Trust Code nor the Restatement (Third) of Trusts presume that the insertion of a spendthrift clause constitutes a material purpose barring modification or termination.

According to California law, the settlor and all beneficiaries may compel the modification or termination of a trust where they all consent, even if the trust is irrevocable. 60 Cal. Jur.3d Trusts §308 (citing California Probate Code §15404). Moreover, the court may grant a petition for modification or termination of an irrevocable trust at the request of all the beneficiaries even if a "material purpose" of the trust has not been accomplished. The test in such cases (adopted by the Restatement (Third) of Trusts §65(2)) is if the reason for modification or termination "outweighs the interest in accomplishing a material purpose of the trust" (Cal. Prob. Code §15403).

Since 1986, California law has authorized the appointment of guardian ad litem to represent a trust beneficiary who lacks capacity (California Probate Code §15405 continues the former

California Probate Code provision of the same number, originally added by 1986 Cal. Stat. Ch. 820 §40, amended by 1987 Cal. Stat. Ch. 128, §9). According to California Probate Code §15405, for purposes of (1) modification or termination upon the consent of all the beneficiaries or (2) modification or termination upon the mutual consent of the settlor and beneficiaries, a guardian ad litem may give consent for any beneficiary who lacks legal capacity, including a minor, or who is an unascertained or unborn person "if it would be appropriate to do so" (Cal. Prob. Code §15405). The statute provides further that the guardian ad litem may rely in the determination "on general family benefit accruing to living members of the beneficiary's family." ***Id.*** **This second provision, which permits a nonpecuniary quid pro quo as the basis for protection of the beneficiaries' interests, is based on Wisconsin statute (Wis. Stat. Ann. §701.12(2) (2004)). Law Revision Commentary following California Probate Code §15404.**

The common law conclusively presumed that all persons were capable of parenthood, regardless of their age or physical condition (called the "fertile octogenarian" doctrine). Therefore, a beneficiary designation in a trust to a class ("children" or "issue") created a class of contingent remaindermen that could preclude premature termination. California statute provides that the fertile octogenarian doctrine is a rebuttable presumption in determining the class of beneficiaries whose consent is necessary to modify or terminate a trust (Cal. Prob. Code §15406). Thus, California courts admit evidence of capacity to parent (e.g., age and physical condition) of the beneficiary (beneficiaries) and thereby are able to approve termination in cases involving little likelihood of additional offspring.

Note that California law differs from that of the Restatement (Third) of Trusts and Uniform Trust Code regarding the effect of a spendthrift provision on trust modification or termination. In California, when a trust validly restrains a beneficiary's interests, courts lack discretion to permit modification or termination of that trust in cases in which all the beneficiaries of an irrevocable trust consent (Cal. Prob. Code §15403(b)). But cf. California Probate Code §15409 (permitting a court to modify or terminate a trust provision because of changed circumstances, even if the trust has a restraint on transfer, if continuation of the trust would impair the trust purposes).

On judicial termination at the request of the beneficiaries when the trust purposes have been accomplished, see Bogert, ***supra,*** **at §1007; on judicial termination at the request of the beneficiaries when the trust purposes have not been accomplished, see** ***id.*** **at §1008.**

§15403. Conditions under which irrevocable trust may be modified or terminated if all beneficiaries consent

(a) Except as provided in subdivision (b), if all beneficiaries of an irrevocable trust consent, they may compel modification or termination of the trust upon petition to the court.

(b) If the continuance of the trust is necessary to carry out a material purpose of the trust, the trust cannot be modified or terminated unless the court, in its discretion, determines that the reason for doing so under the circumstances outweighs the interest in accomplishing a material purpose of the trust. Under this section the court does not have discretion to permit termination of a trust that is subject to a valid restraint on transfer of the beneficiary's interest as provided in Chapter 2 (commencing with Section 15300).

(Stats. 1990 (A.B. 759), ch. 79, §14, effective July 1, 1991.)

§15404. Modification or termination if settlor and all beneficiaries consent

(a) If the settlor and all beneficiaries of a trust consent, they may compel the modification or termination of the trust.

(b) If any beneficiary does not consent to the modification or termination of the trust, upon petition to the court, the other beneficiaries, with the consent of the settlor, may compel a modification or a partial termination of the trust if the interests of the beneficiaries who do not consent are not substantially impaired.

(c) If the trust provides for the disposition of principal to a class of persons described only as "heirs" or "next of kin" of the settlor, or using other words that describe the class of all persons who would take under the rules of intestacy, the court may limit the class of beneficiaries whose consent is needed to compel the modification or termination of the trust to the beneficiaries who are reasonably likely to take under the circumstances.

(Stats. 1990 (A.B. 759), ch. 79, §14, effective July 1, 1991.)

§15405. Authorization for appointment of guardian ad litem to represent beneficiary who lacks capacity

For the purposes of Sections 15403 [modification or termination of irrevocable trust by all beneficiaries] and 15404 [modification or termination of trust by settlor and all beneficiaries], the consent of a beneficiary who lacks legal capacity, including a minor, or who is an unascertained or unborn person may be given in proceedings before the court by a guardian ad litem, if it would be appropriate to do so. In determining whether to give consent, the guardian ad litem may rely on general family benefit accruing to living members of the beneficiary's family as a basis for approving a modification or termination of the trust.

(Stats. 1990 (A.B. 759), ch. 79, §14, effective July 1, 1991.)

§15406. Presumption of fertility is rebuttable in determining class of beneficiaries for consent purposes

In determining the class of beneficiaries whose consent is necessary to modify or terminate a trust pursuant to Section 15403 or 15404, the presumption of fertility is rebuttable.

(Stats. 1990 (A.B. 759), ch. 79, §14, effective July 1, 1991.)

§15408. Trust with an uneconomically low principal

(a) On petition by a trustee or beneficiary, if the court determines that the fair market value of the principal of a trust has become so low in relation to the cost of administration that continuation of the trust under its existing terms will defeat or substantially impair the accomplishment of its purposes, the court may, in its discretion and in a manner that conforms as nearly as possible to the intention of the settlor, order any of the following:

(1) Termination of the trust.

(2) Modification of the trust.

(3) Appointment of a new trustee.

(b) Notwithstanding subdivision (a), if the trust principal does not exceed twenty thousand dollars ($20,000) in value, the trustee has the power to terminate the trust.

(c) The existence of a trust provision restraining transfer of the beneficiary's interest does not prevent application of this section.

(Stats. 1990 (A.B. 759), ch. 79, §14, effective July 1, 1991.)

§15410. Disposition of property upon termination

At the termination of a trust, the trust property shall be disposed of as follows:

(a) In the case of a trust that is revoked by the settlor, as directed by the settlor.

(b) In the case of a trust that is terminated by the consent of the settlor and all beneficiaries, as agreed by the settlor and all beneficiaries.

(c) In any other case, as provided in the trust instrument or in a manner directed by the court that conforms as nearly as possible to the intention of the settlor as expressed in the trust instrument.

(d) If a trust is terminated by the trustee pursuant to subdivision (b) of Section 15408, the trust property may be distributed as determined by the trustee pursuant to the standard provided in subdivision (c) without the need for a court order. Where the trust instrument does not provide a manner of distribution at termination and the settlor's intent is not adequately expressed in the trust instrument, the trustee may distribute the trust property to the living beneficiaries on an actuarial basis.

(Stats. 1990 (A.B. 759), ch. 79, §14, effective July 1, 1991.)

§15800. Limits on the rights of a beneficiary of a revocable trust

Except to the extent that the trust instrument otherwise provides or where the joint action of the settlor and all beneficiaries is required, during the time that a trust is revocable and the person holding the power to revoke the trust is competent:

(a) The person holding the power to revoke, and not the beneficiary, has the rights afforded beneficiaries under this division.

(b) The duties of the trustee are owned to the person holding the power to revoke.

(Stats. 1990 (A.B. 759), ch. 79, §14, effective July 1, 1991.)

§15801. Consent by the beneficiary of a revocable trust

(a) In any case where the consent of a beneficiary may be given or is required to be given before an action may be taken, during the time that a trust is revocable and the person holding the power to revoke the trust is competent, the person holding the power to revoke, and not the beneficiary, has the power to consent or withhold consent.

(b) This section does not apply where the joint consent of the settlor and all beneficiaries is required by statute.

(Stats. 1990 (A.B. 759), ch. 79, §14, effective July 1, 1991.)

§15805. The Attorney General is subject to limitations on the rights of beneficiaries of revocable trusts

Notwithstanding any other provision of law, the Attorney General is subject to the limitations on the rights of beneficiaries of revocable trusts provided by Sections 15800 to 15802, inclusive.

(Stats. 1990 (A.B. 759), ch. 79, §14, effective July 1, 1991.)

IV. Judicial Power to Modify

A court can modify the terms of the trust upon the application of the settlor or one or more beneficiaries. Judicial modification of a trust is the doctrine of "equitable deviation." Courts generally have the power to alter *administrative* provisions of a trust where a circumstance arises that is unknown or unanticipated by the settlor, or where a change is necessary to assure that the trust accomplishes its purposes. Bogert, *supra*, at §§146, 994.

According to the general rule, although the court may modify administrative provisions of the trust, it may *not* modify *distributive* provisions. That is, the court may not introduce new beneficiaries, remove beneficiaries, or change the interests of the beneficiaries. *Id.* at §994. See Estate of Van Deusen, 182 P.2d 565 (Cal. 1947) (holding that an order modifying a distributive provision by allowing an invasion of corpus by the life beneficiaries without the consent of the residuary beneficiaries was error). Nonetheless, a court might approve a compromise agreement among the beneficiaries following litigation that changes the dispositive provisions, provided that the settlement agreement is fair and reasonable. *Van Deusen*, 182 P.2d 565.

The Restatement (Second) of Trusts §167 incorporated the traditional rule by providing for equitable deviation based on changed circumstances that were unknown or unanticipated by the settlor if "compliance would defeat or substantially impair the accomplishment of the purposes of the trust." Commentary explained that a court should not "permit or direct the trustee to deviate from the terms of the trust merely because such deviation would be more advantageous to the beneficiaries than a compliance with such direction." *Id.*, cmt. b. Commentators have criticized the harshness of the rule precluding judicial modification of distributive provisions:

> The Restatement (Second) reflects an outmoded view of the world, based on a sentiment that Adam Smith called "piety to the dead." The Restatement provision assumes that a settlor would not want a deviation if its only purpose were to make trust beneficiaries better off, notwithstanding that most trusts are set up for just that reason—to provide advantages for beneficiaries by way of tax savings, competent management, protection from creditors, and so forth. The trust provisions, created at a given time, presumably aim to advantage the beneficiaries under the circumstances as they existed at that time. No one can see how circumstances will change, but we can reasonably suppose that, whatever happens, settlors would rather hold to the beneficial purposes of their trust than to precise terms that have come to be inconsistent with those purposes, given subsequent events. Trust law needs modernizing in this respect. . . .

Dukeminier & Krier, *supra*, at 1327.

In response to such criticisms, the Restatement (Third) of Trusts §66 liberalizes the traditional rule to permit a court to modify an administrative *or* distributive provision or to direct or permit the trust to deviate from either an administrative *or* distributive provision in cases of unanticipated circumstances where modification or deviation would further the trust purposes. The Commentary suggests that the court may modify or permit deviation by the trustee of provisions governing the management and administration of the trust property (e.g., prohibitions on sale of properties or acquisition of certain investments), or defining the beneficial interests of the beneficiaries (prohibitions on invasion of principal or accumulation of income). *Id.* at §66, cmt. b. The court also may modify the terms so as to require termination. In this event, the court will distribute trust property in accordance with the trust purposes and the settlor's probable intention. *Id.*

Under Restatement (Third) of Trusts §66, it is not required that the situation constitute an emergency or jeopardize the trust purposes. *Id.* at §66, cmt. a. For the classic case permitting judicial modification in cases of emergencies, see Matter of Pulitzer, 249 N.Y.S. 87 (Surr. Ct. 1931), *aff'd mem.*, 260 N.Y.S. 975 (1932). See also Stewart v. Towse, 249 Cal. Rptr. 622 (Ct. App. 1988) (permitting modification to replace designated successor-trustee based on allegations that settlor had lost confidence in trustee because of perceived conflict of interest

and that continuation of trustee would defeat purpose of trust).

The Uniform Trust Code §412(a), similarly, has liberalized the equitable deviation doctrine to permit modification of administrative *or* distributive provisions. Some state statutes also permit modification of distributive provisions. California Probate Code §15409(a) provides that a court may modify either administrative or distributive provisions in cases of changed circumstances. Specifically, upon a petition by a trustee or beneficiary, the court may modify or even terminate the trust if, owing to circumstances unknown or unanticipated by the settlor, "the continuation of the trust under its terms would defeat or substantially impair the accomplishment of the purposes of the trust." In making its decision to modify or terminate the trust, the court must consider restraints on the beneficiary's interests (e.g., spendthrift restrictions); however, the presence of such a restriction does not preclude the court from modifying or terminating the trust. *Id.* at §15409(b). But cf. California Probate Code §15403(b) (providing that a court may not authorize modification or termination of an irrevocable trust "if the continuance of the trust is necessary to carry out a material purpose of the trust" upon consent of all the beneficiaries if the trust has a spendthrift restriction).

§15408. Court may order modification or termination of trust with uneconomically low principal

(a) On petition by a trustee or beneficiary, if the court determines that the fair market value of the principal of a trust has become so low in relation to the cost of administration that continuation of the trust under its existing terms will defeat or substantially impair the accomplishment of its purposes, the court may, in its discretion and in a manner that conforms as nearly as possible to the intention of the settlor, order any of the following:

(1) Termination of the trust.

(2) Modification of the trust.

(3) Appointment of a new trustee.

(b) Notwithstanding subdivision (a), if the trust principal does not exceed twenty thousand dollars ($20,000) in value, the trustee has the power to terminate the trust.

(c) The existence of a trust provision restraining transfer of the beneficiary's interest does not prevent application of this section.

(Stats. 1990 (A.B. 759), ch. 79, §14, effective July 1, 1991.)

§15409. Court may modify or terminate trust in changed circumstances if trust purposes would be impaired

(a) On petition by a trustee or beneficiary, the court may modify the administrative or dispositive provisions of the trust or terminate the trust if, owing to circumstances not known to the settlor and not anticipated by the settlor, the continuation of the trust under its terms would defeat or substantially impair the accomplishment of the purposes of the trust. In this case, if necessary to carry out the purposes of the trust, the court may order the trustee to do acts that are not authorized or are forbidden by the trust instrument.

(b) The court shall consider a trust provision restraining transfer of the beneficiary's interest as a factor in making its decision whether to modify or terminate the trust, but the court is not precluded from exercising its discretion to modify or terminate the trust solely because of a restraint on transfer.

(Stats. 1990 (A.B. 759), ch. 79, §14, effective July 1, 1991.)

§15411. Court may combine similar trusts in some circumstances

If the terms of two or more trusts are substantially similar, on petition by a trustee or beneficiary, the court, for good cause shown, may combine the trusts if the court determines that administration as a single trust will not defeat or substantially impair the accomplishment of the trust purposes or the interests of the beneficiaries.

(Stats. 1990, ch. 79 (A.B. 759), §14, effective July 1, 1991.)

§15412. Court may divide a trust into separate trusts in some circumstances

On petition by a trustee or beneficiary, the court, for good cause shown, may divide a trust into two or more separate trusts, if the court determines that dividing the trust will not defeat or substantially impair the accomplishment of the trust purposes or the interests of the beneficiaries.

(Stats. 1990, ch. 79 (A.B. 759), §14, effective July 1, 1991.)

XI
TRUSTEES

This chapter explores aspects of the fiduciary office, including the selection, appointment, and qualification of trustees; compensation and indemnification of trustees; and resignation and removal of trustees. The chapter then turns to the general standard of conduct imposed by the law on trustees as well as the trustees' duties, powers, and liabilities. Note that the term "fiduciary" refers to both trustees and personal representatives. This chapter addresses only trustees' responsibilities. For a discussion of the responsibilities of personal representatives, see Chapter XIV *infra*.

I. Generally

The settlor may name one trustee or several co-trustees. A trustee's acceptance generally is not essential to the validity of the trust or to the effectiveness of a conveyance in trust. That is, it is possible to create a trust without notice to, or the consent of, a trustee. Although a trustee is an essential element of a valid trust, a familiar maxim is that equity will not permit a trust to fail for want of a trustee. Therefore, if the trust instrument does not name a trustee, or the designated trustee cannot or will not act, the court will appoint a trustee. A trust might fail only if the testator has manifested an intention that the existence of the trust depended on administration by a *particular* trustee. Austin Wakeman Scott, Abridgement of the Law of Trusts §35, at 88 (1960) [hereinafter Scott]. See also Restatement (Third) of Trusts §31.

Courts have held that if the settlor has delivered the subject matter of the trust or a deed of transfer, a trust is validly created at the time of the conveyance, regardless of whether the named trustee has notice or disclaims (refuses to serve). Scott, *supra*, §35 at 89.

Capacity of a trustee refers to the designated person's capacity (1) to take title to the property, (2) to hold title to the property, and (3) to administer the trust property to the same capacity as the beneficial owner. See Restatement (Third) of Trusts §32. Any person who can take title to property may take title to property as a trustee. However, some persons who can take title and hold title cannot administer the trust. For example, minors cannot administer a trust because their contracts are subject to disaffirmance (i.e., are voidable). Also, special requirements may be applicable to nonresident trustees. Some state statutes forbid the appointment of nonresident trustees (or the appointment of nonresidents as executors or administrators). Other state statutes provide that a nonresident can act only with a resident trustee. Bogert, *supra*, at §132.

A trustee may be either an individual or a corporation. Frequently, banks and trust companies are corporations that are chartered to conduct business as trustees, subject to state requirements. Some settlors establish a trust in a different state and designate a foreign corporation as trustee. In such cases, state statutes frequently authorize foreign corporations to transact limited types of business in the state without qualifying to do business within the state. *Id.* See also Restatement (Third) of Trusts §33 ("A corporation has capacity to take and hold property in trust except as limited by law, and to administer trust property and act as trustee to the extent of the powers conferred upon it by law").

Most states that authorize a foreign corporation to administer testamentary trusts subject that foreign corporation to certain requirements. For example, some statutes require the foreign corporation to designate a state officer or other state resident as its agent for purposes of service of process within the state. Some statutes require the foreign corporation to file a bond or deposit cash or securities prior to administering the trust. Some states prohibit a foreign corporation from maintaining a branch in the state or from soliciting trust business within the state. The foreign corporation may have to obtain local letters of trusteeship. *Id.* (On the imposition of these requirements pursuant to California law, see the California Financial Code provisions *infra*.)

In 1999, California enacted California Probate Code §15604 to allow nonprofit charitable corporations to serve as a trustee. However, certain conditions must be met (the corporation must be incorporated in California; the articles authorize the corporation to accept appointments as a trustee; the corporation is exempt from income taxes for the preceding 3 years; the settlor consents to the appointment and the court determines that the trust is in the best interest of the settlor and that the appointment is in the best interest of the settlor and the trust estate). *Id.* at §15604a.

Today, an unincorporated association may serve as trustee if a given jurisdiction recognizes it as a legal entity for such purposes. See Restatement (Third) of Trusts §33(2) ("If a partnership, unincorporated association, or other entity has capacity to take and hold property for its own purposes, it has capacity to take, hold, and administer property in trust"). In contrast, at common law, an unincorporated association could not take or hold legal title to property for its own benefit or in trust for others. Scott, *supra*, §97 at 209. However, a trust would not fail in such cases because the court would appoint a new trustee. See, e.g., Wittmeier v. Heiligenstein, 139 N.E. 871 (Ill. 1923) (holding that a wife's trust to church, to pay her divorced husband $50 a month for his life plus his medical and funeral expenses, was invalid because an unincorporated association could not take as grantee; however, the inability of the trustee to take does not invalidate a deed where the settlor and beneficiary are both competent, and the property is of such a nature that it can be legally placed in trust).

A settlor may serve as trustee of an inter vivos trust that he or she created (as in the case of a trust created by a declaration). (For obvious reasons, a settlor cannot be a trustee of a testamentary trust that the settlor has created!) For a trust created by a declaration, delivery of the property is not required. The settlor merely must manifest an intention to hold the property in trust.

Also, a trust beneficiary can serve as trustee. However, the sole beneficiary may not be the sole trustee because of the merger doctrine. Note that merger does not result if one of several beneficiaries is one of the several trustees, if one of several beneficiaries is the sole trustee, if the sole beneficiary is one of several trustees, or if the group of beneficiaries is identical with the group of trustees. Scott, *supra*, §§99-99.5, at 210-212.

California statute (Cal. Prob. Code §§15600 et seq.) specifies the methods by which a trustee may accept the trust or a modification of the trust: (1) a signature on the trust instrument or on a separate written document, or (2) a knowing exercise of trust powers or performing trust duties. However, this provision is subject to an exception conferring power on a trustee to act in an emergency ("where there is an immediate risk of damage to the trust property") without accepting the trust provided that the "trustee" delivers a written rejection to the settlor or a beneficiary (if the settlor is dead or incompetent) within a reasonable time after acting (Cal. Prob. Code §15600(b)).

According to California law, a trustee may reject the trust provided that the declination is in writing (Cal. Prob. Code §15601(a)). A trustee who does not accept to act within a reasonable period of time is deemed to have rejected the office (Cal. Prob. Code §15601(b)). Declination of the office results in the trustee being excused from liability (Cal. Prob. Code §15601(c)).

The California Probate Code also provides for methods of filling vacancies in the office of trustee. California Probate Code §15643 defines the circumstances that constitute a vacancy. If a vacancy occurs in the office of a co-trustee, the court will not necessarily appoint a new trustee unless the trust instrument so requires (Cal. Prob. Code §15621).

In California, co-trustees must exercise their power *unanimously* unless the trust instrument provides otherwise (Cal. Prob. Code §15620). Note, however, that the Uniform Trust Code §703(a) relaxes the traditional rule ("Co-trustees who are unable to reach a unanimous decision may act by majority decision").

The California Probate Code also specifies the method of compensation of co-trustees (Cal. Prob. Code §15683) (see Section B *infra*) and the duties of co-trustees (Cal. Prob. Code §16013) (see Section IIB *infra*).

If the office of trustee becomes vacant, and the trust instrument fails to provide for a successor trustee or a method for appointing one, a court may appoint a new trustee. Bogert, *supra,* at §32. California law states that if a trust instrument provides a "practical method" of appointing a new trustee, that method will govern (Cal. Prob. Code §15660(b)). The court may appoint the original or lesser number of trustees as allowed in the trust instrument. (Cal. Prob. Code §15660(d)). Also, the court must give consideration to any person nominated as trustee by a beneficiary who has reached at least 14 years of age. *Id.*

§83. "Trust company," defined

"Trust company" means an entity that has qualified to engage in and conduct a trust business in this state.

(Stats. 1990 (A.B. 759), ch. 79, §14, effective July 1, 1991.)

§84. "Trustee," defined

"Trustee" includes an original, additional, or successor trustee, whether or not appointed or confirmed by a court.

(Stats. 1990 (A.B. 759), ch. 79, §14, effective July 1, 1991.)

§15600. Methods of acceptance by trustee

(a) The person named as trustee may accept the trust, or a modification of the trust, by one of the following methods:

(1) Signing the trust instrument or the trust instrument as modified, or signing a separate written acceptance.

(2) Knowingly exercising powers or performing duties under the trust instrument or the trust instrument as modified, except as provided in subdivision (b).

(b) In a case where there is an immediate risk of damage to the trust property, the person named as trustee may act to preserve the trust property without accepting the trust or a modification of the trust, if within a reasonable time after acting the person delivers a written rejection of the trust or the modification of the trust to the settlor or, if the settlor is dead or incompetent, to a beneficiary. This subdivision does not impose a duty on the person named as trustee to act.

(Stats. 1990, (A.B. 759), ch. 79, §14, effective July 1, 1991.)

§15600.5. Public guardian is trustee of last resort; reasonable inquiry required

The public guardian shall not be appointed as a trustee of any trust pursuant to subdivision (d) of Section 15660, unless the court finds, based on reasonable inquiry, that no other qualified person is willing to act as trustee.

(Stats. 1994, (A.B. 2725), ch. 472, §3)

§15601. Rejection of trust by trustee; trustee's liability

(a) A person named as trustee may in writing reject the trust or a modification of the trust.

(b) If the person named as trustee does not accept the trust or a modification of the trust by a method provided in subdivision (a) of Section 15600 within a reasonable time after learning of being named as trustee or of the modification, the person has rejected the trust or the modification.

(c) A person named as trustee who rejects the trust or a modification of the trust is not liable with respect to the rejected trust or modification.

(Stats. 1990, (A.B. 759) ch. 79, §14, effective July 1, 1991.)

§15604. Nonprofit charitable corporation may be appointed as trustee

(a) Notwithstanding any other provision of law, a nonprofit charitable corporation may be appointed as trustee of a trust created pursuant to this division, if all of the following conditions are met:

(1) The corporation is incorporated in this state.

(2) The articles of incorporation specifically authorize the corporation to accept appointments as trustee.

(3) For the three years prior to the filing of a petition under this section, the nonprofit charitable corporation has been exempt from payment of income taxes pursuant to Section 501(c)(3) of the Internal Revenue Code and has served as a private professional conservator in the state.

(4) The settlor or an existing trustee consents to the appointment of the nonprofit corporation as trustee or successor trustee, either in the petition or in a writing signed either before or after the petition is filed.

(5) The court determines the trust to be in the best interest of the settlor.

(6) The court determines that the appointment of the nonprofit corporation as trustee is in the best interest of the settlor and the trust estate.

(b) A petition for appointment of a nonprofit corporation as trustee under this section may be filed by any of the following:

(1) The settlor or the spouse of the settlor.

(2) The nonprofit charitable corporation.

(3) An existing trustee.

(c) The petition shall include in the caption the name of a responsible corporate officer who shall act for the corporation for purposes of this section. If, for any reason, the officer so named ceases to act as the responsible corporate officer for purposes of this section, the corporation shall file with the court a notice containing (1) the name of the successor responsible corporate officer and (2) the date the successor becomes the responsible corporate officer.

(d) The petition shall request that a trustee be appointed for the estate, shall specify the name, address, and telephone number of the proposed trustee and the name, address, and telephone number of the settlor or proposed settlor, and state the reasons why the appointment of the trustee is necessary.

(e) The petition shall set forth, so far as the information is known to the petitioner, the names and addresses of all persons entitled to notice of a conservatorship petition, as specified in subdivision (b) of Section 1821.

(f) Notice of the hearing on the petition shall be given in the same manner as provided in Sections 1822 and 1824.

(g) The trustee appointed by the court pursuant to this section shall do all of the following:

(1) File the required bond for the benefit of the trust estate in the same manner provided for conservators of the estate as set forth in Section 2320. This bond may not be waived, but the court may, in its discretion, permit the filing of a bond in an amount less than would otherwise be required under Section 2320.

(2) Comply with the requirements for registration and filing of annual statements pursuant to Article 4 (commencing with Section 2340) of Chapter 4 of Part 4 of Division 4.

(3) File with the court inventories and appraisals of the trust estate and present its accounts of the trust estate in the manner provided for conservators of the estate set forth in Chapter 7 (commencing with Section 2600) of Part 4 of Division 4.

(4) Be reimbursed for expenses and compensated as trustee in the manner provided for conservators of the estate as described in Chapter 8 (commencing with Section 2640) of Part 4 of Division 4. However, compensation as trustee appointed under this section shall be allowed only for services actually rendered.

(5) Be represented by counsel in all proceedings before the court. Any fee allowed for an attorney for the nonprofit charitable corporation shall be for services actually rendered.

(h) The trustee appointed by the court under this section may be removed by the court, or may resign in accordance with Chapter 9 (commencing with Section 2650) of Part 4 of Division 4. If the nonprofit charitable corporation resigns or is removed by the court, the settlor may appoint another person as successor trustee, or another nonprofit charitable corporation as trustee under this section.

(i) The trustee appointed by the court under this section is bound by the trust instrument created by the settlor, and shall be subject to the duties and responsibilities of a trustee as provided in this code.

(Stats. 1999, ch. 424 (S.B. 1090), §1. Amended by Stats. 2001, ch. 351 (A.B. 479), §2.)

§15620. Unanimity required in actions by cotrustees

Unless otherwise provided in the trust instrument, a power vested in two or more trustees may only be exercised by their unanimous action.

(Stats. 1990 (A.B. 759), ch. 79, §14, effective July 1, 1991.)

§15621. Vacancy of a cotrustee

Unless otherwise provided in the trust instrument, if a vacancy occurs in the office of a cotrustee, the remaining cotrustee or cotrustees may act for the trust as if they are the only trustees.

(Stats. 1990 (A.B. 759), ch. 79, §14, effective July 1, 1991.)

§15622. Temporary incapacity of a cotrustee

Unless otherwise provided in the trust instrument, if a cotrustee is unavailable to perform the duties of the cotrustee because of absence, illness, or other temporary incapacity, the remaining cotrustee or cotrustees may act for the trust, as if they are the only trustees, where necessary to accomplish the purposes of the trust or to avoid irreparable injury to the trust property.

(Stats. 1990 (A.B. 759), ch. 79, §14, effective July 1, 1991.)

§15683. Compensation of cotrustees

Unless the trust instrument otherwise provides or the trustees otherwise agree, if the trust has two or more trustees, the compensation shall be apportioned among the cotrustees according to the services rendered by them.

(Stats. 1990 (A.B. 759), ch. 79, §14, effective July 1, 1991.)

§16013. Duty with respect to cotrustees

If a trust has more than one trustee, each trustee has a duty to do the following:

(a) To participate in the administration of the trust.

(b) To take reasonable steps to prevent a cotrustee from committing a breach of trust or to compel a cotrustee to redress a breach of trust.

(Stats. 1990 (A.B. 759), ch. 79, §14, effective July 1, 1991.)

CALIFORNIA FINANCIAL CODE

§1503. Authorization of foreign corporations to exercise trust powers

No foreign corporation, other than a national banking association or a foreign (other state) state bank that is authorized to conduct a trust business in this state, shall have or exercise the powers of a trust company nor directly or indirectly transact or conduct in this state a trust business as defined in Section 106. However, a foreign corporation that is authorized by its articles to exercise trust powers may act as trustee for the following purposes:

(a) To deliver bonds and receive payments therefor.

(b) To deliver permanent bonds in exchange for temporary bonds of the same issue.

(c) To deliver refunding bonds in exchange for those of a prior issue or issues.

(d) To register bonds or to exchange registered bonds for coupon bonds or coupon bonds for registered bonds.

(e) To pay interest on the bonds, and take up and cancel coupons representing the interest payment.

(f) To redeem and cancel bonds when called for redemption or to pay and cancel bonds when due.

(g) To certify registered bonds for the purpose of exchanging registered bonds for coupon bonds.

A foreign corporation that is authorized by its articles to exercise trust powers may be appointed and may accept appointment and act as trustee under any mortgage, deed of trust, or other instrument securing bonds or other obligations issued or to be issued by any railroad corporation that owns a railroad operating in the State of California and extending into another state.

A foreign corporation exercising in this state the powers conferred by this section shall not establish or maintain directly or indirectly any branch office or agency in this state unless it has complied with all of the applicable provisions of Chapter 13.5 (commencing with Section 1700) or of Chapter 22 (commencing with Section 3800).

(Stats. 1951, ch. 364, p. 903, §1503. Amended by Stats. 1978, ch. 965, p. 2991, §107; Stats. 1979, ch. 373, p. 1289, §97; Stats. 1981, ch. 67, p. 124, §3, effective June 16, 1981; Stats. 1995 (A.B. 1482), ch. 480, §47, effective October 2, 1995.)

§1564. "Common trust funds," defined

(a) For purposes of this section, two or more trust companies shall be deemed to be affiliated if they are members of the same affiliated group, within the meaning of Section 1504 of the Internal Revenue Code.

(b) Any trust company may establish and administer common trust funds composed of property permitted by law for the investment of trust funds, for the purpose of furnishing investments to any one or more of the following: (1) itself, as fiduciary; (2) itself and others, as cofiduciaries; (3) any affiliated trust company including, without limitation, any foreign (other state) affiliated trust company, as fiduciary; and (4) any affiliated trust company including, without limitation, any foreign (other state) affiliated trust company and others, as cofiduciaries. Any trust company may as such fiduciary or cofiduciary invest funds which it lawfully holds for investment in interests in common trust funds administered by itself or by any affiliated trust company including, without limitation, any foreign (other state) affiliated trust company, if such investment is not prohibited by the instrument, judgment, decree, order, or statute creating or governing such fiduciary relationship, and if, in the case of cofiduciaries, the trust company procures the consent of its cofiduciaries to such investment.

(c) Each common trust fund established hereunder shall be treated as an entity separate and distinct from the fiduciary relationships participating therein. No fiduciary in administering a participating fiduciary relationship shall be required to make any apportionment or allocation between the principal and income of this relationship different from that made for the common trust fund. No participating fiduciary relationship, nor any person having an interest in that relationship, shall have or be deemed to have any ownership in any particular property of the common trust fund, but each participating fiduciary relationship shall have a proportionate undivided interest in the fund and its income, and the ownership of all property of the common trust fund shall be in the trustee of the fund.

(d) This section shall apply to fiduciary relationships now in existence or hereafter established, whether the same be revocable or irrevocable. The commissioner, at his or her direction, may make an examination of any common trust fund established hereunder at the times and to the extent as he or she may deem advisable. The provisions of the Corporate Securities Law shall not apply to the creation, administration, or termination of common trust funds, nor to participation therein.

(Stats. 1951, ch. 364, p. 908, §1564. Amended by Stats. 1978, ch. 965, p. 2992, §110.1; Stats. 1991 (A.B. 1693), ch. 419, §1; Stats. 1996 (A.B. 3351), ch. 1064, §211, effective July 1, 1997.)

§1750. Prohibited activities by foreign bank

(a) No foreign (other nation) bank shall transact business in this state except at an agency or branch office that it is licensed to maintain and at which it is permitted by this chapter to transact the business transacted.

(b) Subdivision (a) shall not be deemed to prohibit:

(1) Any foreign (other nation) bank that maintains a federal agency or federal branch in this state from

transacting at the federal agency or federal branch any business that it may be authorized to transact under applicable federal laws and regulations;

(2) Any foreign (other nation) bank from carrying on the activities described in subdivision (d) of Section 191 of the Corporations Code;

(3) Any foreign (other nation) bank that does not maintain an agency or branch office from making in this state loans secured by liens on real property located in this state; or

(4) Any foreign (other nation) bank that does not maintain an agency or branch office from transacting trust business as permitted under Section 1503.

(c) For purposes of subdivision (a), no foreign (other nation) bank shall be deemed to be transacting business in this state merely because a majority-owned subsidiary transacts business in this state.

(Stats. 1981, ch. 67, p. 133, §4, effective June 16, 1981. Amended by Stats. 1995, ch. 480 (A.B. 1482), §70, effective October 2, 1995.)

§3390. Certificate required for engaging in banking business; authorized acts

No person which has not received a certificate from the commissioner authorizing it to engage in the banking business shall solicit or receive deposits, issue certificates of deposit with or without provision for interest, make payments on check, or transact business in the way or manner of a commercial bank, industrial bank, or trust company.

(Stats. 1951, ch. 364, p. 964, §3390. Amended by Stats. 1973, ch. 963, p. 1845, §115; Stats. 1996 (A.B. 3351), ch. 1064, §402, effective July 1, 1997; Stats. 2000 (S.B. 2148), ch. 1015, §29, effective September 30, 2000.)

§3391. Prohibition on advertising without receipt of authorization certificate

No person which has not received a certificate from the commissioner authorizing it to engage in the banking business shall advertise that it is accepting deposits, and issuing notes or certificates therefor, or make use of any office sign, at the place where its business is transacted, having thereon any artificial or corporate name, or other words indicating that the place or office is the place or office of a bank or trust company, that deposits are received there or payments made on check, or any other form of banking business is transacted, nor shall any person make use of or circulate any letterheads, billheads, blank notes, blank receipts, certificates, or circulars, or any written or printed paper, whatever, having thereon any artificial or corporate name or other words indicating that the business is the business of a bank or trust company, or transact business in a way or manner as to lead the public to believe that its business is that of a bank or trust company, except to the extent expressly authorized by this division.

(Stats. 1951, ch. 364, p. 964, §3391. Amended by Stats. 1973, ch. 963, p. 1845, §116; Stats. 1996 (A.B. 3351), ch. 1064, §403, effective July 1, 1997; Stats. 2000 (S.B. 2148), ch. 1015, §30, effective September 30, 2000.)

§3392. Necessity to obtain authorization certificate to engage in business as bank or trust company

No person which has not received a certificate from the commissioner authorizing it to engage in the banking business shall transact business under any name or title which contains the word "bank" or "banker" or "banking" or "industrial bank" or "industrial loan company" or "investment and loan" or "savings bank" or "thrift and loan" or "trust" or "trustee" or "trust company" and which indicates that the business is the business of a bank or trust company. Any building and loan association or savings association having in its corporate name words not clearly indicating the nature of its business shall state, on all signs, letterheads, and advertising matter, "This is a building and loan association" or "This is a savings association" or words to that effect.

(Stats. 1951, ch. 364, p. 964, §3392. Amended by Stats. 1996 (A.B. 3351), ch. 1064, §404, effective July 1, 1997; Stats. 2000 (S.B. 2148), ch. 1015, §31, effective September 30, 2000.)

§3392.5. Exceptions to prohibitions on transacting business or performing activities in state

No provision of Section 3390, 3391, or 3392 prohibits any of the following from transacting any business or performing any activity if it is authorized by applicable law to transact the business or perform the activity and is not prohibited by any applicable law (other than Sections 3390, 3391, and 3392) from transacting the business or performing the activity:

(a) Any California state commercial bank, industrial bank, or trust company.

(b) Any national bank.

(c) Any insured foreign (other state) state bank.

(d) Any foreign (other state) state bank that is licensed by the commissioner under Article 4 (commencing with Section 3860) of Chapter 22 to maintain a facility (as defined in Section 3800) in this state.

(e) Any foreign (other nation) bank that is licensed by the commissioner under Chapter 13.5 (commencing with Section 1700) to maintain an office in this state.

(f) Any foreign (other nation) bank that maintains a federal agency (as defined in subdivision (g) of Section 1700) or federal branch (as defined in subdivision (h) of Section 1700) in this state.

(g) Any California state corporation that is incorporated for the purpose of engaging in, and that is authorized by the commissioner to engage in, business under Article 1 (commencing with Section 3500) of Chapter 19.

(h) Any corporation incorporated under Section 25A of the Federal Reserve Act (12 U.S.C. Sec. 612 et seq.).

(i) Any foreign corporation that is licensed by the commissioner under Article 1 (commencing with Section 3500) of Chapter 19 to maintain an office in this state and to transact at that office business under Article 1 (commencing with Section 3500) of Chapter 19.

(j) Any industrial bank that is organized under the laws of another state of the United States and is insured by the Federal Deposit Insurance Corporation.

(Stats. 1995 (A.B. 1482), ch. 480, §93, effective Oct. 2, 1995. Amended by Stats. 1996 (A.B. 3351), ch. 1064, §405, effective July 1, 1997; Stats. 2000 (S.B. 2148), ch. 1015, §32, effective September 30, 2000.)

§3538. Foreign corporation must make security deposits with state treasurer

Every foreign corporation, before receiving a license to transact business in this state, shall deposit with the State Treasurer of the State of California upon authorization of the commissioner, in trust as security for the depositors with and creditors of such corporation in this state, lawful money of the United States or securities of the kind and character described in Article 3 (commencing at Section 1540) of Chapter 12 of this division, of the value of one hundred thousand dollars ($100,000). Such foreign corporation so long as it shall continue solvent and comply with the laws of this state, may be permitted by the commissioner to collect the interest on the securities so deposited and from time to time to exchange such securities for others, and examine and compare such securities, as provided by said article.

(Stats. 1951, ch. 364, p. 973, §3538. Amended by Stats. 1963, ch. 2036, p. 4250, §22; Stats. 1996, ch. 1064 (A.B. 3351), effective July 1, 1997.)

A. Selection, Appointment, and Qualification

The settlor generally names a trustee. Sometimes, a settlor designates more than one trustee to act. By the terms of the trust, the settlor also can empower a third party to appoint a trustee.

According to California law, if the terms of the trust provide a method to appoint a trustee (or co-trustee) or name a particular person to fill a vacancy in the office of trustee, the vacancy may be filled only as specified in the trust instrument (Cal. Prob. Code §15660(b)).

Most trustees take the office without the need to be appointed by a court. See Restatement (Third) of Trusts §34(1) ("Except as required by statute, a trustee designated by or selected in accordance with the terms of a trust may act without being appointed or confirmed by an order of court"). For trustees who are appointed by a court (as in situations of a vacancy in the office), the court clerk must issue a "certificate" of trustee upon application by the trustee. This certificate is similar to letters issued to a personal representative that provide proof that the individual is qualified to act. Commentary following California Probate Code §15603. The certificate may be useful to assist the trustee in transferring property.

"Qualification" generally refers to the need for the trustee to take an oath and/or post a performance bond. Some states (but not California) require that the trustee take an oath swearing that he or she will faithfully carry out his or her duties. A bond affirms that the trustee will faithfully carry out his or her duties. The court generally sets the amount of the bond, payable by the trustee, based on the value of the trust corpus.

The Restatement (Third) of Trusts §34(3) specifies that "A trustee need not provide a performance bond except as required by statute, trust provision, or court order." California Probate Code §15602 requires a trustee to give

bond only in limited cases (i.e., if the trust instrument requires bond, if the court finds it necessary to protect the beneficiaries' interests, or if the court appoints a trustee who was not designated by the instrument) (§15602(a)(1), (2), (3)). The court has discretion in excusing the requirement of a bond (even if the trust instrument so provides) (§15602(a)(2), and reducing or increasing the amount (*id.*)). No bond is required of trust companies (even if the trust instrument so provides) (§15602(e)).

In Estate of Cibulk, 79 Cal. Rptr. 2d 168 (Ct. App. 1998), a husband (who was executor, testamentary trustee, and lifetime beneficiary of his wife's estate) sought to be excused from posting a trustee's bond. He filed waivers executed by the remainder beneficiaries. The appellate court held that the trial court erred in requiring the husband to post a bond, reasoning that he was the trustee appointed in the trust instrument, the trust instrument did not require bond, and waivers of the bond requirement had been executed by the adult beneficiaries and the guardian ad litem for the minor beneficiaries. The appellate court speculated that the trial court mistakenly believed that a guardian ad litem could only waive the bond requirement with court approval. "However, no beneficiary, whether minor or adult, has a fundamental right to require a trustee's bond." *Cibulk*, 79 Cal. Rptr. 2d at 169.

Former California Probate Code §1127 (repealed) required a bond from testamentary trustees appointed by the probate court to fill a vacancy. However, beneficiaries could waive the requirement if there were no creditors. See Estate of Shapiro, 181 P.2d 117 (Cal. Ct. App. 1947) (holding that beneficiaries could waive Probate Code requirement that a trustee appointed to fill a vacancy in a testamentary trust must give a bond before acting because the requirement is for the benefit of the creditors and beneficiaries and here there were no creditors). See also 60 Cal. Jur.3d Trusts §54.

If no person can be found who is qualified to act as trustee, the court may appoint a public official called a "public guardian" (Cal. Prob. Code §15660.5). A court requires that reasonable inquiry must be taken before a public guardian is appointed as a trustee. (Cal. Prob. Code §15600.5)

§300. Trust company may be appointed as personal representative

A trust company may be appointed to act as a personal representative, guardian or conservator of an estate, or trustee, in the same manner as an individual. A trust company may not be appointed guardian or conservator of the person of a ward or conservatee.

(Stats. 1990 (A.B. 759), ch. 79, §14, effective July 1, 1991.)

§301. Bond may be waived for corporate fiduciary

(a) A trust company appointed to act as a personal representative, or guardian or conservator of an estate, may not be required to give a bond.

(b) The liability of a trust company and the manner of its making of oaths and affidavits are governed by Article 3 (commencing with Section 1540) of Chapter 12 of Division 1 of, and Section 1587 of, the Financial Code.

(Stats. 1990 (A.B. 759), ch. 79, §14, effective July 1, 1991.)

§15602. Circumstances in which trustee is required to give bond

(a) A trustee is not required to give a bond to secure performance of the trustee's duties, unless any of the following circumstances occurs:

(1) A bond is required by the trust instrument.

(2) Notwithstanding a waiver of a bond in the trust instrument, a bond is found by the court to be necessary to protect the interests of beneficiaries or other persons having an interest in the trust.

(3) An individual who is not named as a trustee in the trust instrument is appointed as a trustee by the court.

(b) Notwithstanding paragraph (1) of subdivision (a), the court may excuse a requirement of a bond, reduce or increase the amount of a bond, release a surety, or permit the substitution of another bond with the same or different sureties. The court may not, however, excuse the requirement of a bond for an individual described in paragraph (3) of subdivision (a), except under compelling circumstances. For the purposes of this section, a request by all adult beneficiaries of a trust that bond be waived for an individual described in paragraph (3) of subdivision (a) for their trust is deemed to constitute a compelling circumstance.

(c) If a bond is required, it shall be filed or served and shall be in the amount and with sureties and liabilities ordered by the court.

(d) Except as otherwise provided in the trust instrument or ordered by the court, the cost of the bond shall be charged against the trust.

(e) A trust company may not be required to give a bond, notwithstanding a contrary provision in the trust instrument.
(Stats. 1990 (A.B. 759), ch. 79, §14, effective July 1, 1991. Amended by Stats. 2004 (A.B. 1883 ch. 75, §1.)

§15603. Certificate that trustee is duly appointed

On application by the trustee, the court clerk shall issue a certificate that the trustee is a duly appointed and acting trustee under the trust if the court file shows the incumbency of the trustee.
(Stats. 1990 (A.B. 759), ch. 79, §14, effective July 1, 1991.)

§15604. Appointment of nonprofit charitable corporation as trustee

(a) Notwithstanding any other provision of law, a nonprofit charitable corporation may be appointed as trustee of a trust created pursuant to this division, if all of the following conditions are met:

(1) The corporation is incorporated in this state.

(2) The articles of incorporation specifically authorize the corporation to accept appointments as trustee.

(3) For the three years prior to the filing of a petition under this section, the nonprofit charitable corporation has been exempt from payment of income taxes pursuant to Section 501(c)(3) of the Internal Revenue Code and has served as a private professional conservator in the state.

(4) The settlor or an existing trustee consents to the appointment of the nonprofit corporation as trustee or successor trustee, either in the petition or in a writing signed either before or after the petition is filed.

(5) The court determines the trust to be in the best interest of the settlor.

(6) The court determines that the appointment of the nonprofit corporation as trustee is in the best interest of the settlor and the trust estate.

(b) A petition for appointment of a nonprofit corporation as trustee under this section may be filed by any of the following:

(1) The settlor or the spouse of the settlor.

(2) The nonprofit charitable corporation.

(3) An existing trustee.

(c) The petition shall include in the caption the name of a responsible corporate officer who shall act for the corporation for purposes of this section. If, for any reason, the officer so named ceases to act as the responsible corporate officer for purposes of this section, the corporation shall file with the court a notice containing (1) the name of the successor responsible corporate officer and (2) the date the successor becomes the responsible corporate officer.

(d) The petition shall request that a trustee be appointed for the estate, shall specify the name, address, and telephone number of the proposed trustee and the name, address, and telephone number of the settlor or proposed settlor, and state the reasons why the appointment of the trustee is necessary.

(e) The petition shall set forth, so far as the information is known to the petitioner, the names and addresses of all persons entitled to notice of a conservatorship petition, as specified in subdivision (b) of Section 1821.

(f) Notice of the hearing on the petition shall be given in the same manner as provided in Sections 1822 and 1824.

(g) The trustee appointed by the court pursuant to this section shall do all of the following:

(1) File the required bond for the benefit of the trust estate in the same manner provided for conservators of the estate as set forth in Section 2320. This bond may not be waived, but the court may, in its discretion, permit the filing of a bond in an amount less than would otherwise be required under Section 2320.

(2) Comply with the requirements for registration and filing of annual statements pursuant to Article 4 (commencing with Section 2340) of Chapter 4 of Part 4 of Division 4.

(3) File with the court inventories and appraisals of the trust estate and present its accounts of the trust estate in the manner provided for conservators of the estate set forth in Chapter 7 (commencing with Section 2600) of Part 4 of Division 4.

(4) Be reimbursed for expenses and compensated as trustee in the manner provided for conservators of the estate as described in Chapter 8 (commencing with Section 2640) of Part 4 of Division 4. However, compensation as trustee appointed under this section shall be allowed only for services actually rendered.

(5) Be represented by counsel in all proceedings before the court. Any fee allowed for an attorney for the nonprofit charitable corporation shall be for services actually rendered.

(h) The trustee appointed by the court under this section may be removed by the court, or may resign in accordance with Chapter 9 (commencing with Section 2650) of Part 4 of Division 4. If the nonprofit charitable corporation resigns or is removed by the court, the settlor may appoint another person as successor trustee, or another nonprofit charitable corporation as trustee under this section.

(i) The trustee appointed by the court under this section is bound by the trust instrument created by the settlor, and shall be subject to the duties and responsibilities of a trustee as provided in this code.

(Stats. 1999 (S.B. 1090), ch. 424, §1. Amended by Stats. 2001 (A.B. 479), ch. 3x5, §2.)

§15660. Method of filling vacancy in office of trustee

(a) If the trust has no trustee or if the trust instrument requires a vacancy in the office of a cotrustee to be filled, the vacancy shall be filled as provided in this section.

(b) If the trust instrument provides a practical method of appointing a trustee or names the person to fill the vacancy, the vacancy shall be filled as provided in the trust instrument.

(c) If the vacancy in the office of trustee is not filled as provided in subdivision (b), the vacancy may be filled by a trust company that has agreed to accept the trust on agreement of all adult beneficiaries who are receiving or are entitled to receive income under the trust or to receive a distribution of principal if the trust were terminated at the time the agreement is made. If a beneficiary has a conservator, the conservator may agree to the successor trustee on behalf of the conservatee without obtaining court approval. Without limiting the power of the beneficiary to agree to the successor trustee, if the beneficiary has designated an attorney in fact who has the power under the power of attorney to agree to the successor trustee, the attorney in fact may agree to the successor trustee.

(d) If the vacancy in the office of trustee is not filled as provided in subdivision (b) or (c), on petition of any interested person or any person named as trustee in the trust instrument, the court may, in its discretion, appoint a trustee to fill the vacancy. If the trust provides for more than one trustee, the court may, in its discretion, appoint the original number or any lesser number of trustees. In selecting a trustee, the court shall give consideration to any nomination by the beneficiaries who are 14 years of age or older.

(Stats. 1990 (A.B. 759), ch. 79, §14, effective July 1, 1991. Amended by Stats. 1992, (A.B. 2975), ch. 871, §17.)

§15660.5. Appointment of public guardian as trustee

The public guardian shall not be appointed as a trustee of any trust pursuant to subdivision (d) of Section 15660, unless the court finds, based on reasonable inquiry, that no other qualified person is willing to act as trustee.

(Stats. 1994 (A.B. 2725), ch. 472, §3.)

§17200. Purposes of petitions by trustee or beneficiary, includes appointment, removal, resignation

(a) Except as provided in Section 15800, a trustee or beneficiary of a trust may petition the court under this chapter concerning the internal affairs of the trust or to determine the existence of the trust.

(b) Proceedings concerning the internal affairs of a trust include, but are not limited to, proceedings for any of the following purposes:

(1) Determining questions of construction of a trust instrument.

(2) Determining the existence or nonexistence of any immunity, power, privilege, duty, or right.

(3) Determining the validity of a trust provision.

(4) Ascertaining beneficiaries and determining to whom property shall pass or be delivered upon final or partial termination of the trust, to the extent the determination is not made by the trust instrument.

(5) Settling the accounts and passing upon the acts of the trustee, including the exercise of discretionary powers.

(6) Instructing the trustee.

(7) Compelling the trustee to report information about the trust or account to the beneficiary, if (A) the trustee has failed to submit a requested report or account within 60 days after written request of the beneficiary and (B) no report or account has been made within six months preceding the request.

(8) Granting powers to the trustee.

(9) Fixing or allowing payment of the trustee's compensation or reviewing the reasonableness of the trustee's compensation.

(10) Appointing or removing a trustee.

(11) Accepting the resignation of a trustee.

(12) Compelling redress of a breach of the trust by any available remedy.

(13) Approving or directing the modification or termination of the trust.

(14) Approving or directing the combination or division of trusts.

(15) Amending or conforming the trust instrument in the manner required to qualify a decedent's estate for the charitable estate tax deduction under federal law, including the addition of mandatory governing instrument requirements for a charitable remainder trust as required by final regulations and rulings of the United States Internal Revenue Service.

(16) Authorizing or directing transfer of a trust or trust property to or from another jurisdiction.

(17) Directing transfer of a testamentary trust subject to continuing court jurisdiction from one county to another.

(18) Approving removal of a testamentary trust from continuing court jurisdiction.

(19) Reforming or excusing compliance with the governing instrument of an organization pursuant to Section 16105.

(20) Determining the liability of the trust for any debts of a deceased settlor. However, nothing in this paragraph shall provide standing to bring an action concerning the internal affairs of the trust to a person whose only claim to the assets of the decedent is as a creditor.

(21) Determining petitions filed pursuant to Section 15687 and reviewing the reasonableness of compensation for legal services authorized under that section. In determining the reasonableness of compensation under this paragraph, the court may consider, together with all other relevant circumstances, whether prior approval was obtained pursuant to Section 15687.

(22) If a member of the State Bar of California has transferred the economic interest of his or her practice to a trustee and if the member is a deceased member under Section 9764, a petition may be brought to appoint a practice administrator. The procedures, including, but not limited to, notice requirements, that apply to the appointment of a practice administrator for a deceased member shall apply to the petition brought under this section.

(23) If a member of the State Bar of California has transferred the economic interest of his or her practice to a trustee and if the member is a disabled member under Section 2468, a petition may be brought to appoint a practice administrator. The procedures, including, but not limited to, notice requirements, that apply to the appointment of a practice administrator for a disabled member shall apply to the petition brought under this section.

(c) The court may, on its own moption, set and give notice of an order to show cause why a trustee should not be removed for failing to register in the Statewide Registry under Section 2850.

(Stats. 1990 (A.B. 759), ch. 79, §14, effective July 1, 1991. Amended by Stats. 1991 (S.B. 727), ch. 992, §1; Stats. 1993 (A.B. 21), ch. 293, §7; Stats. 1996 (A.B. 2751), ch. 862, §41; Stats. 1997 (A.B. 1172), ch. 724, §27; Stats. 1998 (A.B. 2069), ch. 682, §13; Stats. 1999 (A.B. 239), ch. 175, §5; Stats. 2003 (S.B. 294) ch 629, §8.)

B. Compensation and Indemnification of Trustees

Trustees are entitled to compensation for their services. In early English law (followed by some American jurisdictions), trustees were expected to serve without compensation unless the terms of the trust provided otherwise. That rule has been changed in all states either by statute or case law. Scott, *supra,* §242 at 513. The amount of the trustee's compensation is fixed either by the terms of the trust instrument, by contract between settlor and trustee, by statute, or by judicial action. Bogert, *supra*, at §975. Trustees may agree to waive compensation.

Most states have statutes that govern the trustee's compensation in cases in which the settlor has not provided for compensation. There are three types of trustee compensation statutes. *Id.* The most common authorizes judicial discretion in providing "reasonable compensation." (The trustee requests a specific amount, and the court determines whether the amount is reasonable.) The second type of statute provides an entitlement to compensation, authorizing compensation from the trust estate without prior court authorization but subject to judicial review upon petition of an interested person. The third basic type of statute sets a fee schedule. *Id.*

The trend is to provide trustees with "reasonable compensation." See Uniform Probate Code §3-719) (personal representative is entitled to "reasonable compensation for his services"); Restatement (Third) of Trusts §38(1) ("A trustee is entitled to reasonable compensation out of the trust estate for services as trustee, unless the terms of the trust provide otherwise or the trustee agrees to forgo compensation"); Uniform Trust Code §708 (trustee is entitled to "compensation that is reasonable under the circumstances" if the terms of the trust do not specify the amount of compensation).

California law follows this trend. See, e.g., Cal. Prob. Code §15681 (if the trust instrument does not specify compensation, the trustee is "entitled to reasonable compensation under the circumstances"). A public guardian who is appointed as a trustee also is entitled to

compensation that is "just and reasonable" (Cal. Prob. Code. §15688).

According to California law, if the trust instrument provides for compensation, the court has discretion to deviate from the stated amount. Statutory guidelines set forth the situations permitting deviation: (1) if the duties of the trustee differ substantially from those contemplated at creation of the trust, (2) the compensation is inequitable or unreasonable, or (3) other extraordinary circumstances call for equitable relief (Cal. Prob. Code §15680(b)).

California Rules of Court, Rule 7. 756 *(infra)*, provides some guidelines to a court in determining the reasonableness of a trustee's compensation. The court may consider such factors as (among others): the complexity and skill of the services rendered, the success of the trustee's administration, the gross income of the trust estate, and the custom in the community. The list is not intended to be exclusive.

If a trust has more than one trustee, the compensation is apportioned among them according to their services (Cal. Prob. Code §15683). Note that, in California, trustees generally receive compensation without judicial approval, unlike personal representatives. However, if a trustee gives himself or herself excessive compensation, this act can be a basis for removal (Cal. Prob. Code §15642(b)(5)). For discussion of removal of trustees, see Section D *infra*.

California statute limits the amount of compensation of a trustee who serves in the dual capacity as trustee and attorney (Cal. Prob. Code §15687(f)). The trustee may receive either the compensation provided by statute for trustees or compensation for legal services performed for the trustee. Certain relatives of the trustee (e.g., parent, child, sibling, spouse) shall not receive compensation for legal services performed for the trustee. An exception to the restrictions is if the trustee is related by blood or marriage to, or is a cohabitant with, the settlor (§15687(c)).

At common law, although trustees were not allowed compensation for their services (unless the trust instrument so provided), they were allowed indemnity (reimbursement) for expenses they properly incurred. Scott, *supra*, §244 at 522. Today, a trustee can be reimbursed from the trust property for expenses that are necessary for carrying out the purposes of the trust. See Restatement (Third) of Trusts §38(2) ("A trustee is entitled to indemnity out of the trust estate for expenses properly incurred in the administration of the trust").

Similarly, in California, a trustee is entitled to reimbursement for "expenditures that were properly incurred in the administration of the trust" (Cal. Prob. Code §15684). The trustee may obtain reimbursement even for expenditures that were not properly incurred in the administration of the trust, to the extent that such expenditures benefited the trust. (Cal. Prob. Code §15684.)

§15680. Trustee's compensation; exercise of judicial discretion; judicial authorization for variance

(a) Subject to subdivision (b), if the trust instrument provides for the trustee's compensation, the trustee is entitled to be compensated in accordance with the trust instrument.

(b) Upon proper showing, the court may fix or allow greater or lesser compensation than could be allowed under the terms of the trust in any of the following circumstances:

(1) Where the duties of the trustee are substantially different from those contemplated when the trust was created.

(2) Where the compensation in accordance with the terms of the trust would be inequitable or unreasonably low or high.

(3) In extraordinary circumstances calling for equitable relief.

(c) An order fixing or allowing greater or lesser compensation under subdivision (b) applies only prospectively to actions taken in administration of the trust after the order is made.

(Stats. 1990 (A.B. 759), ch. 79, §14, effective July 1, 1991.)

§15681. "Reasonable compensation" if trust fails to specify

If the trust instrument does not specify the trustee's compensation, the trustee is entitled to reasonable compensation under the circumstances.

(Stats. 1990 (A.B. 759), ch. 79, §14, effective July 1, 1991.)

§15682. Court may fix periodic compensation

The court may fix an amount of periodic compensation under Sections 15680 and 15681 to continue for as long as the court determines is proper.

(Stats. 1990 (A.B. 759), ch. 79, §14, effective July 1, 1991.)

§15683. Apportionment among cotrustees

Unless the trust instrument otherwise provides or the trustees otherwise agree, if the trust has two or more trustees, the compensation shall be apportioned among the cotrustees according to the services rendered by them.

(Stats. 1990 (A.B. 759), ch. 79, §14, effective July 1, 1991.)

§15684. Reimbursement for expenditures

A trustee is entitled to the repayment out of the trust property for the following:

(a) Expenditures that were properly incurred in the administration of the trust.

(b) To the extent that they benefited the trust, expenditures that were not properly incurred in the administration of the trust.

(Stats. 1990 (A.B. 759), ch. 79, §14, effective July 1, 1991.)

§15685. Trustee may impose lien on trust property

The trustee has an equitable lien on the trust property as against the beneficiary in the amount of advances, with any interest, made for the protection of the trust, and for expenses, losses, and liabilities sustained in the administration of the trust or because of ownership or control of any trust property.

(Stats. 1990, ch. 79 (A.B. 759), §14, effective July 1, 1991.)

§15686. Trustee's fee includes the following

(a) As used in this section, "trustee's fee" includes, but is not limited to, the trustee's periodic base fee, rate of percentage compensation, minimum fee, hourly rate, and transaction charge, but does not include fees for extraordinary services.

(b) A trustee may not charge an increased trustee's fee for administration of a particular trust unless the trustee first gives at least 60 days' written notice of that increased fee to all of the following persons:

(1) Each beneficiary who is entitled to an account under Section 16062.

(2) Each beneficiary who was given the last preceding account.

(3) Each beneficiary who has made a written request to the trustee for notice of an increased trustee's fee and has given an address for receiving notice by mail.

(c) If a beneficiary files a petition under Section 17200 for review of the increased trustee's fee or for removal of the trustee and serves a copy of the petition on the trustee before the expiration of the 60-day period, the increased trustee's fee does not take effect as to that trust until otherwise ordered by the court or the petition is dismissed.

(Stats. 1990 (A.B. 759), ch. 79, §14, effective July 1, 1991. Amended by Stats. 1992 (S.B. 1496), ch. 178, §43.2.)

§15687. Restrictions on dual compensation for attorney acting as trustee

(a) Notwithstanding any provision of a trust to the contrary, a trustee who is an attorney may receive only

(1) the trustee's compensation provided in the trust or otherwise provided in this article or

(2) compensation for legal services performed for the trustee, unless the trustee obtains approval for the right to dual compensation as provided in subdivision (d).

(b) No parent, child, sibling, or spouse of a person who is a trustee, and no law partnership or corporation whose partner, shareholder, or employee is serving as a trustee shall receive any compensation for legal services performed for the trustee unless the trustee waives trustee compensation or unless the trustee obtains approval for the right to dual compensation as provided in subdivision (d).

(c) This section shall not apply if the trustee is related by blood or marriage to, or is a cohabitant with, the settlor.

(d) After full disclosure of the nature of the compensation and relationship of the trustee to all persons receiving compensation under this section, the trustee may obtain approval for dual compensation by either of the following:

(1) An order pursuant to paragraph (21) of subdivision (b) of Section 17200.

(2) Giving 30 days' advance written notice to the persons entitled to notice under Section 17203. Within that 30-day period, any person entitled to notice may object to the proposed action by written notice to the trustee or by filing a petition pursuant to paragraph (21) of subdivision (b) of Section 17200. If the trustee receives this objection during that 30-day period and if the trustee wishes dual compensation, the trustee shall file a petition for approval pursuant to paragraph (21) of subdivision (b) of Section 17200.

(e) Any waiver of the requirements of this section is against public policy and shall be void.

(f) This section applies to services rendered on or after January 1, 1994.

(Stats. 1993 (A.B. 21), ch. 293, §6.3. Amended by Stats. 1995 (A.B. 1466), ch. 730, §10.)

§15688. Compensation of public guardian who is appointed as trustee

Notwithstanding any other provision of this article and the terms of the trust, a public guardian who is appointed as a trustee of a trust pursuant to Section 15660.5 shall be paid from the trust property for all of the following:

(a) Reasonable expenses incurred in the administration of the trust.

(b) Compensation for services of the public guardian and the attorney of the public guardian, and for the filing and processing services of the clerk of the court in the amount the court determines is just and reasonable.

(c) An annual bond fee in the amount of twenty-five dollars ($25) plus one- fourth of 1 percent of the amount of the trust assets greater than ten thousand dollars ($10,000). The amount charged shall be deposited in the county treasury.

(Stats. 1997 (B.S. 696), ch. 93, §3. Amended by Stats. 2002 (S.B. 1316), ch. 784, §581.)

§16243. Trustee has power to pay trust expenses, including reasonable compensation

The trustee has the power to pay taxes, assessments, reasonable compensation of the trustee and of employees and agents of the trust, and other expenses incurred in the collection, care, administration, and protection of the trust.

(Stats. 1990 (A.B. 759), ch. 79, §14, effective July 1, 1991.)

CALIFORNIA RULES OF COURT

Rule 7.756. Compensation of trustees

In determining or approving compensation of a trustee, the court may consider, among other factors, the following:

(1) The gross income of the trust estate;

(2) The success or failure of the trustee's administration;

(3) Any unusual skill, expertise, or experience brought to the trustee's work;

(4) The fidelity or disloyalty shown by the trustee;

(5) The amount of risk and responsibility assumed by the trustee;

(6) The time spent in the performance of the trustee's duties;

(7) The custom in the community where the court is located as to compensation authorized by settlors, as to compensation allowed by the court, or as to charges of corporate trustees for trusts of similar size and complexity; and

(8) Whether the work performed was routine, or required more than ordinary skill or judgment.

(Adopted, effective January 1, 2003.)

C. Resignation and Removal

After a person agrees to serve as trustee, sometimes that trustee may wish to resign. "[I]f the trustee has once accepted the trust, he cannot relieve himself of his duties under the trust, unless he is permitted to resign." Scott, *supra*, §106 at 219. However, the trustee can only resign in accordance with the terms of the trust instrument, or by permission of court or consent of the beneficiaries. Restatement (Third) of Trusts §36. The trust instrument may permit the trustee to resign without the need for judicial proceedings (such as by notice to, or with consent of, the beneficiaries).

Note that resignation does not relieve the trustee from liability for breaches of trust that were committed before the resignation became effective. *Id.*, §36 cmt. d.

California law specifies the methods by which a trustee who has accepted the trust may resign (Cal. Prob. Code §15640). A trustee may resign in a method authorized by the trust instrument (Cal. Prob. Code §15640(a)). If the trust is revocable, a trustee may resign with the consent of the party holding the power to revoke (Cal. Prob. Code §15640(b)). If the trust is irrevocable, a trustee may resign with the consent of all adult beneficiaries who are receiving or have the right to receive trust income or (were the trust to terminate at the time of consent) have a right to principal (Cal. Prob. Code §15640(c)). Finally, a trustee may resign with judicial permission (Cal. Prob. Code §15640(d)).

A trustee also may be removed from office. Absent statutorily enumerated grounds, the issue of removal is in the discretion of the court. The issue is whether the trustee's continuance in office would be detrimental to the trust.

California law specifies the grounds for judicial removal of trustees (i.e., misconduct such as a breach of trust, insolvency or unfitness to administer the trust, hostility among the co-trustees that interferes with the administration of the trust, failure to act, excessive compensation, and status as a disqualified transferee) (Cal. Prob. Code §15642). The trustee may be removed by a settlor, co-trustee, or beneficiary; the court on its own motion; or in accordance with the trust

instrument (Cal. Prob. Code §15642(a)). Courts are reluctant to remove trustees on grounds that were known to the settlor and existed at the time of the trust creation. In Estate v. Gilliland, 140 Cal. Rptr. 795 (Ct. App. 1977), a settlor of a testamentary trust appointed a shareholder and president of a land development corporation as trustee, knowing that a conflict of interest might exist because the trust held notes of the land development corporation. The trustee, however, committed no actual dishonesty or misconduct. Upon an action brought by the beneficiaries, the court held that once the settlor named a trustee, fully aware of possible conflicts of interest posed by the appointment, a court will remove such a trustee only rarely and will never remove him for a potential conflict of interest but only for demonstrated abuse of power that is detrimental to the trust.

Friction between the trustees or between the trustee and beneficiary generally is insufficient to justify removal of the trustee. See, e.g., In re Estate of Beichner, 247 A.2d 779 (Pa. 1968) (holding that hostility displayed toward the trustee was insufficient to remove the trustee). However, as in McDonald v. McDonald, 9 So. 195 (Ala. 1891), removal may be justified if the trustee's continuance would be detrimental to the interests of the trust.

The court has authority to compel the trustee whose removal is sought to surrender the property pending the decision on removal (Cal. Prob. Code §15642(c)). A trustee must receive notice of a removal proceeding in order to defend himself or herself (Cal. Prob. Code §17203).

§15640. Methods of resignation by trustee

A trustee who has accepted the trust may resign only by one of the following methods:

(a) As provided in the trust instrument.

(b) In the case of a revocable trust, with the consent of the person holding the power to revoke the trust.

(c) In the case of a trust that is not revocable, with the consent of all adult beneficiaries who are receiving or are entitled to receive income under the trust or to receive a distribution of principal if the trust were terminated at the time consent is sought. If a beneficiary has a conservator, the conservator may consent to the trustee's resignation on behalf of the conservatee without obtaining court approval. Without limiting the power of the beneficiary to consent to the trustee's resignation, if the beneficiary has designated an attorney in fact who has the power under the power of attorney to consent to the trustee's resignation, the attorney in fact may consent to the resignation.

(d) Pursuant to a court order obtained on petition by the trustee under Section 17200. The court shall accept the trustee's resignation and may make any orders necessary for the preservation of the trust property, including the appointment of a receiver or a temporary trustee.

(Stats. 1990 (A.B. 759), ch. 79, §14, effective July 1, 1991.)

§15641. Liability of a trustee who resigns

The liability for acts or omissions of a resigning trustee or of the sureties on the trustee's bond, if any, is not released or affected in any manner by the trustee's resignation.

(Stats. 1990 (A.B. 759), ch. 79, §14, effective July 1, 1991.)

§15642. Grounds for removal of trustee

(a) A trustee may be removed in accordance with the trust instrument, by the court on its own motion, or on petition of a settlor, cotrustee, or beneficiary under Section 17200.

(b) The grounds for removal of a trustee by the court include the following:

(1) Where the trustee has committed a breach of the trust.

(2) Where the trustee is insolvent or otherwise unfit to administer the trust.

(3) Where hostility or lack of cooperation among cotrustees impairs the administration of the trust.

(4) Where the trustee fails or declines to act.

(5) Where the trustee's compensation is excessive under the circumstances.

(6) Where the sole trustee is a person described in subdivision (a) of Section 21350, whether or not the person is the transferee of a donative transfer by the transferor, unless, based upon any evidence of the intent of the settlor and all other facts and circumstances, which shall be made known to the court, the court finds that it is consistent with the settlor's intent that the trustee continue to serve and that this intent was not the product of fraud, menace, duress, or undue influence. Any waiver by the settlor of this provision is against public policy and shall be void. This paragraph shall not apply to instruments that became irrevocable on or before January 1, 1994. This paragraph shall not apply if any of the following conditions are met:

(A) The settlor is related by blood or marriage to, or is a cohabitant with, any one or more of the trustees, the person who drafted or transcribed the instrument, or the person who caused the instrument to be transcribed.

(B) The instrument is reviewed by an independent attorney who (1) counsels the settlor about the nature of his or her intended trustee designation and (2) signs and delivers to the settlor and the designated trustee a certificate in substantially the following form:

CERTIFICATE OF INDEPENDENT REVIEW

I, ______________________________, have reviewed
(attorney's name)

__________________ and have counseled my client,
(name of instrument)

__________________, fully and privately on the
(name of client)

nature and legal effect of the designation as trustee of

____
(name of trustee)

contained in such instrument. I am so disassociated from the interest of the person named as trustee as to be in a position to advise my client impartially and confidentially as to the consequences of the designation. On the basis of this counsel, I conclude that the designation of a person who would otherwise be subject to removal under paragraph (6) of subdivision (b) of Section 15642 of the Probate Code is clearly the settlor's intent and such intent is not the product of fraud, menace, duress, or undue influence.

______________________________ ____________
(Name of Attorney) (Date)

This independent review and certification may occur either before or after the instrument has been executed, and if it occurs after the date of execution, the named trustee shall not be subject to removal under this paragraph. Any attorney whose written engagement signed by the client is expressly limited to the preparation of a certificate under this subdivision, including the prior counseling, shall not be considered to otherwise represent the client.

(C) After full disclosure of the relationships of the persons involved, the instrument is approved pursuant to an order under Article 10 (commencing with Section 2580) of Chapter 6 of Part 4 of Division 4.

(7) If, as determined under Part 17 (commencing with Section 810) of Division 2, the trustee is substantially unable to manage the trust's financial resources or is otherwise substantially unable to execute properly the duties of the office. When the trustee holds the power to revoke the trust, substantial inability to manage the trust's financial resources or otherwise execute properly the duties of the office may not be proved solely by isolated incidents of negligence or improvidence.

(8) If the trustee is substantially unable to resist fraud or undue influence. When the trustee holds the power to revoke the trust, substantial inability to resist fraud or undue influence may not be proved solely by isolated incidents of negligence or improvidence.

(9) For other good cause.

(c) If, pursuant to paragraph (6) of subdivision (b), the court finds that the designation of the trustee was not consistent with the intent of the settlor or was the product of fraud, menace, duress, or undue influence, the person being removed as trustee shall bear all costs of the proceeding, including reasonable attorney's fees.

(d) If the court finds that the petition for removal of the trustee was filed in bad faith and that removal would be contrary to the settlor's intent, the court may order that the person or persons seeking the removal of the trustee bear all or any part of the costs of the proceeding, including reasonable attorney's fees.

(e) If it appears to the court that trust property or the interests of a beneficiary may suffer loss or injury pending a decision on a petition for removal of a trustee and any appellate review, the court may, on its own motion or on petition of a cotrustee or beneficiary, compel the trustee whose removal is sought to surrender trust property to a cotrustee or to a receiver or temporary trustee. The court may also suspend the powers of the trustee to the extent the court deems necessary.(f) For purposes of this section, the term "related by blood or marriage" shall include persons within the seventh degree.

(Stats. 1990 (A.B. 759), ch. 79, §14, effective July 1, 1991. Amended by Stats. 1993 (A.B. 21), ch. 293, §6; Stats. 1995 (A.B. 1466), ch. 730, §9; Stats. 2006 (A.B. 2042), ch. 84, §1.)

§15643. Circumstances of vacancies in office of trustee

There is a vacancy in the office of trustee in any of the following circumstances:

(a) The person named as trustee rejects the trust.

(b) The person named as trustee cannot be identified or does not exist.

(c) The trustee resigns or is removed.

(d) The trustee dies.

(e) A conservator or guardian of the person or estate of an individual trustee is appointed.

(f) The trustee files a petition for adjudication of bankruptcy or for approval of an arrangement, composition, or other extension under the federal Bankruptcy Code, or a petition filed against the trustee for any of these purposes is approved.

(g) A trust company's charter is revoked or powers are suspended, if the revocation or suspension is to be in effect for a period of 30 days or more.

(h) A receiver is appointed for a trust company if the appointment is not vacated within a period of 30 days.
(Stats. 1990 (A.B. 759), ch. 79, §14, effective July 1, 1991.)

§15644. Former trustee shall deliver property to successor trustee

When a vacancy has occurred in the office of trustee, the former trustee who holds property of the trust shall deliver the trust property to the successor trustee or a person appointed by the court to receive the property and remains responsible for the trust property until it is delivered. A trustee who has resigned or is removed has the powers reasonably necessary under the circumstances to preserve the trust property until it is delivered to the successor trustee and to perform actions necessary to complete the resigning or removed trustee's administration of the trust.
(Stats. 1990 (A.B. 759), ch. 79, §14, effective July 1, 1991.)

§15645. Trustee's refusal to transfer administration of trust

If the trustee of a trust that is not revocable has refused to transfer administration of the trust to a successor trust company on request of the beneficiaries described in subdivision (c) of Section 15640 and the court in subsequent proceedings under Section 17200 makes an order removing the existing trustee and appointing a trust company as successor trustee, the court may, in its discretion, award costs and reasonable attorney's fees incurred by the petitioner in the proceeding to be paid by the trustee or from the trust as ordered by the court.
(Stats. 1990 (A.B. 759), ch. 79, §14, effective July 1, 1991.)

§17203. Notice for trust proceedings

(a) At least 30 days before the time set for the hearing on the petition, the petitioner shall cause notice of hearing to be mailed to all of the following persons:

(1) All trustees.

(2) All beneficiaries, subject to Chapter 2 (commencing with Section 15800) of Part 3.

(3) The Attorney General, if the petition relates to a charitable trust subject to the jurisdiction of the Attorney General.

(b) At least 30 days before the time set for hearing on the petition, the petitioner shall cause notice of the hearing and a copy of the petition to be served in the manner provided in Chapter 4 (commencing with Section 413.10) of Title 5 of Part 2 of the Code of Civil Procedure on any person, other than a trustee or beneficiary, whose right, title, or interest would be affected by the petition and who does not receive notice pursuant to subdivision (a). The court may not shorten the time for giving notice under this subdivision.

(c) If a person to whom notice otherwise would be given has been deceased for at least 40 days, and no personal representative has been appointed for the estate of that person, and the deceased person's right, title, or interest has not passed to any other person pursuant to Division 8 (commencing with Section 13000) or otherwise, notice may instead be given to the following persons:

(1) Each heir and devisee of the decedent, and all persons named as executors of the will of the decedent, so far as known to the petitioner.

(2) Each person serving as guardian or conservator of the decedent at the time of the decedent's death, so far as known to the petitioner.

(Stats. 1990 (A.B. 759), ch. 79, §14, effective July 1, 1991. Amended by Stats. 1992 (A.B. 2974), ch. 871, §20; Stats. 1994 (A.B. 3686), ch. 806, §39; Stats. 1996 (A.B. 2751), ch. 862, §45; Stats. 1997 (A.B. 1172), ch. 724, §28.)

§21350. Enumeration of disqualified transferees of donative transfers

(a) Except as provided in Section 21351, no provision, or provisions, of any instrument shall be valid to make any donative transfer to any of the following:

(1) The person who drafted the instrument.

(2) A person who is related by blood or marriage to, is a domestic partner of, is a cohabitant with, or is an employee of, the person who drafted the instrument.

(3) Any partner or shareholder of any law partnership or law corporation in which the person described in paragraph (1) has an ownership interest, and any employee of that such law partnership or law corporation.

(4) Any person who has a fiduciary relationship with the transferor, including, but not limited to, a conservator or trustee, who transcribes the instrument or causes it to be transcribed.

(5) A person who is related by blood or marriage to, is a domestic partner of, is a cohabitant with, or is an employee of a person who is described in paragraph (4).

(6) A care custodian of a dependent adult who is the transferor.

(7) A person who is related by blood or marriage to, is a domestic partner of, is a cohabitant with, or is an employee of, a person who is described in paragraph (6).

(b) For purposes of this section, "a person who is related by blood or marriage" to a person means all of the following:

(1) The person's spouse or predeceased spouse.

(2) Relatives within the third degree of the person and of the person's spouse.

(3) The spouse of any person described in paragraph (2).

In determining any relationship under this subdivision, Sections 6406, 6407, and Chapter 2 (commencing with Section 6450) of Part 2 of Division 6 shall be applicable.

(c) For purposes of this section, the term "dependent adult" has the meaning as set forth in Section 15610.23 of the Welfare and Institutions Code and also includes those persons who (1) are older than age 64 and (2) would be dependent adults, within the meaning of Section 15610.23, if they were between the ages of 18 and 64. The term "care custodian" has the meaning set forth in Section 15610.17 of Welfare and Institutions Code.

(d) For purposes of this section, "domestic partner" means a domestic partner as defined under Section 297 of the Family Code.

(Stats. 1993 (A.B. 21), ch. 293, §8. Amended by Stats. 1995 (A.B. 1466), ch. 730, §12; Stats. 1996 (S.B. 392), ch. 563, §34; Stats. 1996 (A.B. 2751), ch. 862, §47; Stats. 1997 (A.B. 1172), ch. 724, §33; Stats 2003 (AB 1349) ch. 444 §1.)

§21350.5. Definition of "disqualified person"

For purposes of this part, "disqualified person" means a person specified in subdivision (a) of Section 21350, but only in cases where Section 21351 does not apply.

(Stats. 1995 (A.B. 1466), ch. 730, §13.)

§21351. Exceptions to §21350

Section 21350 does not apply if any of the following conditions are met:

(a) The transferor is related by blood or marriage to, is a cohabitant with, or is the registered domestic partner, pursuant to Division 2.5 (commencing with Section 297) of the Family Code, of the transferee or the person who drafted the instrument. For purposes of this section, "cohabitant" has the meaning set forth in Section 13700 of the Penal Code. This subdivision shall retroactively apply to an instrument that becomes irrevocable on or after July 1, 1993.

(b) The instrument is reviewed by an independent attorney who (1) counsels the client (transferor) about the nature and consequences of the intended transfer, (2) attempts to determine if the intended consequence is the result of fraud, menace, duress, or undue influence, and (3) signs and delivers to the transferor an original certificate in substantially the following form, with a copy delivered to the drafter:

CERTIFICATE OF INDEPENDENT REVIEW

I, ________________,, have reviewed
(attorney's name)

____________________ and counseled my client,
(name of instrument)

____________________________, on the nature and
(name of client)

consequences of the transfer, or transfers, of property to

____
(name of potentially disqualified person)

Contained in the instrument. I am so dissociated from the interest of the transferee as to be in a position to advise my client independently, impartially, and confidentially as to the consequences of the transfer. On the basis of this counsel, I conclude that the transfer, or transfers, in the instrument that otherwise might be invalid under Section 21350 of the Probate Code are valid because the
transfer, or transfers, are not the product of fraud, menace, duress, or undue influence.

____________________________ ______________
(Name of Attorney) (Date)

Any attorney whose written engagement signed by the client is expressly limited solely to the preparation of a certificate under this subdivision, including the prior counseling, shall not be considered to otherwise represent the client.

(c) After full disclosure of the relationships of the persons involved, the instrument is approved pursuant to an order under Article 10 (commencing with Section 2580) of Chapter 6 of Part 4 of Division 4.

(d) The court determines, upon clear and convincing evidence, but not based solely upon the testimony of any person described in subdivision (a) of Section 21350, that the transfer was not the product of fraud, menace, duress, or undue influence. If the court finds that the transfer was the product of fraud, menace, duress, or undue influence, the disqualified person shall bear all costs of the proceeding, including reasonable attorney's fees.

(e) Subdivision (d) shall apply only to the following instruments:

(1) Any instrument other than one making a transfer to a person described in paragraph (1) of subdivision (a) of Section 21350.

(2) Any instrument executed on or before July 1, 1993, by a person who was a resident of this state at the time the instrument was executed.

(3) Any instrument executed by a resident of California who was not a resident at the time the instrument was executed.

(f) The transferee is a federal, state, or local public entity, an entity that qualifies for an exemption from taxation under Section 501(c)(3) or 501(c)(19) of the Internal Revenue Code, or a trust holding an interest for this entity, but only to the extent of the interest of the entity, or the trustee of this trust. This subdivision shall retroactively apply to an instrument that becomes irrevocable on or after July 1, 1993.

(g) For purposes of this section, "related by blood or marriage" shall include persons within the fifth degree or heirs of the transferor.

(h) The transfer does not exceed the sum of three thousand dollars ($3,000). This subdivision shall not apply if the total value of the property in the estate of the transferor does not exceed the amount prescribed in Section 13100.

(i) The transfer is made by an instrument executed by a nonresident of California who was not a resident at the time the instrument was executed, and that was not signed within California.

(Stats. 1993 (A.B. 21), ch. 293, §8. Amended by Stats. 1994 (A.B. 797), ch. 40, §4, effective April 19, 1994; Stats. 1995 (A.B. 1466), ch. 730, §14; Stats. 2002 (S.B. 1575), ch. 412, §1.)

II. Trustee's Standard of Care and Fiduciary Duties

A. Standard of Care

The trustee is required to conform to standards of conduct imposed by law. The standard of care and skill originally was developed by case law. Now, however, these standards of conduct have been codified by statute in most jurisdictions.

The trustee has a duty to manifest the care, skill, prudence, and diligence in the management of the trust as that of an ordinarily prudent person engaged in similar business affairs and with objectives similar to those of the trust in question. Bogert, *supra*, at §541. This is sometimes referred to as the *prudent person standard*. Note that many states, including California, have enacted new prudent investor legislation (discussed *infra*).

Many jurisdictions, influenced by the Uniform Probate Code, have imposed a heightened standard of care on trustees. UPC §7-302 requires that the trustee must observe "the standards in dealing with the trust assets that would be observed by a prudent man dealing with the property of *another*" (emphasis added). This rule changes the former standard of care that required a trustee to observe the standards in dealing with trust assets that would be observed by a prudent man dealing with his or her *own property*.

Professional trustees (i.e., banks, trust companies) are held to a higher standard of care. If a trustee represents that he or she has a higher degree of skill than that possessed by the average individual, the trustee is held to a higher standard of care (UPC §7-302; Cal. Prob. Code §16014). Also, because the prudent person standard is an objective standard, a trustee will not be relieved from liability by arguing that he or she possesses lower-than-normal skill in managing the trust. If a trustee serves without compensation, the trustee is still subject to the requisite standard of care (Cal. Prob. Code §16041).

§16014. Trustee's higher standard based on representation of special skills

(a) The trustee has a duty to apply the full extent of the trustee's skills.

(b) If the settlor, in selecting the trustee, has relied on the trustee's representation of having special skills, the trustee is held to the standard of the skills represented.

(Stats. 1990 (A.B. 759), ch. 79, §14, effective July 1, 1991.)

§16040. Standard of care: reasonable care, skill and caution of a prudent person

(a) The trustee shall administer the trust with reasonable care, skill, and caution under the circumstances then prevailing that a prudent person acting in a like capacity would use in the conduct of an enterprise of like character and with like aims to accomplish the purposes of the trust as determined from the trust instrument.

(b) The settlor may expand or restrict the standard provided in subdivision (a) by express provisions in the trust instrument. A trustee is not liable to a beneficiary for the trustee's good faith reliance on these express provisions.

(c) This section does not apply to investment and management functions governed by the Uniform Prudent Investor Act, Article 2.5 (commencing with Section 16045).
(Stats. 1990 (A.B. 759), ch. 79, §14, effective July 1, 1991. Amended by Stats. 1995 (S.B. 222), ch. 63, §4.)

§16041. Compensation does not affect standard of care

A trustee's standard of care and performance in administering the trust is not affected by whether or not the trustee receives any compensation.
(Stats. 1990 (A.B. 759), ch. 79, §14, effective July 1, 1991.)

§16042. Public guardian's standard of care

(a) Notwithstanding the requirements of this article, Article 2.5 (commencing with Section 16045), and the terms of the trust, all trust funds that come within the custody of the public guardian who is appointed as trustee of the trust pursuant to Section 15660.5 may be deposited or invested in the same manner, and would be subject to the same terms and conditions, as a deposit or investment by the public administrator of funds in the estate of a decedent pursuant to Article 3 (commencing with Section 7640) of Chapter 4 of P art 1 of Division 7.

(b) Upon the deposit or investment of trust property pursuant to subdivision (a), the public guardian shall be deemed to have met the standard of care specified in this article and Article 2.5 (commencing with Section 16045) with respect to this trust property.
(Stats. 1997 (S.B. 696), ch. 93, §4.)

B. Duties Generally

A trustee is subject to various fiduciary duties. If a trustee fails to comply with these duties, he or she can be held personally liable and even may be subject to criminal and/or civil penalties.

The list of trustees' duties in California law is derived largely from the Restatement (Second) of Trusts. 13 Witkin, Summary, Trusts, §61. According to California statute, a trustee has a duty to administer the trust according to the terms of the instrument and the dictates of the law (Cal. Prob. Code §§16000, 16001). For instance, a trustee has a duty "to take reasonable steps to enforce claims that are part of the trust property" (Cal. Prob. Code §16010), and "to take reasonable steps to defend actions that may result in a loss to the trust" (Cal. Prob. Code §16011). During the administration of a revocable living trust, the trustee's primary duty is owed to the settlor (or to another person holding the power of revocation) and not to the beneficiary or beneficiaries (Cal. Prob. Code §16001).

The trustee also has a duty to make the trust property productive (Cal. Prob. Code §16007). As part of this duty, the trustee should invest personal property in appropriate investments. The trustee also has a duty to diversify trust property when prudent to do so, i.e., to place the trust property in different types of assets. The California requirement to diversify is now included in the California version of the Uniform Prudent Investor Act as California Probate Code §16048 (the Act is set forth in Section H *infra*).

The trustee has a duty to keep the beneficiaries informed and to render accountings to them (either directly or via judicial proceedings) (Cal. Prob. Code §§16060-16064) (set forth in Section G *infra*).

In the case of co-trustees, each trustee has a duty to participate in the trust administration and also to take "reasonable steps to prevent a co-trustee from committing a breach of trust or to compel a co-trustee to redress a breach of trust" (Cal. Prob. Code §16013).

For a discussion of the trustee's duties with regard to discretionary powers, see also Chapter XII, Section B2b *infra.*

§16000. Duty to administer trust according to instrument and law

On acceptance of the trust, the trustee has a duty to administer the trust according to the trust instrument and, except to the extent the trust instrument provides otherwise, according to this division.
(Stats. 1990 (A.B. 759), ch. 79, §14, effective July 1, 1991.)

§16001. Trustee's duties regarding revocable trusts

(a) Except as provided in subdivision (b), the trustee of a revocable trust shall follow any written direction acceptable to the trustee given from time to time (1) by the person then having the power to revoke the trust or the part thereof with respect to which the direction is given or (2) by the person to whom the settlor delegates the right to direct the trustee.

(b) If a written direction given under subdivision (a) would have the effect of modifying the trust, the trustee has no duty to follow the direction unless it complies with the requirements for modifying the trust.

(Stats. 1990 (A.B. 759), ch. 79, §14, effective July 1, 1991.)

§16007. Trustee's duty to make trust property productive

The trustee has a duty to make the trust property productive under the circumstances and in furtherance of the purposes of the trust.

(Stats. 1990 (A.B. 759), ch. 79, §14, effective July 1, 1991.)

§16010. Trustee's duty to enforce claims

The trustee has a duty to take reasonable steps to enforce claims that are part of the trust property.

(Stats. 1990 (A.B. 759), ch. 79, §14, effective July 1, 1991.)

§16011. Trustee has duty to defend actions that might result in loss

The trustee has a duty to take reasonable steps to defend actions that may result in a loss to the trust.

(Stats. 1990 (A.B. 759), ch. 79, §14, effective July 1, 1991.)

§16013. Duties of cotrustees

If a trust has more than one trustee, each trustee has a duty to do the following:

(a) To participate in the administration of the trust.

(b) To take reasonable steps to prevent a cotrustee from committing a breach of trust or to compel a cotrustee to redress a breach of trust.

(Stats. 1990 (A.B. 759), ch. 79, §14, effective July 1, 1991.)

§16015. Corporate trustee's services in ordinary course of business does not violate duty of care

The provision of services for compensation by a regulated financial institution or its affiliates in the ordinary course of business either to a trust of which it also acts as trustee or to a person dealing with the trust is not a violation of the duty provided in Section 16002 [duty of loyalty] or 16004 [conflicts of interest]. For the purposes of this section, "affiliate" means a corporation that directly or indirectly through one or more intermediaries controls, is controlled by, or is under common control with another domestic or foreign corporation.

(Stats. 1990 (A.B. 759), ch. 79, §14, effective July 1, 1991.)

§16048. Trustee's duty to diversify

In making and implementing investment decisions, the trustee has a duty to diversify the investments of the trust unless, under the circumstances, it is prudent not to do so.

(Stats. 1995 (S.B. 222), ch. 63, §6.)

§16080. Discretionary powers shall be reasonably exercised

Except as provided in Section 16081, a discretionary power conferred upon a trustee is not left to the trustee's arbitrary discretion, but shall be exercised reasonably.

(Stats. 1990, ch. 79 (A.B. 759), §14, effective July 1, 1991.)

§16081. Fiduciary principles governing trustee's exercise of discretion

(a) Subject to the additional requirements of subdivisions (b), (c), and (d), if a trust instrument confers "absolute," "sole," or "uncontrolled" discretion on a trustee, the trustee shall act in accordance with fiduciary principles and shall not act in bad faith or in disregard of the purposes of the trust.

(b) Notwithstanding the use of terms like "absolute," "sole," or "uncontrolled" by a settlor or a testator, a person who is a beneficiary of a trust that permits the person, either individually or as trustee or cotrustee, to make discretionary distributions of income or principal to or for the benefit of himself or herself pursuant to a standard, shall exercise that power reasonably and in accordance with the standard.

(c) Unless a settlor or a testator clearly indicates that a broader power is intended by express reference to this subdivision, a person who is a beneficiary of a trust that permits the person, as trustee or cotrustee, to make discretionary distributions of income or principal to or for the benefit of himself or herself may exercise that power in his or her favor only for his or her health, education, support, or maintenance within the meaning of Sections 2041 and 2514 of the Internal Revenue Code. Notwithstanding the foregoing and the provisions of Section 15620, if a power to make discretionary distributions of income or principal is conferred upon two or more trustees, the power may be exercised by any trustee who is not a current permissible beneficiary of that power; and provided further that if there is no trustee who is not a current permissible beneficiary of that power, any party in interest may apply to a court of competent jurisdiction to appoint a trustee who is not a current permissible beneficiary of that power, and the power may be exercised by the trustee appointed by the court.

(d) Subdivision (c) does not apply to either of the following:

(1) Any power held by the settlor of a revocable or amendable trust.

(2) Any power held by a settlor's spouse or a testator's spouse who is the trustee of a trust for which a marital deduction, as defined in Section 21520, has been allowed.

(e) Subdivision (c) applies to any of the following:

(1) Any trust executed on or after January 1, 1997.

(2) Any testamentary trust created under a will executed on or after January 1, 1997.

(3) Any irrevocable trust created under a document executed before January 1, 1997, or any revocable trust executed before that date if the settlor was incapacitated as of that date, unless all parties in interest elect affirmatively not to be subject to the application of subdivision (c) through a written instrument delivered to the trustee. That election shall be made on or before the latest of January 1, 1998, three years after the date on which the trust became irrevocable, or, in the case of a revocable trust where the settlor was incapacitated, three years after the date on which the settlor became incapacitated.

(f) Notwithstanding the foregoing, the provisions of subdivision (c) neither create a new cause of action nor impair an existing cause of action that, in either case, relates to any power limited by subdivision (c) that was exercised before January 1, 1997.

(g) For purposes of this section, the term "party in interest" means any of the following persons:

(1) If the trust is revocable and the settlor is incapacitated, the settlor's legal representative under applicable law, or the settlor's attorney-in-fact under a durable power of attorney that is sufficient to grant the authority required under subdivision (c) or (e), as applicable.

(2) If the trust is irrevocable, each trustee, each beneficiary then entitled or authorized to receive income distributions from the trust, or each remainder beneficiary who would be entitled to receive notice of a trust proceeding under Section 15804. Any beneficiary who lacks legal capacity may be represented by the beneficiary's legal representative, attorney-in-fact under a durable power of attorney that is sufficient to grant the authority required under subdivision (c) or (e), as applicable, or in the absence of a legal representative or attorney-in-fact, a guardian ad litem appointed for that purpose.

(Stats. 1990 (A.B. 759), ch. 79, §14, effective July 1, 1991. Amended by Stats. 1996 (S.B. 1907), ch. 410, §1.)

§16082. Person who holds power to appoint or distribute for benefit of others may not use power to discharge obligations of person holding power

Except as otherwise specifically provided in the trust instrument, a person who holds a power to appoint or distribute income or principal to or for the benefit of others, either as an individual or as trustee, may not use the power to discharge the legal obligations of the person holding the power.

(Stats. 1990 (A.B. 759), ch. 79, §14, effective July 1, 1991.)

§16249. Trustee has power to protect trust property in judicial proceedings

The trustee has the power to prosecute or defend actions, claims, or proceedings for the protection of trust property and of the trustee in the performance of the trustee's duties.

(Stats. 1990 (A.B. 759), ch. 79, §14, effective July 1, 1991. Amended by Stats. 1992 (A.B. 2975), ch. 871, §19; Stats. 2001 (S.B. 669), ch. 49, §5.)

§16420. Liability for breach of trust

(a) If a trustee commits a breach of trust, or threatens to commit a breach of trust, a beneficiary or cotrustee of the trust may commence a proceeding for any of the following purposes that is appropriate:

(1) To compel the trustee to perform the trustee's duties.

(2) To enjoin the trustee from committing a breach of trust.

(3) To compel the trustee to redress a breach of trust by payment of money or otherwise.

(4) To appoint a receiver or temporary trustee to take possession of the trust property and administer the trust.

(5) To remove the trustee.

(6) Subject to Section 18100, to set aside acts of the trustee.

(7) To reduce or deny compensation of the trustee.

(8) Subject to Section 18100, to impose an equitable lien or a constructive trust on trust property.

(9) Subject to Section 18100, to trace trust property that has been wrongfully disposed of and recover the property or its proceeds.

(b) The provision of remedies for breach of trust in subdivision (a) does not prevent resort to any other appropriate remedy provided by statute or the common law.

(Stats. 1990 (A.B. 759), ch. 79, §14, effective July 1, 1991.)

§16461. Exculpation of trustee: relief from liability for breach of trust

(a) Except as provided in subdivision (b), the trustee can be relieved of liability for breach of trust by provisions in the trust instrument.

(b) A provision in the trust instrument is not effective to relieve the trustee of liability (1) for breach of trust committed intentionally, with gross negligence, in bad faith, or with reckless indifference to the interest of the beneficiary, or (2) for any profit that the trustee derives from a breach of trust.

(c) subject to subdivision (b), a provision in a trust instrument that releases the trustee from liability if a beneficiary fails to object to an item in an interim or final account or other written report within a specified time period is effective only if all of the following conditions are met:

The account or report sets forth the item.

The period specified in the trust instrument for the beneficiary to object is not less than 180 days, or the trustee elects to follow the procedure provided in subdivision (d).

Written notice in 12-point boldface type is provided to a beneficiary with the account or report in the following form:

NOTICE TO BENEFICIARIES

YOU HAVE [Insert "180 days" or the period specified in the trust agreement, whichever is longer] FROM YOUR RECEIPT OF THIS ACCOUNT OR REPORT TO TAKE AN OBJECTION TO ANY ITEM SET FORTH IN THIS ACCOUNT OR REPORT. ANY OBJECTION YOU MAKE MUST BE IN WRITING; IT MUST BE DELIVERED TO THE TRUSTEE WITHIN THE PERIOD STATED ABOVE; AND IT MUST STATE YOUR OBJECTION. YOUR FAILURE TO DELIVER A WRITEN OBJECTION TO THE TRUSTEE WTIHIN THE PERIOD STATED ABOVE WILL PERMANENTLY PREVENT YOU FROM LATER ASSERTING THIS OBJECTION AGAINST THE TRUSTEE. IF YOU DO MAKE AN OBJECTION TO THE TRUSTEE, THE THREE-YEAR PERIOD PROVIDED IN SECTION 16460 OF THE PROBATE CODE FOR COMMENCEMENT OF LITIGATION WILL APPLY TO CLAIMS BASED ON YOUR OBJECTION AND WILL BEGIN TO RUN ON THE DATE THAT YOU RECEIVE THIS ACCOUNT OR REPORT.

(d) A provision in a trust instrument that provides for a period less than 180 days to object to an item in an account or report shall be ineffective to release the trustee from liability. A trustee of a trust created by an instrument with an ineffective period may elect to be governed by the provisions of subdivision (c) by complying with the requirements of subdivision (c), except that "180 days" shall be substituted in the notice form for the ineffective period.

(e) Subject to subdivision (b), a beneficiary who fails to object in writing to an account or report that complies with the requirements of subdivision (c), within the specified valid period shall be barred from asserting any claim against the trustee regarding an item that is adequately disclosed in the account or report. An item is adequately disclosed if the disclosure regarding the item meets the requirements of paragraph (1) of subdivision (a) of Section 16460.

(f) Except as provided in subdivision (a) of Section 16460, the trustee may not be released from liability as to any claim based on a written objection made by the beneficiary if the objection is delivered to the trustee within the specified, effective period. If a beneficiary has filed a written objection to an account or report that complies with the requirements of subdivision (c) within the specified, valid period that concerns an item that affects any other beneficiary of the trust, any affected beneficiary may join in the objection anytime within the specified, valid period or while the resolution of the objection is pending, whichever is later. This section is not intended to establish a class of beneficiaries for actions on an account and report to provide that the action of one beneficiary is pending, whichever is later. This section is not intended to establish a class of beneficiaries for actions on an account and report or provide that the action of one beneficiary is for the benefit of all beneficiaries. This section does not create a duty for any trustee to notify beneficiaries of objections or resolution of objections.

(g) Provided that a beneficiary has filed a written objection to an account or report that complies with the requirements of subdivision (c) within the specified, valid period, a supplemental written objection may be delivered in the same manner as the objection not later than 180 days after the receipt of the account or report or no later than the period specified in the trust instrument, whichever is longer.

(h) Compliance with subdivision (c) excuses compliance with paragraph (6) of subdivision (a) of Section 16063 for the account or report to which that notice entails.

(i) subject to subdivision (b), if proper notice has been given and a beneficiary has not made a timely objection, the trustee is not liable for any other claims adequately disclosed by any item in the account or report.

(j) Subdivisions (c) to (i), inclusive, apply to all accounts and reports submitted after the effective date of the act adding these subdivisions.

(Stats. 1990 (A.B. 759), ch. 79, §14, effective July 1, 1991. Amended by Stats. 2004 (AB 1990) ch. 538 §1.)

C. Duty to Take Control of and Preserve Trust Property

After the trustee accepts the office, the trustee has a duty to take control of the assets of the trust. This duty signifies that the trustee must locate the property and then ensure that

the property becomes a trust asset (by registering corporate securities or recording real property in the name of the trust, for example). The trustee also has a duty to preserve the trust property. This duty requires that the trustee safeguard the assets by acquiring appropriate insurance (e.g., fire, theft) and placing valuable property in a secure location (e.g., a safe deposit box or safe).

After taking control of the trust property, the trustee has a duty to review the trust assets to make sure that they are appropriate for the trust. This duty is now incorporated in the California version of the Uniform Prudent Investor Act as California Probate Code §16049 (the Act is included as Section H *infra*). The task must be accomplished within a reasonable time after accepting the trusteeship or receiving the trust property. This review entails: (1) disposing of bad investments or investments that the trustee is not permitted to make according to the terms of the trust or state law; and (2) disposing of unproductive property. In addition, the trustee should review the trust property periodically thereafter to determine if the assets continue to be appropriate for the trust, and, if not, the trustee should dispose of these assets as well.

§16006. Trustee's duty to take control and preserve trust property

The trustee has a duty to take reasonable steps under the circumstances to take and keep control of and to preserve the trust property.

(Stats. 1990 (A.B. 759), ch. 79, §14, effective July 1, 1991.)

§16049. Trustee's duty to review assets after acceptance or receipt of property

Within a reasonable time after accepting a trusteeship or receiving trust assets, a trustee shall review the trust assets and make and implement decisions concerning the retention and disposition of assets, in order to bring the trust portfolio into compliance with the purposes, terms, distribution requirements, and other circumstances of the trust, and with the requirements of this chapter.

(Stats. 1995 (S.B. 222), ch. 63, §6.)

D. Duty of Loyalty

The trustee has a duty of undivided loyalty in the administration of the trust. That is, the trustee must administer the trust solely in the interests of the beneficiaries. The duty of loyalty calls for the trustee to exclude consideration of his or her own interests, as well as the interests of third parties.

The trustee must not place himself or herself in a conflict of interest position in which personal interest or that of a third party is adverse to that of the beneficiary or beneficiaries. One type of conflict of interest that a trustee must avoid is "self-dealing." In cases of self-dealing, the trustee acts in such a way as to benefit himself or herself. Examples of prohibited self-dealing include:

- to sell or lease of trust property to oneself as an individual;
- to sell or lease of individual property to the trust;
- (if a corporate trustee) to retain or acquire the corporation's own stock as a trust asset;
- to lend trust assets to oneself as an individual; or
- to acquire an interest in trust property for oneself as an individual.

Bogert, *supra*, at §543.

Most courts adopt a "*no-further-inquiry rule*" and do not consider good faith or fairness as defenses. The strict rule serves as a deterrence against acts of self-dealing. Some defenses have developed: (1) if the act is approved by a court, (2) if the act is authorized by the trust instrument, and (3) if the beneficiaries consent after full disclosure. In some situations, statutes authorize some forms of self-dealing.

If a trustee engages in self-dealing, for example by selling property owned as an individual to the trust, the beneficiary has the choice: to affirm the sale or set it aside. The beneficiary also may require the trustee to account for any personal profit or loss to the trust. 13 Witkin, Summary, Trusts, §63.

According to California law, a trustee may not purchase trust property in his or her individual capacity, even if the purchase is in good faith or if the beneficiary suffers no injury. *Id.* Some exceptions exist to this rule against purchase: (1) if the trust has terminated and the trustee does not take advantage of information acquired as a trustee; (2) if the trustee acts in

good faith, the consideration is fair, and the court authorizes the purchase as being in the interest of the beneficiary; or (3) if the trust instrument authorizes purchase by the trustee. *Id.*

California statute permits one form of self-dealing involving transfers between trusts. That is, by statute, it is not a violation of the prohibition against self-dealing if the trustee under one trust deals with himself or herself as trustee under another. Specifically, a trustee of one trust may sell, exchange, or participate in the sale or exchange of property between the trusts provided that the transaction is fair and reasonable regarding the beneficiaries of both trusts and also if the beneficiaries have notice of all material facts (Cal. Prob. Code §16002).

In addition, a trustee of a trust that has multiple beneficiaries, including successive beneficiaries, has a duty to administer the trust in an impartial manner so as to take into account the interests of all beneficiaries (Cal. Prob. Code §16003). As recently amended, this provision codifies a provision of the Uniform Prudent Investor Act (§6) (1994). 13 Witkin, Summary, Trusts, §170.

The Uniform Trust Code prohibits as self-dealing certain acts involving not only the trustee but also the trustee's relatives, such as: "[a] sale, encumbrance, or other transaction involving the investment or management of trust property" if it is entered into by the trustee with his or her spouse, descendants, siblings, parents, or their spouses. Unif. Trust Code §802(c). See generally Karen E. Boxx, Of Punctilios and Paybacks: The Duty of Loyalty Under the Uniform Trust Code, 67 Mo. L. Rev. 279 (2002).

For a case involving a breach of the duty of loyalty, see Stegemeier v. Magness, 728 A.2d 557 (Del. 1999) (holding that co-administrator and trustee breached their fiduciary duty when they conveyed property to their own corporation; breaches were not cured when a disinterested co-administrator joined in the deeds; and beneficiaries did not have burden of persuasion to show that sale prices of real estate transactions were fair). See also Jason L. Smith, Stegemeier v. Magness: An Analysis of a Trustee's Fiduciary Duty in Self-Interested Transactions, 14 Quinnipiac Prob. L.J. 605 (2000).

§16002. Trustee's duty of loyalty: definition, exception

(a) The trustee has a duty to administer the trust solely in the interest of the beneficiaries.

(b) It is not a violation of the duty provided in subdivision (a) for a trustee who administers two trusts to sell, exchange, or participate in the sale or exchange of trust property between the trusts, if both of the following requirements are met:

(1) The sale or exchange is fair and reasonable with respect to the beneficiaries of both trusts.

(2) The trustee gives to the beneficiaries of both trusts notice of all material facts related to the sale or exchange that the trustee knows or should know.

(Stats. 1990 (A.B. 759), ch. 79, §14, effective July 1, 1991.)

§16003. Trustee has duty to deal impartially with multiple beneficiaries

If a trust has two or more beneficiaries, the trustee has a duty to deal impartially with them and shall act impartially in investing and managing the trust property, taking into account any differing interests of the beneficiaries.

(Stats. 1990 (A.B. 759), ch. 79, §14, effective July 1, 1991. Amended by Stats. 1995 (S.B. 222), ch. 63, §1.)

§16004. Conflicts of interest, defined

(a) The trustee has a duty not to use or deal with trust property for the trustee's own profit or for any other purpose unconnected with the trust, nor to take part in any transaction in which the trustee has an interest adverse to the beneficiary.

(b) The trustee may not enforce any claim against the trust property that the trustee purchased after or in contemplation of appointment as trustee, but the court may allow the trustee to be reimbursed from trust property the amount that the trustee paid in good faith for the claim.

(c) A transaction between the trustee and a beneficiary which occurs during the existence of the trust or while the trustee's influence with the beneficiary remains and by which the trustee obtains an advantage from the beneficiary is presumed to be a violation of the trustee's fiduciary duties. This presumption is a presumption affecting the burden of proof. This subdivision does not apply to the provisions of an agreement between a trustee and a beneficiary relating to the hiring or compensation of the trustee.

(Stats. 1990 (A.B. 759), ch. 79, §14, effective July 1, 1991.)

§16004.5. Trustee may not get waiver of liability as a condition for making distribution or payment

(a) A trustee may not require a beneficiary to relieve the trustee of liability as a condition for making a distribution or payment to, or for the benefit of, the beneficiary, if the distribution or payment is required by the trust instrument.

(b) This section may not be construed as affecting the trustee's right to:

(1) Maintain a reserve for reasonably anticipated expenses, including, but not limited to, taxes, debts, trustee or accounting gees, and costs and expenses of administration.

(2) Seek a voluntary release of discharge of a trustee's liability from the beneficiary.

(3) Require indemnification against a claim by a person or entity, other than a beneficiary referred to in subdivision (a), which may reasonably arise as a result of the distribution.

(4) Withhold any portion of an otherwise required distribution that is reasonably in dispute

(5) Seek court or beneficiary approval of an accounting of trust activities.

(Stats. 2003 (AB 1705) ch. 585 §1.)

§16005. Trustee's duty regarding adverse trusts

The trustee of one trust has a duty not to knowingly become a trustee of another trust adverse in its nature to the interest of the beneficiary of the first trust, and a duty to eliminate the conflict or resign as trustee when the conflict is discovered.

(Stats. 1990 (A.B. 759), ch. 79, §14, effective July 1, 1991.)

E. Duty to Identify and to Segregate Trust Property

The trustee has a duty to earmark the trust property, i.e., to identify and label the trust assets as properly belonging to the trust. The trustee also has a duty to segregate the trust property and not to mingle ("commingle") it with his or her own assets or the assets of other trusts. Earmarking is important because failure to earmark may result in the trustee's personal creditors seizing trust property in the belief that the trustee owns it in his or her individual capacity.

At common law, a trustee was liable for all losses that resulted from failure to earmark. This strict rule has been liberalized, however, to make trustees liable only if the loss resulted from the failure to earmark. Thus, suppose a trustee fails to register corporate securities in the name of the trust (registering them in his or her own name instead) and the stock decreases in value. The trustee will not be liable if the loss was due to economic conditions. However, suppose the trustee fails to register corporate securities in the name of the trust and the trustee's creditor seizes the stock for payment of the trustee's individual debt. Then, the trustee will be liable for the loss.

Some state statutes permit corporate trustees to commingle property from several trusts in a "common trust fund" for ease of management. Such funds permit a trustee to obtain lower costs, for example, on the sale of corporate stock.

CALIFORNIA FINANCIAL CODE

§1564. "Common trust funds," defined

(a) For purposes of this section, two or more trust companies shall be deemed to be affiliated if they are members of the same affiliated group, within the meaning of Section 1504 of the Internal Revenue Code.

(b) Any trust company may establish and administer common trust funds composed of property permitted by law for the investment of trust funds, for the purpose of furnishing investments to any one or more of the following: (1) itself, as fiduciary; (2) itself and others, as cofiduciaries; (3) any affiliated trust company including, without limitation, any foreign (other state) affiliated trust company, as fiduciary; and (4) any affiliated trust company including, without limitation, any foreign (other state) affiliated trust company and others, as cofiduciaries. Any trust company may as such fiduciary or cofiduciary invest funds which it lawfully holds for investment in interests in common trust funds administered by itself or by any affiliated trust company including, without limitation, any foreign (other state) affiliated trust company, if such investment is not prohibited by the instrument, judgment, decree, order, or statute creating or governing such fiduciary relationship, and if, in the case of cofiduciaries, the trust company procures the consent of its cofiduciaries to such investment.

(c) Each common trust fund established hereunder shall be treated as an entity separate and distinct from the fiduciary relationships participating therein. No fiduciary in administering a participating fiduciary relationship shall be required to make any apportionment or allocation between the principal and income of this relationship different from that made for the common trust fund. No participating fiduciary relationship, nor any person having an interest in that relationship, shall have or be deemed to have any ownership in any particular property of the common trust fund, but each participating fiduciary relationship shall have a proportionate undivided interest in the fund and its income, and the ownership of all property of the common trust fund shall be in the trustee of the fund.

(d) This section shall apply to fiduciary relationships now in existence or hereafter established, whether the same be revocable or irrevocable. The commissioner, at his or her direction, may make an examination of any common trust fund established hereunder at the times and to the extent as he or she may deem advisable. The provisions of the Corporate Securities Law shall not apply to the creation, administration, or termination of common trust funds, nor to participation therein.

(Stats. 1951, ch. 364, p. 908, §1564. Amended by Stats. 1978, ch. 965, p. 2992, §110.1; Stats. 1991 (A.B. 1693), ch. 419, §1; Stats. 1996 (A.B. 3351), ch. 1064, §211, effective July 1, 1997.)

CALIFORNIA PROBATE CODE
§16009. Trustee's duty to segregate and identify trust property

The trustee has a duty to do the following:

(a) To keep the trust property separate from other property not subject to the trust.

(b) To see that the trust property is designated as property of the trust.

(Stats. 1990 (A.B. 759), ch. 79, §14, effective July 1, 1991.)

F. Duty with Respect to Delegation

A trustee is not required to perform all acts involved in the administration of a trust. According to the traditional rule, a trustee may delegate *ministerial* duties but may not delegate *discretionary* powers. The revised Restatement (Second) of Trusts §171 cmt f., allows a trustee to delegate discretionary acts in certain circumstances.

The revised Restatement (Second) of Trusts permits a trustee "in appropriate circumstances," to delegate discretionary acts involving "the selection of trust investments or the management of specialized investment programs, and to other activities of administration involving significant judgment." *Id.* The revised Restatement (Second) of Trusts (§171 cmt. h) does, however, require the trustee to define the trust's investment objectives when receiving professional advice. In addition, the trustee must either "formulate or approve of" the trust's investment's programs and strategies. *Id.*

A trend to permit trustees to delegate more of their discretionary duties began in 1964, with the promulgation of the Uniform Trustees' Powers Act. That Act permitted a trustee to employ agents to assist in the performance of the trustee's administrative duties. Such agents could help the trustee by performing any act of administration, whether discretionary or not. The Uniform Trustees' Powers Act was followed by the Uniform Prudent Investor Act (UPIA) in 1994. Taking into consideration modern portfolio theory, the UPIA adopts a "prudent investor standard" to replace the former "prudent person standard" regarding investment decisions—"recognizing that for many individual trustees, delegating some investment authority is actually the prudent approach." Susan N. Gary, Regulating the Management of Charities: Trust Law, Corporate Law, and Tax Law, 21 U. Haw. L. Rev. 593, 601-602 (1999).

The Uniform Trust Code and the revised Restatement (Second) of Trusts adopted the approach of the Uniform Prudent Investor Act in terms of delegation. Both permit trustees to delegate duties and powers to agents to the extent that a prudent trustee would delegate and also require care in the selection and supervision of agents. "A trustee may delegate duties and powers that a prudent trustee of comparable skills could properly delegate under the circumstances." Unif. Trust. Code §807(a) (derived from Uniform Prudent Investor Act §9). Thus, the Uniform Trust Code makes the decision to delegate dependent on the particular facts and circumstances. "For example, delegating some administrative and reporting duties might be prudent for a family trustee but unnecessary for a corporate trustee." Unif. Trust Code §807(a) cmt. Note that the Uniform Trust Code provision applies only to delegation to agents, not to co-trustees (delegation to a co-trustee is set forth in Uniform Trust Code §703(e)).

§16012. Duty to delegate: defined, prohibition, exceptions

(a) The trustee has a duty not to delegate to others the performance of acts that the trustee can reasonably be required personally to perform and may not transfer the office of trustee to another person nor delegate the entire administration of the trust to a cotrustee or other person.

(b) In a case where a trustee has properly delegated a matter to an agent, cotrustee, or other person, the trustee has a duty to exercise general supervision over the person performing the delegated matter.

(c) This section does not apply to investment and management functions under Section 16052.

(Stats. 1990 (A.B. 759), ch. 79, §14, effective July 1, 1991. Amended by Stats. 1995 (S.B. 222), ch. 63, §3.)

G. Duty to Report Information to the Beneficiaries and to Render Accounts

The trustee has a duty to keep the beneficiaries informed and to render accountings to them (either directly or via judicial proceedings) (Cal. Prob. Code §§16060-16064 *infra*). That is, upon the request at the beneficiaries and at reasonable times, the trustee has a duty to give the beneficiary or beneficiaries complete and accurate information relative to the administration of the trust. The purpose of the requirement is to enable a beneficiary to enforce his or her rights.

The duty to inform, as stated in California Probate Code §16060, is derived from UPC §7-303 (1987) and is consistent with prior California case law. Law Revision Commission Comment following California Probate Code §16060. According to the preceding Commentary, while the trustee normally owes the beneficiary to inform, the duty under California Probate Code §16060 is owed to the settlor (or to any other person having the power to revoke) and not to the beneficiaries during the period of time that a revocable trust can be revoked. See also California Probate Code §§15800 and 16064(b).

§15800. Limits on Beneficiary's rights regarding revocable trusts

Except to the extent that the trust instrument otherwise provides or where the joint action of the settlor and all beneficiaries is required, during the time that a trust is revocable and the person holding the power to revoke the trust is competent:

(a) The person holding the power to revoke, and not the beneficiary, has the rights afforded beneficiaries under this division.

(b) The duties of the trustee are owned to the person holding the power to revoke.

(Stats. 1990 (A.B. 759) ch. 79, §14, effective July 1, 1991.)

§16060. Duty to keep beneficiaries reasonably informed

The trustee has a duty to keep the beneficiaries of the trust reasonably informed of the trust and its administration.

(Stats. 1990 (A.B. 759), ch. 79, §14, effective July 1, 1991.)

§16060.5. Terms of the trust, defined

As used in this article, "terms of the trust" means the written trust instrument of an irrevocable trust or those provisions of a written trust instrument in effect at the settlor's death that describe or affect that portion of a trust that has become irrevocable at the death of the settlor. In addition, "terms of the trust" includes, but is not limited to, signatures, amendments, disclaimers, and any directions or instructions to the trustee that affect the disposition of the trust. "Terms of the trust" does not include documents which were intended to affect disposition only while the trust was revocable. If a trust has been completely restated, "terms of the trust" does not include trust instruments or amendments which are superseded by the last restatement before the settlor's death, but it does include amendments executed after the restatement. "Terms of the trust" also includes any document irrevocably exercising a power of appointment over the trust or over any portion of the trust which has become irrevocable.

(Stats. 1997 (A.B. 1172), ch. 724, §21. Amended by Stats. 1998 (A.B.2069), ch. 682, §7; Stats. 2000 (A.B. 460), ch. 34, §2.)

§16061. Trustee shall provide information upon request by beneficiary

Except as provided in Section 16064, on reasonable request by a beneficiary, the trustee shall provide the beneficiary with a report of information about the assets, liabilities, receipts, and disbursements of the trust, the acts of the trustee, and the particulars relating to the administration of the trust relevant to the beneficiary's interest, including the terms of the trust.

(Stats. 1990 (A.B. 759), ch. 79, §14, effective July 1, 1991. Amended by Stats. 1998 (A.B. 2069), ch. 682, §8.)

§16061.5. Trustee shall provide notice when revocable trust becomes irrevocable

(a) When a revocable trust or any portion of a revocable trust becomes irrevocable because of the death of one or more of the settlors of the trust, or because, by the express terms of the trust, the trust becomes irrevocable within one year of the death of a settlor because of a contingency related to the death of one or more of the settlors of the trust, the trustee shall provide a true and complete copy of the terms of the irrevocable trust, or irrevocable portion of the trust, to any beneficiary of the trust who requests it and to any heir of a deceased settlor who requests it.

(b) The trustee shall, for purposes of this section, rely upon any final judicial determination of heirship. However, the trustee shall have discretion to make a good faith determination by any reasonable means of the heirs of a deceased settlor in the absence of a final judicial determination of heirship known to the trustee.

(Stats. 1997 (A.B. 1172), ch. 724, §22. Amended by Stats. 1998 (A.B. 2069), ch. 682, §9; Stats. 2000 (A.B. 460), ch. 34, §3.)

§16061.7. Trustee must notice beneficiary of certain facts: irrevocability and change in trustee

(a) A trustee shall serve a notification by the trustee as described in this section in the following events:

(1) When a revocable trust or any portion thereof becomes irrevocable because of the death of one or more of the settlors of the trust, or because, by the express terms of the trust, the trust becomes irrevocable within one year of the death of a settlor because of a contingency related to the death of one or more of the settlors of the trust.

(2) Whenever there is a change of trustee of an irrevocable trust. The duty to serve the notification by the trustee is the duty of the continuing or successor trustee, and any one cotrustee may serve the notification.

(b) The notification by the trustee required by subdivision (a) shall be served on each of the following:

(1) Each beneficiary of the irrevocable trust or irrevocable portion of the trust, subject to the limitations of Section 15804.

(2) Each heir of the deceased settlor, if the event that requires notification is the death of a settlor or irrevocability within one year of the death of the settlor of the trust by the express terms of the trust because of a contingency related to the death of a settlor.

(3) If the trust is a charitable trust subject to the supervision of the Attorney General, to the Attorney General.

(c) A trustee shall, for purposes of this section, rely upon any final judicial determination of heirship, known to the trustee, but the trustee shall have discretion to make a good faith determination by any reasonable means of the heirs of a deceased settlor in the absence of a final judicial determination of heirship known to the trustee.

(d) The trustee need not provide a copy of the notification by trustee to any beneficiary or heir (1) known to the trustee but who cannot be located by the trustee after reasonable diligence or (2) unknown to the trustee.

(e) The notification by trustee shall be served by mail to the last known address, pursuant to Section 1215, or by personal delivery.

(f) The notification by trustee shall be served not later than 60 days following the occurrence of the event requiring service of the notification by trustee, or 60 days after the trustee became aware of the existence of a person entitled to receive notification by trustee, if that person was not known to the trustee on the occurrence of the event requiring service of the notification. If there is a vacancy in the office of the trustee on the date of the occurrence of the event requiring service of the notification by trustee, or if that event causes a vacancy, then the 60-day period for service of the notification by trustee commences on the date the new trustee commences to serve as trustee.

(g) The notification by trustee shall contain the following information:

(1) The identity of the settlor or settlors of the trust and the date of execution of the trust instrument.

(2) The name, mailing address and telephone number of each trustee of the trust.

(3) The address of the physical location where the principal place of administration of the trust is located, pursuant to Section 17002.

(4) Any additional information that may be expressly required by the terms of the trust instrument.

(5) A notification that the recipient is entitled, upon reasonable request to the trustee, to receive from the trustee a true and complete copy of the terms of the trust.

(h) If the notification by the trustee is served because a revocable trust or any portion of it has become irrevocable because of the death of one or more settlors of the trust, or because, by the express terms of the trust, the trust becomes irrevocable within one year of the death of a settlor because of a contingency related to the death of one or more of the settlors of the trust, the notification by the trustee shall also include a warning, set out in a separate paragraph in not less than 10-point boldface type, or a reasonable equivalent thereof, that states as follows:

"You may not bring an action to contest the trust more than 120 days from the date this notification by the trustee is served upon you or 60 days from the date on which a copy of the terms of the trust is mailed or personally delivered to you during that 120-day period, whichever is later."

(i) Any waiver by a settlor of the requirement of serving the notification by trustee required by this section is against public policy and shall be void.

(j) A trustee may serve a notification by trustee in the form required by this section on any person in addition to those on whom the notification by trustee is required to be served. A trustee is not liable to any person for serving or for not serving the notice on any person in addition to those on whom the notice is required to be served. A trustee is not required to serve a notification by trustee if the event that otherwise requires service of the notification by trustee occurs before January 1, 1998.

(Stats. 1997 (A.B. 1172), ch. 724, §23. Amended by Stats. 1998 (A.B. 2069), ch. 682, §10; Stats. 2000 (A.B. 460), ch. 34, §4; Stats. 2000 (A.B. 1628), ch. 592, §1.)

§16061.8. Trustee's notice serves to alert beneficiary of right to contest trust; limitation period

No person upon whom the notification by the trustee is served pursuant to this chapter may bring an action to contest the trust more than 120 days from the date the notification by the trustee is served upon him or her, or 60 days from the day on which a copy of the terms of the trust is mailed or personally delivered to him or her during that 120-day period, whichever is later.

(Stats. 1997 (A.B. 1172), ch. 724, §24. Amended by Stats. 2000 (A.B. 460), ch. 34, §5; Stats. 2000 (A.B. 1628), ch. 592, §2.)

§16061.9. Liability of trustee who fails to serve notice

(a) A trustee who fails to serve the notification by trustee as required by Section 16061.7 on a beneficiary shall be responsible for all damages, attorney's fees, and costs caused by the failure unless the trustee makes a reasonably diligent effort to comply with that section.

(b) A trustee who fails to serve the notification by trustee as required by Section 16061.7 on an heir who is not a beneficiary and whose identity is known to the trustee shall be responsible for all damages caused to the heir by the failure unless the trustee shows that the trustee made a reasonably diligent effort to comply with that section. For purposes of this subdivision, "reasonably diligent effort" means that the trustee has sent notice by first-class mail to the heir at the heir's last mailing address actually known to the trustee.

(c) A trustee, in exercising discretion with respect to the timing and nature of distributions of trust assets, may consider the fact that the period in which a beneficiary or heir could bring an action to contest the trust has not expired.

(Stats. 2000 (A.B. 460), ch. 34, §6.)

§16062. Trustee's annual accounting; limitations or waivers in trust instrument

(a) Except as otherwise provided in this section and in Section 16064, the trustee shall account at least annually, at the termination of the trust, and upon a change of trustee, to each beneficiary to whom income or principal is required or authorized in the trustee's discretion to be currently distributed.

(b) A trustee of a living trust created by an instrument executed before July 1, 1987, is not subject to the duty to account provided by subdivision (a).

(c) A trustee of a trust created by a will executed before July 1, 1987, is not subject to the duty to account provided by subdivision (a), except that if the trust is removed from continuing court jurisdiction pursuant to Article 2 (commencing with Section 17350) of Chapter 4 of Part 5, the duty to account provided by subdivision (a) applies to the trustee.

(d) Except as provided in Section 16064, the duty of a trustee to account pursuant to former Section 1120.1a of the Probate Code (as repealed by Chapter 820 of the Statutes of 1986), under a trust created by a will executed before July 1, 1977, which has been removed from continuing court jurisdiction pursuant to former Section 1120.1a, continues to apply after July 1, 1987. The duty to account under former Section 1120.1a may be satisfied by furnishing an account that satisfies the requirements of Section 16063.

(e) Any limitation or waiver in a trust instrument of the obligation to account is against public policy and shall be void as to any sole trustee who is a disqualified person as defined in Section 21350.5.

(Stats. 1990 (A.B. 759), ch. 79, §14, effective July 1, 1991. Amended by Stats. 1993 (A.B. 21), ch. 293, §6.5; Stats. 1998 (A.B. 2069), ch. 682, §11; Stats. 2001 (S.B. 662), ch. 159, §165.5.)

§16063. Account shall contain certain information

(a) An account furnished pursuant to Section 16062 shall contain the following information:

(1) A statement of receipts and disbursements of principal and income that have occurred during the last complete fiscal year of the trust or since the last account.

(2) A statement of the assets and liabilities of the trust as of the end of the last complete fiscal year of the trust or as of the end of the period covered by the account.

(3) The trustee's compensation for the last complete fiscal year of the trust or since the last account.

(4) The agents hired by the trustee, their relationship to the trustee, if any, and their compensation, for the last complete fiscal year of the trust or since the last account.

(5) A statement that the recipient of the account may petition the court pursuant to Section 17200 to obtain a court review of the account and of the acts of the trustee.

(6) A statement that claims against the trustee for breach of trust may not be made after the expiration of three years from the date the beneficiary receives an account or report disclosing facts giving rise to the claim.

(b) All accounts filed to be approved by a court shall be presented in the manner provided in Chapter 4 (commencing with Section 1060) of Part 1 of Division 3.

(Stats. 1997 (A.B. 1172), ch. 724, §26.)

§16064. Exceptions to reporting and accounting requirement

The trustee is not required to report information or account to a beneficiary in any of the following circumstances:

(a) To the extent the trust instrument waives the report or account, except that no waiver described in subdivision (e) of Section 16062 shall be valid or enforceable. Regardless of a waiver of accounting in the trust instrument, upon a showing that it is reasonably likely that a material breach of the trust has occurred, the court may compel the trustee to report information about the trust and to account.

(b) In the case of a beneficiary of a revocable trust, as provided in Section 15800, for the period when the trust may be revoked.

(c) As to a beneficiary who has waived in writing the right to a report or account. A waiver of rights under this subdivision may be withdrawn in writing at any time as to the most recent account and future accounts. A waiver has no effect on the beneficiary's right to petition for a report or account pursuant to Section 17200.

(d) Where the beneficiary and the trustee are the same person.

(Stats. 1990 (A.B. 759), ch. 79. §14, effective July 1, 1991. Amended by Stats. 1992 (A.B. 2975), ch. 871, §18; Stats. 1993 (A.B. 21), ch. 293, §6.7.)

H. Uniform Prudent Investor Act

The Uniform Prudent Investor Act (UPIA) was promulgated by the National Conference of Commissioners on Uniform State Laws (NCCUSL) in 1994. UPIA is modeled on the Restatement (Third) of Trusts: Prudent Investor Rule (1992).

NCCUSL promulgated UPIA in order to address shortcomings inherent in the common law rules. For example, common law rules placed severe restrictions on the types of investments in which trustees could invest trust assets. Trustees were precluded from obtaining professional investment help. And a trustee's performance was rated by the performance of each investment individually rather than on the performance of the whole portfolio.

Today, under UPIA, trusts are able to achieve a better rate of return for beneficiaries than at common law. Trustees can better protect the trust corpus by diversification. Trustees can invest to counter the effects of inflation. Trustees can obtain professional investment services. Trustees can take into account the changing character and kinds of assets that are available for investment. Trustees can utilize modern portfolio theory to guide their investment decisions. Trustees are judged on the overall performance of all the trust assets in a trust rather than specific assets. Trustees have a list of factors to consider in making investment decisions, such as "general economic conditions," "possible effect of inflation or deflation," "the expected total return from income and the appreciation of capital," and "other resources of the beneficiaries." A similar prudent person standard applies to executors (Cal. Prob. Code §9600). Approximately 43 jurisdictions have enacted UPIA or are substantially similar (http://nccusl.org/nccusl/uniformact_factsheets/uniformacts-fs-upria.asp (last visited July 5, 2007)).

Note that several duties of trustees are included elsewhere in this Probate Code (e.g., the duty of loyalty, Cal. Prob. Code §16002, and impartial dealings with beneficiaries, Cal. Prob. Code §16003.) Also, some rules that are located elsewhere have been amended to recognize

rules applicable under the UPIA (e.g., the duty not to delegate, Cal. Prob. Code §16012).

§16045. Title, Uniform Prudent Investor Act

This article, together with subdivision (a) of Section 16002 and Section 16003, constitutes the prudent investor rule and may be cited as the Uniform Prudent Investor Act.
(Stats. 1995 (S.B. 222), ch. 63, §6.)

§16046. Trustee owes duty to beneficiaries to comply with prudent investor rule; exception

(a) Except as provided in subdivision (b), a trustee who invests and manages trust assets owes a duty to the beneficiaries of the trust to comply with the prudent investor rule.

(b) The settlor may expand or restrict the prudent investor rule by express provisions in the trust instrument. A trustee is not liable to a beneficiary for the trustee's good faith reliance on these express provisions.
(Stats. 1995 (S.B. 222), ch. 63, §6.)

§16047. Prudent investor standard of care

(a) A trustee shall invest and manage trust assets as a prudent investor would, by considering the purposes, terms, distribution requirements, and other circumstances of the trust. In satisfying this standard, the trustee shall exercise reasonable care, skill, and caution.

(b) A trustee's investment and management decisions respecting individual assets and courses of action must be evaluated not in isolation, but in the context of the trust portfolio as a whole and as a part of an overall investment strategy having risk and return objectives reasonably suited to the trust.

(c) Among circumstances that are appropriate to consider in investing and managing trust assets are the following, to the extent relevant to the trust or its beneficiaries:

(1) General economic conditions.

(2) The possible effect of inflation or deflation.

(3) The expected tax consequences of investment decisions or strategies.

(4) The role that each investment or course of action plays within the overall trust portfolio.

(5) The expected total return from income and the appreciation of capital.

(6) Other resources of the beneficiaries known to the trustee as determined from information provided by the beneficiaries.

(7) Needs for liquidity, regularity of income, and preservation or appreciation of capital.

(8) An asset's special relationship or special value, if any, to the purposes of the trust or to one or more of the beneficiaries.

(d) A trustee shall make a reasonable effort to ascertain facts relevant to the investment and management of trust assets.

(e) A trustee may invest in any kind of property or type of investment or engage in any course of action or investment strategy consistent with the standards of this chapter.
(Stats. 1995 (S.B. 222), ch. 63, §6.)

§16048. Duty to diversify trust investments; exception

In making and implementing investment decisions, the trustee has a duty to diversify the investments of the trust unless, under the circumstances, it is prudent not to do so.
(Stats. 1995 (S.B. 222), ch. 63, §6.)

§16049. Duty to conduct review of assets within reasonable time

Within a reasonable time after accepting a trusteeship or receiving trust assets, a trustee shall review the trust assets and make and implement decisions concerning the retention and disposition of assets, in order to bring the trust portfolio into compliance with the purposes, terms, distribution requirements, and other circumstances of the trust, and with the requirements of this chapter.
(Stats. 1995 (S.B. 222), ch. 63, §6.)

§16050. Trustee may incur appropriate and reasonable costs

In investing and managing trust assets, a trustee may only incur costs that are appropriate and reasonable in relation to the assets, overall investment strategy, purposes, and other circumstances of the trust.
(Stats. 1995 (S.B. 222), ch. 63, §6.)

§16051. Determination of compliance with prudent investor rule

Compliance with the prudent investor rule is determined in light of the facts and circumstances existing at the time of a trustee's decision or action and not by hindsight.
(Stats. 1995 (S.B. 222), ch. 63, §6.)

§16052. Delegation of investment and management functions as prudent

(a) A trustee may delegate investment and management functions as prudent under the circumstances. The trustee shall exercise prudence in the following:

(1) Selecting an agent.

(2) Establishing the scope and terms of the delegation, consistent with the purposes and terms of the trust.

(3) Periodically reviewing the agent's overall performance and compliance with the terms of the delegation.

(b) In performing a delegated function, an agent has a duty to exercise reasonable care to comply with the terms of the delegation.

(c) Except as otherwise provided in Section 16401, a trustee who complies with the requirements of subdivision (a) is not liable to the beneficiaries or to the trust for the decisions or actions of the agent to whom the function was delegated.

(d) By accepting the delegation of a trust function from the trustee of a trust that is subject to the law of this state, an agent submits to the jurisdiction of the courts of this state.

(Stats. 1995 (S.B. 222), ch. 63, §6.)

§16053. Language authorizing application of chapter

The following terms or comparable language in the provisions of a trust, unless otherwise limited or modified, authorizes any investment or strategy permitted under this chapter: "investments permissible by law for investment of trust funds," "legal investments," "authorized investments," "using the judgment and care under the circumstances then prevailing that persons of prudence, discretion, and intelligence exercise in the management of their own affairs, not in regard to speculation but in regard to the permanent disposition of their funds, considering the probable income as well as the probable safety of their capital," "prudent man rule," "prudent trustee rule," "prudent person rule," and "prudent investor rule."

(Stats. 1995 (S.B. 222), ch. 63, §6.)

§16054. Date of application

This article applies to trusts existing on and created after its effective date. As applied to trusts existing on its effective date, this article governs only decisions or actions occurring after that date.

(Stats. 1995 (S.B. 222), ch. 63, §6.)

I. Uniform Principal and Income Allocation

A trustee has a fiduciary obligation to be fair both to the income beneficiaries during the management of the trust and also to the remainder beneficiaries at the termination of the trust. As part of their duties, trustees may be required to allocate income to certain beneficiaries and to pay expenses from particular assets before distribution of the trust property. Trustees must make the proper allocations of assets and charge the proper disbursements to either income or principal.

Model legislation facilitates the difficult tasks of identification of principal versus income, its allocation, and apportionment. The original Uniform Principal and Income Act (UPAIA) was promulgated in 1931 and revised in 1962. The Act was widely adopted by 1997, when a new revision was promulgated.

The purpose of the UPAIA (similar to that of the preceding Acts), is to provide procedures for trustees administering an estate in identifying principal versus income, and to ensure that the settlor's intention is the guiding principle. Importantly, the 1997 revision was necessary in order to enable principal and income allocation rules to accommodate prudent investor rules (the Uniform Prudent Investor Act was promulgated in 1994).

UPAIA is a default statute that operates when the trust instrument is silent. The Act establishes whether specific kinds of assets qualify as principal versus income. Next, the Act simplifies the allocation process by providing that any money received by a fiduciary is income, unless it fits within certain defined categories. The new Act provides for assets that were not within the scope of earlier versions of the Act, such as derivatives, options, deferred payment obligations, and synthetic financial assets. The new legislation also provides better guidelines for apportionment than did earlier versions of the Act. For example, the new Act provides that an income receipt is principal if it is due before a decedent dies (for an estate) or before an income interest begins (for a trust). However, after death or after an income interest begins, the interest is classified as income.

Also, the 1997 Act establishes rules that assure orderly distribution of income when a decedent dies or an income interest ends. Earlier versions of the Act did not address this distribution problem.

Significantly, the 1997 Act also accommodates notions of prudent investment,

modern portfolio theory, and total return that were not in existence at the time of the earlier Acts. The Act provides that a trustee must use prudent investment rules. For example, investment policy should depend upon the trustee's making the appropriate risk/return analysis and reaching investment decisions in light of that analysis. Also, one of the primary contributions of the 1997 Act (UPAIA §104) is to permit a trustee to adjust principal and income as dictated by the prudent investor standard when a trust provides for a fixed income for the income beneficiary. That is, the Act authorizes a trustee to make adjustments between principal and income that may be necessary if the income of a portfolio's total return is too small or too large because of investment decisions made pursuant to the prudent investor rule. The Act provides a list of factors that the trustee shall consider in making adjustment decisions and specifies the circumstances in which such adjustments are prohibited. Section 104 adds an important element of flexibility to the trustee's powers by authorizing adjustment between principal and income instead of merely applying traditional rules.

UPAIA §104 was enacted in California as California Probate Code §16336. However, unlike UPAIA §104(b), the California statute does not mandate consideration of particular factors, but rather specifies that these factors are guidelines subject to the court's discretion (Cal. Prob. Code §16336(g)).

Finally, the 1997 Act has been modernized by the inclusion of a provision that deals with the problem of disbursements made because of environmental laws and by provisions that address imbalances posed by tax laws (i.e., the trustee is given the power to make adjustments between principal and income to correct inequities caused by tax laws).

The California version of the Uniform Principal and Income Act is set forth below.

1. Title, Application, and Definitions

§16320. Title, Uniform Principle and Income Act

This chapter may be cited as the Uniform Principal and Income Act.

(Stats. 1999 (A.B. 846), ch. 145, §5.)

§16321. Application

The definitions in this article govern the construction of this chapter.

(Stats. 1999 (A.B. 846), ch. 145, §5.)

§16322. "Accounting period," defined

"Accounting period" means a calendar year unless another 12-month period is selected by a fiduciary. The term includes a portion of a calendar year or other 12-month period that begins when an income interest begins or ends when an income interest ends.

(Stats. 1999 (A.B. 846), ch. 145, §5.)

§16323. "Fiduciary," defined

"Fiduciary" means a personal representative or a trustee.

(Stats. 1999 (A.B. 846), ch. 145, §5.)

§16324. "Income," defined

"Income" means money or property that a fiduciary receives as current return from a principal asset. The term includes a portion of receipts from a sale, exchange, or liquidation of a principal asset, to the extent provided in Article 5.1 (commencing with Section 16350), 5.2 (commencing with Section 16355), or 5.3 (commencing with Section 16360).

(Stats. 1999 (A.B. 846), ch. 145, §5.)

§16325. "Income beneficiary," defined

"Income beneficiary" means a person to whom net income of a trust is or may be payable.

(Stats. 1999 (A.B. 846), ch. 145, §5.)

§16326. "Income interest," defined

"Income interest" means the right of an income beneficiary to receive all or part of net income, whether the trust requires it to be distributed or authorizes it to be distributed in the trustee's discretion.

(Stats. 1999 (A.B. 846), ch. 145, §5.)

§16327. "Mandatory income interest," defined

"Mandatory income interest" means the right of an income beneficiary to receive net income that the trust requires the fiduciary to distribute.

(Stats. 1999 (A.B. 846), ch. 145, §5.)

§16328. "Net income," defined

"Net income" means the total receipts allocated to income during an accounting period minus the disbursements made from income during the accounting period, plus or minus transfers under this chapter to or from income during the accounting period. During any period in which the trust is

being administered as a unitrust, either pursuant to the powers conferred by Sections 165336.4 to 16336.6, inclusive, or pursuant to the terms of the governing instrument, "net income" means the unitrust amount, if the unitrust amount is no less than 3 percent and no more than 5 percent of the fair market value of the trust assets, whether determined annually or averaged on a multiple year basis.
(Stats. 1999 (A.B. 846), ch. 145, §5. Amended by Stats 2005 (S.B. 754), ch. 100, §1.)

2. General Provisions and Fiduciary Duties

§16335. Allocation between principal and income; exercise of discretion therein

(a) In allocating receipts and disbursements to or between principal and income, and with respect to any other matter within the scope of this chapter, a fiduciary:

(1) Shall administer a trust or decedent's estate in accordance with the trust or the will, even if there is a different provision in this chapter.

(2) May administer a trust or decedent's estate by the exercise of a discretionary power of administration given to the fiduciary by the trust or the will, even if the exercise of the power produces a result different from a result required or permitted by this chapter, and no inference that the fiduciary has improperly exercised the discretion arises from the fact that the fiduciary has made an allocation contrary to a provision of this chapter.

(3) Shall administer a trust or decedent's estate in accordance with this chapter if the trust or the will does not contain a different provision or does not give the fiduciary a discretionary power of administration.

(4) Shall add a receipt or charge a disbursement to principal to the extent that the trust or the will and this chapter do not provide a rule for allocating the receipt or disbursement to or between principal and income.

(b) In exercising a discretionary power of administration regarding a matter within the scope of this chapter, whether granted by a trust, a will, or this chapter, including the trustee's power to adjust under subdivision (a) of Section 16336, and the trustee's power to convert into a unitrust or reconvert or change the unitrust payout percentage pursuant to Sections 16336.4 to 16336.6, inclusive, the fiduciary shall administer the trust or decedent's estate impartially, except to the extent that the trust or the will expresses an intention that the fiduciary shall or may favor one or more of the beneficiaries. The exercise of discretion in accordance with this chapter is presumed to be fair and reasonable to all beneficiaries.

(Stats. 1999 (A.B. 846), ch 145, §5. Amended by Stats. 2005 (S.B. 754), ch. 100, §2.)

§16336. Trustee may make adjustments between principal and income based on guidelines; exceptions

(a) Subject to subdivision (b), a trustee may make an adjustment between principal and income to the extent the trustee considers necessary if all of the following conditions are satisfied:

(1) The trustee invests and manages trust assets under the prudent investor rule.

(2) The trust describes the amount that shall or may be distributed to a beneficiary by referring to the trust's income.

(3) The trustee determines, after applying the rules in subdivision (a) of Section 16335, and considering any power the trustee may have under the trust to invade principal or accumulate income, that the trustee is unable to comply with subdivision (b) of Section 16335.

(b) A trustee may not make an adjustment between principal and income in any of the following circumstances:

(1) Where it would diminish the income interest in a trust (A) that requires all of the income to be paid at least annually to a spouse and (B) for which, if the trustee did not have the power to make the adjustment, an estate tax or gift tax marital deduction would be allowed, in whole or in part.

(2) Where it would reduce the actuarial value of the income interest in a trust to which a person transfers property with the intent to qualify for a gift tax exclusion.

(3) Where it would change the amount payable to a beneficiary as a fixed annuity or a fixed fraction of the value of the trust assets.

(4) Where it would be made from any amount that is permanently set aside for charitable purposes under a will or trust, unless both income and principal are so set aside.

(5) Where possessing or exercising the power to make an adjustment would cause an individual to be treated as the owner of all or part of the trust for income tax purposes, and the individual would not be treated as the owner if the trustee did not possess the power to make an adjustment.

(6) Where possessing or exercising the power to make an adjustment would cause all or part of the trust assets to be included for estate tax purposes in the estate of an individual who has the power to remove a trustee

or appoint a trustee, or both, and the assets would not be included in the estate of the individual if the trustee did not possess the power to make an adjustment.

(7) Where the trustee is a beneficiary of the trust.

(8) During any period in which the trust is being administered as a unitrust pursuant to the trustee's exercise of the power to convert provided in Section 16336.4 or 16336.5, or pursuant to the terms of the governing instrument.

(c) Notwithstanding Section 15620, if paragraph (5), (6), or (7) of subdivision (b) applies to a trustee and there is more than one trustee, a cotrustee to whom the provision does not apply may make the adjustment unless the exercise of the power by the remaining trustee or trustees is not permitted by the trust.

(d) A trustee may release the entire power conferred by subdivision (a) or may release only the power to adjust from income to principal or the power to adjust from principal to income in either of the following circumstances:

(1) If the trustee is uncertain about whether possessing or exercising the power will cause a result described in paragraphs (1) to (6), inclusive, of subdivision (b).

(2) If the trustee determines that possessing or exercising the power will or may deprive the trust of a tax benefit or impose a tax burden not described in subdivision (b).

(e) A release under subdivision (d) may be permanent or for a specified period, including a period measured by the life of an individual.

(f) A trust that limits the power of a trustee to make an adjustment between principal and income does not affect the application of this section unless it is clear from the trust that it is intended to deny the trustee the power of adjustment provided by subdivision (a).

(g) In deciding whether and to what extent to exercise the power to make adjustments under this section, the trustee may consider, but is not limited to, any of the following:

(1) The nature, purpose, and expected duration of the trust.

(2) The intent of the settlor.

(3) The identity and circumstances of the beneficiaries.

(4) The needs for liquidity, regularity of income, and preservation and appreciation of capital.

(5) The assets held in the trust; the extent to which they consist of financial assets, interests in closely held enterprises, tangible and intangible personal property, or real property; the extent to which an asset is used by a beneficiary; and whether an asset was purchased by the trustee or received from the settlor.

(6) The net amount allocated to income under other statutes and the increase or decrease in the value of the principal assets, which the trustee may estimate as to assets for which market values are not readily available.

(7) Whether and to what extent the trust gives the trustee the power to invade principal or accumulate income or prohibit the trustee from invading principal or accumulating income, and the extent to which the trustee has exercised a power from time to time to invade principal or accumulate income.

(8) The actual and anticipated effect of economic conditions on principal and income and effects

(9) The anticipated tax consequences of an adjustment.

(h) Nothing in this section or in this chapter is intended to create or imply a duty to make an adjustment, and a trustee is not liable for not considering whether to make an adjustment or for choosing not to make an adjustment.

(Stats. 1999 (A.B. 846), ch. 145, §5. Amended by Stats. 2005 (S.B. 754), ch. 100, §3.)

§16336.4 Converting a trust into a unitrust

(a) Unless expressly prohibited by the governing instrument, a trustee may convert a trust into a unitrust, as described in this section. A trust that limits the power of the trustee to make an adjustment between principal and income or modify the trust does not effect the application of this section unless it is clear from the governing instrument that it is intended to deny the trustee the power to convert into a unitrust.

(b) The trustee may convert a trust into a unitrust without a court order if all of the following apply:

(1) The conditions set forth in subdivision (a) of Section 16446 are satisfied.

(2) The unitrust proposed by the trustee conforms to the provisions of paragraphs (1) to (8), inclusive, of subdivision (e).

(3) The trustee gives written notice of the trustee's intenion to convert the trust into a unitrust and furnishes the information required by subdivision (c). The notice shall comply with the requirements of Chapter 5 (commencing with Section 16500), including notice to a beneficiary who is a minor and to the minor's guarding, if any.

(4) No beneficiary objects to the proposed action in a writing delivered to the trustee within the period prescribed by subdivision (d) of Section 16502 or a

longer period as is specified in the notice described in subdivision (c).

(c) The notice describe in paragraph (3) of subdivision (b) shall include a copy of Sections 16336.4 to 16336.7 inclusive, and all the following information:

(1) A statement that the trust hsall be administered in accordance with the provisions of subdivision (e) and the effective date of the conversion.

(2) A description of the methods to be used for determining the fair market value of trust assets.

(3) The amount actually distributed to the income beneficiary during the previous accounting year of the trust.

(4) The amount that would have been distributed to the income beneficiary during the previous accounting year of the trust had the trustee's proposed changes been in effect during that entire year.

(5) The discretionary decisions the trustee proposes to make as of the conversion date pursuant to subdivision (f).

(d) In deciding whether to exercise the power conferred by this section, a trustee may consider, among other things, the factors set forth in subdivision (g) of Section 16336.

(e) Except to the extent that the court orders otherwise or the parties agree otherwise pursuant to Section 16336.5 after a trust is converted to a unitrust, all of the following shall apply:

(1) The trustee shall make regular distributions in accordance with the governing instrument construed in accordance with the provisions of this section.

(2) The term "income" in the governing instrument shall mean annual distribution, the unitrust amount, equal to 4 percent, which is the payout percentage, of the net fair market value of the trust's assets, whether those assets would be considered income or principal under other provisions of this chapter, averaged over the lessor of: (A) the three proceeding years, or (B) the period during which the trust has been in existence.

(3) During each accounting year of the trust following its conversion into a unitrust, the trustee shall, as early in the year as is practicable, furnish each income beneficiary with a statement describing the computation of the unitrust amount for that accounting year.

(4) The trustee shall determine the net fair market value of each asset held in the trust no less often than annually. However, the following property shall not be included in determining the unitrust amount:

(A) Any resident property or any tangible personal property, that, as of the first business day of the current accounting year, one or more current beneficiaries of the trust have or have had the right to occupy, or have or had had the right to possess or control, other than in his or her capacity as trustee of the trust, which property shall be administered according to other provisions of this chapter as though no conversion to a unitrust has occurred.

(B) Any asset specifically devised to a beneficiary to he extent necessary, in the trustee's reasonable judgment, to avoid a material risk of exhausting other trust assets prior to termination of the trust. All net income generated by a specifically devised asset excluded from the unitrust computation pursuant to this subdivision shall be accumulated or distributed by the trustee according to the rules otherwise applicable o that net income pursuant to other provisions of this chapter.

(C) Any asset while held in a testator's estate or a terminating trust.

(5) The initrust amount, as otherwise computed pursuant to this subdivision, shall be reduced proportionately for any material distribution made to accomplish a partial termination of the trust required by he governing instrument or made as a result of the exercise of a power of appointment or withdrawal, other than distributions of the unitrust amount, and shall be increased proportionately for the receipt of any material addition to the trust, other than a receipt that represents a return on investment, during the period considered in paragraph (2) in computing the unitrust amount. For the purpose of this paragraph, a distribution or an addition shall be "material" if the net value of the distribution or addition, when combined with all prior distributions made or additions received during the same accounting year, exceeds 10 percent of the value of the assets used to compute the unitrust amount as of the most recent prior valuation date. The trustee may, in the reasonable exercise of his or her discretion, adjust the unitrust amount to this subdivision even if the distributions or additions are not sufficient o meet the definition or materially set forth in the preceding sentence.

(6) In the case of a short year in which a beneficiary's right to payments commences or ceases, the trustee shall prorate the unitrust amount on a daily basis.

(7) Unless otherwise provided by the governing instrument ot determined by the trustee, the unitrust amount shall be considered paid in the following order from the following sources:

(A) From the net taxable income, determined as if the trust ere other than a unitrust.

(B) From net realized short-term capital gains.

(C) From net realized long-term capital gains.

(D) From tax-exempt and other income.

(E) From principal of the trust.

(8) Expenses that would be deducted from income if the trust were not a unitrust may not be deducted from the unitrust amount.

(f) The trustee shall determine, in the trustee's discretion, all of the following matters related to administration of a unitrust created pursuant to this section:

(1) The effective date of a conversion to a unitrust.

(2) The frequency of payments in satisfaction of the unitrust amount.

(3) Whether to value the trust's assets annually or more frequently.

(4) What valuation dates to use.

(5) How to value nonliquid assets.

(6) The characterization of the unitrust payout for income tax reporting purposes. However, the trustee's characterization shall be consistent.

(7) Any other matters that the trustee deems appropriate for the proper functioning of the unitrust.

(g) The conversion into a unitrust shall not affect a provision in the governing instrument directing or authorizing the trustee to distribute principal or authorizing the exercise of a power of appointment over or withdrawal of all or a portion or the principal.

(h) A trustee may not convert a trust into a unitrust in any of the following circumstances:

(1) If payment of the unitrust amount would change the amount payable to a beneficiary as a fixed annuity or a fixed fraction of the value of the trust assets.

(2) If the unitrust distribution would be made from any amount that is permanently set aside for charitable purposes under the governing instrument and for which a federal statute or gift tax deduction has been taken, unless both income and principal are set aside.

(3) If possessing or exercising the power to convert would cause an individual to be treated as the owner of all or part of the trust for federal income tax purposes, and the individual would not be treated as the owner if the trustee did not possess the power to convert.

(4) If possessing or exercising the power to convert would cause all or part of the trust assets to be subject to federal estate or gift tax with respect to an individual, and the asses would not be subject to federal estate or fight tax with respect to the individual if the trustee the power to convert.

(5) If the conversion would result in the disallowance of a federal estate tax or fight tax marital deduction that would be allowed if the trustee did not have the power to convert.

(i) If paragraph (3) or (4) of subdivision (h) applies to a trustee and there is more than one trustee, a cotrustee to whom the provision does not apply may convert the trust unless that exercise of the power by the remaining trustee is prohibited by the governing instrument. If paragraph (3) or (4) of subdivision (h) applies to all the trustees, the court may order the conversion as provided in subdivision (b) of Section 16446.5.

(j) A trustee may release the power conferred by this section to convert to a unitrust if (1) the trustee is uncertain about whether possessing or exercising the power will cause a result described in paragraph (3), (4), or (5) of subdivision (h), or (2) the trustee determines that possessing or exercising the power will or may deprive the trust of a tax benefit or impose a tax burden not described in subdivision (h). The release may be permanent or for a specified period, including a period measured by the life or an individual.

(Stats. 2005 (S.B. 754), ch. 100, §4.)

§16336.5. Additional ways to convert a trust into a unitrust

(a) The trustee may convert a trust into a unitrust upon terms other than hose set forth in subdivision (e) of Section 16336.4, without court order, in all of the following apply:

(1) The conditions set forth in subdivision (a) of Section 16336 are satisfied.

(2) The trustee gives written notice of the trustee's intention to concert the trust into a unitrust and furnishes the information required by subdivision (c) of Section 16336.4. The notice shall comply with the requirements of Chapter 5 (commencing with Section 16500), including notice to a beneficiary who is a minor and to the minor's guardian, if any.

(3) The payout percentage to be adopted is at least 3 percent and no greater than 5 percent.

(4) All beneficiaries entitled to notice under Section 16501 consent in writing to the proposed action after having been furnished with the notice described in subdivision (c) of Section 16336.4.

(b) The court may order the conversion of a trust into a unitrust as provided in this subdivision.

(1)(A) The trustee may petition the court to approve the conversion to a unitrust for any one of the following reasons:

(i) A beneficiary timely objects to a proposed conversion to a unitrust.

(ii) The trustee proposes to make the conversion upon terms other than those described in subdivision (e) of Section 16336.4.

(iii) Paragraph (3) or (4) or subdivision (h) of Section 16336.4 applies to all currently acting trustees.

(iv) IF the trustee determines, in its discretion, that a petition is advisable.

(B) In no event, however, may the court authorize conversion to a unitrust with a payout percentage of less than 3 percent or greater than 5 percent of the fair market value of the trust assets.

(2) A beneficiary may petition the court to order the conversion.

(3) The court shall approve the conversion proposed by the trustee or direct the conversion requested by the beneficiary if the conditions set forth in subdivision (a) of Section 16336 are satisfied and the court concludes that conversion of the trust on the terms proposed will enable the trustee to better comply with the provisions of subdivision (b) of Section 16335.

(4) In deciding whether to approve a proposed conversion or direct a requested conversion, the court may consider, among other factors, those described in subdivision (g) of Section 16336.

(Stats. 2005 (S.B. 754), ch. 100, §5.)

§16336.6. Trustee may reconvert the trust from a unitrust

Unless expressly prohibited by the governing instrument, a trustee may reconvert the trust from a unitrust or change the payout percentage of a unitrust.

(a) A trustee may make the reconversion or change in payout percentage without a court order if all of the following conditions are satisfied:

(1) At least thee years have elapsed since the most recent conversion to a unitrust.

(2) The trustee determines that reconversion or change in payout percentage would enable the trustee to better comply with the provisions of subdivision (b) of Section 16335.

(3) One of the following notice requirements is satisfied.

(A) In the case of a proposed reconversion, the trustee gives notice of the trustee's intention to convert that complies with the requirements of Section 5)commencing with Section 16500) and no beneficiary objects o the proposed action in a writing delivered to the trustee within the period prescribed by subdivision (d) of Section 16502. The trustee's notice shall include the information described in subdivision (3) and (4) of subdivision (c) of Section 16336.4.

(B) In the case of a proposed change in payout percentage, the trustee gives written notice stating the new percentage that the trustee proposes to adopt, which notice shall comply with the requirements of Chapter 5 (commencing with Section 16500), and no beneficiary objects to the proposed action in a writing delivered to the trustee within the period prescribed by subdivision (d) of Section 16502.

(b) The trustee may make the conversion or change in payout percentage at any time pursuant to court order provided that: (1) the court determines that reconversion or change in payout percentage will enable the trustee to better comply with the provisions of subdivision (b) of Section 16335, and (2) in the case of a change in payout percentage, the new payout percentage is at least 3 percent and no greater than 5 percent. The court may enter an order pursuant to this subdivision upon the petition of the trustee of any beneficiary.

(Stats. 2005 (S.B. 754), ch. 100, §6.)

§16336.7. No duty to convert or reconvert a trust

(a) Sections 16336.4-16336.6, inclusive, shall not impose any duty on the trustee to convert or reconvert a trust or to consider a conversion or reconversion

(b) Subdivision (b) of Section 16503 applies to all actions pursuant o Sections 16336.4 to 16336.6, inclusive, for which notice of proposed action is given in compliance with Chapter 5 (commencing with Section 16500), including a notice to a beneficiary who is a minor and to the minor's guardian, if any.

(Stats. 2005 (S.B. 754), ch. 100, §7.)

§16337. Trustee may give notice of proposed action

(a) A trustee may give a notice of proposed action regarding a matter governed in Chapter 5 (commencing with Section 16500). For the purpose of this section, a proposed action includes a course of action and a decision not to take action.

(Stats. 1999 (A.B. 846), ch. 145, §5. Amended by Stats. 2004 (S.B. 1021), ch. 54, §1.)

§16338. Proceedings regarding exercise of trustee's discretion to make an adjustment

In a proceeding with respect to a trustee's exercise or nonexercise of the power to make an adjustment under

Section 16336, the sole remedy is to direct, deny, or revise an adjustment between principal and income. In a proceeding with respect to a trustee's exercise or nonexercise or a power conferred by Sections 16336.4 to 16336.6, inclusive, the sole remedy is to obtain an order directing the trustee to convert the trust to a unitrust, to reconvert from a unitrust, to change the distribution percentage, or to order any administrative procedures the court determines to be necessary or helpful for the proper functioning of the trust.

(Stats. 1999 (A.B. 846), ch. 145, §5. Amended by Stats. 2005 (S.B. 754), ch. 100 §8.)

§16339. Application

This chapter applies to every trust or decedent's estate existing on or after January 1, 2000, except as otherwise expressly provided in the trust or will or in this chapter.

(Stats. 1999 (A.B. 846), ch. 145, §5.)

3. Decedent's Estate or Terminating Income Interest

§16340. Rules that apply after decedent's death or termination of income interest

After the decedent's death, in the case of a decedent's estate, or after an income interest in a trust ends, the following rules apply:

(a) If property is specifically given to a beneficiary, by will or trust, the fiduciary of the estate or of the terminating income interest shall distribute the net income and principal receipts to the beneficiary who is to receive the property, subject to the following rules:

(1) The net income and principal receipts from the specifically given property are determined by including all of the amounts the fiduciary receives or pays with respect to the property, whether the amounts accrued or became due before, on, or after the decedent's death or an income interest in a trust ends, and by making a reasonable provision for amounts the fiduciary believes the estate or terminating income interest may become obligated to pay after the property is distributed.

(2) The fiduciary may not reduce income and principal receipts from the specifically given property on account of a payment described in Section 16370 or 16371, to the extent that the will, the trust, or Section 12002 requires payment from other property or to the extent that the fiduciary recovers the payment from a third person.

(b) The fiduciary shall distribute to a beneficiary who receives a pecuniary amount, whether outright or in trust, the interest or any other amount provided by the will, the trust, or Chapter 8 (commencing with Section 12000) of Part 10 of Division 7, from the remaining net income determined under subdivision (c) or from principal to the extent that net income is insufficient.

(c) The fiduciary shall determine the remaining net income of the decedent's estate or terminating income interest as provided in this chapter and by doing the following:

(1) Including in net income all income from property used to discharge liabilities.

(2) Paying from income or principal, in the fiduciary's discretion, fees of attorneys, accountants, and fiduciaries, court costs and other expenses of administration, and interest on death taxes, except that the fiduciary may pay these expenses from income of property passing to a trust for which the fiduciary claims an estate tax marital or charitable deduction only to the extent that the payment of these expenses from income will not cause the reduction or loss of the deduction.

(3) Paying from principal all other disbursements made or incurred in connection with the settlement of a decedent's estate or the winding up of a terminating income interest, including debts, funeral expenses, disposition of remains, family allowances, and death taxes and related penalties that are apportioned to the estate or terminating income interest by the will, the trust, or Division 10 (commencing with Section 20100).

(d) After distributions required by subdivision (b), the fiduciary shall distribute the remaining net income determined under subdivision (c) in the manner provided in Section 16341 to all other beneficiaries.

(e) For purposes of this section, a reference in Chapter 8 (commencing with Section 12000) of Part 10 of Division 7 to the date of the testator's death means the date of the settlor's death or of the occurrence of some other event on which the distributee's right to receive the gift depends.

(Stats. 1999 (A.B. 846), ch. 145, §5.)

§16341. Beneficiary's portion of net income

(a) Each beneficiary described in subdivision (d) of Section 16340 is entitled to receive a portion of the net income equal to the beneficiary's fractional interest in undistributed principal assets, using values as of the distribution dates and without reducing the values by any unpaid principal obligations.

(b) If a fiduciary does not distribute all of the collected but undistributed net income to each beneficiary as of a distribution date, the fiduciary shall maintain appropriate records showing the interest of each beneficiary in that net income.

(c) The distribution date for purposes of this section may be the date as of which the fiduciary calculates the value of the assets if that date is reasonably near the date on which assets are actually distributed.

(Stats. 1999 (A.B. 846), ch. 145, §5.)

§16345. Date for beneficiary's entitlement to net income and for asset becoming subject to trust

(a) An income beneficiary is entitled to net income from the date on which the income interest begins. An income interest begins on the date specified in the trust or, if no date is specified, on the date an asset becomes subject to a trust or successive income interest.

(b) An asset becomes subject to a trust at the following times:

(1) In the case of an asset that is transferred to a trust during the transferor's life, on the date it is transferred to the trust.

(2) In the case of an asset that becomes subject to a trust by reason of a will, even if there is an intervening period of administration of the testator's estate, on the date of the testator's death.

(3) In the case of an asset that is transferred to a fiduciary by a third party because of the individual's death, on the date of the individual's death.

(c) An asset becomes subject to a successive income interest on the day after the preceding income interest ends, as determined under subdivision (d), even if there is an intervening period of administration to wind up the preceding income interest.

(d) An income interest ends on the day before an income beneficiary dies, or another terminating event occurs, or on the last day of a period during which there is no beneficiary to whom a trustee may distribute income.

(Stats. 1999 (A.B. 846), ch. 145, §5.)

§16346. Trustee shall allocate income receipt or disbursement based on specified due dates

(a) A trustee shall allocate an income receipt or disbursement other than one to which subdivision (a) of Section 16340 applies to principal if its due date occurs before a decedent dies in the case of an estate or before an income interest begins in the case of a trust or successive income interest.

(b) A trustee shall allocate an income receipt or disbursement to income if its due date occurs on or after the date on which a decedent dies or an income interest begins and it is a periodic due date. An income receipt or disbursement shall be treated as accruing from day to day if its due date is not periodic or it has no due date. The portion of the receipt or disbursement accruing before the date on which a decedent dies or an income interest begins shall be allocated to principal and the balance shall be allocated to income.

(c) An item of income or an obligation is due on the date the payer is required to make a payment. If a payment date is not stated, there is no due date for the purposes of this chapter. Distributions to shareholders or other owners from an entity to which Section 16350 applies are deemed to be due on the date fixed by the entity for determining who is entitled to receive the distribution or, if no date is fixed, on the declaration date for the distribution. A due date is periodic for receipts or disbursements that must be paid at regular intervals under a lease or an obligation to pay interest or if an entity customarily makes distributions at regular intervals.

(Stats. 1999 (A.B. 846), ch. 145, §5.)

§16347. "Undistributed income," defined; payment to mandatory income beneficiary

(a) For the purposes of this section, "undistributed income" means net income received before the date on which an income interest ends. The term does not include an item of income or expense that is due or accrued or net income that has been added or is required to be added to principal by the trust.

(b) Except as provided in subdivision (c), on the date when a mandatory income interest ends, the trustee shall pay to a mandatory income beneficiary who survives that date, or to the estate of a deceased mandatory income beneficiary whose death causes the interest to end, the beneficiary's share of the undistributed income that is not disposed of under the trust.

(c) If immediately before the income interest ends, the beneficiary under subdivision (b) has an unqualified power to revoke more than 5 percent of the trust, the undistributed income from the portion of the trust that may be revoked shall be added to principal.

(d) When a trustee's obligation to pay a fixed annuity or a fixed fraction of the value of the trust's assets ends, the trustee shall prorate the final payment.

(Stats. 1999 (A.B. 846), ch. 145, §5.)

4. Allocation of Receipts During Administration of Trust: Receipts from Entities

§16350. Allocation of receipts to income or principal

(a) For the purposes of this section, "entity" means a corporation, partnership, limited liability company, regulated investment company, real estate investment trust, common trust fund, or any other organization in which a trustee has an interest other than a trust or decedent's estate to which Section 16351 applies, a business or activity to which Section 16352 applies, or an asset-backed security to which Section 16367 applies.

(b) Except as otherwise provided in this section, a trustee shall allocate to income money received from an entity.

(c) A trustee shall allocate to principal the following receipts from an entity:

(1) Property other than money.

(2) Money received in one distribution or a series of related distributions in exchange for part or all of a trust's interest in the entity.

(3) Money received in total or partial liquidation of the entity.

(4) Money received from an entity that is a regulated investment company or a real estate investment trust if the money distributed is a capital gain dividend for federal income tax purposes.

(d) For purposes of paragraph (3) of subdivision (c):

(1) Money is received in partial liquidation (A) to the extent that the entity, at or near the time of a distribution, indicates that it is a distribution in partial liquidation, or (B) if the total amount of money and property received by all owners, collectively, in a distribution or series of related distributions is greater than 20 percent of the entity's gross assets, as shown by the entity's yearend financial statements immediately preceding the initial receipt. If that receipt is allocated between December 2, 2004, and the operative date of the act adding this sentence, a trustee shall not b liable for allocating the receipt to income if the amount received by the trustee, when considered together with the amount received by all the owners, collectively, exceeds 20% of the entity's gross assets, but the amount received by the trustee does not exceed 20 percent of the entity's gross assets.

(2) Money is not received in partial liquidation, nor may it be taken into account under clause (B) of paragraph (1), to the extent that it does not exceed the amount of income tax that a trustee or beneficiary is required to pay on taxable income of the entity that distributes the money.

(e) A trustee may rely on a statement made by an entity about the source or character of a distribution if the statement is made at or near the time of distribution by the entity's board of directors or other person or group of persons authorized to exercise powers to pay money or transfer property comparable to those of a corporation's board of directors.

(Stats. 1999 (A.B. 846), ch. 145, §5; Amended by Stats. (S.B. 296) ch. 51, §1, effective July 18, 2005.)

§16351. Allocation to income or principal of amounts received from specified trusts or estates

A trustee shall allocate to income an amount received as a distribution of income from a trust or a decedent's estate (other than an interest in an investment entity) in which the trust has an interest other than a purchased interest, and shall allocate to principal an amount received as a distribution of principal from the trust or estate.

(Stats. 1999 (A.B. 846), ch. 145, §5.)

§16352. Trustee may provide separate accounting records for business or other activity

(a) If a trustee who conducts a business or other activity determines that it is in the best interest of all the beneficiaries to account separately for the business or other activity instead of accounting for it as part of the trust's general accounting records, the trustee may maintain separate accounting records for its transactions, whether or not its assets are segregated from other trust assets.

(b) A trustee who accounts separately for a business or other activity may determine the extent to which its net cash receipts must be retained for working capital, the acquisition or replacement of fixed assets, and its other reasonably foreseeable needs, and the extent to which the remaining net cash receipts are accounted for as principal or income in the trust's general accounting records. If a trustee sells assets of the business or other activity, other than in the ordinary course of the business or other activity, the trustee shall account for the net amount received as principal in the trust's general accounting records to the extent the trustee determines that the amount received is no longer required in the conduct of the business or other activity.

(c) Businesses and other activities for which a trustee may maintain separate accounting records include the following:

(1) Retail, manufacturing, service, and other traditional business activities.

(2) Farming.

(3) Raising and selling livestock and other animals.

(4) Managing rental properties.

(5) Extracting minerals and other natural resources.

(6) Timber operations.

(7) Activities to which Section 16366 applies.

(Stats. 1999 (A.B. 846), ch. 145, §5.)

5. Allocation of Receipts During Administration of Trust: Receipts Not Normally Apportioned

§16355. Trustee shall allocate to principal as provided

A trustee shall allocate to principal:

(a) To the extent not allocated to income under this chapter, assets received from a transferor during the transferor's lifetime, a decedent's estate, a trust with a terminating income interest, or a payer under a contract naming the trust or its trustee as beneficiary.

(b) Subject to any contrary rules in this article and in Articles 5.1 (commencing with Section 16350) and 5.3 (commencing with Section 16360), money or other property received from the sale, exchange, liquidation, or change in form of a principal asset, including realized profit.

(c) Amounts recovered from third parties to reimburse the trust because of disbursements described in paragraph (7) of subdivision (a) of Section 16371 or for other reasons to the extent not based on the loss of income.

(d) Proceeds of property taken by eminent domain, but a separate award made for the loss of income with respect to an accounting period during which a current income beneficiary had a mandatory income interest is income.

(e) Net income received in an accounting period during which there is no beneficiary to whom a trustee may or must distribute income.

(f) Other receipts allocated to principal as provided in Article 5.3 (commencing with Section 16360).

(Stats. 1999 (A.B. 846), ch. 145, §5.)

§16356. Trustee shall allocate amounts received from rental property as provided

Unless the trustee accounts for receipts from rental property pursuant to Section 16352, the trustee shall allocate to income an amount received as rent of real or personal property, including an amount received for cancellation or renewal of a lease. An amount received as a refundable deposit, including a security deposit or a deposit that is to be applied as rent for future periods, shall be added to principal and held subject to the terms of the lease, and is not available for distribution to a beneficiary until the trustee's contractual obligations have been satisfied with respect to that amount.

(Stats. 1999 (A.B. 846), ch. 145, §5.)

§16357. Allocation of interest on obligation to pay money

(a) An amount received as interest, whether determined at a fixed, variable, or floating rate, on an obligation to pay money to the trustee, including an amount received as consideration for prepaying principal, shall be allocated to income without any provision for amortization of premium.

(b) An amount received from the sale, redemption, or other disposition of an obligation to pay money to the trustee more than one year after it is purchased or acquired by the trustee, including an obligation whose purchase price, or its value when it is otherwise acquired, is less than its value at maturity, shall be allocated to principal. If the obligation matures within one year after it is purchased or acquired by the trustee, an amount received in excess of its purchase price, or its value when it is otherwise acquired, shall be allocated to income.

(c) This section does not apply to an obligation to which Section 16361, 16362, 16363, 16364, 16366, or 16367 applies.

(Stats. 1999 (A.B. 846), ch. 145, §5.)

§16358. Allocation of life insurance policy proceeds and other contracts insuring against certain losses

(a) Except as otherwise provided in subdivision (b), a trustee shall allocate to principal the proceeds of a life insurance policy or other contract in which the trust or its trustee is named as beneficiary, including a contract that insures the trust or its trustee against loss for damage to, destruction of, or loss of title to a trust asset. The trustee shall allocate dividends on an insurance policy to income if the premiums on the policy are paid from income, and to principal if the premiums are paid from principal.

(b) A trustee shall allocate to income proceeds of a contract that insures the trustee against loss of occupancy or other use by an income beneficiary, loss of income, or, subject to Section 16352, loss of profits from a business.

(c) This section does not apply to a contract to which Section 16361 applies.

(Stats. 1999 (A.B. 846), ch. 145, §5.)

6. Allocation of Receipts During Administration of Trust: Receipts Normally Apportioned

§16360. Trustee may allocate entire amount to principal if allocation would be insubstantial

(a) If a trustee determines that an allocation between principal and income required by Section 16361, 16362, 16363, 16364, or 16367 is insubstantial, the trustee may allocate the entire amount to principal unless one of the circumstances described in subdivision (b) of Section 16336 applies to the allocation. This power may be exercised by a cotrustee in the circumstances described in subdivision (c) of Section 16336 and may be released for the reasons and in the manner provided in subdivisions (d) and (e) of Section 16336.

(b) An allocation is presumed to be insubstantial in either of the following cases:

(1) Where the amount of the allocation would increase or decrease net income in an accounting period, as determined before the allocation, by less than 10 percent.

(2) Where the value of the asset producing the receipt for which the allocation would be made is less than 10 percent of the total value of the trust's assets at the beginning of the accounting period.

(c) Nothing in this section imposes a duty on the trustee to make an allocation under this section, and the trustee is not liable for failure to make an allocation under this section.

(Stats. 1999 (A.B. 846), ch. 145, §5.)

§16361. Payments characterized as interest or dividend shall be allocated to income; allocation of other payments; excess allocation to income in order to obtain estate tax marital deduction

(a) In this section, "payment" means a payment that a trustee may receive over a fixed number of years or during the life of one or more individuals because of services rendered or property transferred to the payer in exchange for future payments. The term includes a payment made in money or property from the payer's general assets or from a separate fund created by the payer, including a private or commercial annuity, an individual retirement account, and a pension, profit-sharing, stock-bonus, or stock-ownership plan.

(b) To the extent that a payment is characterized as interest or a dividend or a payment made in lieu of interest or a dividend, a trustee shall allocate it to income. The trustee shall allocate to principal the balance of the payment and any other payment received in the same accounting period that is not characterized as interest, a dividend, or an equivalent payment.

(c) If no part of a payment is characterized as interest, a dividend, or an equivalent payment, and all or part of the payment is required to be made, a trustee shall allocate to income 10 percent of the part that is required to be made during the accounting period and the balance to principal. If no part of a payment is required to be made or the payment received is the entire amount to which the trustee is entitled, the trustee shall allocate the entire payment to principal. For purposes of this subdivision, a payment is not "required to be made" to the extent that it is made because the trustee exercises a right of withdrawal.

(d) If, to obtain an estate tax marital deduction for a trust, a trustee shall allocate more of a payment to income than provided by this section, the trustee shall allocate to income the additional amount necessary to obtain the marital deduction.

(e) This section does not apply to payments to which Section 16362 applies.

(Stats. 1999 (A.B. 846), ch. 145, §5.)

§16362. Allocation of receipts from liquidating assets

(a) In this section, "liquidating asset" means an asset whose value will diminish or terminate because the asset is expected to produce receipts for a period of limited duration. The term includes a leasehold, patent, copyright, royalty right, and right to receive payments under an arrangement that does not provide for the payment of interest on the unpaid balance. The term does not include a payment subject to Section 16361, resources subject to Section 16363, timber subject to Section 16364, an activity subject to Section 16366, an asset subject to Section 16367, or any asset for which the trustee establishes a reserve for depreciation under Section 16372.

(b) A trustee shall allocate to income 10 percent of the receipts from a liquidating asset and the balance to principal.

(Stats. 1999 (A.B. 846), ch. 145, §5.)

§16363. Allocation of receipts from mineral interests and other natural resources

(a) To the extent that a trustee accounts for receipts from an interest in minerals or other natural resources pursuant to this section, the trustee shall allocate them as follows:

(1) If received as a nominal bonus, nominal delay rental, or nominal annual rent on a lease, a receipt shall be allocated to income.

(2) If received from a production payment, a receipt shall be allocated to income if and to the extent that the agreement creating the production payment provides a factor for interest or its equivalent. The balance shall be allocated to principal.

(3) If an amount received as a royalty, shut-in-well payment, take-or-pay payment, bonus, or delay rental is more than nominal, 90 percent shall be allocated to principal and the balance to income.

(4) If an amount is received from a working interest or any other interest in mineral or other natural resources not described in paragraph (1), (2), or (3), 90 percent of

the net amount received shall be allocated to principal and the balance to income.

(b) An amount received on account of an interest in water that is renewable shall be allocated to income. If the water is not renewable, 90 percent of the amount shall be allocated to principal and the balance to income.

(c) This chapter applies whether or not a decedent or donor was extracting minerals, water, or other natural resources before the interest became subject to the trust.

(Stats. 1999 (A.B. 846), ch. 145, §5.)

§16364. Allocation of receipts from sale of timber and related products

(a) To the extent that a trustee accounts for receipts from the sale of timber and related products pursuant to this section, the trustee shall allocate the net receipts as follows:

(1) To income to the extent that the amount of timber removed from the land does not exceed the rate of growth of the timber during the accounting periods in which a beneficiary has a mandatory income interest.

(2) To principal to the extent that the amount of timber removed from the land exceeds the rate of growth of the timber or the net receipts are from the sale of standing timber.

(3) To or between income and principal if the net receipts are from the lease of timberland or from a contract to cut timber from land owned by a trust, by determining the amount of timber removed from the land under the lease or contract and applying the rules in paragraphs (1) and (2).

(4) To principal to the extent that advance payments, bonuses, and other payments are not allocated pursuant to paragraph (1), (2), or (3).

(b) In determining net receipts to be allocated under subdivision (a), a trustee shall deduct and transfer to principal a reasonable amount for depletion.

(c) This chapter applies whether or not a decedent or transferor was harvesting timber from the property before it became subject to the trust.

(Stats. 1999 (A.B. 846), ch. 145, §5.)

§16365. Trustee may take action of increasing income in order to obtain marital deduction

(a) If a marital deduction is allowed for all or part of a trust whose assets consist substantially of property that does not provide the spouse with sufficient income from or use of the trust assets, and if the amounts that the trustee transfers from principal to income under Section 16336 and distributes to the spouse from principal pursuant to the terms of the trust are insufficient to provide the spouse with the beneficial enjoyment required to obtain the marital deduction, the spouse may require the trustee to make property productive of income or convert it into productive property or exercise the power under subdivision (a) of Section 16336 within a reasonable time. The trustee may decide which action or combination of actions to take.

(b) In cases not governed by subdivision (a), proceeds from the sale or other disposition of a trust asset are principal without regard to the amount of income the asset produces during any accounting period.

(Stats. 1999 (A.B. 846), ch. 145, §5.)

§16366. Allocation of receipts and disbursements made in connection with transactions in derivatives; options to buy or sell property

(a) In this section, "derivative" means a contract or financial instrument or a combination of contracts and financial instruments that gives a trust the right or obligation to participate in some or all changes in the price of a tangible or intangible asset or group of assets, or changes in a rate, an index of prices or rates, or other market indicator for an asset or a group of assets.

(b) To the extent that a trustee does not account under Section 16352 for transactions in derivatives, the trustee shall allocate to principal receipts from and disbursements made in connection with those transactions.

(c) If a trustee grants an option to buy property from the trust, whether or not the trust owns the property when the option is granted, grants an option that permits another person to sell property to the trust, or acquires an option to buy property for the trust or an option to sell an asset owned by the trust, and the trustee or other owner of the asset is required to deliver the asset if the option is exercised, an amount received for granting the option shall be allocated to principal. An amount paid to acquire the option shall be paid from principal. A gain or loss realized upon the exercise of an option, including an option granted to a settlor of the trust for services rendered, shall be allocated to principal.

(Stats. 1999 (A.B. 846), ch. 145, §5.)

§16367. Allocation of payments from collateral financial assets and payments in exchange for interest in asset-backed security

(a) In this section, "asset-backed security" means an asset whose value is based upon the right it gives the owner to receive distributions from the proceeds of financial assets that provide collateral for the security. The term includes an asset that gives the owner the right to receive from the collateral financial assets only the interest or other current return or only the proceeds other than interest or current return. The term does not include an asset to which Section 16350 or 16361 applies.

(b) If a trust receives a payment from interest or other current return and from other proceeds of the collateral financial assets, the trustee shall allocate to income the portion of the payment which the payer identifies as being from interest or other current return and shall allocate the balance of the payment to principal.

(c) If a trust receives one or more payments in exchange for the trust's entire interest in an asset-backed security in one accounting period, the trustee shall allocate the payments to principal. If a payment is one of a series of payments that will result in the liquidation of the trust's interest in the security over more than one accounting period, the trustee shall allocate 10 percent of the payment to income and the balance to principal.

(Stats. 1999 (A.B. 846), ch. 145, §5.)

7. Allocation of Disbursements During Administration of Trust

§16370. Trustee shall make the following disbursements from income

A trustee shall make the following disbursements from income to the extent that they are not disbursements to which paragraph (2) or (3) of subdivision (c) of Section 16340 applies:

(a) Except as otherwise ordered by the court, one-half of the regular compensation of the trustee and of any person providing investment advisory or custodial services to the trustee.

(b) Except as otherwise ordered by the court, one-half of all expenses for accountings, judicial proceedings, or other matters that involve both the income and remainder interests.

(c) All of the other ordinary expenses incurred in connection with the administration, management, or preservation of trust property and the distribution of income, including interest, ordinary repairs, regularly recurring taxes assessed against principal, and expenses of a proceeding or other matter that concerns primarily the income interest.

(d) All recurring premiums on insurance covering the loss of a principal asset or the loss of income from or use of the asset.

(Stats. 1999 (A.B. 846), ch. 145, §5.)

§16371. Trustee shall make the following disbursements from principal

(a) A trustee shall make the following disbursements from principal:

(1) Except as otherwise ordered by the court, the remaining one-half of the disbursements described in subdivisions (a) and (b) of Section 16370.

(2) Except as otherwise ordered by the court, all of the trustee's compensation calculated on principal as a fee for acceptance, distribution, or termination, and disbursements made to prepare property for sale.

(3) Payments on the principal of a trust debt.

(4) Expenses of a proceeding that concerns primarily principal, including a proceeding to construe the trust or to protect the trust or its property.

(5) Premiums paid on a policy of insurance not described in subdivision (d) of Section 16370 of which the trust is the owner and beneficiary.

(6) Estate, inheritance, and other transfer taxes, including penalties, apportioned to the trust.

(7) Disbursements related to environmental matters, including reclamation, assessing environmental conditions, remedying and removing environmental contamination, monitoring remedial activities and the release of substances, preventing future releases of substances, collecting amounts from persons liable or potentially liable for the costs of those activities, penalties imposed under environmental laws or regulations and other payments made to comply with those laws or regulations, statutory or common law claims by third parties, and defending claims based on environmental matters.

(b) If a principal asset is encumbered with an obligation that requires income from that asset to be paid directly to the creditor, the trustee shall transfer from principal to income an amount equal to the income paid to the creditor in reduction of the principal balance of the obligation.

(Stats. 1999 (A.B. 846), ch. 145, §5.)

§16372. Trustee may transfer from income to principal portion of net cash receipts from asset subject to depreciation

(a) For purposes of this section, "depreciation" means a reduction in value due to wear, tear, decay, corrosion, or gradual obsolescence of a fixed asset having a useful life of more than one year.

(b) A trustee may transfer from income to principal a reasonable amount of the net cash receipts from a principal asset that is subject to depreciation, under generally accepted accounting principles, but may not transfer any amount for depreciation under this section in any of the following circumstances:

(1) As to the portion of real property used or available for use by a beneficiary as a residence or of tangible personal property held or made available for the personal use or enjoyment of a beneficiary.

(2) During the administration of a decedent's estate.

(3) If the trustee is accounting under Section 16352 for the business or activity in which the asset is used.

(c) An amount transferred from income to principal need not be held as a separate fund.

(Stats. 1999 (A.B. 846), ch. 145, §5.)

§16373. Trustee may transfer from income to principal in anticipation of principal disbursement

(a) If a trustee makes or expects to make a principal disbursement described in this section, the trustee may transfer an appropriate amount from income to principal in one or more accounting periods to reimburse principal or to provide a reserve for future principal disbursements.

(b) Principal disbursements to which subdivision (a) applies include the following, but only to the extent that the trustee has not been and does not expect to be reimbursed by a third party:

(1) An amount chargeable to income but paid from principal because it is unusually large, including extraordinary repairs.

(2) A capital improvement to a principal asset, whether in the form of changes to an existing asset or the construction of a new asset, including special assessments.

(3) Disbursements made to prepare property for rental, including tenant allowances, leasehold improvements, and broker's commissions.

(4) Periodic payments on an obligation secured by a principal asset to the extent that the amount transferred from income to principal for depreciation is less than the periodic payments.

(5) Disbursements described in paragraph (7) of subdivision (a) of Section 16371.

(c) If the asset whose ownership gives rise to the disbursements becomes subject to a successive income interest after an income interest ends, a trustee may continue to transfer amounts from income to principal as provided in subdivision (a).

(Stats. 1999 (A.B. 846), ch. 145, §5.)

§16374. Allocation of taxes required to be paid by trustee

(a) A tax required to be paid by a trustee based on receipts allocated to income shall be paid from income.

(b) A tax required to be paid by a trustee based on receipts allocated to principal shall be paid from principal, even if the tax is called an income tax by the taxing authority.

(c) A tax required to be paid by a trustee on the trust's share of an entity's taxable income shall be paid proportionately as follows:

(1) From income to the extent that receipts from the entity are allocated to income.

(2) From principal to the extent that both of the following apply:

(A) Receipts from the entity are allocated to principal.

(B) The trust's share of the entity's taxable income exceeds the total receipts described in paragraph (1) and subparagraph (A).

(d) For purposes of this section, receipts allocated to principal or income shall be reduced by the amount distributed to a beneficiary from principal or income for which the trust receives a deduction in calculating the tax.

(Stats. 1999 (A.B. 846), ch. 145, §5.)

§16375. Fiduciary may make adjustments between principal and interest to obtain tax benefits

(a) A fiduciary may make adjustments between principal and income to offset the shifting of economic interests or tax benefits between income beneficiaries and remainder beneficiaries that arise from any of the following:

(1) Elections and decisions, other than those described in subdivision (b), that the fiduciary makes from time to time regarding tax matters.

(2) An income tax or any other tax that is imposed upon the fiduciary or a beneficiary as a result of a transaction involving or a distribution from the estate or trust.

(3) The ownership by a decedent's estate or trust of an interest in an entity whose taxable income, whether or not distributed, is includable in the taxable income of the estate, trust, or a beneficiary.

(b) If the amount of an estate tax marital deduction or charitable contribution deduction is reduced because a fiduciary deducts an amount paid from principal for income tax purposes instead of deducting it for estate tax purposes, and as a result estate taxes paid from principal are increased and income taxes paid by a decedent's estate, trust, or beneficiary are decreased, each estate, trust, or beneficiary that benefits from the decrease in income tax shall reimburse the principal from which the increase in estate tax is paid. The total reimbursement must equal the increase in the estate tax to the extent that the principal used to pay the increase would have qualified for a marital deduction or charitable contribution deduction but for the payment. The proportionate share of the reimbursement for each estate, trust, or beneficiary whose income taxes are reduced must be the same as its proportionate share of the total decrease in income tax. An estate or trust shall reimburse principal from income.

(Stats. 1999 (A.B. 846), ch. 145, §5.)

III. Trustees' Powers

A trustee must have a broad range of powers to carry out the acts that are necessary in the management of trust property. Such powers include, among others, the power to buy; sell; lease; borrow and lend money; encumber trust property; develop land; make repairs or improvements; continue a business that is part of the trust property; and insure trust property.

Traditionally, the settlor enumerated in the trust instrument the list of powers granted to a trustee. The enumeration of powers has now been codified in many states.

Some trust powers also may be implied by the circumstances. Further, a court may grant additional powers beyond those authorized by the trust instrument or by statute, and also restrict those same powers.

A trust instrument may provide for mandatory powers for a trustee (i.e., requiring the trustee to take a certain action). Or, the trustee may have discretionary powers (permitting the trustee to use judgment in the use of a power).

California law specifies trustees' powers in California Probate Code §§16200-16249. Many of these provisions were derived from the Uniform Trustees' Powers Act, promulgated in 1964, but not widely adopted.

A. Generally

§16200. General powers without court authorization

A trustee has the following powers without the need to obtain court authorization:

(a) The powers conferred by the trust instrument.

(b) Except as limited in the trust instrument, the powers conferred by statute.

(c) Except as limited in the trust instrument, the power to perform any act that a trustee would perform for the purposes of the trust under the standard of care provided in Section 16040 or 16047.

(Stats. 1990 (A.B. 759), ch. 79, §14, effective July 1, 1991. Amended by Stats. 1995 (S.B. 222), ch. 63, §7.)

§16201. Court has power to relieve trustee from restrictions under trust instrument

This chapter does not affect the power of a court to relieve a trustee from restrictions on the exercise of powers under the trust instrument.

(Stats. 1990 (A.B. 759), ch. 79, §14, effective July 1, 1991.)

§16202. Exercise of power is subject to fiduciary duties

The grant of a power to a trustee, whether by the trust instrument, by statute, or by the court, does not in itself require or permit the exercise of the power. The exercise of a power by a trustee is subject to the trustee's fiduciary duties.

(Stats. 1990 (A.B. 759), ch. 79, §14, effective July 1, 1991.)

§16203. References to repealed provisions

An instrument that incorporates the powers provided in former Section 1120.2 (repealed by Chapter 820 of the Statutes of 1986) shall be deemed to refer to the powers provided in Article 2 (commencing with Section 16220). For this purpose, the trustee's powers under former Section 1120.2 are not diminished and the trustee is not required to obtain court approval for exercise of a power for which court approval was not required by former law.

(Stats. 1990 (A.B. 759), ch. 79, §14, effective July 1, 1991.)

B. Specific Powers of Trustees

§16220. Trustee has power to collect and hold property

The trustee has the power to collect, hold, and retain trust property received from a settlor or any other person until, in the judgment of the trustee, disposition of the property should be made. The property may be retained even though it includes property in which the trustee is personally interested.

(Stats. 1990 (A.B. 759), ch. 79, §14, effective July 1, 1991.)

§16221. Trustee has power to accept additions to trust

The trustee has the power to accept additions to the property of the trust from a settlor or any other person.

(Stats. 1990 (A.B. 759), ch. 79, §14, effective July 1, 1991.)

§16222. Trustee has power to continue business

(a) Subject to subdivision (b), the trustee has the power to continue or participate in the operation of any business or other enterprise that is part of the trust property and may effect incorporation, dissolution, or other change in the form of the organization of the business or enterprise.

(b) Except as provided in subdivision (c), the trustee may continue the operation of a business or other enterprise only as authorized by the trust instrument or by the court. For the purpose of this subdivision, the lease of four or fewer residential units is not considered to be the operation of a business or other enterprise.

(c) The trustee may continue the operation of a business or other enterprise for a reasonable time pending a court hearing on the matter or pending a sale of the business or other enterprise.

(d) The limitation provided in subdivision (b) does not affect any power to continue or participate in the operation of a business or other enterprise that the trustee has under a trust created by an instrument executed before July 1, 1987.

(Stats. 1990 (A.B. 759), ch. 79, §14, effective July 1, 1991.)

§16224. Trustee has power to invest in obligations of United States government

(a) In the absence of an express provision to the contrary in a trust instrument, where the instrument directs or permits investment in obligations of the United States government, the trustee has the power to invest in those obligations directly or in the form of an interest in a money market mutual fund registered under the Investment Company Act of 1940 (15 U.S.C. Sec. 80a-1 et seq.) or an investment vehicle authorized for the collective investment of trust funds pursuant to Section 9.18 of Part 9 of Title 12 of the Code of Federal Regulations, the portfolios of which are limited to United States government obligations maturing not later than five years from the date of investment or reinvestment and to repurchase agreements fully collateralized by United States government obligations.

(b) This section applies only to trusts created on or after January 1, 1985.

(Stats. 1990 (A.B. 759), ch. 79, §14, effective July 1, 1991.)

§16225. Trustee has power to deposit trust funds in specified financial institutions

(a) The trustee has the power to deposit trust funds at reasonable interest in any of the following accounts:

(1) An insured account in a financial institution.

(2) To the extent that the account is collateralized, an account in a bank, an account in an insured savings and loan association, or an account in an insured credit union.

(b) A trustee may deposit trust funds pursuant to subdivision (a) in a financial institution operated by, or that is an affiliate of, the trustee. For the purpose of this subdivision, "affiliate" means a corporation that directly or indirectly through one or more intermediaries controls, is controlled by, or is under common control with another domestic or foreign corporation.

(c) This section does not limit the power of a trustee in a proper case to deposit trust funds in an account described in subdivision (a) that is subject to notice or other conditions respecting withdrawal prescribed by law or governmental regulation.

(d) The court may authorize the deposit of trust funds in an account described in subdivision (a) in an amount greater than the maximum insured or collateralized amount.

(e) Nothing in this section prevents the trustee from holding an amount of trust property reasonably necessary for the orderly administration of the trust in the form of cash or in a checking account without interest.

(Stats. 1990 (A.B. 759), ch. 79, §14, effective July 1, 1991.)

§16226. Trustee has power to acquire or dispose of property

The trustee has the power to acquire or dispose of property, for cash or on credit, at public or private sale, or by exchange.

(Stats. 1990 (A.B. 759), ch. 79, §14, effective July 1, 1991.)

§16227. Trustee has power to manage trust property

The trustee has the power to manage, control, divide, develop, improve, exchange, partition, change the character of, or abandon trust property or any interest therein.

(Stats. 1990 (A.B. 759), ch. 79, §14, effective July 1, 1991.)

§16228. Trustee has power to encumber, mortgage, or pledge trust property

The trustee has the power to encumber, mortgage, or pledge trust property for a term within or extending beyond the term of the trust in connection with the exercise of any power vested in the trustee.

(Stats. 1990 (A.B. 759), ch. 79, §14, effective July 1, 1991.)

§16229. Trustee has power to make repairs or improvements

The trustee has the power to do any of the following:

(a) Make ordinary or extraordinary repairs, alterations, or improvements in buildings or other trust property.

(b) Demolish any improvements.

(c) Raze existing or erect new party walls or buildings.

(Stats. 1990 (A.B. 759), ch. 79, §14, effective July 1, 1991.)

§16230. Trustee has power to develop land

The trustee has the power to do any of the following:

(a) Subdivide or develop land.

(b) Dedicate land to public use.

(c) Make or obtain the vacation of plats and adjust boundaries.

(d) Adjust differences in valuation on exchange or partition by giving or receiving consideration.

(e) Dedicate easements to public use without consideration.

(Stats. 1990 (A.B. 759), ch. 79, §14, effective July 1, 1991.)

§16231. Trustee has power to enter into leases

The trustee has the power to enter into a lease for any purpose as lessor or lessee with or without the option to purchase or renew and for a term within or extending beyond the term of the trust.

(Stats. 1990 (A.B. 759), ch. 79, §14, effective July 1, 1991.)

§16232. Trustee has power to enter into mineral leases

The trustee has the power to enter into a lease or arrangement for exploration and removal of gas, oil, or other minerals or geothermal energy, and to enter into a community oil lease or a pooling or unitization agreement, and for a term within or extending beyond the term of the trust.

(Stats. 1990 (A.B. 759), ch. 79, §14, effective July 1, 1991.)

§16233. Trustee has power to grant options

The trustee has the power to grant an option involving disposition of trust property or to take an option for the acquisition of any property, and an option may be granted or taken that is exercisable beyond the term of the trust.

(Stats. 1990 (A.B. 759), ch. 79, §14, effective July 1, 1991.)

§16234. Trustee has power to exercise voting rights regarding corporate shares

With respect to any shares of stock of a domestic or foreign corporation, any membership in a nonprofit corporation, or any other property, a trustee has the power to do any of the following:

(a) Vote in person, and give proxies to exercise, any voting rights with respect to the shares, memberships, or property.

(b) Waive notice of a meeting or give consent to the holding of a meeting.

(c) Authorize, ratify, approve, or confirm any action that could be taken by shareholders, members, or property owners.

(Stats. 1990 (A.B. 759), ch. 79, §14, effective July 1, 1991.)

§16235. Trustee has power to pay calls and assessments

The trustee has the power to pay calls, assessments, and any other sums chargeable or accruing against or on account of securities.

(Stats. 1990 (A.B. 759), ch. 79, §14, effective July 1, 1991.)

§16236. Trustee has power to sell or exercise stock subscriptions and conversions

The trustee has the power to sell or exercise stock subscription or conversion rights.

(Stats. 1990 (A.B. 759), ch. 79, §14, effective July 1, 1991.)

§16237. Trustee has power to consent to a change in form of business

The trustee has the power to consent, directly or through a committee or other agent, to the reorganization, consolidation, merger, dissolution, or liquidation of a corporation or other business enterprise, and to participate in voting trusts, pooling arrangements, and foreclosures, and in connection therewith, to deposit securities with and transfer title and delegate discretion to any protective or other committee as the trustee may deem advisable.

(Stats. 1990 (A.B. 759), ch. 79, §14, effective July 1, 1991.)

§16238. Trustee has power to hold securities in certain forms

The trustee has the power to hold a security in the name of a nominee or in other form without disclosure of the trust so that title to the security may pass by delivery.

(Stats. 1990 (A.B. 759), ch. 79, §14, effective July 1, 1991.)

§16239. Trustee has power to deposit securities in securities depository

The trustee has the power to deposit securities in a securities depository, as defined in Section 30004 of the Financial Code, which is licensed under Section 30200 of the Financial Code or is exempt from licensing by Section 30005 or 30006 of the Financial Code. The securities may be held by the securities depository in the manner authorized by Section 775 of the Financial Code.

(Stats. 1990 (A.B. 759), ch. 79, §14, effective July 1, 1991.)

§16240. Trustee has power to insure trust property and trustee

The trustee has the power to insure the property of the trust against damage or loss and to insure the trustee against liability with respect to third persons.

(Stats. 1990 (A.B. 759), ch. 79, §14, effective July 1, 1991.)

§16241. Trustee has power to borrow money

The trustee has the power to borrow money for any trust purpose to be repaid from trust property. The lender may include, but is not limited to, a bank holding company, affiliate, or subsidiary of the trustee.

(Stats. 1990 (A.B. 759), ch. 79, §14, effective July 1, 1991.)

§16242. Trustee has power to pay and settle claims

The trustee has the power to do any of the following:

(a) Pay or contest any claim.

(b) Settle a claim by or against the trust by compromise, arbitration, or otherwise.

(c) Release, in whole or in part, any claim belonging to the trust.

(Stats. 1990 (A.B. 759), ch. 79, §14, effective July 1, 1991.)

§16243. Trustee has power to pay trust expenses

The trustee has the power to pay taxes, assessments, reasonable compensation of the trustee and of employees and agents of the trust, and other expenses incurred in the collection, care, administration, and protection of the trust.

(Stats. 1990 (A.B. 759), ch. 79, §14, effective July 1, 1991.)

§16244. Trustee has power to make loans to beneficiary

The trustee has the following powers:

(a) To make loans out of trust property to the beneficiary on terms and conditions that the trustee determines are fair and reasonable under the circumstances.

(b) To guarantee loans to the beneficiary by encumbrances on trust property.

(Stats. 1990 (A.B. 759), ch. 79, §14, effective July 1, 1991.)

§16245. Trustee has power to make distributions

The trustee has the power to pay any sum of principal or income distributable to a beneficiary, without regard to whether the beneficiary is under a legal disability, by paying the sum to the beneficiary or by paying the sum to another person for the use or benefit of the beneficiary. Any sum distributable under this section to a custodian under the California Uniform Transfers to Minors Act (Part 9 (commencing with Section 3900)) shall be subject to Section 3906.

(Stats. 1990 (A.B. 759), ch. 79, §14, effective July 1, 1991. Amended by Stats. 1996 (A.B. 2751), ch. 862, §39.)

§16246. Trustee has power to effect nature and value of distributions

The trustee has the power to effect distribution of property and money in divided or undivided interests and to adjust resulting differences in valuation. A distribution in kind may be made pro rata or non pro rata, and may be made pursuant to any written agreement providing for a non pro rata division of the aggregate value of the community property assets or quasi- community property assets, or both.

(Stats. 1990 (A.B. 759), ch. 79, §14, effective July 1, 1991. Amended by Stats. 1998 (A.B. 2069), ch. 682, §12.)

§16247. Trustee has power to hire

The trustee has the power to hire persons, including accountants, attorneys, auditors, investment advisers, appraisers (including probate referees appointed pursuant to Section 400), or other agents, even if they are associated or affiliated with the trustee, to advise or assist the trustee in the performance of administrative duties.

(Stats. 1990 (A.B. 759), ch. 79, §14, effective July 1, 1991. Amended by Stats. 1994 (A.B. 3686), ch. 806 §38.)

§16248. Trustee has power to execute and deliver instruments

The trustee has the power to execute and deliver all instruments which are needed to accomplish or facilitate the exercise of the powers vested in the trustee.

(Stats. 1990 (A.B. 759), ch. 79, §14, effective July 1, 1991.)

§16249. Trustee has power to prosecute or defend actions

The trustee has the power to prosecute or defend actions, claims, or proceedings for the protection of trust property and of the trustee in the performance of the trustee's duties.

(Stats. 1990 (A.B. 759), ch. 79, §14, effective July 1, 1991. Amended by Stats. 1992 (A.B. 2975), ch. 871, §19; Stats. 2001 (S.B. 669), ch. 49, §5.)

IV. Liability of Trustees to Beneficiaries

A. Liability for Breach of Trust

A trustee's violation of any duty that the trustee owes the beneficiary is a breach of trust (Cal. Prob. Code §16400). Trustees are liable for failures to perform their duties and abuses of their powers. 60 Cal. Jur.3d Trusts §244 (citing In re Estate of Reith, 77 P. 942 (Cal. 1904)).

A range of remedies are available for breach of trust, including: compelling the trustee to perform duties, enjoining the trustee from committing the breach of trust, compelling the trustee to redress the breach, appointing a receiver to take possession of the trust property, reducing or denying the trustee's compensation, and removing the trustee (Cal. Prob. Code §16420).

A beneficiary also may sue any third parties who participate in the breach of trust with the trustee. The liability of the third party is directly to the beneficiaries and is not derived through the trustee. 60 Cal. Jur.3d Trusts §244 (citing City of Atascardero v. Merrill Lynch, Pierce, Fenner & Smith. 80 Cal. Rptr. 2d 329 (Ct. App. 1998)).

In general, a trustee is not liable for a co-trustee's breach of trust (Cal. Prob. Code §16402(a)). However, a co-trustee may be liable if the trustee (1) participates in the breach; (2) improperly delegates administration to the co-trustee; (3) approves, knowingly acquiesces in, or conceals the breach; (4) negligently enables the breach; or (5) fails to take reasonable steps to compel the co-trustee to redress the breach where the trustee knew or reasonably should have known of the breach (Cal. Prob. Code §16402(b)). See generally John A. Hartog, A Trustee's Crime & Punishment: Managing Fiduciary Liability Under the California Uniform Prudent Investor Act, Practicing Law Institute (Sept. 1998).

Many of the California statutory provisions *infra* on the trustee's liability for breaches of trust are drawn from the Restatement (Second) of Trusts (1957). The provision on a trustee's liability for the acts of an agent (Cal. Prob. Code §16401) has been amended to make it consistent with California Probate Code §16052 (delegation of investment and management functions), part of the Uniform Prudent Investor Act (1994).

§16400. Breach of trust is a violation of duty owed to beneficiary

A violation by the trustee of any duty that the trustee owes the beneficiary is a breach of trust.

(Stats. 1990 (A.B. 759), ch. 79, §14, effective July 1, 1991.)

§16401. Trustee's liability for acts of agents

(a) Except as provided in subdivision (b), the trustee is not liable to the beneficiary for the acts or omissions of an agent.

(b) Under any of the circumstances described in this subdivision, the trustee is liable to the beneficiary for an act or omission of an agent employed by the trustee in the administration of the trust that would be a breach of the trust if committed by the trustee:

(1) Where the trustee directs the act of the agent.

(2) Where the trustee delegates to the agent the authority to perform an act that the trustee is under a duty not to delegate.

(3) Where the trustee does not use reasonable prudence in the selection of the agent or the retention of the agent selected by the trustee.

(4) Where the trustee does not periodically review the agent's overall performance and compliance with the terms of the delegation.

(5) Where the trustee conceals the act of the agent.

(6) Where the trustee neglects to take reasonable steps to compel the agent to redress the wrong in a case where the trustee knows of the agent's acts or omissions.

(c) The liability of a trustee for acts or omissions of agents that occurred before July 1, 1987, is governed by prior law and not by this section.

(Stats. 1990 (A.B. 759), ch. 79, §14, effective July 1, 1991. Amended by Stats. 1995 (S.B. 222), ch. 63, §9.)

§16402. Trustee's liability for acts of cotrustees

(a) Except as provided in subdivision (b), a trustee is not liable to the beneficiary for a breach of trust committed by a cotrustee.

(b) A trustee is liable to the beneficiary for a breach committed by a cotrustee under any of the following circumstances:

(1) Where the trustee participates in a breach of trust committed by the cotrustee.

(2) Where the trustee improperly delegates the administration of the trust to the cotrustee.

(3) Where the trustee approves, knowingly acquiesces in, or conceals a breach of trust committed by the cotrustee.

(4) Where the trustee negligently enables the cotrustee to commit a breach of trust.

(5) Where the trustee neglects to take reasonable steps to compel the cotrustee to redress a breach of trust in a case where the trustee knows or has information from which the trustee reasonably should have known of the breach.

(c) The liability of a trustee for acts or omissions of a cotrustee that occurred before July 1, 1987, is governed by prior law and not by this section.

(Stats. 1990 (A.B. 759), ch. 79, §14, effective July 1, 1991.)

§16403. Trustee's liability for acts of predecessors

(a) Except as provided in subdivision (b), a successor trustee is not liable to the beneficiary for a breach of trust committed by a predecessor trustee.

(b) A successor trustee is liable to the beneficiary for breach of trust involving acts or omissions of a predecessor trustee in any of the following circumstances:

(1) Where the successor trustee knows or has information from which the successor trustee reasonably should have known of a situation constituting a breach of trust committed by the predecessor trustee and the successor trustee improperly permits it to continue.

(2) Where the successor trustee neglects to take reasonable steps to compel the predecessor trustee to deliver the trust property to the successor trustee.

(3) Where the successor trustee neglects to take reasonable steps to redress a breach of trust committed by the predecessor trustee in a case where the successor trustee knows or has information from which the successor trustee reasonably should have known of the predecessor trustee's breach.

(c) The liability of a trustee for acts or omissions of a predecessor trustee that occurred before July 1, 1987, is governed by prior law and not by this section.

(Stats. 1990 (A.B. 759), ch. 79, §14, effective July 1, 1991.)

B. Remedies for Breach of Trust

§16420. Actions for trustee's breach of trust

(a) If a trustee commits a breach of trust, or threatens to commit a breach of trust, a beneficiary or cotrustee of the trust may commence a proceeding for any of the following purposes that is appropriate:

(1) To compel the trustee to perform the trustee's duties.

(2) To enjoin the trustee from committing a breach of trust.

(3) To compel the trustee to redress a breach of trust by payment of money or otherwise.

(4) To appoint a receiver or temporary trustee to take possession of the trust property and administer the trust.

(5) To remove the trustee.

(6) Subject to Section 18100, to set aside acts of the trustee.

(8) Subject to Section 18100, to impose an equitable lien or a constructive trust on trust property.

(9) Subject to Section 18100, to trace trust property that has been wrongfully disposed of and recover the property or its proceeds.

(b) The provision of remedies for breach of trust in subdivision (a) does not prevent resort to any other appropriate remedy provided by statute or the common law.

(Stats. 1990 (A.B. 759), ch. 79, §14, effective July 1, 1991.)

§16421. Remedies are exclusively in equity

The remedies of a beneficiary against the trustee are exclusively in equity.

(Stats. 1990 (A.B. 759), ch. 79, §14, effective July 1, 1991.)

C. Measure of Liability for Breach of Trust

§16440. Extent of trustee's liability for breach of trust; effect of good faith

(a) If the trustee commits a breach of trust, the trustee is chargeable with any of the following that is appropriate under the circumstances:

(1) Any loss or depreciation in value of the trust estate resulting from the breach of trust, with interest.

(2) Any profit made by the trustee through the breach of trust, with interest.

(3) Any profit that would have accrued to the trust estate if the loss of profit is the result of the breach of trust.

(b) If the trustee has acted reasonably and in good faith under the circumstances as known to the trustee, the court, in its discretion, may excuse the trustee in whole or in part from liability under subdivision (a) if it would be equitable to do so.

(Stats. 1990 (A.B. 759), ch. 79, §14, effective July 1, 1991.)

§16441. Trustee's liability for interest; effect of good faith

(a) If the trustee is liable for interest pursuant to Section 16440, the trustee is liable for the greater of the following amounts:

(1) The amount of interest that accrues at the legal rate on judgments in effect during the period when the interest accrued.

(2) The amount of interest actually received.

(b) If the trustee has acted reasonably and in good faith under the circumstances as known to the trustee, the court, in its discretion, may excuse the trustee in whole or in part from liability under subdivision (a) if it would be equitable to do so.

(Stats. 1990 (A.B. 759), ch. 79, §14, effective July 1, 1991. Amended by Stats. 1998 (S.B. 1841), ch. 77, §5.)

§16442. Availability of other statutory or common law remedies

The provisions in this article for liability of a trustee for breach of trust do not prevent resort to any other remedy available under the statutory or common law.

(Stats. 1990 (A.B. 759), ch. 79, §14, effective July 1, 1991.)

D. Limitations and Exculpation

§16460. Effect of adequate disclosure on existence of claims

(a) Unless a claim is previously barred by adjudication, consent, limitation, or otherwise:

(1) If a beneficiary has received an interim or final account in writing, or other written report, that adequately discloses the existence of a claim against the trustee for breach of trust, the claim is barred as to that beneficiary unless a proceeding to assert the claim is commenced within three years after receipt of the account or report. An account or report adequately discloses existence of a claim if it provides sufficient information so that the beneficiary knows of the claim or reasonably should have inquired into the existence of the claim.

(2) If an interim or final account in writing or other written report does not adequately disclose the existence of a claim against the trustee for breach of trust or if a beneficiary does not receive any written account or report, the claim is barred as to that beneficiary unless a proceeding to assert the claim is commenced within three years after the beneficiary discovered, or reasonably should have discovered, the subject of the claim.

(b) For the purpose of subdivision (a), a beneficiary is deemed to have received an account or report, as follows:

(1) In the case of an adult who is reasonably capable of understanding the account or report, if it is received by the adult personally.

(2) In the case of an adult who is not reasonably capable of understanding the account or report, if it is received by the person's legal representative, including a guardian ad litem or other person appointed for this purpose.

(3) In the case of a minor, if it is received by the minor's guardian or, if the minor does not have a guardian, if it is received by the minor's parent so long as the parent does not have a conflict of interest.

(c) A written account or report under this section may, but need not, satisfy the requirements of Section 16061 or 16063 or any other provision.

(Stats. 1990 (A.B. 759), ch. 79. §14, effective July 1, 1991. Amended by Stats. 1996 (A.B. 2751), ch. 872, §40.)

§16461. Exculpation of trustee; relief of trustee from liability by trust instrument

(a) Except as provided in subdivision (b) (c), or (d), the trustee can be relieved of liability for breach of trust by provisions in the trust instrument.

(b) A provision in the trust instrument is not effective to relieve the trustee of liability (1) for breach of trust committed intentionally, with gross negligence, in bad faith, or with reckless indifference to the interest of the beneficiary, or (2) for any profit that the trustee derives from a breach of trust.

(c) Subject to subdivision (b), a provision in a trust instrument that releases the trustee from liability if a beneficiary fails to object to an item in an interim or final account or other written report within a specified time period is effective only if all or the following conditions are met:

(1) The account or report sets forth the item.

(2) The period specified in the trust instrument for the beneficiary to object is not less than 180 days, or the trustee elects to follow the procedure provided in subdivision (d).

(3) Written notice in 12-point boldface type is provided to a beneficiary with the account or report in the following form:

NOTICE TO BENEFICIARIES

YOU HAVE [Insert "180 days" or the period specified in the trust agreement, whichever is longer] FROM YOUR RECEIPT OF

THIS ACCOUNT OR REPORT TO TAKE AN OBJECTION TO ANY ITEM SET FORTH IN THIS ACCOUNT OR REPORT. ANY OBJECTION YOU MAKE MUST BE IN WRITING; IT MUST BE DELIVERED TO THE TRUSTEE WITHIN THE PERIOD STATED ABOVE; AND IT MUST STATE YOUR OBJECTION. YOUR FAILURE TO DELIVER A WRITEN OBJECTION TO THE TRUSTEE WTIHIN THE PERIOD STATED ABOVE WILL PERMANENTLY PREVENT YOU FROM LATER ASSERTING THIS OBJECTION AGAINST THE TRUSTEE. IF YOU DO MAKE AN OBJECTION TO THE TRUSTEE, THE THREE-YEAR PERIOD PROVIDED IN SECTION 16460 OF THE PROBATE CODE FOR COMMENCEMENT OF LITIGATION WILL APPLY TO CLAIMS BASED ON YOUR OBJECTION AND WILL BEGIN TO RUN ON THE DATE THAT YOU RECEIVE THIS ACCOUNT OR REPORT.

(d) A provision in a trust instrument that provides for a period less than 180 days to object to an item in an account or report shall be ineffective to release the trustee from liability. A trustee of a trust created by an instrument with an ineffective period may elect to be governed by the provisions of subdivision (c) by complying with the requirements of subdivision (c), except that "180 days" shall be substituted in the notice form for the ineffective period.

(e) Subject to subdivision (b), a beneficiary who fails to object in writing to an account or report that complies with the requirements of subdivision (c), within the specified valid period shall be barred from asserting any claim against the trustee regarding an item that is adequately disclosed in the account or report. An item is adequately disclosed if the disclosure regarding the item meets the requirements of paragraph (1) of subdivision (a) of Section 16460.

(f) Except as provided in subdivision (a) of Section 16460, the trustee may not be released from liability as to any claim based on a written objection made by the beneficiary if the objection is delivered to the trustee within the specified, effective period. If a beneficiary has filed a written objection to an account or report that complies with the requirements of subdivision (c) within the specified, valid period that concerns an item that affects any other beneficiary of the trust, any affected beneficiary may join in the objection anytime within the specified, valid period or while the resolution of the objection is pending, whichever is later. This section is not intended to establish a class of beneficiaries for actions on an account and report to provide that the action of one beneficiary is pending, whichever is later. This section is not intended to establish a class of beneficiaries for actions on an account and report or provide that the action of one beneficiary is for the benefit of all beneficiaries. This section does not create a duty for any trustee to notify beneficiaries of objections or resolution of objections.

(g) Provided that a beneficiary has filed a written objection to an account or report that complies with the requirements of subdivision (c) within the specified, valid period, a supplemental written objection may be delivered in the same manner as the objection not later than 180 days after the receipt of the account or report or no later than the period specified in the trust instrument, whichever is longer.

(h) Compliance with subdivision (c) excuses compliance with paragraph (6) of subdivision (a) of Section 16063 for the account or report to which that notice entails.

(i) subject to subdivision (b), if proper notice has been given and a beneficiary has not made a timely objection, the trustee is not liable for any other claims adequately disclosed by any item in the account or report.

(j) Subdivisions (c) to (i), inclusive, apply to all accounts and reports submitted after the effective date of the act adding these subdivisions.

(Stats. 1990 (A.B. 759), ch. 79, §14, effective July 1, 1991. Amended by Stats. 2004 (A.B. 1990), ch. 538, §1.)

§16462. Trustee's liability to beneficiary of revocable trusts for acts performed pursuant to settlor's written instructions

(a) Notwithstanding Section 16461, a trustee of a revocable trust is not liable to a beneficiary for any act performed or omitted pursuant to written directions from the person holding the power to revoke, including a person to whom the power to direct the trustee is delegated.

(b) Subdivision (a) applies to a trust that is revocable in part with respect to the interest of the beneficiary in that part of the trust property.

(Stats. 1990 (A.B. 759), ch. 79, §14, effective July 1, 1991.)

§16463. Effect of beneficiary's consent on liability of trustee

(a) Except as provided in subdivisions (b) and (c), a beneficiary may not hold the trustee liable for an act or omission of the trustee as a breach of trust if the beneficiary consented to the act or omission before or at the time of the act or omission.

(b) The consent of the beneficiary does not preclude the beneficiary from holding the trustee liable for a breach of trust in any of the following circumstances:

(1) Where the beneficiary was under an incapacity at the time of the consent or of the act or omission.

(2) Where the beneficiary at the time consent was given did not know of his or her rights and of the material facts (A) that the trustee knew or should have known and (B) that the trustee did not reasonably believe that the beneficiary knew.

(3) Where the consent of the beneficiary was induced by improper conduct of the trustee.

(c) Where the trustee has an interest in the transaction adverse to the interest of the beneficiary, the consent of the beneficiary does not preclude the beneficiary from holding the trustee liable for a breach of trust under any of the circumstances described in subdivision (b) or where the transaction to which the beneficiary consented was not fair and reasonable to the beneficiary.

(Stats. 1990 (A.B. 759), ch. 79, §14, effective July 1, 1991.)

§16464. Effect of beneficiary's release or contract as discharge of trustee's liability

(a) Except as provided in subdivision (b), a beneficiary may be precluded from holding the trustee liable for a breach of trust by the beneficiary's release or contract effective to discharge the trustee's liability to the beneficiary for that breach.

(b) A release or contract is not effective to discharge the trustee's liability for a breach of trust in any of the following circumstances:

(1) Where the beneficiary was under an incapacity at the time of making the release or contract.

(2) Where the beneficiary did not know of his or her rights and of the material facts (A) that the trustee knew or reasonably should have known and (B) that the trustee did not reasonably believe that the beneficiary knew.

(3) Where the release or contract of the beneficiary was induced by improper conduct of the trustee.

(4) Where the transaction involved a bargain with the trustee that was not fair and reasonable.

(Stats. 1990 (A.B. 759), ch. 79, §14, effective July 1, 1991.)

§16465. Effect of affirmation by beneficiary on liability of trustee

(a) Except as provided in subdivision (b), if the trustee, in breach of trust, enters into a transaction that the beneficiary may at his or her option reject or affirm, and the beneficiary affirms the transaction, the beneficiary shall not thereafter reject it and hold the trustee liable for any loss occurring after the trustee entered into the transaction.

(b) The affirmance of a transaction by the beneficiary does not preclude the beneficiary from holding a trustee liable for a breach of trust if, at the time of the affirmance, any of the following circumstances existed:

(1) The beneficiary was under an incapacity.

(2) The beneficiary did not know of his or her rights and of the material facts (A) that the trustee knew or reasonably should have known and (B) that the trustee did not reasonably believe that the beneficiary knew.

(3) The affirmance was induced by improper conduct of the trustee.

(4) The transaction involved a bargain with the trustee that was not fair and reasonable.

(Stats. 1990 (A.B. 759), ch. 79, §14, effective July 1, 1991.)

V. Liability of Trustees to Third Persons

A trustee often must deal with third parties during the administration of the trust. Such transactions may result in claims asserted by third parties against the trustee in the trustee's representative or individual capacity. Statutes regulate the nature and extent of the trustee's liability to third parties.

According to California statute, a trustee may be liable for claims based on contract, tort, or those involving the ownership or control of trust property (Cal. Prob. Code §§18000, 18001, 18002). In some cases, the trustee may be personally liable (i.e., liable in his or her individual capacity). For example, a trustee may be personally liable on a contract entered into during the administration of the trust, if the trustee entered into the agreement in the trustee's fiduciary capacity without disclosing the trustee's fiduciary capacity or identifying the trust in the contract (Cal. Prob. Code §18100). On the other hand, a trustee is personally liable for obligations regarding ownership or control of trust property only if the trustee is personally at fault (*id.*).

§18000. Personal liability of trustee; exception

(a) Unless otherwise provided in the contract or in this chapter, a trustee is not personally liable on a contract properly entered into in the trustee's fiduciary capacity in the course of administration of the trust unless the trustee fails to reveal the trustee's representative capacity or identify the trust in the contract.

(b) The personal liability of a trustee on a contract entered into before July 1, 1987, is governed by prior law and not by this section.

(Stats. 1990 (A.B. 759), ch. 79, §14, effective July 1, 1991.)

§18001. Trustee is personally liable for obligations regarding ownership/ control of trust property if personally at fault

A trustee is personally liable for obligations arising from ownership or control of trust property only if the trustee is personally at fault.

(Stats. 1990 (A.B. 759), ch. 79, §14, effective July 1, 1991.)

§18002. Trustee is personally liable for torts regarding trust administration if personally at fault

A trustee is personally liable for torts committed in the course of administration of the trust only if the trustee is personally at fault.

(Stats. 1990 (A.B. 759), ch. 79, §14, effective July 1, 1991.)

§18003. Liability of dissenting cotrustees

(a) A cotrustee who does not join in exercising a power held by three or more cotrustees is not liable to third persons for the consequences of the exercise of the power.

(b) A dissenting cotrustee who joins in an action at the direction of the majority cotrustees is not liable to third persons for the action if the dissenting cotrustee expresses the dissent in writing to any other cotrustee at or before the time the action is taken.

(c) This section does not excuse a cotrustee from liability for failure to discharge the cotrustee's duties as a trustee.

(Stats. 1990 (A.B. 759), ch. 79, §14, effective July 1, 1991.)

§18004. Proceeding against the trustee on contract or tort claims

A claim based on a contract entered into by a trustee in the trustee's representative capacity, on an obligation arising from ownership or control of trust property, or on a tort committed in the course of administration of the trust may be asserted against the trust by proceeding against the trustee in the trustee's representative capacity, whether or not the trustee is personally liable on the claim.

(Stats. 1990 (A.B. 759), ch. 79, §14, effective July 1, 1991.)

§18005. Proceedings for determination of liability between trust estate and trustee personally

The question of liability as between the trust estate and the trustee personally may be determined in a proceeding under Section 17200.

(Stats. 1990 (A.B. 759), ch. 79, §14, effective July 1, 1991.)

§18100. Obligations of third persons dealing with, or assisting, a trustee

With respect to a third person dealing with a trustee or assisting a trustee in the conduct of a transaction, if the third person acts in good faith and for a valuable consideration and without actual knowledge that the trustee is exceeding the trustee's powers or improperly exercising them:

(a) The third person is not bound to inquire whether the trustee has power to act or is properly exercising a power and may assume without inquiry the existence of a trust power and its proper exercise.

(b) The third person is fully protected in dealing with or assisting the trustee just as if the trustee has and is properly exercising the power the trustee purports to exercise.

(Stats. 1990 (A.B. 759), ch. 79, §14, effective July 1, 1991.)

§18100.5. Trustee may present certification of trust to establish trust; certification reliance

(a) The trustee may present a certification of trust to any person in lieu of providing a copy of the trust instrument to establish the existence or terms of the trust. A certification of trust may be executed by the trustee voluntarily or at the request of the person with whom the trustee is dealing.

(b) The certification of trust may confirm the following facts or contain the following information:

(1) The existence of the trust and date of execution of the trust instrument.

(2) The identity of the settlor or settlors and the currently acting trustee or trustees of the trust.

(3) The powers of the trustee.

(4) The revocability or irrevocability of the trust and the identity of any person holding any power to revoke the trust.

(5) When there are multiple trustees, the signature authority of the trustees, indicating whether all, or less than all, of the currently acting trustees are required to sign in order to exercise various powers of the trustee.

(6) The trust identification number, whether a social security number or an employer identification number.

(7) The manner in which title to trust assets should be taken.

(8) The legal description of any interest in real property held in the trust.

(c) The certification shall contain a statement that the trust has not been revoked, modified, or amended in any manner which would cause the representations contained in the certification of trust to be incorrect and shall contain a statement that it is being signed by all of the currently acting trustees of the trust. The certification shall be in the form of an acknowledged declaration signed by all currently acting trustees of the trust. The certification signed by the currently acting trustee may be recorded in the office of the county recorder in the county where all or a portion of real property is located.

(d) The certification of trust may, but is not required to, include excerpts from the original trust documents, any amendments hereto, and any other documents evidencing or pertaining to the succession of successor trustees. The certification of trust shall not be required to contain the dispositive provisions of the trust which set forth the distribution of the trust estate.

(e) A person whose interest is, or may be, affected by the certification of trust may require that the trustee offering or recording the certification of trust provide copies of those excerpts from the original trust documents, any amendments thereto, and any other documents which designate, evidence, or pertain to the succession of the trustee or confer upon the trustee the power to act in the pending transaction, or both. Nothing in this section is intended to require or imply an obligation to provide the dispositive provisions of the trust or the entire trust and amendments thereto.

(f) A person who acts in reliance upon a certification of trust without actual knowledge that the representations contained therein are incorrect is not liable to any person for so acting. A person who does not have actual knowledge that the facts contained in the certification of trust are incorrect may assume without inquiry the existence of the facts contained in the certification of trust. Actual knowledge shall not be inferred solely from the fact that a copy of all or part of the trust instrument is held by the person relying upon the trust certification. Any transaction, and any lien created thereby, entered into by the trustee and a person acting in reliance upon a certification of trust shall be enforceable against the trust assets. However, if the person has actual knowledge that the trustee is acting outside the scope of the trust, then the transaction is not enforceable against the trust assets. Nothing contained herein shall limit the rights of the beneficiaries of the trust against the trustee.

(g) A person's failure to demand a certification of trust does not affect the protection provided that person by Section 18100, and no inference as to whether that person has acted in good faith may be drawn from the failure to demand a certification of trust. Nothing in this section is intended to create an implication that a person is liable for acting in reliance upon a certification of trust under circumstances where the requirements of this section are not satisfied.

(h) Except when requested by a beneficiary or in the context of litigation concerning a trust and subject to the provisions of subdivision (e), any person making a demand for the trust documents in addition to a certification of trust to prove facts set forth in the certification of trust acceptable to the third party shall be liable for damages, including attorney's fees, incurred as a result of the refusal to accept the certification of trust in lieu of the requested documents if the court determines that the person acted in bad faith in requesting the trust documents.

(i) Any person may record a certification of trust that relates to an interst in real property in the office of the county recorder in any count y in which all or a portion of the real property is located. The county recorder shall impose any fee prescribed by law for recording that document sufficient to cover all costs incurred by the country in recording the document. The recorded certification of trust shall be a public reord of the real property involved. The subdivision does not create a requirement to record a certification of trust in conjunction with the recordation of a transfer of title or real property involving a trust.

(Stats. 1993 (A.B. 1249), ch. 530, §2. Amended by Stats. 2004 (A.B. 1848) ch. 136 §1.)

§18101. Third party is not required to ensure proper application of property delivered to trustee

A third person who acts in good faith is not bound to ensure the proper application of trust property paid or delivered to the trustee.

(Stats. 1990 (A.B. 759), ch. 79, §14, effective July 1, 1991.)

§18102. Third party's transactions with former trustees

If a third person acting in good faith and for a valuable consideration enters into a transaction with a former trustee without knowledge that the person is no longer a trustee, the third person is fully protected just as if the former trustee were still a trustee.

(Stats. 1990 (A.B. 759), ch. 79, §14, effective July 1, 1991.)

§18103. Effect on purchaser if trust omitted from grant of real property

If an express trust relating to real property is not contained or declared in the grant to the trustee, or in an instrument signed by the trustee and recorded in the same office with the grant to the trustee, the grant shall be deemed absolute in favor of a person dealing with the trustee in good faith and for a valuable consideration.

(Stats. 1990 (A.B. 759), ch. 79, §14, effective July 1, 1991.)

§18104. Effect on real property transactions if beneficiary is undisclosed

(a) If an interest in or lien or encumbrance on real property is conveyed, created, or affected by an instrument in favor of a person in trust but no beneficiary is indicated in the instrument, it is presumed that the person holds the interest, lien, or encumbrance absolutely and free of the trust. This is a presumption affecting the burden of proof. In an action or proceeding involving the interest, lien, or encumbrance instituted against the person, the person shall be deemed the only necessary representative of the undisclosed beneficiary and of the original grantor or settlor and anyone claiming under them. A judgment is binding upon and conclusive against these persons as to all matters finally adjudicated in the judgment.

(b) An instrument executed by the person holding an interest, lien, or encumbrance described in subdivision (a), whether purporting to be the act of that person in his or her own right or in the capacity of a trustee, is presumed to affect the interest, lien, or encumbrance according to the tenor of the instrument. This is a presumption affecting the burden of proof. Upon the recording of the instrument in the county where the land affected by the instrument is located, the presumption is conclusive in favor of a person acting in good faith and for valuable consideration.

(Stats. 1990 (A.B. 759), ch. 79, §14, effective July 1, 1991.)

XII
Beneficiaries

This chapter explores the nature and extent of the beneficiary's interest. It addresses the rights of a beneficiary to enforce a beneficial interest. Then the chapter turns to the transferability of the beneficial interests and the susceptibility of these interests to the claims of creditors.

I. Nature of the Beneficiary's Interest

A. Generally

A private express trust requires a definite beneficiary or beneficiaries. The reason for this requirement is that a trust must have ascertainable beneficiaries in order to enforce it. (Note that charitable trusts are not subject to the rule requiring definite beneficiaries because charitable trusts are enforced by the state Attorney General rather than the courts.)

A trust may be created for a single beneficiary or several beneficiaries. In the case of several beneficiaries, it is common to have successive beneficiaries, i.e., one or more beneficiaries who are entitled to the enjoyment of the trust property in succession.

A trust may be created for an unborn beneficiary. "[A] trust can be created in favor of a person who has not yet come into existence as long as there is a possibility that he may come into existence." Austin Wakeman Scott & William Franklin Fratcher, The Law of Trusts §112.3 at 166 (4th ed., 1987) [hereinafter Scott & Fratcher]. Also, a trust can be created for a minor. A minor has capacity to take and hold title to property even though the minor cannot manage the property. Legal entities such as corporations or partnerships may be beneficiaries of trusts provided they are empowered by state law to take and hold title to property. Further, the settlor can designate as trust beneficiaries the members of a class ("my children," "my nephews and nieces") provided that the class members are ascertainable. On class gifts, see Chapter XV *infra*.

If the settlor fails to name a beneficiary, the trust fails, and a resulting trust arises. In some cases, a beneficiary who is not specifically named in the instrument may be identified by resort to extrinsic facts, such as by use of the "doctrine of facts or acts of independent significance." (For discussion of this doctrine, see Chapter V *supra*.)

The settlor also may be the beneficiary of the trust—either the sole beneficiary or one of several beneficiaries. (For example, it is common for a settlor to transfer property in trust to pay the income to the settlor for life and then, on the settlor's death, to convey the property to other beneficiaries.) The fact that the settlor is the sole beneficiary does not render the trust invalid. However, a settlor cannot create a trust to insulate himself or herself from creditors' claims. (For discussion of the ability of a settlor to terminate a trust when he or she is the sole beneficiary, see Chapter X *supra*.) Although the settlor can be the sole beneficiary of a trust, a sole trustee cannot be the sole beneficiary. Bogert, *supra*, at §129. In the latter case, the doctrine of merger applies (i.e., the legal and beneficial interests would merge), and the trust fails.

Note that California Probate Code §15209(b) expressly states that the merger doctrine does not apply when there are multiple settlors, at least one of which is a trustee, and one or more of those settlors are also beneficiaries during the lifetime of the settlors. See Torrey Pines Bank v. Hoffman, 231 Cal. App. 3d 308 (4th Dis. 1991) where merger did not apply to a family trust in which the married settlors acted as settlors, trustees, and beneficiaries.

CALIFORNIA PROBATE CODE
§24. "Beneficiary," defined

"Beneficiary" means a person to whom a donative transfer of property is made or that person's successor in interest, and:

(a) As it relates to the intestate estate of a decedent, means an heir.

(b) As it relates to the testate estate of a decedent, means a devisee.

(c) As it relates to a trust, means a person who has any present or future interest, vested or contingent.

(d) As it relates to a charitable trust, includes any person entitled to enforce the trust.

(Stats. 1990 (A.B. 759), ch. 79, §14, effective July 1, 1991.)

§15205. Trust requires the designation of a beneficiary

(a) A trust, other than a charitable trust, is created only if there is a beneficiary.

(b) The requirement of subdivision (a) is satisfied if the trust instrument provides for either of the following:

(a) A trust, other than a charitable trust, is created only if there is a beneficiary.

(b) The requirement of subdivision (a) is satisfied if the trust instrument provides for either of the following:

(1) A beneficiary or class of beneficiaries that is ascertainable with reasonable certainty or that is sufficiently described so it can be determined that some person meets the description or is within the class.

(2) A grant of a power to the trustee or some other person to select the beneficiaries based on a standard or in the discretion of the trustee or other person.

(Stats. 1990 (A.B. 759), ch. 79, §14, effective July 1, 1991.)

§15209. Exception to doctrine of merger

If a trust provides for one or more successor beneficiaries after the death of the settlor, the trust is not invalid, merged, or terminated in either of the following circumstances:

(a) Where there is one settlor who is the sole trustee and the sole beneficiary during the settlor's lifetime.

(b) Where there are two or more settlors, one or more of whom are trustees, and the beneficial interest in the trust is in one or more of the settlors during the lifetime of the settlors.

(Stats. 1990 (A.B. 759), ch. 79, §14, effective July 1, 1991.)

B. Disclaimer by the Beneficiary

A beneficiary does not have to accept the property interest given by the settlor. Refusal of an inheritance is termed "disclaimer" or "renunciation." One of the primary reasons for a beneficiary (or an heir) to disclaim his or her gift is to reduce tax liabilities.

State law generally specifies the requirements for disclaimer by a beneficiary (or an heir), such as the interests that may be disclaimed and the procedure for doing so. A beneficiary has a reasonable time after notification of the creation of the trust to accept or disclaim the beneficial interest in the trust. The beneficiary must accept or disclaim the whole trust. A disclaimer relates back to the date of trust creation. In the event of a disclaimer, the disclaimed property passes as if the beneficiary predeceased the settlor. A disclaimer is irrevocable (Cal. Prob. Code §281).

CALIFORNIA PROBATE CODE

§260. Definitions herein govern construction

Unless the provision or context otherwise requires, the definitions in this chapter govern the construction of this part.

(Stats. 1990 (A.B. 759), ch. 79, §14, effective July 1, 1991.)

§262. "Beneficiary," defined

"Beneficiary" means the person entitled, but for the person's disclaimer, to take an interest.

(Stats. 1990 (A.B. 759), ch. 79, §14, effective July 1, 1991.)

§263. "Creator of the interest," defined

(a) "Creator of the interest" means a person who establishes, declares, creates, or otherwise brings into existence an interest.

(b) "Creator of the interest" includes, but is not limited to, the following:

(1) With respect to an interest created by intestate succession, the person dying intestate.

(2) With respect to an interest created under a will, the testator.

(3) With respect to an interest created under a trust, the settlor.

(4) With respect to an interest created by succession to a disclaimed interest, the disclaimant of the disclaimed interest.

(5) With respect to an interest created by virtue of an election to take against a will, the testator.

(6) With respect to an interest created by creation of a power of appointment, the donor.

(7) With respect to an interest created by exercise or nonexercise of a power of appointment, the donee.

(8) With respect to an interest created by an inter vivos gift, the donor.

(9) With respect to an interest created by surviving the death of a depositor of a Totten trust account or P.O.D. account, the deceased depositor.

(10) With respect to an interest created under an insurance or annuity contract, the owner, the insured, or the annuitant.

(11) With respect to an interest created by surviving the death of another joint tenant, the deceased joint tenant.

(12) With respect to an interest created under an employee benefit plan, the employee or other owner of an interest in the plan.

(13) With respect to an interest created under an individual retirement account, annuity, or bond, the owner.

(Stats. 1990 (A.B. 759), ch. 79, §14, effective July 1, 1991.)

§264. "Disclaimant," defined

"Disclaimant" means a beneficiary who executes a disclaimer on his or her own behalf or a person who executes a disclaimer on behalf of a beneficiary.

(Stats. 1990 (A.B. 759), ch. 79, §14, effective July 1, 1991.)

§265. "Disclaimer," defined

"Disclaimer" means any writing which declines, refuses, renounces, or disclaims any interest that would otherwise be taken by a beneficiary.

(Stats. 1990 (A.B. 759), ch. 79, §14, effective July 1, 1991.)

§266. "Employee benefit plan," defined

"Employee benefit plan" includes, but is not limited to, any pension, retirement, death benefit, stock bonus, or profit-sharing plan, system, or trust.

(Stats. 1990 (A.B. 759), ch. 79, §14, effective July 1, 1991.)

§267. "Interest," defined

(a) "Interest" includes the whole of any property, real or personal, legal or equitable, or any fractional part, share, or particular portion or specific assets thereof, or any estate in any such property, or any power to appoint, consume, apply, or expend property, or any other right, power, privilege, or immunity relating to property.

(b) "Interest" includes, but is not limited to, an interest created in any of the following manners:

(1) By intestate succession.

(2) Under a will.

(3) Under a trust.

(4) By succession to a disclaimed interest.

(5) By virtue of an election to take against a will.

(6) By creation of a power of appointment.

(7) By exercise or nonexercise of a power of appointment.

(8) By an inter vivos gift, whether outright or in trust.

(9) By surviving the death of a depositor of a Totten trust account or P.O.D. account.

(10) Under an insurance or annuity contract.

(11) By surviving the death of another joint tenant.

(12) Under an employee benefit plan.

(13) Under an individual retirement account, annuity, or bond.

(14) Any other interest created by any testamentary or inter vivos instrument or by operation of law.

(Stats. 1990 (A.B. 759), ch. 79, §14, effective July 1, 1991.)

§275. Beneficiary may disclaim by filing disclaimer

A beneficiary may disclaim any interest, in whole or in part, by filing a disclaimer as provided in this part.

(Stats. 1990 (A.B. 759), ch. 79, §14, effective July 1, 1991.)

§276. Conservator may file disclaimer for conservatee

A disclaimer on behalf of a conservatee shall be made by the conservator of the estate of the conservatee pursuant to a court order obtained under Article 10 (commencing with Section 2580) of Chapter 6 of Part 4 of Division 4 authorizing or requiring the conservator to execute and file the disclaimer.

(Stats. 1990 (A.B. 759), ch. 79, §14, effective July 1, 1991.)

§277. Guardian may file disclaim on behalf of minor or personal representative may file on behalf of decedent

(a) A disclaimer on behalf of a minor shall be made by the guardian of the estate of the minor if one has been appointed or, if none has been appointed, by a guardian ad litem of the minor. A disclaimer by a guardian is not effective unless made pursuant to a court order obtained under this section.

(b) A disclaimer on behalf of a decedent shall be made by the personal representative of the decedent. Except as provided in Part 6 (commencing with Section 10400) of Division 7, a disclaimer by a guardian or personal representative is not effective unless made pursuant to a court order obtained under this section.

(c) A petition for an order authorizing or requiring a guardian or personal representative to execute and file a disclaimer shall be filed in the superior court in the county in which the estate of the minor or decedent is administered or, if there is no administration, the superior court in any county in which administration would be proper. The petition may be filed by the guardian, personal representative, or other interested person.

(d) The petition shall:

(1) Identify the creator of the interest.

(2) Describe the interest to be disclaimed.

(3) State the extent of the disclaimer.

(4) Identify the person or persons the petitioner believes would take the interest in the event of the disclaimer.

(e) Notice of the hearing on the petition shall be given as follows:

(1) If the petition is for an order authorizing or requiring the guardian of the estate of a minor to execute and file the disclaimer, notice of the hearing on the petition shall be given for the period and in the manner provided in Chapter 3 (commencing with Section 1460) of Part 1 of Division 4 to all of the persons required to be given notice under that chapter.

(2) If the petition is for an order authorizing or requiring the personal representative of a decedent to execute and file the disclaimer, notice of the hearing on the petition shall be given as provided in Section 1220.

(3) If the petition is for an order authorizing or requiring a guardian ad litem of a minor to execute and file the disclaimer, notice of the hearing on the petition shall be given to the persons and in the manner that the court shall by order direct.

(f) After hearing, the court in its discretion may make an order authorizing or requiring the guardian or personal representative to execute and file the disclaimer if the court determines, taking into consideration all of the relevant circumstances, that the minor or decedent as a prudent person would disclaim the interest if he or she had the capacity to do so.

(Stats. 1990 (A.B. 759), ch. 79, §14, effective July 1, 1991.)

§278. Requirements for valid disclaimer

The disclaimer shall be in writing, shall be signed by the disclaimant, and shall:

(a) Identify the creator of the interest.

(b) Describe the interest to be disclaimed.

(c) State the disclaimer and the extent of the disclaimer.

(Stats. 1990 (A.B. 759), ch. 79, §14, effective July 1, 1991.)

§279. Effectiveness of disclaimer

(a) A disclaimer to be effective shall be filed within a reasonable time after the person able to disclaim acquires knowledge of the interest.

(b) In the case of any of the following interests, a disclaimer is conclusively presumed to have been filed within a reasonable time if it is filed within nine months after the death of the creator of the interest or within nine months after the interest becomes indefeasibly vested, whichever occurs later:

(1) An interest created under a will.

(2) An interest created by intestate succession.

(3) An interest created pursuant to the exercise or nonexercise of a testamentary power of appointment.

(4) An interest created by surviving the death of a depositor of a Totten trust account or P.O.D. account.

(5) An interest created under a life insurance or annuity contract.

(6) An interest created by surviving the death of another joint tenant.

(7) An interest created under an employee benefit plan.

(8) An interest created under an individual retirement account, annuity, or bond.

(c) In the case of an interest created by a living trust, an interest created by the exercise of a presently exercisable power of appointment, an outright inter vivos gift, a power of appointment, or an interest created or increased by succession to a disclaimed interest, a disclaimer is conclusively presumed to have been filed within a reasonable time if it is filed within nine months after whichever of the following times occurs latest:

(1) The time of the creation of the trust, the exercise of the power of appointment, the making of the gift, the creation of the power of appointment, or the disclaimer of the disclaimed property.

(2) The time the first knowledge of the interest is acquired by the person able to disclaim.

(3) The time the interest becomes indefeasibly vested.

(d) In case of an interest not described in subdivision (b) or (c), a disclaimer is conclusively presumed to have been filed within a reasonable time if it is filed within nine months after whichever of the following times occurs later:

(1) The time the first knowledge of the interest is acquired by the person able to disclaim.

(2) The time the interest becomes indefeasibly vested.

(e) In the case of a future estate, a disclaimer is conclusively presumed to have been filed within a reasonable time if it is filed within whichever of the following times occurs later:

(1) Nine months after the time the interest becomes an estate in possession.

(2) The time specified in subdivision (b), (c), or (d), whichever is applicable.

(f) If the disclaimer is not filed within the time provided in subdivision (b), (c), (d), or (e), the disclaimant has the burden of establishing that the disclaimer was filed within a reasonable time after the disclaimant acquired knowledge of the interest.

(Stats. 1990 (A.B. 759), ch. 79, §14, effective July 1, 1991.)

§280. Place for filing disclaimer

(a) A disclaimer shall be filed with any of the following:

(1) The superior court in the county in which the estate of the decedent is administered or, if there is no administration of the decedent's estate, the superior court in any county in which administration of the estate of the decedent would be proper.

(2) The trustee, personal representative, other fiduciary, or person responsible for distributing the interest to the beneficiary.

(3) Any other person having custody or possession of or legal title to the interest.

(4) The creator of the interest.

(b) If a disclaimer made pursuant to this part affects real property or an obligation secured by real property and the disclaimer is acknowledged and proved in like manner as a grant of real property, the disclaimer may be recorded in like manner and with like effect as a grant of real property, and all statutory provisions relating to the recordation or nonrecordation of conveyances of real property and to the effect thereof apply to the disclaimer with like effect, without regard to the date when the disclaimer was filed pursuant to subdivision (a). Failure to file a disclaimer pursuant to subdivision (a) which is recorded pursuant to this subdivision does not affect the validity of any transaction with respect to the real property or the obligation secured thereby, and the general laws on recording and its effect govern any such transaction.

(Stats. 1990 (A.B. 759), ch. 79, §14, effective July 1, 1991.)

§281. An effective disclaimer is irrevocable and binding

A disclaimer, when effective, is irrevocable and binding upon the beneficiary and all persons claiming by, through, or under the beneficiary, including creditors of the beneficiary.

(Stats. 1990 (A.B. 759), ch. 79, §14, effective July 1, 1991.)

§282. Disposition of disclaimed interest

(a) Unless the creator of the interest provides for a specific disposition of the interest in the event of a disclaimer, the interest disclaimed shall descend, go, be distributed, or continue to be held

(1) as to a present interest, as if the disclaimant had predeceased the creator of the interest or

(2) as to a future interest, as if the disclaimant had died before the event determining that the taker of the interest had become finally ascertained and the taker's interest indefeasibly vested. A disclaimer relates back for all purposes to the date of the death of the creator of the disclaimed interest or the determinative event, as the case may be.

(b) Notwithstanding subdivision (a), where the disclaimer is filed on or after January 1, 1985:

(1) The beneficiary is not treated as having predeceased the decedent for the purpose of determining the generation at which the division of the estate is to be made under Part 6 (commencing with Section 240) or other provision of a will, trust, or other instrument.

(2) The beneficiary of a disclaimed interest is not treated as having predeceased the decedent for the purpose of applying subdivision (d) of Section 6409 or subdivision (b) of Section 6410.

(Stats. 1990 (A.B. 759), ch. 79, §14, effective July 1, 1991.)

§283. Disclaimer is not a fraudulent transfer by beneficiary

A disclaimer is not a fraudulent transfer by the beneficiary under Chapter 1 (commencing with Section 3439) of Title 2 of Part 2 of Division 4 of the Civil Code.

(Stats. 1990 (A.B. 759), ch. 79, §14, effective July 1, 1991.)

§284. Person may file written waiver of right to disclaim

A person who could file a disclaimer under this part may instead file a written waiver of the right to disclaim. The waiver shall specify the interest to which the waiver applies. Upon being filed as provided in Section 280, the waiver is irrevocable and is binding upon the beneficiary and all persons claiming by, through, or under the beneficiary.

(Stats. 1990 (A.B. 759), ch. 79, §14, effective July 1, 1991.)

§285. Beneficiary may not disclaim after having accepted interest

(a) A disclaimer may not be made after the beneficiary has accepted the interest sought to be disclaimed.

(b) For the purpose of this section, a beneficiary has accepted an interest if any of the following occurs before a disclaimer is filed with respect to that interest:

(1) The beneficiary, or someone acting on behalf of the beneficiary, makes a voluntary assignment, conveyance, encumbrance, pledge, or transfer of the interest or part thereof, or contracts to do so; provided, however, that a beneficiary will not have accepted an interest if the beneficiary makes a gratuitous conveyance or transfer of the beneficiary's entire interest in property to the person or persons who would have received the property had the beneficiary made an otherwise qualified disclaimer pursuant to this part.

(2) The beneficiary, or someone acting on behalf of the beneficiary, executes a written waiver under Section 284 of the right to disclaim the interest.

(3) The beneficiary, or someone acting on behalf of the beneficiary, accepts the interest or part thereof or benefit thereunder.

(4) The interest or part thereof is sold at a judicial sale.

(c) An acceptance does not preclude a beneficiary from thereafter disclaiming all or part of an interest if both of the following requirements are met:

(1) The beneficiary became entitled to the interest because another person disclaimed an interest.

(2) The beneficiary or other person acting on behalf of the beneficiary at the time of the acceptance had no knowledge of the interest to which the beneficiary so became entitled.

(d) The acceptance by a joint tenant of the joint tenancy interest created when the joint tenancy is created is not an acceptance by the joint tenant of the interest created when the joint tenant survives the death of another joint tenant.

(Stats. 1990 (A.B. 759), ch. 79, §14, effective July 1, 1991. Amended by Stats. 1994 (A.B. 3686), ch. 806, §3.)

§286. Right to disclaim exists regardless of spendthrift or other restrictions

The right to disclaim exists regardless of any limitation imposed on the interest of a beneficiary in the nature of an expressed or implied spendthrift provision or similar restriction.

(Stats. 1990 (A.B. 759), ch. 79, §14, effective July 1, 1991.)

§287. Effect of date of creation of interest

An interest created before January 1, 1984, that has not been accepted may be disclaimed after December 31, 1983, in the manner provided in this part, but no interest that arose before January 1, 1984, in a person other than the beneficiary may be destroyed or diminished by any action of the disclaimant taken pursuant to this part.

(Stats. 1990 (A.B. 759), ch. 79, §14, effective July 1, 1991.)

§288. Exclusive means of disclaiming an interest

This part does not limit or abridge any right a person may have under any other law to assign, convey, or release any property or interest, but after December 31, 1983, an interest that would otherwise be taken by a beneficiary may be declined, refused, renounced, or disclaimed only as provided in this part.

(Stats. 1990 (A.B. 759), ch. 79, §14, effective July 1, 1991.)

§295. Effect of federal law

Notwithstanding any other provision of this part, if as a result of a disclaimer or transfer the disclaimed or transferred interest is treated pursuant to the provisions of Title 26 of the United States Code, as now or hereafter amended, or any successor statute thereto, and the regulations promulgated thereunder, as never having been transferred to the beneficiary, then the disclaimer or transfer is effective as a disclaimer under this part.

(Stats. 1990 (A.B. 759), ch. 79, §14, effective July 1, 1991.)

C. Beneficiaries' Rights

1. General Limitations

The beneficiaries' rights in revocable trusts may be limited until after the death of the settlor (or other person holding the power to revoke the trust). When the settlor of a revocable trust is alive, only the settlor (or the holder of a power of revocation) has the right to enforce the trust (Cal. Prob. Code §§15800 et seq.). Similarly, the duty to inform and render accounts to the beneficiaries is owed to the settlor or person holding the power to revoke during the period when the trust is revocable, and not to the beneficiary. Law Revision Comment following California Probate Code §16060. Note that these limitations do not eliminate the rights of beneficiaries (in conjunction with the settlor) to modify or terminate the trust (Cal. Prob. Code §§15800, 15404, 15410). (Law Revision Commission Comment following California Probate Code §15800.)

Until recently, California trustees were required to notify beneficiaries and heirs whenever a trust became irrevocable. Former California Probate Code §16061.7 required a trustee to notify (by providing a copy of the "terms of the trust" according to Cal. Prob. Code §16060.5) any beneficiary or heir whenever a trust became irrevocable for any reason. The notification was accompanied by a warning that a time limit existed on the beneficiary's or heir's ability to contest the trust. The duty to notify beneficiaries and heirs was required even if the settlor was still alive. Stemming from concern about settlors' privacy, the California legislature enacted new legislation in 2000 (amending California Probate Code §16061.7) to limit the circumstances requiring notification.

California Probate Code §16061.7 now requires that a trustee provide a copy only if the trust becomes irrevocable for one of two

reasons: (1) if the trust becomes irrevocable as a result of the death of the settlor; or (2) if the trust becomes irrevocable based on a scheme within the trust instrument that specifies a date within one year before or after the settlor's death. See generally Erik R. Beauchamp, "It's My Money 'Til I Die": When Trustees Must Notify Heirs and Beneficiaries Concerning a Trust That Has Become Irrevocable, 32 McGeorge L. Rev. 670, 679-680 (2001).

§15800. Limitations on beneficiaries' rights

Except to the extent that the trust instrument otherwise provides or where the joint action of the settlor and all beneficiaries is required, during the time that a trust is revocable and the person holding the power to revoke the trust is competent:

(a) The person holding the power to revoke, and not the beneficiary, has the rights afforded beneficiaries under this division.

(b) The duties of the trustee are owed to the person holding the power to revoke.

(Stats. 1990 (A.B. 759), ch. 79, §14, effective July 1, 1991.)

§15801. Power to consent or withhold consent

(a) In any case where the consent of a beneficiary may be given or is required to be given before an action may be taken, during the time that a trust is revocable and the person holding the power to revoke the trust is competent, the person holding the power to revoke, and not the beneficiary, has the power to consent or withhold consent.

(b) This section does not apply where the joint consent of the settlor and all beneficiaries is required by statute.

(Stats. 1990 (A.B. 759), ch. 79, §14, effective July 1, 1991.)

§15802. Person who may receive notice

Notwithstanding any other statute, during the time that a trust is revocable and the person holding the power to revoke the trust is competent, a notice that is to be given to a beneficiary shall be given to the person holding the power to revoke and not to the beneficiary.

(Stats. 1990 (A.B. 759), ch. 79, §14, effective July 1, 1991.)

§15803. Rights of holder of power of appointment

The holder of a presently exercisable general power of appointment or power to withdraw property from the trust has the rights of a person holding the power to revoke the trust that are provided by Sections 15800 to 15802, inclusive, to the extent of the holder's power over the trust property.

(Stats. 1990 (A.B. 759), ch. 79, §14, effective July 1, 1991.)

§15804. Sufficiency of notice

(a) Subject to subdivisions (b) and (c), it is sufficient compliance with a requirement in this division that notice be given to a beneficiary, or to a person interested in the trust, if notice is given as follows:

(1) Where an interest has been limited on any future contingency to persons who will compose a certain class upon the happening of a certain event without further limitation, notice shall be given to the persons in being who would constitute the class if the event had happened immediately before the commencement of the proceeding or if there is no proceeding, if the event had happened immediately before notice is given.

(2) Where an interest has been limited to a living person and the same interest, or a share therein, has been further limited upon the happening of a future event to the surviving spouse or to persons who are or may be the distributees, heirs, issue, or other kindred of the living person, notice shall be given to the living person.

(3) Where an interest has been limited upon the happening of any future event to a person, or a class of persons, or both, and the interest, or a share of the interest, has been further limited upon the happening of an additional future event to another person, or a class of persons, or both, notice shall be given to the person or persons in being who would take the interest upon the happening of the first of these events.

(b) If a conflict of interest involving the subject matter of the trust proceeding exists between a person to whom notice is required to be given and a person to whom notice is not otherwise required to be given under subdivision (a), notice shall also be given to persons not otherwise entitled to notice under subdivision (a) with respect to whom the conflict of interest exists.

(c) Nothing in this section affects any of the following:

(1) Requirements for notice to a person who has requested special notice, a person who has filed notice of appearance, or a particular person or entity required by statute to be given notice.

(2) Availability of a guardian ad litem pursuant to Section 1003.

(d) As used in this section, "notice" includes other papers.

(Stats. 1990 (A.B. 759), ch. 79, §14, effective July 1, 1991. Amended by Stats. 1992 (S.B. 1496), ch. 178, §43.4.)

§15805. Attorney General is subject to limitations on beneficiary rights

Notwithstanding any other provision of law, the Attorney General is subject to the limitations on the rights of beneficiaries of revocable trusts provided by Sections 15800 to 15802, inclusive.

(Stats. 1990 (A.B. 759), ch. 79, §14, effective July 1, 1991.)

§16060.5. "Terms of the trust," defined

As used in his article, "terms of the trust" means the written trust instrument of an irrevocable trust or those provisions of a written trust instrument in effect at the settlor's death that describe or affect that portion of a trust that has become irrevocable at the death of the settlor. In addition, "terms of the trust" includes, but is not limited to, signatures, amendments, disclaimers, and any directions or instructions to the trustee that affect the disposition of the trust. "Terms of the trust" does not include documents which were intended to affect disposition only while the trust was irrevocable. If a trust has been completely restated, "terms of the trust" does not include trust instruments or amendments which are superseded by the last restatement before the settlor's death, but it does include amendments executed after the restatement. "Terms of the trust" also includes any document irrevocably exercising a power of appointment over the trust or over any portion of the trust which has become irrevocable.

(Stats. 1997 (A.B. 1172), ch. 724 §21. Amended by Stats. 1998 (A.B. 2069), ch. 682, §7; Stats. 2000 (A.B. 460), ch. 34, §2.)

§16061. Trustee shall provide information upon request by beneficiary

Except as provided in Section 16064, on reasonable request by a beneficiary, the trustee shall provide the beneficiary with a report of information about the assets, liabilities, receipts, and disbursements of the trust, the acts of the trustee, and the particulars relating to the administration of the trust relevant to the beneficiary's interest, including the terms of the trust.

(Stats. 1990 (A.B. 759), ch. 79, §14, effective July 1, 1991. Amended by Stats. 1998 (A.B. 2069), ch. 682, §8.)

§16061.5. Trustee shall provide notice when revocable trust becomes irrevocable

(a) When a revocable trust or any portion of a revocable trust becomes irrevocable because of the death of one or more of the settlors of the trust, or because, by the express terms of the trust, the trust becomes irrevocable within one year of the death of a settlor because of a contingency related to the death of one or more of the settlors of the trust, the trustee shall provide a true and complete copy of the terms of the irrevocable trust, or irrevocable portion of the trust, to any beneficiary of the trust who requests it and to any heir of a deceased settlor who requests it.

(b) The trustee shall, for purposes of this section, rely upon any final judicial determination of heirship. However, the trustee shall have discretion to make a good faith determination by any reasonable means of the heirs of a deceased settlor in the absence of a final judicial determination of heirship known to the trustee.

(Stats. 1997 (A.B. 1172), ch. 724, §22. Amended by Stats. 1998 (A.B. 2069), ch. 682, §9; Stats. 2000 (A.B. 460), ch. 34, §3.)

§16061.7. Trustee must notice beneficiary of certain facts: irrevocability and change in trustee

(a) A trustee shall serve a notification by the trustee as described in this section in the following events:

(1) When a revocable trust or any portion thereof becomes irrevocable because of the death of one or more of the settlors of the trust, or because, by the express terms of the trust, the trust becomes irrevocable within one year of the death of a settlor because of a contingency related to the death of one or more of the settlors of the trust.

(2) Whenever there is a change of trustee of an irrevocable trust. The duty to serve the notification by the trustee is the duty of the continuing or successor trustee, and any one cotrustee may serve the notification.

(b) The notification by the trustee required by subdivision (a) shall be served on each of the following:

(1) Each beneficiary of the irrevocable trust or irrevocable portion of the trust, subject to the limitations of Section 15804.

(2) Each heir of the deceased settlor, if the event that requires notification is the death of a settlor or irrevocability within one year of the death of the settlor of the trust by the express terms of the trust because of a contingency related to the death of a settlor.

(3) If the trust is a charitable trust subject to the supervision of the Attorney General, to the Attorney General.

(c) A trustee shall, for purposes of this section, rely upon any final judicial determination of heirship, known to the trustee, but the trustee shall have discretion to make a good faith determination by any reasonable means of the heirs of a deceased settlor in the absence of a final judicial determination of heirship known to the trustee.

(d) The trustee need not provide a copy of the notification by trustee to any beneficiary or heir (1) known to the trustee but who cannot be located by the trustee after reasonable diligence or (2) unknown to the trustee.

(e) The notification by trustee shall be served by mail to the last known address, pursuant to Section 1215, or by personal delivery.

(f) The notification by trustee shall be served not later than 60 days following the occurrence of the event requiring service of the notification by trustee, or 60 days after the trustee became aware of the existence of a person entitled to receive notification by trustee, if that person was not known to the trustee on the occurrence of the event requiring service of the notification. If there is a vacancy in the office of the trustee on the date of the occurrence of the event requiring service of the notification by trustee, or if that event causes a vacancy, then the 60-day period for service of the notification by trustee commences on the date the new trustee commences to serve as trustee.

(g) The notification by trustee shall contain the following information:

(1) The identity of the settlor or settlors of the trust and the date of execution of the trust instrument.

(2) The name, mailing address and telephone number of each trustee of the trust.

(3) The address of the physical location where the principal place of administration of the trust is located, pursuant to Section 17002.

(4) Any additional information that may be expressly required by the terms of the trust instrument.

(5) A notification that the recipient is entitled, upon reasonable request to the trustee, to receive from the trustee a true and complete copy of the terms of the trust.

(h) If the notification by the trustee is served because a revocable trust or any portion of it has become irrevocable because of the death of one or more settlors of the trust, or because, by the express terms of the trust, the trust becomes irrevocable within one year of the death of a settlor because of a contingency related to the death of one or more of the settlors of the trust, the notification by the trustee shall also include a warning, set out in a separate paragraph in not less than 10-point boldface type, or a reasonable equivalent thereof, that states as follows:

> "You may not bring an action to contest the trust more than 120 days from the date this notification by the trustee is served upon you or 60 days from the date on which a copy of the terms of the trust is mailed or personally delivered to you during that 120-day period, whichever is later."

(i) Any waiver by a settlor of the requirement of serving the notification by trustee required by this section is against public policy and shall be void.

(j) A trustee may serve a notification by trustee in the form required by this section on any person in addition to those on whom the notification by trustee is required to be served. A trustee is not liable to any person for serving or for not serving the notice on any person in addition to those on whom the notice is required to be served. A trustee is not required to serve a notification by trustee if the event that otherwise requires service of the notification by trustee occurs before January 1, 1998.

(Stats. 1997 (A.B. 1172), ch. 724, §23. Amended by Stats. 1998 (A.B. 2069), ch. 682, §10; Stats. 2000 (A.B. 460), ch. 34, §4; Stats. 2000 (A.B. 1628), ch. 592, §1.)

§16061.8. Trustee's notice serves to alert beneficiary of right to contest trust; limitation period

No person upon whom the notification by the trustee is served pursuant to this chapter may bring an action to contest the trust more than 120 days from the date the notification by the trustee is served upon him or her, or 60 days from the day on which a copy of the terms of the trust is mailed or personally delivered to him or her during that 120-day period, whichever is later.

(Stats. 1997 (A.B. 1172), ch. 724, §24. Amended by Stats. 2000 (A.B. 460), ch. 34, §5; Stats. 2000 (A.B. 1628), ch. 592, §2.)

2. Restrictions on Voluntary and Involuntary Transfers

a. Voluntary Transfer

The beneficiary of a trust generally can transfer his or her equitable interest in the trust. However, if the beneficiary is an income beneficiary, the beneficiary may transfer only his or her interest in the trust income because the transferee cannot acquire a greater estate than that possessed by the beneficiary.

The beneficiary can transfer the equitable interest either inter vivos or by will, in whole or in part, either absolutely or in trust. Thus, the beneficiary's interest is freely alienable unless the interest is made inalienable either by the terms of the trust or by statute. Scott & Fratcher, *supra*, §132, at 4-5. It is now held that the beneficiary has an interest in property and not

merely a right of action against the trustee. *Id.*, §132 at 3.

To transfer an interest in a trust, the beneficiary must manifest an intention to transfer the interest either by express words or otherwise. The beneficiary can transfer his or her interest without the consent of, or notice to, the trustee unless the terms of the trust provide otherwise. *Id.*, §136 at 19. However, if the trustee does not have notice of the transfer, the trustee is under no liability for continuing to make payments to the original beneficiary.

The California Probate Code restricts any donative transfers to two groups:

- persons who drafted the instrument (or caused it to be drafted) if (1) the transferee occupies a fiduciary relationship with the transferor or (2) is related by blood or marriage, or co-habits with, or is an employee of the person who drafted the instrument (or caused the instrument to be drafted) (Cal. Prob. Code §21350); or
- persons who are in a position to take advantage of the transferee, such as a conservatee or trustee who caused the instrument to be transcribed or a custodian of a dependent adult (Cal. Prob. Code §21350).

For exceptions to the above, see California Probate Code §21351. See also Estate of Shinkle, 119 Cal. Rptr. 2d 42 (Ct. App. 2002) (holding that ombudsperson in a long-term facility was disqualified as a transferee due to his status as a "care custodian"; even after the termination of the relationship with a particular resident); 60 Cal. Jur.3d Wills §427. On restrictions to transferees who are also draftspersons, see Chapter IV *supra*.

b. Involuntary Transfer

The beneficiary's interest also may be subject to involuntary transfer. That is, creditors of a beneficiary generally can reach the beneficiary's interest. According to the modern trend, trust assets are increasingly available to creditors. Creditors can enforce their claims by several means, including attachment, garnishment, or execution. 60 Cal. Jur.3d Trusts, §125 (citing Houghton v. Pacific Southwest Trust & Sav. Bank, 295 P. 1079 (Cal. Ct. App. 1931)). However, the creditor acquires only the same rights as the beneficiary.

Certain types of trusts contain restrictions on the beneficiary's interest. The most common type of protective trust is the spendthrift trust. In a spendthrift trust (more accurately, a spendthrift provision in a trust), the beneficiary's interest is not subject to either voluntary alienation by the beneficiary or involuntary alienation in the form of attachment by creditors. Such a provision also prevents a beneficiary from requesting that the trust be terminated prematurely. 60 Cal. Jur.3d Trusts §129. Other types of trusts with spendthrift-like restrictions are discussed *infra*.

Spendthrift trusts have been recognized by California case law since 1898. See Seymour v. McAvoy, 53 P. 946, 947 (Cal. 1898) (holding that a creditor could not attach trust property in the hands of a widow and child because spendthrift restrictions are accepted "by the great weight of authority in America," and reasoning that such provisions need not be express but may be implied from the settlor's intention). Now, such trusts are authorized by statute (Cal. Prob. Code §§15300 et seq.).

In California, spendthrift trusts are subject to certain statutory qualifications: (1) creditors may reach only a portion of the interest that is payable to the beneficiary (in order to protect the beneficiary) (Cal. Prob. Code §15306.5), and (2) such trusts may not be created to insulate the settlor from creditors (Cal. Prob. Code §15304(c)). Note that in the latter case, California Probate Code §15304(a) invalidates only the spendthrift restriction and not the trust.

In regard to the first qualification above, although creditors can satisfy money judgments from payments that are made to a spendthrift beneficiary, a court order on behalf of a judgment creditor may not require a trustee to pay an amount exceeding 25 percent of the payment that would have been made to the beneficiary (Cal. Prob. Code §15306.5(b)). In addition, a court order may not require a trustee to pay an amount that would make it impossible to support the beneficiary (or the support of dependents) (Cal. Prob. Code §15306.5(c)).

Finally, the aggregate of all orders for satisfaction of money judgments against the beneficiary's interest (i.e., obligations due to judgment creditors including obligations for spousal and child support) may not exceed 25 percent of the payment that otherwise would be made to the beneficiary (Cal. Prob. Code §15306.5(f)).

The significance of the spendthrift restriction, from the perspective of a creditor, is that the beneficiary's interest is not subject to enforcement of a money judgment until the beneficiary receives that interest (Cal. Prob. Code §15300) ("the beneficiary's interest in income under the trust . . . is not subject to enforcement of a money judgment *until paid to the beneficiary*") (emphasis added). Thus, according to California case law, once the beneficiary of a spendthrift trust receives his or her interest in the trust income or property, creditors can reach it. Kelly v. Kelly, 79 P.2d 1059 (Cal. 1938) (holding that after the beneficiary of a spendthrift trust has received the trust property, his creditor who was his ex-wife suing pursuant to a property settlement, may reach it because he could dispose of it as he wishes).

Note that the interest of a beneficiary in a spendthrift trust (or a trust for support) can be reached in satisfaction of a money judgment for child or spousal support (Cal. Prob. Code §15305). "As a general rule, the beneficiary should not be permitted to have the enjoyment of the interest under the trust while neglecting to support his or her dependents." Law Revision Commission Comment following California Probate Code §15305. The California legislature added this provision in 1986, based on a Wisconsin statute. Under prior California law, a court had discretion whether or not to permit a creditor to reach the beneficiary's interest in a trust (including a spendthrift trust) in satisfaction of obligations for child or spousal support. The amount under prior law was limited to the amount that could have been applied to child or spousal support on a like amount of earnings. *Id.* Currently, the court has discretion, pursuant to California Probate Code §15305, as to how much of the amount payable to the beneficiary should be applied for support and how much the beneficiary should receive. *Id.*

A beneficiary has the right to disclaim an interest in a spendthrift trust. Thus, a disclaimer of a spendthrift trust does not constitute a prohibited voluntary transfer (Cal. Prob. Code §§286, 15309).

Some trusts are similar to spendthrift trusts in terms of the imposition of restrictions on the ability of creditors to attach a beneficial interest. For example, the California Probate Code authorizes trusts for the beneficiary's education or support. According to California Probate Code §15302, if a trust provides that the trustee must pay income or principal (or both) for the beneficiary's education or support, then the beneficiary's interest, to the extent that it is necessary for the beneficiary's education or support, is not subject to the enforcement of a money judgment until paid to the beneficiary. The determination of the amount necessary for education or support is based on factors derived from case law, including: the standard of living to which the beneficiary and the beneficiary's family is accustomed, the manner in which the beneficiary has been reared and the beneficiary's habits, the beneficiary's background, the number and health of the beneficiary's dependents, and the beneficiary's own health. Relevant evidence includes cost of living, cost of housing, medical expenses, wages of employees, reasonable entertainment, and other reasonably necessary expenses. 60 Cal. Jur.3d Trusts §140.

Discretionary trusts are another type of protective trust. In cases of discretionary trusts, a trustee has discretion regarding the beneficiary's receipt of his or her interest in the trust. That is, the trustee has discretion regarding how much, if any, income to give a beneficiary from the trust.

A settlor may provide that the trustee has "absolute" or "sole" discretion, or, alternatively, the trust instrument may limit the trustee's discretion. The trustee must exercise that discretion reasonably subject to judicial oversight under an abuse-of-discretion standard. In California, if a trust instrument fails to articulate a broader standard, the power to distribute income or principle is limited to providing for the "health, education, support or maintenance" of the beneficiary (Cal. Prob. Code §16081(b)).

According to the California Probate Code, if a trust is a discretionary trust (providing that the trustee must pay to a beneficiary so much of the income or principal or both according to the trustee's discretion), then a creditor cannot compel an allocation to the beneficiary through control of the trustee's discretion (Cal. Prob. Code §15303(a)). The provision applies regardless of whether the trust instrument provides a standard for the exercise of the trustee's discretion (Cal. Prob. Code §15303(c)).

§15300. Beneficiary's interest in income may not be transferred if trust instrument so provides

Except as provided in Sections 15304 to 15307, inclusive, if the trust instrument provides that a beneficiary's interest in income is not subject to voluntary or involuntary transfer, the beneficiary's interest in income under the trust may not be transferred and is not subject to enforcement of a money judgment until paid to the beneficiary.

(Stats. 1990 (A.B. 759), ch. 79, §14, effective July 1, 1991.)

§15301. Beneficiary's interest in principal may not be transferred if trust instrument so provides

(a) Except as provided in subdivision (b) and in Sections 15304 to 15307, inclusive, if the trust instrument provides that a beneficiary's interest in principal is not subject to voluntary or involuntary transfer, the beneficiary's interest in principal may not be transferred and is not subject to enforcement of a money judgment until paid to the beneficiary.

(b) After an amount of principal has become due and payable to the beneficiary under the trust instrument, upon petition to the court under Section 709.010 of the Code of Civil Procedure by a judgment creditor, the court may make an order directing the trustee to satisfy the money judgment out of that principal amount. The court in its discretion may issue an order directing the trustee to satisfy all or part of the judgment out of that principal amount.

(Stats. 1990 (A.B. 759), ch. 79, §14, effective July 1, 1991.)

§15302. Beneficiary's interest in income or principal in trust for education/support

Except as provided in Sections 15304 to 15307, inclusive, if the trust instrument provides that the trustee shall pay income or principal or both for the education or support of a beneficiary, the beneficiary's interest in income or principal or both under the trust, to the extent the income or principal or both is necessary for the education or support of the beneficiary, may not be transferred and is not subject to the enforcement of a money judgment until paid to the beneficiary.

(Stats. 1990 (A.B. 759), ch. 79, §14, effective July 1, 1991.)

§15303. Power to compel trustee to pay income or principal in a trust when payment is subject to trustee's discretion

(a) If the trust instrument provides that the trustee shall pay to or for the benefit of a beneficiary so much of the income or principal or both as the trustee in the trustee's discretion sees fit to pay, a transferee or creditor of the beneficiary may not compel the trustee to pay any amount that may be paid only in the exercise of the trustee's discretion.

(b) If the trustee has knowledge of the transfer of the beneficiary's interest or has been served with process in a proceeding under Section 709.010 of the Code of Civil Procedure by a judgment creditor seeking to reach the beneficiary's interest, and the trustee pays to or for the benefit of the beneficiary any part of the income or principal that may be paid only in the exercise of the trustee's discretion, the trustee is liable to the transferee or creditor to the extent that the payment to or for the benefit of the beneficiary impairs the right of the transferee or creditor. This subdivision does not apply if the beneficiary's interest in the trust is subject to a restraint on transfer that is valid under Section 15300 or 15301.

(c) This section applies regardless of whether the trust instrument provides a standard for the exercise of the trustee's discretion.

(d) Nothing in this section limits any right the beneficiary may have to compel the trustee to pay to or for the benefit of the beneficiary all or part of the income or principal.

(Stats. 1990 (A.B. 759), ch. 79, §14, effective July 1, 1991.)

§15304. Restraint is invalid in cases in which settlor is also beneficiary

(a) If the settlor is a beneficiary of a trust created by the settlor and the settlor's interest is subject to a provision restraining the voluntary or involuntary transfer of the settlor's interest, the restraint is invalid against transferees or creditors of the settlor. The invalidity of the restraint on transfer does not affect the validity of the trust.

(b) If the settlor is the beneficiary of a trust created by the settlor and the trust instrument provides that the trustee shall pay income or principal or both for the education or support of the beneficiary or gives the trustee discretion to determine the amount of income or principal or both to be paid to or for the benefit of the settlor, a transferee or creditor of the settlor may reach the maximum amount that the trustee could pay to or for the benefit of the settlor under the trust instrument, not exceeding the amount of the settlor's proportionate contribution to the trust.

(Stats. 1990 (A.B. 759), ch. 79, §14, effective July 1, 1991.)

§15305. Court may order trustee to satisfy claims for child or spousal support from beneficiary's interest

(a) As used in this section, "support judgment" means a money judgment for support of the trust beneficiary's spouse or former spouse or minor child.

(b) If the beneficiary has the right under the trust to compel the trustee to pay income or principal or both to or for the benefit of the beneficiary, the court may, to the extent that the court determines it is equitable and reasonable under the circumstances of the particular case, order the trustee to satisfy all or part of the support judgment out of all or part of those payments as they become due and payable, presently or in the future.

(c) Whether or not the beneficiary has the right under the trust to compel the trustee to pay income or principal or both to or for the benefit of the beneficiary, the court may, to the extent that the court determines it is equitable and reasonable under the circumstances of the particular case, order the trustee to satisfy all or part of the support judgment out of all or part of future payments that the trustee, pursuant to the exercise of the trustee's discretion, determines to make to or for the benefit of the beneficiary.

(d) This section applies to a support judgment notwithstanding any provision in the trust instrument.

(Stats. 1990 (A.B. 759), ch. 79, §14, effective July 1, 1991.)

§15305.5. Court may order trustee to satisfy restitution judgment

(a) As used in this section, "restitution judgment" means a judgment awarding restitution for the commission of a felony or a money judgment for damages incurred as a result of conduct for which the defendant was convicted of a felony.

(b) If the beneficiary has the right under the trust to compel the trustee to pay income or principal or both to or for the benefit of the beneficiary, the court may, to the extent that the court determines it is equitable and reasonable under the circumstances of the particular case, order the trustee to satisfy all or part of the restitution judgment out of all or part of those payments as they become due and payable, presently or in the future.

(c) Whether or not the beneficiary has the right under the trust to compel the trustee to pay income or principal or both to or for the benefit of the beneficiary, the court may, to the extent that the court determines it is equitable and reasonable under the circumstances of the particular case, order the trustee to satisfy all or part of the restitution judgment out of all or part of future payments that the trustee, pursuant to the exercise of the trustee's discretion, determines to make to or for the benefit of the beneficiary.

(d) This section applies to a restitution judgment notwithstanding any provision in the trust instrument.

(Stats. 1991 (A.B. 534), ch. 175, §1.)

§15306. Court may order trustee to satisfy beneficiary's liability for public support

(a) Notwithstanding any provision in the trust instrument, if a statute of this state makes the beneficiary liable for reimbursement of this state or a local public entity in this state for public support furnished to the beneficiary or to the beneficiary's spouse or minor child, upon petition to the court under Section 709.010 of the Code of Civil Procedure by the appropriate state or local public entity or public official, to the extent the court determines it is equitable and reasonable under the circumstances of the particular case, the court may do the following:

(1) If the beneficiary has the right under the trust to compel the trustee to pay income or principal or both to or for the benefit of the beneficiary, order the trustee to satisfy all or part of the liability out of all or part of the payments as they become due, presently or in the future.

(2) Whether or not the beneficiary has the right under the trust to compel the trustee to pay income or principal or both to or for the benefit of the beneficiary, order the trustee to satisfy all or part of the liability out of all or part of the future payments that the trustee, pursuant to the exercise of the trustee's discretion, determines to make to or for the benefit of the beneficiary.

(3) If the beneficiary is a settlor or the spouse or minor child of the settlor and the beneficiary does not have the right under the trust to compel the trustee to pay income or principal or both to or for the benefit of the beneficiary, to the extent that the trustee has the right to make payments of income or principal or both to or for the beneficiary pursuant to the exercise of the trustee's discretion, order the trustee to satisfy all or part of the liability without regard to whether the trustee has then exercised or may thereafter exercise the discretion in favor of the beneficiary.

(b) Subdivision (a) does not apply to any trust that is established for the benefit of an individual who has a disability that substantially impairs the individual's ability to provide for his or her own care or custody and constitutes a substantial handicap. If, however, the trust results in the individual being ineligible for needed public social services under Division 9 (commencing With Section 10000) of the

Welfare and Institutions Code, this subdivision is not applicable and the provisions of subdivision (a) are to be applied.

(Stats. 1990 (A.B. 759), ch. 79, §14, effective July 1, 1991.)

§15306.5. Court may order trustee to satisfy judgment creditor out of payments to which beneficiary is entitled; limitations

(a) Notwithstanding a restraint on transfer of the beneficiary's interest in the trust under Section 15300 or 15301, and subject to the limitations of this section, upon a judgment creditor's petition under Section 709.010 of the Code of Civil Procedure, the court may make an order directing the trustee to satisfy all or part of the judgment out of the payments to which the beneficiary is entitled under the trust instrument or that the trustee, in the exercise of the trustee's discretion, has determined or determines in the future to pay to the beneficiary.

(b) An order under this section may not require that the trustee pay in satisfaction of the judgment an amount exceeding 25 percent of the payment that otherwise would be made to, or for the benefit of, the beneficiary.

(c) An order under this section may not require that the trustee pay in satisfaction of the judgment any amount that the court determines is necessary for the support of the beneficiary and all the persons the beneficiary is required to support.

(d) An order for satisfaction of a support judgment, as defined in Section 15305, has priority over an order to satisfy a judgment under this section. Any amount ordered to be applied to the satisfaction of a judgment under this section shall be reduced by the amount of an order for satisfaction of a support judgment under Section 15305, regardless of whether the order for satisfaction of the support judgment was made before or after the order under this section.

(e) If the trust gives the trustee discretion over the payment of either principal or income of a trust, or both, nothing in this section affects or limits that discretion in any manner. The trustee has no duty to oppose a petition to satisfy a judgment under this section or to make any claim for exemption on behalf of the beneficiary. The trustee is not liable for any action taken, or omitted to be taken, in compliance with any court order made under this section.

(f) Subject to subdivision (d), the aggregate of all orders for satisfaction of money judgments against the beneficiary's interest in the trust may not exceed 25 percent of the payment that otherwise would be made to, or for the benefit of, the beneficiary.

(Stats. 1990 (A.B. 759), ch. 79, §14, effective July 1, 1991.)

§15307. Income in excess of amount for education and support may be applied to satisfaction of money judgment

Notwithstanding a restraint on transfer of a beneficiary's interest in the trust under Section 15300 or 15301, any amount to which the beneficiary is entitled under the trust instrument or that the trustee, in the exercise of the trustee's discretion, has determined to pay to the beneficiary in excess of the amount that is or will be necessary for the education and support of the beneficiary may be applied to the satisfaction of a money judgment against the beneficiary. Upon the judgment creditor's petition under Section 709.010 of the Code of Civil Procedure, the court may make an order directing the trustee to satisfy all or part of the judgment out of the beneficiary's interest in the trust.

(Stats. 1990 (A.B. 759), ch. 79, §14, effective July 1, 1991.)

§15308. Court order is subject to modification

Any order entered by a court under Section 15305, 15306, 15306.5, or 15307 is subject to modification upon petition of an interested person filed in the court where the order was made.

(Stats. 1990 (A.B. 759), ch. 79, §14, effective July 1, 1991.)

§15309. Disclaimer shall not be considered a transfer

A disclaimer or renunciation by a beneficiary of all or part of his or her interest under a trust shall not be considered a transfer under Section 15300 or 15301.

(Stats. 1990 (A.B. 759), ch. 79, §14, effective July 1, 1991.)

§16080. Discretionary powers to be exercised reasonably

Except as provided in Section 16081, a discretionary power conferred upon a trustee is not left to the trustee's arbitrary discretion, but shall be exercised reasonably.

(Stats. 1990 (A.B. 759), ch. 79, §14, effective July 1, 1991.)

§16081. Fiduciary principles governing trustee's exercise of discretion

(a) Subject to the additional requirements of subdivisions (b), (c), and (d), if a trust instrument confers "absolute," "sole," or "uncontrolled" discretion on a trustee, the trustee shall act in accordance with fiduciary principles and shall not act in bad faith or in disregard of the purposes of the trust.

(b) Notwithstanding the use of terms like "absolute," "sole," or "uncontrolled" by a settlor or a testator, a person who is a beneficiary of a trust that permits the person, either individually or as trustee or cotrustee, to make discretionary distributions of income or principal to or for the benefit of himself or herself pursuant to a standard, shall exercise that power reasonably and in accordance with the standard.

(c) Unless a settlor or a testator clearly indicates that a broader power is intended by express reference to this subdivision, a person who is a beneficiary of a trust that permits the person, as trustee or cotrustee, to make discretionary distributions of income or principal to or for the benefit of himself or herself may exercise that power in his or her favor only for his or her health, education, support, or maintenance within the meaning of Sections 2041 and 2514 of the Internal Revenue Code. Notwithstanding the foregoing and the provisions of Section 15620, if a power to make discretionary distributions of income or principal is conferred upon two or more trustees, the power may be exercised by any trustee who is not a current permissible beneficiary of that power; and provided further that if there is no trustee who is not a current permissible beneficiary of that power, any party in interest may apply to a court of competent jurisdiction to appoint a trustee who is not a current permissible beneficiary of that power, and the power may be exercised by the trustee appointed by the court.

(d) Subdivision (c) does not apply to either of the following:

(1) Any power held by the settlor of a revocable or amendable trust.

(2) Any power held by a settlor's spouse or a testator's spouse who is the trustee of a trust for which a marital deduction, as defined in Section 21520, has been allowed.

(e) Subdivision (c) applies to any of the following:

(1) Any trust executed on or after January 1, 1997.

(2) Any testamentary trust created under a will executed on or after January 1, 1997.

(3) Any irrevocable trust created under a document executed before January 1, 1997, or any revocable trust executed before that date if the settlor was incapacitated as of that date, unless all parties in interest elect affirmatively not to be subject to the application of subdivision (c) through a written instrument delivered to the trustee. That election shall be made on or before the latest of January 1, 1998, three years after the date on which the trust became irrevocable, or, in the case of a revocable trust where the settlor was incapacitated, three years after the date on which the settlor became incapacitated.

(f) Notwithstanding the foregoing, the provisions of subdivision (c) neither create a new cause of action nor impair an existing cause of action that, in either case, relates to any power limited by subdivision (c) that was exercised before January 1, 1997.

(g) For purposes of this section, the term "party in interest" means any of the following persons:

(1) If the trust is revocable and the settlor is incapacitated, the settlor's legal representative under applicable law, or the settlor's attorney-in-fact under a durable power of attorney that is sufficient to grant the authority required under subdivision (c) or (e), as applicable.

(2) If the trust is irrevocable, each trustee, each beneficiary then entitled or authorized to receive income distributions from the trust, or each remainder beneficiary who would be entitled to receive notice of a trust proceeding under Section 15804. Any beneficiary who lacks legal capacity may be represented by the beneficiary's legal representative, attorney-in-fact under a durable power of attorney that is sufficient to grant the authority required under subdivision (c) or (e), as applicable, or in the absence of a legal representative or attorney-in-fact, a guardian ad litem appointed for that purpose.

(Stats. 1990 (A.B. 759), ch. 79, §14, effective July 1, 1991. Amended by Stats. 1996 (S.B. 1907), ch. 410, §1.)

§21350. Limitations on donative transfers

(a) Except as provided in Section 21351, no provision, or provisions, of any instrument shall be valid to make any donative transfer to any of the following:

(1) The person who drafted the instrument.

(2) A person who is related by blood or marriage to, is a domestic partner of, is a cohabitant with, or is an employee of, the person who drafted the instrument.

(3) Any partner or shareholder of any law partnership or law corporation in which the person described in paragraph (1) has an ownership interest, and any employee of that law partnership or law corporation.

(4) Any person who has a fiduciary relationship with the transferor, including, but not limited to, a conservator or trustee, who transcribes the instrument or causes it to be transcribed.

(5) A person who is related by blood or marriage to, is a domestic partner of, is a cohabitant with, or is an employee of a person who is described in paragraph (4).

(6) A care custodian of a dependent adult who is the transferor.

(7) A person who is related by blood or marriage to, is a domestic partner of, is a cohabitant with, or is an employee of, a person who is described in paragraph (6).

(b) For purposes of this section, a person who is related by blood or marriage to a person means all of the following:

(1) The person's spouse or predeceased spouse.

(2) Relatives within the third degree of a person and of the person's spouse.

(3) The spouse of any person described in paragraph (2).

In determining any relationship under this subdivision, Sections 6406, 6407, and Chapter 2 (commencing with Section 6450) of Part 2 of Division 6 shall be applicable.

(c) For purposes of this section, the term "dependent adult" has the meaning set forth in Section 15610.23 of the Welfare and Institutions Code and also includes those persons who (1) are older than 64 and (2) would be dependent adults, within the meaning of Section 15610.13, if they were between the ages of 18 and 64. The term "care custodian" has the meaning as set forth in Section 15610.17 of the Welfare and Institutions Code.

(d) For purposes of this section, "domestic partner" means a domestic partner as defined under Section 297 of the Family Code.

(Stats. 1993 (A.B. 21), ch. 293, §8. Amended by Stats. 1995 (A.B. 1466), ch. 730, §12; Stats. 1996 (S.B.392), ch. 563, §34; (A.B. 2751), ch. 862, §47; Stats. 1997 (A.B. 1172), ch. 724, §33; Stats. 2003 (A.B.1349), ch. 444, §1.)

§21351. Exemptions to limitations

Section 21350 does not apply if any of the following conditions are met:

(a) The transferor is related by blood or marriage to, is a cohabitant with, or is the registered domestic partner, pursuant to Division 2.5 (commencing with Section 297) of the Family Code, of the transferee or the person who drafted the instrument. For purposes of this section, "cohabitant" has the meaning set forth in Section 13700 of the Penal Code. The subdivision shall retroactively apply to an instrument that becomes irrevocable on or after July 1, 1993.

(b) The instrument is reviewed by an independent attorney who (1) counsels the client (transferor about the nature and consequences of the intended transfer, (2) attempts to determine if the intended consequence is the result of fraud, menace, duress, or undue influence, and (3) signs.

CERTIFICATE OF INDEPENDENT REVIEW

I, ___________________,, have reviewed
(attorney's name)

___________________ and counseled my client,
(name of instrument)

___________________, on the nature and consequences of the
(name of client)

Transfer, or transfers, of property to

____
(name of potentially disqualified person)

Contained in the instrument. I am so dissociated from the interest of the transferee as to be in a position to advise my client independently, impartially, and confidentially as to the consequences of the transfer. On the basis of this counsel, I conclude that the transfer, or transfers, in the instrument that otherwise might be invalid under Section 21350 of the Probate Code are valid because the transfer, or transfers, are not the product of fraud, menace, duress, or undue influence.

___________________ ___________________
(Name of Attorney) (Date)

Any attorney whose written engagement signed by the client is expressly limited solely to the preparation of a certificate under this subdivision, including the prior counseling, shall not be considered to otherwise represent the client.

(c) After full disclosure of the relationships of the persons involved, the instrument is approved pursuant to an order under Article 10 (commencing with Section 2580) of Chapter 6 of Part 4 of Division 4.

(d) The court determines, upon clear and convincing evidence, but not solely upon the testimony of any person described in subdivision (a) of Section 21450, that the transfer was not the product of fraud, menace, duress, or undue influence. IF the court finds that the transfer was the product of fraud, menace, duress, or undue influence, the disqualified person shall bear the costs of the proceeding, including reasonable attorney's fees.

(e) Subdivision (d) shall apply only to the following instruments:

(1) Any instrument other than one making a transfer to a person described in paragraph (1) of subdivision (a) of Section 21450.

(2) Any instrument executed on or before July 1, 1993, by a person who was a resident of this state at the time the instrument was executed.

(3) Any instrument executed by a resident of California who was not a resident at the time the instrument was executed.

(f) The transferee is a federal, state, or local public entity, an entity that qualifies for an exemption from taxation under Section 50(c)(3) or 501(c)(19) of the Internal Revenue Code, or a trust holding an interest for this entity, but only to the extent of the interest of the entity, or the trustee of this trust.

This subdivision shall retroactively apply to an instrument that becomes irrevocable on or after July 1, 1993.

(g) For purposes of this section, "related by blood or marriage" shall include persons within the fifth degree or heirs of the transferor.

(h) The transfer does not exceed the sum of three thousand dollars ($3,000). This subdivision shall not apply if the total value of the property in the estate of the transferor does not exceed the amount prescribed in Section 13100.

(i) The transfer is made by an instrument executed by a nonresident to California who was not a resident at the time the instrument was executed, and that was not signed within California.

(Stats. 1993 (A.B. 21), ch. 293, §8. Amended by Stats. 1994 (A.B. 797), ch. 40, §4, effective April 19, 1994; Stats. 1995 (A.B. 1466), ch. 730, §14; Stats. 2002 (S.B. 1575), ch. 412, §1.)

CALIFORNIA CODE OF CIVIL PROCEDURE

§709.010. Method of enforcement of money judgment against interest in trust

(a) As used in this section, "trust" has the meaning provided in Section 82 of the Probate Code.

(b) The judgment debtor's interest as a beneficiary of a trust is subject to enforcement of a money judgment only upon petition under this section by a judgment creditor to a court having jurisdiction over administration of the trust as prescribed in Part 5 (commencing with Section 17000) of Division 9 of the Probate Code. The judgment debtor's interest in the trust may be applied to the satisfaction of the money judgment by such means as the court, in its discretion, determines are proper, including but not limited to imposition of a lien on or sale of the judgment debtor's interest, collection of trust income, and liquidation and transfer of trust property by the trustee.

(c) Nothing in this section affects the limitations on the enforcement of a money judgment against the judgment debtor's interest in a trust under Chapter 2 (commencing with Section 15300) of Part 2 of Division 9 of the Probate Code, and the provisions of this section are subject to the limitations of that chapter.

(Stats. 1982, ch. 1364, p. 5207, §2, effective July 1, 1983. Amended by Stats. 1984, ch. 493, §1; Stats. 1984, ch. 892, §2.5; Stats. 1986, ch. 820, §18, effective July 1, 1987.)

II. Remedies of the Beneficiary

Statutes often specify the remedies available to beneficiaries for a trustee's breach of trust. California law sets forth the nature and extent of a trustee's liability to the beneficiaries in California Probate Code §§16400 et seq. For a discussion of the beneficiaries' remedies, see Chapter XI, Section IV *supra*.

XIII
CHARITABLE TRUSTS

This chapter explores the general nature of charitable trusts, the definition of charitable purposes, the rules applicable to charitable trustees and beneficiaries, the special rules regarding modification of charitable trusts (the "cy pres" doctrine), the constitutional limits (race- and gender-based) on testamentary gifts for charitable purposes, and the enforcement of charitable trusts.

I. Introduction

A. Definition of Charity

Courts frequently have to determine whether a particular gift is "charitable" based on a theoretical definition or purpose. Often, construction of the terms "charity" and "charitable purposes" arises in cases involving exemption from state property taxes. Bogert, *supra*, at §361.

The meaning of "charitable" under both federal and state tax law is distinct from the definition of "charitable" in trust law. In reality, however, the American law of charitable trusts is intimately connected with the statutory requirements for charitable tax exemption. Ilana H. Eisenstein, Comment, Keeping Charity in Charitable Trust Law: The Barnes Foundation and the Case for Consideration of Public Interest in Administration of Charitable Trusts, 151 U. Pa. L. Rev. 1747, 1760-1761 (2003).

A *charitable trust* is a trust established by a settlor for the benefit of the community. California law defines "charitable trust" (Cal. Bus. & Prof. Code §16100(a)) by reference to the Internal Revenue Code definition (IRC §4947(a)). A *charitable gift* is a gift for a general public use. 12 Cal. Jur.3d Charities §1. A definition of "charity" is provided in California's charitable solicitation law (Cal. Bus. & Prof. Code §17510.2 (d)).

Definitions of the term "charitable" in tax law are extremely influential (although not always dispositive) in judicial determinations of the validity of charitable trusts and charitable purposes. The definition of "charity" for purposes of charitable trusts generally is broader than the definition used by the Internal Revenue Service. McGovern & Kurtz, *supra*, §9.7 at 390. In order for a charitable trust to acquire tax-exempt status under federal income tax law, the trust must comply with requirements specified by the Internal Revenue Code. Various sections of the Internal Revenue Code and Treasury regulations issued thereunder specify the types of organizations and charitable purposes that qualify for tax-exempt status.

Note that courts have validated charitable trusts by determining that various synonyms used by settlors (e.g., "benevolent," "beneficent," "eleemosynary") have the same meaning as the term "charitable." 12 Cal. Jur.3d Charities §1. See also People v. Cogswell, 45 P. 270, 271 (Cal. 1896) ("'Eleemosynary' has come in the law to be interchangeable with the word 'charitable'"). Nor do the beneficiaries of a charitable trust have to be poor.

B. Origins of Charitable Trusts

Charitable trusts have been traced as far back as the fourteenth century. In 1601, Parliament codified the law of charitable trusts with the enactment of the Statute of Charitable Uses, 43 Eliz., c. 4 (Eng.). The Statute had two objectives: to enumerate those trust purposes that could qualify as charitable, and to provide for a method of investigation and enforcement of charitable trusts.

The public attitude toward charitable trusts has changed through American history, as explained below:

> The American law of trusts was inherited from British common law, and with it came the taint of British aristocracy. In the early republic, many states adopted highly restrictive laws regulating charitable trusts because they saw them as remnants of colonial law. Until the late nineteenth century, "charity was associated with privilege, with the dead hand, with established churches, with massive wealth in perpetuity"—with distinctly un-American ideals. Only the wealthy could afford to create enduring foundations; thus, such entities were

> considered part and parcel of the problems of inherited privilege.
>
> In the latter part of the nineteenth century, however, American attitudes toward charity began to change. Philanthropy came to be seen as a substitute for government action and socialist values. Greater reverence for private property and individualism led to increased respect for donors and their wishes. The rise of the great philanthropists, particularly Andrew Carnegie and John D. Rockefeller, created a new public perception that private wealth could be a "public trust" benefiting all society, rather than simply a marker of elite privilege. These changes led to more favorable treatment of charitable trusts and greater respect for philanthropists and their charitable designs.

Eisenstein, *supra*, at 1756.

In the nineteenth century, the United States Supreme Court examined the validity of charitable trusts. In Trustees of Philadelphia Baptist Ass'n v. Hart's Executors, 17 U.S. (4 Wheat.) 1 (1819), the Court determined whether a private trust established for charitable purposes was invalid for lack of a definite beneficiary when the jurisdiction had repealed the Statute of Charitable Uses. In 1790, a Virginia citizen, Silas Hart, executed a will bequeathing property to "the Baptist Association [as] a perpetual fund for the education of youths of the Baptist denomination, who shall appear promising for the ministry. . . ." In 1792, Virginia, like many American states in post-Revolutionary America, had repealed all statutes derived from English laws, including the Statute of Charitable Uses. Thus, in 1795, when the testator died, the jurisdiction had no legislation recognizing charitable trusts. The Supreme Court held that Virginia's repeal of the Statute of Charitable Uses deprived the Chancery Court of power to enforce the trust, and that there was no known common law validating such private trusts established for charitable purposes and having no definite beneficiaries.

The Court revisited the issue of the validity of charitable trusts in Vidal v. Girard's Executors, 43 U.S. (2 How.) 127 (1844). Banker Stephen Girard bequeathed his $7 million estate to the City of Philadelphia to establish a school for poor, white male orphans. His heirs challenged the will. The Statute of Charitable Uses, although not repealed (as in Virginia), was not in force in Pennsylvania. Justice Story, the noted scholar of equity jurisprudence, held that recognition of charitable trusts did not depend on enactment by the jurisdiction of the English Statute of Charitable Uses. Based on historical analysis, Story explained that charitable trusts had been enforced in Chancery long before enactment of the Statute of Charitable Uses. That decision effectively overruled *Trustees of Philadelphia Baptist Association* and validated charitable trusts.

C. Private Express Trusts Distinguished

Charitable trusts manifest some similarities to, as well as differences from, private express trusts. Like private express trusts, charitable trusts arise from the intention of a settlor to create a trust. A charitable trust may be created by use of the same methods as those to create private express trusts, and may be inter vivos or testamentary.

However, charitable trusts benefit the community rather than individuals. They are not subject to the definite beneficiaries rule. In fact, they must have *indefinite beneficiaries*. They are enforced by the state Attorney General (rather than the beneficiaries). Also, they constitute an exception to the Rule Against Perpetuities, which limits the duration of private express trusts, and therefore may continue indefinitely.

Finally, charitable trusts receive tax advantages.

> A charitable trust benefits from tax-exempt status in two ways. First, the organization itself does not incur tax liabilities on any income earned or on property or assets held. Second, income tax deductibility and estate tax benefits encourage donors to give money to an established charitable organization or to found a new charitable trust.

Eisenstein, supra, at 1760.

CALIFORNIA BUSINESS AND PROFESSIONS CODE

§17510.2. Definitions of terms

(a) As used in this article, "solicitation for charitable purposes," means any request, plea, entreaty, demand, or invitation, or attempt thereof, to give money or property, in connection with which any of the following applies:

(1) Any appeal is made for charitable purposes.

(2) The name of any charity, philanthropic or charitable organization is used or referred to in any such appeal as an inducement for making any such gift.

(3) Any statement is made to the effect that the gift or any part thereof will go to or be used for any charitable purpose or organization.

(4) The name of any organization of law enforcement personnel, firefighters, or other persons who protect the public safety is used or referred to as an inducement for transferring any money or property, unless the only expressed or implied purpose of the solicitation is for the sole benefit of the actual active membership of the organization.

(b) As used in this article, "sales solicitation for charitable purposes" means the sale of, offer to sell, or attempt to sell any advertisement, advertising space, book, card, chance, coupon device, magazine subscription, membership, merchandise, ticket of admission or any other thing or service in connection with which any of the following applies:

(1) Any appeal is made for charitable purposes.

(2) The name of any charity, philanthropic or charitable organization is used or referred to in any such appeal as an inducement for making any such sale.

(3) Any statement is made to the effect that the whole or any part of the proceeds from the sale will go to or be used for any charitable purpose or organization.

(4) The name of any organization of law enforcement personnel, firefighters, or other persons who protect the public safety is used or referred to as an inducement for transferring any money or property, unless the only expressed or implied purpose of the sales solicitation is for the sole benefit of the actual active membership of the organization.

(c) A solicitation for charitable purposes, or a sale, offer or attempt to sell for charitable purposes, shall include the making or disseminating or causing to be made or disseminated before the public in this state, in any newspaper or other publication, or any advertising device, or by public outcry or proclamation, or in any other manner or means whatsoever any such solicitation.

(d) For purposes of this article, "charity" shall include any person who, or any nonprofit community organization, fraternal, benevolent, educational, philanthropic, or service organization, or governmental employee organization which, solicits or obtains contributions solicited from the public for charitable purposes or holds any assets for charitable purposes.

(Stats. 1972, ch. 1113, p. 2122, §1. Amended by Stats. 1980, ch. 1267, p. 4292, §2; Stats. 1984, ch. 187, §1; Stats. 1998, ch. 445 (A.B. 1810), §1.)

CALIFORNIA PROBATE CODE
§16100. "Charitable trust," defined

As used in this article, the following definitions shall control:

(a) "Charitable trust" means a charitable trust as described in Section 4947(a)(1) of the Internal Revenue Code.

(b) "Private foundation" means a private foundation as defined in Section 509 of the Internal Revenue Code.

(c) "Split-interest trust" means a split-interest trust as described in Section 4947(a)(2) of the Internal Revenue Code. *(Stats. 1990 (A.B. 759), ch. 79, §14, effective July 1, 1991.)*

INTERNAL REVENUE CODE
§501. Organizations exempt from taxation

(a) Exemption from taxation.—An organization described in subsection (c) or (d) or section 401(a) shall be exempt from taxation under this subtitle unless such exemption is denied under section 502 or 503.

(b) Tax on unrelated business income and certain other activities.—An organization exempt from taxation under subsection (a) shall be subject to tax to the extent provided in parts II, III, and VI of this subchapter, but (notwithstanding parts II, III, and VI of this subchapter) shall be considered an organization exempt from income taxes for the purpose of any law which refers to organizations exempt from income taxes.

(c) List of exempt organizations.—The following organizations are referred to in subsection (a):

(1) Any corporation organized under Act of Congress which is an instrumentality of the United States but only if such corporation—

(A) is exempt from Federal income taxes—

(i) under such Act as amended and supplemented before July 18, 1984, or

(ii) under this title without regard to any provision of law which is not contained in this title and which is not contained in a revenue Act, or

(B) is described in subsection (l).

(2) Corporations organized for the exclusive purpose of holding title to property, collecting income therefrom, and turning over the entire amount thereof, less expenses, to an organization which itself is exempt under this section. Rules similar to the rules of subparagraph (G) of paragraph (25) shall apply for purposes of this paragraph.

(3) Corporations, and any community chest, fund, or foundation, organized and operated exclusively for

religious, charitable, scientific, testing for public safety, literary, or educational purposes, or to foster national or international amateur sports competition (but only if no part of its activities involve the provision of athletic facilities or equipment), or for the prevention of cruelty to children or animals, no part of the net earnings of which inures to the benefit of any private shareholder or individual, no substantial part of the activities of which is carrying on propaganda, or otherwise attempting, to influence legislation (except as otherwise provided in subsection (h)), and which does not participate in, or intervene in (including the publishing or distributing of statements), any political campaign on behalf of (or in opposition to) any candidate for public office.

. . . .

(August 16, 1954, ch. 736, 68A Stat. 163; March 13, 1956, ch. 83, §5(2), 70 Stat. 49; April 22, 1960, Pub. L. 86-428, §1, 74 Stat. 54; July 14, 1960, Pub. L. 86-667, §1, 74 Stat. 534; Oct. 16, 1962, Pub. L. 87-834, §8(d), 76 Stat. 997; Feb. 2, 1966, Pub. L. 89-352, §1, 80 Stat. 4; Nov. 8, 1966, Pub. L. 89-800, §6(a), 80 Stat. 1515; June 28, 1968, Pub. L. 90-364, Title I, §109(a), 82 Stat. 269; December 30, 1969, Pub. L. 91-172, Title I, §§101(j)(3) to (6), 121(b)(5)(A), (6)(A), 83 Stat. 526, 527, 541; December 31, 1970, Pub. L. 91-618, §1, 84 Stat. 1855; August 29, 1972, Pub. L. 92-418, §1(a), 86 Stat. 656; June 8, 1974, Pub. L. 93-310, §3(a), 88 Stat. 235; January 3, 1975, Pub. L. 93-625, §10(c), 88 Stat. 2119; Oct. 4, 1976, Pub. L. 94-455, Title XIII, §§1307(a)(1), (d)(1)(A), 1312(a), 1313(a), Title XIX, §1906(b)(13)(A), Title XXI, §§2113(a), 2134(b), 90 Stat. 1720, 1727, 1730, 1834, 1907, 1927; Oct. 20, 1976, Pub. L. 94-568, §§1(a), 2(a), 90 Stat. 2697; Feb. 10, 1978, Pub. L. 95-227, §4(a), 92 Stat. 15; August 15, 1978, Pub. L. 95-345, §1(a), 92 Stat. 481; Nov. 6, 1978, Pub. L. 95-600, Title VII, §703(b)(2), (g)(2)(B), 92 Stat. 2939, 2940; April 1, 1980, Pub. L. 96-222, Title I, §108(b)(2)(B), 94 Stat. 226; September 26, 1980, Pub. L. 96-364, Title II, §209(a), 94 Stat. 1290; December 24, 1980, Pub. L. 96-601, §3(a), 94 Stat. 3496; December 28, 1980, Pub. L. 96-605, Title I, §106(a), 94 Stat. 3523; December 29, 1981, Pub. L. 97-119, Title I, §103(c)(1), 95 Stat. 1638; September 3, 1982, Pub. L. 97-248, Title II, §286(a), Title III, §354(a), (b), 96 Stat. 569, 640, 641; January 12, 1983, Pub. L. 97-448, Title III, §306(b)(5), 96 Stat. 2406; July 18, 1984, Pub. L. 98-369, Div. A, Title X, §§1032(a), 1079, Div. B, Title VIII, §2813(b), 98 Stat. 1033, 1056, 1206; April 7, 1986, Pub. L. 99-272, Title XI, §11012(b), 100 Stat. 260; Oct. 22, 1986, Pub. L. 99-514, Title X, §§1012(a), 1024(b), Title XI, §§1109(a), 1114(b)(14), Title XVI, §1603(a), Title XVIII, §§1879(k)(1), 1899A(15), 100 Stat. 2390, 2406, 2435, 2451, 2768, 2909, 2959; December 22, 1987, Pub. L. 100-203, Title X, §10711(a)(2), 101 Stat. 1330-464; Nov. 10, 1988, Pub. L. 100-647, Title I, §§1010(b)(4), 1011(c)(7)(D), 1016(a)(1)(A), (2) to (4), 1018(u)(14), (15), (34), Title II, §2003(a)(1), (2), Title VI, §6202(a), 102 Stat. 3451, 3458, 3573, 3574, 3590, 3592, 3597 to 3598, 3730; August 9, 1989, Pub. L. 101-73, Title XIV, §1402(a), 103 Stat. 550; Oct. 24, 1992, Pub. L. 102-486, Title XIX, §1940(a), 106 Stat. 3034; August 10, 1993, Pub. L. 103-66, Title XIII, §13146(a), (b), 107 Stat. 443; July 30, 1996, Pub. L. 104-168, Title XIII, §1311(b)(1), 110 Stat. 1478; August 20, 1996, Pub. L. 104-188, Title I, §§1114(a), 1704(j)(5), 110 Stat. 1759, 1882; August 21, 1996, Pub. L. 104-191, Title III, §§341(a), 342(a), 110 Stat. 2070; August 5, 1997, Pub. L. 105-33, Title IV, §4041(a), 111 Stat. 360; August 5, 1997, Pub. L. 105-34, Title I, §101(c), Title IX, §§963(a), (b), 974(a), 111 Stat. 799, 892, 898; July 22, 1998, Pub. L. 105-206, Title VI, §6023(6), (7), 112 Stat. 825; June 7, 2001, Pub. L. 107-16, Title VI, §611(d)(3)(C), 115 Stat. 98; December 21, 2001, Pub. L. 107-90, Title II, §202, 115 Stat. 890; November 11, 2003, Pub. L. 108-121, Title 1 §§105(a), 108(a), 117 Stat. 1338, 1339; April 10, 2004, Pub. L. 108-218, Title II, 206(a), (b), 118 Stat. 610; October 22, 2004, Pub. L. 108-357, Title III, Subititle B, §319(a), (b), 118 Stat. 1470; August 8, 2004, P.L. 109-58, Title XIII, Subtitle A, §1304(a), (b) 110 Stat. 997. Amended by December 21, 2005, Pub. L. 109-135, Title IV, Subititle A, §412(bb), (cc), 110 Stat. 2639; Aug. 17, 2006, Pub. L. 109-280, Title VIII, §862(a), Title XII, §1220(a), 120 Stat. 1021, 1086.)

§4947. Charitable trust defined; certain nonexempt trusts

(a) Application of tax.—

(1) Charitable trusts.—For purposes of part II of subchapter F of chapter 1 (other than section 508(a), (b), and (c)) and for purposes of this chapter, a trust which is not exempt from taxation under section 501(a), all of the unexpired interests in which are devoted to one or more of the purposes described in section 170(c)(2)(B), and for which a deduction was allowed under section 170, 545(b)(2), 556(b)(2), 642(c), 2055, 2106(a)(2), or 2522 (or the corresponding provisions of prior law), shall be treated as an organization described in section 501(c)(3). For purposes of section 509(a)(3)(A), such a trust shall be treated as if organized on the day on which it first becomes subject to this paragraph.

(2) Split-interest trusts.—In the case of a trust which is not exempt from tax under section 501(a), not all of the unexpired interests in which are devoted to one or more of the purposes described in section 170(c)(2)(B), and which

has amounts in trust for which a deduction was allowed under section 170, 545(b)(2), 556(b)(2), 642(c), 2055, 2106(a)(2), or 2522, section 507 (relating to termination of private foundation status), section 508(e) (relating to governing instruments) to the extent applicable to a trust described in this paragraph, section 4941 (relating to taxes on self-dealing), section 4943 (relating to taxes on excess business holdings) except as provided in subsection (b)(3), section 4944 (relating to investments which jeopardize charitable purpose) except as provided in subsection (b)(3), and section 4945 (relating to taxes on taxable expenditures) shall apply as if such trust were a private foundation. This paragraph shall not apply with respect to—

(A) any amounts payable under the terms of such trust to income beneficiaries, unless a deduction was allowed under section 170(f)(2)(B), 2055(e)(2)(B), or 2522(c)(2)(B),

(B) any amounts in trust other than amounts for which a deduction was allowed under section 170, 545(b)(2), 556(b)(2), 642(c), 2055, 2106(a)(2), or 2522, if such other amounts are segregated from amounts for which no deduction was allowable, or

(C) any amounts transferred in trust before May 27, 1969.

(3) Segregated amounts.—For purposes of paragraph (2)(B), a trust with respect to which amounts are segregated shall separately account for the various income, deduction, and other items properly attributable to each of such segregated amounts.

(b) Special rules.—

(1) Regulations.—The Secretary shall prescribe such regulations as may be necessary to carry out the purposes of this section.

(2) Limit to segregated amounts.—If any amounts in the trust are segregated within the meaning of subsection (a)(2)(B) of this section, the value of the net assets for purposes of subsections (c)(2) and (g) of section 507 shall be limited to such segregated amounts.

(3) Sections 4943 and 4944.—Sections 4943 and 4944 shall not apply to a trust which is described in subsection (a)(2) if—

(A) all the income interest (and none of the remainder interest) of such trust is devoted solely to one or more of the purposes described in section 170(c)(2)(B), and all amounts in such trust for which a deduction was allowed under section 170, 545(b)(2), 556(b)(2), 642(c), 2055, 2106(a)(2), or 2522 have an aggregate value not more than 60 percent of the aggregate fair market value of all amounts in such trusts, or

(B) a deduction was allowed under section 170, 545(b)(2), 556(b)(2), 642(c), 2055, 2106(a)(2), or 2522 for amounts payable under the terms of such trust to every remainder beneficiary but not to any income beneficiary.

(4) Section 507.—The provisions of section 507(a) shall not apply to a trust which is described in subsection (a)(2) by reason of a distribution of qualified employer securities (as defined in section 664(g)(4)) to an employee stock ownership plan (as defined in section 4975(e)(7)) in a qualified gratuitous transfer (as defined by section 664(g)).

(December 30, 1969, Pub. L. 91-172, Title I, §101(b), 83 Stat. 517. Amended by October 4, 1976, Pub. L. 94-455, Title XIX, §1906(b) (13) (A), 90 Stat. 1834; August 5, 1997, Pub. L. 105-34, Title XV, §1530(c)(9), , 111 Stat. 1079; June 7, 2001, Pub. L. 107-16, Title V, §542(e)(4), , 115 Stat. 85; October 22, 2004, Pub. L. 109-357, Title IV, §413(c)(30), 118 Stat. 1509.)

TREASURY REGULATION 26 C.F.R. §1.501(c)(3)-1

. . .

(d) Exempt purposes—

(1) In general. (i) An organization may be exempt as an organization described in section 501(c)(3) if it is organized and operated exclusively for one or more of the following purposes:

(a) Religious,
(b) Charitable,
(c) Scientific,
(d) Testing for public safety,
(e) Literary,
(f) Educational, or
(g)Prevention of cruelty to children or animals.

(ii) An organization is not organized or operated exclusively for one or more of the purposes specified in subdivision (i) of this subparagraph unless it serves a public rather than a private interest. Thus, to meet the requirement of this subdivision, it is necessary for an organization to establish that it is not organized or operated for the benefit of private interests such as designated individuals, the creator or his family, shareholders of the organization, or persons controlled, directly or indirectly, by such private interests.

(iii) Since each of the purposes specified in subdivision (i) of this subparagraph is an exempt purpose in itself, an organization may be exempt if it is organized and operated exclusively for any one or more of such purposes. If, in fact, an organization is organized and operated exclusively for an exempt purpose or purposes, exemption will be granted to such an organization regardless of the purpose or purposes specified in its application for exemption. For example, if an organization claims exemption on the ground that it is educational, exemption will not be denied if, in fact, it is charitable.

(2) **Charitable defined**. The term 'charitable' is used in section 501(c)(3) in its generally accepted legal sense and is therefore, not to be construed as limited by the separate enumeration in section 501(c)(3) of other tax-exempt purposes which may fall within the broad outlines of 'charity' as developed by judicial decisions. Such terms include: Relief of the poor and distressed or of the underprivileged; advancement of religion; advancement of education or science; erection or maintenance of public buildings, monuments, or works, lessening of the burdens of Government; and promotion of social welfare by organizations designed to accomplish any of the above purposes, or (i) to lessen neighborhood tensions; (ii) to eliminate prejudice and discrimination; (iii) to defend human and civil rights secured by law; or (iv) to combat community deterioration and juvenile delinquency. The fact that an organization which is organized and operated for the relief of indigent persons may receive voluntary contributions from the persons intended to be relieved will not necessarily prevent such organizations from being exempt as an organization organized and operated exclusively for charitable purposes. The fact that an organization, in carrying out its primary purpose, advocates social or civic changes or presents opinion on controversial issues with the intention of molding public opinion or creating public sentiment to an acceptance of its views does not preclude such organization from qualifying under section 501(c)(3) so long as it is not an 'action' organization of any one of the types described in paragraph (c)(3) of this section.

(November 26, 1960, T.D. 6500, 25 FR 11737. Amended by January 11, 1961, T.D. 6525, 26 R 189; December 12, 1967, T.D. 6939, 32 FR 17661; August 16, 1967, T.D. 7428, 41 FR 34620; August 31, 1990, T.D. 8308, 55 FR 35587.)

D. Application of Law to Charitable Trusts

California trust law applies both to private express trusts and to charitable trusts (Cal. Prob. Code §15004). Charitable trusts may be created by the same methods as private express trusts (Cal. Prob. Code §15200).

CALIFORNIA PROBATE CODE

§15000. Title

This division shall be known and may be cited as the Trust Law.

(Stats. 1990 (A.B. 759), ch. 79, §14, effective July 1, 1991.)

§15001. Application

Except as otherwise provided by statute:

(a) This division applies to all trusts regardless of whether they were created before, on, or after July 1, 1987.

(b) This division applies to all proceedings concerning trusts commenced on or after July 1, 1987.

(c) This division applies to all proceedings concerning trusts commenced before July 1, 1987, unless in the opinion of the court application of a particular provision of this division would substantially interfere with the effective conduct of the proceedings or the rights of the parties and other interested persons, in which case the particular provision of this division does not apply and prior law applies.

(Stats. 1990 (A.B. 759), ch. 79, §14, effective July 1, 1991.)

§15002. Common law applies to state

Except to the extent that the common law rules governing trusts are modified by statute, the common law as to trusts is the law of this state.

(Stats. 1990 (A.B. 759), ch. 79, §14, effective July 1, 1991.)

§15004. Application to charitable trusts

Unless otherwise provided by statute, this division applies to charitable trusts that are subject to the jurisdiction of the Attorney General to the extent that the application of the provision is not in conflict with the Uniform Supervision of Trustees for Charitable Purposes Act, Article 7 (commencing with Section 12580) of Chapter 6 of Part 2 of Division 3 of Title 2 of the Government Code.

(Stats. 1990 (A.B. 759), ch. 79, §14, effective July 1, 1991.)

§15200. Methods of creating a trust

Subject to other provisions of this chapter, a trust may be created by any of the following methods:

(a) A declaration by the owner of property that the owner holds the property as trustee.

(b) A transfer of property by the owner during the owner's lifetime to another person as trustee.

(c) A transfer of property by the owner, by will or by other instrument taking effect upon the death of the owner, to another person as trustee.

(d) An exercise of a power of appointment to another person as trustee.

(e) An enforceable promise to create a trust.

(Stats. 1990 (A.B. 759), ch. 79, §14, effective July 1, 1991.)

§15204. Trusts with indefinite or general purposes

A trust created for an indefinite or general purpose is not invalid for that reason if it can be determined with reasonable certainty that a particular use of the trust property comes within that purpose.

(Stats. 1990 (A.B. 759), ch. 79, §14, effective July 1, 1991.)

II. Charitable Purposes

The Preamble to the English Statute of Charitable Uses enumerated several purposes that were recognized as charitable. Courts frequently refer to that list to identify those purposes that are charitable. Courts generally hold that any purpose is charitable that falls within a type designated in the Preamble, or that is analogous thereto (although the original list was not intended to be complete). As recognized by the Statute of Charitable Uses, charitable purposes include the following:

> The relief of aged, impotent and poor people; the maintenance of maimed and sick soldiers and mariners; the support of schools of learning, free schools, and scholars of universities; repairs of bridges, ports, havens, causeways, churches, seabanks, and highways; education and preferment of orphans; the relief, stock, and maintenance of houses of correction; marriage of poor maids; aid and help of young tradesmen, handicraftsmen, and persons decayed; relief or redemption of prisoners and captives; aid of poor inhabitants concerning payments of fifteenths, setting out of soldiers, and other taxes.

43 Eliz. c. 4 (1601). Gradually, courts have enlarged the scope of charitable purposes.

Definitions of charitable purposes in both the Restatements and the Uniform Trust Code are derived from the Statute of Charitable Uses. According to Uniform Trust Code §405(a), a charitable trust may be created for the following charitable purposes: the relief of poverty; the advancement of education or religion; the promotion of health, governmental, or municipal purposes; or other purposes the accomplishment of which is beneficial to the community. The above rule restates the charitable purposes listed in the Restatement (Third) of Trusts §28 and the Restatement (Second) of Trusts §368.

The determination of whether the settlor's purpose is charitable is made by a court. That is, the settlor's opinion of whether a purpose is charitable is irrelevant. Shenandoah Valley Nat'l Bank v. Taylor, 63 S.E.2d 786 (Va. 1951) (holding that a charitable trust was invalid as an educational trust, despite the fact that the testator had directed that payments be made to school children at Easter and Christmas to be used in furtherance of their education).

Charitable trusts are subject to the restriction that the trust purpose must not be illegal or contrary to public policy. Unif. Trust Code §404 ("A trust may be created only to the extent its purposes are lawful, not contrary to public policy, and possible to achieve. A trust and its terms must be for the benefit of its beneficiaries."). See also Restatement (Third) of Trusts §29 ("An intended trust or trust provision is invalid if: (a) its purpose is unlawful or its performance calls for the commission of a criminal or tortious act; (b) it violates rules relating to perpetuities; or (c) it is contrary to public policy").

If the settlor states a general charitable purpose, and neglects to set forth either a specific purpose or beneficiary (ies), the court may select the particular purpose or beneficiary (ies) or delegate the task to a trustee. Unif. Trust Code §405(b).

Charitable trusts must be dedicated exclusively to charitable objectives, even if only for a period of time (e.g., charitable remainder trust). As explained above, a charitable trust has to be for a charitable purpose. However, a trust can be both charitable and noncharitable simultaneously. Such trusts are termed *split-interest trusts*. A common type of such trusts is a private express trust for the settlor's surviving spouse for life, followed by a charitable

remainder trust devoting the remainder to a charitable organization.

Trusts to satisfy a personal whim of the donor do not have sufficient community benefit. For the same reason, trusts that are established to disseminate beliefs that are either irrational or inconsequential are not valid.

California statutes address only a few charitable purposes expressly. Statutes authorize persons to make gifts of property in trust for founding, endowing, and maintaining within the state any university, college, school, seminary of learning, mechanical institute, museum, botanical garden, public park, art gallery, or public library (Cal. Educ. Code §§21100 et seq.; §§21140 et seq.). The donor also may provide, in the instrument creating the gift, for all matters necessary to carry out the purposes of the gift (e.g., by establishing scholarships) (Cal. Educ. Code §21103). 12 Cal. Jur.3d Charities §11.

CALIFORNIA EDUCATION CODE

§21100. Authority for charitable trusts to educational institutions

Any person desiring in his lifetime to promote the public welfare by founding, endowing, and maintaining within this state a university, college, school, seminary of learning, mechanical institute, museum, botanic garden, public park, or gallery of art, or any or all thereof, may, for such purposes, by grant in writing convey to a trustee, or any number of trustees, named in the grant, and to their successors, any property, real or personal, belonging to him and situated within this state. If he is married and the property is community property, then both husband and wife shall join in the grant.

(Stats. 1976, ch. 1010, §2, effective April 30, 1977.)

§21101. Grantor may designate items

The grantor may designate in the grant:

(a) The nature, object, and purposes of the institution to be founded, endowed, and maintained.

(b) The name by which it shall be known.

(c) The powers and duties of the trustees, and the manner in which they shall account, and to whom, if accounting is required. Such powers and duties shall not be exclusive of other powers and duties which may be necessary to enable the trustees to fully carry out the objects of the grant.

(d) The mode and manner, and by whom, the successors to the trustee or trustees named in the grant are to be appointed.

(e) Such rules and regulations for the management of the property conveyed as the grantor may elect to prescribe. Such rules shall, unless the grantor otherwise prescribes, be deemed advisory only, and shall not preclude the trustees from making such changes as new conditions may from time to time require.

(f) The place where and the time when the buildings necessary and proper for the institution shall be erected, and the character and extent thereof.

(Stats. 1976, ch. 1010, §2, effective April 30, 1977.)

§21102. Grantor may also provide for other provisions to carry out purposes

The grantor may also provide for all other things necessary and proper to carry out the purposes of the grant, and especially may provide for the trades and professions which shall be taught in the institution, and the terms upon which deserving scholars of the public and private schools of the various counties of this state may be admitted to all the privileges of the institution, as a reward for meritorious conduct and good scholarship.

(Stats. 1976, ch. 1010, §2, effective April 30, 1977.)

§21103. Grantor may provide for scholarships

The grantor may also provide for maintaining free scholarships for children of persons who have rendered service to or who have died in the service of the state and for maintaining free scholarships for children of mechanics, tradesmen, and laborers, who have died without leaving means sufficient to give their children a practical education, fitting them for the useful trades or arts.

(Stats. 1976, ch. 1010, §2, effective April 30, 1977.)

§21104. Grantor may provide for attendance by students and others at lectures and other functions

The grantor may also provide the terms and conditions upon which students in the public and private schools, and other deserving persons, may, without cost to themselves, attend the lectures of any university established, and also the terms and conditions upon which the museums, art galleries, and conservatories of music, connected with any such institution, shall be open to all deserving persons without charge, and without their becoming students of the institution.

(Stats. 1976, ch. 1010, §2, effective April 30, 1977.)

§21140. Grantor may provide for gift to library, museum or art gallery

Any person intending in his lifetime or by will or trust deed, to operate after his death, to found, maintain, and perpetuate in this state a public library, museum, gallery of art, or any or all thereof, for the diffusion of mechanical, scientific,

artistic, and general knowledge, may for that purpose, convey in writing by words denoting a gift or grant to one or more trustees named in the gift or grant, and to their successors, any library or collection of books and works, for the public library, or any museum, or gallery of art in this state.
(Stats. 1976, ch. 1010, §2, effective April 30, 1977.)

§21142. Grantor may convey additional real property for other necessary purposes to maintain institution

The grantor may also in like manner, convey by grant to the trustee or trustees any real property within this state belonging to him, which may be necessary or proper for the erection and maintenance of buildings suitable to the institution, and the buildings erected thereon, with grounds, conveniently adjacent thereto, and other lands, tenements, and hereditaments for the purpose of producing an income for the support and maintenance of the institutions and any collateral burdens which may be imposed by the terms of the foundation as part and parcel of the regulations for its conduct, and also personal property of all descriptions, which may subserve the purposes of the institution and maintenance of the library, museum, or gallery of art.
(Stats. 1976, ch. 1010, §2, effective April 30, 1977.)

III. Beneficiaries

Charitable trusts are exempt from the rule applicable to private express trusts (Cal. Prob. Code §15205) requiring definite beneficiaries. Whereas definite beneficiaries are necessary to enforce a private express trust, the state Attorney General is the public representative charged with the enforcement of charitable trusts.

Actually, the more narrow the class of beneficiaries, the more likely a charitable trust runs the danger of being invalid.

> If the trust provides for the distribution of charitable benefits to a single individual, or a very small group of definite persons, it can be said that the public or community benefit is nonexistent or so small as to be negligible. Here the type of benefit to be given by the trust is appropriate for a charitable trust, but the benefit is not to be so widely distributed as to make the trust one of general interest. Illustrations of this type of case are to be found in trusts to educate a particular named person, or to prepare a designated relative of the settlor for the ministry. These trusts provide some educational or religious benefits, but not to such an extent as to give the state any interest in the enforcement of the trust.

Bogert, *supra*, at §363.

§15205. Designation of beneficiary

(a) A trust, other than a charitable trust, is created only if there is a beneficiary.

(b) The requirement of subdivision (a) is satisfied if the trust instrument provides for either of the following:

(1) A beneficiary or class of beneficiaries that is ascertainable with reasonable certainty or that is sufficiently described so it can be determined that some person meets the description or is within the class.

(2) A grant of a power to the trustee or some other person to select the beneficiaries based on a standard or in the discretion of the trustee or other person.

(Enacted Stats. 1990, ch. 79, §14 (A.B. 759), effective July 1, 1991.)

IV. Trustees

Trustees of charitable trusts are charged with fulfilling the trust purposes for the designated class of beneficiaries and in accordance with the settlor's intent. The duties of trustees of charitable trusts are similar to those of private express trusts. However, the trustees of charitable trusts may be subject to additional statutory duties.

The California Probate Code specifies some of these additional duties of charitable trustees (Cal. Prob. Code §§16100 et seq.). These statutory duties apply to trustees of charitable trusts, private foundations, and split-interest trusts. These duties are implied in instruments creating every trust to which the statutes apply (Cal. Prob. Code §16104). Any provision of the instrument that is inconsistent with the statutes is without effect (*id.*).

For example, the trustee must act in accordance with certain provisions of the Internal Revenue Code, i.e., the trustee must distribute income and principal in a manner that will not subject the trust property to federal taxation; the trustee must not engage in self-dealing as defined in the Internal Revenue Code; the trustee must not retain any excess business

holdings as defined in the Internal Revenue Code; and the trustee must not make investments in any manner that will subject the trust property to federal taxation nor make any taxable expenditure as defined in the Internal Revenue Code (Cal. Prob. Code §§16101, 16102). 12 Cal. Jur.3d Charities §44. See also the discussion of Enforcement, *infra* this chapter Section VI.B.

In a famous case of trustee misconduct, a Hawaii probate court reorganized one of the nation's richest charitable trusts by removal of four of the five trustees of the Kamehameha Schools Bishop Estate (and acceptance of the resignation of the fifth). The charitable trust was established over a century ago by the will of Princess Bernice Pauahi Bishop, the last descendant of Hawaiian King Kamehameha. The princess devised 400,000 acres of land in a charitable trust for the education of Hawaiian children.

On the case of In re Estate of Bishop, see Robert Mahealani M. Seto & Lynne Marie Kohm, Of Princesses, Charities, Trustees, and Fairytales: A Lesson of the Simple Wishes of Princess Bernice Pauahi Bishop, 21 Haw. L. Rev. 393 (1999); Robert Whitman & Kumar Paturi, Improving Mechanisms for Resolving Complaints of Powerless Trust Beneficiaries, 16 Quinnipiac Prob. L.J. 64, 81-84 (2002) (discussing Bishop litigation).

§16100. Definitions

As used in this article, the following definitions shall control:

(a) "Charitable trust" means a charitable trust as described in Section 4947(a)(1) of the Internal Revenue Code.

(b) "Private foundation" means a private foundation as defined in Section 509 of the Internal Revenue Code.

(c) "Split-interest trust" means a split-interest trust as described in Section 4947(a)(2) of the Internal Revenue Code.

(Stats. 1990 (A.B. 759), ch. 79, §14, effective July 1, 1991.)

§16101. Distribution of income under charitable trust or private foundation

During any period when a trust is deemed to be a charitable trust or a private foundation, the trustee shall distribute its income for each taxable year (and principal if necessary) at a time and in a manner that will not subject the property of the trust to tax under Section 4942 of the Internal Revenue Code.

(Stats. 1990 (A.B. 759), ch. 79, §14, effective July 1, 1991.)

§16102. Restrictions on trustees under charitable trust, private foundation, or split-interest trust

During any period when a trust is deemed to be a charitable trust, a private foundation, or a split-interest trust, the trustee shall not do any of the following:

(a) Engage in any act of self-dealing as defined in Section 4941(d) of the Internal Revenue Code.

(b) Retain any excess business holdings as defined in Section 4943(c) of the Internal Revenue Code.

(c) Make any investments in such manner as to subject the property of the trust to tax under Section 4944 of the Internal Revenue Code.

(d) Make any taxable expenditure as defined in Section 4945(d) of the Internal Revenue Code.

(Stats. 1990 (A.B. 759), ch. 79, §14, effective July 1, 1991.)

§16103. Exceptions applicable to split-interest trusts

With respect to split-interest trusts:

(a) Subdivisions (b) and (c) of Section 16102 do not apply to any trust described in Section 4947(b)(3) of the Internal Revenue Code.

(b) Section 16102 does not apply with respect to any of the following:

(1) Any amounts payable under the terms of such trust to income beneficiaries, unless a deduction was allowed under Section 170(f)(2)(B), 2055(e)(2)(B), or 2522(c)(2)(B) of the Internal Revenue Code.

(2) Any amounts in trust other than amounts for which a deduction was allowed under Section 170, 545(b)(2), 556(b)(2), 642(c), 2055, 2106(a)(2), or 2522 of the Internal Revenue Code, if the amounts are segregated, as that term is defined in Section 4947(a)(3) of the Internal Revenue Code, from amounts for which no deduction was allowable.

(3) Any amounts irrevocably transferred in trust before May 27, 1969.

(Stats. 1990 (A.B. 759), ch. 79, §14, effective July 1, 1991.)

§16104. Prior provisions are implied in applicable trust instruments

The provisions of Sections 16101, 16102, and 16103 shall be deemed to be contained in the instrument creating every trust to which this article applies. Any provision of the instrument inconsistent with or contrary to this article is without effect.

(Stats. 1990 (A.B. 759), ch. 79, §14, effective July 1, 1991.)

§16105. Proceedings

(a) A proceeding contemplated by Section 101(l)(3) of the federal Tax Reform Act of 1969 (Public Law 91-172) [26 U.S.C.A. §4940 note] may be commenced pursuant to Section 17200 by the organization involved. All specifically named beneficiaries of the organization and the Attorney General shall be parties to the proceedings. Notwithstanding Section 17000, this provision is not exclusive and does not limit any jurisdiction that otherwise exists.

(b) If an instrument creating a trust affected by this section has been recorded, a notice of pendency of judicial proceedings under this section shall be recorded in a similar manner within 10 days from the commencement of the proceedings. A duly certified copy of any final judgment or decree in the proceedings shall be similarly recorded.

(Stats. 1990 (A.B. 759), ch. 79, §14, effective July 1, 1991.)

§21540. Fiduciary must comply with construed charitable remainder unitrusts and annuity trusts

If an instrument indicates the transferor's intention to comply with the Internal Revenue Code requirements for a charitable remainder unitrust or a charitable remainder annuity trust as each is defined in Section 664 of the Internal Revenue Code, the provisions of the instrument, including any power, duty, or discretionary authority given to a fiduciary, shall be construed to comply with the charitable deduction provisions of Section 2055 or Section 2522 of the Internal Revenue Code and the charitable remainder trust provisions of Section 664 of the Internal Revenue Code in order to conform to that intent. In no event shall the fiduciary take an action or have a power that impairs the charitable deduction. The provisions of the instrument may be augmented in any manner consistent with Section 2055(e) or Section 2522(c) of the Internal Revenue Code on a petition provided for in Section 17200.

(Stats 1990 (A.B. 759), ch 79, §14, effective July 1, 1991.)

§21541. Fiduciary must comply with construed charitable lead trusts

If an instrument indicates the transferor's intention to comply with the requirements for a charitable lead trust as described in Section 170(f)(2)(B) and Section 2055(e) (2) or Section 2522(c)(2) of the Internal Revenue Code, the provisions of the instrument, including any power, duty, or discretionary authority given to a fiduciary, shall be construed to comply with the provisions of that section in order to conform to that intent. In no event shall the fiduciary take any action or have any power that impairs the charitable deduction. The provisions of the instrument may be augmented in any manner consistent with that intent upon a petition provided for in Section 17200.

(Stats 1990 (A.B. 759), ch. 79 §14, effective July 1, 1991.)

V. Modification

Under the *cy pres doctrine* [pronounced "see prey" and rhymes with "repay"], when a charitable trust becomes impossible or impracticable, a court will substitute another beneficiary in a manner that approaches the original purpose as closely as possible. The cy pres rule allows the court to direct the disposition of the trust property for a related charitable purpose, keeping as closely as possible to the settlor's intent. Witkin, Summary, Trusts, at §288. The doctrine confers flexibility on charitable trusts to meet changing social conditions. The name "cy pres" is derived from the Norman French expression meaning "so near" (si près).

Application of the doctrine depends on two requirements: (1) the original purpose has become impossible or impracticable, or unforeseen changed circumstances would defeat or substantially impair the accomplishment of the trust purposes, and (2) the settlor had a general charitable intent. Most courts interpret narrowly the requirement that the original purpose has become impossible or impracticable. According to the second requirement, courts will not apply the cy pres doctrine if the testator would have preferred that the gift fail if the original purpose could not be accomplished. However, "courts almost never find that a donor did not exhibit general charitable intent." Bernstein, *supra*, at 1771.

The cy pres doctrine differs from the power of equitable deviation applicable to private express trusts. The cy pres doctrine is unique to charitable trusts. Courts have the power to change the administration of both charitable and private trusts as to time and methods of payments and other features of trust administration, and thus to sanction a deviation from the terms in many ways. However, the power to permit deviation does not extend (as

does the cy pres doctrine) to altering the trust beneficiaries and the size of their interests and thus to revise the gifts that the settlor intended. Bogert, *supra*, at §431.

Although the origins of the cy pres doctrine are unclear, it has been suggested that ecclesiastic judges struggled to save gifts for the benefit of the Church or other religious institutions. *Id.* Because donors often made death-bed charitable gifts to ensure their salvation, "it was natural that chancery, with its ecclesiastical bias, should think that the testator would have desired the substitution of any other similar plan which would bring about a result similar to the original gift." *Id.*

In England, two forms of the cy pres doctrine existed: judicial and prerogative. The latter power, exercisable by the Crown, has never been recognized in this country. Aversion to the prerogative power stemmed from "association of the doctrine with royal abuses." Bernstein, *supra*, at 1771. See, e.g., DaCosta v. De Pas, Amb. 228 (1754) (applying the prerogative power to direct that a gift to educate Jews in their religion should be applied to instruct children in a foundling hospital in the Christian religion).

Most states recognize the cy pres doctrine by case law. A few jurisdictions recognize the doctrine by statute (Cal. Prob. Code §§15407, 15410).

Certain limitations on the cy pres doctrine exist. Courts will not apply the doctrine if the settlor has provided in the trust instrument that, should the charitable gift fail, the trust shall terminate and cy pres should not be applied. In this case, the trust res passes to the settlor or the settlor's successors via a resulting trust. Nor will a court apply the cy pres doctrine if the settlor provided for an alternative charitable disposition should the original charitable gift prove impossible or impracticable. Burr v. Brooks, 393 N.E.2d 1091 (Ill. Ct. App. 1979).

The doctrine may apply when the charitable trust is frustrated either at the beginning of the trust or else subsequently during the administration of the trust.

A famous case, Estate of Buck, 35 Cal. Rptr. 2d 442 (Ct. App. 1994), involved a charitable trust established by Beryl Buck and her husband to benefit the needy residents of a particular California county, Marin County. The trustees unsuccessfully attempted to use the cy pres doctrine to broaden the terms to include a 5-county area. In response to this (and other cases), one scholar has issued a "call for a departure from the 'pure' model of cy pres, which adheres as rigidly as possible to the donor's original intent, and for adoption of one of several modified versions, each of which would allow some consideration of public interest or charitable efficiency." Bernstein, *supra*, at 1771.

In another recent case, Obermeyer v. Bank of America, 140 S.W.3d 18 (Mo. 2004), a St. Louis dentist created a trust with a remainder interest (after the death of his nieces and nephews) to the Washington University Dental School. However, upon the death of the last designated niece and nephew, the university had closed the Dental School. In an action for declaratory relief by the settlor's heirs, the trial court determined that the settler had manifested a general charitable intent and applied the cy pres doctrine in favor of Washington University to establish a chair in the dentist's name.

See generally Rob Atkinson, Reforming Cy Pres Reform, 44 Hastings L. J. 1111 (1993); Evelyn Brody, The Limits of Charity Fiduciary Law, 57 Md. L. Rev. 1400 (1998); W. Dudley McCarter, Charitable Trusts Are Favorites of Equity, 60 J. Mo. Bar 213 (2004); Note, Phantom Selves: The Search for a General Charitable Intent in the Application of the Cy Pres Doctrine, 40 Stan. L. Rev. 973 (1988).

§11603. Designation of alternate distributees

(a) If the court determines that the requirements for distribution are satisfied, the court shall order distribution of the decedent's estate, or such portion as the court directs, to the persons entitled thereto.

(b) The order shall:

(1) Name the distributees and the share to which each is entitled.

(2) Provide that property distributed subject to a limitation or condition, including, but not limited to, an option granted under Chapter 16 (commencing with Section 9960) of Part 5, is distributed to the distributees subject to the terms of the limitation or condition.

(c) If the whereabouts of a distributee named in the order is unknown, the order shall provide for alternate distributees and the share to which each is entitled. The alternate distributees shall be the persons, to the extent known or reasonably ascertainable, who would be entitled under the decedent's will or under the laws of intestate succession if the distributee named in the order had predeceased the decedent, or in the case of a devise for a charitable purpose, under the doctrine of cy pres. If the distributee named in the order does not claim the share to which the distributee is entitled within five years after the date of the order, the distributee is deemed to have predeceased the decedent for the purpose of this section and the alternate distributees are entitled to the share as provided in the order.

(Stats. 1990 (A.B. 759), ch. 79, §14, effective July 1, 1991. Amended by Stats. 2000 (A.B. 791), ch. 17, §4.6.)

§15410. Disposition of property upon termination of trusts generally

At the termination of a trust, the trust property shall be disposed of as follows:

(a) In the case of a trust that is revoked by the settlor, as directed by the settlor.

(b) In the case of a trust that is terminated by the consent of the settlor and all beneficiaries, as agreed by the settlor and all beneficiaries.

(c) In any other case, as provided in the trust instrument or in a manner directed by the court that conforms as nearly as possible to the intention of the settlor as expressed in the trust instrument.

(d) If a trust is terminated by the trustee pursuant to subdivision (b) of Section 15408 [trust with uneconomically low principal], the trust property may be distributed as determined by the trustee pursuant to the standard provided in subdivision (c) without the need for a court order. Where the trust instrument does not provide a manner of distribution at termination and the settlor's intent is not adequately expressed in the trust instrument, the trustee may distribute the trust property to the living beneficiaries on an actuarial basis.

(Stats. 1990 (A.B. 759), ch. 79, §14, effective July 1, 1991.)

VI. Enforcement

A. Judicial

Charitable trusts may be subject to constitutional limitations. Courts may refuse to enforce charitable trusts that discriminate on the basis of race or gender, reasoning that such trusts violate the Equal Protection Clause. Traditionally, courts viewed charitable trusts that discriminated on the basis of race or gender as private arrangements. They held that "private discrimination" was permissible provided it did not implicate the Constitution. Specifically, such trusts were considered private arrangements if they did not involve state action (such as public officials who served as their trustees).

Increasingly, however, courts have been prone to invalidate some types of discriminatory charitable trusts, especially those that discriminate on the basis of race. The last case to uphold a racially discriminatory charitable trust was First National Bank v. Danforth, 523 S.W.2d 808 (Mo. 1975), *cert. denied sub nom.* Sutt v. First Nat'l Bank, 421 U.S. 992 (1975).

The law concerning racially discriminatory charitable trusts has been influenced by two cases: In re Girard Coll. Trusteeship, 138 A.2d 844 (Pa. 1958), *cert. denied*, 357 U.S. 570 (1958), and Evans v. Newton, 382 U.S. 296 (1966). James W. Colliton, Race and Sex Discrimination in Charitable Trusts, 12 Cornell J.L. & Pub. Pol'y 274, 278 (2003). In the *Girard College* case, a settlor established an institution, with the city of Philadelphia as trustee, to provide for the training of "poor male white orphan children." In the latter case, a settlor gave property, naming the city of Macon, Georgia, as trustee, to be used as a park for white people only.

In the *Girard College* case, the United States Supreme Court held that the trust violated the Fourteenth Amendment. Pennsylvania v. Bd. of Dirs. of City Trusts, 353 U.S. 230 (1957). The Pennsylvania Supreme Court affirmed the orphan's court decision that substituted private trustees in an effort to remedy the constitutional shortcoming. Despite this effort, the Third Circuit Court of Appeals found impermissible state involvement. Pennsylvania v. Brown, 392 F.2d 120 (3d. Cir. 1968).

In Evans v. Newton, the Georgia court tried a similar strategy to remedy the constitutional problem by appointing private individuals to replace the public trustees. The United States Supreme Court rejected this ploy, finding that the trust still violated the Constitution because the park benefitted by municipal services (police protection, garbage collection, etc.). In Evans v. Abney, 396 U.S. 435 (1970), the Supreme Court

affirmed the state court decision that the trust failed and the property reverted to the settlor's heirs.

Since these cases, courts have refused to uphold racially discriminatory trusts. See, e.g., Connecticut Bank & Trust Co. v. Johnson Memorial Hospital, 294 A.2d 586 (Conn. 1972) (invalidating a trust to provide Medicare for whites only); Coffee v. Rice University, 408 S.W.2d 269 (Tex. Civ. App. 1966) (upholding a jury verdict allowing the university trustees to admit nonwhite students); Grant v. Medlock, 349 S.E.2d 655 (S.C. Ct. App. 1986) (eliminating a racial restriction in a trust establishing a home for the aged for only white persons); Home for Incurables of Baltimore City v. University of Maryland Medical System Corp., 797 A.2d 746 (Md. 2002) (invalidating a restriction in a trust created for the benefit of Keswick Home to provide accommodations for only white patients) (all cited and discussed in Colliton, *supra*, at 282-286).

However, the judicial response to gender-based charitable trusts has not been as uniform. With rare exception, courts have upheld such trusts. For example, cases in the late 1970s and early 1980s "demonstrate the willingness of courts . . . to permit sex discrimination in charitable trusts" (Colliton, *supra*, at 289). In Shapiro v. Columbia Union National Bank, 576 S.W.2d 310 (Mo. 1978), the court upheld a trust providing scholarships for boys, reasoning that there was no state action despite the fact that state university officials processed scholarship applications and made tentative awards subject to the private trustee's approval. And, in In re Estate of Wilson, 452 N.E.2d 1228 (N.Y. 1983), the court upheld trusts establishing a scholarship fund for "young men," permitted them to continue without the involvement of public officials, despite state action consisting of significant involvement on the part of public officials in certifying and selecting the beneficiaries.

In contrast, in a subsequent case, the Supreme Court of New Hampshire eliminated the trust provisions that limited scholarships to male public high school students. In In re Certain Scholarship Funds, 575 A.2d 1325 (N.H. 1990), the court based its decision on the equal protection clause of the state constitution and the state cy pres statute. See also Ebitz v. Pioneer National Bank, 361 N.E.2d 225 (Mass. 1977) (affirming a decision interpreting a charitable trust for "worthy and ambitious young men" to include women).

One commentator argues that both sexually discriminatory and racially discriminatory trusts violate public policy and should not be enforced under traditional trust law. Colliton, *supra*. He bases his argument on the fact that charitable trusts are "essentially public entities that serve public purposes" (*id.* at 292), and benefit from generous treatment by the law (in the form of exemptions from federal income taxation, application of the cy pres doctrine, and freedom from limitations of the Rule Against Perpetuities) (*id.* at 293).

Recent developments have occurred in litigation surrounding one of the most famous charitable trusts. The Bishop Trust (aforementioned in Section IV *supra*) is an educational trust created by the will of Hawaiian Princess Bernice Pauahi Bishop to establish a school in Hawaii for children of native Hawaiian ancestry. The school has an endowment exceeding $6 billion, and an enrollment of 6,700 students with campuses on three islands. See Adam Liptak, Prestigious Private Schools Settle Rights Suit by a Non-Hawaiian, N.Y. Times, May 15, 2007, at A16.

In Doe v. Kamehameha Schools, 470 F.3d 827 (9th Cir. 2006), a prospective student, who was a non-native Hawaiian, challenged the schools' preferential admissions policy, alleging that he was denied admission based on his race in violation of 42 U.S.C. §1981. The Ninth Circuit Court of Appeals upheld the policy, ruling that the school had the right to offer admissions preference to Native Hawaiian applicants to remedy past discrimination suffered by the indigenous people of Hawaii. In May 2007, a settlement was reached in the case, thereby avoiding review by the United States Supreme Court. Liptak, *supra*.

A recent California case explores the issue of enforcement of a charitable trust. In L.B. Research & Ed. Foundation v. UCLA Foundation, 130 Cal. App.4th 171 (Ct. App. 2005), a donor signed an agreement to contribute $1 million to endow a chair at a medical school, subject to various conditions. The donor later sued the donee, alleging that the latter failed to comply with the conditions. The trial court held that the donor lacked standing. However, the Court of Appeal disagreed, holding that a donor or a third-party beneficiary has standing to enforce the terms of a charitable trust notwithstanding the power of the Attorney General to enforce the trust. Further, the court determined that the intention of the transferor governs whether a contribution constitutes a charitable trust or a conditional charitable gift.

B. Governmental

In most jurisdictions, the state Attorney General is authorized to investigate charitable trusts to ensure that their charitable purposes are being effectuated. Some states authorize enforcement by a similar public official or administrative agency.

> The history and purposes of this standing doctrine make clear that public enforcement is predicated on the paramount importance of the public interest in the administration of charitable trusts. The attorney general acts under the parens *patriae* power, which has its roots in the "ancient powers of guardianship over persons under disability and of protectorship of the public interest." This power, historically held by the English king, has been adopted in the United States by state and federal governments through common law and state statutes.

Bernstein, *supra*, at 1766. For example, California Probate Code §17210 codifies the rule that the Attorney General stands in the place of the beneficiaries of a charitable trust for enforcement purposes.

In addition to the Attorney General, most states permit parties with a "special interest" to sue to enforce the fiduciary duty of charitable trustees. To qualify, a party must prove that he or she is entitled to benefit from the trust and that such entitlement is different from that of the public. Jurisdictions vary in the persons they recognize as parties with "special interests." However, absent statutory authorization, standing generally does not extend to the next of kin, taxpayers, or the settlor. Bernstein, *supra*, at 1766. See also Restatement (Second) of Trusts §391 ("A suit can be maintained for the enforcement of a charitable trust by the Attorney General or other public officer, or by a co-trustee, or by a person who has a special interest in the enforcement of the charitable trust, but not by persons who have no special interest or by the settlors or his heirs, personal representatives or next-of-kin"); Restatement (Third) of Trusts §405(c) ("The settlor of a charitable trust, among others, may maintain a proceeding to enforce the trust").

State law often specifies the duties and responsibilities of the Attorney General vis à vis charitable trusts. In order to improve enforcement of charitable trusts, California passed the Supervision of Trustees and Fundraisers for Charitable Purposes Act (Cal. Govt. Code §§12580 et seq.), based on the Uniform Supervision of Trustees for Charitable Purposes Act, 7C U.L.A. 372 (2000) (promulgated by the National Conference on Uniform State Laws in 1954). See also Unif. Fiduciaries Act §1 U.L.A. 372 (2002). Whenever a will with a charitable trust is offered for probate, a copy of the will must be provided to the Attorney General (Cal. Govt. Code §12593). A similar requirement applies to anyone recording an inter vivos transfer for charitable purposes.

The state Attorney General may require persons (including trustees) to produce records (Cal. Govt. Code §§12588, 12589). The Attorney General must be notified about charitable devises or charitable trusts with nonresident trustees or without identified devisees (Cal. Prob. Code §8111) and about proceedings regarding charitable trusts (Cal. Prob. Code §19024). The Attorney General must maintain a public register of charitable corporations, charitable trusts, and their trustees (Cal. Govt. Code §§12584, 12590). Charitable trustees must file a copy of their governing instruments (Cal. Govt. Code §12585), and also must file periodic reports regarding the trust assets and their administration (Cal. Govt. Code §§12586, 12587). State agencies that receive applications for tax exemptions for trusts must report such applications annually to the state Attorney General (Cal. Govt. Code §12594). Commercial fundraisers for charitable purposes also must

register with the Attorney General before soliciting or receiving funds, and, in addition, must file an annual financial report (Cal. Govt. Code §12599).

For an interesting case involving the attorney general's role in the supervision of a charitable trust, see In re Milton Hershey School Trust, 807 A.2d 324 (Pa. Commw. Ct. 2002) (granting the state attorney general's request for an injunction to the sale of the trust's controlling interest in Hershey Foods Corp.). On the eligibility to serve as a charitable trustee, see In re Estate of Coleman, 317 A.2d 631 (Pa. 1974) (holding that the settlor's requirement that spouses of charitable trustees must be Protestant was an unreasonable condition, unrelated to the settlor's charitable intentions, and not appropriate for judicial enforcement).

On the validity of California charitable trusts, see People v. Cogswell, 45 P. 270 (Cal. 1896) (upholding a charitable trust to establish and maintain a polytechnic college to give boys and girls of the state of California a practical training in the mechanical arts and industries, reasoning that there was ample evidence to warrant the holding that the settlor's wife freely agreed to and executed the trust); Estate of Schloss, 363 P.2d 875 (Cal. 1961) (upholding validity of residuary gift to named trustees to be held as perpetual charitable fund in trust with income to be paid to charitable use to promote progress of mankind, particularly among people who were in accord with teachings of named church, and finding that order removing trustees was void).

For discussion of charitable trusts, see generally Alison Manolovici Cody, Success in New Jersey: Using the Charitable Trust Doctrine to Preserve Women's Reproductive Services When Hospitals Become Catholic, 57 N.Y.U. Ann. Surv. Am. L. 323 (2000); James J. Fishman, Improving Charitable Accountability, 62 Md. L. Rev. 218 (2003); Robert Mahealani M. Seto & Lynne Marie Kohm, Of Princesses, Charities, Trustees, and Fairytales: A Lesson of the Simple Wishes of Princess Bernice Pauahi Bishop, 21 Haw. L. Rev. 393 (1999); Jennifer L. Komoroski, Note, The Hershey Trust's Quest to Diversify: Redefining the State Attorney General's Role When Charitable Trusts Wish to Diversify, 45 Wm. & Mary L. Rev. 1769 (2004).

CALIFORNIA GOVERNMENT CODE

§12580. Title

This article may be cited as the Supervision of Trustees and Fundraisers for Charitable Purposes Act.

(Stats. 1959, ch. 1258, p. 3396, §2, effective June 30, 1959. Amended by Stats. 1998 (A.B. 1810), ch. 445, §2.)

§12581. Application

This article applies to all charitable corporations, unincorporated associations, trustees, and other legal entities holding property for charitable purposes, commercial fundraisers for charitable purposes, fundraising counsel for charitable purposes, and commercial coventurers, over which the state or the Attorney General has enforcement or supervisory powers. The provisions of this article shall not apply to any committee as defined in Section 82013 which is required to and does file any statement pursuant to the provisions of Article 2 (commencing with Section 84200) of Chapter 4 of Title 9.

(Stats. 1959, ch. 1258, p. 3396, §2, effective June 30, 1959. Amended by Stats. 1978, ch. 1287, p. 4213, §28; Stats. 1998 (A.B. 1810), ch. 445, §3; Stats. 2004 (S.B. 1262), ch. 919, §2.)

§12581.2. "Solicitation," defined

As used in this article, "solicitation" or "soliciting" for charitable purposes means any request, plea, entreaty, demand, or invitation, or attempt thereof, to give money or property, in connection with which any of the following applies:

(a) Any appeal is made for charitable purposes.

(b) The name of any charity, philanthropic or charitable organization, is used or referred to in any such appeal as an inducement for making any such gift.

(c) Any statement is made to the effect that the gift or any part thereof will go to or be used for any charitable purpose or organization.

(d) The name of any organization of law enforcement personnel, firefighters or other persons who protect the public safety is used or referred to as an inducement for transferring any money or property, unless the only expressed or implied purpose of the solicitation is for the sole benefit of the actual active membership of the organization.

(Stats. 1998 (A.B. 1810), ch. 445, §4.)

§12582. "Trustee," defined

"Trustee" means (a) any individual, group of individuals, corporation, unincorporated association, or other legal entity holding property in trust pursuant to any charitable trust, (b) any corporation or unincorporated association which has

accepted property to be used for a particular charitable corporate purpose as distinguished from the general purposes of the corporation or unincorporated association, and (c) a corporation or unincorporated association formed for the administration of a charitable trust, pursuant to the directions of the settlor or at the instance of the trustee.
(Stats. 1959, ch. 1258, p. 3396, §4, effective June 30, 1959. Amended by Stats. 2004 (S.B. 1262), ch. 919, §3.)

§12582.1. "Charitable corporation," defined

"Charitable corporation" means any nonprofit corporation organized under the laws of this State for charitable or eleemosynary purposes and any similar foreign corporation doing business or holding property in this State for such purposes.
(Stats. 1959, ch. 1258, p. 3396, §4, effective June 30, 1959.)

§12583. Exemption of certain trustees

The filing, registration, and reporting provisions of this article do not apply to the United States, any state, territory, or possession of the United States, the District of Columbia, the Commonwealth of Puerto Rico, or to any of their agencies or governmental subdivisions, to any religious corporation sole or other religious corporation or organization that holds property for religious purposes, or to any officer, director, or trustee thereof who holds property for like purposes, to a cemetery corporation regulated under Chapter 19 (commencing with Section 9600) of Division 3 of the Business and Professions Code, or to any committee as defined in Section 82013 that is required to and does file any statement pursuant to Article 2 (commencing with Section 84200) of Chapter 4 of Title 9, or to a charitable corporation or unincorporated association organized and operated primarily as a religious organization, educational institution, hospital, or a health care service plan licensed pursuant to Section 1349 of the Health and Safety Code.
(Stats. 1959, ch. 1258, p. 3396, §2, effective June 30, 1959. Amended by Stats. 1978, ch. 1287, p. 4213, §29; Stats. 1979, ch. 186, §1; Stats. 1997 (S.B. 73), ch. 892, §12; 2004 (S.B. 1262), ch. 919, §4.)

§12584. Attorney General shall establish a register of charitable corporations and trustees

The Attorney General shall establish and maintain a register of charitable corporations, unincorporated associations, and trustees subject to this article and of the particular trust or other relationship under which they hold property for charitable purposes and, to that end, may conduct whatever investigation is necessary, and shall obtain from public records, court officers, taxing authorities, trustees, and other sources, whatever information, copies of instruments, reports, and records are needed for the establishment and maintenance of the register.
(Stats. 1959, ch. 1258, p. 3397, §2, effective June 30, 1959. Amended byStats. 2004 (S.B. 1262), ch. 919, §5.)

§12585. Charitable corporation and trustees shall file copy of articles of incorporation or instrument providing for trustee's title, powers or duties

(a) Every charitable corporation, unincorporated association, and trustee subject to this article shall file with the Attorney General an initial registration form, under oath, setting forth information and attaching documents prescribed in accordance with rules and regulations of the Attorney General, within 30 days after the corporation, unincorporated association, or trustee initially receives property. A trustee is not required to register as long as the charitable interest in a trust is a future interest, but shall do so within 30 days after any charitable interest in a trust becomes a present interest.

(b) The Attorney General shall adopt rules and regulations as to the contents of the initial registration form and the manner of executing and filing that document or documents.
(Stats. 1959, ch. 1258, p. 3397, §2, effective June 30, 1959; Stats. 2004 (S.B. 1262), ch. 919, §6; Stats. 2006 (A.B. 2303), ch. 567, §18.)

§12586. Charitable corporations and trustees shall file periodic written reports regarding trust assets and administration

(a) Except as otherwise provided and except corporate trustees which are subject to the jurisdiction of the Commissioner of Financial Institutions of the State of California under Division 1 (commencing with Section 99) of the Financial Code or to the Comptroller of the Currency of the United States, every charitable corporation, unincorporated association, and trustee subject to this article shall, in addition to filing copies of the instruments previously required, file with the Attorney General periodic written reports, under oath, setting forth information as to the nature of the assets held for charitable purposes and the administration thereof by the corporation, unincorporated association, or trustee, in accordance with rules and regulations of the Attorney General.

(b) The Attorney General shall make rules and regulations as to the time for filing reports, the contents thereof, and the manner of executing and filing them. The Attorney General may classify trusts and other relationships concerning property held for a charitable purpose as to purpose, nature of assets, duration of the trust or other relationship, amount of assets, amounts to be devoted to charitable purposes, nature of trustee, or otherwise, and may establish different rules for the different classes as to time and nature of the reports required to the ends (1) that he or she shall receive reasonably current, periodic reports as to all charitable trusts or other relationships of a similar nature, which will enable him or her to ascertain whether they are being properly administered, and (2) that periodic reports shall not unreasonably add to the expense of the administration of charitable trusts and similar relationships. The Attorney General may suspend the filing of reports as to a particular charitable trust or relationship for a reasonable, specifically designated time upon written application of the trustee filed with the Attorney General and after the Attorney General has filed in the register of charitable trusts a written statement that the interests of the beneficiaries will not be prejudiced thereby and that periodic reports are not required for proper supervision by his or her office.

(c) A copy of an account filed by the trustee in any court having jurisdiction of the trust or other relationship, if the account substantially complies with the rules and regulations of the Attorney General, may be filed as a report required by this section.

(d) The first report for a trust or similar relationship hereafter established, unless the filing thereof is suspended as herein provided, shall be filed not later than four months and 15 days following the close of the first calendar or fiscal year in which any part of the income or principal is authorized or required to be applied to a charitable purpose. If any part of the income or principal of a trust previously established is authorized or required to be applied to a charitable purpose at the time this article takes effect, the first report shall be filed at the close of the calendar or fiscal year in which it was registered with the Attorney General or not later than four months and 15 days following the close of such calendar or fiscal period.

(e) Every charitable corporation, unincorporated association, and trustee required to file reports with the Attorney General pursuant to this section that receives or accrues in any fiscal year gross revenue of two million dollars ($ 2,000,000) or more, exclusive of grants from, and contracts for services with, governmental entities for which the governmental entity requires an accounting of the funds received, shall do the following:

(1) Prepare annual financial statements using generally accepted accounting principles that are audited by an independent certified public accountant in conformity with generally accepted auditing standards. For any nonaudit services performed by the firm conducting the audit, the firm and its individual auditors shall adhere to the standards for auditor independence set forth in the latest revision of the Government Auditing Standards, issued by the Comptroller General of the United States (the Yellow Book). The Attorney General may, by regulation, prescribe standards for auditor independence in the performance of nonaudit services, including standards different from those set forth in the Yellow Book. If a charitable corporation or unincorporated association that is required to prepare an annual financial statement pursuant to this subdivision is under the control of another organization, the controlling organization may prepare a consolidated financial statement. The audited financial statements shall be available for inspection by the Attorney General and by members of the public no later than nine months after the close of the fiscal year to which the statements relate. A charity shall make its annual audited financial statements available to the public in the same manner that is prescribed for IRS Form 990 by the latest revision of Section 6104(d) of the Internal Revenue Code and associated regulation.

(2) If it is a corporation, have an audit committee appointed by the board of directors. The audit committee may include persons who are not members of the board of directors, but the member or members of the audit committee shall not include any members of the staff, including the president or chief executive officer and the treasurer or chief financial officer. If the corporation has a finance committee, it must be separate from the audit committee. Members of the finance committee may serve on the audit committee; however, the chairperson of the audit committee may not be a member of the finance committee and members of the finance committee shall constitute less than one-half of the membership of the audit committee. Members of the audit committee shall not receive any compensation from the corporation in excess of the compensation, if any, received by members of the board of directors for service on the board and shall not have a material financial interest in any entity doing business with the corporation. Subject to the supervision of the board of directors, the audit committee shall be responsible for recommending to the board of directors the retention and termination of the independent auditor and may negotiate the independent auditor's compensation, on behalf of the board of directors. The audit committee shall confer with the auditor to satisfy its members that the financial affairs of the corporation are in order, shall review and determine whether to accept the audit, shall assure that any nonaudit services performed by the auditing firm conform with standards for auditor independence referred to in paragraph (1), and shall approve performance of nonaudit services by the auditing firm. If the charitable corporation that is required to have an audit committee pursuant to this subdivision is under the control of another corporation, the audit committee

may be part of the board of directors of the controlling corporation.

(f) If, independent of the audit requirement set forth in paragraph (1) of subdivision (e), a charitable corporation, unincorporated association, or trustee required to file reports with the Attorney General pursuant to this section prepares financial statements that are audited by a certified public accountant, the audited financial statements shall be available for inspection by the Attorney General and shall be made available to members of the public in conformity with paragraph (1) of subdivision (e).

(g) The board of directors of a charitable corporation or unincorporated association, or an authorized committee of the board, and the trustee or trustees of a charitable trust shall review and approve the compensation, including benefits, of the president or chief executive officer and the treasurer or chief financial officer to assure that it is just and reasonable. This review and approval shall occur initially upon the hiring of the officer, whenever the term of employment, if any, of the officer is renewed or extended, and whenever the officer's compensation is modified. Separate review and approval shall not be required if a modification of compensation extends to substantially all employees. If a charitable corporation is affiliated with other charitable corporations, the requirements of this section shall be satisfied if review and approval is obtained from the board, or an authorized committee of the board, of the charitable corporation that makes retention and compensation decisions regarding a particular individual.

(Stats. 1959, ch. 1258, p. 3397, §2, effective June 30, 1959. Amended by Stats. 1976, ch. 1320, p. 5919, §6; Stats. 1978, ch. 1346, p. 4409, §8; Stats. 1996 (A.B. 3351), ch. 1064, §786, effective July 1, 1997; Stats. 2004 (S.B. 1262), ch. 919, §7.)

§12586.1. Assessment of late fees

In addition to a registration fee, a charitable corporation or trustee, commercial fundraiser, fundraising counsel, or coventurer may be assessed a late fee or an additional fee of twenty-five dollars ($25) for each month or part of the month after the date on which the registration statement and financial report were due to be filed or after the period of extension granted for the filing if the charitable corporation or trustee, commercial fundraiser, fundraising counsel, or coventurer does any of the following:

(a) Exists and operates in California without being registered.

(b) Solicits contributions in California without being registered or, if applicable, bonded.

(c) Fails to file its first report no later than four months and 15 days following the close of each calendar or fiscal year and has not requested an extension of time to file the annual report.

(d) Fails to file its subsequent annual report no later than four months and 15 days following the close of each calendar or fiscal year subsequent to the filing of the first report and has not requested an extension of time to file the annual report.

(e) Fails to file its annual registration/renewal form within the time specified by the Attorney General irrespective of other report filing requirements.

(f) Fails to correct the deficiencies in its registration or annual report within 10 days of receipt of written notice of those deficiencies.

(Stats. 2000 (S.B. 2015), ch. 475, §1.)

§12586.2. Funds collected by Attorney General shall be used for charitable trust enforcement

All fines, penalties, attorney's fees, if any, as authorized by law, and costs of investigation paid to the Attorney General pursuant to Section 12598 shall be used by the Department of Justice solely for the administration of the Attorney General's charitable trust enforcement responsibilities.

(Stats. 2000 (S.B. 2015), ch. 475, §1.)

§12587. Attorney General may make additional rules and regulations

The Attorney General may make additional rules and regulations necessary for the administration of this article, provided that any assessment of an annual registration or renewal fee from charitable trustees and corporations, commercial fundraisers, fundraising counsel, and commercial coventurers subject to this article, authorized by statute or regulation, shall be used by the Department of Justice solely to operate and maintain the Attorney General's Registry of Charitable Trusts and provide public access via the Internet to reports filed with the Attorney General.

(Stats. 1959, ch. 1258, p. 3398, §2, effective June 30, 1959; Stats. 1998 (A.B. 1810), ch. 445, §5.)

§12587.1. Establishment of the Registry of Charitable Trust Fund

(a) The Registry of Charitable Trusts Fund is hereby established in the State Treasury, to be administered by the Department of Justice.

(b) Notwithstanding any other provision of law, all registration fees, registration renewal fees, and late fees or other fees paid to the Department of Justice pursuant to this article, Section 2850 of the Probate Code, or Section 320.5 of the Penal Code, shall be deposited in the Registry of Charitable Trusts Fund.

(c) Moneys in the fund, upon appropriation by the Legislature, shall be used by the Attorney General solely to operate and maintain the Attorney General's Registry of

Charitable Trusts and Registry of Conservators, Guardians, and Trustees, and provide public access via the Internet to reports filed with the Attorney General.
(Stats 2005 (A.B. 139), ch 74, §33, effective July 19, 2005; Stats. 2006 (A.B. 1806), ch. 69, §4, effective July 12, 2006.)

§12588. Attorney General may investigate transactions of charitable corporations and trustees to ensure that charitable purposes are effectuated

The Attorney General may investigate transactions and relationships of corporations and trustees subject to this article for the purpose of ascertaining whether or not the purposes of the corporation or trust are being carried out in accordance with the terms and provisions of the articles of incorporation or other instrument. He may require any agent, trustee, fiduciary, beneficiary, institution, association, or corporation, or other person to appear, at a named time and place, in the county designated by the Attorney General, where the person resides or is found, to give information under oath and to produce books, memoranda, papers, documents of title, and evidence of assets, liabilities, receipts, or disbursements in the possession or control of the person ordered to appear.
(Stats. 1959, ch. 1258, p. 3398, §2, effective June 30, 1959.)

§12589. Attorney General shall issue order setting forth time and place when attendance required

When the Attorney General requires the attendance of any person, as provided in Section 12588, he shall issue an order setting forth the time when and the place where attendance is required and shall cause the same to be delivered to or sent by registered mail to the person at least 14 days before the date fixed for attendance. Such order shall have the same force and effect as a subpoena and, upon application of the Attorney General, obedience to the order may be enforced by the superior court in the county where the person receiving it resides or is found, in the same manner as though the notice were a subpoena. The court, after hearing, for cause, and upon application of any person aggrieved by the order, shall have the right to alter, amend, revise, suspend or postpone all or any part of its provisions.
(Stats. 1959, ch. 1258, p. 3398, §2, effective June 30, 1959.)

§12590. Public may inspect instruments for charitable purposes that are filed with Attorney General

Subject to reasonable rules and regulations adopted by the Attorney General, the register, copies of instruments, and the reports filed with the Attorney General shall be open to public inspection. The Attorney General shall withhold from public inspection any instrument so filed whose content is not exclusively for charitable purposes.
(Stats. 1959, ch. 1258, p. 3399, §2, effective June 30, 1959.)

§12591. Attorney General must be party to proceedings to modify or terminate charitable trust

The Attorney General may institute appropriate proceedings to secure compliance with this article and to invoke the jurisdiction of the court. The powers and duties of the Attorney General provided in this article are in addition to his existing powers and duties. Nothing in this article shall impair or restrict the jurisdiction of any court with respect to any of the matters covered by it, except that no court shall have jurisdiction to modify or terminate any trust of property for charitable purposes unless the Attorney General is a party to the proceedings.
(Stats. 1959, ch. 1258, p. 3399, §2, effective June 30, 1959.)

§12591.1. Penalties for intent to deceive or defraud any charity or individual

(a) Any person who violates any provision of this article with intent to deceive or defraud any charity or individual is liable for a civil penalty not exceeding ten thousand dollars ($10,000).

(b) Except as provided in subdivision (d), any person who violates any other provision of this article is liable for a civil penalty, as follows:

(1) For the first offense, a fine not exceeding one thousand dollars ($1,000).

(2) For any subsequent offense, a fine not exceeding two thousand five hundred dollars ($2,500).

(c) Any offense committed under this article involving a solicitation may be deemed to have been committed at either the place at which the solicitation was initiated or at the place where the solicitation was received.

(d) Any person who violates only subdivision (c), (d), (e), or (f) of Section 12586.1 shall not be liable for a civil penalty under subdivision (b) if the person (1) has not received reasonable notice of the violation and (2) has not been given a reasonable opportunity to correct the violation. The Attorney General shall notify in writing a person who violates only subdivisions (c), (d), (e), or (f) of Section 12586.1 that he or she has 30 days to correct the violation.

(e) The recovery of a civil penalty pursuant to this section precludes assessment of a late fee pursuant to Section 12586.1 for the same offense.
(Stats. 2000 (S.B. 2015), ch. 475, §3.)

§12591.2. Attorney General may accept assurances of voluntary compliance

In any case where the Attorney General has authority to institute an action or proceeding under this article, he or she may accept an assurance of voluntary compliance through which any person alleged to be engaged in any method, act, or practice in violation of this article agrees to discontinue that method, act, or practice. The assurance may, among other terms, include a stipulation of a voluntary payment by the person of the cost of the investigation or of an amount to be held in escrow pending the outcome of an action or as restitution to aggrieved persons, or both. The assurance of voluntary compliance shall not be considered an admission of a violation for any purpose. The assurance of compliance shall be in writing and shall be filed with a superior court in this state for approval and if approved shall thereafter be filed with the clerk of the court. Matters closed may at any time be reopened by the court for further proceedings in the public interest. In the event of an alleged violation, the Attorney General may, at his or her discretion, either initiate contempt proceedings or proceed as if the assurance of voluntary compliance has not been accepted.

(Stats. 2000 (S.B. 2015), ch. 475, §4.)

§12592. Application

This article shall apply regardless of any contrary provisions of any instrument.

(Stats. 1959, ch. 1258, p. 3399, §2, effective June 30, 1959.)

§12593. Person offering instrument for probate with charitable trust must furnish copies of instruments and records to Attorney General

Every person who offers for probate any instrument which establishes a testamentary trust of property for charitable purposes or who records in any county or city and county any inter vivos transfer of property for charitable purposes shall furnish a copy of such document to the Attorney General. The custodian of the records of a court having jurisdiction of probate matters or of charitable trusts shall furnish such copies of papers, records and files of his office relating to the subject of this article as the Attorney General requires.

(Stats. 1959, ch. 1258, p. 3399, §2, effective June 30, 1959.)

§12594. State officials must file with Attorney General a list of applications for tax exemption

Every officer, agency, board, or commission of this State receiving applications for exemption from taxation of any corporation, charitable trust or similar relationship in which the corporation or trustee is subject to this article shall annually file with the Attorney General a list of all applications received during the year.

(Stats. 1959, ch. 1258, p. 3399, §2, effective June 30, 1959.)

§12595. Construction of Act

This act shall be so construed as to effectuate its general purpose to make uniform the law of those states which enact it.

(Stats. 1959, ch. 1258, p. 3399, §2, effective June 30, 1959.)

§12596. Attorney General has 10 years to bring cause of action

Any action brought by the Attorney General against trustees or other persons holding property in trust for charitable purposes or against any charitable corporation or any director or officer thereof to enforce a charitable trust or to impress property with a trust for charitable purposes or to recover property or the proceeds thereof for and on behalf of any charitable trust or corporation, may be brought at any time within ten (10) years after the cause of action shall have accrued.

(Stats. 1965, ch. 1129, p. 2776, §1.)

§12597. Defendants shall pay reasonable expenses incurred by state in investigation and prosecution

In any proceeding brought by the Attorney General to secure compliance with the provisions of Sections 12584 to 12587, inclusive, or any regulation issued pursuant thereto, the judgment, if in favor of the state, shall provide that the person having the responsibility or duty to comply with such provisions on behalf of any charitable trust or charitable corporation, shall pay the reasonable expense necessarily incurred by the state in the investigation and prosecution of such action.

(Stats. 1969, ch. 490, p. 1098, §1.)

§12598. Supervision and enforcement of charitable trusts by Attorney General

(a) The primary responsibility for supervising charitable trusts in California, for ensuring compliance with trusts and articles of incorporation, and for protection of assets held by charitable trusts and public benefit corporations, resides in the Attorney General. The Attorney General has broad powers under common law and California statutory law to carry out these charitable trust enforcement responsibilities. These powers include, but are not limited to, charitable trust enforcement actions under all of the following:

(1) This article.

(2) Title 8 (commencing with Section 2223) of Part 4 of Division 3 of the Civil Code.

(3) Division 2 (commencing with Section 5000) of Title 1 of the Corporations Code.

(4) Sections 8111, 11703, 15004, 15409, 15680 to 15685, inclusive, 16060 to 16062, inclusive, 16064, and 17200 to 17210, inclusive, of the Probate Code.

(5) Chapter 5 (commencing with Section 17200) of Part 2 of Division 7 of the Business and Professions Code, and Sections 17500 and 17535 of the Business and Professions Code.

(6) Sections 319, 326.5, and 532d of the Penal Code.

(b) The Attorney General shall be entitled to recover from defendants named in a charitable trust enforcement action all reasonable attorney's fees and actual costs incurred in conducting that action, including, but not limited to, the costs of auditors, consultants, and experts employed or retained to assist with the investigation, preparation, and presentation in court of the charitable trust enforcement action.

(c) Attorney's fees and costs shall be recovered by the Attorney General pursuant to court order. When awarding attorneys' fees and costs, the court shall order that the attorney's fees and costs be paid by the charitable organization and the individuals named as defendants in or otherwise subject to the action, in a manner that the court finds to be equitable and fair.

(d) Upon a finding by the court that a lawsuit filed by the Attorney General was frivolous or brought in bad faith, the court may award the defendant charity the costs of that action.

(e)(1) The Attorney General may refuse to register or may revoke or suspend the registration of a charitable corporation or trustee, commercial fundraiser, fundraising counsel, or coventurer whenever the Attorney General finds that the charitable corporation or trustee, commercial fundraiser, fundraising counsel, or coventurer has violated or is operating in violation of any provisions of this article.

(2) All actions of the Attorney General shall be taken subject to the rights authorized pursuant to Chapter 4.5 (commencing with Section 11400) of Part 1 of Division 3 of Title 2.

(Stats. 1987, ch. 892, §2. Amended by Stats. 1988, ch. 1199, §15, effective July 1, 1989; Stats. 2000, ch. 475 (S.B. 2015), §5; Stats. 2003, ch. 159 (A.B. 1759), §6, effective August 2, 2003; Stats. 2004 (A.B. 3082), ch. 183, §144.)

§12599. "Commercial fundraiser for charitable purposes," defined

(a) "Commercial fundraiser for charitable purposes" means any individual, corporation, unincorporated association, or other legal entity who for compensation does any of the following:

(1) Solicits funds, assets, or property in this state for charitable purposes.

(2) As a result of a solicitation of funds, assets, or property in this state for charitable purposes, receives or controls the funds, assets, or property solicited for charitable purposes.

(3) Employs, procures, or engages any compensated person to solicit, receive, or control funds, assets, or property for charitable purposes.

A commercial fundraiser for charitable purposes shall include any person, association of persons, corporation, or other entity that obtains a majority of its inventory for sale by the purchase, receipt, or control for resale to the general public, of salvageable personal property solicited by an organization qualified to solicit donations pursuant to Section 148.3 of the Welfare and Institutions Code.

A commercial fundraiser for charitable purposes shall not include a "trustee" as defined in Section 12582 or 12583, a "charitable corporation" as defined in Section 12582.1, or any employee thereof. A commercial fundraiser for charitable purposes shall not include an individual who is employed by or under the control of a commercial fundraiser for charitable purposes registered with the Attorney General. A commercial fundraiser for charitable purposes shall not include any federally insured financial institution that holds as a depository funds received as a result of a solicitation for charitable purposes.

As used in this section, "charitable purposes" includes any solicitation in which the name of any organization of law enforcement personnel, firefighters, or other persons who protect the public safety is used or referred to as an inducement for transferring any funds, assets, or property, unless the only expressed or implied purpose of the solicitation is for the sole benefit of the actual active membership of the organization.

(b) A commercial fundraiser for charitable purposes shall, prior to soliciting any funds, assets, or property, including salvageable personal property, in California for charitable purposes, or prior to receiving and controlling any funds, assets, or property, including salvageable personal property, as a result of a solicitation in this state for charitable purposes, register with the Attorney General's Registry of Charitable Trusts on a registration form provided by the Attorney General. Renewals of registration shall be filed with the Registry of Charitable Trusts by January 15 of each calendar year in which the commercial fundraiser for charitable purposes does business and shall be effective for one year. A registration or renewal fee of two hundred dollars ($200) shall be required for registration of a commercial fundraiser for charitable purposes, and shall be payable by certified or cashier's check to the Attorney General's Registry of Charitable Trusts at the time of registration or renewal. The Attorney General may adjust the annual registration or renewal fee, or means of payment, as needed pursuant to this section. The Attorney General's Registry of Charitable Trusts may grant extensions of time to file annual registration as required, pursuant to subdivision (b) of Section 12586. No separate fee shall be charged by the Attorney General for electronic registration, electronic renewal, or electronic repayment of fees.

(c) A commercial fundraiser for charitable purposes shall file with the Attorney General's Registry of Charitable Trusts an annual financial report on a form provided by the Attorney General, accounting for all funds collected pursuant to any solicitation for charitable purposes during the preceding calendar year. The annual financial report shall be filed with the Attorney General's Registry of Charitable Trusts no later than 30 days after the close of the preceding calendar year.

(d) The contents of the forms for annual registration and annual financial reporting by commercial fundraisers for charitable purposes shall be established by the Attorney General in a manner consistent with the procedures set forth in subdivisions (a) and (b) of Section 12586. The annual financial report shall require a detailed, itemized accounting of funds, assets, or property, solicited for charitable purposes on behalf of each charitable organization exempt from taxation under Section 501(c)(3) of the Internal Revenue Code or for each charitable purpose during the accounting period, and shall include, among other data, the following information for funds, assets, or property, solicited by the commercial fundraiser for charitable purposes:

(1) Total revenue.

(2) The fee or commission charged by the commercial fundraiser for charitable purposes.

(3) Salaries paid by the commercial fundraiser for charitable purposes to its officers and employees.

(4) Fundraising expenses.

(5) Distributions to the identified charitable organization or purpose.

(6) The names and addresses of any director, officer, or employee of the commercial fundraiser for charitable purposes who is a director, officer, or employee of any charitable organization listed in the annual financial report.

(e) A commercial fundraiser for charitable purposes that obtains a majority of its inventory for sale by the purchase, receipt, or control for resale to the general public, of salvageable personal property solicited by an organization qualified to solicit donations pursuant to Section 148.3 of the Welfare and Institutions Code shall file with the Attorney General's Registry of Charitable Trusts, and not with the sheriff of any county, an annual financial report on a form provided by the Attorney General that is separate and distinct from forms filed by other commercial fundraisers for charitable purposes pursuant to subdivisions (c) and (d).

(f) It shall be unlawful for any commercial fundraiser for charitable purposes to solicit funds in this state for charitable purposes unless the commercial fundraiser for charitable purposes has complied with the registration or annual renewal and financial reporting requirements of this article. Failure to comply with these registration or annual renewal and financial reporting requirements shall be grounds for injunction against solicitation in this state for charitable purposes and other civil remedies provided by law.

(g) A commercial fundraiser for charitable purposes is a constructive trustee for charitable purposes as to all funds collected pursuant to solicitation for charitable purposes and shall account to the Attorney General for all funds. A commercial fundraiser for charitable purposes is subject to the Attorney General's supervision and enforcement over charitable funds and assets to the same extent as a trustee for charitable purposes under this article.

(h) Not less than 10 working days prior to the commencement of each solicitation campaign, event, or service, or not later than commencement of solicitation for solicitations to aid victims of emergency hardship or disasters, a commercial fundraiser for charitable purposes shall file with the Attorney General's Registry of Charitable Trusts a notice on a form prescribed by the Attorney General that sets forth all of the following:

(1) The name, address, and telephone number of the commercial fundraiser for charitable purposes.

(2) The name, address, and telephone number of the charitable organization with whom the commercial fundraiser has contracted.

(3) The fundraising methods to be used.

(4) The projected dates when performance under the contract will commence and terminate.

(5) The name, address, and telephone number of the person responsible for directing and supervising the work of the commercial fundraiser under the contract.

(i) There shall be a written contract between a commercial fundraiser for charitable purposes and a charitable organization for each solicitation campaign, event, or service, that shall be signed by the authorized contracting officer for the commercial fundraiser and by an official of the charitable organization who is authorized to sign by the organization's governing body. The contract shall be available for inspection by the Attorney General and shall contain all of the following provisions:

(1) The legal name and address of the charitable organization as registered with the Registry of Charitable Trusts, unless the charitable organization is exempt from registration.

(2) A statement of the charitable purpose for which the solicitation campaign, event, or service is being conducted.

(3) A statement of the respective obligations of the commercial fundraiser and the charitable organization.

(4) If the commercial fundraiser is to be paid a fixed fee, a statement of the fee to be paid to the commercial fundraiser and a good faith estimate of what percentage the fee will constitute of the total contributions received. The contract shall clearly disclose the assumptions upon which the estimate is based, and the stated assumptions shall be based upon all of the relevant facts known to the commercial fundraiser regarding the solicitation to be conducted by the commercial fundraiser.

(5) If a percentage fee is to be paid to the commercial fundraiser, a statement of the percentage of the total contributions received that will be remitted to or retained by the charitable organization, or, if the solicitation involves the sale of goods or services or the sale of admissions to a fundraising event, the percentage of the purchase price that will be remitted to the charitable organization. The stated percentage shall be calculated by subtracting from contributions received and sales receipts not only the commercial fundraiser's fee, but also any additional amounts that the charitable organization is obligated to pay as fundraising costs.

(6) The effective and termination dates of the contract and the date solicitation activity is to commence within the state.

(7) A provision that requires that each contribution in the control or custody of the commercial fundraiser shall in its entirety and within five working days of its receipt comply with either of the following:

(A) Be deposited in an account at a bank or other federally insured financial institution that is solely in the name of the charitable organization and over which the charitable organization has sole control of withdrawals.

(B) Be delivered to the charitable organization in person, by United States express mail, or by another method of delivery providing for overnight delivery.

(8) A statement that the charitable organization exercises control and approval over the content and frequency of any solicitation.

(9) If the commercial fundraiser proposes to make any payment in cash or in kind to any person or legal entity to secure any person's attendance at, or sponsorship, approval, or endorsement of, a charity fundraising event, the maximum dollar amount of those payments shall be set forth in the contract. "Charity fundraising event" means any gathering of persons, including, but not limited to, a party, banquet, concert, or show, that is held for the purpose or claimed purpose of raising funds for any charitable purpose or organization.

(10) A provision that includes all of the following statements:

(A) The charitable organization has the right to cancel the contract without cost, penalty, or liability for a period of 10 days following the date on which the contract is executed; that the charitable organization may cancel the contract by serving a written notice of cancellation on the commercial fundraiser; that, if mailed, service shall be by certified mail, return receipt requested, and cancellation shall be deemed effective upon the expiration of five calendar days from the date of mailing; that any funds collected after effective notice that the contract has been canceled shall be deemed to be held in trust for the benefit of the charitable organization without deduction for costs or expenses of any nature; and that the charitable organization shall be entitled to recover all funds collected after the date of cancellation.

(11) A provision that, following the initial 10-day cancellation period, the charitable organization may terminate the contract by giving 30 days' written notice; that, if mailed, service of the notice shall be by certified mail, return receipt requested, and shall be deemed effective upon the expiration of five calendar days from the date of mailing; and that, in the event of termination under this subdivision, the charitable organization shall be liable for services provided by the commercial fundraiser up to 30 days after the effective service of the notice.

(12) A provision that, following the initial 10-day cancellation period, the charitable organization may terminate the contract at any time upon written notice, without payment or compensation of any kind to the commercial fundraiser, if the commercial fundraiser or its agents, employees, or representatives (A) make any material misrepresentations in the course of solicitations or with respect to the charitable organization, (B) are found by the charitable organization to have been convicted of a crime arising from the conduct of a solicitation for a charitable organization or purpose punishable as a

misdemeanor or a felony, or (C) otherwise conduct fundraising activities in a manner that causes or could cause public disparagement of the charitable organization's good name or good will.

(13) Any other information required by the regulations of the Attorney General.

(j) It shall be unlawful for a commercial fundraiser for charitable purposes to not disclose the percentage of total fundraising expenses of the fundraiser upon receiving a written or oral request from a person solicited for a contribution for a charitable purpose. "Percentage of total fundraising expenses," as used in this section, means the ratio of the total expenses of the fundraiser to the total revenue received by the fundraiser for the charitable purpose for which funds are being solicited, as reported on the most recent financial report filed with the Attorney General's Registry of Charitable Trusts. A commercial fundraiser shall disclose this information in writing within five working days from receipt of a request by mail or facsimile. A commercial fundraiser shall orally disclose this information immediately upon a request made in person or in a telephone conversation and shall follow this response with a written disclosure within five working days. Failure to comply with the requirements of this subdivision shall be grounds for an injunction against solicitation in this state for charitable purposes and other civil remedies provided by law.

(k) If the Attorney General issues a report to the public containing information obtained from registration forms or financial report forms filed by commercial fundraisers for charitable purposes, there shall be a separate section concerning commercial fundraisers for charitable purposes that obtain a majority of their inventory for sale by the purchase, receipt, or control for resale to the general public, of salvageable personal property solicited by an organization qualified to solicit donations pursuant to Section 148.3 of the Welfare and Institutions Code. The report shall include an explanation of the distinctions between these thrift store operations and other types of commercial fundraising.

(l) No person may act as a commercial fundraiser for charitable purposes if that person, any officer or director of that person's business, any person with a controlling interest in the business, or any person the commercial fundraiser employs, engages, or procures to solicit for compensation, has been convicted by a court of any state or the United States of a crime arising from the conduct of a solicitation for a charitable organization or purpose punishable as a misdemeanor or felony.

(m) A commercial fundraiser for charitable purposes shall not solicit in the state on behalf of a charitable organization unless that charitable organization is registered or is exempt from registration with the Attorney General's Registry of Charitable Trusts.

(n) If any provision of this section or the application thereof to any person or circumstances is held invalid, that invalidity shall not affect any other provision or application of this section that can be given effect without the invalid provision or application, and to this end the provisions of this section are severable.

(Stats. 1989, ch. 307, §2. Amended by Stats. 1991 (A.B. 2099), ch. 1150, §2; Stats. 1992 (A.B. 3066), ch. 249, §1; Stats. 1992 (S.B. 1682), ch. 511, §2.5; Stats. 1998 (A.B. 1810), ch. 445, §6; Stats. 2004 (S.B. 1262), ch. 919, §8; Stats. 2005 (S.B. 1108), ch. 22, §79.)

§12599.1. Definition of "fundraising counsel for charitable purposes"; obligations

(a) "Fundraising counsel for charitable purposes" is defined as any individual, corporation, unincorporated association, or other legal entity who is described by all of the following:

(1) For compensation plans, manages, advises, counsels, consults, or prepares material for, or with respect to, the solicitation in this state of funds, assets, or property for charitable purposes.

(2) Does not solicit funds, assets, or property for charitable purposes.

(3) Does not receive or control funds, assets, or property solicited for charitable purposes in this state.

(4) Does not employ, procure, or engage any compensated person to solicit, receive, or control funds, assets, or property for charitable purposes.

(b) "Fundraising counsel for charitable purposes" does not include any of the following:

(1) An attorney, investment counselor, or banker who in the conduct of that person's profession advises a client when actually engaged in the giving of legal, investment, or financial advice.

(2) A trustee as defined in Section 12582 or 12583.

(3) A charitable corporation as defined in Section 12582.1, or any employee thereof.

(4) A person employed by or under the control of a fundraising counsel for charitable purposes, as defined in subdivision (a).

(5) A person, corporation, or other legal entity, engaged as an independent contractor directly by a trustee or a charitable corporation, that prints, reproduces, or distributes written materials prepared by a trustee, a charitable corporation, or any employee thereof, or that performs artistic or graphic services with respect to written materials prepared by a trustee, a charitable corporation, or any employee thereof, provided that the independent contractor does not perform any of the activities described in paragraph (1) of subdivision (a).

(6) A person whose total annual gross compensation for performing any activity described in paragraph (1) of subdivision (a) does not exceed twenty-five thousand dollars ($ 25,000).

(c) A fundraising counsel for charitable purposes shall, prior to managing, advising, counseling, consulting, or preparing material for, or with respect to, the solicitation in this state of funds, assets, or property for charitable purposes, register with the Attorney General's Registry of Charitable Trusts on a registration form provided by the Attorney General. Renewals of registration shall be filed with the Registry of Charitable Trusts by January 15 of each calendar year in which the fundraising counsel for charitable purposes does business and shall be effective for one year.

A registration or renewal fee of two hundred dollars ($ 200) shall be required for registration of a fundraising counsel for charitable purposes, and shall be payable by certified or cashier's check to the Attorney General's Registry of Charitable Trusts at the time of registration and renewal. The Attorney General may adjust the annual registration or renewal fee as needed pursuant to this section. The Attorney General's Registry of Charitable Trusts may grant extensions of time to file annual registration as required, pursuant to subdivision (b) of Section 12586.

(d) A fundraising counsel for charitable purposes shall file annually with the Attorney General's Registry of Charitable Trusts on a form provided by the Attorney General, a report listing each person, corporation, unincorporated association, or other legal entity for whom the fundraising counsel has performed any services described in paragraph (1) of subdivision (a), and a statement certifying that the fundraising counsel had a written contract with each listed person, corporation, unincorporated association, or other legal entity that complied with the requirements of subdivision (f).

(e) Not less than 10 working days prior to the commencement of the performance of any service for a charitable organization by a fundraising counsel for charitable purposes, or not later than commencement of solicitation for solicitations to aid victims of emergency hardship or disasters, the fundraising counsel shall file with the Attorney General's Registry of Charitable Trusts a notice on a form prescribed by the Attorney General that sets forth all of the following:

(1) The name, address, and telephone number of the fundraising counsel for charitable purposes.

(2) The name, address, and telephone number of the charitable organization with whom the fundraising counsel has contracted.

(3) The projected dates when performance under the contract will commence and terminate.

(4) The name, address, and telephone number of the person responsible for directing and supervising the work of the fundraising counsel under the contract.

(f) There shall be a written contract between a fundraising counsel for charitable purposes and a charitable organization for each service to be performed by the fundraising counsel for the charitable organization, that shall be signed by the authorized contracting officer for the fundraising counsel and by an official of the charitable organization who is authorized to sign by the organization's governing body. The contract shall be available for inspection by the Attorney General and shall contain all of the following provisions:

(1) The legal name and address of the charitable organization as registered with the Registry of Charitable Trusts unless the charitable organization is exempt from registration.

(2) A statement of the charitable purpose for which the solicitation campaign is being conducted.

(3) A statement of the respective obligations of the fundraising counsel and the charitable organization.

(4) A clear statement of the fees and any other form of compensation, including commissions and property, that will be paid to the fundraising counsel.

(5) The effective and termination dates of the contract and the date services will commence with respect to solicitation in this state of contributions for a charitable organization.

(6) A statement that the fundraising counsel will not at any time solicit funds, assets, or property for charitable purposes, receive or control funds, assets, or property solicited for charitable purposes, or employ, procure, or engage any compensated person to solicit, receive, or control funds, assets, or property for charitable purposes.

(7) A statement that the charitable organization exercises control and approval over the content and frequency of any solicitation.

(8) A provision that the charitable organization has the right to cancel the contract without cost, penalty, or liability for a period of 10 days following the date on which the contract is executed; that the charitable organization may cancel the contract by serving a written notice of cancellation on the fundraising counsel; and that, if mailed, service shall be by certified mail, return receipt requested, and cancellation shall be deemed effective upon the expiration of five calendar days from the date of mailing.

(9) A provision that, following the initial 10-day cancellation period, the charitable organization may terminate the contract by giving 30 days' written notice; that, if mailed, service of the notice shall be by certified mail, return receipt requested, and shall be deemed effective upon the expiration of five calendar days from the date of mailing; and that, in the event of termination under this subdivision, the charitable organization shall be liable for services provided by the fundraising counsel to the effective date of the termination.

(10) Any other information required by the regulations of the Attorney General.

(g) It shall be unlawful for any fundraising counsel for charitable purposes to manage, advise, counsel, consult, or prepare material for, or with respect to, the solicitation in this state of funds, assets, or property for charitable purposes unless the fundraising counsel for charitable purposes has complied with the registration or annual renewal and financial reporting requirements of this article.

(h) A fundraising counsel for charitable purposes is subject to the Attorney General's supervision and enforcement to the same extent as a trustee for charitable purposes under this article.

(i) If any provision of this section or the application thereof to any person or circumstances is held invalid, that invalidity shall not affect other provisions or application of this section which can be given effect without the invalid provision or application, and to this end the provisions of this section are severable.

(Stats. 1998 (A.B. 1810), ch. 445, §7. Amended by Stats. 2004 (S.B. 1262), ch. 919, §9.)

§12599.2. "Commercial coventurer," defined

(a) "Commercial coventurer" is defined as any person who, for profit, is regularly and primarily engaged in trade or commerce other than in connection with the raising of funds, assets, or property for charitable organizations or charitable purposes, and who represents to the public that the purchase or use of any goods, services, entertainment, or any other thing of value will benefit a charitable organization or will be used for a charitable purpose.

(b) A commercial coventurer is a trustee as defined in Section 12582. Notwithstanding the requirements of Sections 12585 and 12586, a commercial coventurer is not required to register or file periodic reports with the Attorney General provided that the commercial coventurer:

(1) Has a written contract with a trustee or charitable corporation subject to this article, signed by two officers of the trustee or charitable corporation, prior to representing to the public that the purchase or use of any goods, services, entertainment, or any other thing of value will benefit the trustee or charitable corporation or will be used for a charitable purpose.

(2) Within 90 days after commencement of those representations, and at the end of each successive 90-day period during which the representations are made, transfers to that trustee or charitable corporation subject to this article all funds, assets, or property received as a result of the representations.

(3) Provides in conjunction with each transfer required by paragraph (2) a written accounting to the trustee or charitable corporation subject to this article of all funds, assets, or property received sufficient to enable the trustee or charitable corporation (A) to determine that representations made to the public on its behalf have been adhered to accurately and completely, and (B) to prepare its periodic report filed with the Attorney General pursuant to Section 12586.

(c) A commercial coventurer that does not meet the requirements of paragraphs (1), (2), and (3) of subdivision (b) shall register and report to the Attorney General on forms required by the Attorney General. An annual registration or renewal fee of two hundred dollars ($200) shall be required for registration or renewal of registration of a commercial coventurer, and shall be payable by certified or cashier's check to the Attorney General's Registry of Charitable Trusts at the time of registration or renewal. The Attorney General may adjust the annual registration or renewal fee as needed pursuant to this section.

(Stats. 1998 (A.B. 1810), ch. 445, §8.)

§12599.3. Charitable organizations and commercial fundraisers for charitable purposes

(a) A contract between a charitable organization and a commercial fundraiser for charitable purposes or fundraising counsel for charitable purposes shall be voidable by the charitable organization unless the commercial fundraiser or the fundraising counsel is registered with the Attorney General's Registry of Charitable Trusts prior to the commencement of the solicitation.

(b) Whenever a charitable organization contracts with a commercial fundraiser for charitable purposes or fundraising counsel for charitable purposes, the charitable organization shall have the right to cancel the contract without cost, penalty, or liability for a period of 10 days following the date on which the contract is executed. Any provision in the contract that is intended to waive this right of cancellation shall be void and unenforceable.

(c) A charitable organization may cancel a contract pursuant to subdivision (b) by serving a written notice of cancellation on the fundraising counsel or commercial fundraiser. If mailed, service shall be by certified mail, return receipt requested, and cancellation shall be deemed effective upon the expiration of five calendar days from the date of mailing. The notice shall be sufficient if it indicates that the charitable organization does not intend to be bound by the contract.

(d) Whenever a charitable organization cancels a contract pursuant to this section, it shall mail a duplicate copy of the notice of cancellation to the Attorney General's Registry of Charitable Trusts.

(e) Any funds collected after effective notice that a contract has been canceled shall be deemed to be held in trust for the benefit of the charitable organization without deduction for costs or expenses of any nature. A charitable organization shall be entitled to recover all funds collected after the date of cancellation.

(f) Following the initial 10-day cancellation period, a charitable organization may terminate a contract with a commercial fundraiser for charitable purposes or a fundraising counsel for charitable purposes by giving 30 days' written notice. If mailed, service of the notice shall be by certified mail, return receipt requested, and shall be deemed effective upon the expiration of five calendar days from the date of mailing. In the event of termination under this subdivision, the charitable organization shall be liable for services provided by the commercial fundraiser or fundraising counsel up to 30 days after the effective service of the notice.

(g) Following the initial 10-day cancellation period, a charitable organization may terminate at any time upon written notice a contract with a commercial fundraiser for charitable purposes or a fundraising counsel for charitable purposes, without payment or compensation of any kind to the commercial fundraiser or fundraising counsel, if the commercial fundraiser or the fundraising counsel, or their agents, employees, or representatives

(1) make any material misrepresentations in the course of solicitations or with respect to the charitable organization,

(2) are found by the charitable organization to have been convicted of a crime arising from the conduct of a solicitation for a charitable organization or purpose that is punishable as a felony or misdemeanor, or

(3) otherwise conduct fundraising activities in a manner that causes or could cause public disparagement of the charitable organization's good name or good will.

(Stats. 2004 (S.B. 1262), ch 919, §10.)

§12599.5. Applications for registration of commercial fundraiser for charitable purposes must be accompanied by cash deposit or bond

Each application for registration or renewal of registration under subdivision (b) of Section 12599 shall be accompanied by a cash deposit or by a bond issued by an admitted surety in favor of the State of California and in a form acceptable to the Attorney General. The cash deposit or bond shall be in the amount of twenty-five thousand dollars ($25,000) and shall be for the benefit of any person damaged as a result of malfeasance or misfeasance in the conduct of the activities specified in subdivision (a) of Section 12599. The bond may be in the form of a rider to a larger blanket liability bond.

(Stats. 1991 (A.B. 838), ch. 569, §1.)

§12599.6. Misrepresentation of purpose of organization or nature or purpose of beneficiary

(a) Charitable organizations and commercial fundraisers for charitable purposes shall not misrepresent the purpose of the charitable organization or the nature or purpose or beneficiary of a solicitation. A misrepresentation may be accomplished by words or conduct or failure to disclose a material fact.

(b) A charitable organization must establish and exercise control over its fundraising activities conducted for its benefit, including approval of all written contracts and agreements, and must assure that fundraising activities are conducted without coercion.

(c) A charitable organization shall not enter into any contract or agreement with, or employ, any commercial fundraiser for charitable purposes or fundraising counsel for charitable purposes unless that commercial fundraiser or fundraising counsel is registered with the Attorney General's Registry of Charitable Trusts or, if not registered, agrees to register prior to the commencement of any solicitation.

(d) A charitable organization shall not enter into any contract or agreement with, or raise any funds for, any charitable organization required to be registered pursuant to this act unless that charitable organization is registered with the Attorney General's Registry of Charitable Trusts or, if not registered, agrees to register prior to the commencement of the solicitation.

(e) Each contribution in the control or custody of a commercial fundraiser for charitable purposes shall in its entirety and within five working days of receipt (1) be deposited in an account at a bank or other federally insured financial institution that is solely in the name of the charitable organization on whose behalf the contribution was solicited and over which the charitable organization has sole control of withdrawals or, (2) be delivered to the charitable organization in person, by Express Mail, or by another method of delivery providing for overnight delivery.

(f) Regardless of injury, the following acts and practices are prohibited in the planning, conduct, or execution of any solicitation or charitable sales promotion:

(1) Operating in violation of, or failing to comply with, any of the requirements of this act or regulations or orders of the Attorney General, or soliciting contributions after registration with the Attorney General's Registry of Charitable Trusts has expired or has been suspended or revoked.

(2) Using any unfair or deceptive acts or practices or engaging in any fraudulent conduct that creates a likelihood of confusion or misunderstanding.

(3) Using any name, symbol, emblem, statement, or other material stating, suggesting, or implying to a reasonable person that the contribution is to or for the benefit of a particular charitable organization when that is not the fact.

(4) Misrepresenting or misleading anyone in any manner to believe that the person on whose behalf a solicitation or charitable sales promotion is being conducted is a charitable organization or that the proceeds of the solicitation or charitable sales promotion will be used for charitable purposes when that is not the fact.

(5) Misrepresenting or misleading anyone in any manner to believe that any other person sponsors, endorses, or approves a charitable solicitation or charitable sales promotion when that person has not given consent in writing to the use of the person's name for these purposes.

(6) Misrepresenting or misleading anyone in any manner to believe that goods or services have endorsement, sponsorship, approval, characteristics, ingredients, uses, benefits, or qualities that they do not have or that a person has endorsement, sponsorship, approval, status, or affiliation that the person does not have.

(7) Using or exploiting the fact of registration with the Attorney General's Registry of Charitable Trusts so as to lead any person to believe that the registration in any manner constitutes an endorsement or approval by the Attorney General. The use of the following statement is not prohibited:

"The official registration and financial information regarding (insert the legal name of the charity as registered with the Registry of Charitable Trusts) can be obtained from the Attorney General's Web site at http://caag.state.ca.us/charities/. Registration does not imply endorsement."

(8) Representing directly or by implication that a charitable organization will receive an amount greater than the actual net proceeds reasonably estimated to be retained by the charity for its use.

(9) With respect to solicitations by commercial fundraisers for charitable purposes on behalf of law enforcement personnel, firefighters, or other persons who protect the public safety, issuing, offering, giving, delivering, or distributing any honorary membership cards, courtesy cards, or similar cards, or any stickers, emblems, plates, or other items that could be used for display on a motor vehicle, and that suggest affiliation with, or endorsement by any public safety personnel or a group comprising such personnel.

(10)(A) Soliciting for advertising to appear in a for-profit publication that relates to, purports to relate to, or that could reasonably be construed to relate to, any charitable purpose without making the following disclosures at the time of solicitation:

(i) The publication is a for-profit, commercial enterprise.

(ii) The true name of the solicitor and the fact that the solicitor is a professional solicitor.

(iii) The publication is not affiliated with or sponsored by any charitable organization.

(B) Where a sale of advertising has been made, the solicitor, prior to accepting any money for the sale, shall make to the purchaser the disclosures required by subparagraph (A) in written form and in conspicuous type.

(11) Representing that any part of the contributions solicited by a charitable organization will be given or donated to any other charitable organization unless that organization has consented in writing to the use of its name prior to the solicitation. The written consent shall be signed by one authorized officer, director, or trustee of the charitable organization.

(12) Representing that tickets to events will be donated for use by another, unless all of the following requirements have been met:

(A) The charitable organization or commercial fundraiser has commitments, in writing, from charitable organizations stating that they will accept donated tickets and specifying the number of tickets they are willing to accept.

(B) The donated tickets will not, when combined with other ticket donations, exceed either of the following:

(i) The number of ticket commitments the charitable organization or commercial fundraiser has received from charitable organizations.

(ii) The total attendance capacity of the site of the event.

(g) A ticket commitment from a charitable organization alone, as described in subdivision (i), does not constitute written consent to use of the organization's name in the solicitation campaign.

(Stats. 2004 (S.B. 1262), ch 919, §11.)

CALIFORNIA PROBATE CODE

§8111. Charitable devise or trust without designated devisee or resident trustee; service on Attorney General

If the decedent's will involves or may involve a testamentary trust of property for charitable purposes other than a charitable trust with a designated trustee resident in this state, or involves or may involve a devise for charitable purposes without an identified devisee, notice of hearing accompanied by a copy of the petition and of the will shall be served on the Attorney General as provided in Section 1209.

(Stats.1990, c. 79 (A.B.759), § 14, operative July 1, 1991.)

§ 17210. Charitable trusts; petition by attorney general

In a case involving a charitable trust subject to the jurisdiction of the Attorney General, the Attorney General may petition under this chapter.

(Stats. 1990 (A.B.759), ch. 79, § 14, operative July 1, 1991.)

§19024. Notice of hearing; persons not petitioners

At least 30 days before the time set for the hearing on the petition, the petitioner shall cause notice of the time and place of the hearing, together with a copy of the petition, to be mailed to each of the following persons who is not a petitioner:

(a) All trustees of the trust and of any other trusts to which an allocation of liability may be approved by the court pursuant to the petition.

(b) All beneficiaries affected.

(c) The personal representative of the deceased settlor's estate, if any is known to the trustee.

(d) The Attorney General, if the petition relates to a charitable trust subject to the jurisdiction of the Attorney General, unless the Attorney General waives notice.

(Stats. 1991 (S.B.727), ch. 992, §3.)

§19030. Attorney General may petition in cases involving charitable trusts

In a case involving a charitable trust subject to the jurisdiction of the Attorney General, the Attorney General may petition under this chapter ["Petition for Approval and Settlement of Claims Against Deceased Settlor," i.e., the allowance, compromise, or settlement of any claims for which trust property may be liable].

(Stats. 1991 (S.B. 727), ch. 992, §3.)

VII. Restrictions on Charitable Trusts

At common law, the Statute of Mortmain (7 Edw. 1, stat. 2, c. 13 (1279)) restricted gifts to charity. The California mortmain statute (Cal. Prob. Code §41) was repealed by the legislature on November 4, 1971, effective March 4, 1972.

Today, all mortmain statutes have been repealed by statute or declared unconstitutional either on equal protection or due process grounds. Restatement (Third) of Property, §9.6, cmt. C.

For further discussion of mortmain statutes, see Chapter II, Section V(C) *supra*.

XIV
FIDUCIARY ADMINISTRATION

This chapter explores the fundamentals of fiduciary administration. It explores issues of jurisdiction, probate of a will (for testate estates), appointment of a personal representative, the tasks of the personal representative, and the disposition of estates without administration (or with simplified administration).

I. Generally

Before a court may assert authority over a decedent's estate, the court must have jurisdiction. Probate jurisdiction in California is vested in the superior court (Cal. Prob. Code §7050). A petitioner must establish the requisite jurisdictional facts (e.g., findings as to date and place of death, domicile of decedent in California at time of death, location of decedent's property in California at time of death) before the court may proceed on any matter concerning estate administration (Cal. Prob. Code §§7051, 7052).

§7050. Superior court has jurisdiction over estate administration

The superior court has jurisdiction of proceedings under this code concerning the administration of the decedent's estate.
(Stats. 1990 (A.B. 759), ch. 79, §14, effective July 1, 1991. Amended by Stats. 1994 (A.B. 3686), ch. 806, §22.)

§7051. Venue is county of domicile for California domiciliaries

If the decedent was domiciled in this state at the time of death, the proper county for proceedings concerning administration of the decedent's estate is the county in which the decedent was domiciled, regardless of where the decedent died.
(Stats. 1990 (A.B. 759), ch. 79, §14, effective July 1, 1991.)

§7052. Venue for nondomiciliary decedents is county where property is located

If the decedent was not domiciled in this state at the time of death, the proper county for proceedings under this code concerning the administration of the decedent's estate is one of the following:

(a) If property of the nondomiciliary decedent is located in the county in which the nondomiciliary decedent died, the county in which the nondomiciliary decedent died.

(b) If no property of the nondomiciliary decedent is located in the county in which the nondomiciliary decedent died or if the nondomiciliary decedent did not die in this state, any county in which property of the nondomiciliary decedent is located, regardless of where the nondomiciliary decedent died. If property of the nondomiciliary decedent is located in more than one county, the proper county is the county in which a petition for ancillary administration is first filed, and the court in that county has jurisdiction of the administration of the estate.
(Stats. 1990 (A.B. 759), ch. 79, §14, effective July 1, 1991.)

§7060. Grounds for disqualification of judge in probate proceedings

(a) In addition to any other ground provided by law for disqualification of a judge, a judge is disqualified from acting in proceedings under this code concerning the administration of the decedent's estate, except to order the transfer of a proceeding as provided in Article 3 (commencing with Section 7070), if any of the following circumstances exist:

(1) The judge is interested as a beneficiary or creditor.

(2) The judge is named as executor or trustee in the will.

(3) The judge is otherwise interested.

(b) A judge who participates in any manner in the drafting or execution of a will, including acting as a witness to the will, is disqualified from acting in any proceeding prior to and including the admission of the will to probate or in any proceeding involving its validity or interpretation.

(c) The amendments made to former Section 303 by Section 27 of Chapter 923 of the Statutes of 1987 do not apply in any proceeding commenced prior to July 1, 1988.
(Stats. 1990 (A.B. 759), ch. 79, §14, effective July 1, 1991.)

§7070. Lack of qualified judge leads to transfer to another county

The court or judge shall order a proceeding under this code concerning the administration of the decedent's estate transferred to another county if there is no judge of the court in which the proceeding is pending who is qualified to act. This section does not apply if a judge qualified to act is assigned by the chairman of the Judicial Council to sit in the county and hear the proceeding.

(Stats. 1990 (A.B. 759), ch. 79, §14, effective July 1, 1991.)

§7071. Choice of county to transfer proceeding

Transfer of a proceeding under this article shall be to another county in which property of the decedent is located or, if there is no other county in which property of the decedent is located, to an adjoining county.

(Stats. 1990 (A.B. 759), ch. 79, §14, effective July 1, 1991.)

§7072. Proceeding may be retransferred to original county

Upon petition of the personal representative or other interested person before entry of the order for final distribution of the estate, a proceeding transferred under this article may be retransferred to the court in which the proceeding was originally commenced if the court determines that both of the following conditions are satisfied:

(a) Another person has become judge of the court where the proceeding was originally commenced who is not disqualified to act in the administration of the estate.

(b) The convenience of the parties interested would be promoted by the retransfer.

(Stats. 1990 (A.B. 759), ch. 79, §14, effective July 1, 1991.)

§7220. Motion for new trial is limited to certain cases

In proceedings under this code concerning the administration of the decedent's estate, a motion for a new trial may be made only in the following cases:

(a) Contest of a will or revocation of probate of a will.

(b) Cases in which a right to jury trial is expressly granted, whether or not the case was tried by a jury.

(Stats. 1990 (A.B. 759), ch. 79, §14, effective July 1, 1991.)

§7250. Final judgment releases personal representative and sureties from claims of heirs or devisees

(a) When a judgment or order made pursuant to the provisions of this code concerning the administration of the decedent's estate becomes final, it releases the personal representative and the sureties from all claims of the heirs or devisees and of any persons affected thereby based upon any act or omission directly authorized, approved, or confirmed in the judgment or order. For the purposes of this section, "order" includes an order settling an account of the personal representative, whether an interim or final account.

(b) Nothing in this section affects any order, judgment, or decree made, or any action taken, before July 1, 1988. The validity of any action taken before July 1, 1988, is determined by the applicable law in effect before July 1, 1988, and not by this section.

(c) This section shall not apply where the judgment or order is obtained by fraud or conspiracy or by misrepresentation contained in the petition or account or in the judgment as to any material fact. For purposes of this subdivision, misrepresentation includes, but shall not be limited to, the omission of a material fact.

(Stats. 1990 (A.B. 759), ch. 79, §14, effective July 1, 1991. Amended by Stats. 1993 (A.B. 516), ch. 794, §2.)

§7260. "Transaction" defined

As used in this article, "transaction" means a transaction affecting title to property in the estate, including, but not limited to, the following:

(a) In the case of real property, a conveyance (including a sale, option, or order confirming a sale or option), a lease, the creation of a mortgage, deed of trust, or other lien or encumbrance, the setting apart of a probate homestead, or the distribution of property.

(b) In the case of personal property, a transfer of the property or the creation of a security interest or other lien on the property.

(Stats. 1990 (A.B. 759), ch. 79, §14, effective July 1, 1991.)

§7261. Court-ordered real property transaction shall be stated in instrument

If a transaction affecting real property in the estate is executed by the personal representative in accordance with the terms of a court order, the instrument shall include a statement that the transaction is made by authority of the order authorizing or directing the transaction and shall give the date of the order.

(Stats. 1990 (A.B. 759), ch. 79, §14, effective July 1, 1991.)

§7262. Court-ordered transaction by personal representative has same effect as that of decedent

A transaction executed by the personal representative in accordance with an order authorizing or directing the transaction has the same effect as if the decedent were living at the time of the transaction and had carried it out in person while having legal capacity to do so.

(Stats. 1990 (A.B. 759), ch. 79, §14, effective July 1, 1991.)

§7263. Personal representative shall record order affecting title to real property

If an order is made setting apart a probate homestead, confirming a sale or making a distribution of real property, or determining any other matter affecting title to real property in the estate, the personal representative shall record a certified copy of the order in the office of the county recorder in each county in which any portion of the real property is located.

(Stats. 1990 (A.B. 759), ch. 79, §14, effective July 1, 1991.)

§7280. Federal government has certain rights where federal allowance is made to estate

Where compensation, pension, insurance, or other allowance is made or awarded by a department or bureau of the United States government to a decedent's estate, the department or bureau has the same right as an interested person to do any of the following:

(a) Request special notice.

(b) Commence and prosecute an action on the bond of a personal representative.

(c) Contest an account of a personal representative.

(Stats. 1990 (A.B. 759), ch. 79, §14, effective July 1, 1991.)

II. Opening Estate Administration

"Probate" refers to the court-supervised administration of a decedent's estate (for a decedent who died testate (with a valid will) or intestate (without a valid will)). For a decedent who died testate, probate proceedings are initiated by the filing of a petition for probate of the decedent's will and for letters testamentary. For a decedent who died intestate, probate proceedings are initiated by a petition for letters of administration.

The stages of estate administration include: probating the will (for testate decedents), appointing a personal representative, marshalling the assets, conducting an inventory and appraisement, determining and paying the decedent's debts, and transferring title to the estate property to the beneficiaries or heirs.

Not all of a decedent's property is subject to probate. For example, inter vivos trusts, joint tenancy property, and life insurance proceeds pass outside the estate. Probate also may be avoided regarding a decedent's real and personal property that passes outright to a surviving spouse (by will or intestate succession) pursuant to a spousal set-aside proceeding (Cal. Prob. Code §§13650 et seq.). In addition, summary distribution proceedings may occur in cases involving estates below a statutorily designated amount (see Section VI *infra*).

A. Generally

§7000. Passage of decedent's property passes either to devisee or intestate heirs

Subject to Section 7001, title to a decedent's property passes on the decedent's death to the person to whom it is devised in the decedent's last will or, in the absence of such a devise, to the decedent's heirs as prescribed in the laws governing intestate succession.

(Stats. 1990 (A.B. 759), ch. 79, §14, effective July 1, 1991.)

§7001. Decedent's property is administered under Probate Code subject to rights of beneficiaries and creditors

The decedent's property is subject to administration under this code, except as otherwise provided by law, and is subject to the rights of beneficiaries, creditors, and other persons as provided by law.

(Stats. 1990 (A.B. 759), ch. 79, §14, effective July 1, 1991.)

§8000. Any interested person may commence proceedings for estate administration, to appoint personal representative and probate will

(a) At any time after a decedent's death, any interested person may commence proceedings for administration of the estate of the decedent by a petition to the court for an order determining the date and place of the decedent's death and for either or both of the following:

(1) Appointment of a personal representative.

(2) Probate of the decedent's will.

(b) A petition for probate of the decedent's will may be made regardless of whether the will is in the petitioner's possession or is lost, destroyed, or beyond the jurisdiction of the state.

(Stats. 1990 (A.B. 759), ch. 79, §14, effective July 1, 1991.)

§8001. Executor may waive right to appointment as personal representative by failure to petition in timely fashion

Unless good cause for delay is shown, if a person named in a will as executor fails to petition the court for administration of the estate within 30 days after the person has knowledge of the death of the decedent and that the person is named as executor, the person may be held to have waived the right to appointment as personal representative.

(Stats. 1990 (A.B. 759), ch. 79, §14, effective July 1, 1991.)

§8002. Petition shall contain jurisdictional facts and attachment of will

(a) The petition shall contain all of the following information:

(1) The date and place of the decedent's death.

(2) The street number, street, and city, or other address, and the county, of the decedent's residence at the time of death.

(3) The name, age, address, and relation to the decedent of each heir and devisee of the decedent, so far as known to or reasonably ascertainable by the petitioner.

(4) The character and estimated value of the property in the estate.

(5) The name of the person for whom appointment as personal representative is petitioned.

(b) If the decedent left a will:

(1) The petitioner shall attach to the petition a photographic copy of the will. In the case of a holographic will or other will of which material provisions are handwritten, the petitioner shall also attach a typed copy of the will.

(2) If the will is in a foreign language, the petitioner shall attach an English language translation. On admission of the will to probate, the court shall certify to a correct translation into English, and the certified translation shall be filed with the will.

(3) The petition shall state whether the person named as executor in the will consents to act or waives the right to appointment.

(Stats. 1990 (A.B. 759), ch. 79, §14, effective July 1, 1991.)

§8003. Time for hearing; petitioner shall serve and publish notice

(a) The hearing on the petition shall be set for a day not less than 15 nor more than 30 days after the petition is filed. At the request of the petitioner made at the time the petition is filed, the hearing on the petition shall be set for a day not less than 30 nor more than 45 days after the petition is filed. The court may not shorten the time for giving the notice of hearing under this section.

(b) The petitioner shall serve and publish notice of the hearing in the manner prescribed in Chapter 2 (commencing with Section 8100).

(Stats. 1990 (A.B. 759), ch. 79, §14, effective July 1, 1991.)

§8004. Grounds for contesting appointment of personal representative

(a) If appointment of the personal representative is contested, the grounds of opposition may include a challenge to the competency of the personal representative or the right to appointment. If the contest asserts the right of another person to appointment as personal representative, the contestant shall also file a petition and serve notice in the manner provided in Article 2 (commencing with Section 8110) of Chapter 2, and the court shall hear the two petitions together.

(b) If a will is contested, the applicable procedure is that provided in Article 3 (commencing with Section 8250) of Chapter 3.

(Stats. 1990 (A.B. 759), ch. 79, §14, effective July 1, 1991.)

§8005. Court shall make order establishing jurisdiction, admitting will to probate, appointing personal representative

(a) At the hearing on the petition, the court may examine and compel any person to attend as a witness concerning any of the following matters:

(1) The time, place, and manner of the decedent's death.

(2) The place of the decedent's domicile and residence at the time of death.

(3) The character and value of the decedent's property.

(4) Whether or not the decedent left a will.

(b) The following matters shall be established:

(1) The jurisdictional facts, including:

(A) The date and place of the decedent's death.

(B) That the decedent was domiciled in this state or left property in this state at the time of death.

(C) The publication of notice under Article 3 (commencing with Section 8120) of Chapter 2.

(2) The existence or nonexistence of the decedent's will.

(3) That notice of the hearing was served as provided in Article 2 (commencing with Section 8110) of Chapter 2.

(Stats. 1990 (A.B. 759), ch. 79, §14, effective July 1, 1991.)

§8006. After establishment of jurisdictional facts, court shall make order determining time and place of death and jurisdiction, admitting will to probate, and appointing personal representative

(a) If the court finds that the matters referred to in paragraph (1) of subdivision (b) of Section 8005 are established, the court shall make an order determining the time and place of the decedent's death and the jurisdiction of the court. Where appropriate and on satisfactory proof, the order shall admit the decedent's will to probate and appoint a personal representative. The date the will is admitted to probate shall be included in the order.

(b) If through defect of form or error the matters referred to in paragraph (1) of subdivision (b) of Section 8005 are incorrectly stated in the petition but actually are established, the court has and retains jurisdiction to correct the defect or error at any time. No such defect or error makes void an order admitting the will to probate or appointing a personal representative or an order made in any subsequent proceeding.

(Stats. 1990 (A.B. 759), ch. 79, §14, effective July 1, 1991.)

§8007. Order admitting will or appointing personal representative is conclusive determination of court's jurisdiction; exceptions

(a) Except as provided in subdivision (b), an order admitting a will to probate or appointing a personal representative, when it becomes final, is a conclusive determination of the jurisdiction of the court and cannot be collaterally attacked.

(b) Subdivision (a) does not apply in either of the following cases:

(1) The presence of extrinsic fraud in the procurement of the court order.

(2) The court order is based on the erroneous determination of the decedent's death.

(Stats. 1990 (A.B. 759), ch. 79, §14, effective July 1, 1991.)

B. Notice

1. Notice in Probate Proceedings Generally

The petitioner must give notice of probate proceedings to interested parties. Proper notice is a prerequisite to the establishment of probate court subject matter jurisdiction (Cal. Prob. Code §§8005(b)(1)(C), 8124).

The importance of the giving of proper notice was highlighted in In Estate of Buckley, 183 Cal. Rptr. 281 (Ct. App. 1982), in which the decedent's two sons filed a petition for probate of the will and issuance of letters of administration with the will annexed (the will had named decedent's son-in-law as executor). The decedent's daughter (and wife of the named executor) filed an objection to the appointment. The probate court granted the sons' petition and appointed them as administrators with the will annexed. Subsequently, the decedent's daughter filed a petition to vacate the orders regarding the petition for probate and issuance of letters, alleging deficiencies in the performance of the personal representatives' duties, including the failure to file an affidavit showing publication of notice of death and of petition to administer the estate in compliance with California Probate Code §333 (now repealed).

The Court of Appeal held that: (1) the probate court does not have power to hear matters where the statutory requirements have not been met; and (2) the failure of the administrator to publish notice rendered void the order appointing him as administrator.

California Probate Code §§1200 et seq. govern notice generally in probate proceedings. However, because probate is a process involving many stages, proceedings in each stage may require the establishment of jurisdiction and the giving of proper notice. Therefore, additional Probate Code sections govern the specific requirements for giving of proper notice for the various stages (e.g., Cal. Prob. Code §§8003(b), 8100-8125), (pertaining to the opening of estate administration).

Further, proper notice must comply with the requirements of due process. That is, publication of notice does not satisfy due process when the personal representative knows or could reasonably ascertain the identity and addresses of persons interested in the estate (beneficiaries, heirs, creditors). Mullane v. Central Hanover Bank, 339 U.S. 306 (1950) (requiring notice that is reasonably calculated under the circumstances to inform interested parties of the pendency of the action and provide them with a reasonable opportunity to be heard; Tulsa v. Pope, 485 U.S. 478 (1988) (requiring *Mullane* notice to creditors)).

Any person interested in the estate (e.g., beneficiary, heir, creditor, trust beneficiary) may file a request with the court clerk for special notice (Cal. Prob. Code §1250). Special notice may be requested regarding the following matters: (1) petitions filed in the administration proceeding, inventories, and appraisals of estate property; (2) objections to an appraisal; (3) accounts of a personal representative; and (4) reports of the status of estate administration (Cal. Prob. Code §1250(c)).

§1200. Applicability of part

(a) Except as otherwise provided in this code, this part governs notice required or permitted under this code.

(b) This part does not apply to notice under a particular provision to the extent that the particular provision is inconsistent with this part.

(c) This part does not apply to the giving of a particular notice where the notice was delivered, mailed, posted, or first published before July 1, 1991. The applicable law in effect before July 1, 1991, continues to apply to the giving of that notice, notwithstanding its repeal.

(Stats. 1990 (A.B. 759), ch. 79, §14, effective July 1, 1991.)

§1201. Person need not give notice to oneself or joining party

If a person is required to give notice, the person required to give the notice need not give the notice to himself or herself or to any other person who joins in the petition.

(Stats. 1990 (A.B. 759), ch. 79, §14, effective July 1, 1991.)

§1202. Court may require additional notice if notice is insufficient

Where the court determines that the notice otherwise required is insufficient in the particular circumstances, the court may require that further or additional notice, including a longer period of notice, be given.

(Stats. 1990 (A.B. 759), ch. 79, §14, effective July 1, 1991.)

§1203. Court may shorten time for giving notice of hearing upon good cause

(a) Subject to subdivision (b), unless the particular provision governing the notice of hearing provides that the time for giving notice may not be shortened, the court may, for good cause, shorten the time for giving a notice of hearing.

(b) Unless the particular provision governing the publication of notice of hearing otherwise provides, the court may not shorten the time for publication of notice of hearing.

(Stats. 1990 (A.B. 759), ch. 79, §14, effective July 1, 1991. Amended by Stats. 1991 (S.B. 896), ch. 82, §2.5, effective July 1, 1991.)

§1204. Waiver of notice

A person, including a guardian ad litem, guardian, conservator, trustee, or other fiduciary, may waive notice by a writing signed by the person or the person's attorney and filed in the proceeding.

(Stats. 1990 (A.B. 759), ch. 79, §14, effective July 1, 1991.)

§1205. No further notice required for continuance or postponement of hearing

If a hearing is continued or postponed, no further notice of the continued or postponed hearing is required unless ordered by the court.

(Stats. 1990 (A.B. 759), ch. 79, §14, effective July 1, 1991.)

§1206. Persons who are entitled to notice

(a) Subject to subdivision (b), where notice is required to be given to known heirs or known devisees, notice shall be given to the following persons:

(1) If the estate is an intestate estate, to the heirs named in the petition for letters of administration and to any additional heirs who become known to the person giving the notice prior to the giving of the notice.

(2) If the estate is a testate estate, to the devisees named in the petition for probate of the will and to any additional devisees who become known to the person giving the notice prior to the giving of the notice.

(b) Notice need not be given to a person under subdivision (a) if the person's interest has been satisfied pursuant to court order or as evidenced by the person's written receipt.

(Stats. 1990 (A.B. 759), ch. 79, §14, effective July 1, 1991.)

§1207. Persons not entitled to notice

(a) Subject to subdivision (b), where notice is required to be given to a decedent's beneficiaries, devisees, or heirs, notice need not be given to a person who, because of a possible parent-child relationship between a stepchild and a stepparent or between a foster child and a foster parent, may be (1) an heir of the decedent or (2) a member of a class to which a devise is made.

(b) Subdivision (a) does not apply where the person required to give the notice has actual knowledge of facts that a person would reasonably believe give rise under Section 6454 to the parent-child relationship between the stepchild and the stepparent or between the foster child and the foster parent.

(Stats. 1990 (A.B. 759), ch. 79, §14, effective July 1, 1991. Amended by Stats. 1993 (A.B. 1137), ch. 529, §1.)

§1208. Notice to trust beneficiaries is not required if given to trust or trustee

(a) Except as provided in subdivision (b), if notice is required to be given to a trust or trustee, notice to trust beneficiaries is not required.

(b) Subject to subdivision (c), where the personal representative and the trustee are the same person, or where no trustee has been appointed, notice shall be given to (1) each person to whom income or principal would be required or authorized in the trustee's discretion to be currently distributed if the trust were in effect, or (2) if there are no such persons, to each person who, under the terms of the trust, would be entitled to any distribution if the trust were terminated at the time the notice is required to be given.

(c) Notice to trust beneficiaries is not required under subdivision (b) where the trust has more than one trustee and

notice is given to a cotrustee who is not a personal representative.
(Stats. 1990 (A.B. 759), ch. 79, §14, effective July 1, 1991. Amended by Stats. 1992 (A.B. 2975), ch. 871, §5; Stats. 1995 (A.B. 1466), ch. 730, §2.)

§1209. Notice to State of California shall be given to Attorney General

(a) Where notice is required to be given to the State of California, the notice shall be given to the Attorney General.

(b) Where notice is required to be given to the Attorney General, the notice shall be mailed to the Attorney General at the office of the Attorney General at Sacramento, California.
(Stats. 1990 (A.B. 759), ch. 79, §14, effective July 1, 1991.)

§1210. Notice to guardians and conservators

If an interested person has a guardian or conservator of the estate who resides in this state, personal service on the guardian or conservator of any process, notice, or court order concerning a decedent's estate is equivalent to service on the ward or conservatee, and it is the duty of the guardian or conservator to attend to the interests of the ward or conservatee in the matter. The guardian or conservator may appear for the ward or conservatee and waive any process, notice, or order to show cause that a person not under legal disability might waive.
(Stats. 1990 (A.B. 759), ch. 79, §14, effective July 1, 1991.)

§1211. Form of notice where type of notice not otherwise prescribed

If a notice is required by this code and no other type of notice is prescribed by law, by the Judicial Council, or by the court or judge, the notice shall be in substantially the following form:

SUPERIOR COURT OF THE STATE OF CALIFORNIA FOR THE (CITY AND) COUNTY OF ____________

Estate of ______________________ No. ______

NOTICE OF HEARING

(If to be published, describe purport or character of the notice to be given.)

Notice is hereby given that (name of petitioner and representative capacity, if any) has filed herein a (nature of petition, application, report, or account), reference to which is made for further particulars, and that the time and place of hearing the same has been set for _________ (date) ___________, at ____ .m., in the courtroom (of Department No. _________, if any) of said court, at (the courthouse, or state other location of the court), in the City of _________, California.

Dated _________

______________________________________,
Clerk

By ______________________, Deputy Clerk

(Stats. 1990 (A.B. 759), ch. 79, §14, effective July 1, 1991.)

§1212. Notice if address is not known

Unless the court dispenses with the notice, if the address of the person to whom a notice or other paper is required to be mailed or delivered is not known, notice shall be given as the court may require in the manner provided in Section 413.30 of the Code of Civil Procedure.
(Stats. 1990 (A.B. 759), ch. 79, §14, effective July 1, 1991.)

§1213. Notice shall be mailed to surety who has filed court bond

(a) The following persons shall mail a notice, as described in Section 1211, to a surety who has filed a court bond in a proceeding:

(1) A person who files a petition to surcharge.

(2) A person who files an objection to an account.

(3) A person who files a petition to suspend or remove a guardian, conservator, or personal representative.

(4) An attorney who files a motion to withdraw from representation of a guardian, conservator, or personal representative.

(b) Within five days after entry of an order to suspend or remove a guardian, conservator, or personal representative, the person who filed a petition to suspend or remove a guardian or, if the order to suspend or remove a guardian, conservator, or personal representative was issued upon a motion by the court, the court, shall notify the surety who has filed a court bond of the order by first-class mail, postage prepaid.

(c) The notice required by this section shall be mailed to the address listed on the surety bond.

(d) Notwithstanding subdivisions (a) and (b), notice is not required to a surety pursuant to this section if the surety bond is for a guardian, conservator, or personal representative who is not the subject of the petition, motion, or order described in this section.
(Stats. 1997 (S.B. 792), ch. 198, §1.)

§1214. Notice shall also be given to attorney if person is represented

If a notice or other paper is required or permitted to be mailed, delivered, served, or otherwise given to a person who is represented by an attorney of record, the notice or other paper shall also be mailed to this attorney, unless otherwise specified in a request for special notice.

(Stats. 1999 (A.B. 1051), ch. 263, §2.)

§1215. Requirements for mailing of notice

Unless otherwise expressly provided:

(a) If a notice or other paper is required or permitted to be mailed to a person, the notice or other paper shall be mailed as provided in this section or personally delivered as provided in Section 1216.

(b) The notice or other paper shall be sent by:

(1) First-class mail if the person's address is within the United States. First-class mail includes certified, registered, and express mail.

(2) Airmail if the person's address is not within the United States.

(c) The notice or other paper shall be deposited for collection in the United States mail, in a sealed envelope, with postage paid, addressed to the person to whom it is mailed.

(d) Subject to Section 1212, the notice or other paper shall be addressed to the person at the person's place of business or place of residence.

(e) When the notice or other paper is deposited in the mail, mailing is complete and the period of notice is not extended.

(Stats. 1990 (A.B. 759), ch. 79, §14, effective July 1, 1991. Amended by Stats. 1990 (S.B. 1775), ch. 710, §5, effective July 1, 1991.)

§1216. Notice that may be mailed may be delivered by personal delivery

(a) If a notice or other paper is required or permitted to be mailed to a person, it may be delivered personally to that person. Personal delivery as provided in this section satisfies a provision that requires or permits a notice or other paper to be mailed.

(b) Personal delivery pursuant to this section is complete when the notice or other paper is delivered personally to the person who is to receive it.

(Stats. 1990 (A.B. 759), ch. 79, §14, effective July 1, 1991.)

§1217. Manner of notice if manner not statutorily specified

If a notice or other paper is required to be served or otherwise given and no other manner of giving the notice or other paper is specified by statute, the notice or other paper shall be mailed or personally delivered as provided in this chapter.

(Stats. 1990 (A.B. 759), ch. 79, §14, effective July 1, 1991.)

§1220. Requirements for notice of hearing

(a) When notice of hearing is required to be given as provided in this section:

(1) At least 15 days before the time set for the hearing, the petitioner or the person filing the report, account, or other paper shall cause notice of the time and place of the hearing to be mailed to the persons required to be given notice.

(2) Unless the statute requiring notice specifies the persons to be given notice, notice shall be mailed to all of the following:

(A) The personal representative.

(B) All persons who have requested special notice in the estate proceeding pursuant to Section 1250.

(3) Subject to Section 1212, the notice shall be addressed to the person required to be given notice at the person's place of business or place of residence.

(b) Subject to subdivision (c), nothing in this section excuses compliance with the requirements for notice to a person who has requested special notice pursuant to Chapter 6 (commencing with Section 1250).

(c) The court for good cause may dispense with the notice otherwise required to be given to a person as provided in this section.

(Stats. 1990 (A.B. 759), ch. 79, §14, effective July 1, 1991. Amended by Stats. 1990 (S.B. 1775), ch. 710, §6, effective July 1, 1991; Stats. 1994 (A.B. 3686), ch. 806, §7.)

§1221. Provisions for giving notice absent specific provisions

Where notice of hearing is required but no other period or manner is prescribed by statute, unless the period or manner of giving the notice is ordered by the court or judge, the notice of hearing shall be given for the period and in the manner provided in Section 1220.

(Stats. 1990 (A.B. 759), ch. 79, §14, effective July 1, 1991.)

§1230. Requirements for posting notice

Where notice of hearing is required to be posted as provided in this section:

(a) At least 15 days before the time set for the hearing, the court clerk shall cause a notice of the time and place of the hearing to be posted at the courthouse of the county where the proceedings are pending. If court is held at a place other than the county seat, the notice may be posted either at the courthouse of the county where the proceedings are pending or at the building where the court is held.

(b) The posted notice of hearing shall state all of the following:

(1) The name of the estate.

(2) The name of the petitioner.

(3) The nature of the petition, referring to the petition for further particulars.

(4) The time and place of the hearing of the petition.

(Stats. 1990 (A.B. 759), ch. 79, §14, effective July 1, 1991.)

§1240. Authorization of issuance of citation

Where use of a citation is authorized or required by statute, a citation may be issued by the court clerk on the application of any party, without a court order, except in cases where an order is expressly required by law.

(Stats. 1990 (A.B. 759), ch. 79, §14, effective July 1, 1991.)

§1241. Requirements for citation

The citation shall be directed to the person to be cited, signed by the court clerk, and issued under the seal of the court. The citation shall contain the title of the proceeding, a brief statement of the nature of the proceeding, and a direction that the person cited appear at a time and place specified.

(Stats. 1990 (A.B. 759), ch. 79, §14, effective July 1, 1991.)

§1242. Service of citation

The citation shall be served on the person cited in the manner provided in Chapter 4 (commencing with Section 413.10) of Title 5 of Part 2 of the Code of Civil Procedure. Except as otherwise provided by statute, the citation shall be served at least five days before its return day.

(Stats. 1990 (A.B. 759), ch. 79, §14, effective July 1, 1991.)

§1250. Procedure for requests for special notice

(a) At any time after the issuance of letters in a proceeding under this code for the administration of a decedent's estate, any person interested in the estate, whether as devisee, heir, creditor, beneficiary under a trust, or as otherwise interested, may in person or by attorney, file with the court clerk a written request for special notice.

(b) The request for special notice shall be so entitled and shall set forth the name of the person and the address to which notices shall be sent.

(c) Special notice may be requested of one or more of the following matters:

(1) Petitions filed in the administration proceeding.

(2) Inventories and appraisals of property in the estate, including any supplemental inventories and appraisals.

(3) Objections to an appraisal.

(4) Accounts of a personal representative.

(5) Reports of status of administration.

(d) Special notice may be requested of any matter in subdivision (c) by describing it, or of all the matters in subdivision (c) by referring generally to "the matters described in subdivision (c) of Section 1250 of the Probate Code" or by using words of similar meaning.

(e) A copy of the request shall be personally delivered or mailed to the personal representative or to the attorney for the personal representative. If personally delivered, the request is effective when it is delivered. If mailed, the request is effective when it is received.

(f) When the original of the request is filed with the court clerk, it shall be accompanied by a written admission or proof of service.

(Stats. 1990 (A.B. 759), ch. 79, §14, effective July 1, 1991.)

§1251. Modification or withdrawal of requests for special notice

A request for special notice under this chapter may be modified or withdrawn in the same manner as provided for the making of the initial request.

(Stats. 1990 (A.B. 759), ch. 79, §14, effective July 1, 1991.)

§1252. Requirement of written notice of filing

(a) Unless the court makes an order dispensing with the notice, if a request has been made pursuant to Section 1250 for special notice of a hearing, the person filing the petition, report, account, or other paper shall give written notice of the filing, together with a copy of the petition, report, account, or other paper, and the time and place set for the hearing, by mail to the person named in the request at the address set forth in the request, at least 15 days before the time set for the hearing.

(b) If a request has been made pursuant to Section 1250 for special notice of the filing of an inventory and appraisal of the estate or of the filing of any other paper that does not require a hearing, the inventory and appraisal or other paper shall be mailed not later than 15 days after the inventory and appraisal or other paper is filed with the court.

(Stats. 1990 (A.B. 759), ch. 79, §14, effective July 1, 1991.)

§1260. Proof of giving notice; finding

(a) If notice of a hearing is required, proof of giving notice of the hearing shall be made to the satisfaction of the court at or before the hearing.

(b) If it appears to the satisfaction of the court that notice has been regularly given or that the party entitled to notice has waived it, the court shall so find in its order.

(c) The finding described in subdivision (b), when the order becomes final, is conclusive on all persons.
(Stats. 1990 (A.B. 759), ch. 79, §14, effective July 1, 1991.)

§1261. Requirement for proof of mailing

Proof of mailing may be made in the manner prescribed in Section 1013a of the Code of Civil Procedure.
(Stats. 1990 (A.B. 759), ch. 79, §14, effective July 1, 1991.)

§1262. Requirement for proof of publication

Proof of publication may be made by the affidavit of the publisher or printer, or the foreman or principal clerk of the publisher or printer, showing the time and place of publication.
(Stats. 1990 (A.B. 759), ch. 79, §14, effective July 1, 1991.)

§1263. Requirement for proof of posting

Proof of posting may be made by the affidavit of the person who posted the notice.
(Stats. 1990 (A.B. 759), ch. 79, §14, effective July 1, 1991.)

§1264. Requirement for proof of personal delivery

Proof of notice by personal delivery may be made by the affidavit of the person making the delivery showing the time and place of delivery and the name of the person to whom delivery was made.
(Stats. 1990 (A.B. 759), ch. 79, §14, effective July 1, 1991.)

§1265. Proof of notice at hearing

Proof of notice, however given, may be made by evidence presented at the hearing.
(Stats. 1990 (A.B. 759), ch. 79, §14, effective July 1, 1991.)

2. Notice for Purposes of Commencing Administration

The petitioner must serve and publish notice of the petition to administer the estate (Cal. Prob. Code §8120). The notice must be published in a newspaper of general circulation in the city where the decedent resided at the time of death or where the property is located (Cal. Prob. Code §8121).

§8100. Form of notice of hearing to open administration

The notice of hearing of a petition for administration of a decedent's estate, whether served under Article 2 (commencing with Section 8110) or published under Article 3 (commencing with Section 8120), shall state substantially as follows:

NOTICE OF PETITION TO ADMINISTER ESTATE OF
_______________, ESTATE NO. _________

To all heirs, beneficiaries, creditors, and contingent creditors of ____________ and persons who may be otherwise interested in the will or estate, or both:

A petition has been filed by ____________ in the Superior Court of California, County of ____________, requesting that ____________ be appointed as personal representative to administer the estate of ______ [and for probate of the decedent's will, which is available for examination in the court file].

[The petition requests authority to administer the estate under the Independent Administration of Estates Act. This will avoid the need to obtain court approval for many actions taken in connection with the estate. However, before taking certain actions, the personal representative will be required to give notice to interested persons unless they have waived notice or have consented to the proposed action. The petition will be granted unless good cause is shown why it should not be.]

The petition is set for hearing in Dept. No. ____________
at ______________________________________ (Address)
on __________________________ (Date of hearing) at
____________ (Time of hearing).

IF YOU OBJECT to the granting of the petition, you should appear at the hearing and state your objections or file written objections with the court before the hearing. Your appearance may be in person or by your attorney.

IF YOU ARE A CREDITOR or a contingent creditor of the deceased, you must file your claim with the court and mail a copy to the personal representative appointed by the court within four months from the date of first issuance of letters as provided in Section 9100 of the California Probate Code. The time for filing claims will not expire before four months from the date of the hearing noticed above.

YOU MAY EXAMINE the file kept by the court. If you are interested in the estate, you may request special notice of the filing of an inventory and appraisal of estate assets or of any petition or account as provided in Section 1250 of the California Probate Code.

____
(Name and address of petitioner or petitioner's attorney)

(Stats. 1990 (A.B. 759), ch. 79, §14, effective July 1, 1991.)

§8110. Petitioner shall serve notice of hearing at least 15 days before hearing; recipients

At least 15 days before the hearing of a petition for administration of a decedent's estate, the petitioner shall serve notice of the hearing by mail or personal delivery on all of the following persons:

(a) Each heir of the decedent, so far as known to or reasonably ascertainable by the petitioner.

(b) Each devisee, executor, and alternative executor named in any will being offered for probate, regardless of whether the devise or appointment is purportedly revoked in a subsequent instrument.

(Stats. 1990 (A.B. 759), ch. 79, §14, effective July 1, 1991. Amended by Stats. 1996 (S.B. 392), ch. 563, §22.)

§8111. Petitioner must serve notice on Attorney General in cases of charitable devise or trust without designated devisee or resident trustee

If the decedent's will involves or may involve a testamentary trust of property for charitable purposes other than a charitable trust with a designated trustee resident in this state, or involves or may involve a devise for charitable purposes without an identified devisee, notice of hearing accompanied by a copy of the petition and of the will shall be served on the Attorney General as provided in Section 1209.

(Stats. 1990 (A.B. 759), ch. 79, §14, effective July 1, 1991.)

§8112. Personal representative shall give notice to creditors and public entities with claims

A general personal representative shall give notice of administration of the estate of the decedent to creditors under Chapter 2 (commencing with Section 9050), and to public entities under Chapter 5 (commencing with Section 9200), of Part 4.

(Stats. 1990 (A.B. 759), ch. 79, §14, effective July 1, 1991.)

§8113. Notice of foreign citizen's death shall be given to diplomat or consul in some cases

If a citizen of a foreign country dies without leaving a will or leaves a will without naming an executor, or if it appears that property will pass to a citizen of a foreign country, notice shall be given to a recognized diplomatic or consular official of the foreign country maintaining an office in the United States.

(Stats. 1990 (A.B. 759), ch. 79, §14, effective July 1, 1991.)

§8120. Notice of hearing shall be published as well as served

In addition to service of the notice of hearing as provided in Article 2 (commencing with Section 8110), notice of hearing of a petition for administration of a decedent's estate shall also be published before the hearing in the manner provided in this article.

(Stats. 1990 (A.B. 759), ch. 79, §14, effective July 1, 1991.)

§8121. Publication date of notice of hearing; number of publications; type of newspaper

(a) The first publication date of the notice shall be at least 15 days before the hearing. Three publications in a newspaper published once a week or more often, with at least five days intervening between the first and last publication dates, not counting the publication dates, are sufficient.

(b) Notice shall be published in a newspaper of general circulation in the city where the decedent resided at the time of death, or where the decedent's property is located if the court has jurisdiction under Section 7052. If there is no such newspaper, or if the decedent did not reside in a city, or if the property is not located in a city, then notice shall be published in a newspaper of general circulation in the county which is circulated within the area of the county in which the decedent resided or the property is located. If there is no such newspaper, notice shall be published in a newspaper of general circulation published in this state nearest to the county seat of the county in which the decedent resided or the property is located, and which is circulated within the area of the county in which the decedent resided or the property is located.

(c) For purposes of this section, "city" means a charter city as defined in Section 34101 of the Government Code or a general law city as defined in Section 34102 of the Government Code.

(Stats. 1990 (A.B. 759), ch. 79, §14, effective July 1, 1991.)

§8122. Effect of good faith attempt to comply with notice requirements

The Legislature finds and declares that, to be most effective, notice of hearing should be published in compliance with Section 8121. However, the Legislature recognizes the possibility that in unusual cases due to confusion over jurisdictional boundaries or oversight such notice may inadvertently be published in a newspaper that does not satisfy Section 8121. Therefore, to prevent a minor error in publication from invalidating what would otherwise be a proper proceeding, the Legislature further finds and declares that notice published in a good faith attempt to comply with Section 8121 is sufficient to provide notice of hearing and to establish jurisdiction if the court expressly finds that the notice was published in a newspaper of general circulation published within the county and widely circulated within a true cross-section of the area of the county in which the decedent resided or the property was located in substantial compliance with Section 8121.

(Stats. 1990 (A.B. 759), ch. 79, §14, effective July 1, 1991.)

§8123. Type size of notice

The caption of a notice under this article shall be in 8 point type or larger and the text shall be in 7 point type or larger.

(Stats. 1990 (A.B. 759), ch. 79, §14, effective July 1, 1991.)

§8124. Affidavit showing due publication is prerequisite for hearing petition to open administration

A petition for administration of a decedent's estate shall not be heard by the court unless an affidavit showing due publication of the notice of hearing has been filed with the court. The affidavit shall contain a copy of the notice and state the date of its publication.

(Stats. 1990 (A.B. 759), ch. 79, §14, effective July 1, 1991.)

§8125. Subsequent publication may omit creditor and contingent creditor information

Notwithstanding Section 8100, after the notice of hearing is published and an affidavit filed, any subsequent publication of the notice ordered by the court may omit the information for creditors and contingent creditors.

(Stats. 1990 (A.B. 759), ch. 79, §14, effective July 1, 1991.)

III. Probate of Will

A. Production of Will

Before the will can be probated, it must be located. The will may have been in the decedent's possession, in the office of the attorney who supervised the execution of the will, or in the executor's possession.

Some testators keep their wills in safe deposit boxes in financial institutions. California Probate Code §331 provides that a person with a key (and who provides proof of identity and proof of death) may obtain access to the box, before issuance of letters, in order to search for a will and burial instructions. When the safe deposit box is opened, an employee of the financial institution has the duty to keep a record of the person's identity; to permit the person to make an inventory of its contents; to make a photocopy of all wills and trust instruments therein that are removed, and keep the photocopy in the safe deposit box until the contents of the box are removed by the personal representative of the estate or other legally authorized person; and to permit the person to remove burial instructions and any testamentary instruments. *Id.* at §331(d). Attorneys who hold estate planning documents also have statutorily defined duties regarding their safekeeping (Cal. Prob. Code §§700 et seq., Section B *infra*).

The custodian of a will has a statutory duty (within 30 days after learning of the testator's death, unless a petition for probate is filed earlier) to deliver the will to the superior court clerk of the county in which the estate may be administered and to mail a copy to the named executor (or to a named beneficiary if the executor's location is unknown) (Cal. Prob. Code §8200). If the custodian delivers the will to the superior court clerk of a county where no probate proceedings are pending, the court may order the will transferred to the county where such proceedings are pending (Cal. Prob. Code §8203).

CALIFORNIA PROBATE CODE
§331. Safe deposit box

(a) This section applies only to a safe deposit box in a financial institution held by the decedent in the decedent's sole name, or held by the decedent and others where all are deceased. Nothing in this section affects the rights of a surviving coholder.

(b) A person who has a key to the safe deposit box may, before letters have been issued, obtain access to the safe deposit box only for the purposes specified in this section by providing the financial institution with both of the following:

(1) Proof of the decedent's death. Proof shall be provided by a certified copy of the decedent's death certificate or by a written statement of death from the coroner, treating physician, or hospital or institution where the decedent died.

(2) Reasonable proof of the identity of the person seeking access. Reasonable proof of identity is provided for the purpose of this paragraph if the requirements of Section 13104 are satisfied.

(c) The financial institution has no duty to inquire into the truth of any statement, declaration, certificate, affidavit, or document offered as proof of the decedent's death or proof of identity of the person seeking access.

(d) When the person seeking access has satisfied the requirements of subdivision (b), the financial institution shall do all of the following:

(1) Keep a record of the identity of the person.

(2) Permit the person to open the safe deposit box under the supervision of an officer or employee of the financial institution, and to make an inventory of its contents.

(3) Make a photocopy of all wills and trust instruments removed from the safe deposit box, and keep the photocopy in the safe deposit box until the contents of the box are removed by the personal representative of the estate or other legally authorized person. The financial institution may charge the person given access a reasonable fee for photocopying.

(4) Permit the person given access to remove instructions for the disposition of the decedent's remains, and, after a photocopy is made, to remove the wills and trust instruments.

(e) The person given access shall deliver all wills found in the safe deposit box to the clerk of the superior court and mail or deliver a copy to the person named in the will as executor or beneficiary as provided in Section 8200.

(f) Except as provided in subdivision (d), the person given access shall not remove any of the contents of the decedent's safe deposit box.

(Stats. 1991 (S.B. 271), ch. 1055, §15.)

§8200. Duties and liability of custodian of will

(a) Unless a petition for probate of the will is earlier filed, the custodian of a will shall, within 30 days after having knowledge of the death of the testator, do both of the following:

(1) Deliver the will to the clerk of the superior court of the county in which the estate of the decedent may be administered. No fee shall be charged for compliance with the requirement of this paragraph.

(2) Mail a copy of the will to the person named in the will as executor, if the person's whereabouts is known to the custodian, or if not, to a person named in the will as a beneficiary, if the person's whereabouts is known to the custodian.

(b) A custodian of a will who fails to comply with the requirements of this section is liable for all damages sustained by any person injured by the failure.

(c) The clerk shall release a copy of a will delivered under this section for attachment to a petition for probate of the will or otherwise on receipt of payment of the required fee and either a court order for production of the will or a certified copy of a death certificate of the decedent.

(Stats. 1990 (A.B. 759), ch. 79, §14, effective July 1, 1991. Amended by Stats. 1994 (A.B. 3686), ch. 806, §25.)

§8201. Court shall order production of will

If, on petition to the superior court of the county in which the estate of the decedent is being or may be administered alleging that a person has possession of a decedent's will, the court is satisfied that the allegation is true, the court shall order the person to produce the will.

(Stats. 1990 (A.B. 759), ch. 79, §14, effective July 1, 1991.)

§8202. Court may admit certified copy of will detained in court of other state or country

If the will of a person who was domiciled in this state at the time of death is detained in a court of any other state or country and cannot be produced for probate in this state, a certified photographic copy of the will may be admitted to probate in this state with the same force and effect as the original will. The same proof shall be required as if the original will were produced.

(Stats. 1990 (A.B. 759), ch. 79, §14, effective July 1, 1991.)

§8203. Court may order transfer of wills between counties

If a will has been delivered to the clerk of the superior court in a county in which no proceeding is pending to administer the testator's estate, that court may order the will transferred to the clerk of the superior court in a county in which such a proceeding is pending. A petition for the transfer may be presented and heard without notice, but shall not be granted without proof that a copy of the petition has been mailed to the petitioner and any persons who have requested special notice in the proceeding in the court to which the will is to be transferred. The petition and order shall include the case number of the proceeding in the court to which transfer is prayed. Certified copies of the petition, any supporting documents, and the order shall be transmitted by the clerk along with the original will, and these copies shall be filed in the proceeding by the clerk of the recipient court.

(Stats. 1992 (A.B. 2975), ch. 871, §10.)

B. Attorney's Duties Regarding Safekeeping of Estate Planning Documents

An attorney has certain duties regarding the safekeeping of estate planning documents (wills, trusts and trust amendments, powers of attorney, nomination of conservator, etc.). Such duties are specified in California Probate Code §§700 et seq. Attorneys who safeguard wills and

other estate planning documents must use "ordinary care" to preserve such documents (Cal. Prob. Code §710). The standard of care is reduced to "slight care" if: the attorney has informed the client (with proper notice and acknowledgment by the client, pursuant to Cal. Prob. Code §715) of the need to keep the attorney informed as to changes of address, the attorney has mailed a reclamation notice to the client, and the client fails to reclaim the document (Cal. Prob. Code §716).

§700. Applicability of chapter

Unless the provision or context otherwise requires, the definitions in this chapter govern the construction of this part.

(Stats. 1993 (A.B. 209), ch. 519, §4.)

§701. "Attorney," defined

"Attorney" means an individual licensed to practice law in this state.

(Stats. 1993 (A.B. 209), ch. 519, §4.)

702. "Deposit," defined

"Deposit" means delivery of a document by a depositor to an attorney for safekeeping or authorization by a depositor for an attorney to retain a document for safekeeping.

(Stats. 1993 (A.B. 209), ch. 519, §4.)

§703. "Depositor," defined

"Depositor" means a natural person who deposits the person's document with an attorney.

(Stats. 1993 (A.B. 209), ch. 519, §4.)

§704. "Document," defined

"Document" means any of the following:

(a) A signed original will, declaration of trust, trust amendment, or other document modifying a will or trust.

(b) A signed original power of attorney.

(c) A signed original nomination of conservator.

(d) Any other signed original instrument that the attorney and depositor agree in writing to make subject to this part.

(Stats. 1993 (A.B. 209), ch. 519, §4.)

§710. Ordinary duty of care for safekeeping of documents; places of safekeeping

If a document is deposited with an attorney, the attorney, and a successor attorney that accepts transfer of the document, shall use ordinary care for preservation of the document on and after July 1, 1994, whether or not consideration is given, and shall hold the document in a safe, vault, safe deposit box, or other secure place where it will be reasonably protected against loss or destruction.

(Stats. 1993 (A.B. 209), ch. 519, §4.)

§711. Attorney shall give notice of loss if document is lost or destroyed; methods of giving notice

If a document deposited with an attorney is lost or destroyed, the attorney shall give notice of the loss or destruction to the depositor by one of the following methods:

(a) By mailing the notice to the depositor's last known address.

(b) By the method most likely to give the depositor actual notice.

(Stats. 1993 (A.B. 209), ch. 519, §4.)

§712. Attorney's liability for loss or destruction of documents

Notwithstanding failure of an attorney to satisfy the standard of care required by Section 710 or 716, the attorney is not liable for loss or destruction of the document if the depositor has actual notice of the loss or destruction and a reasonable opportunity to replace the document, and the attorney offers without charge either to assist the depositor in replacing the document, or to prepare a substantially similar document and assist in its execution.

(Stats. 1993 (A.B. 209), ch. 519, §4.)

§713. Responsibilities of attorney who accepts document for deposit

The acceptance by an attorney of a document for deposit imposes no duty on the attorney to do either of the following:

(a) Inquire into the content, validity, invalidity, or completeness of the document, or the correctness of any information in the document.

(b) Provide continuing legal services to the depositor or to any beneficiary under the document. This subdivision does not affect the duty, if any, of the drafter of the document to provide continuing legal services to any person.

(Stats. 1993 (A.B. 209), ch. 519, §4.)

§714. Attorney may charge expenses for safekeeping of documents

(a) If so provided in a written agreement signed by the depositor, an attorney may charge the depositor for compensation and expenses incurred in safekeeping or delivery of a document deposited with the attorney.

(b) No lien arises for the benefit of an attorney on a document deposited with the attorney, whether before or after its transfer, even if provided by agreement.
(Stats. 1993 (A.B. 209), ch. 519, §4.)

§715. Form of written notice to depositor

An attorney may give written notice to a depositor, and obtain written acknowledgment from the depositor, in the following form:

NOTICE AND ACKNOWLEDGMENT

To: ______________________________
(Name of depositor)

____
(Address)

____
(City, state, and ZIP)

I have accepted your will or other estate planning document for safekeeping. I must use ordinary care for preservation of the document.

You must keep me advised of any change in your address shown above. If you do not and I cannot return this document to you when necessary, I will no longer be required to use ordinary care for preservation of the document, and I may transfer it to another attorney, or I may transfer it to the clerk of the superior court of the county of your last known domicile, and give notice of the transfer to the State Bar of California.

____
(Signature of attorney)

____
(Address of attorney)

____
(City, state, ZIP)

My address shown above is correct. I understand that I must keep you advised of any change in this address.

Dated: ____________ ______________________________
(Signature of depositor)

(Stats. 1993 (A.B. 209), ch. 519, §4.)

§716. Cases involving minimal duty of care by attorney

Notwithstanding Section 710, if an attorney has given written notice to the depositor, and has obtained written acknowledgment from the depositor, in substantially the form provided in Section 715, and the requirements of subdivision (a) of Section 732 are satisfied, the attorney, and a successor attorney that accepts transfer of a document, shall use at least slight care for preservation of a document deposited with the attorney.
(Stats. 1993 (A.B. 209), ch. 519, §4.)

§720. Depositor may terminate deposit

A depositor may terminate a deposit on demand, in which case the attorney shall deliver the document to the depositor.
(Stats. 1993 (A.B. 209), ch. 519, §4.)

§730. Attorney may terminate deposit

An attorney with whom a document has been deposited, or to whom a document has been transferred pursuant to this article, may terminate the deposit only as provided in this article.
(Stats. 1993 (A.B. 209), ch. 519, §4.)

§731. Methods of termination of deposit by attorney

An attorney may terminate the deposit by one of the following methods:

(a) Personal delivery of the document to the depositor.

(b) Mailing the document to the depositor's last known address, by registered or certified mail with return receipt requested, and receiving a signed receipt.

(c) The method agreed on by the depositor and attorney.
(Stats. 1993 (A.B. 209), ch. 519, §4.)

§732. Methods of terminating deposit by transfer

(a) An attorney may terminate a deposit under this section if the attorney has mailed notice to reclaim the document to the depositor's last known address and the depositor has failed to reclaim the document within 90 days after the mailing.

(b) Subject to subdivision (f), an attorney may terminate a deposit under this section by transferring the document to another attorney. All documents transferred under this subdivision shall be transferred to the same attorney.

(c) Subject to subdivision (f), if an attorney is deceased, lacks legal capacity, or is no longer an active member of the State Bar, a deposit may be terminated under this section by transferring the document to the clerk of the superior court of the county of the depositor's last known domicile. The attorney shall advise the clerk that the document is being transferred pursuant to Section 732.

(d) An attorney may not accept a fee or compensation from a transferee for transferring a document under this section. An attorney may charge a fee for receiving a document under this section.

(e) Transfer of a document by an attorney under this section is not a waiver or breach of any privilege or confidentiality associated with the document, and is not a violation of the rules of professional conduct. If the document is privileged under Article 3 (commencing with Section 950) of Chapter 4 of Division 8 of the Evidence Code, the document remains privileged after the transfer.

(f) If the document is a will and the attorney has actual notice that the depositor has died, the attorney may terminate a deposit only as provided in Section 734.

(Stats. 1993 (A.B. 209), ch. 519, §4.)

§733. Attorney shall give notice of transfer of documents to State Bar

(a) An attorney transferring one or more documents under Section 732 shall mail notice of the transfer to the State Bar of California. The notice shall contain all of the following information:

(1) The name of the depositor.

(2) The date of the transfer.

(3) The name, address, and State Bar number of the transferring attorney.

(4) Whether any documents are transferred to an attorney, and the name, address, and State Bar number of the attorney to whom the documents are transferred.

(5) Whether any documents are transferred to a superior court clerk.

(b) The State Bar shall record only one notice of transfer for each transferring attorney. The State Bar shall prescribe the form for the notice of transfer. On request by any person, the State Bar shall give that person information in the notice of transfer. At its sole election, the State Bar may give the information orally or in writing.

(Stats. 1993 (A.B. 209), ch. 519, §4.)

§734. Attorney may terminate deposit after death of depositor by delivery to decedent's personal representative

(a) In cases not governed by subdivision (b) or (c), after the death of the depositor an attorney may terminate a deposit by personal delivery of the document to the depositor's personal representative.

(b) If the document is a will and the attorney has actual notice that the depositor has died but does not have actual notice that a personal representative has been appointed for the depositor, an attorney may terminate a deposit only as provided in Section 8200.

(c) If the document is a trust, after the death of the depositor an attorney may terminate a deposit by personal delivery of the document either to the depositor's personal representative or to the trustee named in the document.

(Stats. 1993 (A.B. 209), ch. 519, §4.)

§735. Attorney's law partner may terminate deposit of document after death or lack of legal capacity of attorney

(a) If the attorney is deceased or lacks legal capacity, a deposit may be terminated as provided in this article by the attorney's law partner, by a shareholder of the attorney's law corporation, or by a lawyer or nonlawyer employee of the attorney's firm, partnership, or corporation.

(b) If the attorney lacks legal capacity and there is no person to act under subdivision (a), a deposit may be terminated by the conservator of the attorney's estate or by an attorney in fact acting under a durable power of attorney. A conservator of the attorney's estate may act without court approval.

(c) If the attorney is deceased and there is no person to act under subdivision (a), a deposit may be terminated by the attorney's personal representative.

(d) If a person authorized under this section terminates a deposit as provided in Section 732, the person shall give the notice required by Section 733.

(Stats. 1993 (A.B. 209), ch. 519, §4.)

C. Proof of Will

California law specifies that a will may be admitted to probate based on the testimony of only one of the subscribing witnesses (Cal. Prob. Code §8220) if the proceeding is uncontested. Alternatively, the court may admit evidence by either affidavit of the subscribing witness to which is attached a photographic copy of the will, or else by an affidavit in the original will that includes or incorporates an attestation clause. The latter affidavit, based on the UPC provision, is called a "self-proving will." On self-proving wills, see generally Chapter III, Section II L *supra*.

If no subscribing witness is available ("availability" is determined according to the meaning of California Evidence Code §240), the court may permit proof of the will by proof of the testator's handwriting plus: (1) the handwriting of one of the subscribing witnesses *or* (2) receipt in evidence of *either* a writing in the will bearing the signatures of all the subscribing witnesses *or* else an affidavit of a person with personal

knowledge of the circumstances surrounding the will execution (Cal. Prob. Code §8221).

§8220. Will may be proved on evidence of one subscribing witness or affidavit or deposition

Unless there is a contest of a will:

(a) The will may be proved on the evidence of one of the subscribing witnesses only, if the evidence shows that the will was executed in all particulars as prescribed by law.

(b) Evidence of execution of a will may be received by an affidavit of a subscribing witness to which there is attached a photographic copy of the will, or by an affidavit in the original will that includes or incorporates the attestation clause.

(c) If no subscribing witness resides in the county, but the deposition of a witness can be taken elsewhere, the court may direct the deposition to be taken. On the examination, the court may authorize a photographic copy of the will to be made and presented to the witness, and the witness may be asked the same questions with respect to the photographic copy as if the original will were present.

(Stats. 1990 (A.B. 759), ch. 79, §14, effective July 1, 1991.)

§8221. Court may permit proof of testator's handwriting plus other evidence if subscribing witness unavailable

If no subscribing witness is available as a witness within the meaning of Section 240 of the Evidence Code, the court may, if the will on its face conforms to all requirements of law, permit proof of the will by proof of the handwriting of the testator and one of the following:

(a) Proof of the handwriting of any one subscribing witness.

(b) Receipt in evidence of one of the following documents reciting facts showing due execution of the will:

(1) A writing in the will bearing the signatures of all subscribing witnesses.

(2) An affidavit of a person with personal knowledge of the circumstances of the execution.

(Stats. 1990 (A.B. 759), ch. 79, §14, effective July 1, 1991.)

§8222. Proof of holographic will

A holographic will may be proved in the same manner as other writings.

(Stats. 1990 (A.B. 759), ch. 79, §14, effective July 1, 1991.)

§8223. Proof of lost or destroyed will

The petition for probate of a lost or destroyed will shall include a written statement of the testamentary words or their substance. If the will is proved, the provisions of the will shall be set forth in the order admitting the will to probate.

(Stats. 1990 (A.B. 759), ch. 79, §14, effective July 1, 1991.)

§8224. Preserving witness's testimony by reduction to writing

The testimony of each witness in a proceeding concerning the execution or provisions of a will, the testamentary capacity of the decedent, and other issues of fact, may be reduced to writing, signed by the witness, and filed, whether or not the will is contested. The testimony so preserved, or an official reporter's transcript of the testimony, is admissible in evidence in any subsequent proceeding concerning the will if the witness has become unavailable as a witness within the meaning of Section 240 of the Evidence Code.

(Stats. 1990 (A.B. 759), ch. 79, §14, effective July 1, 1991.)

§8225. Clerk shall record admission of will to probate; filing of will

When the court admits a will to probate, that fact shall be recorded in the minutes by the clerk and the will shall be filed.

(Stats. 1990 (A.B. 759), ch. 79, §14, effective July 1, 1991.)

§8226. Conclusiveness of admission of will to probate

(a) If no person contests the validity of a will or petitions for revocation of probate of the will within the time provided in this chapter, admission of the will to probate is conclusive, subject to Section 8007.

(b) Subject to subdivision (c), a will may be admitted to probate notwithstanding prior admission to probate of another will or prior distribution of property in the proceeding. The will may not affect property previously distributed, but the court may determine how any provision of the will affects property not yet distributed and how any provision of the will affects provisions of another will.

(c) If the proponent of a will has received notice of a petition for probate or a petition for letters of administration for a general personal representative, the proponent of the will may petition for probate of the will only within the later of either of the following time periods:

(1) One hundred twenty days after issuance of the order admitting the first will to probate or determining the decedent to be intestate.

(2) Sixty days after the proponent of the will first obtains knowledge of the will.

(Stats. 1990 (A.B. 759), ch. 79, §14, effective July 1, 1991. Amended by Stats. 1997 (A.B. 1172), ch. 724, §19.)

CALIFORNIA EVIDENCE CODE

§240. "Unavailable as a witness," defined

(a) Except as otherwise provided in subdivision (b), "unavailable as a witness" means that the declarant is any of the following:

(1) Exempted or precluded on the ground of privilege from testifying concerning the matter to which his or her statement is relevant.

(2) Disqualified from testifying to the matter.

(3) Dead or unable to attend or to testify at the hearing because of then existing physical or mental illness or infirmity.

(4) Absent from the hearing and the court is unable to compel his or her attendance by its process.

(5) Absent from the hearing and the proponent of his or her statement has exercised reasonable diligence but has been unable to procure his or her attendance by the court's process.

(b) A declarant is not unavailable as a witness if the exemption, preclusion, disqualification, death, inability, or absence of the declarant was brought about by the procurement or wrongdoing of the proponent of his or her statement for the purpose of preventing the declarant from attending or testifying.

(c) Expert testimony which establishes that physical or mental trauma resulting from an alleged crime has caused harm to a witness of sufficient severity that the witness is physically unable to testify or is unable to testify without suffering substantial trauma may constitute a sufficient showing of unavailability pursuant to paragraph (3) of subdivision (a). As used in this section, the term "expert" means a physician and surgeon, including a psychiatrist, or any person described by subdivision (b), (c), or (e) of Section 1010.

The introduction of evidence to establish the unavailability of a witness under this subdivision shall not be deemed procurement of unavailability, in absence of proof to the contrary.

(Stats. 1965, ch. 299, §2, effective January 1, 1967. Amended by Stats. 1984, ch. 401, §1; Stats. 1988, ch. 485, §1.)

D. Contest of Will

California Probate Code §§8250 et seq. specify the procedure for filing an objection to probate of the will. A will contest is a challenge to the validity of a decedent's will. Such a challenge may occur either before or after admission of the will to probate: if before admission, to preclude admission of the will to probate (Cal. Prob. Code §§8250-8254) or, if after admission, to revoke probate (Cal. Prob. Code §§8270-8272).

The Code specifies the applicable burden of proof: proponents of the will have the burden of proof of due execution; contestants have the burden of proof of lack of testamentary intent or capacity or revocation (Cal. Prob. Code §8252). There is no right to a jury trial, in general, in the probate court (Cal. Prob. Code §825) or, specifically for will contests (Cal. Prob. Code §8252(b)). See Ross & Grant, Cal. Prob. Prac., *supra,* at §15:229. On the right to jury trial generally in probate matters, see also Chapter IV, Section V, *supra*.

Several statutory restrictions apply to will contests. Provisions regulate the persons who may bring such contests, the grounds for a contest, and the time within which the petitioner must commence the action. Any interested party may contest a will (Cal. Prob. Code §§1043, 8004(b), 8270(a)). The term "interested party" is defined as the spouse, children, heirs, beneficiaries, and creditors of the decedent, as well as any other person having a property right in or claim against a trust or estate (Cal. Prob. Code §48(a)). Case law requires that the interested party have "such a pecuniary interest in the devolution of the testator's estate as would be impaired or defeated by the probate of the will or be benefited by setting it aside" (Estate of Weber, 280 Cal. Rptr. 22, 25 (Ct. App. 1991) (citing Estate of Marler, 306 P.2d 105 (Cal. Ct. App. 1957)). That is, a will contestant must show that his or her share of the distribution would be increased if the contest is successful. In *Weber*, a mother's will contained a residuary clause that divided her assets equally between her son and daughter. The court dismissed the son's will contest, saying that "Even if Jack were successful in challenging the will, the result would be the same. Because Sonya [mother] left no surviving spouse, her estate would be divided between her children, Ruth and Jack. (§6402, subd. (a).) Thus, it would appear Jack cannot benefit by pursuing the will contest." *Weber*, 280 Cal. Rptr. at 23 n4.

Beneficiaries under an earlier will (whose interests are impaired by a later will) have

standing to contest a later will. Similarly, beneficiaries under a later will (whose rights may be impaired by probate of an earlier will) have standing to contest probate of the earlier will. Ross & Grant, Cal. Prob. Prac., *supra*, at §15:34.

An executor who is appointed as a personal representative has an obligation to defend the will against contests (Cal. Prob. Code §8250(b)).

Will contests generally are disfavored by the law. "This attitude is evidenced by rigid evidentiary requirements, the relatively low percentage of contests that prevail, and the 1988 Code revisions eliminating the right to a jury trial." Ross & Grant, Cal. Prob. Prac., *supra,* at §15:81.

The Probate Code also governs the law applicable to no-contest clauses (will provisions that penalize an heir or beneficiary who brings an unsuccessful challenge to a will) (Cal. Prob. Code §§21300-21308). Whether an action is a "contest" within the meaning of a particular no-contest clause depends upon the circumstances of the particular case and the language used (Cal. Prob. Code §21300).

Beginning in 2000, the California legislature evidenced its dissatisfaction with no-contest clauses by amending applicable law with the addition of California Probate Code §21305, which required for the first time that certain enumerated actions be expressly identified in the no-contest clause as violations to constitute a contest. In 2002, the legislature further restricted the application of no-contest clauses (Stats. 2000, ch. 150, §2). The California Law Revision Commission is presently considering further reform of the enforcement of no-contest clauses with its recommendation of proposed California Probate Code §§21333 and 21335 to make such clauses unenforceable, effective January 1, 2010. As this book goes to press, the proposal is still under consideration. See Minutes of Meeting, California Law Revision Commission, Sacramento, CA, April 26, 2007, p. 6.

A beneficiary may apply for a determination of whether a proposed action would constitute a contest under the no-contest clause of a decedent's will (Cal. Prob. Code §21320). This statute is called a "safe harbor provision" and the proceeding is referred to as a "safe harbor proceeding." To illustrate, in Estate of Kaila, 94 Cal. App. 4th 1122 (2001), a beneficiary petitioned for a determination of whether her proposed action to enforce an alleged domestic partnership agreement between herself and the (male) testator would be a contest under the no-contest clause of a will. After the trial court denied her petition, the appellate court reversed and remanded, holding that extrinsic evidence was admissible to interpret the no-contest clause (i.e., whether it was intended to apply to her) and that the admission of extrinsic evidence to interpret the clause did not preclude a safe harbor proceeding. However, in the unlikely event that the merits of the proposed action had to be reached on remand, the safe harbor protection would be lost.

See also In re Estate of Rossi, 42 Cal. Rptr. 3d 244 (Ct. App. 2006) (holding that son's proposed challenge to an amendment to his father's will on the ground of undue influence did not violate the no-contest clauses of his father's will and trust); Zwirn v. Schweizer, 36 Cal. Rptr. 3d 527 (Ct. App. 2005) (holding that beneficiary's effort to enforce oral contract between decedent and her husband was not within the creditor's claim exception to Probate Code §21305, and therefore constituted a contest that violated the no-contest clause).

No-contest clauses are not enforceable against a beneficiary who brings (with reasonable cause) a contest on grounds of forgery and/or revocation of the instrument (Cal. Prob. Code §21306), and who brings (with probable cause) a contest of a provision benefiting a person who drafted or transcribed the will or other instrument (Cal. Prob. Code §21307) or who gave directions to the draftsperson concerning dispositive or other substantive contents of the provision or directed inclusion of the no-contest clause in the instrument (unless the decedent instructed the inclusion of the provision) (*id.*) or acted as a witness to the will or other instrument (*id.*).

In addition (as explained above), certain actions are statutorily excluded as will contests, unless the no-contest clause provides otherwise: filing a creditor's claim, an action to determine the character (separate, community, etc.) of property, challenging the validity of an instrument other than the instrument containing

the no-contest clause, or a petition for settlement or compromise affecting the terms of the instrument containing the no-contest clause (Cal. Prob. Code §21305(a)).

If a will contest succeeds, the no-contest clause falls. A contestant who is barred from challenging the will by virtue of a no-contest clause may have other remedies. Such remedies include a proceeding to determine distribution rights (Cal. Prob. Code §§11700 et seq.); an action to specifically enforce decedent's contract; a proceeding to determine adverse claims to title or possession (Cal. Prob. Code §850); an action on a contract to make a particular will or devise; or objections to accounting and distribution (Cal. Prob. Code §§11600 et seq.). Ross & Grant, Cal. Prob. Prac., *supra*, §§14:106, 15:3.

On will contests, see also Chapter IV *supra* on testamentary capacity.

CALIFORNIA PROBATE CODE

§48. "Interested person," defined

(a) Subject to subdivision (b), "interested person" includes any of the following:

(1) An heir, devisee, child, spouse, creditor, beneficiary, and any other person having a property right in or claim against a trust estate or the estate of a decedent which may be affected by the proceeding.

(2) Any person having priority for appointment as personal representative.

(3) A fiduciary representing an interested person.

(b) The meaning of "interested person" as it relates to particular persons may vary from time to time and shall be determined according to the particular purposes of, and matter involved in, any proceeding.

(Stats. 1990, ch. 79, §14 (A.B. 759), effective July 1, 1991.)

§8250. Will contestant shall file objection to probate; procedure; executor's duty to defend

(a) When a will is contested under Section 8004, the contestant shall file with the court an objection to probate of the will. Thereafter, a summons shall be issued and served, with a copy of the objection, on the persons required by Section 8110 to be served with notice of hearing of a petition for administration of the decedent's estate. The summons shall be issued and served as provided in Chapter 4 (commencing with Section 413.10) of Title 5 of Part 2 of the Code of Civil Procedure. The summons shall contain a direction that the persons summoned file with the court a written pleading in response to the contest within 30 days after service of the summons.

(b) A person named as executor in the will is under no duty to defend a contest until the person is appointed personal representative.

(Stats. 1990 (A.B. 759), ch. 79, §14, effective July 1, 1991. Amended by Stats. 1998 (A.B. 2801), ch. 581, §24.)

§8251. Answer and demurrer; failure to respond in timely fashion to summons

(a) The petitioner and any other interested person may jointly or separately answer the objection or demur to the objection within the time prescribed in the summons.

(b) Demurrer may be made on any of the grounds of demurrer available in a civil action. If the demurrer is sustained, the court may allow the contestant a reasonable time, not exceeding 15 days, within which to amend the objection. If the demurrer is overruled, the petitioner and other interested persons may, within 15 days thereafter, answer the objection.

(c) If a person fails timely to respond to the summons:

(1) The case is at issue notwithstanding the failure and the case may proceed on the petition and other documents filed by the time of the hearing, and no further pleadings by other persons are necessary.

(2) The person may not participate further in the contest, but the person's interest in the estate is not otherwise affected. Nothing in this paragraph precludes further participation by the petitioner.

(3) The person is bound by the decision in the proceeding.

(Stats. 1990 (A.B. 759), ch. 79, §14, effective July 1, 1991.)

§8252. Proponents of will have burden of proof of due execution; contestants have burden of proof of lack of testamentary capacity or revocation

(a) At the trial, the proponents of the will have the burden of proof of due execution. The contestants of the will have the burden of proof of lack of testamentary intent or capacity, undue influence, fraud, duress, mistake, or revocation. If the will is opposed by the petition for probate of a later will revoking the former, it shall be determined first whether the later will is entitled to probate.

(b) The court shall try and determine any contested issue of fact that affects the validity of the will.

(Stats. 1990 (A.B. 759), ch. 79, §14, effective July 1, 1991.)

§8253. Production and examination of subscribing witnesses

At the trial, each subscribing witness shall be produced and examined. If no subscribing witness is available as a witness within the meaning of Section 240 of the Evidence Code, the court may admit the evidence of other witnesses to prove the due execution of the will.

(Stats. 1990 (A.B. 759), ch. 79, §14, effective July 1, 1991.)

§8254. Court may make appropriate orders admitting or rejecting will

The court may make appropriate orders, including orders sustaining or denying objections, and shall render judgment either admitting the will to probate or rejecting it, in whole or in part, and appointing a personal representative.

(Stats. 1990 (A.B. 759), ch. 79, §14, effective July 1, 1991.)

§21300. Definitions applicable to no contest clauses

As used in this part:

(a) "Contest" means any action identified in a "no contest clause" as a violation of the clause. The term includes both direct and indirect contests.

(b) "Direct contest" in an instrument or in this chapter means a pleading in a proceeding in any court alleging the invalidity of an instrument or one or more of its terms based on one or more of the following grounds:

(1) Revocation.

(2) Lack of capacity.

(3) Fraud.

(4) Misrepresentation.

(5) Menace.

(6) Duress.

(7) Undue influence.

(8) Mistake.

(9) Lack of due execution.

(10) Forgery.

(c) "Indirect contest" means a pleading in a proceeding in any court that indirectly challenges the validity of an instrument or one or more of its terms based on any other ground not contained in subdivision (b), and that does not contain any of those grounds.

(d) "No contest clause" means a provision in an otherwise valid instrument that, if enforced, would penalize a beneficiary if the beneficiary files a contest with the court.

(Stats. 1990 (A.B. 759), ch. 79, §14, effective July 1, 1991. Amended by Stats. 2002 (S.B. 1878), ch. 150, §1.)

§21301. Common law also governs enforcement of no contest clauses

This part is not intended as a complete codification of the law governing enforcement of a no contest clause. The common law governs enforcement of a no contest clause to the extent this part does not apply.

(Stats. 1990 (A.B. 759), ch. 79, §14, effective July 1, 1991.)

§21302. Contrary provision in instrument is inapplicable

This part applies notwithstanding a contrary provision in the instrument.

(Stats. 1990 (A.B. 759), ch. 79, §14, effective July 1, 1991.)

§21303. No contest clause is enforceable against a contestant according to will

Except to the extent otherwise provided in this part, a no contest clause is enforceable against a beneficiary who brings a contest within the terms of the no contest clause.

(Stats. 1990 (A.B. 759), ch. 79, §14, operative July 1, 1991.)

§21304. No contest clauses shall be strictly construed

In determining the intent of the transferor, a no contest clause shall be strictly construed.

(Stats. 1990 (A.B. 759), ch. 79, §14, effective July 1, 1991.)

§21305. Certain actions do not constitute a contest

(a) For instruments executed on or after January 1, 2001, the following actions do not constitute a contest unless expressly identified in the no contest clause as a violation of the clause:

(1) The filing of a creditor's claim or prosecution of an action based upon it.

(2) An action or proceeding to determine the character, title, or ownership of property.

(3) A challenge to the validity of an instrument, contract, agreement, beneficiary designation, or other document, other than the instrument containing the no contest clause.

(b) Except as provided in subdivision (d), notwithstanding anything to the contrary in any instrument, the following proceedings do not violate a no contest clause as a matter of public policy:

(1) A pleading seeking relief under Chapter 3 (commencing with Section 15400) of Part 2 of Division 9.

(2) A pleading under Part 3 (commencing with Section 1800) of Division 4.

(3) A pleading under Part 2 (commencing with Section 4100) of Division 4.5.

(4) A pleading regarding an order annulling a marriage of the person who executed the instrument containing the no contest clause.

(5) A pleading pursuant to Section 2403.

(6) A pleading challenging the exercise of a fiduciary power.

(7) A pleading regarding the appointment of a fiduciary or the removal of a fiduciary.

(8) A pleading regarding an accounting or report of a fiduciary.

(9) A pleading regarding the interpretation of the instrument containing the no contest clause or an instrument or other document expressly identified in the no contest clause.

(10) A pleading regarding the approval of a settlement or compromise whether or not it affects the terms of an instrument.

(11) A pleading regarding the reformation of an instrument to carry out the intention of the person creating the instrument.

(12) A petition to compel an accounting or report of a fiduciary, if that accounting or report is not waived by the instrument. If the instrument waives an accounting or report of a fiduciary, a petition to determine if subdivision (a) of Section 16064 applies does not constitute a violation of a no contest clause.

(c) Subdivision (a) does not apply to a codicil or amendment to an instrument that was executed on or after January 1, 2001, unless the codicil or amendment adds a no contest clause or amends a no contest clause contained in an instrument executed before January 1, 2001.

(d) Subdivision (b) shall apply only to instruments of decedents dying on or after January 1, 2001, and to documents that become irrevocable on or after January 1, 2001. However, paragraphs (9), (11), and (12) of subdivision (b) shall only apply to instruments of decedents dying on or after January 1, 2003, and to documents that become irrevocable on or after January 1, 2003.

(e) The provisions of paragraphs (6), (9), and (11) of subdivision (b) do not apply if the court finds that the filing of the pleading is a direct contest of an instrument or any of its terms, as defined in Section 21300.

(f) The term "pleading" in subdivision (b) includes a petition, complaint, response, objection, or other document filed with the court that expresses the position of a party to the proceedings.

(Stats. 2000 (A.B. 1491), ch. 17, §5. Amended by Stats. 2002 (S.B. 1878), ch. 150, §2.)

§21306. No contest clauses are not enforceable for certain contests brought with reasonable cause

(a) A no contest clause is not enforceable against a beneficiary to the extent the beneficiary, with reasonable cause, brings a contest that is limited to one or more of the following grounds:

(1) Forgery.

(2) Revocation.

(3) An action to establish the invalidity of any transfer described in Section 21350.

(b) "Reasonable cause" is defined for the purposes of this section to mean that the party filing the action, proceeding, contest, or objections has possession of facts that would cause a reasonable person to believe that the allegations and other factual contentions in the matter filed with the court may be proven or, if specifically so identified, are likely to be proven after a reasonable opportunity for further investigation or discovery.

(Stats. 1990 (A.B. 759), ch. 79, §14, effective July 1, 1991. Amended by Stats. 1995 (A.B. 1466), ch. 730, §11; Stats. 2000 (A.B. 1491), ch. 17, §6.)

§21307. No contest clause is unenforceable if beneficiary contests a provision that benefits certain persons

A no contest clause is not enforceable against a beneficiary to the extent the beneficiary, with probable cause, contests a provision that benefits any of the following persons:

(a) A person who drafted or transcribed the instrument.

(b) A person who gave directions to the drafter of the instrument concerning dispositive or other substantive contents of the provision or who directed the drafter to include the no contest clause in the instrument, but this subdivision does not apply if the transferor affirmatively instructed the drafter to include the contents of the provision or the no contest clause.

(c) A person who acted as a witness to the instrument.

(Stats. 1990 (A.B. 759), ch. 79, §14, effective July 1, 1991.)

§21308. Statute of limitations

The statute of limitations for the commencement of any motion, petition, or other act referred to in subdivision (a) of Section 21320 shall be tolled beginning with the date the application for the court's determination under subdivision (a) of Section 21320 is made and ending with the date the court's determination becomes final.

(Stats. 1992 (A.B. 2975), ch. 871, §21.)

§21320. Beneficiary may apply to court for determination of whether an act constitutes a contest

(a) If an instrument containing a no contest clause is or has become irrevocable, a beneficiary may apply to the court for a determination of whether a particular motion, petition, or other act by the beneficiary, including, but not limited to, creditor claims under Part 4 (commencing with Section 9000) of Division 7, Part 8 (commencing with Section 19000) of Division 9, an action pursuant to Section 21305, and an action under Part 7 (commencing with Section 21700) of Division 11, would be a contest within the terms of the no contest clause.

(b) A no contest clause is not enforceable against a beneficiary to the extent an application under subdivision (a) is limited to the procedure and purpose described in subdivision (a).

(c) A determination under this section of whether a proposed motion, petition, or other act by the beneficiary violates a no contest clause may not be made if a determination of the merits of the motion, petition, or other act by the beneficiary is required.

(d) A determination of whether Section 21306 or 21307 would apply in a particular case may not be made under this section.

(Stats. 1990 (A.B. 759), ch. 79, §14, effective July 1, 1991. Amended by Stats. 1994 (A.B. 797), ch. 40, §3, effective January 1, 1995; Stats. 2000 (A.B. 1491), ch. 17, §7; Stats. 2002 (S.B. 1878), ch. 150, §3; Stats. 2004 (A.B. 3082) ch. 183, §282.)

§21321. Venue for proceedings pending for administration of transferor's estate and where no proceedings are pending

(a) If a proceeding is pending for administration of the transferor's estate, an application under Section 21320 shall be filed in the court in which the proceeding is pending.

(b) If no proceeding is pending for administration of the transferor's estate and the transferor is deceased, an application under Section 21320 may be filed in the superior court in any county in which administration of the transferor's estate would be proper or, if none, in any county in which property affected by the transfer is located or, if none, in any county in this state.

(c) If no proceeding is pending for administration of the transferor's estate and the transferor is living and resides in this state, an application under Section 21320 shall be filed in the superior court in the county in which the transferor resides.

(d) If no proceeding is pending for administration of the transferor's estate and the transferor is living but does not reside in this state, an application under Section 21320 may be filed in the superior court in the county in which property affected by the transfer is located or, if none, in any county in this state.

(e) Notwithstanding any other provision of this section, if the instrument containing the no contest clause is a trust, an application under Section 21320 shall be filed in the court having jurisdiction over the trust under Chapter 1 (commencing with Section 17000) of Part 5 of Division 9.

(Stats. 1990 (A.B. 759), ch. 79, §14, effective July 1, 1991.)

§ 21322. Notice if proceedings pending for administration of transferor's estate and if no proceedings are pending

(a) If a proceeding is pending for administration of the transferor's estate, notice of the hearing on an application under Section 21320 shall be given as provided in Section 1220 to all of the following persons:

(1) Each person listed in Section 1220.

(2) Each beneficiary named in the instrument containing the no contest clause whose interest could be adversely affected by the application.

(3) The Attorney General, if the instrument containing the no contest clause (A) involves or may involve a testamentary trust of property for charitable purposes other than a charitable trust with a designated trustee resident in this state or (B) involves or may involve a devise for charitable purposes without an identified devisee.

(b) If no proceeding is pending for administration of the transferor's estate, at least 30 days before the hearing on an application under Section 21320, the applicant shall serve notice of the hearing in the manner provided in Section 415.10 or 415.30 of the Code of Civil Procedure on all of the following persons:

(1) Each beneficiary named in the instrument containing the no contest clause whose interest could be affected by the application.

(2) Each executor, trustee, or other fiduciary named in the instrument containing the no contest clause.

(3) The Attorney General, if the instrument containing the no contest clause (A) involves or may involve a testamentary trust of property for charitable purposes other than a charitable trust with a designated trustee resident in this state or (B) involves or may involve a devise for charitable purposes without an identified devisee.

(Stats. 1990 (A.B. 759), ch. 79, §14, effective July 1, 1991.)

E. Revocation of Probate

Interested persons may petition the court to revoke the probate of a will (Cal. Prob. Code §8270). There is a statute of limitations on post probate contests. Petitioners have 120 days after admission of the will to probate in order to petition for revocation of probate (*id.*). Revocation of the probate of a will terminates the powers of the personal representative (Cal. Prob. Code §8272).

A person who was a party to a will contest filed before probate may not file a petition to revoke probate (Cal. Prob. Code §8270(a)). Similarly, a party who had actual notice of a preprobate will contest in time to have joined in that action may not file a petition to revoke probate (*id.*). An interested contestant who has notice of a pending preprobate contest should *intervene* in the pending contest rather than await the outcome of the proceeding while intending to bring a second contest. Ross & Grant, Cal. Prob. Prac., *supra*, at §15:47.

§8270. Time period to petition for revocation of probate

(a) Within 120 days after a will is admitted to probate, any interested person, other than a party to a will contest and other than a person who had actual notice of a will contest in time to have joined in the contest, may petition the court to revoke the probate of the will. The petition shall include objections setting forth written grounds of opposition.

(b) Notwithstanding subdivision (a), a person who was a minor or who was incompetent and had no guardian or conservator at the time a will was admitted to probate may petition the court to revoke the probate of the will at any time before entry of an order for final distribution.

(Stats. 1990 (A.B. 759), ch. 79, §14, effective July 1, 1991.)

§8271. Summons shall be directed to personal representative, heirs and devisees

(a) On the filing of the petition, a summons shall be directed to the personal representative and to the heirs and devisees of the decedent, so far as known to the petitioner. The summons shall contain a direction that the persons summoned file with the court a written pleading in response to the petition within 30 days after service of the summons. Failure of a person timely to respond to the summons precludes the person from further participation in the revocation proceeding, but does not otherwise affect the person's interest in the estate.

(b) The summons shall be issued and served with a copy of the petition and proceedings had as in the case of a contest of the will.

(c) If a person fails timely to respond to the summons:

(1) The case is at issue notwithstanding the failure and the case may proceed on the petition and other documents filed by the time of the hearing, and no further pleadings by other persons are necessary.

(2) The person may not participate further in the contest, but the person's interest in the estate is not otherwise affected.

(3) The person is bound by the decision in the proceeding.

(Stats. 1990 (A.B. 759), ch. 79, §14, effective July 1, 1991. Amended by Stats. 1998 (A.B. 2801), ch. 581, §25.)

§8272. Sufficiency of proof will lead to revocation of probate and termination of powers of personal representative

(a) If it appears on satisfactory proof that the will should be denied probate, the court shall revoke the probate of the will.

(b) Revocation of probate of a will terminates the powers of the personal representative. The personal representative is not liable for any otherwise proper act done in good faith before the revocation, nor is any transaction void by reason of the revocation if entered into with a third person dealing in good faith and for value.

(Stats. 1990 (A.B. 759), ch. 79, §14, effective July 1, 1991.)

IV. Appointment of Personal Representative

A. Types of Personal Representative

A personal representative is an officer of the court and acts in a fiduciary capacity. A personal representative who administers the estate of a decedent generally is one of the following: (1) an "executor" named by a decedent in his or her will, (2) an "administrator with the will annexed" (if no executor is named or none is willing or able to act), (3) an "administrator" if the decedent dies without a valid will, (4) a "special administrator" if required by an emergency, or (5) a public administrator if no personal representative is appointed and the decedent appears to have died without beneficiaries or heirs.

1. Executors

An executor who is named in the decedent's will has the right to be appointed personal representative unless he or she declines to act or is statutorily disqualified. Ross & Grant, Cal. Prob. Prac., *supra,* at §3:331.

A person is statutorily disqualified to act as personal representative if he or she is (1) a minor (Cal. Prob. Code §§8402, 8424); (2) an incompetent (i.e., "subject to a conservatorship of the estate or is otherwise incapable of executing, or is otherwise unfit to execute, the duties of the office")(Cal. Prob. Code §8402); (3) subject to removal under California Probate Code §8502 for misuse of funds, incapable of executing the duties of office, neglect of the estate, for the protection of the estate or interested persons, or any other cause provided by statute) *(id.)*; (4) a nonresident of the United States (*id.*); or (5) a surviving partner of the decedent if an interested person objects to the appointment (*id.*). (California Probate Code §8402 is set forth in Section B1 *infra.*)

By will, the testator also may nominate someone to designate an executor or co-executor, or successor executor or co-executor (Cal. Prob. Code §8422). If the testator names more than one person to serve as executor, the court may appoint fewer persons than those named (Cal. Prob. Code §8425).

Any interested person may challenge the appointment of an executor. Sometimes, the contestant may request that the court appoint the contestant instead as personal representative (by filing for letters of administration with the will annexed). The court considers such objections at the hearing for probate of the will (Cal Prob. Code §8004 *supra* in Section IIA).

A trust company may be appointed as a personal representative (Cal. Prob. Code §300). Bond is not generally required when a trust company is appointed as a personal representative (Cal. Prob. Code §301). A trust company also may be appointed as a trustee or as a guardian or conservator of an estate. However, a trust company may not be appointed as a guardian or conservator of the person (Cal. Prob. Code §300). Guardianship or conservatorship has two components: a guardian or conservator of the estate (involving financial affairs) and a guardian or conservator of the person (involving personal decisionmaking).

§300. Trust company may be appointed as personal representative, guardian of estate or trustee

A trust company may be appointed to act as a personal representative, guardian or conservator of an estate, or trustee, in the same manner as an individual. A trust company may not be appointed guardian or conservator of the person of a ward or conservatee.

(Stats. 1990 (A.B. 759), ch. 79, §14, effective July 1, 1991.)

§301. Bond may be waived for corporate fiduciary

(a) A trust company appointed to act as a personal representative, or guardian or conservator of an estate, may not be required to give a bond.

(b) The liability of a trust company and the manner of its making of oaths and affidavits are governed by Article 3 (commencing with Section 1540) of Chapter 12 of Division 1 of, and Section 1587 of, the Financial Code.

(Stats. 1990 (A.B. 759), ch. 79, §14, effective July 1, 1991.)

§8420. Executor has right to appointment as personal representative

The person named as executor in the decedent's will has the right to appointment as personal representative.

(Stats. 1990 (A.B. 759), ch. 79, §14, effective July 1, 1991.)

§8421. Person intended as executor by terms of will has right to appointment

If a person is not named as executor in a will but it appears by the terms of the will that the testator intended to commit the execution of the will and the administration of the estate to the person, the person is entitled to appointment as personal representative in the same manner as if named as executor.

(Stats. 1990 (A.B. 759), ch. 79, §14, effective July 1, 1991.)

§8422. Testator may confer a power by will to designate executor or coexecutor

(a) The testator may by will confer on a person the power to designate an executor or coexecutor, or successor executor or coexecutor. The will may provide that the persons so designated may serve without bond.

(b) A designation shall be in writing and filed with the court. Unless the will provides otherwise, if there are two or more holders of the power to designate, the designation shall be unanimous, unless one of the holders of the power is unable or unwilling to act, in which case the remaining holder or holders may exercise the power.

(c) Except as provided in this section, an executor does not have authority to name a coexecutor, or a successor executor or coexecutor.

(Stats. 1990 (A.B. 759), ch. 79, §14, effective July 1, 1991.)

§8423. Court may appoint successor trust company as executor

If the executor named in the will is a trust company that has sold its business and assets to, has consolidated or merged with, or is in any manner provided by law succeeded by, another trust company, the court may, and to the extent required by the Banking Law (Division 1 (commencing with Section 99) of the Financial Code) shall, appoint the successor trust company as executor.

(Stats. 1990 (A.B. 759), ch. 79, §14, effective July 1, 1991.)

§8424. Minor may not be named as executor

(a) If a person named as executor is under the age of majority and there is another person named as executor, the other person may be appointed and may administer the estate until the majority of the minor, who may then be appointed as coexecutor.

(b) If a person named as executor is under the age of majority and there is no other person named as executor, another person may be appointed as personal representative, but the court may revoke the appointment on the majority of the minor, who may then be appointed as executor.

(Stats. 1990 (A.B. 759), ch. 79, §14, effective July 1, 1991.)

§8425. Court may appoint fewer persons than those named in will as executors

If the court does not appoint all the persons named in the will as executors, those appointed have the same authority to act in every respect as all would have if appointed.

(Stats. 1990 (A.B. 759), ch. 79, §14, effective July 1, 1991.)

2. Administrators with the Will Annexed

An "administrator with the will annexed" is the personal representative who is appointed by the court in cases in which: (1) the decedent left a will but did not name an executor in the will, (2) the named executor does not desire to act, or (3) the named executor is unable to act (e.g., because of being incapacitated). This administrator is also called an "administrator CTA" (*cum testamento annexo*).

§8440. "Administrator with the will annexed," defined

An administrator with the will annexed shall be appointed as personal representative if no executor is named in the will or if the sole executor or all the executors named in the will have waived the right to appointment or are for any reason unwilling or unable to act.

(Stats. 1990 (A.B. 759), ch. 79, §14, effective July 1, 1991.)

§8441. Priority for appointment as administrator with the will annexed

(a) Except as provided in subdivision (b), persons and their nominees are entitled to appointment as administrator with the will annexed in the same order of priority as for appointment of an administrator.

(b) A person who takes under the will has priority over a person who does not, but the court in its discretion may give priority to a person who does not take under the will if the person is entitled to a statutory interest that is a substantially greater portion of the estate than the devise to the person who takes under the will and the priority appears appropriate under the circumstances. A person who takes more than 50 percent of the value of the estate under the will or the person's nominee, or the nominee of several persons who together take more than 50 percent of the value of the estate under the will, has priority over other persons who take under the will.

(Stats. 1990 (A.B. 759), ch. 79, §14, effective July 1, 1991.)

§8442. Administrator with the will annexed has same authority as executor

(a) Subject to subdivision (b), an administrator with the will annexed has the same authority over the decedent's estate as an executor named in the will would have.

(b) If the will confers a discretionary power or authority on an executor that is not conferred by law and the will does not extend the power or authority to other personal representatives, the power or authority shall not be deemed to be conferred on an administrator with the will annexed, but the court in its discretion may authorize the exercise of the power or authority.

(Stats. 1990 (A.B. 759), ch. 79, §14, effective July 1, 1991.)

3. Administrators

An administrator is the personal representative who is appointed to administer the estate of a decedent who dies intestate. Since 2001, a domestic partner has the same right as a surviving spouse to priority of appointment to administer the estate of a deceased partner (Cal. Prob. Code §§8461, 8462,

8465). The surviving spouse or domestic partner occupies the highest order of priority, followed by children, and then the grandchildren of the decedent (Cal. Prob. Code §8461(a), (b)).

Spouses and domestic partners retain their priority only if they are entitled either to succeed to all or part of the estate (Cal. Prob. Code §8462(a)) or to take by will or succession from another decedent entitled to succeed to all or part of the estate (Cal. Prob. Code §8462(b)). According to Probate Code section 8463, if a surviving spouse has initiated an action for legal separation, annulment, or dissolution and was living apart from the decedent at the time of death, the survivor loses his or her priority (Cal. Prob. Code §8463). Although section 8463 does not explicitly apply to domestic partners, the broad grant of equal rights and responsibilities to domestic partners in Family Code section 297.5 suggests that Probate Code section 8463 does, in fact, apply to domestic partners as well.

Two or more persons may have equal priority. For example, if the decedent had several children and died without a surviving spouse or domestic partner, the children would have equal priority. In such a case, the court can appoint one or more of the children as administrator(s). Alternatively, if the children disagree as to whom shall act, the court can appoint the public administrator or a disinterested person in the same or next lower priority class (Cal. Prob. Code §8467).

§8460. Administrator is personal representative of intestate decedent

(a) If the decedent dies intestate, the court shall appoint an administrator as personal representative.

(b) The court may appoint one or more persons as administrator.

(Stats. 1990 (A.B. 759), ch. 79, §14, effective July 1, 1991.)

§8461. Persons who may be appointed as administrator of decedent's estate

Subject to the provisions of this article, a person in the following relation to the decedent is entitled to appointment as administrator in the following order of priority:

(a) Surviving spouse or domestic partner as defined in Section 37.

(b) Children.

(c) Grandchildren.

(d) Other issue.

(e) Parents.

(f) Brothers and sisters.

(g) Issue of brothers and sisters.

(h) Grandparents.

(i) Issue of grandparents.

(j) Children of a predeceased spouse or domestic partner.

(k) Other issue of a predeceased spouse or domestic partner.

(l) Other next of kin.

(m) Parents of a predeceased spouse or domestic partner.

(n) Issue of parents of a predeceased spouse or domestic partner.

(o) Conservator or guardian of the estate acting in that capacity at the time of death who has filed a first account and is not acting as conservator or guardian for any other person.

(p) Public administrator.

(q) Creditors.

(r) Any other person.

(Stats. 1990 (A.B. 759), ch. 79, §14, effective July 1, 1991. Amended by Stats. 1990 (S.B. 1775), ch. 710, §20, effective July 1, 1991; Stats. 2001 (A.B. 25), ch. 893, §53.)

§8462. Conditions of priority for surviving spouse or domestic partner

The surviving spouse or domestic partner of the decedent, a relative of the decedent, or a relative of a predeceased spouse or domestic partner of the decedent, has priority under Section 8461 only if one of the following conditions is satisfied:

(a) The surviving spouse, domestic partner, or relative is entitled to succeed to all or part of the estate.

(b) The surviving spouse, domestic partner, or relative either takes under the will of, or is entitled to succeed to all or part of the estate of, another deceased person who is entitled to succeed to all or part of the estate of the decedent.

(Stats. 1990 (A.B. 759), ch. 79, §14, effective July 1, 1991. Amended by Stats. 2001 (A.B. 25), ch. 893, §54.)

§8463. Surviving spouse loses priority if living apart and party to action for separate maintenance, annulment, or dissolution

If the surviving spouse is a party to an action for separate maintenance, annulment, or dissolution of the marriage of the decedent and the surviving spouse, and was living apart from the decedent on the date of the decedent's death, the surviving spouse has priority next after brothers and sisters and not the priority prescribed in Section 8461.

(Stats. 1990 (A.B. 759), ch. 79, §14, effective July 1, 1991.)

§8464. Court may appoint guardian or conservator

If a person otherwise entitled to appointment as administrator is a person under the age of majority or a person for whom a guardian or conservator of the estate has been appointed, the court in its discretion may appoint the guardian or conservator or another person entitled to appointment.

(Stats. 1990 (A.B. 759), ch. 79, §14, effective July 1, 1991.)

§8465. Court may appoint nominee of person entitled to appointment

(a) The court may appoint as administrator a person nominated by a person otherwise entitled to appointment or by the guardian or conservator of the estate of a person otherwise entitled to appointment. The nomination shall be made in writing and filed with the court.

(b) If a person making a nomination for appointment of an administrator is the surviving spouse or domestic partner, child, grandchild, other issue, parent, brother or sister, or grandparent of the decedent, the nominee has priority next after those in the class of the person making the nomination.

(c) If a person making a nomination for appointment of an administrator is other than a person described in subdivision (b), the court in its discretion may appoint either the nominee or a person of a class lower in priority to that of the person making the nomination, but other persons of the class of the person making the nomination have priority over the nominee.

(Stats. 1990 (A.B. 759), ch. 79, §14, effective July 1, 1991. Amended by Stats. 2001 (A.B. 25), ch. 893, §55.)

§8466. Court may deny appointment of creditor

If a person whose only priority is that of a creditor claims appointment as administrator, the court in its discretion may deny the appointment and appoint another person.

(Stats. 1990 (A.B. 759), ch. 79, §14, effective July 1, 1991.)

§8467. Court discretion to appoint in case of equal priority

If several persons have equal priority for appointment as administrator, the court may appoint one or more of them, or if such persons are unable to agree, the court may appoint the public administrator or a disinterested person in the same or the next lower class of priority as the persons who are unable to agree.

(Stats. 1990 (A.B. 759), ch. 79, §14, effective July 1, 1991.)

§8468. Appointment in cases of failure to claim appointment as administrator

If persons having priority fail to claim appointment as administrator, the court may appoint any person who claims appointment.

(Stats. 1990 (A.B. 759), ch. 79, §14, effective July 1, 1991.)

§8469. Court may appoint conservator or guardian serving at time of death

(a) For good cause, the court may allow the priority given by Section 8461 to a conservator or guardian of the estate of the decedent serving in that capacity at the time of death that has not filed a first account, or that is acting as guardian or conservator for another person, or both.

(b) If the petition for appointment as administrator requests the court to allow the priority permitted by subdivision (a), the petitioner shall, in addition to the notice otherwise required by statute, serve notice of the hearing by mail or personal delivery on the public administrator.

(Stats. 1990 (S.B. 1775), ch. 710, §21, effective July 1, 1991.)

4. Special Administrators

A special administrator is the personal representative who is appointed by the court in special circumstances, such as when there is an immediate need for appointment of a representative (Cal. Prob. Code §8540). The special administrator is intended to act temporarily on behalf of the estate and often for limited purposes.

California Probate Code §8540 does not specify the specific grounds for appointment of a special administrator but merely provides for appointment if "the circumstances of the estate require the immediate appointment of a personal representative . . ." However, the need for a special administrator generally arises when (1) there are problems with issuance of letters testamentary or letters of administrator (e.g., letters have not yet issued, letters are defective, or have been revoked), or (2) when there is a vacancy in the office of a general personal representative (e.g., if the executor or administrator dies, resigns, or is removed or has his or her powers suspended), or (3) if there is a will contest pending. California Probate Code

provisions §§8540-8547 govern appointment of special administrators.

A court may grant the special administrator the same powers as a general personal representative (Cal. Prob. Code §8545). However, more commonly, a special administrator's authority is limited and restricted to situations giving rise to the need for special administration.

§8540. Circumstances may require immediate appointment

(a) If the circumstances of the estate require the immediate appointment of a personal representative, the court may appoint a special administrator to exercise any powers that may be appropriate under the circumstances for the preservation of the estate.

(b) The appointment may be for a specified term, to perform particular acts, or on any other terms specified in the court order.

(Stats. 1990 (A.B. 759), ch. 79, §14, effective July 1, 1991.)

§8541. Notice in case of appointment of special administrator

(a) Appointment of a special administrator may be made at any time without notice or on such notice to interested persons as the court deems reasonable.

(b) In making the appointment, the court shall ordinarily give preference to the person entitled to appointment as personal representative. The court may appoint the public administrator.

(c) In the case of an appointment to perform a particular act, request for approval of the act may be included in the petition for appointment, and approval may be made on the same notice and at the same time as the appointment.

(d) The court may act, if necessary, to remedy any errors made in the appointment.

(Stats. 1990 (A.B. 759), ch. 79, §14, effective July 1, 1991.)

§8542. Conditions for issuance of letters to special administrator

(a) The clerk shall issue letters to the special administrator after both of the following conditions are satisfied:

(1) The special administrator gives any bond that may be required by the court under Section 8480.

(2) The special administrator takes the usual oath attached to or endorsed on the letters.

(b) Subdivision (a) does not apply to the public administrator.

(c) The letters of a special administrator appointed to perform a particular act shall include a notation of the particular act the special administrator was appointed to perform.

(Stats. 1990 (A.B. 759), ch. 79, §14, effective July 1, 1991.)

§8543. Bond requirement may be waived if will or beneficiaries waive requirement

Subject to subdivision (b) of Section 8481, the court shall direct that no bond be given in either of the following cases:

(a) The will waives the requirement of a bond and the person named as executor in the will is appointed special administrator.

(b) All beneficiaries waive in writing the requirement of a bond and the written waivers are attached to the petition for appointment of the special administrator. This paragraph does not apply if the will requires a bond.

(Stats. 1990 (A.B. 759), ch. 79, §14, effective July 1, 1991.)

§8544. Powers of special administrator to perform particular acts

(a) Except to the extent the order appointing a special administrator prescribes terms, the special administrator has the power to do all of the following without further order of the court:

(1) Take possession of all of the real and personal property of the estate of the decedent and preserve it from damage, waste, and injury.

(2) Collect all claims, rents, and other income belonging to the estate.

(3) Commence and maintain or defend suits and other legal proceedings.

(4) Sell perishable property.

(b) Except to the extent the order prescribes terms, the special administrator has the power to do all of the following on order of the court:

(1) Borrow money, or lease, mortgage, or execute a deed of trust on real property, in the same manner as an administrator.

(2) Pay the interest due or all or any part of an obligation secured by a mortgage, lien, or deed of trust on property in the estate, where there is danger that the holder of the security may enforce or foreclose on the obligation and the property exceeds in value the amount of the obligation. This power may be ordered only on petition of the special administrator or any interested person, with any notice that the court deems proper, and shall remain in effect until appointment of a successor personal representative. The order may also direct that interest not yet accrued be paid as it becomes due, and the order shall remain in effect and cover the future interest unless and

until for good cause set aside or modified by the court in the same manner as for the original order.

(3) Exercise other powers that are conferred by order of the court.

(c) Except where the powers, duties, and obligations of a general personal representative are granted under Section 8545, the special administrator is not a proper party to an action on a claim against the decedent.

(d) A special administrator appointed to perform a particular act has no duty to take any other action to protect the estate.

(Stats. 1990 (A.B. 759), ch. 79, §14, effective July 1, 1991.)

§8545. Court may grant special administrator same powers as general personal representative

(a) Notwithstanding Section 8544, the court may grant a special administrator the same powers, duties, and obligations as a general personal representative where to do so appears proper. Notwithstanding Section 8541, if letters have not previously been issued to a general personal representative, the grant shall be on the same notice required under Section 8003 for appointment of a personal representative, unless the appointment is made at a hearing on a petition for appointment of a general personal representative and the notice of that petition required under Section 8003 has been given.

(b) Subject to Section 8543, the court may require as a condition of the grant that the special administrator give any additional bond that the court deems proper. From the time of approving and filing any required additional bond, the special administrator shall have the powers, duties, and obligations of a general personal representative.

(c) If a grant is made under this section, the letters shall recite that the special administrator has the powers, duties, and obligations of a general personal representative.

(Stats. 1990 (A.B. 759), ch. 79, §14, effective July 1, 1991. Amended by Stats. 1994 (A.B. 3686), ch. 806, §28.)

§8546. Powers of special administrator cease upon issuance of letters to general personal representative

(a) The powers of a special administrator cease on issuance of letters to a general personal representative or as otherwise directed by the court.

(b) The special administrator shall promptly deliver to the general personal representative:

(1) All property of the estate in the possession of the special administrator. The court may authorize the special administrator to complete a sale or other transaction affecting property in the possession of the special administrator.

(2) A list of all creditor claims of which the special administrator has knowledge. The list shall show the name and address of each creditor, the amount of the claim, and what action has been taken with respect to the claim. A copy of the list shall be filed in the court.

(c) The special administrator shall account in the same manner as a general personal representative is required to account. If the same person acts as both special administrator and general personal representative, the account of the special administrator may be combined with the first account of the general personal representative.

(Stats. 1990 (A.B. 759), ch. 79, §14, effective July 1, 1991.)

§8547. Court shall fix compensation of special administrator

(a) Subject to the limitations of this section, the court shall fix the compensation of the special administrator and the compensation of the attorney of the special administrator.

(b) The compensation of the special administrator shall not be allowed until the close of administration, unless the general personal representative joins in the petition for allowance of the special administrator's compensation or the court in its discretion so allows. Compensation for extraordinary services of a special administrator may be allowed on settlement of the final account of the special administrator. The total compensation paid to the special administrator and general personal representative shall not, together, exceed the sums provided in Part 7 (commencing with Section 10800) for compensation for the ordinary and extraordinary services of a personal representative. If the same person does not act as both special administrator and general personal representative, the compensation shall be divided in such proportions as the court determines to be just or as may be agreed to by the special administrator and general personal representative.

(c) The total compensation paid to the attorneys both of the special administrator and the general personal representative shall not, together, exceed the sums provided in Part 7 (commencing with Section 10800) as compensation for the ordinary and extraordinary services of attorneys for personal representatives. When the same attorney does not act for both the special administrator and general personal representative, the compensation shall be divided between the attorneys in such proportions as the court determines to be just or as agreed to by the attorneys.

(d) Compensation of an attorney for extraordinary services to a special administrator may be awarded in the same manner and subject to the same standards as for extraordinary services to a general personal representative, except that the award of compensation to the attorney may be made on settlement of the final account of the special administrator.

(Stats. 1990 (A.B. 759), ch. 79, §14, effective July 1, 1991. Amended by Stats. 1990 (S.B. 1775), ch. 710, §22, effective July 1, 1991.)

5. Public Administrators

The court may appoint a "public administrator" to administer an estate in some circumstances if no personal representative has been appointed. The need for a public administrator may arise if an estate "sits idle because no representative has been appointed and there are no known heirs." Ross & Grant, Cal. Prob. Prac., *supra*, at §2:24. In cases of small estates (if the value of the estate is less than $20,000), the public administrator may resort to procedures for summary disposition without the need for a court order (Cal. Prob. Code §7660(a)(2)).

The public administrator bears responsibility for paying the decedent's debts. Thereafter, the public administrator may distribute any remaining property to any known beneficiaries or heirs provided that the distribution occurs 4 months after the court has authorized the public administrator to act or after the public administrator takes possession or control of the estate. If there are no known beneficiaries or heirs, the public administrator must deposit the balance of the estate with the county treasurer for use in the general fund. For balances exceeding $5000, the public administrator must give the State Controller written notice (Cal. Prob. Code §7663). California Probate Code §§7600 et seq. (some provisions omitted) regulate the appointment and management of a public administrator.

In In re Conservatorship of Key, 35 Cal. Rptr. 3d 859 (Ct. App. 2005), the court of appeals upheld the constitutionality of California Probate Code §7642. An executor of a conservatee's estate, who challenged the statute as a violation of the Fifth Amendment takings clause and procedural due process, objected to the manner in which the public guardian allocated interest earned on the pooled conservatorship estates to each individual estate.

§7601. Duty of public administrator to take possession or control of property

(a) If no personal representative has been appointed, the public administrator of a county shall take prompt possession or control of property of a decedent in the county that is deemed by the public administrator to be subject to loss, injury, waste, or misappropriation, or that the court orders into the possession or control of the public administrator after notice to the public administrator as provided in Section 1220.

(b) If property described in subdivision (a) is beyond the ability of the public administrator to take possession or control, the public administrator is not liable for failing to take possession or control of the property.

(Stats. 1990 (A.B. 759), ch. 79, §14, effective July 1, 1991. Amended by Stats. 2004 (A.B. 2689), ch. 888 §2.)

§7602. Duty of public administrator to search for property, will, and instructions for deposition of remains

(a) A public administrator who is authorized to take possession or control of property of a decedent under this article shall make a prompt search for other property, a will, and instructions for disposition of the decedent's remains.

(b) If a will is found, the public administrator or custodian of the will shall deliver the will as provided in Section 8200.

(c) If instructions for disposition of the decedent's remains are found, the public administrator shall promptly deliver the instructions to the person upon whom the right to control disposition of the decedent's remains devolves as provided in Section 7100 of the Health and Safety Code.

(d) If other property is located, the public administrator shall take possession or control of any property that, in the sole discretion of the public administrator, is deemed to be subject to loss, injury, waste, or misappropriation and that is located anywhere in this state or that is subject to the laws of this state. The public administrator does not have any liability for loss, injury, waste, or misappropriation of property of which he or she is unable to take possession or control.

(Stats. 1990 (A.B. 759), ch. 79 §14, effective July 1, 1991. Amended by Stats. 2004 (AB 2687), ch. 888, §3.)

§7621. Public administrator as personal representative

(a) Except as otherwise provided in this section, appointment of the public administrator as personal representative shall be made, and letters issued, in the same manner and pursuant to the same procedure as for appointment of and issuance of letters to personal representatives generally.

(b) Appointment of the public administrator may be made on the court's own motion, after notice to the public administrator as provided in Section 1220.

(c) Letters may be issued to "the public administrator" of the county without naming the public administrator.

(d) The public administrator's oath and official bond are in lieu of the personal representative's oath and bond. Every estate administered under this chapter shall be charged an annual bond fee in the amount of twenty-five dollars ($25) plus one-fourth of one percent of the amount of an estate greater than ten thousand dollars ($10,000). The amount charged is an expense of administration and that amount shall be deposited in the county treasury. If a successor personal representative is appointed, the amount of the bond fee shall be prorated over the period of months during which the public administrator acted as personal representative. Upon final distribution by the public administrator, any amount of bond charges in excess of one year shall be a prorated charge to the estate.

(Stats. 1990 (A.B. 759), ch 79 §14, effective July 1, 1991. Amended by Stats. 1995 (A.B. 128), ch 160 §1.)

§7640. Deposit with financial institution or county treasurer

(a) The public administrator shall, upon receipt, deposit all money of the estate in an insured account in a financial institution or with the county treasurer of the county in which the proceedings are pending.

(b) Upon deposit under this section the public administrator is discharged from further responsibility for the money deposited until the public administrator withdraws the money.

(Stats. 1990 (A.B. 759), ch. 79, §14, effective July 1, 1991.)

§7641. Withdrawals funds for administration

Money deposited in a financial institution or with the county treasurer under this article may be withdrawn upon the order of the public administrator when required for the purposes of administration.

(Stats. 1990 (A.B. 759), ch. 79, §14, effective July 1, 1991.)

§7642. Payment of interest and dividends

(a) The public administrator shall credit each estate with the highest rate of interest or dividends that the estate would have received if the funds available for deposit had been individually and separately deposited.

(b) Interest or dividends credited to the account of the public administrator in excess of the amount credited to the estates pursuant to subdivision (a) shall be deposited in the county general fund.

(Stats. 1990 (A.B. 759), ch 79, §14, effective July 1, 1991.)

§7660. Public Administrator's power to dispose of the estate

(a) If a public administrator takes possession or control of an estate pursuant to this chapter, the public administrator may, acting as personal representative of the estate, summarily dispose of the estate in the manner provided in this article in either of the following circumstances:

(1) The total value of the property in the decedent's estate does not exceed the amount prescribed in Section 13100. The authority provided by this paragraph may be exercised only upon order of the court. The order may be made upon ex parte application. The fee to be allowed to the clerk for the filing of the application is one hundred eighty dollars ($180). The authority for this summary administration of the estate shall be evidenced by a court order for summary disposition.

(2) The total value of the property in the decedent's estate does not exceed thirty thousand dollars ($30,000). The authority provided by this paragraph may be exercised without court authorization.

(A) A public administrator who is authorized to summarily dispose of property of a decedent pursuant to this paragraph may issue a written certification of Authority for Summary Administration. The written certification is effective for 30 days after the date of issuance.

(B) A financial institution, government or private agency, retirement fund administrator, insurance company, licensed securities dealer, or other person shall, without the necessity of inquiring into the truth of the written certification of Authority for Summary Administration and without court order or letters being issued do all of the following:

(i) Provide the public administrator complete information concerning any property held in the name of the decedent, including the names and addresses of any beneficiaries or joint owners.

(ii) Grant the public administrator access to a safe-deposit box or storage facility rented in the name of the decedent for the purpose of inspection and removal of property of the decedent. Costs and expenses incurred in accessing a safe-deposit box or storage facility shall be borne by the estate of the decedent.

(iii) Surrender to the public administrator any property of the decedent that is held or controlled by the financial institution, agency, retirement fund administrator, insurance company, licensed securities dealer, or other person.

(C) Receipt by a financial institution, government or private agency, retirement fund administrator, insurance company, licensed securities dealer, or other person of the written certification provided by this article shall do both of the following:

(i) Constitute sufficient acquittance for providing information or granting access to a safe-deposit box or a storage facility and for surrendering any property of the decedent.

(ii) Fully discharge the financial institution, government or private agency, retirement fund administrator, insurance company, licensed securities dealer, or other person from liability for any act or omission of the public administrator with respect to the property, a safe-deposit box, or a storage facility.

(b) Summary disposition may be made notwithstanding the existence of the decedent's will, if the will does not name an executor or if the named executor refuses to act.

(c) Nothing in this article precludes the public administrator from filing a petition with the court under any other provision of this code concerning the administration of the decedent's estate.

(d) Petitions filed pursuant to this article shall contain the information required by Section 8002.

(e) If a public administrator takes possession or control of an estate pursuant to this chapter, this article conveys the authority of a personal representative as described in Section 9650 to the public administrator to summarily dispose of the estates pursuant to the procedures described in paragraphs (1) and (2) of subdivision (a).

(f) The fee charged under paragraph (1) of subdivision (a) shall be distributed as provided in Section 68085.4 of the Government Code. When an application is filed under that paragraph, no other fees shall be charged in addition to the uniform filing fee provided for in Section 68085.4 of the Government Code.

(Stats. 1990 (A.B. 759), ch. 79, §14, effective July 1, 1991. Amended by Stats 1997 (A.B. 1165), ch 63 § 1; Stats. 1997 (S.B. 696), ch 93, §2.5; Stats 2004 (A.B. 2687), ch. 888, §7; Stats. 2005 (A.B. 145), ch 75 §149; effective July 19, 2005, operative January 1, 2006.)

§7661. Public Administrator's power to collect and sell property

A public administrator acting under authority of this article may:

(a) Withdraw money or take possession of any other property of the decedent that is in the possession or control of a financial institution, government or private agency, retirement fund administrator, insurance company, licensed securities dealer, or other person.

(b) Collect any debts owed to the decedent, including, but not limited to, any rents, issues, or profits from the real and personal property in the estate until the estate is distributed.

(c) Sell any personal property of the decedent, including, but not limited to, stocks, bonds, mutual funds and other types of securities. Sales may be made with or without notice, as the public administrator elects. Title to the property sold passes without the need for confirmation by the court.

(d) Sell any real property of the decedent . The sale shall be accomplished through one of the following procedures:

(1) The sale may be conducted subject to Article 6 (commencing with Section 10300) of Chapter 18 of Part 5.

(2) With approval specified in the original court order for summary disposition of the estate, the sale of real property may be accomplished using a Notice of Proposed Action according to the following requirements:

(A) The publication of the sale shall be accomplished according to Sections 10300 to 10307, inclusive.

(B) The appraisal of the property and determination of the minimum sale price of 90 percent of the appraised value shall be accomplished according to Section 10309.

(C) If an offer meets the approval of the public administrator and the offered price is at least 90 percent of the appraised value, a notice of proposed action shall be made according to Sections 10581 to 10588, inclusive. If objection is not made to the notice of proposed action, the sale may be completed without a court confirmation of the sale. The sale may be consummated by recording a public administrator's deed and a copy of the court order for summary disposition that authorized the use of the notice of proposed action.

(D) If an objection to the notice of proposed action is made pursuant to Section 10587, the sale shall be confirmed in court according to Sections 10308 to 10316, inclusive. The sale may be consummated by recording an administrator's deed and a copy of the court order confirming the sale.

(E) If objection to the notice of proposed action is not made under Section 10587, the public administrator may still elect to have the sale confirmed in court according to Sections 10308 to 10316, inclusive, if the public administrator deems that is in the best interest of the estate. Title to the property sold passes with the public administrator's deed.

(Stats. 1990 (A.B. 759), ch 79, §14, effective July 1, 1991. Amended by Stats. 2004 (A.B. 2687), ch. 888, §8.)

§7662. Order of payments from estate

The public administrator acting under authority of this article shall pay out the money of the estate in the order prescribed in Section 11420, for expenses of administration, charges against the estate, and claims presented to the public administrator before distribution of the decedent's property pursuant to Section 7663. A creditor whose claim is paid under this section is not liable for contribution to a creditor whose claim is presented after the payment.

(Stats. 1990 (A.B. 759), ch. 79, §14, effective July 1, 1991. Amended by Stats. 1990 (S.B. 1775), ch. 710, §18, effective July 1, 1991; Stats. 1991 (S.B. 896), ch. 82, §23, effective July 1, 1991.)

§7663. Duty of public administrator to distribute property

(a) After payment of debts pursuant to Section 7662, but in no case before four months after court authorization of the public administrator to act under this article or after the public administrator takes possession or control of the estate, the public administrator shall distribute to the decedent's beneficiaries any money or other property of the decedent remaining in the possession of the public administrator.

(b) If there are no beneficiaries, the public administrator shall deposit the balance with the county treasurer for use in the general fund of the county, subject to Article 3 (commencing with Section 50050) of Chapter 1 of Part 1 of Division 1 of Title 5 of the Government Code. If the amount deposited exceeds five thousand dollars ($ 5,000), the public administrator shall at the time of the deposit give the Controller written notice of the information specified in Section 1311 of the Code of Civil Procedure.

(Stats. 1990 (A.B. 759), ch. 79, §14, effective July 1, 1991. Amended by Stats. 1990 (S.B. 1774), ch. 324, §2, effective July 16, 1990, effective July 1, 1991; Stats. 1996 (S.B. 1582), ch. 401, § 2.)

§7665. Duty of public administrator to file statements showing property, deposition of, receipts, and records of expenditures

(a) The public administrator shall file with the clerk a statement showing the property of the decedent that came into possession of the public administrator and the disposition made of the property, together with receipts for all distributions. This subdivision does not apply to proceedings under paragraph (2) of subdivision (a) of Section 7660.

(b) The public administrator shall maintain a file of all receipts and records of expenditures for a period of three years after disposition of the property pursuant to Section 7663.

(Stats. 1990 (A.B. 759), ch. 79, §14, effective July 1, 1991.)

6. Nonresident Personal Representatives

The personal representative is not required to be a resident of California. The decedent's will might name an executor who lives outside the state of California. Or, the court might appoint a California personal representative who subsequently moves to another state. However, nonresident personal representatives are subject to special requirements.

California Probate Code §§8570-8577 apply to nonresident personal representatives. In cases of nonresident personal representatives, the court may require bond even if the will waives the bond requirement (Cal. Prob. Code §8571). The nonresident personal representative must notify the court of his or her permanent address and any changes of address (Cal. Prob. Code §8573). Failure to do so is grounds for removal (Cal. Prob. Code §8577). Note that a nonresident of the *United States* is not authorized to serve as personal representative (Cal. Prob. Code §8402). The Secretary of State is appointed agent for service of notices in any proceedings involving nonresident personal representatives (Cal. Prob. Code §§8572, 8574).

§8570. Nonresident personal representative; defined

As used in this article, "nonresident personal representative" means a nonresident of this state appointed as personal representative, or a resident of this state appointed as personal representative who later removes from and resides without this state.

(Stats. 1990 (A.B. 759), ch. 79, §14, effective July 1, 1991. Amended by Stats. 1991 (S.B. 271), ch. 1055, §22.)

§8571. Nonresident personal representative may be required to give a bond

Notwithstanding any other provision of this chapter and notwithstanding a waiver of a bond, the court in its discretion may require a nonresident personal representative to give a bond in an amount determined by the court.

(Stats. 1990 (A.B. 759), ch. 79, §14, effective July 1, 1991.)

§8572. The Secretary of State as attorney for service

(a) Acceptance of appointment by a nonresident personal representative is equivalent to and constitutes an irrevocable and binding appointment by the nonresident personal representative of the Secretary of State to be the attorney of the personal representative for the purpose of this article. The appointment of the nonresident personal representative also applies to any personal representative of a deceased nonresident personal representative.

(b) All lawful processes, and notices of motion under Section 377.41 of the Code of Civil Procedure, in an action or proceeding against the nonresident personal representative with respect to the estate or founded on or arising out of the acts or omissions of the nonresident personal representative in that capacity may be served on the Secretary of State as the attorney for service of the nonresident personal representative.

(Stats. 1990 (A.B. 759), ch. 79, §14, effective July 1, 1991. Amended by Stats. 1993 (A.B. 2211), ch. 589, §129.)

§8573. Nonresident personal representative's permanent address

A nonresident personal representative shall sign and file with the court a statement of the permanent address of the nonresident personal representative. If the permanent address is changed, the nonresident personal representative shall promptly file in the same manner a statement of the change of address.

(Stats. 1990 (A.B. 759), ch. 79, §14, effective July 1, 1991.)

§8574. Service of Process or notice of motion

(a) Service of process or notice of a motion under Section 377.41 of the Code of Civil Procedure in any action or proceeding against the nonresident personal representative shall be made by delivering to and leaving with the Secretary of State two copies of the summons and complaint or notice of motion and either of the following:

(1) A copy of the statement by the nonresident personal representative under Section 8573.

(2) If the nonresident personal representative has not filed a statement under Section 8573, a copy of the letters issued to the nonresident personal representative together with a written statement signed by the party or attorney of the party seeking service that sets forth an address for use by the Secretary of State.

(b) The Secretary of State shall promptly mail by registered mail one copy of the summons and complaint or notice of motion to the nonresident personal representative at the address shown on the statement delivered to the Secretary of State.

(c) Personal service of process, or notice of motion, on the nonresident personal representative wherever found shall be the equivalent of service as provided in this section.

(Stats. 1990 (A.B. 759), ch. 79, §14, effective July 1, 1991. Amended by Stats. 1993 (A.B. 2211), ch. 589, §129.)

§8575. Proof of service

Proof of compliance with Section 8574 shall be made in the following manner:

(a) In the event of service by mail, by certificate of the Secretary of State, under official seal, showing the mailing. The certificate shall be filed with the court from which process issued.

(b) In the event of personal service outside this state, by the return of any duly constituted public officer qualified to serve like process, or notice of motion, of and in the jurisdiction where the nonresident personal representative is found, showing the service to have been made. The return shall be attached to the original summons, or notice of motion, and filed with the court from which process issued.

(Stats. 1990 (A.B. 759), ch. 79, §14, effective July 1, 1991. Amended by Stats. 1991 (S.B. 271), ch. 1055, §23.)

§8576. Time limits for service

(a) Except as provided in this section, service made under Section 8574 has the same legal force and validity as if made personally in this state.

(b) A nonresident personal representative served under Section 8574 may appear and answer the complaint within 30 days from the date of service.

(c) Notice of motion shall be served on a nonresident personal representative under Section 8574 not less than 30 days before the date of the hearing on the motion.

(Stats. 1990 (A.B. 759), ch. 79, §14, effective July 1, 1991).

§8577. Failure to file statement of address may lead to removal from office

(a) Failure of a nonresident personal representative to comply with Section 8573 is cause for removal from office.

(b) Nothing in this section limits the liability of, or the availability of any other remedy against, a nonresident personal representative who is removed from office under this section.

(Stats. 1990 (A.B. 759), ch. 79, §14, effective July 1, 1991.)

B. Qualification, Appointment, and Removal

All states specify the persons who are entitled to appointment as personal representatives. Such persons have power to administer an estate after they have been appointed by the court. The appointment becomes effective following issuance of letters testamentary (for the estate of a decedent who died testate) or letters of administration (for the estate of a decedent who died intestate). Before the issuance of letters, the personal representative may have to take an oath to perform faithfully the duties of the office (Cal. Prob. Code §8403) and also to file a bond with the court (Cal. Prob. Code §8480).

1. Generally

§8400. Power to administer estate begins with appointment upon issuance of letters

(a) A person has no power to administer the estate until the person is appointed personal representative and the appointment becomes effective. Appointment of a personal representative becomes effective when the person appointed is issued letters.

(b) Subdivision (a) applies whether or not the person is named executor in the decedent's will, except that a person named executor in the decedent's will may, before the appointment is made or becomes effective, pay funeral expenses and take necessary measures for the maintenance and preservation of the estate.

(c) The order appointing a personal representative shall state in capital letters on the first page of the order, in at least 12point type, the following:

"WARNING: THIS APPOINTMENT IS NOT EFFECTIVE UNTIL LETTERS HAVE ISSUED."

(Stats. 1990 (A.B. 759), ch. 79, §14, effective July 1, 1991. Amended by Stats. 1996 (A.B. 2751), ch. 862, §16.)

§8401. Petitioner for appointment may deposit property in financial institution

(a) Notwithstanding Section 8400, a petitioner for appointment as personal representative may deliver property in the petitioner's possession to a trust company or financial institution for deposit, or allow a trust company or financial institution to retain on deposit property already in its possession, as provided in Chapter 3 (commencing with Section 9700) of Part 5.

(b) The petitioner shall obtain and file with the court a written receipt including the agreement of the trust company or financial institution that the property on deposit, including any earnings thereon, shall not be allowed to be withdrawn except on order of the court.

(c) In receiving and retaining property under this section, the trust company or financial institution is protected to the same extent as though it had received the property from a person who had been appointed personal representative.

(Stats. 1990 (A.B. 759), ch. 79, §14, effective July 1, 1991.)

§8402. Persons not eligible for appointment as personal representative

(a) Notwithstanding any other provision of this chapter, a person is not competent to act as personal representative in any of the following circumstances:

(1) The person is under the age of majority.

(2) The person is subject to a conservatorship of the estate or is otherwise incapable of executing, or is otherwise unfit to execute, the duties of the office.

(3) There are grounds for removal of the person from office under Section 8502.

(4) The person is not a resident of the United States.

(5) The person is a surviving partner of the decedent and an interested person objects to the appointment.

(b) Paragraphs (4) and (5) of subdivision (a) do not apply to a person named as executor or successor executor in the decedent's will.

(Stats. 1990 (A.B. 759), ch. 79, §14, effective July 1, 1991.)

§8403. Personal representative shall take oath to perform duties

(a) Before letters are issued, the personal representative shall take and subscribe an oath to perform, according to law, the duties of the office. The oath may be taken and dated on or after the time the petition for appointment as personal representative is signed, and may be filed with the clerk at any time after the petition is granted.

(b) The oath constitutes an acceptance of the office and shall be attached to or endorsed on the letters.

(Stats. 1990 (A.B. 759), ch. 79, §14, effective July 1, 1991.)

§8404. Personal representative shall file statement of duties and liabilities

(a) Before letters are issued, the personal representative (other than a trust company or a public administrator) shall file an acknowledgment of receipt of a statement of duties and liabilities of the office of personal representative. The statement shall be in the form prescribed by the Judicial Council.

(b) The court may by local rule require the acknowledgment of receipt to include the personal representative's birth date and driver's license number, if any, provided that the court ensures their confidentiality.

(c) The statement of duties and liabilities prescribed by the Judicial Council does not supersede the law on which the statement is based.

(Stats. 1990 (A.B. 759), ch. 79, §14, effective July 1, 1991. Amended by Stats. 1994 (A.B. 3686), ch. 806, §26.)

§8405. Contents of letters testamentary or letters of administration: county, name, type of representative, authorization under IAEA

Letters shall be signed by the clerk under the seal of the court and shall include:

(a) The county from which the letters are issued.

(b) The name of the person appointed as personal representative and whether the personal representative is an executor, administrator, administrator with the will annexed, or special administrator.

(c) A notation whether the personal representative is authorized to act under the Independent Administration of Estates Act (Part 6 (commencing with Section 10400) of Division 7), and if so authorized whether the independent administration authority includes or excludes the power to do any of the following:

(1) Sell real property.

(2) Exchange real property.

(3) Grant an option to purchase real property.

(4) Borrow money with the loan secured by an encumbrance upon real property.

(Stats. 1990 (A.B. 759), ch. 79, §14, effective July 1, 1991.)

2. Bond

As a general rule, a personal representative is required to give bond before issuance of letters (Cal. Prob. Code §8480). The bond is conditioned on the personal representative's faithful execution of his or her duties (*id.* at §8480(b)). The will may waive the requirement of a bond. The beneficiaries also may waive this requirement if they do so in writing (Cal. Prob. Code §8481(a)). However, the court may require bond for good cause even if waived by the will or the beneficiaries (Cal. Prob. Code §8481(b)).

If several persons are appointed as personal representatives, each must satisfy the bond requirement (absent waiver of the requirement) (Cal. Prob. Code §8480(a)). The court may require a separate bond from each of them or require a joint and several bond (*id.*).

§8480. General requirement of a bond by the personal representative before issuance of letters

(a) Except as otherwise provided by statute, every person appointed as personal representative shall, before letters are issued, give a bond approved by the court. If two or more persons are appointed, the court may require either a separate bond from each or a joint and several bond. If a joint bond is furnished, the liability on the bond is joint and several.

(b) The bond shall be for the benefit of interested persons and shall be conditioned on the personal representative's faithful execution of the duties of the office according to law.

(c) If the person appointed as personal representative fails to give the required bond, letters shall not be issued. If the person appointed as personal representative fails to give a new, additional, or supplemental bond, or to substitute a sufficient surety, under court order, the person may be removed from office.

(Stats. 1990 (A.B. 759), ch. 79, §14, effective July 1, 1991. Amended by Stats. 1998 (S.B. 1841), ch. 77, §3.)

§8481. Bond requirement may be waived by will or by beneficiaries

(a) A bond is not required in either of the following cases:

(1) The will waives the requirement of a bond.

(2) All beneficiaries waive in writing the requirement of a bond and the written waivers are attached to the petition for appointment of a personal representative. This paragraph does not apply if the will requires a bond.

(b) Notwithstanding the waiver of a bond by a will or by all the beneficiaries, on petition of any interested person or on its own motion, the court may for good cause require that a bond be given, either before or after issuance of letters.

(Stats. 1990 (A.B. 759), ch. 79, §14, effective July 1, 1991.)

§8482. Judicial discretion to fix amount of bond; additional bond required before confirming sale of real property

(a) The court in its discretion may fix the amount of the bond, but the amount of the bond shall be not more than the sum of:

(1) The estimated value of the personal property.

(2) The probable annual gross income of the estate.

(3) If independent administration is granted as to real property, the estimated value of the decedent's interest in the real property.

(b) Notwithstanding subdivision (a), if the bond is given by an admitted surety insurer, the court may establish a fixed minimum amount for the bond, based on the minimum premium required by the admitted surety insurer.

(c) If the bond is given by personal sureties, the amount of the bond shall be twice the amount fixed by the court under subdivision (a).

(d) Before confirming a sale of real property the court shall require such additional bond as may be proper, not exceeding the maximum requirements of this section, treating the expected proceeds of the sale as personal property.

(Stats. 1990 (A.B. 759), ch. 79, §14, effective July 1, 1991.)

§8483. Determination of amount of bond if personal representative deposits money or securities in an insured account

(a) This section applies where property in the estate has been deposited pursuant to Chapter 3 (commencing with Section 9700) of Part 5 on condition that the property, including any earnings thereon, will not be withdrawn except on authorization of the court.

(b) In a proceeding to determine the amount of the bond of the personal representative (whether at the time of appointment or subsequently), on production of a receipt showing the deposit of property of the estate in the manner described in subdivision (a), the court may order that the property shall not be withdrawn except on authorization of the court and may, in its discretion, do either of the following:

(1) Exclude the property in determining the amount of the required bond or reduce the amount of the bond to an amount the court determines is reasonable.

(2) If a bond has already been given or the amount fixed, reduce the amount to an amount the court determines is reasonable.

(Stats. 1990 (A.B. 759), ch. 79, §14, effective July 1, 1991.)

§8484. Petition to reduce amount of bond shall include affidavit

If a personal representative petitions to have the amount of the bond reduced, the petition shall include an affidavit setting forth the condition of the estate and notice of hearing shall be given as provided in Section 1220.

(Stats. 1990 (A.B. 759), ch. 79, §14, effective July 1, 1991.)

§8485. Personal representative may petition for substitution or release of a surety

A personal representative who petitions for substitution or release of a surety shall file with the petition an account in the form provided in Section 10900. The court shall not order a substitution or release unless the account is approved.

(Stats. 1990 (A.B. 759), ch. 79, §14, effective July 1, 1991.)

§8486. Personal representative allowed reasonable cost of bond annually

The personal representative shall be allowed the reasonable cost of the bond for every year it remains in force.

(Stats. 1990 (A.B. 759), ch. 79, §14, effective July 1, 1991.)

§8487. Application of Bond and Undertaking Law

The provisions of the Bond and Undertaking Law (Chapter 2 (commencing with Section 995.010) of Title 14 of Part 2 of the Code of Civil Procedure) apply to a bond given under this division, except to the extent this division is inconsistent.

(Stats. 1990 (A.B. 759), ch. 79, §14, effective July 1, 1991.)

§8488. Action against sureties on breach of a condition of the bond; limitation of actions

(a) In case of a breach of a condition of the bond, an action may be brought against the sureties on the bond for the use and benefit of the decedent's estate or of any person interested in the estate.

(b) No action may be maintained against the sureties on the bond of the personal representative unless commenced within four years from the discharge or removal of the personal representative or within four years from the date the order surcharging the personal representative becomes final, whichever is later.

(c) In any case, and notwithstanding subdivision (c) of Section 7250, no action may be maintained against the sureties on the bond unless commenced within six years from the date the judgment under Section 7250 or the later of the orders under subdivision (b) of this section becomes final.

(Stats. 1990 (A.B. 759), ch. 79, §14, effective July 1, 1991. Amended by Stats. 1993 (A.B. 516), ch. 794, §3; Stats. 1994 (A.B. 3686), ch. 806, §27.)

3. Removal of Personal Representative

Sometimes, interested persons may desire removal of the personal representative. Removal can be accomplished following a petition to the court for an order of removal. Alternatively, the court on its own motion may seek removal of the personal representative to protect the estate or interested persons (Cal. Prob. Code §8500). California Probate Code §§8500-8525 and §9614 govern resignation, removal, and suspension of the powers of the personal representative, and the appointment of successors. See also Ross & Grant, Cal. Prob. Prac., *supra,* at §§14:452, 14:452.1.

The Probate Code specifies several of the grounds for removal of a personal representative, including: misuse of funds, lack of capacity to execute the duties of office, neglect of the estate, the need to protect the estate or interested persons, or any other cause provided by statute (Cal. Prob. Code §8502).

Grounds for removal that qualify as "other statutory grounds" under California Probate Code §8502(e)) include:

1) **failure to fulfill the requirements of the Independent Administration of Estates Act (i.e., legislation permitting estate management with minimal supervision), such as by failing to give the required notice of an action or taking action without the requisite court approval (Cal. Prob. Code §§10589, 10592);**
2) **failure to file an inventory and appraisal in a timely fashion (Cal. Prob. Code §8804);**

3) failure to post court-ordered bond (Cal. Prob. Code §8480(c));
4) failure to appear and file a required account, or evading personal service of a contempt citation for failure to do so (Cal. Prob. Code §§11051, 11052);
5) adjudication of contempt for disobeying a court order (Cal. Prob. Code §8505(a));
6) replacement by another person who has a superior right to appointment as administrator (i.e., a higher order of statutory priority) when the latter petitions for removal (Cal. Prob. Code §8503(a));
7) subsequent probate of a will naming an executor following the appointment of the administrator of the intestate estate (Cal. Prob. Code §8504);
8) a nonresident personal representative's failure to file an address statement (Cal Prob. Code §§8573, 8577(a));
9) the failure to attend the hearing on the petition for removal or to answer questions concerning estate administration (Cal. Prob. Code §8500(c)); or
10) a conflict of interest when removal is necessary for the protection of the estate or interested persons (Cal. Prob. Code §8502(d)).

Ross & Grant, Cal. Prob. Prac., *supra*, at §14:466

§8500. Any interested person may petition for removal of personal representative; court also may initiate removal hearing

(a) Any interested person may petition for removal of the personal representative from office. A petition for removal may be combined with a petition for appointment of a successor personal representative under Article 7 (commencing with Section 8520). The petition shall state facts showing cause for removal.

(b) On a petition for removal, or if the court otherwise has reason to believe from the court's own knowledge or from other credible information, whether on the settlement of an account or otherwise, that there are grounds for removal, the court shall issue a citation to the personal representative to appear and show cause why the personal representative should not be removed. The court may suspend the powers of the personal representative and may make such orders as are necessary to deal with the property pending the hearing.

(c) Any interested person may appear at the hearing and file a written declaration showing that the personal representative should be removed or retained. The personal representative may demur to or answer the declaration. The court may compel the attendance of the personal representative and may compel the personal representative to answer questions, on oath, concerning the administration of the estate. Failure to attend or answer is cause for removal of the personal representative from office.

(d) The issues shall be heard and determined by the court. If the court is satisfied from the evidence that the citation has been duly served and cause for removal exists, the court shall remove the personal representative from office.

(Stats. 1990 (A.B. 759), ch. 79, §14, effective July 1, 1991.)

§8501. Court shall revoke letters upon removal from office

On removal of a personal representative from office, the court shall revoke any letters issued to the personal representative, and the authority of the personal representative ceases.

(Stats. 1990 (A.B. 759), ch. 79, §14, effective July 1, 1991.)

§8502. Grounds for removal of personal representative

A personal representative may be removed from office for any of the following causes:

(a) The personal representative has wasted, embezzled, mismanaged, or committed a fraud on the estate, or is about to do so.

(b) The personal representative is incapable of properly executing the duties of the office or is otherwise not qualified for appointment as personal representative.

(c) The personal representative has wrongfully neglected the estate, or has long neglected to perform any act as personal representative.

(d) Removal is otherwise necessary for protection of the estate or interested persons.

(e) Any other cause provided by statute.

(Stats. 1990 (A.B. 759), ch. 79, §14, effective July 1, 1991.)

§8503. Administrator may be removed upon petition of person with higher priority

(a) Subject to subdivision (b), an administrator may be removed from office on the petition of the surviving spouse or a relative of the decedent entitled to succeed to all or part of the estate, or the nominee of the surviving spouse or relative, if such person is higher in priority than the administrator.

(b) The court in its discretion may refuse to grant the petition:

(1) Where the petition is by a person or the nominee of a person who had actual notice of the proceeding in which the administrator was appointed and an opportunity to contest the appointment.

(2) Where to do so would be contrary to the sound administration of the estate.

(Stats. 1990 (A.B. 759), ch. 79, §14, effective July 1, 1991.)

§8504. Personal representative shall be removed if later will is admitted to probate

(a) After appointment of an administrator on the ground of intestacy, the personal representative shall be removed from office on the later admission to probate of a will.

(b) After appointment of an executor or administrator with the will annexed, the personal representative shall be removed from office on admission to probate of a later will.

(Stats. 1990 (A.B. 759), ch. 79, §14, effective July 1, 1991.)

§8505. Personal representative may be removed if found in contempt

(a) A personal representative may be removed from office if the personal representative is found in contempt for disobeying an order of the court.

(b) Notwithstanding any other provision of this article, a personal representative may be removed from office under this section by a court order reciting the facts and without further showing or notice.

(Stats. 1990 (A.B. 759), ch. 79, §14, effective July 1, 1991.)

§9614. Court may suspend powers of personal representative as to specific property, circumstances or duties

(a) On petition of an interested person, the court may suspend the powers of the personal representative in whole or in part, for a time, as to specific property or circumstances or as to specific duties of the office, or may make any other order to secure proper performance of the duties of the personal representative, if it appears to the court that the personal representative otherwise may take some action that would jeopardize unreasonably the interest of the petitioner. Persons with whom the personal representative may transact business may be made parties.

(b) The matter shall be set for hearing within 10 days unless the parties agree otherwise. Notice as the court directs shall be given to the personal representative and attorney of record, if any, and to any other parties named in the petition.

(c) The court may, in its discretion, if it determines that the petition was brought unreasonably and for the purpose of hindering the personal representative in the performance of the duties of the office, assess attorney's fees against the petitioner and make the assessment a charge against the interest of the petitioner.

(Stats. 1990 (A.B. 759), ch. 79, §14, effective July 1, 1991.)

4. Filling Vacancies in Office of Personal Representative

California Probate Code §§8520-8525 regulate the filling of vacancies in the office of personal representative. A personal representative may resign at any time (Cal. Prob. Code §8520). The court need not fill a vacancy of one of several personal representatives (Cal. Prob. Code §8521). A resigning personal representative remains liable until his or her accounts are settled and the estate property is delivered to the successor representative (or court-designated receiver) (Cal. Prob. Code §8525). See also Ross & Grant, Cal. Prob. Prac., *supra*, at §14:453.

§8520. Vacancy in the office of personal representative

A vacancy occurs in the office of a personal representative who resigns, dies, or is removed from office under Article 6 (commencing with Section 8500), or whose authority is otherwise terminated.

(Stats 1990 (A.B. 759), ch. 79, §14, effective July 1, 1991.)

§8521. Vacancy occurs; remaining personal representatives' duties

(a) Unless the will provides otherwise or the court in its discretion orders otherwise, if a vacancy occurs in the office of fewer than all personal representatives, the remaining personal representatives shall complete the administration of the estate.

(b) The court, on the filing of a petition alleging that a vacancy has occurred in the office of fewer than all personal representatives, may order the clerk to issue appropriate amended letters to the remaining personal representatives.

(Stats 1990 (A.B. 759), ch. 79, §14, effective July 1, 1991.)

§8522. Vacancy in the offices of all personal representatives

(a) If a vacancy occurs in the office of a personal representative and there are no other personal representatives, the court shall appoint a successor personal representative.

(b) Appointment of a successor personal representative shall be made on petition and service of notice on interested persons in the manner provided in Article 2 (commencing with Section 8110) of Chapter 2, and shall be subject to the

same priority as for an original appointment of a personal representative. The personal representative of a deceased personal representative is not, as such, entitled to appointment as successor personal representative.
(Stats 1990 (A.B. 759), ch. 79, §14, effective July 1, 1991.)

§8523. Protection of estate during vacancy

The court may make orders that are necessary to deal with the estate of the decedent between the time a vacancy occurs in the office of personal representative and appointment of a successor. Those orders may include appointment of a special administrator.
(Stats 1990 (A.B. 759), ch. 79, §14, effective July 1, 1991.)

§8524. Successor personal representative's duties and powers

(a) A successor personal representative is entitled to demand, sue for, recover and collect all the estate of the decedent remaining unadministered, and may prosecute to final judgment any suit commenced by the former personal representative before the vacancy.

(b) No notice, process, or claim given to or served on the former personal representative need be given to or served on the successor in order to preserve any position or right the person giving the notice or filing the claim may thereby have obtained or preserved with reference to the former personal representative.

(c) Except as provided in subdivision (b) of Section 8442 (authority of administrator with will annexed) or as otherwise ordered by the court, the successor personal representative has the powers and duties in respect to the continued administration that the former personal representative would have had.
(Stats 1990 (A.B. 759), ch. 79, §14, effective July 1, 1991.)

§8525. Effect of vacancy on acts of personal representative

(a) The acts of the personal representative before a vacancy occurs are valid to the same extent as if no vacancy had later occurred.

(b) The liability of a personal representative whose office is vacant, or of the surety on the bond, is not discharged, released, or affected by the vacancy or by appointment of a successor, but continues until settlement of the accounts of the personal representative and delivery of all the estate of the decedent to the successor personal representative or other person appointed by the court to receive it. The personal representative shall render an account of the administration within the time that the court directs.
(Stats 1990 (A.B. 759), ch. 79, §14, effective July 1, 1991.)

C. Compensation

The personal representative receives compensation for fulfilling his or her responsibilities. If the personal representative has rendered "ordinary services," the compensation is based on the value of the estate (Cal. Prob. Code §10800). On the other hand, if the personal representative has rendered "extraordinary services," the court may authorize additional compensation (Cal. Prob. Code §10811).

The fee for the personal representative (executor and administrator) is the same as that for the attorney for the estate. Both fees are based on a statutory fee schedule applicable to the performance of ordinary services (Cal. Prob. Code §§10800, 10810). The schedule provides for 4 percent on the first $100,000 of the amount of the estate, 3 percent on the next $100,000, 2 percent on the next $800,000, 1 percent on the next $9 million dollars, half of 1 percent on the next $15 million dollars, and a reasonable amount to be determined by the court for amounts above $25 million dollars.

The statutory fee schedule is not applicable if the will specifies the compensation (Cal. Prob. Code §§10802, 10812). Furthermore, any agreement between the personal representative and the attorney that provides for higher compensation is void (Cal. Prob. Code §10803).

In some cases, a personal representative may be an attorney. However, a personal representative who is an attorney cannot serve in a dual function (as both the personal representative and estate attorney) and thereby receive dual compensation, absent prior judicial authorization (and subject to the court's finding that the arrangement is "to the advantage, benefit, and best interests of the decedent's estate") (Cal. Prob. Code §10804).

§10800. Personal representative shall receive compensation based on value of estate for ordinary services

(a) Subject to the provisions of this part, for ordinary services the personal representative shall receive compensation based on the value of the estate accounted for by the personal representative, as follows:

(1) Four percent on the first one hundred thousand dollars ($100,000).

(2) Three percent on the next one hundred thousand dollars ($100,000).

(3) Two percent on the next eight hundred thousand dollars ($800,000).

(4) One percent on the next nine million dollars ($9,000,000).

(5) One-half of one percent on the next fifteen million dollars ($15,000,000).

(6) For all amounts above twenty-five million dollars ($25,000,000), a reasonable amount to be determined by the court.

(b) For the purposes of this section, the value of the estate accounted for by the personal representative is the total amount of the appraisal value of property in the inventory, plus gains over the appraisal value on sales, plus receipts, less losses from the appraisal value on sales, without reference to encumbrances or other obligations on estate property.

(Stats. 1990 (A.B. 759), ch. 79, §14, effective July 1, 1991. Amended by Stats. 1991 (S.B. 896), ch. 82, §27, effective July 1, 1991; Stats. 2001 (A.B. 232), ch. 699, §2.)

§10801. Court may allow additional compensation; personal representative may employ tax experts

(a) Subject to the provisions of this part, in addition to the compensation provided by Section 10800, the court may allow additional compensation for extraordinary services by the personal representative in an amount the court determines is just and reasonable.

(b) The personal representative may also employ or retain tax counsel, tax auditors, accountants, or other tax experts for the performance of any action which such persons, respectively, may lawfully perform in the computation, reporting, or making of tax returns, or in negotiations or litigation which may be necessary for the final determination and payment of taxes, and pay from the funds of the estate for such services.

(Stats. 1990 (A.B. 759), ch. 79, §14, effective July 1, 1991. Amended by Stats. 1991 (S.B. 896), ch. 82, §28, effective July 1, 1991.)

§10802. Personal representative shall receive compensation as specified in will

(a) Except as otherwise provided in this section, if the decedent's will makes provision for the compensation of the personal representative, the compensation provided by the will shall be the full and only compensation for the services of the personal representative.

(b) The personal representative may petition the court to be relieved from a provision of the will that provides for the compensation of the personal representative.

(c) Notice of the hearing on the petition shall be given as provided in Section 1220 to all of the following persons:

(1) Each person listed in Section 1220.

(2) Each known heir whose interest in the estate would be affected by the petition.

(3) Each known devisee whose interest in the estate would be affected by the petition.

(4) The Attorney General, at the office of the Attorney General in Sacramento, if any portion of the estate is to escheat to the state and its interest in the estate would be affected by the petition.

(d) If the court determines that it is to the advantage of the estate and in the best interest of the persons interested in the estate, the court may make an order authorizing compensation for the personal representative in an amount greater than provided in the will.

(Stats. 1990 (A.B. 759), ch. 79, §14, effective July 1, 1991.)

§10803. Agreement between personal representative and heir for higher compensation is void

An agreement between the personal representative and an heir or devisee for higher compensation than that provided by this part is void.

(Stats. 1990 (A.B. 759), ch. 79, §14, effective July 1, 1991.)

§10804. Personal representative who is an attorney shall not be compensated as attorney; exception

Notwithstanding any provision in the decedent's will, a personal representative who is an attorney shall be entitled to receive the personal representative's compensation as provided in this part, but shall not receive compensation for services as the attorney for the personal representative unless the court specifically approves the right to the compensation in advance and finds that the arrangement is to the advantage, benefit, and best interests of the decedent's estate.

(Stats. 1990 (A.B. 759), ch. 79, §14, effective July 1, 1991. Amended by Stats. 1993 (A.B. 21), ch. 293, §5; Stats. 1996 (S.B. 392), ch. 563, §26; Stats. 2001 (A.B. 232), ch. 699, §3.)

§10805. Compensation shall be apportioned between two or more personal representatives

If there are two or more personal representatives, the personal representative's compensation shall be apportioned among the personal representatives by the court according to the services actually rendered by each personal representative or as agreed to by the personal representatives.

(Stats. 1990 (A.B. 759), ch. 79, §14, effective July 1, 1991.)

§10810. Attorney for personal representative shall receive compensation based on value of estate for ordinary services

(a) Subject to the provisions of this part, for ordinary services the attorney for the personal representative shall receive compensation based on the value of the estate accounted for by the personal representative, as follows:

(1) Four percent on the first one hundred thousand dollars ($100,000).

(2) Three percent on the next one hundred thousand dollars ($100,000).

(3) Two percent on the next eight hundred thousand dollars ($800,000).

(4) One percent on the next nine million dollars ($9,000,000).

(5) One-half of 1 percent on the next fifteen million dollars ($15,000,000).

(6) For all amounts above twenty-five million dollars ($25,000,000), a reasonable amount to be determined by the court.

(b) For the purposes of this section, the value of the estate accounted for by the personal representative is the total amount of the appraisal of property in the inventory, plus gains over the appraisal value on sales, plus receipts, less losses from the appraisal value on sales, without reference to encumbrances or other obligations on estate property.

(Stats. 1991 (S.B. 896), ch. 82, §30, effective July 1, 1991. Amended by Stats. 2001 (A.B. 232), ch. 699, §4.)

§10811. Court may allow additional compensation for extraordinary services by attorney for personal representative; contingent fee sometimes permitted

(a) Subject to the provisions of this part, in addition to the compensation provided by Section 10810, the court may allow additional compensation for extraordinary services by the attorney for the personal representative in an amount the court determines is just and reasonable.

(b) Extraordinary services by the attorney for which the court may allow compensation include services by a paralegal performing the extraordinary services under the direction and supervision of an attorney. The petition for compensation shall set forth the hours spent and services performed by the paralegal.

(c) An attorney for the personal representative may agree to perform extraordinary service on a contingent fee basis subject to the following conditions:

(1) The agreement is written and complies with all the requirements of Section 6147 of the Business and Professions Code.

(2) The agreement is approved by the court following a hearing noticed as provided in Section 10812.

(3) The court determines that the compensation provided in the agreement is just and reasonable and the agreement is to the advantage of the estate and in the best interests of the persons who are interested in the estate.

(Stats. 1991 (S.B. 896), ch. 82, §30, effective July 1, 1991. Amended by Stats. 1993 (A.B. 908), ch. 527, §4.)

§10812. Attorney for personal representative shall receive compensation as specified in will

(a) Except as otherwise provided in this section, if the decedent's will makes provision for the compensation of the attorney for the personal representative, the compensation provided by the will shall be the full and only compensation for the services of the attorney for the personal representative.

(b) The personal representative or the attorney for the personal representative may petition the court to be relieved from a provision of the will that provides for the compensation of the attorney for the personal representative.

(c) Notice of the hearing on the petition shall be given as provided in Section 1220 to all of the following persons:

(1) Each person listed in Section 1220.

(2) Each known heir whose interest in the estate would be affected by the petition.

(3) Each known devisee whose interest in the estate would be affected by the petition.

(4) The Attorney General, at the office of the Attorney General in Sacramento, if any portion of the estate is to escheat to the state and its interest in the estate would be affected by the petition.

(5) If the court determines that it is to the advantage of the estate and in the best interest of the persons interested in the estate, the court may make an order authorizing compensation of the attorney for the personal representative in an amount greater than provided in the will.

(Stats. 1991 (S.B. 896), ch. 82, §30, effective July 1, 1991.)

§10813. Agreement between personal representative and attorney for higher compensation is void

An agreement between the personal representative and the attorney for higher compensation for the attorney than that provided by this part is void.

(Stats. 1991 (S.B. 896), ch. 82, §30, effective July 1, 1991.)

§10814. Compensation shall be apportioned between two or more attorneys

If there are two or more attorneys for the personal representative, the attorney's compensation shall be apportioned among the attorneys by the court according to the services actually rendered by each attorney or as agreed to by the attorneys.

(Stats. 1991 (S.B. 896), ch. 82, §30, effective July 1, 1991.)

§10830. Personal representative or attorney may petition for part of compensation; hearing

(a) At any time after four months from the issuance of letters:

(1) The personal representative may file a petition requesting an allowance on the compensation of the personal representative.

(2) The personal representative or the attorney for the personal representative may file a petition requesting an allowance on the compensation of the attorney for the personal representative.

(b) Notice of the hearing on the petition shall be given as provided in Section 1220 to all of the following:

(1) Each person listed in Section 1220.

(2) Each known heir whose interest in the estate would be affected by the payment of the compensation.

(3) Each known devisee whose interest in the estate would be affected by the payment of the compensation.

(4) The Attorney General, at the office of the Attorney General in Sacramento, if any portion of the estate is to escheat to the state and its interest in the estate would be affected by the petition.

(c) On the hearing, the court may make an order allowing the portion of the compensation of the personal representative or the attorney for the personal representative, as the case may be, on account of services rendered up to that time, that the court determines is proper. The order shall authorize the personal representative to charge against the estate the amount allowed.

(Stats. 1990 (A.B. 759), ch. 79, §14, effective July 1, 1991. Amended by Stats. 1990 (S.B. 1775), ch. 710, §35, effective July 1, 1991.)

§10831. Personal representative or attorney may petition for order fixing compensation upon filing of final account and order for final distribution

(a) At the time of the filing of the final account and petition for an order for final distribution:

(1) The personal representative may petition the court for an order fixing and allowing the personal representative's compensation for all services rendered in the estate proceeding.

(2) The personal representative or the attorney for the personal representative may petition the court for an order fixing and allowing the compensation, of the attorney for all services rendered in the estate proceeding.

(b) The request for compensation may be included in the final account or the petition for final distribution or may be made in a separate petition.

(c) Notice of the hearing on the petition shall be given as provided in Section 1220 to all of the following:

(1) Each person listed in Section 1220.

(2) Each known heir whose interest in the estate would be affected by the payment of the compensation.

(3) Each known devisee whose interest in the estate would be affected by the payment of the compensation.

(4) The Attorney General, at the office of the Attorney General in Sacramento, if any portion of the estate is to escheat to the state and its interest in the estate would be affected by the petition.

(d) On the hearing, the court shall make an order fixing and allowing the compensation for all services rendered in the estate proceeding. In the case of an allowance to the personal representative, the order shall authorize the personal representative to charge against the estate the amount allowed, less any amount previously charged against the estate pursuant to Section 10830. In the case of the attorney's compensation the order shall require the personal representative to pay the attorney out of the estate the amount allowed, less any amount paid to the attorney out of the estate pursuant to Section 10830.

(Stats. 1990 (A.B. 759), ch. 79, §14, effective July 1, 1991. Amended by Stats. 1990 (S.B. 1775), ch. 710, §36, effective July 1, 1991.)

§10832. Court may allow compensation to personal representative or attorney for extraordinary services before final distribution

Notwithstanding Sections 10830 and 10831, the court may allow compensation to the personal representative or to the attorney for the personal representative for extraordinary services before final distribution when any of the following requirements is satisfied:

(a) It appears likely that administration of the estate will continue, whether due to litigation or otherwise, for an unusually long time.

(b) Present payment will benefit the estate or the beneficiaries of the estate.

(c) Other good cause is shown.

(Stats. 1990 (A.B. 759), ch. 79, §14, effective July 1, 1991. Amended by Stats. 1994 (A.B. 3686), ch. 806, §33.)

§10850. Part inapplicable to proceedings commenced before July 1, 1991

(a) This part does not apply in any proceeding for administration of a decedent's estate commenced before July 1, 1991.

(b) Notwithstanding its repeal, the applicable law in effect before July 1, 1991, governing the subject matter of this part continues to apply in any proceeding for administration of a decedent's estate commenced before July 1, 1991.

(Stats. 1990 (A.B. 759), ch. 79, §14, effective July 1, 1991. Amended by Stats. 1990 (S.B. 1775), ch. 710, §37, effective July 1, 1991.)

V. Tasks of Personal Representative

A. Estate Management

The personal representative is charged with preserving and managing estate assets for the benefit of beneficiaries, heirs, and creditors. To accomplish this task, the personal representative has many tasks to perform during administration of the estate, such as marshalling the assets, conducting an inventory and appraisement, paying creditors' claims, and making preliminary and final distributions of the assets.

"Marshaling assets" involves "the process of discovering, identifying, and taking possession and control of the decedent's assets so they may be managed and administered in an orderly fashion, used to pay taxes, creditors' claims and expenses of administration, and, ultimately, distributed to the estate beneficiaries." Ross & Grant, Cal. Prob. Prac., *supra,* at §6.0. After assets are marshaled, the assets that are subject to probate administration must be reported to the court (inventoried) and appraised.

Statutes govern the personal representative's responsibilities regarding various acts of estate management, including the making of deposits and investments; borrowing funds; sales, leases, and exchanges of property, and other forms of property dispositions (Cal. Prob. Code §§9600 et seq. and §§850 et seq.).

In the performance of his or her duties, the personal representative is subject to a fiduciary obligation. That is, the representative has the duty to exercise "ordinary care and diligence" in managing the estate (Cal. Prob. Code §9600). A court makes the determination as to "ordinary care and diligence" by examining all the circumstances of a particular estate (*id.* at §9600(a)).

1. General Provisions

§9600. Personal representative's duty to exercise ordinary care and diligence

(a) The personal representative has the management and control of the estate and, in managing and controlling the estate, shall use ordinary care and diligence. What constitutes ordinary care and diligence is determined by all the circumstances of the particular estate.

(b) The personal representative:

(1) Shall exercise a power to the extent that ordinary care and diligence require that the power be exercised.

(2) Shall not exercise a power to the extent that ordinary care and diligence require that the power not be exercised.

(Stats. 1990 (A.B. 759), ch. 79, §14, effective July 1, 1991.)

§9601. Extent of liability for breach of fiduciary duty

(a) If a personal representative breaches a fiduciary duty, the personal representative is chargeable with any of the following that is appropriate under the circumstances:

(1) Any loss or depreciation in value of the decedent's estate resulting from the breach of duty, with interest.

(2) Any profit made by the personal representative through the breach of duty, with interest.

(3) Any profit that would have accrued to the decedent's estate if the loss of profit is the result of the breach of duty.

(b) If the personal representative has acted reasonably and in good faith under the circumstances as known to the personal representative, the court, in its discretion, may excuse the personal representative in whole or in part from liability under subdivision (a) if it would be equitable to do so.

(Stats. 1990 (A.B. 759), ch. 79, §14, effective July 1, 1991.)

§9602. Liability for interest; excuse from liability

(a) If the personal representative is liable for interest pursuant to Section 9601, the personal representative is liable for the greater of the following amounts:

(1) The amount of interest that accrues at the legal rate on judgments.

(2) The amount of interest actually received.

(b) If the personal representative has acted reasonably and in good faith under the circumstances as known to the personal representative, the court, in its discretion, may excuse the personal representative in whole or in part from liability under subdivision (a) if it would be equitable to do so.

(Stats. 1990 (A.B. 759), ch. 79, §14, effective July 1, 1991. Amended by Stats. 1998 (S.B. 1841), ch. 77, §4.)

§9603. Resort to other statutory or common law remedies

The provisions of Sections 9601 and 9602 for liability of a personal representative for breach of a fiduciary duty do not prevent resort to any other remedy available against the personal representative under the statutory or common law.

(Stats. 1990 (A.B. 759), ch. 79, §14, effective July 1, 1991.)

§9604. Personal representative is not personally liable for decedent's debts absent agreement

No personal representative is chargeable upon a special promise to answer in damages for a liability of the decedent or to pay a debt of the decedent out of the personal representative's own estate unless the agreement for that purpose, or some memorandum or note thereof, is in writing and is signed by one of the following:

(a) The personal representative.

(b) Some other person specifically authorized by the personal representative in writing to sign the agreement or the memorandum or note.

(Stats. 1990 (A.B. 759), ch. 79, §14, effective July 1, 1991.)

§9605. Appointment of personal representative does not discharge claims of decedent against appointee

Appointment of a person as personal representative does not discharge any claim the decedent has against the person.

(Stats. 1990 (A.B. 759), ch. 79, §14, effective July 1, 1991.)

§9606. Personal representative is not personally liable on an instrument absent failure to reveal representative capacity or to identify estate in instrument

Unless otherwise provided in the instrument or in this division, a personal representative is not personally liable on an instrument, including but not limited to a note, mortgage, deed of trust, or other contract, properly entered into in the personal representative's fiduciary capacity in the course of administration of the estate unless the personal representative fails to reveal the personal representative's representative capacity or identify the estate in the instrument.

(Stats. 1990 (A.B. 759), ch. 79, §14, effective July 1, 1991.)

§9610. Personal representative may exercise powers and duties without court authorization absent specific requirement therefor

Unless this part specifically provides a proceeding to obtain court authorization or requires court authorization, the powers and duties set forth in this part may be exercised by the personal representative without court authorization, instruction, approval, or confirmation. Nothing in this section precludes the personal representative from seeking court authorization, instructions, approval, or confirmation.

(Stats. 1990 (A.B. 759), ch. 79, §14, effective July 1, 1991.)

§9611. Court may provide authorization and instruction of personal representative, and confirmation of acts

(a) In all cases where no other procedure is provided by statute, upon petition of the personal representative, the court may authorize and instruct the personal representative, or approve and confirm the acts of the personal representative, in the administration, management, investment, disposition, care, protection, operation, or preservation of the estate, or the incurring or payment of costs, fees, or expenses in connection therewith. Section 9613 does not preclude a petition for instructions under this section.

(b) Notice of the hearing on the petition shall be given as provided in Section 1220.

(Stats. 1990 (A.B. 759), ch. 79, §14, effective July 1, 1991.)

§9613. Court may make orders directing personal representative upon petition and showing of harm

(a) On petition of any interested person, and upon a showing that if the petition is not granted the estate will suffer great or irreparable injury, the court may direct the personal representative to act or not to act concerning the estate. The order may include terms and conditions the court determines are appropriate under the circumstances.

(b) Notice of the hearing on the petition shall be given as provided in Section 1220.

(Stats. 1990 (A.B. 759), ch. 79, §14, effective July 1, 1991.)

§9614. Court may suspend powers of personal representative as to specific property, circumstances or duties

(a) On petition of an interested person, the court may suspend the powers of the personal representative in whole or in part, for a time, as to specific property or circumstances or as to specific duties of the office, or may make any other order to secure proper performance of the duties of the personal representative, if it appears to the court that the personal representative otherwise may take some action that would jeopardize unreasonably the interest of the petitioner. Persons with whom the personal representative may transact business may be made parties.

(b) The matter shall be set for hearing within 10 days unless the parties agree otherwise. Notice as the court directs shall be given to the personal representative and attorney of record, if any, and to any other parties named in the petition.

(c) The court may, in its discretion, if it determines that the petition was brought unreasonably and for the purpose of hindering the personal representative in the performance of the duties of the office, assess attorney's fees against the petitioner and make the assessment a charge against the interest of the petitioner.

(Stats. 1990 (A.B. 759), ch. 79, §14, effective July 1, 1991.)

§9620. Personal representative may refer disputes with third parties to judge

If there is a dispute relating to the estate between the personal representative and a third person, the personal representative may do either of the following:

(a) Enter into an agreement in writing with the third person to refer the dispute to a temporary judge designated in the agreement. The agreement shall be filed with the clerk, who shall thereupon, with the approval of the court, enter an order referring the matter to the designated person. The temporary judge shall proceed promptly to hear and determine the matter in controversy by summary procedure, without pleadings or discovery. The decision of the designated person is subject to Section 632 of the Code of Civil Procedure. Judgment shall be entered on the decision and shall be as valid and effective as if rendered by a judge of the court in an action against the personal representative or the third person commenced by ordinary process.

(b) Enter into an agreement in writing with the third person that a judge, pursuant to the agreement and with the written consent of the judge, both filed with the clerk within the time specified in Section 9353 for bringing an independent suit on the matter in dispute, may hear and determine the dispute pursuant to the procedure provided in subdivision (a).

(Stats. 1990 (A.B. 759), ch. 79, §14, effective July 1, 1991.)

§9621. Personal representative may enter into written agreements to submit disputes to arbitration

If there is a dispute relating to the estate between the personal representative and a third person, the personal representative may enter into an agreement in writing with the third person to submit the dispute to arbitration under Title 9 (commencing with Section 1280) of Part 3 of the Code of Civil Procedure. The agreement is not effective unless it is first approved by the court and a copy of the approved agreement is filed with the court. Notice of the hearing on the petition for approval of the agreement shall be given as provided in Section 1220. The order approving the agreement may be made ex parte.

(Stats. 1990 (A.B. 759), ch. 79, §14, effective July 1, 1991.)

§9630. Powers and duties of co-executors or co-administrators; unanimity required if two; majority if more than two

(a) Subject to subdivisions (b), (c), and (d):

(1) Where there are two personal representatives, both must concur to exercise a power.

(2) Where there are more than two personal representatives, a majority must concur to exercise a power.

(b) If one of the joint personal representatives dies or is removed or resigns, the powers and duties continue in the remaining joint personal representatives as if they were the only personal representatives until further appointment is made by the court.

(c) Where joint personal representatives have been appointed and one or more are (1) absent from the state and unable to act, or (2) otherwise unable to act, or (3) legally disqualified from serving, the court may, by order made with or without notice, authorize the remaining joint personal representatives to act as to all matters embraced within its order.

(d) Where there are two or more personal representatives, any of them may:

(1) Oppose a petition made by one or more of the other personal representatives or by any other person.

(2) Petition the court for an order requiring the personal representatives to take a specific action for the benefit of the estate or directing the personal representatives not to take a specific action. If a procedure is provided by statute for a petition to authorize the specific action by the personal representatives, the petitioner shall file the petition under the provision relating to that procedure. Otherwise, the petitioner shall file the petition under Section 9611.

(Stats. 1990 (A.B. 759), ch. 79, §14, effective July 1, 1991.)

§9631. Extent of liability for breach of fiduciary duty involving more than one personal representative

(a) Except as provided in subdivision (b), where there is more than one personal representative, one personal representative is not liable for a breach of fiduciary duty committed by another of the personal representatives.

(b) Where there is more than one personal representative, one personal representative is liable for a breach of fiduciary duty committed by another of the personal representatives under any of the following circumstances:

(1) Where the personal representative participates in a breach of fiduciary duty committed by the other personal representative.

(2) Where the personal representative improperly delegates the administration of the estate to the other personal representative.

(3) Where the personal representative approves, knowingly acquiesces in, or conceals a breach of fiduciary duty committed by the other personal representative.

(4) Where the personal representative's negligence enables the other personal representative to commit a breach of fiduciary duty.

(5) Where the personal representative knows or has information from which the personal representative reasonably should have known of the breach of fiduciary duty by the other personal representative and fails to take reasonable steps to compel the other personal representative to redress the breach.

(c) The liability of a personal representative for a breach of fiduciary duty committed by another of the personal representatives that occurred before July 1, 1988, is governed by prior law and not by this section.

(Stats. 1990 (A.B. 759), ch. 79, §14, effective July 1, 1991.)

§9640. Part does not limit personal representative's authority under IAEA

Nothing in this part limits or restricts any authority granted to a personal representative under the Independent Administration of Estates Act (Part 6 (commencing with Section 10400)) to administer the estate under that part.

(Stats. 1990 (A.B. 759), ch. 79, §14, effective July 1, 1991.)

§9645. Continuation of actions; exception

(a) Subject to subdivisions (b) and (c), any petition or other matter filed or commenced before July 1, 1988, shall be continued under this part, so far as applicable, except where the court determines that application of a particular provision of this part would substantially interfere with the rights of the parties or other interested persons, in which case the particular provision of this part does not apply and the applicable law in effect before July 1, 1988, applies.

(b) Nothing in this part affects any order, judgment, or decree made, or any action taken, before July 1, 1988.

(c) Notwithstanding the enactment of this part:

(1) An order, judgment, or decree made before July 1, 1988, shall continue in full force and effect in accordance with its terms or until modified or terminated by the court.

(2) The validity of an order, judgment, or decree made before July 1, 1988, is determined by the applicable law in effect before July 1, 1988, and not by this part.

(3) The validity of any action taken before July 1, 1988, is determined by the applicable law in effect before July 1, 1988, and not by this part.

(Stats. 1990 (A.B. 759), ch. 79, §14, effective July 1, 1991.)

§9650. Powers and duties of personal representatives to take possession of property, collect debts, pay taxes

(a) Except as provided by statute and subject to subdivision (c):

(1) The personal representative has the right to, and shall take possession or control of, all the property of the decedent to be administered in the decedent's estate and shall collect all debts due to the decedent or the estate. The personal representative is not accountable for any debts that remain uncollected without his or her fault.

(2) The personal representative is entitled to receive the rents, issues, and profits from the real and personal property in the estate until the estate is distributed.

(b) The personal representative shall pay taxes on, and take all steps reasonably necessary for the management, protection, and preservation of, the estate in his or her possession.

(c) Real property or tangible personal property may be left with or surrendered to the person presumptively entitled to it unless or until, in the judgment of the personal representative,

possession of the property by the personal representative will be necessary for purposes of administration. The person holding the property shall surrender it to the personal representative on request by the personal representative.
(Stats. 1990 (A.B. 759), ch. 79, §14, effective July 1, 1991.)

§9651. Personal representative not civilly or criminally liable for good faith possession of property; entitlement to compensation for services

(a) A personal representative who in good faith takes into possession real or personal property, and reasonably believes that the property is part of the estate of the decedent, is not:

(1) Criminally liable for so doing.

(2) Civilly liable to any person for so doing.

(b) The personal representative shall make reasonable efforts to determine the true nature of, and title to, the property so taken into possession.

(c) During his or her possession, the personal representative is entitled to receive all rents, issues, and profits of the property. If the property is later determined not to be part of the estate of the decedent, the personal representative shall deliver the property, or cause it to be delivered, to the person legally entitled to it, together with all rents, issues, and profits of the property received by the personal representative, less any expenses incurred in protecting and maintaining the property and in collecting rents, issues, and profits. The personal representative may request court approval before delivering the property pursuant to this subdivision.

(d) The court may allow the personal representative reasonable compensation for services rendered in connection with the duties specified in this section as to property later determined not to be part of the estate of the decedent, if the court makes one of the following findings:

(1) The services were of benefit to the estate. If the court makes this finding, the compensation and the expenses and costs of litigation, including attorney's fees of the attorney hired by the personal representative to handle the matter, are a proper expense of administration.

(2) The services were essential to preserve, protect, and maintain the property. If the court makes this finding, the court shall award compensation and the expenses and costs of litigation, including attorney's fees of the attorney hired by the personal representative to handle the matter, as an expense deductible from the rents, issues, and profits received by the personal representative, or, if these are insufficient, as a lien against the property.

(Stats. 1990 (A.B. 759), ch. 79, §14, effective July 1, 1991.)

§9652. Personal representative shall invest cash in interest-bearing accounts

(a) Except as provided in subdivisions (b) and (c), the personal representative shall keep all cash in his or her possession invested in interest-bearing accounts or other investments authorized by law.

(b) The requirement of subdivision (a) does not apply to the amount of cash that is reasonably necessary for orderly administration of the estate.

(c) The requirement of subdivision (a) does not apply to the extent that the testator's will otherwise provides.

(Stats. 1990 (A.B. 759), ch. 79, §14, effective July 1, 1991.)

§9653. Personal representative shall commence action to recover property fraudulently conveyed, gifts in view of impending death, or transfers to designated beneficiaries on death

(a) On application of a creditor of the decedent or the estate, the personal representative shall commence and prosecute an action for the recovery of real or personal property of the decedent for the benefit of creditors if the personal representative has insufficient assets to pay creditors and the decedent during lifetime did any of the following with respect to the property:

(1) Made a conveyance of the property, or any right or interest in the property, that is fraudulent as to creditors under the Uniform Fraudulent Transfer Act (Chapter 1 (commencing with Section 3439) of Title 2 of Part 2 of Division 4 of the Civil Code).

(2) Made a gift of the property in view of impending death.

(3) Made a direction to transfer a vehicle, undocumented vessel, manufactured home, mobilehome, commercial coach, truck camper, or floating home to a designated beneficiary on the decedent's death pursuant to Section 18102.2 of the Health and Safety Code, or Section 5910.5 or 9916.5 of the Vehicle Code, and the property has been transferred as directed.

(b) A creditor making application under this section shall pay such part of the costs and expenses of the suit and attorney's fees, or give an undertaking to the personal representative for that purpose, as the personal representative and the creditor agree, or, absent an agreement, as the court or judge orders.

(c) The property recovered under this section shall be sold for the payment of debts in the same manner as if the decedent had died seized or possessed of the property. The proceeds of the sale shall be applied first to payment of the costs and expenses of suit, including attorney's fees, and then

to payment of the debts of the decedent in the same manner as other property in possession of the personal representative. After all the debts of the decedent have been paid, the remainder of the proceeds shall be paid to the person from whom the property was recovered. The property may be sold in its entirety or in such portion as necessary to pay the debts.
(Stats. 1990 (A.B. 759), ch. 79, §14, effective July 1, 1991. Amended by Stats. 1991 (S.B. 271), ch. 1055, §27, effective January 1, 1993.)

§9654. Heirs and devisees may maintain actions for possession of property or to quiet title

The heirs or devisees may themselves, or jointly with the personal representative, maintain an action for possession of property or to quiet title to property against any person except the personal representative.
(Stats. 1990 (A.B. 759), ch. 79, §14, effective July 1, 1991.)

§9655. Personal representative may take certain actions regarding corporate stock

With respect to a share of stock of a domestic or foreign corporation held in the estate, a membership in a nonprofit corporation held in the estate, or other property held in the estate, a personal representative may do any one or more of the following:

(a) Vote in person, and give proxies to exercise, any voting rights with respect to the share, membership, or other property.

(b) Waive notice of a meeting or give consent to the holding of a meeting.

(c) Authorize, ratify, approve, or confirm any action which could be taken by shareholders, members, or property owners.
(Stats. 1990 (A.B. 759), ch. 79, §14, effective July 1, 1991.)

§9656. Personal representative may insure property against loss or damage

The personal representative may insure the property of the estate against damage or loss and may insure himself or herself against liability to third persons.
(Stats. 1990 (A.B. 759), ch. 79, §14, effective July 1, 1991.)

§9657. Personal representative must not make profit from increase of estate

The personal representative shall not make profit by the increase, nor suffer loss by the decrease or destruction without his or her fault, of any part of the estate.
(Stats. 1990 (A.B. 759), ch. 79, §14, effective July 1, 1991.)

2. Investments and Purchase of Property

§9730. Personal representative may make permissible investments of estate money

Pending distribution of the estate, the personal representative may invest money of the estate in possession of the personal representative in any one or more of the following:

(a) Direct obligations of the United States, or of the State of California, maturing not later than one year from the date of making the investment.

(b) An interest in a money market mutual fund registered under the Investment Company Act of 1940 (15 U.S.C. Sec. 80a1, et seq.) or an investment vehicle authorized for the collective investment of trust funds pursuant to Section 9.18 of Part 9 of Title 12 of the Code of Federal Regulations, the portfolios of which are limited to United States government obligations maturing not later than five years from the date of investment and to repurchase agreements fully collateralized by United States government obligations.

(c) Units of a common trust fund described in Section 1564 of the Financial Code. The common trust fund shall have as its objective investment primarily in short term fixed income obligations and shall be permitted to value investments at cost pursuant to regulations of the appropriate regulatory authority.
(Stats. 1990 (A.B. 759), ch. 79, §14, effective July 1, 1991.)

§9731. Court may order that personal representative invest in United States or state securities

(a) Pending distribution of the estate, upon a showing that it is to the advantage of the estate, the court may order that money of the estate in possession of the personal representative be invested in securities of the United States or of this state.

(b) To obtain an order under this section, the personal representative or any interested person shall file a petition stating the types of securities that are proposed to be purchased and the advantage to the estate of the purchase.

(c) Notice of the hearing on the petition shall be given as provided in Section 1220.
(Stats. 1990 (A.B. 759), ch. 79, §14, effective July 1, 1991.)

§9732. Court may order manner of investment as provided by will

(a) The court may order that money of the estate in possession of the personal representative be invested in any manner provided by the will if all of the following conditions are satisfied:

(1) The time for filing claims has expired.

(2) All debts (as defined in Section 11401) have been paid or are sufficiently secured by mortgage or otherwise, or there is sufficient cash in the estate aside from the money to be invested to pay all the debts, or the court is otherwise satisfied that all the debts will be paid.

(3) The estate is not in a condition to be finally distributed.

(b) To obtain an order under this section, the personal representative or any interested person shall file a petition showing the general condition of the estate and the types of investments that are proposed to be made.

(c) Notice of the hearing on the petition shall be given as provided in Section 1220. In addition, the petitioner shall cause notice of the hearing and a copy of the petition to be mailed to all known devisees of property which is proposed to be invested. Where the property proposed to be invested is devised to a trust or trustee, notice of the hearing and a copy of the petition shall be mailed to the trustee or, if the trustee has not yet accepted the trust, to the person named in the will as trustee. Mailing pursuant to this subdivision shall be to the person's last known address as provided in Section 1220.

(d) If no objection has been filed by an interested person, the court may make an order authorizing or directing the personal representative to invest such portion of the money of the estate as the court deems advisable in the types of investments proposed in the petition and authorized by the will. If there is no objection by an interested person and no substantial reason why some or all of the investment powers given by the will should not be exercised, the court shall make the order. The order may be for a limited period or until the administration of the estate is completed. Upon petition of the personal representative or any interested person, the order may be renewed, modified, or terminated at any time.

(Stats. 1990 (A.B. 759), ch. 79, §14, effective July 1, 1991.)

[California Probate Code §§9733-9737 (authorizing the court to order the personal representative to purchase an annuity, to exercise option rights, to purchase securities or commodities required to perform an incomplete contract of sale by the decedent, to exercise subscription rights, etc.) are omitted.]

3. Operation of Decedent's Business

§9760. Personal representative may continue decedent's business if continuation works to advantage of estate and best interest of interested persons; need for court authorization

(a) As used in this section, "decedent's business" means an unincorporated business or venture in which the decedent was engaged or which was wholly or partly owned by the decedent at the time of the decedent's death, but does not include a business operated by a partnership in which the decedent was a partner.

(b) If it is to the advantage of the estate and in the best interest of the interested persons, the personal representative, with or without court authorization, may continue the operation of the decedent's business; but the personal representative may not continue the operation of the decedent's business for a period of more than six months from the date letters are first issued to a personal representative unless a court order has been obtained under this section authorizing the personal representative to continue the operation of the business.

(c) The personal representative or any interested person may file a petition requesting an order (1) authorizing the personal representative to continue the operation of the decedent's business or (2) directing the personal representative to discontinue the operation of the decedent's business. The petition shall show the advantage to the estate and the benefit to the interested persons of the order requested. Notice of the hearing on the petition shall be given as provided in Section 1220.

(d) If a petition is filed under this section, the court may make an order that either:

(1) Authorizes the personal representative to continue the operation of the decedent's business to such an extent and subject to such restrictions as the court determines to be to the advantage of the estate and in the best interest of the interested persons.

(2) Directs the personal representative to discontinue the operation of the decedent's business within the time specified in, and in accordance with the provisions of, the order.

(Stats. 1990 (A.B. 759), ch. 79, §14, effective July 1, 1991.)

§9761. Court may order surviving partner to render account

If a partnership existed between the decedent and another person at the time of the decedent's death, on application of the personal representative, the court may order any surviving partner to render an account pursuant to Section 15510, 15634, or 16807 of the Corporations Code. An order under this section may be enforced by the court's power to punish for contempt.

(Stats. 1990 (A.B. 759), ch. 79, §14, effective July 1, 1991. Amended by Stats. 2003 (A.B. 167), ch. 32, §8.)

§9762. Personal representative may continue as a general or limited partner upon court authorization

(a) After authorization by order of court upon a showing that it would be to the advantage of the estate and in the best interest of the interested persons, the personal representative may continue as a general or a limited partner in any partnership in which the decedent was a general partner at the time of death. In its order, the court may specify any terms and conditions of the personal representative's participation as a partner that the court determines are to the advantage of the estate and in the best interest of the interested persons, but any terms and conditions that are inconsistent with the terms of any written partnership agreement are subject to the written consent of all of the surviving partners.

(b) If there is a written partnership agreement permitting the decedent's personal representative to participate as a partner, the personal representative has all the rights, powers, duties, and obligations provided in the written partnership agreement, except as otherwise ordered by the court pursuant to subdivision (a).

(c) If there is not a written partnership agreement, the personal representative has the rights, powers, duties, and obligations that the court specifies in its order pursuant to subdivision (a).

(d) To obtain an order under this section, the personal representative or any interested person shall file a petition showing that the order requested would be to the advantage of the estate and in the best interest of the interested persons. Notice of the hearing on the petition shall be given as provided in Section 1220. In addition, unless the court otherwise orders, the petitioner, not less than 15 days before the hearing, shall cause notice of hearing and a copy of the petition to be mailed to each of the surviving general partners at his or her last known address.

(Stats. 1990 (A.B. 759), ch. 79, §14, effective July 1, 1991.)

§9763. Personal representative may commence and maintain actions against surviving partners

(a) If the decedent was a general partner, the personal representative may commence and maintain any action against the surviving partner that the decedent could have commenced and maintained.

(b) The personal representative may exercise the decedent's rights as a limited partner as provided in Section 15675 of the Corporations Code.

(Stats. 1990 (A.B. 759), ch. 79, §14, effective July 1, 1991.)

§9764. Persons who may petition for another attorney to take control of files and assets of practice of deceased attorney

(a) The personal representative of the estate of a deceased attorney who was engaged in a practice of law at the time of his or her death or other person interested in the estate may bring a petition for appointment of an active member of the State Bar of California to take control of the files and assets of the practice of the deceased member.

(b) The petition may be filed and heard on such notice that the court determines is in the best interests of the estate of the deceased member. If the petition alleges that the immediate appointment of a practice administrator is required to safeguard the interests of the estate, the court may dispense with notice only if the personal representative is the petitioner or has joined in the petition or has otherwise waived notice of hearing on the petition.

(c) The petition shall indicate the powers sought for the practice administrator from the list of powers set forth in Section 6185 of the Business and Professions Code. These powers shall be specifically listed in the order appointing the practice administrator.

(d) The petition shall allege the value of the assets that are to come under the control of the practice administrator, including, but not limited by the amount of funds in all accounts used by the deceased member. The court shall require the filing of a surety bond in the amount of the value of the personal property to be filed with the court by the practice administrator. No action may be taken by the practice administrator unless a bond has been fully filed with the court.

(e) The practice administrator shall not be the attorney representing the personal representative.

(f) The court shall appoint the attorney nominated by the deceased member in a writing, including, but not limited to, the deceased member's will, unless the court concludes that the appointment of the nominated person would be contrary to the best interests of the estate or would create a conflict of interest with any of the clients of the deceased member.

(g) The practice administrator shall be compensated only upon order of the court making the appointment for his or her reasonable and necessary services. The law practice shall be the source of the compensation for the practice administrator unless the assets are insufficient in which case, the compensation of the practice administrator shall be charged against the assets of the estate as a cost of administration. The practice administrator shall also be entitled to reimbursement of his or her costs.

(h) Upon conclusion of the services of the practice administrator, the practice administrator shall render an accounting and petition for its approval by the superior court making the appointment. Upon settlement of the accounting, the practice administrator shall be discharged and the surety on his or her bond exonerated.

(i) For the purposes of this section, the person appointed to take control of the practice of the deceased member shall be referred to as the "practice administrator" and the decedent shall be referred to as the "deceased member."

(Stats. 1998 (A.B. 2069), ch. 682, §5.)

[Provisions have been omitted regarding: authorization of the personal representative to dispose of or abandon personal property where the cost of collecting and safeguarding the property would exceed its market value (Cal. Prob. Code §§9780-9788); authorization of the personal representative to borrow money, refinance, and encumber property (Cal. Prob. Code §§9800-9807); authorization of the personal representative to settle and release claims and extend, renew, or modify obligations (Cal. Prob. Code §§9830-9839); authorization of the personal representative to accept a deed to property which is subject to a mortgage in lieu of foreclosure of the mortgage or to give a partial satisfaction of a mortgage or to cause a partial reconveyance to be executed by a trustee under a trust deed held by the estate (Cal. Prob. Code §§9850-9851); authorization of the personal representative to dedicate or convey real property to governmental entities (Cal. Prob. Code §§9900-9901); authorization of the personal representative to grant an option to purchase real property of the estate (Cal. Prob. Code §§9960-9966); authorization of the personal representative to transfer or convey property to the person given the option to purchase it by the will (Cal. Prob. Code §§9980-9983).

4. Actions and Proceedings By or Against the Personal Representative

§9820. Personal representative may commence, maintain and defend actions

The personal representative may:

(a) Commence and maintain actions and proceedings for the benefit of the estate.

(b) Defend actions and proceedings against the decedent, the personal representative, or the estate.

(Stats. 1990 (A.B. 759), ch. 79, §14, effective July 1, 1991.)

§9822. Personal representative may bring actions on bond of former personal representative

The personal representative may bring an action on the bond of any former personal representative of the same estate, for the use and benefit of all interested persons.

(Stats. 1990 (A.B. 759), ch. 79, §14, effective July 1, 1991.)

§9823. Personal representative may bring partition action

(a) If the decedent leaves an undivided interest in any property, an action for partition of the property may be brought against the personal representative.

(b) The personal representative may bring an action against the other cotenants for partition of any property in which the decedent left an undivided interest.

(Stats. 1990 (A.B. 759), ch. 79, §14, effective July 1, 1991.)

5. Personal Representative or Representative's Attorney's Purchase of Claims or Estate Property

§9880. Certain purchases or interests prohibited by personal representative or representative's attorney

Except as provided in this chapter, neither the personal representative nor the personal representative's attorney may do any of the following:

(a) Purchase any property of the estate or any claim against the estate, directly or indirectly.

(b) Be interested in any such purchase.

(Stats. 1990 (A.B. 759), ch. 79, §14, effective July 1, 1991.)

§9881. Court may authorize personal representative or representative's attorney to purchase property of estate subject to conditions

Upon a petition filed under Section 9883, the court may make an order under this section authorizing the personal representative or the personal representative's attorney to purchase property of the estate if all of the following requirements are satisfied:

(a) Written consent to the purchase is signed by (1) each known heir whose interest in the estate would be affected by the proposed purchase and (2) each known devisee whose interest in the estate would be affected by the proposed purchase.

(b) The written consents are filed with the court.

(c) The purchase is shown to be to the advantage of the estate.

(Stats. 1990 (A.B. 759), ch. 79, §14, effective July 1, 1991.)

§9882. Court may authorize personal representative or representative's attorney to purchase property of estate if will so authorizes

Upon a petition filed under Section 9883, the court may make an order under this section authorizing the personal representative or the personal representative's attorney to purchase property of the estate if the will of the decedent authorizes the personal representative or the personal representative's attorney to purchase the property.

(Stats. 1990 (A.B. 759), ch. 79, §14, effective July 1, 1991.)

§9883. Petition; confirmation of sale; persons eligible to receive notice of hearing; court order authorizing purchase

(a) The personal representative may file a petition requesting that the court make an order under Section 9881 or 9882. The petition shall set forth the facts upon which the request for the order is based.

(b) If court confirmation of the sale is required, the court may make its order under Section 9881 or 9882 at the time of the confirmation.

(c) Notice of the hearing on the petition shall be given as provided in Section 1220 to all of the following persons:

(1) Each person listed in Section 1220.

(2) Each known heir whose interest in the estate would be affected by the proposed purchase.

(3) Each known devisee whose interest in the estate would be affected by the proposed purchase.

(d) If the court is satisfied that the purchase should be authorized, the court shall make an order authorizing the purchase upon the terms and conditions specified in the order, and the personal representative may execute a conveyance or transfer according to the terms of the order. Unless otherwise provided in the will or in the order of the court, the sale of the property shall be made in the same manner as the sale of other estate property of the same nature.

(Stats. 1990 (A.B. 759), ch. 79, §14, effective July 1, 1991.)

§9884. Some purchases pursuant to contract are permitted

This chapter does not prohibit the purchase of property of the estate by the personal representative or the personal representative's attorney pursuant to a contract in writing made during the lifetime of the decedent if the contract is one that can be specifically enforced and the requirements of Part 19 (commencing with Section 850) of Division 2 are satisfied.

(Stats. 1990 (A.B. 759), ch. 79, §14, effective July 1, 1991. Amended by Stats. 2003 (A.B. 167), ch. 32, §9.)

§9885. Personal representative may exercise option to purchase estate property if given in will

This chapter does not prevent the exercise by the personal representative or the personal representative's attorney of an option to purchase property of the estate given in the will of the decedent if the requirements of Chapter 17 (commencing with Section 9980) are satisfied.

(Stats. 1990 (A.B. 759), ch. 79, §14, effective July 1, 1991.)

[California Probate Code §§9940 et seq. (omitted) authorize the personal representative to lease real property. California Probate Code §§10000-10382 (omitted) regulate the conditions for the sale of personal property and real property of the estate.]

B. Inventory and Appraisal

The personal representative must file a document called "an inventory and appraisal." This document constitutes a public record of all assets that are owned by the decedent as of the date of death that are subject to probate administration (Cal. Prob. Code §§8802, 8850(a)). The primary purposes of the inventory and appraisal are to advise the beneficiaries and heirs of the assets and their value; and to enable the court to determine such matters as bond, family allowance, etc. Before the repeal of California's inheritance tax in 1982, one of the purposes of the inventory and appraisal was to facilitate computation of state inheritance taxes.

California Probate Code §§8800 et seq. govern the procedures for preparation and filing of the inventory and appraisal. The inventory and appraisal is due within four months after issuance of letters (Cal. Prob. Code §8800(b)), but the deadline may be extended with leave of court if "additional time is reasonable under the circumstances" (*id.*). If an asset is discovered subsequently (after the four-month period), the personal representative must file a supplemental inventory and appraisal (Cal. Prob. Code §8801). This supplemental document must be filed

within four months after the personal representative acquires knowledge of the newly discovered asset (*id.*). A personal representative may file a partial inventory and appraisal but the final complete document nonetheless must be filed before the expiration of the four-month period (absent extension of the deadline) (*id.* at §8801(c)). The inventory must show the portions of the estate property that are community, quasi-community, and separate property of the decedent (Cal. Prob. Code §8850(c)).

The personal representative has the task of appraising only some estate assets (such as cash, accounts in financial institutions, money market funds, mutual funds, stocks, bonds, etc.) (Cal. Prob. Code §8901). A probate referee appraises all assets other than those appraised by the personal representative (i.e., assets that generally are more difficult to value) (Cal. Prob. Code §8902(b)). (Probate referees are appointed by the State Controller and designated by a probate court judge.) The personal representative must provide the probate referee with necessary information to facilitate the latter's appraisal (Cal. Prob. Code §8902(a)). Statutory provisions govern the computation of the probate referee's fees which are payable from the estate (Cal. Prob. Code §§8960, 8961, 8963, 8964). On a showing of "good cause," the court may waive the probate referee's appraisal (Cal. Prob. Code §8903 (a)). For unique items of personal property, the personal representative may choose to have an independent expert conduct the appraisal (Cal. Prob. Code §8904(a)).

Any interested person may file written objections to an appraisal by the personal representative, probate referee, or an independent expert (Cal. Prob. Code §8906(a)). The court will hold a hearing on such objections (*id.* at §8906(b)). At the hearing, the court may make any orders that it finds appropriate (e.g., order a new appraisal) (Cal. Prob. Code §8906(e)).

§8800. Personal representative must file inventory and appraisal within 4 months after issuance of letters

(a) The personal representative shall file with the court clerk an inventory of property to be administered in the decedent's estate together with an appraisal of property in the inventory. An inventory and appraisal shall be combined in a single document.

(b) The inventory and appraisal shall be filed within four months after letters are first issued to a general personal representative. The court may allow such further time for filing an inventory and appraisal as is reasonable under the circumstances of the particular case.

(c) The personal representative may file partial inventories and appraisals where appropriate under the circumstances of the particular case, but all inventories and appraisals shall be filed before expiration of the time allowed under subdivision (b).

(d) Concurrent with the filing of the inventory and appraisal pursuant to this section, the personal representative shall also file a certification that the requirements of Section 480 of the Revenue and Taxation Code either:

(1) Are not applicable because the decedent owned no real property in California at the time of death.

(2) Have been satisfied by the filing of a change in ownership statement with the county recorder or assessor of each county in California in which the decedent owned property at the time of death.

(Stats. 1990 (A.B. 759), ch. 79, §14, effective July 1, 1991. Amended by Stats. 1992 (S.B. 1639), ch. 1180, §1.)

§8801. Personal representative must file supplemental inventory and appraisal for property omitted from prior document

If the personal representative acquires knowledge of property to be administered in the decedent's estate that is not included in a prior inventory and appraisal, the personal representative shall file a supplemental inventory and appraisal of the property in the manner prescribed for an original inventory and appraisal. The supplemental inventory and appraisal shall be filed within four months after the personal representative acquires knowledge of the property. The court may allow such further time for filing a supplemental inventory and appraisal as is reasonable under the circumstances of the particular case.

(Stats. 1990 (A.B. 759), ch. 79, §14, effective July 1, 1991.)

§8802. Inventory and appraisal must list each item and state fair market value at time of death

The inventory and appraisal shall separately list each item and shall state the fair market value of the item at the time of the decedent's death in monetary terms opposite the item.

(Stats. 1990 (A.B. 759), ch. 79, §14, effective July 1, 1991.)

§8803. Personal representative must mail copy to persons requesting special notice

On the filing of an inventory and appraisal or a supplemental inventory and appraisal, the personal representative shall, pursuant to Section 1252, mail a copy to each person who has requested special notice.

(Stats. 1990 (A.B. 759), ch. 79, §14, effective July 1, 1991.)

§8804. Consequences of failure to file inventory and appraisal by deadline

If the personal representative refuses or negligently fails to file an inventory and appraisal within the time allowed under this chapter, upon petition of an interested person:

(a) The court may compel the personal representative to file an inventory and appraisal pursuant to the procedure prescribed in Chapter 4 (commencing with Section 11050) of Part 8.

(b) The court may remove the personal representative from office.

(c) The court may impose on the personal representative personal liability for injury to the estate or to an interested person that directly results from the refusal or failure. The liability may include attorney's fees, in the court's discretion. Damages awarded pursuant to this subdivision are a liability on the bond of the personal representative, if any.

(Stats. 1990 (A.B. 759), ch. 79, §14, effective July 1, 1991.)

§8850. Contents of inventory and appraisal; specification of property to be included

(a) The inventory, including partial and supplemental inventories, shall include all property to be administered in the decedent's estate.

(b) The inventory shall particularly specify the following property:

(1) Money owed to the decedent, including debts, bonds, and notes, with the name of each debtor, the date, the sum originally payable, and the endorsements, if any, with their dates. The inventory shall also specify security for the payment of money to the decedent, including mortgages and deeds of trust. If security for the payment of money is real property, the inventory shall include the recording reference or, if not recorded, a legal description of the real property.

(2) A statement of the interest of the decedent in a partnership, appraised as a single item.

(3) All money and other cash items, as defined in Section 8901, of the decedent.

(c) The inventory shall show, to the extent ascertainable by the personal representative, the portions of the property that are community, quasi community, and separate property of the decedent.

(Stats. 1990 (A.B. 759), ch. 79, §14, effective July 1, 1991.)

§8851. Personal representative must include devise in will of debt or demand; effect of testamentary discharge or devise of debt or demand

The discharge or devise in a will of any debt or demand of the testator against the executor or any other person is not valid against creditors of the testator, but is a specific devise of the debt or demand. The debt or demand shall be included in the inventory. If necessary, the debt or demand shall be applied in the payment of the debts of the testator. If not necessary for that purpose, the debt or demand shall be distributed in the same manner and proportion as other specific devises.

(Stats. 1990 (A.B. 759), ch. 79, §14, effective July 1, 1991.)

§8852. Personal representative must take oath regarding inventory; disagreement among personal representatives regarding inventory

(a) The personal representative shall take and subscribe an oath that the inventory contains a true statement of the property to be administered in the decedent's estate of which the personal representative has knowledge, and particularly of money of the decedent and debts or demands of the decedent against the personal representative. The oath shall be endorsed upon or attached to the inventory.

(b) If there is more than one personal representative, each shall take and subscribe the oath. If the personal representatives are unable to agree as to property to be included in the inventory, any personal representative may petition for a court order determining whether the property is to be administered in the decedent's estate. The determination shall be made pursuant to the procedure provided in Part 19 (commencing with Section 850) or Division 2 or, if there is an issue of property belonging or passing to the surviving spouse, pursuant to Chapter 5 (commencing with Section 13650) of Part 2 of Division 8.

(Stats. 1990 (A.B. 759), ch. 79, §14, effective July 1, 1991.Amended by Stats. 2003 (A.B. 167), ch. 32, §7.)

§8870. Court may order interrogatories or examination in court; consequences of failure to comply

(a) On petition by the personal representative or an interested person, the court may order that a citation be issued to a person to answer interrogatories, or to appear before the court and be examined under oath, or both, concerning any of the following allegations:

(1) The person has wrongfully taken, concealed, or disposed of property in the estate of the decedent.

(2) The person has knowledge or possession of any of the following:

(A) A deed, conveyance, bond, contract, or other writing that contains evidence of or tends to disclose the right, title, interest, or claim of the decedent to property.

(B) A claim of the decedent.

(C) A lost will of the decedent.

(b) If the person does not reside in the county in which the estate is being administered, the superior court either of the county in which the person resides or of the county in which the estate is being administered may issue a citation under this section.

(c) Disobedience of a citation issued pursuant to this section may be punished as a contempt of the court issuing the citation.

(d) Notice to the personal representative of a proceeding under subdivision (a) shall be given for the period and in the manner provided in Section 1220. Other persons requesting notice of the hearing pursuant to Section 1250 shall be notified by the person filing the petition as set forth in Section 1252.

(Stats. 1990 (A.B. 759), ch. 79, §14, effective July 1, 1991. Amended by Stats. 1996 (S.B. 392), ch. 563, §23.)

§8871. Interrogatories and answers must be in writing and filed with court

Interrogatories may be put to a person cited to answer interrogatories pursuant to Section 8870. The interrogatories and answers shall be in writing. The answers shall be signed under penalty of perjury by the person cited. The interrogatories and answers shall be filed with the court.

(Stats. 1990 (A.B. 759), ch. 79, §14, effective July 1, 1991.)

§8872. Witnesses may be produced and examined

(a) At an examination witnesses may be produced and examined on either side.

(b) If upon the examination it appears that the allegations of the petition are true, the court may order the person to disclose the person's knowledge of the facts to the personal representative.

(c) If upon the examination it appears that the allegations of the petition are not true, the person's necessary expenses, including a reasonable attorney's fee, shall be charged against the petitioner or allowed out of the estate, in the discretion of the court.

(Stats. 1990 (A.B. 759), ch. 79, §14, effective July 1, 1991.)

§8873. Court may require person controlling property in estate to appear and give accounting; contempt

(a) On petition by the personal representative, the court may issue a citation to a person who has possession or control of property in the decedent's estate to appear before the court and make an account under oath of the property and the person's actions with respect to the property.

(b) Disobedience of a citation issued pursuant to this section may be punished as a contempt of the court issuing the citation.

(Stats. 1990 (A.B. 759), ch. 79, §14, effective July 1, 1991.)

§8900. Persons who must make appraisal

The appraisal of property in the inventory shall be made by the personal representative, probate referee, or independent expert as provided in this chapter.

(Stats. 1990 (A.B. 759), ch. 79, §14, effective July 1, 1991.)

§8901. Personal representative shall appraise the following property

The personal representative shall appraise the following property, excluding items whose fair market value is, in the opinion of the personal representative, an amount different from the face value of the property:

(a) Money and other cash items. As used in this subdivision, a "cash item" is a check, draft, money order, or similar instrument issued on or before the date of the decedent's death that can be immediately converted to cash.

(b) The following checks issued after the date of the decedent's death:

(1) Checks for wages earned before death.

(2) Refund checks, including tax and utility refunds, and Medicare, medical insurance, and other health care reimbursements and payments.

(c) Accounts (as defined in Section 21) in financial institutions.

(d) Cash deposits and money market mutual funds, as defined in subdivision (b) of Section 9730, whether in a financial institution or otherwise, including a brokerage cash account. All other mutual funds, stocks, bonds, and other securities shall be appraised pursuant to Sections 8902 to 8909, inclusive.

(e) Proceeds of life and accident insurance policies and retirement plans and annuities payable on death in lump sum amounts.

(Stats. 1990 (A.B. 759), ch. 79, §14, effective July 1, 1991. Amended by Stats. 1994 (A.B. 3686), ch. 806, §30.)

§8902. Probate referee shall appraise all property other than that appraised by personal representative; representative must deliver inventory with supporting data

Except as otherwise provided by statute:

(a) The personal representative shall deliver the inventory to the probate referee designated by the court, together with necessary supporting data to enable the probate referee to make an appraisal of the property in the inventory to be appraised by the probate referee.

(b) The probate referee shall appraise all property other than that appraised by the personal representative.

(Stats. 1990 (A.B. 759), ch. 79, §14, effective July 1, 1991.)

§8903. Waiver of probate referee's appraisal

(a) The court may, for good cause, waive appraisal by a probate referee in the manner provided in this section.

(b) The personal representative may apply for a waiver together with the petition for appointment of the personal representative or together with another petition, or may apply for a waiver in a separate petition filed in the administration proceedings, but the application may not be made later than the time the personal representative delivers the inventory to the probate referee, if a probate referee has been designated. A copy of the proposed inventory and appraisal and a statement that sets forth the good cause that justifies the waiver shall be attached to the petition.

(c) The hearing on the waiver shall be not sooner than 15 days after the petition is filed. Notice of the hearing on the petition, together with a copy of the petition and a copy of the proposed inventory and appraisal, shall be given as provided in Section 1220 to all of the following persons:

(1) Each person listed in Section 1220.

(2) Each known heir whose interest in the estate would be affected by the waiver.

(3) Each known devisee whose interest in the estate would be affected by the waiver.

(4) The Attorney General, at the office of the Attorney General in Sacramento, if any portion of the estate is to escheat to the state and its interest in the estate would be affected by the waiver.

(5) The probate referee, if a probate referee has been designated.

(d) A probate referee to whom notice is given under this section may oppose the waiver. If the opposition fails and the court determines the opposition was made without substantial justification, the court shall award litigation expenses, including reasonable attorney's fees, against the probate referee. If the opposition succeeds, the court may designate a different probate referee to appraise property in the estate.

(e) If the petition is granted, the inventory and appraisal attached to the petition shall be filed pursuant to Section 8800.

(Stats. 1990 (A.B. 759), ch. 79, §14, effective July 1, 1991.)

§8904. Appraisal of special item of tangible personal property by independent expert

(a) A unique, artistic, unusual, or special item of tangible personal property that would otherwise be appraised by the probate referee may, at the election of the personal representative, be appraised by an independent expert qualified to appraise the item.

(b) The personal representative shall make the election provided in subdivision (a) by a notation on the inventory delivered to the probate referee indicating the property to be appraised by an independent expert. The probate referee may, within five days after delivery of the inventory, petition for a court determination whether the property to be appraised by an independent expert is a unique, artistic, unusual, or special item of tangible personal property. If the petition fails and the court determines that the petition was made without substantial justification, the court shall award litigation expenses, including reasonable attorney's fees, against the probate referee.

(Stats. 1990 (A.B. 759), ch. 79, §14, effective July 1, 1991.)

§8905. Appraiser must sign appraisal and take oath

A person who appraises property, whether a personal representative, probate referee, or independent expert, shall sign the appraisal as to property appraised by that person, and shall take and subscribe an oath that the person has truly, honestly, and impartially appraised the property to the best of the person's ability.

(Stats. 1990 (A.B. 759), ch. 79, §14, effective July 1, 1991.)

§8906. Objection to appraisal

(a) At any time before the hearing on the petition for final distribution of the estate, the personal representative or an interested person may file with the court a written objection to the appraisal.

(b) The clerk shall fix a time, not less than 15 days after the filing, for a hearing on the objection.

(c) The person objecting shall give notice of the hearing, together with a copy of the objection, as provided in Section 1220. If the appraisal was made by a probate referee, the person objecting shall also mail notice of the hearing and a copy of the objection to the probate referee at least 15 days before the date set for the hearing.

(d) The person objecting to the appraisal has the burden of proof.

(e) Upon completion of the hearing, the court may make any orders that appear appropriate. If the court determines the objection was filed without reasonable cause or good faith, the court may order that the fees of the personal representative and attorney and any costs incurred for defending the appraisal be made a charge against the person filing the objection.

(Stats. 1990 (A.B. 759), ch. 79, §14, effective July 1, 1991.)

§8907. Compensation for extraordinary services not available to personal representative or attorney for appraisals

Neither the personal representative nor the attorney for the personal representative is entitled to receive compensation for extraordinary services by reason of appraising any property in the estate.

(Stats. 1990 (A.B. 759), ch. 79, §14, effective July 1, 1991. Amended by Stats. 1991 (S.B. 896), ch. 82, §24, effective July 1, 1991.)

§8908. Probate referee must provide appraisal report, backup data, justification of appraisal upon demand

A probate referee who appraises property in the estate shall, upon demand by the personal representative or by a beneficiary:

(a) Provide any appraisal report or backup data in the possession of the probate referee used by the referee to appraise an item of property. The probate referee shall not disclose any information that is required by law to be confidential. The probate referee shall provide the appraisal report or backup data without charge. The cost of providing the appraisal report or backup data shall not be allowed as an expense of appraisal but is included in the commission for services of the probate referee.

(b) Justify the appraisal of an item of property if the appraisal is contested, whether by objection pursuant to Section 8906, by tax audit, or otherwise. The probate referee may be entitled to an additional fee for services provided to justify the appraisal, to be agreed upon by the personal representative or beneficiary and referee. If the personal representative or beneficiary and the probate referee are unable to agree, the court shall determine what fee, if any, is appropriate.

(Stats. 1990 (A.B. 759), ch. 79, §14, effective July 1, 1991.)

§8909. Probate referee must retain appraisal reports and backup data for 3 years

A probate referee who appraises property in an estate shall retain possession of all appraisal reports and backup data used by the referee to appraise the property for a period of three years after the appraisal is filed. The probate referee shall, during the three-year period, offer the personal representative the reports and data used by the referee to appraise the property and deliver the reports and data to the personal representative on request. Any reports and data not requested by the personal representative may be destroyed at the end of the three-year period without further notice.

(Stats. 1990 (A.B. 759), ch. 79, §14, effective July 1, 1991.)

§8920. Court designation of probate referee

The probate referee, when designated by the court, shall be among the persons appointed by the Controller to act as a probate referee for the county. If there is no person available who is able to act or if, pursuant to authority of Section 8922 or otherwise, the court does not designate a person appointed for the county, the court may designate a probate referee from another county.

(Stats. 1990 (A.B. 759), ch. 79, §14, effective July 1, 1991.)

§8921. Court may designate person requested by personal representative upon showing of good cause

The court may designate a person requested by the personal representative as probate referee, on a showing by the personal representative of good cause for the designation. The following circumstances are included within the meaning of good cause, as used in this section:

(a) The probate referee has recently appraised the same property that will be appraised in the administration proceeding.

(b) The probate referee will be making related appraisals in another proceeding.

(c) The probate referee has recently appraised similar property in another proceeding.

(Stats. 1990 (A.B. 759), ch. 79, §14, effective July 1, 1991.)

§8922. Court has authority not to designate particular person as probate referee

The court has authority and discretion not to designate a particular person as probate referee even though appointed by the Controller to act as a probate referee for the county.

(Stats. 1990 (A.B. 759), ch. 79, §14, effective July 1, 1991.)

§8923. Persons who are ineligible as probate referee

The court may not designate as probate referee any of the following persons:

(a) The court clerk.

(b) A partner or employee of the judge or commissioner who orders the designation.

(c) The spouse of the judge or commissioner who orders the designation.

(d) A person, or the spouse of a person, who is related within the third degree either (1) to the judge or commissioner who orders the designation or (2) to the spouse of the judge or commissioner who orders the designation.

(Stats. 1990 (A.B. 759), ch. 79, §14, effective July 1, 1991.)

§8924. Court shall remove designated probate referee in some circumstances

(a) The court shall remove the designated probate referee in any of the following circumstances:

(1) The personal representative shows cause, including incompetence or undue delay in making the appraisal, that in the opinion of the court warrants removal of the probate referee. The showing shall be made at a hearing on petition of the personal representative. The personal representative shall mail notice of the hearing on the petition to the probate referee at least 15 days before the date set for the hearing.

(2) The personal representative has the right to remove the first probate referee who is designated by the court. No cause need be shown for removal under this paragraph. The personal representative may exercise the right at any time before the personal representative delivers the inventory to the probate referee. The personal representative shall exercise the right by filing an affidavit or declaration under penalty of perjury with the court and mailing a copy to the probate referee. Thereupon, the court shall remove the probate referee without any further act or proof.

(3) Any other cause provided by statute.

(b) Upon removal of the probate referee, the court shall designate another probate referee in the manner prescribed in Section 8920.

(Stats. 1990 (A.B. 759), ch. 79, §14, effective July 1, 1991.)

§8940. Probate referee shall promptly appraise property in inventory and make status report

(a) The probate referee shall promptly and with reasonable diligence appraise the property scheduled for appraisal by the probate referee in the inventory that the personal representative delivers to the referee.

(b) The probate referee shall, not later than 60 days after delivery of the inventory, do one of the following:

(1) Return the completed appraisal to the personal representative.

(2) Make a report of the status of the appraisal. The report shall show the reason why the property has not been appraised and an estimate of the time needed to complete the appraisal. The report shall be delivered to the personal representative and filed with the court.

(Stats. 1990 (A.B. 759), ch. 79, §14, effective July 1, 1991.)

§8941. Hearing on status report of appraisal

(a) The court shall, on petition of the personal representative or probate referee, or may, on the court's own motion, hear the report of the status of the appraisal. The court may issue a citation to compel the personal representative or the probate referee to attend the hearing.

(b) If the probate referee does not make the report of the status of the appraisal within the time required by this article or prescribed by the court, the court shall, on petition of the personal representative or may, on its own motion, cite the probate referee to appear before the court and show the reason why the property has not been appraised.

(c) Upon the hearing, the court may order any of the following:

(1) That the appraisal be completed within a time that appears reasonable.

(2) That the probate referee be removed. Upon removal of the probate referee the court shall designate another probate referee in the manner prescribed in Section 8920.

(3) That the commission of the probate referee be reduced by an amount the court deems appropriate, regardless of whether the commission otherwise allowable under the provisions of Sections 8960 to 8964 would be reasonable compensation for the services rendered.

(4) That the personal representative deliver to the probate referee all information necessary to allow the probate referee to complete the appraisal. Failure to comply with such an order is grounds for removal of the personal representative.

(5) Such other orders as may be appropriate.

(Stats. 1990 (A.B. 759), ch. 79, §14, effective July 1, 1991.)

§8960. Commission and expenses for services of probate referee shall be paid from estate; priority of payment

(a) The commission and expenses provided by this article as compensation for the services of the probate referee shall be paid from the estate.

(b) The probate referee may not withhold the appraisal until the commission and expenses are paid, but shall deliver the appraisal to the personal representative promptly upon completion.

(c) The commission and expenses of the probate referee are an expense of administration, entitled to the priority for payment provided by Section 11420, and shall be paid in the course of administration.

(Stats. 1990 (A.B. 759), ch. 79, §14, effective July 1, 1991.)

§8961. Computation of commission for probate referee; eligible expenses

As compensation for services the probate referee shall receive all of the following:

(a) A commission of one-tenth of one percent of the total value of the property for each estate appraised, subject to Section 8963. The commission shall be computed excluding property appraised by the personal representative pursuant to Section 8901 or by an independent expert pursuant to Section 8904.

(b) Actual and necessary expenses for each estate appraised. The referee shall file with, or list on, the inventory and appraisal a verified account of the referee's expenses.

(Stats. 1990 (A.B. 759), ch. 79, §14, effective July 1, 1991.)

§8963. Range of compensation for probate referee

(a) Notwithstanding Section 8961 and subject to subdivision (b), the commission of the probate referee shall in no event be less than seventy-five dollars ($75) nor more than ten thousand dollars ($10,000) for any estate appraised.

(b) Upon application of the probate referee, the court may allow a commission in excess of ten thousand dollars ($10,000) if the court determines that the reasonable value of the referee's services exceeds that amount. Notice of the hearing under this subdivision shall be given as provided in Section 1220 to all of the following persons:

(1) Each person listed in Section 1220.

(2) Each known heir whose interest in the estate would be affected by the petition.

(3) Each known devisee whose interest in the estate would be affected by the petition.

(4) The Attorney General, at the office of the Attorney General in Sacramento, if any portion of the estate is to escheat to the state and its interest in the estate would be affected by the petition.

(5) Each person who has requested special notice of petitions filed in the proceeding.

(Stats. 1990 (A.B. 759), ch. 79, §14, effective July 1, 1991.)

§8964. Allocation of compensation for multiple probate referees

If more than one probate referee appraises or participates in the appraisal of property in the estate, each is entitled to the share of the commission agreed upon by the referees or, absent an agreement, that the court allows. In no case shall the total commission for all referees exceed the maximum commission that would be allowable for a single referee.

(Stats. 1990 (A.B. 759), ch. 79, §14, effective July 1, 1991.)

§8980. Applicable law for inventories delivered for appraisal before July 1, 1989

If an inventory is delivered to a probate referee for appraisal before July 1, 1989, all matters relating to the appraisal by the referee, including the property to be included in the appraisal, waiver of the appraisal, and compensation of the referee, are governed by the applicable law in effect before July 1, 1989, and are not governed by this chapter.

(Stats. 1990 (A.B. 759), ch. 79, §14, effective July 1, 1991.)

C. Payment of Creditors' Claims

Certain statutory requirements regulate the procedure for payment of creditors' claims against the decedent. Creditors must file their claims in the manner specified. Compliance with these statutory regulations is a prerequisite to the creditor's ability to maintain a subsequent action on the claim. If the creditor does not file a claim in a timely manner, the claim will be barred (Cal. Prob. Code §9002). Short claim periods facilitate the expeditious settlement of estates.

Claims are defined as demands for payment regarding particular liabilities of the decedent that arise (1) in contract, tort, or otherwise; (2) for taxes incurred before the decedent's death (whether assessed before or after the decedent's death, other than property taxes and assessments secured by real property liens); and (3) for funeral expenses (Cal. Prob. Code §9000(a)). However, claims do not include title disputes (*id.* at §9000(b)).

The personal representative has the responsibility to give proper notice to creditors. A *"nonclaim period"* begins running upon the filing of the personal representative's petition for issuance of letters testamentary (or letters of administration) and the provision of proper notice to creditors. The provision of notice informs creditors of the need to file their claims. In compliance with statutory and constitutional

requirements, proper notice consists of notice by publication as well as, in some cases, personal notice (Cal. Prob. Code §9001(a)). Personal service is required for those creditors who are known and reasonably ascertainable. Tulsa Professional Collection Servs., Inc. v. Pope, 485 U.S. 478 (1988).

"Known" creditors are those of whom the personal representative has knowledge, i.e., "if the personal representative is aware that the creditor has demanded payment from the decedent or the estate" (Cal. Prob. Code §9050(a)). In addition, the personal representative has a statutory duty toward those creditors who are "reasonably ascertainable" by making "reasonable diligent efforts to identify" them (Cal. Prob. Code §9053(d)). In some circumstances, the personal representative is not required to notify known creditors, e.g., if the creditor already has filed a claim or the creditor has demanded payment (i.e., less formally than filing a claim) which the personal representative has determined to treat as a claim (Cal. Prob. Code §9054).

Creditors who are given proper notice must file their claims before (the later of the following two periods): four months after issuance of letters or 60 days after the personal representative gave notice to the creditor (Cal. Prob. Code §9100). Claims that are not filed timely are forever barred (Cal. Prob. Code §9002), absent a statutory exception (discussed below).

A claim may be filed by a creditor or a person acting on his or her behalf (Cal. Prob. Code §9150(a)). The creditor must file the claim with the court and serve a copy on the personal representative (*id.* at §9150(b)). If the personal representative has not yet been appointed, the creditor must serve the representative when the latter is appointed (*id.*). The creditor must serve a copy on the personal representative within the requisite time period: the later of 30 days after filing the claim with the court or four months after issuance of letters to a general personal representative (*id.* at §9150(c)).

Creditors' demand for payment must be supported by an affidavit (Cal. Prob. Code §9151). The affidavit must state: (1) the claim is a "just" claim; (2) the facts supporting the claim, the amount of the claim, and that all payments on and offsets to the claim have been credited (if the claim is due); (3) if the claim is not due or contingent, or the amount is not yet ascertainable, the facts supporting the claim; and (4) if the affidavit is made by a person other than the creditor, the reason it is not made by the creditor (*id.* at Cal. Prob. Code §9151(a)).

The personal representative may request additional supporting proof to support the creditor's claim (*id.* at §9151(b)).

The personal representative may allow the claim in whole or part (Cal. Prob. Code §9255(a)). The representative must put his or her allowance or rejection of the claim in writing (Cal. Prob. Code §9250(b)). In addition, the representative must file the allowance or rejection with the court clerk and give notice to the creditor (*id.*).

A creditor who is dissatisfied with the personal representative's actions may choose to bring an action (Cal. Prob. Code §9255(b)). If the personal representative (or the court) does not act on a claim in a timely fashion (within 30 days after the claim is filed), the creditor may treat this failure to act as a rejection, thereby entitling the creditor to institute legal action (Cal. Prob. Code §9256). Claims that are allowed by the personal representative are presented to the court for approval (Cal. Prob. Code §9251). Court approval is not necessary if the personal representative is acting pursuant to the Independent Administration of Estates Act (see Section VII E *infra*).

Some recourse is available to some creditors whose claims are not properly filed within the requisite time period. Some creditors are entitled to petition for late claim relief pursuant to California Probate Code §9103 if two conditions are met: (1) the personal representative failed to send proper notice to the creditor, and the late claim petition was filed within 60 days after the creditor had actual knowledge of the administration of the estate; and (2) the creditor lacked knowledge of the facts reasonably giving rise to the existence of the claim more than 30 days prior to the time for filing a claim, and the late claim petition was filed within 60 days after the creditor had actual knowledge of both of the following: (a) the existence of the facts reasonably giving rise to the existence of the claim, and (b) the

administration of the estate (Cal. Prob. Code §9103).

According to the general rule, after an estate is closed (i.e., after the court orders the payments of debts and distribution pursuant to the representative's final accounting and petition for distribution), unpaid creditors have no recourse against those creditors who were paid or from distributees. This rule is subject to a limited exception for some creditors. That is, for those creditors who do not petition for late claim relief, if they are known or reasonably ascertainable, they may proceed against the estate distributees if the following conditions are met: if the claim is not merely conjectural (Cal. Prob. Code §9392(a)); if proper notice was not given to the creditor and neither the creditor nor the attorney representing the creditor has actual knowledge of the administration of the estate before the time the court made an order for final distribution of the property; and if the statute of limitations applicable to the claim under §366.2 of the Code of Civil Procedure has not expired at the time of commencement of an action under this section (Cal. Prob. Code §9392(b)). (General statutes of limitations applicable to civil suits are distinct from the short nonclaim period. For example, California Code of Civil Procedure §366.2 (*infra*) provides a one-year statute of limitations for actions on claims against the decedent that survive the decedent's death. A personal representative may not allow claims that are barred by the general statute of limitations (Cal. Prob. Code §§9103(b), 9253).)

Distributees have limited protection against creditors in such cases. Distributees may be held liable only if the creditor's claim cannot be satisfied from the estate (Cal. Prob. Code §9392(b)), and liability is limited to a "pro rata" portion of the claim (based on the share of the estate received by the distributee) (*id.*). Further, if a distributee has transferred his or her share to a bona fide purchaser, the latter is protected (Cal. Prob. Code §9392).

Special rules apply in cases in which personal representatives (or the representative's attorney) have claims against the estate because of the possibility of conflicts of interest (Cal. Prob. Code §9252(a)). In such cases, the court clerk must present the claim to the court for court approval (Cal. Prob. Code §9252(a)). On the rules for handling other special types of creditors' claims (e.g., public entities), see Ross & Grant, Cal. Prob. Prac., *supra*, at §§8:126-8:178.

Finally, a personal representative who fails to give proper notice to a known or reasonably ascertainable creditor in bad faith may be held personally liable (Cal. Prob. Code §§9053(b)(1), 11429(b)).

§9000. "Claim" defined

As used in this division:

(a) "Claim" means a demand for payment for any of the following, whether due, not due, accrued or not accrued, or contingent, and whether liquidated or unliquidated:

(1) Liability of the decedent, whether arising in contract, tort, or otherwise.

(2) Liability for taxes incurred before the decedent's death, whether assessed before or after the decedent's death, other than property taxes and assessments secured by real property liens.

(3) Liability of the estate for funeral expenses of the decedent.

(b) "Claim" does not include a dispute regarding title of a decedent to specific property alleged to be included in the decedent's estate.

(Stats. 1990 (A.B. 759), ch. 79, §14, effective July 1, 1991. Amended by Stats. 1996 (A.B. 2751), ch. 862, §17.)

§9001. Publication of notice and giving of notice of administration constitutes notice to creditors

(a) The publication of notice under Section 8120 and the giving of notice of administration of the estate of the decedent under Chapter 2 (commencing with Section 9050) constitute notice to creditors of the requirements of this part.

(b) Nothing in subdivision (a) affects a notice or request to a public entity required by Chapter 5 (commencing with Section 9200).

(Stats. 1990 (A.B. 759), ch. 79, §14, effective July 1, 1991.)

§9002. All claims shall be filed as provided or forever barred

Except as otherwise provided by statute:

(a) All claims shall be filed in the manner and within the time provided in this part.

(b) A claim that is not filed as provided in this part is barred.

(Stats. 1990 (A.B. 759), ch. 79, §14, effective July 1, 1991.)

§9003. Claims shall be included among debts to be paid in course of administration

A claim that is established under this part shall be included among the debts to be paid in the course of administration.

(Stats. 1990 (A.B. 759), ch. 79, §14, effective July 1, 1991.)

§9004. Application of law

(a) This part does not apply in any proceeding for administration of a decedent's estate commenced before July 1, 1988.

(b) The applicable law in effect before July 1, 1988, governing the subject matter of this part continues to apply in any proceeding for administration of a decedent's estate commenced before July 1, 1988, notwithstanding its repeal by Chapter 923 of the Statutes of 1987.

(Stats. 1990 (A.B. 759), ch. 79, §14, effective July 1, 1991.)

§9050. Types of creditors who must be given notice: known or reasonably ascertainable creditors

(a) Subject to Section 9054, the personal representative shall give notice of administration of the estate to the known or reasonably ascertainable creditors of the decedent. The notice shall be given as provided in Section 1215. For the purpose of this subdivision, a personal representative has knowledge of a creditor of the decedent if the personal representative is aware that the creditor has demanded payment from the decedent or the estate.

(b) The giving of notice under this chapter is in addition to the publication of the notice under Section 8120.

(Stats. 1990 (A.B. 759), ch. 79, §14, effective July 1, 1991. Amended by Stats. 1990 (S.B. 1855), ch. 140, §6.1, effective July 1, 1991; Stats. 1991 (S.B. 896), ch. 82, §25, effective July 1, 1991; Stats. 1996 (A.B. 2751), ch. 862, §18.)

§9051. Notice shall be given within certain time: 4 months after issuance of letters or 30 days after knowledge (whichever is later)

The notice shall be given within the later of:

(a) Four months after the date letters are first issued.

(b) Thirty days after the personal representative first has knowledge of the creditor.

(Stats. 1990 (A.B. 759), ch. 79, §14, effective July 1, 1991. Amended by Stats. 1990 (S.B. 1855), ch. 140, §7.1, effective July 1, 1991; Stats. 1996 (A.B. 2751), ch. 862, §19.)

§9052. Form of notice to creditors

The notice shall be in substantially the following form:

NOTICE OF ADMINISTRATION OF ESTATE OF

______________________, DECEDENT

Notice to creditors:

Administration of the estate of ____________ (deceased) has been commenced by ____________ (personal representative) in Estate No. _____ in the Superior Court of California, County of ____________. You must file your claim with the court and mail or deliver a copy to the personal representative within the last to occur of four months after ____________ (the date letters were issued to the personal representative), or 60 days after the date this notice was mailed to you or, in the case of personal delivery, 60 days after the date this notice was delivered to you, as provided in Section 9100 of the California Probate Code, or you must petition to file a late claim as provided in Section 9103 of the California Probate Code. Failure to file a claim with the court and serve a copy of the claim on the personal representative will, in most instances, invalidate your claim. A claim form may be obtained from the court clerk. For your protection, you are encouraged to file your claim by certified mail, with return receipt requested.

______________________ ______________________

(Date of mailing this notice) (Name and address of personal representative or attorney)

(Stats. 1990 (A.B. 759), ch. 79, §14, effective July 1, 1991. Amended by Stats. 1990 (S.B. 1855), ch. 140, ch. 140, §8.1, effective July 1, 1991; Stats. 1996 (A.B. 2751), ch. 862, §20.)

§9053. Liability of personal representative for giving or failing to give notice

(a) If the personal representative believes that notice to a particular creditor is or may be required by this chapter and gives notice based on that belief, the personal representative is not liable to any person for giving the notice, whether or not required by this chapter.

(b) If the personal representative fails to give notice required by this chapter, the personal representative is not liable to any person for the failure, unless a creditor establishes all of the following:

(1) The failure was in bad faith.

(2) The creditor had no actual knowledge of the administration of the estate before expiration of the time for filing a claim, and payment would have been made on the creditor's claim in the course of administration if the claim had been properly filed.

(3) Within 16 months after letters were first issued to a general personal representative, the creditor did both of the following:

(A) Filed a petition requesting that the court in which the estate was administered make an order determining the liability of the personal representative under this subdivision.

(B) At least 30 days before the hearing on the petition, caused notice of the hearing and a copy of the petition to be served on the personal representative in the manner provided in Chapter 4 (commencing with Section 413.10) of Title 5 of Part 2 of the Code of Civil Procedure.

(c) Nothing in this section affects the liability of the estate, if any, for the claim of a creditor, and the personal representative is not liable for the claim to the extent it is paid out of the estate or could be paid out of the estate pursuant to Section 9103.

(d) A personal representative has a duty to make reasonably diligent efforts to identify reasonably ascertainable creditors of the decedent.

(Stats. 1990 (A.B. 759), ch. 79, §14, effective July 1, 1991. Amended by Stats. 1991 (S.B. 271), ch. 1055, §24; Stats. 1996 (A.B. 2751), ch. 862, §21; Stats. 1999 (A.B. 1051), ch. 263, §4.)

§9054. Conditions under which no notice to creditor is required

Notwithstanding Section 9050, the personal representative need not give notice to a creditor even though the personal representative has knowledge of the creditor if any of the following conditions is satisfied:

(a) The creditor has filed a claim as provided in this part.

(b) The creditor has demanded payment and the personal representative elects to treat the demand as a claim under Section 9154.

(Stats. 1990 (A.B. 759), ch. 79, §14, effective July 1, 1991.)

§9100. Expiration date for filing creditors' claims

(a) A creditor shall file a claim before expiration of the later of the following times:

(1) Four months after the date letters are first issued to a general personal representative.

(2) Sixty days after the date notice of administration is given to the creditor. Nothing in this paragraph extends the time provided in Section 366.2 of the Code of Civil Procedure.

(b) A reference in another statute to the time for filing a claim means the time provided in paragraph (1) of subdivision (a).

(c) Nothing in this section shall be interpreted to extend or toll any other statute of limitations or to revive a claim that is barred by any statute of limitations. The reference in this subdivision to a "statute of limitations" includes Section 366.2 of the Code of Civil Procedure.

(Stats. 1990 (A.B. 759), ch. 79, §14, effective July 1, 1991. Amended by Stats. 1990 (S.B. 1855), ch. 140, §9.1, effective July 1, 1991; Stats. 1996 (A.B. 2751), ch. 862, §22; Stats. 1999 (A.B. 1051), ch. 263, §5.)

§9101. Vacancy in office of personal representative does not extend time for filing

A vacancy in the office of the personal representative that occurs before expiration of the time for filing a claim does not extend the time.

(Stats. 1990 (A.B. 759), ch. 79, §14, effective July 1, 1991.)

§9102. Claim is timely if filed before expiration of time

A claim that is filed before expiration of the time for filing the claim is timely even if acted on by the personal representative or by the court after expiration of the time.

(Stats. 1990 (A.B. 759), ch. 79, §14, effective July 1, 1991.)

§9103. Court may approve some claims filed after expiration of time; late claim relief

(a) Upon petition by a creditor or the personal representative, the court may allow a claim to be filed after expiration of the time for filing a claim provided in Section 9100 if either of the following conditions is satisfied:

(1) The personal representative failed to send proper and timely notice of administration of the estate to the creditor, and that petition is filed within 60 days after the creditor has actual knowledge of the administration of the estate.

(2) The creditor had no knowledge of the facts reasonably giving rise to the existence of the claim more than 30 days prior to the time for filing a claim as provided in Section 9100, and the petition is filed within 60 days after the creditor has actual knowledge of both of the following:

(A) The existence of the facts reasonably giving rise to the existence of the claim.

(B) The administration of the estate.

(b) Notwithstanding subdivision (a), the court shall not allow a claim to be filed under this section after the court makes an order for final distribution of the estate. Nothing in this subdivision authorizes allowance or approval of a claim barred by, or extends the time provided in, Section 366.2 of the Code of Civil Procedure.

(c) The court may condition the claim on terms that are just and equitable, and may require the appointment or reappointment of a personal representative if necessary. The court may deny the creditor's petition if a payment to general creditors has been made and it appears that the filing or establishment of the claim would cause or tend to cause unequal treatment among creditors.

(d) Regardless of whether the claim is later established in whole or in part, payments otherwise properly made before a claim is filed under this section are not subject to the claim. Except to the extent provided in Section 9392 and subject to Section 9053, the personal representative or payee is not liable on account of the prior payment. Nothing in this subdivision limits the liability of a person who receives a preliminary distribution of property to restore to the estate an amount sufficient for payment of the distributee's proper share of the claim, not exceeding the amount distributed.

(e) Notice of hearing on the petition shall be given as provided in Section 1220.

(Stats. 1990 (A.B. 759), ch. 79, §14, effective July 1, 1991. Amended by Stats. 1990 (S.B. 1855), ch. 140, §10.1, effective July 1, 1991; Stats. 1991 (S.B. 271), ch. 1055, §25; Stats. 1992 (S.B. 1496), ch. 178, §34; Stats. 1996 (A.B. 2751), ch. 862, §23.)

§9104. Creditor may amend or revise a claim

(a) Subject to subdivision (b), if a claim is filed within the time provided in this chapter, the creditor may later amend or revise the claim. The amendment or revision shall be filed in the same manner as the claim.

(b) An amendment or revision may not be made to increase the amount of the claim after the time for filing a claim has expired. An amendment or revision to specify the amount of a claim that, at the time of filing, was not due, was contingent, or was not yet ascertainable, is not an increase in the amount of the claim within the meaning of this subdivision.

(c) An amendment or revision may not be made for any purpose after the earlier of the following times:

(1) The time the court makes an order for final distribution of the estate.

(2) One year after letters are first issued to a general personal representative.

(Stats. 1990 (A.B. 759), ch. 79, §14, effective July 1, 1991.)

§9150. Creditors shall file their claims with court and serve copy on personal representative

(a) A claim may be filed by the creditor or a person acting on behalf of the creditor.

(b) A claim shall be filed with the court and a copy shall be served on the personal representative, or on a person who is later appointed and qualified as personal representative.

(c) Service of the claim on the personal representative shall be made within the later of 30 days of the filing of the claim or four months after letters issue to a personal representative with general powers. Service shall not be required after the claim has been allowed or rejected.

(d) If the creditor does not file the claim with the court and serve the claim on the personal representative as provided in this section, the claim shall be invalid.

(Stats. 1990 (A.B. 759), ch. 79, §14, effective July 1, 1991. Amended by Stats. 1996 (A.B. 2751), ch. 862, §24.)

§9151. Creditor's claim must be supported by affidavit

(a) A claim shall be supported by the affidavit of the creditor or the person acting on behalf of the creditor stating:

(1) The claim is a just claim.

(2) If the claim is due, the facts supporting the claim, the amount of the claim, and that all payments on and offsets to the claim have been credited.

(3) If the claim is not due or contingent, or the amount is not yet ascertainable, the facts supporting the claim.

(4) If the affidavit is made by a person other than the creditor, the reason it is not made by the creditor.

(b) The personal representative may require satisfactory vouchers or proof to be produced to support the claim. An original voucher may be withdrawn after a copy is provided. If a copy is provided, the copy shall be attached to the claim.

(Stats. 1990 (A.B. 759), ch. 79, §14, effective July 1, 1991.)

§9152. Claim based on written instruments must have document attached to claim

(a) If a claim is based on a written instrument, either the original or a copy of the original with all endorsements shall be attached to the claim. If a copy is attached, the original instrument shall be exhibited to the personal representative or court or judge on demand unless it is lost or destroyed, in which case the fact that it is lost or destroyed shall be stated in the claim.

(b) If the claim or a part of the claim is secured by a mortgage, deed of trust, or other lien that is recorded in the office of the recorder of the county in which the property subject to the lien is located, it is sufficient to describe the mortgage, deed of trust, or lien and the recording reference for the instrument that created the mortgage, deed of trust, or other lien.

(Stats. 1990 (A.B. 759), ch. 79, §14, effective July 1, 1991.)

§9153. Claim forms

A claim form adopted by the Judicial Council shall inform the creditor that the claim must be filed with the court and a

copy mailed or delivered to the personal representative. The claim form shall include a proof of mailing or delivery of a copy of the claim to the personal representative, which may be completed by the creditor.
(Stats. 1990 (A.B. 759), ch. 79, §14, effective July 1, 1991.)

§9154. Conditions for waiver of formal defects in creditor's timely written demand for payment

(a) Notwithstanding any other provision of this part, if a creditor makes a written demand for payment within four months after the date letters are first issued to a general personal representative, the personal representative may waive formal defects and elect to treat the demand as a claim that is filed and established under this part by paying the amount demanded before the expiration of 30 days after the four-month period if all of the following conditions are satisfied:

(1) The debt was justly due.

(2) The debt was paid in good faith.

(3) The amount paid was the true amount of the indebtedness over and above all payments and offsets.

(4) The estate is solvent.

(b) Nothing in this section limits application of (1) the doctrines of waiver, estoppel, laches, or detrimental reliance or (2) any other equitable principle.
(Stats. 1990 (A.B. 759), ch. 79, §14, effective July 1, 1991.)

[Some provisions of California Probate Code §§9200 et seq., which set forth requirements for claims by public entities, have been omitted.]

§9202. Notice to Director of Health Services of death of person receiving public health care

(a) Not later than 90 days after the date letters are first issued to a general personal representative, the general personal representative or estate attorney shall give the Director of Health Services notice of the decedent's death in the manner provided in Section 215 if the general personal representative knows or has reason to believe that the decedent received health care under Chapter 7 (commencing with Section 14000) or Chapter 8 (commencing with Section 14200) of Part 3 of Division 9 of the Welfare and Institutions Code, or was the surviving spouse of a person who received that health care. The director has four months after notice is given in which to file a claim.

(b) Not later than 90 days after the date letters are first issued to a general personal representative, the general personal representative or estate attorney shall give the Director of the California Victim Compensation and Government Claims Board notice of the decedent's death in the manner provided in Section 216 if the general personal representative or estate attorney knows or has reason to believe that an heir is confined in a prison or facility under the jurisdiction of the Department of Corrections or the Department of the Youth Authority or confined in any county or city jail, road camp, industrial farm, or other local correctional facility. The director of the board shall have four months after that notice is received in which to pursue collection of any outstanding restitution fines or orders.
(Stats. 1990 (A.B. 759), ch. 79, §14, effective July 1, 1991. Amended by Stats. 1993 (S.B. 35), ch. 69, §5, effective June 30, 1993; Stats. 2005 (S.B. 972), ch. 238, §4.)

§9250. Personal representative must allow or reject claim in whole or part, and in writing; form

(a) When a claim is filed, the personal representative shall allow or reject the claim in whole or in part.

(b) The allowance or rejection shall be in writing. The personal representative shall file the allowance or rejection with the court clerk and give notice to the creditor as provided in Part 2 (commencing with Section 1200) of Division 3, together with a copy of the allowance or rejection.

(c) The allowance or rejection shall contain the following information:

(1) The name of the creditor.

(2) The total amount of the claim.

(3) The date of issuance of letters.

(4) The date of the decedent's death.

(5) The estimated value of the decedent's estate.

(6) The amount allowed or rejected by the personal representative.

(7) Whether the personal representative is authorized to act under the Independent Administration of Estates Act (Part 6 (commencing with Section 10400)).

(8) A statement that the creditor has three months in which to act on a rejected claim.

(d) The Judicial Council may prescribe an allowance or rejection form, which may be part of the claim form. Use of a form prescribed by the Judicial Council is deemed to satisfy the requirements of this section.

(e) This section does not apply to a demand the personal representative elects to treat as a claim under Section 9154.
(Stats. 1990 (A.B. 759), ch. 79, §14, effective July 1, 1991. Amended by Stats. 1999 (A.B. 1051), ch. 263, §6.)

§9251. Requisite actions of personal representative not authorized to act under Independent Administration of Estates Act

If the personal representative is not authorized to act under the Independent Administration of Estates Act (Part 6 (commencing with Section 10400)):

(a) Immediately on the filing of the allowance of a claim, the clerk shall present the claim and allowance to the court or judge for approval or rejection.

(b) On presentation of a claim and allowance, the court or judge may, in its discretion, examine the creditor and others on oath and receive any evidence relevant to the validity of the claim. The court or judge shall endorse on the claim whether the claim is approved or rejected and the date.

(Stats. 1990 (A.B. 759), ch. 79, §14, effective July 1, 1991.)

§9252. Claim of personal representative or attorney of personal representative who is creditor of decedent

(a) If the personal representative or the attorney for the personal representative is a creditor of the decedent, the clerk shall present the claim to the court or judge for approval or rejection. The court or judge may in its discretion require the creditor to file a petition and give notice of hearing.

(b) If the court or judge approves the claim, the claim is established and shall be included with other established claims to be paid in the course of administration.

(c) If the court or judge rejects the claim, the personal representative or attorney may bring an action against the estate. Summons shall be served on the judge, who shall appoint an attorney at the expense of the estate to defend the action.

(Stats. 1990 (A.B. 759), ch. 79, §14, effective July 1, 1991.)

§9253. Claims barred by statutes limitations

A claim barred by the statute of limitations may not be allowed by the personal representative or approved by the court or judge.

(Stats. 1990 (A.B. 759), ch. 79, §14, effective July 1, 1991.)

§9254. Interested person may contest validity of claim

(a) The validity of an allowed or approved claim may be contested by any interested person at any time before settlement of the report or account of the personal representative in which it is first reported as an allowed or approved claim. The burden of proof is on the contestant, except where the personal representative has acted under the Independent Administration of Estates Act (Part 6 (commencing with Section 10400)), in which case the burden of proof is on the personal representative.

(b) Subdivision (a) does not apply to a claim established by a judgment.

(Stats. 1990 (A.B. 759), ch. 79, §14, effective July 1, 1991.)

§9255. Personal representative may allow a claim in whole or part; creditor may bring action upon refusal to accept partial payment

(a) The personal representative may allow a claim, or the court or judge may approve a claim, in part. The allowance or approval shall state the amount for which the claim is allowed or approved.

(b) A creditor who refuses to accept the amount allowed or approved in satisfaction of the claim may bring an action on the claim in the manner provided in Chapter 8 (commencing with Section 9350). The creditor may not recover costs in the action unless the creditor recovers an amount greater than that allowed or approved.

(Stats. 1990 (A.B. 759), ch. 79, §14, effective July 1, 1991.)

§9256. Refusal or neglect to act on claim shall be deemed notice of rejection

If within 30 days after a claim is filed the personal representative or the court or judge has refused or neglected to act on the claim, the refusal or neglect may, at the option of the creditor, be deemed equivalent to giving a notice of rejection on the 30th day.

(Stats. 1990 (A.B. 759), ch. 79, §14, effective July 1, 1991.)

§9300. Payment of money judgments against decedent or against personal representative on claims against decedent or estate

(a) Except as provided in Section 9303, after the death of the decedent all money judgments against the decedent or against the personal representative on a claim against the decedent or estate are payable in the course of administration and are not enforceable against property in the estate of the decedent under the Enforcement of Judgments Law (Title 9 (commencing with Section 680.010) of Part 2 of the Code of Civil Procedure).

(b) Subject to Section 9301, a judgment referred to in subdivision (a) shall be filed in the same manner as other claims.

(Stats. 1990 (A.B. 759), ch. 79, §14, effective July 1, 1991.)

§9301. Final judgment conclusively establishes validity of amount of claim

When a money judgment against a personal representative in a representative capacity becomes final, it conclusively

establishes the validity of the claim for the amount of the judgment. The judgment shall provide that it is payable out of property in the decedent's estate in the course of administration. An abstract of the judgment shall be filed in the administration proceedings.
(Stats. 1990 (A.B. 759), ch. 79, §14, effective July 1, 1991.)

§9302. Enforcement of judgments for possession or sale of property

(a) Notwithstanding the death of the decedent, a judgment for possession of property or a judgment for sale of property may be enforced under the Enforcement of Judgments Law (Title 9 (commencing with Section 680.010) of Part 2 of the Code of Civil Procedure). Nothing in this subdivision authorizes enforcement under the Enforcement of Judgments Law against any property in the estate of the decedent other than the property described in the judgment for possession or sale.

(b) After the death of the decedent, a demand for money that is not satisfied from the property described in a judgment for sale of property shall be filed as a claim in the same manner as other claims and is payable in the course of administration.
(Stats. 1990 (A.B. 759), ch. 79, §14, effective July 1, 1991.)

§9303. Enforcement of execution liens

If property of the decedent is subject to an execution lien at the time of the decedent's death, enforcement against the property may proceed under the Enforcement of Judgments Law (Title 9 (commencing with Section 680.010) of Part 2 of the Code of Civil Procedure) to satisfy the judgment. The levying officer shall account to the personal representative for any surplus. If the judgment is not satisfied, the balance of the judgment remaining unsatisfied is payable in the course of administration.
(Stats. 1990 (A.B. 759), ch. 79, §14, effective July 1, 1991.)

§9304. Conversion of attachment liens into judgment liens

(a) An attachment lien may be converted into a judgment lien on property in the estate subject to the attachment lien, with the same priority as the attachment lien, in either of the following cases:

(1) Where the judgment debtor dies after entry of judgment in an action in which the property was attached.

(2) Where a judgment is entered after the death of the defendant in an action in which the property was attached.

(b) To convert the attachment lien into a judgment lien, the levying officer shall, after entry of judgment in the action in which the property was attached and before the expiration of the attachment lien, do one of the following:

(1) Serve an abstract of the judgment, and a notice that the attachment lien has become a judgment lien, on the person holding property subject to the attachment lien.

(2) Record or file, in any office where the writ of attachment and notice of attachment are recorded or filed, an abstract of the judgment and a notice that the attachment lien has become a judgment lien. If the attached property is real property, the plaintiff or the plaintiff's attorney may record the required abstract and notice with the same effect as if recorded by the levying officer.

(c) After the death of the decedent, any members of the decedent's family who were supported in whole or in part by the decedent may claim an exemption provided in Section 487.020 of the Code of Civil Procedure for property levied on under the writ of attachment if the right to the exemption exists at the time the exemption is claimed. The personal representative may claim the exemption on behalf of members of the decedent's family. The claim of exemption may be made at any time before the time the abstract and notice are served, recorded, or filed under subdivision (b) with respect to the property claimed to be exempt. The claim of exemption shall be made in the same manner as an exemption is claimed under Section 482.100 of the Code of Civil Procedure.
(Stats. 1990 (A.B. 759), ch. 79, §14, effective July 1, 1991.)

§9350. Application of article to payment of claims in litigation

This article applies to any claim other than a claim on an action or proceeding pending against the decedent at the time of death.
(Stats. 1990 (A.B. 759), ch. 79, §14, effective July 1, 1991.)

§9351. Rejection of claim is prerequisite to commencement of action against personal representative

An action may not be commenced against a decedent's personal representative on a cause of action against the decedent unless a claim is first filed as provided in this part and the claim is rejected in whole or in part.
(Stats. 1990 (A.B. 759), ch. 79, §14, effective July 1, 1991.)

§9352. Tolling of statute of limitations

(a) The filing of a claim or a petition under Section 9103 to file a claim tolls the statute of limitations otherwise applicable to the claim until allowance, approval, or rejection.

(b) The allowance or approval of a claim in whole or in part further tolls the statute of limitations during the administration of the estate as to the part allowed or approved.
(Stats. 1990 (A.B. 759), ch. 79, §14, effective July 1, 1991. Amended by Stats. 1991 (S.B. 271), ch. 1055, §26.)

§9353. Rejected claim is barred regardless of statute of limitations; exceptions

(a) Regardless of whether the statute of limitations otherwise applicable to a claim will expire before or after the following times, a claim rejected in whole or in part is barred as to the part rejected unless, within the following times, the creditor commences an action on the claim or the matter is referred to a referee or to arbitration:

(1) If the claim is due at the time the notice of rejection is given, three months after the notice is given.

(2) If the claim is not due at the time the notice of rejection is given, three months after the claim becomes due.

(b) The time during which there is a vacancy in the office of the personal representative shall be excluded from the period determined under subdivision (a).
(Stats. 1990 (A.B. 759), ch. 79, §14, effective July 1, 1991.)

§9354. Venue for action on claims in county where estate administration is pending; notice; liability

(a) In addition to any other county in which an action may be commenced, an action on the claim may be commenced in the county in which the proceeding for administration of the decedent's estate is pending.

(b) The plaintiff shall file a notice of the pendency of the action with the court clerk in the estate proceeding, together with proof of giving a copy of the notice to the personal representative as provided in Section 1215. Personal service of a copy of the summons and complaint on the personal representative is equivalent to the filing and giving of the notice. Any property distributed under court order, or any payment properly made, before the notice is filed and given is not subject to the claim. The personal representative, distributee, or payee is not liable on account of the prior distribution or payment.

(c) The prevailing party in the action shall be awarded court costs and, if the court determines that the prosecution or defense of the action against the prevailing party was unreasonable, the prevailing party shall be awarded reasonable litigation expenses, including attorney's fees.
(Stats. 1990 (A.B. 759), ch. 79, §14, effective July 1, 1991.)

§9370. Conditions for continuation of action pending against decedent at time of death

(a) An action or proceeding pending against the decedent at the time of death may not be continued against the decedent's personal representative unless all of the following conditions are satisfied:

(1) A claim is first filed as provided in this part.

(2) The claim is rejected in whole or in part.

(3) Within three months after the notice of rejection is given, the plaintiff applies to the court in which the action or proceeding is pending for an order to substitute the personal representative in the action or proceeding. This paragraph applies only if the notice of rejection contains a statement that the plaintiff has three months within which to apply for an order for substitution.

(b) No recovery shall be allowed in the action against property in the decedent's estate unless proof is made of compliance with this section.
(Stats. 1990 (A.B. 759), ch. 79, §14, effective July 1, 1991.)

§9390. Actions to establish decedent's liability if decedent was protected by insurance

(a) An action to establish the decedent's liability for which the decedent was protected by insurance may be commenced or continued under Section 550, and a judgment in the action may be enforced against the insurer, without first filing a claim as provided in this part.

(b) Unless a claim is first made as provided in this part, an action to establish the decedent's liability for damages outside the limits or coverage of the insurance may not be commenced or continued under Section 550.

(c) If the insurer seeks reimbursement under the insurance contract for any liability of the decedent, including, but not limited to, deductible amounts in the insurance coverage and costs and attorney's fees for which the decedent is liable under the contract, an insurer defending an action under Section 550 shall file a claim as provided in this part. Failure to file a claim is a waiver of reimbursement under the insurance contract for any liability of the decedent.
(Stats. 1990 (A.B. 759), ch. 79, §14, effective July 1, 1991. Amended by Stats. 1990 (S.B. 1775), ch. 710, §23, effective July 1, 1991.)

§9391. Prerequisite to commencement of enforcement action by holder of mortgage or other lien on decedent's property without first filing claim

Except as provided in Section 10361, the holder of a mortgage or other lien on property in the decedent's estate, including, but not limited to, a judgment lien, may commence an action to enforce the lien against the property that is subject to the lien, without first filing a claim as provided in this part, if in the complaint the holder of the lien expressly waives all recourse against other property in the estate. Section 366.2 of the Code of Civil Procedure does not apply to an action under this section. The personal representative shall have the authority to seek to enjoin any action of the lienholder to enforce a lien against property that is subject to the lien.

(Stats. 1990 (A.B. 759), ch. 79, §14, effective July 1, 1991. Amended by Stats. 1990 (S.B. 1855), ch. 140, § 2.1, effective July 1, 1991; Stats. 1992 (S.B. 1496), ch. 178, §35; Stats. 1996 (S.B. 392), ch. 563, §24; Stats. 1996 (A.B. 2751), ch. 862, §25.)

§9392. Conditions under which distributee is personally liable for claims of creditors who did not first file claim

(a) Subject to subdivision (b), a person to whom property is distributed is personally liable for the claim of a creditor, without a claim first having been filed, if all of the following conditions are satisfied:

(1) The identity of the creditor was known to, or reasonably ascertainable by, a general personal representative within four months after the date letters were first issued to the personal representative, and the claim of the creditor was not merely conjectural.

(2) Notice of administration of the estate was not given to the creditor under Chapter 2 (commencing with Section 9050) and neither the creditor nor the attorney representing the creditor in the matter has actual knowledge of the administration of the estate before the time the court made an order for final distribution of the property.

(3) The statute of limitations applicable to the claim under Section 366.2 of the Code of Civil Procedure has not expired at the time of commencement of an action under this section.

(b) Personal liability under this section is applicable only to the extent the claim of the creditor cannot be satisfied out of the estate of the decedent and is limited to a pro rata portion of the claim of the creditor, based on the proportion that the value of the property distributed to the person out of the estate bears to the total value of all property distributed to all persons out of the estate. Personal liability under this section for all claims of all creditors shall not exceed the value of the property distributed to the person out of the estate. As used in this section, the value of property is the fair market value of the property on the date of the order for distribution, less the amount of any liens and encumbrances on the property at that time.

(c) Nothing in this section affects the rights of a purchaser or encumbrancer of property in good faith and for value from a person who is personally liable under this section.

(Stats. 1990 (S.B. 1855), ch. 140, §13.1, effective July 1, 1991. Amended by Stats. 1992 (S.B. 1496), ch. 178, §36.)

§9399. Application of chapter to actions commenced before July 1, 1989

(a) This chapter does not apply to an action commenced before July 1, 1989.

(b) The applicable law in effect before July 1, 1989, continues to apply to an action commenced before July 1, 1989, notwithstanding its repeal by Chapter 1199 of the Statutes of 1988.

(Stats. 1990 (A.B. 759), ch. 79, §14, effective July 1, 1991.)

CALIFORNIA CODE OF CIVIL PROCEDURE

§366.2. Statute of limitations for contracts, torts, etc. after the death of alleged wrongdoer

(a) If a person against whom an action may be brought on a liability of the person, whether arising in contract, tort, or otherwise, and whether accrued or not accrued, dies before the expiration of the applicable limitations period, and the cause of action survives, an action may be commenced within one year after the date of death, and the limitations period that would have been applicable does not apply.

(b) The limitations period provided in this section for commencement of an action shall not be tolled or extended for any reason except as provided in any of the following, where applicable:

(1) Sections 12, 12a, and 12b of this code.

(2) Part 4 (commencing with Section 9000) of Division 7 of the Probate Code (creditor claims in administration of estates of decedents).

(3) Part 8 (commencing with Section 19000) of Division 9 of the Probate Code (payment of claims, debts, and expenses from revocable trust of deceased settlor).

(4) Part 3 (commencing with Section 21300) of Division 11 of the Probate Code (no contest clauses).

(c) This section applies to actions brought on liabilities of persons dying on or after January 1, 1993.

(Stats. 1992 (S.B. 1496), ch. 178, §8. Amended by Stats. 1993 (A.B. 1704), ch. 151, §2, effective July 19, 1993; Stats. 1994 (A.B. 797), ch. 40, §1, effective January 1, 1995; Stats. 1996, (A.B. 2751), ch. 862, §1; Stats. 1998 (A.B. 2801), ch. 581, §1; Stats. 2006 (A.B. 2864), ch. 221, §1.)

D. Payment of Decedent's Debts

In some cases, an estate does not have sufficient funds to provide for payment of all of the decedent's debts. In such situations, the

California Probate Code specifies an order of priority in which debts are to be paid. The statute accords the highest priority to expenses of estate administration (e.g., compensation for the personal representative and the representative's attorney). Next come funeral expenses; last illness expenses; family allowance; claims for wages of the decedent's employees; obligations secured by a mortgage, deed of trust, or other lien; and all other debts (Cal. Prob. Code §11420).

The personal representative may pay some debts without the need to obtain prior court approval (e.g., funeral and last illness expenses, family allowance, and claims for the decedent's employees' wages) (Cal. Prob. Code §11421). However, before making payments for these debts, the personal representative must first make sure that there are sufficient funds to pay for the expenses of administration (*id.*). For all other debts, the personal representative must obtain court approval—which is forthcoming generally after expiration of the nonclaim period and pursuant to settlement of an account (Cal. Prob. Code §11422).

CALIFORNIA PROBATE CODE

§11400. Application of definitions

Unless the provision or context otherwise requires, the definitions in this article govern the construction of this part.

(Stats. 1990 (A.B. 759), ch. 79, §14, effective July 1, 1991.)

§11401. "Debt," defined

"Debt" means:

(a) A claim that is established under Part 4 (commencing with Section 9000) or that is otherwise payable in the course of administration.

(b) An expense of administration.

(c) A charge against the estate including, but not limited to, taxes, expenses of last illness, and family allowance.

(Stats. 1990 (A.B. 759), ch. 79, §14, effective July 1, 1991.)

§11402. "Wage claim," defined

"Wage claim" means a claim for wages, not exceeding two thousand dollars ($2,000), of each employee of the decedent for work done or personal services rendered within 90 days before the death of the decedent.

(Stats. 1990 (A.B. 759), ch. 79, §14, effective July 1, 1991.)

§11405. Application of part to proceedings for administration commenced before July 1, 1988

(a) This part does not apply in any proceeding for the administration of a decedent's estate commenced before July 1, 1988.

(b) The applicable law in effect before July 1, 1988, governing the subject matter of this part continues to apply in any proceeding for administration of a decedent's estate commenced before July 1, 1988, notwithstanding its repeal by Chapter 923 of the Statutes of 1987.

(Stats. 1990 (A.B. 759), ch. 79, §14, effective July 1, 1991.)

§11420. Order of priority of debts: debts owed to U.S., expenses of administration, etc.

(a) Debts shall be paid in the following order of priority among classes of debts, except that debts owed to the United States or to this state that have preference under the laws of the United States or of this state shall be given the preference required by such laws:

(1) Expenses of administration. With respect to obligations secured by mortgage, deed of trust, or other lien, including, but not limited to, a judgment lien, only those expenses of administration incurred that are reasonably related to the administration of that property by which obligations are secured shall be given priority over these obligations.

(2) Obligations secured by a mortgage, deed of trust, or other lien, including, but not limited to, a judgment lien, in the order of their priority, so far as they may be paid out of the proceeds of the property subject to the lien. If the proceeds are insufficient, the part of the obligation remaining unsatisfied shall be classed with general debts.

(3) Funeral expenses.

(4) Expenses of last illness.

(5) Family allowance.

(6) Wage claims.

(7) General debts, including judgments not secured by a lien and all other debts not included in a prior class.

(b) Except as otherwise provided by statute, the debts of each class are without preference or priority one over another. No debt of any class may be paid until all those of prior classes are paid in full. If property in the estate is insufficient to pay all debts of any class in full, each debt in that class shall be paid a proportionate share.

(Stats. 1990 (A.B. 759), ch. 79, §14, effective July 1, 1991. Amended by Stats. 1996 (A.B. 2751), ch. 862, §33.)

§11421. Personal representative shall pay debts after covering administration expenses when there are sufficient funds

Subject to Section 11420, as soon as the personal representative has sufficient funds, after retaining sufficient funds to pay expenses of administration, the personal representative shall pay the following:

(a) Funeral expenses.

(b) Expenses of last illness.

(c) Family allowance.

(d) Wage claims.

(Stats. 1990 (A.B. 759), ch. 79, §14, effective July 1, 1991.)

§11422. Payment of debt is not required until ordered by court; exceptions

(a) Except as provided in Section 11421, the personal representative is not required to pay a debt until payment has been ordered by the court.

(b) On the settlement of any account of the personal representative after the expiration of four months after the date letters are first issued to a general personal representative, the court shall order payment of debts, as the circumstances of the estate permit. If property in the estate is insufficient to pay all of the debts, the order shall specify the amount to be paid to each creditor.

(c) If the estate will be exhausted by the payment ordered, the account of the personal representative constitutes a final account, and notice of hearing shall be the notice given for the hearing of a final account. The personal representative is entitled to a discharge when the personal representative has complied with the terms of the order.

(d) Nothing in this section precludes settlement of an account of a personal representative for payment of a debt made without prior court authorization.

(Stats. 1990 (A.B. 759), ch. 79, §14, effective July 1, 1991.)

§11423. Accrual of interest on debt

(a) Interest accrues on a debt from the date the court orders payment of the debt until the date the debt is paid. Interest accrues at the legal rate on judgments.

(b) Notwithstanding subdivision (a), in the case of a debt based on a written contract, interest accrues at the rate and in accordance with the terms of the contract. The personal representative may, by order of the court, pay all or part of the interest accumulated and unpaid at any time when there are sufficient funds, whether the debt is then due or not.

(c) Notwithstanding subdivision (a), in the case of a debt for unpaid taxes or any other debt for which interest is expressly provided by statute, interest accrues at the rate and in accordance with the terms of the statute.

(Stats. 1990 (A.B. 759), ch. 79, §14, effective July 1, 1991.)

§11424. Personal representative's liability for failure to pay debt

The personal representative shall pay a debt to the extent of the order for payment of the debt, and is liable personally and on the bond, if any, for failure to make the payment.

(Stats. 1990 (A.B. 759), ch. 79, §14, effective July 1, 1991.)

§11428. Personal representative shall deposit payment with county treasurer for debts unpayable because creditor cannot be found

(a) If an estate is in all other respects ready to be closed, and it appears to the satisfaction of the court, on affidavit or evidence taken in open court, that a debt has not been and cannot be paid because the creditor cannot be found, the court or judge shall make an order fixing the amount of the payment and directing the personal representative to deposit the payment with the county treasurer of the county in which the proceeding is pending.

(b) The county treasurer shall give a receipt for the deposit, for which the county treasurer is liable on the official bond. The receipt shall be treated by the court or judge in favor of the personal representative with the same force and effect as if executed by the creditor.

(c) A deposit with the county treasurer under the provisions of this section shall be received, accounted for, and disposed of as provided by Section 1444 of the Code of Civil Procedure. A deposit in the State Treasury under the provisions of this section shall be deemed to be made under the provisions of Article 1 (commencing with Section 1440) of Chapter 6 of Title 10 of Part 3 of the Code of Civil Procedure.

(Stats. 1990 (A.B. 759), ch. 79, §14, effective July 1, 1991.)

§11429. Unpaid creditor has no right of contribution among creditors

(a) Where the accounts of the personal representative have been settled and an order made for the payment of debts and distribution of the estate, a creditor who is not paid, whether or not included in the order for payment, has no right to require contribution from creditors who are paid or from distributees, except to the extent provided in Section 9392.

(b) Nothing in this section precludes recovery against the personal representative personally or on the bond, if any, by a creditor who is not paid, subject to Section 9053.

(Stats. 1990 (A.B. 759), ch. 79, §14, effective July 1, 1991. Amended by Stats. 1990 (S.B. 1855), ch. 140, §14.1, effective July 1, 1991.)

§11440. Persons may petition to allocate debt

If it appears that a debt of the decedent has been paid or is payable in whole or in part by the surviving spouse, or that a debt of the surviving spouse has been paid or is payable in whole or in part from property in the decedent's estate, the personal representative, the surviving spouse, or a beneficiary may, at any time before an order for final distribution is made, petition for an order to allocate the debt.

(Stats. 1990 (A.B. 759), ch. 79, §14, effective July 1, 1991.)

§11441. Contents of petition

The petition shall include a statement of all of the following:

(a) All debts of the decedent and surviving spouse known to the petitioner that are alleged to be subject to allocation and whether paid in whole or part or unpaid.

(b) The reason why the debts should be allocated.

(c) The proposed allocation and the basis for allocation alleged by the petitioner.

(Stats. 1990 (A.B. 759), ch. 79, §14, effective July 1, 1991.)

§11442. Allocation affected by value of separate and community property where no inventory and appraisal provided

If it appears from the petition that allocation would be affected by the value of the separate property of the surviving spouse and any community property and quasi-community property not administered in the estate and if an inventory and appraisal of the property has not been provided by the surviving spouse, the court shall make an order to show cause why the information should not be provided.

(Stats. 1990 (A.B. 759), ch. 79, §14, effective July 1, 1991.)

§11443. Petitioner shall give notice of hearing on show cause order

The petitioner shall give notice of the hearing as provided in Section 1220, together with a copy of the petition and the order to show cause, if any.

(Stats. 1990 (A.B. 759), ch. 79, §14, effective July 1, 1991.)

§11444. Court shall order allocation of debt provided in agreement between personal representative and surviving spouse

(a) The personal representative and the surviving spouse may provide for allocation by agreement and, on a determination by the court that the agreement substantially protects the rights of interested persons, the allocation provided in the agreement shall be ordered by the court.

(b) In the absence of an agreement, each debt subject to allocation shall first be characterized by the court as separate or community, in accordance with the laws of the state applicable to marital dissolution proceedings. Following that characterization, the debt or debts shall be allocated as follows:

(1) Separate debts of either spouse shall be allocated to that spouse's separate property assets, and community debts shall be allocated to the spouses' community property assets.

(2) If a separate property asset of either spouse is subject to a secured debt that is characterized as that spouse's separate debt, and the net equity in that asset available to satisfy that secured debt is less than that secured debt, the unsatisfied portion of that secured debt shall be treated as an unsecured separate debt of that spouse and allocated to the net value of that spouse's other separate property assets.

(3) If the net value of either spouse's separate property assets is less than that spouse's unsecured separate debt or debts, the unsatisfied portion of the debt or debts shall be allocated to the net value of that spouse's one-half share of the community property assets. If the net value of that spouse's one half share of the community property assets is less than that spouse's unsatisfied unsecured separate debt or debts, the remaining unsatisfied portion of the debt or debts shall be allocated to the net value of the other spouse's one-half share of the community property assets.

(4) If a community property asset is subject to a secured debt that is characterized as a community debt, and the net equity in that asset available to satisfy that secured debt is less than that secured debt, the unsatisfied portion of that secured debt shall be treated as an unsecured community debt and allocated to the net value of the other community property assets.

(5) If the net value of the community property assets is less than the unsecured community debt or debts, the unsatisfied portion of the debt or debts shall be allocated equally between the separate property assets of the decedent and the surviving spouse. If the net value of either spouse's separate property assets is less than that

spouse's share of the unsatisfied portion of the unsecured community debt or debts, the remaining unsatisfied portion of the debt or debts shall be allocated to the net value of the other spouse's separate property assets.

(c) For purposes of this section:

(1) The net value of either spouse's separate property asset shall refer to its fair market value as of the date of the decedent's death, minus the date-of-death balance of any liens and encumbrances on that asset that have been characterized as that spouse's separate debts.

(2) The net value of a community property asset shall refer to its fair market value as of the date of the decedent's death, minus the date-of-death balance of any liens and encumbrances on that asset that have been characterized as community debts.

(3) In the case of a nonrecourse debt, the amount of that debt shall be limited to the net equity in the collateral, based on the fair market value of the collateral as of the date of the decedent's death, that is available to satisfy that debt. For the purposes of this paragraph, "nonrecourse debt" means a debt for which the debtor's obligation to repay is limited to the collateral securing the debt, and for which a deficiency judgment against the debtor is not permitted by law.

(d) Notwithstanding the foregoing provisions of this section, the court may order a different allocation of debts between the decedent's estate and the surviving spouse if the court finds a different allocation to be equitable under the circumstances.

(e) Nothing contained in this section is intended to impair or affect the rights of third parties. If a personal representative or the surviving spouse incurs any damages or expense, including attorney's fees, on account of the nonpayment of a debt that was allocated to the other party pursuant to subdivision (b), or as the result of a debt being misallocated due to fraud or intentional misrepresentation by the other party, the party incurring damages shall be entitled to recover from the other party for damages or expense deemed reasonable by the court that made the allocation.

(Stats. 1990 (A.B. 759), ch. 79, §14, effective July 1, 1991. Amended by Stats. 2001 (S.B. 668), ch. 72, §1.)

§11445. Court shall make order directing payment of allocated shares

On making a determination as provided in this chapter, the court shall make an order that:

(a) Directs the personal representative to make payment of the amounts allocated to the estate by payment to the surviving spouse or creditors.

(b) Directs the personal representative to charge amounts allocated to the surviving spouse against any property or interests of the surviving spouse that are in the possession or control of the personal representative. To the extent that property or interests of the surviving spouse in the possession or control of the personal representative are insufficient to satisfy the allocation, the court order shall summarily direct the surviving spouse to pay the allocation to the personal representative.

(Stats. 1990 (A.B. 759), ch. 79, §14, effective July 1, 1991.)

§11446. Allocation of last illness and funeral expenses

Notwithstanding any other statute, funeral expenses and expenses of last illness shall be charged against the estate of the decedent and shall not be allocated to, or charged against the community share of, the surviving spouse, whether or not the surviving spouse is financially able to pay the expenses and whether or not the surviving spouse or any other person is also liable for the expenses.

(Stats. 1990 (A.B. 759), ch. 79, §14, effective July 1, 1991.)

§11460. Definitions of terms: contingent, disputed, not due

As used in this chapter:

(a) A debt is "contingent" if it is established under Part 4 (commencing with Section 9000) in either a fixed or an uncertain amount and will become absolute on occurrence of a stated event other than the passage of time. The term includes a secured obligation for which there may be recourse against property in the estate, other than the property that is the security, if the security is insufficient.

(b) A debt is "disputed" if it is a claim rejected in whole or in part under Part 4 (commencing with Section 9000) and is not barred under Section 9353 as to the part rejected.

(c) A debt is "not due" if it is established under Part 4 (commencing with Section 9000) and will become due on the passage of time. The term includes a debt payable in installments.

(Stats. 1991 (S.B. 271), ch. 1055, §31.)

§11461. Court may make or modify order regarding certain types of debts

When all other debts have been paid and the estate is otherwise in a condition to be closed, on petition by an interested person, the court may make or modify an order or a combination of orders under this chapter that the court in its discretion determines is appropriate to provide adequately for a debt that is contingent, disputed, or not due, if the debt becomes absolute, established, or due.

Notice of the hearing on the petition shall be given as provided in Section 1220 to the creditor whose debt is contingent, disputed, or not due, as well as to the persons provided in Section 11601.

(Stats. 1991 (S.B. 271), ch. 1055, §31.)

§11462. Court shall approve agreements of interested persons

Notwithstanding any other provision of this chapter, if the court determines that all interested persons agree to the manner of providing for a debt that is contingent, disputed, or not due and that the agreement reasonably protects all interested persons and will not extend administration of the estate unreasonably, the court shall approve the agreement.

(Stats. 1991 (S.B. 271), ch. 1055, §31.)

§11463. Court may order account deposited in financial institution and withdrawable only on court order

The court may order an amount deposited in a financial institution, as provided in Chapter 3 (commencing with Section 9700) of Part 5, that would be payable if a debt that is contingent, disputed, or not due, were absolute, established, or due. The order shall provide that the amount deposited is subject to withdrawal only upon authorization of the court, to be paid to the creditor when the debt becomes absolute, established, or due, or to be distributed in the manner provided in Section 11642 if the debt does not become absolute or established.

(Stats. 1991 (S.B. 271), ch. 1055, §31.)

§11464. Court may order distribution subject to assumption of liability

(a) The court may order property in the estate distributed to a person entitled to it under the final order for distribution, if the person files with the court an assumption of liability for a contingent or disputed debt as provided in subdivision (b). The court may impose any other conditions the court in its discretion determines are just, including that the distributee give a security interest in all or part of the property distributed or that the distributee give a bond in an amount determined by the court.

(b) As a condition for an order under subdivision (a), each distributee shall file with the court a signed and acknowledged agreement assuming personal liability for the contingent or disputed debt and consenting to jurisdiction within this state for the enforcement of the debt if it becomes absolute or established. The personal liability of each distributee shall not exceed the fair market value on the date of distribution of the property received by the distributee, less the amount of liens and encumbrances. If there is more than one distributee, the personal liability of the distributees is joint and several.

(c) If the debt becomes absolute or established, it may be enforced against each distributee in the same manner as it could have been enforced against the decedent if the decedent had not died. In an action based on the debt, the distributee may assert any defense, cross-complaint, or setoff that would have been available to the decedent if the decedent had not died.

(d) The statute of limitations applicable to a contingent debt is tolled from the time the creditor's claim is filed until 30 days after the order for distribution becomes final. The signing of an agreement under subdivision (b) neither extends nor revives any limitation period.

(Stats. 1991 (S.B. 271), ch. 1055, §31.)

§11465. Court may order appointment of trustee to receive payment for certain debts

(a) The court may order that a trustee be appointed to receive payment for a debt that is contingent, disputed, or not due. The court in determining the amount paid to the trustee shall compute the present value of the debt, giving consideration to a reasonable return on the amount to be invested. The trustee shall invest the payment in investments that would be proper for a personal representative or as authorized in the order.

(b) The trustee shall pay the debt as provided in the order. On completion of payment, any excess in possession of the trustee shall be distributed in the manner provided in Section 11642.

(Stats. 1991 (S.B. 271), ch. 1055, §31.)

§11466. Court may order distribution subject to bond

The court may order property in the estate distributed to a person entitled to it under the final order for distribution, if the person gives a bond conditioned on payment by the person of the amount of a contingent or disputed debt that becomes absolute or established. The amount of the bond shall be determined by the court, not to exceed the fair market value on the date of distribution of the property received by the distributee, less the amount of liens and encumbrances. In the case of a disputed debt or in the case of a contingent debt where litigation is required to establish the contingency, the cost of the bond is recoverable from the unsuccessful party as a cost of litigation.

(Stats. 1991 (S.B. 271), ch. 1055, §31.)

§11467. Court may order continuation of administration until resolution of certain debts

The court may order that the administration of the estate continue until the contingency, dispute, or passage of time of a debt that is contingent, disputed, or not due is resolved.

(Stats. 1991 (S.B. 271), ch. 1055, §31.)

E. Accounting

The personal representative must file periodic accounts with the court. "The accountings periodically filed by an estate representative allow the court to examine the record of the estate's administration (receipts, claims, and disbursements, etc.) and afford the court the opportunity to pass on the propriety and reasonableness of the representative's stewardship of the estate's assets." Ross & Grant, Cal. Prob. Prac., *supra*, at §16:91.

At such accountings, the personal representative also may petition to distribute some or all of the estate. Proceedings on accountings furnish interested persons an opportunity to object to various actions taken by the personal representative.

Several types of accounts exist: interim accounts, optional accounts, and final accounts. The representative may be required to file an interim account if requested by the court or any interested person (Cal. Prob. Code §10950(a)); if the representative ends his or her tenure in office (e.g., by resignation, absconding, removal, or death) (Cal. Prob. Code §§10952, 10953); or if the representative becomes incapacitated (Cal. Prob. Code §10953).

The representative also may file optional accounts at any time (Cal. Prob. Code §10950). Such an accounting may be advisable for a representative who wishes to obtain court approval regarding the performance of certain acts in order to be discharged from liability. The personal representative must file a final account and petition for final distribution when the estate is ready to be closed (Cal. Prob. Code §10951).

The accounting requirement (i.e., for interim or final accounts) may be waived. That is, a personal representative is not obligated to file a required account if each person who is entitled to distribution executes and files a written waiver or a written acknowledgment that the person's interest has been satisfied, or if adequate provision has made for satisfaction in full of the person's interest (Cal. Prob. Code §10954). Even if a distributee files a waiver, the personal representative must still file a report revealing his or her compensation (and that of the attorneys for the estate) (Cal. Prob. Code §10954). The court has recourse to the contempt power to compel a personal representative to file an accounting (Cal. Prob. Code §11050).

§10900. Account shall include financial statement and report of administration

(a) An account shall include both a financial statement and a report of administration as provided in Chapter 4 (commencing with Section 1060) of Part 1 of Division 3, and this section.

(b) The statement of liabilities in the report of administration shall include the following information:

(1) Whether notice to creditors was given under Section 9050.

(2) Creditor claims filed, including the date of filing the claim, the name of the claimant, the amount of the claim, and the action taken on the claim.

(3) Creditor claims not paid, satisfied, or adequately provided for. As to each such claim, the statement shall indicate whether the claim is due and the date due, the date any notice of rejection was given, and whether the creditor has brought an action on the claim. The statement shall identify any real or personal property that is security for the claim, whether by mortgage, deed of trust, lien, or other encumbrance.

(c) The amendments to this section made by Assembly Bill 2751 of the 199596 Regular Session shall become operative on July 1, 1997.

(Stats. 1990 (A.B. 759), ch. 79, §14, effective July 1, 1991. Amended by Stats. 1990 (S.B. 1775), ch. 710, §38, effective July 1, 1991; Stats. 1996 (A.B. 2751), ch. 862, §30, effective July 1, 1997.)

§10901. Personal representative shall produce documents supporting accounts

On court order, or on request by an interested person filed with the clerk and a copy served on the personal representative, the personal representative shall produce for inspection and audit by the court or interested person the documents specified in the order or request that support an account.

(Stats. 1990 (A.B. 759), ch. 79, §14, effective July 1, 1991.)

§10902. Personal representative may incorporate by reference any accounting provided by conservator or guardian of deceased person

When a personal representative receives assets from the conservator of a deceased conservatee or the guardian of a deceased ward, the personal representative may incorporate by reference any accounting provided by the conservator or guardian for the decedent for the period subsequent to the date of death, and the personal representative is entitled to rely on the accounting by such other fiduciary, and shall not have a duty to independently investigate or verify the transactions reported in such an account.

(Stats. 1996 (A.B. 2751), ch. 862, §32, effective July 1, 1997.)

§10950. Court may order account at any time

(a) On its own motion or on petition of an interested person, the court may order an account at any time.

(b) The court shall order an account on petition of an interested person made more than one year after the last account was filed or, if no previous account has been filed, made more than one year after issuance of letters to the personal representative.

(c) The court order shall specify the time within which the personal representative must file an account.

(Stats. 1990 (A.B. 759), ch. 79, §14, effective July 1, 1991.)

§10951. Personal representative shall file final account and petition for final distribution order when estate is ready to be closed

The personal representative shall file a final account and petition for an order for final distribution of the estate when the estate is in a condition to be closed.

(Stats. 1990 (A.B. 759), ch. 79, §14, effective July 1, 1991.)

§10952. Account required upon termination of personal representative's authority

A personal representative who resigns or is removed from office or whose authority is otherwise terminated shall, unless the court extends the time, file an account not later than 60 days after termination of authority. If the personal representative fails to so file the account, the court may compel the account pursuant to Chapter 4 (commencing with Section 11050).

(Stats. 1990 (A.B. 759), ch. 79, §14, effective July 1, 1991.)

§10953. Successor personal representative; responsibilities; compensation

(a) As used in this section:

(1) "Incapacitated" means lack of capacity to serve as personal representative.

(2) "Legal representative" means the personal representative of a deceased personal representative or the conservator of the estate of an incapacitated personal representative.

(b) If a personal representative dies or becomes incapacitated and a legal representative is appointed for the deceased or incapacitated personal representative, the legal representative shall not later than 60 days after appointment, unless the court extends the time, file an account of the administration of the deceased or incapacitated personal representative.

(c) If a personal representative dies or becomes incapacitated and no legal representative is appointed for the deceased or incapacitated personal representative, or if the personal representative absconds, the court may compel the attorney for the deceased, incapacitated, or absconding personal representative or attorney of record in the estate proceeding to file an account of the administration of the deceased, incapacitated, or absconding personal representative.

(d) The legal representative or attorney shall exercise reasonable diligence in preparing an account under this section. Verification of the account may be made on information and belief. The court shall settle the account as in other cases. The court shall allow reasonable compensation to the legal representative or the attorney for preparing the account. The amount allowed is a charge against the estate that was being administered by the deceased, incapacitated, or absconding personal representative. Legal services for which compensation shall be allowed to the attorney under this subdivision include those services rendered by any paralegal performing the services under the direction and supervision of an attorney. The petition or application for compensation shall set forth the hours spent and services performed by the paralegal.

(Stats. 1990 (A.B. 759), ch. 79, §14, effective July 1, 1991.)

§10954. Personal representative is not required to account in some circumstances

(a) Notwithstanding any other provision of this part, the personal representative is not required to file an account if any of the following conditions is satisfied as to each person entitled to distribution from the estate:

(1) The person has executed and filed a written waiver of account or a written acknowledgment that the person's interest has been satisfied.

(2) Adequate provision has been made for satisfaction in full of the person's interest. This paragraph does not

apply to a residuary devisee or a devisee whose interest in the estate is subject to abatement, payment of expenses, or accrual of interest or income.

(b) A waiver or acknowledgment under subdivision (a) shall be executed as follows:

(1) If the person entitled to distribution is an adult and competent, by that person.

(2) If the person entitled to distribution is a minor, by a person authorized to receive money or property belonging to the minor. If the waiver or acknowledgment is executed by a guardian of the estate of the minor, the waiver or acknowledgment may be executed without the need to obtain approval of the court in which the guardianship proceeding is pending.

(3) If the person entitled to distribution is a conservatee, by the conservator of the estate of the conservatee. The waiver or acknowledgment may be executed without the need to obtain approval of the court in which the conservatorship proceeding is pending.

(4) If the person entitled to distribution is a trust, by the trustee, but only if the named trustee's written acceptance of the trust is filed with the court. In the case of a trust that is subject to the continuing jurisdiction of the court pursuant to Chapter 4 (commencing with Section 17300) of Part 5 of Division 9, the waiver or acknowledgment may be executed without the need to obtain approval of the court.

(5) If the person entitled to distribution is an estate, by the personal representative of the estate. The waiver or acknowledgment may be executed without the need to obtain approval of the court in which the estate is being administered.

(6) If the person entitled to distribution is incapacitated, unborn, unascertained, or is a person whose identity or address is unknown, or is a designated class of persons who are not ascertained or are not in being, and there is a guardian ad litem appointed to represent the person entitled to distribution, by the guardian ad litem.

(7) If the person entitled to distribution has designated an attorney in fact who has the power under the power of attorney to execute the waiver or acknowledgment, by either of the following:

(A) The person entitled to distribution if an adult and competent.

(B) The attorney in fact.

(c) Notwithstanding subdivision (a):

(1) The personal representative shall file a final report of administration at the time the final account would otherwise have been required. The final report shall include the amount of compensation paid or payable to the personal representative and to the attorney for the personal representative and shall set forth the basis for determining the amounts.

(2) A creditor whose interest has not been satisfied may petition under Section 10950 for an account.

(Stats. 1990 (A.B. 759), ch. 79, §14, effective July 1, 1991. Amended by Stats. 1990 (S.B. 1775), ch. 710, §39, effective July 1, 1991.)

§11000. Persons who are entitled to receive notice of hearing; contents

(a) The personal representative shall give notice of the hearing as provided in Section 1220 to all of the following persons:

(1) Each person listed in Section 1220.

(2) Each known heir whose interest in the estate would be affected by the account.

(3) Each known devisee whose interest in the estate would be affected by the account.

(4) The Attorney General, at the office of the Attorney General in Sacramento, if any portion of the estate is to escheat to the state and its interest would be affected by the account.

(5) If the estate is insolvent, each creditor who has filed a claim that is allowed or approved but is unpaid in whole or in part.

(b) If the petition for approval of the account requests allowance of all or a portion of the compensation of the personal representative or the attorney for the personal representative, the notice of hearing shall so state.

(c) If the account is a final account and is filed together with a petition for an order for final distribution of the estate, the notice of hearing shall so state.

(Stats. 1990 (A.B. 759), ch. 79, §14, effective July 1, 1991. Amended by Stats. 1990 (S.B. 1775), ch. 710, §40, effective July 1, 1991.)

§11001. Matters relating to an account may be contested for cause

All matters relating to an account may be contested for cause shown, including, but not limited to:

(a) The validity of an allowed or approved claim not reported in a previous account and not established by judgment.

(b) The value of property for purposes of distribution.

(c) Actions taken by the personal representative not previously authorized or approved by the court, subject to Section 10590 (Independent Administration of Estates Act).

(Stats. 1990 (A.B. 759), ch. 79, §14, effective July 1, 1991.)

§11002. Court may conduct any hearing necessary to settle the account and appoint referees to examine the account

(a) The court may conduct any hearing that may be necessary to settle the account, and may cite the personal representative to appear before the court for examination.

(b) The court may appoint one or more referees to examine the account and make a report on the account, subject to confirmation by the court. The court may allow a reasonable compensation to the referee to be paid out of the estate.

(c) The court may make any orders that the court deems necessary to effectuate the provisions of this section.

(Stats. 1990 (A.B. 759), ch. 79, §14, effective July 1, 1991.)

§11003. Court may award costs and attorneys fees if contest was without reasonable cause and in bad faith

(a) If the court determines that the contest was without reasonable cause and in bad faith, the court may award against the contestant the compensation and costs of the personal representative and other expenses and costs of litigation, including attorney's fees, incurred to defend the account. The amount awarded is a charge against any interest of the contestant in the estate and the contestant is personally liable for any amount that remains unsatisfied.

(b) If the court determines that the opposition to the contest was without reasonable cause and in bad faith, the court may award the contestant the costs of the contestant and other expenses and costs of litigation, including attorney's fees, incurred to contest the account. The amount awarded is a charge against the compensation or other interest of the personal representative in the estate and the personal representative is liable personally and on the bond, if any, for any amount that remains unsatisfied.

(Stats. 1990 (A.B. 759), ch. 79, §14, effective July 1, 1991.)

§11004. Personal representative shall be allowed necessary expenses

The personal representative shall be allowed all necessary expenses in the administration of the estate, including, but not limited to, necessary expenses in the care, management, preservation, and settlement of the estate.

(Stats. 1990 (A.B. 759), ch. 79, §14, effective July 1, 1991.)

§11005. Court shall allow payment of debts without claim filed in certain circumstances

If a debt has been paid within the time prescribed in Section 9154 but without a claim having been filed and established in the manner prescribed by statute, in settling the account the court shall allow the amount paid if all of the following are proven:

(a) The debt was justly due.

(b) The debt was paid in good faith.

(c) The amount paid did not exceed the amount reasonably necessary to satisfy the indebtedness.

(d) The estate is solvent.

(Stats. 1990 (A.B. 759), ch. 79, §14, effective July 1, 1991.)

§11050. Personal representative shall be subject to contempt for failure to file account

Subject to the provisions of this chapter, if the personal representative does not file a required account, the court shall compel the account by punishment for contempt.

(Stats. 1990 (A.B. 759), ch. 79, §14, effective July 1, 1991.)

§11051. Personal representative shall be required to appear and show cause

(a) A citation shall be issued, served, and returned, requiring a personal representative who does not file a required account to appear and show cause why the personal representative should not be punished for contempt.

(b) If the personal representative purposefully evades personal service of the citation, the personal representative shall be removed from office.

(Stats. 1990 (A.B. 759), ch. 79, §14, effective July 1, 1991.)

§11052. Personal representative also may be removed from office for failure to appear and file account

If the personal representative does not appear and file a required account, after having been duly cited, the personal representative may be punished for contempt or removed from office, or both, in the discretion of the court.

(Stats. 1990 (A.B. 759), ch. 79, §14, effective July 1, 1991.)

F. Distribution

A personal representative is permitted to make a preliminary distribution of an estate before the time for closing and distributing the estate. California Probate Code §§11600 et seq. authorize preliminary distributions of an estate (upon notice and a hearing), after 2 months following the issuance of letters to a personal representative. The personal representative or any interested person may petition the court for an order for a preliminary (or final) distribution (Cal. Prob. Code §11600). The representative makes such distributions typically when the

distributees' entitlement to estate property is not in dispute.

Preliminary distributions generally are not approved by the court unless the period for filing creditors' claims has expired, or a bond is furnished, and if distribution may be made "without loss to creditors or injury to the estate or any interested person" (Cal. Prob. Code §11621(a)). Ross & Grant, Cal. Prob. Prac., *supra*, at §16:11.

Several reasons exist for preliminary distributions of estates. These include: (1) they facilitate earlier enjoyment of the property by beneficiaries or heirs in the face of the delays of estate administration; (2) they favor public policy preference for speedy distribution of probate estates; (3) they shift responsibility for maintenance and protection of estate property from the representative to the designated beneficiaries; (4) they save the estate money by avoiding the statutorily mandated accrual of interest on pecuniary legacies that begin 1 year after the date of death (Cal. Prob. Code §12003); (5) those preliminary distributions in partial satisfaction of residuary bequests or to fund a testamentary trust may have income tax advantages; and (6) they may be preferable to the payment of a family allowance (for example, if assets would have to be sold to fund the allowance). *Id.,* at §16:2.1.

The court may require a bond (given by the distributee and filed with the court) in some cases of preliminary distribution. If a preliminary distribution occurs before 4 months have elapsed following issuance of letters (i.e., if the period for filing creditors' claims has not expired), the court *must* require a bond (Cal. Prob. Code §11622(a)). However, after that time, the bond is at the court's discretion (*id.* at §11622(b)). The bond is conditioned on the distributee's paying his or her proper share of the debts of the estate (*id.* at §11622(c)). Notice of a distribution must be given to designated persons (Cal. Prob. Code §11601).

The personal representative (i.e., a nonpetitioning representative) or interested person may oppose the petition for preliminary distribution (Cal. Prob. Code §11602). Creditors do not qualify as persons with a direct pecuniary interest who may oppose the petition. Ross & Grant, Cal. Prob. Prac., *supra*, at §16:64.

In some cases, a personal representative may petition to administer the estate under the Independent Administration of Estates Act (IAEA) (i.e., legislation that permits some acts of estate administration with only minimal judicial supervision). A representative acting pursuant to the IAEA may make a distribution that does not exceed 50 percent of the net value (as statutorily defined) of the estate (Cal. Prob. Code §11623). Distributions under the IAEA still require court approval; however, they may be made without notice and a hearing (*id.*). The IAEA is discussed in Section VII E *infra.*

When the personal representative has paid the decedent's debts (or if the estate is insolvent), and the estate is in a condition to be closed, he or she files a petition for final distribution of the estate (Cal. Prob. Code §11640(a)). California Probate Code §§12200 et seq. (Section G, *infra*) govern closing the estate.

1. Preliminary Distribution

§11600. Personal representative may petition for preliminary or final distribution

The personal representative or an interested person may petition the court under this chapter for an order for preliminary or final distribution of the decedent's estate to the persons entitled thereto.

(Stats. 1990 (A.B. 759), ch. 79, §14, effective July 1, 1991.)

§11601. Persons who must receive notice of petition

Notice of the hearing on the petition shall be given as provided in Section 1220 to all of the following persons:

(a) Each person listed in Section 1220.

(b) Each known heir whose interest in the estate would be affected by the petition.

(c) Each known devisee whose interest in the estate would be affected by the petition.

(d) The Attorney General, at the office of the Attorney General in Sacramento, if any portion of the estate is to escheat to the state and its interest in the estate would be affected by the petition.

(e) The Controller, if property is to be distributed to the state because there is no known beneficiary or if property is to be distributed to a beneficiary whose whereabouts is

unknown. A copy of the latest account filed with the court shall be served on the Controller with the notice.
(Stats. 1990 (A.B. 759), ch. 79, §14, effective July 1, 1991.)

§11602. Persons who may oppose petition

The personal representative or any interested person may oppose the petition.
(Stats. 1990 (A.B. 759), ch. 79, §14, effective July 1, 1991.)

§11603. Court shall order distribution of decedent's estate; contents of order

(a) If the court determines that the requirements for distribution are satisfied, the court shall order distribution of the decedent's estate, or such portion as the court directs, to the persons entitled thereto.

(b) The order shall:

(1) Name the distributees and the share to which each is entitled.

(2) Provide that property distributed subject to a limitation or condition, including, but not limited to, an option granted under Chapter 16 (commencing with Section 9960) of Part 5, is distributed to the distributees subject to the terms of the limitation or condition.

(c) If the whereabouts of a distributee named in the order is unknown, the order shall provide for alternate distributees and the share to which each is entitled. The alternate distributees shall be the persons, to the extent known or reasonably ascertainable, who would be entitled under the decedent's will or under the laws of intestate succession if the distributee named in the order had predeceased the decedent, or in the case of a devise for a charitable purpose, under the doctrine of cy pres. If the distributee named in the order does not claim the share to which the distributee is entitled within five years after the date of the order, the distributee is deemed to have predeceased the decedent for the purpose of this section and the alternate distributees are entitled to the share as provided in the order.
(Stats. 1990 (A.B. 759), ch. 79, §14, effective July 1, 1991. Amended by Stats. 2000 (A.B. 1491), ch. 17, §4.6.)

§11604. Distribution to persons other than beneficiary, such as transferees of beneficiary

(a) This section applies where distribution is to be made to any of the following persons:

(1) The transferee of a beneficiary.

(2) Any person other than a beneficiary under an agreement, request, or instructions of a beneficiary or the attorney in fact of a beneficiary.

(b) The court on its own motion, or on motion of the personal representative or other interested person or of the public administrator, may inquire into the circumstances surrounding the execution of, and the consideration for, the transfer, agreement, request, or instructions, and the amount of any fees, charges, or consideration paid or agreed to be paid by the beneficiary.

(c) The court may refuse to order distribution, or may order distribution on any terms that the court deems just and equitable, if the court finds either of the following:

(1) The fees, charges, or consideration paid or agreed to be paid by a beneficiary are grossly unreasonable.

(2) The transfer, agreement, request, or instructions were obtained by duress, fraud, or undue influence.

(d) Notice of the hearing on the motion shall be served on the beneficiary and on the persons described in subdivision (a) at least 15 days before the hearing in the manner provided in Section 415.10 or 415.30 of the Code of Civil Procedure.
(Stats. 1990 (A.B. 759), ch. 79, §14, effective July 1, 1991.)

§11604.5. Distribution of decedent's estate to transferee for value; written agreement terms and conditions

(a) This section applies when distribution from a decedent's estate is made to a transferee for value who acquires any interest of a beneficiary in exchange for cash or other consideration.

(b) For purposes of this section, a transferee for value is a person who satisfies both of the following criteria:

(1) He or she purchases the interest from a beneficiary for consideration pursuant to a written agreement.

(2) He or she, directly or indirectly, regularly engages in the purchase of beneficial interests in estates for consideration.

(c) This section does not apply to any of the following:

(1) A transferee who is a beneficiary of the estate or a person who has a claim to distribution from the estate under another instrument or by intestate succession.

(2) A transferee who is either the registered domestic partner of the beneficiary, or is related by blood, marriage, or adoption to the beneficiary or the decedent.

(3) A transaction made in conformity with the California Finance Lenders Law (Division 9 (commencing with Section 22000) of the Financial Code) and subject to regulation by the Department of Corporations.

(4) A transferee who is engaged in the business of locating missing or unknown heirs and who acquires an interest from a beneficiary solely in exchange for providing information or services associated with locating the heir or beneficiary.

(d) A written agreement is effective only if all of the following conditions are met:

(1) The executed written agreement is filed with the court not later than 30 days following the date of its execution or, if administration of the decedent's estate has not commenced, then within 30 days of issuance of the letters of administration or letters testamentary, but in no event later than 15 days prior to the hearing on the petition for final distribution. Prior to filing or serving that written agreement, the transferee for value shall redact any personally identifying information about the beneficiary, other than the name and address of the beneficiary, and any financial information provided by the beneficiary to the transferee for value on the application for cash or other consideration, from the agreement.

(2) If the negotiation or discussion between the beneficiary and the transferee for value leading to the execution of the written agreement by the beneficiary was conducted in a language other than English, the beneficiary shall receive the written agreement in English, together with a copy of the agreement translated into the language in which it was negotiated or discussed. The written agreement and the translated copy, if any, shall be provided to the beneficiary.

(3) The documents signed by, or provided to, the beneficiary are printed in at least 10-point type.

(4) The transferee for value executes a declaration or affidavit attesting that the requirements of this section have been satisfied, and the declaration or affidavit is filed with the court within 30 days of execution of the written agreement or, if administration of the decedent's estate has not commenced, then within 30 days of issuance of the letters of administration or letters testamentary, but in no event later than 15 days prior to the hearing on the petition for final distribution.

(5) Notice of the assignment is served on the personal representative or the attorney of record for the personal representative within 30 days of execution of the written agreement or, if general or special letters of administration or letters testamentary have not been issued, then within 30 days of issuance of the letters of administration or letters testamentary, but in no event later than 15 days prior to the hearing on the petition for final distribution.

(e) The written agreement shall include the following terms, in addition to any other terms:

(1) The amount of consideration paid to the beneficiary.

(2) A description of the transferred interest.

(3) If the written agreement so provides, the amount by which the transferee for value would have its distribution reduced if the beneficial interest assigned is distributed prior to a specified date.

(4) A statement of the total of all costs or fees charged to the beneficiary resulting from the transfer for value, including, but not limited to, transaction or processing fees, credit report costs, title search costs, due diligence fees, filing fees, bank or electronic transfer costs, or any other fees or costs. If all the costs and fees are paid by the transferee for value and are included in the amount of the transferred interest, then the statement of costs need not itemize any costs or fees. This subdivision shall not apply to costs, fees, or damages arising out of a material breach of the agreement or fraud by or on the part of the beneficiary.

(f) A written agreement shall not contain any of the following provisions and, if any such provision is included, that provision shall be null and void:

(1) A provision holding harmless the transferee for value, other than for liability arising out of fraud by the beneficiary.

(2) A provision granting to the transferee for value agency powers to represent the beneficiary's interest in the decedent's estate beyond the interest transferred.

(3) A provision requiring payment by the beneficiary to the transferee for value for services not related to the written agreement or services other than the transfer of interest under the written agreement.

(4) A provision permitting the transferee for value to have recourse against the beneficiary if the distribution from the estate in satisfaction of the beneficial interest is less than the beneficial interest assigned to the transferee for value, other than recourse for any expense or damage arising out of the material breach of the agreement or fraud by the beneficiary.

(g) The court on its own motion, or on the motion of the personal representative or other interested person, may inquire into the circumstances surrounding the execution of, and the consideration for, the written agreement to determine that the requirements of this section have been satisfied.

(h) The court may refuse to order distribution under the written agreement, or may order distribution on any terms that the court considers equitable, if the court finds that the transferee for value did not substantially comply with the requirements of this section, or if the court finds that any of the following conditions existed at the time of transfer:

(1) The fees, charges, or consideration paid or agreed to be paid by the beneficiary were grossly unreasonable.

(2) The transfer of the beneficial interest was obtained by duress, fraud, or undue influence.

(i) In addition to any remedy specified in this section, for any willful violation of the requirements of this section found to be committed in bad faith, the court may require the transferee for value to pay to the beneficiary up to twice the value paid for the assignment.

(j) Notice of the hearing on any motion brought under this section shall be served on the beneficiary and on the transferee for value at least 15 days before the hearing in the manner provided in Section 415.10 or 415.30 of the Code of Civil Procedure.

(k) If the decedent's estate is not subject to a pending court proceeding under the Probate Code in California, but is the subject of a probate proceeding in another state, the transferee for value shall not be required to submit to the court a copy of the written agreement as required under paragraph (1) of subdivision (d). If the written agreement is entered into in California or if the beneficiary is domiciled in California, that written agreement shall otherwise conform to the provisions of subdivisions (d), (e), and (f) in order to be effective.

(Stats 2005 (SB 390), ch. 438, §1.)

§11605. Final order is conclusive

When a court order made under this chapter becomes final, the order binds and is conclusive as to the rights of all interested persons.

(Stats. 1990 (A.B. 759), ch. 79, §14, effective July 1, 1991.)

§11620. Petition for preliminary distribution must be filed more than 2 months after issuance of letters

A petition for an order for preliminary distribution of all, or a portion of, the share of a decedent's estate to which a beneficiary is entitled may not be filed unless at least two months have elapsed after letters are first issued to a general personal representative.

(Stats. 1990 (A.B. 759), ch. 79, §14, effective July 1, 1991.)

§11621. Court shall order distribution absent loss to creditors or injury to estate

(a) The court shall order distribution under this article if at the hearing it appears that the distribution may be made without loss to creditors or injury to the estate or any interested person.

(b) The order for distribution shall be stayed until any bond required by the court is filed.

(Stats. 1990 (A.B. 759), ch. 79, §14, effective July 1, 1991.)

§11622. Court shall require bond in cases of early distribution

(a) If the court orders distribution before four months have elapsed after letters are first issued to a general personal representative, the court shall require a bond. The bond shall be in the amount of the distribution.

(b) If the court orders distribution after four months have elapsed after letters are first issued to a general personal representative, the court may require a bond. The bond shall be in the amount the court orders.

(c) Any bond required by the court shall be given by the distributee and filed with the court. The bond shall be conditioned on payment of the distributee's proper share of the debts of the estate, not exceeding the amount distributed.

(Stats. 1990 (A.B. 759), ch. 79, §14, effective July 1, 1991.)

§11623. Preliminary distribution for independently administered estate

(a) Notwithstanding Section 11601, if authority is granted to administer the estate without court supervision under the Independent Administration of Estates Act, Part 6 (commencing with Section 10400):

(1) The personal representative may petition the court for an order for preliminary distribution on notice as provided in Section 1220. Notwithstanding subdivision (c) of Section 1220, the court may not dispense with notice unless the time for filing creditor claims has expired.

(2) The aggregate of all property distributed under this section shall not exceed 50 percent of the net value of the estate. For the purpose of this subdivision, "net value of the estate" means the excess of the value of the property in the estate, as determined by all inventories and appraisals on file with the court, over the total amount of all creditor claims and of all liens and encumbrances recorded or known to the personal representative not included in a creditor claim, excluding any estate tax lien occasioned by the decedent's death.

(b) Nothing in this section limits the authority of the personal representative to make preliminary distribution under other provisions of this chapter, whether or not authority is granted to administer the estate under the Independent Administration of Estates Act, Part 6 (commencing with Section 10400).

(Stats. 1990 (A.B. 759), ch. 79, §14, effective July 1, 1991. Amended by Stats. 1990 (S.B. 1775), ch. 710, §41, effective July 1, 1991; Stats. 1991 (S.B. 896), ch. 82, §30.5, effective July 1, 1991.)

§11624. Costs of proceeding for preliminary distribution

The costs of a proceeding under this article shall be paid by the distributee or the estate in proportions determined by the court.

(Stats. 1990 (A.B. 759), ch. 79, §14, effective July 1, 1991.)

2. Final Distribution

California Probate Code §11640 specifies the requirements for a final distribution. The court may order a final distribution of the estate after the personal representative's final account has been settled (or waived), all debts have been paid (unless the estate is insolvent), and the estate is ready to be closed (*id.*).

§11640. Order for final distribution if debts have been paid or estate insolvent; court shall determine ademption by satisfaction and advancements

(a) When all debts have been paid or adequately provided for, or if the estate is insolvent, and the estate is in a condition to be closed, the personal representative shall file a petition for, and the court shall make, an order for final distribution of the estate.

(b) The court shall hear and determine and resolve in the order all questions arising under Section 21135 (ademption by satisfaction) or Section 6409 (advancements).

(c) If debts remain unpaid or not adequately provided for or if, for other reasons, the estate is not in a condition to be closed, the administration may continue for a reasonable time, subject to Chapter 1 (commencing with Section 12200) of Part 11 (time for closing estate).

(Stats. 1990 (A.B. 759), ch. 79, §14, effective July 1, 1991. Amended by Stats. 2002 (A.B. 1784), ch. 138, §9.)

§11641. Personal representative may distribute property

When an order settling a final account and for final distribution is entered, the personal representative may immediately distribute the property in the estate to the persons entitled to distribution, without further notice or proceedings.

(Stats. 1990 (A.B. 759), ch. 79, §14, effective July 1, 1991.)

§11642. Distribution of property acquired or discovered after order made

Any property acquired or discovered after the court order for final distribution is made shall be distributed in the following manner:

(a) If the order disposes of the property, distribution shall be made in the manner provided in the order. The court may, in an appropriate case, require a supplemental account and make further instructions relating to the property.

(b) If the order does not dispose of the property, distribution shall be made either (1) in the manner ordered by the court on a petition for instructions or (2) under Section 12252 (administration after discharge) if the personal representative has been discharged.

(Stats. 1990 (A.B. 759), ch. 79, §14, effective July 1, 1991.)

G. Closing the Estate

If the personal representative does not file a petition for final distribution within a statutorily specified time, the representative must file a report on the status of the estate administration (Cal. Prob. Code §12220). Such a report advises interested persons and the court of the condition of the estate, reasons for the delay in closing the estate, and provides an estimate of the time needed to close administration (Cal. Prob. Code §12201(a)).

If the personal representative does not file either a petition for final distribution or the requisite status report within the applicable time period, the court may hold a hearing at which time it will require the representative to appear and disclose the condition of the estate and the reasons for the representative's failure to close the estate (Cal. Prob. Code §12202). Such a hearing may have several outcomes: (1) the court may order the continuation of estate administration, (2) the court may compel the representative to file a petition for final distribution (*id.*), (3) the court may reduce the compensation of the representative (and/or the personal representative's attorney) (Cal. Prob. Code §12205), and/or (4) the court may order the personal representative's removal from office (Cal. Prob. Code §12204).

After a personal representative has complied with the terms of the order for final distribution, the personal representative is entitled to be discharged from liability (Cal. Prob. Code §12250). Sometimes, however, estate property may be discovered after an estate has been closed. If such a discovery necessitates subsequent administration of the estate, the court will again appoint a personal representative. In such cases, the person who was formerly appointed as personal representative has priority of appointment (Cal. Prob. Code §12252(a)).

§12200. Time for closing the estate and petitioning for final distribution order

The personal representative shall either petition for an order for final distribution of the estate or make a report of status of administration not later than the following times:

(a) In an estate for which a federal estate tax return is not required, within one year after the date of issuance of letters.

(b) In an estate for which a federal estate tax return is required, within 18 months after the date of issuance of letters.

(Stats. 1990 (A.B. 759), ch. 79, §14, effective July 1, 1991.)

§12201. Contents of report of status of administration

If a report of status of administration is made under Section 12200:

(a) The report shall show the condition of the estate, the reasons why the estate cannot be distributed and closed, and an estimate of the time needed to close administration of the estate.

(b) The report shall be filed with the court. Notice of hearing of the report shall be given as provided in Section 1220 to persons then interested in the estate, and shall include a statement in not less than 10point boldface type or a reasonable equivalent thereof if printed, or in all capital letters if not printed, in substantially the following words:

"YOU HAVE THE RIGHT TO PETITION FOR AN ACCOUNT UNDER SECTION 10950 OF THE CALIFORNIA PROBATE CODE."

(c) On the hearing of the report, the court may order either of the following:

(1) That the administration of the estate continue for the time and on the terms and conditions that appear reasonable, including an account under Section 10950, if the court determines that continuation of administration is in the best interests of the estate or of interested persons.

(2) That the personal representative shall petition for final distribution.

(Stats. 1990 (A.B. 759), ch. 79, §14, effective July 1, 1991.)

§12202. Court may require personal representative to appear to show condition of estate and reasons for failure to make distribution

(a) The court may, on petition of any interested person or on its own motion, for good cause shown on the record, cite the personal representative to appear before the court and show the condition of the estate and the reasons why the estate cannot be distributed and closed.

(b) On the hearing of the citation, the court may either order the administration of the estate to continue or order the personal representative to petition for final distribution, as provided in Section 12201.

(Stats. 1990 (A.B. 759), ch. 79, §14, effective July 1, 1991. Amended by Stats. 1996 (S.B. 392), ch. 563, §28.)

§12203. Continuance of administration to pay family allowance is not generally in best interests of estate; exceptions

(a) For purposes of this chapter, continuation of the administration of the estate in order to pay a family allowance is not in the best interests of the estate or interested persons unless the court determines both of the following:

(1) The family allowance is needed by the recipient to pay for necessaries of life, including education so long as pursued to advantage.

(2) The needs of the recipient for continued family allowance outweigh the needs of the decedent's beneficiaries whose interests would be adversely affected by continuing the administration of the estate for this purpose.

(b) Nothing in this section shall be construed to authorize continuation of a family allowance beyond the time prescribed in Section 6543.

(c) Nothing in this section limits the power of the court to order a preliminary distribution of the estate.

(Stats. 1990 (A.B. 759), ch. 79, §14, effective July 1, 1991.)

§12204. Noncompliance of personal representative with order is grounds for removal

Failure of the personal representative to comply with an order made under this chapter is grounds for removal from office.

(Stats. 1990 (A.B. 759), ch. 79, §14, effective July 1, 1991.)

§12205. Court may reduce compensation of personal representative or attorney in some cases

(a) The court may reduce the compensation of the personal representative or the attorney for the personal representative by an amount the court determines to be appropriate if the court makes all of the following determinations:

(1) The time taken for administration of the estate exceeds the time required by this chapter or prescribed by the court.

(2) The time taken was within the control of the personal representative or attorney whose compensation is being reduced.

(3) The delay was not in the best interest of the estate or interested persons.

(b) An order under this section reducing compensation may be made regardless of whether the compensation otherwise allowable under Part 7 (commencing with Section 10800) would be reasonable compensation for the services rendered by the personal representative or attorney.

(c) An order under this section may be made at any of the following hearings:

(1) The hearing for final distribution.

(2) The hearing for an allowance on the compensation of the personal representative or attorney.

(d) In making a determination under this section, the court shall take into account any action taken under Section 12202 as a result of a previous delay.

(Stats. 1990 (A.B. 759), ch. 79, §14, effective July 1, 1991. Amended by Stats. 1990 (S.B. 1775), ch. 710, §42, effective July 1, 1991.)

§12206. Time limit on administration in will is directory only

A limitation in a will of the time for administration of an estate is directory only and does not limit the power of the personal representative or the court to continue administration of the estate beyond the time limitation in the will if the continuation is necessary.

(Stats. 1990 (A.B. 759), ch. 79, §14, effective July 1, 1991.)

§12250. Court shall discharge personal representative upon compliance with final distribution order

(a) When the personal representative has complied with the terms of the order for final distribution and has filed the appropriate receipts or the court has excused the filing of a receipt as provided in Section 11753, the court shall, on ex parte petition, make an order discharging the personal representative from all liability incurred thereafter.

(b) Nothing in this section precludes discharge of the personal representative for distribution made without prior court order, so long as the terms of the order for final distribution are satisfied.

(Stats. 1990 (A.B. 759), ch. 79, §14, effective July 1, 1991.)

§12251. Personal representative may petition to close estate and for discharge if no property subject to administration

(a) At any time after appointment of a personal representative and whether or not letters have been issued, if it appears there is no property of any kind belonging to the estate and subject to administration, the personal representative may petition for the termination of further proceedings and for discharge of the personal representative. The petition shall state the facts required by this subdivision.

(b) Notice of the hearing on the petition shall be given as provided in Section 1220 to all interested persons.

(c) If it appears to the satisfaction of the court on the hearing that the facts stated in the petition are true, the court shall make an order terminating the proceeding and discharging the personal representative.

(Stats. 1990 (A.B. 759), ch. 79, §14, effective July 1, 1991.)

§12252. Appointment of personal representative for subsequent administration for after-discovered property

If subsequent administration of an estate is necessary after the personal representative has been discharged because other property is discovered or because it becomes necessary or proper for any cause:

(a) The court shall appoint as personal representative the person entitled to appointment in the same order as is directed in relation to an original appointment, except that the person who served as personal representative at the time of the order of discharge has priority.

(b) Notice of hearing of the appointment shall be given as provided in Section 1220 to the person who served as personal representative at the time of the order of discharge and to other interested persons. If property has been distributed to the State of California, a copy of any petition for subsequent appointment of a personal representative and the notice of hearing shall be given as provided in Section 1220 to the Controller.

(Stats. 1990 (A.B. 759), ch. 79, §14, effective July 1, 1991.)

VI. Nondomiciliary Decedents

Estates are generally administered at the place of the decedent's domicile (termed *"principal"* or *"domiciliary" administration*). However, in order to satisfy the policy of protection of creditors' rights, assets must be administered in each state in which they are found at the decedent's death. As a result, sometimes administration occurs in locations other than that of the decedent's domicile. Nondomiciliary administration is termed *"ancillary" administration.*

California Probate Code §§12500 et seq. govern proceedings in the state of California that involve the administration of an estate of a nondomiciliary decedent. A nondomiciliary decedent is defined as a decedent who is a domiciliary of another state or a foreign nation (Cal. Prob. Code §12505).

§12500. Application of chapter

Unless the provision or context otherwise requires, the definitions in this chapter govern the construction of this part.

(Stats. 1990 (A.B. 759), ch. 79, §14, effective July 1, 1991.)

§12501. "Ancillary administration," defined

"Ancillary administration" means proceedings in this state for administration of the estate of a nondomiciliary decedent.

(Stats. 1990 (A.B. 759), ch. 79, §14, effective July 1, 1991.)

§12502. "Foreign nation," defined

"Foreign nation" means a jurisdiction other than a state of the United States.

(Stats. 1990 (A.B. 759), ch. 79, §14, effective July 1, 1991.)

§12503. "Foreign nation personal representative," defined

"Foreign nation personal representative" means a personal representative appointed in a jurisdiction other than a state of the United States.

(Stats. 1990 (A.B. 759), ch. 79, §14, effective July 1, 1991.)

§12504. "Local personal representative," defined

"Local personal representative" means a nondomiciliary decedent's personal representative appointed in this state.

(Stats. 1990 (A.B. 759), ch. 79, §14, effective July 1, 1991.)

§12505. "Nondomiciliary decedent," defined

"Nondomiciliary decedent" means a person who dies domiciled in a sister state or foreign nation.

(Stats. 1990 (A.B. 759), ch. 79, §14, effective July 1, 1991.)

§12506. "Sister state," defined

"Sister state" means a state other than this state.

(Stats. 1990 (A.B. 759), ch. 79, §14, effective July 1, 1991.)

§12507. "Sister state personal representative," defined

"Sister state personal representative" means a personal representative appointed in a sister state.

(Stats. 1990 (A.B. 759), ch. 79, §14, effective July 1, 1991.)

§12510. Persons who may commence ancillary administration proceeding

Any interested person, or a sister state or foreign nation personal representative, may commence an ancillary administration proceeding by a petition to the court for either or both of the following:

(a) Probate of the nondomiciliary decedent's will.

(b) Appointment of a local personal representative.

(Stats. 1990 (A.B. 759), ch. 79, §14, effective July 1, 1991.)

§12511. Venue for ancillary administration

The proper county for an ancillary administration proceeding under this chapter is the county determined pursuant to Section 7052.

(Stats. 1990 (A.B. 759), ch. 79, §14, effective July 1, 1991.)

§12512. Notice of an ancillary administration proceeding

Notice of an ancillary administration proceeding shall be given and, except as provided in Article 2 (commencing with Section 12520), the same proceedings had as in the case of a petition for probate of a will or appointment of a personal representative of a person who dies domiciled in this state.

(Stats. 1990 (A.B. 759), ch. 79, §14, effective July 1, 1991.)

§12513. Priority is given to personal representative for nondomiciliary decedent who is appointed by court of sister state

If the decedent dies while domiciled in a sister state, a personal representative appointed by a court of the decedent's domicile has priority over all other persons except where the decedent's will nominates a different person to be the personal representative in this state. The sister state personal representative may nominate another person as personal representative and the nominee has the same priority as the sister state personal representative.

(Stats. 1990 (A.B. 759), ch. 79, §14, effective July 1, 1991.)

§12520. Application of Article to probate of will that is admitted to probate in a sister state or foreign nation

(a) If a nondomiciliary decedent's will has been admitted to probate in a sister state or foreign nation and satisfies the requirements of this article, probate of the will in an ancillary administration proceeding is governed by this article.

(b) If a nondomiciliary decedent's will has been admitted to probate in a sister state or foreign nation, but does not satisfy the requirements of this article, the will may be probated in an ancillary administration proceeding pursuant to Part 2 (commencing with Section 8000).

(Stats. 1990 (A.B. 759), ch. 79, §14, effective July 1, 1991.)

§12521. Contents of petition for probate of a nondomiciliary decedent's will

(a) A petition for probate of a nondomiciliary decedent's will under this article shall include both of the following:

(1) The will or an authenticated copy of the will.

(2) An authenticated copy of the order admitting the will to probate in the sister state or foreign nation or other evidence of the establishment or proof of the will in accordance with the law of the sister state or foreign nation.

(b) As used in this section, "authenticated copy" means a copy that satisfies the requirements of Article 2 (commencing with Section 1530) of Chapter 2 of Division 11 of the Evidence Code.

(Stats. 1990 (A.B. 759), ch. 79, §14, effective July 1, 1991.)

§12522. Court shall admit to probate a will that was established in a sister state

If a will of a nondomiciliary decedent was admitted to probate, or established or proved, in accordance with the laws of a sister state, the court shall admit the will to probate in this state, and may not permit a contest or revocation of probate, unless one or more of the following are shown:

(a) The determination in the sister state is not based on a finding that at the time of death the decedent was domiciled in the sister state.

(b) One or more interested parties were not given notice and an opportunity for contest in the proceedings in the sister state.

(c) The determination in the sister state is not final.

(Stats. 1990 (A.B. 759), ch. 79, §14, effective July 1, 1991.)

§12523. Court shall admit to probate a will that was established in foreign nation

(a) Except as provided in subdivision (b), if a will of a nondomiciliary decedent was admitted to probate, or established or proved, in accordance with the laws of a foreign nation, the court shall admit the will to probate in this state, and may not permit a contest or revocation of probate, if it appears from the order admitting the will to probate in the foreign nation, or otherwise appears, that all of the following conditions are satisfied:

(1) The determination in the foreign nation is based on a finding that at the time of death the decedent was domiciled in the foreign nation.

(2) All interested parties were given notice and an opportunity for contest in the proceedings in the foreign nation.

(3) The determination in the foreign nation is final.

(b) The court may refuse to admit the will, even though it is shown to satisfy the conditions provided in subdivision (a), where the order admitting the will was made under a judicial system that does not provide impartial tribunals or procedures compatible with the requirements of due process of law.

(Stats. 1990 (A.B. 759), ch. 79, §14, effective July 1, 1991.)

§12524. Nondomiciliary decedent's probated will has same effect as domiciliary's probated will

A nondomiciliary decedent's will admitted to probate under this article has the same force and effect as the will of a person who dies while domiciled in this state that is admitted to probate in this state.

(Stats. 1990 (A.B. 759), ch. 79, §14, effective July 1, 1991.)

§12530. Other Code provisions are applicable to ancillary administration proceeding

Except to the extent otherwise provided in this chapter, ancillary administration of a decedent's estate is subject to all other provisions of this code concerning the administration of the decedent's estate, including, but not limited to, opening estate administration, inventory and appraisal, creditor claims, estate management, independent administration, compensation, accounts, payment of debts, distribution, and closing estate administration.

(Stats. 1990 (A.B. 759), ch. 79, §14, effective July 1, 1991.)

§12540. Court may make order for preliminary or final distribution to sister state personal representative

(a) If a person dies while domiciled in a sister state, the court in an ancillary administration proceeding may make an order for preliminary or final distribution of all or part of the decedent's personal property in this state to the sister state personal representative if distribution is in the best interest of the estate or interested persons.

(b) The court order shall be made in the manner and pursuant to the procedure provided in, and is subject to the provisions of, Chapter 1 (commencing with Section 11600) of Part 10.

(Stats. 1990 (A.B. 759), ch. 79, §14, effective July 1, 1991.)

§12541. Real property in nondomiciliary decedent's estate may be sold

If necessary to make distribution pursuant to this article, real property in the nondomiciliary decedent's estate may be sold and the court may order the proceeds to be distributed to the sister state personal representative. The sale shall be made in the same manner as other sales of real property of a decedent.

(Stats. 1990 (A.B. 759), ch. 79, §14, effective July 1, 1991.)

§12542. Distribution for insolvent estate in a sister state

If the nondomiciliary decedent's estate in the sister state where the decedent was domiciled is insolvent, distribution may be made only to the sister state personal representative and not to the beneficiaries.

(Stats. 1990 (A.B. 759), ch. 79, §14, effective July 1, 1991.)

§12570. Sister state personal representative may use affidavit procedure

If a nondomiciliary decedent's property in this state satisfies the requirements of Section 13100, a sister state personal representative may, without petitioning for ancillary administration, use the affidavit procedure provided by Chapter 3 (commencing with Section 13100) of Part 1 of Division 8 to collect personal property of the decedent.

(Stats. 1990 (A.B. 759), ch. 79, §14, effective July 1, 1991.)

§12571. Governing provisions for transfer of personal property to sister state personal representative

The effect of payment, delivery, or transfer of personal property to the sister state personal representative pursuant to this chapter, and the effect of failure to do so, are governed by Chapter 3 (commencing with Section 13100) of Part 1 of Division 8.

(Stats. 1990 (A.B. 759), ch. 79, §14, effective July 1, 1991.)

§12572. Sister state personal representative may bring action against holder of property

The sister state personal representative may bring an action against a holder of the decedent's property, and may be awarded attorney's fees, as provided in subdivision (b) of Section 13105.

(Stats. 1990 (A.B. 759), ch. 79, §14, effective July 1, 1991.)

§12573. Liability of sister state personal representative

A sister state personal representative who takes property by affidavit under this chapter is not liable as a person to whom payment, delivery, or transfer of the decedent's property is made under Section 13109 or 13110 to the extent that the sister state personal representative restores the property to the nondomiciliary decedent's estate in the sister state in compliance with Section 13111.

(Stats. 1990 (A.B. 759), ch. 79, §14, effective July 1, 1991.)

§12590. Submission of sister state personal representative to jurisdiction

A sister state personal representative or foreign nation personal representative submits personally in a representative capacity to the jurisdiction of the courts of this state in any proceeding relating to the estate by any of the following actions:

(a) Filing a petition for ancillary administration.

(b) Receiving money or other personal property pursuant to Chapter 3 (commencing with Section 12570). Jurisdiction under this subdivision is limited to the amount of money and the value of personal property received.

(c) Doing any act in this state as a personal representative that would have given this state jurisdiction over the personal representative as an individual.

(Stats. 1990 (A.B. 759), ch. 79, §14, effective July 1, 1991.)

§12591. Extent of jurisdiction over sister state personal representative

A sister state personal representative or foreign nation personal representative is subject to the jurisdiction of the courts of this state in a representative capacity to the same extent that the nondomiciliary decedent was subject to jurisdiction at the time of death.

(Stats. 1990 (A.B. 759), ch. 79, §14, effective July 1, 1991.)

VII. Disposition of Estates Without (or with Simplified) Administration

A decedent's estate may qualify for summary probate proceedings in some situations. Summary probate results in the disposition of the decedent's assets without the necessity for lengthy, costly probate proceedings. These proceedings generally permit the collection and transfer of certain property without administration.

The primary situations in California law that give rise to summary probate proceedings are: (1) small estate set-sides, (2) court orders determining succession to property, (3) affidavit procedures for the collection or transfer of personal property and for real property of small value, (4) determination or confirmation of property passing or belonging to surviving spouse, and (5) proceedings under the Independent Administration of Estates Act.

A. Small Estates Set-Aside

California Probate Code §§6600 et seq. provide for the filing of a petition setting aside the decedent's estate to the surviving spouse and minor children, provided that the net value of the estate does not exceed $20,000. The small estate set-aside procedure insures support for the dependent surviving spouse and minor children at the death of a breadwinner who possesses a small estate. "This right to have a small estate set aside effectively forecloses the rights of a third person to inherit or otherwise receive a part of that estate under the decedent's will." Law Revision Commission Comment to California Probate Code §6602. According to California Probate Code §6600(a), which defines the term "decedent's estate," real property located outside California is not included in the determination of the estate or its value.

The court has considerable discretion in making the order for small estate set-asides, and may even withhold the set-aside to an eligible spouse. In its determination, the court may consider such factors as: the needs of the surviving spouse and minor children, liens and encumbrances, creditors' claims, the needs of heirs or devisees, the intent of the decedent "as expressed in inter vivos and testamentary transfers or by other means," and other relevant considerations (Cal. Prob. Code §6609(b)). The remarriage of a surviving spouse raises a presumption that the survivor no longer needs the setting aside of the small estate. *Id.*

The petition may be filed independently or concurrently with a petition for probate or for administration and at any time prior to entry of an order for final distribution (Cal. Prob. Code §6605). The petition may be filed by the surviving spouse, child, guardian, or personal representative (Cal. Prob. Code §6606).

§6600. "Decedent's estate," defined

(a) Subject to subdivision (b), for the purposes of this chapter, "decedent's estate" means all the decedent's personal property, wherever located, and all the decedent's real property located in this state.

(b) For the purposes of this chapter:

(1) Any property or interest or lien thereon which, at the time of the decedent's death, was held by the decedent as a joint tenant, or in which the decedent had a life or other interest terminable upon the decedent's death, shall be excluded in determining the estate of the decedent or its value.

(2) A multiple-party account to which the decedent was a party at the time of the decedent's death shall be excluded in determining the estate of the decedent or its value, whether or not all or a portion of the sums on deposit are community property, to the extent that the sums on deposit belong after the death of the decedent to a surviving party, P.O.D. payee, or beneficiary. As used in this paragraph, the terms "multiple-party account," "party," "P.O.D. payee," and "beneficiary" have the meanings given those terms in Article 2 (commencing with Section 5120) of Chapter 1 of Part 2 of Division 5.

(Stats. 1990 (A.B. 759), ch. 79, §14, effective July 1, 1991.)

§6601. "Minor child," defined

As used in this chapter, "minor child" means a child of the decedent who was under the age of 18 at the time of the decedent's death and who survived the decedent.

(Stats. 1990 (A.B. 759), ch. 79, §14, effective July 1, 1991.)

§6602. Maximum value of $20,000 for summary probate proceeding

A petition may be filed under this chapter requesting an order setting aside the decedent's estate to the decedent's surviving spouse and minor children, or one or more of them, as provided in this chapter, if the net value of the decedent's estate, over and above all liens and encumbrances at the date of death and over and above the value of any probate homestead interest set apart out of the decedent's estate under Section 6520, does not exceed twenty thousand dollars ($20,000).

(Stats. 1990 (A.B. 759), ch. 79, §14, effective July 1, 1991.)

§6603. Venue for summary probate proceeding

The petition shall be filed in the superior court of a county in which the estate of the decedent may be administered.

(Stats. 1990 (A.B. 759), ch. 79, §14, effective July 1, 1991.)

§6604. Contents of petition for summary probate proceeding

(a) The petition shall allege that this chapter applies and request that an order be made setting aside the estate of the decedent as provided in this chapter.

(b) The petition shall include the following:

(1) If proceedings for administration of the estate are not pending, the facts necessary to determine the county in which the estate of the decedent may be administered.

(2) The name, age, address, and relation to the decedent of each heir and devisee of the decedent, so far as known to the petitioner.

(3) A specific description and estimate of the value of the decedent's estate and a list of all liens and encumbrances at the date of death.

(4) A specific description and estimate of the value of any of the decedent's real property located outside this state that passed to the surviving spouse and minor children of the decedent, or any one or more of them, under the will of the decedent or by intestate succession.

(5) A specific description and estimate of the value of any of the decedent's property described in subdivision (b) of Section 6600 that passed to the surviving spouse and minor children of the decedent, or any one or more of them, upon the death of the decedent.

(6) A designation of any property as to which a probate homestead is set apart out of the decedent's estate under Section 6520.

(7) A statement of any unpaid liabilities for expenses of the last illness, funeral charges, and expenses of administration.

(8) The requested disposition of the estate of the decedent under this chapter and the considerations that justify the requested disposition.

(Stats. 1990 (A.B. 759), ch. 79, §14, effective July 1, 1991.)

§6605. Procedure for filing petition for summary probate

(a) If proceedings for the administration of the estate of the decedent are pending, a petition under this chapter shall be filed in those proceedings without the payment of an additional fee.

(b) If proceedings for the administration of the estate of the decedent have not yet been commenced, a petition under this chapter may be filed concurrently with a petition for the probate of the decedent's will or for administration of the estate of the decedent, or, if no petition for probate or for administration is being filed, a petition under this chapter may be filed independently.

(c) A petition may be filed under this chapter at any time prior to the entry of the order for final distribution of the estate.

(Stats. 1990 (A.B. 759), ch. 79, §14, effective July 1, 1991.)

§6606. Persons who may file petition for summary probate

(a) A petition may be filed under this chapter by any of the following:

(1) The person named in the will of the decedent as executor.

(2) The surviving spouse of the decedent.

(3) The guardian of a minor child of the decedent.

(4) A child of the decedent who was a minor at the time the decedent died.

(5) The personal representative if a personal representative has been appointed for the decedent's estate.

(b) The guardian of a minor child of the decedent may file the petition without authorization or approval of the court in which the guardianship proceeding is pending.

(Stats. 1990 (A.B. 759), ch. 79, §14, effective July 1, 1991.)

§6607. Notice of hearing for summary probate

(a) Where proceedings for the administration of the estate of the decedent are not pending when the petition is filed under this chapter and the petition under this chapter is not joined with a petition for the probate of the decedent's will or for administration of the estate of the decedent, the petitioner shall give notice of the hearing on the petition as provided in Section 1220 to (1) each person named as executor in the decedent's will and to (2) each heir or devisee of the decedent, if known to the petitioner. A copy of the petition shall be sent with the notice of hearing to the surviving spouse, each child, and each devisee who is not petitioning.

(b) If the petition under this chapter is filed with a petition for the probate of the decedent's will or with a petition for administration of the estate of the deceased spouse, notice of the hearing on the petition shall be given to the persons and in the manner prescribed by Section 8003 and shall be included in the notice required by that section.

(c) If proceedings for the administration of the estate of the decedent are pending when the petition is filed under this chapter and the hearing of the petition for probate of the will or administration of the estate of the decedent is set for a day more than 15 days after the filing of the petition filed under this chapter, the petition under this chapter shall be set for hearing at the same time as the petition for probate of the will or for administration of the estate, and notice of hearing on the petition filed under this chapter shall be given by the petitioner as provided in Section 1220. If the hearing of the petition for probate of the will or for administration of the estate is not set for hearing for a day more than 15 days after the filing of the petition under this chapter, (1) the petition filed under this chapter shall be set for hearing at least 15 days after the date on which it is filed, (2) notice of the hearing on the petition filed under this chapter shall be given by the petitioner as provided in Section 1220, and (3) if the petition for probate of the will or for administration of the estate has not already been heard, that petition shall be continued until that date and heard at the same time unless the court otherwise orders.

(Stats. 1990 (A.B. 759), ch. 79, §14, effective July 1, 1991.)

§6608. Personal representative shall file inventory and appraisal

If a petition is filed under this chapter, the personal representative, or the petitioner if no personal representative has been appointed, shall file with the clerk of the court, prior to the hearing of the petition, an inventory and appraisal made as provided in Part 3 (commencing with Section 8800) of Division 7. The personal representative or the petitioner, as the case may be, may appraise the assets which a personal representative could appraise under Section 8901.

(Stats. 1990 (A.B. 759), ch. 79, §14, effective July 1, 1991.)

§6609. Court shall make order unless inequitable under the circumstances

(a) If the court determines that the net value of the decedent's estate, over and above all liens and encumbrances at the date of death of the decedent and over and above the value of any probate homestead interest set apart out of the decedent's estate under Section 6520, does not exceed twenty thousand dollars ($20,000) as of the date of the decedent's death, the court shall make an order under this section unless the court determines that making an order under this section would be inequitable under the circumstances of the particular case.

(b) In determining whether to make an order under this section, the court shall consider the needs of the surviving spouse and minor children, the liens and encumbrances on the property of the decedent's estate, the claims of creditors, the needs of the heirs or devisees of the decedent, the intent of the decedent with respect to the property in the estate and the estate plan of the decedent as expressed in inter vivos and testamentary transfers or by other means, and any other relevant considerations. If the surviving spouse has remarried at the time the petition is heard, it shall be presumed that the needs of the surviving spouse do not justify the setting aside of the small estate, or any portion thereof, to the surviving spouse. This presumption is a presumption affecting the burden of proof.

(c) Subject to subdivision (d), if the court makes an order under this section, the court shall assign the whole of the decedent's estate, subject to all liens and encumbrances on property in the estate at the date of the decedent's death, to the surviving spouse and the minor children of the decedent, or any one or more of them.

(d) If there are any liabilities for expenses of the last illness, funeral charges, or expenses of administration that are unpaid at the time the court makes an order under this section, the court shall make such orders as are necessary so that those unpaid liabilities are paid.

(e) Title to property in the decedent's estate vests absolutely in the surviving spouse, minor children, or any or all of them, as provided in the order, subject to all liens and encumbrances on property in the estate at the date of the decedent's death, and there shall be no further proceedings in the administration of the decedent's estate unless additional property in the decedent's estate is discovered.

(Stats. 1990 (A.B. 759), ch. 79, §14, effective July 1, 1991.)

§6610. Effect of final order: conclusive on all persons

Upon becoming final, an order under Section 6609 shall be conclusive on all persons, whether or not they are then in being.

(Stats. 1990 (A.B. 759), ch. 79, §14, effective July 1, 1991.)

§6611. Personal liability for unsecured debts of decedent following summary probate

(a) Subject to the limitations and conditions specified in this section, the person or persons in whom title vested pursuant to Section 6609 are personally liable for the unsecured debts of the decedent.

(b) The personal liability of a person under this section does not exceed the fair market value at the date of the decedent's death of the property title to which vested in that person pursuant to Section 6609, less the total of all of the following:

(1) The amount of any liens and encumbrances on that property.

(2) The value of any probate homestead interest set apart under Section 6520 out of that property.

(3) The value of any other property set aside under Section 6510 out of that property.

(c) In any action or proceeding based upon an unsecured debt of the decedent, the surviving spouse of the decedent, the child or children of the decedent, or the guardian of the minor child or children of the decedent, may assert any defense, cross-complaint, or setoff which would have been available to the decedent if the decedent had not died.

(d) If proceedings are commenced in this state for the administration of the estate of the decedent and the time for filing claims has commenced, any action upon the personal liability of a person under this section is barred to the same extent as provided for claims under Part 4 (commencing with Section 9000) of Division 7, except as to the following:

(1) Creditors who commence judicial proceedings for the enforcement of the debt and serve the person liable under this section with the complaint therein prior to the expiration of the time for filing claims.

(2) Creditors who have or who secure an acknowledgment in writing of the person liable under this section that that person is liable for the debts.

(3) Creditors who file a timely claim in the proceedings for the administration of the estate of the decedent.

(e) Section 366.2 of the Code of Civil Procedure applies in an action under this section.

(Stats. 1990 (A.B. 759), ch. 79, §14, effective July 1, 1991. Amended by Stats. 1990, ch. 140 (S.B. 1855), §4.1, effective July 1, 1991. Amended by Stats. 1992, ch. 178 (S.B. 1496), §32.)

§6612. Court may determine *not* to make an order for summary probate

If a petition filed under this chapter is filed with a petition for the probate of the decedent's will or for administration of the estate of the decedent and the court determines not to make an order under Section 6609, the court shall act on the petition for probate of the decedent's will or for administration of the estate of the decedent in the same manner as if no petition had been filed under this chapter, and the estate shall then be administered in the same manner as if no petition had been filed under this chapter.

(Stats. 1990 (A.B. 759), ch. 79, §14, effective July 1, 1991.)

§6613. Attorneys' fees shall be determined by attorney and client, not subject to court approval

The attorney's fees for services performed in connection with the filing of a petition and the obtaining of a court order under this chapter shall be determined by private agreement between the attorney and the client and are not subject to approval by the court. If there is no agreement between the attorney and the client concerning the attorney's fees for services performed in connection with the filing of a petition and obtaining of a court order under this chapter and there is a dispute concerning the reasonableness of the attorney's fees for those services, a petition may be filed with the court in the same proceeding requesting that the court determine the reasonableness of the attorney's fees for those services. If there is an agreement between the attorney and the client concerning the attorney's fees for services performed in connection with the filing of a petition and obtaining a court order under this chapter and there is a dispute concerning the meaning of the agreement, a petition may be filed with the court in the same proceeding requesting that the court determine the dispute.

(Stats. 1990 (A.B. 759), ch. 79, §14, effective July 1, 1991.)

§6614. Effective date of application

Sections 6600 to 6613, inclusive, do not apply if the decedent died before July 1, 1987. If the decedent died before July 1, 1987, the case continues to be governed by the law applicable to the case prior to July 1, 1987.

(Stats. 1990 (A.B. 759), ch. 79, §14, effective July 1, 1991.)

§6615. References to repealed provisions

A reference in any statute of this state or in a written instrument, including a will or trust, to a provision of former Sections 640 to 647.5, inclusive, repealed by Chapter 783 of the Statutes of 1986, shall be deemed to be a reference to the comparable provisions of this chapter.

(Stats. 1990 (A.B. 759), ch. 79, §14, effective July 1, 1991.)

B. Affidavit Procedure for Collection and Transfer of Personal Property and for Real Property of Small Value

California Probate Code §§13000-13054 specify the definitions and general provisions applicable to the collection or transfer of small estates without administration, including the use of an affidavit procedure for collection or transfer of personal property and for collection and transfer of real property of small value, as well as securing court orders determining succession to property. Specific regulations are set forth below that are applicable to the affidavit procedure for collection and transfer of *personal property* (Cal. Prob. Code §§13100-13116) and the affidavit procedure for *real property* of small value (Cal. Prob. Code §§13200-13210). For the specific regulations applicable to court orders determining succession to property, see Section C *infra*.

1. Affidavit Procedure for Collection and Transfer of Personal Property

§13000. Definitions govern construction of Part

Unless the provision or context otherwise requires, the definitions in this chapter govern the construction of this part.

(Stats. 1990 (A.B. 759), ch. 79, §14, effective July 1, 1991.)

§13002. "Holder of the decedent's property," defined

"Holder of the decedent's property" or "holder" means, with respect to any particular item of property of the decedent, the person owing money to the decedent, having custody of tangible personal property of the decedent, or acting as registrar or transfer agent of the evidences of a debt, obligation, interest, right, security, or chose in action belonging to the decedent.

(Stats. 1990 (A.B. 759), ch. 79, §14, effective July 1, 1991.)

§13004. "Particular item of property," defined

(a) "Particular item of property" means :

Particular item of property

(1) Particular personal property of the decedent which is sought to be collected, received, or transferred by the successor of the decedent under Chapter 3 (commencing with Section 13100) .

(2) Particular real property of the decedent, or particular real and personal property of the decedent, for which the successor of the decedent seeks a court order determining succession under Chapter 4 (commencing with Section 13150).

(3) Particular real property of the decedent with respect to which the successor of the decedent files an affidavit of succession under Chapter 5 (commencing with Section 13200).

(b) Subject to subdivision (a), "particular item of property" includes all interests specified in Section 62.

(Stats. 1990 (A.B. 759), ch. 79, §14, effective July 1, 1991. Amended by Stats. 1991 (S.B. 271), ch. 1055, §32.)

§13005. "Property of the decedent," defined

"Property of the decedent," "decedent's property," "money due the decedent," and similar phrases, include property that becomes part of the decedent's estate on the decedent's death, whether by designation of the estate as beneficiary under an insurance policy on the decedent's life or under the decedent's retirement plan, or otherwise.

(Stats. 1991 (S.B. 271), ch. 1055, §33.)

§13006. "Successor of the decedent," defined

"Successor of the decedent" means:

(a) If the decedent died leaving a will, the sole beneficiary or all of the beneficiaries who succeeded to a particular item of property of the decedent under the decedent's will. For the purposes of this part, a trust is a beneficiary under the decedent's will if the trust succeeds to the particular item of property under the decedent's will.

(b) If the decedent died without a will, the sole person or all of the persons who succeeded to the particular item of property of the decedent under Sections 6401 and 6402 or, if the law of a sister state or foreign nation governs succession to the particular item of property, under the law of the sister state or foreign nation.

(Stats. 1990 (A.B. 759), ch. 79, §14, effective July 1, 1991. Amended by Stats. 1991 (S.B. 271), ch. 1055, §34.)

§13007. "Proceeding," defined

"Proceeding" means either that a petition is currently pending in this state for administration of a decedent's estate under Division 7 (commencing with Section 7000), a special administrator for the decedent's estate has been appointed in this state and is now serving, or a personal representative for the decedent's estate has been appointed in this state with general powers. "Proceeding" does not include a petition for administration which was dismissed without the appointment of a personal representative, any proceeding under Division 8 (commencing with Section 13000), or any action or proceeding in another state.

(Stats. 1992 (A.B. 2975), ch. 871, §15.)

§13050. Property that is excluded in determining property or estate of decedent or its value

(a) For the purposes of this part:

(1) Any property or interest or lien thereon which, at the time of the decedent's death, was held by the decedent as a joint tenant, or in which the decedent had a life or other interest terminable upon the decedent's death, or which was held by the decedent and passed to the decedent's surviving spouse pursuant to Section 13500, shall be excluded in determining the property or estate of the decedent or its value. This excluded property shall include, but not be limited to, property in a trust revocable by the decedent during his or her lifetime.

(2) A multiple-party account to which the decedent was a party at the time of the decedent's death shall be excluded in determining the property or estate of the decedent or its value, whether or not all or a portion of the sums on deposit are community property, to the extent that the sums on deposit belong after the death of the decedent to a surviving party, P.O.D. payee, or beneficiary. For the purposes of this paragraph, the terms "multiple-party account," "party," "P.O.D. payee," and "beneficiary" are defined in Article 2 (commencing with Section 5120) of Chapter 1 of Part 2 of Division 5.

(b) For the purposes of this part, all of the following property shall be excluded in determining the property or estate of the decedent or its value:

(1) Any vehicle registered under Division 3 (commencing with Section 4000) of the Vehicle Code or

titled under Division 16.5 (commencing with Section 38000) of the Vehicle Code.

(2) Any vessel numbered under Division 3.5 (commencing with Section 9840) of the Vehicle Code.

(3) Any manufactured home, mobilehome, commercial coach, truck camper, or floating home registered under Part 2 (commencing with Section 18000) of Division 13 of the Health and Safety Code.

(c) For the purposes of this part, the value of the following property shall be excluded in determining the value of the decedent's property in this state:

(1) Any amounts due to the decedent for services in the armed forces of the United States.

(2) The amount, not exceeding five thousand dollars ($5,000), of salary or other compensation, including compensation for unused vacation, owing to the decedent for personal services from any employment.

(Stats. 1990 (A.B. 759), ch. 79, §14, effective July 1, 1991. Amended by Stats. 1996 (S.B. 392), ch. 563, §29.)

§13051. Persons who may act: guardian or conservator; trustee; custodian; sister state personal representative

For the purposes of this part:

(a) The guardian or conservator of the estate of a person entitled to any of the decedent's property may act on behalf of the person without authorization or approval of the court in which the guardianship or conservatorship proceeding is pending.

(b) The trustee of a trust may act on behalf of the trust. In the case of a trust that is subject to continuing jurisdiction of the court pursuant to Chapter 4 (commencing with Section 17300) of Part 5 of Division 9, the trustee may act on behalf of the trust without the need to obtain approval of the court.

(c) If the decedent's will authorizes a custodian under the Uniform Gifts to Minors Act or the Uniform Transfers to Minors Act of any state to receive a devise to a beneficiary , the custodian may act on behalf of the beneficiary until such time as the custodianship terminates.

(d) A sister state personal representative may act on behalf of the beneficiaries as provided in Chapter 3 (commencing with Section 12570) of Part 13 of Division 7.

(e) The attorney in fact authorized under a durable power of attorney may act on behalf of the beneficiary giving the power of attorney.

(Stats. 1990 (A.B. 759), ch. 79, §14, effective July 1, 1991. Amended by Stats. 1991 (S.B. 271), ch. 1055, §35.)

§13052. Date of valuation of property: date of death

In making an appraisal for the purposes of this part, the probate referee shall use the date of the decedent's death as the date of valuation of the property.

(Stats. 1990 (A.B. 759), ch. 79, §14, effective July 1, 1991.)

§13053. Application of part

(a) Except as provided in subdivision (b), this part applies whether the decedent died before, on, or after July 1, 1987.

(b) This part does not apply and the law in effect at the time of payment, delivery, or transfer shall apply if the payment, delivery, or transfer was made prior to July 1, 1987, pursuant to former Probate Code Sections 630 to 632, inclusive, repealed by Chapter 783 of the Statutes of 1986.

(Stats. 1990 (A.B. 759), ch. 79, §14, effective July 1, 1991.)

§13054. References to former Probate Code provisions are deemed references to comparable provisions herein

A reference in any statute of this state or in a written instrument, including a will or trust, to a provision of former Sections 630 to 632, inclusive, repealed by Chapter 783, Statutes of 1986, shall be deemed to be a reference to the comparable provisions of Chapter 3 (commencing with Section 13100).

(Stats. 1990 (A.B. 759), ch. 79, §14, effective July 1, 1991.)

§13100. Successor may collect or transfer personal property without letters or awaiting probate if estate, real and personal, is under $100,000

Excluding the property described in Section 13050, if the gross value of the decedent's real and personal property in this state does not exceed one hundred thousand dollars ($100,000) and if 40 days have elapsed since the death of the decedent, the successor of the decedent may, without procuring letters of administration or awaiting probate of the will, do any of the following with respect to one or more particular items of property:

(a) Collect any particular item of property that is money due the decedent.

(b) Receive any particular item of property that is tangible personal property of the decedent.

(c) Have any particular item of property that is evidence of a debt, obligation, interest, right, security, or chose in action belonging to the decedent transferred, whether or not secured by a lien on real property.

(Stats. 1990 (A.B. 759), ch. 79, §14, effective July 1, 1991. Amended by Stats. 1996 (A.B. 2146), ch. 86, §4; Stats. 1996 (A.B. 2751), ch. 862, §34.)

§13101. Contents of affidavit or declaration to be furnished to holder of decedent's property

(a) To collect money, receive tangible personal property, or have evidences of a debt, obligation, interest, right, security, or chose in action transferred under this chapter, an affidavit or a declaration under penalty of perjury under the laws of this state shall be furnished to the holder of the decedent's property stating all of the following:

(1) The decedent's name.

(2) The date and place of the decedent's death.

(3) "At least 40 days have elapsed since the death of the decedent, as shown in a certified copy of the decedent's death certificate attached to this affidavit or declaration."

(4) Either of the following, as appropriate:

(A) "No proceeding is now being or has been conducted in California for administration of the decedent's estate."

(B) "The decedent's personal representative has consented in writing to the payment, transfer, or delivery to the affiant or declarant of the property described in the affidavit or declaration."

(5) "The current gross fair market value of the decedent's real and personal property in California, excluding the property described in Section 13050 of the California Probate Code, does not exceed one hundred thousand dollars ($100,000)."

(6) A description of the property of the decedent that is to be paid, transferred, or delivered to the affiant or declarant.

(7) The name of the successor of the decedent (as defined in Section 13006 of the California Probate Code) to the described property.

(8) Either of the following, as appropriate:

(A) "The affiant or declarant is the successor of the decedent (as defined in Section 13006 of the California Probate Code) to the decedent's interest in the described property."

(B) "The affiant or declarant is authorized under Section 13051 of the California Probate Code to act on behalf of the successor of the decedent (as defined in Section 13006 of the California Probate Code) with respect to the decedent's interest in the described property."

(9) "No other person has a superior right to the interest of the decedent in the described property."

(10) "The affiant or declarant requests that the described property be paid, delivered, or transferred to the affiant or declarant."

(11) "The affiant or declarant affirms or declares under penalty of perjury under the laws of the State of California that the foregoing is true and correct."

(b) Where more than one person executes the affidavit or declaration under this section, the statements required by subdivision (a) shall be modified as appropriate to reflect that fact.

(c) If the particular item of property to be transferred under this chapter is a debt or other obligation secured by a lien on real property and the instrument creating the lien has been recorded in the office of the county recorder of the county where the real property is located, the affidavit or declaration shall satisfy the requirements both of this section and of Section 13106.5.

(d) A certified copy of the decedent's death certificate shall be attached to the affidavit or declaration.

(e) If the decedent's personal representative has consented to the payment, transfer, or delivery of the described property to the affiant or declarant, a copy of the consent and of the personal representative's letters shall be attached to the affidavit or declaration.

(Stats. 1990 (A.B. 759), ch. 79, §14, effective July 1, 1991. Amended by Stats. 1991 (S.B. 271), ch. 1055, §36; Stats. 1996 (A.B. 2146), ch. 86, §5; Stats. 1996 (A.B. 2751), ch. 862, §35.)

§13102. Evidence of property ownership shall be presented with affidavit or declaration

(a) If the decedent had evidence of ownership of the property described in the affidavit or declaration and the holder of the property would have had the right to require presentation of the evidence of ownership before the duty of the holder to pay, deliver, or transfer the property to the decedent would have arisen, the evidence of ownership, if available, shall be presented with the affidavit or declaration to the holder of the decedent's property.

(b) If the evidence of ownership is not presented to the holder pursuant to subdivision (a), the holder may require, as a condition for the payment, delivery, or transfer of the property, that the person presenting the affidavit or declaration provide the holder with a bond or undertaking in a reasonable amount determined by the holder to be sufficient to indemnify the holder against all liability, claims, demands, loss, damages, costs, and expenses that the holder may incur or suffer by reason of the payment, delivery, or transfer of the property. Nothing in this subdivision precludes the holder and the person presenting the affidavit or declaration from dispensing with the requirement that a bond or undertaking be provided and instead entering into an agreement satisfactory to the holder concerning the duty of the person presenting the affidavit or declaration to indemnify the holder.

(Stats. 1990 (A.B. 759), ch. 79, §14, effective July 1, 1991.)

§13103. Affidavit or declaration shall be accompanied by inventory and appraisal for estates including real property

If the estate of the decedent includes any real property in this state, the affidavit or declaration shall be accompanied by an inventory and appraisal of the real property. The inventory and appraisal of the real property shall be made as provided in Part 3 (commencing with Section 8800) of Division 7. The appraisal shall be made by a probate referee selected by the affiant or declarant from those probate referees appointed by the Controller under Section 400 to appraise property in the county where the real property is located.

(Stats. 1990 (A.B. 759), ch. 79, §14, effective July 1, 1991.)

§13104. Proof of identity of person executing affidavit or declaration

(a) Reasonable proof of the identity of each person executing the affidavit or declaration shall be provided to the holder of the decedent's property.

(b) Reasonable proof of identity is provided for the purposes of this section if both of the following requirements are satisfied:

(1) The person executing the affidavit or declaration is personally known to the holder.

(2) The person executes the affidavit or declaration in the presence of the holder.

(c) If the affidavit or declaration is executed in the presence of the holder, a written statement under penalty of perjury by a person personally known to the holder affirming the identity of the person executing the affidavit or declaration is reasonable proof of identity for the purposes of this section.

(d) If the affidavit or declaration is executed in the presence of the holder, the holder may reasonably rely on any of the following as reasonable proof of identity for the purposes of this section:

(1) An identification card or driver's license issued by the Department of Motor Vehicles of this state that is current or was issued during the preceding five years.

(2) A passport issued by the Department of State of the United States that is current or was issued during the preceding five years.

(3) Any of the following documents if the document is current or was issued during the preceding five years and contains a photograph and description of the person named on it, is signed by the person, and bears a serial or other identifying number:

(A) A passport issued by a foreign government that has been stamped by the United States Immigration and Naturalization Service.

(B) A driver's license issued by a state other than California.

(C) An identification card issued by a state other than California.

(D) An identification card issued by any branch of the armed forces of the United States.

(e) For the purposes of this section, a notary public's certificate of acknowledgment identifying the person executing the affidavit or declaration is reasonable proof of identity of the person executing the affidavit or declaration.

(f) Unless the affidavit or declaration contains a notary public's certificate of acknowledgment of the identity of the person, the holder shall note on the affidavit or declaration either that the person executing the affidavit or declaration is personally known or a description of the identification provided by the person executing the affidavit or declaration.

(Stats. 1990 (A.B. 759), ch. 79, §14, effective July 1, 1991.)

§13105. Entitlement to property by persons executing affidavit or declaration as decedent's successor

(a) If the requirements of Sections 13100 to 13104, inclusive, are satisfied:

(1) The person or persons executing the affidavit or declaration as successor of the decedent are entitled to have the property described in the affidavit or declaration paid, delivered, or transferred to them.

(2) A transfer agent of a security described in the affidavit or declaration shall change the registered ownership on the books of the corporation from the decedent to the person or persons executing the affidavit or declaration as successor of the decedent.

(b) If the holder of the decedent's property refuses to pay, deliver, or transfer any personal property or evidence thereof to the successor of the decedent within a reasonable time, the successor may recover the property or compel its payment, delivery, or transfer in an action brought for that purpose against the holder of the property. If an action is brought against the holder under this section, the court shall award reasonable attorney's fees to the person or persons bringing the action if the court finds that the holder of the decedent's

property acted unreasonably in refusing to pay, deliver, or transfer the property to them as required by subdivision (a).
(Stats. 1990 (A.B. 759), ch. 79, §14, effective July 1, 1991.)

§13106. Receipt of affidavit or declaration discharges property holder from liability

(a) If the requirements of Sections 13100 to 13104, inclusive, are satisfied, receipt by the holder of the decedent's property of the affidavit or declaration constitutes sufficient acquittance for the payment of money, delivery of property, or changing registered ownership of property pursuant to this chapter and discharges the holder from any further liability with respect to the money or property. The holder may rely in good faith on the statements in the affidavit or declaration and has no duty to inquire into the truth of any statement in the affidavit or declaration.

(b) If the requirements of Sections 13100 to 13104, inclusive, are satisfied, the holder of the decedent's property is not liable for any taxes due to this state by reason of paying money, delivering property, or changing registered ownership of property pursuant to this chapter.
(Stats. 1990 (A.B. 759), ch. 79, §14, effective July 1, 1991.)

§13106.5. Conditions for recording affidavit or declaration

(a) If the particular item of property transferred under this chapter is a debt or other obligation secured by a lien on real property and the instrument creating the lien has been recorded in the office of the county recorder of the county where the real property is located, the affidavit or declaration described in Section 13101 shall be recorded in the office of the county recorder of that county and, in addition to the contents required by Section 13101, shall include both of the following:

(1) The recording reference of the instrument creating the lien.

(2) A notary public's certificate of acknowledgment identifying each person executing the affidavit or declaration.

(b) The transfer under this chapter of the debt or obligation secured by a lien on real property has the same effect as would be given to an assignment of the right to collect the debt or enforce the obligation. The recording of the affidavit or declaration under subdivision (a) shall be given the same effect as is given under Sections 2934 and 2935 of the Civil Code to recording an assignment of a mortgage and an assignment of the beneficial interest under a deed of trust.

(c) If a deed of trust upon the real property was given to secure the debt and the requirements of subdivision (a) and of Sections 13100 to 13103, inclusive, are satisfied:

(1) The trustee under the deed of trust may rely in good faith on the statements made in the affidavit or declaration and has no duty to inquire into the truth of any statement in the affidavit or declaration.

(2) A person acting in good faith and for a valuable consideration may rely upon a recorded reconveyance of the trustee under the deed of trust.

(d) If a mortgage upon the real property was given to secure the debt and the requirements of subdivision (a) and of Sections 13100 to 13103, inclusive, are satisfied, a person acting in good faith and for a valuable consideration may rely upon a recorded discharge of the mortgage executed by the person or persons executing the affidavit or declaration as successor of the decedent or by their successors in interest.
(Stats. 1990 (A.B. 759), ch. 79, §14, effective July 1, 1991.)

§13107. Personal representative shall present affidavit or declaration to court in some cases

Where the money or property claimed in an affidavit or declaration presented under this chapter is that of a deceased heir or devisee of a deceased person whose estate is being administered in this state, the personal representative of the person whose estate is being administered shall present the affidavit or declaration to the court in which the estate is being administered. The court shall direct the personal representative to pay the money or deliver the property to the person or persons identified by the affidavit or declaration as the successor of the decedent to the extent that the order for distribution determines that the deceased heir or devisee was entitled to the money or property under the will or the laws of succession.
(Stats. 1990 (A.B. 759), ch. 79, §14, effective July 1, 1991.)

§13107.5. Substitution of parties without issuance of letters or probate if action against decedent pending

Where the money or property claimed in an affidavit or declaration executed under this chapter is the subject of a pending action or proceeding in which the decedent was a party, the successor of the decedent shall, without procuring letters of administration or awaiting probate of the will, be substituted as a party in place of the decedent by making a motion under Article 3 (commencing with Section 377.30) of Chapter 4 of Title 2 of Part 2 of the Code of Civil Procedure. The successor of the decedent shall file the affidavit or declaration with the court when the motion is made. For the purpose of Article 3 (commencing with Section 377.30) of Chapter 4 of Title 2 of Part 2 of the Code of Civil Procedure, a successor of the decedent who complies with this chapter shall be considered as a successor in interest of the decedent.

(Stats. 1991 (S.B. 271), ch. 1055, §37. Amended by Stats. 1992 (S.B. 1496), ch. 178, §39.)

§13108. Conditions for use of procedure

(a) The procedure provided by this chapter may be used only if one of the following requirements is satisfied:

(1) No proceeding for the administration of the decedent's estate is pending or has been conducted in this state.

(2) The decedent's personal representative consents in writing to the payment, transfer, or delivery of the property described in the affidavit or declaration pursuant to this chapter.

(b) Payment, delivery, or transfer of a decedent's property pursuant to this chapter does not preclude later proceedings for administration of the decedent's estate.

(Stats. 1990 (A.B. 759), ch. 79, §14, effective July 1, 1991. Amended by Stats. 1991 (S.B. 271), ch. 1055, §38.)

§13109. Liability for unsecured debts of decedent

A person to whom payment, delivery, or transfer of the decedent's property is made under this chapter is personally liable, to the extent provided in Section 13112, for the unsecured debts of the decedent. Any such debt may be enforced against the person in the same manner as it could have been enforced against the decedent if the decedent had not died. In any action based upon the debt, the person may assert any defenses, cross-complaints, or setoffs that would have been available to the decedent if the decedent had not died. Nothing in this section permits enforcement of a claim that is barred under Part 4 (commencing with Section 9000) of Division 7. Section 366.2 of the Code of Civil Procedure applies in an action under this section.

(Stats. 1990 (A.B. 759), ch. 79, §14, effective July 1, 1991. Amended by Stats. 1990 (S.B. 1855), ch. 140, §15.1, effective July 1, 1991; Stats. 1992 (S.B. 1496), ch. 178, §40.)

§13110. Liability of persons who received property to those persons having superior rights

(a) Except as provided in subdivision (b), each person to whom payment, delivery, or transfer of the decedent's property is made under this chapter is personally liable to the extent provided in Section 13112 to any person having a superior right by testate or intestate succession from the decedent.

(b) In addition to any other liability the person has under this section and Sections 13109, 13111, and 13112, any person who fraudulently secures the payment, delivery, or transfer of the decedent's property under this chapter is liable to the person having such a superior right for three times the fair market value of the property. For the purposes of this subdivision, the "fair market value of the property" is the fair market value of the property paid, delivered, or transferred to the person liable under this subdivision, valued as of the time the person liable under this subdivision presents the affidavit or declaration under this chapter to the holder of the decedent's property, less any liens and encumbrances on that property at that time.

(c) An action to impose liability under this section is forever barred three years after the affidavit or declaration is presented under this chapter to the holder of the decedent's property, or three years after the discovery of the fraud, whichever is later. The three-year period specified in this subdivision is not tolled for any reason.

(Stats. 1990 (A.B. 759), ch. 79, §14, effective July 1, 1991. Amended by Stats. 1991 (S.B. 271), ch. 1055, §39.)

§13111. Liability of persons who received property in some cases

(a) Subject to the provisions of this section, if proceedings for the administration of the decedent's estate are commenced in this state, or if the decedent's personal representative has consented to the payment, transfer, or delivery of the decedent's property under this chapter and the personal representative later requests that the property be restored to the estate, each person to whom payment, delivery, or transfer of the decedent's property is made under this chapter is liable for:

(1) The restitution of the property to the estate if the person still has the property, together with (A) the net income the person received from the property and (B) if the person encumbered the property after it was delivered or transferred to the person, the amount necessary to satisfy the balance of the encumbrance as of the date the property is restored to the estate.

(2) The restitution to the estate of the fair market value of the property if the person no longer has the property, together with (A) the net income the person received from the property and (B) interest on the fair market value of the property from the date of disposition at the rate payable on a money judgment. For the purposes of this subdivision, the "fair market value of the property" is the fair market value, determined as of the time of the disposition of the property, of the property paid, delivered, or transferred to the person under this chapter, less any liens and encumbrances on the property at that time.

(b) Subject to subdivision (c) and subject to any additional liability the person has under Sections 13109 to 13112, inclusive, if the person fraudulently secured the payment, delivery, or transfer of the decedent's property under this chapter, the person is liable under this section for restitution to the decedent's estate of three times the fair market value of the property. For the purposes of this subdivision, the "fair market value of the property" is the fair market value, determined as of the time the person liable under this subdivision presents the affidavit or declaration under this chapter, of the property paid, delivered, or transferred to the person under this chapter, less the amount of any liens and encumbrances on the property at that time.

(c) The property and amount required to be restored to the estate under this section shall be reduced by any property or amount paid by the person to satisfy a liability under Section 13109 or 13110.

(d) An action to enforce the liability under this section may be brought only by the personal representative of the estate of the decedent. In an action to enforce the liability under this section, the court's judgment may enforce the liability only to the extent necessary to protect the interests of the heirs, devisees, and creditors of the decedent.

(e) An action to enforce the liability under this section is forever barred three years after presentation of the affidavit or declaration under this chapter to the holder of the decedent's property, or three years after the discovery of the fraud, whichever is later. The three-year period specified in this subdivision is not tolled for any reason.

(f) In the case of a nondomiciliary decedent, restitution under this section shall be made to the estate in an ancillary administration proceeding.

(Stats. 1990 (A.B. 759), ch. 79, §14, effective July 1, 1991. Amended by Stats. 1991 (S.B. 271), ch. 1055, §40.)

§13112. Exemption from liability of persons who received property in some cases

(a) A person to whom payment, delivery, or transfer of the decedent's property has been made under this chapter is not liable under Section 13109 or 13110 if proceedings for the administration of the decedent's estate are commenced in this state, and the person satisfies the requirements of Section 13111.

(b) Except as provided in subdivision (b) of Section 13110, the aggregate of the personal liability of a person under Sections 13109 and 13110 shall not exceed the fair market value, valued as of the time the affidavit or declaration is presented under this chapter, of the property paid, delivered, or transferred to the person under this chapter, less the amount of any liens and encumbrances on that property at that time, together with the net income the person received from the property and, if the property has been disposed of, interest on the fair market value of the property accruing from the date of disposition at the rate payable on a money judgment. For the purposes of this subdivision, "fair market value of the property" has the same meaning as defined in paragraph (2) of subdivision (a) of Section 13111.

(Stats. 1990 (A.B. 759), ch. 79, §14, effective July 1, 1991.)

§13113. Remedies are in addition to other available remedies for fraud or intentional wrongdoing

The remedies available under Sections 13109 to 13112, inclusive, are in addition to any remedies available by reason of any fraud or intentional wrongdoing.

(Stats. 1990 (A.B. 759), ch. 79, §14, effective July 1, 1991.)

§13114. Public administrator and coroner may refuse to deliver property in some cases

(a) A public administrator who has taken possession or control of property of a decedent under Article 1 (commencing with Section 7600) of Chapter 4 of Part 1 of Division 7 may refuse to pay money or deliver property pursuant to this chapter if payment of the costs and fees described in Section 7604 has not first been made or adequately assured to the satisfaction of the public administrator.

(b) A coroner who has property found upon the body of a decedent, or who has taken charge of property of the decedent pursuant to Section 27491.3 of the Government Code, may refuse to pay or deliver the property pursuant to this chapter if payment of the reasonable costs of holding or safeguarding the property has not first been made or adequately assured to the satisfaction of the coroner.

(Stats. 1990 (A.B. 759), ch. 79, §14, effective July 1, 1991.)

§13115. Prohibition on use of procedure to obtain possession or transfer of real property

The procedure provided in this chapter may not be used to obtain possession or the transfer of real property.

(Stats. 1990 (A.B. 759), ch. 79, §14, effective July 1, 1991.)

§13116. Procedure is additional and supplemental to other procedures

The procedure provided in this chapter is in addition to and supplemental to any other procedure for (1) collecting money due to a decedent, (2) receiving tangible personal property of a decedent, or (3) having evidence of ownership of property of a decedent transferred. Nothing in this chapter restricts or limits the release of tangible personal property of a decedent pursuant to any other provision of law. This section is declaratory of existing law.

(Stats. 1990 (A.B. 759), ch. 79, §14, effective July 1, 1991.)

2. Affidavit Procedure for Transfer of Real Property of Small Value

§13200. Procedure for filing affidavit for real property of small value; contents of affidavit; service

(a) No sooner than six months from the death of a decedent, a person or persons claiming as successor of the decedent to a particular item of property that is real property may file in the superior court in the county in which the decedent was domiciled at the time of death, or if the decedent was not domiciled in this state at the time of death, then in any county in which real property of the decedent is located, an affidavit in the form prescribed by the Judicial Council pursuant to Section 1001 stating all of the following:

(1) The name of the decedent.

(2) The date and place of the decedent's death.

(3) A legal description of the real property and the interest of the decedent therein.

(4) The name and address of each person serving as guardian or conservator of the estate of the decedent at the time of the decedent's death, so far as known to the affiant.

(5) "The gross value of all real property in the decedent's estate located in California, as shown by the inventory and appraisal attached to this affidavit, excluding the real property described in Section 13050 of the California Probate Code, does not exceed twenty thousand dollars ($20,000)."

(6) "At least six months have elapsed since the death of the decedent as shown in a certified copy of decedent's death certificate attached to this affidavit."

(7) Either of the following, as appropriate:

(A) "No proceeding is now being or has been conducted in California for administration of the decedent's estate."

(B) "The decedent's personal representative has consented in writing to use of the procedure provided by this chapter."

(8) "Funeral expenses, expenses of last illness, and all unsecured debts of the decedent have been paid."

(9) "The affiant is the successor of the decedent (as defined in Section 13006 of the Probate Code) and to the decedent's interest in the described property, and no other person has a superior right to the interest of the decedent in the described property."

(10) "The affiant declares under penalty of perjury under the law of the State of California that the foregoing is true and correct."

(b) For each person executing the affidavit, the affidavit shall contain a notary public's certificate of acknowledgment identifying the person.

(c) There shall be attached to the affidavit an inventory and appraisal of the decedent's real property in this state, excluding the real property described in Section 13050. The inventory and appraisal of the real property shall be made as provided in Part 3 (commencing with Section 8800) of Division 7. The appraisal shall be made by a probate referee selected by the affiant from those probate referees appointed by the Controller under Section 400 to appraise property in the county where the real property is located.

(d) If the affiant claims under the decedent's will and no estate proceeding is pending or has been conducted in California, a copy of the will shall be attached to the affidavit.

(e) A certified copy of the decedent's death certificate shall be attached to the affidavit. If the decedent's personal representative has consented to the use of the procedure provided by this chapter, a copy of the consent and of the personal representative's letters shall be attached to the affidavit.

(f) The affiant shall mail a copy of the affidavit and attachments to any person identified in paragraph (4) of subdivision (a).

(Stats. 1990 (A.B. 759), ch. 79, §14, effective July 1, 1991. Amended by Stats. 1991 (S.B. 271), ch. 1055, §48; Stats. 1996 (A.B. 2146), ch. 86, §9.)

§13201. Fee for filing affidavit

Notwithstanding any other provision of law, the total fee for the filing of an affidavit under Section 13200 and the issuance of one certified copy of the affidavit under Section 13202 as provided in subdivision (b) of Section 70626 of the Government Code.

(Stats. 1990 (A.B. 759), ch. 79, §14, effective July 1, 1991. Amended by Stats. 2005 (A.B. 145), ch. 75, §150, effective July 19, 2005, effective January 1, 2006.)

§13202. County clerk shall file affidavit and attachments and then issue certified copy to be recorded

Upon receipt of the affidavit and the required fee, the court clerk, upon determining that the affidavit is complete and has the required attachments, shall file the affidavit and attachments and shall issue a certified copy of the affidavit without the attachments. The certified copy shall be recorded in the office of the county recorder of the county where the real property is located. The county recorder shall index the certified copy in the index of grantors and grantees. The decedent shall be indexed as the grantor and each person designated as a successor to the property in the certified copy shall be indexed as a grantee.

(Stats. 1990 (A.B. 759), ch. 79, §14, effective July 1, 1991.)

§13203. Rights and protections of good faith purchaser

(a) A person acting in good faith and for a valuable consideration with a person designated as a successor of the decedent to a particular item of property in a certified copy of an affidavit issued under Section 13202 and recorded in the county in which the real property is located has the same rights and protections as the person would have if each person designated as a successor in the recorded certified copy of the affidavit had been named as a distributee of the real property in an order for distribution that had become final.

(b) The issuance and recording of a certified copy of an affidavit under this chapter does not preclude later proceedings for administration of the decedent's estate.

(Stats. 1990 (A.B. 759), ch. 79, §14, effective July 1, 1991.)

§13204. Persons designated successors in affidavit are personally liable for decedent's unsecured debts

Each person who is designated as a successor of the decedent in a certified copy of an affidavit issued under Section 13202 is personally liable to the extent provided in Section 13207 for the unsecured debts of the decedent. Any such debt may be enforced against the person in the same manner as it could have been enforced against the decedent if the decedent had not died. In any action based upon the debt, the person may assert any defense, cross-complaint, or setoff that would have been available to the decedent if the decedent had not died. Nothing in this section permits enforcement of a claim that is barred under Part 4 (commencing with Section 9000) of Division 7. Section 366.2 of the Code of Civil Procedure applies in an action under this section.

(Stats. 1990 (A.B. 759), ch. 79, §14, effective July 1, 1991. Amended by Stats. 1990 (S.B. 1855), ch. 140, §17.1, effective July 1, 1991; Stats. 1992 (S.B. 1496), ch. 178, §42.)

§13205. Persons designated successors in affidavit are personally liable to persons having superior right by testate or intestate succession

(a) Except as provided in subdivision (b), each person who is designated as a successor of the decedent in a certified copy of any affidavit issued under Section 13202 is personally liable to the extent provided in Section 13207 to any person having a superior right by testate or intestate succession from the decedent.

(b) In addition to any other liability the person has under this section and Sections 13204, 13206, and 13207, if the person fraudulently executed or filed the affidavit under this chapter, the person is liable to the person having a superior right for three times the fair market value of the property. For the purposes of this subdivision, the "fair market value of the property" is the fair market value, determined as of the time the certified copy of the affidavit was issued under Section 13202, of the property the person liable took under the certified copy of the affidavit to which the other person has a superior right, less any liens and encumbrances on the property at that time.

(c) An action to impose liability under this section is forever barred three years after the certified copy of the affidavit is issued under Section 13202, or three years after the discovery of the fraud, whichever is later. The three-year period specified in this subdivision is not tolled for any reason.

(Stats. 1990 (A.B. 759), ch. 79, §14, effective July 1, 1991. Amended by Stats. 1991(S.B. 271), ch. 1055, §49.)

§13206. Liability of successors of decedent in some cases

(a) Subject to subdivisions (b), (c), (d), and (e), if proceedings for the administration of the decedent's estate are commenced, or if the decedent's personal representative has consented to use of the procedure provided by this chapter and the personal representative later requests that the property be restored to the estate, each person who is designated as a successor of the decedent in a certified copy of an affidavit issued under Section 13202 is liable for:

(1) The restitution to the decedent's estate of the property the person took under the certified copy of the affidavit if the person still has the property, together with (A) the net income the person received from the property and (B) if the person encumbered the property after the certified copy of the affidavit was issued, the amount necessary to satisfy the balance of the encumbrance as of the date the property is restored to the estate.

(2) The restitution to the decedent's estate of the fair market value of the property if the person no longer has the property, together with (A) the net income the person received from the property prior to disposing of it and (B) interest from the date of disposition at the rate payable on a money judgment on the fair market value of the property. For the purposes of this paragraph, the "fair

market value of the property" is the fair market value, determined as of the time of the disposition of the property, of the property the person took under the certified copy of the affidavit, less the amount of any liens and encumbrances on the property at the time the certified copy of the affidavit was issued.

(b) Subject to subdivision (d), if the person fraudulently executed or filed the affidavit under this chapter, the person is liable under this section for restitution to the decedent's estate of three times the fair market value of the property. For the purposes of this subdivision, the "fair market value of the property" is the fair market value, determined as of the time the certified copy of the affidavit was issued, of the property the person took under the certified copy of the affidavit, less the amount of any liens and encumbrances on the property at that time.

(c) Subject to subdivision (d), if proceedings for the administration of the decedent's estate are commenced and a person designated as a successor of the decedent in a certified copy of an affidavit issued under Section 13202 made a significant improvement to the property taken by the person under the certified copy of the affidavit in the good faith belief that the person was the successor of the decedent to that property, the person is liable for whichever of the following the decedent's estate elects:

(1) The restitution of the property, as improved, to the estate of the decedent upon the condition that the estate reimburse the person making restitution for (A) the amount by which the improvement increases the fair market value of the property restored, determined as of the time of restitution, and (B) the amount paid by the person for principal and interest on any liens or encumbrances that were on the property at the time the certified copy of the affidavit was issued.

(2) The restoration to the decedent's estate of the fair market value of the property, determined as of the time of the issuance of the certified copy of the affidavit under Section 13202, less the amount of any liens and encumbrances on the property at that time, together with interest on the net amount at the rate payable on a money judgment running from the date of the issuance of the certified copy of the affidavit.

(d) The property and amount required to be restored to the estate under this section shall be reduced by any property or amount paid by the person to satisfy a liability under Section 13204 or 13205.

(e) An action to enforce the liability under this section may be brought only by the personal representative of the estate of the decedent. In an action to enforce the liability under this section, the court's judgment may enforce the liability only to the extent necessary to protect the interests of the heirs, devisees, and creditors of the decedent.

(f) An action to enforce the liability under this section is forever barred three years after the certified copy of the affidavit is issued under Section 13202, or three years after the discovery of the fraud, whichever is later. The three-year period specified in this subdivision is not tolled for any reason.

(Stats. 1990 (A.B. 759), ch. 79, §14, effective July 1, 1991. Amended by Stats. 1991 (S.B. 271), ch. 1055, §50.)

§13207. Exemption of successors of decedent from certain liability

(a) A person designated as a successor of the decedent in a certified copy of an affidavit issued under Section 13202 is not liable under Section 13204 or 13205 if proceedings for the administration of the decedent's estate are commenced, or if the decedent's personal representative has consented to use of the procedure provided by this chapter and the personal representative later requests that the property be restored to the estate, and the person satisfies the requirements of Section 13206.

(b) Except as provided in subdivision (b) of Section 13205, the aggregate of the personal liability of a person under Sections 13204 and 13205 shall not exceed the sum of the following:

(1) The fair market value at the time of the issuance of the certified copy of the affidavit under Section 13202 of the decedent's property received by that person under this chapter, less the amount of any liens and encumbrances on the property at that time .

(2) The net income the person received from the property .

(3) If the property has been disposed of, interest on the fair market value of the property from the date of disposition at the rate payable on a money judgment. For the purposes of this paragraph, "fair market value of the property" has the same meaning as defined in paragraph (2) of subdivision (a) of Section 13206.

(Stats. 1990 (A.B. 759), ch. 79, §14, effective July 1, 1991. Amended by Stats. 1991 (S.B. 271), ch. 1055, §51.)

§13208. Remedies are in addition to other available remedies for fraud or intentional wrongdoing

The remedies available under Sections 13204 to 13207, inclusive, are in addition to any remedies available by reason of any fraud or intentional wrongdoing.

(Stats. 1990 (A.B. 759), ch. 79, §14, effective July 1, 1991.)

§13210. Requirements for use of procedure provided

The procedure provided by this chapter may be used only if one of the following requirements is satisfied:

(a) No proceeding for the administration of the decedent's estate is pending or has been conducted in this state.

(b) The decedent's personal representative consents in writing to use of the procedure provided by this chapter.

(Stats. 1991 (S.B. 271), ch. 1055, §52.)

C. Court Order Determining Succession to Property

California Probate Code §§13150-13158 authorize a procedure for obtaining, without the need for a probate proceeding, a court order determining that *real property* of the decedent passes to certain persons either by intestate or testate succession. The prerequisites for use of the procedure include:

(1) the gross value of the decedent's real and personal property (with some exceptions) in California is less than $60,000,

(2) no estate administration proceedings are pending,

(3) the decedent died leaving real property in California and 40 days have elapsed since death,

(4) all successors to the real property (by testate or intestate succession) have joined in the petition,

(5) the petition is accompanied by an inventory and appraisal by a probate referee, and

(6) the requisite notice is given.

Law Revision Commission Comment to California Probate Code §13150.

§13150. Conditions for use of procedure provided by chapter

The procedure provided by this chapter may be used only if one of the following requirements is satisfied:

(a) No proceeding is being or has been conducted in this state for administration of the decedent's estate.

(b) The decedent's personal representative consents in writing to use of the procedure provided by this chapter to determine that real property of the decedent is property passing to the petitioners.

(Stats. 1990 (A.B. 759), ch. 79, §14, effective July 1, 1991. Amended by Stats. 1991 (S.B. 271), ch. 1055, §42.)

§13151. Successor to interest in real property may file petition requesting determination of succession if estate consists of real and personal property worth less than $100,000

Exclusive of the property described in Section 13050, if a decedent dies leaving real property in this state and the gross value of the decedent's real and personal property in this state does not exceed one hundred thousand dollars ($100,000) and 40 days have elapsed since the death of the decedent, the successor of the decedent to an interest in a particular item of property that is real property, without procuring letters of administration or awaiting the probate of the will, may file a petition in the superior court of the county in which the estate of the decedent may be administered requesting a court order determining that the petitioner has succeeded to that real property. A petition under this chapter may include an additional request that the court make an order determining that the petitioner has succeeded to personal property described in the petition.

(Stats. 1990 (A.B. 759), ch. 79, §14, effective July 1, 1991. Amended by Stats. 1991 (S.B. 271), ch. 1055, §43; Stats. 1996 (A.B. 2146), ch. 86, §6; Stats. 1996 (A.B. 2751), ch. 862, §36.)

§13152. Contents of petition requesting determination of succession; requirement of attached inventory and appraisal

(a) The petition shall be verified by each petitioner, shall contain a request that the court make an order under this chapter determining that the property described in the petition is property passing to the petitioner, and shall state all of the following:

(1) The facts necessary to determine that the petition is filed in the proper county.

(2) The gross value of the decedent's real and personal property in this state, excluding the property described in Section 13050, as shown by the inventory and appraisal attached to the petition, does not exceed one hundred thousand dollars ($100,000).

(3) A description of the particular item of real property in this state which the petitioner alleges is property of the decedent passing to the petitioner, and a description of the personal property which the petitioner alleges is property of the decedent passing to the petitioner if the requested order also is to include a determination that the described personal property is property passing to the petitioner.

(4) The facts upon which the petitioner bases the allegation that the described property is property passing to the petitioner.

(5) Either of the following, as appropriate:

(A) A statement that no proceeding is being or has been conducted in this state for administration of the decedent's estate.

(B) A statement that the decedent's personal representative has consented in writing to use of the procedure provided by this chapter.

(6) Whether estate proceedings for the decedent have been commenced in any other jurisdiction and, if so, where those proceedings are pending or were conducted.

(7) The name, age, address, and relation to the decedent of each heir and devisee of the decedent, the names and addresses of all persons named as executors of the will of the decedent, and, if the petitioner is the trustee of a trust that is a devisee under the will of the decedent, the names and addresses of all persons interested in the trust, as determined in cases of future interests pursuant to paragraph (1), (2), or (3) of subdivision (a) of Section 15804, so far as known to any petitioner.

(8) The name and address of each person serving as guardian or conservator of the estate of the decedent at the time of the decedent's death, so far as known to any petitioner.

(b) There shall be attached to the petition an inventory and appraisal in the form set forth in Section 8802 of the decedent's real and personal property in this state, excluding the property described in Section 13050. The appraisal shall be made by a probate referee selected by the petitioner from those probate referees appointed by the Controller under Section 400 to appraise property in the county where the real property is located. The appraisal shall be made as provided in Part 3 (commencing with Section 8800) of Division 7. The petitioner may appraise the assets which a personal representative could appraise under Section 8901.

(c) If the petitioner bases his or her claim to the described property upon the will of the decedent, a copy of the will shall be attached to the petition.

(d) If the decedent's personal representative has consented to use of the procedure provided by this chapter, a copy of the consent shall be attached to the petition.

(Stats. 1990 (A.B. 759), ch. 79, §14, effective July 1, 1991. Amended by Stats. 1991 (S.B. 271), ch. 1055, §44; Stats. 1996 (A.B. 2146), ch. 86, §7; Stats. 1996 (A.B. 2751), ch. 862, §37.)

§13153. Notice of hearing shall be given

Notice of the hearing shall be given as provided in Section 1220 to each of the persons named in the petition pursuant to Section 13152.

(Stats. 1990 (A.B. 759), ch. 79, §14, effective July 1, 1991.)

§13154. Court shall make order determining succession and for transfer of property; conditions

(a) If the court makes the determinations required under subdivision (b), the court shall issue an order determining (1) that real property, to be described in the order, of the decedent is property passing to the petitioners and the specific property interest of each petitioner in the described property and (2) if the petition so requests, that personal property, to be described in the order, of the decedent is property passing to the petitioners and the specific property interest of each petitioner in the described property.

(b) The court may make an order under this section only if the court makes all of the following determinations:

(1) The gross value of the decedent's real and personal property in this state, excluding the property described in Section 13050, does not exceed one hundred thousand dollars ($100,000).

(2) Not less than 40 days have elapsed since the death of the decedent.

(3) Whichever of the following is appropriate:

(A) No proceeding is being or has been conducted in this state for administration of the decedent's estate.

(B) The decedent's personal representative has consented in writing to use of the procedure provided by this chapter.

(4) The property described in the order is property of the decedent passing to the petitioner.

(c) If the petition has attached an inventory and appraisal that satisfies the requirements of subdivision (b) of Section 13152, the determination required by paragraph (1) of subdivision (b) of this section shall be made on the basis of the verified petition and the attached inventory and appraisal, unless evidence is offered by a person opposing the petition that the gross value of the decedent's real and personal property in this state, excluding the property described in Section 13050, exceeds one hundred thousand dollars ($100,000).

(Stats. 1990 (A.B. 759), ch. 79, §14, effective July 1, 1991. Amended by Stats. 1991 (S.B. 271), ch. 1055, §45; Stats. 1996 (A.B. 2146), ch. 86, §8.)

§13155. Final order is conclusive

Upon becoming final, an order under this chapter determining that property is property passing to the petitioner is conclusive on all persons, whether or not they are in being.

(Stats. 1990 (A.B. 759), ch. 79, §14, effective July 1, 1991. Amended by Stats. 1991 (S.B. 271), ch. 1055, §46.)

§13156. Petitioner who receives decedent's property is liable for decedent's unsecured debts; limitation on liability; defenses

(a) Subject to subdivisions (b), (c), and (d), the petitioner who receives the decedent's property pursuant to an order under this chapter is personally liable for the unsecured debts of the decedent.

(b) The personal liability of any petitioner shall not exceed the fair market value at the date of the decedent's death of the property received by that petitioner pursuant to an order under this chapter, less the amount of any liens and encumbrances on the property.

(c) In any action or proceeding based upon an unsecured debt of the decedent, the petitioner may assert any defense, cross-complaint, or setoff which would have been available to the decedent if the decedent had not died.

(d) Nothing in this section permits enforcement of a claim that is barred under Part 4 (commencing with Section 9000) of Division 7.

(e) Section 366.2 of the Code of Civil Procedure applies in an action under this section.

(Stats. 1990 (A.B. 759), ch. 79, §14, effective July 1, 1991. Amended by Stats. 1990 (S.B. 1855), ch. 140, §16.1, effective July 1, 1991; Stats. 1992 (S.B. 1496), ch. 178, §41.)

§13157. Attorneys' fees shall be determined by private agreement; not subject to court approval

The attorney's fees for services performed in connection with the filing of a petition and obtaining a court order under this chapter shall be determined by private agreement between the attorney and the client and are not subject to approval by the court. If there is no agreement between the attorney and the client concerning the attorney's fees for services performed in connection with the filing of a petition and obtaining of a court order under this chapter and there is a dispute concerning the reasonableness of the attorney's fees for those services, a petition may be filed with the court in the same proceeding requesting that the court determine the reasonableness of the attorney's fees for those services. If there is an agreement between the attorney and the client concerning the attorney's fees for services performed in connection with the filing of a petition and obtaining a court order under this chapter and there is a dispute concerning the meaning of the agreement, a petition may be filed with the court in the same proceeding requesting that the court determine the dispute.

(Stats. 1990 (A.B. 759), ch. 79, §14, effective July 1, 1991.)

§13158. Compliance still required regarding affidavit procedure for personal property collection or transfer

Nothing in this chapter excuses compliance with Chapter 3 (commencing with Section 13100) by the holder of the decedent's personal property if an affidavit or declaration is furnished as provided in that chapter.

(Stats. 1991 (S.B. 271), ch. 1055, §47.)

D. Passage of Property to Surviving Spouse Without Administration

Probate administration may be avoided in some cases of succession by the surviving spouse. Specifically, the California Probate Code provides for a summary procedure in situations in which community and/or quasi-community property passes to the survivor from the decedent (either by will or intestate succession), or already belongs to the surviving spouse, or the decedent's separate property passes to the surviving spouse.

Although a decedent's property that passes by testate or intestate succession to the surviving spouse does so without the necessity for court proceedings, a judicial determination and order provides a *formal declaration* that such property has rightfully passed to the surviving spouse. The Probate Code authorizes a procedure that enables property qualifying for the "set-aside" to be "determined" (i.e., for property passing to the surviving spouse) and "confirmed" (for community or quasi-community property already belonging to the surviving spouse) to the surviving spouse without formal administration (Cal. Prob. Code §13650).

Most spouses who qualify for a spousal set-aside decide to proceed with the procedure for a spousal property order, even though the procedure is optional. Ross & Grant, Cal. Prob. Prac., *supra*, at §4:54. The set-aside procedure is especially helpful for purposes of clearing title, clarifying which property is subject to administration (when only part of the estate requires administration), and determining the value of property to establish the surviving spouse's liability to creditors. *Id.*

§13500. Administration not necessary when decedent dies intestate leaving property passing to surviving spouse or dies testate devising all or part of property to surviving spouse

Except as provided in this chapter, when a husband or wife dies intestate leaving property that passes to the surviving spouse under Section 6401, or dies testate and by his or her will devises all or a part of his or her property to the surviving spouse, the property passes to the survivor subject to the provisions of Chapter 2 (commencing with Section 13540) and Chapter 3 (commencing with Section 13550), and no administration is necessary.

(Stats. 1990 (A.B. 759) ch. 79, §14, effective July 1, 1991.)

§13501. Following property is subject to administration

Except as provided in Chapter 6 (commencing with Section 6600) of Division 6 and in Part 1 (commencing with Section 13000) of this division, the following property of the decedent is subject to administration under this code:

(a) Property passing to someone other than the surviving spouse under the decedent's will or by intestate succession.

(b) Property disposed of in trust under the decedent's will.

(c) Property in which the decedent's will limits the surviving spouse to a qualified ownership. For the purposes of this subdivision, a devise to the surviving spouse that is conditioned on the spouse surviving the decedent by a specified period of time is not a "qualified ownership" interest if the specified period of time has expired.

(Stats. 1990 (A.B. 759), ch. 79, §14, effective July 1, 1991.)

§13502. Following property is subject to administration upon election of surviving spouse

(a) Upon the election of the surviving spouse or the personal representative, guardian of the estate, or conservator of the estate of the surviving spouse, all or a portion of the following property may be administered under this code:

(1) The one-half of the community property that belongs to the decedent under Section 100, the one-half of the quasi-community property that belongs to the decedent under Section 101, and the separate property of the decedent.

(2) The one-half of the community property that belongs to the surviving spouse under Section 100 and the one-half of the quasi-community property that belongs to the surviving spouse under Section 101.

(b) The election shall be made by a writing specifically evidencing the election filed in the proceedings for the administration of the estate of the deceased spouse within four months after the issuance of letters, or within any further time that the court may allow upon a showing of good cause, and before entry of an order under Section 13656.

(Stats. 1990 (A.B. 759), ch. 79, §14, effective July 1, 1991.)

§13502.5. Court may order that property be subject to administration

(a) Upon a petition by the personal representative of a decedent and a showing of good cause, the court may order that a pecuniary devise to the surviving spouse, or a fractional interest passing to the surviving spouse in any property in which the remaining fraction is subject to the administration, may be administered under this code, except to the extent that it has passed by inheritance as determined by an order pursuant to Chapter 5 (commencing with Section 13650).

(b) Notice of this petition shall be given as provided in Section 1220 to the person designated in that section and to the surviving spouse.

(Stats. 1992 (A.B. 2975), ch. 871, §16.)

§13503. Surviving spouse may file an election to transfer certain property to trustee under decedent's will

(a) The surviving spouse or the personal representative, guardian of the estate, or conservator of the estate of the surviving spouse may file an election and agreement to have all or part of the one-half of the community property that belongs to the surviving spouse under Section 100 and the one-half of the quasi-community property that belongs to the surviving spouse under Section 101 transferred by the surviving spouse or the surviving spouse's personal representative, guardian, or conservator to the trustee under the will of the deceased spouse or the trustee of an existing trust identified by the will of the deceased spouse, to be administered and distributed by the trustee.

(b) The election and agreement shall be filed in the proceedings for the administration of the estate of the deceased spouse and before the entry of the order for final distribution in the proceedings.

(Stats. 1990 (A.B. 759), ch. 79, §14, effective July 1, 1991.)

§13504. Community property held in revocable trust is governed by trust provision

Notwithstanding the provisions of this part, community property held in a revocable trust described in Section 761 of the Family Code is governed by the provisions, if any, in the trust for disposition in the event of death.

(Stats. 1990 (A.B. 759), ch. 79, §14, operative July 1, 1991. Amended by Stats. 1994 (A.B. 2208), ch. 1269, §61.6.)

§13505. Application of part

This part applies whether the deceased spouse died before, on, or after July 1, 1987.

(Stats. 1990 (A.B. 759), ch. 79, §14, effective July 1, 1991.)

§13506. References to former Probate Code provisions deemed references to comparable provisions herein

A reference in any statute of this state or in a written instrument, including a will or trust, to a provision of former Sections 202 to 206, inclusive, of the Probate Code (as repealed by Chapter 527 of the Statutes of 1984) or former Sections 649.1 to 649.5, inclusive, or Sections 650 to 658, inclusive, of the Probate Code (as repealed by Chapter 783 of the Statutes of 1986) shall be deemed to be a reference to the comparable provision of this part.

(Stats. 1990 (A.B. 759), ch. 79, §14, effective July 1, 1991.)

§13540. Surviving spouse has power to deal with and dispose of community or quasi-community real property 40 days after death of decedent

(a) Except as provided in Section 13541, after 40 days from the death of a spouse, the surviving spouse or the personal representative, guardian of the estate, or conservator of the estate of the surviving spouse has full power to sell, convey, lease, mortgage, or otherwise deal with and dispose of the community or quasi-community real property, and the right, title, and interest of any grantee, purchaser, encumbrancer, or lessee shall be free of rights of the estate of the deceased spouse or of devisees or creditors of the deceased spouse to the same extent as if the property had been owned as the separate property of the surviving spouse.

(b) The surviving spouse or the personal representative, guardian of the estate, or conservator of the estate of the surviving spouse may record, prior to or together with the instrument that makes a disposition of property under this section, an affidavit of the facts that establish the right of the surviving spouse to make the disposition.

(c) Nothing in this section affects or limits the liability of the surviving spouse under Sections 13550 to 13553, inclusive, and Chapter 3.5 (commencing with Section 13560).

(Stats. 1990 (A.B. 759), ch. 79, §14, effective July 1, 1991. Amended by Stats. 1991 (S.B. 271), ch. 1055, §54; Stats. 1994 (A.B. 3686), ch. 806, §36.)

§13541. Exceptions to surviving spouse's power to dispose of community or quasi-community real property

(a) Section 13540 does not apply to a sale, conveyance, lease, mortgage, or other disposition that takes place after a notice that satisfies the requirements of this section is recorded in the office of the county recorder of the county in which real property is located.

(b) The notice shall contain all of the following:

(1) A description of the real property in which an interest is claimed.

(2) A statement that an interest in the property is claimed by a named person under the will of the deceased spouse.

(3) The name or names of the owner or owners of the record title to the property.

(c) There shall be endorsed on the notice instructions that it shall be indexed by the recorder in the name or names of the owner or owners of record title to the property, as grantor or grantors, and in the name of the person claiming an interest in the property, as grantee.

(d) A person shall not record a notice under this section for the purpose of slandering title to the property. If the court in an action or proceeding relating to the rights of the parties determines that a person recorded a notice under this section for the purpose of slandering title, the court shall award against the person the cost of the action or proceeding, including a reasonable attorney's fee, and the damages caused by the recording.

(Stats. 1990 (A.B. 759), ch. 79, §14, effective July 1, 1991. Amended by Stats. 1991 (S.B. 271), ch. 1055, §55.)

§13542. Application of former Probate Code provisions

The repeal of former Section 649.2 by Chapter 783 of the Statutes of 1986 does not affect any sale, lease, mortgage, or other transaction or disposition of real property made prior to July 1, 1987, to which that section applied, and such a sale, lease, mortgage, or other transaction or disposition shall continue to be governed by the provisions of former Section 649.2 notwithstanding the repeal of that section.

(Stats. 1990 (A.B. 759), ch. 79, §14, effective July 1, 1991.)

§13545. Surviving spouse's power to deal with securities

(a) After the death of a spouse, the surviving spouse, or the personal representative, guardian of the estate, or conservator of the estate of the surviving spouse has full power to sell, assign, pledge, or otherwise deal with and dispose of community or quasi-community property securities registered in the name of the surviving spouse alone, and the right, title, and interest of any purchaser, assignee, encumbrancer, or other transferee shall be free of the rights of the estate of the deceased spouse or of devisees or creditors of the deceased spouse to the same extent as if the deceased spouse had not died.

(b) Nothing in this section affects or limits the liability of a surviving spouse under Sections 13550 to 13553, inclusive, and Chapter 3.5 (commencing with Section 13560).

(Stats. 1991 (S.B. 271), ch. 1055, §56.)

§13550. Personal liability of surviving spouse for debts chargeable against property

Except as provided in Sections 11446, 13552, 13553, and 13554, upon the death of a married person, the surviving spouse is personally liable for the debts of the deceased spouse chargeable against the property described in Section 13551 to the extent provided in Section 13551.

(Stats. 1990 (A.B. 759), ch. 79, §14, effective July 1, 1991.)

§13551. Limitation of liability for debts of deceased spouse

The liability imposed by Section 13550 shall not exceed the fair market value at the date of the decedent's death, less the amount of any liens and encumbrances, of the total of the following:

(a) The portion of the one-half of the community and quasi-community property belonging to the surviving spouse under Sections 100 and 101 that is not exempt from enforcement of a money judgment and is not administered in the estate of the deceased spouse.

(b) The portion of the one-half of the community and quasi-community property belonging to the decedent under Sections 100 and 101 that passes to the surviving spouse without administration.

(c) The separate property of the decedent that passes to the surviving spouse without administration.

(Stats. 1990 (A.B. 759), ch. 79, §14, effective July 1, 1991.)

§13552. Limitation of actions; exceptions

If proceedings are commenced in this state for the administration of the estate of the deceased spouse and the time for filing claims has commenced, any action upon the liability of the surviving spouse pursuant to Section 13550 is barred to the same extent as provided for claims under Part 4 (commencing with Section 9000) of Division 7, except as to the following:

(a) Creditors who commence judicial proceedings for the enforcement of the debt and serve the surviving spouse with the complaint therein prior to the expiration of the time for filing claims.

(b) Creditors who have or who secure the surviving spouse's acknowledgment in writing of the liability of the surviving spouse for the debts.

(c) Creditors who file a timely claim in the proceedings for the administration of the estate of the deceased spouse.

(Stats. 1990 (A.B. 759), ch. 79, §14, effective July 1, 1991.)

§13553. Exemption of surviving spouse from liability

The surviving spouse is not liable under this chapter if all the property described in paragraphs (1) and (2) of subdivision (a) of Section 13502 is administered under this code.

(Stats. 1990 (A.B. 759), ch. 79, §14, effective July 1, 1991.)

§13554. Enforcement of debt against surviving spouse; defenses

(a) Except as otherwise provided in this chapter, any debt described in Section 13550 may be enforced against the surviving spouse in the same manner as it could have been enforced against the deceased spouse if the deceased spouse had not died.

(b) In any action or proceeding based upon the debt, the surviving spouse may assert any defense, cross-complaint, or setoff which would have been available to the deceased spouse if the deceased spouse had not died.

(c) Section 366.2 of the Code of Civil Procedure applies in an action under this section.

(Stats. 1990 (A.B. 759), ch. 79, §14, effective July 1, 1991. Amended by Stats. 1990 (S.B. 1855), ch. 140, §18.1, effective July 1, 1991; Stats. 1992 (S.B. 1496), ch. 178, §43.)

§13560. Definition of "decedent's property"

For the purposes of this chapter, "decedent's property" means the one-half of the community property that belongs to the decedent under Section 100 and the one-half of the quasi-community property that belongs to the decedent under Section 101.

(Stats. 1991 (S.B. 271), ch. 1055, §57.)

§13561. Liability of surviving spouse to person having superior right; limitation of actions

(a) If the decedent's property is in the possession or control of the surviving spouse at the time of the decedent's death, the surviving spouse is personally liable to the extent provided in Section 13563 to any person having a superior right by testate succession from the decedent.

(b) An action to impose liability under this section is forever barred three years after the death of the decedent. The three-year period specified in this subdivision is not tolled for any reason.

(Stats. 1991 (S.B. 271), ch. 1055, §57.)

§13562. Liability of surviving spouse if estate proceedings have commenced

(a) Subject to subdivisions (b), (c), and (d), if proceedings for the administration of the decedent's estate are commenced, the surviving spouse is liable for:

(1) The restitution to the decedent's estate of the decedent's property if the surviving spouse still has the decedent's property, together with (A) the net income the surviving spouse received from the decedent's property and (B) if the surviving spouse encumbered the decedent's property after the date of death, the amount necessary to satisfy the balance of the encumbrance as of the date the decedent's property is restored to the estate.

(2) The restitution to the decedent's estate of the fair market value of the decedent's property if the surviving spouse no longer has the decedent's property, together with (A) the net income the surviving spouse received from the decedent's property prior to disposing of it and (B) interest from the date of disposition at the rate payable on a money judgment on the fair market value of the decedent's property. For the purposes of this paragraph, the "fair market value of the decedent's property" is the fair market value of the decedent's property, determined as of the time of the disposition of the decedent's property, less the amount of any liens and encumbrances on the decedent's property at the time of the decedent's death.

(b) Subject to subdivision (c), if proceedings for the administration of the decedent's estate are commenced and the surviving spouse made a significant improvement to the decedent's property in the good faith belief that the surviving spouse was the successor of the decedent to the decedent's property, the surviving spouse is liable for whichever of the following the decedent's estate elects:

(1) The restitution of the decedent's property, as improved, to the estate of the decedent upon the condition that the estate reimburse the surviving spouse for (A) the amount by which the improvement increases the fair market value of the decedent's property restored, valued as of the time of restitution, and (B) the amount paid by the surviving spouse for principal and interest on any liens or encumbrances that were on the decedent's property at the time of the decedent's death.

(2) The restoration to the decedent's estate of the fair market value of the decedent's property, valued as of the time of the decedent's death, excluding the amount of any liens and encumbrances on the decedent's property at that time, together with interest on the net amount at the rate payable on a money judgment running from the date of the decedent's death.

(c) The property and amount required to be restored to the estate under this section shall be reduced by any property or amount paid by the surviving spouse to satisfy a liability under Chapter 3 (commencing with Section 13550).

(d) An action to enforce the liability under this section may be brought only by the personal representative of the estate of the decedent. In an action to enforce the liability under this section, the court's judgment may enforce the liability only to the extent necessary to protect the interests of the heirs, devisees, and creditors of the decedent.

(e) An action to enforce the liability under this section is forever barred three years after the death of the decedent. The three-year period specified in this subdivision is not tolled for any reason.

(Stats. 1991 (S.B. 271), ch. 1055, §57.)

§13563. Limitation on surviving spouse's liability

(a) The surviving spouse is not liable under Section 13561 if proceedings for the administration of the decedent's estate are commenced and the surviving spouse satisfies the requirements of Section 13562.

(b) The aggregate of the personal liability of the surviving spouse under Section 13561 shall not exceed the sum of the following:

(1) The fair market value at the time of the decedent's death, less the amount of any liens and encumbrances on the decedent's property at that time, of the portion of the decedent's property that passes to any person having a superior right by testate succession from the decedent.

(2) The net income the surviving spouse received from the portion of the decedent's property that passes to any person having a superior right by testate succession from the decedent.

(3) If the decedent's property has been disposed of, interest on the fair market value of the portion of the decedent's property that passes to any person having a superior right by testate succession from the decedent from the date of disposition at the rate payable on a money judgment. For the purposes of this paragraph, "fair market value" is fair market value, determined as of the time of disposition of the decedent's property, less the amount of any liens and encumbrances on the decedent's property at the time of the decedent's death.

(Stats. 1991 (S.B. 271), ch. 1055, §57.)

§13564. Other remedies are not affected

The remedies available under Sections 13561 to 13563, inclusive, are in addition to any remedies available by reason of any fraud or intentional wrongdoing.

(Stats. 1991 (S.B. 271), ch. 1055, §57.)

§13600. Surviving spouse may collect salary or other compensation owed decedent; ceiling

(a) At any time after a husband or wife dies, the surviving spouse or the guardian or conservator of the estate of the surviving spouse may, without procuring letters of administration or awaiting probate of the will, collect salary or other compensation owed by an employer for personal services of the deceased spouse, including compensation for unused vacation, not in excess of five thousand dollars ($5,000) net.

(b) Not more than five thousand dollars ($5,000) net in the aggregate may be collected by or for the surviving spouse under this chapter from all of the employers of the decedent.

(c) For the purposes of this chapter, a guardian or conservator of the estate of the surviving spouse may act on behalf of the surviving spouse without authorization or approval of the court in which the guardianship or conservatorship proceeding is pending.

(d) The five thousand dollar ($5,000) net limitation set forth in subdivisions (a) and (b) does not apply to the surviving spouse or the guardian or conservator of the estate of the surviving spouse of a firefighter or peace officer described in subdivision (a) of Section 22820 of the Government Code.

(e) On January 1, 2003, and on January 1 of each year thereafter, the maximum net amount of salary or compensation payable under subdivisions (a) and (b) to the surviving spouse or the guardian or conservator of the estate of the surviving spouse may be adjusted to reflect any increase in the cost of living occurring after January 1 of the immediately preceding year. The United States city average of the "Consumer Price Index for all Urban Consumers," as published by the United States Bureau of Labor Statistics, shall be used as the basis for determining the changes in the cost of living. The cost-of-living increase shall equal or exceed 1 percent before any adjustment is made. The net amount payable may not be decreased as a result of the cost-of-living adjustment.

(Stats. 1990 (A.B. 759), ch. 79, §14, effective July 1, 1991. Amended by Stats. 2002 (A.B. 2059), ch. 733, §2, effective September 20, 2002.; Stats. 2004 (S.B. 626), ch. 69, §35, effective June 1, 2004.)

§13601. Contents of affidavit or declaration to collect compensation owed decedent

(a) To collect salary or other compensation under this chapter, an affidavit or a declaration under penalty of perjury under the laws of this state shall be furnished to the employer of the deceased spouse stating all of the following:

(1) The name of the decedent.

(2) The date and place of the decedent's death.

(3) Either of the following, as appropriate:

(A) "The affiant or declarant is the surviving spouse of the decedent."

(B) "The affiant or declarant is the guardian or conservator of the estate of the surviving spouse of the decedent."

(4) "The surviving spouse of the decedent is entitled to the earnings of the decedent under the decedent's will or by intestate succession and no one else has a superior right to the earnings."

(5) "No proceeding is now being or has been conducted in California for administration of the decedent's estate."

(6) "Sections 13600 to 13605, inclusive, of the California Probate Code require that the earnings of the decedent, including compensation for unused vacation, not in excess of five thousand dollars ($ 5,000) net, be paid promptly to the affiant or declarant."

(7) "Neither the surviving spouse, nor anyone acting on behalf of the surviving spouse, has a pending request to collect compensation owed by another employer for personal services of the decedent under Sections 13600 to 13605, inclusive, of the California Probate Code."

(8) "Neither the surviving spouse, nor anyone acting on behalf of the surviving spouse, has collected any compensation owed by an employer for personal services of the decedent under Sections 13600 to 13605, inclusive, of the California Probate Code except the sum of -------- dollars ($ --) which was collected from --------."

(9) "The affiant or declarant requests that he or she be paid the salary or other compensation owed by you for personal services of the decedent, including compensation for unused vacation, not to exceed five thousand dollars ($ 5,000) net, less the amount of -------- dollars ($ ----) which was previously collected."

(10) "The affiant or declarant affirms or declares under penalty of perjury under the laws of the State of California that the foregoing is true and correct."

(b) Reasonable proof of the identity of the surviving spouse shall be provided to the employer. If a guardian or conservator is acting for the surviving spouse, reasonable proof of the identity of the guardian or conservator shall also be provided to the employer. Proof of identity that is sufficient under Section 13104 is sufficient proof of identity for the purposes of this subdivision.

(c) If a person presenting the affidavit or declaration is a person claiming to be the guardian or conservator of the estate of the surviving spouse, the employer shall be provided with reasonable proof, satisfactory to the employer, of the appointment of the person to act as guardian or conservator of the estate of the surviving spouse.

(Stats. 1990 (A.B. 759), ch. 79, §14, effective July 1, 1991. Amended by Stats. 2003 ((A.B. 167), ch. 32, §13.)

§13602. Employer shall promptly pay decedent's earnings

If the requirements of Section 13600 are satisfied, the employer to whom the affidavit or declaration is presented shall promptly pay the earnings of the decedent, including compensation for unused vacation, not in excess of five thousand dollars ($5,000) net, to the person presenting the affidavit or declaration.

(Stats. 1990 (A.B. 759), ch. 79, §14, effective July 1, 1991.)

§13603. Affidavit or declaration discharges employers' liability

If the requirements of Section 13601 are satisfied, receipt by the employer of the affidavit or declaration constitutes sufficient acquittance for the compensation paid pursuant to this chapter and discharges the employer from any further liability with respect to the compensation paid. The employer may rely in good faith on the statements in the affidavit or declaration and has no duty to inquire into the truth of any statement in the affidavit or declaration.

(Stats. 1990 (A.B. 759), ch. 79, §14, effective July 1, 1991.)

§13604. Surviving spouse may bring action if employer refuses to pay

(a) If the employer refuses to pay as required by this chapter, the surviving spouse may recover the amount the surviving spouse is entitled to receive under this chapter in an action brought for that purpose against the employer.

(b) If an action is brought against the employer under this section, the court shall award reasonable attorney's fees to the surviving spouse if the court finds that the employer acted unreasonably in refusing to pay as required by this chapter.

(Stats. 1990 (A.B. 759), ch. 79, §14, effective July 1, 1991.)

§13605. Effect of chapter on rights of heirs or devisees; liability for payment; fraudulent transactions

(a) Nothing in this chapter limits the rights of the heirs or devisees of the deceased spouse. Payment of a decedent's compensation pursuant to this chapter does not preclude later proceedings for administration of the decedent's estate.

(b) Any person to whom payment is made under this chapter is answerable and accountable therefor to the personal representative of the decedent's estate and is liable for the amount of the payment to any other person having a superior right to the payment received. In addition to any other liability the person has under this section, a person who fraudulently secures a payment under this chapter is liable to a person having a superior right to the payment for three times the amount of the payment.

(Stats. 1990 (A.B. 759), ch. 79, §14, effective July 1, 1991.)

§13606. Procedure does not preclude other methods of collecting compensation

The procedure provided in this chapter is in addition to, and not in lieu of, any other method of collecting compensation owed to a decedent.

(Stats. 1990 (A.B. 759), ch. 79, §14, effective July 1, 1991.)

§13650. Surviving spouse or personal representative may file petition requesting order that administration is not necessary

(a) A surviving spouse or the personal representative, guardian of the estate, or conservator of the estate of the surviving spouse may file a petition in the superior court of the county in which the estate of the deceased spouse may be administered requesting an order that administration of all or part of the estate is not necessary for the reason that all or part of the estate is property passing to the surviving spouse. The petition may also request an order confirming the ownership of the surviving spouse of property belonging to the surviving spouse under Section 100 or 101.

(b) To the extent of the election, this section does not apply to property that the petitioner has elected, as provided in Section 13502, to have administered under this code.

(c) A guardian or conservator may file a petition under this section without authorization or approval of the court in which the guardianship or conservatorship proceeding is pending.

(Stats. 1990 (A.B. 759), ch. 79, §14, effective July 1, 1991.)

§13651. Contents of petition for order that administration is not necessary

(a) A petition filed pursuant to Section 13650 shall allege that administration of all or a part of the estate of the deceased spouse is not necessary for the reason that all or a part of the estate is property passing to the surviving spouse, and shall set forth all of the following information:

(1) If proceedings for the administration of the estate are not pending, the facts necessary to determine the county in which the estate of the deceased spouse may be administered.

(2) A description of the property of the deceased spouse which the petitioner alleges is property passing to the surviving spouse, including the trade or business name of any property passing to the surviving spouse that consists of an unincorporated business or an interest in an unincorporated business which the deceased spouse was operating or managing at the time of death, subject to any written agreement between the deceased spouse and the surviving spouse providing for a non pro rata division of the aggregate value of the community property assets or quasi-community assets, or both.

(3) The facts upon which the petitioner bases the allegation that all or a part of the estate of the deceased spouse is property passing to the surviving spouse.

(4) A description of any interest in the community property or quasi-community property, or both, which the petitioner requests the court to confirm to the surviving spouse as belonging to the surviving spouse pursuant to Section 100 or 101, subject to any written agreement between the deceased spouse and the surviving spouse providing for a non pro rata division of the aggregate value of the community property assets or quasi-community assets, or both.

(5) The name, age, address, and relation to the deceased spouse of each heir and devisee of the deceased spouse, the names and addresses of all persons named as executors of the will of the deceased spouse, and the names and addresses of all persons appointed as personal representatives of the deceased spouse, which are known to the petitioner.

Disclosure of any written agreement between the deceased spouse and the surviving spouse providing for a non pro rata division of the aggregate value of the community property assets or quasi-community property assets, or both, or the affirmative statement that this agreement does not exist. If a dispute arises as to the division of the community property assets or quasi-community property assets, or both, pursuant to this agreement, the court shall determine the division subject to terms and conditions or other remedies that appear equitable under the circumstances of the case, taking into account the rights of all interested persons.

(b) If the petitioner bases the allegation that all or part of the estate of the deceased spouse is property passing to the surviving spouse upon the will of the deceased spouse, a copy of the will shall be attached to the petition.

(c) If the petitioner bases the description of the property of the deceased spouse passing to the surviving spouse or the property to be confirmed to the surviving spouse, or both, upon a written agreement between the deceased spouse and the surviving spouse providing for a non pro rata division of the aggregate value of the community property assets or quasi-community assets, or both, a copy of the agreement shall be attached to the petition.

(Stats. 1990 (A.B. 759), ch. 79, §14, effective July 1, 1991. Amended by Stats. 1998 (A.B. 2069), ch. 682, §6.)

§13652. Additional fee not necessary if proceedings pending

If proceedings for the administration of the estate of the deceased spouse are pending, a petition under this chapter shall be filed in those proceedings without the payment of an additional fee.

(Stats. 1990 (A.B. 759), ch. 79, §14, effective July 1, 1991.)

§13653. Petition may be filed with petition for probate or administration if proceedings are not pending

If proceedings for the administration of the estate of the deceased spouse are not pending, a petition under this chapter may, but need not, be filed with a petition for probate of the will of the deceased spouse or for administration of the estate of the deceased spouse.

(Stats. 1990 (A.B. 759), ch. 79, §14, effective July 1, 1991.)

§13654. Petition does not preclude admission of will to probate or appointment of personal representative

The filing of a petition under this chapter does not preclude the court from admitting the will of the deceased spouse to probate or appointing a personal representative of the estate of the deceased spouse upon the petition of any person legally entitled, including any petition for probate of the will or for administration of the estate which is filed with a petition filed under this chapter.

(Stats. 1990 (A.B. 759), ch. 79, §14, effective July 1, 1991.)

§13655. Notice of hearing shall be given as provided

(a) If proceedings for the administration of the estate of the deceased spouse are pending at the time a petition is filed under this chapter, or if the proceedings are not pending and if the petition filed under this chapter is not filed with a petition for probate of the deceased spouse's will or for administration of the estate of the deceased spouse, notice of the hearing on the petition filed under this chapter shall be given as provided in Section 1220 to all of the following persons:

(1) Each person listed in Section 1220 and each person named as executor in any will of the deceased spouse.

(2) All devisees and known heirs of the deceased spouse and, if the petitioner is the trustee of a trust that is a devisee under the will of the decedent, all persons interested in the trust, as determined in cases of future interests pursuant to paragraph (1), (2), or (3) of subdivision (a) of Section 15804.

(b) The notice specified in subdivision (a) shall also be mailed as provided in subdivision (a) to the Attorney General, addressed to the office of the Attorney General at Sacramento, if the petitioner bases the allegation that all or part of the estate of the deceased spouse is property passing to the surviving spouse upon the will of the deceased spouse and the will involves or may involve either of the following:

(1) A testamentary trust of property for charitable purposes other than a charitable trust with a designated trustee, resident in this state.

(2) A devise for a charitable purpose without an identified devisee or beneficiary.

(Stats. 1990 (A.B. 759), ch. 79, §14, effective July 1, 1991. Amended by Stats. 1996 (S.B. 392), ch. 563, §30.)

§13656. Court shall issue order upon determination that all of decedent's property passes to surviving spouse

(a) If the court finds that all of the estate of the deceased spouse is property passing to the surviving spouse, the court shall issue an order describing the property, determining that the property is property passing to the surviving spouse, and determining that no administration is necessary. The court may issue any further orders which may be necessary to cause delivery of the property or its proceeds to the surviving spouse.

(b) If the court finds that all or part of the estate of the deceased spouse is not property passing to the surviving spouse, the court shall issue an order (1) describing any property which is not property passing to the surviving spouse, determining that that property does not pass to the surviving spouse and determining that that property is subject to administration under this code and (2) describing the property, if any, which is property passing to the surviving spouse, determining that that property passes to the surviving spouse, and determining that no administration of that property is necessary. If the court determines that property passes to the surviving spouse, the court may issue any further orders which may be necessary to cause delivery of that property or its proceeds to the surviving spouse.

(c) If the petition filed under this chapter includes a description of the interest of the surviving spouse in the community or quasi-community property, or both, which belongs to the surviving spouse pursuant to Section 100 or 101 and the court finds that the interest belongs to the surviving spouse, the court shall issue an order describing the property and confirming the ownership of the surviving spouse and may issue any further orders which may be necessary to cause ownership of the property to be confirmed in the surviving spouse.

(Stats. 1990 (A.B. 759), ch. 79, §14, effective July 1, 1991.)

§13657. Final order is conclusive

Upon becoming final, an order under Section 13656 (1) determining that property is property passing to the surviving spouse or (2) confirming the ownership of the surviving spouse of property belonging to the surviving spouse under Section 100 or 101 shall be conclusive on all persons, whether or not they are in being.

(Stats. 1990 (A.B. 759), ch. 79, §14, effective July 1, 1991.)

§13658. Surviving spouse shall file list of creditors if property consists of unincorporated businesses

If the court determines that all or a part of the property passing to the surviving spouse consists of an unincorporated business or an interest in an unincorporated business which the deceased spouse was operating or managing at the time of death, the court shall require the surviving spouse to file a list of all of the known creditors of the business and the amounts owing to each of them. The court may issue any order necessary to protect the interests of the creditors of the business, including, but not limited to, the filing of (1) an undertaking and (2) an inventory and appraisal in the form provided in Section 8802 and made as provided in Part 3 (commencing with Section 8800) of Division 7.

(Stats. 1990 (A.B. 759), ch. 79, §14, effective July 1, 1991.)

§13659. Inventory and appraisal are not required

Except as provided in Section 13658, no inventory and appraisal of the estate of the deceased spouse is required in a proceeding under this chapter. However, within three months after the filing of a petition under this chapter, or within such further time as the court or judge for reasonable cause may allow, the petitioner may file with the clerk of the court an inventory and appraisal made as provided in Part 3 (commencing with Section 8800) of Division 7. The petitioner may appraise the assets which a personal representative could appraise under Section 8901.

(Stats. 1990 (A.B. 759), ch. 79, §14, effective July 1, 1991.)

§13660. Attorneys' fees pursuant to agreement are not subject to court approval

The attorney's fees for services performed in connection with the filing of a petition and obtaining of a court order under this chapter shall be determined by private agreement between the attorney and the client and are not subject to approval by the court. If there is no agreement between the attorney and the client concerning the attorney's fees for services performed in connection with the filing of a petition and obtaining of a court order under this chapter and there is a dispute concerning the reasonableness of the attorney's fees for those services, a petition may be filed with the court in the same proceeding requesting that the court determine the reasonableness of the attorney's fees for those services. If there is an agreement between the attorney and the client concerning the attorney's fees for services performed in connection with the filing of a petition and obtaining a court order under this chapter and there is a dispute concerning the meaning of the agreement, a petition may be filed with the court in the same proceeding requesting that the court determine the dispute.

(Stats. 1990 (A.B. 759), ch. 79, §14, effective July 1, 1991.)

E. Independent Administration of Estates Act

The Independent Administration of Estates Act (IAEA) (Cal. Prob. Code §§10400 et seq.) was originally enacted in 1974. A personal representative has the option of proceeding to administer the estate under the IAEA unless the will precludes this alternative (Cal. Prob. Code §10404). The purpose of the IAEA is to simplify estate administration in order to save time and money. Authority under the IAEA enables the personal representative to exercise a broad range of administrative powers without court supervision.

In order to invoke the act, the personal representative must first file a petition requesting authority to act pursuant to the legislation. The representative may request full authority to act under the IAEA (Cal. Prob. Code §10402) (authorizing "all the powers granted under this part") or limited authority (Cal. Prob. Code §10403) (containing certain restrictions on the representative's powers regarding the sale or exchange of real property, granting an option to purchase real property, and borrowing money with the loan secured by an encumbrance on real property).

The classification of the personal representative's powers under the IAEA falls into three categories: (1) actions requiring court supervision despite the grant of IAEA authority (Cal. Prob. Code §10501); (2) actions that may be taken only after giving notice (Cal. Prob. Code §§10510-10538) but will require court supervision if an interested party files a timely objection; and (3) actions that may be taken without giving notice of proposed action and, hence, without court supervision in all cases (Cal. Prob. Code §§10550-10564). Ross & Grant, Cal. Prob. Prac., *supra*, at §9:19.

Specifically, California Probate Code §10501 mandates court supervision for IAEA representatives for the following acts: allowance of compensation for the personal representative or the estate attorney; settlement of accounts; preliminary and final distributions and discharge; actions regarding estate property (e.g., sale, exchange, granting options to purchase) to or by the personal representative or the estate attorney for the personal representative; allowance, payment, or compromise of claims of the personal representative, or the attorney for the personal representative, against the estate (or by the estate against the personal representative or against the estate attorney); and extension, renewal, or modification of the terms of a debt or other obligation of the personal representative, or the estate attorney, owing to or in favor of the decedent or the estate.

Of course, a personal representative has the option of requesting court authorization for a given act, pursuant to California Probate Code §9610 (set forth in Section VA1 *supra*), even if the IAEA does not specifically require it. Personal representatives might choose to secure

court authorization because of the concern about liability: those representatives who take action under the IAEA without court supervision are not discharged from liability under California Probate Code §7250(a) (set forth in Section I *supra*) until the settlement of their accounts reporting IAEA transactions.

Interested persons who disagree with the representative's proposed actions may file objections. They may apply to the court which may then grant an order restraining the action (Cal. Prob. Code §10588). Or objectants may deliver or mail a written objection to the personal representative. In the latter case, the personal representative's recourse is to submit the proposed action for court approval (Cal. Prob. Code §10589).

Personal representatives who have authority under the IAEA are still bound by the general fiduciary standard of care. That is, pursuant to California Probate Code §9600, they must exercise "ordinary care and diligence" in the management and control of the estate. See, e.g., Estate of Davis, 268 Cal. Rptr. 384, 390 (Ct. App. 1990) ("Nothing within the act even remotely suggests an IAEA administrator does not have the same fiduciary duties as an administrator under any other Probate Code section").

§10400. Title

This part shall be known and may be cited as the Independent Administration of Estates Act.

(Stats. 1990 (A.B. 759), ch. 79, §14, effective July 1, 1991.)

§10401. "Court supervision," defined

As used in this part, "court supervision" means the judicial order, authorization, approval, confirmation, or instructions that would be required if authority to administer the estate had not been granted under this part.

(Stats. 1990 (A.B. 759), ch. 79, §14, effective July 1, 1991.)

§10402. "Full authority," defined

As used in this part, "full authority" means authority to administer the estate under this part that includes all the powers granted under this part.

(Stats. 1990 (A.B. 759), ch. 79, §14, effective July 1, 1991.)

§10403. "Limited authority," defined

As used in this part, "limited authority" means authority to administer the estate under this part that includes all the powers granted under this part except the power to do any of the following:

(a) Sell real property.

(b) Exchange real property.

(c) Grant an option to purchase real property.

(d) Borrow money with the loan secured by an encumbrance upon real property.

(Stats. 1990 (A.B. 759), ch. 79, §14, effective July 1, 1991.)

§10404. Will provision may preclude independent administration

The personal representative may not be granted authority to administer the estate under this part if the decedent's will provides that the estate shall not be administered under this part.

(Stats. 1990 (A.B. 759), ch. 79, §14, effective July 1, 1991.)

§10405. Special administrator may be granted authority to administer estate under Act

A special administrator may be granted authority to administer the estate under this part if the special administrator is appointed with, or has been granted, the powers of a general personal representative.

(Stats. 1990 (A.B. 759), ch. 79, §14, effective July 1, 1991.)

§10406. Authority of personal representative granted independent administration under prior law

(a) Subject to subdivision (b), this part applies in any case where authority to administer the estate is granted under this part or where independent administration authority was granted under prior law.

(b) If the personal representative was granted independent administration authority prior to July 1, 1988, the personal representative may use that existing authority on and after July 1, 1988, to borrow money on a loan secured by an encumbrance upon real property, whether or not that existing authority includes the authority to sell real property.

(Stats. 1990 (A.B. 759), ch. 79, §14, effective July 1, 1991. Amended by Stats. 1990 (S.B. 1775), ch. 710, §28, effective July 1, 1991.)

§10450. Personal representative must petition for authority for independent administration of estate

(a) To obtain authority to administer the estate under this part, the personal representative shall petition the court for that authority either in the petition for appointment of the personal representative or in a separate petition filed in the estate proceedings.

(b) The petition may request either of the following:

(1) Full authority to administer the estate under this part.

(2) Limited authority to administer the estate under this part.

(Stats. 1990 (A.B. 759), ch. 79, §14, effective July 1, 1991.)

§10451. Contents of notice of hearing on petition to administer estate under Act

(a) If the authority to administer the estate under this part is requested in the petition for appointment of the personal representative, notice of the hearing on the petition shall be given for the period and in the manner applicable to the petition for appointment.

(b) Where proceedings for the administration of the estate are pending at the time a petition is filed under Section 10450, notice of the hearing on the petition shall be given as provided in Section 1220 to all of the following persons:

(1) Each person listed in Section 1220.

(2) Each known heir whose interest in the estate would be affected by the petition.

(3) Each known devisee whose interest in the estate would be affected by the petition.

(4) Each person named as executor in the will of the decedent.

(c) The notice of hearing of the petition for authority to administer the estate under this part, whether included in the petition for appointment or in a separate petition, shall include the substance of the following statement: "The petition requests authority to administer the estate under the Independent Administration of Estates Act. This will avoid the need to obtain court approval for many actions taken in connection with the estate. However, before taking certain actions, the personal representative will be required to give notice to interested persons unless they have waived notice or have consented to the proposed action. Independent administration authority will be granted unless good cause is shown why it should not be."

(Stats. 1990 (A.B. 759), ch. 79, §14, effective July 1, 1991.)

§10452. Objections to requests to administer estate under Act

Unless an interested person objects as provided in Section 1043 to the granting of authority to administer the estate under this part and the court determines that the objecting party has shown good cause why the authority to administer the estate under this part should not be granted, the court shall grant the requested authority. If the objecting party has shown good cause why only limited authority should be granted, the court shall grant only limited authority.

(Stats. 1990 (A.B. 759), ch. 79, §14, effective July 1, 1991.)

§10453. Court has discretion to fix amount of bond of personal representative

(a) If the personal representative is otherwise required to file a bond and has full authority, the court, in its discretion, shall fix the amount of the bond at not more than the estimated value of the personal property, the estimated value of the decedent's interest in the real property authorized to be sold under this part, and the probable annual gross income of the estate, or, if the bond is to be given by personal sureties, at not less than twice that amount.

(b) If the personal representative is otherwise required to file a bond and has limited authority, the court, in its discretion, shall fix the amount of the bond at not more than the estimated value of the personal property and the probable annual gross income of the estate, or, if the bond is to be given by personal sureties, at not less than twice that amount.

(Stats. 1990 (A.B. 759), ch. 79, §14, effective July 1, 1991.)

§10454. Interested person may file petition requesting modification or revocation of authority of personal representative

(a) Any interested person may file a petition requesting that the court make either of the following orders:

(1) An order revoking the authority of the personal representative to continue administration of the estate under this part.

(2) An order revoking the full authority of the personal representative to administer the estate under this part and granting the personal representative limited authority to administer the estate under this part.

(b) The petition shall set forth the basis for the requested order.

(c) Notice of the hearing on the petition shall be given as provided in Section 1220. In addition, the personal representative shall be served with a copy of the petition and a notice of the time and place of the hearing at least 15 days prior to the hearing. Service on the personal representative shall be made in the manner provided in Section 415.10 or 415.30 of the Code of Civil Procedure or in such manner as may be authorized by the court.

(d) If the court determines that good cause has been shown, the court shall make an order revoking the authority of the personal representative to continue administration of the estate under this part. Upon the making of the order, new letters shall be issued without the notation described in subdivision (c) of Section 8405.

(e) If the personal representative was granted full authority and the court determines that good cause has been shown, the court shall make an order revoking the full authority and granting the personal representative limited authority. Upon the making of the order, new letters shall be issued with the notation described in subdivision (c) of Section 8405 that is required where the authority granted is limited authority.
(Stats. 1990 (A.B. 759), ch. 79, §14, effective July 1, 1991.)

§10500. Authority of personal representative to administer estate without court supervision; representative may request supervision

(a) Subject to the limitations and conditions of this part, a personal representative who has been granted authority to administer the estate under this part may administer the estate as provided in this part without court supervision, but in all other respects the personal representative shall administer the estate in the same manner as a personal representative who has not been granted authority to administer the estate under this part.

(b) Notwithstanding subdivision (a), the personal representative may obtain court supervision as provided in this code of any action to be taken by the personal representative during administration of the estate.
(Stats. 1990 (A.B. 759), ch. 79, §14, effective July 1, 1991.)

§10501. Personal representative is required to obtain court supervision for certain actions; exceptions

(a) Notwithstanding any other provision of this part, whether the personal representative has been granted full authority or limited authority, a personal representative who has obtained authority to administer the estate under this part is required to obtain court supervision, in the manner provided in this code, for any of the following actions:

(1) Allowance of the personal representative's compensation.

(2) Allowance of compensation of the attorney for the personal representative.

(3) Settlement of accounts.

(4) Subject to Section 10520, preliminary and final distributions and discharge.

(5) Sale of property of the estate to the personal representative or to the attorney for the personal representative.

(6) Exchange of property of the estate for property of the personal representative or for property of the attorney for the personal representative.

(7) Grant of an option to purchase property of the estate to the personal representative or to the attorney for the personal representative.

(8) Allowance, payment, or compromise of a claim of the personal representative, or the attorney for the personal representative, against the estate.

(9) Compromise or settlement of a claim, action, or proceeding by the estate against the personal representative or against the attorney for the personal representative.

(10) Extension, renewal, or modification of the terms of a debt or other obligation of the personal representative, or the attorney for the personal representative, owing to or in favor of the decedent or the estate.

(b) Notwithstanding any other provision of this part, a personal representative who has obtained only limited authority to administer the estate under this part is required to obtain court supervision, in the manner provided in this code, for any of the following actions:

(1) Sale of real property.

(2) Exchange of real property.

(3) Grant of an option to purchase real property.

(4) Borrowing money with the loan secured by an encumbrance upon real property.

(c) Paragraphs (5) to (10), inclusive, of subdivision (a) do not apply to a transaction between the personal representative as such and the personal representative as an individual where all of the following requirements are satisfied:

(1) Either (A) the personal representative is the sole beneficiary of the estate or (B) all the known heirs or devisees have consented to the transaction.

(2) The period for filing creditor claims has expired.

(3) No request for special notice is on file or all persons who filed a request for special notice have consented to the transaction.

(4) The claim of each creditor who filed a claim has been paid, settled, or withdrawn, or the creditor has consented to the transaction.
(Stats. 1990 (A.B. 759), ch. 79, §14, effective July 1, 1991. Amended by Stats. 1990 (S.B. 1775), ch. 710, §29, effective July 1, 1991; Stats. 1992 (S.B. 1496), ch. 178, §37.)

§10502. Powers of personal representative are subject to certain limitations and may be restricted by will

(a) Subject to the conditions and limitations of this part and to Section 9600, a personal representative who has been granted authority to administer the estate under this part has the powers described in Article 2 (commencing with Section

10510), Article 3 (commencing with Section 10530), and Article 4 (commencing with Section 10550).

(b) The will may restrict the powers that the personal representative may exercise under this part.

(Stats. 1990 (A.B. 759), ch. 79, §14, effective July 1, 1991.)

§10503. Sale of estate property under Act; court confirmation not required

Subject to the limitations and requirements of this part, when the personal representative exercises the authority to sell property of the estate under this part, the personal representative may sell the property either at public auction or private sale, and with or without notice, for such price, for cash or on credit, and upon such terms and conditions as the personal representative may determine, and the requirements applicable to court confirmation of sales of real property (including, but not limited to, publication of notice of sale, court approval of agents' and brokers' commissions, sale at not less than 90 percent of appraised value, and court examination into the necessity for the sale, advantage to the estate and benefit to interested persons, and efforts of the personal representative to obtain the highest and best price for the property reasonably attainable), and the requirements applicable to court confirmation of sales of personal property, do not apply to the sale.

(Stats. 1990 (A.B. 759), ch. 79, §14, effective July 1, 1991.)

§10510. Personal representative may exercise powers only if notice requirements are satisfied

The personal representative may exercise the powers described in this article only if the requirements of Chapter 4 (commencing with Section 10580) (notice of proposed action procedure) are satisfied.

(Stats. 1990 (A.B. 759), ch. 79, §14, effective July 1, 1991.)

§10511. Personal representative has power to sell or exchange estate real property

The personal representative who has full authority has the power to sell or exchange real property of the estate.

(Stats. 1990 (A.B. 759), ch. 79, §14, effective July 1, 1991.)

§10512. Personal representative has power to sell or incorporate business

The personal representative has the power to sell or incorporate any of the following:

(a) An unincorporated business or venture in which the decedent was engaged at the time of the decedent's death.

(b) An unincorporated business or venture which was wholly or partly owned by the decedent at the time of the decedent's death.

(Stats. 1990 (A.B. 759), ch. 79, §14, effective July 1, 1991.)

§10513. Personal representative has power to abandon tangible personal property

The personal representative has the power to abandon tangible personal property where the cost of collecting, maintaining, and safeguarding the property would exceed its fair market value.

(Stats. 1990 (A.B. 759), ch. 79, §14, effective July 1, 1991.)

§10514. Personal representative has power to borrow or encumber property

(a) Subject to subdivision (b), the personal representative has the following powers:

(1) The power to borrow.

(2) The power to place, replace, renew, or extend any encumbrance upon any property of the estate.

(b) Only a personal representative who has full authority has the power to borrow money with the loan secured by an encumbrance upon real property.

(Stats. 1990 (A.B. 759), ch. 79, §14, effective July 1, 1991.)

§10515. Personal representative has power to grant option to purchase estate real property

The personal representative who has full authority has the power to grant an option to purchase real property of the estate for a period within or beyond the period of administration.

(Stats. 1990 (A.B. 759), ch. 79, §14, effective July 1, 1991.)

§10516. Personal representative has power to transfer property to person exercising option to purchase as provided by will

If the will gives a person the option to purchase real or personal property and the person has complied with the terms and conditions stated in the will, the personal representative has the power to convey or transfer the property to the person.

(Stats. 1990 (A.B. 759), ch. 79, §14, effective July 1, 1991.)

§10517. Personal representative has power to convey or transfer real or personal property to complete decedent's contract

The personal representative has the power to convey or transfer real or personal property to complete a contract entered into by the decedent to convey or transfer the property.

(Stats. 1990 (A.B. 759), ch. 79, §14, effective July 1, 1991.)

§10518. Personal representative has power to determine claims to property

The personal representative has the power to allow, compromise, or settle any of the following:

(a) A third-party claim to real or personal property if the decedent died in possession of, or holding title to, the property.

(b) The decedent's claim to real or personal property title to or possession of which is held by another.

(Stats. 1990 (A.B. 759), ch. 79, §14, effective July 1, 1991.)

§10519. Personal representative has power to make disclaimers

The personal representative has the power to make a disclaimer.

(Stats. 1990 (A.B. 759), ch. 79, §14, effective July 1, 1991.)

§10520. Personal representative has power to make preliminary distributions after time for filing claims expired

If the time for filing claims has expired and it appears that the distribution may be made without loss to creditors or injury to the estate or any interested person, the personal representative has the power to make preliminary distributions of the following:

(a) Income received during administration to the persons entitled under Chapter 8 (commencing with Section 12000) of Part 10.

(b) Household furniture and furnishings, motor vehicles, clothing, jewelry, and other tangible articles of a personal nature to the persons entitled to the property under the decedent's will, not to exceed an aggregate fair market value to all persons of fifty thousand dollars ($50,000) computed cumulatively through the date of distribution. Fair market value shall be determined on the basis of the inventory and appraisal.

(c) Cash to general pecuniary devisees entitled to it under the decedent's will, not to exceed ten thousand dollars ($10,000) to any one person.

(Stats. 1992 (S.B. 1496), ch. 178, §38.)

§10530. Personal representative may exercise certain powers without notice

Except to the extent that this article otherwise provides, the personal representative may exercise the powers described in this article without giving notice of proposed action under Chapter 4 (commencing with Section 10580).

(Stats. 1990 (A.B. 759), ch. 79, §14, effective July 1, 1991.)

§10531. Personal representative has power to manage and control estate property, including allocations of principal and income

(a) The personal representative has the power to manage and control property of the estate, including making allocations and determinations under the Uniform Principal and Income Act, Chapter 3 (commencing with Section 16320) of Part 4 of Division 9. Except as provided in subdivision (b), the personal representative may exercise this power without giving notice of proposed action under Chapter 4 (commencing with Section 10580).

(b) The personal representative shall comply with the requirements of Chapter 4 (commencing with Section 10580) in any case where a provision of Chapter 3 (commencing with Section 10500) governing the exercise of a specific power so requires.

(Stats. 1990 (A.B. 759), ch. 79, §14, effective July 1, 1991. Amended by Stats. 1999 (A.B. 846), ch. 145, §3.)

§10532. Personal representative has power to enter contracts with or without notice

(a) The personal representative has the power to enter into a contract in order to carry out the exercise of a specific power granted by this part, including, but not limited to, the powers granted by Sections 10531 and 10551. Except as provided in subdivision (b), the personal representative may exercise this power without giving notice of proposed action under Chapter 4 (commencing with Section 10580).

(b) The personal representative shall comply with the requirements of Chapter 4 (commencing with Section 10580) where the contract is one that by its provisions is not to be fully performed within two years, except that the personal representative is not required to comply with those requirements if the personal representative has the unrestricted right under the contract to terminate the contract within two years.

(c) Nothing in this section excuses compliance with the requirements of Chapter 4 (commencing with Section 10580) when the contract is made to carry out the exercise of a specific power and the provision that grants that power requires compliance with Chapter 4 (commencing with Section 10580) for the exercise of the power.

(Stats. 1990 (A.B. 759), ch. 79, §14, effective July 1, 1991.)

§10533. Personal representative has power to make deposits and investments

(a) The personal representative has the power to do all of the following:

(1) Deposit money belonging to the estate in an insured account in a financial institution in this state.

(2) Invest money of the estate in any one or more of the following:

(A) Direct obligations of the United States, or of the State of California, maturing not later than one year from the date of making the investment.

(B) An interest in a money market mutual fund registered under the Investment Company Act of 1940 (15 U.S.C. Sec. 80a1, et seq.) or an investment vehicle authorized for the collective investment of trust funds pursuant to Section 9.18 of Part 9 of Title 12 of the Code of Federal Regulations, the portfolios of which are limited to United States government obligations maturing not later than five years from the date of investment and to repurchase agreements fully collateralized by United States government obligations.

(C) Units of a common trust fund described in Section 1564 of the Financial Code. The common trust fund shall have as its objective investment primarily in short term fixed income obligations and shall be permitted to value investments at cost pursuant to regulations of the appropriate regulatory authority.

(D) Eligible securities for the investment of surplus state moneys as provided for in Section 16430 of the Government Code.

(3) Invest money of the estate in any manner provided by the will.

(b) Except as provided in subdivision (c), the personal representative may exercise the powers described in subdivision (a) without giving notice of proposed action under Chapter 4 (commencing with Section 10580).

(c) The personal representative shall comply with the requirements of Chapter 4 (commencing with Section 10580) where the personal representative exercises the power to make any investment pursuant to the power granted by subparagraph (D) of paragraph (2) of subdivision (a) or paragraph (3) of subdivision (a), except that the personal representative may invest in direct obligations of the United States, or of the State of California, maturing not later than one year from the date of making the investment without complying with the requirements of Chapter 4 (commencing with Section 10580).

(Stats. 1990 (A.B. 759), ch. 79, §14, effective July 1, 1991.)

§10534. Personal representative has power of continuation of partnership or other business

(a) Subject to the partnership agreement and the provisions of the Uniform Partnership Act of 1994 (Chapter 5 (commencing with Section 16001) of Title 2 of the Corporations Code), the personal representative has the power to continue as a general partner in any partnership in which the decedent was a general partner at the time of death.

(b) The personal representative has the power to continue operation of any of the following:

(1) An unincorporated business or venture in which the decedent was engaged at the time of the decedent's death.

(2) An unincorporated business or venture which was wholly or partly owned by the decedent at the time of the decedent's death.

(c) Except as provided in subdivision (d), the personal representative may exercise the powers described in subdivisions (a) and (b) without giving notice of proposed action under Chapter 4 (commencing with Section 10580).

(d) The personal representative shall comply with the requirements of Chapter 4 (commencing with Section 10580) if the personal representative continues as a general partner under subdivision (a), or continues the operation of any unincorporated business or venture under subdivision (b), for a period of more than six months from the date letters are first issued to a personal representative.

(Stats. 1990 (A.B. 759), ch. 79, §14, effective July 1, 1991. Amended by Stats. 2003 A.B. 167), ch. 32, §11.)

§10535. Personal representative has power to pay reasonable family allowance without notice

(a) The personal representative has the power to pay a reasonable family allowance. Except as provided in subdivision (b), the personal representative may exercise this power without giving notice of proposed action under Chapter 4 (commencing with Section 10580).

(b) The personal representative shall comply with the requirements of Chapter 4 (commencing with Section 10580) for all of the following:

(1) Making the first payment of a family allowance.

(2) Making the first payment of a family allowance for a period commencing more than 12 months after the death of the decedent.

(3) Making any increase in the amount of the payment of a family allowance.

(Stats. 1990 (A.B. 759), ch. 79, §14, effective July 1, 1991.)

§10536. Personal representative has power to lease estate property for exploration, production or removal of minerals, oil or gas, without notice

(a) The personal representative has the power to enter as lessor into a lease of property of the estate for any purpose (including, but not limited to, exploration for and production or removal of minerals, oil, gas, or other hydrocarbon substances or geothermal energy, including a community oil lease or a pooling or unitization agreement) for such period, within or beyond the period of administration, and for such rental or royalty or both, and upon such other terms and conditions as the personal representative may determine. Except as provided in subdivisions (b) and (c), the personal representative may exercise this power without giving notice of proposed action under Chapter 4 (commencing with Section 10580).

(b) The personal representative shall comply with the requirements of Chapter 4 (commencing with Section 10580) where the personal representative enters into a lease of real property for a term in excess of one year. If the lease gives the lessee the right to extend the term of the lease, the lease shall be considered as if the right to extend has been exercised.

(c) The personal representative shall comply with the requirements of Chapter 4 (commencing with Section 10580) where the personal representative enters into a lease of personal property and the lease is one described in subdivision (b) of Section 10532.

(Stats. 1990 (A.B. 759), ch. 79, §14, effective July 1, 1991.)

§10537. Personal representative has power to sell or exchange estate personal property without notice

(a) The personal representative has the power to sell personal property of the estate or to exchange personal property of the estate for other property upon such terms and conditions as the personal representative may determine. Except as provided in subdivision (b), the personal representative shall comply with the requirements of Chapter 4 (commencing with Section 10580) in exercising this power.

(b) The personal representative may exercise the power granted by subdivision (a) without giving notice of proposed action under Chapter 4 (commencing with Section 10580) in case of the sale or exchange of any of the following:

(1) A security sold on an established stock or bond exchange.

(2) A security designated as a national market system security on an inter-dealer quotation system, or subsystem thereof, by the National Association of Securities Dealers, Inc., sold through a broker-dealer registered under the Securities Exchange Act of 1934 [15 U.S.C.A. § 78a et seq.] during the regular course of business of the broker-dealer.

(3) Personal property referred to in Section 10202 or 10259 when sold for cash.

(4) A security described in Section 10200 surrendered for redemption or conversion.

(Stats. 1990 (A.B. 759), ch. 79, §14, effective July 1, 1991.)

§10538. Personal representative has power to grant exclusive right to sell property

(a) The personal representative has the following powers:

(1) The power to grant an exclusive right to sell property for a period not to exceed 90 days.

(2) The power to grant to the same broker one or more extensions of an exclusive right to sell property, each extension being for a period not to exceed 90 days.

(b) Except as provided in subdivision (c), the personal representative may exercise the powers described in subdivision (a) without giving notice of proposed action under Chapter 4 (commencing with Section 10580).

(c) The personal representative shall comply with the requirements of Chapter 4 (commencing with Section 10580) where the personal representative grants to the same broker an extension of an exclusive right to sell property and the period of the extension, together with the periods of the original exclusive right to sell the property and any previous extensions of that right, is more than 270 days.

(Stats. 1990 (A.B. 759), ch. 79, §14, effective July 1, 1991.)

§10550. Personal representative may exercise subsequently designated powers without giving notice

The personal representative may exercise the powers described in this article without giving notice of proposed action under Chapter 4 (commencing with Section 10580).

(Stats. 1990 (A.B. 759), ch. 79, §14, effective July 1, 1991.)

§10551. Powers under Act are in addition to those other powers that a personal representative can exercise without giving notice

In addition to the powers granted to the personal representative by other sections of this chapter, the personal representative has all the powers that the personal representative could exercise without court supervision under this code if the personal representative had not been granted authority to administer the estate under this part.

(Stats. 1990 (A.B. 759), ch. 79, §14, effective July 1, 1991.)

§10552. Personal representative has power to allow or reject claims of or against estate, settle or release claims

The personal representative has the power to do all of the following:

(a) Allow, pay, reject, or contest any claim by or against the estate.

(b) Compromise or settle a claim, action, or proceeding by or for the benefit of, or against, the decedent, the personal representative, or the estate.

(c) Release, in whole or in part, any claim belonging to the estate to the extent that the claim is uncollectible.

(d) Allow a claim to be filed after the expiration of the time for filing the claim.

(Stats. 1990 (A.B. 759), ch. 79, §14, effective July 1, 1991. Amended by Stats. 1996 (A.B. 2751), ch. 862, §29.)

§10553. Personal representative has power to commence and maintain or defend actions and proceedings against decedent or estate

The personal representative has the power to do all of the following:

(a) Commence and maintain actions and proceedings for the benefit of the estate.

(b) Defend actions and proceedings against the decedent, the personal representative, or the estate.

(Stats. 1990 (A.B. 759), ch. 79, §14, effective July 1, 1991.)

§10554. Personal representative has power to modify obligation to or in favor of decedent

The personal representative has the power to extend, renew, or in any manner modify the terms of an obligation owing to or in favor of the decedent or the estate.

(Stats. 1990 (A.B. 759), ch. 79, §14, effective July 1, 1991.)

§10555. Personal representative has power to transfer or convey property

The personal representative has the power to convey or transfer property in order to carry out the exercise of a specific power granted by this part.

(Stats. 1990 (A.B. 759), ch. 79, §14, effective July 1, 1991.)

§10556. Personal representative has power to pay taxes, assessments or expenses

The personal representative has the power to pay all of the following:

(a) Taxes and assessments.

(b) Expenses incurred in the collection, care, and administration of the estate.

(Stats. 1990 (A.B. 759), ch. 79, §14, effective July 1, 1991.)

§10557. Personal representative has power to purchase annuity

The personal representative has the power to purchase an annuity from an insurer admitted to do business in this state to satisfy a devise of an annuity or other direction in the will for periodic payments to a devisee.

(Stats. 1990 (A.B. 759), ch. 79, §14, effective July 1, 1991.)

§10558. Personal representative has power to exercise an option

The personal representative has the power to exercise an option right that is property of the estate.

(Stats. 1990 (A.B. 759), ch. 79, §14, effective July 1, 1991.)

§10559. Personal representative has power to purchase securities or commodities to perform contract of sale

The personal representative has the power to purchase securities or commodities required to perform an incomplete contract of sale where the decedent died having sold but not delivered securities or commodities not owned by the decedent.

(Stats. 1990 (A.B. 759), ch. 79, §14, effective July 1, 1991.)

§10560. Personal representative has power to hold security in name of nominee

The personal representative has the power to hold a security in the name of a nominee or in any other form without disclosure of the estate, so that title to the security may pass by delivery.

(Stats. 1990 (A.B. 759), ch. 79, §14, effective July 1, 1991.)

§10561. Personal representative has power to exercise security subscription or conversion rights

The personal representative has the power to exercise security subscription or conversion rights.

(Stats. 1990 (A.B. 759), ch. 79, §14, effective July 1, 1991.)

§10562. Personal representative has power to repair and improve property

The personal representative has the power to make repairs and improvements to real and personal property of the estate.

(Stats. 1990 (A.B. 759), ch. 79, §14, effective July 1, 1991.)

§10563. Personal representative has power to accept deed or deed in trust in lieu of foreclosure

The personal representative has the power to accept a deed to property which is subject to a mortgage or deed of trust in lieu of foreclosure of the mortgage or sale under the deed of trust.

(Stats. 1990 (A.B. 759), ch. 79, §14, effective July 1, 1991.)

§10564. Personal representative has power to give partial satisfaction of mortgage or cause partial reconveyance under deed of trust

The personal representative has the power to give a partial satisfaction of a mortgage or to cause a partial reconveyance to be executed by a trustee under a deed of trust held by the estate.

(Stats. 1990 (A.B. 759), ch. 79, §14, effective July 1, 1991.)

§10580. Personal representative shall give notice as required

(a) A personal representative who has been granted authority to administer the estate under this part shall give notice of proposed action as provided in this chapter prior to the taking of the proposed action without court supervision if the provision of Chapter 3 (commencing with Section 10500) giving the personal representative the power to take the action so requires. Nothing in this subdivision authorizes a personal representative to take an action under this part if the personal representative does not have the power to take the action under this part.

(b) A personal representative who has been granted authority to administer the estate under this part may give notice of proposed action as provided in this chapter even if the provision of Chapter 3 (commencing with Section 10500) giving the personal representative the power to take the action permits the personal representative to take the action without giving notice of proposed action. Nothing in this subdivision requires the personal representative to give notice of proposed action where not required under subdivision (a) or authorizes a personal representative to take any action that the personal representative is not otherwise authorized to take.

(Stats. 1990 (A.B. 759), ch. 79, §14, effective July 1, 1991.)

§10581. Certain parties must receive notice

Except as provided in Sections 10582 and 10583, notice of proposed action shall be given to all of the following:

(a) Each known devisee whose interest in the estate would be affected by the proposed action.

(b) Each known heir whose interest in the estate would be affected by the proposed action.

(c) Each person who has filed a request under Chapter 6 (commencing with Section 1250) of Part 2, of Division 3 for special notice of petitions filed in the administration proceeding.

(d) The Attorney General, at the office of the Attorney General in Sacramento, if any portion of the estate is to escheat to the state and its interest in the estate would be affected by the proposed action.

(Stats. 1990 (A.B. 759), ch. 79, §14, effective July 1, 1991.)

§10582. Notice need not be given to party consenting to action in writing

Notice of proposed action need not be given to any person who consents in writing to the proposed action. The consent may be executed at any time before or after the proposed action is taken.

(Stats. 1990 (A.B. 759), ch. 79, §14, effective July 1, 1991.)

§10583. Notice need not be given to a party who waives the right to notice

(a) Notice of proposed action need not be given to any person who, in writing, waives the right to notice of proposed action with respect to the particular proposed action. The waiver may be executed at any time before or after the proposed action is taken. The waiver shall describe the particular proposed action and may waive particular aspects of the notice, such as the delivery, mailing, or time requirements of Section 10586, or the giving of the notice in its entirety for the particular proposed action.

(b) Notice of proposed action need not be given to any person who has executed the Statutory Waiver of Notice of Proposed Action Form prescribed by the Judicial Council and in that form has made either of the following:

(1) A general waiver of the right to notice of proposed action.

(2) A waiver of the right to notice of proposed action for all transactions of a type which includes the particular proposed action.

(Stats. 1990 (A.B. 759), ch. 79, §14, effective July 1, 1991.)

§10584. Revocation of waiver of notice

(a) A waiver or consent may be revoked only in writing and is effective only when the writing is received by the personal representative.

(b) A copy of the revocation may be filed with the court, but the effectiveness of the revocation is not dependent upon a copy being filed with the court.

(Stats. 1990 (A.B. 759), ch. 79, §14, effective July 1, 1991.)

§10585. Contents of notice of proposed action

(a) The notice of proposed action shall state all of the following:

(1) The name and mailing address of the personal representative.

(2) The person and telephone number to call to get additional information.

(3) The action proposed to be taken, with a reasonably specific description of the action. Where the proposed action involves the sale or exchange of real property, or the granting of an option to purchase real property, the

notice of proposed action shall state the material terms of the transaction, including, if applicable, the sale price and the amount of, or method of calculating, any commission or compensation paid or to be paid to an agent or broker in connection with the transaction.

(4) The date on or after which the proposed action is to be taken.

(b) The notice of proposed action may be given using the most current Notice of Proposed Action form prescribed by the Judicial Council.

(c) If the most current form prescribed by the Judicial Council is not used to give notice of proposed action, the notice of proposed action shall satisfy all of the following requirements:

(1) The notice of proposed action shall be in substantially the same form as the form prescribed by the Judicial Council.

(2) The notice of proposed action shall contain the statements described in subdivision (a).

(3) The notice of proposed action shall contain a form for objecting to the proposed action in substantially the form set out in the Judicial Council form.

(Stats. 1990 (A.B. 759), ch. 79, §14, effective July 1, 1991.)

§10586. Mail or delivery of notice of proposed action

The notice of proposed action shall be mailed or personally delivered to each person required to be given notice of proposed action not less than 15 days before the date specified in the notice of proposed action on or after which the proposed action is to be taken. If mailed, the notice of proposed action shall be addressed to the person at the person's last known address. Sections 1215 and 1216 apply to the mailing or delivery of the notice of proposed action.

(Stats. 1990 (A.B. 759), ch. 79, §14, effective July 1, 1991.)

§10587. Any person entitled to notice may object to proposed action as provided

(a) Any person entitled to notice of proposed action under Section 10581 may object to the proposed action as provided in this section.

(b) The objection to the proposed action is made by delivering or mailing a written objection to the proposed action to the personal representative at the address stated in the notice of proposed action. The person objecting to the proposed action either may use the Judicial Council form or may make the objection in any other writing that identifies the proposed action with reasonable certainty and indicates that the person objects to the taking of the proposed action.

(c) The personal representative is deemed to have notice of the objection to the proposed action if it is delivered or received at the address stated in the notice of proposed action before whichever of the following times is the later:

(1) The date specified in the notice of proposed action on or after which the proposed action is to be taken.

(2) The date the proposed action is actually taken.

(Stats. 1990 (A.B. 759), ch. 79, §14, effective July 1, 1991.)

§10588. Any person entitled to notice may apply for restraining order prohibiting action without court supervision

(a) Any person who is entitled to notice of proposed action for a proposed action described in subdivision (a) of Section 10580, or any person who is given notice of a proposed action described in subdivision (b) of Section 10580, may apply to the court having jurisdiction over the proceeding for an order restraining the personal representative from taking the proposed action without court supervision. The court shall grant the requested order without requiring notice to the personal representative and without cause being shown for the order.

(b) The personal representative is deemed to have notice of the restraining order if it is served upon the personal representative in the same manner as is provided for in Section 415.10 or 415.30 of the Code of Civil Procedure, or in the manner authorized by the court, before whichever of the following times is the later:

(1) The date specified in a notice of proposed action on or after which the proposed action is to be taken.

(2) The date the proposed action is actually taken.

(Stats. 1990 (A.B. 759), ch. 79, §14, effective July 1, 1991.)

§10589. Personal representative who is under notice of objection or restraining order must undertake action with court supervision

(a) If the proposed action is one that would require court supervision if the personal representative had not been granted authority to administer the estate under this part and the personal representative has notice of a written objection made under Section 10587 to the proposed action or a restraining order issued under Section 10588, the personal representative shall, if the personal representative desires to take the proposed action, take the proposed action under the provisions of this code dealing with court supervision of that kind of action.

(b) If the proposed action is one that would not require court supervision even if the personal representative had not been granted authority to administer the estate under this part but the personal representative has given notice of the proposed action and has notice of a written objection made under Section 10587 to the proposed action or a restraining order issued under Section 10588, the personal representative shall, if he or she desires to take the proposed action, request instructions from the court concerning the proposed action. The personal representative may take the proposed action only under such order as may be entered by the court.

(c) A person who objects to a proposed action as provided in Section 10587 or serves a restraining order issued under Section 10588 in the manner provided in that section shall be given notice of any hearing on a petition for court authorization or confirmation of the proposed action.

(Stats. 1990 (A.B. 759), ch. 79, §14, effective July 1, 1991. Amended by Stats. 1991 (S.B. 896), ch. 82, §26, effective July 1, 1991.)

§10590. Right to have court review proposed action

(a) Except as provided in subdivision (c), only a person described in Section 10581 has a right to have the court review the proposed action after it has been taken or otherwise to object to the proposed action after it has been taken. Except as provided in subdivisions (b) and (c), a person described in Section 10581 waives the right to have the court review the proposed action after it has been taken, or otherwise to object to the proposed action after it has been taken, if either of the following circumstances exists:

(1) The person has been given notice of a proposed action, as provided in Sections 10580 to 10586, inclusive, and fails to object as provided in subdivision (d).

(2) The person has waived notice of or consented to the proposed action as provided in Sections 10582 to 10584, inclusive.

(b) Unless the person has waived notice of or consented to the proposed action as provided in Sections 10582 to 10584, inclusive, the court may review the action taken upon motion of a person described in Section 10581 who establishes that he or she did not actually receive the notice of proposed action before the time to object under subdivision (d) expires.

(c) The court may review the action of the personal representative upon motion of an heir or devisee who establishes all of the following:

(1) At the time the notice was given, the heir or devisee lacked capacity to object to the proposed action or was a minor.

(2) No notice of proposed action was actually received by the guardian, conservator, or other legal representative of the heir or devisee.

(3) The guardian, conservator, or other legal representative did not waive notice of proposed action.

(4) The guardian, conservator, or other legal representative did not consent to the proposed action.

(d) For the purposes of this section, an objection to a proposed action is made only by one or both of the following methods:

(1) Delivering or mailing a written objection as provided in Section 10587 within the time specified in subdivision (c) of that section.

(2) Serving a restraining order obtained under Section 10588 in the manner prescribed and within the time specified in subdivision (b) of that section.

(Stats. 1990 (A.B. 759), ch. 79, §14, effective July 1, 1991.)

§10591. Failure of personal representative to comply with requirements does not affect validity of action

(a) The failure of the personal representative to comply with subdivision (a) of Section 10580 and with Sections 10581, 10585, 10586, and 10589, and the taking of the action by the personal representative without such compliance, does not affect the validity of the action so taken or the title to any property conveyed or transferred to bona fide purchasers or the rights of third persons who, dealing in good faith with the personal representative, changed their position in reliance upon the action, conveyance, or transfer without actual notice of the failure of the personal representative to comply with those provisions.

(b) No person dealing with the personal representative has any duty to inquire or investigate whether or not the personal representative has complied with the provisions listed in subdivision (a).

(Stats. 1990 (A.B. 759), ch. 79, §14, effective July 1, 1991.)

§10592. Court may remove personal representative from office for failure to give notice

(a) In a case where notice of proposed action is required by this chapter, the court in its discretion may remove the personal representative from office unless the personal representative does one of the following:

(1) Gives notice of proposed action as provided in this chapter.

(2) Obtains a waiver of notice of proposed action as provided in this chapter.

(3) Obtains a consent to the proposed action as provided in this chapter.

(b) The court in its discretion may remove the personal representative from office if the personal representative takes a proposed action in violation of Section 10589.

(Stats. 1990 (A.B. 759), ch. 79, §14, effective July 1, 1991.)

XV
Special Constructional Problems of Wills, Trusts, and Other Instruments

This chapter explores those constructional problems involving certain dispositive provisions that arise because of changes either in particular estate assets after the will is executed (i.e., loss or destruction of an asset), or life changes among the beneficiaries (i.e., births and deaths). It examines such distributive problems as ademption, satisfaction, abatement, and exoneration. It also addresses constructional problems in the determination of beneficiaries, such as lapse and class gifts.

The California legislature broadened constructional rules in 1994 revisions to the California Probate Code to extend beyond wills (former Cal. Prob. Code §§6140 et seq.) to include "at-death transfers" (i.e., wills, trusts, deeds, and other instruments).

I. Introduction: Classification of Testamentary Gifts

For purposes of resolving some constructional problems, it is helpful to understand the classification of testamentary gifts. Such gifts may be classified as follows:

- specific gift, i.e., a transfer of specifically identifiable property ("I leave my pearl necklace to my niece Alice");
- general gift, i.e., a transfer from the general assets of the estate ("I leave $5000 to my nephew Bob");
- demonstrative gift, i.e., a general gift, payable from a specific source ("I leave $10,000 to my daughter-in-law Carole, payable out of my brokerage account at Charles Schwab, and if this is insufficient then out of my other property");
- residuary gift, i.e., the property that remains after all specific and general gifts have been made ("I give the residue of my estate to my husband Daniel").

"It is often a question of testamentary construction whether legacies are general or specific, [and] what they include, if specific. . . ." 25 Cal. Jur.3d Decedents' Estates §833.

Specific devises are accorded preferential treatment in some regards (such as abatement). In addition, the beneficiary of a specific devise has the right to income on the property dating from the testator's date of death, less expenses during administration (Cal. Prob. Code §12002(b)). If this income is not sufficient to pay the expenses attributable to the property, the shortfall is payable from the estate assets, but is a charge on the devise and becomes a lien on the property if paid or accrued more than 1 year after the testator's death (Cal. Prob. Code §12002(c)). (This statute is set forth in Section C *infra.*)

The testator need not use any particular wording to create a valid residuary clause that bequeaths property to a residuary legatee. In Estate of Plummer, 324 P.2d 346 (Cal. Ct. App. 1958), the decedent executed a holographic will, disinheriting her heirs and providing that her estate be divided among her named friends because she wanted "my friends to be remembered." The appellate court ruled that the residue of the estate would be distributed to the designated friends and not to decedent's first cousins, reasoning that no particular mode of expression is necessary to constitute a residuary bequest. Furthermore, the residuary disposition need not be placed last in the will.

§12002. Specific devices; income and expenses

(a) Except as provided in this section, a specific devise does not bear interest.

(b) A specific devise carries with it income on the devised property from the date of death, less expenses attributable to the devised property during administration of the estate. For purposes of this section, expenses attributable to property are expenses that result directly from the use or ownership of the property, including property tax and tax on the income from the property, but excluding estate and generation-skipping transfer taxes.

(c) If income of specifically devised property is not sufficient to pay expenses attributable to the property, the deficiency shall be paid out of the estate until the property is distributed to the devisee or the devisee takes possession of or occupies the property, whichever occurs first. To the extent a deficiency paid out of the estate is attributable to the period that commences one year after the testator's death, whether paid during or after expiration of the one year period following the date of death, the amount paid is a charge against the share of the devisee, and the personal representative has an equitable lien on the specifically devised property as against the devisee in the amount paid.

(d) If specifically devised property is sold during administration of the estate, the devisee is entitled to the net income from the property until the date of sale, and to interest on the net sale proceeds thereafter, but no interest accrues during the first year after the testator's death.

(Stats. 1990 (A.B. 759), ch. 79, §14, operative July 1, 1991.)

§21117. Classification of devises: specific, general, demonstrative gifts

At death transfers are classified as follows:

(a) A specific gift is a transfer of specifically identifiable property.

(b) A general gift is a transfer from the general assets of the transferor that does not give specific property.

(c) A demonstrative gift is a general gift that specifies the fund or property from which the transfer is primarily to be made.

(d) A general pecuniary gift is a pecuniary gift within the meaning of Section 21118.

(e) An annuity is a general pecuniary gift that is payable periodically.

(f) A residuary gift is a transfer of property that remains after all specific and general gifts have been satisfied.

(Stats. 1994 (A.B. 3686), ch. 806, §41. Amended by Stats. 2002 (A.B. 1784), ch. 138, §26.)

II. Constructional Problems in the Disposition of Property

A. Ademption Doctrine

Ademption occurs when a specific gift that was the subject of an at-death transfer is not in the transferor's estate at death. Several events may lead to ademption. Ademption may occur if:

- **the decedent made a gift of the property during his or her lifetime (to the recipient or to another person) (sometimes referred to as "ademption by satisfaction"),**
- **if the gift was destroyed during the decedent's lifetime (sometimes referred to as "ademption by extinction"), or**
- **if the property underwent a change in form.**

Ross & Grant, Cal. Prob. Prac., *supra*, at §16:543. If a specific gift of real or personal property is not in the estate at death, the property is adeemed, i.e., the distributee's rights are extinguished. That is, the distributee has no right to other estate property (or money).

California Probate Code §§21132-21139 govern the distributee's rights. Because of the harshness of the ademption doctrine (resulting in extinguishing the gift), the legislature enacted these statutory provisions with "the intent to avoid ademption by providing statutory rules of construction favoring 'nonademption.'" Ross & Grant, Cal. Prob. Prac., *supra*, at §16:559.

Ademption issues frequently arise in regard to gifts of shares of corporate stock. Sometimes, the number of shares in an estate differs from that designated in the testamentary gift. The difference in shares might result from either the decedent's actions or the corporation's acts. For example, the decedent may have sold some of the shares of the stock before death or the corporation may have issued a stock dividend or stock split.

California Probate Code §21132 applies to changes in the form of securities. If the decedent intended to make a specific gift of the securities, the recipient is entitled to: (1) any additional or other securities of the same entity owned by the decedent (if the corporation initiated the action); (2) any securities of another entity that were acquired by means of a merger, consolidation, reorganization, or similar action; and (3) additional securities of the entity owned by the decedent as a result of a reinvestment plan. The section is based on Uniform Probate Code §2605 (1990), and is consistent with prior California case law. Law Revision Commission Commentary following California Probate Code §21132.

Property that is the subject of a specific gift may no longer be in the estate because of the

occurrence of certain common events: sale, eminent domain, an insurable loss, or foreclosure. Sometimes, the decedent was not fully paid or compensated prior to his or her death. In such cases, California Probate Code §21333 provides that the designated beneficiary is entitled to: any unpaid balance of the purchase price or eminent domain award, any unpaid proceeds from life insurance, or any property acquired as a result of the foreclosure.

A special rule applies if the decedent was placed under a conservatorship after executing the transfer instrument. If the specific property that was the subject of the gift was sold by the conservator, the transferee has the right to a cash award equal to the net sale price of the property (Cal. Prob. Code §21134). The rationale for the above rule is: "Because of the conservatorship, the transferor is unable to make a new transfer instrument to account for the change in form; and absent this rule, the conservator would, in effect, be able to determine distribution of the estate." Ross & Grant, Cal. Prob. Prac., *supra*, at §15:556. An exception applies if the conservatorship terminates because the transferor has regained competence and the transferor survives for at least a year (Cal. Prob. Code §21134(c)). The exception may be explained because the transferor "now competent, can execute a new transfer instrument to account for the change in form of the gifted property." Ross & Grant, Cal. Prob. Prac., *supra*, at §15:558.

§21132. Ademption change in form rules: additional securities acquired by transferor after execution of instrument are included in gift

(a) If a transferor executes an instrument that makes an at death transfer of securities and the transferor then owned securities that meet the description in the instrument, the transfer includes additional securities owned by the transferor at death to the extent the additional securities were acquired by the transferor after the instrument was executed as a result of the transferor's ownership of the described securities and are securities of any of the following types:

(1) Securities of the same organization acquired by reason of action initiated by the organization or any successor, related, or acquiring organization, excluding any acquired by exercise of purchase options.

(2) Securities of another organization acquired as a result of a merger, consolidation, reorganization, or other distribution by the organization or any successor, related, or acquiring organization.

(3) Securities of the same organization acquired as a result of a plan of reinvestment.

(b) Distributions in cash before death with respect to a described security are not part of the transfer.

(Stats. 2002 (A.B. 1784), ch. 138, §33.)

§21133. Ademption doctrine: effect on distributee's rights for unpaid proceeds

A recipient of an at death transfer of a specific gift has a right to the property specifically given, to the extent the property is owned by the transferor at the time the gift takes effect in possession or enjoyment, and all of the following:

(a) Any balance of the purchase price (together with any security agreement) owing from a purchaser to the transferor at the time the gift takes effect in possession or enjoyment by reason of sale of the property.

(b) Any amount of an eminent domain award for the taking of the property unpaid at the time the gift takes effect in possession or enjoyment.

(c) Any proceeds unpaid at the time the gift takes effect in possession or enjoyment on fire or casualty insurance on or other recovery for injury to the property.

(d) Property owned by the transferor at the time the gift takes effect in possession or enjoyment and acquired as a result of foreclosure, or obtained in lieu of foreclosure, of the security interest for a specifically given obligation.

(Stats. 1994 (A.B. 3686), §41. Amended by Stats. 2002 (A.B. 1784), ch. 138, §34.)

§21134. Ademption doctrine: right of recipient of property that is sold or mortgaged by conservator

(a) Except as otherwise provided in this section, if after the execution of the instrument of gift specifically given property is sold or mortgaged by a conservator or by an agent acting within the authority of a durable power of attorney for an incapacitated principal, the transferee of the specific gift has the right to a general pecuniary gift equal to the net sale price of, or the amount of the unpaid loan on, the property.

(b) Except as otherwise provided in this section, if an eminent domain award for the taking of specifically given property is paid to a conservator or to an agent acting within the authority of a durable power of attorney for an incapacitated principal, or if the proceeds on fire or casualty insurance on, or recovery for injury to, specifically gifted property are paid to a conservator or to an agent acting within the authority of a durable power of attorney for an incapacitated principal, the recipient of the specific gift has the right to a general pecuniary gift equal to the eminent domain award or the insurance proceeds or recovery.

(c) For the purpose of the references in this section to a conservator, this section does not apply if, after the sale, mortgage, condemnation, fire, or casualty, or recovery, the conservatorship is terminated and the transferor survives the termination by one year.

(d) For the purpose of the references in this section to an agent acting with the authority of a durable power of attorney for an incapacitated principal, (1) "incapacitated principal" means a principal who is an incapacitated person, (2) no adjudication of incapacity before death is necessary, and (3) the acts of an agent within the authority of a durable power of attorney are presumed to be for an incapacitated principal.

(e) The right of the transferee of the specific gift under this section shall be reduced by any right the transferee has under Section 21133.

(Stats. 1994 (A.B. 3686), §41. Amended by Stats. 2002 (A.B. 1784), ch. 138, §35.)

B. Satisfaction Doctrine

Inter vivos gifts from the decedent to his or her heirs or beneficiaries sometimes may be deemed in "satisfaction" (in part or in whole) of the at-death transfer. The applicable intestate doctrine is termed "advancement," and requires either the decedent's written contemporaneous declaration of an intent to deduct the gift from the heir's share of the estate or the heir's written acknowledgment that the gift is to be deducted (discussed in Chapter I, Section V *supra*).

The testate doctrine is termed "satisfaction." For the doctrine of satisfaction to apply, California Probate Code §21135 requires:

- **a testamentary declaration of intent that the inter vivos gift will be deducted from the testamentary gift, or**
- **the transferor's contemporaneous written statement of intent that the gift is to be deducted from the testamentary gift, or**
- **the transferee's written acknowledgment that the gift is in satisfaction of the testamentary gift.**

The doctrine is sometimes referred to as "ademption by satisfaction."

If the decedent specifies the value of the inter vivos gift in his or her contemporaneous written declaration (or the heir specifies the value in his or her contemporaneous written acknowledgment), that valuation is conclusive. This rule applies to both the advancement and satisfaction doctrines (Cal. Prob. Code §§6409(c), 21135(c)). Absent such proof, the gift is valued as of the time the heir or transferee came into possession or enjoyment of the gift or as of the time of decedent's death, whichever occurs first (Cal. Prob. Code §§6409(b), 21135(b)).

§6409. Advancements; conditions and terms

(a) If a person dies intestate as to all or part of his or her estate, property the decedent gave during lifetime to an heir is treated as an advancement against that heir's share of the intestate estate only if one of the following conditions is satisfied:

(1) The decedent declares in a contemporaneous writing that the gift is an advancement against the heir's share of the estate or that its value is to be deducted from the value of the heir's share of the estate.

(2) The heir acknowledges in writing that the gift is to be so deducted or is an advancement or that its value is to be deducted from the value of the heir's share of the estate.

(b) Subject to subdivision (c), the property advanced is to be valued as of the time the heir came into possession or enjoyment of the property or as of the time of death of the decedent, whichever occurs first.

(c) If the value of the property advanced is expressed in the contemporaneous writing of the decedent, or in an acknowledgment of the heir made contemporaneously with the advancement, that value is conclusive in the division and distribution of the intestate estate.

(d) If the recipient of the property advanced fails to survive the decedent, the property is not taken into account in computing the intestate share to be received by the recipient's issue unless the declaration or acknowledgment provides otherwise.

(Stats. 1990 (A.B. 759). ch 79, §14, effective July 1, 1991. Amended by Stats 2002 (A.B. 1784), ch 138, §8.)

§21135. Satisfaction doctrine: conditions

(a) Property given by a transferor during his or her lifetime to a person is treated as a satisfaction of an at death transfer to that person in whole or in part only if one of the following conditions is satisfied:

(1) The instrument provides for deduction of the lifetime gift from the at death transfer.

(2) The transferor declares in a contemporaneous writing that the gift is in satisfaction of the at death transfer or that its value is to be deducted from the value of the at death transfer.

(3) The transferee acknowledges in writing that the gift is in satisfaction of the at death transfer or that its value is to be deducted from the value of the at death transfer.

(4) The property given is the same property that is the subject of a specific gift to that person.

(b) Subject to subdivision (c), for the purpose of partial satisfaction, property given during lifetime is valued as of the time the transferee came into possession or enjoyment of the property or as of the time of death of the transferor, whichever occurs first.

(c) If the value of the gift is expressed in the contemporaneous writing of the transferor, or in an acknowledgment of the transferee made contemporaneously with the gift, that value is conclusive in the division and distribution of the estate.

(d) If the transferee fails to survive the transferor, the gift is treated as a full or partial satisfaction of the gift, as the case may be, in applying Sections 21110 and 21111 unless the transferor's contemporaneous writing provides otherwise.

(Stats. 1994 (A.B. 3686), §41. Amended by Stats. 2002 (A.B. 1784), ch. 138, §36.)

§21139. Rules are not exhaustive and not intended to increase incidence of ademption

The rules stated in Sections 21133 to 21135, inclusive, are not exhaustive, and nothing in those sections is intended to increase the incidence of ademption under the law of this state.

(Stats. 1994 (A.B. 3686), §41. Amended by Stats. 2002 (A.B. 1784), ch. 138, §40.)

§21140. Application

This part applies to all instruments, regardless of when they were executed.

(Stats. 1994 (A.B. 3686), §41. Amended by Stats. 2002 (A.B. 1784), ch. 138, §41.)

C. Abatement

The abatement doctrine is triggered when the assets in the testator's estate are insufficient to satisfy all of the testamentary gifts. Abatement provides a method by which the shares of some or all beneficiaries are reduced. Abatement problems most frequently occur because the value of the estate has been depleted by payments of debts, expenses of estate administration, taxes, expenses of last illness, funeral and/or burial costs, or the assertion of statutory rights by a spouse or pretermitted heir.

Most states specify, by case law or statute, an order of abatement that applies in the absence of any contrary indication in the will as to how devises shall be reduced. The usual order of abatement is: (1) intestate property is reduced first; then (2) residuary gifts; (3) general gifts; and (4) specific gifts and demonstrative gifts are reduced last. Within each category, gifts also abate ratably, e.g., each general gift would be reduced proportionately (e.g., Cal. Prob. Code §21403).

The common law distinguished between real and personal property. That is, at common law, personal property in a given category was exhausted before reduction of real property from that category. Modern statutes generally reject this distinction See, e.g., Cal. Prob. Code §21401 (providing for no priority for abatement purposes between real and personal property). Some states (but not California) provide preferential treatment for spouses, i.e., gifts to the testator's spouse abate last.

The UPC also follows the normal order of abatement when a pretermitted child claims a share. However, the UPC follows a special rule of abatement if the need arises because a spouse claims an elective share. In such cases, the UPC departs from the general rule and authorizes pro rata abatement (UPC §§2-210, 3-902(a)). California statute authorizes pro rata abatement in cases of omitted spouses (in the antenuptial will situation) (Cal. Prob. Code §21612(2)) and omitted children (Cal. Prob. Code §21623(2)).

According to California law, the personal representative must follow the Probate Code's abatement rules to determine the order of estate assets to liquidate (Cal. Prob. Code §§10003, 21400-21406). However, first, the representative must determine if the decedent has specified the assets to be used for abatement purposes, or if the decedent's plan would be impaired by following the statutory order of abatement (Cal.

Prob. Code §21400). In such cases, the shares of beneficiaries abate as necessary to effectuate the instrument, plan, or purpose. If neither of the preceding situations occur, then the representative reduces the beneficiaries' shares according to the following order of priority: (1) intestate property, (2) residuary gifts, (3) general gifts to nonrelatives, (4) general gifts to relatives, (5) specific gifts to nonrelatives, (6) specific gifts to relatives (Cal. Prob. Code §21402). The term "relatives" is defined as persons who would be intestate heirs, including those persons considered to be decedent's children or parents by virtue of provisions such as California Probate Code §§6450-6455 (i.e., adoptive parents, foster parents, and stepparents) if the decedent had died intestate and there were no other persons having priority (Cal. Prob. Code §21402(b)). Ross & Grant, Cal. Prob. Prac., *supra*, at §7:98.

In cases of abatement, the court must fix the amount each distributee has to contribute. Then, the personal representative must reduce each person's share by the designated amount (Cal. Prob. Code §21405(a)). According to the general rule, specific gifts abate last (i.e., the beneficiary of a specific gift receives the most protection). In accordance with that policy, California law provides that if a specific gift must be abated, the distributee is permitted to satisfy the obligation from the beneficiary's other property (rather than from the specifically devised gift) (§21405(b)).

For abatement purposes, demonstrative gifts (and gifts of annuities) are treated as specific gifts to the extent they are satisfied out of the property designated by the grantor for that purpose, but as general gifts to the extent they are satisfied out of other property (Cal. Prob. Code §21403(b)).

§10000. When personal representative may sell estate property

Subject to the limitations, conditions, and requirements of this chapter, the personal representative may sell real or personal property of the estate in any of the following cases:

(a) Where the sale is necessary to pay debts, devises, family allowance, expenses of adminis-tration, or taxes.

(b) Where the sale is to the advantage of the estate and in the best interest of the interested persons.

(c) Where the property is directed by the will to be sold.

(d) Where authority is given in the will to sell the property.

(Stats. 1990 (A.B. 759), ch. 79, §14, effective July 1, 1991.)

§10001. Court ordering the sale of property

(a) If the personal representative neglects or refuses to sell the property, any interested person may petition the court for an order requiring the personal representative to sell real or personal property of the estate in any of the following cases:

(1) Where the sale is necessary to pay debts, devises, family allowance, expenses of administration, or taxes.

(2) Where the sale is to the advantage of the estate and in the best interest of the interested persons.

(3) Where the property is directed by the will to be sold.

(b) Notice of the hearing on the petition shall be given as provided in Section 1220.

(c) Notice of the hearing on the petition also shall be given to the personal representative by citation served at least five days before the hearing.

(Stats. 1990 (A.B. 759), ch. 79, §14, effective July 1, 1991.)

§10002. Will directions as to the mode of sale

(a) Subject to subdivision (b), if directions are given in the will as to the mode of selling or the particular property to be sold, the personal representative shall comply with those directions.

(b) If the court determines that it would be to the advantage of the estate and in the best interest of the interested persons, the court may make an order relieving the personal representative of the duty to comply with the directions in the will. The order shall specify the mode and the terms and conditions of selling or the particular property to be sold, or both. The personal representative or any interested person may file a petition for an order under this subdivision. Notice of the hearing on the petition shall be given as provided in Section 1220.

(Stats. 1990 (A.B. 759), ch. 79, §14, effective July 1, 1991.)

§10003. Discretion of personal representative as to property to be sold and mode of selling

Subject to Part 4 (commencing with Section 21400) of Division 11 and to Sections 10001 and 10002, if estate property is required or permitted to be sold, the personal representative may:

(a) Use discretion as to which property to sell first.

(b) Sell the entire interest of the estate in the property or any lesser interest therein.

(c) Sell the property either at public auction or private sale.

(Stats. 1990 (A.B. 759), ch. 79, §14, effective July 1, 1991.)

§12002. Specific devise: special provisions regarding interest, and charges against devisee's share

(a) Except as provided in this section, a specific devise does not bear interest.

(b) A specific devise carries with it income on the devised property from the date of death, less expenses attributable to the devised property during administration of the estate. For purposes of this section, expenses attributable to property are expenses that result directly from the use or ownership of the property, including property tax and tax on the income from the property, but excluding estate and generation skipping transfer taxes.

(c) If income of specifically devised property is not sufficient to pay expenses attributable to the property, the deficiency shall be paid out of the estate until the property is distributed to the devisee or the devisee takes possession of or occupies the property, whichever occurs first. To the extent a deficiency paid out of the estate is attributable to the period that commences one year after the testator's death, whether paid during or after expiration of the one year period following the date of death, the amount paid is a charge against the share of the devisee, and the personal representative has an equitable lien on the specifically devised property as against the devisee in the amount paid.

(d) If specifically devised property is sold during administration of the estate, the devisee is entitled to the net income from the property until the date of sale, and to interest on the net sale proceeds thereafter, but no interest accrues during the first year after the testator's death.

(Stats. 1990 (A.B. 759), ch. 79, §14, effective July 1, 1991.)

§21400. Beneficiaries' shares abate as necessary to effectuate intent

Notwithstanding any other provision of this part, if the instrument provides for abatement, or if the transferor's plan or if the purpose of the transfer would be defeated by abatement as provided in this part, the shares of beneficiaries abate as is necessary to effectuate the instrument, plan, or purpose.

(Stats. 1990 (A.B. 759), ch. 79, §14, effective July 1, 1991.)

§21401. No priority for abatement purposes between real and personal property

Except as provided in Sections 21612 (omitted spouse) and 21623 (omitted children) and in Division 10 (commencing with Section 20100) (proration of taxes), shares of beneficiaries abate as provided in this part for all purposes, including payment of the debts, expenses, and charges specified in Section 11420, satisfaction of gifts, and payment of expenses on specifically devised property pursuant to Section 12002, and without any priority as between real and personal property.

(Stats. 1990 (A.B. 759), ch. 79, §14, effective July 1, 1991. Amended by Stats. 2003 (A.B. 167), ch. 32, §15.)

§21402. Order of abatement: intestate property, residue, general, specific gifts

(a) Shares of beneficiaries abate in the following order:

(1) Property not disposed of by the instrument.

(2) Residuary gifts.

(3) General gifts to persons other than the transferor's relatives.

(4) General gifts to the transferor's relatives.

(5) Specific gifts to persons other than the transferor's relatives.

(6) Specific gifts to the transferor's relatives.

(b) For purposes of this section, a "relative" of the transferor is a person to whom property would pass from the transferor under Section 6401 or 6402 (intestate succession) if the transferor died intestate and there were no other person having priority.

(Stats. 1990 (A.B. 759), ch. 79, §14, effective July 1, 1991.)

§21403. Beneficiaries' shares abate pro rata within each class

(a) Subject to subdivision (b), shares of beneficiaries abate pro rata within each class specified in Section 21402.

(b) Gifts of annuities and demonstrative gifts are treated as specific gifts to the extent they are satisfied out of the fund or property specified in the gift and as general gifts to the extent they are satisfied out of property other than the fund or property specified in the gift.

(Stats. 1990 (A.B. 759), ch. 79, §14, effective July 1, 1991.)

§21404. Directive for exoneration precludes abatement of other specific gift for that purpose

If an instrument requires property that is the subject of a specific gift to be exonerated from a mortgage, deed of trust, or other lien, a specific gift of other property does not abate for the purpose of exonerating the encumbered property.

(Stats. 1990 (A.B. 759), ch. 79, §14, effective July 1, 1991.)

§21405. Court shall fix amount for abatement; representative shall reduce distributees' shares accordingly

(a) In any case in which there is abatement when a distribution is made during estate administration, the court shall fix the amount each distributee must contribute for abatement. The personal representative shall reduce the distributee's share by that amount.

(b) If a specific gift must be abated, the beneficiary of the specific gift may satisfy the contribution for abatement out of the beneficiary's property other than the property that is the subject of the specific gift.

(Stats. 1990 (A.B. 759), ch. 79, §14, effective July 1, 1991.)

§21406. Application

(a) This part does not apply to a gift made before July 1, 1989. In the case of a gift made before July 1, 1989, the law that would have applied had this part not been enacted shall apply.

(b) For purposes of this section a gift by will is made on the date of the decedent's death.

(Stats. 1990 (A.B. 759), ch. 79, §14, effective July 1, 1991.)

§21612. Manner of satisfying spouse's share; order of abatement

(a) Except as provided in subdivision (b), in satisfying a share provided by this chapter:

(1) The share will first be taken from the decedent's estate not disposed of by will or trust, if any.

(2) If that is not sufficient, so much as may be necessary to satisfy the share shall be taken from all beneficiaries of decedent's testamentary instruments in proportion to the value they may respectively receive. The proportion of each beneficiary's share that may be taken pursuant to this subdivision shall be determined based on values as of the date of the decedent's death.

(b) If the obvious intention of the decedent in relation to some specific gift or devise or other provision of a testamentary instrument would be defeated by the application of subdivision (a), the specific devise or gift or provision may be exempted from the apportionment under subdivision (a), and a different apportionment, consistent with the intention of the decedent, may be adopted.

(Stats. 1997 (A.B. 1172), ch. 724, §34. Amended by Stats. 2003 (A.B. 167), ch. 32, §17.)

[Note that California Probate Code §§21610-21612 apply to surviving spouses who are omitted from the decedent's testamentary instruments because the marriage occurred after execution of the instruments.]

§21623. Omitted child's share; role of decedent's intention

(a) Except as provided in subdivision (b), in satisfying a share provided by this chapter:

(1) The share will first be taken from the decedent's estate not disposed of by will or trust, if any.

(2) If that is not sufficient, so much as may be necessary to satisfy the share shall be taken from all beneficiaries of decedent's testamentary instruments in proportion to the value they may respectively receive. The proportion of each beneficiary's share that may be taken pursuant to this subdivision shall be determined based on values as of the date of the decedent's death.

(b) If the obvious intention of the decedent in relation to some specific gift or devise or other provision of a testamentary instrument would be defeated by the application of subdivision (a), the specific devise or gift or provision of a testamentary instrument may be exempted from the apportionment under subdivision (a), and a different apportionment, consistent with the intention of the decedent, may be adopted.

(Stats. 1997 (A.B. 1172), ch. 724, §34. Amended by Stats. 2003 (A.B. 167), ch. 32, §16.)

D. Exoneration

At common law, a presumption of exoneration applied when a will contained a specific devise of property that was subject to a loan (e.g., a mortgage). That is, the common law included a rebuttable presumption that such obligations should be discharged by the personal representative from the assets of the estate before he or she distributed the asset to the devisee. The devisee of encumbered property would take the property free of the encumbrance. In California, this presumption applied unless the will specified a contrary intent. In re De Bernal's Estate, 131 P. 375 (Cal. 1913).

The modern trend reverses the presumption, adopting a nonexoneration rule. For example, the UPC provides that a devise passes *subject to* any mortgage interest (i.e., without the right of exoneration), and that any general testamentary directive to pay debts is not applicable (UPC §2-607). Similarly, California Probate Code §21131, based on the UPC provision, reverses the prior California case law rule. Law Revision

Commission Commentary following California Probate Code §21131.

§21131. Nonexoneration rule: specific gifts subject to a mortgage pass without right of exoneration

A specific gift passes the property transferred subject to any mortgage, deed of trust, or other lien existing at the date of death, without right of exoneration, regardless of a general directive to pay debts contained in the instrument.

(Stats. 1994 (A.B. 3686), ch. 806, §41. Amended by Stats. 2002 (A.B. 1784), ch. 138, §31.)

III. Constructional Problems in the Determination of Beneficiaries

A. Lapse

Testamentary gifts to a beneficiary who predeceases the testator lapse, i.e., fail. The common law made a distinction between *void* gifts and *lapsed* gifts. A testamentary gift was *void* if the devisee predeceased the testator by dying *before* execution of the will. If the devisee predeceased the testator by dying *after* execution of the will but before the death of the testator, the gift *lapsed*. In modern usage, both situations generally qualify as lapse. "The distinction [between void and lapsed gifts] is of no consequence in modern law, and is not perpetuated in [the Restatement (Third) of Property]. Both types are subsumed herein under the term 'lapsed devises.'" Restatement (Third) Property: Wills, *supra*, at §5.5 cmt. a. A lapsed gift passes to (1) a designated alternative beneficiary, (2) if no alternative beneficiary has been named, to a residuary beneficiary, or, (3) if neither of the above, then by intestacy.

All states today have "anti-lapse" statutes. Anti-lapse statutes specify substitute takers for lapsed testamentary gifts. Anti-lapse statutes typically provide that the devised property passes to the *issue* of the deceased devisee provided the issue survive the testator. The statutes are based on presumed intent. Statutes do not apply if the deceased devisee died without descendants. Restatement (Third) Property: Wills, *supra*, at §5.5 cmt. e. Generally, issue more remote than children take by representation. McGovern & Kurtz, *supra*, §8.3 at 329. See also Restatement (Third) Property: Wills, *supra*, at §5.5 cmt. d.

Statutes vary in terms of the requisite familial relationship *between the testator and the predeceased beneficiary* that evoke application of the anti-lapse doctrine. That is, statutes vary in terms of those who qualify as "protected devisees." Some anti-lapse statutes are narrow and avoid lapse only if the predeceased protected devisee was a descendant of the testator (i.e., child or grandchild). However, most anti-lapse statutes define the requisite familial relationship more broadly. These statutes avoid lapse if the predeceased protected devisee was a grandparent of the testator or a descendant of grandparents. Restatement (Third) of Property: Wills, *supra*, at §5.5 cmt. c. See, e.g., UPC §2-603(b) (applying to devises to the testator's grandparent or a descendant of the testator's grandparent). Some statutes are so broad that they avoid lapse if the predeceased beneficiary is kin of the testator's *spouse*. See, e.g., UPC §2-603(b)(applying to devises to a predeceased stepchild of the testator).

Note that anti-lapse statutes do not apply if the testator has expressed a contrary intent. According to the Restatement (Third) of Property: Wills, *supra*, at §5.5 cmt. f., many anti-lapse statutes recognize a contrary intent only if expressed in the will. The revised Uniform Probate Code §2-601, however, allows the admission of extrinsic evidence on the question of contrary intent.

Testamentary gifts may fail for other reasons than because the beneficiary predeceases the testator. For example, lapse also may arise if a beneficiary is disqualified (i.e., due to disclaimer, divorce, or homicide), or if the beneficiary is an interested witness. In such cases, even though the beneficiary survives the testator, statutes may provide for substitute takers. McGovern & Kurtz, *supra*, §8.3 at 333.

California statute addresses the situation of lapse. According to California Probate Code §21110(a), if a transferee predeceases the transferor (either is dead when the instrument is executed or dies thereafter), the issue of the predeceased transferee take in the latter's place (in the manner provided in California Probate Code §240 dealing with representation).

"Transferee" is defined as a person who is "kindred of the transferor or kindred of a surviving, deceased, or former spouse of the transferor" (Cal. Prob. Code §21110(c)). In Estate of Dye, 112 Cal. Rptr. 2d 362 (Ct. App. 2001), the decedent and his second wife signed reciprocal form wills, leaving their property to each other, with no residuary clause. Decedent's second wife predeceased him. She had one son who was adopted by decedent, but the decedent had two children by his prior marriage who had been adopted out. The adopted-in son argued (inter alia) that the decedent's gift to his wife did not lapse. The appellate court disagreed and also found that the anti-lapse statute did not apply. That is, the court reasoned that, according to California Probate Code §211010(c), issue of a predeceased transferee take only if the transferee is "kindred of the transferor." Because decedent's second wife was married to him, she was not "kindred" to decedent and, therefore, did not qualify as a "transferee" under the antilapse statute.

The California Probate Code also addresses the lapse of a residuary gift. If the transferor gives a residuary gift to two or more persons and the share of a residuary transferee fails for any reason without the transferor having provided for an alternative disposition, the failed share passes to the other transferees in proportion to their other interest in the residuary gift (Cal. Prob. Code §21111(b)).

§21108. Devise of interest to heirs or next of kin; common law rule of worthier title rejected

The law of this state does not include (a) the common law rule of worthier title that a transferor cannot devise an interest to his or her own heirs or (b) a presumption or rule of interpretation that a transferor does not intend, by a transfer to his or her own heirs or next of kin, to transfer an interest to them. The meaning of a transfer of a legal or equitable interest to a transferor's own heirs or next of kin, however designated, shall be determined by the general rules applicable to the interpretation of instruments.

(Stats. 1994 (A.B. 3686), ch. 806, §41. Amended by Stats. 2002 (A.B. 1784), ch. 138, §17.)

§21109. Lapse doctrine: transferee who predeceases transferor does not take under instrument

(a) A transferee who fails to survive the transferor of an at death transfer or until any future time required by the instrument does not take under the instrument.

(b) If it cannot be determined by clear and convincing evidence that the transferee survived until a future time required by the instrument, it is deemed that the transferee did not survive until the required future time.

(Stats. 1994 (A.B. 3686), ch. 806, §41. Amended by Stats. 2002 (A.B. 1784), ch. 138, §18.)

§21110. Antilapse provision substitutes issue of predeceased transferee

(a) Subject to subdivision (b), if a transferee is dead when the instrument is executed, or fails or is treated as failing to survive the transferor or until a future time required by the instrument, the issue of the deceased transferee take in the transferee's place in the manner provided in Section 240. A transferee under a class gift shall be a transferee for the purpose of this subdivision unless the transferee's death occurred before the execution of the instrument and that fact was known to the transferor when the instrument was executed.

(b) The issue of a deceased transferee do not take in the transferee's place if the instrument expresses a contrary intention or a substitute disposition. A requirement that the initial transferee survive the transferor or survive for a specified period of time after the death of the transferor constitutes a contrary intention. A requirement that the initial transferee survive until a future time that is related to the probate of the transferor's will or administration of the estate of the transferor constitutes a contrary intention.

(c) As used in this section, "transferee" means a person who is kindred of the transferor or kindred of a surviving, deceased, or former spouse of the transferor.

(Stats. 1994 (A.B. 3686), ch. 806, §41. Amended by Stats. 2002 (A.B. 1784), ch. 138, §19.)

§21111. Effect of failed or lapsed transfers

(a) Except as provided in subdivision (b) and subject to Section 21110, if a transfer fails for any reason, the property is transferred as follows:

(1) If the transferring instrument provides for an alternative disposition in the event the transfer fails, the property is transferred according to the terms of the instrument.

(2) If the transferring instrument does not provide for an alternative disposition but does provide for the transfer of a residue, the property becomes a part of the residue transferred under the instrument.

(3) If the transferring instrument does not provide for an alternative disposition and does not provide for the transfer of a residue, or if the transfer is itself a residuary gift, the property is transferred to the decedent's estate.

(b) Subject to Section 21110, if a residuary gift or a future interest is transferred to two or more persons and the share of a transferee fails for any reason, and no alternative disposition is provided, the share passes to the other transferees in proportion to their other interest in the residuary gift or the future interest.

(c) A transfer of "all my estate" or words of similar import is a residuary gift for purposes of this section.

(d) If failure of a future interest results in an intestacy, the property passes to the heirs of the transferor determined pursuant to Section 21114.

(Stats. 1994 (A.B. 3686), ch. 806, §41. Amended by Stats. 1996, ch. 563 (S.B. 392), §32; Stats. 2001 (A.B. 873), ch. 417, §11; Stats. 2002, ch. 138 (A.B. 1784), §20.)

§21112. Transfers referring to "issue"

A condition in a transfer of a present or future interest that refers to a person's death "with" or "without" issue, or to a person's "having" or "leaving" issue or no issue, or a condition based on words of similar import, is construed to refer to that person's being dead at the time the transfer takes effect in enjoyment and to that person either having or not having, as the case may be, issue who are alive at the time of enjoyment.

(Stats. 1994 (A.B. 3686), ch. 806, §41. Amended by Stats. 2002 (A.B. 1784), ch. 138, §21.)

B. Class Gifts

Sometimes, a testator devises a gift to a designated *class* of beneficiaries. For example, class gift language applies to bequests to such aggregate groups as "children," or "nephews and nieces." A class gift is a gift to a group, without naming the takers individually.

Sometimes, a testator may devise property to both a group and individuals, i.e., "to my nephews and nieces, John, Thomas, and Barbara." The aggregate designation suggests a class gift, but the testator's naming of the relatives individually contradicts the former designation. Some cases hold that such a gift is treated as one to named individuals (i.e., not as a class gift). However, courts are divided on the issue. McGovern & Kurtz, *supra*, §8.3 at 332.

Once the determination is made that the testator intended a class gift, special rules are applicable. For example, if any class member predeceases the decedent without issue, the share of that predeceased devisee passes to the other members of the class. However, if the predeceased class member dies leaving issue surviving, then his or her issue take the share of the predeceased devisee, based on most anti-lapse statutes (UPC §2-603(a)(4); Cal. Prob. Code §21110(a)). See also McGovern & Kurtz, *supra*, §8.3, at 332.

The UPC would save the gift for the issue of the predeceased class member in cases where the class member died *before* or after the execution of the instrument (UPC §2-603(a)(4)). (Recall that a gift was void at common law if the class member was already dead.) However, under California law, if a transferor makes a gift to a predeceased transferee using class gift language, the issue of the predeceased transferee are substituted for the latter *unless* the transferee died before execution of the instrument (i.e., unless the gift was void at common law) and that fact was known to the transferor when the instrument was executed (Cal. Prob. Code §21110(a)). Further, "[w]ith respect to a class gift of a future interest, Section 21109 must be read together with Section 21114. If the transferee fails to survive but is properly related to the transferor or the transferor's spouse, the antilapse statute may substitute the transferee's issue." Law Revision Commission Commentary following California Probate Code §21109.

Another rule applicable to class gifts is that membership in the class includes afterborn persons (persons born after execution of the will) who satisfy the class description. California's "rule of convenience," subject to common law exceptions, specifies that, for purposes of a class gift, the class closes (and its membership is determined) at the death of the testator, provided that at least one member of the class is then living.

According to California law, those persons who are half bloods, adopted, nonmarital children, stepchildren, and foster children are included in class gift language (Cal. Prob. Code §21115(a)). This rule is subject to an exception that bases the child's eligibility to inherit on whether the child lived while a minor as a

member of the household of the natural or adoptive parent or of that of the parent's parent, brother, sister, spouse, or surviving spouse (Cal. Prob. Code §21115(b)).

§21110. Antilapse provision substitutes issue of predeceased transferee; application of antilapse statute to class gift

(a) Subject to subdivision (b), if a transferee is dead when the instrument is executed, or fails or is treated as failing to survive the transferor or until a future time required by the instrument, the issue of the deceased transferee take in the transferee's place in the manner provided in Section 240. A transferee under a class gift shall be a transferee for the purpose of this subdivision unless the transferee's death occurred before the execution of the instrument and that fact was known to the transferor when the instrument was executed.

(b) The issue of a deceased transferee do not take in the transferee's place if the instrument expresses a contrary intention or a substitute disposition. A requirement that the initial transferee survive the transferor or survive for a specified period of time after the death of the transferor constitutes a contrary intention. A requirement that the initial transferee survive until a future time that is related to the probate of the transferor's will or administration of the estate of the transferor constitutes a contrary intention.

(c) As used in this section, "transferee" means a person who is kindred of the transferor or kindred of a surviving, deceased, or former spouse of the transferor.

(Stats. 1994 (A.B. 3686), ch. 806, §41. Amended by Stats. 2002 (A.B. 1784), ch. 138, §19.)

[California Probate Code §§21111 and 21112 are set forth in Chapter V, Section I, *supra*.]

§21114. Class gift to "heirs," "next of kin," "relatives," etc.

(a) If a statute or instrument provides for transfer of a present or future interest to, or creates a present or future interest in, a designated person's "heirs," "heirs at law," "next of kin," or "family," or words of similar import, the transfer is to the persons, including the state under Section 6800, and in the shares that would succeed to the designated person's intestate estate under the intestate succession law of the transferor's domicile, if the designated person died when the transfer is to take effect in enjoyment. If the designated person's surviving spouse is living but is remarried at the time the transfer is to take effect in enjoyment, the surviving spouse is not an heir of the designated person for purposes of this section.

(b) As used in this section, "designated person" includes the transferor.

(Stats. 1994 (A.B. 3686), ch. 806, §41. Amended by Stats. 2002 (A.B. 1784), ch. 138, §23.)

§21115. Class gifts: inclusion of halfbloods, adoptees, nonmarital children, stepchildren, foster children

(a) Except as provided in subdivision (b), halfbloods, adopted persons, persons born out of wedlock, stepchildren, foster children, and the issue of these persons when appropriate to the class, are included in terms of class gift or relationship in accordance with the rules for determining relationship and inheritance rights for purposes of intestate succession.

(b) In construing a transfer by a transferor who is not the natural parent, a person born to the natural parent shall not be considered the child of that parent unless the person lived while a minor as a regular member of the household of the natural parent or of that parent's parent, brother, sister, spouse, or surviving spouse. In construing a transfer by a transferor who is not the adoptive parent, a person adopted by the adoptive parent shall not be considered the child of that parent unless the person lived while a minor (either before or after the adoption) as a regular member of the household of the adopting parent or of that parent's parent, brother, sister, or surviving spouse.

(c) Subdivisions (a) and (b) shall also apply in determining:

(1) Persons who would be kindred of the transferor or kindred of a surviving, deceased, or former spouse of the transferor under Section 21110.

(2) Persons to be included as issue of a deceased transferee under Section 21110.

(3) Persons who would be the transferor's or other designated person's heirs under Section 21114.

(d) The rules for determining intestate succession under this section are those in effect at the time the transfer is to take effect in enjoyment.

(Stats. 1994 (A.B. 3686), ch. 806, §41. Amended by Stats. 2002 (A.B. 1784), ch. 138, §24.)

XVI
Health Care Decisionmaking: Planning for Disability and Death

Considerable public attention has focused in recent years on the issue of health care decisionmaking, including the withdrawal of treatment for terminally ill individuals or other persons who lose the capacity to control their own treatment. This chapter explores the statutory provisions that are applicable to persons who wish to plan for both disability (in terms of health care and property management) and for death.

I. Legal Determination of Mental Capacity

Medical and legal personnel sometimes need to determine whether a person has the legal capacity to make a particular decision or act. The statutory basis for such determinations in California is the Due Process in Competence Determination Act (Cal. Prob. Code §§810 et seq.). The Act includes a rebuttable presumption of mental capacity (Cal. Prob. Code §810(a)). Note that a person may have a mental or physical disability and still be legally competent to make certain decisions: enter into contracts, convey property, marry, make medical decisions, execute wills or trusts (Cal. Prob. Code §810(b)).

California Probate Code §§810 and 811 specify the standards that apply to judicial determinations of incapacity. Such a determination must be based on evidence of a deficit in one or more of the person's mental functions rather than on a diagnosis of the person's mental or physical disorder (Cal. Prob. Code §810(c)), and must be supported by evidence as to at least one of the following mental functions: alertness and attention, information processing, thought processes, and ability to modulate mood and affect (Cal. Prob. Code §811(a)). Furthermore, there must be evidence of a correlation between the deficit(s) and the decision or acts in question (Cal. Prob. Code §811(a)).

The Probate Code also governs the standards to determine the individual's capacity to give *informed consent* to proposed medical treatment. According to California Probate Code §813, a person has the capacity to give informed consent to a proposed medical treatment if the person can do all of the following: respond knowingly and intelligently to queries about that medical treatment; participate in that treatment decision by means of a rational thought process; and understand certain medical treatment information (i.e., the nature and seriousness of the disorder; nature of the recommended medical treatment; degree and duration of benefits and risks of medical intervention; and the nature, risks, and benefits of any reasonable alternatives).

§810. Judicial determination of capabilities of persons with mental or physical disorders

The Legislature finds and declares the following:

(a) For purposes of this part, there shall exist a rebuttable presumption affecting the burden of proof that all persons have the capacity to make decisions and to be responsible for their acts or decisions.

(b) A person who has a mental or physical disorder may still be capable of contracting, conveying, marrying, making medical decisions, executing wills or trusts, and performing other actions.

(c) A judicial determination that a person is totally without understanding, or is of unsound mind, or suffers from one or more mental deficits so substantial that, under the circumstances, the person should be deemed to lack the legal capacity to perform a specific act, should be based on evidence of a deficit in one or more of the person's mental functions rather than on a diagnosis of a person's mental or physical disorder.

(Stats. 1995 (S.B. 730), ch. 842, §2. Amended by Stats. 1998 (A.B. 2801), ch. 581, §19.)

§811. Deficits in particular mental functions

(a) A determination that a person is of unsound mind or lacks the capacity to make a decision or do a certain act, including, but not limited to, the incapacity to contract, to make a conveyance, to marry, to make medical decisions, to execute wills, or to execute trusts, shall be supported by evidence of a deficit in at least one of the following mental functions, subject to subdivision (b), and evidence of a correlation between the deficit or deficits and the decision or acts in question:

(1) Alertness and attention, including, but not limited to, the following:

(A) Level of arousal or consciousness.

(B) Orientation to time, place, person, and situation.

(C) Ability to attend and concentrate.

(2) Information processing, including, but not limited to, the following:

(A) Short- and long-term memory, including immediate recall.

(B) Ability to understand or communicate with others, either verbally or otherwise.

(C) Recognition of familiar objects and familiar persons.

(D) Ability to understand and appreciate quantities.

(E) Ability to reason using abstract concepts.

(F) Ability to plan, organize, and carry out actions in one's own rational self-interest.

(G) Ability to reason logically.

(3) Thought processes. Deficits in these functions may be demonstrated by the presence of the following:

(A) Severely disorganized thinking.

(B) Hallucinations.

(C) Delusions.

(D) Uncontrollable, repetitive, or intrusive thoughts.

(4) Ability to modulate mood and affect. Deficits in this ability may be demonstrated by the presence of a pervasive and persistent or recurrent state of euphoria, anger, anxiety, fear, panic, depression, hopelessness or despair, helplessness, apathy or indifference, that is inappropriate in degree to the individual's circumstances.

(b) A deficit in the mental functions listed above may be considered only if the deficit, by itself or in combination with one or more other mental function deficits, significantly impairs the person's ability to understand and appreciate the consequences of his or her actions with regard to the type of act or decision in question.

(c) In determining whether a person suffers from a deficit in mental function so substantial that the person lacks the capacity to do a certain act, the court may take into consideration the frequency, severity, and duration of periods of impairment.

(d) The mere diagnosis of a mental or physical disorder shall not be sufficient in and of itself to support a determination that a person is of unsound mind or lacks the capacity to do a certain act.

(e) This part applies only to the evidence that is presented to, and the findings that are made by, a court determining the capacity of a person to do a certain act or make a decision, including, but not limited to, making medical decisions. Nothing in this part shall affect the decisionmaking process set forth in Section 1418.8 of the Health and Safety Code, nor increase or decrease the burdens of documentation on, or potential liability of, health care providers who, outside the judicial context, determine the capacity of patients to make a medical decision.

(Stats. 1995 (S.B. 730), ch. 842, §2. Amended by Stats. 1998 (A.B. 2801), ch. 581, §19.)

§812. Standard for determination of capacity to make decisions: ability to understand and appreciate

Except where otherwise provided by law, including, but not limited to, Section 813 and the statutory and decisional law of testamentary capacity, a person lacks the capacity to make a decision unless the person has the ability to communicate verbally, or by any other means, the decision, and to understand and appreciate, to the extent relevant, all of the following:

(a) The rights, duties, and responsibilities created by, or affected by the decision.

(b) The probable consequences for the decisionmaker and, where appropriate, the persons affected by the decision.

(c) The significant risks, benefits, and reasonable alternatives involved in the decision.

(Stats. 1996 (S.B. 1650), ch. 178, §5.)

§813. Judicial determination of capacity to give informed consent to medical treatment

(a) For purposes of a judicial determination, a person has the capacity to give informed consent to a proposed medical treatment if the person is able to do all of the following:

(1) Respond knowingly and intelligently to queries about that medical treatment.

(2) Participate in that treatment decision by means of a rational thought process.

(3) Understand all of the following items of minimum basic medical treatment information with respect to that treatment:

(A) The nature and seriousness of the illness, disorder, or defect that the person has.

(B) The nature of the medical treatment that is being recommended by the person's health care providers.

(C) The probable degree and duration of any benefits and risks of any medical intervention that is being recommended by the person's health care providers, and the consequences of lack of treatment.

(D) The nature, risks, and benefits of any reasonable alternatives.

(b) A person who has the capacity to give informed consent to a proposed medical treatment also has the capacity to refuse consent to that treatment.

(Stats. 1995 (S.B. 730), ch. 842, §5. Amended by Stats. 1996 (S.B. 1650), ch. 178, §6.)

II. Powers of Attorney

A power of attorney is an agency relationship that enables one person to act in the place of another. The person who grants authority is termed the "principal," whereas the person who is given the authority to act is termed the "agent" or "attorney-in-fact." (The term "attorney-in-fact" merely signifies an agent, not a lawyer.)

An agency relationship, in some ways, is similar to a trust. For example, an agent is a fiduciary, like a trustee. However, whereas a trustee has powers that are implied by common law or statute, agency law "only sparingly implies powers and strictly construes express powers." William M. McGovern, Jr., Trusts, Custodianships, and Durable Powers of Attorney, 27 Real Prop., Prob. & Trust J. 33 (1992) (cited in McGovern & Kurtz, *supra*, §9.3 at 351). Moreover, a trust can function as a will substitute, but a power of attorney cannot. McGovern & Kurtz, *supra*, §9.3 at 351.

According to the traditional rule, an agent's powers terminate at the death or incapacity of the principal. Therefore, an agency relationship cannot be used for health care planning when the principal became incapacitated. A "durable" power of attorney is required that will not be affected by the disability of the principal. The principal must execute the durable power while legally competent. Note that a durable power survives disability but not death; it terminates at the death of the principal (although acts of an agent who does not have knowledge of the principal's death may be binding). *Id.* (citing UPC §5-504).

Many states have enacted statutes to enable a person to nominate a guardian prior to disability and to provide for health care decisionmaking in the event of incapacity. Common devices include a durable power of attorney (such as "durable powers of attorney for health care") as well as the "living will" (a document executed with formalities resembling a will). Living wills are discussed in Section III, *infra*.

To address the need for planning for health care, disability, and death, the National Conference of Commissioners on Uniform State Laws (NCCUSL) promulgated a series of uniform acts. NCCUSL approved the Uniform Durable Power of Attorney Act in 1979 and revised it in 1987. That Act subsequently was included in revisions of the Uniform Probate Code (Article V, Part V). Most states (including California) have adopted this legislation although with some variations. The California version of this uniform Act is set forth *infra*.

In 1982, NCCUSL promulgated the Model Health-Care Consent Act, which addressed broad issues of consent to treatment but not issues involving the dying patient. That legislation enables a person to transfer health care decisionmaking to a health care representative. To address the specific issues facing dying patients, the Uniform Law Commissioners approved the Uniform Rights of the Terminally Ill Act in 1985 (amended in 1989).

In 1988, NCCUSL adopted the Uniform Statutory Power of Attorney Act (USPAA) to provide a standardized form to facilitate the creation of a power of attorney. The Uniform Law Commissioners approved USPAA in recognition of the problem that agents bearing power-of-attorney documents often have their powers refused or disregarded in transactions on a principal's behalf. This difficulty frequently necessitates the need for an agent to seek judicial enforcement of his or her legitimately exercised powers. USPAA includes a comprehensive list of powers for an agent, enabling a principal to choose (by a check-off list) the desired specific or general powers. Fewer than a dozen states adopted this legislation. California is among those states that have adopted the legislation. California's version of the USPAA is set forth in Section F below. Although health care decisionmaking issues are not expressly included among USPAA powers, Section 2 of the Act and the form itself permit the power of attorney to remain in effect after the

disability of the principal if that is permitted by other laws of the state.

At the same time that NCCUSL was addressing patients' self-determination in health care decisionmaking, the federal government also enacted legislation on the subject. In 1990, Congress enacted the Patient Self-Determination Act (PSDA), 42 U.S.C. §1395cc (f)(2000). The PSDA makes the provision of information about advance directives to patients in health care facilities a condition for the receipt of federal Medicare funds to health care facilities.

Finally, in 1993, NCCUSL approved the Uniform Health-Care Decisions Act (UHCDA), which assists persons and the medical profession to designate a health care agent to choose a particular course of medical treatment. It addresses the general problem of health care decisionmaking and the specific issue of the withdrawal of life support. The legislation is designed to promote uniformity among the various state statutes by replacing existing living will, power of attorney for health care, and family health care consent statutes (California has not yet adopted this Act).

A. General Provisions

California's Power of Attorney Law (Cal. Prob. Code §§4000 et seq.) is applicable to durable powers of attorney (other than powers of attorney for health care); statutory form powers of attorney; and any other power of attorney that incorporates or refers to the Power of Attorney Law or its provisions (Cal. Prob. Code §4050(a)(1)-(3)). Ross & Grant, Cal. Prob. Prac., *supra*, at §l:54. Powers of attorney for health care are regulated by the Health Care Decisions Law (Cal. Prob. Code §§4600 et seq., set forth in Section III *infra*).

§4000. Power of Attorney Law

This division may be cited as the Power of Attorney Law.

(Stats. 1994 (S.B. 1907), ch. 307, §16.)

§4001. Uniform Durable Power of Attorney Act

Sections 4124, 4125, 4126, 4127, 4206, 4304, and 4305 may be cited as the Uniform Durable Power of Attorney Act.

(Stats. 1994 (S.B. 1907), ch. 307, §16.)

§4010. Definitions

Unless the provision or context otherwise requires, the definitions in this chapter govern the construction of this division.

(Stats. 1994 (S.B. 1907), ch. 307, §16.)

§4014. "Attorney-in-fact," defined

(a) "Attorney-in-fact" means a person granted authority to act for the principal in a power of attorney, regardless of whether the person is known as an attorney-in-fact or agent, or by some other term.

(b) "Attorney-in-fact" includes a successor or alternate attorney-in-fact and a person delegated authority by an attorney-in-fact.

(Stats. 1994 (S.B. 1907), ch. 307, §16.)

§4018. "Durable power of attorney," defined

"Durable power of attorney" means a power of attorney that satisfies the requirements for durability provided in Section 4124.

(Stats. 1994 (S.B. 1907), ch. 307, §16.)

§4022. "Power of attorney," defined

"Power of attorney" means a written instrument, however denominated, that is executed by a natural person having the capacity to contract and that grants authority to an attorney infact. A power of attorney may be durable or nondurable.

(Stats. 1994 (S.B. 1907), ch. 307, §16.)

§4026. "Principal," defined

"Principal" means a natural person who executes a power of attorney.

(Stats. 1994 (S.B. 1907), ch. 307, §16.)

§4030. "Springing power of attorney," defined

"Springing power of attorney" means a power of attorney that by its terms becomes effective at a specified future time or on the occurrence of a specified future event or contingency, including, but not limited to, the subsequent incapacity of the principal. A springing power of attorney may be a durable power of attorney or a nondurable power of attorney.

(Stats. 1994 (S.B. 1907), ch. 307, §16.)

§4034. "Third person," defined

"Third person" means any person other than the principal or attorney-in-fact.

(Stats. 1994 (S.B. 1907), ch. 307, §16.)

§4050. Application of division to particular powers of attorney

(a) This division applies to the following:

(1) Durable powers of attorney, other than powers of attorney for health care governed by Division 4.7 (commencing with Section 4600).

(2) Statutory form powers of attorney under Part 3 (commencing with Section 4400).

(3) Any other power of attorney that incorporates or refers to this division or the provisions of this division.

(b) This division does not apply to the following:

(1) A power of attorney to the extent that the authority of the attorney-in-fact is coupled with an interest in the subject of the power of attorney.

(2) Reciprocal or interinsurance exchanges and their contracts, subscribers, attorneys-in-fact, agents, and representatives.

(3) A proxy given by an attorney-in-fact to another person to exercise voting rights.

(c) This division is not intended to affect the validity of any instrument or arrangement that is not described in subdivision (a).

(Stats. 1994 (S.B. 1907), ch. 307, §16. Amended by Stats. 1999 (A.B. 891), ch. 658, §27, effective July 1, 2000.)

§4051. Agency law generally applies to powers of attorney

Except where this division provides a specific rule, the general law of agency, including Article 2 (commencing with Section 2019) of Chapter 2 of Title 6 of, and Title 9 (commencing with Section 2295) of, Part 4 of Division 3 of the Civil Code, applies to powers of attorney.

(Stats. 1994 (S.B. 1907), ch. 307, §16.)

§4052. Conditions for application of Power of Attorney Law

(a) If a power of attorney provides that the Power of Attorney Law of this state governs the power of attorney or otherwise indicates the principal's intention that the Power of Attorney Law of this state governs the power of attorney, this division governs the power of attorney and applies to acts and transactions of the attorney-in-fact in this state or outside this state where any of the following conditions is satisfied:

(1) The principal or attorney-in-fact was domiciled in this state when the principal executed the power of attorney.

(2) The authority conferred on the attorney-in-fact relates to property, acts, or transactions in this state.

(3) The acts or transactions of the attorney-in-fact occurred or were intended to occur in this state.

(4) The principal executed the power of attorney in this state.

(5) There is otherwise a reasonable relationship between this state and the subject matter of the power of attorney.

(b) If subdivision (a) does not apply to the power of attorney, this division governs the power of attorney and applies to the acts and transactions of the attorney-in-fact in this state where either of the following conditions is satisfied:

(1) The principal was domiciled in this state when the principal executed the power of attorney.

(2) The principal executed the power of attorney in this state.

(c) A power of attorney described in this section remains subject to this division despite a change in domicile of the principal or the attorney-in-fact, or the removal from this state of property that was the subject of the power of attorney.

(Stats. 1994 (S.B. 1907), ch. 307, §16.)

§4053. Validity of durable power of attorney executed in another state

A durable power of attorney executed in another state or jurisdiction in compliance with the law of that state or jurisdiction or the law of this state is valid and enforceable in this state to the same extent as a durable power of attorney executed in this state, regardless of whether the principal is a domiciliary of this state.

(Stats. 1994 (S.B. 1907), ch. 307, §16.)

§4054. Application of Division; execution date

Except as otherwise provided by statute:

(a) On and after January 1, 1995, this division applies to all powers of attorney regardless of whether they were executed before, on, or after January 1, 1995.

(b) This division applies to all proceedings concerning powers of attorney commenced on or after January 1, 1995.

(c) This division applies to all proceedings concerning powers of attorney commenced before January 1, 1995, unless the court determines that application of a particular provision of this division would substantially interfere with the effective conduct of the proceedings or the rights of the parties and other interested persons, in which case the particular provision of this division does not apply and prior law applies.

(d) Nothing in this division affects the validity of a power of attorney executed before January 1, 1995, that was valid under prior law.

(Stats. 1994 (S.B. 1907), ch. 307, §16. Amended by Stats. 1995 (S.B. 984), ch. 300, §3, effective August 3, 1995.)

§4100. Application of Part: applicable to all powers of attorney except statutory form powers

This part applies to all powers of attorney under this division, subject to any special rules applicable to statutory form powers of attorney under Part 3 (commencing with Section 4400).

(Stats. 1994 (S.B. 1907), ch. 307, §16. Amended by Stats. 1999 (A.B. 891), ch. 658, §28, effective July 1, 2000.)

§4101. Principal may limit application of statute; exclusions

(a) Except as provided in subdivision (b), the principal may limit the application of any provision of this division by an express statement in the power of attorney or by providing an inconsistent rule in the power of attorney.

(b) A power of attorney may not limit either the application of a statute specifically providing that it is not subject to limitation in the power of attorney or a statute concerning any of the following:

(1) Warnings or notices required to be included in a power of attorney.

(2) Operative dates of statutory enactments or amendments.

(3) Execution formalities.

(4) Qualifications of witnesses.

(5) Qualifications of attorneys-in-fact.

(6) Protection of third persons from liability.

(Stats. 1994 (S.B. 1907), ch. 307, §16.)

§4102. Requirements for validity of printed form of durable power of attorney

Notwithstanding Section 4128:

(a) Except as provided in subdivision (b), on and after January 1, 1995, a printed form of a durable power of attorney may be sold or otherwise distributed if it satisfies the requirements of former Section 2510.5 of the Civil Code.

(b) A printed form of a durable power of attorney printed on or after January 1, 1986, that is sold or otherwise distributed in this state for use by a person who does not have the advice of legal counsel shall comply with former Section 2510 of the Civil Code or with Section 4128 of this code.

(c) A durable power of attorney executed on or after January 1, 1995, using a printed form that complies with subdivision (b) of former Section 2400 of the Civil Code, as enacted by Chapter 511 of the Statutes of 1981, or with former Section 2510 of the Civil Code, is as valid as if it had been executed using a printed form that complies with Section 4128 of this code.

(Stats. 1994 (S.B. 1907), ch. 307, §16.)

B. Creation and Effect of Powers of Attorney

§4120. Capacity to execute power of attorney

A natural person having the capacity to contract may execute a power of attorney.

(Stats. 1994 (S.B. 1907), ch. 307, §16.)

§4121. Conditions for legal sufficiency of power of attorney

A power of attorney is legally sufficient if all of the following requirements are satisfied:

(a) The power of attorney contains the date of its execution.

(b) The power of attorney is signed either (1) by the principal or (2) in the principal's name by another adult in the principal's presence and at the principal's direction.

(c) The power of attorney is either (1) acknowledged before a notary public or (2) signed by at least two witnesses who satisfy the requirements of Section 4122.

(Stats. 1994 (S.B. 1907), ch. 307, §16. Amended by Stats. 1999 (A.B. 891), ch. 658, §29, effective July 1, 2000.)

§4122. Qualifications and duties of witnesses to power of attorney

If the power of attorney is signed by witnesses, as provided in Section 4121, the following requirements shall be satisfied:

(a) The witnesses shall be adults.

(b) The attorney-in-fact may not act as a witness.

(c) Each witness signing the power of attorney shall witness either the signing of the instrument by the principal or the principal's acknowledgment of the signature or the power of attorney.

(Stats. 1994 (S.B. 1907), ch. 307, §16. Amended by Stats. 1999 (A.B. 891), ch. 658, §29, effective July 1, 2000.)

§4123. Principal may grant authority to attorney-in-fact for all or some purposes regarding property, personal care, etc.

(a) In a power of attorney under this division, a principal may grant authority to an attorney-in-fact to act on the principal's behalf with respect to all lawful subjects and purposes or with respect to one or more express subjects or purposes. The attorney-in-fact may be granted authority with regard to the principal's property, personal care, or any other matter.

(b) With regard to property matters, a power of attorney may grant authority to make decisions concerning all or part of the principal's real and personal property, whether owned by the principal at the time of the execution of the power of attorney or thereafter acquired or whether located in this state or elsewhere, without the need for a description of each item or parcel of property.

(c) With regard to personal care, a power of attorney may grant authority to make decisions relating to the personal care of the principal, including, but not limited to, determining where the principal will live, providing meals, hiring household employees, providing transportation, handling mail, and arranging recreation and entertainment.

(Stats. 1994 (S.B. 1907), ch. 307, §16. Amended by Stats. 1999 (A.B. 891), ch. 658, §29, effective July 1, 2000; Stats. 2001 (A.B. 1278), ch. 230, §2.)

§4124. Durable power of attorney: defined and requisite language

A durable power of attorney is a power of attorney by which a principal designates another person as attorney-in-fact in writing and the power of attorney contains any of the following statements:

(a) "This power of attorney shall not be affected by subsequent incapacity of the principal."

(b) "This power of attorney shall become effective upon the incapacity of the principal."

(c) Similar words showing the intent of the principal that the authority conferred shall be exercisable notwithstanding the principal's subsequent incapacity.

(Stats. 1994 (S.B. 1907), ch. 307, §16.)

§4125. Acts of attorney-in-fact bind principal and successors in interest as if principal had capacity

All acts done by an attorney-in-fact pursuant to a durable power of attorney during any period of incapacity of the principal have the same effect and inure to the benefit of and bind the principal and the principal's successors in interest as if the principal had capacity.

(Stats. 1994 (S.B. 1907), ch. 307, §16.)

§4126. Principal may nominate conservator or guardian pursuant to durable power of attorney

(a) A principal may nominate, by a durable power of attorney, a conservator of the person or estate or both, or a guardian of the person or estate or both, for consideration by the court if protective proceedings for the principal's person or estate are thereafter commenced.

(b) If the protective proceedings are conservatorship proceedings in this state, the nomination has the effect provided in Section 1810 and the court shall give effect to the most recent writing executed in accordance with Section 1810, whether or not the writing is a durable power of attorney.

(Stats. 1994 (S.B. 1907), ch. 307, §16.)

§4127. Termination of power of attorney

Unless a power of attorney states a time of termination, the authority of the attorney-in-fact is exercisable notwithstanding any lapse of time since execution of the power of attorney.

(Stats. 1994 (S.B. 1907), ch. 307, §16.)

§4128. Warning statement required to person executing durable power of attorney via printed forms

(a) Subject to subdivision (b), a printed form of a durable power of attorney that is sold or otherwise distributed in this state for use by a person who does not have the advice of legal counsel shall contain, in not less than 10-point boldface type or a reasonable equivalent thereof, the following warning statements:

Notice to Person Executing Durable Power of Attorney

A durable power of attorney is an important legal document. By signing the durable power of attorney, you are authorizing another person to act for you, the principal. Before you sign this durable power of attorney, you should know these important facts:

Your agent (attorney-in-fact) has no duty to act unless you and your agent agree otherwise in writing.

This document gives your agent the powers to manage, dispose of, sell, and convey your real and personal property, and to use your property as security if your agent borrows money on your behalf. This document does not give your agent the power to accept or receive any of your property, in trust or otherwise, as a gift, unless you specifically authorize the agent to accept or receive a gift. Your agent will have the right to receive reasonable payment for services provided under this durable power of attorney unless you provide otherwise in this power of attorney.

The powers you give your agent will continue to exist for your entire lifetime, unless you state that the durable power of attorney will last for a shorter period of time or unless you otherwise terminate the durable power of attorney. The powers you give your agent in this durable power of attorney will continue to exist even if you can no longer make your own decisions respecting the management of your property.

You can amend or change this durable power of attorney only by executing a new durable power of attorney or by executing an amendment through the same formalities as an original. You have the right to revoke or terminate this durable power of attorney at any time, so long as you are competent.

This durable power of attorney must be dated and must be acknowledged before a notary public or signed by two witnesses. If it is signed by two witnesses, they must witness either (1) the signing of the power of attorney or (2) the principal's signing or acknowledgment of his or her signature. A durable power of attorney that may affect real property should be acknowledged before a notary public so that it may easily be recorded.

You should read this durable power of attorney carefully. When effective, this durable power of attorney will give your agent the right to deal with property that you now have or might acquire in the future. The durable power of attorney is important to you. If you do not understand the durable power of attorney, or any provision of it, then you should obtain the assistance of an attorney or other qualified person.

Notice to Person Accepting the Appointment as Attorney-in-Fact

By acting or agreeing to act as the agent (attorney-in-fact) under this power of attorney you assume the fiduciary and other legal responsibilities of an agent. These responsibilities include:

1. The legal duty to act solely in the interest of the principal and to avoid conflicts of interest.

2. The legal duty to keep the principal's property separate and distinct from any other property owned or controlled by you.

You may not transfer the principal's property to yourself without full and adequate consideration or accept a gift of the principal's property unless this power of attorney specifically authorizes you to transfer property to yourself or accept a gift of the principal's property. If you transfer the principal's property to yourself without specific authorization in the power of attorney, you may be prosecuted for fraud and/or embezzlement. If the principal is 65 years of age or older at the time that the property is transferred to you without authority, you may also be prosecuted for elder abuse under Penal Code Section 368. In addition to criminal prosecution, you may also be sued in civil court.

I have read the foregoing notice and I understand the legal and fiduciary duties that I assume by acting or agreeing to act as the agent (attorney-in-fact) under the terms of this power of attorney.

Date:

____

(Signature of agent)

____

(Print name of agent)

(b) Nothing in subdivision (a) invalidates any transaction in which a third person relied in good faith on the authority created by the durable power of attorney.

(c) This section does not apply to a statutory form power of attorney under Part 3 (commencing with Section 4400).

(Stats. 1994 (S.B. 1907), ch. 307, §16. Amended by Stats. 1999 (A.B. 891), ch. 658, §32, effective July 1, 2000; Stats. 2000 (S.B. 1869), ch. 999, §1.)

§4129. Springing power of attorney: definition and effectiveness

(a) In a springing power of attorney, the principal may designate one or more persons who, by a written declaration under penalty of perjury, have the power to determine conclusively that the specified event or contingency has occurred. The principal may designate the attorney-in-fact or another person to perform this function, either alone or jointly with other persons.

(b) A springing power of attorney containing the designation described in subdivision (a) becomes effective when the person or persons designated in the power of attorney execute a written declaration under penalty of perjury that the specified event or contingency has occurred, and any person may act in reliance on the written declaration without liability to the principal or to any other person, regardless of whether the specified event or contingency has actually occurred.

(c) This section applies to a power of attorney whether executed before, on, or after January 1, 1991, if the power of attorney contains the designation described in subdivision (a).

(d) This section does not provide the exclusive method by which a power of attorney may be limited to take effect on the occurrence of a specified event or contingency.

(Stats. 1994 (S.B. 1907), ch. 307, §16.)

§4130. Validity of multiple powers of attorney

(a) If a principal grants inconsistent authority to one or more attorneys-in-fact in two or more powers of attorney, the authority granted last controls to the extent of the inconsistency.

(b) This section is not subject to limitation in the power of attorney.

(Stats. 1994 (S.B. 1907), ch. 307, §16.)

C. Modification and Revocation of Powers of Attorney

§4150. Conditions for modifications of powers of attorney

(a) A principal may modify a power of attorney as follows:

(1) In accordance with the terms of the power of attorney.

(2) By an instrument executed in the same manner as a power of attorney may be executed.

(b) An attorney-in-fact or third person who does not have notice of the modification is protected from liability as provided in Chapter 5 (commencing with Section 4300).

(Stats. 1994 (S.B. 1907), ch. 307, §16. Amended by Stats. 1995 (S.B. 984), ch. 300, §4, effective August 3, 1995.)

§4151. Revocation of power of attorney

(a) A principal may revoke a power of attorney as follows:

(1) In accordance with the terms of the power of attorney.

(2) By a writing. This paragraph is not subject to limitation in the power of attorney.

(b) An attorney-in-fact or third person who does not have notice of the revocation is protected from liability as provided in Chapter 5 (commencing with Section 4300).

(Stats. 1994 (S.B. 1907), ch. 307, §16. Amended by Stats. 1995, ch. 300 (S.B. 984), ch. 300, §5, effective August 3, 1995.)

§4152. Events that terminate authority of attorney-in-fact

(a) Subject to subdivision (b), the authority of an attorney-in-fact under a power of attorney is terminated by any of the following events:

(1) In accordance with the terms of the power of attorney.

(2) Extinction of the subject or fulfillment of the purpose of the power of attorney.

(3) Revocation of the attorney-in-fact's authority, as provided in Section 4153.

(4) Death of the principal, except as to specific authority permitted by statute to be exercised after the principal's death.

(5) Removal of the attorney-in-fact.

(6) Resignation of the attorney-in-fact.

(7) Incapacity of the attorney-in-fact, except that a temporary incapacity suspends the attorney-in-fact's authority only during the period of the incapacity.

(8) Dissolution or annulment of the marriage of the attorney-in-fact and principal, as provided in Section 4154.

(9) Death of the attorney-in-fact.

(b) An attorney-in-fact or third person who does not have notice of an event that terminates the power of attorney or the authority of an attorney-in-fact is protected from liability as provided in Chapter 5 (commencing with Section 4300).

(Stats. 1994 (S.B. 1907), ch. 307, §16. Amended by Stats. 1995, ch. 300 (S.B. 984), ch. 300, §6, effective August 3, 1995.)

§4153. Methods of revocation of authority of attorney-in-fact

(a) The authority of an attorney-in-fact under a power of attorney may be revoked as follows:

(1) In accordance with the terms of the power of attorney.

(2) Where the principal informs the attorney-in-fact orally or in writing that the attorney-in-fact's authority is revoked or when and under what circumstances it is revoked. This paragraph is not subject to limitation in the power of attorney.

(3) Where the principal's legal representative, with approval of the court as provided in Section 4206, informs the attorney-in-fact in writing that the attorney-in-fact's authority is revoked or when and under what circumstances it is revoked. This paragraph is not subject to limitation in the power of attorney.

(b) An attorney-in-fact or third person who does not have notice of the revocation is protected from liability as provided in Chapter 5 (commencing with Section 4300).

(Stats. 1994 (S.B. 1907), ch. 307, §16. Amended by Stats. 1995, ch. 300 (S.B. 984), ch. 300, §6, effective August 3, 1995.)

§4154. Effect of principal's dissolution or annulment on designation of spouse as attorney-in-fact

(a) If after executing a power of attorney the principal's marriage to the attorney-in-fact is dissolved or annulled, the principal's designation of the former spouse as an attorney-in-fact is revoked.

(b) If the attorney-in-fact's authority is revoked solely by subdivision (a), it is revived by the principal's remarriage to the attorney-in-fact.

(Stats. 1994 (S.B. 1907), ch. 307, §16.)

§4155. Effect of incapacity of principal under a nondurable power of attorney: notice of incapacity, extent of liability

(a) Subject to subdivision (b), the authority of an attorney-in-fact under a nondurable power of attorney is terminated by the incapacity of the principal to contract.

(b) An attorney-in-fact or third person who does not have notice of the incapacity of the principal is protected from liability as provided in Chapter 5 (commencing with Section 4300).

(c) This section is not subject to limitation in the power of attorney.

(Stats. 1994 (S.B. 1907), ch. 307, §16. Amended by Stats. 1995 (S.B. 984), ch. 300, §6, effective August 3, 1995.)

D. Attorneys-in-Fact

1. Qualifications and Authority

§4200. Attorney-in-fact must have capacity to contract

Only a person having the capacity to contract is qualified to act as an attorney-in-fact.

(Stats. 1994 (S.B. 1907), ch. 307, §16.)

§4201. Unqualified person not relieved of duties

Designating an unqualified person as an attorney-in-fact does not affect the immunities of third persons nor relieve the unqualified person of any applicable duties to the principal or the principal's successors.

(Stats. 1994 (S.B. 1907), ch. 307, §16.)

§4202. Authority and liability of multiple attorneys-in-fact

(a) A principal may designate more than one attorney-in-fact in one or more powers of attorney.

(b) Authority granted to two or more attorneys-in-fact is exercisable only by their unanimous action.

(c) If a vacancy occurs, the remaining attorneys-in-fact may exercise the authority conferred as if they are the only attorneys-in-fact.

(d) If an attorney-in-fact is unavailable because of absence, illness, or other temporary incapacity, the other attorneys-in-fact may exercise the authority under the power of attorney as if they are the only attorneys-in-fact, where necessary to accomplish the purposes of the power of attorney or to avoid irreparable injury to the principal's interests.

(e) An attorney-in-fact is not liable for the actions of other attorneys-in-fact, unless the attorney-in-fact participates in, knowingly acquiesces in, or conceals a breach of fiduciary duty committed by another attorney-in-fact.

(Stats. 1994 (S.B. 1907), ch. 307, §16.)

§4203. Principal may designate successor attorneys-in-fact

(a) A principal may designate one or more successor attorneys-in-fact to act if the authority of a predecessor attorney-in-fact terminates.

(b) The principal may grant authority to another person, designated by name, by office, or by function, including the initial and any successor attorneysin fact, to designate at any time one or more successor attorneys-in-fact.

(c) A successor attorney-in-fact is not liable for the actions of the predecessor attorney-in-fact.

(Stats. 1994 (S.B. 1907), ch. 307, §16. Amended by Stats. 1999 (A.B. 891), ch. 658, §33, effective July 1, 2000.)

§4204. Compensation and reimbursement

An attorney-in-fact is entitled to reasonable compensation for services rendered to the principal as attorney-in-fact and to reimbursement for reasonable expenses incurred as a result of acting as attorney-in-fact.

(Stats. 1994 (S.B. 1907), ch. 307, §16.)

§4205. Attorney-in-fact may delegate authority

(a) An attorney-in-fact may revocably delegate authority to perform mechanical acts to one or more persons qualified to exercise the authority delegated.

(b) The attorney-in-fact making a delegation remains responsible to the principal for the exercise or nonexercise of the delegated authority.

(Stats. 1994 (S.B. 1907), ch. 307, §16.)

§4206. Attorney-in-fact may be liable to court-appointed fiduciary as well as principal

(a) If, following execution of a durable power of attorney, a court of the principal's domicile appoints a conservator of the estate, guardian of the estate, or other fiduciary charged with the management of all of the principal's property or all of the principal's property except specified exclusions, the attorney-in-fact is accountable to the fiduciary as well as to the principal. Except as provided in subdivision (b), the fiduciary has the same power to revoke or amend the durable power of attorney that the principal would have had if not incapacitated, subject to any required court approval.

(b) If a conservator of the estate is appointed by a court of this state, the conservator can revoke or amend the durable power of attorney only if the court in which the conservatorship proceeding is pending has first made an order authorizing or requiring the fiduciary to modify or revoke the durable power of attorney and the modification or revocation is in accord with the order.

(c) This section is not subject to limitation in the power of attorney.

(Stats. 1994 (S.B. 1907), ch. 307, §16. Amended by Stats. 1999 (A.B. 891), ch. 658, §34, effective July 1, 2000.)

§4207. Methods of resignation

(a) An attorney-in-fact may resign by any of the following means:

(1) If the principal is competent, by giving notice to the principal.

(2) If a conservator has been appointed, by giving notice to the conservator.

(3) On written agreement of a successor who is designated in the power of attorney or pursuant to the terms of the power of attorney to serve as attorney-in-fact.

(4) Pursuant to a court order.

(b) This section is not subject to limitation in the power of attorney.

(Stats. 1994 (S.B. 1907), ch. 307, §16.)

2. Duties of Attorneys-in-Fact

§4230. Limitations on duty of attorney-in-fact to exercise authority

(a) Except as provided in subdivisions (b) and (c), a person who is designated as an attorney-in-fact has no duty to exercise the authority granted in the power of attorney and is not subject to the other duties of an attorney-in-fact, regardless of whether the principal has become incapacitated, is missing, or is otherwise unable to act.

(b) Acting for the principal in one or more transactions does not obligate an attorney-in-fact to act for the principal in a subsequent transaction, but the attorney-in-fact has a duty to complete a transaction that the attorney-in-fact has commenced.

(c) If an attorney-in-fact has expressly agreed in writing to act for the principal, the attorney-in-fact has a duty to act pursuant to the terms of the agreement. The agreement to act on behalf of the principal is enforceable against the attorney-in-fact as a fiduciary regardless of whether there is any consideration to support a contractual obligation.

(Stats. 1994 (S.B. 1907), ch. 307, §16.)

§4231. Standard of care in dealing with principal's property

(a) Except as provided in subdivisions (b) and (c), in dealing with property of the principal, an attorney-in-fact shall observe the standard of care that would be observed by a prudent person dealing with property of another and is not limited by any other statute restricting investments by fiduciaries.

(b) If an attorney-in-fact is not compensated, the attorney-in-fact is not liable for a loss to the principal's property unless the loss results from the attorney-in-fact's bad faith, intentional wrongdoing, or gross negligence.

(c) An attorney-in-fact who has special skills or expertise or was designated as an attorney-in-fact on the basis of representations of special skills or expertise shall observe the standard of care that would be observed by others with similar skills or expertise.

(Stats. 1994 (S.B. 1907), ch. 307, §16.)

§4232. Duty to avoid conflicts of interest

(a) An attorney-in-fact has a duty to act solely in the interest of the principal and to avoid conflicts of interest.

(b) An attorney-in-fact is not in violation of the duty provided in subdivision (a) solely because the attorney-in-fact also benefits from acting for the principal, has conflicting interests in relation to the property, care, or affairs of the principal, or acts in an inconsistent manner regarding the respective interests of the principal and the attorney-in-fact.

(Stats. 1994, ch. 307 (S.B. 1907), §16.)

§4233. Duty to keep principal's property separate and distinct from other property

(a) The attorney-in-fact shall keep the principal's property separate and distinct from other property in a manner adequate to identify the property clearly as belonging to the principal.

(b) An attorney-in-fact holding property for a principal complies with subdivision (a) if the property is held in the name of the principal or in the name of the attorney-in-fact as attorney-in-fact for the principal.

(Stats. 1994 (S.B. 1907), ch. 307, §16.)

§4234. Duty to keep regular contact and communicate with principal

(a) To the extent reasonably practicable under the circumstances, an attorney infact has a duty to keep in regular contact with the principal, to communicate with the principal, and to follow the instructions of the principal.

(b) With court approval, the attorney-in-fact may disobey instructions of the principal.

(Stats. 1994 (S.B. 1907), ch. 307, §16.)

§4235. Consultation regarding principal's incapacity

If the principal becomes wholly or partially incapacitated, or if there is a question concerning the capacity of the principal to give instructions to and supervise the attorney-in-fact, the attorney-in-fact may consult with a person previously designated by the principal for this purpose, and may also consult with and obtain information needed to carry out the attorney-in-fact's duties from the principal's spouse, physician, attorney, accountant, a member of the principal's family, or other person, business entity, or government agency with respect to matters to be undertaken on the principal's behalf and affecting the principal's personal affairs, welfare, family, property, and business interests. A person from whom information is requested shall disclose relevant information to the attorney-in-fact. Disclosure under this section is not a waiver of any privilege that may apply to the information disclosed.

(Stats. 1994 (S.B. 1907), ch. 307, §16.)

§4236. Duty to keep records and limited duty to make account of transactions

(a) The attorney-in-fact shall keep records of all transactions entered into by the attorney-in-fact on behalf of the principal.

(b) The attorney-in-fact does not have a duty to make an account of transactions entered into on behalf of the principal, except in the following circumstances:

(1) At any time requested by the principal.

(2) Where the power of attorney requires the attorney-in-fact to account and specifies to whom the account is to be made.

(3) On request by the conservator of the estate of the principal while the principal is living.

(4) On request by the principal's personal representative or successor in interest after the death of the principal.

(5) Pursuant to court order.

(c) The following persons are entitled to examine and copy the records kept by the attorney-in-fact:

(1) The principal.

(2) The conservator of the estate of the principal while the principal is living.

(3) The principal's personal representative or successor in interest after the death of the principal.

(4) Any other person, pursuant to court order.

(d) This section is not subject to limitation in the power of attorney.

(Stats. 1994 (S.B. 1907), ch. 307, §16.)

§4237. Duty to apply special skills

An attorney-in-fact with special skills has a duty to apply the full extent of those skills.

(Stats. 1994 (S.B. 1907), ch. 307, §16.)

§4238. Duty to deliver property and records upon termination of authority

(a) On termination of an attorney-in-fact's authority, the attorney-in-fact shall promptly deliver possession or control of the principal's property as follows:

(1) If the principal is not incapacitated, to the principal or as directed by the principal.

(2) If the principal is incapacitated, to the following persons with the following priority:

(A) To a qualified successor attorney-in-fact.

(B) As to any community property, to the principal's spouse.

(C) To the principal's conservator of the estate or guardian of the estate.

(3) In the case of the death of the principal, to the principal's personal representative, if any, or the principal's successors.

(b) On termination of an attorney-in-fact's authority, the attorney-in-fact shall deliver copies of any records relating to transactions undertaken on the principal's behalf that are requested by the person to whom possession or control of the property is delivered.

(c) Termination of an attorney-in-fact's authority does not relieve the attorney-in-fact of any duty to render an account of actions taken as attorney infact.

(d) The attorney-in-fact has the powers reasonably necessary under the circumstances to perform the duties provided by this section.

(Stats. 1994 (S.B. 1907), ch. 307, §16.)

3. Authority of Attorneys-in-Fact

The principal's designation of the power provides the extent of the agent's authority. The principal can grant general authority without limitation (Cal. Prob. Code §4261). However, certain acts must be expressly authorized, such as the creation, modification, or revocation of a trust (Cal. Prob. Code §4264(a)); funding a trust with the principal's property (Cal. Prob. Code §4264(b)); making or revoking a gift of the principal's property (Cal. Prob. Code §4264(c)); exercising the principal's right to disclaim a property interest (Cal. Prob. Code §4264(d)); creating or changing survivorship interests in the principal's property (Cal. Prob. Code

§4264(e)); designating or changing the designation of beneficiaries to receive any property, benefit, or contract right on the principal's death (Cal. Prob. Code §4264(f)); and making a loan to the attorney-in-fact (Cal. Prob. Code §4264(g)). Ross & Grant, Cal. Prob. Prac., *supra*, §1:57.2. Note that a power of attorney may not authorize an attorney-in-fact to "make, publish, declare, amend or revoke the principal's will" (Cal. Prob. Code §4265).

California case law recognizes a limited exception to the rule requiring express authorization for certain acts. An "amanuensis rule" provides that where the grantor gives express authority to the signing of the grantor's name to a deed, the person signing the grantor's name is not deemed an agent but rather is regarded as a mere tool or instrument (or amanuensis) of the grantor so that the signature is deemed to be that of the grantor. The rule applies when an agent, acting with mechanical and not discretionary authority, signs an instrument outside of the principal's presence. In Estate of Stephens, 122 Cal. Rptr. 2d 358 (Cal. 2002), a decedent orally instructed his daughter to sign his name on a grant deed that vested title to his residence in himself and her as joint tenants. She did so outside of his presence, and he later ratified the conveyance. The court held that the deed was valid because the daughter-as-signatory was acting merely as amanuensis.

§4260. Application; exclusion regarding statutory form powers

This article does not apply to statutory form powers of attorney under Part 3 (commencing with Section 4400).

(Stats. 1994 (S.B. 1907), ch. 307, §16. Amended by Stats. 1999 (A.B. 891), ch. 658, §35, effective July 1, 2000.)

§4261. "General authority," defined

If a power of attorney grants general authority to an attorney-in-fact and is not limited to one or more express actions, subjects, or purposes for which general authority is conferred, the attorney-in-fact has all the authority to act that a person having the capacity to contract may carry out through an attorney-in-fact specifically authorized to take the action.

(Stats. 1994 (S.B. 1907), ch. 307, §16.)

§4262. "Limited authority," defined

Subject to this article, if a power of attorney grants limited authority to an attorney-in-fact, the attorney-in-fact has the following authority:

(a) The authority granted in the power of attorney, as limited with respect to permissible actions, subjects, or purposes.

(b) The authority incidental, necessary, or proper to carry out the granted authority.

(Stats. 1994 (S.B. 1907), ch. 307, §16.)

§4263. Power of attorney may incorporate by reference other statutes

(a) A power of attorney may grant authority to the attorney-in-fact by incorporating powers by reference to another statute, including, but not limited to, the following:

(1) Powers of attorneys-in-fact provided by the Uniform Statutory Form Power of Attorney Act (Part 3 (commencing with Section 4400)).

(2) Powers of guardians and conservators provided by Chapter 5 (commencing with Section 2350) and Chapter 6 (commencing with Section 2400) of Part 4 of Division 4.

(3) Powers of trustees provided by Chapter 2 (commencing with Section 16200) of Part 4 of Division 9.

(b) Incorporation by reference to another statute includes any amendments made to the incorporated provisions after the date of execution of the power of attorney.

(Stats. 1994 (S.B. 1907), ch. 307, §16.)

§4264. Certain acts require express authorization in power of attorney

A power of attorney may not be construed to grant authority to an attorney-in-fact to perform any of the following acts unless expressly authorized in the power of attorney:

(a) Create, modify, or revoke a trust.

(b) Fund with the principal's property a trust not created by the principal or a person authorized to create a trust on behalf of the principal.

(c) Make or revoke a gift of the principal's property in trust or otherwise.

(d) Exercise the right to make a disclaimer on behalf of the principal. This subdivision does not limit the attorney-in-fact's authority to disclaim a detrimental transfer to the principal with the approval of the court.

(e) Create or change survivorship interests in the principal's property or in property in which the principal may have an interest.

(f) Designate or change the designation of beneficiaries to receive any property, benefit, or contract right on the principal's death.

(g) Make a loan to the attorney-in-fact.
(Stats. 1994 (S.B. 1907), ch. 307, §16.)

§4265. Certain acts may not be authorized by power of attorney

A power of attorney may not authorize an attorney-in-fact to make, publish, declare, amend, or revoke the principal's will.
(Stats. 1994 (S.B. 1907), ch. 307, §16. Amended by Stats. 1999 (A.B. 891), ch. 658, §36, effective July 1, 2000.)

§4266. Grant of authority does not require exercise of that authority; fiduciary duties

The grant of authority to an attorney-in-fact, whether by the power of attorney, by statute, or by the court, does not in itself require or permit the exercise of the power. The exercise of authority by an attorney-in-fact is subject to the attorney-in-fact's fiduciary duties.
(Stats. 1994 (S.B. 1907), ch. 307, §16.)

E. Relations with Third Persons

§4300. Third parties shall accord attorney-in-fact same rights and privileges of principal

A third person shall accord an attorney-in-fact acting pursuant to the provisions of a power of attorney the same rights and privileges that would be accorded the principal if the principal were personally present and seeking to act. However, a third person is not required to honor the attorney-in-fact's authority or conduct business with the attorney-in-fact if the principal cannot require the third person to act or conduct business in the same circumstances.
(Stats. 1994 (S.B. 1907), ch. 307, §16.)

§4301. Third party may rely on attorney-in-fact's acts, transactions or decisions

A third person may rely on, contract with, and deal with an attorney-in-fact with respect to the subjects and purposes encompassed or expressed in the power of attorney without regard to whether the power of attorney expressly authorizes the specific act, transaction, or decision by the attorney-in-fact.
(Stats. 1994 (S.B. 1907), ch. 307, §16.)

§4302. Third party may require attorney-in-fact to provide identification, signature specimens and other information

When requested to engage in transactions with an attorney-in-fact, a third person, before incurring any duty to comply with the power of attorney, may require the attorney-in-fact to provide identification, specimens of the signatures of the principal and the attorney-in-fact, and any other information reasonably necessary or appropriate to identify the principal and the attorney infact and to facilitate the actions of the third person in transacting business with the attorney-in-fact. A third person may require an attorney-in-fact to provide the current and permanent residence addresses of the principal before agreeing to engage in a transaction with the attorney-in-fact.
(Stats. 1994 (S.B. 1907), ch. 307, §16.)

§4303. Third party is not liable to principal or another for good faith reliance on power of attorney

(a) A third person who acts in good faith reliance on a power of attorney is not liable to the principal or to any other person for so acting if all of the following requirements are satisfied:

(1) The power of attorney is presented to the third person by the attorney-in-fact designated in the power of attorney.

(2) The power of attorney appears on its face to be valid.

(3) The power of attorney includes a notary public's certificate of acknowledgment or is signed by two witnesses.

(b) Nothing in this section is intended to create an implication that a third person is liable for acting in reliance on a power of attorney under circumstances where the requirements of subdivision (a) are not satisfied. Nothing in this section affects any immunity that may otherwise exist apart from this section.
(Stats. 1994 (S.B. 1907), ch. 307, §16.)

§4304. Death or incapacity of principal does not revoke agency as to either agent or third party who acts in good faith and without actual knowledge of principal's death

(a) The death of a principal who has executed a power of attorney, whether durable or nondurable, does not revoke or terminate the agency as to the attorney-in-fact or a third person who, without actual knowledge of the principal's death, acts in good faith under the power of attorney. Any action so taken, unless otherwise invalid or unenforceable, binds the principal's successors in interest.

(b) The incapacity of a principal who has previously executed a nondurable power of attorney does not revoke or terminate the agency as to the attorney-in-fact or a third

person who, without actual knowledge of the incapacity of the principal, acts in good faith under the power of attorney. Any action so taken, unless otherwise invalid or unenforceable, binds the principal and the principal's successors in interest.
(Stats. 1994 (S.B. 1907), ch. 307, §16.)

§4305. Affidavit stating that acts were undertaken without knowledge of revoked power or principal's death or incapacity is conclusive proof of nonrevocation or nontermination of power

(a) As to acts undertaken in good faith reliance thereon, an affidavit executed by the attorney-in-fact under a power of attorney, whether durable or nondurable, stating that, at the time of the exercise of the power, the attorney-in-fact did not have actual knowledge of the termination of the power of attorney or the attorney-in-fact's authority by revocation or of the principal's death or incapacity is conclusive proof of the nonrevocation or nontermination of the power at that time. If the exercise of the power of attorney requires execution and delivery of any instrument that is recordable, the affidavit when authenticated for record is likewise recordable.

(b) This section does not affect any provision in a power of attorney for its termination by expiration of time or occurrence of an event other than express revocation or a change in the principal's capacity.
(Stats. 1994 (S.B. 1907), ch. 307, §16.)

§4306. Liability for refusal to accept attorney-in-fact's authority referred to in affidavit

(a) If an attorney-in-fact furnishes an affidavit pursuant to Section 4305, whether voluntarily or on demand, a third person dealing with the attorney-in-fact who refuses to accept the exercise of the attorney-in-fact's authority referred to in the affidavit is liable for attorney's fees incurred in an action or proceeding necessary to confirm the attorney-in-fact's qualifications or authority, unless the court determines that the third person believed in good faith that the attorney-in-fact was not qualified or was attempting to exceed or improperly exercise the attorney-in-fact's authority.

(b) The failure of a third person to demand an affidavit pursuant to Section 4305 does not affect the protection provided the third person by this chapter, and no inference as to whether a third person has acted in good faith may be drawn from the failure to demand an affidavit from the attorney-in-fact.
(Stats. 1994 (S.B. 1907), ch. 307, §16.)

§4307. Certified copy of power of attorney has same effect as original power of attorney

(a) A copy of a power of attorney certified under this section has the same force and effect as the original power of attorney.

(b) A copy of a power of attorney may be certified by any of the following:

(1) An attorney authorized to practice law in this state.

(2) A notary public in this state.

(3) An official of a state or of a political subdivision who is authorized to make certifications.

(c) The certification shall state that the certifying person has examined the original power of attorney and the copy and that the copy is a true and correct copy of the original power of attorney.

(d) Nothing in this section is intended to create an implication that a third person may be liable for acting in good faith reliance on a copy of a power of attorney that has not been certified under this section.
(Stats. 1994 (S.B. 1907), ch. 307, §16. Amended by Stats. 1995 (S.B. 984), ch. 300, §9, effective August 3, 1995.)

§4308. Knowledge of third parties conducting activities through employees

(a) A third person who conducts activities through employees is not charged under this chapter with actual knowledge of any fact relating to a power of attorney, nor of a change in the authority of an attorney-in-fact, unless both of the following requirements are satisfied:

(1) The information is received at a home office or a place where there is an employee with responsibility to act on the information.

(2) The employee has a reasonable time in which to act on the information using the procedure and facilities that are available to the third person in the regular course of its operations.

(b) Knowledge of an employee in one branch or office of an entity that conducts business through branches or multiple offices is not attributable to an employee in another branch or office.
(Stats. 1994 (S.B. 1907), ch. 307, §16.)

§4309. Third parties need not engage in future transactions with attorneys-in-fact if latter has breached prior agreements

Nothing in this chapter requires a third person to engage in any transaction with an attorney-in-fact if the attorney-in-

fact has previously breached any agreement with the third person.
(Stats. 1994 (S.B. 1907), ch. 307, §16.)

§4310. Financial institution need not open deposit account for, or make loan to, attorney-in-fact if principal is not a customer

Without limiting the generality of Section 4300, nothing in this chapter requires a financial institution to open a deposit account for a principal at the request of an attorney-in-fact if the principal is not currently a depositor of the financial institution or to make a loan to the attorney-in-fact on the principal's behalf if the principal is not currently a borrower of the financial institution.
(Stats. 1994 (S.B. 1907), ch. 307, §16.)

F. Uniform Statutory Form Power of Attorney

As explained above, USPAA provides a form for powers of attorney that any principal may use to designate an agent. A person must fill in blank spaces in order to designate the name of the principal and agent, and execute this form by the addition of signatures and a notarial attestation.

The statutory form includes a list of transactions that any principal can choose in order to delegate powers to an agent. The principal need only initial the transaction categories (such as "real property transactions" and/or "tangible personal property transactions") for an agent to conduct. If the principal wishes to execute a general power of attorney, the principal can specify one general category that incorporates all 15 categories of transactions. USPAA also specifies the authority of an agent under each of the 15 categories of transactions.

§4400. Uniform Statutory Form Power of Attorney Act

This part may be cited as the Uniform Statutory Form Power of Attorney Act.
(Stats. 1994 (S.B. 1907), ch. 307, §16.)

§4401. Statutory form

The following statutory form power of attorney is legally sufficient when the requirements of Section 4402 are satisfied:

UNIFORM STATUTORY FORM
POWER OF ATTORNEY
(California Probate Code Section 4401)

NOTICE: THE POWERS GRANTED BY THIS DOCUMENT ARE BROAD AND SWEEPING. THEY ARE EXPLAINED IN THE UNIFORM STATUTORY FORM POWER OF ATTORNEY ACT (CALIFORNIA PROBATE CODE SECTIONS 4400-4465). IF YOU HAVE ANY QUESTIONS ABOUT THESE POWERS, OBTAIN COMPETENT LEGAL ADVICE. THIS DOCUMENT DOES NOT AUTHORIZE ANYONE TO

MAKE MEDICAL AND OTHER HEALTH-CARE DECISIONS FOR YOU. YOU MAY REVOKE THIS POWER OF ATTORNEY IF YOU LATER WISH TO DO SO.

I ____
(your name and address)

appoint ____
(name and address of the person appointed, or of each person appointed if you want to designate more than one)

as my agent (attorney-in-fact) to act for me in any lawful way with respect to the following initialed subjects:

TO GRANT ALL OF THE FOLLOWING POWERS, INITIAL THE LINE IN FRONT OF (N) AND IGNORE THE LINES IN FRONT OF THE OTHER POWERS.
TO GRANT ONE OR MORE, BUT FEWER THAN ALL, OF THE FOLLOWING POWERS, INITIAL THE LINE IN FRONT OF EACH POWER YOU ARE GRANTING.

TO WITHHOLD A POWER, DO NOT INITIAL THE LINE IN FRONT OF IT. YOU MAY, BUT NEED NOT, CROSS OUT EACH POWER WITHHELD.

INITIAL
_____ (A) Real property transactions.
_____ (B) Tangible personal property transactions.
_____ (C) Stock and bond transactions.
_____ (D) Commodity and option transactions.
_____ (E) Banking and other financial institution transactions.
_____ (F) Business operating transactions.
_____ (G) Insurance and annuity transactions.
_____ (H) Estate, trust, and other beneficiary transac- tions.
_____ (I) Claims and litigation.
_____ (J) Personal and family maintenance.

_____ (K) Benefits from social security, medicare, medicaid, or other governmental programs, or civil or military service.
_____ (L) Retirement plan transactions.
_____ (M) Tax matters.
_____ (N) ALL OF THE POWERS LISTED ABOVE.

YOU NEED NOT INITIAL ANY OTHER LINES IF YOU INITIAL LINE (N).

SPECIAL INSTRUCTIONS:

ON THE FOLLOWING LINES YOU MAY GIVE SPECIAL INSTRUCTIONS LIMITING OR EXTENDING THE POWERS GRANTED TO YOUR AGENT.

____
____
____
____
____
____
____
____

UNLESS YOU DIRECT OTHERWISE ABOVE, THIS POWER OF ATTORNEY IS EFFECTIVE IMMEDIATELY AND WILL CONTINUE UNTIL IT IS REVOKED.

This power of attorney will continue to be effective even though I become incapacitated.

STRIKE THE PRECEDING SENTENCE IF YOU DO NOT WANT THIS POWER OF ATTORNEY TO CONTINUE IF YOU BECOME INCAPACITATED.

EXERCISE OF POWER OF ATTORNEY WHERE MORE THAN ONE AGENT DESIGNATED

If I have designated more than one agent, the agents are to act

____

IF YOU APPOINTED MORE THAN ONE AGENT AND YOU WANT EACH AGENT TO BE ABLE TO ACT ALONE WITHOUT THE OTHER AGENT JOINING, WRITE THE WORD "SEPARATELY" IN THE BLANK SPACE ABOVE. IF YOU DO NOT INSERT ANY WORD IN THE BLANK SPACE, OR IF YOU INSERT THE WORD "JOINTLY", THEN ALL OF YOUR AGENTS MUST ACT OR SIGN TOGETHER.

I agree that any third party who receives a copy of this document may act under it. A third party may seek identification. Revocation of the power of attorney is not effective as to a third party until the third party has actual knowledge of the revocation. I agree to indemnify the third party for any claims that arise against the third party because of reliance on this power of attorney.

Signed this ___ day of _________, 19___

____

(your signature)

State of ____________ County of __________________

BY ACCEPTING OR ACTING UNDER THE APPOINTMENT, THE AGENT ASSUMES THE FIDUCIARY AND OTHER LEGAL RESPONSIBILITIES OF AN AGENT.

[Include certificate of acknowledgment of notary public in compliance with Section 1189 of the Civil Code or other applicable law.]

(Stats. 1994 (S.B. 1907), ch. 307, §16. Amended by Stats. 2005 (S.B. 158), ch. 251, §1.)

§4402. Conditions for legal sufficiency of statutory form

A statutory form power of attorney under this part is legally sufficient if all of the following requirements are satisfied:

(a) The wording of the form complies substantially with Section 4401. A form does not fail to comply substantially with Section 4401 merely because the form does not include the provisions of Section 4401 relating to designation of co-agents. A form does not fail to comply substantially with Section 4401 merely because the form uses the sentence "Revocation of the power of attorney is not effective as to a third party until the third party learns of the revocation" in place of the sentence "Revocation of the power of attorney is not effective as to a third party until the third party has actual knowledge of the revocation," in which case the form shall be interpreted as if it contained the sentence "Revocation of the power of attorney is not effective as to a third party until the third party has actual knowledge of the revocation."

(b) The form is properly completed.

(c) The signature of the principal is acknowledged.

(Stats. 1994 (S.B. 1907), ch. 307, §16. Amended by Stats. 1995, ch. 300 (S.B. 984), ch. 300, §10, effective August 3, 1995.)

§4403. Limitation of powers on form

If the line in front of (N) of the statutory form under Section 4401 is initialed, an initial on the line in front of any other power does not limit the powers granted by line (N)

(Stats. 1994 (S.B. 1907), ch. 307, §16.)

§4404. Language showing principal's intent to render power of attorney as durable

A statutory form power of attorney legally sufficient under this part is durable to the extent that the power of attorney contains language, such as "This power of attorney will continue to be effective even though I become incapacitated," showing the intent of the principal that the power granted may be exercised notwithstanding later incapacity.

(Stats. 1994 (S.B. 1907), ch. 307, §16.)

§4405. Statutory form may contain provision designating person to determine occurrence of event or contingency

(a) A statutory form power of attorney under this part that limits the power to take effect upon the occurrence of a specified event or contingency, including, but not limited to, the incapacity of the principal, may contain a provision designating one or more persons who, by a written declaration under penalty of perjury, have the power to determine conclusively that the specified event or contingency has occurred.

(b) A statutory form power of attorney that contains the provision described in subdivision (a) becomes effective when the person or persons designated in the power of attorney execute a written declaration under penalty of perjury that the specified event or contingency has occurred, and any person may act in reliance on the written declaration without liability to the principal or to any other person, regardless whether the specified event or contingency has actually occurred.

(c) The provision described in subdivision (a) may be included in the "Special Instructions" portion of the form set forth in Section 4401.

(d) Subdivisions (a) and (b) do not provide the exclusive method by which a statutory form power of attorney under this part may be limited to take effect upon the occurrence of a specified event or contingency.

(Stats. 1994 (S.B. 1907), ch. 307, §16.)

§4406. Third person may be compelled to honor agent's authority under power of attorney; attorney's fees

(a) If a third person to whom a properly executed statutory form power of attorney under this part is presented refuses to honor the agent's authority under the power of attorney within a reasonable time, the third person may be compelled to honor the agent's authority under the power of attorney in an action brought against the third person for this purpose, except that the third person may not be compelled to honor the agent's authority if the principal could not compel the third person to act in the same circumstances.

(b) If an action is brought under this section, the court shall award attorney's fees to the agent if the court finds that the third person acted unreasonably in refusing to accept the agent's authority under the statutory form power of attorney.

(c) For the purpose of subdivision (b), and without limiting any other grounds that may constitute a reasonable refusal to accept an agent's authority under a statutory form power of attorney, a third person shall not be deemed to have acted unreasonably in refusing to accept an agent's authority if the refusal is authorized or required by state or federal statute or regulation.

(d) Notwithstanding subdivision (c), a third person's refusal to accept an agent's authority under a statutory form power of attorney under this part shall be deemed unreasonable if the only reason for the refusal is that the power of attorney is not on a form prescribed by the third person to whom the power of attorney is presented.

(e) The remedy provided in this section is cumulative and nonexclusive.

(Stats. 1994 (S.B. 1907), ch. 307, §16.)

§4407. Application of Division to statutory form power of attorney

Unless there is a conflicting provision in this part, in which case the provision of this part governs, the other provisions of this division apply to a statutory form power of attorney.

(Stats. 1994 (S.B. 1907), ch. 307, §16.)

§4408. Other forms may be used but none of provisions of this Part apply to other forms

Nothing in this part affects or limits the use of any other form for a power of attorney. A form that complies with the requirements of any law other than the provisions of this part may be used instead of the form set forth in Section 4401, and none of the provisions of this part apply if the other form is used.

(Stats. 1994 (S.B. 1907), ch. 307, §16.)

§4409. Validity of statutory short form powers of attorney executed under prior law

(a) A statutory short form power of attorney executed before, on, or after the repeal of Chapter 3 (commencing with Section 2450) of Title 9 of Part 4 of Division 3 of the Civil Code by Chapter 986 of the Statutes of 1990, using a form that complied with former Section 2450 of the Civil Code, as originally enacted by Chapter 602 of the Statutes of 1984, or as amended by Chapter 403 of the Statutes of 1985, is as valid as if Chapter 3 (commencing with Section 2450) of Title 9 of

Part 4 of Division 3 of the Civil Code had not been repealed by, and former Section 2511 of the Civil Code amended by, Chapter 986 of the Statutes of 1990.

(b) A statutory form power of attorney executed before, on, or after the repeal of Chapter 3.5 (commencing with Section 2475) of Title 9 of Part 4 of Division 3 of the Civil Code by the act that enacted this section, using a form that complied with the repealed chapter of the Civil Code is as valid as if that chapter had not been repealed.

(Stats. 1994 (S.B. 1907), ch. 307, §16. Amended by Stats. 1995 (S.B. 984), ch. 300, §11, effective August 3, 1995.)

§4450. Powers covered by statutory form power of attorney

By executing a statutory form power of attorney with respect to a subject listed in Section 4401, the principal, except as limited or extended by the principal in the power of attorney, empowers the agent, for that subject, to do all of the following:

(a) Demand, receive, and obtain by litigation or otherwise, money or other thing of value to which the principal is, may become, or claims to be entitled, and conserve, invest, disburse, or use anything so received for the purposes intended.

(b) Contract in any manner with any person, on terms agreeable to the agent, to accomplish a purpose of a transaction, and perform, rescind, reform, release, or modify the contract or another contract made by or on behalf of the principal.

(c) Execute, acknowledge, seal, and deliver a deed, revocation, mortgage, lease, notice, check, release, or other instrument the agent considers desirable to accomplish a purpose of a transaction.

(d) Prosecute, defend, submit to arbitration, settle, and propose or accept a compromise with respect to, a claim existing in favor of or against the principal or intervene in litigation relating to the claim.

(e) Seek on the principal's behalf the assistance of a court to carry out an act authorized by the power of attorney.

(f) Engage, compensate, and discharge an attorney, accountant, expert witness, or other assistant.

(g) Keep appropriate records of each transaction, including an accounting of receipts and disbursements.

(h) Prepare, execute, and file a record, report, or other document the agent considers desirable to safeguard or promote the principal's interest under a statute or governmental regulation.

(i) Reimburse the agent for expenditures properly made by the agent in exercising the powers granted by the power of attorney.

(j) In general, do any other lawful act with respect to the subject.

(Stats. 1994 (S.B. 1907), ch. 307, §16.)

§4451. Real property transactions covered by statutory form power of attorney

In a statutory form power of attorney, the language granting power with respect to real property transactions empowers the agent to do all of the following:

(a) Accept as a gift or as security for a loan, reject, demand, buy, lease, receive, or otherwise acquire, an interest in real property or a right incident to real property.

(b) Sell, exchange, convey with or without covenants, quitclaim, release, surrender, mortgage, encumber, partition, consent to partitioning, subdivide, apply for zoning, rezoning, or other governmental permits, plat or consent to platting, develop, grant options concerning, lease, sublease, or otherwise dispose of, an interest in real property or a right incident to real property.

(c) Release, assign, satisfy, and enforce by litigation or otherwise, a mortgage, deed of trust, encumbrance, lien, or other claim to real property which exists or is asserted.

(d) Do any act of management or of conservation with respect to an interest in real property, or a right incident to real property, owned, or claimed to be owned, by the principal, including all of the following:

(1) Insuring against a casualty, liability, or loss.

(2) Obtaining or regaining possession, or protecting the interest or right, by litigation or otherwise.

(3) Paying, compromising, or contesting taxes or assessments, or applying for and receiving refunds in connection with them.

(4) Purchasing supplies, hiring assistance or labor, and making repairs or alterations in the real property.

(e) Use, develop, alter, replace, remove, erect, or install structures or other improvements upon real property in or incident to which the principal has, or claims to have, an interest or right.

(f) Participate in a reorganization with respect to real property or a legal entity that owns an interest in or right incident to real property and receive and hold shares of stock or obligations received in a plan of reorganization, and act with respect to them, including all of the following:

(1) Selling or otherwise disposing of them.

(2) Exercising or selling an option, conversion, or similar right with respect to them.

(3) Voting them in person or by proxy.

(g) Change the form of title of an interest in or right incident to real property.

(h) Dedicate to public use, with or without consideration, easements or other real property in which the principal has, or claims to have, an interest or right.
(Stats. 1994 (S.B. 1907), ch. 307, §16.)

§4452. Tangible personal property transactions covered by statutory form power of attorney

In a statutory form power of attorney, the language granting power with respect to tangible personal property transactions empowers the agent to do all of the following:

(a) Accept as a gift or as security for a loan, reject, demand, buy, receive, or otherwise acquire ownership or possession of tangible personal property or an interest in tangible personal property.

(b) Sell, exchange, convey with or without covenants, release, surrender, mortgage, encumber, pledge, hypothecate, create a security interest in, pawn, grant options concerning, lease, sublease to others, or otherwise dispose of tangible personal property or an interest in tangible personal property.

(c) Release, assign, satisfy, or enforce by litigation or otherwise, a mortgage, security interest, encumbrance, lien, or other claim on behalf of the principal, with respect to tangible personal property or an interest in tangible personal property.

(d) Do an act of management or conservation with respect to tangible personal property or an interest in tangible personal property on behalf of the principal, including all of the following:

(1) Insuring against casualty, liability, or loss.

(2) Obtaining or regaining possession, or protecting the property or interest, by litigation or otherwise.

(3) Paying, compromising, or contesting taxes or assessments or applying for and receiving refunds in connection with taxes or assessments.

(4) Moving from place to place.

(5) Storing for hire or on a gratuitous bailment.

(6) Using, altering, and making repairs or alterations.

(Stats. 1994 (S.B. 1907), ch. 307, §16.)

§4453. Stock and bond transactions covered by statutory form power of attorney

In a statutory form power of attorney, the language granting power with respect to stock and bond transactions empowers the agent to do all of the following:

(a) Buy, sell, and exchange stocks, bonds, mutual funds, and all other types of securities and financial instruments except commodity futures contracts and call and put options on stocks and stock indexes.

(b) Receive certificates and other evidences of ownership with respect to securities.

(c) Exercise voting rights with respect to securities in person or by proxy, enter into voting trusts, and consent to limitations on the right to vote.
(Stats. 1994 (S.B. 1907), ch. 307, §16.)

§4454. Commodity and option transactions covered by statutory form power of attorney

In a statutory form power of attorney, the language granting power with respect to commodity and option transactions empowers the agent to do all of the following:

(a) Buy, sell, exchange, assign, settle, and exercise commodity futures contracts and call and put options on stocks and stock indexes traded on a regulated option exchange.

(b) Establish, continue, modify, and terminate option accounts with a broker.
(Stats. 1994 (S.B. 1907), ch. 307, §16.)

§4455. Banking and other financial institution transactions covered by statutory form power of attorney

In a statutory form power of attorney, the language granting power with respect to banking and other financial institution transactions empowers the agent to do all of the following:

(a) Continue, modify, and terminate an account or other banking arrangement made by or on behalf of the principal.

(b) Establish, modify, and terminate an account or other banking arrangement with a bank, trust company, savings and loan association, credit union, thrift company, industrial loan company, brokerage firm, or other financial institution selected by the agent.

(c) Hire or close a safe deposit box or space in a vault.

(d) Contract to procure other services available from a financial institution as the agent considers desirable.

(e) Withdraw by check, order, or otherwise money or property of the principal deposited with or left in the custody of a financial institution.

(f) Receive bank statements, vouchers, notices, and similar documents from a financial institution and act with respect to them.

(g) Enter a safe deposit box or vault and withdraw or add to the contents.

(h) Borrow money at an interest rate agreeable to the agent and pledge as security personal property of the principal necessary in order to borrow, pay, renew, or extend the time of payment of a debt of the principal.

(i) Make, assign, draw, endorse, discount, guarantee, and negotiate promissory notes, checks, drafts, and other negotiable or nonnegotiable paper of the principal, or payable to the principal or the principal's order, receive the cash or other proceeds of those transactions, and accept a draft drawn by a person upon the principal and pay it when due.

(j) Receive for the principal and act upon a sight draft, warehouse receipt, or other negotiable or nonnegotiable instrument.

(k) Apply for and receive letters of credit, credit cards, and traveler's checks from a financial institution, and give an indemnity or other agreement in connection with letters of credit.

(l) Consent to an extension of the time of payment with respect to commercial paper or a financial transaction with a financial institution.

(Stats. 1994 (S.B. 1907), ch. 307, §16.)

§4456. Business operating transactions covered by statutory form power of attorney

In a statutory form power of attorney, the language granting power with respect to business operating transactions empowers the agent to do all of the following:

(a) Operate, buy, sell, enlarge, reduce, and terminate a business interest.

(b) To the extent that an agent is permitted by law to act for a principal and subject to the terms of the partnership agreement:

(1) Perform a duty or discharge a liability and exercise a right, power, privilege, or option that the principal has, may have, or claims to have, under a partnership agreement, whether or not the principal is a partner.

(2) Enforce the terms of a partnership agreement by litigation or otherwise.

(3) Defend, submit to arbitration, settle, or compromise litigation to which the principal is a party because of membership in the partnership.

(c) Exercise in person or by proxy, or enforce by litigation or otherwise, a right, power, privilege, or option the principal has or claims to have as the holder of a bond, share, or other instrument of similar character, and defend, submit to arbitration, settle, or compromise litigation to which the principal is a party because of a bond, share, or similar instrument.

(d) With respect to a business owned solely by the principal:

(1) Continue, modify, renegotiate, extend, and terminate a contract made with an individual or a legal entity, firm, association, or corporation by or on behalf of the principal with respect to the business before execution of the power of attorney.

(2) Determine the policy of the business as to (A) the location of its operation, (B) the nature and extent of its business, (C) the methods of manufacturing, selling, merchandising, financing, accounting, and advertising employed in its operation, (D) the amount and types of insurance carried, and (E) the mode of engaging, compensating, and dealing with its accountants, attorneys, and other agents and employees.

(3) Change the name or form of organization under which the business is operated and enter into a partnership agreement with other persons or organize a corporation to take over all or part of the operation of the business.

(4) Demand and receive money due or claimed by the principal or on the principal's behalf in the operation of the business, and control and disburse the money in the operation of the business.

(e) Put additional capital into a business in which the principal has an interest.

(f) Join in a plan of reorganization, consolidation, or merger of the business.

(g) Sell or liquidate a business or part of it at the time and upon the terms the agent considers desirable.

(h) Represent the principal in establishing the value of a business under a buy-out agreement to which the principal is a party.

(i) Prepare, sign, file, and deliver reports, compilations of information, returns, or other papers with respect to a business which are required by a governmental agency or instrumentality or which the agent considers desirable, and make related payments.

(j) Pay, compromise, or contest taxes or assessments and do any other act which the agent considers desirable to protect the principal from illegal or unnecessary taxation, fines, penalties, or assessments with respect to a business, including attempts to recover, in any manner permitted by law, money paid before or after the execution of the power of attorney.

(Stats. 1994 (S.B. 1907), ch. 307, §16.)

§4457. Insurance and annuity transactions covered by statutory form power of attorney

In a statutory form power of attorney, the language granting power with respect to insurance and annuity transactions empowers the agent to do all of the following:

(a) Continue, pay the premium or assessment on, modify, rescind, release, or terminate a contract procured by or on behalf of the principal which insures or provides an annuity to either the principal or another person, whether or not the principal is a beneficiary under the contract.

(b) Procure new, different, and additional contracts of insurance and annuities for the principal and the principal's spouse, children, and other dependents, and select the amount, type of insurance or annuity, and mode of payment.

(c) Pay the premium or assessment on, modify, rescind, release, or terminate a contract of insurance or annuity procured by the agent.

(d) Designate the beneficiary of the contract, but the agent may be named a beneficiary of the contract, or an extension, renewal, or substitute for it, only to the extent the agent was named as a beneficiary under a contract procured by the principal before executing the power of attorney.

(e) Apply for and receive a loan on the security of the contract of insurance or annuity.

(f) Surrender and receive the cash surrender value.

(g) Exercise an election.

(h) Change the manner of paying premiums.

(i) Change or convert the type of insurance contract or annuity as to any insurance contract or annuity with respect to which the principal has or claims to have a power described in this section.

(j) Change the beneficiary of a contract of insurance or annuity, but the agent may not be designated a beneficiary except to the extent permitted by subdivision (d).

(k) Apply for and procure government aid to guarantee or pay premiums of a contract of insurance on the life of the principal.

(l) Collect, sell, assign, hypothecate, borrow upon, or pledge the interest of the principal in a contract of insurance or annuity.

(m) Pay from proceeds or otherwise, compromise or contest, and apply for refunds in connection with, a tax or assessment levied by a taxing authority with respect to a contract of insurance or annuity or its proceeds or liability accruing by reason of the tax or assessment.

(Stats. 1994 (S.B. 1907), ch. 307, §16.)

§4458. Estate, trust and other beneficiary transactions covered by statutory power of attorney

In a statutory form power of attorney, the language granting power with respect to estate, trust, and other beneficiary transactions, empowers the agent to act for the principal in all matters that affect a trust, probate estate, guardianship, conservatorship, escrow, custodianship, or other fund from which the principal is, may become, or claims to be entitled, as a beneficiary, to a share or payment, including the power to do all of the following:

(a) Accept, reject, disclaim, receive, receipt for, sell, assign, release, pledge, exchange, or consent to a reduction in or modification of a share in or payment from the fund.

(b) Demand or obtain by litigation or otherwise money or other thing of value to which the principal is, may become, or claims to be entitled by reason of the fund.

(c) Initiate, participate in, and oppose litigation to ascertain the meaning, validity, or effect of a deed, will, declaration of trust, or other instrument or transaction affecting the interest of the principal.

(d) Initiate, participate in, and oppose litigation to remove, substitute, or surcharge a fiduciary.

(e) Conserve, invest, disburse, and use anything received for an authorized purpose.

(f) Transfer an interest of the principal in real property, stocks, bonds, accounts with financial institutions, insurance, and other property, to the trustee of a revocable trust created by the principal as settlor.

(Stats. 1994 (S.B. 1907), ch. 307, §16.)

§4459. Claims and litigation covered by statutory form power of attorney

In a statutory form power of attorney, the language with respect to claims and litigation empowers the agent to do all of the following:

(a) Assert and prosecute before a court or administrative agency a claim, claim for relief, cause of action, counterclaim, cross-complaint, or offset, and defend against an individual, a legal entity, or government, including suits to recover property or other thing of value, to recover damages sustained by the principal, to eliminate or modify tax liability, or to seek an injunction, specific performance, or other relief.

(b) Bring an action to determine adverse claims, intervene in litigation, and act as amicus curiae.

(c) In connection with litigation:

(1) Procure an attachment, garnishment, libel, order of arrest, or other preliminary, provisional, or intermediate relief and use any available procedure to effect, enforce, or satisfy a judgment, order, or decree.

(2) Perform any lawful act, including acceptance of tender, offer of judgment, admission of facts, submission of a controversy on an agreed statement of facts, consent to examination before trial, and binding the principal in litigation.

(d) Submit to arbitration, settle, and propose or accept a compromise with respect to a claim or litigation.

(e) Waive the issuance and service of process upon the principal, accept service of process, appear for the principal, designate persons upon whom process directed to the principal may be served, execute and file or deliver stipulations on the principal's behalf, verify pleadings, seek appellate review, procure and give surety and indemnity bonds, contract and pay for the preparation and printing of records and briefs, receive and execute and file or deliver a consent, waiver, release, confession of judgment, satisfaction of judgment, notice, agreement, or other instrument in connection with the prosecution, settlement, or defense of a claim or litigation.

(f) Act for the principal with respect to bankruptcy or insolvency proceedings, whether voluntary or involuntary, concerning the principal or some other person, or with respect to a reorganization proceeding, or with respect to an assignment for the benefit of creditors, receivership, or application for the appointment of a receiver or trustee which affects an interest of the principal in property or other thing of value.

(g) Pay a judgment against the principal or a settlement made in connection with litigation and receive and conserve money or other thing of value paid in settlement of or as proceeds of a claim or litigation.

(Stats. 1994 (S.B. 1907), ch. 307, §16.)

§4460. Personal and family maintenance covered by statutory form power of attorney

In a statutory form power of attorney, the language granting power with respect to personal and family maintenance empowers the agent to do all of the following:

(a) Do the acts necessary to maintain the customary standard of living of the principal, the principal's spouse, children, and other individuals customarily or legally entitled to be supported by the principal, including providing living quarters by purchase, lease, or other contract, or paying the operating costs, including interest, amortization payments, repairs, and taxes on premises owned by the principal and occupied by those individuals.

(b) Provide for the individuals described in subdivision (a) all of the following:

(1) Normal domestic help.

(2) Usual vacations and travel expenses.

(3) Funds for shelter, clothing, food, appropriate education, and other current living costs.

(c) Pay for the individuals described in subdivision (a) necessary medical, dental, and surgical care, hospitalization, and custodial care.

(d) Continue any provision made by the principal, for the individuals described in subdivision (a), for automobiles or other means of transportation, including registering, licensing, insuring, and replacing them.

(e) Maintain or open charge accounts for the convenience of the individuals described in subdivision (a) and open new accounts the agent considers desirable to accomplish a lawful purpose.

(f) Continue payments incidental to the membership or affiliation of the principal in a church, club, society, order, or other organization and continue contributions to those organizations.

(Stats. 1994 (S.B. 1907), ch. 307, §16.)

§4461. Benefits from social security or other governmental program covered by statutory form power of attorney

In a statutory form power of attorney, the language granting power with respect to benefits from social security, medicare, medicaid, or other governmental programs, or civil or military service, empowers the agent to do all of the following:

(a) Execute vouchers in the name of the principal for allowances and reimbursements payable by the United States or a foreign government or by a state or subdivision of a state to the principal, including allowances and reimbursements for transportation of the individuals described in subdivision (a) of Section 4460, and for shipment of their household effects.

(b) Take possession and order the removal and shipment of property of the principal from a post, warehouse, depot, dock, or other place of storage or safekeeping, either governmental or private, and execute and deliver a release, voucher, receipt, bill of lading, shipping ticket, certificate, or other instrument for that purpose.

(c) Prepare, file, and prosecute a claim of the principal to a benefit or assistance, financial or otherwise, to which the principal claims to be entitled, under a statute or governmental regulation.

(d) Prosecute, defend, submit to arbitration, settle, and propose or accept a compromise with respect to any benefits the principal may be entitled to receive.

(e) Receive the financial proceeds of a claim of the type described in this section, conserve, invest, disburse, or use anything received for a lawful purpose.

(Stats. 1994 (S.B. 1907), ch. 307, §16.)

§4462. Retirement plan transactions covered by statutory form power of attorney

In a statutory form power of attorney, the language granting power with respect to retirement plan transactions empowers the agent to do all of the following:

(a) Select payment options under any retirement plan in which the principal participates, including plans for self-employed individuals.

(b) Designate beneficiaries under those plans and change existing designations.

(c) Make voluntary contributions to those plans.

(d) Exercise the investment powers available under any self-directed retirement plan.

(e) Make rollovers of plan benefits into other retirement plans.

(f) If authorized by the plan, borrow from, sell assets to, and purchase assets from the plan.

(g) Waive the right of the principal to be a beneficiary of a joint or survivor annuity if the principal is a spouse who is not employed.

(Stats. 1994 (S.B. 1907), ch. 307, §16.)

§4463. Tax matters covered by statutory form power of attorney

In a statutory form power of attorney, the language granting power with respect to tax matters empowers the agent to do all of the following:

(a) Prepare, sign, and file federal, state, local, and foreign income, gift, payroll, Federal Insurance Contributions Act returns, and other tax returns, claims for refunds, requests for extension of time, petitions regarding tax matters, and any other tax-related documents, including receipts, offers, waivers, consents (including consents and agreements under Internal Revenue Code Section 2032A or any successor section), closing agreements, and any power of attorney required by the Internal Revenue Service or other taxing authority with respect to a tax year upon which the statute of limitations has not run and to the tax year in which the power of attorney was executed and any subsequent tax year.

(b) Pay taxes due, collect refunds, post bonds, receive confidential information, and contest deficiencies determined by the Internal Revenue Service or other taxing authority.

(c) Exercise any election available to the principal under federal, state, local, or foreign tax law.

(d) Act for the principal in all tax matters for all periods before the Internal Revenue Service and any other taxing authority.

(Stats. 1994 (S.B. 1907), ch. 307, §16.)

§4464. Powers are exercisable regarding after-acquired property and regardless of where power of attorney is executed

The powers described in this chapter are exercisable equally with respect to an interest the principal has when the statutory form power of attorney is executed or acquires later, whether or not the property is located in this state, and whether or not the powers are exercised or the power of attorney is executed in this state.

(Stats. 1994 (S.B. 1907), ch. 307, §16.)

§4465. Statutory form power of attorney does not empower agent to modify or revoke trust absent express grant of authority

A statutory form power of attorney under this part does not empower the agent to modify or revoke a trust created by the principal unless that power is expressly granted by the power of attorney. If a statutory form power of attorney under this part empowers the agent to modify or revoke a trust created by the principal, the trust may only be modified or revoked by the agent as provided in the trust instrument.

(Stats. 1994 (S.B. 1907), ch. 307, §16.)

G. Judicial Proceedings Concerning Powers of Attorney

§4500. Power of attorney can be exercised without Judicial intervention

A power of attorney is exercisable free of judicial intervention, subject to this part.

(Stats. 1999 (A.B. 891), ch. 658, §37, effective July 1, 2000.)

§4501. Remedies are cumulative and not exclusive

The remedies provided in this part are cumulative and not exclusive of any other remedies provided by law.

(Stats. 1999 (A.B. 891), ch. 658, §37, effective July 1, 2000.)

§4502. Power of attorney may not limit operation of law except as provided

Except as provided in Section 4503, this part is not subject to limitation in the power of attorney.

(Stats. 1999 (A.B. 891), ch. 658, §37, effective July 1, 2000.)

§4503. Power of attorney may eliminate authority to petition court for enumerated purposes

(a) Subject to subdivision (b), a power of attorney may expressly eliminate the authority of a person listed in Section 4540 to petition the court for any one or more of the purposes enumerated in Section 4541 if both of the following requirements are satisfied:

(1) The power of attorney is executed by the principal at a time when the principal has the advice of a lawyer authorized to practice law in the state where the power of attorney is executed.

(2) The principal's lawyer signs a certificate stating in substance:

"I am a lawyer authorized to practice law in the state where this power of attorney was executed, and the principal was my client at the time this power of attorney was executed. I have advised my client concerning his or her rights in connection with this power of attorney and the applicable law and the consequences of signing or not signing this power of attorney, and my client, after being so advised, has executed this power of attorney."

(b) A power of attorney may not limit the authority of the attorney-in-fact, the principal, the conservator of the person or estate of the principal, or the public guardian to petition under this part.

(Stats. 1999 (A.B. 891), ch. 658, §37, effective July 1, 2000.)

§4504. No right to jury trial

There is no right to a jury trial in proceedings under this division.

(Stats. 1999 (A.B. 891), ch. 658, §37, effective July 1, 2000.)

§4505. Application of Division 3

Except as otherwise provided in this division, the general provisions in Division 3 (commencing with Section 1000) apply to proceedings under this division.

(Stats. 1999 (A.B. 891), ch. 658, §37, effective July 1, 2000.)

§4520. Superior court has jurisdiction under Division

(a) The superior court has jurisdiction in proceedings under this division.

(b) The court in proceedings under this division is a court of general jurisdiction and the court, or a judge of the court, has the same power and authority with respect to the proceedings as otherwise provided by law for a superior court, or a judge of the superior court, including, but not limited to, the matters authorized by Section 128 of the Code of Civil Procedure.

(Stats. 1999 (A.B. 891), ch. 658, §37, effective July 1, 2000.)

§4521. Exercise of jurisdiction subject to Code of Civil Procedure provision

The court may exercise jurisdiction in proceedings under this division on any basis permitted by Section 410.10 of the Code of Civil Procedure.

(Stats. 1999 (A.B. 891), ch. 658, §37, effective July 1, 2000.)

§4522. Attorney-in-fact is subject to personal jurisdiction in this state

Without limiting Section 4521, a person who acts as an attorney-in-fact under a power of attorney governed by this division is subject to personal jurisdiction in this state with respect to matters relating to acts and transactions of the attorney-in-fact performed in this state or affecting property or a principal in this state.

(Stats. 1999 (A.B. 891), ch. 658, §37, effective July 1, 2000.)

§4523. Venue

The proper county for commencement of a proceeding under this division shall be determined in the following order of priority:

(a) The county in which the principal resides.

(b) The county in which the attorney-in-fact resides.

(c) A county in which property subject to the power of attorney is located.

(d) Any other county that is in the principal's best interest.

(Stats. 1999 (A.B. 891), ch. 658, §37, effective July 1, 2000.)

§4540. Persons eligible to file petition

Subject to Section 4503, a petition may be filed under this part by any of the following persons:

(a) The attorney-in-fact.

(b) The principal.

(c) The spouse of the principal.

(d) A relative of the principal.

(e) The conservator of the person or estate of the principal.

(f) The court investigator, described in Section 1454, of the county where the power of attorney was executed or where the principal resides.

(g) The public guardian of the county where the power of attorney was executed or where the principal resides.

(h) The personal representative or trustee of the principal's estate.

(i) The principal's successor in interest.

(j) A person who is requested in writing by an attorney-in-fact to take action.

(k) Any other interested person or friend of the principal.

(Stats. 1999 (A.B. 891), ch. 658, §37, effective July 1, 2000.)

§4541. Petition may be filed for various purposes

A petition may be filed under this part for any one or more of the following purposes:

(a) Determining whether the power of attorney is in effect or has terminated.

(b) Passing on the acts or proposed acts of the attorney-in-fact, including approval of authority to disobey the principal's instructions pursuant to subdivision (b) of Section 4234.

(c) Compelling the attorney-in-fact to submit the attorney-in-fact's accounts or report the attorney-in-fact's acts as attorney-in-fact to the principal, the spouse of the principal, the conservator of the person or the estate of the principal, or to any other person required by the court in its discretion, if the attorney-in-fact has failed to submit an accounting or report within 60 days after written request from the person filing the petition.

(d) Declaring that the authority of the attorney-in-fact is revoked on a determination by the court of all of the following:

(1) The attorney in fact has violated or is unfit to perform the fiduciary duties under the power of attorney.

(2) At the time of the determination by the court, the principal lacks the capacity to give or to revoke a power of attorney.

(3) The revocation of the attorney-in-fact's authority is in the best interest of the principal or the principal's estate.

(e) Approving the resignation of the attorney-in-fact:

(1) If the attorney-in-fact is subject to a duty to act under Section 4230, the court may approve the resignation, subject to any orders the court determines are necessary to protect the principal's interests.

(2) If the attorney-in-fact is not subject to a duty to act under Section 4230, the court shall approve the resignation, subject to the court's discretion to require the attorney-in-fact to give notice to other interested persons.

(f) Compelling a third person to honor the authority of an attorney-in-fact.

(Stats. 1999 (A.B. 891), ch. 658, §37, effective July 1, 2000.)

§4542. Petitioner commences proceeding by filing petition

A proceeding under this part is commenced by filing a petition stating facts showing that the petition is authorized under this part, the grounds of the petition, and, if known to the petitioner, the terms of the power of attorney.

(Stats. 1999 (A.B. 891), ch. 658, §37, effective July 1, 2000.)

§4543. Court may dismiss petition if not reasonably necessary to protect principal's interest

The court may dismiss a petition if it appears that the proceeding is not reasonably necessary for the protection of the interests of the principal or the principal's estate and shall stay or dismiss the proceeding in whole or in part when required by Section 410.30 of the Code of Civil Procedure [infra].

(Stats. 1999 (A.B. 891), ch. 658, §37, effective July 1, 2000.)

§4544. Petitioner shall serve notice of time and place of hearing

(a) Subject to subdivision (b), at least 15 days before the time set for hearing, the petitioner shall serve notice of the time and place of the hearing, together with a copy of the petition, on the following:

(1) The attorney-in-fact if not the petitioner.

(2) The principal if not the petitioner.

(b) In the case of a petition to compel a third person to honor the authority of an attorney-in-fact, notice of the time and place of the hearing, together with a copy of the petition, shall be served on the third person in the manner provided in Chapter 4 (commencing with Section 413.10) of Title 5 of Part 2 of the Code of Civil Procedure.

(Stats. 1999 (A.B. 891), ch. 658, §37, effective July 1, 2000.)

§4545. Court has discretion to award attorney's fees

In a proceeding under this part commenced by the filing of a petition by a person other than the attorney-in-fact, the court may in its discretion award reasonable attorney's fees to one of the following:

(a) The attorney-in-fact, if the court determines that the proceeding was commenced without any reasonable cause.

(b) The person commencing the proceeding, if the court determines that the attorney-in-fact has clearly violated the fiduciary duties under the power of attorney or has failed without any reasonable cause or justification to submit accounts or report acts to the principal or conservator of the estate or of the person, as the case may be, after written request from the principal or conservator.

(Stats. 1999 (A.B. 891), ch. 658, §37, effective July 1, 2000.)

CALIFORNIA CODE OF CIVIL PROCEDURE

§410.10. Basis for exercise of jurisdiction

A court of this state may exercise jurisdiction on any basis not inconsistent with the Constitution of this state or of the United States.

(Stats. 1969, ch. 1610, p. 3363, §3, effective July 1, 1970.)

§410.30. Court must stay or dismiss action in interest of substantial justice

(a) When a court upon motion of a party or its own motion finds that in the interest of substantial justice an action should be heard in a forum outside this state, the court shall stay or dismiss the action in whole or in part on any conditions that may be just.

(b) The provisions of Section 418.10 do not apply to a motion to stay or dismiss the action by a defendant who has made a general appearance.

(Stats. 1969, ch. 1610, p. 3363, §3, effective July 1, 1970. Amended by Stats. 1972, ch. 601, §1; Stats. 1986, ch. 968,

§4, effective September 22, 1986; Stats. 1972, ch. 601, §1, effective January 1, 1992.)

III. Power of Attorney for Health Care Decisionmaking

Beginning in the 1970s, many states enacted statutes authorizing *living wills*. A living will is a document that includes written instructions regarding health care (i.e., end-of-life decisions) in the event of an individual's becoming incapacitated. California was the first state to enact a living will statute, entitled "The Natural Death Act." Jeanine Lewis, Chapter 658: California's Health Care Decisions Act, 31 McGeorge L. Rev. 501, 509 (2000). The Natural Death Act had several restrictions: concurring diagnoses by two physicians, time constraints regarding the execution and term of the directive, and attestation by two unrelated individuals who would not profit from the declarant's death. *Id.*

Similar to living will legislation in many other jurisdictions, the California Act was limited to those individuals who had a terminal illness. The famous case of In re Quinlan, 355 A.2d 647 (N.J. 1976), first brought to light the possibility that people who were in comas might also desire to put into effect their advance directives. In recognition of this problem, in 1991, the California legislature broadened the scope of the Act by adding the term "permanent unconsciousness" to the conditions that set in motion advance directives, adding nutrition and hydration to the treatment that could be withdrawn, prohibiting recognition of a living will for pregnant patients, and deleting time limitations on the validity of an advance directive. Lewis, *supra,* at 509.

The California legislature enacted another law addressing self-determination in health care decisionmaking. In 1983, the legislature enacted the durable power of attorney for health care (former Cal. Civ. Code §§2430-2443). This power of attorney was a written document permitting a person to appoint a surrogate to make health care decisions on behalf of the declarant who became incapacitated. As originally enacted, the durable power of attorney for health care was effective for 7 years. Subsequent revisions in 1991, however, eliminated the time limitation.

California case law involving health care decisionmaking by incapacitated persons follows New Jersey's case In re Quinlan, *supra*. According to California case law, incapacitated persons have the right to refuse medical treatment if a surrogate decisionmaker determines that such refusal is in the patient's best interests. Lewis, *supra*, at 515. Moreover, in the determination of cessation of life support, California courts consider a patient's prior informal statements regarding withdrawal of life support, as well as medical advice regarding the course of treatment that is in the patient's best interests. *Id.* In this regard, California courts are more liberal than those jurisdictions that require higher standards of proof of the patient's wishes. See Cruzan v. Missouri Department of Health, 497 U.S. 261 (1990) (holding that states may require clear and convincing evidence of the patient's wishes).

In 1999, the California legislature enacted the Health Care Decisions Law (Cal. Prob. Code §§4600 et seq.) to address the shortcomings of prior law. The Act repeals both the Natural Death Act and the Durable Power of Attorney for Health Care, combining the power of attorney for health care, individual health care instructions, and anatomical gifts laws. The Act provides uniform standards to govern health care for incapacitated persons. It facilitates the process by providing an optional statutory form for persons to utilize.

The new legislation substitutes the term "power of attorney for health care" for the former "durable power of attorney for health care." The power of attorney for health care continues the earlier attestation requirements (date of execution and two witnesses or notarizing the principal's signature). According to California Probate Code §4650 (*infra*), an adult has "the fundamental right to control the decisions relating to his or her own health care, including the decision to have life-sustaining treatment withheld or withdrawn."

A. General Provisions

CALIFORNIA PROBATE CODE
§4600. Short title

This division may be cited as the Health Care Decisions Law.

(Stats. 1999 (A.B. 891), ch. 658, §39, effective July 1, 2000.)

§4603. Definitions govern construction of this Division

Unless the provision or context otherwise requires, the definitions in this chapter govern the construction of this division.

(Stats. 1999 (A.B. 891), ch. 658, §39, effective July 1, 2000.)

§4605. "Advance health care directive," defined

"Advance health care directive" or "advance directive" means either an individual health care instruction or a power of attorney for health care.

(Stats. 1999 (A.B. 891), ch. 658, §39, effective July 1, 2000.)

§4607. "Agent," defined

(a) "Agent" means an individual designated in a power of attorney for health care to make a health care decision for the principal, regardless of whether the person is known as an agent or attorney-in-fact, or by some other term.(b) "Agent" includes a successor or alternate agent.

(Stats. 1999 (A.B. 891), ch. 658, §39, effective July 1, 2000.)

§4609. "Capacity," defined

"Capacity" means a person's ability to understand the nature and consequences of a decision and to make and communicate a decision, and includes in the case of proposed health care, the ability to understand its significant benefits, risks, and alternatives.

(Stats. 1999 (A.B. 891), ch. 658, §39, effective July 1, 2000. Amended by Stats. 2001 (A.B. 1278), ch. 230, §3.)

§4611. "Community care facility," defined

"Community care facility" means a "community care facility" as defined in Section 1502 of the Health and Safety Code

(Stats. 1999 (A.B. 891), ch. 658, §39, effective July 1, 2000.)

§4613. "Conservator," defined

"Conservator" means a court-appointed conservator having authority to make a health care decision for a patient.

(Stats. 1999 (A.B. 891), ch. 658, §39, effective July 1, 2000.)

§4615. "Health care," defined

"Health care" means any care, treatment, service, or procedure to maintain, diagnose, or otherwise affect a patient's physical or mental condition.

(Stats. 1999 (A.B. 891), ch. 658, §39, effective July 1, 2000.)

§4617. "Health care decision," defined

"Health care decision" means a decision made by a patient or the patient's agent, conservator, or surrogate, regarding the patient's health care, including the following:

(a) Selection and discharge of health care providers and institutions.

(b) Approval or disapproval of diagnostic tests, surgical procedures, and programs of medication.

(c) Directions to provide, withhold, or withdraw artificial nutrition and hydration and all other forms of health care, including cardiopulmonary resuscitation.

(Stats. 1999 (A.B. 891), ch. 658, §39, effective July 1, 2000.)

§4619. "Health care institution," defined

"Health care institution" means an institution, facility, or agency licensed, certified, or otherwise authorized or permitted by law to provide health care in the ordinary course of business.

(Stats. 1999 (A.B. 891), ch. 658, §39, effective July 1, 2000.)

§4621. "Health care provider," defined

"Health care provider" means an individual licensed, certified, or otherwise authorized or permitted by the law of this state to provide health care in the ordinary course of business or practice of a profession.

(Stats. 1999 (A.B. 891), ch. 658, §39, effective July 1, 2000.)

§4623. "Individual health care instruction," defined

"Individual health care instruction" or "individual instruction" means a patient's written or oral direction concerning a health care decision for the patient.

(Stats. 1999 (A.B. 891), ch. 658, §39, effective July 1, 2000.)

§4625. "Patient," defined

"Patient" means an adult whose health care is under consideration, and includes a principal under a power of attorney for health care and an adult who has given an individual health care instruction or designated a surrogate.

(Stats. 1999 (A.B. 891), ch. 658, §39, effective July 1, 2000.)

§4627. "Physician," defined

"Physician" means a physician and surgeon licensed by the Medical Board of California or the Osteopathic Medical Board of California.

(Stats. 1999 (A.B. 891), ch. 658, §39, effective July 1, 2000.)

§4629. "Power of attorney for health care," defined

"Power of attorney for health care" means a written instrument designating an agent to make health care decisions for the principal.

(Stats. 1999 (A.B. 891), ch. 658, §39, effective July 1, 2000.)

§4631. "Primary physician," defined

"Primary physician" means a physician designated by a patient or the patient's agent, conservator, or surrogate, to have primary responsibility for the patient's health care or, in the absence of a designation or if the designated physician is not reasonably available or declines to act as primary physician, a physician who undertakes the responsibility.

(Stats. 1999 (A.B. 891), ch. 658, §39, effective July 1, 2000.)

§4633. "Principal," defined

"Principal" means an adult who executes a power of attorney for health care.

(Stats. 1999 (A.B. 891), ch. 658, §39, effective July 1, 2000.)

§4635. "Reasonably available," defined

"Reasonably available" means readily able to be contacted without undue effort and willing and able to act in a timely manner considering the urgency of the patient's health care needs.

(Stats. 1999 (A.B. 891), ch. 658, §39, effective July 1, 2000.)

§4637. "Residential care facility for the elderly," defined

"Residential care facility for the elderly" means a "residential care facility for the elderly" as defined in Section 1569.2 of the Health and Safety Code.

(Stats. 1999 (A.B. 891), ch. 658, §39, effective July 1, 2000.)

§4639. "Skilled nursing facility," defined

"Skilled nursing facility" means a "skilled nursing facility" as defined in Section 1250 of the Health and Safety Code.

(Stats. 1999 (A.B. 891), ch. 658, §39, effective July 1, 2000.)

§4641. "Supervising health care provider," defined

"Supervising health care provider" means the primary physician or, if there is no primary physician or the primary physician is not reasonably available, the health care provider who has undertaken primary responsibility for a patient's health care.

(Stats. 1999 (A.B. 891), ch. 658, §39, effective July 1, 2000.)

§4643. "Surrogate," defined

"Surrogate" means an adult, other than a patient's agent or conservator, authorized under this division to make a health care decision for the patient.

(Stats. 1999 (A.B. 891), ch. 658, §39, effective July 1, 2000.)

§4650. Legislative findings regarding human dignity and privacy; court normally not proper forum for decisionmaking

The Legislature finds the following:

(a) In recognition of the dignity and privacy a person has a right to expect, the law recognizes that an adult has the fundamental right to control the decisions relating to his or her own health care, including the decision to have life-sustaining treatment withheld or withdrawn.

(b) Modern medical technology has made possible the artificial prolongation of human life beyond natural limits. In the interest of protecting individual autonomy, this prolongation of the process of dying for a person for whom continued health care does not improve the prognosis for recovery may violate patient dignity and cause unnecessary pain and suffering, while providing nothing medically necessary or beneficial to the person.

(c) In the absence of controversy, a court is normally not the proper forum in which to make health care decisions, including decisions regarding life-sustaining treatment.

(Stats. 1999 (A.B. 891), ch. 658, §39, effective July 1, 2000.)

§4651. Application to health care decisions for adults who lack capacity; exemptions

(a) Except as otherwise provided, this division applies to health care decisions for adults who lack capacity to make health care decisions for themselves.

(b) This division does not affect any of the following:

(1) The right of an individual to make health care decisions while having the capacity to do so.

(2) The law governing health care in an emergency.

(3) The law governing health care for unemancipated minors.

(Stats. 1999 (A.B. 891), ch. 658, §39, effective July 1, 2000.)

§4652. Scope of consent

This division does not authorize consent to any of the following on behalf of a patient:

(a) Commitment to or placement in a mental health treatment facility.

(b) Convulsive treatment (as defined in Section 5325 of the Welfare and Institutions Code).

(c) Psychosurgery (as defined in Section 5325 of the Welfare and Institutions Code).

(d) Sterilization.

(e) Abortion.

(Stats. 1999 (A.B. 891), ch. 658, §39, effective July 1, 2000.)

§4653. Division does not authorize mercy killing, assisted suicide, or euthanasia

Nothing in this division shall be construed to condone, authorize, or approve mercy killing, assisted suicide, or euthanasia. This division is not intended to permit any affirmative or deliberate act or omission to end life other than withholding or withdrawing health care pursuant to an advance health care directive, by a surrogate, or as otherwise provided, so as to permit the natural process of dying.

(Stats. 1999 (A.B. 891), ch. 658, §39, effective July 1, 2000.)

§4654. Division does not authorize health care contrary to generally accepted health care standards

This division does not authorize or require a health care provider or health care institution to provide health care contrary to generally accepted health care standards applicable to the health care provider or health care institution.

(Stats. 1999 (A.B. 891), ch. 658, §39, effective July 1, 2000.)

§4655. No presumption concerning intention of patient without directive

(a) This division does not create a presumption concerning the intention of a patient who has not made or who has revoked an advance health care directive.

(b) In making health care decisions under this division, a patient's attempted suicide shall not be construed to indicate a desire of the patient that health care be restricted or inhibited.

(Stats. 1999 (A.B. 891), ch. 658, §39, effective July 1, 2000.)

§4656. Effect of death resulting from withholding or withdrawing health care: not suicide or homicide

Death resulting from withholding or withdrawing health care in accordance with this division does not for any purpose constitute a suicide or homicide or legally impair or invalidate a policy of insurance or an annuity providing a death benefit, notwithstanding any term of the policy or annuity to the contrary.

(Stats. 1999 (A.B. 891), ch. 658, §39, effective July 1, 2000.)

§4657. Presumption of capacity to make health care decision

A patient is presumed to have the capacity to make a health care decision, to give or revoke an advance health care directive, and to designate or disqualify a surrogate. This presumption is a presumption affecting the burden of proof.

(Stats. 1999 (A.B. 891), ch. 658, §39, effective July 1, 2000.)

§4658. Primary physician shall make determination regarding patient's capacity

Unless otherwise specified in a written advance health care directive, for the purposes of this division, a determination that a patient lacks or has recovered capacity, or that another condition exists that affects an individual health care instruction or the authority of an agent or surrogate, shall be made by the primary physician.

(Stats. 1999 (A.B. 891), ch. 658, §39, effective July 1, 2000.)

§4659. Persons excluded from making health care decisions

(a) Except as provided in subdivision (b), none of the following persons may make health care decisions as an agent under a power of attorney for health care or a surrogate under this division:

(1) The supervising health care provider or an employee of the health care institution where the patient is receiving care.

(2) An operator or employee of a community care facility or residential care facility where the patient is receiving care.

(b) The prohibition in subdivision (a) does not apply to the following persons:

(1) An employee, other than the supervising health care provider, who is related to the patient by blood, marriage, or adoption, or is a registered domestic partner of the patient.

(2) An employee, other than the supervising health care provider, who is employed by the same health care institution, community care facility, or residential care facility for the elderly as the patient.

(c) A conservator under the Lanterman-Petris-Short Act (Part 1 (commencing with Section 5000) of Division 5 of the Welfare and Institutions Code) may not be designated as an agent or surrogate to make health care decisions by the conservatee, unless all of the following are satisfied:

(1) The advance health care directive is otherwise valid.

(2) The conservatee is represented by legal counsel.

(3) The lawyer representing the conservatee signs a certificate stating in substance:

"I am a lawyer authorized to practice law in the state where this advance health care directive was executed, and the principal or patient was my client at the time this advance directive was executed. I have advised my client

concerning his or her rights in connection with this advance directive and the applicable law and the consequences of signing or not signing this advance directive, and my client, after being so advised, has executed this advance directive."
(Stats. 1999 (A.B. 891), ch. 658, §39, effective July 1, 2000. Amended by Stats. 2001 (A.B. 1278), ch. 230, §4.)

§4660. Copy of directive has same effect as original

A copy of a written advance health care directive, revocation of an advance directive, or designation or disqualification of a surrogate has the same effect as the original.
(Stats. 1999 (A.B. 891), ch. 658, §39, effective July 1, 2000.)

§4665. Application of division

Except as otherwise provided by statute:

(a) On and after July 1, 2000, this division applies to all advance health care directives, including, but not limited to, durable powers of attorney for health care and declarations under the Natural Death Act (former Chapter 3.9 (commencing with Section 7185) of Part 1 of Division 7 of the Health and Safety Code), regardless of whether they were given or executed before, on, or after July 1, 2000.

(b) This division applies to all proceedings concerning advance health care directives commenced on or after July 1, 2000.

(c) This division applies to all proceedings concerning written advance health care directives commenced before July 1, 2000, unless the court determines that application of a particular provision of this division would substantially interfere with the effective conduct of the proceedings or the rights of the parties and other interested persons, in which case the particular provision of this division does not apply and prior law applies.

(d) Nothing in this division affects the validity of an advance health care directive executed before July 1, 2000, that was valid under prior law.

(e) Nothing in this division affects the validity of a durable power of attorney for health care executed on a printed form that was valid under prior law, regardless of whether execution occurred before, on, or after July 1, 2000.
(Stats. 1999 (A.B. 891), ch. 658, §39, effective July 1, 2000.)

B. Uniform Health Care Decisions Act

1. Advance Health Care Directives

The most common type of advance health care directive is the "power of attorney for health care" that designates an agent to make health care decisions for the principal. California Probate Code §§4670 et seq. govern powers of attorney for health care. Any adult who has legal capacity may give an individual health care instruction. The instruction may be given orally or in writing, and may be limited to take effect on the occurrence of a specified condition (Cal. Prob. Code §4670).

According to California Probate Code §4680, a power of attorney for health care must meet the formal execution requirements of California Probate Code §4673 (specifying the requirements for execution of advance health care directives, including the date of its execution, signature by the patient or a proxy who signs in the patient's presence and at the patient's direction, and either two witnesses or acknowledgment before a notary public).

The powers granted in a power of attorney for health care may pertain to the principal's personal care, "including, but not limited to, determining where the principal will live, providing meals, hiring household employees, providing transportation, handling mail, and arranging recreation and entertainment" (Cal. Prob. Code §4671(b)).

a. General Provisions

As explained above, a person who has capacity may make health care decisions (Cal. Prob. Code §4670). Such decisions include: the selection and discharge of health care providers and institutions; approval or disapproval of diagnostic tests, surgical procedures, and programs of medication; and directions to provide, withhold, or withdraw artificial nutrition and hydration and all other forms of health care, including cardiopulmonary resuscitation (Cal. Prob. Code §4617, *supra*).

Many states have requirements for witnessing advance directives. The requirement of "disinterested witnesses" is analogous to the requirement in the will context. One commentator, however, criticizes the former requirement and urges its abolition:

> Where both relatives and health care professionals are disqualified from witnessing, it is difficult for patients to execute a directive during a physician visit, and the opportunity to promote end of life discussions between doctors and patients is lost.

Ben Kusmin, Note and Comment, Swing Low, Sweet Chariot: Abandoning the Disinterested Witness Requirement for Advance Directives, 32 Am.J.L. & Med. 93, 95 (2006).

§4670. Persons with capacity may give oral or written individual health care instruction

An adult having capacity may give an individual health care instruction. The individual instruction may be oral or written. The individual instruction may be limited to take effect only if a specified condition arises.

(Stats. 1999 (A.B. 891), ch. 658, §39, effective July 1, 2000.)

§4671. Adults with capacity may execute power of attorney for health care

(a) An adult having capacity may execute a power of attorney for health care, as provided in Article 2 (commencing with Section 4680). The power of attorney for health care may authorize the agent to make health care decisions and may also include individual health care instructions.

(b) The principal in a power of attorney for health care may grant authority to make decisions relating to the personal care of the principal, including, but not limited to, determining where the principal will live, providing meals, hiring household employees, providing transportation, handling mail, and arranging recreation and entertainment.

(Stats. 1999 (A.B. 891), ch. 658, §39, effective July 1, 2000.)

§4672. Written advance health care directive may nominate conservator or guardian

(a) A written advance health care directive may include the individual's nomination of a conservator of the person or estate or both, or a guardian of the person or estate or both, for consideration by the court if protective proceedings for the individual's person or estate are thereafter commenced.

(b) If the protective proceedings are conservatorship proceedings in this state, the nomination has the effect provided in Section 1810 and the court shall give effect to the most recent writing executed in accordance with Section 1810, whether or not the writing is a written advance health care directive.

(Stats. 1999 (A.B. 891), ch. 658, §39, effective July 1, 2000.)

§4673. Conditions for legal sufficiency of directive

(a) A written advance health care directive is legally sufficient if all of the following requirements are satisfied:

(1) The advance directive contains the date of its execution.

(2) The advance directive is signed either by the patient or in the patient's name by another adult in the patient's presence and at the patient's direction.

(3) The advance directive is either acknowledged before a notary public or signed by at least two witnesses who satisfy the requirements of Sections 4674 and 4675.

(b) An electronic advance health care directive or power of attorney for health care is legally sufficient if the requirements in subdivision (a) are satisfied, except that for the purposes of paragraph (3) of subdivision (a), an acknowledgment before a notary public shall be required, and if a digital signature is used, it meets all of the following requirements:

(1) The digital signature either meets the requirements of Section 16.5 of the Government Code and Chapter 10 (commencing with Section 22000) of Division 7 of Title 2 of the California Code of Regulations or the digital signature uses an algorithm approved by the National Institute of Standards and Technology.

(2) The digital signature is unique to the person using it.

(3) The digital signature is capable of verification.

(4) The digital signature is under the sole control of the person using it.

(5) The digital signature is linked to data in such a manner that if the data are changed, the digital signature is invalidated.

(6) The digital signature persists with the document and not by association in separate files.

(7) The digital signature is bound to a digital certificate.

(Stats. 1999 (A.B. 891), ch. 658, §39, effective July 1, 2000; Stats. 2006 (A.B. 2805), ch. 579, §1, effective September 28, 2006.)

§4674. Requirements for witnessing advance health care directive

If the written advance health care directive is signed by witnesses, as provided in Section 4673, the following requirements shall be satisfied:

(a) The witnesses shall be adults.

(b) Each witness signing the advance directive shall witness either the signing of the advance directive by the patient or the patient's acknowledgment of the signature or the advance directive.

(c) None of the following persons may act as a witness:

(1) The patient's health care provider or an employee of the patient's health care provider.

(2) The operator or an employee of a community care facility.

(3) The operator or an employee of a residential care facility for the elderly.

(4) The agent, where the advance directive is a power of attorney for health care.

(d) Each witness shall make the following declaration in substance:

"I declare under penalty of perjury under the laws of California (1) that the individual who signed or acknowledged this advance health care directive is personally known to me, or that the individual's identity was proven to me by convincing evidence, (2) that the individual signed or acknowledged this advance directive in my presence, (3) that the individual appears to be of sound mind and under no duress, fraud, or undue influence, (4) that I am not a person appointed as agent by this advance directive, and (5) that I am not the individual's health care provider, an employee of the individual's health care provider, the operator of a community care facility, an employee of an operator of a community care facility, the operator of a residential care facility for the elderly, nor an employee of an operator of a residential care facility for the elderly."

(e) At least one of the witnesses shall be an individual who is neither related to the patient by blood, marriage, or adoption, nor entitled to any portion of the patient's estate upon the patient's death under a will existing when the advance directive is executed or by operation of law then existing.

(f) The witness satisfying the requirement of subdivision (e) shall also sign the following declaration in substance:

"I further declare under penalty of perjury under the laws of California that I am not related to the individual executing this advance health care directive by blood, marriage, or adoption, and, to the best of my knowledge, I am not entitled to any part of the individual's estate upon his or her death under a will now existing or by operation of law."

(g) The provisions of this section applicable to witnesses do not apply to a notary public before whom an advance health care directive is acknowledged.

(Stats. 1999 (A.B. 891), ch. 658, §39, effective July 1, 2000.)

§4675. Requirements for witnesses of directives of patients in skilled nursing facilities

(a) If an individual is a patient in a skilled nursing facility when a written advance health care directive is executed, the advance directive is not effective unless a patient advocate or ombudsman, as may be designated by the Department of Aging for this purpose pursuant to any other applicable provision of law, signs the advance directive as a witness, either as one of two witnesses or in addition to notarization. The patient advocate or ombudsman shall declare that he or she is serving as a witness as required by this subdivision. It is the intent of this subdivision to recognize that some patients in skilled nursing facilities are insulated from a voluntary decisionmaking role, by virtue of the custodial nature of their care, so as to require special assurance that they are capable of willfully and voluntarily executing an advance directive.

(b) A witness who is a patient advocate or ombudsman may rely on the representations of the administrators or staff of the skilled nursing facility, or of family members, as convincing evidence of the identity of the patient if the patient advocate or ombudsman believes that the representations provide a reasonable basis for determining the identity of the patient.

(Stats. 1999 (A.B. 891), ch. 658, §39, effective July 1, 2000.)

§4676. Validity of instruments from another state or jurisdiction

(a) A written advance health care directive or similar instrument executed in another state or jurisdiction in compliance with the laws of that state or jurisdiction or of this state, is valid and enforceable in this state to the same extent as a written advance directive validly executed in this state.

(b) In the absence of knowledge to the contrary, a physician or other health care provider may presume that a written advance health care directive or similar instrument, whether executed in another state or jurisdiction or in this state, is valid.

(Stats. 1999 (A.B. 891), ch. 658, §39, effective July 1, 2000.)

§4677. Health care provider may not require execution or revocation of directive as condition for providing health care

A health care provider, health care service plan, health care institution, disability insurer, self-insured employee welfare plan, or nonprofit hospital plan or a similar insurance plan may not require or prohibit the execution or revocation of an advance health care directive as a condition for providing health care, admission to a facility, or furnishing insurance.

(Stats. 1999 (A.B. 891), ch. 658, §39, effective July 1, 2000.)

§4678. Authorized person has same right as patient to request and consent to disclosure of medical information

Unless otherwise specified in an advance health care directive, a person then authorized to make health care decisions for a patient has the same rights as the patient to request, receive, examine, copy, and consent to the disclosure of medical or any other health care information.

(Stats. 1999 (A.B. 891), ch. 658, §39, effective July 1, 2000.)

b. Powers of Attorney for Health Care

A power of attorney for health care is valid if it meets certain requirements for execution, including the date of its execution, signatures by either (1) the patient or (2) a proxy (another adult who signs in the patient's name in the patient's presence and at the patient's direction), and (3) either acknowledged before a notary public or signed by at least two witnesses (Cal. Prob. Code §4673).

§4680. Legal sufficiency of power of attorney for health care

A power of attorney for health care is legally sufficient if it satisfies the requirements of Section 4673.

(Stats. 1999 (A.B. 891), ch. 658, §39, effective July 1, 2000.)

§4681. Principal may impose limitations on statutory authority

(a) Except as provided in subdivision (b), the principal may limit the application of any provision of this division by an express statement in the power of attorney for health care or by providing an inconsistent rule in the power of attorney.

(b) A power of attorney for health care may not limit either the application of a statute specifically providing that it is not subject to limitation in the power of attorney or a statute concerning any of the following:

(1) Statements required to be included in a power of attorney.

(2) Operative dates of statutory enactments or amendments.

(3) Formalities for execution of a power of attorney for health care.

(4) Qualifications of witnesses.

(5) Qualifications of agents.

(6) Protection of third persons from liability.

(Stats. 1999 (A.B. 891), ch. 658, §39, effective July 1, 2000.)

§4682. Authority of agent for health care depends on principal's lack of capacity

Unless otherwise provided in a power of attorney for health care, the authority of an agent becomes effective only on a determination that the principal lacks capacity, and ceases to be effective on a determination that the principal has recovered capacity.

(Stats. 1999 (A.B. 891), ch. 658, §39, effective July 1, 2000.)

§4683. Scope of agent's authority during principal's life and at death

Subject to any limitations in the power of attorney for health care:

(a) An agent designated in the power of attorney may make health care decisions for the principal to the same extent the principal could make health care decisions if the principal had the capacity to do so.

(b) The agent may also make decisions that may be effective after the principal's death, including the following:

(1) Making a disposition under the Uniform Anatomical Gift Act (Chapter 3.5 (commencing with Section 7150) of Part 1 of Division 7 of the Health and Safety Code).

(2) Authorizing an autopsy under Section 7113 of the Health and Safety Code.

(3) Directing the disposition of remains under Section 7100 of the Health and Safety Code.

(4) Authorizing the release of the records of the principal to the extent necessary for the agent to fulfill his or her duties as set forth in this division.

(Stats. 1999 (A.B. 891), ch. 658, §39, effective July 1, 2000. Amended by Stats. 2006 (S.B. 1307), ch. 249, §2.)

§4684. Agent shall make decisions per instructions and in principal's best interests

An agent shall make a health care decision in accordance with the principal's individual health care instructions, if any, and other wishes to the extent known to the agent. Otherwise, the agent shall make the decision in accordance with the agent's determination of the principal's best interest. In determining the principal's best interest, the agent shall consider the principal's personal values to the extent known to the agent.

(Stats. 1999 (A.B. 891), ch. 658, §39, effective July 1, 2000.)

§4685. Agent has priority in making health care decisions

Unless the power of attorney for health care provides otherwise, the agent designated in the power of attorney who is known to the health care provider to be reasonably available and willing to make health care decisions has priority over any other person in making health care decisions for the principal.

(Stats. 1999 (A.B. 891), ch. 658, §39, effective July 1, 2000.)

§4686. Lapse of time since execution of power of attorney is irrelevant

Unless the power of attorney for health care provides a time of termination, the authority of the agent is exercisable notwithstanding any lapse of time since execution of the power of attorney.

(Stats. 1999 (A.B. 891), ch. 658, §39, effective July 1, 2000.)

§4687. Agent has rights apart from power of attorney

Nothing in this division affects any right the person designated as an agent under a power of attorney for health care may have, apart from the power of attorney, to make or participate in making health care decisions for the principal.
(Stats. 1999 (A.B. 891), ch. 658, §39, effective July 1, 2000.)

§4688. Law of agency applies absent statutory rule under Division

Where this division does not provide a rule governing agents under powers of attorney, the law of agency applies.
(Stats. 1999 (A.B. 891), ch. 658, §39, effective July 1, 2000.)

§4689. Agent cannot make health care decision if principal objects

Nothing in this division authorizes an agent under a power of attorney for health care to make a health care decision if the principal objects to the decision. If the principal objects to the health care decision of the agent under a power of attorney, the matter shall be governed by the law that would apply if there were no power of attorney for health care.
(Stats. 1999 (A.B. 891), ch. 658, §39, effective July 1, 2000.)

§4690. Agent may consult with others to determine incapacity of principal

(a) If the principal becomes wholly or partially incapacitated, or if there is a question concerning the capacity of the principal, the agent may consult with a person previously designated by the principal for this purpose, and may also consult with and obtain information needed to carry out the agent's duties from the principal's spouse, physician, supervising health care provider, attorney, a member of the principal's family, or other person, including a business entity or government agency, with respect to matters covered by the power of attorney for health care.

(b) Except as set forth in subdivision (c) [FN1], a person described in subdivision (a) from whom information is requested shall disclose information that the agent requires to carry out his or her duties. Disclosure under this section is not a waiver of any privilege that may apply to the information disclosed.

[FN1] Subdivision (c) not present in enrolled bill.
(Stats. 1999 (A.B. 891), ch. 658, §39, effective July 1, 2000. Amended by Stats. 2006 (S.B. 1307), ch. 249, §3.)

c. Revocation of Advance Directives

A patient who has capacity may revoke an advance directive. The method of revocation is specified by California Probate Code §4695, requiring a signed writing or oral notification to the health care provider. A health care provider who has notice of the revocation of an advance directive has a duty to communicate the fact of revocation to the supervising health care provider and to any health care institution that is providing care to the patient (Cal. Prob. Code §4696). Divorce revokes the designation of the former spouse as an agent to make health care decisions (Cal. Prob. Code §4697); however, the authority may be revived by the parties' remarriage to each other (Cal. Prob. Code §4697(b)). Further, a later advance directive revokes an earlier one only to the extent of any conflicts between the two directives (Cal. Prob. Code §4698).

§4695. Patient with capacity may revoke advance directives; method of revocation

(a) A patient having capacity may revoke the designation of an agent only by a signed writing or by personally informing the supervising health care provider.

(b) A patient having capacity may revoke all or part of an advance health care directive, other than the designation of an agent, at any time and in any manner that communicates an intent to revoke.
(Stats. 1999 (A.B. 891), ch. 658, §39, effective July 1, 2000.)

§4696. Health care provider must communicate fact of revocation

A health care provider, agent, conservator, or surrogate who is informed of a revocation of an advance health care directive shall promptly communicate the fact of the revocation to the supervising health care provider and to any health care institution where the patient is receiving care.
(Stats. 1999 (A.B. 891), ch. 658, §39, effective July 1, 2000.)

§4697. Effect of dissolution of marriage on designation of former spouse as agent

(a) If after executing a power of attorney for health care the principal's marriage to the agent is dissolved or annulled, the principal's designation of the former spouse as an agent to make health care decisions for the principal is revoked.

(b) If the agent's authority is revoked solely by subdivision (a), it is revived by the principal's remarriage to the agent.
(Stats. 1999 (A.B. 891), ch. 658, §39, effective July 1, 2000.)

§4698. Effect of conflicting directives

An advance health care directive that conflicts with an earlier advance directive revokes the earlier advance directive to the extent of the conflict.

(Stats. 1999 (A.B. 891), ch. 658, §39, effective July 1, 2000.)

§4700. No particular form is required

The form provided in Section 4701 may, but need not, be used to create an advance health care directive. The other sections of this division govern the effect of the form or any other writing used to create an advance health care directive. An individual may complete or modify all or any part of the form in Section 4701.

(Stats. 1999 (A.B. 891), ch. 658, §39, effective July 1, 2000.)

§4701. Statutory form

The statutory advance health care directive form is as follows:

ADVANCE HEALTH CARE DIRECTIVE

(California Probate Code Section 4701)

Explanation

You have the right to give instructions about your own health care. You also have the right to name someone else to make health care decisions for you. This form lets you do either or both of these things. It also lets you express your wishes regarding donation of organs and the designation of your primary physician. If you use this form, you may complete or modify all or any part of it. You are free to use a different form.

Part 1 of this form is a power of attorney for health care. Part 1 lets you name another individual as agent to make health care decisions for you if you become incapable of making your own decisions or if you want someone else to make those decisions for you now even though you are still capable. You may also name an alternate agent to act for you if your first choice is not willing, able, or reasonably available to make decisions for you. (Your agent may not be an operator or employee of a community care facility or a residential care facility where you are receiving care, or your supervising health care provider or employee of the health care institution where you are receiving care, unless your agent is related to you or is a coworker.)

Unless the form you sign limits the authority of your agent, your agent may make all health care decisions for you. This form has a place for you to limit the authority of your agent. You need not limit the authority of your agent if you wish to rely on your agent for all health care decisions that may have to be made. If you choose not to limit the authority of your agent, your agent will have the right to:

(a) Consent or refuse consent to any care, treatment, service, or procedure to maintain, diagnose, or otherwise affect a physical or mental condition.

(b) Select or discharge health care providers and institutions.

(c) Approve or disapprove diagnostic tests, surgical procedures, and programs of medication.

(d) Direct the provision, withholding, or withdrawal of artificial nutrition and hydration and all other forms of health care, including cardiopulmonary resuscitation.

(e) Make anatomical gifts, authorize an autopsy, and direct disposition of remains.

Part 2 of this form lets you give specific instructions about any aspect of your health care, whether or not you appoint an agent. Choices are provided for you to express your wishes regarding the provision, withholding, or withdrawal of treatment to keep you alive, as well as the provision of pain relief. Space is also provided for you to add to the choices you have made or for you to write out any additional wishes. If you are satisfied to allow your agent to determine what is best for you in making end-of-life decisions, you need not fill out Part 2 of this form.

Part 3 of this form lets you express an intention to donate your bodily organs and tissues following your death.

Part 4 of this form lets you designate a physician to have primary responsibility for your health care.

After completing this form, sign and date the form at the end. The form must be signed by two qualified witnesses or acknowledged before a notary public. Give a copy of the signed and completed form to your physician, to any other health care providers you may have, to any health care institution at which you are receiving care, and to any health care agents you have named. You should talk to the person you have named as agent to make sure that he or she understands your wishes and is willing to take the responsibility.

You have the right to revoke this advance health care directive or replace this form at any time.

* * * * *

PART 1

POWER OF ATTORNEY FOR HEALTH CARE

(1.1) DESIGNATION OF AGENT: I designate the following individual as my agent to make health care decisions for me:

____

(name of individual you choose as agent)

____

(address) (city) (state) (ZIP Code)

____

(home phone) (work phone)

OPTIONAL: If I revoke my agent's authority or if my agent is not willing, able, or reasonably available to make a health care decision for me, I designate as my first alternate agent:

____

(name of individual you choose as first alternate agent)

____

(address) (city) (state) (ZIP Code)

____

(home phone) (work phone)

OPTIONAL: If I revoke the authority of my agent and first alternate agent or if neither is willing, able, or reasonably available to make a health care decision for me, I designate as my second alternate agent:

____

(name of individual you choose as second alternate agent)

____

(address) (city) (state) (ZIP Code)

____

(home phone) (work phone)

(1.2) AGENT'S AUTHORITY: My agent is authorized to make all health care decisions for me, including decisions to provide, withhold, or withdraw artificial nutrition and hydration and all other forms of health care to keep me alive, except as I state here:

____

____

____

(Add additional sheets if needed.)

(1.3) WHEN AGENT'S AUTHORITY BECOMES EFFECTIVE: My agent's authority becomes effective when my primary physician determines that I am unable to make my own health care decisions unless I mark the following box. If I mark this box [ ], my agent's authority to make health care decisions for me takes effect immediately.

(1.4) AGENT'S OBLIGATION: My agent shall make health care decisions for me in accordance with this power of attorney for health care, any instructions I give in Part 2 of this form, and my other wishes to the extent known to my agent. To the extent my wishes are unknown, my agent shall make health care decisions for me in accordance with what my agent determines to be in my best interest. In determining my best interest, my agent shall consider my personal values to the extent known to my agent.

(1.5) AGENT'S POSTDEATH AUTHORITY: My agent is authorized to make anatomical gifts, authorize an autopsy, and direct disposition of my remains, except as I state here or in Part 3 of this form:

____

____

____

(Add additional sheets if needed.)

(1.6) NOMINATION OF CONSERVATOR: If a conservator of my person needs to be appointed for me by a court, I nominate the agent designated in this form. If that agent is not willing, able, or reasonably available to act as conservator, I nominate the alternate agents whom I have named, in the order designated.

PART 2
INSTRUCTIONS FOR HEALTH CARE

If you fill out this part of the form, you may strike any wording you do not want.

(2.1) END-OF-LIFE DECISIONS: I direct that my health care providers and others involved in my care provide, withhold, or withdraw treatment in accordance with the choice I have marked below:

[ ] (a) Choice Not To Prolong Life

I do not want my life to be prolonged if (1) I have an incurable and irreversible condition that will result in my death within a relatively short time, (2) I become unconscious and, to a reasonable degree of medical certainty, I will not regain consciousness, or (3) the likely risks and burdens of treatment would outweigh the expected benefits, OR

[ ] (b) Choice To Prolong Life

I want my life to be prolonged as long as possible within the limits of generally accepted health care standards.

(2.2) RELIEF FROM PAIN: Except as I state in the following space, I direct that treatment for alleviation of pain or discomfort be provided at all times, even if it hastens my death:

____

____

(Add additional sheets if needed.)

(2.3) OTHER WISHES: (If you do not agree with any of the optional choices above and wish to write your own, or if you wish to add to the instructions you have given above, you may do so here.) I direct that:

____

____

(Add additional sheets if needed.)

PART 3
DONATION OF ORGANS AT DEATH
(OPTIONAL)

(3.1) Upon my death (mark applicable box):
[ ] (a) I give any needed organs, tissues, or parts, OR
[ ] (b) I give the following organs, tissues, or parts only.[1]

____

(c) My gift is for the following purposes (strike any of[2] the following you do not want):
(1) Transplant
(2) Therapy
(3) Research
(4) Education

PART 4
PRIMARY PHYSICIAN
(OPTIONAL)

(4.1) I designate the following physician as my primary[3] physician:

____
(name of physician)

____
(address) (city) (state) (ZIP Code)

____
(phone)

OPTIONAL: If the physician I have designated above is not willing, able, or reasonably available to act as my primary physician, I designate[4] the following physician as my primary physician:

____
(name of physician)

____
(address) (city) (state) (ZIP Code)

____
(phone)

*****

PART 5

(5.1) EFFECT OF COPY: A copy of this form has the same effect as[5] the original.

(5.2) SIGNATURE: Sign and date the form here[6]:

______________________ ______________________
(date) (sign your name)

______________________ ______________________
(address) (print your name)

____
(city) (state)

(5.3) STATEMENT OF WITNESSES: I declare under penalty of perjury under the laws of California (1) that the individual who signed or acknowledged this advance health care directive is personally known to me, or that the individual's identity was proven to me by convincing evidence, (2) that the individual signed or acknowledged this advance directive in my presence, (3) that the individual appears to be of sound mind and under no duress, fraud, or undue influence, (4) that I am not a person appointed as agent by this advance directive, and (5) that I am not the individual's health care provider, an employee of the individual's health care provider, the operator of a community care facility, an employee of an operator of a community care facility, the operator of a residential care facility for the elderly, nor an employee of an operator of a residential care facility for the elderly.

First witness Second witness

______________________ ______________________
(print name) (print name)

______________________ ______________________
(address) (address)

______________________ ______________________
(city) (state) (city) (state)

_______________ _______________
(signature of witness) (signature of witness)

_______________ _______________
(date) (date)

(5.4) ADDITIONAL STATEMENT OF WITNESSES: At least one of the above witnesses must also sign the following declaration:
I further declare under penalty of perjury under the laws of California that I am not related to the individual executing this advance health care directive by blood, marriage, or adoption, and to the best of my knowledge, I am not entitled to any part of the individual's estate upon his or her death under a will now existing or by operation of law.

_______________ _______________
(signature of witness) (signature of witness)

PART 6
SPECIAL WITNESS REQUIREMENT

(6.1) The following statement is required only if you are a patient in a skilled nursing facility—a health care facility that provides the following basic services: skilled nursing care and supportive care to patients whose primary need is for availability of skilled nursing care on an extended basis. The patient advocate or ombudsman must sign the following statement:

STATEMENT OF PATIENT ADVOCATE
OR OMBUDSMAN

I declare under penalty of perjury under the laws of California that I am a patient advocate or ombudsman as designated by the State Department of Aging and that I am serving as a witness as required by Section 4675 of the Probate Code.

_______________ _______________
(date) (sign your name)

_______________ _______________
(address) (print your name)

____
(city) (state)

(Stats. 1999 (A.B. 891), ch. 658, §39, effective July 1, 2000.)

2. Health Care Surrogates

§4711. Method of designation of surrogate for health care decisions; expiration and revocation

(a) A patient may designate an adult as a surrogate to make health care decisions by personally informing the supervising health care provider. The designation of a surrogate shall be promptly recorded in the patient's health care record.

(b) Unless the patient specifies a shorter period, a surrogate designation under subdivision (a) is effective only during the course of treatment or illness or during the stay in the health care institution when the surrogate designation is made, or for 60 days, whichever period is shorter.

(c) The expiration of a surrogate designation under subdivision (b) does not affect any role the person designated under subdivision (a) may have in making health care decisions for the patient under any other law or standards of practice.

(d) If the patient has designated an agent under a power of attorney for health care, the surrogate designated under subdivision (a) has priority over the agent for the period provided in subdivision (b), but the designation of a surrogate does not revoke the designation of an agent unless the patient communicates the intention to revoke in compliance with subdivision (a) of Section 4695.

(Stats. 1999 (A.B. 891), ch. 658, §39, effective July 1, 2000. Amended by Stats. 2001 (A.B. 1278), ch. 230, §5.)

§4714. Surrogate shall make decisions based on patient's best interests

A surrogate, including a person acting as a surrogate, shall make a health care decision in accordance with the patient's individual health care instructions, if any, and other wishes to the extent known to the surrogate. Otherwise, the surrogate shall make the decision in accordance with the surrogate's determination of the patient's best interest. In determining the patient's best interest, the surrogate shall consider the patient's personal values to the extent known to the surrogate.

(Stats. 1999 (A.B. 891), ch. 658, §39, effective July 1, 2000.)

§4715. Person may disqualify another person from acting as surrogate

A patient having capacity at any time may disqualify another person, including a member of the patient's family, from acting as the patient's surrogate by a signed writing or by personally informing the supervising health care provider of the disqualification.

(Stats. 1999, ch. 658 (A.B. 891), §39, effective July 1, 2000.)

§4716. Spouse or domestic partner may make health care decisions

(a) If a patient lacks the capacity to make a health care decision, the patient's domestic partner shall have the same authority as a spouse has to make a health care decision for his or her incapacitated spouse. This section may not be construed to expand or restrict the ability of a spouse to make a health care decision for an incapacitated spouse.

(b) For the purposes of this section, the following definitions shall apply:

(1) "Capacity" has the same meaning as defined in Section 4609.

(2) "Health care" has the same meaning as defined in Section 4615.

(3) "Health care decision" has the same meaning as defined in Section 4617.

(4) "Domestic partner" has the same meaning as that term is used in Section 297 of the Family Code.

(Stats. 2001 (A.B. 25), ch. 893, §49.)

§4717. The hospital shall make reasonable effort to contact person who has the authority to make health care decisions for unconscious or incapable patient

(a) Notwithstanding any other provision of law, within 24 hours of the arrival in the emergency department of a general acute care hospital of a patient who is unconscious or otherwise incapable of communication, the hospital shall make reasonable efforts to contact the patient's agent, surrogate, or a family member or other person the hospital reasonably believes has the authority to make health care decisions on behalf of the patient. A hospital shall be deemed to have made reasonable efforts, and to have discharged its duty under this section, if it does all of the following:

(1) Examines the personal effects, if any, accompanying the patient and any medical records regarding the patient in its possession, and reviews any verbal or written report made by emergency medical technicians or the police, to identify the name of any agent, surrogate, or a family member or other person the hospital reasonably believes has the authority to make health care decisions on behalf of the patient.

(2) Contacts or attempts to contact any agent, surrogate, or a family member or other person the hospital reasonably believes has the authority to make health care decisions on behalf of the patient, as identified in paragraph (1).

(3) Contacts the Secretary of State directly or indirectly, including by voice mail or facsimile, to inquire whether the patient has registered an advance health care directive with the Advance Health Care Directive Registry, if the hospital finds evidence of the patient's Advance Health Care Directive Registry identification card either from the patient or from the patient's family or authorized agent.

(b) The hospital shall document in the patient's medical record all efforts made to contact any agent, surrogate, or a family member or other person the hospital reasonably believes has the authority to make health care decisions on behalf of the patient.

(c) Application of this section shall be suspended during any period in which the hospital implements its disaster and mass casualty program, or its fire and internal disaster program.

(Stats 2001 (S.B. 751), ch. 329 §1, known as Prob C §4716. Amended and renumbered by Stats 2004 (A.B. 2445), ch 882, §2.)

3. Duties of Health Care Providers

The Health Care Decisions Law imposes certain duties on health care providers. For example, the provider has the duty to:

- **promptly communicate to the patient the health care decision and the identity of the decisionmaker (Cal. Prob. Code §4730);**
- **record the existence (or revocation) of an advance health care directive and the designation (or disqualification) of a surrogate in the patient's record (Cal. Prob. Code §4731); and**
- **comply with a health care instruction made by the patient and to comply with a health care decision made by a surrogate decisionmaker (Cal. Prob. Code §4733).**

Two exceptions exist to the duty to comply with health care instructions made by a patient or a surrogate. A health care provider may decline to comply with a health care instruction or decision for reasons of conscience (Cal. Prob. Code §4734), and a health care provider may decline to comply with a health care instruction that is medically ineffective (Cal. Prob. Code §4735). In the event that the provider declines to comply, the provider has the duty to: inform the patient, if possible, and surrogate; make reasonable efforts to assist in the transfer of the patient to another health care provider or

institution that is willing to comply with the instruction or decision; provide continuing care to the patient until a transfer can be accomplished; and continue appropriate pain relief and other palliative care (Cal. Prob. Code §4736).

§4730. Health care provider shall communicate decision to patient

Before implementing a health care decision made for a patient, a supervising health care provider, if possible, shall promptly communicate to the patient the decision made and the identity of the person making the decision.

(Stats. 1999 (A.B. 891), ch. 658, §39, effective July 1, 2000.)

§4731. Health care provider has duty to record certain information and notify agent of revocation

(a) A supervising health care provider who knows of the existence of an advance health care directive, a revocation of an advance health care directive, or a designation or disqualification of a surrogate, shall promptly record its existence in the patient's health care record and, if it is in writing, shall request a copy. If a copy is furnished, the supervising health care provider shall arrange for its maintenance in the patient's health care record.

(b) A supervising health care provider who knows of a revocation of a power of attorney for health care or a disqualification of a surrogate shall make a reasonable effort to notify the agent or surrogate of the revocation or disqualification.

(Stats. 1999 (A.B. 891), ch. 658, §39, effective July 1, 2000.)

§4732. Primary physician has duty to record information regarding patient's capacity

A primary physician who makes or is informed of a determination that a patient lacks or has recovered capacity, or that another condition exists affecting an individual health care instruction or the authority of an agent, conservator of the person, or surrogate, shall promptly record the determination in the patient's health care record and communicate the determination to the patient, if possible, and to a person then authorized to make health care decisions for the patient.

(Stats. 1999 (A.B. 891), ch. 658, §39, effective July 1, 2000.)

§4733. Health care provider has duty to comply with health care instructions

Except as provided in Sections 4734 and 4735, a health care provider or health care institution providing care to a patient shall do the following:

(a) Comply with an individual health care instruction of the patient and with a reasonable interpretation of that instruction made by a person then authorized to make health care decisions for the patient.

(b) Comply with a health care decision for the patient made by a person then authorized to make health care decisions for the patient to the same extent as if the decision had been made by the patient while having capacity.

(Stats. 1999 (A.B. 891), ch. 658, §39, effective July 1, 2000.)

§4734. Exception: health care provider may decline to comply with health care instruction due to conscience

(a) A health care provider may decline to comply with an individual health care instruction or health care decision for reasons of conscience.

(b) A health care institution may decline to comply with an individual health care instruction or health care decision if the instruction or decision is contrary to a policy of the institution that is expressly based on reasons of conscience and if the policy was timely communicated to the patient or to a person then authorized to make health care decisions for the patient.

(Stats. 1999 (A.B. 891), ch. 658, §39, effective July 1, 2000.)

§4735. Exception: health care provider may decline to comply with health care instruction that is medically ineffective

A health care provider or health care institution may decline to comply with an individual health care instruction or health care decision that requires medically ineffective health care or health care contrary to generally accepted health care standards applicable to the health care provider or institution.

(Stats. 1999 (A.B. 891), ch. 658, §39, effective July 1, 2000.)

§4736. Duties of health care provider who declines to comply

A health care provider or health care institution that declines to comply with an individual health care instruction or health care decision shall do all of the following:

(a) Promptly so inform the patient, if possible, and any person then authorized to make health care decisions for the patient.

(b) Unless the patient or person then authorized to make health care decisions for the patient refuses assistance, immediately make all reasonable efforts to assist in the transfer of the patient to another health care provider or institution that is willing to comply with the instruction or decision.

(c) Provide continuing care to the patient until a transfer can be accomplished or until it appears that a transfer cannot be accomplished. In all cases, appropriate pain relief and other palliative care shall be continued.

(Stats. 1999 (A.B. 891), ch. 658, §39, effective July 1, 2000.)

4. Immunities and Liabilities

If a health care provider acts in good faith and in accordance with generally accepted standards of health care, the provider is not subject to civil or criminal liability for either complying with a health care decision by a decisionmaking that the provider believes has authority or, conversely, declining to comply with a health care decision based on a belief that the decisionmaker lacked authority (Cal. Prob. Code §4740(a), (b)). Moreover, the health care provider is relieved from liability, again, if acting in good faith and in accordance with generally accepted standards of health care, for complying with an advance directive on the assumption that the directive was valid when made and has not been revoked or terminated (*id.* at §4740(c)).

Nonetheless, if a health care provider intentionally violates the Act, he or she is liable for civil damages ($2500 or actual damages, whichever is greater) in addition to reasonable attorney's fees (Cal. Prob. Code §4742 (a)). The penalty for intentionally falsifying or concealing a written advance health care directive (or coercing a person to give, revoke, or not to give an advance health care directive) is more severe: damages of $10,000 or actual damages, whichever is greater, in addition to reasonable attorney's fees (*id.* at §4742 (b)). Finally, a person may be prosecuted for homicide for altering a written advance health care directive, or concealing or withholding knowledge of the revocation of a directive, if that act results in hastening a patient's death (Cal. Prob. Code §4743).

§4740. Health care provider has immunity from civil or criminal liability if acting in good faith and according to accepted standards

A health care provider or health care institution acting in good faith and in accordance with generally accepted health care standards applicable to the health care provider or institution is not subject to civil or criminal liability or to discipline for unprofessional conduct for any actions in compliance with this division, including, but not limited to, any of the following conduct:

(a) Complying with a health care decision of a person that the health care provider or health care institution believes in good faith has the authority to make a health care decision for a patient, including a decision to withhold or withdraw health care.

(b) Declining to comply with a health care decision of a person based on a belief that the person then lacked authority.

(c) Complying with an advance health care directive and assuming that the directive was valid when made and has not been revoked or terminated.

(d) Declining to comply with an individual health care instruction or health care decision, in accordance with Sections 4734 to 4736, inclusive.

(Stats. 1999 (A.B. 891), ch. 658, §39, effective July 1, 2000.)

§4741. Agent or surrogate has immunity from civil or criminal liability for decisionmaking in good faith

A person acting as agent or surrogate under this part is not subject to civil or criminal liability or to discipline for unprofessional conduct for health care decisions made in good faith.

(Stats. 1999 (A.B. 891), ch. 658, §39, effective July 1, 2000.)

§4742. Damages for intentional violations and acts

(a) A health care provider or health care institution that intentionally violates this part is subject to liability to the aggrieved individual for damages of two thousand five hundred dollars ($2,500) or actual damages resulting from the violation, whichever is greater, plus reasonable attorney's fees.

(b) A person who intentionally falsifies, forges, conceals, defaces, or obliterates an individual's advance health care directive or a revocation of an advance health care directive without the individual's consent, or who coerces or fraudulently induces an individual to give, revoke, or not to give an advance health care directive, is subject to liability to that individual for damages of ten thousand dollars ($10,000) or actual damages resulting from the action, whichever is greater, plus reasonable attorney's fees.

(c) The damages provided in this section are cumulative and not exclusive of any other remedies provided by law.

(Stats. 1999 (A.B. 891), ch. 658, §39, effective July 1, 2000.)

§4743. Criminal liability for altering or forging health care directive

Any person who alters or forges a written advance health care directive of another, or willfully conceals or withholds personal knowledge of a revocation of an advance directive, with the intent to cause a withholding or withdrawal of health care necessary to keep the patient alive contrary to the desires of the patient, and thereby directly causes health care necessary to keep the patient alive to be withheld or withdrawn and the death of the patient thereby to be hastened, is subject to prosecution for unlawful homicide as provided in Chapter 1 (commencing with Section 187) of Title 8 of Part 1 of the Penal Code.

(Stats. 1999 (A.B. 891), ch. 658, §39, effective July 1, 2000.)

IV. Judicial Proceedings Regarding Health Care Directives

§4750. Health care directive is effective absent judicial intervention

Subject to this division:

(a) An advance health care directive is effective and exercisable free of judicial intervention.

(b) A health care decision made by an agent for a principal is effective without judicial approval.

(c) A health care decision made by a surrogate for a patient is effective without judicial approval.

(Stats. 1999 (A.B. 891), ch. 658, §39, effective July 1, 2000.)

§4751. Remedies are cumulative and not exclusive

The remedies provided in this part are cumulative and not exclusive of any other remedies provided by law.

(Stats. 1999 (A.B. 891), ch. 658, §39, effective July 1, 2000.)

§4752. Ability to limit judicial intervention

Except as provided in Section 4753, this part is not subject to limitation in an advance health care directive.

(Stats. 1999 (A.B. 891), ch. 658, §39, effective July 1, 2000.)

§4753. Requirements for directive to limit ability of person to petition court

(a) Subject to subdivision (b), an advance health care directive may expressly eliminate the authority of a person listed in Section 4765 to petition the court for any one or more of the purposes enumerated in Section 4766, if both of the following requirements are satisfied:

(1) The advance directive is executed by an individual having the advice of a lawyer authorized to practice law in the state where the advance directive is executed.

(2) The individual's lawyer signs a certificate stating in substance:

"I am a lawyer authorized to practice law in the state where this advance health care directive was executed, and __________ [insert name] was my client at the time this advance directive was executed. I have advised my client concerning his or her rights in connection with this advance directive and the applicable law and the consequences of signing or not signing this advance directive, and my client, after being so advised, has executed this advance directive."

(b) An advance health care directive may not limit the authority of the following persons to petition under this part:

(1) The conservator of the person, with respect to a petition relating to an advance directive, for a purpose specified in subdivision (b) or (d) of Section 4766.

(2) The agent, with respect to a petition relating to a power of attorney for health care, for a purpose specified in subdivision (b) or (c) of Section 4766.

(Stats. 1999 (A.B. 891), ch. 658, §39, effective July 1, 2000.)

§4754. Right to jury trial

There is no right to a jury trial in proceedings under this division.

(Stats. 1999 (A.B. 891), ch. 658, §39, effective July 1, 2000.)

§4755. Application of provisions in Division 3

Except as otherwise provided in this division, the general provisions in Division 3 (commencing with Section 1000) apply to proceedings under this division.

(Stats. 1999 (A.B. 891), ch. 658, §39, effective July 1, 2000.)

§4760. Superior court has jurisdiction

(a) The superior court has jurisdiction in proceedings under this division.

(b) The court in proceedings under this division is a court of general jurisdiction and the court, or a judge of the court, has the same power and authority with respect to the proceedings as otherwise provided by law for a superior court, or a judge of the superior court, including, but not limited to, the matters authorized by Section 128 of the Code of Civil Procedure.

(Stats. 1999 (A.B. 891), ch. 658, §39, effective July 1, 2000.)

4761. Exercise of jurisdiction limited by Code of Civil Procedure provision

The court may exercise jurisdiction in proceedings under this division on any basis permitted by Section 410.10 of the Code of Civil Procedure.

(Stats. 1999 (A.B. 891), ch. 658, §39, effective July 1, 2000.)

§4762. Agent or surrogate is subject to personal jurisdiction for acts affecting patient

Without limiting Section 4761, a person who acts as an agent under a power of attorney for health care or as a surrogate under this division is subject to personal jurisdiction in this state with respect to matters relating to acts and transactions of the agent or surrogate performed in this state or affecting a patient in this state.

(Stats. 1999 (A.B. 891), ch. 658, §39, effective July 1, 2000.)

§4763. Venue

The proper county for commencement of a proceeding under this division shall be determined in the following order of priority:

(a) The county in which the patient resides.

(b) The county in which the agent or surrogate resides.

(c) Any other county that is in the patient's best interest.

(Stats. 1999 (A.B. 891), ch. 658, §39, effective July 1, 2000.)

§4765. Persons eligible to file petition

Subject to Section 4753, a petition may be filed under this part by any of the following persons:

(a) The patient.

(b) The patient's spouse, unless legally separated.

(c) A relative of the patient.

(d) The patient's agent or surrogate.

(e) The conservator of the person of the patient.

(f) The court investigator, described in Section 1454, of the county where the patient resides.

(g) The public guardian of the county where the patient resides.

(h) The supervising health care provider or health care institution involved with the patient's care.

(i) Any other interested person or friend of the patient.

(Stats. 1999 (A.B. 891), ch. 658, §39, effective July 1, 2000.)

§4766. Petition may be filed for the following purposes

A petition may be filed under this part for any one or more of the following purposes:

(a) Determining whether or not the patient has capacity to make health care decisions.

(b) Determining whether an advance health care directive is in effect or has terminated.

(c) Determining whether the acts or proposed acts of an agent or surrogate are consistent with the patient's desires as expressed in an advance health care directive or otherwise made known to the court or, where the patient's desires are unknown or unclear, whether the acts or proposed acts of the agent or surrogate are in the patient's best interest.

(d) Declaring that the authority of an agent or surrogate is terminated, upon a determination by the court that the agent or surrogate has made a health care decision for the patient that authorized anything illegal or upon a determination by the court of both of the following:

(1) The agent or surrogate has violated, has failed to perform, or is unfit to perform, the duty under an advance health care directive to act consistent with the patient's desires or, where the patient's desires are unknown or unclear, is acting (by action or inaction) in a manner that is clearly contrary to the patient's best interest.

(2) At the time of the determination by the court, the patient lacks the capacity to execute or to revoke an advance health care directive or disqualify a surrogate.

(e) Compelling a third person to honor individual health care instructions or the authority of an agent or surrogate.

(Stats. 1999 (A.B. 891), ch. 658, §39, effective July 1, 2000. Amended by Stats. 2001 (A.B. 1278), ch. 230, §7.)

§4767. Commencement of proceeding by filing a petition

A proceeding under this part is commenced by filing a petition stating facts showing that the petition is authorized under this part, the grounds of the petition, and, if known to the petitioner, the terms of any advance health care directive in question.

(Stats. 1999 (A.B. 891), ch. 658, §39, effective July 1, 2000.)

§4768. Conditions for dismissal of petition

The court may dismiss a petition if it appears that the proceeding is not reasonably necessary for the protection of the interests of the patient and shall stay or dismiss the proceeding in whole or in part when required by Section 410.30 of the Code of Civil Procedure.

(Stats. 1999 (A.B. 891), ch. 658, §39, effective July 1, 2000.)

§4769. Petitioner shall serve notice of time and place of hearing

(a) Subject to subdivision (b), at least 15 days before the time set for hearing, the petitioner shall serve notice of the time and place of the hearing, together with a copy of the petition, on the following:

(1) The agent or surrogate, if not the petitioner.

(2) The patient, if not the petitioner.

(b) In the case of a petition to compel a third person to honor individual health care instructions or the authority of an agent or surrogate, notice of the time and place of the hearing, together with a copy of the petition, shall be served on the third person in the manner provided in Chapter 4 (commencing with Section 413.10) of Title 5 of Part 2 of the Code of Civil Procedure.

(Stats. 1999 (A.B. 891), ch. 658, §39, effective July 1, 2000. Amended by Stats. 2001 (A.B. 1278), ch. 230, §8.)

§4770. Court may issue temporary order prescribing health care until disposition of petition

The court in its discretion, on a showing of good cause, may issue a temporary order prescribing the health care of the patient until the disposition of the petition filed under Section 4766. If a power of attorney for health care is in effect and a conservator (including a temporary conservator) of the person is appointed for the principal, the court that appoints the conservator in its discretion, on a showing of good cause, may issue a temporary order prescribing the health care of the principal, the order to continue in effect for the period ordered by the court but in no case longer than the period necessary to permit the filing and determination of a petition filed under Section 4766.

(Stats. 1999 (A.B. 891), ch. 658, §39, effective July 1, 2000.)

§4771. Court has discretion to award attorney's fees

In a proceeding under this part commenced by the filing of a petition by a person other than the agent or surrogate, the court may in its discretion award reasonable attorney's fees to one of the following:

(a) The agent or surrogate, if the court determines that the proceeding was commenced without any reasonable cause.

(b) The person commencing the proceeding, if the court determines that the agent or surrogate has clearly violated the duties under the advance health care directive.

(Stats. 1999 (A.B. 891), ch. 658, §39, effective July 1, 2000.)

V. Requests to Forgo Resuscitative Measures

The Health Care Decisions Law also governs the individual's request to forgo resuscitative measures. Such requests must be in writing and signed by the patient (or authorized surrogate decisionmaker), as well as a physician (Cal. Prob. Code §4780(a)(1)). A health care provider who honors such a request is immune from civil and criminal liability, provided that the provider believes in good faith that the action or decision is consistent with the Health Care Decisions Law, and has no knowledge that the decision would be inconsistent with a decision that the patient would have made in similar circumstances (Cal. Prob. Code §4782). Note, however, that the Health Care Decisions Law is not intended to permit acts or omissions other than withholding or withdrawing health care pursuant to an advance directive. That is, the legislation shall not be construed to "condone, authorize, or approve mercy killing, assisted suicide or euthanasia" (Cal. Prob. Code §4653).

§4780. Definitions

(a) As used in this part:

(1) "Request to forgo resuscitative measures" means a written document, signed by (A) an individual, or a legally recognized surrogate health care decisionmaker, and (B) a physician, that directs a health care provider to forgo resuscitative measures for the individual.

(2) "Request to forgo resuscitative measures" includes a prehospital "do not resuscitate" form as developed by the Emergency Medical Services Authority or other substantially similar form.

(b) A request to forgo resuscitative measures may also be evidenced by a medallion engraved with the words "do not resuscitate" or the letters "DNR," a patient identification number, and a 24-hour toll-free telephone number, issued by a person pursuant to an agreement with the Emergency Medical Services Authority.

(Stats. 1999 (A.B. 891), ch. 658, §39, effective July 1, 2000.)

§4781. "Health care provider," defined

As used in this part, "health care provider" includes, but is not limited to, the following:

(a) Persons described in Section 4621.

(b) Emergency response employees, including, but not limited to, firefighters, law enforcement officers, emergency medical technicians I and II, paramedics, and employees and volunteer members of legally organized and recognized volunteer organizations, who are trained in accordance with standards adopted as regulations by the Emergency Medical Services Authority pursuant to Sections 1797.170, 1797.171, 1797.172, 1797.182, and 1797.183 of the Health and Safety Code to respond to medical emergencies in the course of performing their volunteer or employee duties with the organization.

(Stats. 1999 (A.B. 891), ch. 658, §39, effective July 1, 2000.)

§4782. Conditions under which health care provider who honors request to forgo resuscitative measures is immune from criminal or civil liability or other sanction

A health care provider who honors a request to forgo resuscitative measures is not subject to criminal prosecution, civil liability, discipline for unprofessional conduct, administrative sanction, or any other sanction, as a result of his or her reliance on the request, if the health care provider (a) believes in good faith that the action or decision is consistent with this part, and (b) has no knowledge that the action or decision would be inconsistent with a health care decision that the individual signing the request would have made on his or her own behalf under like circumstances.

(Stats. 1999 (A.B. 891), ch. 658, §39, effective July 1, 2000.)

§4783. Contents of forms

(a) Forms for requests to forgo resuscitative measures printed after January 1, 1995, shall contain the following:

> "By signing this form, the surrogate acknowledges that this request to forgo resuscitative measures is consistent with the known desires of, and with the best interest of, the individual who is the subject of the form."

(b) A substantially similar printed form is valid and enforceable if all of the following conditions are met:

(1) The form is signed by the individual, or the individual's legally recognized surrogate health care decisionmaker, and a physician.

(2) The form directs health care providers to forgo resuscitative measures.

(3) The form contains all other information required by this section.

(Stats. 1999 (A.B. 891), ch. 658, §39, effective July 1, 2000.)

§4784. Presumption of validity of request to forgo resuscitative measures

In the absence of knowledge to the contrary, a health care provider may presume that a request to forgo resuscitative measures is valid and unrevoked.

(Stats. 1999 (A.B. 891), ch. 658, §39, effective July 1, 2000.)

§4785. Part applies regardless of whether patient is within or outside of hospital

This part applies regardless of whether the individual executing a request to forgo resuscitative measures is within or outside a hospital or other health care institution.

(Stats. 1999 (A.B. 891), ch. 658, §39, effective July 1, 2000.)

§4786. Effect on other laws relating to health care decisionmaking

This part does not repeal or narrow laws relating to health care decisionmaking.

(Stats. 1999 (A.B. 891), ch. 658, §39, effective July 1, 2000.)

§4800. Establishment of central registry system

(a) The Secretary of State shall establish a registry system through which a person who has executed a written advance health care directive may register in a central information center, information regarding the advance directive, making that information available upon request to any health care provider, the public guardian, or the legal representative of the registrant. A request for information pursuant to this section shall state the need for the information.

(b) The Secretary of State shall respond by the close of business on the next business day to a request for information made pursuant to Section 4717 by the emergency department of a general acute care hospital.

(c) Information that may be received is limited to the registrant's name, social security number, driver's license number, or other individual identifying number established by law, if any, address, date and place of birth, the registrant's advance health care directive, an intended place of deposit or safekeeping of a written advance health care directive, and the name and telephone number of the agent and any alternative agent. Information that may be released upon request may not include the registrant's social security number except when necessary to verify the identity of the registrant.

(d) When the Secretary of State receives information from a registrant, the secretary shall issue the registrant an Advance Health Care Directive Registry identification card indicating that an advance health care directive, or information regarding an advance health care directive, has been deposited with the registry. Costs associated with issuance of the card shall be offset by the fee charged by the Secretary of State to receive and register information at the registry.

(e) The Secretary of State, at the request of the registrant or his or her legal representative, shall transmit the information received regarding the written advance health care directive to the registry system of another jurisdiction as identified by the registrant, or his or her legal representative.

(f) The Secretary of State shall charge a fee to each registrant in an amount such that, when all fees charged to registrants are aggregated, the aggregated fees do not exceed the actual cost of establishing and maintaining the registry.
(Stats. 1999 (A.B. 891), ch. 658, §39, effective July 1, 2000. Amended by Stats. 2004 (A.B. 2445), ch. 882, §3.)

§4801. Establishment of procedures to verify identities of health care providers requesting information

The Secretary of State shall establish procedures to verify the identities of health care providers, the public guardian, and other authorized persons requesting information pursuant to Section 4800. No fee shall be charged to any health care provider, the public guardian, or other authorized person requesting information pursuant to Section 4800.
(Stats. 1999 (A.B. 891), ch. 658, §39, effective July 1, 2000.)

§4802. Establishment of procedures to advise registrants of certain matters

The Secretary of State shall establish procedures to advise each registrant of the following:

(a) A health care provider may not honor a written advance health care directive until it receives a copy from the registrant.

(b) Each registrant must notify the registry upon revocation of the advance directive.

(c) Each registrant must reregister upon execution of a subsequent advance directive.
(Stats. 1999 (A.B. 891), ch. 658, §39, effective July 1, 2000.)

§4803. Failure to register with Secretary of States does not effect validity of directive

Failure to register with the Secretary of State does not affect the validity of any advance health care directive.
(Stats. 1999 (A.B. 891), ch. 658, §39, effective July 1, 2000.)

§4804. Registration does not limit ability to revoke directive

Registration with the Secretary of State does not affect the ability of the registrant to revoke the registrant's advance health care directive or a later executed advance directive, nor does registration raise any presumption of validity or superiority among any competing advance directives or revocations.
(Stats. 1999 (A.B. 891), ch. 658, §39, effective July 1, 2000.)

§4805. Effect of chapter on duties of health care providers to request or provide information

Nothing in this chapter shall be construed to require a health care provider to request from the registry information about whether a patient has executed an advance health care directive. Nothing in this chapter shall be construed to affect the duty of a health care provider to provide information to a patient regarding advance health care directives pursuant to any provision of federal law.
(Stats. 1999 (A.B. 891), ch. 658, §39, effective July 1, 2000. Amended by Stats. 2004 (A.B. 2005), ch. 882, §4.)

4806. Advance Directives and Terminal Illness Decisions Program

(a) The Secretary of State shall work with the State Department of Health Services and the office of the Attorney General to develop information about end of life care, advance health care directives, and registration of the advance health care directives at the registry established pursuant to subdivision (a) of Section 4800. This information shall be developed utilizing existing information developed by the office of the Attorney General.

(b) Links to the information specified in subdivision (a) and to the registry shall be available on the Web sites of the Secretary of State, the State Department of Health Services, the office of the Attorney General, the Department of Managed Health Care, the Department of Insurance, the Board of Registered Nursing, and the Medical Board of California.
(Stats. 2005 (A.B. 1676), ch. 434, §3.)

PART II

~

RESTATEMENT (THIRD) OF PROPERTY: WILLS AND OTHER DONATIVE TRANSFERS, VOLS. 1 & 2 (1999, 2003)

RESTATEMENT (THIRD) OF PROPERTY: WILLS AND OTHER DONATIVE TRANSFERS, VOLS. 1 & 2 (1999, 2003)

TABLE OF CONTENTS

RESTATEMENT (THIRD) OF PROPERTY: WILLS AND OTHER DONATIVE TRANSFERS, vol. 1 (1999)

Chapter 1: DEFINITIONS AND BASIC PRINCIPLES

§1.1 Probate Estate

(a) A decedent's "probate estate" is the estate subject to administration under applicable laws relating to decedents' estates. The probate estate consists of property owned by the decedent at death and property acquired by the decedent's estate at or after the decedent's death.

(b) The "net probate estate" is the probate estate after deduction for family, exempt property, and homestead allowances, claims against the estate (including funeral expenses and expenses of administration), and taxes for which the estate is liable. Subject to overriding claims and rights provided by applicable law, such as the right of the decedent's surviving spouse to take an elective share or to elect other marital rights, the decedent's net probate estate passes to the decedent's heirs or devisees by intestate or testate succession.

§1.2 Requirement of Surviving the Decedent

An individual who fails to survive the decedent cannot take as an heir or a devisee.

§1.3 Noncitizens

Except as otherwise provided by applicable statute, the fact that an individual, or an individual through whom he or she claims, is not or was not a citizen of the United States does not disqualify the individual from acquiring or transmitting property through testate or intestate succession

Chapter 2: INTESTACY

§2.1 General Principles and Definitions

(a) A decedent who dies without a valid will dies intestate. A decedent who dies with a valid will that does not dispose of all of the decedent's net probate estate dies partially intestate.

(b) The decedent's intestate estate, consisting of that part of the decedent's net probate estate that is not disposed of by a valid will, passes at the decedent's death to the decedent's heirs as provided by statute.

§2.2 Intestate Share of Surviving Spouse

An intestate decedent's surviving spouse takes a share of the intestate estate as provided by statute. The exact share differs among the states. Not infrequently, the spouse takes the entire intestate estate if the decedent leaves no surviving descendants or parents and, in some states, if the decedent also leaves no other specified relative such as a descendant of a parent. Older statutes tend to reduce the spouse's share to a fraction such as one-half or one-third when the decedent leaves a surviving descendant or another specified relative. Under the Revised Uniform Probate Code, the surviving spouse takes either the entire intestate estate or a specified lump sum plus a specified percentage of the excess, if any, depending on what other relatives survive the decedent.

§2.3 Intestate Share of Surviving Descendants

(a) An intestate decedent's surviving descendants take the entire intestate estate if the decedent leaves no surviving spouse, and they take any portion of the intestate estate not passing to the surviving spouse if the decedent leaves a surviving spouse.

(b) The decedent's surviving descendants take by representation. There are several systems of representation.

§2.4 Intestate Share of Surviving Ancestors and Collateral Relatives

(a) If an intestate decedent leaves no surviving spouse and no surviving descendants, nearly all intestacy statutes grant the intestate estate to the second parentela (the decedent's surviving parents or, if deceased, to the parent's surviving descendants) and if no member of the second parentela survives the decedent, to the third parentela (the decedent's grandparents or, if deceased, to the grandparent's surviving descendants).

(b) If no member of the second or third parentela survives the decedent, the intestacy statutes diverge, but most follow one of two patterns. Either the intestate estate escheats to the state, or the intestate estate passes per capita to the decedent's nearest kindred as determined by the civil-law method, with the relatives having the nearer common ancestor taking exclusively under some statutes. Under statutes of the latter sort, the estate escheats to the state only if the decedent leaves no surviving kindred.

§2.5 Parent and Child Relationship

For purposes of intestate succession by, from, or through an individual:

(1) An individual is the child of his or her genetic parents, whether or not they are married to each other, except as otherwise provided in paragraph (2) or (5) or as other facts and circumstances warrant a different result.

(2) An adopted individual is a child of his or her adoptive parent or parents.

(A) If the adoption removes the child from the families of both of the genetic parents, the child is not a child of either genetic parent.

(B) If the adoption is by a relative of either genetic parent, or by the spouse or surviving spouse of such a relative, the individual remains a child of both genetic parents.

(C) If the adoption is by a stepparent, the adopted stepchild is not only a child of the adoptive stepparent but is also a child of the genetic parent who is married to the stepparent. Under several intestacy statutes, including the Uniform Probate Code, the adopted stepchild is also a child of the other genetic parent for purposes of inheritance from and through that parent, but not for purposes of inheritance from or through the child.

(3) A stepchild who is not adopted by his or her stepparent is not the stepparent's child.

(4) A foster child is not the child of his or her foster parent or parents.

(5) A parent who has refused to acknowledge or has abandoned his or her child, or a person whose parental rights have been terminated, is barred from inheriting from or through the child.

§2.6 Advancements

An inter vivos gift made by an intestate decedent to an individual who, at the decedent's death, is an heir is treated as an advancement against the heir's intestate share if the decedent indicated in a contemporaneous writing, or if the heir acknowledged in writing, that the gift was so to operate.

§2.7 Negative Wills

A decedent's will may expressly exclude or limit the right of an individual or class to succeed to property of the decedent passing by intestate succession.

Chapter 3: EXECUTION OF WILLS

§3.1 Attested Wills

A will is validly executed if it is in writing and is signed by the testator and by a specified number of attesting witnesses under procedures provided by applicable law.

§3.2 Holographic Wills

Statutes in many states provide that a will, though unwitnessed, is validly executed if it is written in the testator's handwriting and signed by the testator, and, under some statutes, dated in the testator's handwriting.

§3.3 Excusing Harmless Errors

A harmless error in executing a will may be excused if the proponent establishes by clear and convincing evidence that the decedent adopted the document as his or her will.

Comment

. . . b. Excusing harmless errors. . . . The requirement of a writing is so fundamental to the purpose of the execution formalities that it cannot be excused as harmless under the principle of this Restatement. Only a harmless error in executing a document can be excused under this Restatement.

Among the defects in execution that can be excused, the lack of a signature is the hardest to excuse. An unsigned will raises a serious but not insuperable doubt about whether the testator adopted the document as his or her will. A particularly attractive case for excusing the lack of the testator's signature is a crossed will case, in which, by mistake, a wife signs her husband's will and the husband signs his wife's will. Because attestation makes a more modest contribution to the purpose of the formalities, defects in compliance with attestation procedures are more easily excused. . . .

c. Scope of harmless-error rule. The harmless-error rule established in this section applies not only to defective execution but also to the validity of attempts to revoke a will or to revive a revoked will, topics covered in Chapter 4. . . .

§3.4 Republication by Codicil

A will is treated as if it were executed when its most recent codicil was executed, whether or not the codicil expressly republishes the prior will, unless the effect of so treating it would be inconsistent with the testator's intent.

§3.5 Integration of Multiple Pages or Writings Into a Single Will

To be treated as part of a page or other writing must be present when the will is executed and must be intended to be part of the will.

§3.6 Incorporation by Reference

A writing that is not valid as a will but is in existence when a will is executed may be incorporated by reference into the will if the will manifests an intent to incorporate the writing and the writing to be incoporated is identified with reasonable certainty.

§3.7 Independent Significance

The meaning of a dispositive or other provision may be supplied or affected by an external circumstance referred to in the will, unless the external circumstance has no significance apart from its effect upon the will.

§3.8 Pour-Over Devises

(a) A "pour-over" devise is a provision in a will that (i) adds property to an inter vivos trust or (ii) funds a trust that was not funded during the testator's lifetime but whose terms are in a trust instrument that was executed during the testator's lifetime.

(b) A pour-over devise may be validated by statute, by incorporation by reference, or by independent significance.

§3.9 Testamentary Disposition by Unattested Writing

When permitted by statute, a will may devise property as provided in a separate unattested writing even though the writing has no independent significance and does not satisfy the requirements for incorporation by reference.

Chapter 4: REVOCATION OF WILLS

§4.1 Revocation of Wills

(a) A testator may revoke his or her will in whole or in part by subsequent will or by revocatory act.

(b) The dissolution of the testator's marraige is a change in circumstance that presumptively revokes any provision in the testator's will in favor of his or her former spouse. Neither marriage nor marriage followed by birth of issue is a chance in circumstance that revokes a will or any part of a will.

Comment

. . . *j. Presumption if lost or mutilated will traced to testator's possession.* If a will is traced to the testator's possession and cannot be found after death, there are three plausible explanations for its absence: The testator destroyed it with the intent to revoke; the will was accidentally destroyed or lost; or the will was wrongfully destroyed or suppressed by someone dissatisfied with its terms. Of these plausible explanations, the law presumes that the testator destroyed the will with intent to revoke it.

If a will is traced to the testator's possession and it is found after death with a revocatory act performed on it, . . . the law presumes that the testator performed the act on the will with intent to revoke it.

The presumption that the testator destroyed the will or performed some other revocatory act on it with intent to revoke is rebuttable. . . .

l. Act performed by another. Even if the testator did not perform a revocatory act on the will with intent to revoke, the will is still revoked by act if the testator directed another to perform the act and if the other person performed the act in the testator's presence. . . .

m. Revocation of codicil by act—effect on will. The revocation by act of a codicil to a will does not revoke the will, but the revocation is presumed to revive portions of the will that the codicil revoked. See §4.2, Comment g.

n. Revocation of will by act—effect on codicil. The revocation of a will by act does not revoke a codicil to the will. If the codicil depends on the revoked will for its meaning, however, the codicil may have no effect as a matter of construction. . . .

§4.2 Revival of Revoked Wills

(a) A will that was revoked by a later will is revived if the testator: (i) reexecuted the previously revoked will; (ii) executed a codicil indicating an intent to revive the previously revoked will; (iii) revoked the revoking will by act intending to revive the previously revoked will; or (iv) revoked the revoking will by another, later will whose terms indicate an intent to revive the previously revoked will.

(b) A will that was revoked by act is revived if the testator: (i) reexecuted the will; (ii) executed a codicil indicating an intent to revive the previously revoked will; or (iii) performed an act on the will that clearly and convincingly demonstrates an intent to reverse the revocation.

(c) A testamentary provision that was revoked by dissolution of the testator's marriage is revived if: (i) the testator remarried the former spouse, reexecuted the will, or executed a codicil indicating an intent to revive the previously revoked provision; or (ii) the dissolution of hte marriage is nullified.

§4.3 Ineffective Revocation (Dependent Relative Revocation)

(a) A partial or complete revocation of a will is presumptively ineffective if the testator made the revocation:

(1) in connection with an attempt to achieve a dispositive objective that fails under applicable law, or

(2) because of a false assumption of law, or because of a false belief about an objective fact, that is either recited in the revoking instrument or established by clear and convincing evidence.

(b) The presumption established in subsection (a) is rebutted if allowing the revocation to remain in effect would be more consistent with the testator's probable intention.

Chapter 5: POST-EXECUTION EVENTS AFFECTING WILLS

§5.1 Classification of Devises

Devises are classified as specific, general, demonstrative, or residuary:

(1) A specific devise is a testamentary disposition of a specifically identified asset.

(2) A general devise is a testamentary disposition, usually of a specified amount of money or quantity of property, that is payable from the general assets of the estate.

(3) A demonstrative devise is a testamentary disposition, usually of a specified amount of money or quantity of property, that is primarily payable from a designated source, but is secondarily payable from the general assets of the estate to the extent that the primary source is insufficient.

(4) A residuary devise is a testamentary disposition of property of the testator's net probate estate not disposed of by a specific, general, or demonstrative devise.

§5.2 Failure ("Ademption") of Specific Devises by Extinction

(a) If specifically devised property, in its original or in a changed form, is in the testator's estate at death, the devisee is entitled to the specifically devised property.

(b) If specifically devised property is not in the testator's estate at death, the devisee is entitled to any proceeds unpaid at death of (i) any sale, (ii) any condemnation award, or (iii) any insurance on or other recovery for damage to or loss of the property.

(c) Subject to subsection (b), if specifically devised property is not in the testator's estate at death, the specific devise fails unless failure of the devise would be inconsistent with the testator's intent.

§5.3 Effect of Stock Splits, Stock Dividends, and Other Distributions on Devises of a Specified Number of Securities

A devise of a specified number of securities carries with it any additional securities acquired by the testator after executing the will to the extent that the post-execution acquisitions resulted from the testator's ownership of the described securities.

§5.4 Ademption by Satisfaction

An inter vivos gift made by a testator to a devisee or to a member of the devisee's family adeems the devise by satisfaction, in whole or in part, if the testator indicated in a contemporaneous writing, or if the devisee acknowledged in writing, that the gift was so to operate.

§5.5 Antilapse Statutes

Antilapse statutes typically provide, as a rebuttable rule of construction, that devises to certain relatives who predecease the testator pass to specified substitute takers, usually the descendants of the predeceased devisee who survive the testator.

Comment

. . . Antilapse statutes establish a strong rule of construction, designed to carry out probable intent. They are based on the constructional preference against disinheriting a line of descent, which in turn implements the constructional preference for preserving equality among different lines of descent. . . .

h. Contrary intent; survival language. An often litigated question is whether language requiring the devisee to survive the testator, without more, constitutes a sufficient expression of a contrary intent to defeat the antilapse statute. The majority view is that such language signifies a contrary intent. Because such a survival provision is often boiler-plate form-book language, the testator may not understand that such language could disinherit the line of descent headed by the deceased devisee. When the testator is older than the devisee and hence does not expect the devisee to die first, or if the devisee was childless when the will was executed, it seems especially unlikely that a provision requiring the devisee to survive the testator was intended to disinherit the devisee's descendants. . . .

. . . As indicated [*supra*], antilapse statutes are based on the constructional preference against disinheriting a line of descent. As explained in §11.3, . . . that constructional preference

is strongest when applied to direct descendants of the donor (sometimes called *lineal* descendants). The preference . . . becomes somewhat weaker the farther removed the ancestor is to the donor. . . .

o. Lapse in the residue; rejection of the no-residue-of-a-residue rule. For the purpose of determining what happens to the share of a residuary devisee who fails to survive the testator, a residuary clause that devises the residue to two or more persons is treated as if it created a class gift, even if the devise is not in the form of a class gift. The contrary rule, sometimes called the *no-residue-of-a-residue rule*, is not followed in modern statutory law, including the Uniform Probate Code, nor in this Restatement. Thus, if an antilapse statute does not apply, the share of a residuary devisee that fails for any reason passes to the other residuary devisee, or if more than one, to the other residuary devisees in proportion to the interest of each in the remaining part of the residue. A residuary devise lapses and passes to intestacy only if an antilapse statute does not apply and no residuary devisee survives the testator. . . .

RESTATEMENT (THIRD) OF PROPERTY: WILLS AND OTHER DONATIVE TRANSFERS, vol. 2 (2003)

Chapter 6: GIFTS

§6.1 Requirements Applicable to All Gifts of Property

(a) To make a gift of property, the donor must transfer an ownership interest to the donee without consideration and with donative intent.

(b) Acceptance by the donee is required for a gift to become complete. Acceptance is presumed, subject to the donee's right to refuse or disclaim.

§6.2 Gifts of Personal Property

The transfer of personal property, necessary to perfect a gift, may be made

(1) by delivering the property to the donee or

(2) by inter vivos donative document.

§6.3 Gifts of Land

The transfer of land, necessary to perfect a gift, must be evidenced in a writing that is executed in compliance with the formalities required by the applicable statute of frauds.

Chapter 7: WILL SUBSTITUTES

§7.1 Will Substitute—Definition and Validity

(a) A will substitute is an arrangement respecting property or contract rights that is established during the donor's life, under which (1) the right to possession or enjoyment of the property or to a contractual payment shifts outside of probate to the donee at the donor's death; and (2) substantial lifetime rights of dominion, control, possession, or enjoyment are retained by the donor.

(b) To be valid, a will substitute need not be executed in compliance with the statutory formalities required for a will.

§7.2 Application of Will Doctrines to Will Substitutes

Although a will substitute need not be executed in compliance with the statutory formalities required for a will, such an arrangement is, to the extent appropriate, subject to substantive restrictions on testation and to rules of construction and other rules applicable to testamentary dispositions.

Comment

. . . A will substitute is subject to [wills'] rules of construction only to the extent appropriate. . . .

Historically, some of the rules of construction were formulated only for wills because wills then constituted the principal means of transmitting property at death. Some rules of construction were placed in the probate code, which led the legislature to draft them as rules applicable to wills. As will substitutes have proliferated and become alternative means of passing property at death, legislatures and courts have sometimes been slow to expand the scope of these rules to transactions to which they should be fully applicable in policy. This Restatement (along with Restatement Third, Trusts, the Revised Uniform Probate Code, and the Uniform Trust Code) moves toward the policy of unifying the law of wills and will substitutes. . . .

Chapter 8: INVALIDITY DUE TO THE DONOR'S INCAPACITY OR ANOTHER'S WRONGDOING

A. Donor's Capacity

§8.1 Requirement of Mental Capacity
§8.2 Incapacity Due to Minority

B. Protection Against Wrongdoing

§8.3 Undue Influence, Duress, or Fraud
§8.4 Homicide—The Slayer Rule

C. No Contest Clauses

§8.5 No Contest Clauses

§8.1 Requirement of Mental Capacity

(a) A person must have mental capacity in order to make or revoke a donative transfer.

(b) If the donative transfer is in the form of a will, a revocable will substitute, or a revocable gift, the testator or donor must be capable of knowing and understanding in a general way the nature and extent of his or her property, the natural objects of his or her bounty, and the disposition that he or she is making of that property, and must also be capable of relating these documents to one another and forming an orderly desire regarding the disposition of that property.

(c) If the donative transfer is in the form of an irrevocable gift, the donor must have the mental capacity necessary to make or revoke a will and must also be capable of understanding the effect that the gift may have on the future financial security of the donor and of anyone who may be dependent on the donor.

§8.2 Incapacity Due to Minority

(a) A minor does not have capacity to make a will. A purported will made by a minor is void.

(b) A minor does not have capacity to make a gift. A purported gift made by a minor is voidable, not void. Before reaching majority, the minor may disaffirm the gift. After reaching minority, the minor may either disaffirm or ratify the gift. The failure to disaffirm within a reasonable time after reaching majority constitutes a ratification of the gift.

(c) For purposes of this section, a "minor" is a person who has not reached the age of majority or the age of capacity for the purpose in question and who is not emancipated. The age of majority is 18, unless an applicable statute provides otherwise.

§8.3 Undue Influence, Duress, or Fraud

(a) A donative transfer is invalid to the extent that it was procured by undue influence, duress, or fraud.

(b) A donative transfer is procured by undue influence if the wrongdoer exerted such influence over the donor that it overcame the donor's free will and cuased the donor to make a donative transfer that the donor would not otherwise have made.

(c) A donative transfer is procured by duress if the wrongdoer threatened to perform or did perform a wrongful act that coerced the donor into making a donative transfer that the donor would not otherwise have made.

(d) A donative transfer is procured by fraud if the wrongdoer knowingly or recklessly made a false representation to the donor about a material fact that was intended to and did lead the donor to make a donative transfer that the donor would not otherwise have made.

§8.4 Homicide—The Slayer Rule

(a) A slayer is denied any right to benefit from the wrong. For purposes of this section, a slayer is a person who, without legal excuse or justification, is responsible for the felonious and intentional killing of another.

(b) Whether or not a person is a slayer is determined in a civil proceeding under the preponderance of the evidence standard rather than beyond a reasonable doubt. For purposes of the civil proceeding, however, a final judgment of conviction for the felonious and intentional killing of the decedent in a criminal proceeding conclusively establishes the convicted person as the decedent's slayer.

§8.5 No Contest Clauses

A provision in a donative document purporting to rescind a donative transfer to, or a fiduciary appointment of, any person who institutes a proceeding challenging the validity of all or part of the donative document is enforceable unless probable cause existed for instituting the proceeding.

Comment

a. Scope. . . This section only addresses the validity of a no contest clause that pertains to proceedings that challenge the validity of a donative document (or a portion of such a document). A clause that purports to prohibit beneficiaries from enforcing fiduciary duties owed to the beneficiaries by trustees or other fiduciaries does not fall within the scope of this section. Although sometimes couched as a no contest clause, such a measure functions as an exculpation clause and is governed by the standards applying to such clauses. . .

d. Construction of no contest clauses. No contest clauses are construed narrowly, consistent with their terms. The institution of a proceeding to contest a will or other donative transfer, or to challenge a particular provision, upon any of the grounds within the scope of the no contest clause, normally violates the clause. In the absence of specific language to the contrary, the clause should be construed to be violated regardless of whether the action is subsequently withdrawn immediately after its institution, prior to a hearing, at the trial, or at any time thereafter. The mere filing of a paper that is intended solely to procure time to ascertain the facts upon which the decision to institute a proceeding must rest should not be construed to constitute the institution of an action to contest or to challenge. . . .

A suit to construe, reform, or modify the language of a donative document is not a contest of the document and hence is not a violation of a no contest clause, unless the construction, reformation, or modification advocated by the person bringing the suit would invalidate the donative document or any of its provisions. . . . A proceeding brought by a beneficiary for the purpose of resolving an ambiguity, or for reforming or modifying the document, valid under all possible constructions or valid under the construction advocated by the beneficiary, is not a contest as that term is used in this section. In such a case, the beneficiary is seeking merely to determine and to protect the donor's intention and is not seeking to circumvent it. . . .

i. Donative transfers other than wills. This section applies to no contest clauses in all donative documents, not only in wills. No contest clauses have traditionally appeared more frequently in wills than in other donative documents. With the increase in the use of revocable inter vivos trusts as will substitutes, no contest clauses and clauses restraining challenges of particular provisions in those trusts serve the same purpose as do such clauses in wills, and the same test applies to determine the validity of those clauses in the two comparable situations. . . .

Chapter 9: PROTECTIONS AGAINST DISINHERITANCE

A. Protections Against Unintentional Disinheritance

B. Protections Against Unintentional Disinheritance

§9.1 Surviving Spouse's Elective Share—Noncommunity Property States Other Than Those That Have Adopted a Revised Uniform Probate-Code Type Statute

(a) In nearly all of the non-community property states, the decedent's surviving spouse is entitled to elect a share of the decedent's property. The exact share differs among the states. The predominant share in the states that have not adopted a Revised Uniform Probate Code-type statute is one-third.

(b) In a state whose statute subjects the decedent's probate estate and specified nonprobate assets to the elective share, the elective-share fraction is applied to the sum of the value of the probate estate and the value of the specified nonprobate assets.

(c) In a state whose statute subjects the decedent's "estate" to the elective share, the elective share is applied to the value of the decedent's estate which, for purposes of calculating the elective share, includes (i) the value of the decedent's probate estate, (ii) the value of property owned or owned in substance by the decedent immediately before death that passed outside of probate at the decedent's death to donees other than the surviving spouse, and (iii) the value of irrevocable gifts to donees other than the surviving spouse made by the decedent in anticipation of imminent death.

§9.2 Surviving Spouse's Elective Share Under the Revised Uniform Probate Code

(a) Under the Revised Uniform Probate Code, the decedent's surviving spouse is entitled to an elective-share amount calculated by applying a specified percentage to the augmented estate. The percentage increases with the length of the marriage until it reaches a maximum of 50 percent, which is the percentage applicable to a marriage that has lasted 15 years or longer.

(b) The augmented estate consists of the sum of four components:

(1) the value of the decedent's net probate estate;

(2) the value of the decedent's nonprobate transfers to persons other than the surviving spouse;

(3) the value of the decedent's nonprobate transfers to the surviving spouse; and

(4) the value of the surviving spouse's net assets at the decedent's death, plus the surviving spouse's nonprobate transfers to others.

(c) In satisfying the elective-share amount, the decedent's probate and nonprobate transfers to the surviving spouse and the marital portion of the surviving spouse's assets are applied first. If these amounts equal or exceed the elective-share amount, the surviving spouse is not entitled to an additional amount. If the elective-share amount is not satisfied from these terms, the decedent's probate and nonprobate transfers to others are proportionately liable to satisfy the balance.

§9.3 Before-Tax Treatment of an Election

The amount of the elective share is calculated by applying the elective-share fraction or percentage to the estate or augmented estate without reduction by the amount of any tax liability imposed on (i) the decedent's estate by an applicable estate or similar transfer tax or (ii) the recipients of property from a decedent's estate by an applicable inheritance or similar tax.

§9.4 Premarital or Marital Agreement

(a) The elective share and other statutory rights accruing to a surviving spouse may be waived, wholly or partially, or otherwise altered, before or during marriage, by a written agreement that was signed by both parties. An agreement that was entered into before marriage is a premarital agreement. An agreement that was entered into during marriage is a marital agreement. Consideration is not necessary to the enforcement of a premarital or a marital agreement.

(b) For a premarital or marital agreement to be enforceable against the surviving spouse, the enforcing party must show that the surviving spouse's consent was informed and was not obtained by undue influence or duress.

(c) A rebuttable presumption arises that the requirements of subsection (b) are satisfied, shifting the burden of proof to the surviving spouse to show that his or her consent was not informed or was obtained under undue influence or duress, if the enforcing party shows that:

(1) before the agreement's execution, (i) the surviving spouse knew, at least approximately, the decedent's assets and asset values, income, and liabilities; or (ii) the decedent or his or her representative provided in timely fashion to the surviving spouse a written statement accurately disclosing the decedent's significant assets and asset values, income, and liabilities; and either

(2) the surviving spouse was represented by independent legal counsel; or

(3) if the surviving spouse was not represented by independent legal counsel, (i) the decedent or the decedent's representative advised the surviving spouse, in timely fashion, to obtain independent legal counsel, and if the surviving spouse was needy, offered to pay for the costs of the surviving spouse's representation; and (ii) the agreement stated, in language easily understandable by an adult of ordinary intelligence with no legal training, the nature of any rights or claims otherwise arising at death that were altered by the agreement, and the nature of that alteration.

§9.5 Protection of Surviving Spouse Against Unintentional Disinheritance by a Premarital Will

(a) Under the Original or Revised Uniform Probate Code, the testator's surviving spouse is entitled to a specified share of the testator's estate if the testator's will was executed before the marriage unless:

(1) the will or other evidence indicates that the will was made in contemplation of the marriage;

(2) the will expresses the intention that it be effective notwithstanding any subsequent marriage; or

(3) the testator provided for the spouse by transfer outside the will and the intent that the transfer be in lieu of a testamentary provision is shown by the testator's statements or is reasonably inferred from the amount of the transfer or other evidence.

(b) Under the Original Uniform Probate Code, the surviving spouse's share is the share that the spouse would have received if the testator had died intestate, but the spouse is only entitled to that share if the premarital will fails to provide for the surviving spouse. In satisfying the spouse's share, the devises made by the premarital will will abate according to the rules of abatement for the payment of claims.

(c) Under the Revised Uniform Probate Code, the surviving spouse's share is the share that the spouse would have received if the testator had died intestate as to that portion of the testator's estate, if any, that is not devised to the testator's children of a prior marriage or their descendants (or that does not pass to such descendants under an antilapse or other statute). Any devise in the premarital will to the surviving spouse counts toward satisfying the spouse's entitlement.

§9.6 Protection of Child or Descendant Against Unintentional Disinheritance

(a) A child of the testator, or under some statutes a descendant of the testator, who was not provided for in the testator's will may be entitled to a specified share of the testator's estate as provided by statute. Most of the statutes, including the Original and Revised Uniform Probate Code, only protect a child who was born or adopted after the will was executed.

(b) A child of the testator who was not provided for in the testator's will because the testator thought that the child was dead may be entitled to a specified share of the testator's estate as provided by statute.

(c) The omitted child or descendant is entitled to the specified share unless a contrary intent or other statutory exception is established.

§9.7 Mortmain Abolished

Any rule that a charitable devise is invalid if it exceeds a certain proportion of the testator's estate or if it is contained in a will that was executed within a certain time before the testator's death is abolished.

Chapter 10: GENERAL PRINCIPLES

§10.1 Donor's Intention Controls the Meaning of a Donative Document and Is Given Effect to the Maximum Extent Allowable by Law

The controlling consideration in determining the meaning of a donative document is the donor's intention. The donor's intention is given effect to the maximum extent allowable by law.

§10.2 Permissible Evidence for Determining Donor's Intention

In seeking to determine the donor's intention, all relevant evidence, whether direct or circumstantial, may be considered, including the text of the donative document and relevant extrinsic evidence.

Chapter 11: RESOLVING AMBIGUITIES

§11.1 Ambiguity Defined

An ambiguity in a donative document is an uncertainty in meaning that is revealed by the text or by extrinsic evidence other than direct evidence of intention contradicting the plain meaning of the text.

§11.2 Resolving Ambiguities in Accordance with the Donor's Intention

(a) An ambiguity to which no rule of construction or constructional preference applies is resolved by construing the text of the donative document in accordance with the donor's intention, to the extent that the donor's intention is established by a preponderance of the evidence.

(b) Ambiguities to which no rule of construction or constructional preference applies include those arising when:

(1) the text or extrinsic evidence (other than direct evidence contradicting the plain meaning of the text) reveals a mistaken description of persons or property.

(2) the text reveals an apparent mistaken inclusion or omission.

(3) extrinsic evidence (other than direct evidence contradicting the plain meaning of the text) reveals that the donor's personal usage differs from the ordinary meaning of a term used in the text.

Comment on Subsection (a)

d. Extrinsic evidence. Once an ambiguity, patent, or latent is established, direct as well as circumstantial evidence of the donor's intention may be considered in resolving the ambiguity in accordance with the donor's intention. . . .

e. Construction by fiduciary or other payor. In resolving an ambiguity in a donative document, the construction placed on the document by the fiduciary (or other payor) is not entitled to a presumption of correctness in litigation. The court resolves the matter de novo. The position is different, however, if the donative document grants the fiduciary (or other payor) authority to resolve questions of construction and provides that the fiduciary's decision shall be binding on all interested parties. In such cases, the clause does not make the fiduciary's decision controlling but does entitle it to a strong presumption of correctness that is to be set aside only if it is arbitrary or made in bad faith. On the analogous question of reviewing a fiduciary's decisions regarding the exercise of discretionary distributive powers, see Restatement Third, Trusts §50. . . .

§11.3 Rules of Construction and Constructional Preferences

(a) An ambiguity to which a rule of construction applies is resolved by the rule of construction, unless evidence establishes that the donor had a different intention.

(b) In the absence of an applicable rule of construction, an ambiguity to which a constructional preference applies is resolved by the constructional preference, unless evidence establishes that the donor had a different intention. If conflicting constructional preferences apply, the constructional preference that is most persuasive in the circumstances prevails unless evidence establishes that the donor had a different intention.

(c) The foundational constructional preference is for the construction that is more in accord with common intention than other plausible constructions. Constructional preferences derived from the preference for common intention include the constructional preferences for:

(1) the construction that is more in accord with the donor's general dispositive plan than other plausible constructions.

(2) the construction that renders the document more effective than other plausible constructions, including the construction that favors completeness of disposition and the construction that avoids illegality.

(3) the construction that favors family members over non-family members, the construction that favors close family members over more remote family members, and the construction that does not disinherit a line of descent.

(4) the construction that gives more favorable tax consequences than other plausible constructions.

(5) the construction that accords with the transferor's contractual obligations.

(6) the construction that is more in accord with public policy than other plausible constructions.

Comment on Subsections (a) and (b)

. . . *b. Constructional preferences distinguished from rules of construction.* Constructional preferences are general in nature. They provide general guidance for construing a wide variety of ambiguities in donative documents. Because of their generality, more than one constructional preference can apply to a particular ambiguity. Usually, the overlapping constructional preferences point to the same result, but not always; they sometimes conflict.

Rules of construction are specific in nature. They provide guidance for resolving specific situations or construing specific terms. Rules of construction are derived from one or more constructional preferences. For example, the rule of construction embodied in the antilapse statutes is derived from the constructional preference for avoiding disinheritance of a line of descent. The rule of construction that presumes an intent to include adopted children in class gifts is derived from the constructional preferences for the construction that carries out common intention and for the construction that accords with public policy. Because rules of construction, in contrast to constructional preferences, address relatively delimited problems, rules of construction ought not to overlap or conflict with one another within the law of a given jurisdiction.

Once a constructional preference or a set of overlapping constructional preferences have crystallized into a rule of construction, the rule of construction becomes the exclusive source of attributed intention for resolving ambiguities to which it applies, displacing the antecedent constructional preferences. To the extent that antecedent constructional preferences conflict with one another when applied to the type of ambiguity at issue, the conflict is resolved by adopting the rule of construction. The rule of construction is based upon the constructional preference or preferences deemed to carry the most weight for that situation. Thus, an ambiguity to which a rule of construction applies is resolved by considering only the rule of construction together with evidence of the donor's intention. Antecedent constructional preferences are no longer considered.

c. "Construction" versus "interpretation." As noted in §10.1, Comment b, this Restatement uses the word "construction" to designate the final product of the process of determining the meaning of a donative document (apart from exceptional cases in which reformation or modification is warranted (see Chapter 12)). Textwriters and courts sometimes state that there are two distinct processes involved in determining the meaning of a donative document. Under this conception, "interpretation" refers to the process of searching for the donor's actual intention by looking to the text of the document and extrinsic evidence. "Construction" refers to the process of attributing intention from constructional preferences and rules of construction. The process of interpretation is sometimes thought to occur first, followed by construction only when interpretation fails.

Interpretation and construction are not completely distinct processes, however, nor are they applied sequentially. Interpretation and construction are part of a single process. Distinguishing between actual and attributed intention is useful in determining which governs if the two conflict. Actual intention, when sufficiently established, always overcomes attributed intention. The key notion, however, is "when sufficiently established." Although constructional preferences and rules of construction are sometimes referred to as "default rules," this does not mean that they only govern in default of evidence of actual intention. The term, properly understood, means that they govern in default of sufficiently persuasive evidence of contrary actual intention.

In deciding whether actual intention is sufficiently established to overcome attributed intention, the process of construction requires all factors to be brought to bear simultaneously and conflicting factors to be considered against each other. This is a single process. Take, for example, a case in which there is an applicable constructional preference or rule of construction. It would misdescribe the process to say that the constructional preference or rule of construction ought to be consulted only if there is *no* evidence of actual intention. Rather, the constructional preference or rule of construction is considered together with any evidence of actual intention. Evidence of actual intention may itself consist of conflicting elements, some supporting the constructional preference or rule of construction and some contradicting it.

d. Considering a constructional preference or a rule of construction with evidence of actual intention. Because the primary objective of construction is to give effect to actual intention, to the extent that actual intention can be established, constructional preferences and rules of construction yield when a different intention is found. In determining whether the donor's actual intention overcomes a constructional preference or rule of construction, both the text of the document read as an entirety and extrinsic evidence of the donor's intention may be considered, as described in §10.2, unless consideration of extrinsic evidence is precluded by statute. . . . Extrinsic evidence and inferences derived from the text of the document tending to support as well as tending to overcome a constructional preference or a rule of construction must be considered as part of a single process. The single nature of this process is described in Comment c.

Sometimes a codified rule of construction provides that it prevails unless the donative document, another specified document, or one of a list of specified documents expressly provides otherwise. Since constructional preferences are seldom codified, it is uncommon to find a similar statutory provision regarding a constructional preference. Nevertheless, if a statute provides that a particular constructional preference or rule of construction can only be rebutted by an express statement in a document, extrinsic evidence may not be considered to support, rebut, or contradict the constructional preference or rule of construction. If, however, the elements prescribed in §12.1 are satisfied, the appropriate document can be reformed to insert language into its text expressly stating an intention contrary to the constructional preference or rule of construction. . . .

Some constructional preferences and rules of construction have more force and are therefore more difficult to rebut than others. Because constructional preferences are general in nature, two or more constructional preferences might apply in a given case and point to the same result or to differing results. If such overlapping constructional preferences lead to the same result, they reinforce each other and are more difficult to rebut. If they lead to differing results, they tend to neutralize each other unless the trier of fact determines that one is more weighty than the other in the particular case. The ambiguity in such a case is resolved by considering each of the constructional preferences together with evidence of the donor's intention to determine which resolution of the ambiguity is the most persuasive in the circumstances.

A rule of construction based on one or more strong constructional preferences is especially difficult to rebut. For example, because the rule of construction reflected in antilapse statutes derives from the strong constructional preference against disinheriting a line of descent, antilapse Statutes are especially difficult to rebut. . . .

Chapter 12: REFORMING AND MODIFYING DONATIVE DOCUMENTS

§12.1 Reforming Donative Documents to Correct Mistakes

A donative document, though unambiguous, may be reformed to conform the text to the donor's intention if it is established by clear and convincing evidence (1) that a mistake of fact or law, whether in expression or inducement, affected specific terms of the document; and (2) what the donor's intention was. In determining whether these elements have been established by clear and convincing evidence, direct evidence of intention contradicting the plain meaning of the text as well as other evidence of intention may be considered.

Comment

. . . *b. Rationale.* When a donative document is unambiguous, evidence suggesting that the terms of the document vary from intention is inherently suspect but possibly correct. The law deals with situations of inherently suspicious but possibly correct evidence in either of two ways. One is to exclude the evidence altogether, in effect denying a remedy in cases in which the evidence is genuine and persuasive. The other is to consider the evidence, but guard against giving effect to fraudulent or mistaken evidence by imposing an above-normal standard of proof. In choosing between exclusion and high-safeguard allowance of extrinsic evidence, this Restatement adopts the latter. Only high-safeguard allowance of extrinsic evidence achieves the primary objective of giving effect to the donor's intention. To this end, the full range of direct and circumstantial evidence relevant to the donor's intention described in §10.2 may be considered in a reformation action.

Equity rests the rationale for reformation on two related grounds: giving effect to the donor's intention and preventing unjust enrichment. . . .

c. Historical background. The reformation doctrine for donative documents other than wills is well established. Equity has long recognized that deeds of gifts, inter vivos trusts, life insurance contracts, and other donative documents can be reformed if it is established by clear and convincing evidence: (1) that a mistake of fact or law, whether in expression or inducement, affected specific terms of the document; and (2) what the donor's intention was. Reformation of these documents is granted, on an adequate showing of proof, even after the death of the donor.

This action unifies the law of wills and will substitutes by applying to wills the standards that govern other donative documents. Until recently, courts have not allowed reformation of wills. The denial of a reformation remedy for wills was predicated on observance of the Statute of Wills, which requires that wills be executed in accordance with certain formalities. See §3.1. Reforming a will, it was feared, would often require inserting language that was not executed in accordance with the statutory formalities. Section 11.2, however, authorizes inserting language to resolve *ambiguities* in accordance with the donor's intention. [M]odern authority is moving away from insistence on strict compliance with the statutory formalities on the question of initial execution of wills. Section 3.3 adopts the position that a harmless error in executing a will may be excused "if the proponent establishes by clear and convincing evidence that the decedent adopted the document as his or her will." See also Restatement Second, Property (Donative Transfers) §33.1, Comment g. The Revised Uniform Probate Code §2-503 also adopts a harmless-error rule. Under the Revised UPC, a document or writing on a document that was not executed in compliance with the statutory formalities is treated as if it had been properly executed "if the proponent of the document or writing establishes by clear and convincing evidence that the decedent intended the document or writing to constitute . . . the decedent's will. . . ."

The trend away from insisting on strict compliance with statutory formalities is based on a growing acceptance of the broader principle that mistake, whether in execution or in expression, should not be allowed to defeat intention. A common principle underlies the principle of this section, which authorizes reformation of unambiguous donative documents (including wills) to correct mistakes, and the movement (1) to excuse defective execution under §3.3 and (2) to authorize insertion of language to resolve ambiguities in donative documents under §11.2.

The important difference between §11.2 and this section is the burden of proof. Ambiguity shows that the donative document contains an inadequate expression of the donor's intention. Here, because there is no ambiguity, clear and convincing evidence is required to establish that the document does not adequately express intention. . . .

d. Plain-meaning rule disapproved. The so-called plain-meaning rule is disapproved to the extent that the rule purports to exclude extrinsic evidence of the donor's intention. . . .

§12.2 Modifying Donative Documents to Achieve Donor's Tax Objectives

A donative document may be modified, in a manner that does not violate the donor's probable intention, to achieve the donor's tax objectives.

Comment

a. Scope note. . . The term "modification" rather than "reformation" is used in this section to distinguish the situation covered here from the situation covered by §12.1, in which the donative document fails to express the donor's original, particularized intention. . . .

PART III

~

RESTATEMENT (THIRD) OF TRUSTS, VOLS. 1 & 2 (2003)

Restatement (Third) of Trusts, Vols. 1 & 2 (2003)

TABLE OF CONTENTS

CHAPTER 8. TRUST PROPERTY

- §40. Any Property May Be Trust Property
- §41. Expectancies; Nonexistent Property Interests
- §42. Extent and Nature of Trustee's Title

CHAPTER 9. BENEFICIARIES

- §43. Persons Who May Be Beneficiaries
- §44. Definite-Beneficiary Requirement
- §45. Members of a Definite Class as Beneficiaries
- §46. Members of an Indefinite Class as Beneficiaries
- §47. Trusts for Noncharitable Purposes
- §48. Beneficiaries Defined; Incidental Benefits

Part 4. Nature of Beneficiaries' Rights and Interests

CHAPTER 10. EXTENT AND ENFORCEABILITY OF BENEFICIAL INTERESTS

- §49. Extent of Beneficiaries' Interests
- §50. Enforcement and Construction of Discretionary Interests

CHAPTER 11. VOLUNTARY AND INVOLUNTARY TRANFSERS OF BENEFICIAL INTERESTS; GENERAL PRINCIPLES

- §51. Voluntary Transfers Inter Vivos
- §52. Intention to Transfer
- §53. Need for a Writing
- §54. Effect of Successive Transfers
- §55. Transfers at Death
- §56. Rights of Beneficiary's Creditors
- §57. Forfeiture for Voluntary or Involuntary Alienation
- §58. Spendthrift Trusts: Validity and General Effect
- §59. Spendthrift Trusts: Exceptions for Particular Types of Claims
- §60. Transfer or Attachment of Discretionary Interests

Part 5. Modification and Termination of Trusts

CHAPTER 13. MODIFICATION AND TERMINATION OF TRUSTS

- §61. Completion of Period or Purpose for Which Trust Created
- §62. Rescission and Reformation
- §63. Power of Settlor to Revoke or Modify
- §64. Termination or Modification by Trustee, Beneficiary, or Third Party
- §65. Termination or Modification by Consent of Beneficiaries
- §66. Power of Court to Modify: Unanticipated Circumstances
- §67. Failure of Designated Charitable Purpose: The Doctrine of Cy Pres
- §68. Dividing and Combining Trusts
- §69. MergerPart

Part 1. Nature, Characteristics, and Types of Trusts

Chapter 1: DEFINITIONS AND DISTINCTIONS

§1. Scope of this Restatement
§2. Definition of Trust
§3. Settlor, Trust Property, Trustee, and Beneficiary
§4. Terms of the Trust
§5. Trusts and Other Relationships
§6. Active and Passive Trusts; The Statute of Uses

§1. Scope of this Restatement

Trusts dealt with in this Restatement include:

(a) trusts as defined in §2;
(b) charitable trusts (see §28); and
(c) resulting trusts (see §§7, 8, and 9).

§2. Definition of Trust

A trust, as the term is used in this Restatement when not qualified by the word "resulting" or "constructive," is a fiduciary relationship with respect to property, arising from a manifestation of intention to create that relationship and subjecting the person who holds title to the property to duties to deal with it for the benefit of charity or for one or more persons, at least one of whom is not the sole trustee.

Comment

b. Fiduciary relationship*. . . .* Despite the differences in the legal circumstances and responsibilities of various fiduciaries, one characteristic is common to all: A person in a fiduciary relationship to another is under a duty to act for the benefit of the other as to matters within the scope of the relationship. (Fiduciary duties may, in the circumstances of certain trust relationships, technically exist but not be effectively enforceable; the situation arises to the extent the trustee holds a power of revocation or a presently exercisable general power of appointment or withdrawal. . . .)

d. Title, ownership, and interests. . . . Although trust beneficiaries have equitable title, a trustee's title to trust property may be either legal or equitable. Although it is usually true (and is, unfortunately, often stated without qualification in cases and texts) that the trustee has legal title, in some instances the trustee will hold only an equitable title. . . .

f. The elements of a trust. In the strict, traditional sense, a trust involves three elements: (1) a trustee, who holds the trust property and is subject to duties to deal with it for the benefit of one or more others; (2) one or more beneficiaries, to whom and for whose benefit the trustee owes the duties with respect to the trust property; and (3) trust property, which is held by the trustee for the beneficiaries. In a more comprehensive sense, the trust purpose is often included in discussions of the elements of trusts, as in Part 3 (specifically Chapter 6) of this Restatement.

Although all of these elements are present in a complete trust, either or both of elements (1) and (2) above may be temporarily absent without destroying the trust or preventing its creation. . . .

§3. Settlor, Trust Property, Trustee, and Beneficiary

(1) The person who creates a trust is the settlor.

(2) The property held in trust is the trust property.

(3) The person who holds property in trust is the trustee.

(4) A person for whose benefit property is held in trust is a beneficiary.

§4. Terms of the Trust

The phrase "terms of the trust" means the manifestation of intention of the settlor with respect to the trust provisions expressed in a manner that admits of its proof in judicial proceedings.

Comment

d. Trusts created inter vivos by written instrument. If a trust is created by a transaction inter vivos and is evidenced by a written instrument, the terms of the trust are determined by the provisions of the governing instrument as interpreted in light of all the relevant circumstances and such direct evidence of the intention of the settlor with respect to the trust as is not denied consideration because of a statute of frauds, the parol-evidence rule, or some other rule of law. On the statutes of frauds, see §§22-24 (and cf. §20), and on the parol-evidence rule, see §21. See generally Restatement Third, Property (Wills and Other Donative Transfers) §10.2 and §§11.1-11.3.

The "provisions of the governing instrument" include the terms of any statute incorporated or made applicable by other provisions of that instrument. . . .

f. Trusts created by court order. If a trust is established by an order of court and is to be administered as an express trust, the terms of the trust are determined by the provisions of the court order as interpreted in accordance with general rules governing interpretation of judgments.

g. Trusts created by statute. Some forms of trusts that are created by statute, especially public retirement systems or pension funds, and sometimes public land trusts, school land trusts, or trusts for benefit of native populations, are administered as express trusts, the terms of which are either set forth in the statute or are supplied by the default rules of general trust law. . . .

§5. Trusts and Other Relationships

The following are not trusts:

(a) successive legal estates;

(b) decedents' estates;

(c) guardianships and conservatorships;

(d) receiverships and bankruptcy trusteeships;

(e) durable powers of attorney and other agencies;

(f) bailments and leases;

(g) corporations, partnerships, and other business associations;

(h) conditions and equitable charges;

(i) contracts to convey or certain contracts for the benefit of third parties;

(j) assignments or partial assignments of choses in action;

(k) relationships of debtors to creditors;

(l) mortgages, deeds of trust, pledges, liens, and other security arrangements.

§6. Active and Passive Trusts; The Statute of Uses

(1) A trust is active if, by the terms of the trust, the trustee has affirmative duties to perform; a trust is passive if the trustee's sole duty is not to interfere with the enjoyment of the trust property by the beneficiaries.

(2) A beneficiary of a passive trust is entitled to receive, upon demand, transfer of the property passively held for that beneficiary.

(3) If the Statute of Uses or similar statute applies to property of a trust, the trustee's title to that property is extinguished and the title is held by the beneficiary or beneficiaries in accordance with the equitable interests of each.

Chapter 2: RESULTING TRUSTS

§7. Nature and Definition of Resulting Trusts

A resulting trust is a reversionary, equitable interest implied by law in property that is held by a transferee, in whole or in part, as trustee for the transferor or the transferor's successors in interest.

§8. When Express Trust Fails in Whole or in Part

Where the owner of property makes a donative transfer and manifests an intention that the transferee is to hold the property in trust but the intended trust fails in whole or in part, or the trust is or will be fully performed without exhausting or fully utilizing the trust estate, the transferee holds the trust estate or the appropriate portion or interest therein on resulting trust for the transferor or the transferor's successors in interest, unless

(a) the transferor manifested an intention that a resulting trust should not arise, or

(b) the trust fails for illegality and the policy against permitting unjust enrichment of a transferee is outweighed by the policy against giving relief to one who has entered into an illegal transaction.

Comment

a. In general. . . . [If] a deed or will is ineffective to transfer title to the property to the intended trustee or a substitute trustee, no resulting trust arises by reason of the failure of the intended inter vivos or testamentary trust. The title to the property remains (with no need of the resulting-trust device) either in the would-be transferor or in the personal representative or beneficiaries of the testator's estate.

a(1). Successors in interest defined. If a testamentary disposition is not a residuary disposition, the decedent's successors in interest are normally determined by the residuary provisions of the will. Otherwise—that is, if the will contains no applicable residuary clause or if the trust disposition is itself residuary and there is no alternative disposition—the successors in interest are the testator's intestate successors, specifically the decedent's heirs at law.

If a testamentary trust comes into operation but thereafter is fully performed, or subsequently fails in whole or in part, the trustee then holds the appropriate property or interests on resulting trust for the testator's successors in interest. The initial step in determining these successors is as stated in the preceding paragraph. This is because the testator died leaving this reversionary interest to (that is, the possibility of a resulting trust later arising for) those original residuary or intestate successors from the very outset. Then, when the resulting trust eventually occurs, the interests of those various successors will have to be traced, if and as necessary, through possible subsequent assignments, insolvency proceedings, and decedents' estates, and ultimately then into the hands of the initial successors' respective successors in interest, who at the time of the resulting trust will also be successors in interest to the testator. In any of the foregoing situations, the successor in interest (or one of the successors) may be the State, for want of other successors.

Similarly, if an inter vivos express trust comes into existence but later is fully performed or wholly or partially fails, the reversionary interest based on this possibility remained in the settlor from the outset. If the settlor is dead when the resulting trust arises, and if the reversion has by then been voluntarily or involuntarily alienated, the successors in interest are determined by tracing the retained interest through the settlor's estate, or assignments or insolvency proceedings, and onward into the hands of the current interest holders, essentially as described in the preceding paragraph. The beneficiaries of the resulting trust are those so determined. . . .

§9. Purchase-Money Resulting Trusts

(1) Except as stated in Subsection (2), where a transfer of property is made to one person and the purchase price is paid by another, a resulting trust arises in favor of the person by whom the purchase price is paid unless

(a) the latter manifests an intention that no resulting trust should arise, or

(b) the transfer is made to accomplish an unlawful purpose, in which case a resulting trust does not arise if the policy against unjust enrichment of the transferee is outweighed by the policy against giving relief to a person who has entered into an illegal transaction.

(2) Where a transfer of property is made to one person and the purchase price is paid by another and the transferee is a spouse, descendant, or other natural object of the bounty of the person by whom the purchase price is paid, a resulting trust does not arise unless the latter manifests an intention that the transferee should not have the beneficial interest in the property.

Part 2. Creation of Trusts

Chapter 3: BASIC PRINCIPLES AND REQUIREMENTS

§10. Methods of Creating a Trust

Except as prevented by the doctrine of merger (§69), a trust may be created by:

(a) a transfer by the will of a property owner to another person as trustee for one or more persons; or

(b) a transfer inter vivos by a property owner to another person as trustee for one or more persons; or

(c) a declaration by an owner of property that he or she holds that property as trustee for one or more persons; or

(d) an exercise of a power of appointment by appointing property to a person as trustee for one or more persons who are objects of the power; or

(e) a promise or beneficiary designation that creates enforceable rights in a person who immediately or later holds those rights as trustee, or who pursuant to those rights later receives property as trustee, for one or more persons.

Comment

Comment on Clause (c)

e. Declaration of trust. If the owner of property declares himself or herself trustee of the property for the benefit of one or more others, or for the declarant and one or more others, a trust is created, even though there is no transfer of the title to the trust property to another and even though no consideration is received for the declaration. . . .

A statute of frauds may require a signed writing in order for a declaration of trust to be enforceable. See §22. . . .

[E]xcept as precluded by statute, a trust may be established by the settlor's signing of an instrument that begins, essentially, "I hereby declare myself trustee of the property listed in Schedule A attached hereto" or "O, as settlor, hereby transfers to O, as trustee, the property listed in the attached Schedule A," even though in either case the document is not supported at the time of execution, or by the time of the settlor's death or incompetency, by other acts or other documents of transfer or title. In short, the trust instrument may serve as an instrument of transfer (i.e., as a "deed" of gift or conveyance). . . .

Comment on Clause (e)

g. Trust created by enforceable promise or beneficiary designation. Where a property owner makes a nonbinding promise to create a trust in the future, no trust is thereby created. If the property owner later establishes the trust by inter vivos or testamentary transfer or by declaration, the trust is created by the transfer or declaration (see Comments d and e) and not by the promise.

Similarly, when a property owner makes a contractually binding promise to establish a trust by inter vivos or testamentary transfer or by declaration and later performs by making the promised transfer or declaration, ordinarily the trust is created at the time of performance, whether the transfer or declaration is made voluntarily or involuntarily. In this situation, the trust and the trustee's fiduciary duties ordinarily come into existence at the time of the settlor's performance and not at the time the binding promise is made. . . .

If, however, a person makes or causes to be made an enforceable promise to pay money or transfer property to another as trustee, and if the person (with the expressed or implied acceptance of the intended trustee) also manifests an intention immediately to create a trust of the promisee's rights, a trust is created at the time of the contract, with a chose in action (the rights under that contract) then being held for the beneficiaries by the trustee. . . .

§11. Capacity of a Settlor to Create a Trust

(1) A person has capacity to create a trust by will to the same extent that the person has capacity to devise or bequeath the property free of trust.

(2) A person has capacity to create a revocable inter vivos trust by transfer to another or by declaration to the same extent that the person has capacity to create a trust by will.

(3) A person has capacity to create an irrevocable inter vivos trust by transfer to another or by declaration to the same extent that the person has capacity to transfer the property inter vivos free of trust in similar circumstances.

(4) A person has capacity to create a trust by exercising a power of appointment to the same extent that the person has capacity to create a trust of his or her own property under Subsection (1), (2), or (3) above, as appropriate to the type of transfer and trust being created.

(5) Under some circumstances, an agent under a durable power of attorney or the legal representative of a property owner who is under disability may create a trust on behalf of the property owner.

Comment

Comment on Subsection (3)

c. Irrevocable inter vivos trusts. A property owner who has capacity to transfer property by outright gift inter vivos ordinarily has capacity to create an irrevocable trust during life. A property owner who does not have the capacity to make a gift lacks capacity to establish an irrevocable trust.

Rules concerning gift-making capacity are not peculiar to the law of trusts and are not within the scope of this Restatement. See generally Restatement Third, Property (Wills and Other Donative Transfers) §8.1, Comment d. In general, however, this is a standard slightly higher than that for a will because, in addition to factors that testators must be capable of understanding, irrevocable donative transfers during life require an ability to understand the effects the disposition may have on the future financial security of the settlor/donor and of those who may be dependent on him or her.

Some irrevocable inter vivos trusts, however, are not donative, or at least not entirely. Trusts are sometimes created as a result of negotiations, as in the case of a trust that is established as part of a commercial transaction or in settlement of an adversary legal proceeding, such as an action for divorce. For these situations, higher standards are normally appropriate. Again, however, these rules are not peculiar to the law of trusts and are not within the scope of this Restatement. See generally Restatement Second, Contracts §12, on capacity to contract. . . .

Comment on Subsection (5)

f. Acts on behalf of owner under disability. Transfers of property belonging to minors and legally incompetent adults may be made in the course of managing their financial affairs by their guardians, conservators, or other legal representatives, or by the agent (attorney in fact) of an incompetent adult appointed and acting under a durable power of attorney executed before the principal's incapacity. The legal representative or holder of a durable power of attorney may also make charitable and other inter vivos gifts of the property of a minor or incompetent person, including gift-transfers in trust, but only to the extent authorized by the appropriate court or, expressly or impliedly, by the terms of the durable power.

Ordinarily, under principles of "substituted judgment" . . ., a court may authorize a legal representative to make such transfers of the minor's or mentally incompetent person's property as would be reasonable as a matter of the property owner's personal, family, tax, and estate-planning objectives. Under many statutes, however, by express provision or judicial interpretation, courts do not have power to authorize legal representatives to make wills for minors or legally incompetent persons. Similarly, under many durable-power-of-attorney statutes, it is not legally permissible for the terms of a durable power to authorize an agent to make a will for an incapacitated principal.

Nevertheless, even under statutes that preclude the making of wills for persons under legal disability, a court or the terms of a durable power may for some purposes authorize a legal representative or agent to create, amend, or revoke, or to transfer additional property to, a revocable trust or other will-substitute arrangement. See Uniform Trust Code §602(e) and (f); and compare generally Restatement Third, Property (Wills and Other Donative Transfers) §8.1, Comments k and l, and Restatement Second, Property (Donative Transfers) §§34.4(2) and 34.5. For example, despite a restriction against making a will for an incompetent person, it is proper for a court or principal to authorize a legal representative or agent to establish, modify, or enlarge a revocable inter vivos trust to serve purposes that are financially advantageous to the estate, such as probate avoidance and managerial efficiency.

The trust's distributive provisions, however, present more sensitive issues, which turn on the policy underlying the typical statute's will-making prohibition. Distributions directed or authorized by the provisions of a revocable trust established by a legal representative or agent must be consistent either: (i) with inter vivos gifts the legal representative or agent could be empowered to make directly (supra); or (ii) with post-death dispositions that, under the statute, the court may, or the terms of the durable power may and do, authorize the legal representative or agent to make of the affected property of the incompetent person.

In the second situation (alternative (ii), above), the effect of a statutory prohibition against will making by legal representatives or agents depends on the reasons underlying that prohibition. The underlying policy may reflect a narrow purpose (based on efficiency and tradition) of precluding the use of a particular device (a will) that relies on the safeguards of probate and of specific, well-established statutory formalities; or the will-making prohibition may instead manifest a more general, substantive policy against post-death dispositions by these fiduciaries that would alter the plan of disposition established by intestate succession or by an existing will executed by a person who has subsequently become incompetent.

The breadth and generality of the latter policy would ordinarily apply by analogy (cf. §25(2) and Comments d and e thereto) to limit the post-death distributive provisions of a revocable inter vivos trust created by a legal representative or agent to dispositions that conform to the disposition of the affected property that would result, as the case may be, by operation of law or under the incompetent person's existing estate plan. Any departure from that pre-incompetency scheme of disposition would then be permissible only to the extent the adversely affected, expectant beneficiaries consent to relinquish some or all of their expected interests.

On the other hand, if the underlying policy is a narrow one that applies only to the making of wills by legal representatives or agents, and not to their use of will substitutes, the foregoing limitations on post-death distributive provisions (preceding paragraph) do not apply to the creation of revocable trusts by these fiduciaries.

Ultimately, the nature and breadth of the policy indicated by a will-making prohibition are matters of statutory interpretation. Durable-power-of-attorney legislation and principles of substituted judgment under conservatorship, guardianship, and other such statutes are designed to preserve for persons under disability much of the flexibility in financial management and planning that other property owners enjoy. Estate planning is fundamental to the objectives ordinarily implicit in such statutes; and sound, flexible planning requires actions that reflect not only the property owner's evolving circumstances and likely objectives but also changes in the law and in the personal and financial circumstances of potential beneficiaries. Furthermore, these statutes allow donative dispositions only with court authorization or as a result of authorization granted by a competent principal, with judicial scrutiny available for cases in which it is alleged that an agent's fiduciary authority has been exceeded or abused.

Accordingly, prohibitions against will making are generally to be strictly construed to prevent only the use of a particular device, the will, and not as reflecting a more general, substantive policy that extends to and prohibits the use of other methods of planning and accomplishing properly justified post-death disposition of estates of persons under disability.

In many states, the general preference for narrow construction is reinforced by statutes that, while prohibiting the making of wills, expressly enable a court or principal to authorize the use or amendment of certain other post-death dispositions or will substitutes. Some such statutes, for example, refer specifically to creating, amending, or enlarging revocable trusts, whereas other statutes or sections may authorize the closely related actions of selecting or changing post-death beneficial rights—such as beneficiary designations and payment options—under life insurance policies, retirement plans, and the like.

A conservator, guardian, or other legal representative or an agent under a durable power of attorney may be authorized by court or the terms of a durable power to exercise a settlor's expressed or implied rights to withdraw funds or amend terms of a revocable trust in accordance with the foregoing principles applicable to the creation of revocable trusts by these fiduciaries. That is, legal representatives and agents may be authorized to exercise the incompetent settlor's reserved powers not only in circumstances and ways that are appropriate to the current needs of the settlor and the settlor's family but also as appropriate to the settlor's estate-planning objectives, based on (i) the principles of substituted judgment or the terms of the durable power and on (ii) what is proper in light of the policies underlying any applicable statutory prohibition against the making of wills by such fiduciaries. . . .

§12. Trust Creation Induced by Undue Influence, Duress, Fraud, or Mistake

A transfer in trust or declaration of trust can be set aside, or the terms of a trust can be reformed, upon the same grounds as those upon which a transfer of property not in trust can be set aside or reformed.

§13. Intention to Create Trust

A trust is created only if the settlor properly manifests an intention to create a trust relationship.

§14. Notice and Acceptance Not Required to Create Trust

A trust can be created without notice to or acceptance by any beneficiary or trustee.

§15. Consideration Not Required to Create Trust

The owner of property can create a trust of the property by will or by declaration or transfer inter vivos, whether or not consideration is received for doing so.

§16. Ineffective Inter Vivos Transfers

(1) If a property owner undertakes to make a donative inter vivos disposition in trust by transferring property to another as trustee, an express trust is not created if the property owner fails during life to complete the contemplated transfer of the property. In some circumstances, however, the trust intention of such a property owner who dies or becomes incompetent may be given effect by constructive trust in order to prevent unjust enrichment of the property owner's successors in interest.

(2) If a property owner intends to make an outright gift inter vivos but fails to make the transfer that is required in order to do so, the gift intention will not be given effect by treating it as a declaration of trust.

Comment

b. Intended inter vivos transfer to another as trustee: Effective or ineffective? When an owner of property intends to create an inter vivos trust other than by declaration, the owner must transfer the property to the intended trustee. If the property owner attempts to make a transfer in trust but the intended transfer is not effective, no express trust is created.

An intended or contemplated transfer in trust may be ineffective for a number of reasons. The transfer may not be completed for want of delivery of the subject matter or instrument of transfer; or it may be ineffective because a would-be settlor does not own the intended trust property at the time of the purported transfer. In cases of these types, no trust is created. In the latter of these situations, however, actions of the would-be settlor after acquiring the intended trust property, considered together with the initial manifestation of trust intent, may serve to perfect the transfer and thereby create the trust at the later time. . . .

In the first of the above-mentioned situations, where there has been no delivery, the title to the property ordinarily (but see Comment c) remains in the owner free of trust. Even when an owner of property surrenders possession of it or of a document of transfer in a manner that otherwise would be sufficient to transfer the property to a trustee, if the property owner does not intend to make a presently effective transfer there is no transfer of the title. Accordingly, no trust is created and the owner retains title to the property, ordinarily free of trust. Again, however, subsequent actions of the property owner, considered together with the initial manifestation of trust intention, may constitute delivery, thereby completing the transfer and bringing the trust into being.

On the other hand, delivery sufficient to pass title to a trustee, like transfers to others as donees of outright gifts, may occur without handing over the property or an instrument of transfer to the intended trustee. Thus, a delivery may be made in escrow or may be accomplished by acts of constructive or symbolic delivery performed with the requisite intention to make a present transfer. . . .

Furthermore, if the owner of property transfers it to another with the intention that it be held immediately in trust, a trust may then arise even though by the terms of the trust the settlor reserves the power to revoke and modify the trust in whole or in part. . . . Similarly, a declaration of trust is not incomplete, nor is it a mere expression of an intention to create a trust in the future, simply because of the declarant's reservation of power to revoke and amend (§25(1)). In either of these situations the revocable inter vivos trust may be created even though the terms of the revocable trust also include the reservation to the settlor of a life interest in the property, and even though the transfer or declaration of trust thereby serves primarily as a substitute for a will (*id.*). . . .

Unless the contrary is expressly provided in an applicable statute, or is necessarily implied from its provisions, formalities prescribed for the creation of a recordable document, or otherwise for protection of or from third parties, need not be satisfied in order to make a valid donative transfer, that is, one that is effective as between the transferor and the transferee(s). See Restatement Second, Property (Donative Transfers) §32.3, Comment a.

Good practice certainly calls for the use of additional formalities and the taking of appropriate further steps, such as changes of registration, or the execution and recordation of deeds to land. Nevertheless, a writing signed by the settlor, or a trust agreement signed by the settlor and trustee, manifesting the settlor's present intention thereby to transfer specified property (such as all property listed on an attached schedule) is sufficient to create a trust. . . .

The rights and interests of transferees may be later perfected with respect to third parties, and for the protection of third parties, by steps taken by the settlor or, even following the settlor's death or incompetency, by court order or other procedures appropriate to the circumstances and applicable law or practice. Compare also the discussion of declarations of trust. . . . §10, Comment e.

c. Incomplete transfer sometimes given effect by constructive trust. Sometimes an attempted inter vivos transfer is ineffective to create an express trust even though the property owner has taken all the steps that would be required of the owner personally in order to implement the transfer in the intended manner. In such a case, the acts and circumstances may nevertheless satisfy the underlying legal policy of determining, by objective and reliable evidence, that the property owner had arrived at a definite, considered intention to create a trust. . . .

Cases of this type may arise because the title to intended trust property remains in a would-be settlor as a result of some technical defect or incompleteness in the intended transfer. For example, a person named as trustee may be dead or otherwise incapable of taking title to the intended trust property. . . . Similarly, an intended transfer may remain incomplete because an essentially ministerial act has not been performed. For example, a property owner may have placed property in the hands of his or her own agent with instruction to complete delivery promptly or as soon as conveniently possible (or at some time or upon the occurrence of some event that would have been expected to occur soon within the property owner's lifetime) but without need of further direction or action by the property owner.

In these various situations, if the property owner becomes legally incompetent or dies, it may be appropriate for a court of equity to compel the legal representative of the incompetent property owner or the deceased property owner's successors in interest to transfer property upon the intended trust. Provided the property owner had not expressly or impliedly by inaction manifested an intention to retain or reacquire the property free of trust, a constructive trust may be enforced to prevent the unjust enrichment that would occur if the property owner's successors in interest were allowed to retain or acquire property that is satisfactorily shown to have been intended to benefit others. This is so even though, at the time of death or incompetency, the property owner personally had the right to terminate or modify the agent's authority or to refuse to correct a defect in the intended transfer. [S]ee generally and compare Restatement of Restitution §164.

In some of these cases, of course, it may be difficult to determine whether the property owner had formed a sufficiently definite intention presently to proceed with the creation of the trust, or whether the owner had simply manifested an intention gratuitously to create a trust at some future time. Such questions are inevitably ones for interpretation. The critical issue in these cases is likely to be whether or not, under the chosen manner of making the transfer, it had been contemplated that the property owner personally would take some further action or make some further manifestation of intention before the transfer to the intended trustee was to be completed. Events and circumstances, however, may provide a negative answer to this question and satisfy the underlying policies by supplying both the evidentiary certainty and the likelihood of deliberation that support carrying out a trust intention. Thus, in a given situation the steps actually taken may supply the objective, reliable manifestations of intention needed to show that the now deceased or legally incompetent property owner had made a serious, definite decision to proceed with a transfer in trust (whether revocable or irrevocable), with no showing that this objective had been abandoned. . . .

Illustrations . . .

7. O, the owner of Blackacre, executes a deed by which she might convey Blackacre to T as trustee for B for life, remainder to B's issue. Because of her imminent departure on a business trip to Europe, O hands the deed to her financial adviser, A, asking him to act as her agent to make delivery to T as soon as A has an opportunity to do so. O dies in an automobile accident in Europe shortly after arriving there and before A has an opportunity to make delivery to T. Although O could have telephoned A immediately before her death to terminate his authority as her agent, and although title to Blackacre remained in A, O's personal representative or other successors in interest can be compelled to transfer Blackacre to T in trust for the intended purposes and beneficiaries.

The result in Illustration 7 is not based on dilatory conduct on the part of A or otherwise confined to cases that invite application of the maxim that equity treats as done what ought to have been done. . . .

Chapter 4: FORMALITIES: TRUSTS CREATED BY WILL

§17. Creation of Testamentary Trusts

§17. Creation of Testamentary Trusts

(1) A testamentary trust is one created by a valid will.

(2) Except as provided in §19, a trust is created by a will if the intention to create the trust and other elements essential to the creation of a testamentary trust (ordinarily, identification of the trust property, the beneficiaries, and the purposes of the trust) can be ascertained from

(a) the will itself; or

(b) an existing instrument properly incorporated by reference into the will; or

(c) facts referred to in the will that have significance apart from their effect upon the disposition of the property bequeathed or devised by the will.

§18. Secret Trusts

(1) Where a testator devises or bequeaths property to a person in reliance on the devisee's or legatee's expressed or implied agreement to hold the property upon a particular trust, no express trust is created, but the devisee or legatee holds the property upon a constructive trust for the agreed purposes and persons.

(2) Where a property owner dies intestate relying upon the expressed or implied agreement of an intestate successor to hold upon a particular trust the property acquired by intestate succession, no express trust is created, but the intestate successor holds the property upon a constructive trust for the agreed purposes and persons.

Comment

a. In general. Sometimes decedents by will or intestate succession leave property to a devisee or intestate successor who has agreed to hold the property upon a particular trust pursuant to an expressed or implied agreement with the decedent, but the terms of the trust (and often the intention to create a trust) do not appear in a will. (The term "devisee," here and generally today, includes "legatee.")

Where the person dies intestate, or the testator's will manifests no intention to create a trust, the expression "secret trust" is commonly used, as it is in this Restatement. Where the will reveals the intention to create the trust but not its terms, the expression "semi-secret trust" is used, generally and in this Restatement.

When a constructive trust is imposed under the rules stated in this Section in a situation of this type, it arises out of an intended express trust that is unenforceable because of the failure to satisfy the requirements of the Wills Act. In such a case, the testate or intestate successor would be unjustly enriched if permitted to retain the property, and is therefore chargeable as a constructive trustee.

It is arguable that, if a secret-trust agreement is shown, the testate or intestate successor should be chargeable as a constructive trustee (or, in the case of a semi-secret trust, as trustee of a resulting trust) for the estate of the decedent rather than for the intended beneficiaries. This would suffice to prevent the recipient from being unjustly enriched. The same evidence that shows the intended trust, however, also shows that the other (albeit innocent) beneficiaries of the decedent's estate would be unjustly enriched by such a result. In addition, the rule of this Section is supported by the great weight of authority in secret-trust cases . . . and by the lesser risk of unwarranted litigation in the semi-secret-trust cases. . . .

§19. "Pour-Over" Dispositions by Will

Where a will contains a testamentary disposition for the purpose of adding property to an irrevocable or revocable inter vivos trust, or for the purpose of funding a trust pursuant to the terms of an instrument of trust executed but not funded during the testator's lifetime, the intended disposition is effective if and as:

(a) provided by statute;

(b) validated by the doctrine of incorporation by reference or by the doctrine of facts of independent significance; or

(c) the trust instrument, together with the will, either

(i) satisfies an applicable rule of substantial compliance, harmless error, or judicial dispensation, or

(ii) otherwise satisfies the policies underlying the formal safeguards of the applicable Wills Act.

Chapter 5: FORMALITIES: CREATION OF INTER VIVOS TRUSTS

§20. Validity of Oral Inter Vivos Trusts

Except as required by a statute of frauds, a writing is not necessary to create an enforceable inter vivos trust, whether by declaration, by transfer to another as trustee, or by contract.

§21. The Parol-Evidence Rule

(1) In the absence of fraud, duress, undue influence, mistake, or other ground for reformation or rescission, if the owner of property:

(a) transfers it inter vivos to another person by a writing that states that the transferee is to take the property for the transferee's own benefit, extrinsic evidence may not be used to show that the transferee was intended to hold the property in trust; or

(b) transfers it inter vivos to another person by a writing that states that the transferee is to hold the property upon a particular trust, extrinsic evidence may not be used to show that the transferee was intended to hold the property upon a different trust or to take it beneficially; or

(c) by a writing declares that the property owner holds the property upon a particular trust, extrinsic evidence may not be used to show that the owner intended to hold the property upon a different trust or to hold it free of trust.

(2) If the owner of property transfers it inter vivos to another person by a writing that does not state either that the transferee is to take the property for the transferor's own benefit or that the transferee is to hold it upon a particular trust, except as excluded by a statute of frauds or other statute, extrinsic evidence may be used to show that the transferee was to hold the property in trust for either the transferor or one or more third parties, or for some combination of the transferor, the transferee, and one or more third parties.

§22. Writing Required by Statute of Frauds

(1) In order to create an enforceable express inter vivos trust of property for which a statute of frauds requires a writing, the writing must be signed as provided in §23 and must

(a) manifest the trust intention, and

(b) reasonably identify the trust property, the beneficiaries, and the purposes of the trust.

(2) The writing required by a statute of frauds

(a) may consist of several writings,

(b) need not be intended as the expression of a trust, and

(c) continues to satisfy the statute-of-frauds requirement even though later lost or destroyed.

§23 Signing Requirement: When and By Whom?

(1) Where the owner of property declares that he or she holds it upon a trust for which a statute of frauds requires a writing, a writing evidencing the trust as provided in §22 is sufficient to satisfy the statute if it is signed by the declarant

(a) before or at the time of the declaration, or

(b) after the time of the declaration but before the declarant has transferred the property.

(2) Where the owner of property transfers it inter vivos to another person upon an inter vivos trust for which a statute of frauds requires a writing, a writing evidencing the trust as provided in §22 is sufficient to satisfy the statute if it is signed:

(a) by the transferor before or at the time of the transfer; or

(b) by the transferee

(i) before or at the time of the transfer, or

(ii) after the transfer was made to the transferee but before the transferee has transferred the property to a third person.

§24. Result of Noncompliance with Statute of Frauds

(1) Where a property owner creates an oral inter vivos trust for which a statute of frauds requires a writing, the trustee

(a) can properly perform the intended express trust, or

(b) can be compelled to perform the intended express trust if it later becomes enforceable on the basis of part performance.

(2) Where an owner of property transfers it to another upon an inter vivos trust for which a statute of frauds requires a writing, but no writing is properly signed (§23) evidencing the intended trust (§22), and the transferee refuses and cannot be compelled to perform it as an express trust under Clause (b) of Subsection (1), the transferee holds upon a constructive trust for the intended beneficiaries and purposes if

(a) the transfer was procured by fraud, undue influence, or duress, or

(b) the transferee at the time of the transfer was in a confidential relation to the transferor.

(3) Where an owner of property transfers it to another upon an inter vivos trust for which a statute of frauds requires a writing, but no writing is properly signed (§23) evidencing the intended trust (§22) and the rule of Subsection (2) does not apply, and the transferee refuses and cannot be compelled under Clause (b) of Subsection (1) to perform the intended express trust, the transferee can be compelled to hold the property either upon resulting trust or upon constructive trust for the transferor, except when the transferor is incompetent or dead and a constructive trust for the intended beneficiaries and purposes is necessary as a means of preventing unjust enrichment of successors in interest of the transferor.

(4) Where an owner of property orally declares a trust that is unenforceable because of a statute of frauds and cannot be compelled to perform the trust under Clause (b) of Subsection (1), the declarant holds the property free of enforceable trust, except when the declarant is incompetent or dead and a constructive trust for the intended beneficiaries and purposes is necessary as a means of preventing unjust enrichment of successors in interest of the declarant.

§25. Validity and Effect of Revocable Inter Vivos Trust

(1) A trust that is created by the settlor's declaration of trust, or by inter vivos transfer to another, or by beneficiary designation or other payment under a life-insurance policy, employee-benefit or retirement arrangement, or other contract is not rendered testamentary merely because the settlor retains extensive rights such as a beneficial interest for life, powers to revoke and modify the trust, and the right to serve as or control the trustee, or because the trust is funded in whole or in part or comes into existence at or after the death of the settlor, or because the trust is intended to serve as a substitute for a will.

(2) A trust that is not testamentary is not subject to the formal requirements of §17 or to procedures for the administration of a decedent's estate; nevertheless, a trust is ordinarily subject to substantive restrictions on testation and to rules of construction and other rules applicable to testamentary dispositions, and in other respects the property of such a trust is ordinarily treated as though it were owned by the settlor.

Comment

a. Scope, background, and rationale of this Section. Revocable inter vivos (or living) trusts are useful and widely used as a legitimate means of avoiding the costs and delays typically associated with the processes of administering decedents' estates in this country. This is because probate administration is not required for assets transferred to the trustee inter vivos, or for funds payable to the trustee by nonprobate arrangements, such as pension or life insurance beneficiary designations. Assets added to the trust by will, however, are subject to estate administration before they are distributed to the trustee. (On such "pour-over" arrangements, see §19.)

Living trusts also are used as means of providing property management for settlors late in life, often on a contingent or standby basis by settlors who initially at least serve as their own trustees but designate successors to assume responsibility in the event the settlor resigns or becomes incompetent. Thus, for management of the trust estate, the relatively developed principles and processes associated with trust administration (see §§74 and 97, as well as §§76-89) in general are substituted for the heavily court-dependent concepts and procedures of conservatorship.

Occasionally, settlors find additional motivation for the use of revocable trusts rather than wills—reasons such as privacy or, in some states, the avoidance of probate courts' retained jurisdiction over testamentary trusts, with what may be perceived as more intrusive supervision than the relationship of equity courts to inter vivos (or "non-court") trusts. Under some state inheritance-tax systems, tax considerations also may encourage the use of living trusts as receptacles for life insurance proceeds or death benefits under retirement plans.

In short, despite modern efforts to simplify the probate process and the modern and ongoing development of the durable powers of attorney for property management, revocable trusts created by declaration or by transfer to another are often preferred by property owners as means of holding and disposing of their property. Accordingly, the revocable trust is widely used as a legally accepted substitute for the will as the central document of an estate plan, usually in conjunction with pour-over wills (§19) and often with durable powers of attorney . . . , the latter more for trust funding than for asset management.

The law offers a variety of different means of transferring property to others or of creating property rights and interests in beneficiaries, each with its own set of procedures and formalities. These same means are available for creating trusts and conferring equitable property interests on trust beneficiaries, with the declaration of trust offering an additional means of trust creation. See generally §10. Thus, for example, just as it is not necessary to comply with the formalities of Statutes of Wills for a beneficiary to receive insurance proceeds or periodic payments after the death of an insured policy owner, or to receive death benefits under various settlement options under a decedent's pension plan, so, too, may insurance proceeds or plan benefits be paid to a trustee on the death of the insured or plan participant based on the usual policy or plan formalities and without need to comply with those of a Wills Act.

With widespread legislative and judicial endorsement over the years, supported by experience as well as popular interest, the revocable trust has become well established in American law as a socially useful and successful device for property management, especially late in life, and for the disposition of property (outright or in further trust) following the settlor's death. . . .

Issues of formality and procedure aside, however, the availability of nontestamentary methods of making disposition should not mean that substantive policies applicable to testamentary dispositions have no application. Thus, increasingly, statutes and case law in the various states are coming to recognize, as this Restatement provides, that the rights of the spouses and creditors of testators and of settlors of revocable trusts are fundamentally alike, because both the testator and the settlor have retained their complete control over the property that is subject to the will or trust instrument. Similarly, whatever the technicalities of concept and terminology, the interests the revocable-trust beneficiaries will receive on the death of the settlor should, generally at least, receive the same treatment and should be subject to the same rules of construction as the "expectancies" of devisees.

Thus, this Restatement recognizes and gives effect to a property owner's right to choose among different forms and procedures for disposition of property. Yet it seeks to treat functional equivalents similarly, and not to allow choice of form either to provide an escape from serious, substantive policies or to cause the loss of properly relevant aids in essentially constructional matters. Such a policy of treating revocable trusts and their settlors and beneficiaries in like manner to the treatment accorded testators and will beneficiaries, both during life and after the death of the settlor or testator, has long been explicit in the federal income and transfer tax systems. See, e.g., Internal Revenue Code §§671-677 (income tax), §§2036 and 3038 (estate tax), §2511 with Treasury Regulation §25.2511-2(c) (gift tax), and §2652(a) (generation-skipping transfer tax). Early, traditional, and still-developing doctrine in trust and probate law has been neither so clear nor so consistent.

In brief, the fundamental and pervasive policy underlying this Section and related rules of this Restatement is that diverse forms of revocable trusts (i) are valid without compliance with Wills Act formalities but (ii) absent persuasive reason for departure, are subject to the same restrictions (such as spousal rights) and other rules and constructional aids that are applicable to wills. In other substantive respects (such as creditors' rights), the property held in a revocable trust is ordinarily to be treated as if it were property of the settlor and not of the beneficiaries.

Unless a contrary intent is manifested or the rights of the spouses are significantly altered by the trust terms, community property transferred by husband and wife to a jointly created revocable inter vivos trust remains community property. . . .

e. Rights of creditors and other matters. Although a revocable trust is nontestamentary and is therefore not subject to the Wills Act or to the usual procedures of estate administration, property held in the trust is subject to the claims of creditors of the settlor or of the deceased settlor's estate if the same property belonging to the settlor or the estate would be subject to the claims of the creditors, taking account of homestead rights and other exemptions.

This result is not dependent on the trust being "illusory" or "testamentary," or on the transfer being a fraudulent conveyance, but is based on the sound public policy of basing the rights of creditors on the substance rather than the form of the debtor's property rights. Nor is the result affected by the presence of a spendthrift provision in the terms of the trust (see §58(2)) or by whether a creditor's claim arose before or after the transfer.

Whether other assets of the settlor must first be exhausted and other questions involving priority among creditors or among various categories of intended beneficiaries of a deceased debtor are not within the scope of this Restatement. . . .

e(1). Statutory protections against oversight and aids in construction. In addition to the limitations on testamentary disposition represented by statutes discussed in Comment d and less directly by claims of creditors (above), an array of statutes are found throughout the various American jurisdictions that are designed as protections or aids against oversight or inadequacies in the planning and drafting of wills. These statutes often fail specifically to address revocable inter vivos trusts or other will-substitute dispositions. (*Common law* rules or principles of construction normally apply to revocable and irrevocable inter vivos trusts as well as to testamentary trusts.) . . .

Illustrative are pretermitted-heir statutes that, despite differences in their breadth and other details, usually provide intestate shares of a decedent's estate at least for children born after the making of a will that does not by class gift or otherwise make provision, as defined by the statute, for them. Analogous statutes in some states, especially where intestate shares of surviving spouses are significantly greater than their elective shares, make provision in certain circumstances for survivors of marriages entered after the execution of wills.

Other examples include anti-lapse statutes, usually providing substitute gifts for the issue of certain legatees and devisees who predecease testators, and statutes primarily providing for revocation of will provisions for spouses in cases in which divorce occurs after the making of a will.

Statutes of these various types are generally based on legislative judgments concerning probabilities of intention and yield to contrary intent that is shown by types of evidence allowed by the legislation. Sound policy suggests that a property owner's choice of form in using a revocable trust rather than a will as the central instrument of an estate plan should not deprive that property owner and the objects of his or her bounty of appropriate aids and safeguards intended to achieve likely intentions. Thus, although a particular statute of this general type fails to address trusts that are revocable but nontestamentary, the legislation should ordinarily be applied as if trust dispositive provisions that are to be carried out after the settlor's death had been made by will.

e(2). Limits on public benefits and resources. Somewhat analogous problems may arise from quite different types of federal and state legislation or administrative regulations, involving such matters as public benefit programs and governmentally allocated opportunities. Examples range from matters of eligibility and reimbursement for welfare benefits and services to issues about the allocation of entitlements or licenses with respect to water resources, communications media, and the like. . . .

Illustrations

11. W transfers the bulk of her estate to T in trust for W for life, the trust to continue thereafter for the benefit of her husband H for life, with remainder thereafter to be distributed to W's issue. W reserves the power to revoke or amend the trust. A number of years later W and H are divorced; W dies shortly thereafter, and H is still alive. It is provided by statute that a divorce revokes provisions for the former spouse in a will executed before the divorce, with the provisions of the will to be carried out as if the former spouse had predeceased the testator. The provision for H in W's revocable living trust is revoked (see Comment e(1)); the issue are entitled to distribution of the trust property although H is still alive.

12. S owns two ranches, Blackacre and Whiteacre, and her brother B owns a ranch called Greenacre. The Scarce and Subsidized Water Act (SASWA) limits the water allocation each applicant may receive—"directly or indirectly," according to SASWA Regulations. S transfers all of her real and personal property, except for Whiteacre and some personal items, to T in trust for the benefit and use of S during her lifetime, and upon her death to distribute one-half of the trust property to B and the rest to certain nieces and nephews. S reserves the power to revoke or amend the trust. T applies for and obtains a SASWA water allocation for Blackacre. Soon thereafter, S and B also apply for water allocations, respectively, for Whiteacre and Greenacre. For purposes of their eligibility for water allocations, in the absence of an explicit SASWA provision to the contrary, the SASWA allocation to the trust for Blackacre is treated as an allocation to S and not to B (see Comment e(2)). . . .

§26. Tentative ("Totten" or Bank-Account) Trusts

Where a person makes a deposit in an account with a bank or similar financial institution in the depositor's own name "as trustee" or "in trust" for another, the presumption is that the depositor intends to establish a "tentative trust." The depositor may modify or revoke a tentative trust and may, from time to time, withdraw any or all of the funds on deposit. On the death of the depositor, the trust is enforceable by the beneficiary as to any funds then remaining on deposit, unless the depositor has revoked the trust.

. . . *c. Revocation and termination of tentative trust.* A tentative trust can properly be revoked by the depositor at any time during life by a manifestation of intention to do so. No particular formalities are necessary to manifest that intention.

Thus, the trust is terminated by withdrawal of all the funds or by transferring them to a different account. If any part of the deposit is withdrawn during the depositor's lifetime, this operates as a revocation of the trust to the extent of the withdrawal; and the beneficiary will be entitled only to the amount remaining on deposit at the death of the depositor. The nature or terms of the account may be changed by the depositor's direction to the savings institution. In addition, the right to funds remaining in the account at the depositor's death may be changed by agreement between the beneficiary and the depositor. . . .

Where there are multiple depositors, or if there are multiple persons designated as trustees, one of whom is the depositor, it is presumed that there is a right of survivorship between or among the "trustees" of the trust, which remains a tentative trust as long as a trustee and a beneficiary survive. The death of the beneficiary (or of the last survivor of multiple beneficiaries) of a tentative trust prior to the death of the depositor (or last trustee) terminates the trust, even though the depositor (or last trustee) later dies without having manifested an intention to revoke the trust and without having withdrawn the amount on deposit. In such a case, the personal representative of the depositor (or last trustee), not the personal representative of the beneficiary, will be entitled to the amount of deposit; and even an anti-lapse statute that ordinarily applies to other revocable trusts . . . does not apply to tentative trusts. . . .

In the absence of a statute to the contrary, a tentative trust may be revoked in whole or in part by the depositor's will, either by express provision or by necessary implication. The conservator of a depositor who becomes incompetent may, with such court permission as may be required by law, withdraw some or all of the tentative-trust funds as necessary for the welfare of the depositor and appropriate members of his or her family. . . .

d. Creditors' rights, family protection, and rules of will construction. The creditors of a person who establishes a tentative trust can reach the funds on deposit, as may the personal representative of a deceased depositor if assets otherwise available in the estate administration are insufficient to pay debts and funeral, last-illness, and administration expenses.

The tentative trust, like other revocable inter vivos trusts, is subject to restrictions on testamentary disposition and also to pretermitted-heir and omitted-spouse protections. . . .

Part 3. Elements of Trusts

Chapter 6: TRUST PURPOSES

§27. Purposes For Which a Trust Can Be Created

(1) Subject to the rules of §29, a trust may be created for charitable purposes (see §28) or for private purposes, or for a combination of charitable and private purposes.

(2) Subject to the special rules of §§46(2) and 47, a private trust, its terms, and its administration must be for the benefit of its beneficiaries, who must be identified or ascertainable as provided in §44. (On charitable trusts, see §28.)

Comment

Comment on Subsection (1)

a. Charitable and private purposes. Except as provided in §§46(2) and 47 (on certain trust provisions for "indefinite beneficiaries" and "noncharitable purposes," respectively), permissible purposes of trusts that are the subject of this Restatement are confined to those that are charitable ("charitable trusts") and those that are for the benefit of persons who are definite or will be ascertainable in compliance with rules regulating perpetuities ("private trusts"). Furthermore, trust purposes and provisions must not be unlawful or contrary to public policy (§29).

Trusts may have mixed charitable and private purposes. Thus, for example, a trust may be created to provide concurrent benefits for both charitable and private purposes, either by fixed portions or discretionary distributions. More frequently, so-called "split-interest" trusts are created to benefit the settlor or family members for term or life periods and thereafter to benefit charity, or vice versa. . . .

. . . Some purposes that a reasonable individual might believe worthwhile may fall short of the standard of charity for which a charitable trust may be established. On such cases, see §47.

Often the purposes of private trusts are not specified but must be inferred from the interests conferred on the various beneficiaries, whose identities and interests are subject to the requirements of definiteness discussed in Chapter 9 (especially §§44 through 47). . . .

Comment on Subsection (2)

b. Private trusts. The general purpose of a private trust is to benefit identified or identifiable beneficiaries (see §§44-46) in accordance with their respective interests in the trust. Within this general private purpose, a given trust may and most likely will serve multiple objectives or purposes (see *b(1)* below).

The settlor of a particular trust has considerable latitude in specifying the manner in which a trust purpose is to be pursued. In order to be valid, however, administrative and other provisions must reasonably relate to a trust purpose and must not have the effect of diverting the trust's funds or administration from that purpose in support of a purpose that does not meet the private- or charitable-purpose requirement of Subsection (1), as qualified by §47 (on general and specific noncharitable "purpose" trusts). . . .

§28. Charitable Purposes

Charitable trust purposes include:

(a) the relief of poverty;

(b) the advancement of knowledge or education;

(c) the advancement of religion;

(d) the promotion of health;

(e) governmental or municipal purposes; and

(f) other purposes that are beneficial to the community.

General Comment

a. The general nature of charitable trusts and purposes. . . .

The discussion in this Section of dispositions that are charitable does not necessarily provide a complete enumeration of charitable purposes. Other purposes of the same general character are likewise charitable. The common element of charitable purposes is that they are designed to accomplish objects that are beneficial to the community—i.e., to the public or indefinite members thereof—without also serving what amount to private trust purposes . . . . As long as the purposes to which the property of the trust is to be devoted are charitable, however, the motives of the settlor in creating the trust are immaterial.

A trust purpose is charitable if its accomplishment is of such social interest or benefit to the community as to justify permitting the property to be devoted to the purpose in perpetuity and to justify the various other special privileges that are typically allowed to charitable trusts.

There is no fixed standard to determine what purposes are of such interest to the community, for the interests of the community vary with time and place. Trust-law definitions of charity are not limited by those used in federal, state, and local tax law; nor are tax-law definitions necessarily limited to charitable purposes recognized by the trust law. Of the generally agreed purposes stated in this Section, it is Clause (f) (Comment *l*) that provides the greatest flexibility and also presents the most definitional issues at the margin. . . .

a(2). Controversial ideas and unpopular causes. If the general purposes for which a trust is created are such that they may be reasonably thought to promote the social interest of the community, the mere fact that a majority of the people or of the members of a court believe that the particular purpose of the settlor is unwise or not well adapted to its social objective does not prevent the trust from being charitable. Thus, a trust to promote a particular religious doctrine or a particular system of taxation is charitable even though the view to be promoted has but a modest number of adherents. The role of the court in deciding whether a purpose is charitable is not to attempt to decide which of conflicting views of the social or community interest is more beneficial or appropriate but to decide whether the trust purpose or the view to be promoted is sufficiently useful or reasonable to be of such benefit or interest to the community, including through a marketplace of ideas, as to justify the perpetual existence and other privileges of a charitable trust. Thus, a trust to establish a museum to exhibit what a testator regarded as objects of art but which testimony establishes to be of no artistic value, or a trust to publish and distribute a testator's views that are irrational or other writings that are of no literary or educational value, is not charitable. The line between what is charitable and what is not is sometimes a difficult one to draw, for the difference may be one of degree and the line may be drawn differently at different times and in different places. For trusts that do not qualify as either private or charitable trusts, see the limited duration and acceptance of "trusts for noncharitable purposes" in §47. . . .

d. Duration of charitable trusts. A charitable trust is not invalid although by its terms it is to continue for an indefinite or unlimited period of time. This is unlike the rules for private trusts, in which the interests of the beneficiaries must vest within the period of the applicable rule against perpetuities, and under which a provision that a private trust shall be indestructible (i. e., is not to be terminated even upon the consent of all beneficiaries) beyond the period of the rule is invalid. See §29(b) . . . .

Charitable trusts may be of unlimited duration, although dispositions over to charitable purposes following private trusts are subject to the rule against perpetuities, as are dispositions over to private purposes upon termination of charitable trusts. On the other hand, even after the perpetuities period would have expired, a shift over from one charitable purpose or trust to another is permissible because, it is often said, the property is "vested in charity." . . .

e. Trusts with mixed charitable and other purposes. A trust is not invalid, although it might not be a charitable trust, merely because it includes private trust interests (§27(2)) or a "noncharitable purpose" (§47) as well as the designated charitable purpose.

If the charitable and other purposes are distinctly divided either by time or into separate and independent shares, the period or share devoted to charity will be treated as a charitable trust just as if separate trusts had been created for the different purposes. Where there is no such separation by time or by independent shares, the trust is valid, but such a mixed charitable and private trust is subject to the rule against perpetuities as a private trust; and if the trust similarly combines charitable purposes with a noncharitable purpose, the trust is subject to the rules and limitations of noncharitable-purpose trusts under §47. . . .

f. Consistency with law and public policy. Like other trusts, charitable trusts are subject to the rule of §29 that trust purposes and provisions must not be unlawful or contrary to public policy.

It is particularly common, however, for provisions to be included in various types of charitable trusts, especially those created for educational or health purposes or for the relief of poverty, limiting the direct benefits or eligibility to persons of a particular national origin, religion, gender, sexual orientation, age group, political affiliation, or other characteristics or background. Of course, federal and state constitutions, legislation, and other binding expressions of applicable law and policy are to be respected in the administration of trusts and in determining the enforceability of the terms of trusts. These matters, and such implicit issues as what may constitute state action, are beyond the scope of this Restatement. The issue for present purposes, however, remains what provisions of this general type may, as a matter of trust law and policy, be inconsistent with the nature of charitable purposes.

Provisions of these types in charitable trusts are not valid if they involve invidious discrimination (see below). Where a restriction or preference is invalid, or the particular charitable disposition cannot be carried out because the intended recipient refuses to accept it due to a restrictive provision or preference the intended recipient deems objectionable, an issue arises concerning the application of the doctrine of cy pres. See §67. . . .

It is not always possible to state with certainty what constitutes an "invidious" form of discrimination for these purposes. What the law of charitable trusts does or does not allow inevitably varies from time to time and place to place, as well as from context to context. For example, trust-law policies regarding restrictions on gender, sexual orientation, or age are especially sensitive to context, as the scope of more general statutory and constitutional protections evolve in these matters. . . . Some generalizations are nevertheless possible.

When a scholarship or other form of assistance or opportunity is to be awarded on a basis that, for example, explicitly excludes potential beneficiaries on the basis of membership in a particular racial, ethnic, or religious group, the restriction is ordinarily invidious and therefore unenforceable. Thus, a trust to provide land and maintenance for a playground from which Black children are excluded, or a trust to support a scholarship program for which no Roman Catholic may apply, is not enforceable under those terms as a charitable trust. Similarly, although the exclusions are not explicit, a trust to provide research grants for which only "white, Anglo-Saxon Protestants" may apply is invidious and noncharitable.

This does not mean that a criterion such as gender, religion, or national origin may not be used in a charitable trust when it is a reasonable element of a settlor's charitable purpose and charitable motivation. Thus, the requirement that the purpose be of charitable character does not prevent alumnae or friends of a women's college from endowing a professorial chair or library fund for that college, or a Jewish man from leaving money to a university to establish a scholarship program, in the betterment of his religion as he sees it, to enable a rabbi or two each year to study in that university's philosophy department. Nor does it mean that a Norwegian immigrant who became wealthy in this country cannot establish a program of an otherwise charitable nature to aid, solely or by preference, other Norwegian immigrants or the children of Norwegian immigrants. Similarly, the law of charitable trusts as such does not object to what is sometimes called "affirmative action," attempting to respond to a social problem in its own terms, at least as reasonably perceived by a substantial (even if not majority) segment of society or of the affected community. . . .

Comment on Clause (f)

l. Promotion of other purposes beneficial to the community. A trust is charitable if it is established for the promotion of purposes that are of a character sufficiently of interest or beneficial to the community to justify permitting the property to be devoted forever to their accomplishment and to justify whatever other special privileges may be accorded to charitable trusts. . . .

The trusts encompassed by this Comment may involve any of a large, indefinite array of purposes in addition to (or overlapping) those that are dealt with in the preceding Comments but that are nevertheless held to promote the social interests of the community, and are therefore upheld as falling within the scope of charity. It is not possible adequately and accurately to enumerate all purposes of this type, for in deciding whether a particular purpose falls within the present clause, much depends on the time and the place at which the question arises. In each such case, as under some other clauses of this Section, particularly some cases involving purposes that are arguably educational, the question for potential judicial determination is whether at the time when the question arises and in the state in which it arises the purpose is one that might reasonably be held to be of community or social interest. The mere fact that a trust is created for the benefit of members of a community outside the state, however, does not prevent the trust from being charitable. Thus, a trust for the benefit of impoverished residents of another state, or to establish a school or hospital in a foreign country, is charitable.

A trust to prevent or alleviate the suffering of animals is charitable. . . . So also is a trust to establish or support a home or to provide care for stray animals, although a trust to provide for the settlor's own pets is not charitable (see, however, §47). . . .

A trust may be charitable although the accomplishment of the purpose for which the trust is created involves a change in the existing law. If the purpose of the trust is to bring about a change in the law by illegal means, however, such as by revolution, bribery, or illegal lobbying, or bringing improper pressure to bear upon members of the legislature, the purpose is not charitable. Cf. §29. Certainly a trust to promote general improvement in the law, whether by financial support of the work of a law-revision commission or through the support of research projects so directed, is charitable. The mere fact, however, that the purpose of a trust is to advocate and bring about a *particular* change of law does not prevent the purpose from being charitable. . . ..

Although a trust to promote the success of a particular political party is not charitable, the development and dissemination of information advocating or seeking to improve understanding of a particular set of social, economic, or political views is charitable, whether because it is educational (Comment h) or because it contributes to a marketplace of ideas that is beneficial to the community. Thus, on the one hand, a trust the income of which is to be used in the discretion of the chairperson of a political party to assist in the election of members of that party or otherwise to promote its interests is not charitable. On the other hand, if the promotion of a particular cause or socio-economic perspective is charitable, the mere fact that one or another of the political parties advocates that cause or viewpoint does not make the promotion of that cause or set of views noncharitable. Accordingly, a trust to promote a policy either of free trade or of protective tariffs is charitable although different political parties may take different stands on these policies or their current applications. . . .

§29. Purposes and Provisions That Are Unlawful or Against Public Policy

An intended trust or trust provision is invalid if:

(a) its purpose is unlawful or its performance calls for the commission of a criminal or tortious act;

(b) it violates rules relating to perpetuities; or

(c) it is contrary to public policy.

Comment on Clause (a)

b. Voidable transfers contrasted. The types of situations addressed in Clause (a) involve impermissible purposes or provisions of the trust itself. Analogous but different are trusts that may fail in whole or in part because a third party is entitled to set aside the settlor's transfer to the trustee or to reach the property in the trustee's hands. Illustrative are cases in which the settlor's property had been illegally acquired by the settlor and cases in which the settlor's transfer to the trust constitutes a fraudulent transfer under applicable creditors' rights law. . . .

Comment on Clause (c)

i. Nature and rationale of public-policy limits on trust provisions. The rules allowing and limiting the use of trusts, and the time-divided property ownership usually associated with deadhand control, reflect a compromise between free disposition of private property and other values (see §27 and Introductory Note to this Chapter). So also does the rule of Clause (c) of this Section, and ensuing Comments j-l involving trust benefits conditioned upon the beneficiary's future conduct.

The private trust is tolerated, even treasured, in the common-law world for the flexibility it offers to property owners in planning and designing diverse beneficial interests and financial protections over time, individually tailored as the particular property owner deems best to the varied needs, abilities, and circumstances of particular family members and others whom the owner chooses to benefit. Yet these societal and individual advantages are properly to be balanced against other social values and the effects of deadhand control on the subsequent conduct or personal freedoms of others, and also against the burdens a former owner's unrestrained dispositions might place on courts to interpret and enforce individualized interests and conditions.

The simplest examples of trusts or provisions that offend public policy are those that tend to encourage criminal or tortious conduct on the part of beneficiaries. . . .

Policies concerned with deadhand control limit the use of trusts in ways that do not apply to living individuals in the direct disposition of their property. Thus, a policy of fostering free family interaction or privacy between individuals, or simply society's tolerance of human frailty, traditionally exempts acts of property owners (and even their outright dispositions by will) from restrictions that would apply to personally intrusive or socially dubious conditions in the distributive provisions of irrevocable trusts. Furthermore, the "rigor mortis" of deadhand control is not present while a property owner is able to respond to persuasion and evolving circumstances.

Thus, although one is free to give property to another or to withhold it, it does not follow that one may give in trust with whatever terms or conditions one may wish to attach. This is particularly so of provisions that the law views as exerting a socially undesirable influence on the exercise or nonexercise of fundamental rights that significantly affect the personal lives of beneficiaries and often of others as well. See Scope note, Comment i(2), below. Also compare §28, Comment f, on "invidious" restrictions in charitable trusts.

In cases of the types considered in the Comments that follow, simple and precise rules of validity or invalidity frequently cannot be stated. This is particularly so because of the need to weigh the often worthy concerns and objectives of settlors against the objectionable effects or tendencies of conditions attached to beneficial interests, each of which involves specific terms and personal and overall estate-planning contexts that may vary subtly but significantly from situation to situation. Furthermore, in these various situations, remedial flexibility is required to reconcile (i) the policy objection to a provision with (ii) a motive or goal of the settlor that is legally acceptable in whole or in part as an effort to protect the beneficiary's interest or the trust property.

i(1). Consequences of invalidity; reformation. Ordinarily, if a beneficial interest in a trust is to be conferred or is to terminate upon an invalid condition (whether, in form, precedent or subsequent), the interest becomes effective or continues as if the condition had not been imposed, or as if the settlor's requirements or restrictions were satisfied. A different result may be reached, however, to avoid distorting the settlor's underlying general plan for allocating his or her estate among family members. Furthermore, if the settlor provides for a certain disposition in case of a condition's invalidity, that direction will be respected unless it would have the effect of deterring a beneficiary from asserting the rule of this Clause (c) of this Section.

In addition, a provision that is not to be upheld as written but is susceptible of adaptation to accommodate both public-policy concerns and legitimate settlor objectives may be so adapted by the court. The rule allowing reformation under the Comments that follow is rather like the use of equitable approximation (i.e., reformation) in cases of violations of the rule against perpetuities. . . .

i(2). Scope note. The policies restraining deadhand control in Clause (c) of this Section do not apply to outright dispositions conditioned on conduct prior to the death of the testator, or prior to the time a revocable trust becomes irrevocable. See Restatement Second, Property (Donative Transfers) §6.1, Comment c; although the Property Restatement's rules on behavior restraints apply to nontrust as well as trust dispositions in various forms, those rules (as here) only address restraints on "future conduct."

Some of the personal relationships or freedoms considered in Comments j through l may be protected in some fashion by federal or state statutes or constitutions (such as religious freedom). These Comments, however, involve rules and policies of the trust law and limit the purposes and terms of trusts in ways that are not based on statutory or constitutional safeguards, although trust law may be influenced by policies underlying such protections.

j. Family relationships. A trust or a condition or other provision in the terms of a trust is ordinarily (see below) invalid if it tends to encourage disruption of a family relationship or to discourage formation or resumption of such a relationship. See also Restatement Second, Contracts §§189-191.

Thus, a trust provision normally may not terminate a beneficial interest if a beneficiary and spouse who are living apart should resume living together, or confer a beneficial interest upon a beneficiary if he or she obtains a divorce or legal separation. Similarly, a trust provision is ordinarily invalid if it would tend to induce termination of a long-established relationship of cohabitation without marriage.

In addition, a trust provision is ordinarily invalid if it tends seriously to interfere with or inhibit the exercise of a beneficiary's freedom to obtain a divorce (creating a risk, e.g., of encouraging financial dependency upon an abusive relationship) or the exercise of freedom to marry, either by limiting the beneficiary's selection of a spouse or by unduly postponing the time of marriage. A fundamental exception, however, permits termination of a beneficial interest of the settlor's spouse in the event of the spouse's remarriage or, if the restraint is reasonable under all the circumstances . . . , termination of a beneficial interest of the surviving spouse of one who is or would have been a natural object of the settlor's bounty. . . .

The policy against undermining family relationships applies as well to trust provisions that discourage a person from living with or caring for a parent or child or from social interaction with siblings.

Clause (c) of this Section is generally concerned with the objective effects of a provision rather than with the settlor's underlying motive(s). Nevertheless, a subjective inquiry into the settlor's reasons for including a provision in a trust may be relevant. Thus, it may be shown that the settlor's motive was to provide for special needs that might arise in the event of the beneficiary's divorce, or to provide support for a beneficiary until marriage or for a child who feels unable to return to a parent's home. A provision of this type may be upheld despite the incidental influence it may have on the beneficiary's decision(s) affecting a marriage or family relationship. Such a condition may even relieve financial pressure on a beneficiary to remain in or enter a marriage. Similarly, in making or increasing provision for a beneficiary upon divorce from a particular spouse, a settlor may be motivated by reasonable concern over that spouse's financial irresponsibility or an apparent gambling or substance addiction.

The credibility of any such explanation is diminished, however, and its socially undesirable influence aggravated, when the provision does not take the form of discretionary distributions appropriately tailored to the alleged risk or to the beneficiary's needs and the availability of other means of meeting those needs. Moreover, a provision may reflect a mixture of motives or may provide some other basis for finding it invalid as written despite an acceptable purpose. In cases of these various types, a provision may fail in its original form but nevertheless be judicially reformed to accomplish the permissible objectives (possibly with fiduciary discretion over distributions) while removing or minimizing socially undesirable effects. Speculation about a settlor's motives and other difficulties inherent in these cases may be eased by this remedial flexibility under which an all-or-nothing decision is not required. . . .

k. Religious freedom. Individuals are normally free during life to promote their theological views among others, and to create charitable trusts during life or at death to support or advance a chosen religion (see §28, Clause (b)). But the use of private trusts that create financial pressure regarding the future religious choices of beneficiaries is a different matter. A trust provision is ordinarily invalid if its enforcement would tend to restrain the religious freedom of the beneficiary by offering a financial inducement to embrace or reject a particular faith or set of beliefs concerning religion. Illustrative is a provision granting or terminating a beneficial interest only if the beneficiary should adopt or abandon a particular religious faith. . . .

On the other hand, trust provisions would ordinarily be upheld if reasonably designed (or reformed) to protect beneficial interests or trust property from adverse financial implications associated with a beneficiary's present or future religious commitments. . . .

l. Careers and conduct. It is not contrary to public policy for a trust provision to encourage a beneficiary to be a productive member of society or to pursue a particular career or form of training, as long as the effect of the provision is not punitive or so rewarding as to be coercive. Thus, a settlor may validly create a trust or include a provision solely to finance a beneficiary's higher education, or a particular type of education, or to facilitate pursuit of a particular type of career (such as religious or social service) by compensating for the financial services that tend to be associated with the career choice.

Different policy considerations are presented, however, by a provision to distribute the corpus of a trust to its income beneficiary only if the beneficiary becomes a surgeon, or to terminate a beneficiary's interests for abandoning a particular career or for failing to take it up by a stated age. In cases of this type, society's interest in a property owner's freedom of disposition must be weighed against the risk of excessive influence on a personal decision significantly affecting the life of the beneficiary and perhaps others. The social concerns here involve not only the increased risk of an unsuitable decision being made or adhered to by the beneficiary but also the burdens and difficulties of judicial interpretation and enforcement of such interpretations.

Trust provisions intended or likely to induce a change or a continuation of a beneficiary's personal habits or conduct ordinarily are not against public policy. But Compare Comments *j* and *k* above, that where a provision is unnecessarily punitive or unreasonably intrusive into significant personal decisions or interests, or involves an unreasonable restraint on personal associations, the provision may be invalid. . . .

m. Capricious purposes; sound administration of trust. It is against public policy to enforce a trust provision that would divert distributions or administration from the interests of the beneficiaries to other purposes that are capricious or frivolous . . . , detrimental to the community, or otherwise (with limited exceptions . . .) neither private nor charitable in character. See §27.

Similarly, a trust provision may not be enforced if to do so would undermine proper administration of the trust. Thus, a provision that purports to prevent a court from removing a trustee will be disregarded if removal appears appropriate to proper administration of the trust; and an arbitrary restriction on the appointment of trustees or successor trustees may be invalid if not reasonably related to the trust purposes. A provision is also invalid to the extent it purports to relieve the trustee altogether from accountability and the duty to provide information to beneficiaries (see §§82, 83), or to relieve the trustee from liability even for dishonest or reckless acts (see §87, §96, and §§76-79). See generally Chapters 14 through 18, and cf. Restatement Second, Property (Donative Transfers) §9.2 and Restatement Third, Property (Wills and Other Donative Transfers) §8.5.

This principle does not, however, prevent a settlor from prescribing administrative provisions designed to serve a reasonable view of the beneficiaries' best interests or to express a widely even if not generally held view of business ethics or morality. . . .

§30. Impossibility and Indefiniteness

A private trust, or a provision in the terms of a trust, may be unenforceable because of impossibility or indefiniteness.

Chapter 7: THE TRUSTEE

§31. Trust Does Not Fail for Lack of Trustee

A trust does not fail because no trustee is designated or because the designated trustee declines, is unable, or ceases to act, unless the trust's creation or continuation depends on a specific person serving as trustee; a proper court will appoint a trustee as necessary and appropriate (see §34).

§32. Capacity of Individual to Be Trustee

A natural person, including a settlor or beneficiary, has capacity

(a) to take and hold property in trust to the extent the person has capacity to take and hold the property as beneficial owner; and

(b) to administer trust property and act as trustee to the same extent the person would have capacity to deal with the property as beneficial owner.

§33. Corporations and Other Entities as Trustees

(1) A corporation has capacity to take and hold property in trust except as limited by law, and to administer trust property and act as trustee to the extent of the powers conferred upon it by law.

(2) If a partnership, unincorporated association, or other entity has capacity to take and hold property for its own purposes, it has capacity to take, hold, and administer property in trust.

§34. Appointment of Trustees

(1) Except as required by statute, a trustee designated by or selected in accordance with the terms of a trust may act without being appointed or confirmed by an order of court.

(2) If the appointment of a trustee is not provided for or made pursuant to the terms of the trust, the trustee will be appointed by a proper court.

(3) A trustee need not provide a performance bond except as required by statute, trust provision, or court order.

§35. Acceptance or Renunciation of Trusteeship

(1) A designated trustee may accept the trusteeship either by words or by conduct.

(2) A designated trustee who has not accepted the trusteeship may decline it.

§36. Resignation of Trustee

A trustee who has accepted the trust can properly resign:

(a) in accordance with the terms of the trust;

(b) with the consent of all beneficiaries; or

(c) upon terms approved by a proper court.

§37. Removal of Trustee

A trustee may be removed

(a) in accordance with the terms of the trust; or

(b) for cause by a proper court.

Comment

. . .*d. Removal by court; judicial discretion.* A court may remove a trustee whose continuation in that role would be detrimental to the interests of the beneficiaries. See Comment e. The matter is largely left to the discretion of the trial court, but is subject to review for abuse of discretion.

The court may act on the petition of any beneficiary, co-trustee, or other interested party, or on its own motion (see generally §94). The trustee is entitled to due process, with notice and an opportunity to be heard, although the court may suspend a trustee's powers (including, if necessary, by appointing a temporary trustee) pending a removal hearing.

e. Grounds for removal. The following are illustrative, but not exhaustive, of possible grounds for a court to remove a trustee: lack of capacity to administer the trust (see §32); unfitness, whether due to insolvency, diminution of physical vigor or mental acuity, substance abuse, want of skill, or the inability to understand fiduciary standards and duties; acquisition of a conflicting interest (cf. Comment f(1)); refusal or inability to give bond, if bond is required (see §34, Comment a); repeated or flagrant failure or delay in providing proper information or accountings to beneficiaries (see §§82 and 83); the commission of a crime, particularly one involving dishonesty; gross or continued inadequacies in matters of investment (see §§90-92); changes in the place of trust administration, location of beneficiaries, or other developments causing serious geographic inconvenience to the beneficiaries or to the administration of the trust; unwarranted preference to the interests of one or more beneficiaries; a pattern of indifference toward some or all of the beneficiaries; or unreasonable or corrupt failure to cooperate with a co-trustee.

Not every breach of trust warrants removal of the trustee (*cf.* Comment g), but serious or repeated misconduct, even unconnected with the trust itself, may justify removal. . . .

e(1). Friction between trustee and beneficiaries. Friction between the trustee and some of the beneficiaries is not a sufficient ground for removing the trustee unless it interferes with the proper administration of the trust. . . .

f. Trustee named by settlor. The court will less readily remove a trustee named by the settlor than one appointed by a court. . . .

Ordinarily, a court will not remove a trustee named by the settlor upon a ground that was known to the settlor at the time the trustee was designated, even though a court would not itself have appointed that person as trustee. In cases of unfitness to serve (*supra*), however, a court may remove a trustee even upon a ground known to the settlor at the time of designation.

f(1). Conflicting interests. Thus, the fact that the trustee named by the settlor is one of the beneficiaries of the trust, or would otherwise have conflicting interests, is not a sufficient ground for removing the trustee or refusing to confirm the appointment. This is so even though the trustee has broad discretion in matters of distribution and investment.

A trustee's removal may be warranted, however, by a conflict of interests that existed but was unknown to the settlor at the time of the designation, or that came into being at a later time.

Furthermore, when a beneficiary serves as trustee or when other conflict-of-interest situations exist, the conduct of the trustee in the administration of the trust will be subject to especially careful scrutiny. . . .

g. Alternatives to removal of trustee. Courts may grant more limited relief to deal with cases in which removal is not necessary or appropriate.

For example, conflict-of-interest problems might be ameliorated by the appointment of an additional trustee, or by the appointment of a trustee ad litem to handle a specific, conflict-sensitive transaction. . . .

§38. Trustee's Compensation and Indemnification

(1) A trustee is entitled to reasonable compensation out of the trust estate for services as trustee, unless the terms of the trust provide otherwise or the trustee agrees to forgo compensation.

(2) A trustee is entitled to indemnity out of the trust estate for expenses properly incurred in the administration of the trust.

Comment

Comment on Subsection (1)

c. Amount of compensation. . . . The reasonable compensation rule applies where there is no statute dealing with trustee compensation.

Trustees ordinarily receive some compensation periodically and, when the trust terminates, additional compensation for their special responsibilities at that time.

c(1). Determining reasonable compensation. Trial courts have discretion in determining reasonable compensation, but their determinations are subject to review for abuse of discretion.

Local custom is a factor to be considered in determining compensation. Other relevant factors are: the trustee's skill, experience and facilities, and the time devoted to trust duties; the amount and character of the trust property; the degree of difficulty, responsibility, and risk assumed in administering the trust, including in making discretionary distributions; the nature and costs of services rendered by others; and the quality of the trustee's performance.

The amount of compensation received by a trustee is relevant in determining whether certain costs of others' services are reimbursable under Subsection (2). This is particularly so of costs of hiring advisors, agents, and others to render services expected or normally to be performed by the trustee. Conversely, even proper expenses of this type may affect what is reasonable compensation for the trustee. . . . On the requirement that expenses be properly incurred, see generally §88.

Absent a statute so requiring, the trustee's compensation need not be approved by a court, but a trustee who has taken excessive compensation may be ordered to refund it. To make the possibility of judicial review meaningful, beneficiaries should be informed of compensation being taken by the trustee. On the extent to which a trustee is protected by a court decree, or by approval or acquiescence of beneficiaries, see §83 (on accounting) and §§97 (beneficiary consent) and 98 (laches). . . .

e. The terms of the trust. When the terms of a trust provide that the trustee is to receive a certain compensation or no compensation, the trustee's right to compensation is ordinarily governed by that provision. It is a question of interpretation whether such a provision applies also to successor trustees.

If the amount of compensation provided by the terms of the trust is or becomes unreasonably high or unreasonably low, the court may allow a smaller or larger compensation, or may allow the trustee to resign. See §36. . . .

l. Several trustees. When there are two or more co-trustees, compensation that is fixed by statute or trust provision ordinarily is to be divided among them in accordance with the relative value of their services. . . .

In the aggregate, the reasonable fees for multiple trustees may be higher than for a single trustee, because the normal duty of each trustee to participate in all aspects of administration (see §81, and cf. §80) can be expected not only to result in some duplication of effort but also to contribute to the quality of administration. . . .

§39. Exercise of Powers by Multiple Trustees

Unless otherwise provided by the terms of the trust, if there are two trustees their powers may be exercised only by concurrence of both of them, absent an emergency or a proper delegation; but if there are three or more trustees their powers may be exercised by a majority.

Comment

a. Basic rule and rationale. If a trust has two trustees, they must concur in order to exercise powers of the trusteeship. If there are three or more trustees and they disagree, the decision of the majority controls, although when feasible all trustees must be consulted before decisions are made. . . ..

For purposes of this rule, the number of trustees in office at the time of the action is controlling, rather than the original number of trustees. . . .

Traditionally, the majority-rule principle has applied only to charitable trusts; in private trusts all the trustees had to agree in order to take action. Considerations of sound and efficient administration, however, tend to be better served by the rule stated in this Section. This is evidenced not only by widespread drafting practice but also by the fact that most states today provide for majority rule by statute. . . . See also Uniform Trustees Powers Act §6; Uniform Trusts Act (1937) §11; and Uniform Trust Code §703(a).

These statutory provisions and the rule of this Section ordinarily protect a dissenting trustee from liability for an act authorized by the majority, while preserving the co-trustee's duty normally to participate in deliberations and decisionmaking and to act reasonably to prevent a breach of trust. . . .

Chapter 8: TRUST PROPERTY

§40. Any Property May Be Trust Property

Subject to the rule of §29, a trustee may hold in trust any interest in any type of property.

§41. Expectancies; Nonexistent Property Interests

An expectation or hope of receiving property in the future, or an interest that has not come into existence or has ceased to exist, cannot be held in trust.

§42. Extent and Nature of Trustee's Title

Unless a different intention is manifested, or the settlor owned only a lesser interest, the trustee takes a nonbeneficial interest of unlimited duration in the trust property and not an interest limited to the duration of the trust.

Chapter 9: BENEFICIARIES

§43. Persons Who May Be Beneficiaries

A person who would have capacity to take and hold legal title to the intended trust property has capacity to be a beneficiary of a trust of that property; ordinarily, a person who lacks capacity to hold legal title to property may not be a trust beneficiary.

§44. Definite-Beneficiary Requirement

A trust is not created, or if created will not continue, unless the terms of the trust provide a beneficiary who is ascertainable at the time or who may later become ascertainable within the period and terms of the rule against perpetuities.

§45. Members of a Definite Class as Beneficiaries

The members of a definite class of persons can be the beneficiaries of a trust.

§46. Members of an Indefinite Class as Beneficiaries

(1) Except as stated in Subsection (2), where the owner of property transfers it upon intended trust for the members of an indefinite class of persons, no trust is created.

(2) If the transferee is directed to distribute the property to such members of the indefinite class as the transferee shall select, the transferee holds the property in trust with power but no duty to distribute the property to such class members as the transferee may select; to whatever extent the power (presumptively personal) is not exercised, the transferee will then hold for reversionary beneficiaries implied by law.

Comment

Comment on Subsection (1)

b. *Where an equal division is directed among, or a specified amount is to be paid to, all members of the class.* If the only beneficial provision of an intended trust directs the trust property to be divided in equal shares among all of the members of an indefinite class, no member of the class can maintain a proceeding to enforce the intended trust, nor can anyone else. Because the intended trustee is under no enforceable duty to carry out the testator's direction, no trust is created. Moreover, since the total membership of the class cannot be ascertained, it is impossible to make an equal distribution among all of the members of the class, even if the intended trustee wishes to do so.

Similarly, where a testator directs the trustee to pay a specified sum to every member of an indefinite class, the intended trust provision for those class members fails. Accordingly, in these circumstances, the intended trustee holds the property upon resulting trust for the testator's estate.

Although a disposition is expressed simply as a trust for the members of an indefinite class, a literal interpretation would seem doubtful as a matter of transferor intention and (unless the transferor is alive to take by resulting trust) would wholly defeat whatever specific objective the transferor had in mind. An interpretation is therefore preferred that would give the disposition some effect reasonably consistent with the transferor's general objective. Thus, the disposition may be interpreted as intended to create a trust for members of the described class as determined or selected by the designated trustee, in which case the situation falls within Subsection (2). See Comment d. Or, if the disposition is interpreted as one intended to benefit those members of an otherwise indefinite class that are or may become identifiable in a manner described in §44 . . . , a valid trust is created. See §45. . . .

Comment on Subsection (2)

c. Background and comparison: powers of appointment. Subsection (2) addresses situations in which a property owner conveys or devises property to a person who is directed, not merely authorized, by the terms of the intended trust to distribute the property to persons to be selected by the trustee from an indefinite class of intended beneficiaries. This situation is discussed hereafter in Comment d.

Different from those situations and much more frequent are instances of valid transfers in trust for the benefit of definite beneficiaries under which one or more of the beneficiaries, or occasionally a trustee or other person, is granted a power of appointment by which the trust property or remainder may be (i.e., is authorized but not required to be) appointed to or for one or more "objects" (permissible appointees) of the power.

Under well-established doctrine, the objects of powers of appointment may properly consist of classes that are either definite or indefinite; powers of appointment may even be general, with no limit whatever with respect to permissible appointees. . . .

d. Beneficiaries to be selected by trustee. Occasionally, a testator leaves property to another upon an intended trust for members of an indefinite class to be selected by the devisee, intending thereby to impose upon the devisee, as trustee, a duty to make selections and to hold and administer the property in the meantime solely for the members of the class. This presents a problem that differs significantly from that in Comment b but that similarly arises from the requirement that a trust have definite beneficiaries.

d(1). Example. Instead of attempting to create a trust simply for all of the members of an indefinite class (as in Subsection (1) and Comment b), the testator leaves property to a person who, as trustee, is directed to liquidate the property and to distribute all of its proceeds in equal shares to those of the testator's "friends" whom the trustee shall select.

This trust, as written, fails for lack of definite beneficiaries capable of enforcing the intended fiduciary duty of selection. See Reporter's Notes. The settlor's intended trust purpose, however, need not fail altogether: That the trustee cannot be required to select the beneficiaries, and that a court will not direct a recalcitrant trustee to make equal distribution to class members too indefinite to be ascertained, nor even remove and replace the trustee, does not mean that the trustee cannot be allowed to make the selections if willing to do so.

The result of this example is that the devisee holds the property upon a trust, adapted by operation of law, for reversionary beneficiaries (the same persons who would take by resulting trust under §8 if the trust had immediately and completely failed), subject to the interests of potential beneficiaries later to be identified by the devisee's exercise of a nonmandatory power of selection. (On the validity of such a trust, cf. §44, Comments a and c; Comment c, above, on powers of appointment; and §45, Comment g.) Thus, the law simply treats the defective disposition as having a trust effect approximating that stated by the testator. Instead of complete failure, with an immediate resulting trust, there is a legally implied reversion to take effect only in default of selection.

d(2). Rationale. A testator can create a trust expressly for the people who would be his or her own heirs (or residuary beneficiaries), subject to an express power of appointment by which the trustee is allowed to appoint among an indefinite class of objects. (See Comment c.) Or the testator could have created a trust for beneficiaries authorized to be appointed later by the trustee, with either an express gift or one implied by law (a reversionary or "resulting trust" interest) in favor of the testator's estate . . . .

Therefore, if an intended trust that purports to require the trustee to select distributees from an indefinite class (such as "friends") fails as written, then, rather than to have the purpose fail altogether, the testator's purpose would be better served—and no policy of the law is violated (see Comment c)— by treating the will as having created an adapted version of the intended trust. This results in an enforceable trust for a definite though unexpressed (legally implied) class of reversionary beneficiaries, whose interests are subject, by legal adaptation, to a nonmandatory power in the trustee to select other distributees.

In brief, if a devisee can properly make distributions where merely authorized to do so, there is no reason why a devisee should be precluded from doing so where directed to do so. In neither case can the devisee be compelled to make the distributions, but in both cases a willing devisee should be permitted to carry out the testator's intention. This rule also serves to remove (or at least to reduce to technical questions) any issue of whether a particular power was or was not intended by the settlor to be mandatory.

Under the rule of Subsection (2), the primary purpose of the adapted trust will fail only to the extent the trustee (i) refuses to make selections, (ii) selects beneficiaries to receive some of the property but declines to make additional selections, (iii) fails to make selections within the specified time or the otherwise implied "reasonable period" for doing so, or (iv) dies without having exercised the power.

d(3). Selection power presumed personal. The preceding paragraph assumes, as is normally presumed, that the power of selection in any such case (like the typical power of appointment) was intended by the settlor to be personal to the designated trustee. . . .

On the other hand, if the testator in the Example above (Comment d(1)) had designated or provided a means for designating a substitute or successor trustee, the power of selection in the adapted trust would pass to the substitute or successor upon the initially designated trustee's disclaimer, resignation, incapacity, or death before the power is exercised or expires.

Similarly, if no substitute or successor was designated but the testator's intention is shown not to depend on the designated person serving as trustee . . . , then the selection power as well as the trusteeship in the adapted trust would pass to a court-appointed substitute or successor trustee. . . .

g. Enforcement of adapted trust. In no event is the devisee in the situation in Subsection (2) permitted to keep or misappropriate the property. Either the power of selection must be exercised or the trust property must be returned to the settlor's estate. See Comment d.

The heirs or other successors in interest of the settlor can maintain a proceeding to prevent or redress a breach of trust, or to compel the trustee to convey the trust property to them if the power is not exercised within the period specified in the will or, if none is specified, within a reasonable period fixed by the court. Thus, the devisee holds the property upon an enforceable trust for the legally implied reversionary beneficiaries, subject to a power in the devisee (trustee) voluntarily to select and make distribution among members of the class.

A situation may arise in which the named trustee disclaims the office or resigns, dies, or becomes incapacitated before the power in the adapted trust is exercised and, although the power is not personal to that trustee (see Comment d(3)), no substitute or successor is designated in the will. In such a case, either the testator's successors in interest or a person who fits within the class description may petition the court for appointment of another trustee. So may the testator's personal representative if the named trustee in such a case predeceases the testator, as may the personal representative, conservator, or guardian of a trustee who survives the testator but dies or becomes incapacitated before the exercise or expiration of a nonpersonal power. . . .

§47. Trusts for Noncharitable Purposes

(1) If the owner of property transfers it in trust for indefinite or general purposes, not limited to charitable purposes, the transferee holds the property as trustee with the power but not the duty to distribute or apply the property for such purposes; if and to whatever extent the power (presumptively personal) is not exercised, the trustee holds the property for distribution to reversionary beneficiaries implied by law.

(2) If the owner of property transfers it in trust for a specific noncharitable purpose and no definite or ascertainable beneficiary is designated, unless the purpose is capricious, the transferee holds the property as trustee with power, exercisable for a specified or reasonable period of time normally not to exceed 21 years, to apply the property to the designated purpose; to whatever extent the power is not exercised (although this power is *not* presumptively personal), or the property exceeds what reasonably may be needed for the purpose, the trustee holds the property, or the excess, for distribution to reversionary beneficiaries implied by law.

General Comment

a. Scope and basic principles. This Section is concerned with what are often called "purpose" or "honorary" trusts. These are a special form of noncharitable trust in which the purpose as expressed by the settlor is normally unenforceable. Thus, a testator may seek to establish a trust (1) for a noncharitable purpose that is general or indefinite (compare §46(2) dealing with indefinite beneficiaries) or (2) for a specific noncharitable purpose. In either case, for lack of a definite beneficiary, the trust is not enforceable in accordance with its intended terms.

Although reversionary interests arise in these cases by operation of law (compare §§7, 8 on "resulting trusts"), the primary question is whether the intended purpose should fail entirely or whether the devisee who wishes to do so may carry out the intended purpose. That is, does the devisee hold the property in trust for the testator's successors in interest, with a "power" (rather than a duty) to divest those successors in whole or in part by making distributions for the noncharitable purpose? Cf. §46(2) on "adapted trusts" in the private-trust context.

The rule of this Section also applies to trust provisions for either general or definite noncharitable purposes. In either case, there is no definite beneficiary to enforce the particular provision, even if the trust has identifiable express beneficiaries (§§44 and 45) to enforce it in other respects. The provision for the noncharitable purpose is unenforceable as written, leaving again the question of whether that purpose may be carried out through a power, even at the expense of express interests of ascertainable beneficiaries.

These questions are addressed, with affirmative answers, in Subsections (1) and (2) of this Section . . . . The underlying principles are similar to those applicable to the indefinite-beneficiaries situations in §46(2). . . .

The *adapted trust* rule of this Section does not apply to intended trusts for purposes that are capricious (see Comment e) or otherwise contrary to public policy. See generally §29(c).

d(2). Special duration rule: care of pets and graves. An adapted trust is allowed a period reasonably appropriate to accomplish the settlor's legally permissible purpose, although a period specified by the settlor is normally accepted if reasonably related to the purpose. Generally, however, regardless of how the reasonable period is determined, the period may not exceed 21 years, by analogy to the period of the rule against perpetuities. . . .

The 21-year period is neither sacred nor necessarily suitable to all cases of adapted trust powers. If an adapted trust for the care of a pet is worth allowing at all . . . , it makes sense to allow it to continue for the life of the pet, although not a human "life in being" for perpetuities purposes (but see below). Also, a trust power to maintain a grave should be allowed for the lifetime of the decedent's spouse and children or of other concerned individuals designated in the will . . . , all lives in being at the testator's death.

These exceptions to the 21-year limit are based on the special nature of the permissible noncharitable objective and the modest commitment of resources involved. . . .

f. Successor trustee enforcement. In the case of an adapted trust under either Subsection (1) or (2), the devisee may retain the power to direct the distribution or application of trust funds while declining or resigning from the trusteeship. A substitute or successor may be appointed by court, or by other means described in §34 Comments c and c(1).

A proceeding to prevent or redress a breach of trust, or to replace a trustee-power holder, may be brought (i) by the personal representative of the settlor or of a trustee who dies while in office, (ii) by any of the settlor's successors in interest, or (iii) by a person identifiably interested in the purpose of the power, such as the person caring for a pet or a member of the immediate family of a decedent for whom masses, grave care, or a monument is to be provided. . . .

§48. Beneficiaries Defined; Incidental Benefits

A person is a beneficiary of a trust if the settlor manifests an intention to give the person a beneficial interest; a person who merely benefits incidentally from the performance of the trust is not a beneficiary.

Part 4. Nature of Beneficiaries' Rights and Interests

Chapter 10: EXTENT AND ENFORCEABILITY OF BENEFICIAL INTERESTS

§49. Extent of Beneficiaries' Interests

Except as limited by law or public policy (see §29), the extent of the interest of a trust beneficiary depends upon the intention manifested by the settlor.

§50. Enforcement and Construction of Discretionary Interests

(1) A discretionary power conferred upon the trustee to determine the benefits of a trust beneficiary is subject to judicial control only to prevent misinterpretation or abuse of the discretion by the trustee.

(2) The benefits to which a beneficiary of a discretionary interest is entitled, and what may constitute an abuse of discretion by the trustee, depend on the terms of the discretion, including the proper construction of any accompanying standards, and on the settlor's purposes in granting the discretionary power and in creating the trust.

Comment

General Comment

a. Scope of Section. The powers of trustees and the discharge of trusteeship responsibilities regularly involve the exercise of discretion, or fiduciary judgment, with which courts do not interfere except to prevent abuse. . . .

This Section deals with situations in which trustees are granted discretion with respect to beneficiaries' rights to trust benefits. For these situations, the terminology "discretionary trust" or "discretionary interest" is used in this Restatement whether or not the terms of the trust provide standards (see Comments d, e, and f) to limit or guide the trustee's exercise of the discretionary power.

Situations of this type range from the typical power to invade principal for an income beneficiary to the discretionary trust that calls for distributions or applications of income, or of income and principal, for the support of a designated beneficiary (often a surviving spouse, elderly parent, or underage child) or for the benefit of "any one or more" of a group of beneficiaries, such as the settlor's spouse and issue. The trustee may have discretion whether or not to make payments to a particular beneficiary; or the trustee may have discretion only to determine the time, manner, and amount of distributions, pursuant to a particular standard or otherwise. A power's "discretionary" character may be implied from its being attached to a standard, such as a simple direction to pay "amounts appropriate to B's support."

The commentary that follows is concerned not only with the trustee's duties but also with the ability of beneficiaries of these discretionary interests to enforce their rights, and thus with the extent of the beneficiaries' interests. Comments b and c address the limited but important judicial authority to control a trustee's exercise of discretion, while Comments d, e, and f examine the meaning and effects of various standards and omissions frequently encountered in trust terms accompanying a grant of discretion.

A trustee's discretionary power with respect to trust benefits is to be distinguished from a power of appointment. The latter is not subject to fiduciary obligations and may be exercised arbitrarily within the scope of the power. That an appointment may not be made to persons who are not objects (i.e., not permissible appointees) of a power of appointment, see Restatement Second, Property (Donative Transfers) §20.1; "fraud on powers" is discussed in id. §§20.2-20.4; and cf. §§16.1, 16.2 (on contracts to appoint). (Tax law generally does not categorize powers in this manner, and even traditional property-law distinctions between fiduciary powers and powers of appointment may be difficult to draw; this is especially so because a true power of appointment can be conferred upon one who is also a trustee, although a power that runs with the office of trustee is strongly presumed to be a fiduciary power.). . .

Comment on Subsection (1)

b. Judicial review and control of trustee's discretion. A court will not interfere with a trustee's exercise of a discretionary power when that exercise is reasonable and not based on an improper interpretation of the terms of the trust. Thus, judicial intervention is not warranted merely because the court would have differently exercised the discretion. . . .

Furthermore, a court will intervene where the exercise of a power is left to the judgment of a trustee who improperly fails to exercise that judgment. Thus, even where a trustee has discretion whether or not to make any payments to a particular beneficiary, the court will interpose if the trustee, arbitrarily or without knowledge of or inquiry into relevant circumstances, fails to exercise the discretion. . . .

c. Effect of extended discretion. Although the discretionary character of a power of distribution does not ordinarily authorize the trustee to act beyond the bounds of reasonable judgment (Comment b), a settlor may manifest an intention to grant the trustee greater than ordinary latitude in exercising discretionary judgment. How does such an intention affect the duty of the trustee and the role of the court?

It is contrary to sound policy, and a contradiction in terms, to permit the settlor to relieve a "trustee" of all accountability. (Cf. §87, and also §76.) Once it is determined that the authority over trust distributions is held in the role of trustee (contrast nonfiduciary powers mentioned in Comment a), words such as "absolute" or "unlimited" or "sole and uncontrolled" are not interpreted literally. Even under the broadest grant of fiduciary discretion, a trustee must act honestly and in a state of mind contemplated by the settlor. Thus, the court will not permit the trustee to act in bad faith or for some purpose or motive other than to accomplish the purposes of the discretionary power. Except as the power is for the trustee's personal benefit, the court will also prevent the trustee from failing to act, either arbitrarily or from a misunderstanding of the trustee's duty or authority.

Within these limits, it is a matter of interpretation to ascertain the degree to which the settlor's use of language of extended (e.g., "absolute") discretion manifests an intention to relieve the trustee of normal judicial supervision and control in the exercise of a discretionary power over trust distributions. . . .

Comment on Subsection (2)

d. Meaning of frequently used standards. The terms of trusts usually provide some standards or guidelines concerning the purposes the settlor has in mind in creating a discretionary interest. Reasonably definite or objective standards serve to assure a beneficiary some minimum level of benefits, even when other standards are included to grant broad latitude with respect to additional benefits. On the trustee's duty to inform beneficiaries of the bases upon which discretionary distributions have been or will be made, see Comment b.

Sometimes trust terms express no standards or other clear guidance concerning the purposes of a discretionary power, or about the relative priority intended among the various beneficiaries. Even then a general standard of reasonableness, or at least of good-faith judgment, will apply to the trustee (Comment b), based on the extent of the trustee's discretion, the various beneficial interests created, the beneficiaries' circumstances and relationships to the settlor, and the general purposes of the trust.

d(1). General observations. This Comment is concerned with the construction of expressions frequently used in the terms of discretionary powers, and particularly with the types of benefits likely to be encompassed by typical standards. (The manner in which other resources available to a beneficiary relate to various standards is considered hereafter in Comment e; and Comment f discusses multiple beneficiaries or groups as concurrent discretionary distributees.) Presumed meanings yield to findings of actual contrary intention and also may be affected by context and the more general purpose(s) of the trust and the estate plan of which it is a part. See Comment g. Thus, distributions to which a discretionary beneficiary would ordinarily be entitled by a standard might properly be withheld if distribution would divert funds from other beneficiaries or purposes without achieving the purpose of the discretionary power.

d(2). Support or maintenance. The terms "support" and "maintenance" are normally construed as synonyms, even when this treats the terms as redundant. Probably the most common guides used in grants of discretion, these terms are sometimes accompanied by a reference to the beneficiary's accustomed standard of living or station in life. That level of intended support is normally implied from "support" or "maintenance" even without an express reference to the beneficiary's customary lifestyle. Whether this accustomed style is expressed or implied, a lower level of distributions may be justifiable if the trust estate is modest relative to the probable future needs of the beneficiary.

The accustomed manner of living for these purposes is ordinarily that enjoyed by the beneficiary at the time of the settlor's death or at the time an irrevocable trust is created. The distributions appropriate to that lifestyle not only increase to compensate for inflation but also may increase to meet subsequent increases in the beneficiary's needs resulting, for example, from deteriorating health or from added burdens appropriately assumed for the needs of another. See Illustration 5. Also, if a beneficiary becomes accustomed over time to a higher standard of living, that standard may become the appropriate standard of support if consistent with the trust's level of productivity and not inconsistent with an apparent priority among beneficiaries or other purpose of the settlor. Furthermore, distributions allowing the beneficiary an increased standard of living may be appropriate if, in light of the productivity of the trust estate, the eventual result would otherwise favor the remainder beneficiaries over the present beneficiary to a degree unlikely to have been intended by the settlor. "Productivity" for these purposes refers not only to trust income but also to a pattern of appreciation beyond maintenance of purchasing power, such as might result from a growth-oriented investment program. . . .

Under the usual construction of a support standard (supra) it would not be reasonable (Comment b), or even a result contemplated by the settlor (Comment c), for the trustee to provide only bare essentials for a beneficiary who had enjoyed a relatively comfortable lifestyle. (This is so even though the discretionary power is couched in terms of amounts the trustee considers "necessary" for the beneficiary's support.) The standard ordinarily entitles a beneficiary to distributions sufficient for accustomed living expenses, extending to such items as regular mortgage payments, property taxes, suitable health insurance or care, existing programs of life and property insurance, and continuation of accustomed patterns of vacation and of charitable and family giving. Reasonable additional comforts or "luxuries" that are within the means of many individuals of like station in life, such as a special vacation of a type the beneficiary had never before taken, may be borderline as entitlements but would normally be within the permissible range of the trustee's judgment, even without benefit of a grant of extended discretion (Comment c).

Without additional language suggesting a broader standard (infra), however, even with extended discretion, the terms "support" and "maintenance" do not normally encompass payments that are unrelated to support but merely contribute in other ways to a beneficiary's contentment or happiness. Thus, these terms do not authorize distributions to enlarge the beneficiary's personal estate or to enable the making of extraordinary gifts. See Illustration 3; but also compare Comment g.

A support standard normally covers not only the beneficiary's own support but also that of persons for whom provision is customarily made as a part of the beneficiary's accustomed manner of living. This generally includes the support of members of the beneficiary's household and the costs of suitable education (infra) for the beneficiary's children. The beneficiary is entitled also to receive reasonable amounts for the support of a current spouse, and of minor children who reside elsewhere but for whom the beneficiary either chooses or is required to provide support. Additional amounts to cover the beneficiary's support obligation to a former spouse would normally be within the trustee's reasonable discretion. (These matters of construction differ from but may be relevant to the question, discussed in §60, whether a beneficiary's discretionary interest may be reached in satisfaction of claims for spousal or child support.)

d(3). Other standards and supplementary language. Other terms or language may be used with or instead of a support standard to define or guide a trustee's discretionary authority with respect to trust distributions. These provisions may permit or even entitle beneficiaries to receive greater or lesser, or different, benefits than would have been authorized under a support provision standing alone. Sometimes, however, additional language adds little or nothing to what "support" might imply.

Supplementary terminology may affect the degree of generosity appropriate to a beneficiary's support, or it may suggest a special emphasis. For example, the term "education," without elaboration, is ordinarily construed as extending to payment of living expenses as well as fees and other costs of attending an institution of higher education, or the beneficiary's pursuit of a program of trade or technical training, and the like, as may be reasonably suitable to the individual and to the trust funds available for the purpose.

Similarly, without more, references to "health," "medical care," and the like in the terms of a discretionary power may be useful to inform beneficiary expectations or guide an inexperienced trustee, but presumptively they provide merely for health and medical benefits like those normally implied by a support standard. Thus, if the intention is to assure the beneficiary some special form of education, or expensive home care when not cost efficient, further elaboration would be helpful. Even a grant of extended discretion is likely to make it more difficult, if the trustee does not act generously, for a beneficiary to compel a trustee to follow a particular course of action (see Comment c).

Language of "comfort" often accompanies a support standard. Whether modifying support (e.g., "comfortable support" or "support in reasonable comfort") or as an additional standard ("support and comfort"), the normal construction is the same: the language adds nothing to the usual meaning of accustomed support (supra) for a beneficiary whose lifestyle is already at least reasonably comfortable. Such terms, however, would tend to elevate the appropriate standard for a beneficiary whose accustomed lifestyle has been more modest. "Comfort," in isolation, normally has like effect, impliedly referring to a comfortable level of support. On the other hand, stronger language, such as "generous" support, may permit and encourage the trustee to allow, and may even require, some reasonable enhancement of the beneficiary's lifestyle; but it falls short of a "happiness" standard (*infra*) in that the benefits still must normally be support-related. . . .

Although one effect of authorizing distributions for the "benefit," "best interests," or "welfare" of a beneficiary is to suggest a support standard, these terms tend also to authorize discretionary expenditures that fall beyond the usual scope of a purely support-related standard. For example, a "benefit" standard might make it reasonable for a trustee to make substantial distributions to provide a beneficiary with capital needed to start a business. (See also loans to beneficiaries, infra this Comment.) Terms of this type, however, lack the objective quality of a term such as "support." Thus, they may not facilitate a beneficiary's efforts to obtain judicial intervention to compel distributions by the trustee. On the other hand, the presence of less objective terminology in a discretionary standard may diminish the relevance of the beneficiary's other resources, except a parent's obligation to support a minor beneficiary. See Comment e.

The terms of a discretionary standard occasionally include stronger language, such as the word "happiness." Such language suggests an intention that the trustee's judgment be exercised generously and without relatively objective limitation. Although "happiness" alone expresses no objective minimum of entitlements (which to some extent may nevertheless be readily implied), the primary effect of such a term is to immunize from challenge by remainder beneficiaries almost any reasonably affordable distributions. This, however, does not mean that the trustee cannot properly resist any reasonable request by the beneficiary, because the decision remains one within the fiduciary discretion of the trustee. . . .

d(5). Post-death obligations. A question may arise, following the death of the beneficiary of a discretionary interest, whether a support or other standard authorizes or requires the trustee to pay the beneficiary's funeral and last-illness expenses and debts incurred by the beneficiary for support. Ultimately, the question is one of interpretation when the terms of the trust are unclear, with the presumption being that the trustee has discretion to pay these debts and expenses.

A duty to do so is presumed only to the extent that (i) probate estate, revocable trust, and other assets available for these purposes are insufficient or (ii) the trustee, during the beneficiary's lifetime, either agreed to make payment or unreasonably delayed in responding to a claim by the beneficiary for which the terms of the trust would have required payment while the beneficiary was alive. (A deceased beneficiary's estate may also recover distributions the trustee had a duty to make but did not make during the beneficiary's lifetime.)

d(6). Loans to beneficiaries. Sometimes a beneficiary requests funds for a purpose that falls within the reasonable discretion of the trustee but which the applicable standard would not require the trustee to furnish. If the trustee is reluctant for some reason to make the requested distribution, and particularly if the trustee's concern is one of impartiality, the trustee has discretion to make a loan or advance to the beneficiary. The loan need not qualify as a prudent investment under §90 [Restatement Third, Trusts (Prudent Investor Rule) §227]. It is a form of discretionary benefit, and may be made at a market rate of interest or at low or no interest. . . .

e. Significance of beneficiary's other resources. It is important to ascertain whether a trustee, in determining the distributions to be made to a beneficiary under an objective standard (such as a support standard), (i) is *required* to take account of the beneficiary's other resources, (ii) is *prohibited* from doing so, or (iii) is to consider the other resources but has some discretion in the matter. If the trust provisions do not address the question, the general rule of construction presumes the last of these.

Specifically, with several qualifications (below), the presumption is that the trustee is to take the beneficiary's other resources into account in determining whether and in what amounts distributions are to be made, except insofar as, in the trustee's discretionary judgment, the settlor's intended treatment of the beneficiary or the purposes of the trust will in some respect be better accomplished by not doing so.

One qualification is that, if the discretionary power is one to invade principal for (or to distribute additional income to) a beneficiary who is entitled to all or a specific part of the trust income, or to an annuity or unitrust amount, the trustee must take the mandatory distributions into account before making additional payments under the discretionary power. . . .

Another qualification is that, to the extent and for as long as the discretionary interest is intended to provide for the support, education, or health care of a beneficiary (or group of beneficiaries, Comment f) for periods during which a beneficiary probably was not expected to be self-supporting, the usual inference is that the trustee is not to deny or reduce payments for these purposes because of a beneficiary's personal resources. (But contrast the effect of another's duty to support the beneficiary, Comment e(3)).

Furthermore, in cases of nonobjective standards (e.g., "benefit" or "happiness"), other resources have less direct relevance than with regard to additional amounts necessary to maintain an accustomed lifestyle, for example. Those resources, however, may have some bearing on the overall reasonableness of an exercise of the discretionary authority.

As a rule of construction, the above presumption, with its qualifications, does not apply when the settlor expresses a different intent or if the presumption is contrary to purposes or terms of the trust as interpreted in light of circumstances and other evidence of the settlor's intention (§4). Thus, the settlor may manifest an intention that other resources are not to be taken into account (as in an absolute gift of support) or that they must be (as in a provision for payments "only if and as needed" to maintain an accustomed standard of living), with the trustee to have no discretion in the matter. (Contrast, however, the common phrase "necessary for support," which without more normally does not limit the trustee's discretion in this way.) On factors relevant to this question of interpretation, see Comment g.

A grant of extended discretion (Comment c) does not relieve the trustee of a duty to take into account, or of a duty to disregard, a beneficiary's other resources, although the extended discretion is a factor to be considered in the process of interpretation. If, under the general rule of construction, the trustee has discretion in the matter the trustee has greater latitude in exercising that discretion when the settlor has used language of extended discretion in granting the power of distribution. . . .

e(2). What other resources are to be considered? Where a trustee is to take a beneficiary's other resources into account in deciding whether and in what amounts to make discretionary payments to satisfy a standard, those resources normally include the beneficiary's income and other periodic receipts, such as pension or other annuity payments and court-ordered support payments.

A trustee may have discretion, and perhaps a duty, to take account of the principal of the beneficiary's personal estate, depending on the terms and purposes of the discretionary power and other purposes of the trust. . . .

e(4). Public benefits. If a discretionary beneficiary is or may be eligible to receive public benefits, this factor, like the availability of other resources generally, is to be taken into account by the trustee under the usual rule of construction. Thus, to the extent consistent with the terms and purposes of the trust, and allowable by applicable benefits statutes (see Reporter's Notes), the presumption is that the trustee's discretion should be exercised in a manner that will avoid either disqualifying the beneficiary for other benefits or expending trust funds for purposes for which public funds would otherwise be available. . . .

Chapter 11: VOLUNTARY AND INVOLUNTARY TRANFSERS OF BENEFICIAL INTERESTS; GENERAL PRINCIPLES

§51. Voluntary Transfers Inter Vivos

Except as provided in Chapter 12, a beneficiary of a trust can transfer his or her beneficial interest during life to the same extent as a similar legal interest.

§52. Intention to Transfer

(1) To transfer a beneficial interest in a trust, the beneficiary must manifest an intention to make a present transfer; consideration is not essential to such a transfer.

(2) A promise to transfer an interest in the future is enforceable only if the requirements for an enforceable contract are satisfied.

(3) A transfer by a beneficiary can be rescinded upon the same grounds as the transfer of a legal interest.

§53. Need for a Writing

(1) A writing is not necessary to transfer a trust beneficiary's interest.

(2) If a statute requires the assignment of an interest in a trust to be in writing and signed by the assignor, the applicable principles are as stated in §§22-24.

§54. Effect of Success ive Transfers

Where the beneficiary of a trust makes successive transfers of an interest, the first transferee is entitled to the interest unless the subsequent transferee prevails under principles of estoppel.

§55. Transfers at Death

(1) If the interest of a deceased beneficiary of a trust does not terminate or fail by reason of the beneficiary's death, the interest devolves by will or intestate succession in the same manner as a corresponding legal interest.

(2) Where a statute gives a surviving spouse an elective share of the deceased beneficiary's estate, equitable interests of the deceased beneficiary's estate are included in determining that share.

§56. Rights of Beneficiary's Creditors

Except as stated in Chapter 12, creditors of a trust beneficiary, or of a deceased beneficiary's estate, can subject the interest of the beneficiary to the satisfaction of their claims, except insofar as a corresponding legal interest is exempt from creditors' claims.

Comment

a. Scope of Section. . . . The rule of this Section applies to all beneficial interests in a trust. Thus, subject to the rules of Chapter 12 and applicable exemptions (Comment d), creditors may reach a beneficiary's right to receive the trust income or an annuity or unitrust payments. They may also attach a beneficiary's right to discretionary distributions, subject to the practical limitations described in §60. The rule of this Section applies as well to all forms of future interests in trust, except to the extent that a policy of applicable law precludes or limits creditors' access to contingent or other uncertain legal interests. . . .

Creditors may also reach a beneficiary's right to withdraw trust property or to demand distribution of a stated or formula amount . . . , including a power periodically to compel payments of stated or percentage amounts. This power to require periodic distributions (although arguably a series of general powers) is treated for this purpose as an annuity or unitrust interest. . . .

e. Procedure for reaching beneficiary's interest. Except as modified by statute, a creditor can subject the beneficiary's interest to the satisfaction of a claim under the rule of this Section after having attempted to satisfy the claim out of legal interests of the beneficiary, or when it appears that an attempt to do so would be unsuccessful or insufficiently productive.

In the appropriate proceedings, the court will give creditors relief that is fair and reasonable under the circumstances. If the beneficiary has only a right to the trust income or a right periodically to receive ascertainable or discretionary (but see §60) payments, the court will normally direct the trustee to make the payments to the creditor until the claim, with interest, is satisfied. The court, however, may order less than all of the payments to be made to the creditor, leaving some distributions for the actual needs of the beneficiary and his or her family. ("Actual needs" are not based on a "station-in-life" standard of support and require that account also be taken of the beneficiary's other available resources.) . . .

In some circumstances, the court may order a sale of the beneficiary's interest and payment of the creditor's claim from the proceeds. Sale may be appropriate when it appears unlikely that the debt can be satisfied from distribution(s) within a reasonable time, particularly when the beneficiary's interest is a future interest. Even then the uncertainty or remoteness of the interest may be such that its forced sale would produce little relative to its value to the beneficiary, and perhaps also too little to satisfy the creditor's claim. In that case, unless a loan or other arrangement can be obtained, it would be appropriate for the court to grant the creditor a lien on the beneficiary's interest, to be realized if and when it falls into possession. . . .

§57. Forfeiture for Voluntary or Involuntary Alienation

Except with respect to an interest retained by the settlor, the terms of a trust may validly provide that an interest shall terminate or become discretionary upon an attempt by the beneficiary to transfer it or by the beneficiary's creditors to reach it, or upon the bankruptcy of the beneficiary.

§58. Spendthrift Trusts: Validity and General Effect

(1) Except as stated in Subsection (2), and subject to the rules in Comment *b* (ownership equivalence) and §59, if the terms of a trust provide that a beneficial interest shall not be transferable by the beneficiary or subject to claims of the beneficiary's creditors, the restraint on voluntary and involuntary alienation of the interest is valid.

(2) A restraint on the voluntary and involuntary alienation of a beneficial interest retained by the settlor of a trust is invalid.

Comment

General Comment

a. Terminology, background, and scope of Section. The term "spendthrift trust" refers to a trust that restrains voluntary and involuntary alienation of all or any of the beneficiaries' interests. The extent of the protection such a trust offers is considered hereafter in Comment d. Spendthrift protection is not limited to beneficiaries who are legally incompetent or who, as a practical matter, lack the ability to manage their finances in a responsible manner.

A spendthrift trust is to be distinguished from a discretionary trust but may or may not also contain discretionary interests, which are considered in §60 (and §50). A spendthrift restraint may or may not also contain a forfeiture provision of the type discussed in §57. . . .

Spendthrift restraints are not permitted under English law and have been rejected by a few American cases. The vast majority of decisions in this country, however, have accepted the spendthrift trust doctrine essentially as stated above in Subsections (1) and (2) but differ in some matters discussed hereafter in this commentary, and also in matters discussed in §59.

A number of states have enacted legislation codifying the law of spendthrift trusts. A few statutes contain significant departures from the rules stated here, such as by allowing restraints on income but not principal interests or otherwise limiting the extent of the protection allowed (e.g., to the beneficiary's support). Some statutes make all trusts spendthrift trusts unless the settlor provides otherwise, or restrain involuntary but not voluntary alienation with respect to all trusts.

The rules of this Section have long been recognized under federal bankruptcy law. Current Bankruptcy Code §541(c)(2) states that a "restriction on the transfer of a beneficial interest of a debtor in a trust that is enforceable under applicable nonbankruptcy law" is to be honored in bankruptcy. . . .

Comment on Subsection (1)

b. Requirements for a valid spendthrift trust. Subsection (2) invalidates a spendthrift clause to the extent it is intended to apply to any interest of a beneficiary who is also the settlor of the trust. . . .

b(1). Absence of ownership equivalence. An intended spendthrift restraint is also invalid with respect to a nonsettlor's interests in trust property over which the beneficiary has the equivalent of ownership, entitling the beneficiary to demand immediate distribution of the property. . . .

b(2). Restraint on both voluntary and involuntary alienation. A spendthrift trust is one that restrains both voluntary and involuntary alienation.

b(3). Required manifestation of spendthrift intention. The settlor must manifest the intention to create a spendthrift trust. No particular form of wording is necessary for this purpose, as long as the requisite intention can be discerned from the terms of the trust (as defined in §4). It is sufficient if a settlor simply provides that the trust "is to be a spendthrift trust.". . .

d(1). Rights of beneficiary's purported transferees. Persons who have received a purported assignment of a beneficiary's interest in a spendthrift trust do not thereby acquire that beneficial interest. This does not mean, however, that the purported transfer has no effect. The beneficiary's act has the effect of an authorization to the trustee to distribute to the purported transferee whatever distributions the beneficiary is entitled to receive and has purported to assign, but the authorization is revocable at any time. Thus, a spendthrift restraint merely prevents the beneficiary from making an irrevocable transfer of his or her beneficial interest.

A trustee who pays funds to a purported assignee in accordance with a beneficiary's unrevoked assignment is protected, but must cease doing so upon instruction from the beneficiary. A trustee, however, is under no duty either to the beneficiary or to the purported assignee to accept this authorization to act on behalf of the beneficiary. . . .

If the beneficiary of a spendthrift interest purports to transfer it to another for value but later revokes the assignment and the trustee's authority pursuant to it, the beneficiary is liable to that other person. Although that person cannot reach the beneficiary's interest under the trust, satisfaction of the claim can be obtained from other property of the beneficiary or from trust funds after they have been distributed to the beneficiary.

d(2). Rights of beneficiary's creditors. A spendthrift trust protects the income and principal interests of its beneficiaries from the claims of their creditors as long as the income or principal in question is properly held in the trust. . . .

f. Circumstances in which beneficiary is settlor. The rule of Subsection (2) is not limited to cases in which the beneficiary actually conveyed the property to the trust or executed the trust instrument, or was designated as settlor. It is sufficient, for example, that the beneficiary pay the consideration in return for which another transferred the property to fund the trust.

If a beneficiary transfers part of the property or supplies part of the consideration to fund a trust, the beneficiary is ordinarily settlor to the extent of a fractional portion appropriate to reflect his or her proportionate share of the funding. . . .

Where a spendthrift trust is created by the will of one spouse in favor of the other, the surviving spouse does not become the settlor of the trust for purposes of the rule of this Section merely because she or he waives a right to insist on a statutory forced share of the deceased spouse's estate. (See Reporter's Notes on the different treatment of community-property spousal elections.)

f(1). Renunciations. Where the income beneficiary of a residuary trust under the will of another is also designated to receive a specific devise under that will but properly disclaims the devise, the disclaimer is not a transfer to the residuary trust even though it would normally have the effect of enlarging that trust (see §51, Comment f). Thus, the beneficiary is not the settlor of the enlarged portion of the trust, and a spendthrift provision in the trust terms is valid with respect to the beneficiary's life interest in all of the enlarged trust.

If, however, the beneficiary's renunciation is not a proper disclaimer, it would be treated as a transfer (id.); if the devised property then passes to the residuary trust the beneficiary would be treated as settlor to the extent of the property so added.

Similarly, if an income beneficiary of a trust properly disclaims a power of withdrawal or other presently exercisable general power of appointment over all or a portion of the trust estate, the beneficiary has not acquired an equivalent of ownership that invalidates a spendthrift restraint applicable to the income interest in the appointive property under the rule of Comment b; and the disclaimer is not treated as a transfer of the appointive property to the trust . . . to cause the beneficiary to be treated as settlor of the trust or portion thereof.

On the other hand, if the beneficiary had made a belated renunciation or other release (including a lapse, by allowing expiration) of the power, the beneficiary would have the equivalent of ownership until the time of the release, which—as a transfer (*id.*)—would have made the beneficiary settlor of the trust thereafter to the extent of the property previously subject to the power. Thus, any spendthrift restraint that would otherwise be applicable to the beneficiary's interest would be invalid, initially under Comment b and subsequently under this Subsection (2). . . .

§59. Spendthrift Trusts: Exceptions for Particular Types of Claims

The interest of a beneficiary in a valid spendthrift trust can be reached in satisfaction of an enforceable claim against the beneficiary for

(a) support of a child, spouse, or former spouse; or

(b) services or supplies provided for necessities or for the protection of the beneficiary's interest in the trust.

General Comment

a. Scope of the rule. The rule stated in this Section allows certain categories of creditors to reach beneficial interests in spendthrift trusts that are valid under the rule of §58, including discretionary interests in those trusts. The creditor's special advantage in being able to attach a discretionary interest is limited by the nature of the interest, as described in §60.

a(1). Governmental claims. It is implicit in the rule of this Section, as a statement of the common law, that governmental claimants, and other claimants as well, may reach the interest of a beneficiary of a spendthrift trust to the extent provided by federal law or an applicable state statute. Governmental claims and claims under governmentally assisted programs are often granted this special status. . . .

a(2). Other exceptions. The exceptions to spendthrift immunity stated in this Section are not exclusive. Special circumstances or evolving policy may justify recognition of other exceptions, allowing the beneficiary's interest to be reached by certain creditors in appropriate proceedings (on which see §56, Comment e).

In some circumstances, to permit attachment despite the spendthrift restraint may not undermine, and may even support, the protective purposes of the trust or some policy of the law. On the other hand, the advantage thus conferred on select creditors over others who cannot attach the interest but must pursue funds in the hands of the beneficiary, after distribution (see §58, Comment d), is not always appropriate as a matter of fairness and sound policy. Unlike the exceptions in Comments b through d, possible exceptions in situations of this type require case-by-case weighing of relevant considerations or evolving policies.

The nature or a pattern of tortious conduct by a beneficiary, for example, may on policy grounds justify a court's refusal to allow spendthrift immunity to protect the trust interest and the lifestyle of that beneficiary, especially one whose willful or fraudulent conduct or persistently reckless behavior causes serious harm to others. . . .

Comment on Clause (a)

b. Support claims. A beneficial interest in a spendthrift trust can be reached to satisfy an enforceable claim by the beneficiary's spouse or children for support. It can also be reached in satisfaction of a claim by a former spouse for support or alimony (on "compensatory spousal payments," see Reporter's Notes).

Although a spendthrift clause can often be construed as not intended to exclude the beneficiary's dependents, that is neither the rationale nor the limit of this exception to the general effect (§58, Comment d) of spendthrift protection. On public-policy grounds, the beneficiary should not be permitted to enjoy a beneficial interest in a trust while neglecting the support of dependents. The resulting advantage over other creditors (compare §58, Comment d) is also based on policy considerations. . . .

The right to benefits under the spendthrift interest, however, cannot be anticipated by execution sale, even in the case of a future interest. Nor can the support claimant assign to others the rights he or she acquires by attachment.

The beneficiary's interest may be attached through an appropriate proceeding in which the court has equitable discretion to determine whether all or only a portion of the trust distributions should be allocated to the support claimant, taking account of the beneficiary's actual need for some part of the distributions. Compare §56, Comment e. . . .

Comment on Clause (b)

c. Debts incurred for beneficiary's necessities. The interest of a beneficiary of a spendthrift trust can be reached to satisfy an enforceable claim by one, such as a physician or grocer, who renders necessary services or furnishes necessary supplies to the beneficiary. To the extent the person's claim is excessive in amount, however, or if the person has acted officiously, the claim cannot be enforced against the spendthrift interest.

Failure to give enforcement to appropriate claims of this type would tend to undermine the beneficiary's ability to obtain necessary goods and assistance; and a refusal to enforce such claims is not essential to a settlor's purpose of protecting the beneficiary.

d. Debts incurred to protect beneficiary's interest. The interest of a beneficiary in a spendthrift trust can be reached to satisfy an enforceable claim for services rendered or materials furnished to the beneficiary for the purpose of preserving his or her beneficial interest. . . .

§60. Transfer or Attachment of Discretionary Interests

Subject to the rules stated in §§58 and 59 (on spendthrift trusts), if the terms of a trust provide for a beneficiary to receive distributions in the trustee's discretion, a transferee or creditor of the beneficiary is entitled to receive or attach any distributions the trustee makes or is required to make in the exercise of that discretion after the trustee has knowledge of the transfer or attachment. The amounts a creditor can reach may be limited to provide for the beneficiary's needs (Comment *c*), or the amounts may be increased where the beneficiary either is the settlor (Comment *f*) or holds the discretionary power to determine his or her own distributions (Comment *g*).

Comment

a. Scope of the rule. The rule of this Section allows a beneficiary's assignee to receive discretionary distributions to which the beneficiary would otherwise be entitled, and allows creditors of the beneficiary to attach his or her discretionary interest. The rule does not apply if the beneficiary's interest is subject to a valid spendthrift restraint under the rules of §58 unless the situation falls within an exception under §59.

This Section recognizes special rules for discretionary interests retained by a settlor (compare §58(2)) and for trusts in which the beneficiary, as trustee or otherwise, holds the discretionary authority to determine his or her own distributions (compare §58, Comment c). These rules (in Comments f and g, respectively) expand the amount such a beneficiary's creditors may reach.

The rules stated in this Section and its commentary apply to whatever extent a beneficiary's interest is discretionary. Thus, if the beneficiary is entitled to all of the trust's net income but only to principal in the trustee's discretion, the Section applies to the provision for invasion of principal but not to the income interest. Also, the Section prevents the trustee not only from making payments to the beneficiary but also from making "distributions" by applying funds directly for the beneficiary's benefit contrary to the rights of the transferee or creditor. (On the latter, see especially Comment c.)

"Discretionary interests" for purposes of this Section include those encompassed by §50 (see especially §50, Comment a). Thus, this Section applies where trustees are granted discretionary authority over benefits, regardless of whether the trust terms provide simply for the beneficiary's support, provide other or additional standards, or express no standards to limit or guide the trustee's exercise of discretion. For purposes of this Section, however, unlike §50 (see §50, Comment a), discretionary interests also include powers by which beneficiaries who are not trustees may determine their own benefits pursuant to any form of standards, but which are not equivalent to ownership under §58, Comment c. . . .

b. Application to transferees. In the absence of a valid restraint on voluntary alienation, the beneficiary of a discretionary interest can properly assign that interest to another. The assignee, however, acquires only what the beneficiary had. Thus, if the interest is for the designated beneficiary's lifetime, the assignee takes a life interest pur autre vie—that is, for the life of the assigning beneficiary. (See Chapter 11, Introductory

Note.) Standards governing the trustee's exercise of discretion still refer to the assigning beneficiary and his or her circumstances. Thus, to the extent the trustee may refuse or limit payments to or for the beneficiary, the trustee may refuse or limit payments to the assignee.

Whether or not the transferee could compel the trustee to make distributions (see Comments e-e(2)), if the trustee with knowledge of the assignment does make discretionary distributions they must be made to the transferee and not to the beneficiary-assignor. . . .

c. Rights of creditors. In the absence of a valid restraint on involuntary alienation (under §58 or a statute), the creditors of the beneficiary of a discretionary interest may attach that interest and may subject it to the satisfaction of enforceable claims by appropriate process as described in §56, Comment e. The interest, however, is not subject to execution sale. Furthermore, if an expressed or implied purpose of the discretionary interest is to provide for the beneficiary's support, health care, or education, in establishing the portion of each distribution allocated to the payment of claims the court is to take account of the beneficiary's actual needs in maintaining a reasonable level of support, care, and education. (Compare the court's equitable discretion in the spendthrift-trust exception in §59, Comment b, and more generally in §56, Comment e. Also contrast the generous station-in-life standard typical of discretionary "support" provisions, §50, Comment d, and the flexibility a trustee usually has in considering a beneficiary's other resources, §50, Comment e, neither of which is appropriate here.)

If the trustee has been served with process in a proceeding by a creditor to reach the beneficiary's interest, the trustee is personally liable to the creditor for any amount paid to or applied for the benefit of the beneficiary in disregard of the rights of the creditor, in the absence of a valid spendthrift provision (§58) applicable to the creditor (see §59). . . .

e. Can discretionary distributions be compelled by beneficiary's transferee or creditors? A transferee or creditor of a trust beneficiary cannot compel the trustee to make discretionary distributions if the beneficiary personally could not do so. It is rare, however, that the beneficiary's circumstances, the terms of the discretionary power, and the purposes of the trust leave the beneficiary so powerless. The exercise or non-exercise of fiduciary discretion is always subject to judicial review to prevent abuse. What might constitute an abuse, however, is not only affected by the extent of the trustee's discretion, standards applicable to its exercise, and purposes of the trust, but also by the beneficiary's circumstances and the effect discretionary decisions will have on the discretionary beneficiary and on others in relation to the fulfillment of trust purposes. See generally §50 and its commentary, especially Comment d(1). . . .

f. Where discretionary beneficiary is settlor. Where the trustee of an irrevocable trust has discretionary authority to pay to the settlor or apply for the settlor's benefit as much of the income or principal as the trustee may determine appropriate, creditors of the settlor can reach the maximum amount the trustee, in the proper exercise of fiduciary discretion, could pay to or apply for the benefit of the settlor. Where the beneficiary is the settlor of only a portion of the trust, the amount the creditor can reach under this rule is limited to that portion of the trust estate. . . .

g. Where beneficiary holds discretionary power. Sometimes a beneficiary is trustee of the discretionary trust, with authority to determine his or her own benefits. In such a case, a rule similar to that of Comment f applies, with creditors able to reach from time to time the maximum amount the trustee-beneficiary can properly take. As in other nonsettlor-beneficiary situations, the court may reserve a portion of that amount for the beneficiary's actual needs for reasonable support, health care, and education (Comment c). . . .

The rule does not apply, however, if the discretionary power is held jointly with another person who, in exercising the discretionary authority, has fiduciary duties to other beneficiaries of the trust. . . .

Part 5. Modification and Termination of Trusts

Chapter 13: MODIFICATION AND TERMINATION OF TRUSTS

Introductory Note [to Chapter 13] . . .

Liberalized rules and their rationale. At various points throughout this Chapter, traditional rules concerning revocation, termination, and modification are relaxed somewhat, or in some instances clarified, to facilitate the making of changes in the terms of trusts. This reflects both (i) modern trends in legislative policy and judicial decisions and (ii) practical considerations arising from other developments in or affecting estate planning. . . .

As life in the estate-planning world becomes increasingly complex, mainly with changing tax rules and concerns, which tend also to invite the use of longer-term trusts, the parties to trusts and the courts increasingly, and understandably, encounter instances of apparent oversight and human error. . . .

[P]roblems of error and oversight appear to have increased as broader segments of the population have come to recognize the utility of trusts for an expanding variety of purposes, with many settlors relying on advice and implementation not only by less expert or independent members of the legal profession but also by nonlawyers. . . .

Still another set of reasons underlying the selective liberalization of the rules considered in this Chapter is possibly more fundamental: the growing recognition that trusts should serve the beneficiaries' best interests (§27(2); and also the growing recognition that, realistically, this greater flexibility is more likely to aid than to undermine settlor objectives. . . .

§61. Completion of Period or Purpose for Which Trust Created

A trust will terminate in whole or in part upon the expiration of a period or the happening of an event as provided by the terms of the trust; in the absence of such a provision in the terms of the trust, termination will occur in whole or in part when the purpose(s) of the trust or severable portion thereof are accomplished.

§62. Rescission and Reformation

A trust may be rescinded or reformed upon the same grounds as those upon which a transfer of property not in trust may be rescinded or reformed.

Comment

. . . *b. Clarification and correction of terms of trust.* On resolving uncertainties of meaning where the terms of a donative document are ambiguous, see Restatement Third, Property (Wills and Other Donative Transfers) §§11.1-11.3.

Even if the will or other instrument creating a donative testamentary or inter vivos trust is unambiguous, the terms of the trust may be reformed by the court to conform the text to the intention of the settlor if the following are established by clear and convincing evidence: (1) that a mistake of fact or law, whether in expression or inducement, affected the specific terms of the document; and (2) what the settlor's intention was. Restatement Third, Property (Wills and Other Donative Transfers) §12.1 (noting that direct evidence of intention contradicting the plain meaning of the text, as well as other evidence of intention, may be considered).

§63. Power of Settlor to Revoke or Modify

(1) The settlor of an inter vivos trust has power to revoke or modify the trust to the extent the terms of the trust (§4) so provide.

(2) If the settlor has failed expressly to provide whether the trust is subject to a retained power of revocation or amendment, the question is one of interpretation. (See presumptions in Comment *c.*)

(3) Absent contrary provision in the terms of the trust, the settlor's power to revoke or modify the trust can be exercised in any way that provides clear and convincing evidence of the settlor's intention to do so.

Comment

Comment on Subsections (1) and (2)

b. The "terms of the trust." The phrase "terms of the trust" means the settlor's intention concerning the trust provisions, manifested in a manner that admits of its proof in judicial proceedings. See §4.

If the terms of the trust are otherwise expressed in writing but fail to provide whether or to what extent the settlor reserves the power to revoke or modify the trust, the writing is incomplete and its meaning uncertain. Accordingly, the writing does not prevent the admission of extrinsic evidence to prove the settlor's intention to either retain or relinquish power to revoke or amend the trust, or the admission of evidence to prove an intent to limit any such power. . . .

c. Presumptions regarding revocability. Where the settlor has failed expressly to provide whether a trust is subject to revocation or amendment, if the settlor has retained no interest in the trust (other than by resulting trust, §8), it is rebuttably presumed that the settlor has no power to revoke or amend the trust. If, however, the settlor has failed expressly to provide whether the trust is revocable or amendable but has retained an interest in the trust (other than by resulting trust), the presumption is that the trust is revocable and amendable by the settlor. . . .

Comment on Subsection (3)

. . .

i. Where method of revocation or amendment specified. If the terms of the trust reserve to the settlor a power to revoke or amend the trust exclusively by a particular procedure, the settlor can exercise the power only by substantial compliance with the method prescribed. . . .

k. Trust with multiple settlors. If a revocable trust has more than one settlor, unless the terms of the trust provide otherwise, each settlor ordinarily (but see exceptions below) may revoke or amend the trust with regard to that portion of the trust property attributable to the settlor's contribution. . . .

l. Settlor under legal incapacity. Where a settlor who has retained the power to revoke or amend a trust becomes legally incompetent, the power may be exercised by an agent under a durable power of attorney if and to the extent expressly authorized by the terms of the durable power or by the terms of the trust. The agent in such a case acts in a fiduciary capacity and, except as the settlor-principal specifies otherwise, for purposes similar to the substituted-judgment concept in conservatorship law.

Similarly, unless the trust terms provide otherwise, the settlor's power to revoke or amend a revocable trust may be exercised by a conservator, guardian, or other legal representative if and to the extent authorized by the appropriate court. . . .

§64. Termination or Modification by Trustee, Beneficiary, or Third Party

(1) Except as provided in §§65 and 68, the trustee or beneficiaries of a trust have only such power to terminate the trust or to change its terms as is granted by the terms of the trust.

(2) The terms of a trust may grant a third party a power with respect to termination or modification of the trust; such a third-party power is presumed to be held in a fiduciary capacity.

§65. Termination or Modification by Consent of Beneficiaries

(1) Except as stated in Subsection (2), if all of the beneficiaries of an irrevocable trust consent, they can compel the termination or modification of the trust.

(2) If termination or modification of the trust under Subsection (1) would be inconsistent with a material purpose of the trust, the beneficiaries cannot compel its termination or modification except with the consent of the settlor or, after the settlor's death, with authorization of the court if it determines that the reason(s) for termination or modification outweigh the material purpose.

Comment

a. Scope, background, and general principles. With the rule of this Section contrast the rule of §66, which depends upon a finding of unanticipated circumstances but does not require beneficiary consent. . . .

Although Subsection (2) is not a part of the English law, that subsection recognizes the prevalent American view under the so-called Claflin doctrine (Claflin v. Claflin, 149 Mass. 19, 20 N.E. 454 (1889)).

While the rule against perpetuities requires only the timely vesting of interests and does not directly limit the duration of trusts, the rule of Subsection (2) ceases to apply after the perpetuities period has expired, and the Claflin doctrine no longer restricts the beneficiaries' power to terminate or modify the trust under Subsection (1). . . .

Comment on Subsection (1)

b. Requirement that all beneficiaries consent. The rule of Subsection (1) requires that consent be obtained from or on behalf of all potential beneficiaries, including those who lack capacity. This requirement of unanimous consent also includes, for example, beneficiaries who are relatively unlikely ever to receive distributions, those whose interests arise by operation of law (i.e., reversionary, or "resulting trust," interests), and persons who hold powers of appointment under the trust, as well as those who would take in default of the exercise of any but a presently exercisable general power (on which see §74). See generally §48, Comment a, defining trust beneficiary. Also included among those whose consent is required are successors in interest of prior beneficiaries, and the potential unborn (including after-adopted) or unascertainable beneficiaries so often provided for by class description, as in a seemingly simple trust designed to pay income to A for life and then to distribute the principal to A's descendants who are living at her death. . . .

[In some cases], the requirements of Subsection (1) are likely to be difficult to satisfy. The consent of potential beneficiaries who cannot consent for themselves, however, may be provided by guardians ad litem, by court appointed or other legally authorized representatives, or through representation by other beneficiaries under the doctrine of virtual representation. . . .

As a practical matter, however, the necessary consents may not be obtainable in many situations. This is not only because some beneficiaries may dissent from a termination or modification plan but also because of fiduciary inhibitions on the part of those called upon to represent the interests of others. The technical and practical problems of representing others are particularly challenging whenever more is involved than mutually beneficial modification of administrative provisions. . . .

Comment on Subsection (2)

d. The material-purpose restriction. Under the rule of Subsection (2), even all of the beneficiaries acting together ordinarily cannot compel termination of a trust if its continuance is necessary to carry out a material purpose of the trust. Similarly, the beneficiaries ordinarily cannot compel modification of the trust if the modification is inconsistent with a material purpose of the trust.

Because the rights of the beneficiaries are thus limited out of respect for serious objectives that appear to have motivated the settlor in creating the trust, however, the material-purpose restriction does not apply if the settlor is alive, legally competent, and content to waive it. Also, the restriction becomes unimportant and does not apply if the material purpose is no longer relevant or cannot be accomplished in any event. Furthermore, following the death or incapacity of the settlor, an appropriate court may authorize the termination of a trust under this Section if it determines that the reason(s) offered in support of the beneficiaries' petition for termination outweigh, at the time, the concerns or objectives reflected in the material purpose.

The line is not always easy to draw between a "material purpose" on the one hand and, on the other, specific intentions that are deemed less important so that the Claflin doctrine does not protect them. Occasionally, a settlor expressly states in the will, trust agreement, or declaration of trust that a specific purpose is the primary purpose or a material purpose of the trust. Otherwise, the identification and weighing of purposes under this Section frequently involve a relatively subjective process of interpretation and application of judgment to a particular situation, much as purposes or underlying objectives of settlors in other respects are often left to be inferred from specific terms of a trust, the nature of the various interests created, and the circumstances surrounding the creation of the trust. The question is narrower and more focused, although not necessarily easier, when applied to a specific modification rather than to the termination of the trust. . . .

Material purposes are not readily inferred. A finding of such a purpose generally requires some showing of a particular concern or objective on the part of the settlor, such as concern with regard to a beneficiary's management skills, judgment, or level of maturity. Thus, a court may look for some circumstantial or other evidence indicating that the trust arrangement represented to the settlor more than a method of allocating the benefits of property among multiple intended beneficiaries, or a means of offering to the beneficiaries (but not imposing on them) a particular advantage. Sometimes, of course, the very nature or design of a trust suggests its protective nature or some other material purpose. . . .

. . . A trust plan to provide successive enjoyment is not itself sufficient to indicate, for example, that the settlor had a material purpose of depriving the beneficiaries of the property management or otherwise of protecting them from the risks of their own judgment. In the absence of additional circumstances indicating a further purpose, the inference is that the trust was intended merely to allow one or more persons to enjoy the benefits of the property during the period of the trust and to allow the other beneficiary or beneficiaries to receive the property thereafter. . . .

e. Discretionary and spendthrift trusts. If the interests of one or more of the beneficiaries of a trust are subject to restraints on alienation (see §§58, 59), or if the terms of the trust provide support or other discretionary benefits for some or all of the beneficiaries (see §50), this may supply some indication that the settlor had a material purpose—a protective purpose—that would be inconsistent with allowing the beneficiaries to terminate the trust. Nevertheless, spendthrift restrictions are not sufficient in and of themselves to establish, or to create a presumption of, a material purpose that would prevent termination by consent of all of the beneficiaries. This is also true, in many contexts, of discretionary provisions. . . .

§66. Power of Court to Modify: Unanticipated Circumstances

(1) The court may modify an administrative or distributive provision of a trust, or direct or permit the trustee to deviate from an administrative or distributive provision, if because of circumstances not anticipated by the settlor the modification or deviation will further the purposes of the trust.

(2) If a trustee knows or should know of circumstances that justify judicial action under Subsection (1) with respect to an administrative provision, and of the potential of those circumstances to cause substantial harm to the trust or its beneficiaries, the trustee has a duty to petition the court for appropriate modification of or deviation from the terms of the trust.

Comment

Comment on Subsection (1)

a. Scope and purpose of Section. With the rule of this Section, contrast the rule of §65, which requires the consent of all beneficiaries but does not depend on a finding of unanticipated circumstances.

This Section — the so-called "equitable deviation" doctrine — applies to both charitable and private trusts. Although the unanticipated circumstances in cases falling under this Section are likely to be circumstances that have changed since the creation of the trust, the rule of the Section does not require changed circumstances. It is sufficient that the settlor was unaware of the circumstances in establishing the terms of the trust.

It is not necessary under this Section that the situation be so serious as to constitute an "emergency" or to jeopardize the accomplishment of the trust purposes.

The objective of the rule allowing judicial modification (or deviation) and the intended consequences of its application are not to disregard the intention of a settlor. The objective is to give effect to what the settlor's intent probably would have been had the circumstances in question been anticipated.

b. Operation of Section. The terms of the trust that the court may modify, or from which the court may authorize deviation by the trustee, may be provisions governing the management or administration of the trust estate or they may be provisions defining the beneficial interests or entitlements of the various trust beneficiaries. . . .

§67. Failure of Designated Charitable Purpose: The Doctrine of Cy Pres

Unless the terms of the trust provide otherwise, where property is placed in trust to be applied to a designated charitable purpose and it is or becomes unlawful, impossible, or impracticable to carry out that purpose, or to the extent it is or becomes wasteful to apply all of the property to the designated purpose, the charitable trust will not fail but the court will direct application of the property or appropriate portion thereof to a charitable purpose that reasonably approximates the designated purpose.

Comment

a. The cy pres doctrine: background and scope of the rule. The rule stated in this Section is called the doctrine of cy pres. The expression indicates the principle that, when the exact intention of the settlor is not to be carried out, the intention will be given effect "as nearly" as may be. . . .

The cy pres doctrine's modern rationale rests primarily in the perpetual duration allowed charitable trusts and in the resulting risk that designated charitable purposes may become obsolete as the needs and circumstances of society evolve over time, not to mention the sometimes unanticipated extent of decrease or increase in the funds available from a given trust. . . .

b. Contrary intention of settlor. Just as it is against the policy of the trust law to permit wasteful or seriously inefficient use of resources dedicated to charity, trust law also favors an interpretation that would sustain a charitable trust and avoid the return of the trust property to the settlor or successors in interest. . . . Accordingly, when the particular purpose of a charitable trust fails, in whole or in part, the rule of this Section makes the cy pres power applicable (thus presuming the existence of what is often called a general charitable purpose) unless the terms of the trust (defined in §4) express a contrary intention. . . .

A trust provision expressing the settlor's own choice of an alternative charitable purpose will be carried out, without need to apply the cy pres doctrine. . . .

The mere fact that the terms of the trust provide that property shall be devoted "forever" to a particular charitable purpose, or that it shall be devoted "only" to that purpose, or that the property is given "upon condition" that it be applied to that purpose, does not necessarily indicate the absence of a more general charitable commitment on the part of the settlor. Such language may merely emphasize the intention of the settlor that the property should not be applied to other charitable purposes as long as it is practicable to apply it to the specific purpose. Thus, such language alone does not sufficiently express an intention that cy pres should not apply and that the trust is to terminate if it should become illegal, impossible, or impracticable to carry out the particular purpose.

Even though the terms of a trust contain an express provision precluding the application of cy pres to alter the trust purpose, this does not prevent application of the so-called equitable-deviation doctrine of §66 to modify the means by which the purpose is to be accomplished.

c. Causes for failure of designated purpose. Under what circumstances will the particular purpose intended by the settlor not be carried out or continued, so that the court will either modify the trust cy pres or give effect to a trust provision calling for termination? It is not sufficient merely that it can be demonstrated that the trust funds could be better spent on some other purpose. Certainly, however, the particular purpose will fail if it is or becomes illegal or impossible to carry it out, or if the purpose is no longer charitable (as defined in §28, see especially Comment a). The doctrine of cy pres may also be applied, even though it is possible to carry out the particular purpose of the settlor, if to do so would not accomplish the settlor's charitable objective, or would not do so in a reasonable way. In such a case, it is "impracticable" to carry out the particular purpose in the sense in which that word is used in this Section. . . .

c(1). Surplus funds. Another type of case appropriate to the application of cy pres, when not precluded by the terms of the trust, is a situation in which the amount of property held in the trust exceeds what is needed for the particular charitable purpose to such an extent that the continued expenditure of all of the funds for that purpose, although possible to do, would be wasteful. . . .

d. New purpose; manner of cy pres application. In applying the cy pres doctrine, it is sometimes stated that the property must be applied to a purpose as near as possible to that designated by the terms of the intended trust. Increasingly, however, courts have recognized (as does the rule of this Section) that the substitute or supplementary purpose need not be the nearest possible but one reasonably similar or close to the settlor's designated purpose, or "falling within the general charitable purpose" of the settlor. This is especially so when the particular purpose becomes impossible or impracticable of accomplishment long after the creation of the trust or when, among purposes reasonably close to the original, one has a distinctly greater usefulness than the others that have been identified. This more liberal application of cy pres is appropriate both because settlors' probable preferences are almost inevitably a matter of speculation in any event and because it is reasonable to suppose that among relatively similar purposes charitably inclined settlors would tend to prefer those most beneficial to their communities.

In framing a scheme for the application of property cy pres, the court will consider evidence suggesting what the wishes of the settlor probably would have been if the circumstances had been anticipated. Such an assessment may look to whatever evidence is available concerning the attitudes and interests that appear to have motivated the settlor's selection of the particular purpose. Thus, it would be especially appropriate to consult the donor if available. In other situations, the circumstances of the trust's creation may be revealing, as may the settlor's relationships, social or religious affiliations, personal background, charitable-giving history, and the like. For example, a settlor's adviser may be able to reveal that a devise to a particular institution for a specific project or purpose began with a desire to benefit that institution and was then shaped to address some institutional interest, need, or opportunity; or the opposite might be revealed, with the settlor having a strong desire to encourage a particular field of study or research, or a particular charitable activity, and then settling upon an institution that appeared suitable. In the former case, if the precise plan does not work out or the funds prove to be excessive for the purpose, a court would probably decide to look for a different but related subject or activity at the chosen institution. In the latter case, the court would probably decide that the special interest of the settlor should be pursued at a nearby or comparable institution.

The cy pres power is vested in the court, not in the trustee or the Attorney General, who is, however, a necessary party entitled to notice of the proceeding. . . .

§68. Dividing and Combining Trusts

The trustee may divide a trust into two or more trusts or combine two or more trusts into a single trust, if doing so does not adversely affect the rights of any beneficiary or the accomplishment of the trust purposes.

§69. Merger

If the legal title to the trust property and the entire beneficial interest become united in one person, the trust terminates.

PART IV

~

UNIFORM PRINCIPAL AND INCOME ACT (1997, REV. 2000)

UNIFORM PRINCIPAL AND INCOME ACT (1997, REV. 2000)

TABLE OF CONTENTS

UNIFORM PRINCIPAL AND INCOME ACT

Prefatory Note

This revision of the 1931 Uniform Principal and Income Act and the 1962 Revised Uniform Principal and Income Act has two purposes.

One purpose is to revise the 1931 and the 1962 Acts. Revision is needed to support the now widespread use of the revocable living trust as a will substitute, to change the rules in those Acts that experience has shown need to be changed, and to establish new rules to cover situations not provided for in the old Acts, including rules that apply to financial instruments invented since 1962.

The other purpose is to provide a means for implementing the transition to an investment regime based on principles embodied in the Uniform Prudent Investor Act, especially the principle of investing for total return rather than a certain level of "income" as traditionally perceived in terms of interest, dividends, and rents.

Revision of the 1931 and 1962 Acts

The prior Acts and this revision of those Acts deal with four questions affecting the rights of beneficiaries:

(1) How is income earned during the probate of an estate to be distributed to trusts and to persons who receive outright bequests of specific property, pecuniary gifts, and the residue?

(2) When an income interest in a trust begins (i.e., when a person who creates the trust dies or when she transfers property to a trust during life), what property is principal that will eventually go to the remainder beneficiaries and what is income?

(3) When an income interest ends, who gets the income that has been received but not distributed, or that is due but not yet collected, or that has accrued but is not yet due?

(4) After an income interest begins and before it ends, how should its receipts and disbursements be allocated to or between principal and income?

Changes in the traditional sections are of three types: new rules that deal with situations not covered by the prior Acts, clarification of provisions in the 1962 Act, and changes to rules in the prior Acts.

New rules. Issues addressed by some of the more significant new rules include:

(1) The application of the probate administration rules to revocable living trusts after the settlor's death and to other terminating trusts. Articles 2 and 3.

(2) The payment of interest or some other amount on the delayed payment of an outright pecuniary gift that is made pursuant to a trust agreement instead of a will when the agreement or state law does not provide for such a payment. Section 201(3).

(3) The allocation of net income from partnership interests acquired by the trustee other than from a decedent (the old Acts deal only with partnership interests acquired from a decedent). Section 401.

(4) An "unincorporated entity" concept has been introduced to deal with businesses operated by a trustee, including farming and livestock operations, and investment activities in rental real estate, natural resources, timber, and derivatives. Section 403.

(5) The allocation of receipts from discount obligations such as zero-coupon bonds. Section 406(b).

(6) The allocation of net income from harvesting and selling timber between principal and income. Section 412.

(7) The allocation between principal and income of receipts from derivatives, options, and asset-backed securities. Sections 414 and 415.

(8) Disbursements made because of environmental laws. Section 502(a)(7).

(9) Income tax obligations resulting from the ownership of S corporation stock and interests in partnerships. Section 505.

(10) The power to make adjustments between principal and income to correct inequities caused by tax elections or peculiarities in the way the fiduciary income tax rules apply. Section 506.

Clarifications and changes in existing rules. A number of matters provided for in the prior Acts have been changed or clarified in this revision, including the following:

(1) An income beneficiary's estate will be entitled to receive only net income actually received by a trust before the beneficiary's death and not items of accrued income. Section 303.

(2) Income from a partnership is based on actual distributions from the partnership, in the same manner as corporate distributions. Section 401.

(3) Distributions from corporations and partnerships that exceed 20 percent of the entity's gross assets will be principal whether or not intended by the entity to be a partial liquidation. Section 401(d)(2).

(4) Deferred compensation is dealt with in greater detail in a separate section. Section 409.

(5) The 1962 Act rule for "property subject to depletion," (patents, copyrights, royalties, and the like), which provides that a trustee may allocate up to 5 percent of the asset's inventory value to income and the balance to principal, has been replaced by a rule that allocates 90 percent of the amounts received to principal and the balance to income. Section 410.

(6) The percentage used to allocate amounts received from oil and gas has been changed—90 percent of those receipts are allocated to principal and the balance to income. Section 411.

(7) The unproductive property rule has been eliminated for trusts other than marital deduction trusts. Section 413.

(8) Charging depreciation against income is no longer mandatory, and is left to the discretion of the trustee. Section 503.

Coordination with the Uniform Prudent Investor Act

The law of trust investment has been modernized. See Uniform Prudent Investor Act (1994); Restatement (Third) of Trusts: Prudent Investor Rule (1992) (hereinafter Restatement of Trusts 3d: Prudent Investor Rule). Now it is time to update the principal and income allocation rules so the two bodies of doctrine can work well together. This revision deals conservatively with the tension between modern investment theory and traditional income allocation. The starting point is to use the traditional system. If prudent investing of all the assets in a trust viewed as a portfolio and traditional allocation effectuate the intent of the settlor, then nothing need be done. The Act, however, helps the trustee who has made a prudent, modern portfolio-based investment decision that has the initial effect of skewing return from all the assets under management, viewed as a portfolio, as between income and principal beneficiaries. The Act gives that trustee a power to reallocate the portfolio return suitably. To leave a trustee constrained by the traditional system would inhibit the trustee's ability to fully implement modern portfolio theory. . . .

UNIFORM PRINCIPAL AND INCOME ACT [ARTICLE] 1 DEFINITIONS AND FIDUCIARY DUTIES

§101. Short Title

This [Act] May Be Cited as the Uniform Principal and Income Act.

§102. Definitions

In this [Act]:

(1) "Accounting period" means a calendar year unless another 12_month period is selected by a fiduciary. The term includes a portion of a calendar year or other 12_month period that begins when an income interest begins or ends when an income interest ends.

(2) "Beneficiary" includes, in the case of a decedent's estate, an heir [, legatee,] and devisee and, in the case of a trust, an income beneficiary and a remainder beneficiary.

(3) "Fiduciary" means a personal representative or a trustee. The term includes an executor, administrator, successor personal representative, special administrator, and a person performing substantially the same function.

(4) "Income" means money or property that a fiduciary receives as current return from a principal asset. The term includes a portion of receipts from a sale, exchange, or liquidation of a principal asset, to the extent provided in [Article] 4.

(5) "Income beneficiary" means a person to whom net income of a trust is or may be payable.

(6) "Income interest" means the right of an income beneficiary to receive all or part of net income, whether the terms of the trust require it to be distributed or authorize it to be distributed in the trustee's discretion.

(7) "Mandatory income interest" means the right of an income beneficiary to receive net income that the terms of the trust require the fiduciary to distribute.

(8) "Net income" means the total receipts allocated to income during an accounting period minus the disbursements made from income during the period, plus or minus transfers under this [Act] to or from income during the period.

(9) "Person" means an individual, corporation, business trust, estate, trust, partnership, limited liability company, association, joint venture, government; governmental subdivision, agency, or instrumentality; public corporation, or any other legal or commercial entity.

(10) "Principal" means property held in trust for distribution to a remainder beneficiary when the trust terminates.

(11) "Remainder beneficiary" means a person entitled to receive principal when an income interest ends.

(12) "Terms of a trust" means the manifestation of the intent of a settlor or decedent with respect to the trust, expressed in a manner that admits of its proof in a judicial proceeding, whether by written or spoken words or by conduct.

(13) "Trustee" includes an original, additional, or successor trustee, whether or not appointed or confirmed by a court.

Comment

"Income beneficiary." The definitions of income beneficiary (Section 102(5)) and income interest (Section 102(6)) cover both mandatory and discretionary beneficiaries and interests. . . .

"Net income." The reference to "transfers under this Act to or from income" means transfers made under Sections 104(a), 412(b), 502(b), 503(b), 504(a), and 506. . . .

§103. Fiduciary Duties; General Principles

(a) In allocating receipts and disbursements to or between principal and income, and with respect to any matter within the scope of [Articles] 2 and 3, a fiduciary:

(1) shall administer a trust or estate in accordance with the terms of the trust or the will, even if there is a different provision in this [Act];

(2) may administer a trust or estate by the exercise of a discretionary power of administration given to the fiduciary by the terms of the trust or the will, even if the exercise of the power produces a result different from a result required or permitted by this [Act];

(3) shall administer a trust or estate in accordance with this [Act] if the terms of the trust or the will do not contain a different provision or do not give the fiduciary a discretionary power of administration; and

(4) shall add a receipt or charge a disbursement to principal to the extent that the terms of the trust and this [Act] do not provide a rule for allocating the receipt or disbursement to or between principal and income.

(b) In exercising the power to adjust under Section 104(a) or a discretionary power of administration regarding a matter within the scope of this [Act], whether granted by the terms of a trust, a will, or this [Act], a fiduciary shall administer a trust or estate impartially, based on what is fair and reasonable to all of the beneficiaries, except to the extent that the terms of the trust or the will clearly manifest an intention that the fiduciary shall or may favor one or more of the beneficiaries. A determination in accordance with this [Act] is presumed to be fair and reasonable to all of the beneficiaries.

Comment

. . . **Fiduciary discretion.** The general rule is that if a discretionary power is conferred upon a trustee, the exercise of that power is not subject to control by a court except to prevent an abuse of discretion. Restatement (Second) of Trusts §187. The situations in which a court will control the exercise of a trustee's discretion are discussed in the comments to §187. See also id. §233 Comment *p*.

. . . **Duty of impartiality.** Whenever there are two or more beneficiaries, a trustee is under a duty to deal impartially with them. Restatement of Trusts 3d: Prudent Investor Rule §183 (1992). This rule applies whether the beneficiaries' interests in the trust are concurrent or successive. If the terms of the trust give the trustee discretion to favor one beneficiary over another, a court will not control the exercise of such discretion except to prevent the trustee from abusing it. Id. §183, Comment *a*. "The precise meaning of the trustee's duty of impartiality and the balancing of competing interests and objectives inevitably are matters of judgment and interpretation. Thus, the duty and balancing are affected by the purposes, terms, distribution requirements, and other circumstances of the trust, not only at the outset but as they may change from time to time." Id. §232, Comment *c*.

The terms of a trust may provide that the trustee, or an accountant engaged by the trustee, or a committee of persons who may be family members or business associates, shall have the power to determine what is income and what is principal. If the terms of a trust provide that this Act specifically or principal and income legislation in general does not apply to the trust but fail to provide a rule to deal with a matter provided for in this Act, the trustee has an implied grant of discretion to decide the question. Section 103(b) provides that the rule of impartiality applies in the exercise of such a discretionary power to the extent that the terms of the trust do not provide that one or more of the beneficiaries are to be favored. The fact that a person is named an income beneficiary or a remainder beneficiary is not by itself an indication of partiality for that beneficiary.

§104. Trustee's Power to Adjust

(a) A trustee may adjust between principal and income to the extent the trustee considers necessary if the trustee invests and manages trust assets as a prudent investor, the terms of the trust describe the amount that may or must be distributed to a beneficiary by referring to the trust's income, and the trustee determines, after applying the rules in Section 103(a), that the trustee is unable to comply with Section 103(b).

(b) In deciding whether and to what extent to exercise the power conferred by subsection (a), a trustee shall consider all factors relevant to the trust and its beneficiaries, including the following factors to the extent they are relevant:

(1) the nature, purpose, and expected duration of the trust;

(2) the intent of the settlor;

(3) the identity and circumstances of the beneficiaries;

(4) the needs for liquidity, regularity of income, and preservation and appreciation of capital;

(5) the assets held in the trust; the extent to which they consist of financial assets, interests in closely held enterprises, tangible and intangible personal property, or real property; the extent to which an asset is used by a beneficiary; and whether an asset was purchased by the trustee or received from the settlor;

(6) the net amount allocated to income under the other sections of this [Act] and the increase or decrease in the value of the principal assets, which the trustee may estimate as to assets for which market values are not readily available;

(7) whether and to what extent the terms of the trust give the trustee the power to invade principal or accumulate income or prohibit the trustee from invading principal or accumulating income, and the extent to which the trustee has exercised a power from time to time to invade principal or accumulate income;

(8) the actual and anticipated effect of economic conditions on principal and income and effects of inflation and deflation; and

(9) the anticipated tax consequences of an adjustment.

(c) A trustee may not make an adjustment:

(1) that diminishes the income interest in a trust that requires all of the income to be paid at least annually to a spouse and for which an estate tax or gift tax marital deduction would be allowed, in whole or in part, if the trustee did not have the power to make the adjustment;

(2) that reduces the actuarial value of the income interest in a trust to which a person transfers property with the intent to qualify for a gift tax exclusion;

(3) that changes the amount payable to a beneficiary as a fixed annuity or a fixed fraction of the value of the trust assets;

(4) from any amount that is permanently set aside for charitable purposes under a will or the terms of a trust unless both income and principal are so set aside;

(5) if possessing or exercising the power to make an adjustment causes an individual to be treated as the owner of all or part of the trust for income tax purposes, and the

individual would not be treated as the owner if the trustee did not possess the power to make an adjustment;

(6) if possessing or exercising the power to make an adjustment causes all or part of the trust assets to be included for estate tax purposes in the estate of an individual who has the power to remove a trustee or appoint a trustee, or both, and the assets would not be included in the estate of the individual if the trustee did not possess the power to make an adjustment;

(7) if the trustee is a beneficiary of the trust; or

(8) if the trustee is not a beneficiary, but the adjustment would benefit the trustee directly or indirectly.

(d) If subsection (c)(5), (6), (7), or (8) applies to a trustee and there is more than one trustee, a cotrustee to whom the provision does not apply may make the adjustment unless the exercise of the power by the remaining trustee or trustees is not permitted by the terms of the trust.

(e) A trustee may release the entire power conferred by subsection (a) or may release only the power to adjust from income to principal or the power to adjust from principal to income if the trustee is uncertain about whether possessing or exercising the power will cause a result described in subsection (c)(1) through (6) or (c)(8) or if the trustee determines that possessing or exercising the power will or may deprive the trust of a tax benefit or impose a tax burden not described in subsection (c). The release may be permanent or for a specified period, including a period measured by the life of an individual.

(f) Terms of a trust that limit the power of a trustee to make an adjustment between principal and income do not affect the application of this section unless it is clear from the terms of the trust that the terms are intended to deny the trustee the power of adjustment conferred by subsection (a).

Comment

Purpose and Scope of Provision. The purpose of Section 104 is to enable a trustee to select investments using the standards of a prudent investor without having to realize a particular portion of the portfolio's total return in the form of traditional trust accounting income such as interest, dividends, and rents. Section 104(a) authorizes a trustee to make adjustments between principal and income if three conditions are met: (1) the trustee must be managing the trust assets under the prudent investor rule; (2) the terms of the trust must express the income beneficiary's distribution rights in terms of the right to receive "income" in the sense of traditional trust accounting income; and (3) the trustee must determine, after applying the rules in Section 103(a), that he is unable to comply with Section 103(b). In deciding whether and to what extent to exercise the power to adjust, the trustee is required to consider the factors described in Section 104(b), but the trustee may not make an adjustment in circumstances described in Section 104(c).

Section 104 does not empower a trustee to increase or decrease the degree of beneficial enjoyment to which a beneficiary is entitled under the terms of the trust; rather, it authorizes the trustee to make adjustments between principal and income that may be necessary if the income component of a portfolio's total return is too small or too large because of investment decisions made by the trustee under the prudent investor rule. The paramount consideration in applying Section 104(a) is the requirement in Section 103(b) that "a fiduciary must administer a trust or estate impartially, based on what is fair and reasonable to all of the beneficiaries, except to the extent that the terms of the trust or the will clearly manifest an intention that the fiduciary shall or may favor one or more of the beneficiaries." The power to adjust is subject to control by the court to prevent an abuse of discretion. Restatement (Second) of Trusts §187 (1959). See also id. §§183, 232, 233, Comment *p* (1959).

Section 104 will be important for trusts that are irrevocable when a State adopts the prudent investor rule by statute or judicial approval of the rule in Restatement of Trusts 3d: Prudent Investor Rule. Wills and trust instruments executed after the rule is adopted can be drafted to describe a beneficiary's distribution rights in terms that do not depend upon the amount of trust accounting income, but to the extent that drafters of trust documents continue to describe an income beneficiary's distribution rights by referring to trust accounting income, Section 104 will be an important tool in trust administration.

Three conditions to the exercise of the power to adjust. The first of the three conditions that must be met before a trustee can exercise the power to adjust—that the trustee invest and manage trust assets as a prudent investor—is expressed in this Act by language derived from the Uniform Prudent Investor Act, but the condition will be met whether the prudent investor rule applies because the Uniform Act or other prudent investor legislation has been enacted, the prudent investor rule has been approved by the courts, or the terms of the trust require it. Even if a State's legislature or courts have not formally adopted the rule, the Restatement establishes the prudent investor rule as an authoritative interpretation of the common law prudent man rule, referring to the prudent investor rule as a "modest reformulation of the Harvard College dictum and the basic rule of prior Restatements." Restatement of Trusts 3d: Prudent Investor Rule, Introduction, at 5. As a result, there is a basis for concluding that the first condition is satisfied in virtually all States except those in which a trustee is permitted to invest only in assets set forth in a statutory "legal list."

The second condition will be met when the terms of the trust require all of the "income" to be distributed at regular intervals; or when the terms of the trust require a trustee to distribute all of the income, but permit the trustee to decide how much to distribute to each member of a class of beneficiaries; or when the terms of a trust provide that the beneficiary shall receive the greater of the trust accounting income and a fixed dollar amount (an annuity), or of trust accounting income and a fractional share of the value of the trust assets (a unitrust amount). If the trust authorizes the trustee in its discretion to distribute the trust's income to the beneficiary or to accumulate some or all of the income, the condition will be met because the terms of the trust do not permit the trustee to distribute more than the trust accounting income.

To meet the third condition, the trustee must first meet the requirements of Section 103(a), i.e., she must apply the terms of the trust, decide whether to exercise the discretionary powers given to the trustee under the terms of the trust, and must apply the provisions of the Act if the terms of the trust do not contain a different provision or give the trustee discretion. Second, the trustee must determine the extent to which the terms of the trust clearly manifest an intention by the settlor that the trustee may or must favor one or more of the beneficiaries. To the extent that the terms of the trust do not require partiality, the trustee must conclude that she is unable to comply with the duty to administer the trust impartially. To the extent that the terms of the trust do require or permit the trustee to favor the income beneficiary or the remainder beneficiary, the trustee must conclude that she is unable to achieve the degree of partiality required or permitted. If the trustee comes to either conclusion—that she is unable to administer the trust impartially or that she is unable to achieve the degree of partiality required or permitted—she may exercise the power to adjust under Section 104(a).

Impartiality and productivity of income. The duty of impartiality between income and remainder beneficiaries is linked to the trustee's duty to make the portfolio productive of trust accounting income whenever the distribution requirements are expressed in terms of distributing the trust's "income." The 1962 Act implies that the duty to produce income applies on an asset by asset basis because the right of an income beneficiary to receive "delayed income" from the sale proceeds of underproductive property under Section 12 of that Act arises if "any part of principal . . . has not produced an average net income of a least 1 percent per year of its inventory value for more than a year . . . ." Under the prudent investor rule, "[t]o whatever extent a requirement of income productivity exists, . . . the requirement applies not investment by investment but to the portfolio as a whole." Restatement of Trusts 3d: Prudent Investor Rule §227, Comment *i*, at 34. The power to adjust under Section 104(a) is also to be exercised by considering net income from the portfolio as a whole and not investment by investment. Section 413(b) of this Act eliminates the underproductive property rule in all cases other than trusts for which a marital deduction is allowed; the rule applies to a marital deduction trust if the trust's assets "consist substantially of property that does not provide the spouse with sufficient income from or use of the trust assets . . ."—in other words, the section applies by reference to the portfolio as a whole.

While the purpose of the power to adjust in Section 104(a) is to eliminate the need for a trustee who operates under the prudent investor rule to be concerned about the income component of the portfolio's total return, the trustee must still determine the extent to which a distribution must be made to an income beneficiary and the adequacy of the portfolio's liquidity as a whole to make that distribution.

For a discussion of investment considerations involving specific investments and techniques under the prudent investor rule, see Restatement of Trusts 3d: Prudent Investor Rule §227, Comments *k-p*.

Factors to consider in exercising the power to adjust. Section 104(b) requires a trustee to consider factors relevant to the trust and its beneficiaries in deciding whether and to what extent the power to adjust should be exercised. Section 2(c) of the Uniform Prudent Investor Act sets forth circumstances that a trustee is to consider in investing and managing trust assets. The circumstances in Section 2(c) of the Uniform Prudent Investor Act are the source of the factors in paragraphs (3) through (6) and (8) of Section 104(b) (modified where necessary to adapt them to the purposes of this Act) so that, to the extent possible, comparable factors will apply to investment decisions and decisions involving the power to adjust. If a trustee who is operating under the prudent investor rule decides that the portfolio should be composed of financial assets whose total return will result primarily from capital appreciation rather than dividends, interest, and rents, the trustee can decide at the same time the extent to which an adjustment from principal to income may be necessary under Section 104. On the other hand, if a trustee decides that the risk and return objectives for the trust are best achieved by a portfolio whose total return includes interest and dividend income that is sufficient to provide the income beneficiary with the beneficial interest to which the beneficiary is entitled under the terms of the trust, the trustee can decide that it is unnecessary to exercise the power to adjust.

Assets received from the settlor. Section 3 of the Uniform Prudent Investor Act provides that "[a] trustee shall diversify the investments of the trust unless the trustee reasonably determines that, because of special circumstances, the purposes of the trust are better served without diversifying." The special circumstances may include the wish to retain a family business, the benefit derived from deferring liquidation of the asset in order to defer payment of income taxes, or the anticipated capital appreciation from retaining an asset such as undeveloped real estate for a long period. To the extent the trustee retains assets received from the settlor because of special circumstances that overcome the duty to diversify, the trustee may take these circumstances into account in determining whether and to what extent the power to adjust should be exercised to change the results produced by other provisions of this Act that apply to the retained assets. See Section

104(b)(5); Uniform Prudent Investor Act §3, Comment, 7B U.L.A. 18, at 25-26 (Supp. 1997); Restatement of Trusts 3d: Prudent Investor Rule §229 and Comments *a-e*.

Limitations on the power to adjust. The purpose of subsections (c)(1) through (4) is to preserve tax benefits that may have been an important purpose for creating the trust. Subsections (c)(5), (6), and (8) deny the power to adjust in the circumstances described in those subsections in order to prevent adverse tax consequences, and subsection (c)(7) denies the power to adjust to any beneficiary, whether or not possession of the power may have adverse tax consequences.

Under subsection (c)(1), a trustee cannot make an adjustment that diminishes the income interest in a trust that requires all of the income to be paid at least annually to a spouse and for which an estate tax or gift tax marital deduction is allowed; but this subsection does not prevent the trustee from making an adjustment that increases the amount of income paid from a marital deduction trust to the spouse. Subsection (c)(1) applies to a trust that qualifies for the marital deduction because the spouse has a general power of appointment over the trust, but it applies to a qualified terminable interest property (QTIP) trust only if and to the extent that the fiduciary makes the election required to obtain the tax deduction. Subsection (c)(1) does not apply to a so-called "estate" trust. This type of trust qualifies for the marital deduction because the terms of the trust require the principal and undistributed income to be paid to the surviving spouse's estate when the spouse dies; it is not necessary for the terms of an estate trust to require the income to be distributed annually. Reg. §20.2056(c)_2(b)(1)(iii).

Subsection (c)(3) applies to annuity trusts and unitrusts with no charitable beneficiaries as well as to trusts with charitable income or remainder beneficiaries; its purpose is to make it clear that a beneficiary's right to receive a fixed annuity or a fixed fraction of the value of a trust's assets is not subject to adjustment under Section 104(a). Subsection (c)(3) does not apply to any additional amount to which the beneficiary may be entitled that is expressed in terms of a right to receive income from the trust. For example, if a beneficiary is to receive a fixed annuity or the trust's income, whichever is greater, subsection (c)(3) does not prevent a trustee from making an adjustment under Section 104(a) in determining the amount of the trust's income.

If subsection (c)(5), (6), (7), or (8), prevents a trustee from exercising the power to adjust, subsection (d) permits a cotrustee who is not subject to the provision to exercise the power unless the terms of the trust do not permit the cotrustee to do so.

Release of the power to adjust. Section 104(e) permits a trustee to release all or part of the power to adjust in circumstances in which the possession or exercise of the power might deprive the trust of a tax benefit or impose a tax burden. For example, if possessing the power would diminish the actuarial value of the income interest in a trust for which the income beneficiary's estate may be eligible to claim a credit for property previously taxed if the beneficiary dies within ten years after the death of the person creating the trust, the trustee is permitted under subsection (e) to release just the power to adjust from income to principal.

Trust terms that limit a power to adjust. Section 104(f) applies to trust provisions that limit a trustee's power to adjust. Since the power is intended to enable trustees to employ the prudent investor rule without being constrained by traditional principal and income rules, an instrument executed before the adoption of this Act whose terms describe the amount that may or must be distributed to a beneficiary by referring to the trust's income or that prohibit the invasion of principal or that prohibit equitable adjustments in general should not be construed as forbidding the use of the power to adjust under Section 104(a) if the need for adjustment arises because the trustee is operating under the prudent investor rule. Instruments containing such provisions that are executed after the adoption of this Act should specifically refer to the power to adjust if the settlor intends to forbid its use. See generally, Joel C. Dobris, Limits on the Doctrine of Equitable Adjustment in Sophisticated Postmortem Tax Planning, 66 Iowa L. Rev. 273 (1981).

Examples. The following examples illustrate the application of Section 104:

Example (1)—T is the successor trustee of a trust that provides income to A for life, remainder to B. T has received from the prior trustee a portfolio of financial assets invested 20 percent in stocks and 80 percent in bonds. Following the prudent investor rule, T determines that a strategy of investing the portfolio 50 percent in stocks and 50 percent in bonds has risk and return objectives that are reasonably suited to the trust, but T also determines that adopting this approach will cause the trust to receive a smaller amount of dividend and interest income. After considering the factors in Section 104(b), T may transfer cash from principal to income to the extent T considers it necessary to increase the amount distributed to the income beneficiary.

Example (2)—T is the trustee of a trust that requires the income to be paid to the settlor's son C for life, remainder to C's daughter D. In a period of very high inflation, T purchases bonds that pay double-digit interest and determines that a portion of the interest, which is allocated to income under Section 406 of this Act, is a return of capital. In consideration of the loss of value of principal due to inflation and other factors that T considers relevant, T may transfer part of the interest to principal.

Example (3)—T is the trustee of a trust that requires the income to be paid to the settlor's sister E for life, remainder to charity F. E is a retired schoolteacher who is single and has no children. E's income from her social security, pension, and savings exceeds the amount required to provide for her accustomed standard of living. The terms of the trust permit T to invade principal to provide for E's health and to support her in her accustomed manner of living, but do not otherwise indicate that T should favor E or F. Applying the prudent investor rule, T determines that the trust assets should be invested entirely in growth stocks that produce very little dividend income. Even though it is not necessary to invade principal to maintain E's accustomed standard of living, she is entitled to receive from the trust the degree of beneficial enjoyment normally accorded a person who is the sole income beneficiary of a trust, and T may transfer cash from principal to income to provide her with that degree of enjoyment.

Example (4)—T is the trustee of a trust that is governed by the law of State X. The trust became irrevocable before State X adopted the prudent investor rule. The terms of the trust require all of the income to be paid to G for life, remainder to H, and also give T the power to invade principal for the benefit of G for "dire emergencies only." The terms of the trust limit the aggregate amount that T can distribute to G from principal during G's life to 6 percent of the trust's value at its inception. The trust's portfolio is invested initially 50 percent in stocks and 50 percent in bonds, but after State X adopts the prudent investor rule T determines that, to achieve suitable risk and return objectives for the trust, the assets should be invested 90 percent in stocks and 10 percent in bonds. This change increases the total return from the portfolio and decreases the dividend and interest income. Thereafter, even though G does not experience a dire emergency, T may exercise the power to adjust under Section 104(a) to the extent that T determines that the adjustment is from only the capital appreciation resulting from the change in the portfolio's asset allocation. If T is unable to determine the extent to which capital appreciation resulted from the change in asset allocation or is unable to maintain adequate records to determine the extent to which principal distributions to G for dire emergencies do not exceed the 6 percent limitation, T may not exercise the power to adjust. See Joel C. Dobris, Limits on the Doctrine of Equitable Adjustment in Sophisticated Postmortem Tax Planning, 66 Iowa L. Rev. 273 (1981).

Example (5)—T is the trustee of a trust for the settlor's child. The trust owns a diversified portfolio of marketable financial assets with a value of $600,000, and is also the sole beneficiary of the settlor's IRA, which holds a diversified portfolio of marketable financial assets with a value of $900,000. The trust receives a distribution from the IRA that is the minimum amount required to be distributed under the Internal Revenue Code, and T allocates 10 percent of the distribution to income under Section 409(c) of this Act. The total return on the IRA's assets exceeds the amount distributed to the trust, and the value of the IRA at the end of the year is more than its value at the beginning of the year. Relevant factors that T may consider in determining whether to exercise the power to adjust and the extent to which an adjustment should be made to comply with Section 103(b) include the total return from all of the trust's assets, those owned directly as well as its interest in the IRA, the extent to which the trust will be subject to income tax on the portion of the IRA distribution that is allocated to principal, and the extent to which the income beneficiary will be subject to income tax on the amount that T distributes to the income beneficiary.

Example (6)—T is the trustee of a trust whose portfolio includes a large parcel of undeveloped real estate. T pays real property taxes on the undeveloped parcel from income each year pursuant to Section 501(3). After considering the return from the trust's portfolio as a whole and other relevant factors described in Section 104(b), T may exercise the power to adjust under Section 104(a) to transfer cash from principal to income in order to distribute to the income beneficiary an amount that T considers necessary to comply with Section 103(b).

Example (7)—T is the trustee of a trust whose portfolio includes an interest in a mutual fund that is sponsored by T. As the manager of the mutual fund, T charges the fund a management fee that reduces the amount available to distribute to the trust by $2,000. If the fee had been paid directly by the trust, one-half of the fee would have been paid from income under Section 501(1) and the other one-half would have been paid from principal under Section 502(a)(1). After considering the total return from the portfolio as a whole and other relevant factors described in Section 104(b), T may exercise its power to adjust under Section 104(a) by transferring $1,000, or half of the trust's proportionate share of the fee, from principal to income.

§105. Judicial Control of Discretionary Power

(a) The court may not order a fiduciary to change a decision to exercise or not to exercise a discretionary power conferred by this [Act] unless it determines that the decision was an abuse of the fiduciary's discretion. A fiduciary's decision is not an abuse of discretion merely because the court would have exercised the power in a different manner or would not have exercised the power.

(b) The decisions to which subsection (a) applies include:

(1) a decision under Section 104(a) as to whether and to what extent an amount should be transferred from principal to income or from income to principal.

(2) a decision regarding the factors that are relevant to the trust and its beneficiaries, the extent to which the factors are relevant, and the weight, if any, to be given to

those factors, in deciding whether and to what extent to exercise the discretionary power conferred by Section 104(a).

(c) If the court determines that a fiduciary has abused the fiduciary's discretion, the court may place the income and remainder beneficiaries in the positions they would have occupied if the discretion had not been abused, according to the following rules:

(1) To the extent that the abuse of discretion has resulted in no distribution to a beneficiary or in a distribution that is too small, the court shall order the fiduciary to distribute from the trust to the beneficiary an amount that the court determines will restore the beneficiary, in whole or in part, to the beneficiary's appropriate position.

(2) To the extent that the abuse of discretion has resulted in a distribution to a beneficiary which is too large, the court shall place the beneficiaries, the trust, or both, in whole or in part, in their appropriate positions by ordering the fiduciary to withhold an amount from one or more future distributions to the beneficiary who received the distribution that was too large or ordering that beneficiary to return some or all of the distribution to the trust.

(3) To the extent that the court is unable, after applying paragraphs (1) and (2), to place the beneficiaries, the trust, or both, in the positions they would have occupied if the discretion had not been abused, the court may order the fiduciary to pay an appropriate amount from its own funds to one or more of the beneficiaries or the trust or both.

(d) Upon [petition] by the fiduciary, the court having jurisdiction over a trust or estate shall determine whether a proposed exercise or nonexercise by the fiduciary of a discretionary power conferred by this [Act] will result in an abuse of the fiduciary's discretion. If the petition describes the proposed exercise or nonexercise of the power and contains sufficient information to inform the beneficiaries of the reasons for the proposal, the facts upon which the fiduciary relies, and an explanation of how the income and remainder beneficiaries will be affected by the proposed exercise or nonexercise of the power, a beneficiary who challenges the proposed exercise or nonexercise has the burden of establishing that it will result in an abuse of discretion.

Comment

General. All of the discretionary powers in the 1997 Act are subject to the normal rules that govern a fiduciary's exercise of discretion. Section 105 codifies those rules for purposes of the Act so that they will be readily apparent and accessible to fiduciaries, beneficiaries, their counsel, and the courts if and when questions concerning such powers arise.

Section 105 also makes clear that the normal rules governing the exercise of a fiduciary's powers apply to the discretionary power to adjust conferred upon a trustee by Section 104(a). Discretionary provisions authorizing trustees to determine what is income and what is principal have been used in governing instruments for years; Section 2 of the 1931 Uniform Principal and Income Act recognized that practice by providing that "the person establishing the principal may himself direct the manner of ascertainment of income and principal . . . or grant discretion to the trustee or other person to do so. . . ." Section 103(a)(2) also recognizes the power of a settlor to grant such discretion to the trustee. Section 105 applies to a discretionary power granted by the terms of a trust or a will as well as the power to adjust in Section 104(a).

Power to adjust. The exercise of the power to adjust is governed by a trustee's duty of impartiality, which requires the trustee to strike an appropriate balance between the interests of the income and remainder beneficiaries. Section 103(b) expresses this duty by requiring the trustee to "administer a trust or estate impartially, based on what is fair and reasonable to all of the beneficiaries, except to the extent that the terms of the trust or the will clearly manifest an intention that the fiduciary shall or may favor one or more of the beneficiaries." Because this involves the exercise of judgment in circumstances rarely capable of perfect resolution, trustees are not expected to achieve perfection; they are, however, required to make conscious decisions in good faith and with proper motives.

In seeking the proper balance between the interests of the beneficiaries in matters involving principal and income, a trustee's traditional approach has been to determine the settlor's objectives from the terms of the trust, gather the information needed to ascertain the financial circumstances of the beneficiaries, determine the extent to which the settlor's objectives can be achieved with the resources available in the trust, and then allocate the trust's assets between stocks and fixed-income securities in a way that will produce a particular level or range of income for the income beneficiary. The key element in this process has been to determine the appropriate level or range of income for the income beneficiary, and that will continue to be the key element in deciding whether and to what extent to exercise the discretionary power conferred by Section 104(a). If it becomes necessary for a court to determine whether an abuse of the discretionary power to adjust between principal and income has occurred, the criteria should be the same as those that courts have used in the past to determine whether a trustee has abused its discretion in allocating the trust's assets between stocks and fixed-income securities.

A fiduciary has broad latitude in choosing the methods and criteria to use in deciding whether and to what extent to exercise the power to adjust in order to achieve impartiality between income beneficiaries and remainder beneficiaries or the degree of partiality for one or the other that is provided for by the terms of the trust or the will. For example, in deciding what the appropriate level or range of income should be for the income beneficiary and whether to exercise the power, a trustee may use the methods employed prior to the adoption of the 1997 Act in deciding how to allocate trust assets between stocks and fixed-income securities; or may consider the amount that would be distributed each year based on a percentage of the portfolio's value at the beginning or end of an accounting period, or the average portfolio value for several accounting periods, in a manner similar to a unitrust, and may select a percentage that the trustee believes is appropriate for this purpose and use the same percentage or different percentages in subsequent years. The trustee may also use hypothetical portfolios of marketable securities to determine an appropriate level or range of income within which a distribution might fall.

An adjustment may be made prospectively at the beginning of an accounting period, based on a projected return or range of returns for a trust's portfolio, or retrospectively after the fiduciary knows the total realized or unrealized return for the period; and instead of an annual adjustment, the trustee may distribute a fixed dollar amount for several years, in a manner similar to an annuity, and may change the fixed dollar amount periodically. No inference of abuse is to be drawn if a fiduciary uses different methods or criteria for the same trust from time to time, or uses different methods or criteria for different trusts for the same accounting period.

While a trustee must consider the portfolio as a whole in deciding whether and to what extent to exercise the power to adjust, a trustee may apply different criteria in considering the portion of the portfolio that is composed of marketable securities and the portion whose market value cannot be determined readily, and may take into account a beneficiary's use or possession of a trust asset.

Under the prudent investor rule, a trustee is to incur costs that are appropriate and reasonable in relation to the assets and the purposes of the trust, and the same consideration applies in determining whether and to what extent to exercise the power to adjust. In making investment decisions under the prudent investor rule, the trustee will have considered the purposes, terms, distribution requirements, and other circumstances of the trust for the purpose of adopting an overall investment strategy having risk and return objectives reasonably suited to the trust. A trustee is not required to duplicate that work for principal and income purposes, and in many cases the decision about whether and to what extent to exercise the power to adjust may be made at the same time as the investment decisions. To help achieve the objective of reasonable investment costs, a trustee may also adopt policies that apply to all trusts or to individual trusts or classes of trusts, based on their size or other criteria, stating whether and under what circumstances the power to adjust will be exercised and the method of making adjustments; no inference of abuse is to be drawn if a trustee adopts such policies.

General rule. The first sentence of Section 105(a) is from Restatement (Second) of Trusts §187 and Restatement (Third) of Trusts (Tentative Draft No. 2, 1999) §50(1). The second sentence of Section 105(a) derives from Comment e to §187 of the Second Restatement and Comment b to §50 of the Third Restatement.

The reference in Section 105(a) to a fiduciary's decision to exercise or not to exercise a discretionary power underscores a fundamental precept, which is that a fiduciary has a duty to make a conscious decision about exercising or not exercising a discretionary power. Comment b to §50 of the Third Restatement states:

> [A] court will intervene where the exercise of a power is left to the judgment of a trustee who improperly fails to exercise that judgment. Thus, even where a trustee has discretion whether or not to make any payments to a particular beneficiary, the court will interpose if the trustee, arbitrarily or without knowledge of or inquiry into relevant circumstances, fails to exercise the discretion.

Section 105(b) makes clear that the rule of subsection (a) applies not only to the power conferred by Section 104(a) but also to the evaluation process required by Section 104(b) in deciding whether and to what extent to exercise the power to adjust. Under Section 104(b), a trustee is to consider all of the factors that are relevant to the trust and its beneficiaries, including, to the extent the trustee determines they are relevant, the nine factors enumerated in Section 104(b). Section 104(b) derives from Section 2(c) of the Uniform Prudent Investor Act, which lists eight circumstances that a trustee shall consider, to the extent they are relevant, in investing and managing assets. The trustee's decisions about what factors are relevant for purposes of Section 104(b) and the weight to be accorded each of the relevant factors are part of the discretionary decision-making process. As such, these decisions are not subject to change for the purpose of changing the trustee's ultimate decision unless the court determines that there has been an abuse of discretion in determining the relevancy and weight of these factors.

Remedy. The exercise or nonexercise of a discretionary power under the Act normally affects the amount or timing of a distribution to the income or remainder beneficiaries. The primary remedy under Section 105(c) for abuse of discretion is the restoration of the beneficiaries and the trust to the positions they would have occupied if the abuse had not occurred. It draws on a basic principle of restitution that if a person pays money to someone who is not intended to receive it (and in a case to which this Act applies, not intended by the settlor to receive it in the absence of an abuse of discretion by the trustee), that person is entitled to restitution on the ground that the payee would be unjustly enriched if he or she were permitted to retain the payment. See Restatement of Restitution §22

(1937). The objective is to accomplish the restoration initially by making adjustments between the beneficiaries and the trust to the extent possible; to the extent that restoration is not possible by such adjustments, a court may order the trustee to pay an amount to one or more of the beneficiaries, the trust, or both the beneficiaries and the trust. If the court determines that it is not possible in the circumstances to restore them to the their appropriate positions, the court may provide other remedies appropriate to the circumstances. The approach of Section 105(c) is supported by Comment b to §50 of the Third Restatement of Trusts:

When judicial intervention is required, a court may direct the trustee to make or refrain from making certain payments; issue instructions to clarify the standards or guidelines applicable to the exercise of the power; or rescind the trustee's payment decisions, usually directing the trustee to recover amounts improperly distributed and holding the trustee liable for failure or inability to do so. . . .

Advance determinations. Section 105(d) employs the familiar remedy of the trustee's petition to the court for instructions. It requires the court to determine, upon a petition by the fiduciary, whether a proposed exercise or nonexercise of a discretionary power by the fiduciary of a power conferred by the Act would be an abuse of discretion under the general rule of Section 105(a). If the petition contains the information prescribed in the second sentence of subsection (d), the proposed action or inaction is presumed not to result in an abuse, and a beneficiary who challenges the proposal must establish that it will.

Subsection (d) is intended to provide a fiduciary the opportunity to obtain an assurance of finality in a judicial proceeding before proceeding with a proposed exercise or nonexercise of a discretionary power. Its purpose is not, however, to have the court instruct the fiduciary how to exercise the discretion. A fiduciary may also obtain the consent of the beneficiaries to a proposed act or an omission to act, and a beneficiary cannot hold the fiduciary liable for that act or omission unless:

(a) the beneficiary was under an incapacity at the time of such consent or of such act or omission; or

(b) the beneficiary, when he gave his consent, did not know of his rights and of the material facts which the trustee knew or should have known and which the trustee did not reasonably believe that the beneficiary knew; or

(c) the consent of the beneficiary was induced by improper conduct of the trustee.

Restatement (Second) of Trusts §216.

If there are many beneficiaries, including some who are incapacitated or unascertained, the fiduciary may prefer the greater assurance of finality provided by a judicial proceeding that will bind all persons who have an interest in the trust.

[ARTICLE] 2

DECEDENT'S ESTATE OR TERMINATING INCOME INTEREST

§201. Determination and Distribution of Net Income

After a decedent dies, in the case of an estate, or after an income interest in a trust ends, the following rules apply:

(1) A fiduciary of an estate or of a terminating income interest shall determine the amount of net income and net principal receipts received from property specifically given to a beneficiary under the rules in [Articles] 3 through 5 which apply to trustees and the rules in paragraph (5). The fiduciary shall distribute the net income and net principal receipts to the beneficiary who is to receive the specific property.

(2) A fiduciary shall determine the remaining net income of a decedent's estate or a terminating income interest under the rules in [Articles] 3 through 5 which apply to trustees and by:

(A) including in net income all income from property used to discharge liabilities;

(B) paying from income or principal, in the fiduciary's discretion, fees of attorneys, accountants, and fiduciaries; court costs and other expenses of administration; and interest on death taxes, but the fiduciary may pay those expenses from income of property passing to a trust for which the fiduciary claims an estate tax marital or charitable deduction only to the extent that the payment of those expenses from income will not cause the reduction or loss of the deduction; and

(C) paying from principal all other disbursements made or incurred in connection with the settlement of a decedent's estate or the winding up of a terminating income interest, including debts, funeral expenses, disposition of remains, family allowances, and death taxes and related penalties that are apportioned to the estate or terminating income interest by the will, the terms of the trust, or applicable law.

(3) A fiduciary shall distribute to a beneficiary who receives a pecuniary amount outright the interest or any other amount provided by the will, the terms of the trust, or applicable law from net income determined under paragraph (2) or from principal to the extent that net income is insufficient. If a beneficiary is to receive a pecuniary amount outright from a trust after an income interest ends and no interest or other amount is provided for by the terms of the trust or applicable law, the fiduciary shall distribute the interest or other amount to which the beneficiary would be entitled under applicable law if the pecuniary amount were required to be paid under a will.

(4) A fiduciary shall distribute the net income remaining after distributions required by paragraph (3) in the manner described in Section 202 to all other beneficiaries, including a beneficiary who receives a pecuniary amount in trust, even if

the beneficiary holds an unqualified power to withdraw assets from the trust or other presently exercisable general power of appointment over the trust.

(5) A fiduciary may not reduce principal or income receipts from property described in paragraph (1) because of a payment described in Section 501 or 502 to the extent that the will, the terms of the trust, or applicable law requires the fiduciary to make the payment from assets other than the property or to the extent that the fiduciary recovers or expects to recover the payment from a third party. The net income and principal receipts from the property are determined by including all of the amounts the fiduciary receives or pays with respect to the property, whether those amounts accrued or became due before, on, or after the date of a decedent's death or an income interest's terminating event, and by making a reasonable provision for amounts that the fiduciary believes the estate or terminating income interest may become obligated to pay after the property is distributed.

§202. Distribution to Residuary and Remainder Beneficiaries

(a) Each beneficiary described in Section 201(4) is entitled to receive a portion of the net income equal to the beneficiary's fractional interest in undistributed principal assets, using values as of the distribution date. If a fiduciary makes more than one distribution of assets to beneficiaries to whom this section applies, each beneficiary, including one who does not receive part of the distribution, is entitled, as of each distribution date, to the net income the fiduciary has received after the date of death or terminating event or earlier distribution date but has not distributed as of the current distribution date.

(b) In determining a beneficiary's share of net income, the following rules apply:

(1) The beneficiary is entitled to receive a portion of the net income equal to the beneficiary's fractional interest in the undistributed principal assets immediately before the distribution date, including assets that later may be sold to meet principal obligations.

(2) The beneficiary's fractional interest in the undistributed principal assets must be calculated without regard to property specifically given to a beneficiary and property required to pay pecuniary amounts not in trust.

(3) The beneficiary's fractional interest in the undistributed principal assets must be calculated on the basis of the aggregate value of those assets as of the distribution date without reducing the value by any unpaid principal obligation.

(4) The distribution date for purposes of this section may be the date as of which the fiduciary calculates the value of the assets if that date is reasonably near the date on which assets are actually distributed.

(c) If a fiduciary does not distribute all of the collected but undistributed net income to each person as of a distribution date, the fiduciary shall maintain appropriate records showing the interest of each beneficiary in that net income.

(d) A fiduciary may apply the rules in this section, to the extent that the fiduciary considers it appropriate, to net gain or loss realized after the date of death or terminating event or earlier distribution date from the disposition of a principal asset if this section applies to the income from the asset.

Comment

Relationship to prior Acts. Section 202 retains the concept in Section 5(b)(2) of the 1962 Act that the residuary legatees of estates are to receive net income earned during the period of administration on the basis of their proportionate interests in the undistributed assets when distributions are made. It changes the basis for determining their proportionate interests by using asset values as of a date reasonably near the time of distribution instead of inventory values; it extends the application of these rules to distributions from terminating trusts; and it extends these rules to gain or loss realized from the disposition of assets during administration, an omission in the 1962 Act that has been noted by several commentators. . . .

[ARTICLE] 3

APPORTIONMENT AT BEGINNING AND END OF INCOME INTEREST

§301. When Right to Income Begins and Ends

(a) An income beneficiary is entitled to net income from the date on which the income interest begins. An income interest begins on the date specified in the terms of the trust or, if no date is specified, on the date an asset becomes subject to a trust or successive income interest.

(b) An asset becomes subject to a trust:

(1) on the date it is transferred to the trust in the case of an asset that is transferred to a trust during the transferor's life;

(2) on the date of a testator's death in the case of an asset that becomes subject to a trust by reason of a will, even if there is an intervening period of administration of the testator's estate; or

(3) on the date of an individual's death in the case of an asset that is transferred to a fiduciary by a third party because of the individual's death.

(c) An asset becomes subject to a successive income interest on the day after the preceding income interest ends, as determined under subsection (d), even if there is an intervening period of administration to wind up the preceding income interest.

(d) An income interest ends on the day before an income beneficiary dies or another terminating event occurs, or on the last day of a period during which there is no beneficiary to whom a trustee may distribute income.

§302. Apportionment of Receipts and Disbursements When Decedent Dies or Income Interest Begins

(a) A trustee shall allocate an income receipt or disbursement other than one to which Section 201(1) applies to principal if its due date occurs before a decedent dies in the case of an estate or before an income interest begins in the case of a trust or successive income interest.

(b) A trustee shall allocate an income receipt or disbursement to income if its due date occurs on or after the date on which a decedent dies or an income interest begins and it is a periodic due date. An income receipt or disbursement must be treated as accruing from day to day if its due date is not periodic or it has no due date. The portion of the receipt or disbursement accruing before the date on which a decedent dies or an income interest begins must be allocated to principal and the balance must be allocated to income.

(c) An item of income or an obligation is due on the date the payer is required to make a payment. If a payment date is not stated, there is no due date for the purposes of this [Act]. Distributions to shareholders or other owners from an entity to which Section 401 applies are deemed to be due on the date fixed by the entity for determining who is entitled to receive the distribution or, if no date is fixed, on the declaration date for the distribution. A due date is periodic for receipts or disbursements that must be paid at regular intervals under a lease or an obligation to pay interest or if an entity customarily makes distributions at regular intervals.

§303. Apportionment When Income Interest Ends

(a) In this section, "undistributed income" means net income received before the date on which an income interest ends. The term does not include an item of income or expense that is due or accrued or net income that has been added or is required to be added to principal under the terms of the trust.

(b) When a mandatory income interest ends, the trustee shall pay to a mandatory income beneficiary who survives that date, or the estate of a deceased mandatory income beneficiary whose death causes the interest to end, the beneficiary's share of the undistributed income that is not disposed of under the terms of the trust unless the beneficiary has an unqualified power to revoke more than five percent of the trust immediately before the income interest ends. In the latter case, the undistributed income from the portion of the trust that may be revoked must be added to principal.

(c) When a trustee's obligation to pay a fixed annuity or a fixed fraction of the value of the trust's assets ends, the trustee shall prorate the final payment if and to the extent required by applicable law to accomplish a purpose of the trust or its settlor relating to income, gift, estate, or other tax requirements.

[ARTICLE] 4

ALLOCATION OF RECEIPTS DURING ADMINISTRATION OF TRUST

[PART 1 RECEIPTS FROM ENTITIES]

§401. Character of Receipts

(a) In this section, "entity" means a corporation, partnership, limited liability company, regulated investment company, real estate investment trust, common trust fund, or any other organization in which a trustee has an interest other than a trust or estate to which Section 402 applies, a business or activity to which Section 403 applies, or an asset-backed security to which Section 415 applies.

(b) Except as otherwise provided in this section, a trustee shall allocate to income money received from an entity.

(c) A trustee shall allocate the following receipts from an entity to principal:

(1) property other than money;

(2) money received in one distribution or a series of related distributions in exchange for part or all of a trust's interest in the entity;

(3) money received in total or partial liquidation of the entity; and

(4) money received from an entity that is a regulated investment company or a real estate investment trust if the money distributed is a capital gain dividend for federal income tax purposes.

(d) Money is received in partial liquidation:

(1) to the extent that the entity, at or near the time of a distribution, indicates that it is a distribution in partial liquidation; or

(2) if the total amount of money and property received in a distribution or series of related distributions is greater than 20 percent of the entity's gross assets, as shown by the entity's year-end financial statements immediately preceding the initial receipt.

(e) Money is not received in partial liquidation, nor may it be taken into account under subsection (d)(2), to the extent that it does not exceed the amount of income tax that a trustee or beneficiary must pay on taxable income of the entity that distributes the money.

(f) A trustee may rely upon a statement made by an entity about the source or character of a distribution if the statement is made at or near the time of distribution by the entity's board of directors or other person or group of persons authorized to exercise powers to pay money or transfer property comparable to those of a corporation's board of directors.

§402. Distribution from Trust or Estate

A trustee shall allocate to income an amount received as a distribution of income from a trust or an estate in which the trust has an interest other than a purchased interest, and shall allocate to principal an amount received as a distribution of principal from such a trust or estate. If a trustee purchases an interest in a trust that is an investment entity, or a decedent or donor transfers an interest in such a trust to a trustee, Section 401 or 415 applies to a receipt from the trust.

§403. Business and Other Activities Conducted by Trustee

(a) If a trustee who conducts a business or other activity determines that it is in the best interest of all the beneficiaries to account separately for the business or activity instead of accounting for it as part of the trust's general accounting records, the trustee may maintain separate accounting records for its transactions, whether or not its assets are segregated from other trust assets.

(b) A trustee who accounts separately for a business or other activity may determine the extent to which its net cash receipts must be retained for working capital, the acquisition or replacement of fixed assets, and other reasonably foreseeable needs of the business or activity, and the extent to which the remaining net cash receipts are accounted for as principal or income in the trust's general accounting records. If a trustee sells assets of the business or other activity, other than in the ordinary course of the business or activity, the trustee shall account for the net amount received as principal in the trust's general accounting records to the extent the trustee determines that the amount received is no longer required in the conduct of the business.

(c) Activities for which a trustee may maintain separate accounting records include:

(1) retail, manufacturing, service, and other traditional business activities;

(2) farming;

(3) raising and selling livestock and other animals;

(4) management of rental properties;

(5) extraction of minerals and other natural resources;

(6) timber operations; and

(7) activities to which Section 414 applies.

[PART 2 RECEIPTS NOT NORMALLY APPORTIONED]

§404. Principal Receipts

A trustee shall allocate to principal:

(1) to the extent not allocated to income under this [Act], assets received from a transferor during the transferor's lifetime, a decedent's estate, a trust with a terminating income interest, or a payer under a contract naming the trust or its trustee as beneficiary;

(2) money or other property received from the sale, exchange, liquidation, or change in form of a principal asset, including realized profit, subject to this [article];

(3) amounts recovered from third parties to reimburse the trust because of disbursements described in Section 502(a)(7) or for other reasons to the extent not based on the loss of income;

(4) proceeds of property taken by eminent domain, but a separate award made for the loss of income with respect to an accounting period during which a current income beneficiary had a mandatory income interest is income;

(5) net income received in an accounting period during which there is no beneficiary to whom a trustee may or must distribute income; and

(6) other receipts as provided in [Part 3].

§405. Rental Property

To the extent that a trustee accounts for receipts from rental property pursuant to this section, the trustee shall allocate to income an amount received as rent of real or personal property, including an amount received for cancellation or renewal of a lease. An amount received as a refundable deposit, including a security deposit or a deposit that is to be applied as rent for future periods, must be added to principal and held subject to the terms of the lease and is not available for distribution to a beneficiary until the trustee's contractual obligations have been satisfied with respect to that amount.

§406. Obligation to Pay Money

(a) An amount received as interest, whether determined at a fixed, variable, or floating rate, on an obligation to pay money to the trustee, including an amount received as consideration for prepaying principal, must be allocated to income without any provision for amortization of premium.

(b) A trustee shall allocate to principal an amount received from the sale, redemption, or other disposition of an obligation to pay money to the trustee more than one year after it is purchased or acquired by the trustee, including an obligation whose purchase price or value when it is acquired is less than its value at maturity. If the obligation matures within one year after it is purchased or acquired by the trustee, an amount received in excess of its purchase price or its value when acquired by the trust must be allocated to income.

(c) This section does not apply to an obligation to which Section 409, 410, 411, 412, 414, or 415 applies.

§407. Insurance Policies and Similar Contracts

(a) Except as otherwise provided in subsection (b), a trustee shall allocate to principal the proceeds of a life insurance policy or other contract in which the trust or its trustee is named as beneficiary, including a contract that insures the trust or its trustee against loss for damage to, destruction of, or loss of title to a trust asset. The trustee shall allocate dividends on an insurance policy to income if the premiums on the policy are paid from income, and to principal if the premiums are paid from principal.

(b) A trustee shall allocate to income proceeds of a contract that insures the trustee against loss of occupancy or other use by an income beneficiary, loss of income, or, subject to Section 403, loss of profits from a business.

(c) This section does not apply to a contract to which Section 409 applies.

[PART 3 RECEIPTS NORMALLY APPORTIONED]

§408. Insubstantial Allocations Not Required

If a trustee determines that an allocation between principal and income required by Section 409, 410, 411, 412, or 415 is insubstantial, the trustee may allocate the entire amount to principal unless one of the circumstances described in Section 104(c) applies to the allocation. This power may be exercised by a cotrustee in the circumstances described in Section 104(d) and may be released for the reasons and in the manner described in Section 104(e). An allocation is presumed to be insubstantial if:

(1) the amount of the allocation would increase or decrease net income in an accounting period, as determined before the allocation, by less than 10 percent; or

(2) the value of the asset producing the receipt for which the allocation would be made is less than 10 percent of the total value of the trust's assets at the beginning of the accounting period.

§409. Deferred Compensation, Annuities, and Similar Payments

(a) In this section, "payment" means a payment that a trustee may receive over a fixed number of years or during the life of one or more individuals because of services rendered or property transferred to the payer in exchange for future payments. The term includes a payment made in money or property from the payer's general assets or from a separate fund created by the payer, including a private or commercial annuity, an individual retirement account, and a pension, profit-sharing, stock-bonus, or stock-ownership plan.

(b) To the extent that a payment is characterized as interest or a dividend or a payment made in lieu of interest or a dividend, a trustee shall allocate it to income. The trustee shall allocate to principal the balance of the payment and any other payment received in the same accounting period that is not characterized as interest, a dividend, or an equivalent payment.

(c) If no part of a payment is characterized as interest, a dividend, or an equivalent payment, and all or part of the payment is required to be made, a trustee shall allocate to income 10 percent of the part that is required to be made during the accounting period and the balance to principal. If no part of a payment is required to be made or the payment received is the entire amount to which the trustee is entitled, the trustee shall allocate the entire payment to principal. For purposes of this subsection, a payment is not "required to be made" to the extent that it is made because the trustee exercises a right of withdrawal.

(d) If, to obtain an estate tax marital deduction for a trust, a trustee must allocate more of a payment to income than provided for by this section, the trustee shall allocate to income the additional amount necessary to obtain the marital deduction.

(e) This section does not apply to payments to which Section 410 applies.

§410. Liquidating Asset

(a) In this section, "liquidating asset" means an asset whose value will diminish or terminate because the asset is expected to produce receipts for a period of limited duration. The term includes a leasehold, patent, copyright, royalty right, and right to receive payments during a period of more than one year under an arrangement that does not provide for the payment of interest on the unpaid balance. The term does not include a payment subject to Section 409, resources subject to Section 411, timber subject to Section 412, an activity subject to Section 414, an asset subject to Section 415, or any asset for which the trustee establishes a reserve for depreciation under Section 503.

(b) A trustee shall allocate to income 10 percent of the receipts from a liquidating asset and the balance to principal.

§411. Minerals, Water, and Other Natural Resources

(a) To the extent that a trustee accounts for receipts from an interest in minerals or other natural resources pursuant to this section, the trustee shall allocate them as follows:

(1) If received as nominal delay rental or nominal annual rent on a lease, a receipt must be allocated to income.

(2) If received from a production payment, a receipt must be allocated to income if and to the extent that the agreement creating the production payment provides a factor for interest or its equivalent. The balance must be allocated to principal.

(3) If an amount received as a royalty, shut-in-well payment, take-or-pay payment, bonus, or delay rental is more than nominal, 90 percent must be allocated to principal and the balance to income.

(4) If an amount is received from a working interest or any other interest not provided for in paragraph (1), (2), or (3), 90 percent of the net amount received must be allocated to principal and the balance to income.

(b) An amount received on account of an interest in water that is renewable must be allocated to income. If the water is not renewable, 90 percent of the amount must be allocated to principal and the balance to income.

(c) This [Act] applies whether or not a decedent or donor was extracting minerals, water, or other natural resources before the interest became subject to the trust.

(d) If a trust owns an interest in minerals, water, or other natural resources on [the effective date of this [Act]], the trustee may allocate receipts from the interest as provided in this [Act] or in the manner used by the trustee before [the effective date of this [Act]]. If the trust acquires an interest in minerals, water, or other natural resources after [the effective date of this [Act]], the trustee shall allocate receipts from the interest as provided in this [Act].

§412. Timber

(a) To the extent that a trustee accounts for receipts from the sale of timber and related products pursuant to this section, the trustee shall allocate the net receipts:

(1) to income to the extent that the amount of timber removed from the land does not exceed the rate of growth of the timber during the accounting periods in which a beneficiary has a mandatory income interest;

(2) to principal to the extent that the amount of timber removed from the land exceeds the rate of growth of the timber or the net receipts are from the sale of standing timber;

(3) to or between income and principal if the net receipts are from the lease of timberland or from a contract to cut timber from land owned by a trust, by determining the amount of timber removed from the land under the lease or contract and applying the rules in paragraphs (1) and (2); or

(4) to principal to the extent that advance payments, bonuses, and other payments are not allocated pursuant to paragraph (1), (2), or (3).

(b) In determining net receipts to be allocated pursuant to subsection (a), a trustee shall deduct and transfer to principal a reasonable amount for depletion.

(c) This [Act] applies whether or not a decedent or transferor was harvesting timber from the property before it became subject to the trust.

(d) If a trust owns an interest in timberland on [the effective date of this [Act]], the trustee may allocate net receipts from the sale of timber and related products as provided in this [Act] or in the manner used by the trustee before [the effective date of this [Act]]. If the trust acquires an interest in timberland after [the effective date of this [Act]], the trustee shall allocate net receipts from the sale of timber and related products as provided in this [Act].

§413. Property Not Productive of Income

(a) If a marital deduction is allowed for all or part of a trust whose assets consist substantially of property that does not provide the spouse with sufficient income from or use of the trust assets, and if the amounts that the trustee transfers from principal to income under Section 104 and distributes to the spouse from principal pursuant to the terms of the trust are insufficient to provide the spouse with the beneficial enjoyment required to obtain the marital deduction, the spouse may require the trustee to make property productive of income, convert property within a reasonable time, or exercise the power conferred by Section 104(a). The trustee may decide which action or combination of actions to take.

(b) In cases not governed by subsection (a), proceeds from the sale or other disposition of an asset are principal without regard to the amount of income the asset produces during any accounting period.

§414. Derivatives and Options

(a) In this section, "derivative" means a contract or financial instrument or a combination of contracts and financial instruments which gives a trust the right or obligation to participate in some or all changes in the price of a tangible or intangible asset or group of assets, or changes in a rate, an index of prices or rates, or other market indicator for an asset or a group of assets.

(b) To the extent that a trustee does not account under Section 403 for transactions in derivatives, the trustee shall allocate to principal receipts from and disbursements made in connection with those transactions.

(c) If a trustee grants an option to buy property from the trust, whether or not the trust owns the property when the option is granted, grants an option that permits another person to sell property to the trust, or acquires an option to buy property for the trust or an option to sell an asset owned by the trust, and the trustee or other owner of the asset is required to deliver the asset if the option is exercised, an amount received for granting the option must be allocated to principal. An amount paid to acquire the option must be paid from principal. A gain or loss realized upon the exercise of an option, including an option granted to a settlor of the trust for services rendered, must be allocated to principal.

§415. Asset-Backed Securities

(a) In this section, "asset-backed security" means an asset whose value is based upon the right it gives the owner to receive distributions from the proceeds of financial assets that provide collateral for the security. The term includes an asset that gives the owner the right to receive from the collateral financial assets only the interest or other current return or only the proceeds other than interest or current return. The term does not include an asset to which Section 401 or 409 applies.

(b) If a trust receives a payment from interest or other current return and from other proceeds of the collateral financial assets, the trustee shall allocate to income the portion of the payment which the payer identifies as being from interest or other current return and shall allocate the balance of the payment to principal.

(c) If a trust receives one or more payments in exchange for the trust's entire interest in an asset-backed security in one accounting period, the trustee shall allocate the payments to principal. If a payment is one of a series of payments that will result in the liquidation of the trust's interest in the security over more than one accounting period, the trustee shall allocate 10 percent of the payment to income and the balance to principal.

Comment

Scope of section. Typical asset-backed securities include arrangements in which debt obligations such as real estate mortgages, credit card receivables, and auto loans are acquired by an investment trust and interests in the trust are sold to investors. The source for payments to an investor is the money received from principal and interest payments on the underlying debt. An asset-backed security includes an "interest only" or a "principal only" security that permits the investor to receive only the interest payments received from the bonds, mortgages, or other assets that are the collateral for the asset-backed security, or only the principal payments made on those collateral assets. An asset-backed security also includes a security that permits the investor to participate in either the capital appreciation of an underlying security or in the interest or dividend return from such a security, such as the "Primes" and "Scores" issued by Americus Trust. An asset-backed security does not include an interest in a corporation, partnership, or an investment trust described in the Comment to Section 402, whose assets consist significantly or entirely of investment assets. Receipts from an instrument that do not come within the scope of this section or any other section of the Act would be allocated entirely to principal under the rule in Section 103(a)(4), and the trustee may then consider whether and to what extent to exercise the power to adjust in Section 104, taking into account the return from the portfolio as whole and other relevant factors.

[ARTICLE] 5

ALLOCATION OF DISBURSEMENTS DURING ADMINISTRATION OF TRUST

§501. Disbursements from Income

A trustee shall make the following disbursements from income to the extent that they are not disbursements to which Section 201(2)(B) or (C) applies:

(1) one-half of the regular compensation of the trustee and of any person providing investment advisory or custodial services to the trustee;

(2) one-half of all expenses for accountings, judicial proceedings, or other matters that involve both the income and remainder interests;

(3) all of the other ordinary expenses incurred in connection with the administration, management, or preservation of trust property and the distribution of income, including interest, ordinary repairs, regularly recurring taxes assessed against principal, and expenses of a proceeding or other matter that concerns primarily the income interest; and

(4) recurring premiums on insurance covering the loss of a principal asset or the loss of income from or use of the asset.

Comment

Trustee fees. The regular compensation of a trustee or the trustee's agent includes compensation based on a percentage of either principal or income or both.

Insurance premiums. The reference in paragraph (4) to "recurring" premiums is intended to distinguish premiums paid annually for fire insurance from premiums on title insurance, each of which covers the loss of a principal asset. Title insurance premiums would be a principal disbursement under Section 502(a)(5).

Regularly recurring taxes. The reference to "regularly recurring taxes assessed against principal" includes all taxes regularly imposed on real property and tangible and intangible personal property.

§502. Disbursements from Principal

(a) A trustee shall make the following disbursements from principal:

(1) the remaining one-half of the disbursements described in Section 501(1) and (2);

(2) all of the trustee's compensation calculated on principal as a fee for acceptance, distribution, or termination, and disbursements made to prepare property for sale;

(3) payments on the principal of a trust debt;

(4) expenses of a proceeding that concerns primarily principal, including a proceeding to construe the trust or to protect the trust or its property;

(5) premiums paid on a policy of insurance not described in Section 501(4) of which the trust is the owner and beneficiary;

(6) estate, inheritance, and other transfer taxes, including penalties, apportioned to the trust; and

(7) disbursements related to environmental matters, including reclamation, assessing environmental conditions, remedying and removing environmental contamination, monitoring remedial activities and the release of substances, preventing future releases of substances, collecting amounts from persons liable or potentially liable for the costs of those activities, penalties imposed under environmental laws or regulations and other payments made to comply with those laws or regulations, statutory or common law claims by third parties, and defending claims based on environmental matters.

(b) If a principal asset is encumbered with an obligation that requires income from that asset to be paid directly to the creditor, the trustee shall transfer from principal to income an amount equal to the income paid to the creditor in reduction of the principal balance of the obligation.

§503. Transfers from Income to Principal for Depreciation

(a) In this section, "depreciation" means a reduction in value due to wear, tear, decay, corrosion, or gradual obsolescence of a fixed asset having a useful life of more than one year.

(b) A trustee may transfer to principal a reasonable amount of the net cash receipts from a principal asset that is subject to depreciation, but may not transfer any amount for depreciation:

(1) of that portion of real property used or available for use by a beneficiary as a residence or of tangible personal property held or made available for the personal use or enjoyment of a beneficiary;

(2) during the administration of a decedent's estate; or

(3) under this section if the trustee is accounting under Section 403 for the business or activity in which the asset is used.

(c) An amount transferred to principal need not be held as a separate fund.

Comment

Prior Acts. The 1931 Act has no provision for depreciation. Section 13(a)(2) of the 1962 Act provides that a charge shall be made against income for ". . . a reasonable allowance for depreciation on property subject to depreciation under generally accepted accounting principles . . . ." That provision has been resisted by many trustees, who do not provide for any depreciation for a variety of reasons. One reason relied upon is that a charge for depreciation is not needed to protect the remainder beneficiaries if the value of the land is increasing; another is that generally accepted accounting principles may not require depreciation to be taken if the property is not part of a business. The Drafting Committee concluded that the decision to provide for depreciation should be discretionary with the trustee. The power to transfer funds from income to principal that is granted by this section is a discretionary power of administration referred to in Section 103(b), and in exercising the power a trustee must comply with Section 103(b).

One purpose served by transferring cash from income to principal for depreciation is to provide funds to pay the principal of an indebtedness secured by the depreciable property. Section 504(b)(4) permits the trustee to transfer additional cash from income to principal for this purpose to the extent that the amount transferred from income to principal for depreciation is less than the amount of the principal payments.

§504. Transfers from Income to Reimburse Principal

(a) If a trustee makes or expects to make a principal disbursement described in this section, the trustee may transfer an appropriate amount from income to principal in one or more accounting periods to reimburse principal or to provide a reserve for future principal disbursements.

(b) Principal disbursements to which subsection (a) applies include the following, but only to the extent that the trustee has not been and does not expect to be reimbursed by a third party:

(1) an amount chargeable to income but paid from principal because it is unusually large, including extraordinary repairs;

(2) a capital improvement to a principal asset, whether in the form of changes to an existing asset or the construction of a new asset, including special assessments;

(3) disbursements made to prepare property for rental, including tenant allowances, leasehold improvements, and broker's commissions;

(4) periodic payments on an obligation secured by a principal asset to the extent that the amount transferred from income to principal for depreciation is less than the periodic payments; and

(5) disbursements described in Section 502(a)(7).

(c) If the asset whose ownership gives rise to the disbursements becomes subject to a successive income interest after an income interest ends, a trustee may continue to transfer amounts from income to principal as provided in subsection (a).

Comment

Prior Acts. The sources of Section 504 are Section 13(b) of the 1962 Act, which permits a trustee to "regularize distributions," if charges against income are unusually large, by using "reserves or other reasonable means" to withhold sums from income distributions; Section 13(c)(3) of the 1962 Act, which authorizes a trustee to establish an allowance for depreciation out of income if principal is used for extraordinary repairs, capital improvements, and special assessments; and Section 12(3) of the 1931 Act, which permits the trustee to spread income expenses of unusual amount "throughout a series of years." Section 504 contains a more detailed enumeration of the circumstances in which this authority may be used, and includes in subsection (b)(4) the express authority to use income to make principal payments on a mortgage if the depreciation charge against income is less than the principal payments on the mortgage.

§505. Income Taxes

(a) A tax required to be paid by a trustee based on receipts allocated to income must be paid from income.

(b) A tax required to be paid by a trustee based on receipts allocated to principal must be paid from principal, even if the tax is called an income tax by the taxing authority.

(c) A tax required to be paid by a trustee on the trust's share of an entity's taxable income must be paid proportionately:

(1) from income to the extent that receipts from the entity are allocated to income; and

(2) from principal to the extent that:

(A) receipts from the entity are allocated to principal; and

(B) the trust's share of the entity's taxable income exceeds the total receipts described in paragraphs (1) and (2)(A).

(d) For purposes of this section, receipts allocated to principal or income must be reduced by the amount distributed to a beneficiary from principal or income for which the trust receives a deduction in calculating the tax.

§506. Adjustments between Principal and Income Because of Taxes

(a) A fiduciary may make adjustments between principal and income to offset the shifting of economic interests or tax benefits between income beneficiaries and remainder beneficiaries which arise from:

(1) elections and decisions, other than those described in subsection (b), that the fiduciary makes from time to time regarding tax matters;

(2) an income tax or any other tax that is imposed upon the fiduciary or a beneficiary as a result of a transaction involving or a distribution from the estate or trust; or

(3) the ownership by an estate or trust of an interest in an entity whose taxable income, whether or not distributed, is includable in the taxable income of the estate, trust, or a beneficiary.

(b) If the amount of an estate tax marital deduction or charitable contribution deduction is reduced because a fiduciary deducts an amount paid from principal for income tax purposes instead of deducting it for estate tax purposes, and as a result estate taxes paid from principal are increased and income taxes paid by an estate, trust, or beneficiary are decreased, each estate, trust, or beneficiary that benefits from the decrease in income tax shall reimburse the principal from which the increase in estate tax is paid. The total reimbursement must equal the increase in the estate tax to the extent that the principal used to pay the increase would have qualified for a marital deduction or charitable contribution deduction but for the payment. The proportionate share of the reimbursement for each estate, trust, or beneficiary whose income taxes are reduced must be the same as its proportionate share of the total decrease in income tax. An estate or trust shall reimburse principal from income.

[ARTICLE] 6

MISCELLANEOUS PROVISIONS

§601. Uniformity of Application and Construction

In applying and construing this Uniform Act, consideration must be given to the need to promote uniformity of the law with respect to its subject matter among States that enact it.

§602. Severability Clause

If any provision of this [Act] or its application to any person or circumstance is held invalid, the invalidity does not affect other provisions or applications of this [Act] which can be given effect without the invalid provision or application, and to this end the provisions of this [Act] are severable.

§603. Repeal

The following acts and parts of acts are repealed:

(1) ....

(2) ....

(3) ....

§604. Effective Date

This [Act] takes effect on ....

§605. Application of [Act] to Existing Trusts and Estates

This [Act] applies to every trust or decedent's estate existing on [the effective date of this [Act]] except as otherwise expressly provided in the will or terms of the trust or in this [Act].

PART V

~

UNIFORM PROBATE CODE ARTICLE II (1990, AS AMENDED)

UNIFORM PROBATE CODE ARTICLE II (1990, AS AMENDED)

PREFATORY NOTE

The Uniform Probate Code was promulgated in 1969. In 1990, Article II of the Code underwent significant revision. The 1990 revisions are the culmination of a systematic study of the Code conducted by the Joint Editorial Board for the Uniform Probate Code (JEB-UPC) and a special Drafting Committee to Revise Article II. The 1990 revisions concentrate on Article II, which is the article that covers the substantive law of intestate succession; spouse's elective share; omitted spouse and children; probate exemptions and allowances; execution and revocation of wills; will contracts; rules of construction; disclaimers; the effect of homicide and divorce on succession rights; and the rule against perpetuities and honorary trusts.

In the 20 or so years between the original promulgation of the Code and the 1990 revisions, several developments occurred that prompted the systematic round of review. Three themes were sounded: (1) the decline of formalism in favor of intent-serving policies; (2) the recognition that will substitutes and other inter-vivos transfers have so proliferated that they now constitute a major, if not the major, form of wealth transmission; (3) the advent of the multiple-marriage society, resulting in a significant fraction of the population being married more than once and having stepchildren and children by previous marriages and in the acceptance of a partnership or marital-sharing theory of marriage.

The 1990 revisions respond to these themes. The multiple-marriage society and the partnership/marital-sharing theory are reflected in the revised elective-share provisions of Part 2. As the General Comment to Part 2 explains, the revised elective share grants the surviving spouse a right of election that implements the partnership/marital-sharing theory by adjusting the elective share to the length of the marriage.

The children-of-previous-marriages and stepchildren phenomena are reflected most prominently in the revised rules on the spouse's share in intestacy.

The proliferation of will substitutes and other inter-vivos transfers is recognized, mainly, in measures tending to bring the law of probate and nonprobate transfers into greater unison. One aspect of this tendency is reflected in the restructuring of the rules of construction. Rules of construction are rules that supply presumptive meaning to dispositive and similar provisions of governing instruments. Part 6 of the pre-1990 Code contained several rules of construction that applied only to wills. Some of those rules of construction appropriately applied only to wills; provisions relating to lapse, testamentary exercise of a power of appointment, and ademption of a devise by satisfaction exemplify such rules of construction. Other rules of construction, however, properly apply to all governing instruments, not just wills; the provision relating to inclusion of adopted persons in class gift language exemplifies this type of rule of construction. The 1990 revisions divide pre-1990 Part 6 into two parts—Part 6, containing rules of construction for wills only; and Part 7, containing rules of construction for wills and other governing instruments. A few new rules of construction are also added.

In addition to separating the rules of construction into two parts, and adding new rules of construction, the revocation-upon-divorce provision (Section 2-804) is substantially revised so that divorce not only revokes devises, but also nonprobate beneficiary designations, in favor of the former spouse. Another feature of the 1990 revisions is a new section (Section 2-503) that brings the execution formalities for wills more into line with those for nonprobate transfers.

The 1990 Article II revisions also respond to other modern trends. During the period from 1969 to 1990, many developments occurred in the case law and statutory law. Also, many specific topics in probate, estate, and future-interests law were examined in the scholarly literature. The influence of many of these developments is seen in the 1990 revisions of Article II.

ARTICLE II

INTESTACY, WILLS, AND DONATIVE TRANSFERS (1990)

Part 1. Intestate Succession

§2-101. Intestate Estate
§2-102. Share of Spouse
§2-102A. Share of Spouse
§2-103. Share of Heirs Other Than Surviving Spouse
§2-104. Requirement That Heir Survive Decedent for 120 Hours
§2-105. No Taker
§2-106. Representation
§2-107. Kindred of Half Blood
§2-108. Afterborn Heirs
§2-109. Advancements
§2-110. Debts to Decedent
§2-111. Alienage

Part 1. Intestate Succession

General Comment

The pre-1990 Code's basic pattern of intestate succession, contained in Part 1, was designed to provide suitable rules for the person of modest means who relies on the estate plan provided by law. The 1990 revisions are intended to further that purpose, by fine-tuning the various sections and bringing them into line with developing public policy.

The principal features of the 1990 revisions are:

1. So-called negative wills are authorized, under which the decedent who dies intestate, in whole or in part, can by will disinherit a particular heir.

2. A surviving spouse receives the whole of the intestate estate, if the decedent left no surviving descendants and no parents or if the decedent's surviving descendants are also descendants of the surviving spouse and the surviving spouse has no descendants who are not descendants of the decedent. The surviving spouse receives the first $200,000 plus three-fourths of the balance if the decedent left no surviving descendants but a surviving parent. The surviving spouse receives the first $150,000 plus one-half of the balance of the intestate estate, if the decedent's surviving descendants are also descendants of the surviving spouse but the surviving spouse has one or more other descendants. The surviving spouse receives the first $100,000 plus one-half of the balance of the intestate estate, if the decedent has one or more surviving descendants who are not descendants of the surviving spouse.

3. A system of representation called per-capita-at-each-generation is adopted as a means of more faithfully carrying out the underlying premise of the pre-1990 UPC system of representation. Under the per-capita-at-each-generation system, all grandchildren (whose parent has predeceased the intestate) receive equal shares.

4. Although only a modest revision of the section dealing with the status of adopted children and children born of unmarried parents is made at this time, the question is under continuing review and further revisions may be presented in the future.

5. The section on advancements is revised so that it applies to partially intestate estates as well as to wholly intestate estates.

§2-101. Intestate Estate

(a) Any part of a decedent's estate not effectively disposed of by will passes by intestate succession to the decedent's heirs as prescribed in this Code, except as modified by the decedent's will.

(b) A decedent by will may expressly exclude or limit the right of an individual or class to succeed to property of the decedent passing by intestate succession. If that individual or a member of that class survives the decedent, the share of the decedent's intestate estate to which that individual or class would have succeeded passes as if that individual or each member of that class had disclaimed his [or her] intestate share.

§2-102. Share of Spouse

The intestate share of a decedent's surviving spouse is:

(1) the entire intestate estate if:

(i) no descendant or parent of the decedent survives the decedent; or

(ii) all of the decendent's surviving descendants are also descendants of the surviving spouse and there is no other descendant of the surviving spouse who survives the decedent;

(2) the first [$200,000], plus three-fourths of any balance of the intestate estate, if no descendant of the decedent survives the decedent, but a parent of the decedent survivies the decedent;

(3) the first [$150,000], plus one-half of any balance of the intestate estate, if all of the decedent's surviving descendants are also descendants of the surviving spouse and the surviving spouse has one or more surviving descendants who are not descendants of the decedent;

(4) the first [$100,000] plus one-half of any balance of the intestate estate, if one or more of the decedent's surviving descendants are not descendants of the surviving spouse.

[ALTERNATIVE PROVISION FOR COMMUNITY PROPERTY STATES]

§ 2-102A. Share of Spouse

(a) The instestate share of a surviving spouse in separate property is:

(1) the entire intestate estate if:

(i) no descentant or parent of the decedent survives the decedent; or

(ii) all of the decedent's surviving descendants are also descendants of the surviving spouse and there is no other descendant of the surviving spouse who survives the decedent;

(2) The first [$200,000], plus three-fourths of any balance of the intestate estate, if no descendant of the decedent survivies the decedent, but a parent of the decedent survives the decedent;

(3) the first [$150,000], plus one-half of any balance of the intestate estate, if all of the decedent's surviving descendants are also descendants of the surviving spouse and the surviving spouse has one of more surviving descendant's who are not descendants of the decedent;

(4) the first [$100,000], plus one-half of any balance of the intestate estate, if one or more of the decedent's surviving descendants are not descendants of the surviving spouse.

(b) The one-half of community property belonging to the decendent passes to the [surviving spouse] as the intestate share.]

Comment

Purpose and Scope of Revisions. This section is revised to give the surviving spouse a larger share than the pre-1990 UPC. If the decedent leaves no surviving descendants and no surviving parent or if the decedent does leave surviving descendants but neither the decedent nor the surviving spouse has other descendants, the surviving spouse is entitled to all of the decedent's intestate estate.

If the decedent leaves no surviving descendants but does leave a surviving parent, the decedent's surviving spouse receives the first $200,000 plus three-fourths of the balance of the intestate estate.

If the decedent leaves surviving descendants and if the surviving spouse (but not the decedent) has other descendants, and thus the decedent's descendants are unlikely to be the *exclusive* beneficiaries of the surviving spouse's estate, the surviving spouse receives the first $150,000 plus one-half of the balance of the intestate estate. The purpose is to assure the decedent's own descendants of a share in the decedent's intestate estate when the estate exceeds $150,000.

If the decedent has other descendants, the surviving spouse receives $100,000 plus one-half of the balance. In this type of case, the decedent's descendants who are not descendants of the surviving spouse are not natural objects of the bounty of the surviving spouse.

Note that in all the cases where the surviving spouse receives a lump sum plus a fraction of the balance, the lump sums must be understood to be in addition to the probate exemptions and allowances to which the surviving spouse is entitled. . . .

Under the pre-1990 Code, the decedent's surviving spouse received the entire intestate estate only if there were neither surviving descendants nor parents. If there were surviving descendants, the descendants took one-half of the balance of the estate in excess of $50,000 (for example, $25,000 in a $100,000 estate). If there were no surviving descendants, but there was a surviving parent or parents, the parent or parents took that one-half of the balance in excess of $50,000. . .

§2-103. Share of Heirs Other Than Surviving Spouse

Any part of the intestate estate not passing to the decedent's surviving spouse under Section 2-102, or the entire intestate estate if there is no surviving spouse, passes in the following order to the individuals designated below who survive the decedent:

(1) to the decedent's descendants by representation;

(2) if there is no surviving descendant, to the decedent's parents equally if both survive, or to the surviving parent;

(3) if there is no surviving descendant or parent, to the decendant's of the decedent's parents or either of them by representation;

(4) if there is no surviving descendant, parent, or descendant of a parent, but the decedent is survivied by one or more grandparents or descendants of grandparents, half of the estate passes to the decedent's paternal grandparents equally if both survive, or to the surviving paternal grandparent, or to the descendants of the decedent's paternal grandparents or either of them if both are deceased, the descendants taking by representation; and the other half passes to the decedent's maternal relatives in the same manner; but if there is no surviving grandparent or descendant of a grandparent on either the paternal or the materanl side, the entire estate passes to the decedent's relatives on the other side in the same manner as the half.

§2-104. Requirement That Heir Survive Decedent for 120 Hours

An individual who fails to survive the decedent by 120 hours is deemed to have predeceased the decedent for purposes of homestead allowance, exempt property, and intestate succession, and the decedent's heirs are determined accordingly. If it is not established by clear and convincing evidence that an individual who would otherwise be an heir survived the decedent by 120 hours, it is deemed that the individual failed to survive for the required period. This section is not to be applied if its application would result in a taking of intestate estate by the state under Section 2-105.

§2-105. No Taker

If there is no taker under the provisions of this Article, the intestate estate passes to the [state].

§2-106. Representation

(a) [Definitions.] In this section:

(1) "Deceased descendant," "deceased parent," or "deceased grandparent" means a descendant, parent, or grandparent who either predeceased the decedent or is deemed to have predeceased the decedent under Section 2-104.

(2) "Surviving descendant" means a descendant who neither predeceased the decedent nor is deemed to have predeceased the decedent under Section 2-104.

(b) [Decedent's Descendants.] If, under Section 2-103(1), a decedent's intestate estate or a part thereof passes "by representation" to the decedent's descendants, the estate or part thereof is divided into as many equal shares as there are (i) surviving descendants in the generation nearest to the decedent which contains one or more surviving descendants and (ii) deceased descendants in the same generation who left surviving descendants, if any. Each surviving descendant in the nearest generation is allocated one share. The remaining shares, if any, are combined and then divided in the same manner among the surviving descendants of the deceased descendants as if the surviving descendants who were allocated a share and their surviving descendants had predeceased the decedent.

(c) [Descendants of Parents or Grandparents.] If, under Section 2-103(3) or (4), a decedent's intestate estate or a part thereof passes "by representation" to the descendants of the decedent's deceased parents or either of them or to the descendants of the decedent's deceased paternal or maternal grandparents or either of them, the estate or part thereof is divided into as many equal shares as there are (i) surviving descendants in the generation nearest the deceased parents or either of them, or the deceased grandparents or either of them, that contains one or more surviving descendants and (ii) deceased descendants in the same generation who left surviving descendants, if any. Each surviving descendant in the nearest generation is allocated one share. The remaining shares, if any, are combined and then divided in the same manner among the surviving descendants of the deceased descendants as if the surviving descendants who were allocated a share and their surviving descendants had predeceased the decedent.

Comment

Purpose and Scope of Revisions. This section is revised to adopt the system of representation called per-capita-at-each-generation. The per-capita-at-each-generation system is more responsive to the underlying premise of the original UPC system, in that it always provides equal shares to those equally related; the pre-1990 UPC achieved this objective in most but not all cases. . . .

In addition, a recent survey of client preferences, conducted by Fellows of the American College of Trust and Estate Counsel, suggets that the per-capita-at-each-generation system of representation is preferred by most clients. See Young, "Meaning of 'Issue' and 'Descendants,'" 13 ACTEC Probate Notes 225 (1988). The survey results were striking: Of 761 responses, 541 (71%) chose the per-capita-at-each-generation system; 145 (19.1%) chose the per-stirpes system, and 70 (9.2%) chose the pre-1990 UPC system. . . .

§2-107. Kindred of Half Blood

Relatives of the half blood inherit the same share they would inherit if they were of the whole blood.

§2-108. Afterborn Heirs

An individual in gestation at a particular time is treated as living at that time if the individual lives 120 hours or more after birth.

§2-109. Advancements

(a) If an individual dies intestate as to all or a portion of his [or her] estate, property the decedent gave during the decedent's lifetime to an individual who, at the decedent's death, is an heir is treated as an advancement against the heir's intestate share only if (i) the decedent declared in a contemporaneous writing or the heir acknowledged in writing that the gift is an advancement or (ii) the decedent's contemporaneous writing or the heir's written acknowledgment otherwise indicates that the gift is to be taken into account in computing the division and distribution of the decedent's intestate estate.

(b) For purposes of subsection (a), property advanced is valued as of the time the heir came into possession or enjoyment of the property or as of the time of the decedent's death, whichever first occurs.

(c) If the recipient of the property fails to survive the decedent, the property is not taken into account in computing the division and distribution of the decedent's intestate estate, unless the decedent's contemporaneous writing provides otherwise.

§2-110. Debts to Decedent

A debt owed to a decedent is not charged against the intestate share of any individual except the debtor. If the debtor fails to survive the decedent, the debt is not taken into account in computing the intestate share of the debtor's descendants.

§2-111. Alienage

No individual is disqualified to take as an heir because the individual or an individual through whom he [or she] claims is or has been an alien.

§2-112. Dower and Curtesy Abolished

The estates of dower and curtesy are abolished.]

§2-113. Individuals Related to Decedent Through Two Lines

An individual who is related to the decedent through two lines of relationship is entitled to only a single share based on the relationship that would entitle the individual to the larger share.

§2-114. Parent and Child Relationship

(a) Except as provided in subsections (b) and (c), for purposes of intestate succession by, through, or from a person, an individual is the child of his [or her] natural parents, regardless of their marital status. The parent and child relationship may be established under [the Uniform Parentage Act] [applicable state law] [insert appropriate statutory reference].

(b) An adopted individual is the child of his [or her] adopting parent or parents and not of his [or her] natural parents, but adoption of a child by the spouse of either natural parent has no effect on (i) the relationship between the child and that natural parent or (ii) the right of the child or a descendant of the child to inherit from or through the other natural parent.

(c) Inheritance from or through a child by either natural parent or his [or her] kindred is precluded unless that natural parent has openly treated the child as his [or hers], and has not refused to support the child.

Part 2
Elective Share of Surviving Spouse

§ 2-201. Definitions

In this Part:

(1) As used in sections other than Section 2-205, "decedent's nonprobate transfers to others" means the amounts that are included in the augmented estate under Section 2-205.

(2) "Fractional interest in property held in joint tenancy with the right of survivorship," whether the fractional interest is unilaterally severable or not, means the fraction, the numerator of which is one and the denominator of which, if the decedent was a joint tenant, is one plus the number of joint tenants who survive the decedent and which, if the decedent was not a joint tenant, is the number of joint tenants.

(3) "Marriage," as it relates to a transfer by the decedent during marriage, means any marriage of the decedent to the decedent's surviving spouse.

(4) "Nonadverse party" means a person who does not have a substantial beneficial interest in the trust or other property arrangement that would be adversely affected by the exercise or nonexercise of the power that he [or she] possesses respecting the trust or other property arrangement. A person

having a general power of appointment over property is deemed to have a beneficial interest in the property.

(5) "Power" or "power of appointment" includes a power to designate the beneficiary of a beneficiary designation.

(6) "Presently exercisable general power of appointment" means a power of appointment under which, at the time in question, the decedent, whether or not he [or she] then had the capacity to exercise the power, held a power to create a present or future interest in himself [or herself], his [or her] creditors, his [or her] estate, or creditors of his [or her] estate, and includes a power to revoke or invade the principal of a trust or other property arrangement.

(7) "Probate estate" means property that would pass by intestate succession if the decedent died without a valid will.

(8) "Property" includes values subject to a beneficiary designation.

(9) "Right to income" includes a right to payments under a commercial or private annuity, an annuity trust, a unitrust, or a similar arrangement.

(10) "Transfer," as it relates to a transfer by or of the decedent, includes (A) an exercise or release of a presently exercisable general power of appointment held by the decedent, (B) a lapse at death of a presently exercisable general power of appointment held by the decedent, and (C) an exercise, release, or lapse of a general power of appointment that the decedent created in himself [or herself] and of a power described in Section 2-205(2)(ii) that the decedent conferred on a nonadverse party.

Comment

Pre-1990 Provision. The pre-1990 provisions granted the surviving spouse a one-third share of the augmented estate. The one-third fraction was largely a carry over from common-law dower, under which a surviving widow had a one-third interest for life in her deceased husband's life.

Purpose and Scope of Revisions. The revision of this section is the first step in the overall plan of implementing a partnership or marital-sharing theory of marriage, with a support theory back-up.

Subsection (a). Subsection (a) implements the partnership theory by increasing the maximum elective-share percentage of the augmented estate to fifty percent, but by phasing that ultimate entitlement in so that it does not reach the maximum fifty-percent level until the marriage has lasted at least 15 years. If the decedent and the surviving spouse were married to each other more than once, all periods of marriage to eachother are added together for purposes of subsection (a); periods between marriages are not counted.

Subsection (b). Subsection (b) implements the support theory of the elective share by providing a [$50,000] supplemental elective-share amount in case the surviving spouse's assets and other entitlements are below this figure. . . .

§2-202. Elective Share

(a) [Elective-Share Amount.] The surviving spouse of a decedent who dies domiciled in this State has a right of election, under the limitations and conditions stated in this Part, to take an elective-share amount equal to the value of the elective-share percentage of the augmented estate, determined by the length of time the spouse and the decedent were married to each other, in accordance with the following schedule:

If the decedent and the spouse were married to each other:	The elective-share percentage is:
Less than 1 year	Supplemental Amount Only.
1 year but less than 2 years	3% of the augmented estate.
2 years but less than 3 years	6% of the augmented estate.
3 years but less than 4 years	9% of the augmented estate.
4 years but less than 5 years	12% of the augmented estate.
5 years but less than 6 years	15% of the augmented estate.
6 years but less than 7 years	18% of the augmented estate.
7 years but less than 8 years	21% of the augmented estate.
8 years but less than 9 years	24% of the augmented estate.
9 years but less than 10 years	27% of the augmented estate.
10 years but less than 11 years	30% of the augmented estate.
11 years but less than 12 years	34% of the augmented estate.
12 years but less than 13 years	38% of the augmented estate.
13 years but less than 14 years	42% of the augmented estate.
14 years but less than 15 years	46% of the augmented estate.
15 years or more	50% of the augmented estate.

(b) [Supplemental Elective-Share Amount.] If the sum of the amounts described in Sections 2-207, 2-209(a)(1), and that part of the elective-share amount payable from the decedent's probate estate and nonprobate transfers to others under Section 2-209(b) and (c) is less than [$50,000], the surviving spouse is entitled to a supplemental elective-share amount equal to [$50,000], minus the sum of the amounts described in those sections. The supplemental elective-share amount is payable from the decedent's probate estate and from recipients of the decedent's nonprobate transfers to others in the order of priority set forth in Section 2-209(b) and (c).

(c) [Effect of Election on Statutory Benefits.] If the right of election is exercised by or on behalf of the surviving spouse, the surviving spouse's homestead allowance, exempt property, and family allowance, if any, are not charged against but are in addition to the elective-share and supplemental elective-share amounts.

(d) [Non-Domiciliary.] The right, if any, of the surviving spouse of a decedent who dies domiciled outside this State to take an elective share in property in this State is governed by the law of the decedent's domicile at death.

§2-203. Composition of the Augmented Estate

Subject to Section 2-208, the value of the augmented estate, to the extent provided in Sections 2-204, 2-205, 2-206, and 2-207, consists of the sum of the values of all property, whether real or personal; movable or immovable, tangible or intangible, wherever situated, that constitute the decedent's net probate estate, the decedent's nonprobate transfers to others, the decedent's nonprobate transfers to the surviving spouse, and the surviving spouse's property and nonprobate transfers to others.

§2-204. Decedent's Net Probate Estate

The value of the augmented estate includes the value of the decedent's probate estate, reduced by funeral and administration expenses, homestead allowance, family allowances, exempt property, and enforceable claims.

§2-205. Decedent's Nonprobate Transfers to Others

The value of the augmented estate includes the value of the decedent's nonprobate transfers to others, not included under Section 2-204, of any of the following types, in the amount provided respectively for each type of transfer:

(1) Property owned or owned in substance by the decedent immediately before death that passed outside probate at the decedent's death. Property included under this category consists of:

(i) Property over which the decedent alone, immediately before death, held a presently exercisable general power of appointment. The amount included is the value of the property subject to the power, to the extent the property passed at the decedent's death, by exercise, release, lapse, in default, or otherwise, to or for the benefit of any person other than the decedent's estate or surviving spouse.

(ii) The decedent's fractional interest in property held by the decedent in joint tenancy with the right of survivorship. The amount included is the value of the decedent's fractional interest, to the extent the fractional interest passed by right of survivorship at the decedent's death to a surviving joint tenant other than the decedent's surviving spouse.

(iii) The decedent's ownership interest in property or accounts held in POD, TOD, or co-ownership registration with the right of survivorship. The amount included is the value of the decedent's ownership interest, to the extent the decedent's ownership interest passed at the decedent's death to or for the benefit of any person other than the decedent's estate or surviving spouse.

(iv) Proceeds of insurance, including accidental death benefits, on the life of the decedent, if the decedent owned the insurance policy immediately before death or if and to the extent the decedent alone and immediately before death held a presently exercisable general power of appointment over the policy or its proceeds. The amount included is the value of the proceeds, to the extent they were payable at the decedent's death to or for the benefit of any person other than the decedent's estate or surviving spouse.

(2) Property transferred in any of the following forms by the decedent during marriage:

(i) Any irrevocable transfer in which the decedent retained the right to the possession or enjoyment of, or to the income from, the property if and to the extent the decedent's right terminated at or continued beyond the decedent's death. The amount included is the value of the fraction of the property to which the decedent's right related, to the extent the fraction of the property passed outside probate to or for the benefit of any person other than the decedent's estate or surviving spouse.

(ii) Any transfer in which the decedent created a power over income or property, exercisable by the decedent alone or in conjunction with any other person, or exercisable by a nonadverse party, to or for the benefit of the decedent, creditors of the decedent, the decedent's estate, or creditors of the decedent's estate. The amount included with respect to a power over property is the value of the property subject to the power, and the amount included with respect to a power over income is the value of the property that produces or produced the income, to the extent the power in either case was exercisable at the decedent's death to or for the benefit of any person other than the decedent's surviving spouse or to the extent the property passed at the decedent's death, by exercise, release, lapse, in default, or otherwise, to or for the benefit of any person other than the decedent's estate or surviving spouse. If the power is a power over both income and property and the preceding sentence produces different amounts, the amount included is the greater amount.

(3) Property that passed during marriage and during the two-year period next preceding the decedent's death as a result of a transfer by the decedent if the transfer was of any of the following types:

(i) Any property that passed as a result of the termination of a right or interest in, or power over, property that would have been included in the augmented estate under paragraph (1)(i), (ii), or (iii), or under paragraph (2), if the right, interest, or power had not terminated until the decedent's death. The amount included is the value of the property that would have been included under those paragraphs if the property were valued at the time the right, interest, or power terminated, and is included only to the extent the property passed upon termination to or for the benefit of any person other than the decedent or the decedent's estate, spouse, or surviving spouse. As used in this subparagraph, "termination," with respect to a right or interest in property, occurs when the right or interest terminated by the terms of the governing instrument or the decedent transferred or relinquished the right or interest, and, with respect to a power over property, occurs when the power terminated by exercise, release, lapse, default, or otherwise, but, with respect to a power described in paragraph (1)(i), "termination" occurs when the power terminated by exercise or release, but not otherwise.

(ii) Any transfer of or relating to an insurance policy on the life of the decedent if the proceeds would have been included in the augmented estate under paragraph (1)(iv) had the transfer not occurred. The amount included is the value of the insurance proceeds to the extent the proceeds were payable at the decedent's death to or for the benefit of any person other than the decedent's estate or surviving spouse.

(iii) Any transfer of property, to the extent not otherwise included in the augmented estate, made to or for the benefit of a person other than the decedent's surviving spouse. The amount included is the value of the transferred property to the extent the aggregate transfers to any one donee in either of the two years exceeded $10,000.

§2-206. Decedent's Nonprobate Transfers to the Surviving Spouse

Excluding property passing to the surviving spouse under the federal Social Security system, the value of the augmented estate includes the value of the decedent's nonprobate transfers to the decedent's surviving spouse, which consist of all property that passed outside probate at the decedent's death from the decedent to the surviving spouse by reason of the decedent's death, including:

(1) the decedent's fractional interest in property held as a joint tenant with the right of survivorship, to the extent that the decedent's fractional interest passed to the surviving spouse as surviving joint tenant,

(2) the decedent's ownership interest in property or accounts held in co-ownership registration with the right of survivorship, to the extent the decedent's ownership interest passed to the surviving spouse as surviving co-owner, and

(3) all other property that would have been included in the augmented estate under Section 2-205(1) or (2) had it passed to or for the benefit of a person other than the decedent's spouse, surviving spouse, the decedent, or the decedent's creditors, estate, or estate creditors.

§2-207. Surviving Spouse's Property and Nonprobate Transfers to Others

(a) [Included Property.] Except to the extent included in the augmented estate under Section 2-204 or 2-206, the value of the augmented estate includes the value of:

(1) property that was owned by the decedent's surviving spouse at the decedent's death, including:

(i) the surviving spouse's fractional interest in property held in joint tenancy with the right of survivorship,

(ii) the surviving spouse's ownership interest in property or accounts held in co-ownership registration with the right of survivorship, and

(iii) property that passed to the surviving spouse by reason of the decedent's death, but not including the spouse's right to homestead allowance, family allowance, exempt property, or payments under the federal Social Security system; and

(2) property that would have been included in the surviving spouse's nonprobate transfers to others, other than the spouse's fractional and ownership interests included under subsection (a)(1)(i) or (ii), had the spouse been the decedent.

(b) [Time of Valuation.] Property included under this section is valued at the decedent's death, taking the fact that the decedent predeceased the spouse into account, but, for purposes of subsection (a)(1)(i) and (ii), the values of the spouse's fractional and ownership interests are determined immediately before the decedent's death if the decedent was then a joint tenant or a co-owner of the property or accounts. For purposes of subsection (a)(2), proceeds of insurance that would have been included in the spouse's nonprobate transfers to others under Section 2-205(1)(iv) are not valued as if he [or she] were deceased.

(c) [Reduction for Enforceable Claims.] The value of property included under this section is reduced by enforceable claims against the surviving spouse.

§2-208. Exclusions, Valuation, and Overlapping Application

(a) [Exclusions.] The value of any property is excluded from the decedent's nonprobate transfers to others (i) to the extent the decedent received adequate and full consideration in money or money's worth for a transfer of the property or (ii) if the property was transferred with the written joinder of, or if the transfer was consented to in writing by, the surviving spouse.

(b) [Valuation.] The value of property:

(1) included in the augmented estate under Section 2-205, 2-206, or 2-207 is reduced in each category by enforceable claims against the included property; and

(2) includes the commuted value of any present or future interest and the commuted value of amounts payable under any trust, life insurance settlement option, annuity contract, public or private pension, disability compensation, death benefit or retirement plan, or any similar arrangement, exclusive of the federal Social Security system.

(c) [Overlapping Application; No Double Inclusion.] In case of overlapping application to the same property of the paragraphs or subparagraphs of Section 2-205, 2-206, or 2-207, the property is included in the augmented estate under the provision yielding the greatest value, and under only one overlapping provision if they all yield the same value.

§2-209. Sources from Which Elective Share Payable

(a) [Elective-Share Amount Only.] In a proceeding for an elective share, the following are applied first to satisfy the elective-share amount and to reduce or eliminate any contributions due from the decedent's probate estate and recipients of the decedent's nonprobate transfers to others:

(1) amounts included in the augmented estate under Section 2-204 which pass or have passed to the surviving spouse by testate or intestate succession and amounts included in the augmented estate under Section 2-206; and

(2) amounts included in the augmented estate under Section 2-207 up to the applicable percentage thereof. For the purposes of this subsection, the "applicable percentage" is twice the elective-share percentage set forth in the schedule in Section 2-202(a) appropriate to the length of time the spouse and the decedent were married to each other.

(b) [Unsatisfied Balance of Elective-Share Amount; Supplemental Elective-Share Amount.] If, after the application of subsection (a), the elective-share amount is not fully satisfied or the surviving spouse is entitled to a supplemental elective-share amount, amounts included in the decedent's probate estate and in the decedent's nonprobate transfers to others, other than amounts included under Section 2-205(3)(i) or (iii), are applied first to satisfy the unsatisfied balance of the elective-share amount or the supplemental elective-share amount. The decedent's probate estate and that portion of the decedent's nonprobate transfers to others are so applied that liability for the unsatisfied balance of the elective-share amount or for the supplemental elective-share amount is equitably apportioned among the recipients of the decedent's probate estate and of that portion of the decedent's nonprobate transfers to others in proportion to the value of their interests therein.

(c) [Unsatisfied Balance of Elective-Share and Supplemental Elective-Share Amounts.] If, after the application of subsections (a) and (b), the elective-share or supplemental elective-share amount is not fully satisfied, the remaining portion of the decedent's nonprobate transfers to others is so applied that liability for the unsatisfied balance of the elective-share or supplemental elective-share amount is equitably apportioned among the recipients of the remaining portion of the decedent's nonprobate transfers to others in proportion to the value of their interests therein.

§2-210. Personal Liability of Recipients

(a) Only original recipients of the decedent's nonprobate transfers to others, and the donees of the recipients of the decedent's nonprobate transfers to others, to the extent the donees have the property or its proceeds, are liable to make a proportional contribution toward satisfaction of the surviving spouse's elective-share or supplemental elective-share amount. A person liable to make contribution may choose to give up the proportional part of the decedent's nonprobate transfers to him [or her] or to pay the value of the amount for which he [or she] is liable.

(b) If any section or part of any section of this Part is preempted by federal law with respect to a payment, an item of property, or any other benefit included in the decedent's nonprobate transfers to others, a person who, not for value, receives the payment, item of property, or any other benefit is obligated to return the payment, item of property, or benefit, or is personally liable for the amount of the payment or the value of that item of property or benefit, as provided in Section 2-209, to the person who would have been entitled to it were that section or part of that section not preempted.

§2-211. Proceeding for Elective Share; Time Limit

(a) Except as provided in subsection (b), the election must be made by filing in the court and mailing or delivering to the personal representative, if any, a petition for the elective share within nine months after the date of the decedent's death, or within six months after the probate of the decedent's will, whichever limitation later expires. The surviving spouse must give notice of the time and place set for hearing to persons interested in the estate and to the distributees and recipients of portions of the augmented estate whose interests will be adversely affected by the taking of the elective share. Except as provided in subsection (b), the decedent's nonprobate transfers to others are not included within the augmented estate for the purpose of computing the elective-share, if the petition is filed more than nine months after the decedent's death.

(b) Within nine months after the decedent's death, the surviving spouse may petition the court for an extension of time for making an election. If, within nine months after the decedent's death, the spouse gives notice of the petition to all persons interested in the decedent's nonprobate transfers to others, the court for cause shown by the surviving spouse may extend the time for election. If the court grants the spouse's petition for an extension, the decedent's nonprobate transfers to others are not excluded from the augmented estate for the purpose of computing the elective-share and supplemental elective-share amounts, if the spouse makes an election by filing in the court and mailing or delivering to the personal representative, if any, a petition for the elective share within the time allowed by the extension.

(c) The surviving spouse may withdraw his [or her] demand for an elective share at any time before entry of a final determination by the court.

(d) After notice and hearing, the court shall determine the elective-share and supplemental elective-share amounts, and shall order its payment from the assets of the augmented estate or by contribution as appears appropriate under Sections 2-209 and 2-210. If it appears that a fund or property included in the augmented estate has not come into the possession of the personal representative, or has been distributed by the personal representative, the court nevertheless shall fix the liability of any person who has any interest in the fund or property or who has possession thereof, whether as trustee or otherwise. The proceeding may be maintained against fewer than all persons against whom relief could be sought, but no person is subject to contribution in any greater amount than he [or she] would have been under Sections 2-209 and 2-210 had relief been secured against all persons subject to contribution.

(e) An order or judgment of the court may be enforced as necessary in suit for contribution or payment in other courts of this State or other jurisdictions.

§2-212. Right of Election Personal to Surviving Spouse; Incapacitated Surviving Spouse

(a) [Surviving Spouse Must Be Living at Time of Election.] The right of election may be exercised only by a surviving spouse who is living when the petition for the elective share is filed in the court under Section 2-211(a). If the election is not exercised by the surviving spouse personally, it may be exercised on the surviving spouse's behalf by his [or her] conservator, guardian, or agent under the authority of a power of attorney.

(b) [Incapacitated Surviving Spouse.] If the election is exercised on behalf of a surviving spouse who is an incapacitated person, that portion of the elective-share and supplemental elective-share amounts due from the decedent's probate estate and recipients of the decedent's nonprobate transfers to others under Section 2-209(b) and (c) must be placed in a custodial trust for the benefit of the surviving spouse under the provisions of the [Enacting state] Uniform Custodial Trust Act, except as modified below. For the purposes of this subsection, an election on behalf of a surviving spouse by an agent under a durable power of attorney is presumed to be on behalf of a surviving spouse who is an incapacitated person. For purposes of the custodial trust established by this subsection, (i) the electing guardian, conservator, or agent is the custodial trustee, (ii) the surviving spouse is the beneficiary, and (iii) the custodial trust is deemed to have been created by the decedent spouse by written transfer that takes effect at the decedent spouse's death and that directs the custodial trustee to administer the custodial trust as for an incapacitated beneficiary.

(c) [Custodial Trust.] For the purposes of subsection (b), the [Enacting state] Uniform Custodial Trust Act must be applied as if Section 6(b) thereof were repealed and Sections 2(e), 9(b), and 17(a) were amended to read as follows:

(1) Neither an incapacitated beneficiary nor anyone acting on behalf of an incapacitated beneficiary has a power to terminate the custodial trust; but if the beneficiary regains capacity, the beneficiary then acquires the power to terminate the custodial trust by delivering to the custodial trustee a writing signed by the beneficiary declaring the termination. If not previously terminated, the custodial trust terminates on the death of the beneficiary.

(2) If the beneficiary is incapacitated, the custodial trustee shall expend so much or all of the custodial trust property as the custodial trustee considers advisable for the use and benefit of the beneficiary and individuals who were supported by the beneficiary when the beneficiary became incapacitated, or who are legally entitled to support by the beneficiary. Expenditures may be made in the manner, when, and to the extent that the custodial trustee determines suitable and proper, without court order but with regard to other support, income, and property of the beneficiary [exclusive of] [and] benefits of medical or other forms of assistance from any state or federal government or governmental agency for which the beneficiary must qualify on the basis of need.

(3) Upon the beneficiary's death, the custodial trustee shall transfer the unexpended custodial trust property in the following order: (i) under the residuary clause, if any, of the will of the beneficiary's predeceased spouse against whom the elective share was taken, as if that predeceased spouse died immediately after the beneficiary; or (ii) to that predeceased spouse's heirs under Section 2-711 of [this State's] Uniform Probate Code.

[STATES THAT HAVE NOT ADOPTED THE UNIFORM CUSTODIAL TRUST ACT SHOULD ADOPT THE FOLLOWING ALTERNATIVE SUBSECTION (b) AND NOT ADOPT SUBSECTION (b) OR (c) ABOVE]

[(b) [Incapacitated Surviving Spouse.] If the election is exercised on behalf of a surviving spouse who is an incapacitated person, the court must set aside that portion of the elective-share and supplemental elective-share amounts due from the decedent's probate estate and recipients of the decedent's nonprobate transfers to others under Section 2-209(b) and (c) and must appoint a trustee to administer that property for the support of the surviving spouse. For the purposes of this subsection, an election on behalf of a surviving spouse by an agent under a durable power of attorney is presumed to be on behalf of a surviving spouse who is an incapacitated person. The trustee must administer the trust in accordance with the following terms and such additional terms as the court determines appropriate:

(1) Expenditures of income and principal may be made in the manner, when, and to the extent that the trustee determines suitable and proper for the surviving spouse's support, without court order but with regard to other support, income, and property of the surviving spouse [exclusive of] [and] benefits of medical or other forms of assistance from any state or federal government or governmental agency for which the surviving spouse must qualify on the basis of need.

(2) During the surviving spouse's incapacity, neither the surviving spouse nor anyone acting on behalf of the surviving spouse has a power to terminate the trust; but if the surviving spouse regains capacity, the surviving spouse then acquires the power to terminate the trust and acquire full ownership of the trust property free of trust, by delivering to the trustee a writing signed by the surviving spouse declaring the termination.

(3) Upon the surviving spouse's death, the trustee shall transfer the unexpended trust property in the following order: (i) under the residuary clause, if any, of the will of the predeceased spouse against whom the elective share was taken, as if that predeceased spouse died immediately

after the surviving spouse; or (ii) to the predeceased spouse's heirs under Section 2-711.]

§2-213. Waiver of Right to Elect and of Other Rights

(a) The right of election of a surviving spouse and the rights of the surviving spouse to homestead allowance, exempt property, and family allowance, or any of them, may be waived, wholly or partially, before or after marriage, by a written contract, agreement, or waiver signed by the surviving spouse.

(b) A surviving spouse's waiver is not enforceable if the surviving spouse proves that:

(1) he [or she] did not execute the waiver voluntarily; or

(2) the waiver was unconscionable when it was executed and, before execution of the waiver, he [or she]:

(i) was not provided a fair and reasonable disclosure of the property or financial obligations of the decedent;

(ii) did not voluntarily and expressly waive, in writing, any right to disclosure of the property or financial obligations of the decedent beyond the disclosure provided; and

(iii) did not have, or reasonably could not have had, an adequate knowledge of the property or financial obligations of the decedent.

(c) An issue of unconscionability of a waiver is for decision by the court as a matter of law.

(d) Unless it provides to the contrary, a waiver of "all rights," or equivalent language, in the property or estate of a present or prospective spouse or a complete property settlement entered into after or in anticipation of separation or divorce is a waiver of all rights of elective share, homestead allowance, exempt property, and family allowance by each spouse in the property of the other and a renunciation by each of all benefits that would otherwise pass to him [or her] from the other by intestate succession or by virtue of any will executed before the waiver or property settlement.

§2-214. Protection of Payors and Other Third Parties

(a) Although under Section 2-205 a payment, item of property, or other benefit is included in the decedent's nonprobate transfers to others, a payor or other third party is not liable for having made a payment or transferred an item of property or other benefit to a beneficiary designated in a governing instrument, or for having taken any other action in good faith reliance on the validity of a governing instrument, upon request and satisfactory proof of the decedent's death, before the payor or other third party received written notice from the surviving spouse or spouse's representative of an intention to file a petition for the elective share or that a petition for the elective share has been filed. A payor or other third party is liable for payments made or other actions taken after the payor or other third party received written notice of an intention to file a petition for the elective share or that a petition for the elective share has been filed.

(b) A written notice of intention to file a petition for the elective share or that a petition for the elective share has been filed must be mailed to the payor's or other third party's main office or home by registered or certified mail, return receipt requested, or served upon the payor or other third party in the same manner as a summons in a civil action. Upon receipt of written notice of intention to file a petition for the elective share or that a petition for the elective share has been filed, a payor or other third party may pay any amount owed or transfer or deposit any item of property held by it to or with the court having jurisdiction of the probate proceedings relating to the decedent's estate, or if no proceedings have been commenced, to or with the court having jurisdiction of probate proceedings relating to decedents' estates located in the county of the decedent's residence. The court shall hold the funds or item of property, and, upon its determination under Section 2-211(d), shall order disbursement in accordance with the determination. If no petition is filed in the court within the specified time under Section 2-211(a) or, if filed, the demand for an elective share is withdrawn under Section 2-211(c), the court shall order disbursement to the designated beneficiary. Payments or transfers to the court or deposits made into court discharge the payor or other third party from all claims for amounts so paid or the value of property so transferred or deposited.

(c) Upon petition to the probate court by the beneficiary designated in a governing instrument, the court may order that all or part of the property be paid to the beneficiary in an amount and subject to conditions consistent with this Part.

Part 3
Spouse and Children Unprovided for in Wills

§2-301. Entitlement of Spouse; Premarital Will

(a) If a testator's surviving spouse married the testator after the testator executed his [or her] will, the surviving spouse is entitled to receive, as an intestate share, no less than the value of the share of the estate he [or she] would have received if the testator had died intestate as to that portion of the testator's estate, if any, that neither is devised to a child of the testator who was born before the testator married the surviving spouse and who is not a child of the surviving spouse nor is devised to a descendant of such a child or passes under Sections 2-603 or 2-604 to such a child or to a descendant of such a child, unless:

(1) it appears from the will or other evidence that the will was made in contemplation of the testator's marriage to the surviving spouse;

(2) the will expresses the intention that it is to be effective notwithstanding any subsequent marriage; or

(3) the testator provided for the spouse by transfer outside the will and the intent that the transfer be in lieu of a testamentary provision is shown by the testator's

statements or is reasonably inferred from the amount of the transfer or other evidence.

(b) In satisfying the share provided by this section, devises made by the will to the testator's surviving spouse, if any, are applied first, and other devises, other than a devise to a child of the testator who was born before the testator married the surviving spouse and who is not a child of the surviving spouse or a devise or substitute gift under Section 2-603 or 2-604 to a descendant of such a child, abate as provided in Section 3-902.

As amended in 1993.

§ 2-302. Omitted Children

(a) Except as provided in subsection (b), if a testator fails to provide in his [or her] will for any of his [or her] children born or adopted after the execution of the will, the omitted after-born or after-adopted child receives a share in the estate as follows:

(1) If the testator had no child living when he [or she] executed the will, an omitted after-born or after-adopted child receives a share in the estate equal in value to that which the child would have received had the testator died intestate, unless the will devised all or substantially all of the estate to the other parent of the omitted child and that other parent survives the testator and is entitled to take under the will.

(2) If the testator had one or more children living when he [or she] executed the will, and the will devised property or an interest in property to one or more of the then-living children, an omitted after-born or after-adopted child is entitled to share in the testator's estate as follows:

(i) The portion of the testator's estate in which the omitted after-born or after-adopted child is entitled to share is limited to devises made to the testator's then-living children under the will.

(ii) The omitted after-born or after-adopted child is entitled to receive the share of the testator's estate, as limited in subparagraph (i), that the child would have received had the testator included all omitted after-born and after-adopted children with the children to whom devises were made under the will and had given an equal share of the estate to each child.

(iii) To the extent feasible, the interest granted an omitted after-born or after-adopted child under this section must be of the same character, whether equitable or legal, present or future, as that devised to the testator's then-living children under the will.

(iv) In satisfying a share provided by this paragraph, devises to the testator's children who were living when the will was executed abate ratably. In abating the devises of the then-living children, the court shall preserve to the maximum extent possible the character of the testamentary plan adopted by the testator.

(b) Neither subsection (a)(1) nor subsection (a)(2) applies if:

(1) it appears from the will that the omission was intentional; or

(2) the testator provided for the omitted after-born or after-adopted child by transfer outside the will and the intent that the transfer be in lieu of a testamentary provision is shown by the testator's statements or is reasonably inferred from the amount of the transfer or other evidence.

(c) If at the time of execution of the will the testator fails to provide in his [or her] will for a living child solely because he [or she] believes the child to be dead, the child is entitled to share in the estate as if the child were an omitted after-born or after-adopted child.

(d) In satisfying a share provided by subsection (a)(1), devises made by the will abate under Section 3-902.

As amended in 1991 and 1993.

Comment

This section provides for both the case where a child was born or adopted after the execution of the will and not foreseen at the time and thus not provided for in the will, and the rare case where a testator omits one of his or her children because of the mistaken belief that the child is dead.

Basic Purpose and Scope of Revisions. This section is substantially revised. The revisions have two basic objectives. The first basic objective is to provide that a will that devised, under trust or not, all or substantially all of the testator's estate to the other parent of the omitted child prevents an after-born or after-adopted child from taking an intestate share if none of the testator's children was living when he or she executed the will. (Under this rule, the other parent must survive the testator and be entitled to take under the will.)

Under the pre-1990 Code, such a will prevented the omitted child's entitlement only if the testator had one or more children living when he or she executed the will. The rationale for the revised rule is found in the empirical evidence . . . that suggests that even testators with children tend to devise their entire estates to their surviving spouses, especially in smaller estates. The testator's purpose is not to disinherit the children; rather, such a will evidences a purpose to trust the surviving parent to use the property for the benefit of the children, as appropriate. This attitude of trust of the surviving parent carries over to the case where none of the children have been born when the will is executed.

The second basic objective of the revisions is to provide that if the testator had children when he or she executed the will, and if the will made provision for one or more of the then-living children, an omitted after-born or after-adopted child does not take a full intestate share (which might be substantially larger or substantially smaller than given to the living children). Rather, the omitted after-born or after-adopted child participates on a pro rate basis in the property devised, under trust or not, to the then-living children. . . .

Part 4
Exempt Property and Allowances

General Comment

For decedents who die domiciled in this State, this part grants various allowances to the decedent's surviving spouse and certain children. The allowances have priority over unsecured creditors of the estate and persons to whom the estate may be devised by will. If there is a surviving spouse, all of the allowances described in this Part, which (as revised to adjust for inflation) total $25,000, plus whatever is allowed to the spouse for support during administration, normally pass to the spouse. If the surviving spouse and minor or dependent children live apart from one another, the minor or dependent children may receive some of the support allowance. If there is no surviving spouse, minor or dependent children become entitled to the homestead exemption of $15,000 and to support allowances. The exempt property section confers rights on the spouse, if any, or on all children, to $10,000 in certain chattels, or funds if the unencumbered value of chattels is below the $10,000 level. This provision is designed in part to relieve a personal representative of the duty to sell household chattels when there are children who will have them.

These family protection provisions supply the basis for the important small estate provisions of Article III, Part 12.

States adopting the Code may see fit to alter the dollar amounts suggested in these sections, or to vary the terms and conditions in other ways so as to accommodate existing traditions. Although creditors of estates would be aided somewhat if all family exemption provisions relating to probate estates were the same throughout the country, there is probably less need for uniformity of law regarding these provisions than for any of the other parts of this article. Still, it is quite important for all states to limit their homestead, support allowance and exempt property provisions, if any, so that they apply only to estates of decedents who were domiciliaries of the state.

Cross Reference. Notice that under Section 2-104 a spouse or child claiming under this Part must survive the decedent by 120 hours.

§2-401. Applicable Law

This Part applies to the estate of a decedent who dies domiciled in this State. Rights to homestead allowance, exempt property, and family allowance for a decedent who dies not domiciled in this State are governed by the law of the decedent's domicile at death.

§2-402. Homestead Allowance

A decedent's surviving spouse is entitled to a homestead allowance of [$15,000]. If there is no surviving spouse, each minor child and each dependent child of the decedent is entitled to a homestead allowance amounting to [$15,000] divided by the number of minor and dependent children of the decedent. The homestead allowance is exempt from and has priority over all claims against the estate. Homestead allowance is in addition to any share passing to the surviving spouse or minor or dependent child by the will of the decedent, unless otherwise provided, by intestate succession, or by way of elective share.

§2-402A. Constitutional Homestead

The value of any constitutional right of homestead in the family home received by a surviving spouse or child must be charged against the spouse or child's homestead allowance to the extent the family home is part of the decedent's estate or would have been but for the homestead provision of the constitution.]

§2-403. Exempt Property

In addition to the homestead allowance, the decedent's surviving spouse is entitled from the estate to a value, not exceeding $10,000 in excess of any security interests therein, in household furniture, automobiles, furnishings, appliances, and personal effects. If there is no surviving spouse, the decedent's children are entitled jointly to the same value. If encumbered chattels are selected and the value in excess of security interests, plus that of other exempt property, is less than $10,000, or if there is not $10,000 worth of exempt property in the estate, the spouse or children are entitled to other assets of the estate, if any, to the extent necessary to make up the $10,000 value. Rights to exempt property and assets needed to make up a deficiency of exempt property have priority over all claims against the estate, but the right to any assets to make up a deficiency of exempt property abates as necessary to permit earlier payment of homestead allowance and family allowance. These rights are in addition to any benefit or share passing to the surviving spouse or children by the decedent's will, unless otherwise provided, by intestate succession, or by way of elective share.

§2-404. Family Allowance

(a) In addition to the right to homestead allowance and exempt property, the decedent's surviving spouse and minor children whom the decedent was obligated to support and children who were in fact being supported by the decedent are entitled to a reasonable allowance in money out of the estate for their maintenance during the period of administration, which allowance may not continue for longer than one year if the estate is inadequate to discharge allowed claims. The allowance may be paid as a lump sum or in periodic installments. It is payable to the surviving spouse, if living, for the use of the surviving spouse and minor and dependent children; otherwise to the children, or persons having their care and custody. If a minor child or dependent child is not living with the surviving spouse, the allowance may be made partially to the child or his [or her] guardian or other person having the child's care and custody, and partially to the spouse, as their needs may appear. The family allowance is exempt from and has priority over all claims except the homestead allowance.

(b) The family allowance is not chargeable against any benefit or share passing to the surviving spouse or children by the will of the decedent, unless otherwise provided, by intestate succession or by way of elective share. The death of any person entitled to family allowance terminates the right to allowances not yet paid.

§2-405. Source, Determination, and Documentation

(a) If the estate is otherwise sufficient, property specifically devised may not be used to satisfy rights to homestead allowance or exempt property. Subject to this restriction, the surviving spouse, guardians of minor children, or children who are adults may select property of the estate as homestead allowance and exempt property. The personal representative may make those selections if the surviving spouse, the children, or the guardians of the minor children are unable or fail to do so within a reasonable time or there is no guardian of a minor child. The personal representative may execute an instrument or deed of distribution to establish the ownership of property taken as homestead allowance or exempt property. The personal representative may determine the family allowance in a lump sum not exceeding $18,000 or periodic installments not exceeding $1,500 per month for one year, and may disburse funds of the estate in payment of the family allowance and any part of the homestead allowance payable in cash. The personal representative or an interested person aggrieved by any selection, determination, payment, proposed payment, or failure to act under this section may petition the court for appropriate relief, which may include a family allowance other than that which the personal representative determined or could have determined.

(b) If the right to an elective share is exercised on behalf of a surviving spouse who is an incapacitated person, the personal representative may add any unexpended portions payable under the homestead allowance, exempt property, and family allowance to the trust established under Section 2-212(b).

As amended in 1993.

Part 5
Wills, Will Contracts, and Custody and Deposit of Wills

General Comment

Part 5 of Article II is retitled to reflect the fact that it now includes the provisions on will contracts (pre-1990 Section 2-701) and on custody and deposit of wills (pre-1990 Sections 2-901 and 2-902).

Part 5 deals with capacity and formalities for execution and revocation of wills. The basic intent of the pre-1990 sections was to validate wills whenever possible. To that end, the minimum age for making wills was lowered to eighteen, formalities for a written and attested will were reduced, holographic wills written and signed by the testator were authorized, choice of law as to validity of execution was broadened, and revocation by operation of law was limited to divorce or annulment. In addition, the statute also provided for an optional method of execution with acknowledgment before a public officer (the self-proved will).

These measures have been retained, and the purpose of validating wills whenever possible has been strengthened by the addition of a new section, Section 2-503, which allows a will to be upheld despite a harmless error in it execution.

§2-501. Who May Make Will

An individual 18 or more years of age who is of sound mind may make a will.

§2-502. Execution; Witnessed Wills; Holographic Wills

(a) Except as provided in subsection (b) and in Sections 2-503, 2-506, and 2-513, a will must be:

(1) in writing;

(2) signed by the testator or in the testator's name by some other individual in the testator's conscious presence and by the testator's direction; and

(3) signed by at least two individuals, each of whom signed within a reasonable time after he [or she] witnessed either the signing of the will as described in paragraph (2) or the testator's acknowledgment of that signature or acknowledgment of the will.

(b) A will that does not comply with subsection (a) is valid as a holographic will, whether or not witnessed, if the signature and material portions of the document are in the testator's handwriting.

(c) Intent that the document constitute the testator's will can be established by extrinsic evidence, including, for holographic wills, portions of the document that are not in the testator's handwriting.

§2-503. Writings Intended as Wills, etc.

Although a document or writing added upon a document was not executed in compliance with Section 2-502, the document or writing is treated as if it had been executed in compliance with that section if the proponent of the document or writing establishes by clear and convincing evidence that the decedent intended the document or writing to constitute (i) the decedent's will, (ii) a partial or complete revocation of the will, (iii) an addition to or an alteration of the will, or (iv) a partial or complete revival of his [or her] formerly revoked will or of a formerly revoked portion of the will.

Comment

Purpose of New Section. By way of dispensing power, this new section allows the probate court to excuse a harmless error in complying with the formal requirements for executing or revoking a will. The measure accords with legislation in force in the Canadian province of Manitoba and in several Australian jurisdictions. The Uniform Laws Conference of Canada approved a comparable measure for the Canadian Uniform Wills Act in 1987.

Legislation of this sort was enacted in the state of South Australia in 1975. The experience there has been closely studied by a variety of law reform commissions and in the scholarly literature. See, e.g., Law Reform Commission of British Columbia, Report on the Making and Revocation of Wills (1981); New South Wales Law Reform Commission Wills: Execution and Revocation (1986); Langbein, Excusing Harmless Errors in the Execution of Wills: A Report on Australia's Tranquil Revolution in Probate Law, 87 Colum. L. Rev. 1 (1987). A similar measure has been in effect in Israel since 1965 (see British Columbia Report, supra, at 44-46; Langbein, supra, at 48-51).

Consistent with the general trend of the revisions of the UPC, Section 2-503 unifies the law of probate and nonprobate transfers, extending to will formalities the harmless error principle that has long been applied to defective compliance with the formal requirements for nonprobate transfers. See, e.g., Annot., 19 A.L.R.2d 5 (1951) (life insurance beneficiary designation).

Evidence from South Australia suggests that the dispensing power will be applied mainly in two sorts of cases. See Langbein, *supra*, at 15-33. When the testator misunderstands the attestation requirements of Section 2-502(a) and englects to obtain one or both witnesses, new Section 2-503 permits the proponents of the will to prove that the defective execution did not result from irresolution or from circumstances suggesting duress or trickery—in other words, that the defect was harmless to the purpose of the formality. The measure reduces the tension between holographic wills and the two-witness requirement for attested wills under Section 2-502(a). Ordinarily, the testator who attempts to make an attested will but blunders will still have achieved a level of formality that compares favorably with that permitted for holographic wills under the Code.

The other recurrent class of case in which the dispensing power has been invoked in South Australia entails alterations to a previously executed will. Sometimes the testator adds a clause, that is, the testator attempts to interpolate a defectively executed codicil. More frequently, the amendment has the character of a revision—the testator crosses out former text and inserts replacement terms. Lay persons do not always understand that the execution and revocation requirements of Section 2-503 call for fresh execution in order to modify a will; rather, lay persons often think that the original execution has continuing effect.

By placing the burden of proof upon the proponent of a defective instrument, and by requiring the proponent to discharge that burden by clear and convincing evidence (which courts at the trial and appellate levels are urged to police with rigor), Section 2-503 imposes procedural standards appropriate to the seriousness of the issue. Experience in Israel and South Australia strongly supports the view that a dispensing power like Section 2-503 will not breed litigation. Indeed, as an Israeli judge reported to the British Law Reform Commission, the dispensing power "actually prevents a great deal of unnecessary litigation," because it eliminates disputes about technical lapses and limits the zone of dispute to the functional question of whether the instrument correctly expresses the testator's intent. British Columbia Report, *supra*, at 46.

The larger the departure from Section 2-502 formality, the harder it will be to satisfy the court that the instrument reflects the testator's intent. Whereas the South Australian and Israeli courts lightly excuse breaches of the attestation requirements, they have never excused noncompliance with the requirement that a will be in writing, and they have been extremely reluctant to excuse noncompliance with the signature requirement. See Langbein, *supra*, at 23-29, 49-50. The main circumstance in which the South Australian courts have excused signature errors has been in the recurrent class of cases in which two wills are prepared for simultaneous execution by two testators, typically husband and wife, and each mistakenly signs the will prepared for the other. E.g., Estate of Blakely, 32 S.A.S.R. 473 (1983). Recently, the New York Court of Appeals remedied such a case without aid of statute, simply on the ground "what has occurred is so obvious, and what was intended so clear." In re Snide, 52 N.Y.2d 193, 196, 418 N.E.2d 656, 657, 437 N.Y.S.2d 63, 64 (1981).

Section 2-503 means to retain the intent-serving benefits of Section 2-502 formality without inflicting intent-defeating outcomes in cases of harmless error.

Reference. The rule of this section is supported by the Restatement (Second) of Property (Donative Transfers) §33.1 comment g (as approved by the American Law Institute at the 1990 annual meeting).

§2-504. Self-Proved Will

(a) A will may be simultaneously executed, attested, and made self-proved, by acknowledgment thereof by the testator and affidavits of the witnesses, each made before an officer authorized to administer oaths under the laws of the state in which execution occurs and evidenced by the officer's certificate, under official seal, in substantially the following form:

I, _______, the testator, sign my name to this instrument this ____ day of _______, and being first duly sworn, do hereby declare to the undersigned authority that I sign and execute this instrument as my will and that I sign it willingly (or willingly direct another to sign for me), that I execute it as my free and voluntary act for the purposes therein expressed, and that I am eighteen years of age or older, of sound mind, and under no constraint or undue influence.

____
Testator

We, _______, _______, the witnesses, sign our names to this instrument, being first duly sworn, and do hereby declare to the undersigned authority that the testator signs and executes this instrument as [his] [her] will and that [he] [she] signs it willingly (or willingly directs another to sign for [him] [her]), and that each of us, in the presence and hearing of the testator, hereby signs this will as witness to the testator's signing, and that to the best of our knowledge the testator is eighteen years of age or older, of sound mind, and under no constraint or undue influence.

____
Witness

____
Witness

The State of _______
County of _______
Subscribed, sworn to and acknowledged before me by _______, the testator, and subscribed and sworn to before me by _______, and _______, witness, this ____ day of _______.

(Signed) _____________________

____
(Official capacity of officer)

(b) An attested will may be made self-proved at any time after its execution by the acknowledgment thereof by the testator and the affidavits of the witnesses, each made before an officer authorized to administer oaths under the laws of the state in which the acknowledgment occurs and evidenced by the officer's certificate, under the official seal, attached or annexed to the will in substantially the following form:

The State of _______
County of _______
We, _______, _______, and _______, the testator and the witnesses, respectively, whose names are signed to the attached or foregoing instrument, being first duly sworn, do hereby declare to the undersigned authority that the testator signed and executed the instrument as the testator's will and that [he] [she] had signed willingly (or willingly directed another to sign for [him] [her]), and that [he] [she] executed it as [his] [her] free and voluntary act for the purposes therein expressed, and that each of the witnesses, in the presence and hearing of the testator, signed the will as witness and that to the best of [his] [her] knowledge the testator was at that time eighteen years or age or older, of sound mind, and under no constraint or undue influence.

____
Testator

____
Witness

____
Witness

Subscribed, sworn to and acknowledged before me by _______, the testator, and subscribed and sworn to before me by _______, and _______, witnesses, this ____ of _______.

(Seal)

(Signed) _____________________

____
(Official capacity of officer)

(c) A signature affixed to a self-proving affidavit attached to a will is considered a signature affixed to the will, if necessary to prove the will's due execution.

Comment

A self-proved will may be admitted to probate as provided . . . without the testimony of any subscribing witness, but otherwise it is treated no differently from a will not self proved. . . .

A new subsection (c) is added to counteract an unfortunate judicial interpretation of similar self-proving will provisions in a few states, under which a signature on the self-proving affidavit has been held not to constitute a signature on the will, resulting in invalidity of the will in cases where the testator or witnesses got confused and only signed on the self-proving affidavit. . .

§2-505. Who May Witness

(a) An individual generally competent to be a witness may act as a witness to a will.

(b) The signing of a will by an interested witness does not invalidate the will or any provision of it.

§2-506. Choice of Law as to Execution

A written will is valid if executed in compliance with Section 2-502 or 2-503 or if its execution complies with the law at the time of execution of the place where the will is executed, or of the law of the place where at the time of execution or at the time of death the testator is domiciled, has a place of abode, or is a national.

§2-507. Revocation by Writing or by Act

(a) A will or any part thereof is revoked:

(1) by executing a subsequent will that revokes the previous will or part expressly or by inconsistency; or

(2) by performing a revocatory act on the will, if the testator performed the act with the intent and for the purpose of revoking the will or part or if another individual performed the act in the testator's conscious presence and by the testator's direction. For purposes of this paragraph, "revocatory act on the will" includes burning , tearing, canceling, obliterating, or destroying the will or any part of it. A burning, tearing, or canceling is a "revocatory act on the will," whether or not the burn, tear, or cancellation touched any of the words on the will.

(b) If a subsequent will does not expressly revoke a previous will, the execution of the subsequent will wholly revokes the previous will by inconsistency if the testator intended the subsequent will to replace rather than supplement the previous will.

(c) The testator is presumed to have intended a subsequent will to replace rather than supplement a previous will if the subsequent will makes a complete disposition of the testator's estate. If this presumption arises and is not rebutted by clear and convincing evidence, the previous will is revoked; only the subsequent will is operative on the testator's death.

(d) The testator is presumed to have intended a subsequent will to supplement rather than replace a previous will if the subsequent will does not make a complete disposition of the testator's estate. If this presumption arises and is not rebutted by clear and convincing evidence, the subsequent will revokes the previous will only to the extent the subsequent will is inconsistent with the previous will; each will is fully operative on the testator's death to the extent they are not inconsistent.

§2-508. Revocation by Change of Circumstances

Except as provided in Sections 2-803 and 2-804, a change of circumstances does not revoke a will or any part of it.

§2-509. Revival of Revoked Will

(a) If a subsequent will that wholly revoked a previous will is thereafter revoked by a revocatory act under Section 2-507(a)(2), the previous will remains revoked unless it is revived. The previous will is revived if it is evident from the circumstances of the revocation of the subsequent will or from the testator's contemporary or subsequent declarations that the testator intended the previous will to take effect as executed.

(b) If a subsequent will that partly revoked a previous will is thereafter revoked by a revocatory act under Section 2-507(a)(2), a revoked part of the previous will is revived unless it is evident from the circumstances of the revocation of the subsequent will or from the testator's contemporary or subsequent declarations that the testator did not intend the revoked part to take effect as executed.

(c) If a subsequent will that revoked a previous will in whole or in part is thereafter revoked by another, later, will, the previous will remains revoked in whole or in part, unless it or its revoked part is revived. The previous will or its revoked part is revived to the extent it appears from the terms of the later will that the testator intended the previous will to take effect.

§2-510. Incorporation by Reference

A writing in existence when a will is executed may be incorporated by reference if the language of the will manifests this intent and describes the writing sufficiently to permit its identification.

§2-511. Testamentary Additions to Trusts

(a) A will may validly devise property to the trustee of a trust established or to be established (i) during the testator's lifetime by the testator, by the testator and some other person, or by some other person, including a funded or unfunded life insurance trust, although the settlor has reserved any or all rights of ownership of the insurance contracts, or (ii) at the testator's death by the testator's devise to the trustee, if the trust is identified in the testator's will and its terms are set forth in a written instrument, other than a will, executed before, concurrently with, or after the execution of the testator's will or in another individual's will if that other individual has predeceased the testator, regardless of the existence, size, or character of the corpus of the trust. The devise is not invalid because the trust is amendable or revocable, or because the trust was amended after the execution of the will or the testator's death.

(b) Unless the testator's will provides otherwise, property devised to a trust described in subsection (a) is not held under a testamentary trust of the testator, but it becomes a part of the trust to which it is devised, and must be administered and disposed of in accordance with the provisions of the governing instrument setting forth the terms of the trust, including any amendments thereto made before or after the testator's death.

(c) Unless the testator's will provides otherwise, a revocation or termination of the trust before the testator's death causes the devise to lapse.

§2-512. Events of Independent Significance

A will may dispose of property by reference to acts and events that have significance apart from their effect upon the dispositions made by the will, whether they occur before or after the execution of the will or before or after the testator's death. The execution or revocation of another individual's will is such an event.

§2-513. Separate Writing Identifying Devise of Certain Types of Tangible Personal Property

Whether or not the provisions relating to holographic wills apply, a will may refer to a written statement or list to dispose of items of tangible personal property not otherwise specifically disposed of by the will, other than money. To be admissible under this section as evidence of the intended disposition, the writing must be signed by the testator and must describe the items and the devisees with reasonable certainty. The writing may be referred to as one to be in existence at the time of the testator's death; it may be prepared before or after the execution of the will; it may be altered by the testator after its preparation; and it may be a writing that has no significance apart from its effect on the dispositions made by the will.

Comment

Purpose and Scope of Revision. As part of the broader policy of effectuating a testator's intent and of relaxing formalities of execution, this section permits a testator to refer in his or her will toa separate document disposing of tangible personalty other than money. . . .

The language "items of tangible personal property" does not require that the separate document specifically itemize each item of tangible personal property covered. The only requirement is that the document describe the items covered "with reasonable certainty." Consequently, a document referring to "all my tangible personal property other than money" or to "all my tangible personal property located in my office" or using similar catch-all type of language would normally be sufficient.

The separate document disposing of an item or items of personal property may be prepared after execution of the will, so would not come within Section 2-510 on incorporation by reference. It may even be altered from time to time. The only requirement is that the document be signed by the testator. . . . The signature requirement is designed to prevent mere drafts from becoming effective against the testator's wishes. An unsigned document could still be given effect under Section 2-503, however, if the proponent could carry the burden of proving by clear and convincing evidence that the testator intended the document to be effective.

The typical case covered by this section would be a list of personal effects and the persons whom the decedent desired to take specified items. . . .

§2-514. Contracts Concerning Succession

A contract to make a will or devise, or not to revoke a will or devise, or to die intestate, if executed after the effective date of this Article, may be established only by (i) provisions of a will stating material provisions of the contract, (ii) an express reference in a will to a contract and extrinsic evidence proving the terms of the contract, or (iii) a writing signed by the decedent evidencing the contract. The execution of a joint will or mutual wills does not create a presumption of a contract not to revoke the will or wills.

§2-515. Deposit of Will with Court in Testator's Lifetime

A will may be deposited by the testator or the testator's agent with any court for safekeeping, under rules of the court. The will must be sealed and kept confidential. During the testator's lifetime, a deposited will must be delivered only to the testator or to a person authorized in writing signed by the testator to receive the will. A conservator may be allowed to examine a deposited will of a protected testator under procedures designed to maintain the confidential character of the document to the extent possible, and to ensure that it will be resealed and kept on deposit after the examination. Upon being informed of the testator's death, the court shall notify any person designated to receive the will and deliver it to that person on request; or the court may deliver the will to the appropriate court.

§2-516. Duty of Custodian of Will; Liability

After the death of a testator and on request of an interested person, a person having custody of a will of the testator shall deliver it with reasonable promptness to a person able to secure its probate and if none is known, to an appropriate court. A person who wilfully fails to deliver a will is liable to any person aggrieved for any damages that may be sustained by the failure. A person who wilfully refuses or fails to deliver a will after being ordered by the court in a proceeding brought for the purpose of compelling delivery is subject to penalty for contempt of court.

§2-517. Penalty Clause for Contest

A provision in a will purporting to penalize an interested person for contesting the will or instituting other proceedings relating to the estate is unenforceable if probable cause exists for instituting proceedings.

Part 6

Rules of Construction Applicable Only to Wills

General Comment

Parts 6 and 7 address a variety of construction problems that commonly occur in wills, trusts, and other types of governing instruments. All of the "rules" set forth in these parts yield to a finding of a contrary intention and are therefore rebuttable presumptions.

The rules of construction set forth in Part 6 apply only to wills. The rules of construction set forth in Part 7 apply to wills and other governing instruments.

The sections in Part 6 deal with such problems as death before the testator (lapse), the inclusiveness of the will as to property of the testator, effect of failure of a gift in the will, change in form of securities specifically devised, ademption by reason of fire, sale and the like, exoneration, and exercise of a power of appointment by general language in the will.

§2-601. Scope

In the absence of a finding of a contrary intention, the rules of construction in this Part control the construction of a will.

§2-602. Will May Pass All Property and After-Acquired Property

A will may provide for the passage of all property the testator owns at death and all property acquired by the estate after the testator's death.

§2-603. Antilapse; Deceased Devisee; Class Gifts

(a) [Definitions.] In this section:

(1) "Alternative devise" means a devise that is expressly created by the will and, under the terms of the will, can take effect instead of another devise on the happening of one or more events, including survival of the testator or failure to survive the testator, whether an event is expressed in condition-precedent, condition-subsequent, or any other form. A residuary clause constitutes an alternative devise with respect to a nonresiduary devise only if the will specifically provides that, upon lapse or failure, the nonresiduary devise, or nonresiduary devises in general, pass under the residuary clause.

(2) "Class member" includes an individual who fails to survive the testator but who would have taken under a devise in the form of a class gift had he [or she] survived the testator.

(3) "Devise" includes an alternative devise, a devise in the form of a class gift, and an exercise of a power of appointment.

(4) "Devisee" includes (i) a class member if the devise is in the form of a class gift, (ii) an individual or class member who was deceased at the time the testator executed his [or her] will as well as an individual or class member who was then living but who failed to survive the testator, and (iii) an appointee under a power of appointment exercised by the testator's will.

(5) "Stepchild" means a child of the surviving, deceased, or former spouse of the testator or of the donor of a power of appointment, and not of the testator or donor.

(6) "Surviving devisee" or "surviving descendant" means a devisee or a descendant who neither predeceased the testator nor is deemed to have predeceased the testator under Section 2-702.

(7) "Testator" includes the donee of a power of appointment if the power is exercised in the testator's will.

(b) [Substitute Gift.] If a devisee fails to survive the testator and is a grandparent, a descendant of a grandparent, or a stepchild of either the testator or the donor of a power of appointment exercised by the testator's will, the following apply:

(1) Except as provided in paragraph (4), if the devise is not in the form of a class gift and the deceased devisee leaves surviving descendants, a substitute gift is created in the devisee's surviving descendants. They take by representation the property to which the devisee would have been entitled had the devisee survived the testator.

(2) Except as provided in paragraph (4), if the devise is in the form of a class gift, other than a devise to "issue," "descendants," "heirs of the body," "heirs," "next of kin," "relatives," or "family," or a class described by language of similar import, a substitute gift is created in the surviving descendant's of any deceased devisee. The property to which the devisees would have been entitled had all of them survived the testator passes to the surviving devisees and the surviving descendants of the deceased devisees. Each surviving devisee takes the share to which he [or she] would have been entitled had the deceased devisees survived the testator. Each deceased devisee's surviving descendants who are substituted for the deceased devisee take by representation the share to which the deceased devisee would have been entitled had the deceased devisee survived the testator. For the purposes of this paragraph, "deceased devisee" means a class member who failed to survive the testator and left one or more surviving descendants.

(3) For the purposes of Section 2-601, words of survivorship, such as in a devise to an individual "if he survives me," or in a devise to "my surviving children," are not, in the absence of additional evidence, a sufficient indication of an intent contrary to the application of this section.

(4) If the will creates an alternative devise with respect to a devise for which a substitute gift is created by paragraph (1) or (2), the substitute gift is superseded by the alternative devise only if an expressly designated devisee of the alternative devise is entitled to take under the will.

(5) Unless the language creating a power of appointment expressly excludes the substitution of the descendants of an appointee for the appointee, a surviving descendant of a deceased appointee of a power of appointment can be substituted for the appointee under this section, whether or not the descendant is an object of the power.

(c) [More Than One Substitute Gift; Which One Takes.] If, under subsection (b), substitute gifts are created and not superseded with respect to more than one devise and the devises are alternative devises, one to the other, the determination of which of the substitute gifts takes effect is resolved as follows:

(1) Except as provided in paragraph (2), the devised property passes under the primary substitute gift.

(2) If there is a younger-generation devise, the devised property passes under the younger-generation substitute gift and not under the primary substitute gift.

(3) In this subsection:

(i) "Primary devise" means the devise that would have taken effect had all the deceased devisees of the alternative devises who left surviving descendants survived the testator.

(ii) "Primary substitute gift" means the substitute gift created with respect to the primary devise.

(iii) "Younger-generation devise" means a devise that (A) is to a descendant of a devisee of the primary devise, (B) is an alternative devise with respect to the primary devise, (C) is a devise for which a substitute gift is created, and (D) would have taken effect had all the deceased devisees who left surviving descendants survived the testator except the deceased devisee or devisees of the primary devise.

(iv) "Younger-generation substitute gift" means the substitute gift created with respect to the younger-generation devise.

As amended in 1991 and 1993.

§2-604. Failure of Testamentary Provision

(a) Except as provided in Section 2-603, a devise, other than a residuary devise, that fails for any reason becomes a part of the residue.

(b) Except as provided in Section 2-603, if the residue is devised to two or more persons, the share of a residuary devisee that fails for any reason passes to the other residuary devisee, or to other residuary devisees in proportion to the interest of each in the remaining part of the residue.

§2-605. Increase in Devised Securities; Accessions

(a) If a testator executes a will that devises securities and the testator then owned securities that meet the description in the will, the devise includes additional securities owned by the testator at death to the extent the additional securities were acquired by the testator after the will was executed as a result of the testator's ownership of the described securities and are securities of any of the following types:

(1) securities of the same organization acquired by reason of action initiated by the organization or any successor, related, or acquiring organization, excluding any acquired by exercise of purchase options;

(2) securities of another organization acquired as a result of a merger, consolidation, reorganization, or other distribution by the organization or any successor, related, or acquiring organization; or

(3) securities of the same organization acquired as a result of a plan of reinvestment.

(b) Distributions in cash before death with respect to a described security are not part of the devise.

§2-606. Nonademption of Specific Devises; Unpaid Proceeds of Sale, Condemnation, or Insurance; Sale by Conservator or Agent

(a) A specific devisee has a right to the specifically devised property in the testator's estate at death and:

(1) any balance of the purchase price, together with any security agreement, owing from a purchaser to the testator at death by reason of sale of the property;

(2) any amount of a condemnation award for the taking of the property unpaid at death;

(3) any proceeds unpaid at death on fire or casualty insurance on or other recovery for injury to the property;

(4) property owned by the testator at death and acquired as a result of foreclosure, or obtained in lieu of foreclosure, of the security interest for a specifically devised obligation;

(5) real or tangible personal property owned by the testator at death which the testator acquired as a replacement for specifically devised real or tangible personal property; and

(6) unless the facts and circumstances indicate that ademption of the devise was intended by the testator or ademption of the devise is consistent with the testator's manifested plan of distribution, the value of the specifically devised property to the extent the specifically devised property is not in the testator's estate at death and its value or its replacement is not covered by paragraphs (1) through (5).

(b) If specifically devised property is sold or mortgaged by a conservator or by an agent acting within the authority of a durable power of attorney for an incapacitated principal, or if a condemnation award, insurance proceeds, or recovery for injury to the property are paid to a conservator or to an agent acting within the authority of a durable power of attorney for an incapacitated principal, the specific devisee has the right to a general pecuniary devise equal to the net sale price, the amount of the unpaid loan, the condemnation award, the insurance proceeds, or the recovery.

(c) The right of a specific devisee under subsection (b) is reduced by any right the devisee has under subsection (a).

(d) For the purposes of the references in subsection (b) to a conservator, subsection (b) does not apply if after the sale, mortgage, condemnation, casualty, or recovery, it was adjudicated that the testator's incapacity ceased and the testator survived the adjudication by one year.

(e) For the purposes of the references in subsection (b) to an agent acting within the authority of a durable power of attorney for an incapacitated principal, (i) "incapacitated principal" means a principal who is an incapacitated person, (ii) no adjudication of incapacity before death is necessary, and (iii) the acts of an agent within the authority of a durable power of attorney are presumed to be for an incapacitated principal.

§2-607. Nonexoneration

A specific devise passes subject to any mortgage interest existing at the date of death, without right of exoneration, regardless of a general directive in the will to pay debts.

§2-608. Exercise of Power of Appointment

In the absence of a requirement that a power of appointment be exercised by a reference, or by an express or specific reference, to the power, a general residuary clause in a will, or a will making general disposition of all of the testator's property, expresses an intention to exercise a power of appointment held by the testator only if (i) the power is a general power and the creating instrument does not contain a gift if the power is not exercised or (ii) the testator's will manifests an intention to include the property subject to the power.

§2-609. Ademption by Satisfaction

(a) Property a testator gave in his [or her] lifetime to a person is treated as a satisfaction of a devise in whole or in part, only if (i) the will provides for deduction of the gift, (ii) the testator declared in a contemporaneous writing that the gift is in satisfaction of the devise or that its value is to be deducted from the value of the devise, or (iii) the devisee acknowledged in writing that the gift is in satisfaction of the devise or that its value is to be deducted from the value of the devise.

(b) For purposes of partial satisfaction, property given during lifetime is valued as of the time the devisee came into possession or enjoyment of the property or at the testator's death, whichever occurs first.

(c) If the devisee fails to survive the testator, the gift is treated as a full or partial satisfaction of the devise, as appropriate, in applying Sections 2-603 and 2-604, unless the testator's contemporaneous writing provides otherwise.

Part 7

Rules of Construction Applicable to Wills and Other Governing Instruments

General Comment

Part 7 contains rules of construction applicable to wills and other governing instruments, such as deeds, trusts, appointments, beneficiary designations, and so on. Like the rules of construction in Part 6 (which apply only to wills), the rules of construction in this Part yield to a finding of a contrary intention.

Some of the sections in Part 7 are revisions of sections contained in Part 6 of the pre-1990 Code. Although these sections originally applied only to wills, their restricted scope was inappropriate.

Some of the sections in Part 7 are new, having been added to the Code as desirable means of carrying out common intention.

Application to Pre-Existing Governing Instruments. Under Section 8-101(b), for decedents dying after the effective date of enactment, the provisions of this Code apply to governing instruments executed prior to as well as on or after the effective date of enactment. The Joint Editorial Board for the Uniform Probate Code has issued a statement concerning the constitutionality under the Contracts Clause of this feature of the Code. The statement, titled "Joint Editorial Board Statement Regarding the Constitutionality of Changes in Default Rules as Applied to Pre-Existing Documents," can be found at 17 Am.C.Tr. & Est. Couns. Notes 184 (1991) or can be obtained from the headquarters office of the National Conference of Commissioners on Uniform State Laws, 676 N. St. Clair St., Suite 1700, Chicago, IL 60611, Phone 312/915-0195, FAX 312/915-0187.

Historical Note. This General Comment was revised in 1993. For the prior version, see 8 U.L.A. 137 (Supp.1992).

§2-701. Scope

In the absence of a finding of a contrary intention, the rules of construction in this Part control the construction of a governing instrument. The rules of construction in this Part apply to a governing instrument of any type, except as the application of a particular section is limited by its terms to a specific type or types of provision or governing instrument. As amended in 1991.

§2-702. Requirement of Survival by 120 Hours

(a) [Requirement of Survival by 120 Hours Under Probate Code.] For the purposes of this Code, except as provided in subsection (d), an individual who is not established by clear and convincing evidence to have survived an event, including the death of another individual, by 120 hours is deemed to have predeceased the event.

(b) [Requirement of Survival by 120 Hours under Governing Instrument.] Except as provided in subsection (d), for purposes of a provision of a governing instrument that relates to an individual surviving an event, including the death of another individual, an individual who is not established by clear and convincing evidence to have survived the event by 120 hours is deemed to have predeceased the event.

(c) [Co-owners With Right of Survivorship; Requirement of Survival by 120 Hours.] Except as provided in subsection (d), if (i) it is not established by clear and convincing evidence that one of two co-owners with right of survivorship survived the other co-owner by 120 hours, one-half of the property passes as if one had survived by 120 hours and one-half as if the other had survived by 120 hours and (ii) there are more than two co-owners and it is not established by clear and convincing evidence that at least one of them survived the others by 120 hours, the property passes in the proportion that one bears to the whole number of co-owners. For the purposes of this subsection, "co-owners with right of survivorship" includes joint tenants, tenants by the entireties, and other co-owners of property or accounts held under circumstances that entitles one or more to the whole of the property or account on the death of the other or others.

(d) [Exceptions.] Survival by 120 hours is not required if:

(1) the governing instrument contains language dealing explicitly with simultaneous deaths or deaths in a common disaster and that language is operable under the facts of the case;

(2) the governing instrument expressly indicates that an individual is not required to survive an event, including the death of another individual, by any specified period or expressly requires the individual to survive the event by a specified period; but survival of the event or the specified period must be established by clear and convincing evidence;

(3) the imposition of a 120-hour requirement of survival would cause a nonvested property interest or a power of appointment to fail to qualify for validity under Section 2-901(a)(1), (b)(1), or (c)(1) or to become invalid under Section 2-901(a)(2), (b)(2), or (c)(2); but survival must be established by clear and convincing evidence; or

(4) the application of a 120-hour requirement of survival to multiple governing instruments would result in an unintended failure or duplication of a disposition; but survival must be established by clear and convincing evidence.

(e) [Protection of Payors and Other Third Parties.]

(1) A payor or other third party is not liable for having made a payment or transferred an item of property or any other benefit to a beneficiary designated in a governing instrument who, under this section, is not entitled to the payment or item of property, or for having taken any other action in good faith reliance on the beneficiary's apparent entitlement under the terms of the governing instrument, before the payor or other third party received written notice of a claimed lack of entitlement under this section. A payor or other third party is liable for a payment made or other action taken after the payor or other third party received written notice of a claimed lack of entitlement under this section.

(2) Written notice of a claimed lack of entitlement under paragraph (1) must be mailed to the payor's or other third party's main office or home by registered or certified mail, return receipt requested, or served upon the payor or other third party in the same manner as a summons in a civil action. Upon receipt of written notice of a claimed lack of entitlement under this section, a payor or other third party may pay any amount owed or transfer or deposit any item of property held by it to or with the court having jurisdiction of the probate proceedings relating to the decedent's estate, or if no proceedings have been commenced, to or with the court having jurisdiction of probate proceedings relating to decedents' estates located in the county of the decedent's residence. The court shall hold the funds or item of property and, upon its determination under this section, shall order disbursement in accordance with the determination. Payments, transfers, or deposits made to or with the court discharge the payor or other third party from all claims for the value of amounts paid to or items of property transferred to or deposited with the court.

(f) [Protection of Bona Fide Purchasers; Personal Liability of Recipient.]

(1) A person who purchases property for value and without notice, or who receives a payment or other item of property in partial or full satisfaction of a legally enforceable obligation, is neither obligated under this section to return the payment, item of property, or benefit nor is liable under this section for the amount of the payment or the value of the item of property or benefit. But a person who, not for value, receives a payment, item of property, or any other benefit to which the person is not entitled under this section is obligated to return the payment, item of property, or benefit, or is personally liable for the amount of the payment or the value of the item of property or benefit, to the person who is entitled to it under this section.

(2) If this section or any part of this section is preempted by federal law with respect to a payment, an item of property, or any other benefit covered by this section, a person who, not for value, receives the payment, item of property, or any other benefit to which the person is not entitled under this section is obligated to return the payment, item of property, or benefit, or is personally liable for the amount of the payment or the value of the item of property or benefit, to the person who would have been entitled to it were this section or part of this section not preempted.

As amended in 1991 and 1993.

§2-703. Choice of Law as to Meaning and Effect of Governing Instrument

The meaning and legal effect of a governing instrument is determined by the local law of the state selected in the governing instrument, unless the application of that law is contrary to the provisions relating to the elective share described in Part 2, the provisions relating to exempt

property and allowances described in Part 4, or any other public policy of this State otherwise applicable to the disposition.
As amended in 1991 and 1993.

§2-704. Power of Appointment; Meaning of Specific Reference Requirement

If a governing instrument creating a power of appointment expressly requires that the power be exercised by a reference, an express reference, or a specific reference, to the power or its source, it is presumed that the donor's intention, in requiring that the donee exercise the power by making reference to the particular power or to the creating instrument, was to prevent an inadvertent exercise of the power.

§2-705. Class Gifts Construed to Accord with Intestate Succession

(a) Adopted individuals and individuals born out of wedlock, and their respective descendants if appropriate to the class, are included in class gifts and other terms of relationship in accordance with the rules for intestate succession. Terms of relationship that do not differentiate relationships by blood from those by affinity, such as "uncles," "aunts," "nieces," or "nephews", are construed to exclude relatives by affinity. Terms of relationship that do not differentiate relationships by the half blood from those by the whole blood, such as "brothers," "sisters," "nieces," or "nephews", are construed to include both types of relationships.

(b) In addition to the requirements of subsection (a), in construing a dispositive provision of a transferor who is not the natural parent, an individual born to the natural parent is not considered the child of that parent unless the individual lived while a minor as a regular member of the household of that natural parent or of that parent's parent, brother, sister, spouse, or surviving spouse.

(c) In addition to the requirements of subsection (a), in construing a dispositive provision of a transferor who is not the adopting parent, an adopted individual is not considered the child of the adopting parent unless the adopted individual lived while a minor, either before or after the adoption, as a regular member of the household of the adopting parent.

As amended in 1991.

§2-706. Life Insurance; Retirement Plan; Account with POD Designation; Transfer-on-Death Registration; Deceased Beneficiary

(a) [Definitions.] In this section:

(1) "Alternative beneficiary designation" means a beneficiary designation that is expressly created by the governing instrument and, under the terms of the governing instrument, can take effect instead of another beneficiary designation on the happening of one or more events, including survival of the decedent or failure to survive the decedent, whether an event is expressed in condition-precedent, condition-subsequent, or any other form.

(2) "Beneficiary" means the beneficiary of a beneficiary designation under which the beneficiary must survive the decedent and includes (i) a class member if the beneficiary designation is in the form of a class gift and (ii) an individual or class member who was deceased at the time the beneficiary designation was executed as well as an individual or class member who was then living but who failed to survive the decedent, but excludes a joint tenant of a joint tenancy with the right of survivorship and a party to a joint and survivorship account.

(3) "Beneficiary designation" includes an alternative beneficiary designation and a beneficiary designation in the form of a class gift.

(4) "Class member" includes an individual who fails to survive the decedent but who would have taken under a beneficiary designation in the form of a class gift had he [or she] survived the decedent.

(5) "Stepchild" means a child of the decedent's surviving, deceased, or former spouse, and not of the decedent.

(6) "Surviving beneficiary" or "surviving descendant" means a beneficiary or a descendant who neither predeceased the decedent nor is deemed to have predeceased the decedent under Section 2-702.

(b) [Substitute Gift.] If a beneficiary fails to survive the decedent and is a grandparent, a descendant of a grandparent, or a stepchild of the decedent, the following apply:

(1) Except as provided in paragraph (4), if the beneficiary designation is not in the form of a class gift and the deceased beneficiary leaves surviving descendants, a substitute gift is created in the beneficiary's surviving descendants. They take by representation the property to which the beneficiary would have been entitled had the beneficiary survived the decedent.

(2) Except as provided in paragraph (4), if the beneficiary designation is in the form of a class gift, other than a beneficiary designation to "issue," "descendants," "heirs of the body," "heirs," "next of kin," "relatives," or "family," or a class described by language of similar import, a substitute gift is created in the surviving descendants of any deceased beneficiary. The property to which the beneficiaries would have been entitled had all of them survived the decedent passes to the surviving beneficiaries and the surviving descendants of the deceased beneficiaries. Each surviving beneficiary takes the share to which he [or she] would have been entitled had the deceased beneficiaries survived the decedent. Each deceased beneficiary's surviving descendants who are substituted for the deceased beneficiary take by representation the share to which the deceased beneficiary would have been entitled had the deceased beneficiary survived the decedent. For the purposes of this paragraph, "deceased beneficiary" means a class member who failed to survive the decedent and left one or more surviving descendants.

(3) For the purposes of Section 2-701, words of survivorship, such as in a beneficiary designation to an individual "if he survives me," or in a beneficiary designation to "my surviving children," are not, in the absence of additional evidence, a sufficient indication of an intent contrary to the application of this section.

(4) If a governing instrument creates an alternative beneficiary designation with respect to a beneficiary designation for which a substitute gift is created by paragraph (1) or (2), the substitute gift is superseded by the alternative beneficiary designation only if an expressly designated beneficiary of the alternative beneficiary designation is entitled to take.

(c) [More Than One Substitute Gift; Which One Takes.] If, under subsection (b), substitute gifts are created and not superseded with respect to more than one beneficiary designation and the beneficiary designations are alternative beneficiary designations, one to the other, the determination of which of the substitute gifts takes effect is resolved as follows:

(1) Except as provided in paragraph (2), the property passes under the primary substitute gift.

(2) If there is a younger-generation beneficiary designation, the property passes under the younger-generation substitute gift and not under the primary substitute gift.

(3) In this subsection:

(i) "Primary beneficiary designation" means the beneficiary designation that would have taken effect had all the deceased beneficiaries of the alternative beneficiary designations who left surviving descendants survived the decedent.

(ii) "Primary substitute gift" means the substitute gift created with respect to the primary beneficiary designation.

(iii) "Younger-generation beneficiary designation" means a beneficiary designation that (A) is to a descendant of a beneficiary of the primary beneficiary designation, (B) is an alternative beneficiary designation with respect to the primary beneficiary designation, (C) is a beneficiary designation for which a substitute gift is created, and (D) would have taken effect had all the deceased beneficiaries who left surviving descendants survived the decedent except the deceased beneficiary or beneficiaries of the primary beneficiary designation.

(iv) "Younger-generation substitute gift" means the substitute gift created with respect to the younger-generation beneficiary designation.

(d) [Protection of Payors.]

(1) A payor is protected from liability in making payments under the terms of the beneficiary designation until the payor has received written notice of a claim to a substitute gift under this section. Payment made before the receipt of written notice of a claim to a substitute gift under this section discharges the payor, but not the recipient, from all claims for the amounts paid. A payor is liable for a payment made after the payor has received written notice of the claim. A recipient is liable for a payment received, whether or not written notice of the claim is given.

(2) The written notice of the claim must be mailed to the payor's main office or home by registered or certified mail, return receipt requested, or served upon the payor in the same manner as a summons in a civil action. Upon receipt of written notice of the claim, a payor may pay any amount owed by it to the court having jurisdiction of the probate proceedings relating to the decedent's estate or, if no proceedings have been commenced, to the court having jurisdiction of probate proceedings relating to decedents' estates located in the county of the decedent's residence. The court shall hold the funds and, upon its determination under this section, shall order disbursement in accordance with the determination. Payment made to the court discharges the payor from all claims for the amounts paid.

(e) [Protection of Bona Fide Purchasers; Personal Liability of Recipient.]

(1) A person who purchases property for value and without notice, or who receives a payment or other item of property in partial or full satisfaction of a legally enforceable obligation, is neither obligated under this section to return the payment, item of property, or benefit nor is liable under this section for the amount of the payment or the value of the item of property or benefit. But a person who, not for value, receives a payment, item of property, or any other benefit to which the person is not entitled under this section is obligated to return the payment, item of property, or benefit, or is personally liable for the amount of the payment or the value of the item of property or benefit, to the person who is entitled to it under this section.

(2) If this section or any part of this section is preempted by federal law with respect to a payment, an item of property, or any other benefit covered by this section, a person who, not for value, receives the payment, item of property, or any other benefit to which the person is not entitled under this section is obligated to return the payment, item of property, or benefit, or is personally liable for the amount of the payment or the value of the item of property or benefit, to the person who would have been entitled to it were this section or part of this section not preempted.

As amended in 1993.

§2-707. Survivorship with Respect to Future Interests under Terms of Trust; Substitute Takers

(a) [Definitions.] In this section:

(1) "Alternative future interest" means an expressly created future interest that can take effect in possession or enjoyment instead of another future interest on the happening of one or more events, including survival of an event or failure to survive an event, whether an event is expressed in condition-precedent, condition-subsequent, or any other form. A residuary clause in a will does not create

an alternative future interest with respect to a future interest created in a nonresiduary devise in the will, whether or not the will specifically provides that lapsed or failed devises are to pass under the residuary clause.

(2) "Beneficiary" means the beneficiary of a future interest and includes a class member if the future interest is in the form of a class gift.

(3) "Class member" includes an individual who fails to survive the distribution date but who would have taken under a future interest in the form of a class gift had he [or she] survived the distribution date.

(4) "Distribution date," with respect to a future interest, means the time when the future interest is to take effect in possession or enjoyment. The distribution date need not occur at the beginning or end of a calendar day, but can occur at a time during the course of a day.

(5) "Future interest" includes an alternative future interest and a future interest in the form of a class gift.

(6) "Future interest under the terms of a trust" means a future interest that was created by a transfer creating a trust or to an existing trust or by an exercise of a power of appointment to an existing trust, directing the continuance of an existing trust, designating a beneficiary of an existing trust, or creating a trust.

(7) "Surviving beneficiary" or "surviving descendant" means a beneficiary or a descendant who neither predeceased the distribution date nor is deemed to have predeceased the distribution date under Section 2-702.

(b) [Survivorship Required; Substitute Gift.] A future interest under the terms of a trust is contingent on the beneficiary's surviving the distribution date. If a beneficiary of a future interest under the terms of a trust fails to survive the distribution date, the following apply:

(1) Except as provided in paragraph (4), if the future interest is not in the form of a class gift and the deceased beneficiary leaves surviving descendants, a substitute gift is created in the beneficiary's surviving descendants. They take by representation the property to which the beneficiary would have been entitled had the beneficiary survived the distribution date.

(2) Except as provided in paragraph (4), if the future interest is in the form of a class gift, other than a future interest to "issue," "descendants," "heirs of the body," "heirs," "next of kin," "relatives," or "family," or a class described by language of similar import, a substitute gift is created in the surviving descendants of any deceased beneficiary. The property to which the beneficiaries would have been entitled had all of them survived the distribution date passes to the surviving beneficiaries and the surviving descendants of the deceased beneficiaries. Each surviving beneficiary takes the share to which he [or she] would have been entitled had the deceased beneficiaries survived the distribution date. Each deceased beneficiary's surviving descendants who are substituted for the deceased beneficiary take by representation the share to which the deceased beneficiary would have been entitled had the deceased beneficiary survived the distribution date. For the purposes of this paragraph, "deceased beneficiary" means a class member who failed to survive the distribution date and left one or more surviving descendants.

(3) For the purposes of Section 2-701, words of survivorship attached to a future interest are not, in the absence of additional evidence, a sufficient indication of an intent contrary to the application of this section. Words of survivorship include words of survivorship that relate to the distribution date or to an earlier or an unspecified time, whether those words of survivorship are expressed in condition-precedent, condition-subsequent, or any other form.

(4) If a governing instrument creates an alternative future interest with respect to a future interest for which a substitute gift is created by paragraph (1) or (2), the substitute gift is superseded by the alternative future interest only if an expressly designated beneficiary of the alternative future interest is entitled to take in possession or enjoyment.

(c) [More Than One Substitute Gift; Which One Takes.] If, under subsection (b), substitute gifts are created and not superseded with respect to more than one future interest and the future interests are alternative future interests, one to the other, the determination of which of the substitute gifts takes effect is resolved as follows:

(1) Except as provided in paragraph (2), the property passes under the primary substitute gift.

(2) If there is a younger-generation future interest, the property passes under the younger-generation substitute gift and not under the primary substitute gift.

(3) In this subsection:

(i) "Primary future interest" means the future interest that would have taken effect had all the deceased beneficiaries of the alternative future interests who left surviving descendants survived the distribution date.

(ii) "Primary substitute gift" means the substitute gift created with respect to the primary future interest.

(iii) "Younger-generation future interest" means a future interest that (A) is to a descendant of a beneficiary of the primary future interest, (B) is an alternative future interest with respect to the primary future interest, (C) is a future interest for which a substitute gift is created, and (D) would have taken effect had all the deceased beneficiaries who left surviving descendants survived the distribution date except the deceased beneficiary or beneficiaries of the primary future interest.

(iv) "Younger-generation substitute gift" means the substitute gift created with respect to the younger-generation future interest.

(d) [If No Other Takers, Property Passes Under Residuary Clause or to Transferor's Heirs.] Except as provided in subsection (e), if, after the application of subsections (b) and (c), there is no surviving taker, the property passes in the following order:

(1) if the trust was created in a nonresiduary devise in the transferor's will or in a codicil to the transferor's will, the property passes under the residuary clause in the

transferor's will; for purposes of this section, the residuary clause is treated as creating a future interest under the terms of a trust.

(2) if no taker is produced by the application of paragraph (1), the property passes to the transferor's heirs under Section 2-711.

(e) [If No Other Takers and If Future Interest Created by Exercise of Power of Appointment.] If, after the application of subsections (b) and (c), there is no surviving taker and if the future interest was created by the exercise of a power of appointment:

(1) the property passes under the donor's gift-in-default clause, if any, which clause is treated as creating a future interest under the terms of a trust; and

(2) if no taker is produced by the application of paragraph (1), the property passes as provided in subsection (d). For purposes of subsection (d), "transferor" means the donor if the power was a nongeneral power and means the donee if the power was a general power.

As amended in 1993.

§2-708. Class Gifts to "Descendants," "Issue," or "Heirs of the Body"; Form of Distribution if None Specified

If a class gift in favor of "descendants," "issue," or "heirs of the body" does not specify the manner in which the property is to be distributed among the class members, the property is distributed among the class members who are living when the interest is to take effect in possession or enjoyment, in such shares as they would receive, under the applicable law of intestate succession, if the designated ancestor had then died intestate owning the subject matter of the class gift.

§2-709. Representation; Per Capita at Each Generation; Per Stirpes

(a) [Definitions.] In this section:

(1) "Deceased child" or "deceased descendant" means a child or a descendant who either predeceased the distribution date or is deemed to have predeceased the distribution date under Section 2-702.

(2) "Distribution date," with respect to an interest, means the time when the interest is to take effect in possession or enjoyment. The distribution date need not occur at the beginning or end of a calendar day, but can occur at a time during the course of a day.

(3) "Surviving ancestor," "surviving child," or "surviving descendant" means an ancestor, a child, or a descendant who neither predeceased the distribution date nor is deemed to have predeceased the distribution date under Section 2-702.

(b) [Representation; Per Capita at Each Generation.] If an applicable statute or a governing instrument calls for property to be distributed "by representation" or "per capita at each generation," the property is divided into as many equal shares as there are (i) surviving descendants in the generation nearest to the designated ancestor which contains one or more surviving descendants (ii) and deceased descendants in the same generation who left surviving descendants, if any. Each surviving descendant in the nearest generation is allocated one share. The remaining shares, if any, are combined and then divided in the same manner among the surviving descendants of the deceased descendants as if the surviving descendants who were allocated a share and their surviving descendants had predeceased the distribution date.

(c) [Per Stirpes.] If a governing instrument calls for property to be distributed "per stripes," the property is divided into as many equal shares as there are (i) surviving children of the designated ancestor and (ii) deceased children who left surviving descendants. Each surviving child, if any, is allocated one share. The share of each deceased child with surviving descendants is divided in the same manner, with subdivision repeating at each succeeding generation until the property is fully allocated among surviving descendants.

(d) [Deceased Descendant With No Surviving Descendant Disregarded.] For the purposes of subsections (b) and (c), an individual who is deceased and left no surviving descendant is disregarded, and an individual who leaves a surviving ancestor who is a descendant of the designated ancestor is not entitled to a share.

As amended in 1993.

§2-710. Worthier-Title Doctrine Abolished

The doctrine of worthier title is abolished as a rule of law and as a rule of construction. Language in a governing instrument describing the beneficiaries of a disposition as the transferor's "heirs," "heirs at law," "next of kin," "distributees," "relatives," or "family," or language of similar import, does not create or presumptively create a reversionary interest in the transferor.

As amended in 1991.

§2-711. Interests in "Heirs" and Like

If an applicable statute or a governing instrument calls for a present or future distribution to or creates a present or future interest in a designated individual's "heirs," "heirs at law," "next of kin," "relatives," or "family," or language of similar import, the property passes to those persons, including the state, and in such shares as would succeed to the designated individual's intestate estate under the intestate succession law of the designated individual's domicile if the designated individual died when the disposition is to take effect in possession or enjoyment. If the designated individual's surviving spouse is living but is remarried at the time the disposition is to take effect in possession or enjoyment, the surviving spouse is not an heir of the designated individual.

As amended in 1991 and 1993.

Part 8

General Provisions Concerning Probate and Nonprobate Transfers

General Comment

Part 8 contains four general provisions that cut across probate and nonprobate transfers. Section 2-801 incorporates portions of the Uniform Disclaimer of Property Interests Act; these portions replace portions of the narrower Uniform Disclaimer of Transfers By Will, Intestacy or Appointment Act, which had been incorporated into the pre-1990 Code. The broader disclaimer provisions are now appropriate, given the broadened scope of Article II in covering nonprobate as well as probate transfers.

Section 2-802 deals with the effect of divorce and separation on the right to elect against a will, exempt property and allowances, and an intestate share.

Section 2-803 spells out the legal consequence of intentional and felonious killing on the right of the killer to take as heir and under wills and revocable inter-vivos transfers, such as revocable trusts and life-insurance beneficiary designations.

Section 2-804 deals with the consequences of a divorce on the right of the former spouse (and relatives of the former spouse) to take under wills and revocable inter-vivos transfers, such as revocable trusts and life-insurance beneficiary designations.

Application to Pre-Existing Governing Instruments. Under Section 8-101(b), for decedents dying after the effective date of enactment, the provisions of this Code apply to governing instruments executed prior to as well as on or after the effective date of enactment. The Joint Editorial Board for the Uniform Probate Code has issued a statement concerning the constitutionality under the Contracts Clause of this feature of the Code. The statement, titled "Joint Editorial Board Statement Regarding the Constitutionality of Changes in Default Rules as Applied to Pre-Existing Documents," can be found at 17 Am.C.Tr. & Est.Couns. Notes 184 (1991) or can be obtained from the headquarters office of the National Conference of Commissioners on Uniform State Laws, 676 N. St. Clair St., Suite 1700, Chicago, IL 60611, Phone 312/915-0195, FAX 312/915-0187.

Historical Note. This General Comment was revised in 1993. For the prior version, see 8 U.L.A. 156 (Supp.1992).

§2-801. Disclaimer of Property Interests

(a) [Right to Disclaim Interest in Property.] A person, or the representative of a person, to whom an interest in or with respect to property or an interest therein devolves by whatever means may disclaim it in whole or in part by delivering or filing a written disclaimer under this section. The right to disclaim exists notwithstanding (i) any limitation on the interest of the disclaimant in the nature of a spendthrift provision or similar restriction or (ii) any restriction or limitation on the right to disclaim contained in the governing instrument. For purposes of this subsection, the "representative of a person" includes a personal representative of a decedent, a conservator of a disabled person, a guardian of a minor or incapacitated person, and an agent acting on behalf of the person within the authority of a power of attorney.

(b) [Time of Disclaimer.] The following rules govern the time when a disclaimer must be filed or delivered:

(1) If the property or interest has devolved to the disclaimant under a testamentary instrument or by the laws of intestacy, the disclaimer must be filed, if of a present interest, not later than [nine] months after the death of the deceased owner or deceased donee of a power of appointment and, if of a future interest, not later than [nine] months after the event determining that the taker of the property or interest is finally ascertained and his [or her] interest is indefeasibly vested. The disclaimer must be filed in the [probate] court of the county in which proceedings for the administration of the estate of the deceased owner or deceased donee of the power have been commenced. A copy of the disclaimer must be delivered in person or mailed by registered or certified mail, return receipt requested, to any personal representative or other fiduciary of the decedent or donee of the power.

(2) If a property or interest has devolved to the disclaimant under a nontestamentary instrument or contract, the disclaimer must be delivered or filed, if of a present interest, not later than [nine] months after the effective date of the nontestamentary instrument or contract and, if of a future interest, not later than [nine] months after the event determining that the taker of the property or interest is finally ascertained and his [or her] interest is indefeasibly vested. If the person entitled to disclaim does not know of the existence of the interest, the disclaimer must be delivered or filed not later than [nine] months after the person learns of the existence of the interest. The effective date of a revocable instrument or contract is the date on which the maker no longer has power to revoke it or to transfer to himself [or herself] or another the entire legal and equitable ownership of the interest. The disclaimer or a copy thereof must be delivered in person or mailed by registered or certified mail, return receipt requested, to the person who has legal title to or possession of the interest disclaimed.

(3) A surviving joint tenant [or tenant by the entireties] may disclaim as a separate interest any property or interest therein devolving to him [or her] by right of survivorship. A surviving joint tenant [or tenant by the entireties] may disclaim the entire interest in any property or interest therein that is the subject of a joint tenancy [or tenancy by the entireties] devolving to him [or her], if the joint tenancy [or tenancy by the entireties] was created by act of a deceased joint tenant [or tenant by the entireties], the

survivor did not join in creating the joint tenancy [or tenancy by the entireties], and has not accepted a benefit under it.

(4) If real property or an interest therein is disclaimed, a copy of the disclaimer may be recorded in the office of the [Recorder of Deeds] of the county in which the property or interest disclaimed is located.*

* If Torrens system is in effect, add provisions to comply with local law.

(c) [Form of Disclaimer.] The disclaimer must (i) describe the property or interest disclaimed, (ii) declare the disclaimer and extent thereof, and (iii) be signed by the disclaimant.

(d) [Effect of Disclaimer.] The effects of a disclaimer are:

(1) If property or an interest therein devolves to a disclaimant under a testamentary instrument, under a power of appointment exercised by a testamentary instrument, or under the laws of intestacy, and the decedent has not provided for another disposition of that interest, should it be disclaimed, or of disclaimed, or failed interests in general, the disclaimed interest devolves as if the disclaimant had predeceased the decedent, but if by law or under the testamentary instrument the descendants of the disclaimant would share in the disclaimed interest by representation or otherwise were the disclaimant to predecease the decedent, then the disclaimed interest passes by representation, or passes as directed by the governing instrument, to the descendants of the disclaimant who survive the decedent. A future interest that takes effect in possession or enjoyment after the termination of the estate or interest disclaimed takes effect as if the disclaimant had predeceased the decedent. A disclaimer relates back for all purposes to the date of death of the decedent.

(2) If property or an interest therein devolves to a disclaimant under a nontestamentary instrument or contract and the instrument or contract does not provide for another disposition of that interest, should it be disclaimed, or of disclaimed or failed interests in general, the disclaimed interest devolves as if the disclaimant has predeceased the effective date of the instrument or contract, but if by law or under the nontestamentary instrument or contract the descendants of the disclaimant would share in the disclaimed interest by representation or otherwise were the disclaimant to predecease the effective date of the instrument, then the disclaimed interest passes by representation, or passes as directed by the governing instrument, to the descendants of the disclaimant who survive the effective date of the instrument. A disclaimer relates back for all purposes to that date. A future interest that takes effect in possession or enjoyment at or after the termination of the disclaimed interest takes effect as if the disclaimant had died before the effective date of the instrument or contract that transferred the disclaimed interest.

(3) The disclaimer or the written waiver of the right to disclaim is binding upon the disclaimant or person waiving and all persons claiming through or under either of them.

(e) [Waiver and Bar.] The right to disclaim property or an interest therein is barred by (i) an assignment, conveyance, encumbrance, pledge, or transfer of the property or interest, or a contract therefor, (ii) a written waiver of the right to disclaim, (iii) an acceptance of the property or interest or a benefit under it or (iv) a sale of the property or interest under judicial sale made before the disclaimer is made.

(f) [Remedy Not Exclusive.] This section does not abridge the right of a person to waive, release, disclaim, or renounce property or an interest therein under any other statute.

(g) [Application.] An interest in property that exists on the effective date of this section as to which, if a present interest, the time for filing a disclaimer under this section has not expired or, if a future interest, the interest has not become indefeasibly vested or the taker finally ascertained, may be disclaimed within [nine] months after the effective date of this section.

As amended in 1993.

§2-802. Effect of Divorce, Annulment, and Decree of Separation

(a) An individual who is divorced from the decedent or whose marriage to the decedent has been annulled is not a surviving spouse unless, by virtue of a subsequent marriage, he [or she] is married to the decedent at the time of death. A decree of separation that does not terminate the status of husband and wife is not a divorce for purposes of this section.

(b) For purposes of Parts 1, 2, 3, and 4 of this Article, and of Section 3-203, a surviving spouse does not include:

(1) an individual who obtains or consents to a final decree or judgment of divorce from the decedent or an annulment of their marriage, which decree or judgment is not recognized as valid in this State, unless subsequently they participate in a marriage ceremony purporting to marry each to the other or live together as husband and wife;

(2) an individual who, following an invalid decree or judgment of divorce or annulment obtained by the decedent, participates in a marriage ceremony with a third individual; or

(3) an individual who was a party to a valid proceeding concluded by an order purporting to terminate all marital property rights.

§2-803. Effect of Homicide on Intestate Succession, Wills, Trusts, Joint Assets, Life Insurance, and Beneficiary Designations

(a) [Definitions.] In this section:

(1) "Disposition or appointment of property" includes a transfer of an item of property or any other benefit to a beneficiary designated in a governing instrument.

(2) "Governing instrument" means a governing instrument executed by the decedent.

(3) "Revocable," with respect to a disposition, appointment, provision, or nomination, means one under which the decedent, at the time of or immediately before death, was alone empowered, by law or under the governing instrument, to cancel the designation, in favor of the killer, whether or not the decedent was then empowered to designate himself [or herself] in place of his [or her] killer and whether or not the decedent then had capacity to exercise the power.

(b) [Forfeiture of Statutory Benefits.] An individual who feloniously and intentionally kills the decedent forfeits all benefits under this Article with respect to the decedent's estate, including an intestate share, an elective share, an omitted spouse's or child's share, a homestead allowance, exempt property, and a family allowance. If the decedent died intestate, the decedent's intestate estate passes as if the killer disclaimed his [or her] intestate share.

(c) [Revocation of Benefits Under Governing Instruments.] The felonious and intentional killing of the decedent:

(1) revokes any revocable (i) disposition or appointment of property made by the decedent to the killer in a governing instrument, (ii) provision in a governing instrument conferring a general or nongeneral power of appointment on the killer, and (iii) nomination of the killer in a governing instrument, nominating or appointing the killer to serve in any fiduciary or representative capacity, including a personal representative, executor, trustee, or agent; and

(2) severs the interests of the decedent and killer in property held by them at the time of the killing as joint tenants with the right of survivorship [or as community property with the right of survivorship], transforming the interests of the decedent and killer into tenancies in common.

(d) [Effect of Severance.] A severance under subsection (c)(2) does not affect any third-party interest in property acquired for value and in good faith reliance on an apparent title by survivorship in the killer unless a writing declaring the severance has been noted, registered, filed, or recorded in records appropriate to the kind and location of the property which are relied upon, in the ordinary course of transactions involving such property, as evidence of ownership.

(e) [Effect of Revocation.] Provisions of a governing instrument are given effect as if the killer disclaimed all provisions revoked by this section or, in the case of a revoked nomination in a fiduciary or representative capacity, as if the killer predeceased the decedent.

(f) [Wrongful Acquisition of Property.] A wrongful acquisition of property or interest by a killer not covered by this section must be treated in accordance with the principle that a killer cannot profit from his [or her] wrong.

(g) [Felonious and Intentional Killing; How Determined.] After all right to appeal has been exhausted, a judgment of conviction establishing criminal accountability for the felonious and intentional killing of the decedent conclusively establishes the convicted individual as the decedent's killer for purposes of this section. In the absence of a conviction, the court, upon the petition of an interested person, must determine whether, under the preponderance of evidence standard, the individual would be found criminally accountable for the felonious and intentional killing of the decedent. If the court determines that, under that standard, the individual would be found criminally accountable for the felonious and intentional killing of the decedent, the determination conclusively establishes that individual as the decedent's killer for purposes of this section.

(h) [Protection of Payors and Other Third Parties.]

(1) A payor or other third party is not liable for having made a payment or transferred an item of property or any other benefit to a beneficiary designated in a governing instrument affected by an intentional and felonious killing, or for having taken any other action in good faith reliance on the validity of the governing instrument, upon request and satisfactory proof of the decedent's death, before the payor or other third party received written notice of a claimed forfeiture or revocation under this section. A payor or other third party is liable for a payment made or other action taken after the payor or other third party received written notice of a claimed forfeiture or revocation under this section.

(2) Written notice of a claimed forfeiture or revocation under paragraph (1) must be mailed to the payor's or other third party's main office or home by registered or certified mail, return receipt requested, or served upon the payor or other third party in the same manner as a summons in a civil action. Upon receipt of written notice of a claimed forfeiture or revocation under this section, a payor or other third party may pay any amount owed or transfer or deposit any item of property held by it to or with the court having jurisdiction of the probate proceedings relating to the decedent's estate, or if no proceedings have been commenced, to or with the court having jurisdiction of probate proceedings relating to decedents' estates located in the county of the decedent's residence. The court shall hold the funds or item of property and, upon its determination under this section, shall order disbursement in accordance with the determination. Payments, transfers, or deposits made to or with the court discharge the payor or other third party from all claims for the value of amounts paid to or items of property transferred to or deposited with the court.

(i) [Protection of Bona Fide Purchasers; Personal Liability of Recipient.]

(1) A person who purchases property for value and without notice, or who receives a payment or other item of property in partial or full satisfaction of a legally enforceable obligation, is neither obligated under this section to return the payment, item of property, or benefit nor is liable under this section for the amount of the payment or the value of the item of property or benefit. But a person who, not for value, receives a payment, item of property, or any other benefit to which the person is not entitled under this section is obligated to return the payment, item of property, or benefit, or is personally liable for the amount of the payment or the value of the

item of property or benefit, to the person who is entitled to it under this section.

(2) If this section or any part of this section is preempted by federal law with respect to a payment, an item of property, or any other benefit covered by this section, a person who, not for value, receives the payment, item of property, or any other benefit to which the person is not entitled under this section is obligated to return the payment, item of property, or benefit, or is personally liable for the amount of the payment or the value of the item of property or benefit, to the person who would have been entitled to it were this section or part of this section not preempted.

As amended in 1993.

§2-804. Revocation of Probate and Nonprobate Transfers by Divorce; No Revocation by Other Changes of Circumstances

(a) [Definitions.] In this section:

(1) "Disposition or appointment of property" includes a transfer of an item of property or any other benefit to a beneficiary designated in a governing instrument.

(2) "Divorce or annulment" means any divorce or annulment, or any dissolution or declaration of invalidity of a marriage, that would exclude the spouse as a surviving spouse within the meaning of Section 2-802. A decree of separation that does not terminate the status of husband and wife is not a divorce for purposes of this section.

(3) "Divorced individual" includes an individual whose marriage has been annulled.

(4) "Governing instrument" means a governing instrument executed by the divorced individual before the divorce or annulment of his [or her] marriage to his [or her] former spouse.

(5) "Relative of the divorced individual's former spouse" means an individual who is related to the divorced individual's former spouse by blood, adoption, or affinity and who, after the divorce or annulment, is not related to the divorced individual by blood, adoption, or affinity.

(6) "Revocable," with respect to a disposition, appointment, provision, or nomination, means one under which the divorced individual, at the time of the divorce or annulment, was alone empowered, by law or under the governing instrument, to cancel the designation in favor of his [or her] former spouse or former spouse's relative, whether or not the divorced individual was then empowered to designate himself [or herself] in place of his [or her] former spouse or in place of his [or her] former spouse's relative and whether or not the divorced individual then had the capacity to exercise the power.

(b) [Revocation Upon Divorce.] Except as provided by the express terms of a governing instrument, a court order, or a contract relating to the division of the marital estate made between the divorced individuals before or after the marriage, divorce, or annulment, the divorce or annulment of a marriage:

(1) revokes any revocable (i) disposition or appointment of property made by a divorced individual to his [or her] former spouse in a governing instrument and any disposition or appointment created by law or in a governing instrument to a relative of the divorced individual's former spouse, (ii) provision in a governing instrument conferring a general or nongeneral power of appointment on the divorced individual's former spouse or on a relative of the divorced individual's former spouse, and (iii) nomination in a governing instrument, nominating a divorced individual's former spouse or a relative of the divorced individual's former spouse to serve in any fiduciary or representative capacity, including a personal representative, executor, trustee, conservator, agent, or guardian; and

(2) severs the interests of the former spouses in property held by them at the time of the divorce or annulment as joint tenants with the right of survivorship [or as community property with the right of survivorship], transforming the interests of the former spouses into tenancies in common.

(c) [Effect of Severance.] A severance under subsection (b)(2) does not affect any third-party interest in property acquired for value and in good faith reliance on an apparent title by survivorship in the survivor of the former spouses unless a writing declaring the severance has been noted, registered, filed, or recorded in records appropriate to the kind and location of the property which are relied upon, in the ordinary course of transactions involving such property, as evidence of ownership.

(d) [Effect of Revocation.] Provisions of a governing instrument are given effect as if the former spouse and relatives of the former spouse disclaimed all provisions revoked by this section or, in the case of a revoked nomination in a fiduciary or representative capacity, as if the former spouse and relatives of the former spouse died immediately before the divorce or annulment.

(e) [Revival if Divorce Nullified.] Provisions revoked solely by this section are revived by the divorced individual's remarriage to the former spouse or by a nullification of the divorce or annulment.

(f) [No Revocation for Other Change of Circumstances.] No change of circumstances other than as described in this section and in Section 2-803 effects a revocation.

(g) [Protection of Payors and Other Third Parties.]

(1) A payor or other third party is not liable for having made a payment or transferred an item of property or any other benefit to a beneficiary designated in a governing instrument affected by a divorce, annulment, or remarriage, or for having taken any other action in good faith reliance on the validity of the governing instrument, before the payor or other third party received written notice of the divorce, annulment, or remarriage. A payor or other third party is liable for a payment made or other action taken after the payor or other third party received written notice of a claimed forfeiture or revocation under this section.

(2) Written notice of the divorce, annulment, or remarriage under subsection (g)(2) must be mailed to the payor's or other third party's main office or home by registered or certified mail, return receipt requested, or served upon the payor or other third party in the same manner as a summons in a civil action. Upon receipt of written notice of the divorce, annulment, or remarriage, a payor or other third party may pay any amount owed or transfer or deposit any item of property held by it to or with the court having jurisdiction of the probate proceedings relating to the decedent's estate or, if no proceedings have been commenced, to or with the court having jurisdiction of probate proceedings relating to decedents' estates located in the county of the decedent's residence. The court shall hold the funds or item of property and, upon its determination under this section, shall order disbursement or transfer in accordance with the determination. Payments, transfers, or deposits made to or with the court discharge the payor or other third party from all claims for the value of amounts paid to or items of property transferred to or deposited with the court.

(h) [Protection of Bona Fide Purchasers; Personal Liability of Recipient.]

(1) A person who purchases property from a former spouse, relative of a former spouse, or any other person for value and without notice, or who receives from a former spouse, relative of a former spouse, or any other person a payment or other item of property in partial or full satisfaction of a legally enforceable obligation, is neither obligated under this section to return the payment, item of property, or benefit nor is liable under this section for the amount of the payment or the value of the item of property or benefit. But a former spouse, relative of a former spouse, or other person who, not for value, received a payment, item of property, or any other benefit to which that person is not entitled under this section is obligated to return the payment, item of property, or benefit, or is personally liable for the amount of the payment or the value of the item of property or benefit, to the person who is entitled to it under this section.

(2) If this section or any part of this section is preempted by federal law with respect to a payment, an item of property, or any other benefit covered by this section, a former spouse, relative of the former spouse, or any other person who, not for value, received a payment, item of property, or any other benefit to which that person is not entitled under this section is obligated to return that payment, item of property, or benefit, or is personally liable for the amount of the payment or the value of the item of property or benefit, to the person who would have been entitled to it were this section or part of this section not preempted.

As amended in 1993.

Comment

Purpose and Scope of Revision. The revisions of this section, pre-1990 Section 2-508, intend to unify the law of probate and nonprobate transfers. As originally promulgated, pre-1990 Section 2-508 revoked a predivorce devise to the testator's former spouse. The revisions expand the section to cover "will substitutes" such as revocable inter-vivos trusts, life-insurance and retirement-plan beneficiary designations, transfer-on-death accounts, and other revocable dispositions to the former spouse that the divorced individual established before the divorce (or annulment). As revised, this section also effects a severance of the interests of the former spouses in property that they held at the time of the divorce (or annulment) as joint tenants with the right of survivorship; their co-ownership interests become tenancies in common.

As revised, this section is the most comprehensive provision of its kind, but many states have enacted piecemeal legislation tending in the same direction. . . . The courts have also come under increasing pressure to use statutory construction techniques to extend statutes like the pre-1990 version of Section 2-508 to various will substitutes. . . .

Part 9

Statutory Rule Against Perpetuities; Honorary Trusts

Adoption of Uniform Statutory Rule Against Perpetuities

Note that Part 9, Subpart 1, of Revised Article II has also been adopted as the free-standing Uniform Statutory Rule Against Perpetuities. See Volume 8B Uniform Laws Annotated, Master Edition or ULA Database on Westlaw.

SUBPART 1. STATUTORY RULE AGAINST PERPETUITIES

SUBPART 2. [HONORARY TRUSTS]

General Comment

Subpart 1 of this Part incorporates into the Code the Uniform Statutory Rule Against Perpetuities (USRAP or Uniform Statutory Rule) and Subpart 2 contains an optional section on honorary trusts and trusts for pets. Subpart 2 is under continuing review and, after appropriate study, might subsequently be revised to add provisions affecting certain types of commercial transactions respecting land, such as options in gross, that directly or indirectly restrain alienability.

In codifying Subparts 1 and 2, enacting states may deem it appropriate to locate them at some place other than in the probate code.

SUBPART 1. STATUTORY RULE AGAINST PERPETUITIES

General Comment

Simplified Wait-and-See / Deferred-Reformation Approach Adopted. The Uniform Statutory Rule reforms the common-law Rule Against Perpetuities (common-law Rule) by adding a simplified wait-and-see element and a deferred-reformation element.

Wait-and-see is a two-step strategy. Step One (Section 2-901(a)(1)) preserves the validating side of the common-law Rule. By satisfying the common law Rule, a nonvested future interest in property is valid at the moment of its creation. Step Two (Section 2-901(a)(2)) is a salvage strategy for future interests that would have been invalid at common law. Rather than invalidating such interests at creation, wait-and-see allows a period of time, called the permissible vesting period, during which the nonvested interests are permitted to vest according to the trust's terms.

The traditional method of measuring the permissible vesting period has been by reference to lives in being at the creation of the interest (the measuring lives) plus 21 years. There are, however, various difficulties and costs associated with identifying and tracing a set of actual measuring lives to see which one is the survivor and when he or she dies. In addition, it has been documented that the use of actual measuring lives plus 21 years does not produce a period of time that self-adjusts to each disposition, extending dead-hand control no further than necessary in each case; rather, the use of actual measuring lives (plus 21 years) generates a permissible vesting period whose length almost always exceeds by some arbitrary margin the point of actual vesting in cases traditionally validated by the wait-and-see strategy. The actual-measuring-lives approach, therefore, performs a margin-of-safety function. Given this fact, and given the costs and difficulties associated with the actual-measuring-lives approach, the Uniform Statutory Rule forgoes the use of actual measuring lives and uses instead a permissible vesting period of a flat 90 years.

The philosophy behind the 90-year period is to fix a period of time that approximates the average period of time that would traditionally be allowed by the wait-and-see doctrine. The flat-period-of-years method was not used as a means of increasing permissible dead-hand control by lengthening the permissible vesting period beyond its traditional boundaries. In fact, the 90-year period falls substantially short of the absolute maximum period of time that could theoretically be achieved under the common-law Rule itself, by the so-called "twelve-healthy-babies ploy"-a ploy that would average out to a period of about 115 years,[1] 25 years or 27.8% longer than the 90 years allowed by USRAP. The fact that the traditional period roughly averages out to a longish-sounding 90 years is a reflection of a quite different phenomenon: the dramatic increase in longevity that society as a whole has experienced in the course of the twentieth century.

The framers of the Uniform Statutory Rule derived the 90-year period as follows. The first point recognized was that if actual measuring lives were to have been used, the length of the permissible vesting period would, in the normal course of events, be governed by the life of the youngest measuring life. The second point recognized was that no matter what method is used to identify the measuring lives, the youngest measuring life, in standard trusts, is likely to be the transferor's youngest descendant living when the trust was created.[2] The 90-year period was premised on these propositions. Using four hypothetical families deemed to be representative of actual families, the framers of the Uniform Statutory Rule determined that, on average, the transferor's youngest descendant in being at the transferor's death—assuming the transferor's death to occur between ages 60 and 90, which is when 73 percent of the population die—is about 6 years old. See Waggoner, "Perpetuities: A Progress Report on the Draft Uniform Statutory Rule Against Perpetuities," 20 U. Miami Inst. on Est. Plan. Ch. 7 at 7-17 (1986). The remaining life expectancy of a 6-year-old is about 69 years. The 69 years, plus the 21-year tack-on period, gives a permissible vesting period of 90 years.

Acceptance of the 90-year-period Approach under the Federal Generation-skipping Transfer Tax. Federal regulations, to be promulgated by the U.S. Treasury Department under the generation-skipping transfer tax, will accept the Uniform Statutory Rule's 90-year period as a valid approximation of the period that, on average, would be produced by lives in being plus 21 years. See Temp. Treas. Reg. § 26.2601-1(b)(1)(v)(B)(2) (as to be revised). When originally promulgated in 1988, this regulation was prepared without knowledge of the Uniform Statutory Rule Against Perpetuities, which had been promulgated in 1986; as first promulgated, the regulation only recognized a period measured by actual lives in being plus 21 years. After the 90-year approach of the Uniform Statutory Rule was brought to the attention of the U.S. Treasury Department, the Department issued a letter of intent to amend the regulation to treat the 90-year period as the equivalent

[1] Actuarially, the life expectancy of the longest living member of a group of twelve new-born babies is about 94 years; with the 21-year tack-on period, the "twelve-healthy-babies ploy" would produce, on average, a period of about 115 years (94 + 21).

[2] Under §2-707, the descendants of a beneficiary of a future interest are presumptively made substitute beneficiaries, almost certainly making those descendants in being at the creation of the interest measuring lives, were measuring lives to have been used.

of a lives-in-being-plus-21-years period. Letter from Michael J. Graetz, Deputy Assistant Secretary of the Treasury (Tax Policy), to Lawrence J. Bugge, President, National Conference of Commissioners on Uniform State Laws (Nov. 16, 1990). For further discussion of the coordination of the federal generation-skipping transfer tax with the Uniform Statutory Rule, see the Comment to Section 2-901(e), infra, and the Comment to Section 1(e) of the Uniform Statutory Rule Against Perpetuities.

The 90-year Period Will Seldom be Used Up. Nearly all trusts (or other property arrangements) will terminate by their own terms long before the 90-year permissible vesting period expires, leaving the permissible vesting period to extend unused (and ignored) into the future long after the contingencies have been resolved and the property distributed. In the unlikely event that the contingencies have not been resolved by the expiration of the permissible vesting period, Section 2-903 requires the disposition to be reformed by the court so that all contingencies are resolved within the permissible period.

In effect, wait-and-see with deferred reformation operates similarly to a traditional perpetuity saving clause, which grants a margin-of-safety period measured by the lives of the transferor's descendants in being at the creation of the trust or other property arrangement (plus 21 years).

No New Learning Required. The Uniform Statutory Rule does not require the practicing bar to learn a new and unfamiliar set of perpetuity principles. The effect of the Uniform Statutory Rule on the planning and drafting of documents for clients should be distinguished from the effect on the resolution of actual or potential perpetuity-violation cases. The former affects many more practicing lawyers than the latter.

With respect to the planning and drafting end of the practice, the Uniform Statutory Rule requires no modification of current practice and no new learning. *Lawyers can and should continue to use the same traditional perpetuity-saving/termination clause, using specified lives in being plus 21 years, they used before enactment.* Lawyers should not shift to a "later of" type clause that purports to operate upon the *later of* (A) 21 years after the death of the survivor of specified lives in being or (B) 90 years. As explained in more detail in the Comment to Section 2-901, such a clause is not effective. If such a "later of" clause is used in a trust that contains a violation of the common-law rule against perpetuities, Section 2-901(a), by itself, would render the clause ineffective, limit the maximum permissible vesting period to 90 years, and render the trust vulnerable to a reformation suit under Section 2-903. Section 2-901(e), however, saves documents using this type of clause from this fate. By limiting the effect of such clauses to the 21-year period following the death of the survivor of the specified lives, subsection (e) in effect transforms this type of clause into a traditional perpetuity-saving/termination clause, bringing the trust into compliance with the common-law rule against perpetuities and rendering it invulnerable to a reformation suit under Section 2-903.

Far fewer in number are those lawyers (and judges) who have an actual or potential perpetuity-violation case. An actual or potential perpetuity-violation case will arise very infrequently under the Uniform Statutory Rule. When such a case does arise, however, lawyers (or judges) involved in the case will find considerable guidance for its resolution in the detailed analysis contained in the commentary accompanying the Uniform Statutory Rule itself. In short, the detailed analysis in the commentary accompanying the Uniform Statutory Rule need not be part of the general learning required of lawyers in the drafting and planning of dispositive documents for their clients. The detailed analysis is supplied in the commentary for the assistance in the resolution of an actual violation. Only then need that detailed analysis be consulted and, in such a case, it will prove extremely helpful.

General References. Fellows, "Testing Perpetuity Reforms: A Study of Perpetuity Cases 1984-89," 25 Real Prop. Prob. & Tr. J. 597 (1991) (testing the various types of perpetuity reform measures and concluding, on the basis of empirical evidence, that the Uniform Statutory Rule is the best opportunity offered to date for a uniform perpetuity law that efficiently and effectively achieves a fair balance between present and future property owners); Waggoner, "The Uniform Statutory Rule Against Perpetuities: Oregon Joins Up," 26 Willamette L. Rev. 259 (1990) (explaining the operation of the Uniform Statutory Rule); Waggoner, "The Uniform Statutory Rule Against Perpetuities: The Rationale of the 90-Year Waiting Period," 73 Cornell L. Rev. 157 (1988) (explaining the derivation of the 90-year period); Waggoner, "The Uniform Statutory Rule Against Perpetuities," 21 Real Prop., Prob. & Tr. J. 569 (1986) (explaining the theory and operation of the Uniform Statutory Rule).

§2-901. Statutory Rule Against Perpetuities

(a) [Validity of Nonvested Property Interest.] A nonvested property interest is invalid unless:

(1) when the interest is created, it is certain to vest or terminate no later than 21 years after the death of an individual then alive; or

(2) the interest either vests or terminates within 90 years after its creation.

(b) [Validity of General Power of Appointment Subject to a Condition Precedent.] A general power of appointment not presently exercisable because of a condition precedent is invalid unless:

(1) when the power is created, the condition precedent is certain to be satisfied or becomes impossible to satisfy no later than 21 years after the death of an individual then alive; or

(2) the condition precedent either is satisfied or becomes impossible to satisfy within 90 years after its creation.

(c) [Validity of Nongeneral or Testamentary Power of Appointment.] A nongeneral power of appointment or a general testamentary power of appointment is invalid unless:

(1) when the power is created, it is certain to be irrevocably exercised or otherwise to terminate no later than 21 years after the death of an individual then alive; or

(2) the power is irrevocably exercised or otherwise terminates within 90 years after its creation.

(d) [Possibility of Post-death Child Disregarded.] In determining whether a nonvested property interest or a power of appointment is valid under subsection (a)(1), (b)(1), or (c)(1), the possibility that a child will be born to an individual after the individual's death is disregarded.

(e) [Effect of Certain "Later-of" Type Language.] If, in measuring a period from the creation of a trust or other property arrangement, language in a governing instrument (i) seeks to disallow the vesting or termination of any interest or trust beyond, (ii) seeks to postpone the vesting or termination of any interest or trust until, or (iii) seeks to operate in effect in any similar fashion upon, the later of (A) the expiration of a period of time not exceeding 21 years after the death of the survivor of specified lives in being at the creation of the trust or other property arrangement or (B) the expiration of a period of time that exceeds or might exceed 21 years after the death of the survivor of lives in being at the creation of the trust or other property arrangement, that language is inoperative to the extent it produces a period of time that exceeds 21 years after the death of the survivor of the specified lives.

§2-902. When Nonvested Property Interest or Power of Appointment Created

(a) Except as provided in subsections (b) and (c) and in Section 2-905(a), the time of creation of a nonvested property interest or a power of appointment is determined under general principles of property law.

(b) For purposes of Subpart 1 of this Part, if there is a person who alone can exercise a power created by a governing instrument to become the unqualified beneficial owner of (i) a nonvested property interest or (ii) a property interest subject to a power of appointment described in Section 2-901(b) or (c), the nonvested property interest or power of appointment is created when the power to become the unqualified beneficial owner terminates. [For purposes of Subpart 1 of this Part, a joint power with respect to community property or to marital property under the Uniform Marital Property Act held by individuals married to each other is a power exercisable by one person alone.]

(c) For purposes of Subpart 1 of this Part, a nonvested property interest or a power of appointment arising from a transfer of property to a previously funded trust or other existing property arrangement is created when the nonvested property interest or power of appointment in the original contribution was created.

§2-903. Reformation

Upon the petition of an interested person, a court shall reform a disposition in the manner that most closely approximates the transferor's manifested plan of distribution and is within the 90 years allowed by Section 2-901(a)(2), 2-901(b)(2), or 2-901(c)(2) if:

(1) a nonvested property interest or a power of appointment becomes invalid under Section 2-901 (statutory rule against perpetuities);

(2) a class gift is not but might become invalid under Section 2-901 (statutory rule against perpetuities) and the time has arrived when the share of any class member is to take effect in possession or enjoyment; or

(3) a nonvested property interest that is not validated by Section 2-901(a)(1) can vest but not within 90 years after its creation.

§2-904. Exclusions from Statutory Rule Against Perpetuities

Section 2-901 (statutory rule against perpetuities) does not apply to:

(1) a nonvested property interest or a power of appointment arising out of a nondonative transfer, except a nonvested property interest or a power of appointment arising out of (i) a premarital or postmarital agreement, (ii) a separation or divorce settlement, (iii) a spouse's election, (iv) a similar arrangement arising out of a prospective, existing, or previous marital relationship between the parties, (v) a contract to make or not to revoke a will or trust, (vi) a contract to exercise or not to exercise a power of appointment, (vii) a transfer in satisfaction of a duty of support, or (viii) a reciprocal transfer;

(2) a fiduciary's power relating to the administration or management of assets, including the power of a fiduciary to sell, lease, or mortgage property, and the power of a fiduciary to determine principal and income;

(3) a power to appoint a fiduciary;

(4) a discretionary power of a trustee to distribute principal before termination of a trust to a beneficiary having an indefeasibly vested interest in the income and principal;

(5) a nonvested property interest held by a charity, government, or governmental agency or subdivision, if the nonvested property interest is preceded by an interest held by another charity, government, or governmental agency or subdivision;

(6) a nonvested property interest in or a power of appointment with respect to a trust or other property arrangement forming part of a pension, profit-sharing, stock bonus, health, disability, death benefit, income deferral, or other current or deferred benefit plan for one or more employees, independent contractors, or their beneficiaries or spouses, to which contributions are made for the purpose of distributing to or for the benefit of the participants or their beneficiaries or spouses the property, income, or principal in the trust or other property arrangement, except a nonvested

property interest or a power of appointment that is created by an election of a participant or a beneficiary or spouse; or

(7) a property interest, power of appointment, or arrangement that was not subject to the common-law rule against perpetuities or is excluded by another statute of this State.

§2-905. Prospective Application

(a) Except as extended by subsection (b), Subpart 1 of this Part applies to a nonvested property interest or a power of appointment that is created on or after the effective date of Subpart 1 of this Part. For purposes of this section, a nonvested property interest or a power of appointment created by the exercise of a power of appointment is created when the power is irrevocably exercised or when a revocable exercise becomes irrevocable.

(b) If a nonvested property interest or a power of appointment was created before the effective date of Subpart 1 of this Part and is determined in a judicial proceeding, commenced on or after the effective date of Subpart 1 of this Part, to violate this State's rule against perpetuities as that rule existed before the effective date of Subpart 1 of this Part, a court upon the petition of an interested person may reform the disposition in the manner that most closely approximates the transferor's manifested plan of distribution and is within the limits of the rule against perpetuities applicable when the nonvested property interest or power of appointment was created.

§2-906. [Supersession][Repeal]

Subpart 1 of this Part [supersedes the rule of the common law known as the rule against perpetuities][repeals (list statutes to be repealed)].

SUBPART 2. [HONORARY TRUSTS]

[Optional provision for validating and limiting the duration of so-called honorary trusts and trusts for pets.]

§2-907. Honorary Trusts; Trusts for Pets

(a) [Honorary Trust.] Subject to subsection (c), if (i) a trust is for a specific lawful noncharitable purpose or for lawful noncharitable purposes to be selected by the trustee and (ii) there is no definite or definitely ascertainable beneficiary designated, the trust may be performed by the trustee for [21] years but no longer, whether or not the terms of the trust contemplate a longer duration.

(b) [Trust for Pets.] Subject to this subsection and subsection (c), a trust for the care of a designated domestic or pet animal is valid. The trust terminates when no living animal is covered by the trust. A governing instrument must be liberally construed to bring the transfer within this subsection, to presume against the merely precatory or honorary nature of the disposition, and to carry out the general intent of the transferor. Extrinsic evidence is admissible in determining the transferor's intent.

(c) [Additional Provisions Applicable to Honorary Trusts and Trusts for Pets.] In addition to the provisions of subsection (a) or (b), a trust covered by either of those subsections is subject to the following provisions:

(1) Except as expressly provided otherwise in the trust instrument, no portion of the principal or income may be converted to the use of the trustee or to any use other than for the trust's purposes or for the benefit of a covered animal.

(2) Upon termination, the trustee shall transfer the unexpended trust property in the following order:

(i) as directed in the trust instrument;

(ii) if the trust was created in a nonresiduary clause in the transferor's will or in a codicil to the transferor's will, under the residuary clause in the transferor's will; and

(iii) if no taker is produced by the application of subparagraph (i) or (ii), to the transferor's heirs under Section 2-711.

(3) For the purposes of Section 2-707, the residuary clause is treated as creating a future interest under the terms of a trust.

(4) The intended use of the principal or income can be enforced by an individual designated for that purpose in the trust instrument or, if none, by an individual appointed by a court upon application to it by an individual.

(5) Except as ordered by the court or required by the trust instrument, no filing, report, registration, periodic accounting, separate maintenance of funds, appointment, or fee is required by reason of the existence of the fiduciary relationship of the trustee.

(6) A court may reduce the amount of the property transferred, if it determines that that amount substantially exceeds the amount required for the intended use. The amount of the reduction, if any, passes as unexpended trust property under subsection (c)(2).

(7) If no trustee is designated or no designated trustee is willing or able to serve, a court shall name a trustee. A court may order the transfer of the property to another trustee, if required to assure that the intended use is carried out and if no successor trustee is designated in the trust instrument or if no designated successor trustee agrees to serve or is able to serve. A court may also make such other orders and determinations as shall be advisable to carry out the intent of the transferor and the purpose of this section.]

As amended in 1993.

[Part 10, the Uniform International Wills Act, has been omitted.]

Part VI

~

Uniform Prudent Investor Act (1994)

UNIFORM PRUDENT INVESTOR ACT (1994)

PREFATORY NOTE

Over the quarter century from the late 1960s the investment practices of fiduciaries experienced significant change. The Uniform Prudent Investor Act (UPIA) undertakes to update trust investment law in recognition of the alterations that have occurred in investment practice. These changes have occurred under the influence of a large and broadly accepted body of empirical and theoretical knowledge about the behavior of capital markets, often described as "modern portfolio theory."

This Act draws upon the revised standards for prudent trust investment promulgated by the American Law Institute in its Restatement (Third) of Trusts: Prudent Investor Rule (1992) [hereinafter Restatement of Trusts 3d: Prudent Investor Rule; also referred to as 1992 Restatement].

Objectives of the Act. UPIA makes five fundamental alterations in the former criteria for prudent investing. All are to be found in the Restatement of Trusts 3d: Prudent Investor Rule.

(1) The standard of prudence is applied to any investment as part of the total portfolio, rather than to individual investments. In the trust setting the term "portfolio" embraces all the trust's assets. UPIA §2(b).

(2) The tradeoff in all investing between risk and return is identified as the fiduciary's central consideration. UPIA §2(b).

(3) All categoric restrictions on types of investments have been abrogated; the trustee can invest in anything that plays an appropriate role in achieving the risk/return objectives of the trust and that meets the other requirements of prudent investing. UPIA §2(e).

(4) The long familiar requirement that fiduciaries diversify their investments has been integrated into the definition of prudent investing. UPIA §3.

(5) The much criticized former rule of trust law forbidding the trustee to delegate investment and management functions has been reversed. Delegation is now permitted, subject to safeguards. UPIA §9.

Literature. These changes in trust investment law have been presaged in an extensive body of practical and scholarly writing. See especially the discussion and reporter's notes by Edward C. Halbach, Jr., in Restatement of Trusts 3d: Prudent Investor Rule (1992); see also Edward C. Halbach, Jr., Trust Investment Law in the Third Restatement, 27 Real Property, Probate & Trust J. 407 (1992); Bevis Longstreth, Modern Investment Management and the Prudent Man Rule (1986); Jeffrey N. Gordon, The Puzzling Persistence of the Constrained Prudent Man Rule, 62 N.Y.U.L. Rev. 52 (1987); John H. Langbein & Richard A. Posner, The Revolution in Trust Investment Law, 62 A.B.A.J. 887 (1976); Note, The Regulation of Risky Investments, 83 Harvard L. Rev. 603 (1970). A succinct account of the main findings of modern portfolio theory, written for lawyers, is Jonathan R. Macey, An Introduction to Modern Financial Theory (1991) (American College of Trust & Estate Counsel Foundation). A leading introductory text on modern portfolio theory is R.A. Brealey, An Introduction to Risk and Return from Common Stocks (2d ed. 1983).

Legislation. Most states have legislation governing trust-investment law. This Act promotes uniformity of state law on the basis of the new consensus reflected in the Restatement of Trusts 3d: Prudent Investor Rule. Some states have already acted. California, Delaware, Georgia, Minnesota, Tennessee, and Washington revised their prudent investor legislation to emphasize the total-portfolio standard of care in advance of the 1992 Restatement. These statutes are extracted and discussed in Restatement of Trusts 3d: Prudent Investor Rule §227, reporter's note, at 60-66 (1992).

Drafters in Illinois in 1991 worked from the April 1990 "Proposed Final Draft" of the Restatement of Trusts 3d: Prudent Investor Rule and enacted legislation that is closely modeled on the new Restatement. 760 ILCS §5/5 (prudent investing); and §5/5.1 (delegation) (1992). As the Comments to this Uniform Prudent Investor Act reflect, the Act draws upon the Illinois statute in several sections. Virginia revised its prudent investor act in a similar vein in 1992. Virginia Code §26-45.1 (prudent investing) (1992). Florida revised its statute in 1993. Florida Laws, ch. 93-257, amending Florida Statutes §518.11 (prudent investing) and creating §518.112 (delegation). New York legislation drawing on the new Restatement and on a preliminary version of this Uniform Prudent Investor Act was enacted in 1994. N.Y. Assembly Bill 11683-B, Ch. 609 (1994), adding Estates, Powers and Trusts Law §11-2.3 (Prudent Investor Act).

Remedies. This Act does not undertake to address issues of remedy law or the computation of damages in trust matters. Remedies are the subject of a reasonably distinct body of doctrine. See generally Restatement (Second) of Trusts §§197-226A (1959) [hereinafter cited as Restatement of Trusts 2d; also referred to as 1959 Restatement].

Implications for charitable and pension trusts. This Act is centrally concerned with the investment responsibilities arising under the private gratuitous trust, which is the common vehicle for conditioned wealth transfer within the family. Nevertheless, the prudent investor rule also bears on charitable and

pension trusts, among others. "In making investments of trust funds the trustee of a charitable trust is under a duty similar to that of the trustee of a private trust." Restatement of Trusts 2d §389 (1959). The Employee Retirement Income Security Act (ERISA), the federal regulatory scheme for pension trusts enacted in 1974, absorbs trust-investment law through the prudence standard of ERISA §404(a)(1)(B), 29 U.S.C. §1104(a). The Supreme Court has said: "ERISA's legislative history confirms that the Act's fiduciary responsibility provisions 'codif[y] and mak[e] applicable to [ERISA] fiduciaries certain principles developed in the evolution of the law of trusts.'" *Firestone Tire & Rubber Co. v. Bruch*, 489 U.S. 101, 110-11 (1989) (footnote omitted).

Other fiduciary relationships. The Uniform Prudent Investor Act regulates the investment responsibilities of trustees. Other fiduciaries—such as executors, conservators, and guardians of the property—sometimes have responsibilities over assets that are governed by the standards of prudent investment. It will often be appropriate for states to adapt the law governing investment by trustees under this Act to these other fiduciary regimes, taking account of such changed circumstances as the relatively short duration of most executorships and the intensity of court supervision of conservators and guardians in some jurisdictions. The present Act does not undertake to adjust trust-investment law to the special circumstances of the state schemes for administering decedents' estates or conducting the affairs of protected persons.

Although the Uniform Prudent Investor Act by its terms applies to trusts and not to charitable corporations, the standards of the Act can be expected to inform the investment responsibilities of directors and officers of charitable corporations. As the 1992 Restatement observes, "the duties of the members of the governing board of a charitable corporation are generally similar to the duties of the trustee of a charitable trust." Restatement of Trusts 3d: Prudent Investor Rule §379, Comment *b*, at 190 (1992). See also id. §389, Comment *b*, at 190-91 (absent contrary statute or other provision, prudent investor rule applies to investment of funds held for charitable corporations).

UNIFORM PRUDENT INVESTOR ACT

§1. Prudent Investor Rule

(a) Except as otherwise provided in subsection (b), a trustee who invests and manages trust assets owes a duty to the beneficiaries of the trust to comply with the prudent investor rule set forth in this [Act].

(b) The prudent investor rule, a default rule, may be expanded, restricted, eliminated, or otherwise altered by the provisions of a trust. A trustee is not liable to a beneficiary to the extent that the trustee acted in reasonable reliance on the provisions of the trust.

Comment

This section imposes the obligation of prudence in the conduct of investment functions and identifies further sections of the Act that specify the attributes of prudent conduct.

Origins. The prudence standard for trust investing traces back to *Harvard College v. Amory*, 26 Mass. (9 Pick.) 446 (1830). Trustees should "observe how men of prudence, discretion and intelligence manage their own affairs, not in regard to speculation, but in regard to the permanent disposition of their funds, considering the probable income, as well as the probable safety of the capital to be invested." Id. at 461.

Prior legislation. The Model Prudent Man Rule Statute (1942), sponsored by the American Bankers Association, undertook to codify the language of the *Amory* case. See Mayo A. Shattuck, The Development of the Prudent Man Rule for Fiduciary Investment in the United States in the Twentieth Century, 12 Ohio State L.J. 491, at 501 (1951); for the text of the model act, which inspired many state statutes, see id. at 508-09. Another prominent codification of the *Amory* standard is Uniform Probate Code §7-302 (1969), which provides that "the trustee shall observe the standards in dealing with the trust assets that would be observed by a prudent man dealing with the property of another . . . ."

. . . **Objective standard.** The concept of prudence in the judicial opinions and legislation is essentially relational or comparative. It resembles in this respect the "reasonable person" rule of tort law. A prudent trustee behaves as other trustees similarly situated would behave. The standard is, therefore, objective rather than subjective. Sections 2 through 9 of this Act identify the main factors that bear on prudent investment behavior.

Variation. Almost all of the rules of trust law are default rules, that is, rules that the settlor may alter or abrogate. Subsection (b) carries forward this traditional attribute of trust law. Traditional trust law also allows the beneficiaries of the trust to excuse its performance, when they are all capable and not misinformed. Restatement of Trusts 2d §216 (1959).

§2. Standard of Care; Portfolio Strategy; Risk and Return Objectives

(a) A trustee shall invest and manage trust assets as a prudent investor would, by considering the purposes, terms, distribution requirements, and other circumstances of the trust. In satisfying this standard, the trustee shall exercise reasonable care, skill, and caution.

(b) A trustee's investment and management decisions respecting individual assets must be evaluated not in isolation but in the context of the trust portfolio as a whole and as a part of an overall investment strategy having risk and return objectives reasonably suited to the trust.

(c) Among circumstances that a trustee shall consider in investing and managing trust assets are such of the following as are relevant to the trust or its beneficiaries:

(1) general economic conditions;

(2) the possible effect of inflation or deflation;

(3) the expected tax consequences of investment decisions or strategies;

(4) the role that each investment or course of action plays within the overall trust portfolio, which may include financial assets, interests in closely held enterprises, tangible and intangible personal property, and real property;

(5) the expected total return from income and the appreciation of capital;

(6) other resources of the beneficiaries;

(7) needs for liquidity, regularity of income, and preservation or appreciation of capital; and

(8) an asset's special relationship or special value, if any, to the purposes of the trust or to one or more of the beneficiaries.

(d) A trustee shall make a reasonable effort to verify facts relevant to the investment and management of trust assets.

(e) A trustee may invest in any kind of property or type of investment consistent with the standards of this [Act].

(f) A trustee who has special skills or expertise, or is named trustee in reliance upon the trustee's representation that the trustee has special skills or expertise, has a duty to use those special skills or expertise.

Comment

Section 2 is the heart of the Act. Subsections (a), (b), and (c) are patterned loosely on the language of the Restatement of Trusts 3d: Prudent Investor Rule §227 (1992), and on the 1991 Illinois statute, 760 §ILCS 5/5a (1992). Subsection (f) is derived from Uniform Probate Code §7-302 (1969).

Objective standard. Subsection (a) of this Act carries forward the relational and objective standard made familiar in the *Amory* case, in earlier prudent investor legislation, and in the Restatements. Early formulations of the prudent person rule were sometimes troubled by the effort to distinguish between the standard of a prudent person investing for another and investing on his or her own account. The language of subsection (a), by relating the trustee's duty to "the purposes, terms, distribution requirements, and other circumstances of the trust," should put such questions to rest. The standard is the standard of the prudent investor similarly situated.

Portfolio standard. Subsection (b) emphasizes the consolidated portfolio standard for evaluating investment decisions. An investment that might be imprudent standing alone can become prudent if undertaken in sensible relation to other trust assets, or to other nontrust assets. In the trust setting the term "portfolio" embraces the entire trust estate.

Risk and return. Subsection (b) also sounds the main theme of modern investment practice, sensitivity to the risk/return curve. See generally the works cited in the Prefatory Note to this Act, under "Literature." Returns correlate strongly with risk, but tolerance for risk varies greatly with the financial and other circumstances of the investor, or in the case of a trust, with the purposes of the trust and the relevant circumstances of the beneficiaries. A trust whose main purpose is to support an elderly widow of modest means will have a lower risk tolerance than a trust to accumulate for a young scion of great wealth.

Subsection (b) of this Act follows Restatement of Trusts 3d: Prudent Investor Rule §227(a), which provides that the standard of prudent investing "requires the exercise of reasonable care, skill, and caution, and is to be applied to investments not in isolation but in the context of the trust portfolio and as a part of an overall investment strategy, which should incorporate risk and return objectives reasonably suitable to the trust."

Factors affecting investment. Subsection (c) points to certain of the factors that commonly bear on risk/return preferences in fiduciary investing. This listing is nonexclusive. Tax considerations, such as preserving the stepped-up basis on death under Internal Revenue Code §1014 for low-basis assets, have traditionally been exceptionally important in estate planning for affluent persons. Under the present recognition rules of the federal income tax, taxable investors, including trust beneficiaries, are in general best served by an investment strategy that minimizes the taxation incident to portfolio turnover. See generally Robert H. Jeffrey & Robert D. Arnott, Is Your Alpha Big Enough to Cover Its Taxes?, Journal of Portfolio Management 15 (Spring 1993).

Another familiar example of how tax considerations bear upon trust investing: In a regime of pass-through taxation, it may be prudent for the trust to buy lower yielding tax-exempt securities for high-bracket taxpayers, whereas it would ordinarily be imprudent for the trustees of a charitable trust, whose income is tax exempt, to accept the lowered yields associated with tax-exempt securities.

When tax considerations affect beneficiaries differently, the trustee's duty of impartiality requires attention to the competing interests of each of them.

Subsection (c)(8), allowing the trustee to take into account any preferences of the beneficiaries respecting heirlooms or other prized assets, derives from the Illinois act, 760 ILCS §5/5(a)(4) (1992).

Duty to monitor. Subsections (a) through (d) apply both to investing and managing trust assets. "Managing" embraces monitoring, that is, the trustee's continuing responsibility for oversight of the suitability of investments already made as well as the trustee's decisions respecting new investments.

Duty to investigate. Subsection (d) carries forward the traditional responsibility of the fiduciary investor to examine information likely to bear importantly on the value or the security of an investment—for example, audit reports or records of title. E.g., *Estate of Collins*, 72 Cal. App. 3d 663, 139 Cal. Rptr. 644 (1977) (trustees lent on a junior mortgage on unimproved real estate, failed to have land appraised, and accepted an unaudited financial statement; held liable for losses).

Abrogating categoric restrictions. Subsection 2(e) clarifies that no particular kind of property or type of investment is inherently imprudent. Traditional trust law was encumbered with a variety of categoric exclusions, such as prohibitions on junior mortgages or new ventures. In some states legislation created so-called "legal lists" of approved trust investments. The universe of investment products changes incessantly. Investments that were at one time thought too risky, such as equities, or more recently, futures, are now used in fiduciary portfolios. By contrast, the investment that was at one time thought ideal for trusts, the long-term bond, has been discovered to import a level of risk and volatility—in this case, inflation risk—that had not been anticipated. Accordingly, section 2(e) of this Act follows Restatement of Trusts 3d: Prudent Investor Rule in abrogating categoric restrictions. The Restatement says: "Specific investments or techniques are not per se prudent or imprudent. The riskiness of a specific property, and thus the propriety of its inclusion in the trust estate, is not judged in the abstract but in terms of its anticipated effect on the particular trust's portfolio." Restatement of Trusts 3d: Prudent Investor Rule §227, Comment f, at 24 (1992). The premise of subsection 2(e) is that trust beneficiaries are better protected by the Act's emphasis on close attention to risk/return objectives as prescribed in subsection 2(b) than in attempts to identify categories of investment that are per se prudent or imprudent.

The Act impliedly disavows the emphasis in older law on avoiding "speculative" or "risky" investments. Low levels of risk may be appropriate in some trust settings but inappropriate in others. It is the trustee's task to invest at a risk level that is suitable to the purposes of the trust.

The abolition of categoric restrictions against types of investment in no way alters the trustee's conventional duty of loyalty, which is reiterated for the purposes of this Act in Section 5. For example, were the trustee to invest in a second mortgage on a piece of real property owned by the trustee, the investment would be wrongful on account of the trustee's breach of the duty to abstain from self-dealing, even though the investment would no longer automatically offend the former categoric restriction against fiduciary investments in junior mortgages.

Professional fiduciaries. The distinction taken in subsection (f) between amateur and professional trustees is familiar law. The prudent investor standard applies to a range of fiduciaries, from the most sophisticated professional investment management firms and corporate fiduciaries, to family members of minimal experience. Because the standard of prudence is relational, it follows that the standard for professional trustees is the standard of prudent professionals; for amateurs, it is the standard of prudent amateurs. Restatement of Trusts 2d §174 (1959) provides: "The trustee is under a duty to the beneficiary in administering the trust to exercise such care and skill as a man of ordinary prudence would exercise in dealing with his own property; and if the trustee has or procures his appointment as trustee by representing that he has greater skill than that of a man of ordinary prudence, he is under a duty to exercise such skill." Case law strongly supports the concept of the higher standard of care for the trustee representing itself to be expert or professional. See Annot., Standard of Care Required of Trustee Representing Itself to Have Expert Knowledge or Skill, 91 A.L.R. 3d 904 (1979) & 1992 Supp. at 48-49.

The Drafting Committee declined the suggestion that the Act should create an exception to the prudent investor rule (or to the diversification requirement of Section 3) in the case of smaller trusts. The Committee believes that subsections (b) and (c) of the Act emphasize factors that are sensitive to the traits of small trusts; and that subsection (f) adjusts helpfully for the distinction between professional and amateur trusteeship. Furthermore, it is always open to the settlor of a trust under Section 1(b) of the Act to reduce the trustee's standard of care if the settlor deems such a step appropriate. The official comments to the 1992 Restatement observe that pooled investments, such as mutual funds and bank common trust funds, are especially suitable for small trusts. Restatement of Trusts 3d: Prudent Investor Rule §227, Comments *h*, *m*, at 28, 51; reporter's note to Comment *g*, id. at 83.

Matters of proof. Although virtually all express trusts are created by written instrument, oral trusts are known, and accordingly, this Act presupposes no formal requirement that trust terms be in writing. When there is a written trust instrument, modern authority strongly favors allowing evidence extrinsic to the instrument to be consulted for the purpose of ascertaining the settlor's intent. See Uniform Probate Code §2-601 (1990), Comment; Restatement (Third) of Property: Donative Transfers (Preliminary Draft No. 2, ch. 11, Sept. 11, 1992).

§3. Diversification

A trustee shall diversify the investments of the trust unless the trustee reasonably determines that, because of special circumstances, the purposes of the trust are better served without diversifying.

Comment

The language of this section derives from Restatement of Trusts 2d §228 (1959). ERISA insists upon a comparable rule for pension trusts. ERISA §404(a)(1)(C), 29 U.S.C. §1104(a)(1)(C). Case law overwhelmingly supports the duty to diversify. See Annot., Duty of Trustee to Diversify Investments, and

Liability for Failure to Do So, 24 A.L.R. 3d 730 (1969) & 1992 Supp. at 78-79.

The 1992 Restatement of Trusts takes the significant step of integrating the diversification requirement into the concept of prudent investing. Section 227(b) of the 1992 Restatement treats diversification as one of the fundamental elements of prudent investing, replacing the separate section 228 of the Restatement of Trusts 2d. The message of the 1992 Restatement, carried forward in Section 3 of this Act, is that prudent investing ordinarily requires diversification.

Circumstances can, however, overcome the duty to diversify. For example, if a tax-sensitive trust owns an underdiversified block of low-basis securities, the tax costs of recognizing the gain may outweigh the advantages of diversifying the holding. The wish to retain a family business is another situation in which the purposes of the trust sometimes override the conventional duty to diversify.

Rationale for diversification. "Diversification reduces risk . . . [because] stock price movements are not uniform. They are imperfectly correlated. This means that if one holds a well diversified portfolio, the gains in one investment will cancel out the losses in another." Jonathan R. Macey, An Introduction to Modern Financial Theory 20 (American College of Trust and Estate Counsel Foundation, 1991). For example, during the Arab oil embargo of 1973, international oil stocks suffered declines, but the shares of domestic oil producers and coal companies benefitted. Holding a broad enough portfolio allowed the investor to set off, to some extent, the losses associated with the embargo.

Modern portfolio theory divides risk into the categories of "compensated" and "uncompensated" risk. The risk of owning shares in a mature and well-managed company in a settled industry is less than the risk of owning shares in a start-up high-technology venture. The investor requires a higher expected return to induce the investor to bear the greater risk of disappointment associated with the start-up firm. This is compensated risk—the firm pays the investor for bearing the risk. By contrast, nobody pays the investor for owning too few stocks. The investor who owned only international oils in 1973 was running a risk that could have been reduced by having configured the portfolio differently—to include investments in different industries. This is uncompensated risk—nobody pays the investor for owning shares in too few industries and too few companies. Risk that can be eliminated by adding different stocks (or bonds) is uncompensated risk. The object of diversification is to minimize this uncompensated risk of having too few investments. "As long as stock prices do not move exactly together, the risk of a diversified portfolio will be less than the average risk of the separate holdings." R.A. Brealey, An Introduction to Risk and Return from Common Stocks 103 (2d ed. 1983).

There is no automatic rule for identifying how much diversification is enough. The 1992 Restatement says: "Significant diversification advantages can be achieved with a small number of well-selected securities representing different industries . . . . Broader diversification is usually to be preferred in trust investing," and pooled investment vehicles "make thorough diversification practical for most trustees." Restatement of Trusts 3d: Prudent Investor Rule §227, General Note on Comments *e-h*, at 77 (1992). See also Macey, supra, at 23-24; Brealey, supra, at 111-13.

Diversifying by pooling. It is difficult for a small trust fund to diversify thoroughly by constructing its own portfolio of individually selected investments. Transaction costs such as the round-lot (100 share) trading economies make it relatively expensive for a small investor to assemble a broad enough portfolio to minimize uncompensated risk. For this reason, pooled investment vehicles have become the main mechanism for facilitating diversification for the investment needs of smaller trusts.

Most states have legislation authorizing common trust funds; see 3 Austin W. Scott & William F. Fratcher, The Law of Trusts §227.9, at 463-65 n.26 (4th ed. 1988) (collecting citations to state statutes). As of 1992, 35 states and the District of Columbia had enacted the Uniform Common Trust Fund Act (UCTFA) (1938), overcoming the rule against commingling trust assets and expressly enabling banks and trust companies to establish common trust funds. 7 Uniform Laws Ann. 1992 Supp. at 130 (schedule of adopting states). The Prefatory Note to the UCTFA explains: "The purposes of such a common or joint investment fund are to diversify the investment of the several trusts and thus spread the risk of loss, and to make it easy to invest any amount of trust funds quickly and with a small amount of trouble." 7 Uniform Laws Ann. 402 (1985).

Fiduciary investing in mutual funds. Trusts can also achieve diversification by investing in mutual funds. See Restatement of Trusts 3d: Prudent Investor Rule, §227, Comment *m*, at 99-100 (1992) (endorsing trust investment in mutual funds). ERISA §401(b)(1), 29 U.S.C. §1101(b)(1), expressly authorizes pension trusts to invest in mutual funds, identified as securities "issued by an investment company registered under the Investment Company Act of 1940 . . . ."

§4. Duties at Inception of Trusteeship

Within a reasonable time after accepting a trusteeship or receiving trust assets, a trustee shall review the trust assets and make and implement decisions concerning the retention and disposition of assets, in order to bring the trust portfolio into compliance with the purposes, terms, distribution requirements, and other circumstances of the trust, and with the requirements of this [Act].

Comment

Section 4, requiring the trustee to dispose of unsuitable assets within a reasonable time, is old law, codified in Restatement of Trusts 3d: Prudent Investor Rule §229 (1992), lightly revising Restatement of Trusts 2d §230 (1959). The duty extends as well to investments that were proper when purchased but subsequently become improper. Restatement of Trusts 2d §231 (1959). The same standards apply to successor trustees, see Restatement of Trusts 2d §196 (1959).

The question of what period of time is reasonable turns on the totality of factors affecting the asset and the trust. The 1959 Restatement took the view that "[o]rdinarily any time within a year is reasonable, but under some circumstances a year may be too long a time and under other circumstances a trustee is not liable although he fails to effect the conversion for more than a year." Restatement of Trusts 2d §230, comment *b* (1959). The 1992 Restatement retreated from this rule of thumb, saying, "No positive rule can be stated with respect to what constitutes a reasonable time for the sale or exchange of securities." Restatement of Trusts 3d: Prudent Investor Rule §229, comment *b* (1992).

The criteria and circumstances identified in Section 2 of this Act as bearing upon the prudence of decisions to invest and manage trust assets also pertain to the prudence of decisions to retain or dispose of inception assets under this section.

§5. Loyalty

A trustee shall invest and manage the trust assets solely in the interest of the beneficiaries.

Comment

The duty of loyalty is perhaps the most characteristic rule of trust law, requiring the trustee to act exclusively for the beneficiaries, as opposed to acting for the trustee's own interest or that of third parties. The language of Section 4 of this Act derives from Restatement of Trusts 3d: Prudent Investor Rule §170 (1992), which makes minute changes in Restatement of Trusts 2d §170 (1959).

The concept that the duty of prudence in trust administration, especially in investing and managing trust assets, entails adherence to the duty of loyalty is familiar. ERISA §404(a)(1)(B), 29 U.S.C. §1104(a)(1)(B), extracted in the Comment to Section 1 of this Act, effectively merges the requirements of prudence and loyalty. A fiduciary cannot be prudent in the conduct of investment functions if the fiduciary is sacrificing the interests of the beneficiaries.

The duty of loyalty is not limited to settings entailing self-dealing or conflict of interest in which the trustee would benefit personally from the trust. "The trustee is under a duty to the beneficiary in administering the trust not to be guided by the interest of any third person. Thus, it is improper for the trustee to sell trust property to a third person for the purpose of benefitting the third person rather than the trust." Restatement of Trusts 2d §170, comment *q*, at 371 (1959).

No form of so-called "social investing" is consistent with the duty of loyalty if the investment activity entails sacrificing the interests of trust beneficiaries—for example, by accepting below-market returns—in favor of the interests of the persons supposedly benefitted by pursuing the particular social cause. See, e.g., John H. Langbein & Richard Posner, Social Investing and the Law of Trusts, 79 Michigan L. Rev. 72, 96-97 (1980) (collecting authority). For pension trust assets, see generally Ian D. Lanoff, The Social Investment of Private Pension Plan Assets: May it Be Done Lawfully under ERISA?, 31 Labor L.J. 387 (1980). Commentators supporting social investing tend to concede the overriding force of the duty of loyalty. They argue instead that particular schemes of social investing may not result in below-market returns. See, e.g., Marcia O'Brien Hylton, "Socially Responsible" Investing: Doing Good Versus Doing Well in an Inefficient Market, 42 American U.L. Rev. 1 (1992). In 1994 the Department of Labor issued an Interpretive Bulletin reviewing its prior analysis of social investing questions and reiterating that pension trust fiduciaries may invest only in conformity with the prudence and loyalty standards of ERISA §§403-404. Interpretive Bulletin 94-1, 59 Fed. Regis. 32606 (Jun. 22, 1994), to be codified as 29 CFR §2509.94-1. The Bulletin reminds fiduciary investors that they are prohibited from "subordinat[ing] the interests of participants and beneficiaries in their retirement income to unrelated objectives."

§6. Impartiality

If a trust has two or more beneficiaries, the trustee shall act impartially in investing and managing the trust assets, taking into account any differing interests of the beneficiaries.

Comment

The duty of impartiality derives from the duty of loyalty. When the trustee owes duties to more than one beneficiary, loyalty requires the trustee to respect the interests of all the beneficiaries. Prudence in investing and administration requires the trustee to take account of the interests of all the beneficiaries for whom the trustee is acting, especially the conflicts between the interests of beneficiaries interested in income and those interested in principal.

The language of Section 6 derives from Restatement of Trusts 2d §183 (1959); see also id., §232. Multiple beneficiaries may be beneficiaries in succession (such as life and remainder interests) or beneficiaries with simultaneous interests (as when the income interest in a trust is being divided among several beneficiaries).

The trustee's duty of impartiality commonly affects the conduct of investment and management functions in the sphere of principal and income allocations. This Act prescribes no regime for allocating receipts and expenses. The details of such allocations are commonly handled under specialized legislation, such as the Revised Uniform Principal and Income Act (1962) (which is presently under study by the Uniform Law Commission with a view toward further revision).

§7. Investment Costs

In investing and managing trust assets, a trustee may only incur costs that are appropriate and reasonable in relation to the assets, the purposes of the trust, and the skills of the trustee.

§8. Reviewing Compliance

Compliance with the prudent investor rule is determined in light of the facts and circumstances existing at the time of a trustee's decision or action and not by hindsight.

Comment

This section derives from the 1991 Illinois act, 760 ILCS 5/5(a)(2) (1992), which draws upon Restatement of Trusts 3d: Prudent Investor Rule §227, comment *b*, at 11 (1992). Trustees are not insurers. Not every investment or management decision will turn out in the light of hindsight to have been successful. Hindsight is not the relevant standard. In the language of law and economics, the standard is ex ante, not ex post.

§9. Delegation of Investment and Management Functions

(a) A trustee may delegate investment and management functions that a prudent trustee of comparable skills could properly delegate under the circumstances. The trustee shall exercise reasonable care, skill, and caution in:

(1) selecting an agent;

(2) establishing the scope and terms of the delegation, consistent with the purposes and terms of the trust; and

(3) periodically reviewing the agent's actions in order to monitor the agent's performance and compliance with the terms of the delegation.

(b) In performing a delegated function, an agent owes a duty to the trust to exercise reasonable care to comply with the terms of the delegation.

(c) A trustee who complies with the requirements of subsection (a) is not liable to the beneficiaries or to the trust for the decisions or actions of the agent to whom the function was delegated.

(d) By accepting the delegation of a trust function from the trustee of a trust that is subject to the law of this State, an agent submits to the jurisdiction of the courts of this State.

Comment

This section of the Act reverses the much-criticized rule that forbad trustees to delegate investment and management functions. The language of this section is derived from Restatement of Trusts 3d: Prudent Investor Rule §171 (1992), discussed infra, and from the 1991 Illinois act, 760 ILCS §5/5.1(b), (c) (1992).

Former law. The former nondelegation rule survived into the 1959 Restatement: "The trustee is under a duty to the beneficiary not to delegate to others the doing of acts which the trustee can reasonably be required personally to perform." The rule put a premium on the frequently arbitrary task of distinguishing discretionary functions that were thought to be nondelegable from supposedly ministerial functions that the trustee was allowed to delegate. Restatement of Trusts 2d §171 (1959).

The Restatement of Trusts 2d admitted in a comment that "There is not a clear-cut line dividing the acts which a trustee can properly delegate from those which he cannot properly delegate." Instead, the comment directed attention to a list of factors that "may be of importance: (1) the amount of discretion involved; (2) the value and character of the property involved; (3) whether the property is principal or income; (4) the proximity or remoteness of the subject matter of the trust; (5) the character of the act as one involving professional skill or facilities possessed or not possessed by the trustee himself." Restatement of Trusts 2d §171, comment *d* (1959). The 1959 Restatement further said: "A trustee cannot properly delegate to another power to select investments." Restatement of Trusts 2d §171, comment *h* (1959). . . .

The modern trend to favor delegation. The trend of subsequent legislation, culminating in the Restatement of Trusts 3d: Prudent Investor Rule, has been strongly hostile to the nondelegation rule. See John H. Langbein, Reversing the Nondelegation Rule of Trust-Investment Law, 59 Missouri L. Rev. 105 (1994).

The delegation rule of the Uniform Trustee Powers Act. The Uniform Trustee Powers Act (1964) effectively abrogates the nondelegation rule. It authorizes trustees "to employ persons, including attorneys, auditors, investment advisors, or agents, even if they are associated with the trustee, to advise or assist the trustee in the performance of his administrative duties; to act without independent investigation upon their recommendations; and instead of acting personally, to employ one or more agents to perform any act of administration, whether or not discretionary . . . ." Uniform Trustee Powers Act §3(24), 7B Uniform Laws Ann. 743 (1985). The Act has been enacted in 16 states. . . .

The delegation rule of the 1992 Restatement. The Restatement of Trusts 3d: Prudent Investor Rule (1992) repeals the nondelegation rule of Restatement of Trusts 2d §171 (1959), extracted supra, and replaces it with substitute text that reads:

§171. Duty with Respect to Delegation. A trustee has a duty personally to perform the responsibilities of trusteeship except as a prudent person might delegate those responsibilities to others. In deciding whether, to whom, and in what manner to delegate fiduciary authority in the administration of a trust, and thereafter in supervising agents, the trustee is under a duty to the beneficiaries to exercise fiduciary discretion and to act as a prudent person would act in similar circumstances.

Restatement of Trusts 3d: Prudent Investor Rule §171 (1992). The 1992 Restatement integrates this delegation standard into the prudent investor rule of section 227, providing that "the trustee must . . . act with prudence in deciding whether and how to delegate to others . . . ." Restatement of Trusts 3d: Prudent Investor Rule §227(c) (1992).

Protecting the beneficiary against unreasonable delegation. There is an intrinsic tension in trust law between granting trustees broad powers that facilitate flexible and efficient trust administration, on the one hand, and protecting trust beneficiaries from the misuse of such powers on the other hand. A broad set of trustees' powers, such as those found in most lawyer-drafted instruments and exemplified in the Uniform Trustees' Powers Act, permits the trustee to act vigorously and expeditiously to maximize the interests of the beneficiaries in a variety of transactions and administrative settings. Trust law relies upon the duties of loyalty and prudent administration, and upon procedural safeguards such as periodic accounting and the availability of judicial oversight, to prevent the misuse of these powers. Delegation, which is a species of trustee power, raises the same tension. If the trustee delegates effectively, the beneficiaries obtain the advantage of the agent's specialized investment skills or whatever other attributes induced the trustee to delegate. But if the trustee delegates to a knave or an incompetent, the delegation can work harm upon the beneficiaries.

Section 9 of the Uniform Prudent Investor Act is designed to strike the appropriate balance between the advantages and the hazards of delegation. Section 9 authorizes delegation under the limitations of subsections (a) and (b). Section 9(a) imposes duties of care, skill, and caution on the trustee in selecting the agent, in establishing the terms of the delegation, and in reviewing the agent's compliance.

The trustee's duties of care, skill, and caution in framing the terms of the delegation should protect the beneficiary against overbroad delegation. For example, a trustee could not prudently agree to an investment management agreement containing an exculpation clause that leaves the trust without recourse against reckless mismanagement. Leaving one's beneficiaries remediless against willful wrongdoing is inconsistent with the duty to use care and caution in formulating the terms of the delegation. This sense that it is imprudent to expose beneficiaries to broad exculpation clauses underlies both federal and state legislation restricting exculpation clauses, e.g., ERISA §§404(a)(1)(D), 410(a), 29 U.S.C. §§1104(a)(1)(D), 1110(a); New York Est. Powers Trusts Law §11-1.7 (McKinney 1967).

Although subsection (c) of the Act exonerates the trustee from personal responsibility for the agent's conduct when the delegation satisfies the standards of subsection 9(a), subsection 9(b) makes the agent responsible to the trust. The beneficiaries of the trust can, therefore, rely upon the trustee to enforce the terms of the delegation.

Costs. The duty to minimize costs that is articulated in Section 7 of this Act applies to delegation as well as to other aspects of fiduciary investing. In deciding whether to delegate, the trustee must balance the projected benefits against the likely costs. Similarly, in deciding how to delegate, the trustee must take costs into account. The trustee must be alert to protect the beneficiary from "double dipping." If, for example, the trustee's regular compensation schedule presupposes that the trustee will conduct the investment management function, it should ordinarily follow that the trustee will lower its fee when delegating the investment function to an outside manager.

§10. Language Invoking Standard of [Act]

The following terms or comparable language in the provisions of a trust, unless otherwise limited or modified, authorizes any investment or strategy permitted under this [Act]: "investments permissible by law for investment of trust funds," "legal investments," "authorized investments," "using the judgment and care under the circumstances then prevailing that persons of prudence, discretion, and intelligence exercise in the management of their own affairs, not in regard to speculation but in regard to the permanent disposition of their funds, considering the probable income as well as the probable safety of their capital," "prudent man rule," "prudent trustee rule," "prudent person rule," and "prudent investor rule."

§11. Application to Existing Trusts

This [Act] applies to trusts existing on and created after its effective date. As applied to trusts existing on its effective date, this [Act] governs only decisions or actions occurring after that date.

§12. Uniformity of Application and Construction

This [Act] shall be applied and construed to effectuate its general purpose to make uniform the law with respect to the subject of this [Act] among the States enacting it.

§13. Short Title

This [Act] may be cited as the "[Name of Enacting State] Uniform Prudent Investor Act."

§14. Severability

If any provision of this [Act] or its application to any person or circumstance is held invalid, the invalidity does not affect other provisions or applications of this [Act] which can be given effect without the invalid provision or application, and to this end the provisions of this [Act] are severable.

§15. Effective Date

This [Act] takes effect

. . . .

§16. Repeals

The following acts and parts of acts are repealed:

(1)
(2)
(3)

PART VII

~

UNIFORM TRUST CODE

UNIFORM TRUST CODE

Article 7
Office of Trustee

Article 8
Duties and Powers of Trustee

Article 9
Uniform Prudent Investor Act

Article 10
Liability of Trustees and Rights of Persons Dealing with Trustee

Article 11
Miscellaneous Provisions

Uniform Trust Code

PREFATORY NOTE

The Uniform Trust Code (2000) is the first national codification of the law of trusts. The primary stimulus to the Commissioners' drafting of the Uniform Trust Code is the greater use of trusts in recent years, both in family estate planning and in commercial transactions, both in the United States and internationally. This greater use of the trust, and consequent rise in the number of day-to-day questions involving trusts, has led to a recognition that the trust law in many States is thin. It has also led to a recognition that the existing Uniform Acts relating to trusts, while numerous, are fragmentary. The Uniform Trust Code will provide States with precise, comprehensive, and easily accessible guidance on trust law questions. On issues on which States diverge or on which the law is unclear or unknown, the Code will for the first time provide a uniform rule. The Code also contains a number of innovative provisions.

Default rule. Most of the Uniform Trust Code consists of default rules that apply only if the terms of the trust fail to address or insufficiently cover a particular issue. Pursuant to Section 105, a drafter is free to override a substantial majority of the Code's provisions. The exceptions are scheduled in Section 105(b).

Innovative provisions. Much of the Uniform Trust Code is a codification of the common law of trusts. But the Code does contain a number of innovative provisions. Among the more significant are specification of the rules of trust law that are not subject to override in the trust's terms (Section 105), the inclusion of a comprehensive article on representation of beneficiaries (Article 3), rules on trust modification and termination that will enhance flexibility (Sections 410-417), and the inclusion of an article collecting the special rules pertaining to revocable trusts (Article 6).

Models for drafting. While the Uniform Trust Code is the first comprehensive Uniform Act on the subject of trusts, comprehensive trust statutes are already in effect in several States. Notable examples include the statutes in California, Georgia, Indiana, Texas, and Washington, all of which were referred to in the drafting process. Most influential was the 1986 California statute, found at Division 9 of the California Probate Code (Sections 15000 et seq.), which was used by the Drafting Committee as its initial model.

Existing uniform laws on trust law subjects. Certain older Uniform Acts are incorporated into the Uniform Trust Code. Others, addressing more specialized topics, will continue to be available for enactment in free-standing form.

The following Uniform Acts are incorporated into or otherwise superseded by the Uniform Trust Code:

Uniform Probate Code Article VII—Originally approved in 1969, Article VII has been enacted in about 15 jurisdictions. Article VII, although titled "Trust Administration," is a modest statute, addressing only a limited number of topics. Except for its provisions on trust registration, Article VII is superseded by the Uniform Trust Code. Its provisions on jurisdiction are incorporated into Article 2 of the Code, and its provisions on trustee liability to persons other than beneficiaries are replaced by Section 1010.

Uniform Prudent Investor Act (1994) —This Act has been enacted in 35 jurisdictions. This Act, and variant forms enacted in a number of other States, has displaced the older "prudent man" standard, bringing trust law into line with modern investment practice. States that have enacted the Uniform Prudent Investor Act are encouraged to recodify it as part of their enactment of the Uniform Trust Code. A place for this is provided in Article 9.

Uniform Trustee Powers Act (1964)—This Act has been enacted in 16 States. The Act contains a list of specific trustee powers and deals with other selected issues, particularly relations of a trustee with persons other than beneficiaries. The Uniform Trustee Powers Act is outdated and is entirely superseded by the Uniform Trust Code, principally at Sections 815, 816, and 1012. States enacting the Uniform Trust Code should repeal their existing trustee powers legislation.

Uniform Trusts Act (1937)—This largely overlooked Act of similar name was enacted in only six States, none within the past several decades. Despite a title suggesting comprehensive coverage of its topic, this Act, like Article VII of the UPC, addresses only a limited number of topics. These include the duty of loyalty, the registration and voting of securities, and trustee liability to persons other than beneficiaries. States enacting the Uniform Trust Code should repeal this earlier namesake.

The following Uniform Acts are not affected by enactment of the Uniform Trust Code and do not need to be amended or repealed:

Uniform Common Trust Fund Act—Originally approved in 1938, this Act has been enacted in 34 jurisdictions. The Uniform Trust Code does not address the subject of common trust funds. In recent years, many banks have replaced their common trust funds with mutual funds that may also be available to non-trust customers. The Code addresses investment in mutual funds at Section 802(f).

Uniform Custodial Trust Act (1987)—This Act has been enacted in 14 jurisdictions. This Act allows standard trust provisions to be automatically incorporated into the terms of a trust simply by referring to the Act. This Act is not displaced by the Uniform Trust Code but complements it.

Uniform Management of Institutional Funds Act (1972)—This Act has been enacted in 47 jurisdictions. It governs the administration of endowment funds held by charitable, religious, and other eleemosynary institutions. The Uniform Management of Institutional Funds Act establishes a standard of prudence for use of appreciation on assets, provides specific authority for the making of investments, authorizes the delegation of this authority, and specifies a procedure, through either donor consent or court approval, for removing restrictions on the use of donated funds.

Uniform Principal and Income Act (1997)—The 1997 Uniform Principal and Income Act is a major revision of the widely enacted Uniform Act of the same name approved in 1962. Because this Act addresses issues with respect both to decedent's estates and trusts, a jurisdiction enacting the revised Uniform Principal and Income Act may wish to include it either as part of this Code or as part of its probate laws.

Uniform Probate Code—Originally approved in 1969, and enacted in close to complete form in about 20 States but influential in virtually all, the UPC overlaps with trust topics in several areas. One area of overlap, already mentioned, is UPC Article VII. Another area of overlap concerns representation of beneficiaries. UPC Section 1-403 provides principles of representation for achieving binding judicial settlements of matters involving both estates and trusts. The Uniform Trust Code refines these representation principles, and extends them to nonjudicial settlement agreements and to optional notices and consents. See Uniform Trust Code, Section 111 and Article 3. A final area of overlap between the UPC and trust law concerns rules of construction. The UPC, in Article II, Part 7, extends certain of the rules on the construction of wills to trusts and other nonprobate instruments. The Uniform Trust Code similarly extends to trusts the rules on the construction of wills. Unlike the UPC, however, the Trust Code does not prescribe the exact rules. Instead, Section 112 of the Uniform Trust Code is an optional provision applying to trusts whatever rules the enacting jurisdiction already has in place on the construction of wills.

Uniform Statutory Rule Against Perpetuities—Originally approved in 1986, this Act has been enacted in 27 jurisdictions. The Act reforms the durational limit on when property interests, including interests created under trusts, must vest or fail. The Uniform Trust Code does not limit the duration of trusts or alter the time when interests must otherwise vest, but leaves this issue to other state law. The Code may be enacted without change regardless of the status of the perpetuities law in the enacting jurisdiction.

Uniform Supervision of Trustees for Charitable Purposes Act (1954)—This Act, which has been enacted in four States, is limited to mechanisms for monitoring the actions of charitable trustees. Unlike the Uniform Trust Code, the Supervision of Trustees for Charitable Purposes Act does not address the substantive law of charitable trusts.

Uniform Testamentary Additions to Trusts Act—This Act is available in two versions: the 1960 Act, with 24 enactments; and the 1991 Act, with 20 enactments through 1999. As its name suggests, this Act validates pour-over devises to trusts. Because it validates provisions in wills, it is incorporated into the Uniform Probate Code, not into the Uniform Trust Code.

Role of Restatement of Trusts. The Restatement (Second) of Trusts was approved by the American Law Institute in 1957. Work on the Restatement Third began in the late 1980s. The portion of Restatement Third relating to the prudent investor rule and other investment topics was completed and approved in 1990. A tentative draft of the portion of Restatement Third relating to the rules on the creation and validity of trusts was approved in 1996, and the portion relating to the office of trustee, trust purposes, spendthrift provisions and the rights of creditors was approved in 1999. The Uniform Trust Code was drafted in close coordination with the writing of the Restatement Third.

OVERVIEW OF UNIFORM TRUST CODE

The Uniform Trust Code consists of 11 articles. The substance of the Code is focused in the first 10 articles; Article 11 is primarily an effective date provision.

Article 1—General Provisions and Definitions—In addition to definitions, this article addresses miscellaneous but important topics. The Uniform Trust Code is primarily default law. A settlor, subject to certain limitations, is free to draft trust terms departing from the provisions of this Code. The settlor, if minimum contacts are present, may in addition designate the trust's principal place of administration; the trustee, if certain standards are met, may transfer the principal place of administration to another State or country. To encourage nonjudicial resolution of disputes, the Uniform Trust Code provides more certainty for when such settlements are binding. While the Code does not prescribe the exact rules to be applied to the construction of trusts, it does extend to trusts whatever rules the enacting jurisdiction has on the construction of wills. The Uniform Trust Code, although comprehensive, does not legislate on every issue. Its provisions are supplemented by the common law of trusts and principles of equity.

Article 2—Judicial Proceedings—This article addresses selected issues involving judicial proceedings concerning trusts, particularly trusts having contacts with more than one State or country. The courts in the trust's principal place of administration have jurisdiction over both the trustee and the beneficiaries as to any matter relating to the trust. Optional provisions on subject-matter jurisdiction and venue are provided. The minimal coverage of this article was deliberate. The Drafting Committee concluded that most issues related to jurisdiction and procedure are not appropriate to a Trust Code, but are best left to other bodies of law.

Article 3—Representation—This article deals with the representation of beneficiaries and other interested persons, both by fiduciaries (personal representatives, guardians and conservators), and through what is known as virtual representation. The representation principles of the article apply to settlement of disputes, whether by a court or nonjudicially. They apply for the giving of required notices. They apply for the giving of consents to certain actions. The article also authorizes a court to appoint a representative if the court concludes that representation of a person might otherwise be inadequate. The court may appoint a representative to represent and approve a settlement on behalf of a minor, incapacitated, or unborn person or person whose identity or location is unknown and not reasonably ascertainable.

Article 4—Creation, Validity, Modification and Termination of Trust—This article specifies the requirements for creating, modifying and terminating trusts. Most of the requirements relating to creation of trusts (Sections 401 through 409) track traditional doctrine, including requirements of intent, capacity, property, and valid trust purpose. The Uniform Trust Code articulates a three-part classification system for trusts: noncharitable, charitable, and honorary. Noncharitable trusts, the most common type, require an ascertainable beneficiary and a valid purpose. Charitable trusts, on the other hand, by their very nature are created to benefit the public at large. The so-called honorary or purposes trust, although unenforceable at common law, is valid and enforceable under this Code despite the absence of an ascertainable beneficiary. The most common example is a trust for the care of an animal.

Sections 410 through 417 provide a series of interrelated rules on when a trust may be terminated or modified other than by its express terms. The overall objective of these sections is to enhance flexibility consistent with the principle that preserving the settlor's intent is paramount. Termination or modification may be allowed upon beneficiary consent if the court concludes that the trust or a particular provision no longer serves a material purpose or if the settlor concurs; by the court in response to unanticipated circumstances or to remedy ineffective administrative terms; or by the court or trustee if the trust is of insufficient size to justify continued administration under its existing terms. Trusts may be reformed to correct a mistake of law or fact, or modified to achieve the settlor's tax objectives. Trusts may be combined or divided. Charitable trusts may be modified or terminated under cy pres to better achieve the settlor's charitable purposes.

Article 5—Creditor's Claims; Spendthrift and Discretionary Trusts—This article addresses the validity of a spendthrift provision and other issues relating to the rights of creditors to reach the trust to collect a debt. To the extent a trust is protected by a spendthrift provision, a beneficiary's creditor may not reach the beneficiary's interest until distribution is made by the trustee. To the extent not protected by a spendthrift provision, a creditor can reach the beneficiary's interest, subject to the court's power to limit the award. Certain categories of claims are exempt from a spendthrift restriction, including certain governmental claims and claims for child support or alimony. Other issues addressed in this article include creditor claims against discretionary trusts; creditor claims against a settlor, whether the trust is revocable or irrevocable; and the rights of creditors when a trustee fails to make a required distribution within a reasonable time.

Article 6—Revocable Trusts—This short article deals with issues of significance not totally settled under current law. The basic policy of this article and of the Uniform Trust Code in general is to treat the revocable trust as the functional equivalent of a will. The article specifies a standard of capacity, provides that a trust is presumed revocable unless its terms provide otherwise, prescribes the procedure for revocation or amendment of a revocable trust, addresses the rights of beneficiaries during the settlor's lifetime, and provides a statute of limitations on contests.

Article 7—Office of Trustee—This article contains a series of default rules dealing with the office of trustee, all of which may be modified in the terms of the trust. Rules are provided on acceptance of office and bonding. The role of the cotrustee is addressed, including the extent that one cotrustee may delegate to another, and the extent to which one cotrustee can be held liable for actions of another trustee. Also covered are changes in trusteeship, including the circumstances when a vacancy must be filled, the procedure for resignation, the grounds for removal, and the process for appointing a successor trustee. Finally, standards are provided for trustee compensation and reimbursement for expenses.

Article 8—Duties and Powers of Trustee—This article states the fundamental duties of a trustee and enumerates the trustee's powers. The duties listed are not new, although some of the particulars have changed over the years. This article was drafted where possible to conform to the Uniform Prudent Investor Act. The Uniform Prudent Investor Act prescribes a trustee's responsibilities with respect to the management and investment of trust property. This article also addresses a trustee's duties regarding distributions to beneficiaries.

Article 9—Uniform Prudent Investor Act—This article provides a place for a jurisdiction to enact, reenact or codify its version of the Uniform Prudent Investor Act. States adopting the Uniform Trust Code which have previously enacted the Uniform Prudent Investor Act are encouraged to reenact their version of the Prudent Investor Act in this article.

Article 10—Liability of Trustees and Rights of Persons Dealing With Trustees—Sections 1001 through 1009 list the remedies for breach of trust, describe how money damages are to be determined, provide a statute of limitations on claims against a trustee, and specify other defenses, including consent of a beneficiary and recognition of and limitations on the effect of an exculpatory clause. Sections 1010 through 1013 address trustee relations with persons other than beneficiaries. The objective is to encourage third parties to engage in commercial transactions with trustees to the same extent as if the property were not held in trust.

Article 11—Miscellaneous Provisions—The Uniform Trust Code is intended to have the widest possible application, consistent with constitutional limitations. The Code applies not only to trusts created on or after the effective date, but also to trusts in existence on the date of enactment.

The Drafting Committee was assisted by numerous officially designated advisors and observers, representing an array of organizations. In addition to the American Bar Association advisors listed above, advisors and observers who attended a majority of the Drafting Committee meetings include Edward C. Halbach, Jr., Reporter, Restatement (Third) of Trust Law; Kent H. McMahan, American College of Trust and Estate Counsel; Alex Misheff, American Bankers Association; and Lawrence W. Waggoner, Reporter, Restatement (Third) of Property: Wills and Other Donative Transfers. Significant input was also received from the Joint Editorial Board for Uniform Trusts and Estates Acts and the Committee on State Laws of the American College of Trust and Estate Counsel.

Uniform Trust Code

ARTICLE 1

GENERAL PROVISIONS AND DEFINITIONS

The Uniform Trust Code is primarily a default statute. Most of the Code's provisions can be overridden in the terms of the trust. The provisions not subject to override are scheduled in Section 105(b). These include the duty of a trustee to act in good faith and with regard to the purposes of the trust, public policy exceptions to enforcement of spendthrift provisions, the requirements for creating a trust, and the authority of the court to modify or terminate a trust on specified grounds.

The remainder of the article specifies the scope of the Code (Section 102), provides definitions (Section 103), and collects provisions of importance not amenable to codification elsewhere in the Uniform Trust Code. Sections 106 and 107 focus on the sources of law that will govern a trust. Section 106 clarifies that despite the Code's comprehensive scope, not all aspects of the law of trusts have been codified. The Uniform Trust Code is supplemented by the common law of trusts and principles of equity. Section 107 addresses selection of the jurisdiction or jurisdictions whose laws will govern the trust. A settlor, absent overriding public policy concerns, is free to select the law that will determine the meaning and effect of a trust's terms.

Changing a trust's principal place of administration is sometimes desirable, particularly to lower a trust's state income tax. Such transfers are authorized in Section 108. The trustee, following notice to the "qualified beneficiaries," defined in Section 103(12), may without approval of court transfer the principal place of administration to another State or country if a qualified beneficiary does not object and if the transfer is consistent with the trustee's duty to administer the trust at a place appropriate to its purposes, its administration, and the interests of the beneficiaries. The settlor, if minimum contacts are present, may also designate the trust's principal place of administration.

Sections 104 and 109 through 111 address procedural issues. Section 104 specifies when persons, particularly persons who work in organizations, are deemed to have acquired knowledge of a fact. Section 109 specifies the methods for giving notice and excludes from the Code's notice requirements persons whose identity or location is unknown and not reasonably ascertainable. Section 110 allows beneficiaries with remote interests to request notice of actions, such as notice of a trustee resignation, which are normally given only to the qualified beneficiaries.

Section 111 ratifies the use of nonjudicial settlement agreements. While the judicial settlement procedures may be used in all court proceedings relating to the trust, the nonjudicial settlement procedures will not always be available. The terms of the trust may direct that the procedures not be used, or settlors may negate or modify them by specifying their own methods for obtaining consents. Also, a nonjudicial settlement may include only terms and conditions a court could properly approve.

The Uniform Trust Code does not prescribe the rules of construction to be applied to trusts created under the Code. The Code instead recognizes that enacting jurisdictions are likely to take a diversity of approaches, just as they have with respect to the rules of construction applicable to wills. Section 112 accommodates this variation by providing that the State's specific rules on construction of wills, whatever they may be, also apply to the construction of trusts.

§101. Short Title

This [Act] may be cited as the Uniform Trust Code.

§102. Scope

This [Code] applies to express trusts, charitable or noncharitable, and trusts created pursuant to a statute, judgment, or decree that requires the trust to be administered in the manner of an express trust.

§103. Definitions

In this [Code]:

(1) "Action," with respect to an act of a trustee, includes a failure to act.

(2) "Beneficiary" means a person that:

(A) has a present or future beneficial interest in a trust, vested or contingent; or

(B) in a capacity other than that of trustee, holds a power of appointment over trust property.

(3) "Charitable trust" means a trust, or portion of a trust, created for a charitable purpose described in Section 405(a).

(4) "[Conservator]" means a person appointed by the court to administer the estate of a minor or adult individual.

(5) "Environmental law" means a federal, state, or local law, rule, regulation, or ordinance relating to protection of the environment.

(6) "[Guardian]" means a person appointed by the court [, a parent, or a spouse] to make decisions regarding the support, care, education, health, and welfare of a minor or adult individual. The term does not include a guardian ad litem.

(7) "Interests of the beneficiaries" means the beneficial interests provided in the terms of the trust.

(8) "Jurisdiction," with respect to a geographic area, includes a State or country.

(9) "Person" means an individual, corporation, business trust, estate, trust, partnership, limited liability company, association, joint venture, government; governmental subdivision, agency, or instrumentality; public corporation, or any other legal or commercial entity.

(10) "Power of withdrawal" means a presently exercisable general power of appointment other than a power exercisable only upon consent of the trustee or a person holding an adverse interest.

(11) "Property" means anything that may be the subject of ownership, whether real or personal, legal or equitable, or any interest therein.

(12) "Qualified beneficiary" means a beneficiary who, on the date the beneficiary's qualification is determined:

(A) is a distributee or permissible distributee of trust income or principal;

(B) would be a distributee or permissible distributee of trust income or principal if the interests of the distributees described in subparagraph (A) terminated on that date; or

(C)would be a distributee or permissible distributee of trust income or principal if the trust terminated on that date.

(13) "Revocable," as applied to a trust, means revocable by the settlor without the consent of the trustee or a person holding an adverse interest.

(14) "Settlor" means a person, including a testator, who creates, or contributes property to, a trust. If more than one person creates or contributes property to a trust, each person is a settlor of the portion of the trust property attributable to that person's contribution except to the extent another person has the power to revoke or withdraw that portion.

(15) "Spendthrift provision" means a term of a trust which restrains both voluntary and involuntary transfer of a beneficiary's interest.

(16) "State" means a State of the United States, the District of Columbia, Puerto Rico, the United States Virgin Islands, or any territory or insular possession subject to the jurisdiction of the United States. The term includes an Indian tribe or band recognized by federal law or formally acknowledged by a State.

(17) "Terms of a trust" means the manifestation of the settlor's intent regarding a trust's provisions as expressed in the trust instrument or as may be established by other evidence that would be admissible in a judicial proceeding.

(18) "Trust instrument" means an instrument executed by the settlor that contains terms of the trust, including any amendments thereto.

(19) "Trustee" includes an original, additional, and successor trustee, and a cotrustee.

Comment

. . . "Terms of a trust" (paragraph (17)) is a defined term used frequently in the Uniform Trust Code. While the wording of a written trust instrument is almost always the most important determinant of a trust's terms, the definition is not so limited. Oral statements, the situation of the beneficiaries, the purposes of the trust, the circumstances under which the trust is to be administered, and, to the extent the settlor was otherwise silent, rules of construction, all may have a bearing on determining a trust's meaning. See Restatement (Third) of Trusts Section 4 cmt. a (Tentative Draft No. 1, approved 1996); Restatement (Second) of Trusts Section 4 cmt. a (1959). If a trust established by order of court is to be administered as an express trust, the terms of the trust are determined from the court order as interpreted in light of the general rules governing interpretation of judgments. See Restatement (Third) of Trusts Section 4 cmt. f (Tentative Draft No. 1, approved 1996).

A manifestation of a settlor's intention does not constitute evidence of a trust's terms if it would be inadmissible in a judicial proceeding in which the trust's terms are in question. See Restatement (Third) of Trusts Section 4 cmt. b (Tentative Draft No. 1, approved 1996); Restatement (Second) of Trusts Section 4 cmt. b (1959). See also Restatement (Third) Property: Donative Transfers Sections 10.2, 11.1-11.3 (Tentative Draft No. 1, approved 1995). For example, in many states a trust of real property is unenforceable unless evidenced by a writing, although Section 407 of this Code does not so require, leaving this issue to be covered by separate statute if the enacting jurisdiction so elects. Evidence otherwise relevant to determining the terms of a trust may also be excluded under other principles of law, such as the parol evidence rule. . . .

§104. Knowledge

(a) Subject to subsection (b), a person has knowledge of a fact if the person:

(1) has actual knowledge of it;

(2) has received a notice or notification of it; or

(3) from all the facts and circumstances known to the person at the time in question, has reason to know it.

(b) An organization that conducts activities through employees has notice or knowledge of a fact involving a trust only from the time the information was received by an employee having responsibility to act for the trust, or would have been brought to the employee's attention if the organization had exercised reasonable diligence. An organization exercises reasonable diligence if it maintains reasonable routines for communicating significant information to the employee having responsibility to act for the trust and there is reasonable compliance with the routines. Reasonable diligence does not require an employee of the organization to communicate information unless the communication is part of the individual's regular duties or the individual knows a matter involving the trust would be materially affected by the information.

§105. Default and Mandatory Rules

(a) Except as otherwise provided in the terms of the trust, this [Code] governs the duties and powers of a trustee, relations among trustees, and the rights and interests of a beneficiary.

(b) The terms of a trust prevail over any provision of this [Code] except:

(1) the requirements for creating a trust;

(2) the duty of a trustee to act in good faith and in accordance with the purposes of the trust;

(3) the requirement that a trust and its terms be for the benefit of its beneficiaries, and that the trust have a purpose that is lawful, not contrary to public policy, and possible to achieve;

(4) the power of the court to modify or terminate a trust under Sections 410 through 416;

(5) the effect of a spendthrift provision and the rights of certain creditors and assignees to reach a trust as provided in [Article] 5;

(6) the power of the court under Section 702 to require, dispense with, or modify or terminate a bond;

(7) the power of the court under Section 708(b) to adjust a trustee's compensation specified in the terms of the trust which is unreasonably low or high;

(8) except for a qualified beneficiary who has not attained 25 years of age, the duty under Section 813(b)(2) and (3) to notify qualified beneficiaries of an irrevocable trust who have attained 25 years of age of the existence of the trust, of the identity of the trustee, and of their right to request trustee's reports;

(9) the duty under Section 813(a) to respond to the request of a beneficiary of an irrevocable trust for trustee's reports and other information reasonably related to the administration of a trust;

(10) the effect of an exculpatory term under Section 1008;

(11) the rights under Sections 1010 through 1013 of a person other than a trustee or beneficiary;

(12) periods of limitation for commencing a judicial proceeding; [and]

(13) the power of the court to take such action and exercise such jurisdiction as may be necessary in the interests of justice [; and

(14) the subject-matter jurisdiction of the court and venue for commencing a proceeding as provided in Sections 203 and 204].

Comment

Subsection (a) emphasizes that the Uniform Trust Code is primarily a default statute. While this Code provides numerous procedural rules on which a settlor may wish to rely, the settlor is generally free to override these rules and to prescribe the conditions under which the trust is to be administered. With only limited exceptions, the duties and powers of a trustee, relations among trustees, and the rights and interests of a beneficiary are as specified in the terms of the trust.

Subsection (b) lists the items not subject to override in the terms of the trust. . . .

The terms of a trust may not deny a court authority to take such action as necessary in the interests of justice, including requiring that a trustee furnish bond. Subsection (b)(6), (13). . . .

Section 813 imposes a general obligation to keep the beneficiaries informed as well as several specific notice requirements. Subsections (b)(8) and (b)(9) specify limits on the settlor's ability to waive these information requirements. With respect to beneficiaries age 25 or older, a settlor may dispense with all of the requirements of Section 813 except for the duties to inform the beneficiaries of the existence of the trust, of the identity of the trustee, and to provide a beneficiary upon request with such reports as the trustee may have prepared. Among the specific requirements that a settlor may waive include the duty to provide a beneficiary upon request with a copy of the trust instrument (Section 813(b)(1)), and the requirement that the trustee provide annual reports to the qualified beneficiaries (Section 813(c)). The furnishing of a copy of the entire trust instrument and preparation of annual reports may be required in a particular case, however, if such information is requested by a beneficiary and is reasonably related to the trust's administration.

Responding to the desire of some settlors that younger beneficiaries not know of the trust's bounty until they have reached an age of maturity and self-sufficiency, subsection (b)(8) allows a settlor to provide that the trustee need not even inform beneficiaries under age 25 of the existence of the trust. However, pursuant to subsection (b)(9), if the younger beneficiary learns of the trust and requests information, the trustee must respond. More generally, subsection (b)(9) prohibits a settlor from overriding the right provided to a beneficiary in Section 813(a) to request from the trustee of an irrevocable trust copies of trustee reports and other information reasonably related to the trust's administration. . . .

Waiver by a settlor of the trustee's duty to keep the beneficiaries informed of the trust's administration does not otherwise affect the trustee's duties. The trustee remains accountable to the beneficiaries for the trustee's actions.

Neither subsection (b)(8) nor (b)(9) apply to revocable trusts. The settlor of a revocable trust may waive all reporting to the beneficiaries, even in the event the settlor loses capacity. If the settlor is silent about the subject, reporting to the beneficiaries will be required upon the settlor's loss of capacity. See Section 603.

In conformity with traditional doctrine, the Uniform Trust Code limits the ability of a settlor to exculpate a trustee from liability for breach of trust. The limits are specified in Section 1008. Subsection (b)(10) of this section provides a cross-reference. . . .

§106. Common Law of Trusts; Principles of Equity

The common law of trusts and principles of equity supplement this [Code], except to the extent modified by this [Code] or another statute of this State.

§107. Governing Law

The meaning and effect of the terms of a trust are determined by:

(1) the law of the jurisdiction designated in the terms unless the designation of that jurisdiction's law is contrary to a strong public policy of the jurisdiction having the most significant relationship to the matter at issue; or

(2) in the absence of a controlling designation in the terms of the trust, the law of the jurisdiction having the most significant relationship to the matter at issue.

§108. Principal Place of Administration

(a) Without precluding other means for establishing a sufficient connection with the designated jurisdiction, terms of a trust designating the principal place of administration are valid and controlling if:

(1) a trustee's principal place of business is located in or a trustee is a resident of the designated jurisdiction; or

(2) all or part of the administration occurs in the designated jurisdiction.

(b) A trustee is under a continuing duty to administer the trust at a place appropriate to its purposes, its administration, and the interests of the beneficiaries. © Without precluding the right of the court to order, approve, or disapprove a transfer, the trustee, in furtherance of the duty prescribed by subsection (b), may transfer the trust's principal place of administration to another State or to a jurisdiction outside of the United States.

(d) The trustee shall notify the qualified beneficiaries of a proposed transfer of a trust's principal place of administration not less than 60 days before initiating the transfer. The notice of proposed transfer must include:

(1) the name of the jurisdiction to which the principal place of administration is to be transferred;

(2) the address and telephone number at the new location at which the trustee can be contacted;

(3) an explanation of the reasons for the proposed transfer;

(4) the date on which the proposed transfer is anticipated to occur; and

(5) the date, not less than 60 days after the giving of the notice, by which the qualified beneficiary must notify the trustee of an objection to the proposed transfer.

(e) The authority of a trustee under this section to transfer a trust's principal place of administration terminates if a qualified beneficiary notifies the trustee of an objection to the proposed transfer on or before the date specified in the notice.

(f) In connection with a transfer of the trust's principal place of administration, the trustee may transfer some or all of the trust property to a successor trustee designated in the terms of the trust or appointed pursuant to Section 704.

§109. Methods and Waiver of Notice

(a) Notice to a person under this [Code] or the sending of a document to a person under this [Code] must be accomplished in a manner reasonably suitable under the circumstances and likely to result in receipt of the notice or document. Permissible methods of notice or for sending a document include first-class mail, personal delivery, delivery to the person's last known place of residence or place of business, or a properly directed electronic message.

(b) Notice otherwise required under this [Code] or a document otherwise required to be sent under this [Code] need not be provided to a person whose identity or location is unknown to and not reasonably ascertainable by the trustee.

(c) Notice under this [Code] or the sending of a document under this [Code] may be waived by the person to be notified or sent the document.

(d) Notice of a judicial proceeding must be given as provided in the applicable rules of civil procedure.

§110. Others Treated as Qualified Beneficiaries

(a) Whenever notice to qualified beneficiaries of a trust is required under this [Code] , the trustee must also give notice to any other beneficiary who has sent the trustee a request for notice.

(b) A charitable organization expressly designated to receive distributions under the terms of a charitable trust or a person appointed to enforce a trust created for the care of an animal or another noncharitable purpose as provided in Section 408 or 409 has the rights of a qualified beneficiary under this [Code].

(c) The [attorney general of this State] has the rights of a qualified beneficiary with respect to a charitable trust having its principal place of administration in this State.

§111. Nonjudicial Settlement Agreements

(a) For purposes of this section, "interested persons" means persons whose consent would be required in order to achieve a binding settlement were the settlement to be approved by the court.

(b) Except as otherwise provided in subsection (c), interested persons may enter into a binding nonjudicial settlement agreement with respect to any matter involving a trust.

(c) A nonjudicial settlement agreement is valid only to the extent it does not violate a material purpose of the trust and includes terms and conditions that could be properly approved by the court under this [Code] or other applicable law.

(d) Matters that may be resolved by a nonjudicial settlement agreement include:

(1) the interpretation or construction of the terms of the trust;

(2) the approval of a trustee's report or accounting;

(3) direction to a trustee to refrain from performing a particular act or the grant to a trustee of any necessary or desirable power;

(4) the resignation or appointment of a trustee and the determination of a trustee's compensation;

(5) transfer of a trust's principal place of administration; and

(6) liability of a trustee for an action relating to the trust.

(e) Any interested person may request the court to approve a nonjudicial settlement agreement, to determine whether the representation as provided in [Article] 3 was adequate, and to determine whether the agreement contains terms and conditions the court could have properly approved.

Comment

While the Uniform Trust Code recognizes that a court may intervene in the administration of a trust to the extent its jurisdiction is invoked by interested persons or otherwise provided by law (see Section 201(a)), resolution of disputes by nonjudicial means is encouraged. This section facilitates the making of such agreements by giving them the same effect as if approved by the court. To achieve such certainty, however, subsection (c) requires that the nonjudicial settlement must contain terms and conditions that a court could properly approve. Under this section, a nonjudicial settlement cannot be used to produce a result not authorized by law, such as to terminate a trust in an impermissible manner.

Trusts ordinarily have beneficiaries who are minors, incapacitated, unborn or unascertained. Because such beneficiaries cannot signify their consent to an agreement, binding settlements can ordinarily be achieved only through the application of doctrines such as virtual representation or appointment of a guardian ad litem, doctrines traditionally available only in the case of judicial settlements. The effect of this section and the Uniform Trust Code more generally is to allow for such binding representation even if the agreement is not submitted for approval to a court. For the rules on representation, including appointments of representatives by the court to approve particular settlements, see Article 3 . . . .

§112. Rules of Construction

The rules of construction that apply in this State to the interpretation of and disposition of property by will also apply as appropriate to the interpretation of the terms of a trust and the disposition of the trust property.]

Comment

This section is patterned after Restatement (Third) of Trusts Section 25(2) and comment e (Tentative Draft No. 1, approved 1996), although this section, unlike the Restatement, also applies to irrevocable trusts. The revocable trust is used primarily as a will substitute, with its key provision being the determination of the persons to receive the trust property upon the settlor's death. Given this functional equivalence between the revocable trust and a will, the rules for interpreting the disposition of property at death should be the same whether the individual has chosen a will or revocable trust as the individual's primary estate planning instrument. Over the years, the legislatures of the States and the courts have developed a series of rules of construction reflecting the legislative or judicial understanding of how the average testator would wish to dispose of property in cases where the will is silent or insufficiently clear. Few legislatures have yet to extend these rules of construction to revocable trusts, and even fewer to irrevocable trusts, although a number of courts have done so as a matter of judicial construction. See Restatement (Third) of Trusts Section 25, Reporter's Notes to cmt. d and e (Tentative Draft No. 1, approved 1996). . . .

§201. Role of Court in Administration of Trust

(a) The court may intervene in the administration of a trust to the extent its jurisdiction is invoked by an interested person or as provided by law.

(b) A trust is not subject to continuing judicial supervision unless ordered by the court.

(c) A judicial proceeding involving a trust may relate to any matter involving the trust's administration, including a request for instructions and an action to declare rights.

§202. Jurisdiction over Trustee and Beneficiary

(a) By accepting the trusteeship of a trust having its principal place of administration in this State or by moving the principal place of administration to this State, the trustee submits personally to the jurisdiction of the courts of this State regarding any matter involving the trust.

(b) With respect to their interests in the trust, the beneficiaries of a trust having its principal place of administration in this State are subject to the jurisdiction of the courts of this State regarding any matter involving the trust. By accepting a distribution from such a trust, the recipient submits personally to the jurisdiction of the courts of this State regarding any matter involving the trust.

(c) This section does not preclude other methods of obtaining jurisdiction over a trustee, beneficiary, or other person receiving property from the trust.

§203. Subject-Matter Jurisdiction

(a) The [designate] court has exclusive jurisdiction of proceedings in this State brought by a trustee or beneficiary concerning the administration of a trust.

(b) The [designate] court has concurrent jurisdiction with other courts of this State of other proceedings involving a trust.]

§204. Venue

(a) Except as otherwise provided in subsection (b), venue for a judicial proceeding involving a trust is in the [county] of this State in which the trust's principal place of administration is or will be located and, if the trust is created by will and the estate is not yet closed, in the [county] in which the decedent's estate is being administered.

(b) If a trust has no trustee, venue for a judicial proceeding for the appointment of a trustee is in a [county] of this State in which a beneficiary resides, in a [county] in which any trust property is located, and if the trust is created by will, in the [county] in which the decedent's estate was or is being administered.]

§301. Representation: Basic Effect

(a) Notice to a person who may represent and bind another person under this [article] has the same effect as if notice were given directly to the other person.

(b) The consent of a person who may represent and bind another person under this [article] is binding on the person represented unless the person represented objects to the representation before the consent would otherwise have become effective.

(c) Except as otherwise provided in Sections 411 and 602, a person who under this [article] may represent a settlor who lacks capacity may receive notice and give a binding consent on the settlor's behalf.

§302. Representation by Holder of General Testamentary Power of Appointment

To the extent there is no conflict of interest between the holder of a general testamentary power of appointment and the persons represented with respect to the particular question or dispute, the holder may represent and bind persons whose interests, as permissible appointees, takers in default, or otherwise, are subject to the power.

Comment

This section specifies the circumstances under which a holder of a general testamentary power of appointment may receive notices on behalf of and otherwise represent and bind persons whose interests are subject to the power, whether as permissible appointees, takers in default, or otherwise. Such representation is allowed except to the extent there is a conflict of interest with respect to the particular matter or dispute. Typically, the holder of a general testamentary power of appointment is also a life income beneficiary of the trust, oftentimes of a trust intended to qualify for the federal estate tax marital deduction. See I.R.C. Section 2056(b)(5). Without the exception for conflict of interest, the holder of the power could act in a way that could enhance the holder's income interests to the detriment of the appointees or takers in default, whoever they may be.

§303. Representation by Fiduciaries and Parents

To the extent there is no conflict of interest between the representative and the person represented or among those being represented with respect to a particular question or dispute:

(1) a [conservator] may represent and bind the estate that the [conservator] controls;

(2) a [guardian] may represent and bind the ward if a [conservator] of the ward's estate has not been appointed;

(3) an agent having authority to act with respect to the particular question or dispute may represent and bind the principal;

(4) a trustee may represent and bind the beneficiaries of the trust;

(5) a personal representative of a decedent's estate may represent and bind persons interested in the estate; and

(6) a parent may represent and bind the parent's minor or unborn child if a [conservator] or [guardian] for the child has not been appointed.

§304. Representation by Person Having Substantially Identical Interest

Unless otherwise represented, a minor, incapacitated, or unborn individual, or a person whose identity or location is unknown and not reasonably ascertainable, may be represented by and bound by another having a substantially identical interest with respect to the particular question or dispute, but only to the extent there is no conflict of interest between the representative and the person represented.

§305. Appointment of Representative

(a) If the court determines that an interest is not represented under this [article], or that the otherwise available representation might be inadequate, the court may appoint a [representative] to receive notice, give consent, and otherwise represent, bind, and act on behalf of a minor, incapacitated, or unborn individual, or a person whose identity or location is unknown. A [representative] may be appointed to represent several persons or interests.

(b) A [representative] may act on behalf of the individual represented with respect to any matter arising under this [Code], whether or not a judicial proceeding concerning the trust is pending.

(c) In making decisions, a [representative] may consider general benefit accruing to the living members of the individual's family.

ARTICLE 4

CREATION, VALIDITY, MODIFICATION, AND TERMINATION OF TRUST

§401. Methods of Creating Trust

A trust may be created by:

(1) transfer of property to another person as trustee during the settlor's lifetime or by will or other disposition taking effect upon the settlor's death;

(2) declaration by the owner of property that the owner holds identifiable property as trustee; or

(3) exercise of a power of appointment in favor of a trustee.

Comment

. . . The methods specified in this section are not exclusive. Section 102 recognizes that trusts can also be created by special statute or court order. See also Restatement (Third) of Trusts Section 1 cmt. a (Tentative Draft No. 1, approved 1996); Unif. Probate Code Section 2-212 (elective share of incapacitated surviving spouse to be held in trust on terms specified in statute); Unif. Probate Code Section 5-411(a)(4) (conservator may create trust with court approval); Restatement (Second) of Trusts Section 17 cmt. i (1959) (trusts created by statutory right to bring wrongful death action).

A trust can also be created by a promise that creates enforceable rights in a person who immediately or later holds these rights as trustee. See Restatement (Third) of Trusts Section 10(e) (Tentative Draft No. 1, approved 1996). A trust thus created is valid notwithstanding that the trustee may resign or die before the promise is fulfilled. Unless expressly made personal, the promise can be enforced by a successor trustee. For examples of trusts created by means of promises enforceable by the trustee, see Restatement (Third) of Trusts Section 10 cmt. g (Tentative Draft No. 1, approved 1996); Restatement (Second) of Trusts Sections 14 cmt. h, 26 cmt. n (1959).

A trust created by self-declaration is best created by reregistering each of the assets that comprise the trust into the settlor's name as trustee. However, such reregistration is not necessary to create the trust. . . .

§402. Requirements for Creation

(a) A trust is created only if:

(1) the settlor has capacity to create a trust;

(2) the settlor indicates an intention to create the trust;

(3) the trust has a definite beneficiary or is:

(A) a charitable trust;

(B) a trust for the care of an animal, as provided in Section 408; or

(C) a trust for a noncharitable purpose, as provided in Section 409;

(4) the trustee has duties to perform; and

(5) the same person is not the sole trustee and sole beneficiary.

(b) A beneficiary is definite if the beneficiary can be ascertained now or in the future, subject to any applicable rule against perpetuities.

(c) A power in a trustee to select a beneficiary from an indefinite class is valid. If the power is not exercised within a reasonable time, the power fails and the property subject to the power passes to the persons who would have taken the property had the power not been conferred.

§403. Trusts Created in other Jurisdictions

A trust not created by will is validly created if its creation complies with the law of the jurisdiction in which the trust instrument was executed, or the law of the jurisdiction in which, at the time of creation:

(1) the settlor was domiciled, had a place of abode, or was a national;

(2) a trustee was domiciled or had a place of business; or

(3) any trust property was located.

§404. Trust Purposes

A trust may be created only to the extent its purposes are lawful, not contrary to public policy, and possible to achieve. A trust and its terms must be for the benefit of its beneficiaries.

§405. Charitable Purposes; Enforcement

(a) A charitable trust may be created for the relief of poverty, the advancement of education or religion, the promotion of health, governmental or municipal purposes, or other purposes the achievement of which is beneficial to the community.

(b) If the terms of a charitable trust do not indicate a particular charitable purpose or beneficiary, the court may select one or more charitable purposes or beneficiaries. The selection must be consistent with the settlor's intention to the extent it can be ascertained.

(c) The settlor of a charitable trust, among others, may maintain a proceeding to enforce the trust.

§406. Creation of Trust Induced by Fraud, Duress, or Undue Influence

A trust is void to the extent its creation was induced by fraud, duress, or undue influence.

§407. Evidence of Oral Trust

Except as required by a statute other than this [Code], a trust need not be evidenced by a trust instrument, but the creation of an oral trust and its terms may be established only by clear and convincing evidence.

§408. Trust for Care of Animal

(a) A trust may be created to provide for the care of an animal alive during the settlor's lifetime. The trust terminates upon the death of the animal or, if the trust was created to provide for the care of more than one animal alive during the settlor's lifetime, upon the death of the last surviving animal.

(b) A trust authorized by this section may be enforced by a person appointed in the terms of the trust or, if no person is so appointed, by a person appointed by the court. A person having an interest in the welfare of the animal may request the court to appoint a person to enforce the trust or to remove a person appointed.

(c) Property of a trust authorized by this section may be applied only to its intended use, except to the extent the court determines that the value of the trust property exceeds the amount required for the intended use. Except as otherwise provided in the terms of the trust, property not required for the intended use must be distributed to the settlor, if then living, otherwise to the settlor's successors in interest.

§409. Noncharitable Trust without Ascertainable Beneficiary

Except as otherwise provided in Section 408 or by another statute, the following rules apply:

(1) A trust may be created for a noncharitable purpose without a definite or definitely ascertainable beneficiary or for a noncharitable but otherwise valid purpose to be selected by the trustee. The trust may not be enforced for more than [21] years.

(2) A trust authorized by this section may be enforced by a person appointed in the terms of the trust or, if no person is so appointed, by a person appointed by the court.

(3) Property of a trust authorized by this section may be applied only to its intended use, except to the extent the court determines that the value of the trust property exceeds the amount required for the intended use. Except as otherwise provided in the terms of the trust, property not required for the intended use must be distributed to the settlor, if then living, otherwise to the settlor's successors in interest.

§410. Modification or Termination of Trust; Proceedings for Approval or Disapproval

(a) In addition to the methods of termination prescribed by Sections 411 through 414, a trust terminates to the extent the trust is revoked or expires pursuant to its terms, no purpose of the trust remains to be achieved, or the purposes of the trust have become unlawful, contrary to public policy, or impossible to achieve.

(b) A proceeding to approve or disapprove a proposed modification or termination under Sections 411 through 416, or trust combination or division under Section 417, may be commenced by a trustee or beneficiary, and a proceeding to approve or disapprove a proposed modification or termination under Section 411 may be commenced by the settlor. The settlor of a charitable trust may maintain a proceeding to modify the trust under Section 413.

§411. Modification or Termination of Noncharitable Irrevocable Trust by Consent

(a) A noncharitable irrevocable trust may be modified or terminated upon consent of the settlor and all beneficiaries, even if the modification or termination is inconsistent with a material purpose of the trust. A settlor's power to consent to a trust's modification or termination may be exercised by an agent under a power of attorney only to the extent expressly authorized by the power of attorney or the terms of the trust; by the settlor's [conservator] with the approval of the court supervising the [conservatorship] if an agent is not so authorized; or by the settlor's [guardian] with the approval of the court supervising the [guardianship] if an agent is not so authorized and a conservator has not been appointed.

(b) A noncharitable irrevocable trust may be terminated upon consent of all of the beneficiaries if the court concludes that continuance of the trust is not necessary to achieve any material purpose of the trust. A noncharitable irrevocable trust may be modified upon consent of all of the beneficiaries if the court concludes that modification is not inconsistent with a material purpose of the trust.

(c) A spendthrift provision in the terms of the trust is not presumed to constitute a material purpose of the trust.

(d) Upon termination of a trust under subsection (a) or (b), the trustee shall distribute the trust property as agreed by the beneficiaries.

(e) If not all of the beneficiaries consent to a proposed modification or termination of the trust under subsection (a) or (b), the modification or termination may be approved by the court if the court is satisfied that:

(1) if all of the beneficiaries had consented, the trust could have been modified or terminated under this section; and

(2) the interests of a beneficiary who does not consent will be adequately protected.

Comment

. . . The provisions of Article 3 on representation, virtual representation, and the appointment and approval of representatives appointed by the court apply to the determination of whether all beneficiaries have signified consent under this section. The authority to consent on behalf of another person, however, does not include authority to consent over the other person's objection. See Section 301(b). Regarding the persons who may consent on behalf of a beneficiary, see Sections 302 through 305. A consent given by a representative is invalid to the extent there is a conflict of interest between the representative and the person represented. Given this limitation, virtual representation of a beneficiary's interest by another beneficiary pursuant to Section 304 will rarely be available in a trust termination case, although it should be routinely available in cases involving trust modification, such as a grant to the trustee of additional powers. If virtual or other form of representation is unavailable, Section 305 of the Code permits the court to appoint a representative who may give the necessary consent to the proposed modification or termination on behalf of the minor, incapacitated, unborn, or unascertained beneficiary. The ability to use virtual and other forms of representation to consent on a beneficiary's behalf to a trust termination or modification has not traditionally been part of the law, although there are some notable exceptions. Compare Restatement (Second) Section 337(1) (1959) (beneficiary must not be under incapacity), with Hatch v. Riggs National Bank, 361 F.2d 559 (D.C. Cir. 1966) (guardian ad litem authorized to consent on beneficiary's behalf). . . .

§412. Modification or Termination because of Unanticipated Circumstances or Inability to Administer Trust Effectively

(a) The court may modify the administrative or dispositive terms of a trust or terminate the trust if, because of circumstances not anticipated by the settlor, modification or termination will further the purposes of the trust. To the extent practicable, the modification must be made in accordance with the settlor's probable intention.

(b) The court may modify the administrative terms of a trust if continuation of the trust on its existing terms would be impracticable or wasteful or impair the trust's administration.

(c) Upon termination of a trust under this section, the trustee shall distribute the trust property in a manner consistent with the purposes of the trust.

Comment

This section broadens the court's ability to apply equitable deviation to terminate or modify a trust. Subsection (a) allows a court to modify the dispositive provisions of the trust as well as its administrative terms. For example, modification of the dispositive provisions to increase support of a beneficiary might be appropriate if the beneficiary has become unable to provide for support due to poor health or serious injury. Subsection (a) is similar to Restatement (Third) of Trusts Section 66(1) (Tentative Draft No. 3, approved 2001), except that this section, unlike the Restatement, does not impose a duty on the trustee to petition the court if the trustee is aware of circumstances justifying judicial modification. The purpose of the "equitable deviation" authorized by subsection (a) is not to disregard the settlor's intent but to modify inopportune details to effectuate better the settlor's broader purposes. Among other things, equitable deviation may be used to modify administrative or dispositive terms due to the failure to anticipate economic change or the incapacity of a beneficiary. For numerous illustrations, see Restatement (Third) of Trusts Section 66 cmt. b (Tentative Draft No. 3, approved 2001). While it is necessary that there be circumstances not anticipated by the settlor before the court may grant relief under subsection (a), the circumstances may have been in existence when the trust was created. . . .

Subsection (b) broadens the court's ability to modify the administrative terms of a trust. . . . Subsections (a) and (b) are not mutually exclusive. Many situations justifying modification of administrative terms under subsection (a) will also justify modification under subsection (b). Subsection (b) is also an application of the requirement in Section 404 that a trust and its terms must be for the benefit of its beneficiaries. See also Restatement (Third) of Trusts Section 27(2) & cmt. b (Tentative Draft No. 2, approved 1999). Although the settlor is granted considerable latitude in defining the purposes of the trust, the principle that a trust have a purpose which is for the benefit of its beneficiaries precludes unreasonable restrictions on the use of trust property. An owner's freedom to be capricious about the use of the owner's own property ends when the property is impressed with a trust for the benefit of others. See Restatement (Second) of Trusts Section 124 cmt. g (1959). Thus, attempts to impose unreasonable restrictions on the use of trust property will fail. See Restatement (Third) of Trusts Section 27 Reporter's Notes to cmt. b (Tentative Draft No. 2, approved 1999). Subsection (b), unlike subsection (a), does not have a direct precedent in the common law, but various states have insisted on such a measure by statute. See, e.g., Mo. Rev. Stat. Section456.590.1. . . .

§413. Cy Pres

(a) Except as otherwise provided in subsection (b), if a particular charitable purpose becomes unlawful, impracticable, impossible to achieve, or wasteful:

(1) the trust does not fail, in whole or in part;

(2) the trust property does not revert to the settlor or the settlor's successors in interest; and

(3) the court may apply cy pres to modify or terminate the trust by directing that the trust property be applied or distributed, in whole or in part, in a manner consistent with the settlor's charitable purposes.

(b) A provision in the terms of a charitable trust that would result in distribution of the trust property to a noncharitable beneficiary prevails over the power of the court under subsection (a) to apply cy pres to modify or terminate the trust only if, when the provision takes effect:

(1) the trust property is to revert to the settlor and the settlor is still living; or

(2) fewer than 21 years have elapsed since the date of the trust's creation.

Comment

Subsection (a) codifies the court's inherent authority to apply cy pres. The power may be applied to modify an administrative or dispositive term. The court may order the trust terminated and distributed to other charitable entities. Partial termination may also be ordered if the trust property is more than sufficient to satisfy the trust's current purposes. Subsection (a), which is similar to Restatement (Third) of Trusts Section 67 (Tentative Draft No. 3, approved 2001), modifies the doctrine of cy pres by presuming that the settlor had a general charitable intent when a particular charitable purpose becomes impossible or impracticable to achieve. Traditional doctrine did not supply that presumption, leaving it to the courts to determine whether the settlor had a general charitable intent. If such an intent is found, the trust property is applied to other charitable purposes. If not, the charitable trust fails. See Restatement (Second) of Trusts Section 399 (1959). In the great majority of cases the settlor would prefer that the property be used for other charitable purposes. Courts are usually able to find a general charitable purpose to which to apply the property, no matter how vaguely such purpose may have been expressed by the settlor. . . .

§414. Modification or Termination of Uneconomic Trust

(a) After notice to the qualified beneficiaries, the trustee of a trust consisting of trust property having a total value less than [$50,000] may terminate the trust if the trustee concludes that the value of the trust property is insufficient to justify the cost of administration.

(b) The court may modify or terminate a trust or remove the trustee and appoint a different trustee if it determines that the value of the trust property is insufficient to justify the cost of administration.

(c) Upon termination of a trust under this section, the trustee shall distribute the trust property in a manner consistent with the purposes of the trust.

(d) This section does not apply to an easement for conservation or preservation.

§415. Reformation to Correct Mistakes

The court may reform the terms of a trust, even if unambiguous, to conform the terms to the settlor's intention if it is proved by clear and convincing evidence that both the settlor's intent and the terms of the trust were affected by a mistake of fact or law, whether in expression or inducement.

§416. Modification to Achieve Settlor's Tax Objectives

To achieve the settlor's tax objectives, the court may modify the terms of a trust in a manner that is not contrary to the settlor's probable intention. The court may provide that the modification has retroactive effect.

§417. Combination and Division of Trusts

After notice to the qualified beneficiaries, a trustee may combine two or more trusts into a single trust or divide a trust into two or more separate trusts, if the result does not impair rights of any beneficiary or adversely affect achievement of the purposes of the trust.

ARTICLE 5

CREDITOR'S CLAIMS; SPENDTHRIFT AND DISCRETIONARY TRUSTS

§501. Rights of Beneficiary's Creditor or Assignee

To the extent a beneficiary's interest is not protected by a spendthrift provision, the court may authorize a creditor or assignee of the beneficiary to reach the beneficiary's interest by attachment of present or future distributions to or for the benefit of the beneficiary or other means. The court may limit the award to such relief as is appropriate under the circumstances.

§502. Spendthrift Provision

(a) A spendthrift provision is valid only if it restrains both voluntary and involuntary transfer of a beneficiary's interest.

(b) A term of a trust providing that the interest of a beneficiary is held subject to a "spendthrift trust," or words of similar import, is sufficient to restrain both voluntary and involuntary transfer of the beneficiary's interest.

(c) A beneficiary may not transfer an interest in a trust in violation of a valid spendthrift provision and, except as otherwise provided in this [article], a creditor or assignee of the beneficiary may not reach the interest or a distribution by the trustee before its receipt by the beneficiary.

§503. Exceptions to Spendthrift Provision

(a) In this section, "child" includes any person for whom an order or judgment for child support has been entered in this or another State.

(b) Even if a trust contains a spendthrift provision, a beneficiary's child, spouse, or former spouse who has a judgment or court order against the beneficiary for support or maintenance, or a judgment creditor who has provided services for the protection of a beneficiary's interest in the trust, may obtain from a court an order attaching present or future distributions to or for the benefit of the beneficiary.

(c) A spendthrift provision is unenforceable against a claim of this State or the United States to the extent a statute of this State or federal law so provides.

§504. Discretionary Trusts; Effect of Standard

(a) In this section, "child" includes any person for whom an order or judgment for child support has been entered in this or another State.

(b) Except as otherwise provided in subsection (c), whether or not a trust contains a spendthrift provision, a creditor of a beneficiary may not compel a distribution that is subject to the trustee's discretion, even if:

(1) the discretion is expressed in the form of a standard of distribution; or

(2) the trustee has abused the discretion.

(c) To the extent a trustee has not complied with a standard of distribution or has abused a discretion:

(1) a distribution may be ordered by the court to satisfy a judgment or court order against the beneficiary for support or maintenance of the beneficiary's child, spouse, or former spouse; and

(2) the court shall direct the trustee to pay to the child, spouse, or former spouse such amount as is equitable under the circumstances but not more than the amount the trustee would have been required to distribute to or for the benefit of the beneficiary had the trustee complied with the standard or not abused the discretion.

(d) This section does not limit the right of a beneficiary to maintain a judicial proceeding against a trustee for an abuse of discretion or failure to comply with a standard for distribution.

§505. Creditor's Claim Against Settlor

(a) Whether or not the terms of a trust contain a spendthrift provision, the following rules apply:

(1) During the lifetime of the settlor, the property of a revocable trust is subject to claims of the settlor's creditors.

(2) With respect to an irrevocable trust, a creditor or assignee of the settlor may reach the maximum amount that can be distributed to or for the settlor's benefit. If a trust has more than one settlor, the amount the creditor or assignee of a particular settlor may reach may not exceed the settlor's interest in the portion of the trust attributable to that settlor's contribution.

(3) After the death of a settlor, and subject to the settlor's right to direct the source from which liabilities will be paid, the property of a trust that was revocable at the settlor's death is subject to claims of the settlor's creditors, costs of administration of the settlor's estate, the expenses of the settlor's funeral and disposal of remains, and [statutory allowances] to a surviving spouse and children to the extent the settlor's probate estate is inadequate to satisfy those claims, costs, expenses, and [allowances].

(b) For purposes of this section:

(1) during the period the power may be exercised, the holder of a power of withdrawal is treated in the same manner as the settlor of a revocable trust to the extent of the property subject to the power; and

(2) upon the lapse, release, or waiver of the power, the holder is treated as the settlor of the trust only to the extent the value of the property affected by the lapse, release, or waiver exceeds the greater of the amount specified in Section 2041(b)(2) or 2514(e) of the Internal Revenue Code of 1986, or Section 2503(b) of the Internal Revenue Code of 1986, in each case as in effect on [the effective date of this [Code]] [, or as later amended].

§506. Overdue Distribution

Whether or not a trust contains a spendthrift provision, a creditor or assignee of a beneficiary may reach a mandatory distribution of income or principal, including a distribution upon termination of the trust, if the trustee has not made the distribution to the beneficiary within a reasonable time after the designated distribution date.

§507. Personal Obligations of Trustee

Trust property is not subject to personal obligations of the trustee, even if the trustee becomes insolvent or bankrupt.

ARTICLE 6

REVOCABLE TRUSTS

§601. Capacity of Settlor of Revocable Trust

The capacity required to create, amend, revoke, or add property to a revocable trust, or to direct the actions of the trustee of a revocable trust, is the same as that required to make a will.

§602. Revocation or Amendment of Revocable Trust

(a) Unless the terms of a trust expressly provide that the trust is irrevocable, the settlor may revoke or amend the trust. This subsection does not apply to a trust created under an instrument executed before [the effective date of this [Code]].

(b) If a revocable trust is created or funded by more than one settlor:

(1) to the extent the trust consists of community property, the trust may be revoked by either spouse acting alone but may be amended only by joint action of both spouses; and

(2) to the extent the trust consists of property other than community property, each settlor may revoke or amend the trust with regard to the portion of the trust property attributable to that settlor's contribution; and

(3) upon the revocation or amendment of the trust by fewer than all of the settlers, the trustee shall promptly notify the other settlers of the revocation or amendment.

(c) The settlor may revoke or amend a revocable trust:

(1) by substantial compliance with a method provided in the terms of the trust; or

(2) if the terms of the trust do not provide a method or the method provided in the terms is not expressly made exclusive, by:

(A) a later will or codicil that expressly refers to the trust or specifically devises property that would otherwise have passed according to the terms of the trust; or

(B) any other method manifesting clear and convincing evidence of the settlor's intent.

(d) Upon revocation of a revocable trust, the trustee shall deliver the trust property as the settlor directs.

(e) A settlor's powers with respect to revocation, amendment, or distribution of trust property may be exercised by an agent under a power of attorney only to the extent expressly authorized by the terms of the trust or the power.

(f) A [conservator] of the settlor or, if no [conservator] has been appointed, a [guardian] of the settlor may exercise a settlor's powers with respect to revocation, amendment, or distribution of trust property only with the approval of the court supervising the [conservatorship] or [guardianship].

(g) A trustee who does not know that a trust has been revoked or amended is not liable to the settlor or settlor's successors in interest for distributions made and other actions taken on the assumption that the trust had not been amended or revoked.

Comment

. . . Revocation or amendment by will is mentioned in subsection (c) not to encourage the practice but to make clear that it is not precluded by omission. See Restatement (Third) of Property: Will and Other Donative Transfers Section 7.2 cmt. e (Tentative Draft No. 3, approved 2001), which validates revocation or amendment of will substitutes by later will. Situations do arise, particularly in death-bed cases, where revocation by will may be the only practicable method. In such cases, a will, a solemn document executed with a high level of formality, may be the most reliable method for expressing intent. A revocation in a will ordinarily becomes effective only upon probate of the will following the testator's death. For the cases, see Restatement (Third) of Trusts Section 63 Reporter's Notes to cmt. h-i (Tentative Draft No. 3, approved 2001).

A residuary clause in a will disposing of the estate differently than the trust is alone insufficient to revoke or amend a trust. The provision in the will must either be express or the will must dispose of specific assets contrary to the terms of the trust. The substantial body of law on revocation of Totten trusts by will offers helpful guidance. The authority is collected in William H. Danne, Jr., Revocation of Tentative ("Totten") Trust of Savings Bank Account by Inter Vivos Declaration or Will, 46 A.L.R. 3d 487 (1972).

Subsection (c) does not require that a trustee concur in the revocation or amendment of a trust. Such a concurrence would be necessary only if required by the terms of the trust. If the trustee concludes that an amendment unacceptably changes the trustee's duties, the trustee may resign as provided in Section 705. . . .

A settlor's power to revoke is not terminated by the settlor's incapacity. The power to revoke may instead be exercised by an agent under a power of attorney as authorized in subsection (e), by a conservator or guardian as authorized in subsection (f), or by the settlor personally if the settlor regains capacity.

Subsection (e), which is similar to Restatement (Third) of Trusts Section 63 cmt. l (Tentative Draft No. 3, approved 2001), authorizes an agent under a power of attorney to revoke or modify a revocable trust only to the extent the terms of the trust or power of attorney expressly so permit. An express provision is required because most settlors usually intend that the revocable trust, and not the power of attorney, to function as the settlor's principal property management device. The power of attorney is usually intended as a backup for assets not transferred to the revocable trust or to address specific topics, such as the power to sign tax returns or apply for government benefits, which may be beyond the authority of a trustee or are not customarily granted to a trustee.

Subsection (f) addresses the authority of a conservator or guardian to revoke or amend a revocable trust. Under the Uniform Trust Code, a "conservator" is appointed by the court to manage the ward's party, a "guardian" to make decisions with respect to the ward's personal affairs. See Section 103. Consequently, subsection (f) authorizes a guardian to exercise a settlor's power to revoke or amend a trust only if a conservator has not been appointed.

Many state conservatorship statutes authorize a conservator to exercise the settlor's power of revocation with the prior approval of the court supervising the conservatorship. See, e.g., Unif. Probate Code Section 411(a)(4). Subsection (f) ratifies this practice. Under the Code, a conservator may exercise a settlor's power of revocation, amendment, or right to withdraw trust property upon approval of the court supervising the conservatorship. Because a settlor often creates a revocable trust for the very purpose of avoiding conservatorship, this power should be exercised by the court reluctantly. Settlors concerned about revocation by a conservator may wish to deny a conservator a power to revoke. However, while such a provision in the terms of the trust is entitled to considerable weight, the court may override the restriction if it concludes that the action is necessary in the interests of justice. See Section 105(b)(13). . . .

§603. Settlor's Powers; Powers of Withdrawal

(a) While a trust is revocable and the settlor has capacity to revoke the trust, rights of the beneficiaries are subject to the control of, and the duties of the trustee are owed exclusively to, the settlor.

(b) If a revocable trust has more than one settlor, the duties of the trustee are owed to all of the settlors having capacity to revoke the trust.

(c) During the period the power may be exercised, the holder of a power of withdrawal has the rights of a settlor of a revocable trust under this section to the extent of the property subject to the power.

Comment

This section has the effect of postponing enforcement of the rights of the beneficiaries of a revocable trust until the death or incapacity of the settlor or other person holding the power to revoke the trust. This section thus recognizes that the settlor of a revocable trust is in control of the trust and should have the right to enforce the trust.

Pursuant to this section, the duty under Section 813 to inform and report to beneficiaries is owed to the settlor of a revocable trust as long as the settlor has capacity. . . .

If the settlor loses capacity, subsection (a) no longer applies, with the consequence that the rights of the beneficiaries are no longer subject to the settlor's control. The beneficiaries are entitled to request information concerning the trust and the trustee must provide the beneficiaries with annual trustee reports and whatever other information may be required under Section 813. However, because this section may be freely overridden in the terms of the trust, a settlor is free to deny the beneficiaries these rights, even to the point of directing the trustee not to inform them of the existence of the trust. . . .

Subsection (c) makes clear that a holder of a power of withdrawal has the same powers over the trust as the settlor of a revocable trust. Equal treatment is warranted due to the holder's equivalent power to control the trust. For the definition of power of withdrawal, see Section 103(10).

2001 Amendment. By a 2001 amendment, former subsection (b) was deleted. Former subsection (b) provided: "While a trust is revocable and the settlor does not have capacity to revoke the trust, rights of the beneficiaries are held by the beneficiaries." No substantive change was intended by this amendment. Former subsection (b) was superfluous. Rights of the beneficiaries are always held by the beneficiaries unless taken away by some other provision. Subsection (a) grants these rights to the settlor of a revocable trust while the settlor has capacity. Upon a settlor's loss of capacity, these rights are held by the beneficiaries with or without former subsection (b).

§604. Limitation on Action Contesting Validity of Revocable Trust; Distribution of Trust Property

(a) A person may commence a judicial proceeding to contest the validity of a trust that was revocable at the settlor's death within the earlier of:

(1) [three] years after the settlor's death; or

(2) [120] days after the trustee sent the person a copy of the trust instrument and a notice informing the person of the trust's existence, of the trustee's name and address, and of the time allowed for commencing a proceeding.

(b) Upon the death of the settlor of a trust that was revocable at the settlor's death, the trustee may proceed to distribute the trust property in accordance with the terms of the trust. The trustee is not subject to liability for doing so unless:

(1) the trustee knows of a pending judicial proceeding contesting the validity of the trust; or

(2) a potential contestant has notified the trustee of a possible judicial proceeding to contest the trust and a judicial proceeding is commenced within 60 days after the contestant sent the notification.

(c) A beneficiary of a trust that is determined to have been invalid is liable to return any distribution received.

ARTICLE 7

OFFICE OF TRUSTEE

§701. Accepting or Declining Trusteeship

(a) Except as otherwise provided in subsection (c), a person designated as trustee accepts the trusteeship:

(1) by substantially complying with a method of acceptance provided in the terms of the trust; or

(2) if the terms of the trust do not provide a method or the method provided in the terms is not expressly made exclusive, by accepting delivery of the trust property, exercising powers or performing duties as trustee, or otherwise indicating acceptance of the trusteeship.

(b) A person designated as trustee who has not yet accepted the trusteeship may reject the trusteeship. A designated trustee who does not accept the trusteeship within a reasonable time after knowing of the designation is deemed to have rejected the trusteeship.

(c) A person designated as trustee, without accepting the trusteeship, may:

(1) act to preserve the trust property if, within a reasonable time after acting, the person sends a rejection of the trusteeship to the settlor or, if the settlor is dead or lacks capacity, to a qualified beneficiary; and

(2) inspect or investigate trust property to determine potential liability under environmental or other law or for any other purpose.

§702. Trustee's Bond

(a) A trustee shall give bond to secure performance of the trustee's duties only if the court finds that a bond is needed to protect the interests of the beneficiaries or is required by the terms of the trust and the court has not dispensed with the requirement.

(b) The court may specify the amount of a bond, its liabilities, and whether sureties are necessary. The court may modify or terminate a bond at any time.

[(c) A regulated financial-service institution qualified to do trust business in this State need not give bond, even if required by the terms of the trust.]

§703. Cotrustees

(a) Cotrustees who are unable to reach a unanimous decision may act by majority decision.

(b) If a vacancy occurs in a cotrusteeship, the remaining cotrustees may act for the trust.

(c) A cotrustee must participate in the performance of a trustee's function unless the cotrustee is unavailable to perform the function because of absence, illness, disqualification under other law, or other temporary incapacity or the cotrustee has properly delegated the performance of the function to another trustee.

(d) If a cotrustee is unavailable to perform duties because of absence, illness, disqualification under other law, or other temporary incapacity, and prompt action is necessary to achieve the purposes of the trust or to avoid injury to the trust property, the remaining cotrustee or a majority of the remaining cotrustees may act for the trust.

(e) A trustee may not delegate to a cotrustee the performance of a function the settlor reasonably expected the trustees to perform jointly. Unless a delegation was irrevocable, a trustee may revoke a delegation previously made.

(f) Except as otherwise provided in subsection (g), a trustee who does not join in an action of another trustee is not liable for the action.

(g) Each trustee shall exercise reasonable care to:

(1) prevent a cotrustee from committing a serious breach of trust; and

(2) compel a cotrustee to redress a serious breach of trust.

(h) A dissenting trustee who joins in an action at the direction of the majority of the trustees and who notified any cotrustee of the dissent at or before the time of the action is not liable for the action unless the action is a serious breach of trust.

§704. Vacancy in Trusteeship; Appointment of Successor

(a) A vacancy in a trusteeship occurs if:

(1) a person designated as trustee rejects the trusteeship;

(2) a person designated as trustee cannot be identified or does not exist;

(3) a trustee resigns;

(4) a trustee is disqualified or removed;

(5) a trustee dies; or

(6) a [guardian] or [conservator] is appointed for an individual serving as trustee.

(b) If one or more cotrustees remain in office, a vacancy in a trusteeship need not be filled. A vacancy in a trusteeship must be filled if the trust has no remaining trustee.

(c) A vacancy in a trusteeship of a noncharitable trust that is required to be filled must be filled in the following order of priority:

(1) by a person designated in the terms of the trust to act as successor trustee;

(2) by a person appointed by unanimous agreement of the qualified beneficiaries; or

(3) by a person appointed by the court.

(d) A vacancy in a trusteeship of a charitable trust that is required to be filled must be filled in the following order of priority:

(1) by a person designated in the terms of the trust to act as successor trustee;

(2) by a person selected by the charitable organizations expressly designated to receive distributions under the terms of the trust if the [attorney general] concurs in the selection; or

(3) by a person appointed by the court.

(e) Whether or not a vacancy in a trusteeship exists or is required to be filled, the court may appoint an additional trustee or special fiduciary whenever the court considers the appointment necessary for the administration of the trust.

§705. Resignation of Trustee

(a) A trustee may resign:

(1) upon at least 30 days' notice to the qualified beneficiaries, the settlor, if living, and all cotrustees; or

(2) with the approval of the court.

(b) In approving a resignation, the court may issue orders and impose conditions reasonably necessary for the protection of the trust property.

(c) Any liability of a resigning trustee or of any sureties on the trustee's bond for acts or omissions of the trustee is not discharged or affected by the trustee's resignation.

§706. Removal of Trustee

(a) The settlor, a cotrustee, or a beneficiary may request the court to remove a trustee, or a trustee may be removed by the court on its own initiative.

(b) The court may remove a trustee if:

(1) the trustee has committed a serious breach of trust;

(2) lack of cooperation among cotrustees substantially impairs the administration of the trust;

(3) because of unfitness, unwillingness, or persistent failure of the trustee to administer the trust effectively, the court determines that removal of the trustee best serves the interests of the beneficiaries; or

(4) there has been a substantial change of circumstances or removal is requested by all of the qualified beneficiaries, the court finds that removal of the trustee best serves the interests of all of the beneficiaries and is not inconsistent with a material purpose of the trust, and a suitable cotrustee or successor trustee is available.

(c) Pending a final decision on a request to remove a trustee, or in lieu of or in addition to removing a trustee, the court may order such appropriate relief under Section 1001(b) as may be necessary to protect the trust property or the interests of the beneficiaries.

§707. Delivery of Property by Former Trustee

(a) Unless a cotrustee remains in office or the court otherwise orders, and until the trust property is delivered to a successor trustee or other person entitled to it, a trustee who has resigned or been removed has the duties of a trustee and the powers necessary to protect the trust property.

(b) A trustee who has resigned or been removed shall proceed expeditiously to deliver the trust property within the trustee's possession to the cotrustee, successor trustee, or other person entitled to it.

§708. Compensation of Trustee

(a) If the terms of a trust do not specify the trustee's compensation, a trustee is entitled to compensation that is reasonable under the circumstances.

(b) If the terms of a trust specify the trustee's compensation, the trustee is entitled to be compensated as specified, but the court may allow more or less compensation if:

(1) the duties of the trustee are substantially different from those contemplated when the trust was created; or

(2) the compensation specified by the terms of the trust would be unreasonably low or high.

§709. Reimbursement of Expenses

(a) A trustee is entitled to be reimbursed out of the trust property, with interest as appropriate, for:

(1) expenses that were properly incurred in the administration of the trust; and

(2) to the extent necessary to prevent unjust enrichment of the trust, expenses that were not properly incurred in the administration of the trust.

(b) An advance by the trustee of money for the protection of the trust gives rise to a lien against trust property to secure reimbursement with reasonable interest.

ARTICLE 8

DUTIES AND POWERS OF TRUSTEE

§801. Duty to Administer Trust

Upon acceptance of a trusteeship, the trustee shall administer the trust in good faith, in accordance with its terms and purposes and the interests of the beneficiaries, and in accordance with this [Code].

§802. Duty of Loyalty

(a) A trustee shall administer the trust solely in the interests of the beneficiaries.

(b) Subject to the rights of persons dealing with or assisting the trustee as provided in Section 1012, a sale, encumbrance, or other transaction involving the investment or management of trust property entered into by the trustee for the trustee's own personal account or which is otherwise affected by a conflict between the trustee's fiduciary and personal interests is voidable by a beneficiary affected by the transaction unless:

(1) the transaction was authorized by the terms of the trust;

(2) the transaction was approved by the court;

(3) the beneficiary did not commence a judicial proceeding within the time allowed by Section 1005;

(4) the beneficiary consented to the trustee's conduct, ratified the transaction, or released the trustee in compliance with Section 1009; or

(5) the transaction involves a contract entered into or claim acquired by the trustee before the person became or contemplated becoming trustee.

(c) A sale, encumbrance, or other transaction involving the investment or management of trust property is presumed to be affected by a conflict between personal and fiduciary interests if it is entered into by the trustee with:

(1) the trustee's spouse;

(2) the trustee's descendants, siblings, parents, or their spouses;

(3) an agent or attorney of the trustee; or

(4) a corporation or other person or enterprise in which the trustee, or a person that owns a significant interest in the trustee, has an interest that might affect the trustee's best judgment.

(d) A transaction between a trustee and a beneficiary that does not concern trust property but that occurs during the existence of the trust or while the trustee retains significant influence over the beneficiary and from which the trustee obtains an advantage is voidable by the beneficiary unless the trustee establishes that the transaction was fair to the beneficiary.

(e) A transaction not concerning trust property in which the trustee engages in the trustee's individual capacity involves a conflict between personal and fiduciary interests if the transaction concerns an opportunity properly belonging to the trust.

(f) An investment by a trustee in securities of an investment company or investment trust to which the trustee, or its affiliate, provides services in a capacity other than as trustee is not presumed to be affected by a conflict between personal and fiduciary interests if the investment complies with the prudent investor rule of [Article] 9. In addition to its compensation for acting as trustee, the trustee may be compensated by the investment company or investment trust for providing those services out of fees charged to the trust. If the trustee receives compensation from the investment company or investment trust for providing investment advisory or investment management services, the trustee at least annually shall notify the persons entitled under Section 813 to receive a copy of the trustee's annual report of the rate and method by which the compensation was determined.

(g) In voting shares of stock or in exercising powers of control over similar interests in other forms of enterprise, the trustee shall act in the best interests of the beneficiaries. If the trust is the sole owner of a corporation or other form of enterprise, the trustee shall elect or appoint directors or other managers who will manage the corporation or enterprise in the best interests of the beneficiaries.

(h) This section does not preclude the following transactions, if fair to the beneficiaries:

(1) an agreement between a trustee and a beneficiary relating to the appointment or compensation of the trustee;

(2) payment of reasonable compensation to the trustee;

(3) a transaction between a trust and another trust, decedent's estate, or [conservatorship] of which the trustee is a fiduciary or in which a beneficiary has an interest;

(4) a deposit of trust money in a regulated financial-service institution operated by the trustee; or

(5) an advance by the trustee of money for the protection of the trust.

(I) The court may appoint a special fiduciary to make a decision with respect to any proposed transaction that might violate this section if entered into by the trustee.

Comment

. . . Subsection (f) attempts to retain the advantages of mutual funds while at the same time making clear that such investments are subject to traditional fiduciary responsibilities. Nearly all of the States have enacted statutes authorizing trustees to invest in funds from which the trustee might derive additional compensation. Portions of subsection (f) are based on these statutes. Subsection (f) makes clear that such dual investment-fee arrangements are not automatically presumed to involve a conflict between the trustee's personal and fiduciary interests, but subsection (f) does not otherwise waive or lessen a trustee's fiduciary obligations. The trustee, in deciding whether to invest in a mutual fund, must not place its own interests ahead of those of the beneficiaries. The investment decision must also comply with the enacting jurisdiction's prudent investor rule. To obtain the protection afforded by subsection (f), the trustee must disclose at least annually to the beneficiaries entitled to receive a copy of the trustee's annual report the rate and method by which the additional compensation was determined. Furthermore, the selection of a mutual fund, and the resulting delegation of certain of the trustee's functions, may be taken into account under Section 708 in setting the trustee's regular compensation. See also Uniform Prudent Investor Act Sections 7 and 9 and Comments; Restatement (Third) of Trusts: Prudent Investor Rule Section 227 cmt. m (1992). . . .

§803. Impartiality

If a trust has two or more beneficiaries, the trustee shall act impartially in investing, managing, and distributing the trust property, giving due regard to the beneficiaries' respective interests.

Comment

. . . This section is identical to Section 6 of the Uniform Prudent Investor Act, except that this section also applies to all aspects of trust administration and to decisions by a trustee with respect to distributions. The Prudent Investor Act is limited to duties with respect to the investment and management of trust property. The differing beneficial interests for which the trustee must act impartially include those of the current beneficiaries versus those of beneficiaries holding interests in the remainder; and among those currently eligible to receive distributions. In fulfilling the duty to act impartially, the trustee should be particularly sensitive to allocation of receipts and disbursements between income and principal and should consider, in an appropriate case, a reallocation of income to the principal account and vice versa, if allowable under local law. For an example of such authority, see Uniform Principal and Income Act Section 104 (1997).

The duty to act impartially does not mean that the trustee must treat the beneficiaries equally. Rather, the trustee must treat the beneficiaries equitably in light of the purposes and terms of the trust. . . .

§804. Prudent Administration

A trustee shall administer the trust as a prudent person would, by considering the purposes, terms, distributional requirements, and other circumstances of the trust. In satisfying this standard, the trustee shall exercise reasonable care, skill, and caution.

§805. Costs of Administration

In administering a trust, the trustee may incur only costs that are reasonable in relation to the trust property, the purposes of the trust, and the skills of the trustee.

§806. Trustee's Skills

A trustee who has special skills or expertise, or is named trustee in reliance upon the trustee's representation that the trustee has special skills or expertise, shall use those special skills or expertise.

§807. Delegation by Trustee

(a) A trustee may delegate duties and powers that a prudent trustee of comparable skills could properly delegate under the circumstances. The trustee shall exercise reasonable care, skill, and caution in:

(1) selecting an agent;

(2) establishing the scope and terms of the delegation, consistent with the purposes and terms of the trust; and

(3) periodically reviewing the agent's actions in order to monitor the agent's performance and compliance with the terms of the delegation.

(b) In performing a delegated function, an agent owes a duty to the trust to exercise reasonable care to comply with the terms of the delegation.

(c) A trustee who complies with subsection (a) is not liable to the beneficiaries or to the trust for an action of the agent to whom the function was delegated.

(d) By accepting a delegation of powers or duties from the trustee of a trust that is subject to the law of this State, an agent submits to the jurisdiction of the courts of this State.

Comment

. . . This section encourages and protects the trustee in making delegations appropriate to the facts and circumstances of the particular trust. Whether a particular function is delegable is based on whether it is a function that a prudent trustee might delegate under similar circumstances. For example, delegating some administrative and reporting duties might be prudent for a family trustee but unnecessary for a corporate trustee.

This section applies only to delegation to agents, not to delegation to a cotrustee. For the provision regulating delegation to a cotrustee, see Section 703(e). . . .

§808. Powers to Direct

(a) While a trust is revocable, the trustee may follow a direction of the settlor that is contrary to the terms of the trust.

(b) If the terms of a trust confer upon a person other than the settlor of a revocable trust power to direct certain actions of the trustee, the trustee shall act in accordance with an exercise of the power unless the attempted exercise is manifestly contrary to the terms of the trust or the trustee knows the attempted exercise would constitute a serious breach of a fiduciary duty that the person holding the power owes to the beneficiaries of the trust.

(c) The terms of a trust may confer upon a trustee or other person a power to direct the modification or termination of the trust.

(d) A person, other than a beneficiary, who holds a power to direct is presumptively a fiduciary who, as such, is required to act in good faith with regard to the purposes of the trust and the interests of the beneficiaries. The holder of a power to direct is liable for any loss that results from breach of a fiduciary duty.

§809. Control and Protection of Trust Property

A trustee shall take reasonable steps to take control of and protect the trust property.

§810. Recordkeeping and Identification of Trust Property

(a) A trustee shall keep adequate records of the administration of the trust.

(b) A trustee shall keep trust property separate from the trustee's own property.

(c) Except as otherwise provided in subsection (d), a trustee shall cause the trust property to be designated so that the interest of the trust, to the extent feasible, appears in records maintained by a party other than a trustee or beneficiary.

(d) If the trustee maintains records clearly indicating the respective interests, a trustee may invest as a whole the property of two or more separate trusts.

§811. Enforcement and Defense of Claims

A trustee shall take reasonable steps to enforce claims of the trust and to defend claims against the trust.

§812. Collecting Trust Property

A trustee shall take reasonable steps to compel a former trustee or other person to deliver trust property to the trustee, and to redress a breach of trust known to the trustee to have been committed by a former trustee.

§813. Duty to Inform and Report

(a) A trustee shall keep the qualified beneficiaries of the trust reasonably informed about the administration of the trust and of the material facts necessary for them to protect their interests. Unless unreasonable under the circumstances, a trustee shall promptly respond to a beneficiary's request for information related to the administration of the trust.

(b) A trustee:

(1) upon request of a beneficiary, shall promptly furnish to the beneficiary a copy of the trust instrument;

(2) within 60 days after accepting a trusteeship, shall notify the qualified beneficiaries of the acceptance and of the trustee's name, address, and telephone number;

(3) within 60 days after the date the trustee acquires knowledge of the creation of an irrevocable trust, or the date the trustee acquires knowledge that a formerly revocable trust has become irrevocable, whether by the death of the settlor or otherwise, shall notify the qualified beneficiaries of the trust's existence, of the identity of the settlor or settlors, of the right to request a copy of the trust instrument, and of the right to a trustee's report as provided in subsection (c); and

(4) shall notify the qualified beneficiaries in advance of any change in the method or rate of the trustee's compensation.

(c) A trustee shall send to the distributees or permissible distributees of trust income or principal, and to other qualified or nonqualified beneficiaries who request it, at least annually and at the termination of the trust, a report of the trust property, liabilities, receipts, and disbursements, including the source and amount of the trustee's compensation, a listing of the trust assets and, if feasible, their respective market values. Upon a vacancy in a trusteeship, unless a cotrustee remains in office, a report must be sent to the qualified beneficiaries by the former trustee. A personal representative, [conservator], or [guardian] may send the qualified beneficiaries a report on behalf of a deceased or incapacitated trustee.

(d) A beneficiary may waive the right to a trustee's report or other information otherwise required to be furnished under this section. A beneficiary, with respect to future reports and other information, may withdraw a waiver previously given.

Comment

. . . The trustee is under a duty to communicate to a qualified beneficiary information about the administration of the trust that is reasonably necessary to enable the beneficiary to enforce the beneficiary's rights and to prevent or redress a breach of trust. See Restatement (Second) of Trusts Section 173 cmt. c (1959). Ordinarily, the trustee is not under a duty to furnish information to a beneficiary in the absence of a specific request for the information. See Restatement (Second) of Trusts Section 173 cmt. d (1959). Thus, the duty articulated in subsection (a) is ordinarily satisfied by providing the beneficiary with a copy of the annual report mandated by subsection (c). However, special circumstances may require that the trustee provide additional information. For example, if the trustee is dealing with the beneficiary on the trustee's own account, the trustee must communicate material facts relating to the transaction that the trustee knows or should know. See Restatement (Second) of Trusts

Section 173 cmt. d (1959). Furthermore, to enable the beneficiaries to take action to protect their interests, the trustee may be required to provide advance notice of transactions involving real estate, closely-held business interests, and other assets that are difficult to value or to replace. See In re Green Charitable Trust, 431 N.W. 2d 492 (Mich. Ct. App. 1988); Allard v. Pacific National Bank, 663 P.2d 104 (Wash. 1983). The trustee is justified in not providing such advance disclosure if disclosure is forbidden by other law, as under federal securities laws, or if disclosure would be seriously detrimental to the interests of the beneficiaries, for example, when disclosure would cause the loss of the only serious buyer.

Subsection (a) provides a different standard if a beneficiary, whether qualified or not, makes a request for information. In that event, the trustee must promptly comply with the beneficiary's request unless unreasonable under the circumstances. Further supporting the principle that a beneficiary should be allowed to make an independent assessment of what information is relevant to protecting the beneficiary's interest, subsection (b)(1) requires the trustee on request to furnish a beneficiary with a complete copy of the trust instrument and not merely with those portions the trustee deems relevant to the beneficiary's interest. For a case reaching the same result, see Fletcher v. Fletcher, 480 S.E. 2d 488 (Va. Ct. App. 1997). Subsection (b)(1) is contrary to Section 7-303(b) of the Uniform Probate Code, which provides that "[u]pon reasonable request, the trustee shall provide the beneficiary with a copy of the terms of the trust which describe or affect his interest. . . ."

The drafters of this Code decided to leave open for further consideration by the courts the extent to which a trustee may claim attorney-client privilege against a beneficiary seeking discovery of attorney-client communications between the trustee and the trustee's attorney. The courts are split because of the important values that are in tension on this question. . . .

The Uniform Trust Code employs the term "report" instead of "accounting" in order to negate any inference that the report must be prepared in any particular format or with a high degree of formality. The reporting requirement might even be satisfied by providing the beneficiaries with copies of the trust's income tax returns and monthly brokerage account statements if the information on those returns and statements is complete and sufficiently clear. The key factor is not the format chosen but whether the report provides the beneficiaries with the information necessary to protect their interests. For model account forms, together with practical advice on how to prepare reports, see Robert Whitman, Fiduciary Accounting Guide (2d ed. 1998). . .

§814. Discretionary Powers; Tax Savings

(a) Notwithstanding the breadth of discretion granted to a trustee in the terms of the trust, including the use of such terms as "absolute", "sole", or "uncontrolled", the trustee shall exercise a discretionary power in good faith and in accordance with the terms and purposes of the trust and the interests of the beneficiaries.

(b) Subject to subsection (d), and unless the terms of the trust expressly indicate that a rule in this subsection does not apply:

(1) a person other than a settlor who is a beneficiary and trustee of a trust that confers on the trustee a power to make discretionary distributions to or for the trustee's personal benefit may exercise the power only in accordance with an ascertainable standard relating to the trustee's individual health, education, support, or maintenance within the meaning of Section 2041(b)(1)(A) or 2514(c)(1) of the Internal Revenue Code of 1986, as in effect on [the effective date of this [Code]] [, or as later amended]; and

(2) a trustee may not exercise a power to make discretionary distributions to satisfy a legal obligation of support that the trustee personally owes another person.

(c) A power whose exercise is limited or prohibited by subsection (b) may be exercised by a majority of the remaining trustees whose exercise of the power is not so limited or prohibited. If the power of all trustees is so limited or prohibited, the court may appoint a special fiduciary with authority to exercise the power.

(d) Subsection (b) does not apply to:

(1) a power held by the settlor's spouse who is the trustee of a trust for which a marital deduction, as defined in Section 2056(b)(5) or 2523(e) of the Internal Revenue Code of 1986, as in effect on [the effective date of this [Code]] [, or as later amended], was previously allowed;

(2) any trust during any period that the trust may be revoked or amended by its settlor; or

(3) a trust if contributions to the trust qualify for the annual exclusion under Section 2503(c) of the Internal Revenue Code of 1986, as in effect on [the effective date of this [Code]] [, or as later amended].

Comment

Despite the breadth of discretion purportedly granted by the wording of a trust, no grant of discretion to a trustee, whether with respect to management or distribution, is ever absolute. A grant of discretion establishes a range within which the trustee may act. The greater the grant of discretion, the broader the range. Pursuant to subsection (a), a trustee's action must always be in good faith, with regard to the purposes of the trust, and in accordance with the trustee's other duties, including the obligation to exercise reasonable skill, care, and caution. See Sections 801 (duty to administer trust) and 804 (duty to act with prudence). The standard stated in subsection (a) applies only to powers which are to be exercised in a fiduciary as opposed to a nonfiduciary capacity. Regarding the standards for exercising discretion and construing particular language of discretion, see Restatement (Third) of Trusts Section 50 (Tentative

Draft No. 2, approved 1999); Restatement (Second) of Trusts Section 187 (1959). See also Edward C. Halbach, Jr., Problems of Discretion in Discretionary Trusts, 61 Colum. L. Rev. 1425 (1961). An abuse by the trustee of the discretion granted in the terms of the trust is a breach of trust that can result in surcharge. See Section 1001(b) (remedies for breach of trust).

Subsections (b) through (d) rewrite the terms of a trust that might otherwise result in adverse estate and gift tax consequences to a beneficiary-trustee. This Code does not generally address the subject of tax curative provisions. These are provisions that automatically rewrite the terms of trusts that might otherwise fail to qualify for probable intended tax benefits. . . .

§815. General Powers of Trustee

(a) A trustee, without authorization by the court, may exercise:

(1) powers conferred by the terms of the trust; or

(2) except as limited by the terms of the trust:

(A) all powers over the trust property which an unmarried competent owner has over individually owned property;

(B) any other powers appropriate to achieve the proper investment, management, and distribution of the trust property; and

(C) any other powers conferred by this [Code].

(b) The exercise of a power is subject to the fiduciary duties prescribed by this [article].

Comment

This section is intended to grant trustees the broadest possible powers, but to be exercised always in accordance with the duties of the trustee and any limitations stated in the terms of the trust. This broad authority is denoted by granting the trustee the powers of an unmarried competent owner of individually owned property, unlimited by restrictions that might be placed on it by marriage, disability, or cotenancy.

The powers conferred elsewhere in this Code that are subsumed under this section include all of the specific powers listed in Section 816 as well as other powers described elsewhere in this Code. See Sections 108(c) (transfer of principal place of administration), 414(a) (termination of uneconomic trust with value less than $50,000), 417 (combination and division of trusts), 703(e) (delegation to cotrustee), 802(h) (exception to duty of loyalty), 807 (delegation to agent of powers and duties), 810(d) (joint investments), and Article 9 (Uniform Prudent Investor Act). The powers conferred by this Code may be exercised without court approval. If court approval of the exercise of a power is desired, a petition for court approval should be filed.

A power differs from a duty. A duty imposes an obligation or a mandatory prohibition. A power, on the other hand, is a discretion, the exercise of which is not obligatory. The existence of a power, however created or granted, does not speak to the question of whether it is prudent under the circumstances to exercise the power.

§816. Specific Powers of Trustee

Without limiting the authority conferred by Section 815, a trustee may:

(1) collect trust property and accept or reject additions to the trust property from a settlor or any other person;

(2) acquire or sell property, for cash or on credit, at public or private sale;

(3) exchange, partition, or otherwise change the character of trust property;

(4) deposit trust money in an account in a regulated financial-service institution;

(5) borrow money, with or without security, and mortgage or pledge trust property for a period within or extending beyond the duration of the trust;

(6) with respect to an interest in a proprietorship, partnership, limited liability company, business trust, corporation, or other form of business or enterprise, continue the business or other enterprise and take any action that may be taken by shareholders, members, or property owners, including merging, dissolving, or otherwise changing the form of business organization or contributing additional capital;

(7) with respect to stocks or other securities, exercise the rights of an absolute owner, including the right to:

(A) vote, or give proxies to vote, with or without power of substitution, or enter into or continue a voting trust agreement;

(B) hold a security in the name of a nominee or in other form without disclosure of the trust so that title may pass by delivery;

(C) pay calls, assessments, and other sums chargeable or accruing against the securities, and sell or exercise stock subscription or conversion rights; and

(D) deposit the securities with a depositary or other regulated financial-service institution;

(8) with respect to an interest in real property, construct, or make ordinary or extraordinary repairs to, alterations to, or improvements in, buildings or other structures, demolish improvements, raze existing or erect new party walls or buildings, subdivide or develop land, dedicate land to public use or grant public or private easements, and make or vacate plats and adjust boundaries;

(9) enter into a lease for any purpose as lessor or lessee, including a lease or other arrangement for exploration and removal of natural resources, with or without the option to purchase or renew, for a period within or extending beyond the duration of the trust;

(10) grant an option involving a sale, lease, or other disposition of trust property or acquire an option for the acquisition of property, including an option exercisable

beyond the duration of the trust, and exercise an option so acquired;

(11) insure the property of the trust against damage or loss and insure the trustee, the trustee's agents, and beneficiaries against liability arising from the administration of the trust;

(12) abandon or decline to administer property of no value or of insufficient value to justify its collection or continued administration;

(13) with respect to possible liability for violation of environmental law:

(A) inspect or investigate property the trustee holds or has been asked to hold, or property owned or operated by an organization in which the trustee holds or has been asked to hold an interest, for the purpose of determining the application of environmental law with respect to the property;

(B) take action to prevent, abate, or otherwise remedy any actual or potential violation of any environmental law affecting property held directly or indirectly by the trustee, whether taken before or after the assertion of a claim or the initiation of governmental enforcement;

(C) decline to accept property into trust or disclaim any power with respect to property that is or may be burdened with liability for violation of environmental law;

(D) compromise claims against the trust which may be asserted for an alleged violation of environmental law; and

(E) pay the expense of any inspection, review, abatement, or remedial action to comply with environmental law;

(14) pay or contest any claim, settle a claim by or against the trust, and release, in whole or in part, a claim belonging to the trust;

(15) pay taxes, assessments, compensation of the trustee and of employees and agents of the trust, and other expenses incurred in the administration of the trust;

(16) exercise elections with respect to federal, state, and local taxes;

(17) select a mode of payment under any employee benefit or retirement plan, annuity, or life insurance payable to the trustee, exercise rights thereunder, including exercise of the right to indemnification for expenses and against liabilities, and take appropriate action to collect the proceeds;

(18) make loans out of trust property, including loans to a beneficiary on terms and conditions the trustee considers to be fair and reasonable under the circumstances, and the trustee has a lien on future distributions for repayment of those loans;

(19) pledge trust property to guarantee loans made by others to the beneficiary;

(20) appoint a trustee to act in another jurisdiction with respect to trust property located in the other jurisdiction, confer upon the appointed trustee all of the powers and duties of the appointing trustee, require that the appointed trustee furnish security, and remove any trustee so appointed;

(21) pay an amount distributable to a beneficiary who is under a legal disability or who the trustee reasonably believes is incapacitated, by paying it directly to the beneficiary or applying it for the beneficiary's benefit, or by:

(A) paying it to the beneficiary's [conservator] or, if the beneficiary does not have a [conservator], the beneficiary's [guardian];

(B) paying it to the beneficiary's custodian under [the Uniform Transfers to Minors Act] or custodial trustee under [the Uniform Custodial Trust Act], and, for that purpose, creating a custodianship or custodial trust;

(C) if the trustee does not know of a [conservator], [guardian], custodian, or custodial trustee, paying it to an adult relative or other person having legal or physical care or custody of the beneficiary, to be expended on the beneficiary's behalf; or

(D) managing it as a separate fund on the beneficiary's behalf, subject to the beneficiary's continuing right to withdraw the distribution;

(22) on distribution of trust property or the division or termination of a trust, make distributions in divided or undivided interests, allocate particular assets in proportionate or disproportionate shares, value the trust property for those purposes, and adjust for resulting differences in valuation;

(23) resolve a dispute concerning the interpretation of the trust or its administration by mediation, arbitration, or other procedure for alternative dispute resolution;

(24) prosecute or defend an action, claim, or judicial proceeding in any jurisdiction to protect trust property and the trustee in the performance of the trustee's duties;

(25) sign and deliver contracts and other instruments that are useful to achieve or facilitate the exercise of the trustee's powers; and

(26) on termination of the trust, exercise the powers appropriate to wind up the administration of the trust and distribute the trust property to the persons entitled to it.

§817. Distribution Upon Termination

(a) Upon termination or partial termination of a trust, the trustee may send to the beneficiaries a proposal for distribution. The right of any beneficiary to object to the proposed distribution terminates if the beneficiary does not notify the trustee of an objection within 30 days after the proposal was sent but only if the proposal informed the beneficiary of the right to object and of the time allowed for objection.

(b) Upon the occurrence of an event terminating or partially terminating a trust, the trustee shall proceed expeditiously to distribute the trust property to the persons entitled to it, subject to the right of the trustee to retain a reasonable reserve for the payment of debts, expenses, and taxes.

(c) A release by a beneficiary of a trustee from liability for breach of trust is invalid to the extent:

(1) it was induced by improper conduct of the trustee; or

(2) the beneficiary, at the time of the release, did not know of the beneficiary's rights or of the material facts relating to the breach.

ARTICLE 9

UNIFORM PRUDENT INVESTOR ACT

[The Uniform Prudent Investor Act is included as Part VI of this Code.]

General Comment

Because of the widespread adoption of the Uniform Prudent Investor Act, no effort has been made to disassemble and integrate the Uniform Prudent Investor Act into the Uniform Trust Code. States adopting the Uniform Trust Code that have previously enacted the Prudent Investor Act are encouraged to reenact their version of the Prudent Investor Act as Article 9 of the Uniform Trust Code. Reenacting the Uniform Prudent Investor Act as a unit will preserve uniformity with States that have enacted the Uniform Prudent Investor Act in free-standing form.

The Uniform Prudent Investor Act prescribes a series of duties relevant to the investment and management of trust property. The Uniform Trust Code, Article 8 contains duties and powers of a trustee relevant to the investment, administration, and distribution of trust property. There is therefore significant overlap between Article 8 and the Prudent Investor Act. Where the Uniform Prudent Investor Act and Uniform Trust Code are duplicative, enacting jurisdictions are encouraged to enact the Uniform Prudent Investor Act in this article but without the provisions already addressed in Article 8 of the Uniform Trust Code. The duplicative provisions of the Uniform Prudent Investor Act and Article 8 of this Code are as follows:

Prudent Investor Act Article 8
Special skills 2(f) 806
Loyalty 5 802
Impartiality 6 803
Investment costs 7 805
Delegation 9 807

Deleting these duplicative provisions leaves the following sections of the Uniform Prudent Investor Act for enactment in this article:

Section 1 Prudent Investor Rule
Section 2 (a)-(e) Standard of Care; Portfolio Strategy; Risk and
Return Objectives
Section 3 Diversification
Section 4 Duties at Inception of Trusteeship
Section 8 Reviewing Compliance
Section 10 Language Invoking Standard of [Act]

ARTICLE 10

LIABILITY OF TRUSTEES AND RIGHTS OF PERSONS DEALING WITH TRUSTEE

§1001. Remedies for Breach of Trust

(a) A violation by a trustee of a duty the trustee owes to a beneficiary is a breach of trust.

(b) To remedy a breach of trust that has occurred or may occur, the court may:

(1) compel the trustee to perform the trustee's duties;

(2) enjoin the trustee from committing a breach of trust;

(3) compel the trustee to redress a breach of trust by paying money, restoring property, or other means;

(4) order a trustee to account;

(5) appoint a special fiduciary to take possession of the trust property and administer the trust;

(6) suspend the trustee;

(7) remove the trustee as provided in Section 706;

(8) reduce or deny compensation to the trustee;

(9) subject to Section 1012, void an act of the trustee, impose a lien or a constructive trust on trust property, or trace trust property wrongfully disposed of and recover the property or its proceeds; or

(10) order any other appropriate relief.

§1002. Damages for Breach of Trust

(a) A trustee who commits a breach of trust is liable to the beneficiaries affected for the greater of:

(1) the amount required to restore the value of the trust property and trust distributions to what they would have been had the breach not occurred; or

(2) the profit the trustee made by reason of the breach.

(b) Except as otherwise provided in this subsection, if more than one trustee is liable to the beneficiaries for a breach of trust, a trustee is entitled to contribution from the other trustee or trustees. A trustee is not entitled to contribution if the trustee was substantially more at fault than another trustee or if the trustee committed the breach of trust in bad faith or with reckless indifference to the purposes of the trust or the interests of the beneficiaries. A trustee who received a benefit from the breach of trust is not entitled to contribution from another trustee to the extent of the benefit received.

Comment

Subsection (a) is based on Restatement (Third) of Trusts: Prudent Investor Rule Section 205 (1992). If a trustee commits a breach of trust, the beneficiaries may either affirm the transaction or, if a loss has occurred, hold the trustee liable for the amount necessary to compensate fully for the consequences of the breach. This may include recovery of lost income, capital gain, or appreciation that would have resulted from proper administration. Even if a loss has not occurred, the trustee may not benefit from the improper action and is accountable for any profit the trustee made by reason of the breach.

For extensive commentary on the determination of damages, traditionally known as trustee surcharge, with numerous specific applications, see Restatement (Third) of Trusts: Prudent Investor Rule Sections 205-213 (1992). For the use of benchmark portfolios to determine damages, see Restatement (Third) of Trusts:

Prudent Investor Rule Reporter's Notes to Sections 205 and 208-211 (1992). On the authority of a court of equity to reduce or excuse damages for breach of trust, see Restatement (Second) of Trusts Section 205 cmt. g (1959). . . .

§1003. Damages in Absence of Breach

(a) A trustee is accountable to an affected beneficiary for any profit made by the trustee arising from the administration of the trust, even absent a breach of trust.

(b) Absent a breach of trust, a trustee is not liable to a beneficiary for a loss or depreciation in the value of trust property or for not having made a profit.

§1004. Attorney's Fees and Costs

In a judicial proceeding involving the administration of a trust, the court, as justice and equity may require, may award costs and expenses, including reasonable attorney's fees, to any party, to be paid by another party or from the trust that is the subject of the controversy.

§1005. Limitation of Action Against Trustee

(a) A beneficiary may not commence a proceeding against a trustee for breach of trust more than one year after the date the beneficiary or a representative of the beneficiary was sent a report that adequately disclosed the existence of a potential claim for breach of trust and informed the beneficiary of the time allowed for commencing a proceeding.

(b) A report adequately discloses the existence of a potential claim for breach of trust if it provides sufficient information so that the beneficiary or representative knows of the potential claim or should have inquired into its existence.

(c) If subsection (a) does not apply, a judicial proceeding by a beneficiary against a trustee for breach of trust must be commenced within five years after the first to occur of:

(1) the removal, resignation, or death of the trustee;

(2) the termination of the beneficiary's interest in the trust; or

(3) the termination of the trust.

§1006. Reliance on Trust Instrument

A trustee who acts in reasonable reliance on the terms of the trust as expressed in the trust instrument is not liable to a beneficiary for a breach of trust to the extent the breach resulted from the reliance.

Comment

It sometimes happens that the intended terms of the trust differ from the apparent meaning of the trust instrument. This can occur because the court, in determining the terms of the trust, is allowed to consider evidence extrinsic to the trust instrument. See Section 103(17) (definition of "terms of a trust"). Furthermore, if a trust is reformed on account of mistake of fact or law, as authorized by Section 415, provisions of a trust instrument can be deleted or contradicted and provisions not in the trust instrument may be added. The concept of the "terms of a trust," both as defined in this Code and as used in the doctrine of reformation, is intended to effectuate the principle that a trust should be administered and distributed in accordance with the settlor's intent. However, a trustee should also be able to administer a trust with some dispatch and without concern that a reasonable reliance on the terms of the trust instrument is misplaced. This section protects a trustee who so relies on a trust instrument but only to the extent the breach of trust resulted from such reliance. This section is similar to Section 1(b) of the Uniform Prudent Investor Act, which protects a trustee from liability to the extent that the trustee acted in reasonable reliance on the provisions of the trust. . . .

§1007. Event Affecting Administration or Distribution

If the happening of an event, including marriage, divorce, performance of educational requirements, or death, affects the administration or distribution of a trust, a trustee who has exercised reasonable care to ascertain the happening of the event is not liable for a loss resulting from the trustee's lack of knowledge.

§1008. Exculpation of Trustee

(a) A term of a trust relieving a trustee of liability for breach of trust is unenforceable to the extent that it:

(1) relieves the trustee of liability for breach of trust committed in bad faith or with reckless indifference to the purposes of the trust or the interests of the beneficiaries; or

(2) was inserted as the result of an abuse by the trustee of a fiduciary or confidential relationship to the settlor.

(b) An exculpatory term drafted or caused to be drafted by the trustee is invalid as an abuse of a fiduciary or confidential relationship unless the trustee proves that the exculpatory term is fair under the circumstances and that its existence and contents were adequately communicated to the settlor.

§1009. Beneficiary's Consent, Release, or Ratification

A trustee is not liable to a beneficiary for breach of trust if the beneficiary, consented to the conduct constituting the breach, released the trustee from liability for the breach, or ratified the transaction constituting the breach, unless:

(1) the consent, release, or ratification of the beneficiary was induced by improper conduct of the trustee; or

(2) at the time of the consent, release, or ratification, the beneficiary did not know of the beneficiary's rights or of the material facts relating to the breach.

§1010. Limitation on Personal Liability of Trustee

(a) Except as otherwise provided in the contract, a trustee is not personally liable on a contract properly entered into in the trustee's fiduciary capacity in the course of administering the trust if the trustee in the contract disclosed the fiduciary capacity.

(b) A trustee is personally liable for torts committed in the course of administering a trust, or for obligations arising from ownership or control of trust property, including liability for violation of environmental law, only if the trustee is personally at fault.

(c) A claim based on a contract entered into by a trustee in the trustee's fiduciary capacity, on an obligation arising from ownership or control of trust property, or on a tort committed in the course of administering a trust, may be asserted in a judicial proceeding against the trustee in the trustee's fiduciary capacity, whether or not the trustee is personally liable for the claim.

§1011. Interest as General Partner

(a) Except as otherwise provided in subsection (c) or unless personal liability is imposed in the contract, a trustee who holds an interest as a general partner in a general or limited partnership is not personally liable on a contract entered into by the partnership after the trust's acquisition of the interest if the fiduciary capacity was disclosed in the contract or in a statement previously filed pursuant to the [Uniform Partnership Act or Uniform Limited Partnership Act].

(b) Except as otherwise provided in subsection (c), a trustee who holds an interest as a general partner is not personally liable for torts committed by the partnership or for obligations arising from ownership or control of the interest unless the trustee is personally at fault.

(c) The immunity provided by this section does not apply if an interest in the partnership is held by the trustee in a capacity other than that of trustee or is held by the trustee's spouse or one or more of the trustee's descendants, siblings, or parents, or the spouse of any of them.

(d) If the trustee of a revocable trust holds an interest as a general partner, the settlor is personally liable for contracts and other obligations of the partnership as if the settlor were a general partner.]

§1012. Protection of Personal Dealing with Trustee

(a) A person other than a beneficiary who in good faith assists a trustee, or who in good faith and for value deals with a trustee, without knowledge that the trustee is exceeding or improperly exercising the trustee's powers is protected from liability as if the trustee properly exercised the power.

(b) A person other than a beneficiary who in good faith deals with a trustee is not required to inquire into the extent of the trustee's powers or the propriety of their exercise.

(c) A person who in good faith delivers assets to a trustee need not ensure their proper application.

(d) A person other than a beneficiary who in good faith assists a former trustee, or who in good faith and for value deals with a former trustee, without knowledge that the trusteeship has terminated is protected from liability as if the former trustee were still trustee.

(e) Comparable protective provisions of other laws relating to commercial transactions or transfer of securities by fiduciaries prevail over the protection provided by this section.

§1013. Certification of Trust

(a) Instead of furnishing a copy of the trust instrument to a person other than a beneficiary, the trustee may furnish to the person a certification of trust containing the following information:

(1) that the trust exists and the date the trust instrument was executed;

(2) the identity of the settlor;

(3) the identity and address of the currently acting trustee;

(4) the powers of the trustee;

(5) the revocability or irrevocability of the trust and the identity of any person holding a power to revoke the trust;

(6) the authority of cotrustees to sign or otherwise authenticate and whether all or less than all are required in order to exercise powers of the trustee;

(7) the trust's taxpayer identification number; and

(8) the manner of taking title to trust property.

(b) A certification of trust may be signed or otherwise authenticated by any trustee.

(c) A certification of trust must state that the trust has not been revoked, modified, or amended in any manner that would cause the representations contained in the certification of trust to be incorrect.

(d) A certification of trust need not contain the dispositive terms of a trust.

(e) A recipient of a certification of trust may require the trustee to furnish copies of those excerpts from the original trust instrument and later amendments which designate the trustee and confer upon the trustee the power to act in pending transaction.

(f) A person who acts in reliance upon a certification of trust without knowledge that the representations contained therein are incorrect is not liable to any person for so acting and may assume without inquiry the existence of the facts contained in the certification. Knowledge of the terms of the trust may not be inferred solely from the fact that a copy of all or part of the trust instrument is held by the person relying upon the certification.

(g) A person who in good faith enters into a transaction in reliance upon a certification of trust may enforce the transaction against the trust property as if the representations contained in the certification were correct.

(h) A person making a demand for the trust instrument in addition to a certification of trust or excerpts is liable for damages if the court determines that the person did not act in good faith in demanding the trust instrument.

(i) This section does not limit the right of a person to obtain a copy of the trust instrument in a judicial proceeding concerning the trust.

ARTICLE 11

MISCELLANEOUS PROVISIONS

§1101. Uniformity of Application and Construction

In applying and construing this Uniform Act, consideration must be given to the need to promote uniformity of the law with respect to its subject matter among States that enact it.

§1102. Electronic Records and Signatures

The provisions of this [Code] governing the legal effect, validity, or enforceability of electronic records or electronic signatures, and of contracts formed or performed with the use of such records or signatures, conform to the requirements of Section 102 of the Electronic Signatures in Global and National Commerce Act (15 U.S.C. Section 7002) and supersede, modify, and limit the requirements of the Electronic Signatures in Global and National Commerce Act.

§1103. Severability Clause

If any provision of this [Code] or its application to any person or circumstances is held invalid, the invalidity does not affect other provisions or application of this [Code] which can be given effect without the invalid provision or application, and to this end the provisions of this [Code] are severable.

§1104. Effective Date

This [Code] takes effect on ____________________.

§1105. Repeals

The following Acts are repealed:

(1) Uniform Trustee Powers Act;

(2) Uniform Probate Code, Article VII;

(3) Uniform Trusts Act (1937); and

(4) Uniform Prudent Investor Act.

§1106. Application to Existing Relationships

(a) Except as otherwise provided in this [Code], on [the effective date of this [Code]]:

(1) this [Code] applies to all trusts created before, on, or after [its effective date];

(2) this [Code] applies to all judicial proceedings concerning trusts commenced on or after [its effective date];

(3) this [Code] applies to judicial proceedings concerning trusts commenced before [its effective date] unless the court finds that application of a particular provision of this [Code] would substantially interfere with the effective conduct of the judicial proceedings or prejudice the rights of the parties, in which case the particular provision of this [Code] does not apply and the superseded law applies;

(4) any rule of construction or presumption provided in this [Code] applies to trust instruments executed before [the effective date of the [Code]] unless there is a clear indication of a contrary intent in the terms of the trust; and

(5) an act done before [the effective date of the [Code]] is not affected by this [Code].

(b) If a right is acquired, extinguished, or barred upon the expiration of a prescribed period that has commenced to run under any other statute before [the effective date of the [Code]], that statute continues to apply to the right even if it has been repealed or superseded.

GLOSSARY

This glossary gives definitions for key terms and concepts used in this California Probate Code and Related Provisions: Student Edition.

Abatement: The process by which the decedent's estate is reduced (after payment of creditors' claims and other debts) to provide for the payment of all the bequests under the will or to provide for the share of an omitted child or spouse. State statutes specify an order of abatement that sets forth the priority by which certain testamentary gifts will be reduced.

Accelerate (i.e., accelerate a remainder): A situation that results in a future interest becoming possessory. Common events that trigger acceleration of a remainder are disclaimer and the application of a slayer (or unworthy heir) statute.

Acknowledgment (of a will): A situation in which a testator confirms to witnesses that a document is his or her will or that the signature on the will is that of the testator. Many states do not require that the testator actually sign in the witnesses' presence but merely that the testator "acknowledge" his or her will or his or her signature. Acknowledgment generally arises if the testator has signed the will prior to the attestation by witnesses.

Active trust: A trust in which the trustee has affirmative duties to perform in managing the trust property for the benefit of the beneficiaries. An active trust may be distinguished from a passive trust in which the trustee's only responsibility is to hold title to the property. Because a passive trust is not a valid trust, the beneficiary is entitled to the property.

Acts of independent significance: A doctrine that permits a court to admit extrinsic evidence (i.e., evidence outside the will) in order to determine certain beneficiaries and certain property that passes under the testator's will. Reference to events of independent significance allows the testator to make testamentary dispositions based on the occurrence or nonoccurrence of specified acts or facts.

Ademption: A situation that arises when a specific gift that was the subject of an at-death transfer is not found in the transferor's estate at death, causing the testamentary gift to fail. If property is adeemed, the distributee's rights are extinguished, i.e., the distributee has no right to other estate property.

Ademption by extinction: A form of ademption that occurs if the subject of the testamentary gift was destroyed during the decedent's lifetime.

Ademption by satisfaction: A form of ademption that occurs if the decedent made an inter vivos gift of the property that was the subject of the testamentary bequest.

Administration: The process of collecting the decedent's assets, making an inventory and appraisal of the property, paying creditors' claims and other debts, and distributing the remaining property to the heirs or beneficiaries.

Administrator: The personal representative who administers the estate of a decedent who dies intestate (without a will); formerly the term "administratrix" referred to a female in this position but in modern usage, the term "administrator" refers to persons of either gender.

Administrator c.t.a. (**cum testamento annexo*****):*** The personal representative who administers an estate of a decedent who left a will that failed to name an executor or that named an executor who does not wish to serve, is incapacitated, or predeceased the decedent.

Administrator d.b.n. (**de bonis non*****):*** A successor personal representative, i.e., the personal representative who administers estate assets that are not administered, for example, if the appointed representative was not able to complete his or her administration.

Administrator pendente lite: A personal representative who is appointed while litigation is pending.

Adoption: A process which creates legal rights and responsibilities in the adoptive parent(s) and, generally, terminates legal rights and responsibilities in the biological parent(s).

Adult adoption: The process by which one adult adopts another adult; persons may be motivated to resort to adult adoption to create a legally recognized familial relationship for the establishment of inheritance rights and/or decisionmaking in the event of incapacity.

Advance directive: An instrument that conveys the individual's wishes for medical treatment upon incapacity; a "living will" is a form of advance directive.

Advancement: An inter vivos gift of real or personal property that anticipates the recipient's inheritance, i.e., is subtracted from the recipient's share of the decedent's estate.

Affinity: The presence of a relationship based upon marriage, distinguishable from *consanguinity,* which is a relationship based upon blood.

Alienage (inheritance laws based on): Laws that limit the right of a nonresident to inherit property; states increasingly are abolishing such limitations.

Ambiguity: An uncertainty in a testamentary document as to the meaning of a provision that often raises the issue of the admissibility of extrinsic evidence; an ambiguity may be "patent" (i.e., one that appears on the face of a will) or "latent" (one that becomes apparent in attempting to apply the will provision to a particular person or property).

Ambulatory: The characteristic of a testamentary document that enables it to be revised or revoked until the testator's death and that enables it to operate on all property owned by the testator at death.

American Law Institute (ALI): An organization of prominent judges, lawyers, and law professors that aims to promote clarification of the law and to improve its administration; also drafters of the *Restatements of the Law* and the *Principles of the Law of Family Dissolution*.

Ancestor: A person who is related to the decedent in an ascending line (such as a parent), compared to a descendant who is related to the decedent in a descending line (such as a child).

Ancillary administration: A probate proceeding in a jurisdiction where the decedent's property is located that is a jurisdiction other than the testator's domicile (the probate proceeding in the latter jurisdiction is termed *domiciliary administration*).

Animus revocandi: The requisite intent to revoke a will; a valid revocation requires the requisite intent and a legally sufficient act.

Annuity: A contract purchased by a party from an insurance company that obligates the company to make payments for a guaranteed interest rate to a beneficiary.

Ante-Mortem Probate: A method of proving the validity of a will prior to the death of the testator by having the testator physically present for observation and examination.

Antenuptial agreement: A contract (also called a *prenuptial* or *premarital* agreement) that is executed by prospective spouses and that determines the parties' property rights in the event of death or dissolution.

Anticontest clause: A testamentary provision that limits the beneficiary's ability to contest the will by causing a forfeiture of that beneficiary's interest.

Anti-lapse statute: A statute that provides, in the event that a devisee predeceases the testator, for a substitute taker (i.e., the issue of the predeceased devisee).

Appraisal (also appraisement): One of the primary tasks of a personal representative that involves a determination of the estate assets and their value; also the personal representative must file a document called an *inventory and appraisal,* i.e., a public record of all assets that are owned by the decedent as of the date of death and that are subject to probate administration.

Ascendants: Ancestors (also termed "lineal ascendants"); persons who are related to the intestate in an ascending line (such as the decedent's parents or grandparents).

Assignment of an expectancy: The transfer by a potential heir that assigns his or her expected interest in the decedent's estate to someone other than the intestate for consideration; an assignment of an expectancy is not binding on the assignor's issue. *See also* Release (of an expectancy).

Attest: To witness, as of a will.

Attestation: The procedure of signing a will by witnesses.

Attestation clause: A testamentary provision in which the witnesses recite the events of the will execution and other facts (e.g., the testator is of sound mind and not operating under duress); the presence of an attestation clause creates a presumption of due execution.

Attested will: A will that has been signed by witnesses (also referred to as a *formal* will or *formally executed will*), distinguished from a *holographic* will that requires no witnesses.

Attesting witnesses: The persons who witness a will; almost all states today require that a will be signed by two witnesses.

Augmented estate: The elective share of the surviving spouse (as conceptualized by the drafters of the Uniform Probate Code) that includes certain of the decedent's inter vivos nonprobate transfers in order to protect the surviving spouse from disinheritance (i.e., in such a case, the probate estate is "augmented" or increased by certain qualifying inter vivos transfers).

Bank account trust: A special type of savings account that functions as a form of will substitute, enabling the depositor to use the funds during his or her lifetime but to pay the balance to a designated beneficiary upon the death of the depositor, also called a *Totten trust, savings bank trust*, or *tentative trust.*

Beneficial interest: The property owned by a beneficiary of a trust.

Beneficiary: A person who inherits property by a will; also the person who has equitable title to a trust.

Bequeath: The historical term for the act of making a testamentary gift of personal property; modern usage interprets the term more broadly to include real and personal property.

Bequest: The historical term for a testamentary gift of personal property; modern usage interprets the term more broadly to include real and personal property.

Blockbuster will: A will that attempts to control the disposition of nonprobate assets (such as life insurance proceeds, joint tenancy property), i.e., a will that enables the testator to change the conditions and provisions of will substitutes through the use of testamentary instruments.

Bona fide purchaser rule: A doctrine that protects a person who has purchased property in good faith in cases in which the property has been transferred to him or her improperly.

Bond: An obligation to pay money upon the occurrence of some event.

Breach of trust: The performance of an unauthorized act by a fiduciary; a violation of a duty imposed by law or the trust provisions.

Cancellation: A method of revocation of a will by physical act, such as by writing the word "canceled" across the face of the will or by putting an X through a testamentary provision.

Canon law system for counting degrees of kinship: A method of determining degrees of consanguinity for those who qualify as next of kin of an intestate; the process involves counting the steps (generations) from the decedent to the nearest common ancestor and then down to the claimant. Instead of adding these two sums (as in the civil law system), the relevant degree of kinship involved in the calculation is the larger of the two lines of kinship. Specifically, the claimant with the smallest degree count takes the intestate estate. This method is also called the common law system for counting degrees of kinship.

Canons of Descent: Rules developed at common law that established the distributive pattern of real property; according to the Canons of Descent, only the eldest male inherited (termed *primogeniture*) and female children shared equally (as *coparceners*).

Cestui que trust: The historical term for a beneficiary of a trust (derived from Norman French).

Charitable trust: A trust for a charitable purpose, such as the relief of poverty, the advancement of education or religion, the promotion of health, etc.

Civil law system for counting degrees of kinship: A method of determining degrees of consanguinity for those who qualify as next of kin of an intestate; the process involves counting the steps from the decedent to the nearest common ancestor and then down to the claimant. (*Common ancestor* means the ancestor who is shared by the decedent and claimant.) The total is the total number of steps (a step is a generation).

Claflin doctrine: A rule for modification or termination of a trust (based on *Claflin v. Claflin*, 20 N.E. 454 (Mass. 1889)), which requires that all the beneficiaries have the requisite capacity, all consent, and also that the modification/termination will not defeat a material purpose of the trust.

Class gift: A disposition to a group of persons who share a common characteristic (such as "children," "nephews and nieces") in which each member of the class takes an equal share.

Closing of a class: A rule that applies to class gifts that determines the time within which a person must be born to be included in the class, i.e., after a class "closes," persons born after that date cannot share in the class gift.

Co-administrator: A person who serves as administrator with another administrator or administrators.

Codicil: A testamentary document that amends a will and must be executed with the requisite statutory formalities.

Co-executor: A person who serves as executor with another executor or executors.

Collateral relative: A person who is related to the decedent in neither an ascending nor descending line but who is related to the decedent *through* a common ancestor; for example, a sister or brother is related to the decedent through common parents whereas an aunt or uncle is related to the decedent through common grandparents.

Commingling: The mixing of assets of a fiduciary with his or her personal assets without properly identifying the assets; a violation of the duty to earmark or segregate is a breach of trust.

Common law: The body of law based on the English legal system as developed by judicial decisions.

Community property: A marital property regime based on a partnership model in which each spouse is the respective owner of an undivided half interest in all property that was acquired during the marriage.

Competent witness (to a will): A witness who is able to give testimony to establish the validity of a will.

Concurrent ownership: A form of joint ownership of property (i.e., joint tenancy, tenancy by the entireties, tenancy in common).

Conditional will: A will whose effectiveness is conditional upon an event, such as death from a particular cause; if the condition does not occur, then the will is not effective.

Confidential relationship: A personal relationship in which one person reposes considerable trust in another and depends on the latter's advice (including, but not limited to, a relationship such as attorney-client; priest-penitent, etc.); the existence of a confidential relationship may raise a presumption of undue influence in the execution of the will.

Conflict of laws: The determination of which state law will be applied by a court to resolve a dispute.

Consanguinity: The presence of a blood relationship between persons. Degrees of consanguinity determine the takers of an intestate's estate (*degrees* refers to the number of steps or generations between the decedent and the claimant). For example, the decedent's parents are related to the decedent in the first degree of consanguinity, and the decedent's grandparents are related to the decedent in the second degree of consanguinity.

Conscious presence test: The requirement that a witness must sign the will within the testator's hearing, knowledge, and understanding.

Conservator: A person appointed by a court to manage the estate of an incompetent. Note that in California, a person who is appointed to manage the property of a minor is referred to as a *guardian* rather than a conservator.

Construction: The process of assigning a legal consequence to a testamentary provision when the testator's intent cannot be ascertained; distinguished from *interpretation,* which is the process of determining the testator's intent, usually by reliance on the language of the will and/or extrinsic evidence.

Constructive trust: A trust created by operation of law (rather than by the express intent of a settlor); an equitable remedy imposed by a court to prevent unjust enrichment, i.e., to prevent a wrongdoer from enjoying an interest in property that was obtained by his or her wrongful act.

Contestant (of a will): A person who attempts to prove that a will is invalid; distinguished from a *proponent* of a will who advocates probate of a will and who attempts to prove that the will is validly executed.

Contingent remainder: A future interest that may not necessarily take effect; distinguished from vested remainder.

Contractual will: A will that is subject to a contract.

Corpus: The principal of a trust (also referred to as the trust *res*).

Co-trustee: A person who serves as a trustee with another trustee or trustees.

Court trust: A testamentary trust that is subject to the continuing jurisdiction of the probate court.

Creditor: A person to whom the decedent owes money or other obligation; the personal representative of the decedent must give notice to creditors notifying them of the death of the decedent and the opportunity to present their claims.

Curtesy: The husband's right at common law to his deceased wife's real property.

Custodian: A fiduciary who manages property for a minor under the Uniform Transfer to Minors Act.

Cy pres (regarding charitable trusts): The doctrine that permits modification of a charitable trust; derived from the Norman French term *si près*, meaning "as near."

Dead hand control: The decedent's post-mortem attempts, by way of testamentary restrictions, to control a beneficiary's enjoyment of the decedent's wealth.

Decedent: A person who is deceased.

Declaration of trust: A method of trust creation by means of a present "declaration" of the trust by the property owner.

Delusion. See *Insane delusion.*

Demonstrative gift: A testamentary gift, typically of money, that is payable from a particular source but if that source is insufficient, then the gift is payable from the general assets of the estate.

Dependent relative revocation: A doctrine that disregards the revocation of a will that was based on a mistaken belief.

Derangement: Mental aberration or delusion that affects testamentary capacity.

Descendant: A person who is related to the decedent in a descending line (such as a child), compared to an *ascendant* who is related to the decedent in an ascending line (such as a parent); another term for descendant is *issue*.

Descent: The historical term for succession to real property; distinguished from the succession to personal property by *distribution*.

Descent and distribution: At common law, the passage of real property to an intestate's heirs and the passage of personal property to the intestate's next of kin; modern law treats both types of property (real and personal) similarly.

Devise: The historical term for the testamentary disposition of real property; according to modern usage, the term refers to a testamentary disposition of both real and personal property.

Devisee: The historical term for a person who inherited real property under a will; in modern usage, the beneficiary of real or personal property.

Disclaimer: A recipient's refusal or renunciation of a gift or inheritance.

Discretionary trust: A trust in which the trustee has discretion to withhold payment of income and/or principal from the beneficiary.

Dispensing power: The authorization by which probate courts excuse harmless errors, i.e., disregard formal statutory requirements if the courts are satisfied that the testamentary document embodies the intent of the testator.

Dissolution: Modern term for divorce, i.e., the legal termination of marriage.

Distribution: The historical term for the succession to personal property; distinguished from the succession of real property by *descent*.

Doctrine of Worthier Title: A doctrine that converts a remainder or executory interest in the transferor's descendants to a reversion in the transferor.

Domicile: A legal concept that is required for the assertion of jurisdiction in such legal matters as marriage, divorce, custody, adoption, probate, etc.; the place where one intends to live permanently (distinguishable from "residence" where a person lives temporarily).

Domiciliary jurisdiction: A probate proceeding in the jurisdiction in which the decedent is domiciled at the date of death.

Donee: The recipient of a gift or power of appointment.

Donor: A person who gives a gift without receiving consideration.

Double inheritance provision: A statutory provision that prevents a person from taking two shares via intestate succession.

Dower: The provision for the widow at common law, consisting of her entitlement to a life estate in one-third of any real property of which the husband was seised during the marriage and that provided protection against the husband's inter vivos transfers and testamentary dispositions.

Dry trust: A trust (also called a *passive trust*) that confers no active duties on the trustee.

Duplicate wills: An executed duplicate original will.

Durable power: A power of attorney that remains effective upon the grantor's incompetency or disability; a mechanism to permit an agent to make health care decisions for an incompetent.

Duress: The use or threat of violence to the testator (or the testator's family) that induces the testator to execute or revoke a testamentary document.

Duty of loyalty: The trustee's duty of impartiality that prohibits the trustee from favoring his or her own interests, requiring that the trustee remain objective when dealing with the interests of the trust beneficiaries.

Duty to diversify: The trustee's duty to spread the trust property among different investments.

Duty to segregate and earmark: The duty of a trustee to separate trust property from the trustee's own property and to identify the assets of the trust as trust property rather than the trustee's property.

Earmark: The process of identifying the assets of a trust as trust property.

Election: A doctrine that permits a surviving spouse to refuse the decedent's testamentary scheme and to "elect" instead to take his or her statutorily specified share; also a doctrine that permits the surviving spouse to retain any of his or her property that was the subject of the decedent's testamentary gift to a third party.

Elective share: The share specified by statute that enables a surviving spouse to reject the decedent's testamentary plan in favor of a designated share of the decedent's estate; a modern doctrine that replaces the common law doctrines of dower and curtesy.

Equitable adoption: A judicially created equitable remedy that enables a child to inherit from a deceased parent's intestate estate in cases in which a foster parent or stepparent agreed to adopt the child but the adoption was never finalized; sometimes referred to as *virtual adoption*.

Equitable title: The beneficiary's interest in a trust; distinguished from the trustee's interest or legal title.

Equivocation: A description that accurately applies to more than one asset or person and that creates an ambiguity in the interpretation of a term in a will or trust.

ERISA: The acronym for the Employee Retirement Income Security Act, i.e., the federal law that governs retirement benefits.

Escheat: The process of distributing the decedent's assets to the state in cases in which the decedent does not have heirs that are statutorily specified as "next of kin."

Escrow: A deposit (of writing, money, or other property) by a grantor with a third party until the performance of a condition upon which the property is to be delivered to a grantee.

Exculpatory clause: An express provision in a trust instrument by which the settlor alters the usual rules regarding trust investments (e.g., expanding the types of permissible investments) or the applicable standard of care; such clauses will not excuse bad faith.

Executor: The personal representative of the estate of a testate decedent; formerly the term *executrix* referred to a female in this position but in modern usage, the term *executor* refers to persons of either gender.

Exempt personal property: The right of the surviving spouse and minor children to retain certain personal property free from the claims of the decedent's creditors.

Exoneration: The doctrine that provides that the beneficiary of encumbered specific gifts takes free from liens; at common law, exoneration was presumed; today many states and the UPC reverse the presumption and provide for exoneration only if required by the will.

Exordium: An introductory provision in a will that specifies the place of a testator's residence and generally includes an express revocation of all prior wills and codicils.

Expectancy: The interest that a potential heir anticipates receiving from a potential decedent.

Express trust: A trust that is created based on the expressed intent of a settlor distinguished from trusts created by operation of law (i.e., resulting or constructive trusts); express trusts may be either private express trusts or charitable trusts.

Extrinsic evidence: Evidence that is "extrinsic" or outside of (i.e., not on the face of) a testamentary document; rules govern the admissibility of extrinsic evidence to determine the intent of the testator.

Facts of independent significance. *See Independent significance.*

Family allowance: An allowance for the support of the surviving spouse and minor children (sometimes including adult dependent children) for a statutorily designated period of time.

Family consent statute: A statute that facilitates health care decisions in the absence of an advance directive by the ill or incompetent person.

Fertile octogenarian: The presumption that a person is able to have children as long as she or he is alive.

Fiduciary: A person who is entrusted with handling property for another person, such as a personal representative (executor, administrator), trustee, guardian, conservator.

Fiduciary relationship: The relationship that arises between parties requiring a high standard of care when one person places trust in another.

Forced share: The doctrine that enables a surviving spouse to take a certain portion of the decedent's estate if the decedent disinherits the spouse or fails to bequeath the survivor a minimum amount; also called the *elective share*.

Fraud: An intentional misrepresentation that is intended to induce reliance or a promise made without intent to perform.

Fraud in the execution (of a will): Fraud that deceives the testator as to the identity of the instrument or its contents; also called *fraud in the factum*.

Fraud in the inducement (of a will): Fraud that deceives the testator as to some fact that causes the testator to make a will (or will provision) contrary to what the testator would have done if the testator had known the truth.

Fraudulent conveyance: A transfer that is subject to attack by creditors.

Funded trust: An inter vivos trust that holds property which has been transferred to it; distinguished from an *unfunded trust*.

Future interest: An interest in property that does not envisage present possession or enjoyment but rather provides for future enjoyment; examples include a remainder, executory interest, reversion.

General power of appointment: A power regarding the disposition of property that is exercisable in favor of the decedent, the decedent's estate, or his or her creditors.

General devise: A testamentary gift that is payable out of the general estate rather than from particular assets.

Gift: A voluntary transfer, without consideration, that requires donative intent and delivery.

Gift causa mortis: A doctrine that pertains to contemplation-at-death transfers; applicable to a donor who is in fear of imminent death; similar to other gifts (in terms of the requisites of donative intent, delivery, and acceptance) but conditional and revocable.

Grantor: A person who creates an inter vivos trust (also termed a *settlor* or *trustor*).

Guardian: The representative of a minor and/or incompetent (depending on the jurisdiction); guardianship encompasses the dual roles of guardian of the person (a person who makes medical decisions, for example) and guardian of the estate (a person who makes financial decisions).

Guardian ad litem: The judicially appointed representative of a minor or an incompetent (not necessarily an attorney).

Half-blood: A person (such as a half-sister or half-brother) who shares only one common ancestor with the decedent. Most states, as well as the UPC, treat half-bloods as equivalent to relatives of the whole blood for inheritance purposes.

Heir: The historical term for a person who succeeds to the real property of a decedent who dies intestate; according to modern usage, a person who takes either real or personal property by intestate succession.

Holographic will: A handwritten will, valid in some jurisdictions.

Homestead exemption: The protection for the residence used by the decedent's family that exempts it from the claims of the decedent's creditors.

Honorary trust: A trust with no ascertainable human beneficiary in which the trustee has only a moral, but not legal, obligation (e.g., a trust for an animal or the care of a grave).

Hotchpot: The process of equalization by which advancements (inter vivos gifts) are charged against the recipient's ultimate share of the intestate estate.

Illegitimate child. See *Nonmarital child.*

Illusory trust: An invalid trust generally created by a testator to defeat the rights of the surviving spouse.

Incorporation by reference: A doctrine that applies when a testamentary instrument refers to an extrinsic writing in an effort to give the latter testamentary significance; requirements include: (1) the testator must have intended to incorporate the extrinsic writing into the will, (2) the extrinsic writing must be in existence when the testator executed the will, (3) the will must describe sufficiently the extrinsic writing, and (4) the writing must conform to the description in the will.

Independent significance (acts or facts of): A doctrine that allows the testator to make testamentary dispositions based on the occurrence of specified acts or facts that have significance other than to pass property at death (e.g., a bequest of $10,000 "to the person who is my housekeeper at my death").

Insane delusion: A testator must have mental capacity when making a will. The will will be invalid if the testator manifests mental derangement that leads to the disposition of the testator's property differently than had the testator been of sound mind. According to case law, an insane delusion is "the conception of a disordered mind which imagines facts to exist of which there is no evidence and the belief in which is adhered to against all evidence and argument to the contrary, and which cannot be accounted for on any reasonable hypothesis. One cannot be said to act under an insane delusion if his condition of mind results from a belief or inference, however irrational and unfounded, drawn from facts which are shown to exist." In re Nigro's Estate, 52 Cal. Rptr. 128 (Cal. Ct. App. 1966).

Insolvent (estate): An estate in which the liabilities exceed the assets.

Insurance trust: A trust created by a settlor to hold and manage the proceeds of life insurance.

Integration: The process of establishing which writings were intended by the testator to be part of his or her will; the doctrine requires that the testator intended the separate writings to be part of the will and that the separate writings must have been present at the time of execution.

Interested witness: A witness to a will who takes a pecuniary interest under the testator's will.

Interpretation: The process of ascertaining the intent of the parties from the instrument itself; distinguished from the process of *construction* which assigns a legal consequence to the words used by the testator unless extrinsic evidence shows a contrary intention.

In terrorem: A testamentary provision that disinherits any beneficiary who contests a will in an attempt to deter a contest, also sometimes termed an *anticontest clause*.

Inter vivos trust: A trust that is established during the settlor's lifetime as distinguished from a testamentary trust created by a will; also termed a *living trust.*

Intestacy: The state of dying without a will.

Intestate: A decedent who dies without a valid will.

Intestate succession: The manner of distributing a decedent's property if he or she dies without a will.

Inventory and appraisement: A document filed with the court that includes an inventory or list of estate assets and also that determines the value of the assets in the estate.

In vitro fertilization: The process by which an egg from a donor is fertilized and implanted into a woman who will bear the child.

Irrevocable trust: A trust in which the settlor permanently cedes control of the trust property.

Issue: Descendants, including children, grandchildren, and others (of all degrees) in the descending line.

Joint tenancy: A form of concurrent ownership of a nonprobate asset by which each owner enjoys an undivided interest in the property, generally including the feature of a right of survivorship such that the surviving joint tenant(s) succeeds to ownership of the property.

Joint will: A single document that is the will of two or more persons and which is probated on the death of each of the testators.

Lapse: The failure of a testamentary gift to a beneficiary who predeceases the testator; at common law, a lapsed gift was a testamentary gift that fails because the devisee predeceased the testator by dying after execution of the will but before the death of the testator as distinguished from a *void gift* that fails because the devisee predeceased the testator by dying before execution of the will; in modern usage, both situations qualify as *lapse*.

Latent ambiguity: An ambiguity that is apparent in attempting to apply the will provision(s) to a particular person or property, distinguished from a *patent ambiguity* that is apparent on the face of the will. Under the traditional rule, courts admit extrinsic evidence to resolve a latent ambiguity but not a patent ambiguity.

Legacy: A testamentary gift of personal property, usually a sum of money.

Legatee: The historical term for a person who inherits personal property under a will.

Letters of administration: The document that authorizes a personal representative (an administrator) to administer an intestate estate.

Letters testamentary: The document that authorizes a personal representative (an executor) to administer a testate estate.

Life insurance: A contract (and nonprobate asset) in which a policy owner (the insured) pays premiums to an insurance company (the insurer) that agrees to pay a death benefit (proceeds) to a beneficiary upon the death of the insured.

Lineal: An ancestor or descendant who is related to the decedent by consanguinity (and today includes adoptees).

Living trust: Another term for an inter vivos trust.

Living will: A document that includes written instructions regarding health care (i.e., end-of-life decisions) in the event of an individual's becoming incapacitated.

Lost or destroyed will statute: A statute that provides for the probate of a will that is lost or cannot be found at the death of the testator.

Loyalty. See *Duty of loyalty*.

Marital property: Property that is acquired by a husband and wife during the marriage.

Merger: The combination of legal and equitable title that results in termination of the trust.

Mistake in the execution (of a will): A mistake regarding the identity or contents of an instrument that prevents the testator from having the requisite testamentary intent; also called *mistake in the factum*.

Mistake in the inducement (of a will): A mistake that leads the testator to make a will based on some erroneous fact.

Mistake in the revocation (of a will). *See Dependent relative revocation.*

Model Code of Professional Responsibility: The rules (together with the Model Rules of Professional Conduct) promulgated by the American Bar Association that govern the conduct of lawyers.

Model Probate Code (MPC): Model legislation that preceded the Uniform Probate Code.

Model Rules of Professional Conduct: The rules (together with the Model Code of Professional Responsibility) promulgated by the American Bar Association that govern the conduct of lawyers.

Mortmain restriction: A limitation on a testamentary gift to charity that requires the testator (for the gift to be valid) to survive by a certain period of time after executing the will.

Mutual wills: Separate testamentary documents executed by two persons (usually husband and wife) that contain reciprocal or mirror provisions, sometimes referred to as *reciprocal wills.*

Negative beneficiary: A beneficiary who has been disinherited by the decedent's will.

Negative will: A will or will provision that states the testator's intention to disinherit a potential heir.

Next of kin: The persons who take the estate of a decedent who dies intestate.

No contest provision: A provision in a will providing that a beneficiary who contests the will will lose some or all of the benefits under the will; also called an *in terrorem* or *forfeiture clause*.

Nonclaim statute: A statute that provides for the filing of claims of the creditors of a decedent; creditors must file within a statutorily designated period or be forever barred.

Noncourt trust: A trust (such as an inter vivos trust) that is not subject to the continuing jurisdiction of a court but must be brought to the court's attention, distinguished from a court trust (such as a testamentary trust) that is subject to the continuing jurisdiction of a probate court.

Nongeneral power of appointment: A power of appointment regarding the disposition of property that may not be exercised in favor of the powerholder, the powerholder's estate, or powerholder's creditors, as distinguished from a general power of appointment that may be exercised in favor of the foregoing persons; also termed a *limited* or *special power of appointment.*

Nonmarital child: The modern term for a child who is born out of wedlock, formerly termed an illegitimate child.

Nonprobate asset: An asset that passes outside of the decedent's estate (i.e., other than by intestate or testate succession); examples include joint tenancies with rights of survivorship, life insurance, retirement plans, payable-on-death accounts, etc.

Nonresident alien: A person who is not a citizen or resident of the United States.

Nuncupative: An oral will that is declared by a testator during a last illness, before witnesses, and later reduced to writing by a person who was present at the declaration.

Oral trust: A trust that is established by parol (instead of by a writing); oral trusts of real property violate the Statute of Frauds.

Orphan's court: A court with probate jurisdiction in some states (e.g., Pennsylvania).

Parentelic: A system of determining inheritance rights of the next of kin of an intestate that dispenses with counting degrees of kinship and, instead, distributes the estate to the grandparents and their descendants (and if none, to the great-grandparents and their descendants).

Partial intestacy: The situation that arises when a decedent fails to dispose of the entire estate by a valid testamentary instrument; the remainder of the decedent's property passes intestate.

Partial revocation: The testator's revocation of only part of his or her will; the doctrine is not recognized by all jurisdictions (in which case, the will is still effective).

Partition: A judicial proceeding that separates the interests of co-owners of property.

Passive trust: A trust in which the trustee has no active duties and therefore is invalid, also termed a *dry trust.*

Patent ambiguity: An ambiguity that is apparent on the face of the document, as distinguished from a *latent ambiguity* which is only apparent in attempting to apply the will provision(s) to a particular person or property. Under the traditional rule, courts admit extrinsic evidence to resolve a latent ambiguity but not a patent ambiguity.

Payable-on-death (POD) account: An account that is created by means of a contract between the depositor and the financial institution; the balance of which passes outside of probate; also one of the forms of multiple-party accounts.

Pendente lite: During the litigation.

Per capita (distribution): A method of distribution that divides the estate in equal shares among persons who are equally related to the decedent; the applicable method if all of the decedent's children survive the decedent.

Per capita at each generation: The method of estate distribution (followed by the new Uniform Probate Code) of an intestate decedent by representation among descendants in which the division of the estate starts *per capita with representation* (the first division of the estate is at the generation with any living takers); the property is distributed into as many equal shares as there are living members of that generation and deceased members who leave issue then living; however, the shares of deceased members who leave issue then living are combined and then distributed among persons per capita at the next generation among descendants who are either alive or left issue living (and the process repeats until the estate is distributed).

Per capita with representation: The method of distribution of an intestate estate among descendants in which the first division of the estate is at the generation with any living descendants; the property then is divided into as many equal shares as there are living members of that generation and deceased members of that generation who leave issue then living; the share of each deceased member of that generation who leaves issue then living is then divided in the same manner among his or her then living issue.

Personal property set-aside: The personal property of a decedent that is specified by statute and that passes by law to the decedent's surviving spouse and/or children.

Personal representative: The fiduciary who is either an executor or administrator and who performs the tasks of probate administration.

Per stirpes: Literally, by root or stocks; a method of distribution of an intestate estate by representation among descendants, in which a descendant takes the share of his or her predeceased ancestor (the particular version depends on the jurisdiction).

Plain-meaning rule: The doctrine that provides that terms should be given their literal meaning.

Posthumous heir: An heir who was conceived while the intestate was alive but born after the intestate's death. At common law and according to the Uniform Probate Code, posthumous heirs inherit as if they had been born during the decedent's lifetime.

Postnuptial agreement: A contract that is executed by the spouses during the marriage (in contrast to an *antenuptial agreement* that is executed by prospective spouses) that determines the parties' property rights in the event of death or dissolution.

Pour-over will (or will provision): A provision in a will that makes a gift of probate assets to an existing inter vivos trust. Use of this common estate planning measure enables a testator to devise property to a trust even though the trust has been altered subsequently after the execution of the will.

Pour-over trust: The inter vivos trust that receives the probate assets from a pour-over will.

Power: The authority that is conferred (by an instrument or implied by law) on a fiduciary to act.

Power of appointment: The authority conferred upon a person (termed a *donee*) to direct the passage of property; powers may be exercised by will or inter vivos.

Power of attorney: The authority that is conferred by one person (termed a *principal*) upon another person (termed an *attorney in fact*) to perform an act for the principal (who is not necessarily an attorney); a form of agency relationship.

Powerholder: The holder of a power of appointment, also termed the *donee of a power of appointment*.

Precatory language: Directions in an instrument that merely request that an act be performed but that do not impose any legal obligation.

Predeceased: A person who dies before another person (i.e., before the decedent).

Prenuptial agreement. *See Antenuptial agreement.*

Pretermitted heir: A child or other heir who has been unintentionally omitted from the decedent's will.

Pretermitted heir statute: A statute that protects those persons (generally, children) who have been unintentionally omitted from a decedent's will (e.g., a child who was born after the testator executed the will).

Primogeniture: The English rule by which the eldest male descendant inherited real property; abolished by Parliament in the Administration of Estates Act in 1925.

Probate: The process of proving the validity of a will and administering an estate (testate or intestate); also the appropriate court that undertakes these tasks.

Probate asset: An asset that passes by intestate or testate succession.

Probate avoidance: The process of avoiding probate (with its cost and delay) by the use of will substitutes and nonprobate property.

Probate estate: The estate that is subject to administration by a court.

Probate homestead: The real property of a decedent that is selected by a court and set aside for the protection of the surviving spouse and children from attachment by creditors.

Proponent (of a will): A person who is in favor of probating a will and who attempts to prove that the will is validly executed; distinguished from a *contestant* of a will who attempts to prove that the will is invalid.

Pro rata: Proportionately, as in the term *pro rata abatement* in which all the shares of the beneficiaries in a given class are reduced equally.

Proxy: A third party who executes a will (by signing in the testator's presence and at the testator's direction) or revokes a will on behalf of a testator who generally is unable to perform the act.

Prudent person doctrine: Rules that specify a fiduciary's standard of care.

Publication: A statement by a testator to witnesses that a given document is his or her will.

Purchase money resulting trust: A trust created by operation of law that arises when one person purchases property that is titled in the name of another; the titleholder is presumed to hold the property on resulting trust.

Putative spouse: A person who, although not legally married, is treated as a legal spouse for some purposes (i.e., intestate succession) provided that the person has a good faith belief in the validity of the marriage (such as cases in which the partner has not been validly divorced from a former spouse).

Quasi-community property: Property that is treated (i.e., on dissolution or death) as if it were community property because it was acquired by the domiciliary of a community property state while that person was living in a separate property state (i.e., before moving to the community property jurisdiction).

Reciprocity statute: A statute governing the right of a nonresident heir to inherit property from the decedent, providing that the heir may inherit if the law of his or her domicile permits a citizen of our country to inherit from the decedent.

Reformation: The remedial process of correcting a written instrument to conform to the maker's intention.

Release (of an expectancy): The process by which a potential heir releases a potential interest in the decedent's estate to the decedent (prior to the decedent's death) and that enables the heir to receive an early distribution of the owner's property.

Remainder: A type of future interest; a *vested remainder* gives the donee the right to obtain possession of property upon the termination of the preceding estate; a *contingent remainder* permits a donee to obtain possession of the property only if a certain condition (the condition precedent) is satisfied.

Renunciation: The process of declining a testamentary gift or a share of an intestate's estate (also termed *disclaimer*).

Republication: The process of validating an invalid will.

Republication by codicil: A doctrine that updates a will by means of a subsequent codicil; the valid codicil republishes the will (i.e., enabling the will to "speak again" as of the date of the codicil).

Res: The corpus or principal of a trust.

Residuary disposition (residue): A gift of the property that remains in the estate after the payment of debts and the distribution of devises.

Restatements of the Law: Works produced by the American Law Institute that explain current law of a given subject matter.

Resulting trust: A trust created by operation of law that is implied from the circumstances to carry out the parties' intentions; such a trust arises when an express trust fails or provides an incomplete disposition of the trust property, or in the situation of a purchase money resulting trust. *See Purchase money resulting trust.*

Revival: The doctrine that applies upon the revocation of a revoking instrument in order to bring to testamentary life ("revive") a prior will.

Revocable trust: A trust created by a settlor in which the settlor retains the power to revoke and modify the trust.

Revocation (of a will) by operation of law: The revocation of a will when certain circumstances (e.g., divorce) have changed such that it is presumed that the testator would have wished his or her will (or some of its provisions) to be revoked.

Revocation (of a will) by physical act: The revocation of a will by a legally designated method, such as cancellation, obliteration, burning, tearing, or other means of destruction.

Revocation (of a will) by subsequent instrument: The revocation of a prior will (expressly or impliedly) by a subsequent testamentary document.

Right of representation: The heirs take "by right of representation" when they take the share that a predeceased relative would have taken had the aforementioned relative survived.

Rule Against Perpetuities: The statutory formulation that restricts dead hand control involving property; the relevant time period within which an interest must vest depends on the jurisdiction.

Satisfaction: The failure of a testamentary gift because the testator has transferred the property to the beneficiary after the execution of the will and prior to the decedent's death; a doctrine that is analogous to the concept of *advancement* applicable in intestate succession. See also *Ademption by satisfaction.*

Savings bank trust. See *Totten trust.*

Secret trust: A will that makes an absolute gift (i.e., is silent about the existence of a trust) but extrinsic evidence reveals that the beneficiary of the gift was supposed to hold that property in trust for the person indicated by the testator; in such a situation, the court may impose a constructive trust for the person indicated.

Self-proving will: A witnessed will that includes a notarized affidavit in which the testator and witnesses affirm under oath that all the statutory requirements have been fulfilled; a self-proved will facilitates probate by enabling the will to be admitted without the necessity of testimony by subscribing witnesses.

Semi-secret trust: A will that contains a gift in trust but without designation of the terms of the trust; in such a situation, most courts hold that the trust fails and that the property should be distributed via resulting trust.

Settlor: The person who creates a trust, also termed a *trustor* or *grantor*.

Severance: The method by which a joint tenancy is terminated and converted into a tenancy in common.

Simultaneous death statute: Legislation that provides for the distribution of estates when the decedent and the beneficiary both die in the same accident or disaster.

Slayer disqualification: State statutes that prohibit a murderer from inheriting property of the victim.

Soldier's and sailor's will: Wills that are permitted by some states for military personnel and mariners and that dispense with some of the formal requirements (e.g., writing, attestation).

Solemn form probate: Probate administration that is commenced after giving notice to interested persons, also termed *formal probate*; distinguished from common form (or informal) probate that permits probate without the need for notice to interested persons and that begins with an ex parte proceeding.

Specific devise: A gift of a particular item of personal property or parcel of real property.

Spendthrift trust (or clause): A trust (or trust provision) that protects the beneficiary from the claims of creditors by restraining the beneficiary's ability to transfer (voluntarily or involuntarily) the trust property.

Statute of Charitable Uses: Legislation (enacted by Parliament in 1601) that included a list of recognized charitable purposes in its Preamble and also provided a method of enforcement of charitable trusts.

Statute of Distribution: Legislation (enacted by Parliament in 1670) that established the distributive pattern of intestate succession for personal property.

Statute of Frauds: Legislation (enacted by Parliament in 1677) that required a writing for transfers of real property, including testamentary dispositions of real property, and also imposed requirements on testamentary disposition of personal property (but not a writing).

Statute of Uses: Legislation (enacted by Parliament in 1535) that "executed" uses, i.e., transformed equitable estates into legal estates.

Statute of Wills: Legislation (enacted by Parliament in 1540) that created the power to devise real property that was owned by the testator at the time the will was executed.

Statutory fees: Fees that are specified by statute to be paid to a personal representative and attorney for an estate.

Statutory will: A fill-in-the-blank will form that is authorized by state statute.

Stepparent relationship: A relationship that arises when a child's biological parent remarries; generally, only a stepchild who is *adopted* by the new spouse may inherit from or through the stepparent.

Stranger-to-the-adoption rule: A doctrine that treats adopted children as biological children for intestate succession regarding the estates of only their adoptive parent(s) but not that of the estate of any other person who was a nonparty to the adoption (hence, a "stranger to the adoption").

Subscribing witness: A person who signs his or her name to a will to attest to its validity.

Subscription: The requirement that the signatures of witnesses to a will must be located at the end of the document.

Substantial compliance: A doctrine advocated by Professor John Langbein in an influential law review article in 1975, in which he proposed liberalization of the formal requirements for will execution by means of the application of the contract doctrine of substantial compliance to the law of wills; according to this doctrine, fatally defective wills should still be admitted to probate if the will proponent could prove that the functions of the will formalities were satisfied.

Supernumerary: An additional, nonessential, attesting witness; the presence of a supernumerary witness may serve to validate a will in cases in which an essential witness takes a pecuniary benefit under the will.

Super-will. See *Blockbuster will*.

Support trust: A trust containing a provision that restricts the use of trust income, principal, or both to the beneficiary's support (i.e., food, clothing, medical care, and educational expenses).

Surcharge: A remedy to redress a breach of trust by holding the fiduciary personally liable for any resulting loss.

Surplusage approach: The view that permits the probate of a holographic will by disregarding "surplusage," i.e., certain nonessential nonholographic material.

Surrogate's court: The court having probate jurisdiction in some jurisdictions (e.g., New York).

Tentative trust. *See Totten trust.*

Testament: The historical term, derived from Latin, for a will.

Testamentary trust: A trust that is created by the decedent's will, distinguished from an *inter vivos trust* that is created by the settlor during the settlor's lifetime.

Testate succession: The manner of distributing a decedent's property if she or he dies with a will.

Testator: A person who has died, leaving a will. Formerly, a man was termed a *testator,* whereas a woman was termed a *testatrix*. Modern usage refers to persons of either gender as a testator.

Totten trust: A savings account trust (in the form of "X, in trust for Y"), derived from the case of In re Totten (71 N.E. 748 (N.Y. 1904)), in which a surviving beneficiary (or beneficiaries) succeed to the balance in the account upon the death of the depositor; also known as a *tentative trust*.

Tracing: A procedure that permits a trust beneficiary to recover the misappropriated trust property (or its proceeds) from the trustee or a third party unless the property is in the hands of a bona fide purchaser.

Trust: A relationship regarding property in which a person or persons (a trustee or trustees) hold(s) legal title to the trust property and is subject to a fiduciary obligation to manage it on behalf of a beneficiary (or beneficiaries) who hold(s) equitable title.

Trust corpus: The trust property, sometimes termed the *trust res* or *principal* of a trust.

Trustee: The fiduciary who holds legal title to the trust property and administers the trust.

Trustor: The creator of a trust, also called a *settlor* or *grantor*.

Trust res: The trust property, sometimes referred to as the *trust corpus* or *principal* of a trust.

Undue influence: Grounds for invalidating a will when the document is the result of an action that subverts the will of the testator and replaces the will of the testator with that of the person exerting the unfair persuasion.

Unfunded trust. See *Funded trust.*

Universal succession: The manner in which heirs to an intestate estate assume all liabilities for the decedent's taxes, debts, creditor's claims, and distributions to other heirs entitled to property.

Unworthy heir statutes: State statutes that preclude certain "unworthy" persons from inheriting by intestate succession.

Use: The precursor of the modern trust; method of property ownership in which a property owner would convey property to another to hold "for the use" of a beneficiary.

Virtual adoption. See *Equitable adoption.*

Virtual representation: The doctrine by which unrepresented beneficiaries may be bound by a decision of those persons who have substantially identical interests.

Void gift: At common law, a testamentary gift that fails because the devisee predeceased the testator by dying before execution of the will, in contrast to a *lapsed gift* that fails because the devisee predeceased the testator by dying after execution of the will but before the death of the testator; in modern usage, both situations qualify as *lapse*.

Wait-and-see doctrine: An approach under the Rule of Perpetuities that measures the validity of interests not by what might happen, but what in fact actually occurs.

Ward: A person for whom a guardian has been appointed.

Waste: Acts that adversely affect the value of the (trust) property.

Will: A testamentary instrument.

Will contest: A proceeding that is brought by an individual (contestant) seeking to have a will declared invalid (e.g., on grounds of capacity, undue influence, or lack of due execution).

Will contract: An agreement to make or revoke a will, to devise certain property, or to die intestate, or not to contest a will.

Will substitute: A nonprobate form of transmission of property ownership that avoids the need for a will by means of a document that is not formally executed according to states' wills legislation; common will substitutes include inter vivos trusts, joint tenancies with the right of survivorship, and multiple-party accounts.

Wills Act: Legislation (enacted by Parliament in 1837) that prescribed the requirements for testamentary disposition of real and personal property.

Wills legislation: State statutes that prescribe the formalities for executing a will.

Worthier Title. See *Doctrine of Worthier Title.*

TABLE OF CASES

TABLE OF STATUTES

References are to page numbers in this work

INDEX

Abbreviations

CAL. BUS. & PROF.	California Business And Professions Code
CAL. CIV.	California Civil Code
CAL. CIV. PROC.	California Code of Civil Procedure
CAL. EVID.	California Evidence Code
CAL. EDUC.	California Education Code
CAL. FAM.	California Family Code
CAL. FIN.	California Financial Code
CAL. GOVT.	California Government Code
CAL. HEALTH & SAFETY	California Health & Safety Code
CAL. INS.	California Insurance Code
CAL. PENAL	California Penal Code
CAL. PROB.	California Probate Code
CAL. VEH.	California Vehicle Code
CAL. RULES CT.	California Rules of Court
CAL. RULES PROF. CONDUCT	California Rules of Professional Conduct
IRC	Internal Revenue Code
TREAS. REG.	Treasury Regulations
UNIF. PRINCIPLE & INCOME ACT	Uniform Principle and Income Act
UNIF. PROBATE CODE	Uniform Probate Code
UNIF. PRUDENT INVESTOR ACT	Uniform Prudent Investor Act
UNIF. TRUST CODE	Uniform Trust Code

References are to code sections, rules, and pages. Page references are in *italics*.